ARCHBOLD

2017

THIRD SUPPLEMENT TO THE 2017 EDITION

EDITOR

P.J. RICHARDSON, Q.C. (Hon.), LL.M. (LOND.), Dip. Crim. (CANTAB.)
of Gray's Inn and the Inner Temple, Barrister

SUPPLEMENT EDITORS

WILLIAM CARTER, M.A. (OXON.)
of Gray's Inn, Barrister

STEPHEN SHAY, B.A. (OXON.)
of the Middle Temple, Barrister

SWEET & MAXWELL

THOMSON REUTERS

Published in 2017 by Thomson Reuters (Professional) UK Limited, trading as Sweet & Maxwell. Registered in England & Wales. Company number 1679046. Registered office 5 Canada Square, Canary Wharf, London E14 5AQ

Printed and bound by CPI Group (UK) Ltd, Croydon, CR0 4YY

Typeset by Sweet & Maxwell, 5 Canada Square, Canary Wharf, London E14 5AQ

For further information on our products and services, visit:

http://www.sweetandmaxwell.co.uk

No natural forests were destroyed to make this product; only farmed timber was used and replanted.

A CIP catalogue record for this book is available from the British Library

ISBN MAINWORK 9780414056503
ISBN SECOND SUPPLEMENT 9780414059481

SERVICE INFORMATION

The Archbold service

Archbold: Criminal Pleading, Evidence and Practice consists of one main text volume (including the tables and index). This volume is re-issued annually, and is updated by cumulative supplements, the e-update service (see below) and *Archbold Review*.

The supplement

Three cumulative supplements, containing updating material for the main volume, are published in each year as part of the service.

This is the third supplement of 2017.

New material is incorporated into this supplement using the same paragraph numbers as appear in the mainwork. All material new to this supplement is marked in the text by a **bold star in the margin.**   ★

After consulting the main work on any given subject, reference should always be made to the same paragraph number in the current supplement to check that there have been no new developments since the main text volume was published. The supplement will also track material which has been removed or relocated as part of the re-issue process.

The back cover contains a list of all important developments included in this supplement for the first time and where they can be found.

All references in the text to cases, statutes and statutory instruments are contained in the tables printed at the beginning of this supplement.

Sentencing Guidelines and Related Authorities

This year we have introduced a new Sentencing Guidelines Supplement to the Archbold service. This will include the Sentencing Guidelines in full, as they are published by the Sentencing Council as well as including the relevant authorities and an abridged version of the Magistrates' Court sentencing guideline. The original pagination from the guidelines will be retained in the paragraph numbering for easy reference. New guidelines published during the currency of the main work, and new decisions of the courts that are relevant to any extant guidelines will be collected in this supplement pending incorporation into the sentencing supplement which will be reissued once a year with the main work.

Please email smg.archbold@thomson.com with comments/suggestions for any of the Archbold services.

Archbold e-update activation code

As a subscriber to Archbold 2017 you have free and unlimited access to the accompanying weekly e-update service and online archive. If you are a new user accessing the service for the first time then please visit www.sweetandmaxwell.co.uk/archbold where you will be asked to complete a simple short registration process, and to enter the following activation code to start receiving updates:

> AB2017

If you are an existing user of the e-update then your access will automatically be updated for the new edition and there is no need to re-register.

TABLE OF CONTENTS

TABLE OF CONTENTS

ABBREVIATIONS OF LEGISLATION

The following abbreviations have been adopted throughout.

AFA	Armed Forces Act
CAA	Criminal Appeal Act
CDA	Crime and Disorder Act
CDDA	Company Directors Disqualification Act
CEMA	Customs and Excise Management Act
CJA	Criminal Justice Act
CJCA	Criminal Justice and Courts Act
CJCSA	Criminal Justice and Court Services Act
CJIA	Criminal Justice and Immigration Act
CJPA	Criminal Justice and Police Act
CJPOA	Criminal Justice and Public Order Act
CLA	Criminal Law Act
CPIA	Criminal Procedure and Investigations Act
C(S)A	Crime (Sentences) Act
CYPA	Children and Young Persons Act
DTA	Drug Trafficking Act
DTOA	Drug Trafficking Offences Act
ECHR	European Convention on Human Rights
FSMA	Financial Services and Markets Act
LASPOA	Legal Aid, Sentencing and Punishment of Offenders Act
MCA	Magistrates' Courts Act
MHA	Mental Health Act
PACE	Police and Criminal Evidence
PCA	Proceeds of Crime Act
PCCA	Powers of Criminal Courts Act
PCC(S)A	Powers of Criminal Courts (Sentencing) Act
PJA	Police and Justice Act
RIPA	Regulation of Investigatory Powers Act
RSA	Road Safety Act
RSC	Rules of the Supreme Court (Revision)
RTA	Road Traffic Act
RTOA	Road Traffic Offenders Act
SCA	Serious Crime Act
SOA	Sexual Offences Act
SOCPA	Serious Organised Crime and Police Act
VCRA	Violent Crime Reduction Act
YJCEA	Youth Justice and Criminal Evidence Act

TABLE OF STATUTES

References in bold indicate where legislation is reproduced in full

TABLE OF NON-UK LEGISLATION

TABLE OF INTERNATIONAL TREATIES AND CONVENTIONS

References in bold indicate where legislation is reproduced in full

TABLE OF EC REGULATIONS AND DIRECTIVES

TABLE OF STATUTORY INSTRUMENTS

References in bold indicate where legislation is reproduced in full

TABLE OF CASES

TABLE OF NON-UK CASES

TABLE OF PRACTICE DIRECTIONS

Chapter 1

THE INDICTMENT

III. SENDINGS FOR TRIAL

B. Principal Provisions

(2) Sending of cases to the Crown Court

Crime and Disorder Act 1998, ss.50A, 51-51E

Children and young persons

The Sentencing Council for England and Wales has issued a definitive guideline relating to the **★1-25**
overarching principles for sentencing those aged under 18 at the date of conviction (Pt 1). It
includes guidance as to mode of trial decisions. For details thereof, see *post*, Appendix S-29 *et seq.*

D. Mode of Trial for Offences Triable Either Way and Certain Summary Offences

(2) Procedure

(a) *Statutory provisions*

Procedure for determining mode of trial of offences triable either way

Magistrates' Courts Act 1980, ss.24-24D

The Sentencing Council for England and Wales has issued a definitive guideline relating to the **★1-88**
overarching principles for sentencing those aged under 18 at the date of conviction (Pt 1). It
includes guidance as to mode of trial decisions. For details thereof, see *post*, Appendix S-29 *et seq.*

Juvenile charged jointly with adult

The Sentencing Council's 2016 guideline on decisions as to mode of trial (as to which, see the **★1-95**
main work) has been overtaken, so far as it relates to children and young persons, by its definitive
guideline relating to the overarching principles for sentencing those aged under 18 at the date of
conviction (as to which, see *ante*, § 1-88).

(d) *Practice direction*

Criminal Practice Direction II Preliminary Proceedings 9A: Allocation (Mode of Trial)

Criminal Practice Direction II (Preliminary Proceedings) 9A was amended, with effect from **1-114**
November 16, 2016, so as to delete the second and third sentences in direction 9A.1 and the
whole of directions 9A.2 and 9A.3: *Criminal Practice Directions 2015 (Amendment No. 2)*, unreported,
November 16, 2016, Lord Thomas C.J. The effect was merely to mandate a magistrates' court to
make decisions as to mode of trial by reference to the Sentencing Council's guideline on allocation.
For the revised text, see *post*, Appendix B-139.

IV. AGAINST WHOM AN INDICTMENT LIES

B. Exemptions

(10) Offenders assisting investigations and prosecutions

Serious Organised Crime and Police Act 2005, s.71

Assistance by offender: immunity from prosecution

With effect from November 9, 2016, the Secretaries of State for Business, Energy and Industrial **1-161**

1

Strategy, for International Trade and for Exiting the European Union and the Transfer of Functions (Education and Skills) Order 2016 (S.I. 2016 No. 992) amended section 71 of the 2005 Act so as to substitute the words "Secretary of State for Business, Energy and Industrial Strategy", for the words "Secretary of State for Business, Innovation and Skills" in subsections (4)(db), (6A) and (6C).

★ With effect from March 1, 2017, section 71 of the 2005 Act was further amended by the Bank of England and Financial Services (Consequential Amendments) Regulations 2017 (S.I. 2017 No. 80), so as, in subsection (6B), to omit the words "and paragraph 16(1) of Schedule 1ZB", and to insert, after the words "(arrangements for discharging functions)", the words "and paragraph 17(1) of Schedule 6A to the Bank of England Act 1998 (delegation of functions)".

V. THE FORM OF AN INDICTMENT

A. RULES AS TO INDICTMENTS

(2) The procedure rules

1-181   As to a new practice direction supplementing the new Part 10 of the Criminal Procedure Rules 2015 (S.I. 2015 No. 1490), see *post*, Appendix B-149 *et seq.*

(3) Practice directions

1-192   As to a new practice direction that has been updated to take account of the revised Part 10 of the Criminal Procedure Rules 2015 (S.I. 2015 No. 1490), see *post*, Appendix B-149 *et seq.*

1-193   It should be noted that *Criminal Practice Directions II (Preliminary Proceedings) 10B: Voluntary bills of indictment* has not been updated, as anticipated in the main work. This means that the references therein to rule 10.3 of the Criminal Procedure Rules 2015 (S.I. 2015 No. 1490) should now be read as references to rule 10.9 of the substituted Part 10 of those rules (§ 1-190 in the main work).

B. DRAWING THE INDICTMENT

(2) Number of counts

1-197   As to the replacement of *Criminal Practice Direction II (Preliminary Proceedings) 10A*, see *ante*, § 1-192, and *post*, Appendix B-149 *et seq.*

C. CONTENTS

(2) Statement and particulars of offence(s)

Prescribed forms of indictment and their use

1-212   As to the replacement of *Criminal Practice Direction II (Preliminary Proceedings) 10A*, see *ante*, § 1-192, and *post*, Appendix B-149 *et seq.* It should be noted that directions 10A.15 to 10A.20 almost exactly replicate the current paragraphs 10A.4 to 10A.9, save that the reference to signing the indictment has now been omitted.

VII. PREFERRING THE BILL OF INDICTMENT

A. WHEN A BILL OF INDICTMENT MAY BE PREFERRED

Indictment based on sending

1-334   As to the replacement of *Criminal Practice Direction II (Preliminary Proceedings) 10A*, see *ante*, § 1-192, and *post*, Appendix B-149 *et seq.* It should be noted that paragraph 5 of the new practice direction corresponds almost exactly to paragraph 2 of the practice direction that has been replaced, save for the omission of the last sentence and a minor change to the wording of the penultimate sentence that reflects that there is no longer a legal requirement for an indictment to be signed.

Joinder of persons or charges separately sent for trial

As to the replacement of *Criminal Practice Direction II (Preliminary Proceedings) 10A*, see *ante*, § 1-192, and *post*, Appendix B-149 *et seq.* It should be noted that paragraph 5 of the new practice direction corresponds almost exactly to paragraph 2 of the practice direction that has been replaced, save for the omission of the last sentence and a minor change to the wording of the penultimate sentence that reflects that there is no longer a legal requirement for an indictment to be signed.

IX. PROCEEDINGS AGAINST CORPORATIONS AND OTHER BODIES

(2) Deferred prosecutions

Relevant offences

With effect from April 1, 2017 (Policing and Crime Act 2017 (Commencement No. 2) Regulations 2017 (S.I. 2017 No. 482)), Part 2 of Schedule 17 to the Crime and Courts Act 2013 was amended by the Policing and Crime Act 2017, s.150, so as to add an offence under an instrument made under the European Communities Act 1972, s.2(2), for the purpose of implementing, or otherwise in relation to, EU obligations created or arising by or under an EU financial sanctions regulation (as to which, see s.143 of the 2017 Act), an offence under an Act or under subordinate legislation where the offence was created for the purpose of implementing a United Nations financial sanctions resolution (as to which, see *ibid.*), an offence under the Anti-terrorism, Crime and Security Act 2001, Sched. 3, para. 7, an offence under the Counter-Terrorism Act 2008, Sched. 7, para. 30 or 30A, where the offence relates to a requirement of the kind mentioned in paragraph 13 of that schedule, and an offence under the 2008 Act, Sched. 7, para. 31.

Crime and Courts Act 2013, Sched. 17, Pt 1

Court approval of DPA: final hearing

For a case considering the interests of justice test in paragraph 8 of Schedule 17 to the 2013 Act, see *post*, § 1-394.

Application of the principles

Whereas a deferred prosecution agreement can only come into force when it is approved by the Crown Court making a declaration, under paragraph 8(1) of Schedule 17 to the Crime and Courts Act 2013 (§ 1-377 in the main work), that it is in the interests of justice and that the terms are fair, reasonable and proportionate, in deciding whether a proposed agreement is in the interests of justice, the court must consider a number of factors, *viz.* (i) the seriousness of the predicate offence, (ii) the importance of incentivising the exposure and self-reporting of corporate wrongdoing, (iii) the history (or otherwise) of similar conduct, (iv) the attention paid to corporate compliance prior to, at the time of, and subsequent to the offending, (v) the extent to which the entity has changed both in its culture and in relation to relevant personnel, and (vi) the impact of prosecution on employees and others innocent of any misconduct: *Serious Fraud Office v. X.Y.Z. Ltd* [2016] Lloyd's Rep. F.C. 509, Crown Court at Southwark (Sir Brian Leveson P.).

XI. POWERS AND DUTIES OF PARTICULAR PROSECUTION AGENCIES

A. CROWN PROSECUTION SERVICE

(1) Establishment
Prosecution of Offences Act 1985, s.1

R. v. Walker (Triston) is now reported at [2016] 2 Cr.App.R. 24.

B. SERIOUS FRAUD OFFICE

(2) Investigation powers
Criminal Justice Act 1987, s.2

Director's investigation powers

As from a day to be appointed, the Investigatory Powers Act 2016, s.12(1), and Sched. 2, para. 2, amend the CJA 1987, s.2, so as to insert new subsections (10A) and (10B), as follows—

"(10A) Nothing in this section is to be read as enabling a person to secure the disclosure by a telecommunications operator or postal operator of communications data without the consent of the operator.

(10B) In subsection (10A) "communications data", "postal operator" and "telecommunications operator" have the same meanings as in the Investigatory Powers Act 2016 (see sections 261 and 262 of that Act).".

CHAPTER 2

THE CRIMINAL JURISDICTION OF THE CROWN COURT

I. THE CROWN COURT

C. CONSTITUTION

(1) Judges of the Crown Court

Criminal Procedure Rules 2015 (S.I. 2015 No. 1490), r.34.11

Constitution of the Crown Court

★**2-8**   With effect from April 3, 2017, the Criminal Procedure (Amendment) Rules 2017 (S.I. 2017 No. 144) amended rule 34.11 of the 2015 rules, so as: (i) to substitute "(b) if the appeal is from a youth court, each justice of the peace must be qualified to sit as a member of a youth court" for paragraph (1)(b); and (ii) to omit the words "and need not include both a man and a woman" in paragraph (2)(a).

D. ALLOCATION OF BUSINESS AND LOCATION OF CROWN COURT SITTINGS

(2) Practice directions

Criminal Practice Direction XIII Listing E: Allocation of Business within the Crown Court

★**2-22j**   With effect from April 3, 2017, *Criminal Practice Direction XIII (Listing) E* (allocation of business within the Crown Court) (see the main work) is amended by *Criminal Practice Directions 2015 (Amendment No. 4)*, unreported, March 28, 2017, Lord Thomas C.J. ([2017] EWCA Crim. 310), so as to insert the words "; or (iii) a deputy circuit judge to whom the case has been specifically released by the presiding judge" after both paras. E.1(ii) and E.2(ii).

II. THE GENERAL JURISDICTION OF THE CROWN COURT

★**2-34a**   As from a day to be appointed, section 162 of the Policing and Crime Act 2017 inserts a new section 86A into the Courts Act 2003. This requires a person who is a defendant in proceedings in a criminal court to provide his name, date of birth and nationality if required to do so at any stage of proceedings by the court, with supplementary provision to be made by Criminal Procedure Rules. Failure to comply without reasonable excuse is a summary offence.

Courts Act 2003, s.86A

Requirement to give information in criminal proceedings

86A. (1) A person who is a defendant in proceedings in a criminal court must provide his or her name, date of birth and nationality if required to do so at any stage of proceedings by the court.

(2) Criminal Procedure Rules must specify the stages of proceedings at which requirements are to be imposed by virtue of subsection (1) (and may specify other stages of proceedings when such requirements may be imposed).

(3) A person commits an offence if, without reasonable excuse, the person fails to comply with a requirement imposed by virtue of subsection (1), whether by providing false or incomplete information or by providing no information.

4

(4) Information provided by a person in response to a requirement imposed by virtue of subsection (1) is not admissible in evidence in criminal proceedings against that person other than proceedings for an offence under this section.

(5) A person guilty of an offence under subsection (3) is liable on summary conviction to either or both of the following—

    (a) imprisonment for a term not exceeding 51 weeks (or 6 months if the offence was committed before the commencement of section 281(5) of the Criminal Justice Act 2003), or

    (b) a fine.

(6) The criminal court before which a person is required to provide his or her name, date of birth and nationality may deal with any suspected offence under subsection (3) at the same time as dealing with the offence for which the person was already before the court.

(7) In this section a "criminal court" is, when dealing with any criminal cause or matter—

    (a) the Crown Court;

    (b) a magistrates' court.

III. JURISDICTION IN RESPECT OF ACTS PERFORMED ABROAD AND IN RESPECT OF FOREIGN NATIONALS

D. PARTICULAR OFFENCES

(4) Offences connected with aircraft

Civil Aviation Act 1982, s.92

As well as the amendment shown in the main work, section 1 of the Civil Aviation (Amend- **2-59** ment) Act 1996 also amended section 92 of the 1982 Act, so as (i) to insert a new subsection (1B), as follows—

"(1B) Any act or omission punishable under the law in force in any country is an offence under that law for the purposes of subsection (1A) above, however it is described in that law."

and (ii) to insert a further definition in subsection (5), after the definition of "British-controlled aircraft", as follows—

"'foreign aircraft' means any aircraft other than a British-controlled aircraft;".

V. APPELLATE JURISDICTION OF CROWN COURT IN CRIMINAL CASES

B. RIGHTS OF APPEAL TO CROWN COURT

(10) Appeals relating to investigation anonymity orders

The Criminal Procedure (Amendment) Rules 2017 (S.I. 2017 No. 144) amend Part 47 of the **★2-106** Criminal Procedure Rules 2015 (S.I. 2015 No. 1490) by the insertion of a new rule 47.39. In consequence, rules 47.45 to 47.49 are renumbered as rules 47.46 to 47.50 (see *post*, Appendix B-659 *et seq.*).

CHAPTER 3

BAIL, APPEARANCE OF ACCUSED FOR TRIAL, PRESENCE DURING TRIAL

I. BAIL

A. GENERAL

(2) The Bail Act 1976

(c) *Text of the Act*

Bail Act 1976, ss.3AB, 3AC

Electronic monitoring: general provisions

With effect from October 17, 2016, the Criminal Justice (Electronic Monitoring) (Responsible **3-19**

Person) (No. 2) Order 2016 (S.I. 2016 No. 961) specifies, for the purposes of section 3AC(2) of the 1976 Act, a person who is employed by, or a police officer who is a member of, Hertfordshire police force as a description of a person who may be made responsible for the electronic monitoring of persons on bail.

★   With effect from March 13, 2017, the Criminal Justice (Electronic Monitoring) (Responsible Person) Order 2017 (S.I. 2017 No. 235) specifies, for the purposes of section 3AC(2) of the 1976 Act, a person who is employed by Buddi Ltd (Co. No. 05308826) as a description of person who may be made responsible for the electronic monitoring of persons on bail.

Bail Act 1976, s.7

Offence of breach of pre-charge bail conditions relating to travel

★3-50a   Breach of conditions of bail normally gives rise to liability to arrest (see s.7 of the 1976 Act (§ 3-48 in the main work)), but section 68 of the Policing and Crime Act 2017, which came into force on April 3, 2017 (Policing and Crime Act 2017 (Commencement No. 1 and Transitional Provisions) Regulations 2017 (S.I. 2017 No. 399)), creates an offence of breaching certain travel-related conditions on pre-charge bail for those arrested on suspicion of committing an offence listed in section 41(1) or (2) of the Counter-Terrorism Act 2008. Section 69 is an interpretation provision (containing definitions of "travel document" and "port"). The offence is triable either way, with a maximum penalty on conviction on indictment of 12 months' imprisonment.

(7) Place of remand

(b) *Persons under 21 years*

Legal Aid, Sentencing and Punishment of Offenders Act 2012, ss.91-94, 96-99, 102, 107

Conditions etc on remands to local authority accommodation

3-99   With effect from November 30, 2016, the Remand to Local Authority Accommodation (Electronic Monitoring) (Responsible Person) Order 2016 (S.I. 2016 No. 1080) specifies, for the purposes of section 96(2) of the 2012 Act (§ 3-101 in the main work), a person who is employed by Capita Business Services Ltd as a person who may be made responsible for the monitoring of a person who is subject to an electronic monitoring condition that has been imposed as a condition of remand to local authority accommodation under section 93(2) (see the main work).

Further provisions about electronic monitoring

3-101   As to a person who may be responsible for an electronic monitoring condition for the purposes of section 96(2) of the 2012 Act, see *ante*, § 3-99.

(9) Appeal against grant of bail

Bail (Amendment) Act 1993, s.1

Prosecution right of appeal

3-114   With effect from November 9, 2016, the Secretaries of State for Business, Energy and Industrial Strategy, for International Trade and for Exiting the European Union and the Transfer of Functions (Education and Skills) Order 2016 (S.I. 2016 No. 992) amended the Bail (Amendment) Act 1993 (Prescription of Prosecuting Authorities) Order 1994 (S.I. 1994 No. 1438), so as to substitute a reference to "The Secretary of State for Business, Energy and Industrial Strategy" for the reference to "The Secretary of State for Business, Innovation and Skills".

(11) Rules of procedure

Criminal Procedure Rules 2015 (S.I. 2015 No. 1490), Pt 14

When this Part applies

★3-118   With effect from April 3, 2017, rule 14.1 of the 2015 rules was amended by the Criminal Procedure (Amendment No. 2) Rules 2017 (S.I. 2017 No. 282), so as to renumber paragraph (2) as paragraph (3), and to insert a new paragraph (2), as follows—

    "(2) Rules 14.20, 14.21 and 14.22 apply where a magistrates' court can authorise an extension of the period for which a defendant is released on bail before being charged with an offence.".

Exercise of court's powers: general

With effect from April 3, 2017, rule 14.2 of the 2015 rules was amended by the Criminal   **★3-119**
Procedure (Amendment) Rules 2017 (S.I. 2017 No. 144), r.4(a), so as (i) to insert a new sub-
paragraph (d) in paragraph (1), as follows—

> "(d) the court is satisfied that sufficient time has been allowed—
>> (i) for the defendant to consider the information provided by the prosecutor under rule
>> 14.5(2), and
>> (ii) for the court to consider the parties' representations and make the decision required.";

and (ii) in paragraph (5), to insert, after the words "(with help, if necessary)", the words ", and by
reference to the circumstances of the defendant and the case,".

With effect from the same date, rule 14.2 was further amended by S.I. 2017 No. 282 (*ante*, §   **★**
3-118), so as to substitute a new heading (as above), and to insert a new paragraph (7), as follows—

> "(7) This rule does not apply on an application to a magistrates' court to authorise an extension of
> pre-charge bail.".

General duties of court officer

With effect from April 3, 2017, rule 14.4 of the 2015 rules was amended by S.I. 2017 No. 282   **★3-121**
(*ante*, § 3-118), so as (i) to omit "or" at the end of paragraph (1)(b)(i); (ii) to insert "or" at the end
of paragraph (1)(b)(ii); (iii) to insert a new paragraph (1)(b)(iii), as follows—

> "(iii) on an application to which rule 14.21 applies (application to authorise extension of
> pre-charge bail)";

and (iv) to insert a new paragraph (5), as follows—

> "(5) Where the court determines without a hearing an application to which rule 14.21 applies (ap-
> plication to authorise extension of pre-charge bail), the court officer must—
>> (a) if the court allows the application, notify the applicant;
>> (b) if the court refuses the application, notify the applicant and the defendant.".

Prosecutor's representations about bail

With effect from April 3, 2017, rule 14.5 of the 2015 rules was amended by S.I. 2017 No. 144   **★3-122**
(*ante*, § 3-119), r.4(b), so as to substitute paragraph (2), as follows—

> "(2) The prosecutor must as soon as practicable—
>> (a) provide the defendant with all the information in the prosecutor's possession which is
>> material to what the court must decide; and
>> (b) provide the court with the same information.".

Reconsideration of police bail by magistrates' court

With effect from April 3, 2017, rule 14.6 of the 2015 rules was amended by S.I. 2017 No. 282   **★3-123**
(*ante*, § 3-118) so as to substitute a new paragraph (1), as follows—

> "(1) This rule applies where—
>> (a) a party wants a magistrates' court to reconsider a bail decision by a police officer after the
>> defendant is charged with an offence;
>> (b) a defendant wants a magistrates' court to reconsider a bail condition imposed by a police
>> officer before the defendant is charged with an offence.".

New rules 14.20, 14.21 and 14.22 were inserted into the 2015 rules, with effect from April 3,   **★3-134a**
2017, by S.I. 2017 No. 282 (*ante*, § 3-118). They provide for applications to magistrates' courts
under sections 47ZF and 47ZG of the PACE Act 1984 (as to which, see *post*, §§ 3-170g, 3-170h).

**Criminal Procedure Rules 2015 (S.I. 2015 No. 1490), rr.14.20-14.22 (as inserted by the Criminal
Procedure (Amendment No. 2) Rules 2017 (S.I. 2017 No. 282), r.3(h))**

Extension of Bail Before Charge

Exercise of court's powers: extension of pre-charge bail

14.20.—(1) The court must determine an application to which rule 14.21 (application to authorise
extension of pre-charge bail) applies—

    (a) without a hearing, subject to paragraph (2); and

    (b) as soon as practicable, but as a general rule no sooner than the fifth business day after the application was served.

  (2) The court must determine an application at a hearing where—

    (a) if the application succeeds, its effect will be to extend the period for which the defendant is on bail to less than 12 months from the day after the defendant's arrest for the offence and the court considers that the interests of justice require a hearing;

    (b) if the application succeeds, its effect will be to extend that period to more than 12 months from that day and the applicant or the defendant asks for a hearing;

    (c) it is an application to withhold information from the defendant and the court considers that the interests of justice require a hearing.

  (3) Any hearing must be in private.

  (4) Subject to rule 14.22 (application to withhold information from the defendant), at a hearing the court may determine an application in the absence of—

    (a) the applicant;

    (b) the defendant, if the defendant has had at least 5 business days in which to make representations.

  (5) If the court so directs, a party to an application may attend a hearing by live link or telephone.

  (6) The court must not authorise an extension of the period for which a defendant is on bail before being charged unless—

    (a) the applicant states, in writing or orally, that to the best of the applicant's knowledge and belief—

      (i) the application discloses all the information that is material to what the court must decide, and

      (ii) the content of the application is true; or

    (b) the application includes a statement by an investigator of the suspected offence that to the best of that investigator's knowledge and belief those requirements are met.

  (7) Where the statement required by paragraph (6) is made orally—

    (a) the statement must be on oath or affirmation, unless the court otherwise directs; and

    (b) the court must arrange for a record of the making of the statement.

  (8) The court may shorten or extend (even after it has expired) a time limit imposed by this rule or by rule 14.21 (application to authorise extension of pre-charge bail).

Application to authorise extension of pre-charge bail

★3-134b   **14.21.**—(1) This rule applies where an applicant wants the court to authorise an extension of the period for which a defendant is released on bail before being charged with an offence.

  (2) The applicant must—

    (a) apply in writing before the date on which the defendant's pre-charge bail is due to end;

    (b) demonstrate that the applicant is entitled to apply as a constable, a member of staff of the Financial Conduct Authority, a member of the Serious Fraud Office or a Crown Prosecutor;

    (c) serve the application on—

      (i) the court officer, and

      (ii) the defendant; and

    (d) serve on the defendant, with the application, a form of response notice for the defendant's use.

  (3) The application must specify—

    (a) the offence or offences for which the defendant was arrested;

    (b) the date on which the defendant's pre-charge bail began;

    (c) the date and period of any previous extension of that bail;

    (d) the date on which that bail is due to end;

    (e) the conditions of that bail; and

    (f) if different, the bail conditions which are to be imposed if the court authorises an extension, or further extension, of the period for which the defendant is released on pre-charge bail.

  (4) The application must explain—

    (a) the grounds for believing that, as applicable—

      (i) further investigation is needed of any matter in connection with the offence or offences for which the defendant was released on bail, or

      (ii) further time is needed for making a decision as to whether to charge the defendant with that offence or those offences;

(b) the grounds for believing that, as applicable—
  (i) the investigation into the offence or offences for which the defendant was released on bail is being conducted diligently and expeditiously, or
  (ii) the decision as to whether to charge the defendant with that offence or those offences is being made diligently and expeditiously; and
(c) the grounds for believing that the defendant's further release on bail is necessary and proportionate in all the circumstances having regard, in particular, to any conditions of bail imposed.
(5) The application must—
  (a) indicate whether the applicant wants the court to authorise an extension of the defendant's bail for 3 months or for 6 months; and
  (b) if for 6 months, explain why the investigation is unlikely to be completed or the charging decision made, as the case may be, within 3 months.
(6) The application must explain why it was not made earlier where—
  (a) the application is made before the date on which the defendant's bail is due to end; but
  (b) it is not likely to be practicable for the court to determine the application before that date.
(7) A defendant who objects to the application must—
  (a) serve notice on—
    (i) the court officer, and
    (ii) the applicant,
  not more than 5 business days after service of the application; and
  (b) in the notice explain the grounds of the objection.

Application to withhold information from the defendant
14.22.—(1) This rule applies where an application to authorise an extension of pre-charge bail   ★**3-134c** includes an application to withhold information from the defendant.
(2) The applicant must—
  (a) omit that information from the part of the application that is served on the defendant;
  (b) mark the other part to show that, unless the court otherwise directs, it is only for the court; and
  (c) in that other part, explain the grounds for believing that the disclosure of that information would have one or more of the following results—
    (i) evidence connected with an indictable offence would be interfered with or harmed,
    (ii) a person would be interfered with or physically injured,
    (iii) a person suspected of having committed an indictable offence but not yet arrested for the offence would be alerted, or
    (iv) the recovery of property obtained as a result of an indictable offence would be hindered.
(3) At any hearing of an application to which this rule applies—
  (a) the court must first determine the application to withhold information, in the defendant's absence and that of any legal representative of the defendant;
  (b) if the court allows the application to withhold information, then in the following sequence—
    (i) the court must consider representations first by the applicant and then by the defendant, in the presence of both, and
    (ii) the court may consider further representations by the applicant in the defendant's absence and that of any legal representative of the defendant, if satisfied that there are reasonable grounds for believing that information withheld from the defendant would be disclosed during those further representations.
(4) If the court refuses an application to withhold information from the defendant, the applicant may withdraw the application to authorise an extension of pre-charge bail.

B. SPECIFIC PROVISIONS

(1) The Police

(a) *Police and Criminal Evidence Act 1984*

Police and Criminal Evidence Act 1984, s.34

Limitations on police detention
With effect from April 3, 2017 (Policing and Crime Act 2017 (Commencement No. 1 and   ★**3-136**

9

Transitional Provisions) Regulations 2017 (S.I. 2017 No. 399)), section 34 of the 1984 Act was amended by the Policing and Crime Act 2017, s.54(1) to (3), so as (i) in subsection (5), to omit the words from "without" to "the custody officer", and to substitute new paragraphs (a) and (b), as follows—

> "(a) without bail unless subsection (5A) applies, or
> (b) on bail if subsection (5A) applies";

and (ii) to insert a new subsection (5A), as follows—

> "(5A) This subsection applies if—
> (a) it appears to the custody officer—
> (i) that there is need for further investigation of any matter in connection with which the person was detained at any time during the period of the person's detention, or
> (ii) that, in respect of any such matter, proceedings may be taken against the person or the person may be given a youth caution under section 66ZA of the Crime and Disorder Act 1998, and
> (b) the pre-conditions for bail are satisfied.".

Article 5 of S.I. 2017 No. 399 provides that sections 52 to 58, 60 and 62 to 65 of the 2017 Act do not apply in relation to a person in respect of an offence if the person was first arrested for the offence before April 3, 2017, or given a conditional caution in respect of the offence before that date.

★ With effect from April 3, 2017 (S.I. 2017 No. 399 (*ante*)), section 34 of the 1984 Act was further amended by the Policing and Crime Act 2017, s.66(1) and (2), so as to insert new subsections (5B) to (5E), as follows—

> "(5B) Subsection (5C) applies where—
> (a) a person is released under subsection (5), and
> (b) the custody officer determines that—
> (i) there is not sufficient evidence to charge the person with an offence, or
> (ii) there is sufficient evidence to charge the person with an offence but the person should not be charged with an offence or given a caution in respect of an offence.
> (5C) The custody officer must give the person notice in writing that the person is not to be prosecuted.
> (5D) Subsection (5C) does not prevent the prosecution of the person for an offence if new evidence comes to light after the notice was given.
> (5E) In this Part 'caution' includes—
> (a) a conditional caution within the meaning of Part 3 of the Criminal Justice Act 2003;
> (b) a youth conditional caution within the meaning of Chapter 1 of Part 4 of the Crime and Disorder Act 1998;
> (c) a youth caution under section 66ZA of that Act.".

★3-137 With effect from April 3, 2017 (Policing and Crime Act 2017 (Commencement No. 1 and Transitional Provisions) Regulations 2017 (S.I. 2017 No. 399)), section 24B(2) (see the main work) of the CJA 2003 was amended by the Policing and Crime Act 2017, s.66(10). The text of the main work should now read "section 34(1) to (5E)".

Police and Criminal Evidence Act 1984, s.37

Duties of custody officer before charge

★3-141 With effect from April 3, 2017 (Policing and Crime Act 2017 (Commencement No. 1 and Transitional Provisions) Regulations 2017 (S.I. 2017 No. 399)), section 37 of the 1984 Act was amended by the Policing and Crime Act 2017, s.54(4) to (8), so as (i) in subsection (2), to substitute, for the words from "released either" to the end, the words—

> "released—
> (a) without bail unless the pre-conditions for bail are satisfied, or
> (b) on bail if those pre-conditions are satisfied,
> (subject to subsection (3))";

(ii) in subsection (3), to substitute, for the words "so believing", the words "believing that the person's detention without being charged is necessary to secure or preserve evidence relating to an offence for which the person is under arrest or to obtain such evidence by questioning the person"; (iii) in subsection (7), to substitute new paragraphs (b) and (c), as follows—

"(b) shall be released without charge and without bail unless the pre-conditions for bail are satisfied,

(c) shall be released without charge and on bail if those pre-conditions are satisfied but not for the purpose mentioned in paragraph (a), or";

and (iv), in subsection (8A)(b), to substitute, for "(b)", "(c)". For related transitional provision, see *ante*, § 3-136.

With effect from April 3, 2017 (S.I. 2017 No. 399 (*ante*)), section 37 of the 1984 Act was ★ further amended by the Policing and Crime Act 2017, s.66(1) and (3) to (5), so as (i) to insert new subsections (6A) to (6C), as follows—

"(6A) Subsection (6B) applies where—
(a) a person is released under subsection (2), and
(b) the custody officer determines that—
(i) there is not sufficient evidence to charge the person with an offence, or
(ii) there is sufficient evidence to charge the person with an offence but the person should not be charged with an offence or given a caution in respect of an offence.
(6B) The custody officer must give the person notice in writing that the person is not to be prosecuted.
(6C) Subsection (6B) does not prevent the prosecution of the person for an offence if new evidence comes to light after the notice was given.";

and (ii) to insert a new subsection (8ZA) after subsection (8), as follows—

"(8ZA) Where—
(a) a person is released under subsection (7)(b) or (c), and
(b) the custody officer makes a determination as mentioned in subsection (6A)(b),
subsections (6B) and (6C) apply.".

With effect from April 3, 2017 (Policing and Crime Act 2017 (Commencement No. 1 and ★**3-142** Transitional Provisions) Regulations 2017 (S.I. 2017 No. 399)), section 24B(2) of the CJA 2003 (see the main work) was amended by the Policing and Crime Act 2017, s.66(10). The effect is that the second line of the main work should now read "section 37(4) to (6C)".

Police and Criminal Evidence Act 1984, ss.37A–37D

Consultation with the Director of Public Prosecutions

With effect from April 3, 2017 (Policing and Crime Act 2017 (Commencement No. 1 and ★**3-145** Transitional Provisions) Regulations 2017 (S.I. 2017 No. 399)), section 37B of the 1984 Act was amended by the Policing and Crime Act 2017, s.66(1) and (6) to (8), so as (i) to insert a new subsection (5A), as follows—

"(5A) Subsection (5) does not prevent the prosecution of the person for an offence if new evidence comes to light after the notice was given.";

and (ii) to omit subsection (9).

R. v. Walker (Triston) is now reported at 2 Cr.App.R. 24.

Breach of bail following release under section 37(7)(b)

With effect from April 3, 2017 (Policing and Crime Act 2017 (Commencement No. 1 and ★**3-147** Transitional Provisions) Regulations 2017 (S.I. 2017 No. 399)), section 37CA of the 1984 Act was amended by the Policing and Crime Act 2017, s.55(1) to (4), so as (i) in the heading and subsection (1), for "section 37(7)(b)", to substitute "section 37(7)(c)"; (ii) in subsection (2)(b), for the words from "charge, either" to the end, to substitute the words—

"charge,—
(i) without bail unless the pre-conditions for bail are satisfied, or
(ii) on bail if those pre-conditions are satisfied.";

For related transitional provision, see *ante*, § 3-136.

With effect from April 3, 2017 (Policing and Crime Act 2017 (Commencement No. 1 and ★ Transitional Provisions) Regulations 2017 (S.I. 2017 No. 399)), section 37CA of the 1984 Act was further amended by the Policing and Crime Act 2017, s.66(1) and (9), so as to insert new subsections (5) to (7), as follows—

"(5) Subsection (6) applies where–

  (a) a person is released under subsection (2), and

  (b) a custody officer determines that–

      (i) there is not sufficient evidence to charge the person with an offence, or

      (ii) there is sufficient evidence to charge the person with an offence but the person should not be charged with an offence or given a caution in respect of an offence.

(6) The custody officer must give the person notice in writing that the person is not to be prosecuted.

(7) Subsection (6) does not prevent the prosecution of the person for an offence if new evidence comes to light after the notice was given.".

Release on bail under section 37: further provision

★3-148   With effect from April 3, 2017 (Policing and Crime Act 2017 (Commencement No. 1 and Transitional Provisions) Regulations 2017 (S.I. 2017 No. 399)), section 37D of the 1984 Act was amended by the Policing and Crime Act 2017, ss.55(5) and 64(1) to (4), so as (i) in subsection (4A), to substitute, for "section 37(7)(b)", "section 37(7)(c)" (s.55(5)); (ii) to omit subsections (1) to (3) (s.64(1)-(3)); and (iii) in subsections (4), (4A) and (5), to substitute, for "subsection (1) above", "section 47(4A)" (s.64(1), (2) and (4)). For related transitional provision, see *ante*, § 3-136.

★   With effect from the same date, section 24B(5) of the CJA 2003 (see the main work) was amended by the 2017 Act, s.64(8)(b). In consequence, the final four lines of this paragraph in the main work should now be deleted. For related transitional provision, see *ante*, § 3-136.

Police and Criminal Evidence Act 1984, s.39

Responsibilities in relation to persons detained

★3-151   With effect from April 3, 2017 (Policing and Crime Act 2017 (Commencement No. 1 and Transitional Provisions) Regulations 2017 (S.I. 2017 No. 399)), section 39 of the 1984 Act was amended by the Policing and Crime Act 2017, s.75, so as (i) in subsection (2)(a), for the words "a police officer investigating an offence for which that person is in police detention", to substitute the words "another police officer at the police station where the person is in police detention, for the purpose of an interview that is part of the investigation of an offence for which the person is in police detention or otherwise in connection with the investigation of such an offence"; and (ii) to insert new subsections (3A) to (3E), as follows–

"(3A) Subsections (3B) and (3C) apply if the custody officer, in accordance with any code of practice issued under this Act, transfers or permits the transfer of a person in police detention to an officer mentioned in subsection (2)(a) for the purpose of an interview that is to be conducted to any extent by means of a live link by another police officer who is investigating the offence but is not at the police station where the person in police detention is held at the time of the interview.

(3B) The officer who is not at the police station has the same duty as the officer mentioned in subsection (2)(a) to ensure that the person is treated in accordance with the provisions of this Act and of any such codes of practice as are mentioned in subsection (1).

(3C) If the person detained is subsequently returned to the custody of the custody officer, the officer who is not at the police station also has the same duty under subsection (3) as the officer mentioned in subsection (2)(a).

(3D) For the purpose of subsection (3C), subsection (3) applies as if the reference to 'in his custody' were a reference to 'being interviewed' .

(3E) In subsection (3A), 'live link' means an arrangement by which the officer who is not at the police station is able to see and hear, and to be seen and heard by, the person in police detention, any legal representative of that person and the officer who has custody of that person at the police station (and for this purpose any impairment of eyesight or hearing is to be disregarded).".

Police and Criminal Evidence Act 1984, s.40A

Use of telephone for review under s.40

★3-155   With effect from April 3, 2017 (Policing and Crime Act 2017 (Commencement No. 1 and Transitional Provisions) Regulations 2017 (S.I. 2017 No. 399)), section 40A of the 1984 Act is amended by the Policing and Crime Act 2017, s.74(1) and (5), so as, in subsection (2)(a), for "video-conferencing facilities", to substitute the words "a live link", and, in subsection (5), for "video-conferencing facilities", to substitute the words "live link".

Police and Criminal Evidence Act 1984, s.41

Limits on period of detention without charge

With effect from April 3, 2017 (Policing and Crime Act 2017 (Commencement No. 1 and ★**3-156** Transitional Provisions) Regulations 2017 (S.I. 2017 No. 399)), section 41(7) of the 1984 Act was amended by the Policing and Crime Act 2017, s.56(1), so as to substitute, for the words from "time either" to the end, the words—

"time—
> (a) without bail unless the pre-conditions for bail are satisfied, or
> (b) on bail if those pre-conditions are satisfied".

For related transitional provision, see *ante*, § 3-136.

With effect from April 3, 2017 (Policing and Crime Act 2017 (Commencement No. 1 and ★ Transitional Provisions) Regulations 2017 (S.I. 2017 No. 399)), section 41(9) of the 1984 Act was amended by the Policing and Crime Act 2017, s. 65(1) and (3), so as to substitute, for the words from "new" to "since", the words ", since the person's release, new evidence has come to light or an examination or analysis of existing evidence has been made which could not reasonably have been made before". For related transitional provision, see *ante*, § 3-136.

With effect from April 3, 2017 (Policing and Crime Act 2017 (Commencement No. 1 and ★ Transitional Provisions) Regulations 2017 (S.I. 2017 No. 399)), section 41 of the 1984 Act was further amended by the Policing and Crime Act 2017, s.67(1) and (2), so as to insert new subsections (10) to (12), as follows—

"(10) Subsection (11) applies where—
> (a) a person is released under subsection (7), and
> (b) a custody officer determines that—
>> (i) there is not sufficient evidence to charge the person with an offence, or
>> (ii) there is sufficient evidence to charge the person with an offence but the person should not be charged with an offence or given a caution in respect of an offence.

(11) The custody officer must give the person notice in writing that the person is not to be prosecuted.

(12) Subsection (11) does not prevent the prosecution of the person for an offence if new evidence comes to light after the notice was given.".

Police and Criminal Evidence Act 1984, s.42

Authorisation of continued detention

With effect from April 3, 2017 (Policing and Crime Act 2017 (Commencement No. 1 and ★**3-157** Transitional Provisions) Regulations 2017 (S.I. 2017 No. 399)), section 42 of the 1984 Act was amended by the Policing and Crime Act 2017, s.56(2) to (4), so as (i) in subsection (10), to omit the words ", either on bail or without bail"; (ii) in subsection (10), for the words from "time, unless" to the end, to substitute the words—

"time—
> (a) without bail unless the pre-conditions for bail are satisfied, or
> (b) on bail if those pre-conditions are satisfied,
(subject to subsection (10A))";

and (iii) to insert a new subsection (10A), as follows—

"(10A) Subsection (10) does not apply if—
> (a) the person has been charged with an offence, or
> (b) the person's continued detention is authorised or otherwise permitted in accordance with section 43.".

For related transitional provision, see *ante*, § 3-136.

With effect from April 3, 2017 (S.I. 2017 No. 399 (*ante*)), section 42 of the 1984 Act was ★ further amended by the Policing and Crime Act 2017, s.65(1) and (4), so as, in subsection (11), to substitute, for the words from "new" to "since", the words ", since the person's release, new evidence has come to light or an examination or analysis of existing evidence has been made which could not reasonably have been made before". For related transitional provision, see *ante*, § 3-136.

★   With effect from April 3, 2017 (S.I. 2017 No. 399 (*ante*)), section 42 of the 1984 Act was further amended by the Policing and Crime Act 2017, s.67(1) and (3), so as to insert new subsections (12) to (14), as follows—

"(12) Subsection (13) applies where—
    (a) a person is released under subsection (10) , and
    (b) a custody officer determines that—
        (i) there is not sufficient evidence to charge the person with an offence, or
        (ii) there is sufficient evidence to charge the person with an offence but the person should not be charged with an offence or given a caution in respect of an offence.
(13) The custody officer must give the person notice in writing that the person is not to be prosecuted.
(14) Subsection (13) does not prevent the prosecution of the person for an offence if new evidence comes to light after the notice was given.".

For related transitional provision, see *ante*, § 3-136.

As to the modification of section 42 where the functions of a police officer under that section are performed by an officer who is not at the police station where the arrested person is held, see section 45ZA of the 1984 Act (*post*, § 3-162a).

Police and Criminal Evidence Act 1984, s.43

Warrants of further detention

★3-159   With effect from April 3, 2017 (Policing and Crime Act 2017 (Commencement No. 1 and Transitional Provisions) Regulations 2017 (S.I. 2017 No. 399)), section 43 of the 1984 Act was amended by the Policing and Crime Act 2017, s.57(1) to (3), so as (i) in subsection (15), to substitute, for the words "released, either on bail or without bail", the words—

"released—
    (a) without bail unless the pre-conditions for bail are satisfied, or
    (b) on bail if those pre-conditions are satisfied";

and (ii) in subsection (18), to substitute, for the words from "be released" to the end, the words—

", unless the person is charged, be released from police detention upon or before the expiry of the warrant—
    (a) without bail unless the pre-conditions for bail are satisfied, or
    (b) on bail if those pre-conditions are satisfied".

For related transitional provision, see *ante*, § 3-136.

★   With effect from April 3, 2017 (S.I. 2017 No. 399 (*ante*)), section 43(19) of the 1984 Act was amended by the Policing and Crime Act 2017, s.65(1) and (5), so as to substitute, for the words from "new" to "since", the words ", since the person's release, new evidence has come to light or an examination or analysis of existing evidence has been made which could not reasonably have been made before". For related transitional provision, see *ante*, § 3-136.

★   With effect from April 3, 2017 (S.I. 2017 No. 399 (*ante*)), section 43 of the 1984 Act was further amended by the Policing and Crime Act 2017, s.67(1) and (4), so as to insert new subsections (20) to (22), as follows—

"(20) Subsection (21) applies where—
    (a) a person is released under subsection (15) or (18) , and
    (b) a custody officer determines that—
        (i) there is not sufficient evidence to charge the person with an offence, or
        (ii) there is sufficient evidence to charge the person with an offence but the person should not be charged with an offence or given a caution in respect of an offence.
(21) The custody officer must give the person notice in writing that the person is not to be prosecuted.
(22) Subsection (21) does not prevent the prosecution of the person for an offence if new evidence comes to light after the notice was given.".

For related transitional provision, see *ante*, § 3-136.

As to the disapplication of section 43(2)(b) where a live link direction is given, see section 45ZB of the 1984 Act (*post*, § 3-162b).

Police and Criminal Evidence Act 1984, s.44

Extension of warrants of further detention

With effect from April 3, 2017 (Policing and Crime Act 2017 (Commencement No. 1 and **★3-161** Transitional Provisions) Regulations 2017 (S.I. 2017 No. 399)), section 44 of the 1984 Act was amended by the Policing and Crime Act 2017, s.57(4). The amendment mirrors that made to section 43(15) by section 57 of the 2017 Act (as to which, see *ante*, § 3-159). For related transitional provision, see *ante*, § 3-136.

With effect from April 3, 2017 (S.I. 2017 No. 399 (*ante*)), section 44 of the 1984 Act was **★** amended by the Policing and Crime Act 2017, s.67(1) and (5), so as to insert new subsections (9) to (11), as follows—

"(9) Subsection (10) applies where—
    (a) a person is released under subsection (7), and
    (b) a custody officer determines that—
      (i) there is not sufficient evidence to charge the person with an offence, or
      (ii) there is sufficient evidence to charge the person with an offence but the person should
        not be charged with an offence or given a caution in respect of an offence.
(10) The custody officer must give the person notice in writing that the person is not to be prosecuted.
(11) Subsection (10) does not prevent the prosecution of the person for an offence if new evidence comes to light after the notice was given.".

For related transitional provision, see *ante*, § 3-136.

Police and Criminal Evidence Act 1984, s.45

Detention before charge–supplementary

With effect from April 3, 2017 (Policing and Crime Act 2017 (Commencement No. 1 and **★3-162** Transitional Provisions) Regulations 2017 (S.I. 2017 No. 399)), section 45(1) of the 1984 Act is amended by the Policing and Crime Act 2017, s.74(1) and (3), so as to substitute for the words "sections 43 and 44", the words "sections 43, 44 and 45ZB".

Use of live links

With effect from April 3, 2017 (Policing and Crime Act 2017 (Commencement No. 1 and **★3-162a** Transitional Provisions) Regulations 2017 (S.I. 2017 No. 399)), new sections 45ZA (functions of extending detention: use of live links) and 45ZB (warrants of further detention: use of live links) were inserted into the 1984 Act after section 45 by the Policing and Crime Act 2017, s.74(1) and (2). Section 45ZA modifies section 42 (§ 3-157 in the main work) to provide for the use of live link technology in connection with the extension of pre-charge detention when the authorising officer is in a different location to the suspect. Section 45ZB provides that a magistrates' court may give a live link direction for the purpose of the hearing of an application under section 43 (*ibid.*, § 3-159) for a warrant authorising further detention of a person, or the hearing of an application under section 44 (*ibid.*, § 3-161) for an extension of such a warrant, if the same safeguards as those in section 45ZA apply and it is not contrary to the interests of justice to direct that live link is used.

Police and Criminal Evidence Act 1984, ss.45ZA, 45ZB

Use of live links

Functions of extending detention: use of live links

45ZA.—(1) The functions of a police officer under section 42(1) or (2) may be performed, in relation to an arrested person who is held at a police station, by an officer who is not present at the police station but has access to the use of a live link if—
    (a) a custody officer considers that the use of the live link is appropriate,
    (b) the arrested person has had advice from a solicitor on the use of the live link, and
    (c) the appropriate consent to the use of the live link has been given.
(2) In subsection (1)(c), "the appropriate consent" means—
    (a) in relation to a person who has attained the age of 18, the consent of that person;
    (b) in relation to a person who has not attained that age but has attained the age of 14, the
      consent of that person and of his or her parent or guardian;

(c) in relation to a person who has not attained the age of 14, the consent of his or her parent or guardian.

(3) The consent of a person who has not attained the age of 18 (but has attained the age of 14), or who is a vulnerable adult, may only be given in the presence of an appropriate adult.

(4) Section 42 applies with the modifications set out in subsections (5) to (7) below in any case where the functions of a police officer under that section are, by virtue of subsection (1), performed by an officer who is not at the police station where the arrested person is held.

(5) Subsections (5)(b) and (9)(iii) and (iv) of that section are each to be read as if, instead of requiring the officer to make a record, they required the officer to cause another police officer to make a record.

(6) Subsection (6) of that section is to be read as if it required the officer to give the persons mentioned in that subsection an opportunity to make representations—

    (a) if facilities exist for the immediate transmission of written representations to the officer, either in writing by means of those facilities or orally by means of the live link, or

    (b) in any other case, orally by means of the live link.

(7) Subsection (9) of that section is to be read as if the reference in paragraph (b) to the right conferred by section 58 were omitted.

(8) In this section—

    "live link" means an arrangement by which an officer who is not present at the police station where an arrested person is held is able to see and hear, and to be seen and heard by, the arrested person and the arrested person's solicitor (and for this purpose any impairment of eyesight or hearing is to be disregarded);

    "vulnerable adult" means a person aged 18 or over who may have difficulty understanding the purpose of an authorisation under section 42(1) or (2) or anything that occurs in connection with a decision whether to give such an authorisation (whether because of a mental disorder or for any other reason);

    "appropriate adult", in relation to a person who has not attained the age of 18, means—

       (a) the person's parent or guardian or, if the person is in the care of a local authority or voluntary organisation, a person representing that authority or organisation,

       (b) a social worker of a local authority, or

       (c) if no person falling within paragraph (a) or (b) is available, any responsible person aged 18 or over who is not a police officer or a person employed for, or engaged on, police purposes;

    "appropriate adult", in relation to a vulnerable adult, means—

       (a) a relative, guardian or other person responsible for the vulnerable adult's care,

       (b) a person who is experienced in dealing with vulnerable adults but who is not a police officer or a person employed for, or engaged on, police purposes, or

       (c) if no person falling within paragraph (a) or (b) is available, any responsible person aged 18 or over who is not a police officer or a person employed for, or engaged on, police purposes.

(9) In subsection (8), in both definitions of "appropriate adult", "police purposes" has the meaning given by section 101(2) of the Police Act 1996.

Warrants for further detention: use of live links

★**3-162b**   **45ZB.**—(1) A magistrates' court may give a live link direction for the purpose of the hearing of an application under section 43 for a warrant authorising further detention of a person, or the hearing of an application under section 44 for an extension of such a warrant, if—

    (a) a custody officer considers that the use of a live link for that purpose is appropriate,

    (b) the person to whom the application relates has had legal advice on the use of the live link,

    (c) the appropriate consent to the use of the live link has been given, and

    (d) it is not contrary to the interests of justice to give the direction.

(2) In subsection (1)(c), "the appropriate consent" means—

    (a) in relation to a person who has attained the age of 18, the consent of that person;

    (b) in relation to a person who has not attained that age but has attained the age of 14, the consent of that person and of his or her parent or guardian;

    (c) in relation to a person who has not attained the age of 14, the consent of his or her parent or guardian.

(3) Where a live link direction is given, the requirement under section 43(2)(b) for the person to whom the application relates to be brought before the court for the hearing does not apply.

(4) In this section—

"live link direction" means a direction that a live link be used for the purposes of the hearing;

"live link" means an arrangement by which a person (when not in the place where the hearing is being held) is able to see and hear, and to be seen and heard by, the court during a hearing (and for this purpose any impairment of eyesight or hearing is to be disregarded);

"vulnerable adult" means a person aged 18 or over who may have difficulty understanding the purpose of the hearing or what occurs at it (whether because of a mental disorder or for any other reason);

"appropriate adult", in relation to a person aged under 18, means—

> (a) the person's parent or guardian or, if the person is in the care of a local authority or voluntary organisation, a person representing that authority or organisation,
>
> (b) a social worker of a local authority, or
>
> (c) if no person falling within paragraph (a) or (b) is available, any responsible person aged 18 or over who is not a police officer or a person employed for, or engaged on, police purposes;

"appropriate adult", in relation to a vulnerable adult, means—

> (a) a relative, guardian or other person responsible for the appropriate [*sic*] adult's care,
>
> (b) a person who is experienced in dealing with vulnerable adults but who is not a police officer or a person employed for, or engaged on, police purposes, or
>
> (c) if no person falling within paragraph (a) or (b) is available, any responsible person aged 18 or over who is not a police officer or a person employed for, or engaged on, police purposes.

(5) In subsection (4), in both definitions of "appropriate adult", "police purposes" has the meaning given by section 101(2) of the Police Act 1996.

Police and Criminal Evidence Act 1984, s.45A

Use of video-conferencing facilities for decisions about detention

With effect from April 3, 2017 (Policing and Crime Act 2017 (Commencement No. 1 and Transitional Provisions) Regulations 2017 (S.I. 2017 No. 399)), section 45A of the 1984 Act was amended by the Policing and Crime Act 2017, s.74(1) and (4), so as, for the heading, to substitute "Use of live links for other decisions about detention"; (ii) in subsection (1)(b), for the words from "video-conferencing facilities" to the end, to substitute the words "a live link"; (iii) in subsection (3), for the words "the facilities mentioned in subsection (1) above", to substitute the words "a live link"; (iv) in subsection (7), in each of paragraphs (a)(i) and (b), for the words "the video-conferencing facilities", to substitute the words "the live link"; and (v) to substitute a new subsection (10), as follows— ★3-163

> "(10) In this section, 'live link', in relation to any functions, means an arrangement by which the functions may be performed by an officer who is not present at the police station where an arrested person is held but who is able (for the purpose of the functions) to see and hear, and to be seen and heard by, the arrested person and any legal representative of that person (and for this purpose any impairment of eyesight or hearing is to be disregarded).".

Police and Criminal Evidence Act 1984, s.46A

Power of arrest for failure to answer police bail

With effect from April 3, 2017 (Policing and Crime Act 2017 (Commencement No. 1 and Transitional Provisions) Regulations 2017 (S.I. 2017 No. 399)), section 46A(1A) of the 1984 Act was amended by the Policing and Crime Act 2017, s.61(1) and (2), so as to substitute, for the words "section 37, 37C(2)(b) or 37CA(2)(b) above", the words "this Part". ★3-167

Police and Criminal Evidence Act 1984, s.47

Bail after arrest

With effect from April 3, 2017 (Policing and Crime Act 2017 (Commencement No. 1 and Transitional Provisions) Regulations 2017 (S.I. 2017 No. 399)), section 47 of the 1984 Act was amended by the Policing and Crime Act 2017, s.61(1) and (3) to (5), so as (i) in subsection (1A), for the words from "section 37" to "cases", to substitute the words "this Part (except sections 37C(2)(b) and 37CA(2)(b))"; and (ii) in subsections (1B) and (1C), to omit "37,". ★3-169

With effect from April 3, 2017 (S.I. 2017 No. 399) (*ante*)), section 47 of the 1984 Act was ★

further amended by the Policing and Crime Act 2017, s.65(1) and (6), so as, in subsection (2), for the words from "new" to the end, to substitute ", since the person's release, new evidence has come to light or an examination or analysis of existing evidence has been made which could not reasonably have been made before the person's release". For related transitional provision, see *ante*, § 3-136.

★ With effect from April 3, 2017 (S.I. 2017 No. 399) (*ante*)), section 47 of the 1984 Act was further amended by the Policing and Crime Act 2017, s.64(1) and (5) to (7), so as (i) in subsection (3)(c), to insert, at the end, the words "(subject to section 47ZA)"; and (ii) to insert new subsections (4A) to (4E), as follows—

"(4A) Where a person has been granted bail under this Part subject to a duty to attend at a police station, a custody officer may subsequently appoint a different time, or an additional time, at which the person is to attend at the police station to answer bail.

(4B) The custody officer must give the person notice in writing of the exercise of the power under subsection (4A).

(4C) The exercise of the power under subsection (4A) does not affect the conditions of bail (if any).

(4D) A custody officer may not appoint a time for a person's attendance under subsection (4A) which is after the end of the applicable bail period in relation to the person.

(4E) Subsection (4D) is subject to section 47ZL.".

For related transitional provision, see *ante*, § 3-136.

★3-170 With effect from April 3, 2017 (Policing and Crime Act 2017 (Commencement No. 1 and Transitional Provisions) Regulations 2017 (S.I. 2017 No. 399)), section 24B(5) of the CJA 2003 was amended by the Policing and Crime Act 2017, s.64(8)(b). In consequence, "section 47 applies" in the first line in the main work should now read "section 47 (except subss. (4D) and (4E)) applies". For related transitional provision, see *ante*, § 3-136.

Limits on period of bail without charge under Part IV of the Police and Criminal Evidence Act 1984

★3-170a With effect from April 3, 2017 (Policing and Crime Act 2017 (Commencement No. 1 and Transitional Provisions) Regulations 2017 (S.I. 2017 No. 399)), new sections 47ZA to 47ZM were inserted into the 1984 Act after section 47 by the Policing and Crime Act 2017, s.63, which set time limits on pre-charge bail and provide for extensions. For related transitional provision, see *ante*, § 3-136.

Police and Criminal Evidence Act 1984, ss.47ZA-47ZM

Limits on period of bail without charge

★3-170b 47ZA.—(1) This section applies in relation to the power conferred on a custody officer, when releasing a person on bail under this Part, to appoint a time for the person to attend at a police station in accordance with section 47(3)(c).

(2) The power must be exercised so as to appoint a time on the day on which the applicable bail period in relation to the person ends, unless subsection (3) or (4) applies.

(3) This subsection applies where—

(a) at the time of the exercise of the power the person is on bail under this Part in relation to one or more offences other than the relevant offence, and

(b) the custody officer believes that it is appropriate to align the person's attendance in relation to the relevant offence with the person's attendance in relation to the one or more other offences.

(4) This subsection applies where the custody officer believes that a decision as to whether to charge the person with the relevant offence would be made before the end of the applicable bail period in relation to the person.

(5) Where subsection (3) or (4) applies, the power may be exercised so as to appoint a time on a day falling before the end of the applicable bail period in relation to the person.

(6) This section is subject to section 47ZL.

(7) In this section references to attendance are to attendance at a police station in accordance with section 47(3)(c).

(8) In this Part the "relevant offence", in relation to a person, means the offence in respect of which the power mentioned in subsection (1) is exercised in relation to the person.

Applicable bail period: initial limit

★3-170c 47ZB.—(1) In this Part the "applicable bail period", in relation to a person, means—

(a) in an SFO case, the period of 3 months beginning with the person's bail start date, or

(b) in an FCA case or any other case, the period of 28 days beginning with the person's bail start date.

(2) The applicable bail period in relation to a person may be extended under sections 47ZD to 47ZG or treated as extended under section 47ZJ(3).

(3) Subsection (1) and sections 47ZD to 47ZG are subject to sections 47ZL and 47ZM.

(4) For the purposes of this Part—

(a) a person's bail start date is the day after the day on which the person was arrested for the relevant offence,

(b) an "FCA case" is a case in which—

(i) the relevant offence in relation to the person is being investigated by the Financial Conduct Authority, and

(ii) a senior officer confirms that sub-paragraph (i) applies,

(c) an "SFO case" is a case in which—

(i) the relevant offence in relation to the person is being investigated by the Director of the Serious Fraud Office, and

(ii) a senior officer confirms that sub-paragraph (i) applies, and

(d) "senior officer" means a police officer of the rank of superintendent or above.

Applicable bail period: conditions A to D in sections 47ZD to 47ZG

47ZC.—(1) This section applies for the purposes of sections 47ZD to 47ZG. ★**3-170d**

(2) Condition A is that the decision-maker has reasonable grounds for suspecting the person in question to be guilty of the relevant offence.

(3) Condition B is that the decision-maker has reasonable grounds for believing—

(a) in a case where the person in question is or is to be released on bail under section 37(7)(c) or 37CA(2)(b), that further time is needed for making a decision as to whether to charge the person with the relevant offence, or

(b) otherwise, that further investigation is needed of any matter in connection with the relevant offence.

(4) Condition C is that the decision-maker has reasonable grounds for believing—

(a) in a case where the person in question is or is to be released on bail under section 37(7)(c) or 37CA(2)(b), that the decision as to whether to charge the person with the relevant offence is being made diligently and expeditiously, or

(b) otherwise, that the investigation is being conducted diligently and expeditiously.

(5) Condition D is that the decision-maker has reasonable grounds for believing that the release on bail of the person in question is necessary and proportionate in all the circumstances (having regard, in particular, to any conditions of bail which are, or are to be, imposed).

(6) In this section "decision-maker" means—

(a) in relation to a condition which falls to be considered by virtue of section 47ZD, the senior officer in question;

(b) in relation to a condition which falls to be considered by virtue of section 47ZE, the appropriate decision-maker in question;

(c) in relation to a condition which falls to be considered by virtue of section 47ZF or 47ZG, the court in question.

Applicable bail period: extension of initial limit in standard cases

47ZD.—(1) This section applies in relation to a person if— ★**3-170e**

(a) the applicable bail period in relation to the person is the period mentioned in section 47ZB(1)(b),

(b) that period has not ended, and

(c) a senior officer is satisfied that conditions A to D are met in relation to the person.

(2) The senior officer may authorise the applicable bail period in relation to the person to be extended so that it ends at the end of the period of 3 months beginning with the person's bail start date.

(3) Before determining whether to give an authorisation under subsection (2) in relation to a person, the senior officer must arrange for the person or the person's legal representative to be informed that a determination is to be made.

(4) In determining whether to give an authorisation under subsection (2) in relation to a person, the senior officer must consider any representations made by the person or the person's legal representative.

(5) The senior officer must arrange for the person or the person's legal representative to be informed whether an authorisation under subsection (2) has been given in relation to the person.

Applicable bail period: extension of limit in designated cases

★**3-170f**   **47ZE.**–(1) This section applies in relation to a person if—

(a) the person's case is an SFO case, or

(b) a senior officer has authorised an extension of the applicable bail period in relation to the person under section 47ZD.

(2) A qualifying prosecutor may designate the person's case as being an exceptionally complex case (a "designated case").

(3) If an appropriate decision-maker is satisfied that conditions A to D are met in relation to the person in a designated case, the decision-maker may authorise the applicable bail period in relation to the person to be extended so that it ends at the end of the period of 6 months beginning with the person's bail start date.

(4) An appropriate decision-maker is—

(a) a member of staff of the Financial Conduct Authority who is of the description designated for the purposes of this paragraph by the Chief Executive of the Authority (in an FCA case),

(b) a member of the Serious Fraud Office who is of the Senior Civil Service (in an SFO case), or

(c) a qualifying police officer (in any other case).

(5) Before determining whether to give an authorisation under subsection (3) in relation to a person—

(a) the appropriate decision-maker must arrange for the person or the person's legal representative to be informed that a determination is to be made, and

(b) if the appropriate decision-maker is a qualifying police officer, the officer must consult a qualifying prosecutor.

(6) In determining whether to give an authorisation under subsection (3) in relation to a person, the appropriate decision-maker must consider any representations made by the person or the person's legal representative.

(7) The appropriate decision-maker must arrange for the person or the person's legal representative to be informed whether an authorisation under subsection (3) has been given in relation to the person.

(8) Any designation under subsection (2) must be made, and any authorisation under subsection (3) must be given, before the applicable bail period in relation to the person has ended.

(9) In this section—

"qualifying police officer" means a police officer of the rank of commander or assistant chief constable or above, and

"qualifying prosecutor" means a prosecutor of the description designated for the purposes of this section by the Chief Executive of the Financial Conduct Authority, the Director of the Serious Fraud Office or the Director of Public Prosecutions.

Applicable bail period: first extension of limit by court

★**3-170g**   **47ZF.**–(1) This section applies in relation to a person if—

(a) the person's case is an SFO case,

(b) a senior officer has authorised an extension of the applicable bail period in relation to the person under section 47ZD, or

(c) an appropriate decision-maker has authorised an extension of the applicable bail period in relation to the person under section 47ZE.

(2) Before the applicable bail period in relation to the person ends a qualifying applicant may apply to a magistrates' court for it to authorise an extension of the applicable bail period in relation to the person under this section.

(3) If the court is satisfied that—

(a) conditions B to D are met in relation to the person, and

(b) the case does not fall within subsection (7),

it may authorise the applicable bail period to be extended as specified in subsection (4).

(4) The applicable bail period is to end—

(a) in a case falling within subsection (1)(a) or (b), at the end of the period of 6 months beginning with the person's bail start date;

(b) in a case falling within subsection (1)(c), at the end of the period of 9 months beginning with the person's bail start date.

(5) If the court is satisfied that—

(a) conditions B to D are met in relation to the person, and

(b) the case falls within subsection (7),

it may authorise the applicable bail period to be extended as specified in subsection (6).

(6) The applicable bail period is to end—

    (a) in a case falling within subsection (1)(a) or (b), at the end of the period of 9 months beginning with the person's bail start date;

    (b) in a case falling within subsection (1)(c), at the end of the period of 12 months beginning with the person's bail start date.

(7) A case falls within this subsection if the nature of the decision or further investigations mentioned in condition B means that that decision is unlikely to be made or those investigations completed if the applicable bail period in relation to the person is not extended as specified in subsection (6).

(8) In this section "qualifying applicant" means—

    (a) a constable,

    (b) a member of staff of the Financial Conduct Authority who is of the description designated for the purposes of this subsection by the Chief Executive of the Authority,

    (c) a member of the Serious Fraud Office, or

    (d) a Crown Prosecutor.

Applicable bail period: subsequent extensions of limit by court

47ZG.—(1) Subsections (2) to (6) apply where a court has authorised an extension of the applicable ★**3-170h** bail period in relation to a person under section 47ZF.

(2) Before the applicable bail period in relation to the person ends a qualifying applicant may apply to a magistrates' court for it to authorise an extension of the applicable bail period in relation to the person under this section.

(3) If the court is satisfied that—

    (a) conditions B to D are met in relation to the person, and

    (b) the case does not fall within subsection (8),

it may authorise the applicable bail period to be extended as specified in subsection (4).

(4) The applicable bail period is to end at the end of the period of 3 months beginning with the end of the current applicable bail period in relation to the person.

(5) If the court is satisfied that—

    (a) conditions B to D are met in relation to the person, and

    (b) the case falls within subsection (8),

it may authorise the applicable bail period to be extended as specified in subsection (6).

(6) The applicable bail period is to end at the end of the period of 6 months beginning with the end of the current applicable bail period in relation to the person.

(7) Where a court has authorised an extension of the applicable bail period in relation to a person under subsection (3) or (5), a qualifying applicant may make further applications under subsection (2) (and subsections (3) to (6) apply accordingly).

(8) A case falls within this subsection if the nature of the decision or further investigations mentioned in condition B means that that decision is unlikely to be made or those investigations completed if the current applicable bail period in relation to the person is not extended as specified in subsection (6).

(9) For the purposes of this section—

    (a) references to the current applicable bail period in relation to a person are to the applicable bail period applying to the person when the application under this section is made (subject to section 47ZJ(3)), and

    (b) "qualifying applicant" has the same meaning as in section 47ZF.

Sections 47ZF and 47ZG: withholding sensitive information

47ZH.—(1) This section applies where a qualifying applicant makes an application to a magistrates' ★**3-170i** court under section 47ZF or 47ZG in relation to a person.

(2) The qualifying applicant may apply to the court for it to authorise the specified information to be withheld from the person and any legal representative of the person.

(3) The court may grant an application under subsection (2) only if satisfied that there are reasonable grounds for believing that the specified information is sensitive information.

(4) For the purposes of this section information is sensitive information if its disclosure would have one or more of the following results—

    (a) evidence connected with an indictable offence would be interfered with or harmed;

    (b) a person would be interfered with or physically injured;

    (c) a person suspected of having committed an indictable offence but not yet arrested for the offence would be alerted;

    (d) the recovery of property obtained as a result of an indictable offence would be hindered.

(5) In this section "specified information" means the information specified in the application under subsection (2).

Sections 47ZF to 47ZH: proceedings in magistrates' court

★**3-170j**
47ZI.–(1) An application made to a magistrates' court under section 47ZF or 47ZG in relation to a person is to be determined by a single justice of the peace on written evidence unless subsection (2) or (3) applies.

(2) This subsection applies if—

(a) the effect of the application would be to extend the applicable bail period in relation to the person so that it ends at or before the end of the period of 12 months beginning with the person's bail start date, and

(b) a single justice of the peace considers that the interests of justice require an oral hearing.

(3) This subsection applies if—

(a) the effect of the application would be to extend the applicable bail period in relation to the person so that it ends after the end of the period of 12 months beginning with the person's bail start date, and

(b) the person, or the person who made the application, requests an oral hearing.

(4) If subsection (2) or (3) applies, the application is to be determined by two or more justices of the peace sitting otherwise than in open court.

(5) Where an application under section 47ZF or 47ZG in relation to a person is to be determined as mentioned in subsection (4), the justices may direct that the person and any legal representative of the person be excluded from any part of the hearing.

(6) The justices may give a direction under subsection (5) only if satisfied that there are reasonable grounds for believing that sensitive information would be disclosed at the part of the hearing in question.

(7) An application under section 47ZH is to be determined by a single justice of the peace on written evidence unless the justice determines that the interests of justice require an oral hearing.

(8) If the justice makes a determination under subsection (7)—

(a) the application is to be determined by two or more justices of the peace sitting otherwise than in open court, and

(b) the justices hearing the application must direct that the person to whom the application relates and any legal representative of the person be excluded from the hearing.

(9) In this section "sensitive information" has the meaning given in section 47ZH(4).

Sections 47ZF and 47ZG: late applications to magistrates' court

★**3-170k**
47ZJ.–(1) This section applies where—

(a) an application under section 47ZF or 47ZG is made to a magistrates' court before the end of the applicable bail period in relation to a person, but

(b) it is not practicable for the court to determine the application before the end of that period.

(2) The court must determine the application as soon as is practicable.

(3) The applicable bail period in relation to the person is to be treated as extended until the application is determined.

(4) If it appears to the court that it would have been reasonable for the application to have been made in time for it to have been determined by the court before the end of the applicable bail period in relation to the person, it may refuse the application.

Rules

★**3-170l**
47ZK. Criminal Procedure Rules may make provision in connection with applications under sections 47ZF, 47ZG and 47ZH and the proceedings for determining such applications.

Applicable bail period and bail return date: special case of release on bail under section 37(7)(a) or 37C(2)(b)

★**3-170m**
47ZL.–(1) This section applies where a person is released on bail under section 37(7)(a) or 37C(2)(b).

(2) The running of the applicable bail period in relation to the person—

(a) does not begin (in the case of a first release on bail), or

(b) is suspended (in any other case),

(subject to subsection (6)).

(3) Accordingly section 47ZA does not apply to the exercise of the power mentioned in section 47ZA(1) when releasing the person on bail.

(4) Subsections (5) and (6) apply if a DPP request is made in relation to the person.

(5) A custody officer must exercise the power mentioned in section 47(4A) to appoint a different time for the person to attend at the police station (and section 47(4B) to (4D) applies accordingly).

(6) The applicable bail period in relation to the person—

    (a) begins to run on the day on which the DPP request is made (in the case of a first release on bail), or

    (b) resumes running on that day (in any other case).

(7) Subsection (8) applies where—

    (a) a DPP request has been made in relation to the person, and

    (b) the applicable bail period in relation to the person would end before the end of the period of 7 days beginning with the day on which the DPP request was made.

(8) The running of the applicable bail period in relation to the person is suspended for the number of days necessary to secure that the applicable bail period ends at the end of the period of 7 days beginning with the day on which the DPP request was made.

(9) Subsections (10) and (11) apply if the DPP request made in relation to the person is met.

(10) The running of the applicable bail period in relation to the person is suspended.

(11) Accordingly section 47(4D) does not apply to any exercise of the power under section 47(4A).

(12) For the purposes of this section—

    (a) a "DPP request", in relation to a person, means a request by the Director of Public Prosecutions for the further information specified in the request to be provided before the Director decides under section 37B(2) whether there is sufficient evidence to charge the person with the relevant offence,

    (b) a DPP request is met when the further information specified in the request is provided, and

    (c) references to the case of a first release on bail are to a case where the person has not been released on bail in relation to the relevant offence under any other provision of this Part or under section 30A.

Applicable bail period: special cases of release on bail under section 30A and periods in hospital

47ZM.—(1) Subsections (2) and (3) apply where a person was released on bail under section 30A. ★**3-170n**

(2) The period of 28 days mentioned in section 30B(8) in relation to the person is to be treated as being the period of 28 days mentioned in section 47ZB(1)(b) in relation to the person.

(3) Any reference to the relevant offence, in relation to the person, is to be read as a reference to the offence in respect of which the power in section 30A(1) was exercised.

(4) Subsection (5) applies if, at any time on the day on which the applicable bail period in relation to a person would end, the person is in hospital as an in-patient.

(5) The running of the applicable bail period in relation to the person is to be treated as having been suspended for any day on which the patient was in hospital as an in-patient.

Interpretation of references to pre-conditions for bail

With effect from April 3, 2017 (Policing and Crime Act 2017 (Commencement No. 1 and ★**3-171a** Transitional Provisions) Regulations 2017 (S.I. 2017 No. 399)), a new section 50A was inserted into the 1984 Act by the Policing and Crime Act 2017, s.58, which defines the "pre-conditions of bail" that must be satisfied if a person is to be released on bail pre-charge. For related transitional provision, see *ante*, § 3-136.

Police and Criminal Evidence Act 1984, s.50A

Interpretation of references to pre-conditions for bail

50A. For the purposes of this Part the following are the pre-conditions for bail in relation to the release of a person by a custody officer—

    (a) that the custody officer is satisfied that releasing the person on bail is necessary and proportionate in all the circumstances (having regard, in particular, to any conditions of bail which would be imposed), and

    (b) that an officer of the rank of inspector or above authorises the release on bail (having considered any representations made by the person or the person's legal representative).

III. PRESENCE OF THE ACCUSED IN COURT DURING THE TRIAL

B. Limitations

Crime and Disorder Act 1998, ss.57A–57E

Live links for accused's attendance at certain preliminary, sentencing and other hearings

For a new practice direction relating to the use of live link and telephone facilities and sup- **3-226** plementing sections 57A to 57E of the 1998 Act, the introduction of rules 3.2(4) and (5) and 3.3(2)(e), and the substitution of rule 3.5(2)(d), of the 2015 rules by the Criminal Procedure (Amendment No. 2) Rules 2016 (S.I. 2016 No. 705) (as to which, see §§ 4-115, 4-116 in the main work), see *post*, Appendix B-72a *et seq.*

CHAPTER 4

TRIAL

I. PRELIMINARIES

B. HEARING IN OPEN COURT

(1) European Convention on Human Rights and common law

Practical application

★**4-4**   *R. v. Denbigh JJ., ex p. Williams and Evans* (as to which, see the main work) was considered in *R. (O'Connor and Jerrard) v. Aldershot Magistrates' Court, CPS and H.M. Courts and Tribunals Service (Interested Parties)*, 181 J.P. 117, DC. It was held: (i) access to a court building for the purpose of attending a public hearing is a matter of legal right; (ii) the right is not unqualified; first, a court has power to restrict access to the courtroom where necessary in the interests of justice, *e.g.*, to prevent disorder; secondly, section 53 of the Courts Act 2003 empowers a court security officer to exclude or remove persons from court buildings if it is reasonably necessary to do so for the purpose of "enabling court business to be carried on without interference or delay", "maintaining order", or "securing the safety of any person in the court building"; (iii) section 53 does not prevent court managers from taking decisions about whether to exclude a person or group of people from a court building and giving instructions to court security officers to implement such a decision; nor does it prevent Her Majesty's Courts and Tribunal Service from formulating policies about how their staff should respond to situations of actual or threatened disruption; but it leaves no room for some parallel power under which court security officers (or people who are not court security officers) may lawfully exclude a person from a court building on the ground, for example, that they have failed to comply with a condition of entry imposed by Her Majesty's Courts and Tribunal Service as occupier, even though the requirements of section 53 have not been met; (iv) the powers under section 53 may lawfully be exercised without reference to the judiciary; but where a member of the public is seeking to attend a particular hearing and there is a dispute or room for dispute about whether he has the right to do so, that question should be decided by the court concerned at the time the question arises; decisions to exclude members of the public potentially affect the fairness and validity of the court process; it is therefore integral to the court's ability to control its own process that such decisions are taken by the court; (v) if an entire group of people are to be excluded simply because of their affiliation with the group, fairness requires that at least one representative member should be allowed to address the court before a final decision is taken to exclude them from the court building; and (vi) the question of when a hearing ceases to be open to the public is one of fact and degree; where members of the public have been unlawfully excluded from the court, the essential question is whether the nature and extent of the exclusion were such as to deprive the hearing of its open and public character; it is not, however, simply a matter of counting heads.

F. INTERPRETERS

(2) In the course of police investigation

4-59   As to the replacement of Codes C and H (see the main work), and in particular in relation to interpreters, see *post*, § 15-7.

(3) Proving what the accused told the interpreter

4-60   As to the replacement of Code C (see the main work), and in particular in relation to interpreters, see *post*, § 15-7.

G. Representation of the Defendant

(1) Legal representation

As to *R. v. Mills* (as to which, see the main work), see also *R. v. Holloway (Adrian)* [2017] 1 ★**4-68** Cr.App.R. 26, CA, where it was said that a court has no power to appoint an *amicus curiae* "to assist the court" who in truth is appointed to act as a defence advocate and adviser.

K. Limited Discretionary Power to Prevent Prosecution Proceeding

(2) Abuse of process

(c) *Where a stay is necessary to protect the integrity of the criminal justice system*

The decision to institute or continue proceedings

Private prosecutions

A subsequent private prosecution is capable of co-existing with an extant police caution in ★**4-91** respect of the same conduct: *R. (Lowden) v. Gateshead Magistrates' Court* [2017] 4 W.L.R. 43, DC (considering *Hayter v. L.* and *Jones v. Whalley* (as to both of which, see the main work)). Where nothing is said at the time of the caution being administered about the possibility of a private prosecution, whilst this is extremely poor practice, it cannot render a subsequent private prosecution an abuse, although it might be different if the prosecutor had been consulted by the police and had acquiesced in their decision to deal with the matter by way of a caution: *ibid.*

N. Pre-Trial Hearings

(1) The court's case management powers and duties

Criminal Procedure Rules 2015 (S.I. 2015 No. 1490), rr.3.1–3.12

The duty of the court and of the parties

For a new practice direction relating to the use of live link and telephone facilities and sup- **4-115** plementing the introduction of rules 3.2(4) and (5) and 3.3(2)(e) of the 2015 rules by the Criminal Procedure (Amendment No. 2) Rules 2016 (S.I. 2016 No. 705) (as to which, see the main work), see *post*, Appendix B-72a *et seq.*

The court's case management powers

As to rule 3.5(1) and (2)(d) (as to which, see the main work), see a new practice direction relat- **4-116** ing to the use of live link and telephone facilities and supplementing the introduction of rules 3.2(4) and (5) and 3.3(2)(e), and the substitution of rule 3.5(2)(d) of the 2015 rules by the Criminal Procedure (Amendment No. 2) Rules 2016 (S.I. 2016 No. 705) (as to which, see also § 4-115 the main work), see *post*, Appendix B-72a *et seq.*

(2) Plea and trial preparation hearings

Criminal Procedure Rules 2015 (S.I. 2015 No. 1490), rr.3.13–3.25

Application for joint or separate trials, etc.

As to a new practice direction supplementing, *inter alia*, the amendments made to rule 3.21 of **4-120f** the 2015 rules by the Criminal Procedure (Amendment No. 2) Rules 2016 (S.I. 2016 No. 705), see *post*, Appendix B-149 *et seq.*

Arraigning the defendant on the indictment

As to a new practice direction supplementing, *inter alia*, the amendments made to rule 3.24 of **4-121** the 2015 rules by the Criminal Procedure (Amendment No. 2) Rules 2016 (S.I. 2016 No. 705), see *post*, Appendix B-149 *et seq.*

R. Vulnerable Defendants: Special Arrangements

For a case considering the role of the judge when deciding whether to appoint an intermediary **4-162** for the defendant, see *post*, § 8-94.

II. ARRAIGNMENT AND PLEA

B. Plea

(9) Autrefois acquit and autrefois convict

(b) *A man may not be tried for a crime in respect of which he has previously been acquitted or convicted*

Relevant statutory provisions

Offences against the Person Act 1861, ss.44, 45

★**4-188**   Sections 44 and 45 of the 1861 Act (§§ 4-186, 4-187 in the main work) only apply to private prosecutions: *Austen v. CPS*, 181 J.P. 181, DC ([2016] EWHC 2247 (Admin.)).

(d) *Adjudication upon guilt or innocence*

Decisions of foreign courts

4-209   The principle of *ne bis in idem* laid down in Article 54 of the Convention Implementing the Schengen Agreement ("54. A person whose trial has been finally disposed of in one contracting party may not be prosecuted in another contracting party for the same acts provided that, if a penalty has been imposed, it has been enforced, is actually in the process of being enforced or can no longer be enforced under the laws of the sentencing contracting party."), read in light of Article 50 of the Charter of Fundamental Rights of the European Union ("50. No one shall be liable to be tried or punished again in criminal proceedings for an offence for which he or she has already been finally acquitted or convicted within the Union in accordance with the law."), must be interpreted as meaning that a decision of a public prosecutor terminating criminal proceedings and finally closing a criminal investigation, albeit with the possibility of its being reopened or annulled, without any penalties having been imposed, could not be characterised as a final decision for the purposes of those articles when it was clear from the statement of reasons for the decision that the procedure was closed without any detailed investigation having been carried out; the mutual trust between contracting states in their criminal justice systems requires that the competent authorities of one contracting state accept at face value a final decision communicated to them by another contracting state; however, that mutual trust can prosper only if the first contracting state is in a position to satisfy itself, on the basis of the documents provided by the second contracting state, that the decision of the competent authorities of the second state did indeed constitute a final decision, including a determination as to the merits of the case: *Criminal proceedings against Kossowski (Case C-486/14)* [2016] 1 W.L.R. 4393, ECJ (Grand Chamber).

(13) Defendant unfit to plead or take his trial

Criminal Procedure (Insanity) Act 1964, ss.4, 4A

When issue is to be determined

4-234   The capacity of a defendant who has given evidence-in-chief to be cross-examined is part and parcel of his ability to give evidence in his own defence, which, in turn, is a key aspect of "fitness to be tried"; where, therefore, the issue of the appellant's fitness to be cross-examined was raised at the conclusion of his examination-in-chief, the judge was bound to determine it at that juncture, section 4(4) of the 1964 Act (see the main work) stipulating that, once the issue is raised, it "shall be determined as soon as it arises"; continuing with the trial, whatever special arrangements were made, and however beneficial to the defendant they may have appeared, was not an option: *R. v. Orr* [2016] 2 Cr.App.R. 32, CA.

VII. THE JURY

B. Qualification

Juries Act 1974, s.1

4-267   Section 68(1) and (2) of the CJCA 2015 (as to which, see the main work) come into force on

December 1, 2016: Criminal Justice and Courts Act 2015 (Commencement No. 5) Order 2016 (S.I. 2016 No. 896).

Electoral register as basis for selection

Section 68(1) and (3) of the CJCA 2015 (as to which, see the main work) came into force on September 9, 2016: Criminal Justice and Courts Act 2015 (Commencement No. 5) Order 2016 (S.I. 2016 No. 896). **4-270**

IX. TRIAL ON INDICTMENT WITHOUT A JURY

A. FRAUD CASES AND JURY TAMPERING

Criminal Justice Act 2003, ss.44–49

Elaborate jury protection measures are not incompatible *per se* with an accused's right under Article 6 of the ECHR (§ 16-72 in the main work) to be presumed innocent: *Price v. U.K.* (2017) 64 E.H.R.R. 17. The main considerations are the nature, extent, method of application and underlying justification of the particular arrangements made, and the nature of the warning given by the judge to the jury: *ibid.* **★4-331**

B. SAMPLE COUNTS

Domestic Violence, Crime and Victims Act 2004, ss.17–20

As to the replacement of *Criminal Practice Direction II (Preliminary Proceedings) 10A*, see *ante*, § 1-192, and *post*, Appendix B-149 *et seq.* It should be noted that directions 10A.15 to 10A.20 replicate almost exactly the current paragraphs 10A.4 to 10A.9, save that the reference to signing the indictment has now been omitted. **4-341**

XIV. THE DEFENCE CASE

B. WARNING AS TO GIVING OF EVIDENCE BY DEFENDANT

Criminal Justice and Public Order Act 1994, s.35

Effect of accused's silence at trial

The procedure set out in section 35(1) to (3) of the 1994 Act (§ 4-377 in the main work) is not a mere formality; failure to carry out it will, in the absence of a legitimate conclusion that it made no difference, be a material irregularity; the method by which subsection (2) is satisfied is significant; whether or not to give evidence is probably the most important decision that a defendant has to make in the course of his trial; that decision will almost invariably be the subject of close consideration by him in conjunction with his advisers, and it does not depend wholly, or even always mainly, on the risk of adverse inferences; many other considerations are bound to be discussed, *viz.* the damage that may be done by cross-examination and the possibility of opening up further enquiries by the prosecution, which must be balanced against the gains that might be made by giving evidence; thus, what matters is that the defendant has had the necessary advice, and the best way of establishing that is by asking him in open court, as required by subsection (2); an omission to ask is an irregularity; however, where it is clear that the necessary advice has indeed been given, the irregularity will be immaterial to the safety of the conviction; often, if an assertion is made by an appellant to the effect that he has not been given appropriate advice, or has not been able to make an informed decision about a matter of materiality in the trial, and that assertion appears to require investigation, the question will arise whether the appellant is willing to waive privilege in order to enable trial counsel to answer it; however, with or without such waiver, the assertion is normally a necessary starting point: *Wright v. The Queen* [2017] Crim.L.R. 137, PC (considering materially identical Cayman Islands legislation). **4-379**

In *R. v. Mulindwa* (2017) 161(16) S.J. 37, CA, it was said that there is a clear dividing line between evidence from a psychiatrist or psychologist that might legitimately provide the jury with necessary assistance in understanding the presentation of a defendant in the witness box, and ★

impermissible evidence from such witnesses that would amount to no more than an expert's opinion on the credibility or truthfulness of the evidence of the witness, an issue that has to remain exclusively for the jury; the former is permissible because it is designed to enhance the ability of the jury to perform its fact-finding role, while the latter is impermissible because it would have the effect of suborning the jury's role and substituting for it the decision of the expert; where, therefore, it was submitted to the judge that he should rule that for the defendant (who suffered from paranoid schizophrenia) to give evidence would be "undesirable" within the meaning of section 35(1)(b) of the CJPOA 1994 (§ 4-377 in the main work), a psychologist having given evidence on a *voir dire* about the difficulties that might arise if the defendant were to give evidence, and where the judge declined so to rule, his approach had involved no error of law in considering that, were the defendant to give evidence, the difficulties could be addressed by giving the psychologist an opportunity to explain to the jury that certain ways of behaving, or responding to questions, were a feature of the recognised mental illness from which the defendant suffered; such evidence would have provided the jury with the information to enable them to form a view on the reliability of the defendant's evidence as a whole (if he were to give evidence); the defendant had had the best of both worlds as the jury had been presented with the psychologist's evidence, the defence had been able to use it in submitting that the jury should not hold it against him that he had not given evidence, and the judge had referred to it in his direction under section 35; the propriety of a psychologist giving evidence before the defendant was catered for by section 79 of the PACE Act 1984 (*ibid.*, § 4-385).

C. Defence Counsel's Duty

★**4-382**   As to the nature of the advice to be given to a defendant in relation to the issue of whether or not to give evidence, and as to the practice to be followed by his legal representatives where he decides not to give evidence, see *R. v. Good (Alfie)*, unreported, May 17, 2016, CA ([2016] EWCA Crim. 1054) (*post*, Appendix C-54).

XVI. CLOSING SPEECHES AND SUMMING UP

A. Argument as to the Relevant Law

Written directions provided by judge to jury

★**4-418**   In *R. v. Brown* [2017] 3 *Archbold Review* 3, CA ([2017] EWCA Crim. 167), it was said that whilst not every trial requires a written route to verdict, where none is provided, it is all the more important that the legal directions given orally are well structured and defined, with a clear focus on each issue and the evidence that might be relevant to that issue; and there is in rare cases a tipping point that is reached, when, if the law and the defence cases are not properly addressed in a structured way by a judge, a conviction will be rendered unsafe.

D. Structure and Content of Summing Up

(8) Comment

(j) *On a witness's demeanour*

4-466a   For a decision of the Supreme Court of New Zealand considering whether there is an invariable requirement for judges to give demeanour warnings when summing up in cases where credibility is in issue, see *Taniwha v. The Queen*, unreported, September 8, 2016 ([2016] NZSC 123).

(12) Defendant's character

(a) *Good character*

★**4-487**   Neither a bind over, nor the conduct leading to it, will necessarily deprive a defendant with no convictions of his entitlement to an unqualified good character direction; equally, however, a defendant will not be entitled to have a bind over simply ignored when a judge is considering whether or not to treat him as a person of good character, no matter what the circumstances: *R. v. B.* [2017] 3 *Archbold Review* 3, CA ([2017] EWCA Crim. 35) (considering *R. v. Hunter (Nigel)*; *R. v. Saruwu (Joseph)*; *R. v. Johnstone (Ian)*; *R. v. Walker (Alan)*; *R. v. Lonsdale (Paul)* (as to which, see § 4-486 in the main work)).

XVIII. VERDICT

H. Verdict for Lesser Offence than that Charged in the Indictment

(5) When to leave alternative verdict to jury

R. v. Barre is now reported at [2016] Crim.L.R. 768.

★**4-533**

Chapter 5

SENTENCES AND ORDERS ON CONVICTION

II. PRELIMINARIES

(6) Pre-sentence drug testing

Criminal Justice Act 2003, s.161

[Pre-sentence drug testing
   With effect from April 3, 2017 (Policing and Crime Act 2017 (Commencement No. 1 and **★5-28**
Transitional Provisions) Regulations 2017 (S.I. 2017 No. 399)), paragraph (c) in the definition of
"appropriate adult" in section 161 of the 2003 Act was amended by the Policing and Crime Act
2017, s.79(3), so as to substitute, for the words "a person employed by the police", the words "a
person employed for, or engaged on, police purposes; and 'police purposes' has the meaning
given by section 101(2) of the Police Act 1996".

III. GENERAL PRINCIPLES

A. Purposes of Sentencing

(2) Children and young persons

Crime and Disorder Act 1998, s.37

Aim of the youth justice system
   As to a new guideline on the sentencing of those aged under 18, see *post*, § 5-178.   **★5-73**

Children and Young Persons Act 1933, s.44

General considerations
   As to a new guideline on the sentencing of those aged under 18, see *post*, § 5-178.   **★5-75**

B. Determining the Seriousness of an Offence

(1) Statute

Criminal Justice Act 2003, s.143

Previous convictions

Relevance
   In *R. v. Evans*, unreported, January 19, 2016, CA ([2016] EWCA Crim. 31) (an offence of   **5-78**
theft of £210 by grabbing it from a till by a 40-year-old with 67 convictions, mainly for dishonesty,
and mainly for shoplifting), the court stressed that, whilst a sentence outside a relevant guideline
may be justified by reason of an offender's relevant previous convictions, the sentence "must bear
some proportionate relationship to the offence committed and the circumstances of the defend-

ant"; an appropriate balance has to be struck between what a guideline indicates for an offence looked at in isolation and a suitable punishment of any consequence to the particular offender.

(2) Factual basis of sentence

(a) *On conviction following plea of not guilty*

Interpreting the verdict of the jury

★**5-93**   The line of authority starting with *R. v. Stosiek* (see the main work), even as limited by *R. v. Fleury* (*ibid.*), is no longer to be treated as a free-standing principle; rather, it has been subsumed by an approach, according to which (i) if there is only one possible interpretation of the jury's verdict, then the judge must sentence on that basis; (ii) where there is more than one possible interpretation, the judge must make up his own mind, to the criminal standard, as to the factual basis upon which to pass sentence; and (iii) if there is more than one possible interpretation, and the judge is not sure of any of them, then he is obliged to pass sentence on the basis of the interpretation (whether in whole or in relevant part) most favourable to the defendant: *R. v. King* [2017] Crim.L.R. 497, CA ([2017] EWCA Crim. 128).

C. Reduction in Sentence for Guilty Plea

Sentencing guidelines

★**5-124**   Whereas the Sentencing Guidelines Council's guideline on reduction in sentence for a guilty plea (Appendix S-8 *et seq.* in the sentencing supplement) did not distinguish, so far as the amount of any credit is concerned, between a plea that was entered at the door of the court and a plea entered after the trial had begun, and whereas the recommendation was a 10 per cent reduction in either case, that may well have been appropriate in some cases, but sentencers should not have felt constrained by the guideline to give 10 per cent credit for a guilty plea in all circumstances; a judgment was required as to what credit was appropriate; that would require careful assessment of the facts of the particular case, including (particularly in sex cases) the extent to which witnesses had been spared from giving evidence, as well as consideration of the time and costs saved as a result of the plea; the strength of the case against the defendant would also have been relevant; however, that was not a definitive or exhaustive list; all the circumstances needed to be taken into account and there may well have been exceptional cases where no reduction was appropriate: *R. v. S.* [2017] 1 C.App.R.(S.) 41, CA. In light of the new guideline on reductions in sentence for a guilty plea issued by the Sentencing Council for England and Wales (as to which, see *post*, § 5-178), this case is of no future significance, but it has continuing potential relevance to sentences passed before June 1, 2017.

Extent of discount

5-132   It is important to give particular credit to the first defendant to break ranks and plead guilty in a complex and multi-handed case: *R. v. Sanghera* [2016] 2 Cr.App.R.(S.) 15, CA. As to this case, see also Appendix S-959.

★   See *R. v. S.*, *ante*, § 5-124, in relation to sentences imposed before June 1, 2017. As to sentences imposed on or after that date, see now the Sentencing Council's guideline on reduction in sentence for a guilty plea (*post*, Appendix S-28 *et seq.*).

First reasonable opportunity

★**5-133**   As to sentences imposed on or after June 1, 2017, see now the Sentencing Council's guideline on reduction in sentence for a guilty plea (*post*, Appendix S-28 *et seq.*). The new guideline no longer refers to the "first reasonable hearing". Rather it recommends that the maximum discount should be given only to those who plead guilty at "the first stage of proceedings." The first stage will normally be the first hearing at which a plea or indication of plea is sought and recorded by the court.

Withholding the discount

★**5-135**   As to sentences imposed on or after June 1, 2017, see now the Sentencing Council's guideline on reduction in sentence for a guilty plea (*post*, Appendix S-28 *et seq.*).

E. Mitigation

(3) Selected mitigating factors

Age/ill health

No special rule is required where a court is dealing with a defendant of extremely old age; **★5-152** whilst a defendant's diminished life expectancy, age, health and the prospect of dying in prison are factors legitimately to be taken into account in passing sentence, they have to be balanced against the gravity of the offending (including the harm done to victims), and the public interest in setting appropriate punishment for very serious crimes; therefore, whilst courts should make allowance for these matters, and should give the most anxious scrutiny to them, they should be taken into account in a limited way: *R. v. Clarke (Ralph)*; *R. v. Cooper (Peter)* (2017) 161(15) S.J. 37, CA ([2017] EWCA Crim. 393).

Assistance to law enforcement agencies

Assistance in accordance with the 2005 Act

R. v. A.X.N.; R. v. Z.A.R. is now reported at [2016] 2 Cr.App.R.(S.) 33, *sub nom. R. v. N.*   **5-166**

Assistance given otherwise than in accordance with the 2005 Act

R. v. A.X.N.; R. v. Z.A.R. is now reported at [2016] 2 Cr.App.R.(S.) 33, *sub nom. R. v. N.*   **5-169**

F. Sentencing Guidelines

Sentencing Council for England and Wales

The Sentencing Council for England and Wales has issued a definitive guideline relating to the **5-178** imposition of community and custodial sentences. It applies to all offenders over the age of 18 falling to be sentenced on or after February 1, 2017, regardless of the date of the offence. Specifically, it deals with (i) the imposition of community orders, (ii) the imposition of custodial sentences, and (iii) suspended sentences (general guidance). There is also a sentencing decision flowchart, and an annex setting out the fine bands. For details, see *post*, Appendix S-27 *et seq.*

The Sentencing Council for England and Wales has issued new sentencing guidelines for magistrates' courts, which revise, in relation to certain summary offences, the Sentencing Guidelines Council's guidelines. The guidelines apply to all offenders aged 18 or over who are sentenced on or after April 24, 2017, regardless of the date of the offence. For further details, see *post*, §§ 20-228, 32-172, 32-183, Appendix S-11.

The Sentencing Council for England and Wales has issued a new guideline on reduction in **★** sentence for a guilty plea, replacing that issued by the Sentencing Guidelines Council (Appendix S-8). It applies equally in magistrates' courts and the Crown Court, to all individual offenders aged 18 and older, and to organisations, in cases where the first hearing is after May 31, 2017, regardless of the date of the offence. For the details thereof, see *post*, Appendix S-28 *et seq.*

The Sentencing Council for England and Wales has issued a definitive guideline relating to the **★** overarching principles for sentencing those aged under 18 at the date of conviction (Pt 1), and to the sentencing of such persons for sexual offences and robbery (Pts 2 & 3). It applies to all offenders who are sentenced after May 31, 2017, regardless of the date of the offence. For the details thereof, see *post*, Appendix S-29 *et seq.*

The Sentencing Council for England and Wales has issued a consultation guideline on sentencing for offences involving bladed articles and offensive weapons. It covers the sentencing of offenders convicted of having a bladed article or offensive weapon in public or on school premises, of using one to threaten someone, and possession of one in prison (*viz.* offences under the Prison Act 1952, s.40CA (§ 28-195a in the main work), the Prevention of Crime Act 1953, ss.1(1) (*ibid.*, § 24-165) and 1A (*ibid.*, § 24-187), and the CJA 1988, ss.139(1) (*ibid.*, § 24-195), 139A(1) and (2) (*ibid.*, § 24-199), and 139AA(1) (*ibid.*, § 24-203)). It does not cover offences where a knife or other weapon is actually used to harm someone, nor the use or possession of firearms. The consultation closed on January 6, 2017. For the full text of the guideline, see www.sentencingcouncil.org.uk.

The Sentencing Council for England and Wales has issued a consultation guideline on sentencing for failures to surrender to bail or to comply with notification requirements, and breaches of community orders, suspended sentence orders, post-sentence supervision, protective orders (*i.e.* restraining and non-molestation orders), criminal behaviour orders and anti-social behaviour orders, sexual harm prevention orders and sexual offences prevention orders, and disqualifications from acting as a director or from keeping an animal. For the first time, guidance for sentencing for breaches of these orders will require sentencers to take into account the risk of harm as well as actual harm caused by a breach. The consultation closed on January 25, 2017. For the full text of the guideline, see www.sentencingcouncil.org.uk.

★   The Sentencing Council for England and Wales has issued a consultation guideline on intimidatory offences (covering harassment and stalking (Protection from Harassment Act 1997, ss.2 (§ 19-341 in the main work), 2A (*ibid.*, § 19-343), 4 (*ibid.*, § 19-347) and 4A (*ibid.*, § 19-349)), the racially or religiously aggravated forms of those offences (CDA 1998, s.32 (*ibid.*, § 19-350)), disclosing private sexual images (CJCA 2015, s.33 (*ibid.*, § 20-237a)), controlling or coercive behaviour in an intimate or family relationship (SCA 2015, s.76 (*ibid.*, § 19-358)), and threats to kill (Offences against the Person Act 1861, s.16 (*ibid.*, § 19-176))) and domestic abuse (covering all offences that occur within a domestic context such as assault, sexual offences or criminal damage). The consultation closes on June 30, 2017. For the full text of the guideline, see www.sentencingcouncil.org.uk.

For guidance from the Sentencing Council on sentencing for the offence of driving, attempting to drive, or being in charge of, a motor vehicle with a specified controlled drug in the body above the specified limit (RTA 1988, s.5A (§ 32-105 in the main work)), see *post*, § 32-108.

Effect of guidelines

★5-183   As to whether sentencing authorities should be cited on an appeal against sentence, see *R. v. Thelwall*, *post*, § 7-135.

V. COMMUNITY SENTENCES

B. GENERAL RESTRICTIONS

Criminal Justice Act 2003, ss.147-151

Restrictions on imposing community sentences

5-235   The Sentencing Council for England and Wales has issued a definitive guideline relating to the imposition of community and custodial sentences: see *ante*, § 5-178; and *post*, Appendix S-27 *et seq.*

C. COMMUNITY ORDERS

(1) General

Criminal Justice Act 2003, s.177

Community orders

5-240   The Sentencing Council for England and Wales has issued a definitive guideline relating to the imposition of community and custodial sentences: see *ante*, § 5-178; and *post*, Appendix S-27 *et seq.* This includes recommendations as to the requirements that should be attached to community orders.

With effect from October 17, 2016 (Crime and Courts Act 2013 (Commencement No. 15, Transitional and Savings Provisions) Order 2016 (S.I. 2016 No. 962)), Part 4 (paras 11 to 21) of Schedule 16 to the 2013 Act, and section 44 of that Act, so far as relating thereto (see the main work), were brought into force, in relation to the local justice areas of Birmingham and Solihull, Black Country, Central and South West Staffordshire, Coventry and Warwickshire, Leicestershire and Rutland, North Staffordshire, Nottinghamshire, and South East Staffordshire. These provisions will cease to be in force at the end of October 13, 2017 (art. 3). Article 4(1) provides that the provisions commenced do not apply in relation to electronic monitoring requirements imposed by a court in accordance with section 215 (§ 5-266 in the main work) of the CJA 2003 in the aforementioned local justice areas before the commencement date. Article 4(2) provides that article 3 does not affect the continued application after October 13, 2017, of an electronic monitoring requirement imposed by a court in the aforementioned local justice areas on or after the commencement date, and before October 14, 2017; and the provisions commenced continue to have effect after October 13, 2017, in relation to any such requirements imposed during that period.

With effect from March 13, 2017 (Crime and Courts Act 2013 (Commencement No. 17, ★ Transitional and Savings Provisions) Order 2017 (S.I. 2017 No. 236)), Part 4 (paras 11-21) of Schedule 16 to the 2013 Act, and section 44 of that Act, so far as relating thereto (see the main work), were brought into force, in relation to the local justice areas of East London and North London. These provisions will cease to be in force at the end of March 12, 2018 (art. 3). Article 4(1) provides that they do not apply in relation to electronic monitoring requirements imposed by a court in accordance with section 215 (§ 5-266 in the main work) of the CJA 2003 in those local justice areas before the commencement date. Article 4(2) provides that article 3 does not affect the continued application after March 12, 2018, of an electronic monitoring requirement imposed by a court in those local justice areas on or after the commencement date, and before March 13, 2018; and the commenced provisions continue to have effect after March 12, 2018, in relation to any such requirements imposed during that period.

With effect from March 31, 2017, the Legal Aid, Sentencing and Punishment of Offenders Act ★ 2012 (Alcohol Abstinence and Monitoring Requirements) Piloting (Amendment) Order 2017 (S.I. 2017 No. 225) amended the Legal Aid, Sentencing and Punishment of Offenders Act 2012 (Alcohol Abstinence and Monitoring Requirements) Piloting Order 2016 (S.I. 2016 No. 286) (see the main work) to extend the piloting period for a further 12 months.

With effect from May 1, 2017, and until the end of April 30, 2019, the Legal Aid, Sentencing ★ and Punishment of Offenders Act 2012 (Alcohol Abstinence and Monitoring Requirements) Piloting Order 2017 (S.I. 2017 No. 525) brought into force, for all purposes other than application by the AFA 2006, section 76 of the 2012 Act (see the main work), in relation to the local justice areas of Humber, Lincolnshire, and North Yorkshire. Any alcohol abstinence and monitoring requirement imposed before April 30, 2019, will continue to have effect on and after that date. See also *post*, § 5-264.

(3) Requirements available in the case of all offenders
Criminal Justice Act 2003, ss.199-213

Alcohol abstinence and monitoring requirement

With effect from March 31, 2017, the Criminal Justice Act 2003 (Alcohol Abstinence and ★5-264 Monitoring Requirement) (Prescription of Arrangement for Monitoring) Order 2016 (S.I. 2016 No. 327) was amended by the Criminal Justice Act 2003 (Alcohol Abstinence and Monitoring Requirement) (Prescription of Arrangement for Monitoring) (Amendment) Order 2017 (S.I. 2017 No. 234) so as to keep in place until March 31, 2018, the specification that monitoring of compliance with the obligations of an alcohol abstinence and monitoring requirement imposed as part of the extended pilot scheme for section 76 of the LASPOA 2012 (as to which, see § 5-240 in the main work and *ante*) will be through a transdermal electronic tag, fitted to an offender to measure the level of alcohol in his sweat.

With effect from May 1, 2017, the Criminal Justice Act 2003 (Alcohol Abstinence and Monitor- ★ ing Requirement) (Prescription of Arrangement for Monitoring) Order 2017 (S.I. 2017 No. 537) prescribes that the monitoring of compliance with a requirement that is imposed as part of the pilot scheme in Humber, Lincolnshire and North Yorkshire (as to which, see *ante*, § 5-240) will also be through a transdermal electronic tag fitted to the offender to measure the level of alcohol in his sweat.

(5) Electronic monitoring
Criminal Justice Act 2003, s.215

Electronic monitoring requirement

As to the commencement of Part 4 of Schedule 16 (paras 11-21) to the Crime and Courts Act **5-266** 2013 (see the main work), and the transitional provision relating specifically to electronic monitoring requirements imposed by a court in accordance with section 215 of the 2003 Act, see *ante*, § 5-240.

With effect from October 17, 2016, the Criminal Justice (Electronic Monitoring) (Responsible Person) (No. 2) Order 2016 (S.I. 2016 No. 961) specifies, for the purposes of section 215(3) of the 2003 Act, a person who is employed by, or a police officer who is a member of, Hertfordshire police force as a description of a person who may be made responsible for the electronic monitoring of persons subject to an electronic monitoring requirement imposed as part of a community order or suspended sentence order, respectively.

★   With effect from March 13, 2017, the Criminal Justice (Electronic Monitoring) (Responsible Person) Order 2017 (S.I. 2017 No. 235) specifies, for the purposes of section 215(3) of the 2003 Act, a person who is employed by Buddi Ltd (Co. No. 05308826) as a description of person who may be made responsible for the electronic monitoring of persons subject to an electronic monitoring requirement imposed as part of a community order or suspended sentence order, respectively.

Data from electronic monitoring: code of practice

5-267   As to the commencement of Part 4 of Schedule 16 (paras 11-21) to the Crime and Courts Act 2013 (see the main work), see *ante*, § 5-240.

(6) Provisions applying to relevant orders generally
Criminal Justice Act 2003, ss.216-220

Availability of arrangements in local area

5-270   As to the commencement of Part 4 of Schedule 16 (paras 11-21) to the Crime and Courts Act 2013 (see the main work), see *ante*, § 5-240.

D. YOUTH COMMUNITY ORDERS

Introduction

5-278   Attendance centre orders under section 60 of the PCC(S)A 2000 were just one of several "youth community orders" that could be made under that Act. As explained in the main work, however, the sections of the Act that provided for the making of a curfew order (s.37), an exclusion order (s.40A), a supervision order (ss.63, 64 and 67, and Sched. 6) and an action plan order (ss.69-71) were repealed by the CJIA 2008, and these repeals came fully into force on November 30, 2009, except that they continue to apply to offences committed before that date. With the passage of time, it was unlikely that, by the time of publication of the 2013 edition of this work, further reference would need to be made to these provisions. Should it be necessary, however, they can be found in the supplements to the 2012 edition. The position with regard to section 60 is rather different (see the annotations thereto (*post*, § 5-279)).

Powers of Criminal Courts (Sentencing) Act 2000, s.60

Attendance centre orders

5-279   **60.**—(1) Where—

 (a) (subject to 148, 150 and 156 of the Criminal Justice Act 2003) a person aged under *21* [16] is convicted by or before a court of an offence punishable with imprisonment, or

 (b) a court [has power or] would have power, but for section 89 below (restrictions on imprisonment of young offenders and defaulters), to commit a person aged under *21* [16] to prison in default of payment of any sum of money or for failing to do or abstain from doing anything required to be done or left undone, *or*

 (c) *a court has power to commit a person aged at least 21 but under 25 to prison in default of payment of any sum of money,*

the court may, if it has been notified by the Secretary of State that an attendance centre is available for the reception of persons of his description, order him to attend at such a centre, to be specified in the order, for such number of hours as may be so specified.

(2) An order under subsection (1) above is in this Act referred to as an "attendance centre order".

(3) The aggregate number of hours for which an attendance centre order may require a person to attend at an attendance centre shall not be less than 12 except where—

 (a) he is aged under 14; and

 (b) the court is of the opinion that 12 hours would be excessive, having regard to his age or any other circumstances.

(4) The aggregate number of hours shall not exceed 12 except where the court is of the opinion,

having regard to all the circumstances, that 12 hours would be inadequate, and in that case [shall not exceed 24]—

    (a) *shall not exceed 24 where the person is aged under 16; and*

    (b) *shall not exceed 36 where the person is aged 16 or over but under 21 or (where subsection (1)(c) above applies) under 25.*

(5) A court may make an attendance centre order in respect of a person before a previous attendance centre order made in respect of him has ceased to have effect, and may determine the number of hours to be specified in the order without regard—

    (a) to the number specified in the previous order; or

    (b) to the fact that order is still in effect.

(6) An attendance centre order shall not be made unless the court is satisfied that the attendance centre to be specified in it is reasonably accessible to the person concerned, having regard to his age, the means of access available to him and any other circumstances.

(7) The times at which a person is required to attend at an attendance centre shall, as for as practicable, be such as to avoid—

    (a) any conflict with his religious beliefs or with the requirements of any other [youth] community order to which he may be subject; and

    (b) any interference with the times, if any, at which he normally works or attends school or any other educational establishment.

(8) The first time at which the person is required to attend at an attendance centre shall be a time at which the centre is available for his attendance in accordance with the notification of the Secretary of State, and shall be specified in the order.

(9) The subsequent times shall be fixed by the officer in charge of the centre, having regard to the person's circumstances.

(10) A person shall not be required under this section to attend at an attendance centre on more than one occasion on any day, or for more than three hours on any occasion.

(11) Where a court makes an attendance centre order, the clerk of the court shall—

    (a) deliver or send a copy of the order to the officer in charge of the attendance centre specified in it; and

    (b) deliver a copy of the order to the person in respect of whom it is made or send a copy by registered post or the recorded delivery service addressed to his last or usual place of abode.

(12) Where a person ("the defaulter") has been ordered to attend at an attendance centre in default of the payment of any sum of money—

    (a) on payment of the whole sum to any person authorised to receive it, the attendance centre order shall cease to have effect;

    (b) on payment of a part of the sum to any such person, the total number of hours for which the defaulter is required to attend at the centre shall be reduced proportionately, that is to say by such number of complete hours as bears to the total number the proportion most nearly approximating to, without exceeding, the proportion which the part bears to the whole sum.

[This section is printed as amended by the CJA 2003, s.304, and Sched. 32, para. 102(1), (2)(a) (substitution of references to sections 148, 150 and 156 of the 2003 Act for references to corresponding provisions of the 2000 Act, and substitution of "16" for "21" in subs. (1)(a)), and (4) (substitution of "youth community order" for "community order" in subs. (7)); and as amended, as from a day to be appointed, by the CJCSA 2000, s.74 and Sched. 7, para. 173 (insertion of words in first set of square brackets in subs. (1)(b)); and the CJA 2003, s.304, and Sched. 32, paras 90 and 102(1), and (2)(b) and (c), and (3) (substitution of "16" for "21" in subs. (1)(b), omission of subs. (1)(c) and the word "or" immediately preceding it, substitution of words in square brackets for italicised words in subs. (4)). The amendments to subss. (1)(a) and (7) came into force on April 4, 2005: Criminal Justice Act 2003 (Commencement No. 8 and Transitional and Saving Provisions) Order 2005 (S.I. 2005 No. 950), save that, in the case of persons aged 16 or 17 upon conviction, the substitution of "16" for "21" in subs. (1)(a) and the insertion of the word "youth" before "community order" in subs. (7) have no application in relation to offences committed before November 30, 2009, or in relation to any failure to comply with an order made in respect of an offence committed before that date: *ibid.*, Sched. 2, paras 12 and 13. The whole of this section is repealed as from a day to be appointed (as to which, see §§ 5-1, 5-232, 5-233 in the main work) by the CJIA 2008, ss.6(1) and 149, and Sched. 28, Pt 1. To the extent that this repeal relates to subs. (1)(a), it was brought into force on November 30, 2009: Criminal Justice and Immigration Act 2008 (Commencement No. 13 and Transitory Provision) Order 2009 (S.I. 2009 No. 3074).]

5-280   As to the requirements to be complied with before imposing an attendance centre order, see (for offences committed before April 4, 2005) sections 35 and 36 of the PCC(S)A 2000 (§§ 5-189, 5-190 in the supplements to the 2012 edition) (it being a "community order" within that Act), and (for offences committed after that date) section 148 of the CJA 2003 (§ 5-235 in the main work) (it being a "community sentence" within that Act).

It is not entirely clear whether a court may make attendance centre orders on the same occasion in respect of a number of offences with an aggregate in excess of the limits in subsection (4). It is submitted that the better view is that it cannot; section 60(1) appears to be concerned with defining an *occasion* when an attendance centre order may be made. On any such occasion *one* order may be made. Subsection (5) appears to confirm the correctness of this approach: if it were incorrect, subsection (5) would not be needed.

Section 61 gives effect to Schedule 5 (*post*, §§ 5-342 *et seq.*).

F. Enforcement, etc.

(1) Of community orders

Criminal Justice Act 2003, Sched. 8

5-334   As to the commencement of Part 4 of Schedule 16 (paras 11-21) to the Crime and Courts Act 2013 (see the main work), see *ante*, § 5-240.

(2) Of youth community orders

Curfew, exclusion and supervision orders

5-341   As to curfew and exclusion orders, see Schedule 3 to the PCC(S)A 2000 (§§ 5-228 *et seq.* in the supplements to the 2012 edition); and as to supervision orders, see Schedule 7 to that Act (§§ 5-371 *et seq.* in the supplements to the 2012 edition).

Powers of Criminal Courts (Sentencing) Act 2000, Sched. 5

Section 61   SCHEDULE 5

BREACH, REVOCATION AND AMENDMENT OF ATTENDANCE CENTRE ORDERS

Breach of order or attendance centre rules

5-342   1.—(1) Where an attendance centre order is in force and it appears on information to a justice that the offender—
   (a) has failed to attend in accordance with the order, or
   (b) while attending has committed a breach of rules made under section 222(1)(d) or (e) of the Criminal Justice Act 2003 which cannot be adequately dealt with under those rules,
the justice may issue a summons requiring the offender to appear at the place and time specified in the summons or, if the information is in writing and on oath, may issue a warrant for the offender's arrest.

(2) Any summons or warrant issued under this paragraph shall direct the offender to appear or be brought—
   (a) before a magistrates' court acting for the petty sessions area in which the offender resides; or
   (b) if it is not known where the offender resides, before a magistrates' court acting for the petty sessions area in which is situated the attendance centre which the offender is required to attend by the order or by virtue of an order under paragraph 5(1)(b) below.

2.—(1) If it is proved to the satisfaction of the magistrates' court before which an offender appears or is brought under paragraph 1 above that he has failed without reasonable excuse to attend as mentioned in sub-paragraph (1)(a) of that paragraph or has committed such a breach of rules as is mentioned in sub-paragraph (1)(b) of that paragraph, that court may deal with him in any one of the following ways—
   (a) it may impose on him a fine not exceeding £1,000;
   (b) where the attendance centre order was made by a magistrates' court, it may deal with him, for the offence in respect of which the order was made, in any way in which he could have been dealt with for that offence by the court which made the order if the order had not been made; or

(c) where the order was made by the Crown Court, it may commit him to custody or release him on bail until he can be brought or appear before the Crown Court.

(2) Any exercise by the court of its power under sub-paragraph (1)(a) above shall be without prejudice to the continuation of the order.

(3) A fine imposed under sub-paragraph (1)(a) above shall be deemed, for the purposes of any enactment, to be a sum adjudged to be paid by a conviction.

(4) Where a magistrates' court deals with an offender under sub-paragraph (1)(b) above, it shall revoke the attendance centre order if it is still in force.

(5) In dealing with an offender under sub-paragraph (1)(b) above, a magistrates' court—

(a) shall take into account the extent to which the offender has complied with the requirements of the attendance centre order; and

(b) in the case of an offender who has wilfully and persistently failed to comply with those requirements, may impose a custodial sentence notwithstanding anything in section 152(2) of the Criminal Justice Act 2003.

(5A) Where a magistrates' court dealing with an offender under sub-paragraph (1)(a) above would not otherwise have the power to amend the order under paragraph 5(1)(b) below (substitution of different attendance centre), that paragraph has effect as if references to an appropriate magistrates' court were references to the court dealing with an offender.

(6) A person sentenced under sub-paragraph (1)(b) above for an offence may appeal to the Crown Court against the sentence.

(7) A magistrates' court which deals with an offender's case under sub-paragraph (1)(c) above shall send to the Crown Court—

(a) a certificate signed by a justice of the peace giving particulars of the offender's failure to attend or, as the case may be, the breach of the rules which he has committed; and

(b) such other particulars of the case as may be desirable;

and a certificate purporting to be so signed shall be admissible as evidence of the failure or the breach before the Crown Court.

3.—(1) Where by virtue of paragraph 2(1)(c) above the offender is brought or appears before the Crown Court and it is proved to the satisfaction of the court—

(a) that he has failed without reasonable excuse to attend as mentioned in paragraph 1(1)(a) above, or

(b) that he has committed such a breach of rules as is mentioned in paragraph 1(1)(b) above,

that court may deal with him, for the offence in respect of which the order was made, in any way in which it could have dealt with him for that offence if it had not made the order.

(2) Where the Crown Court deals with an offender under sub-paragraph (1) above, it shall revoke the attendance centre order if it is still in force.

(3) In in dealing with an offender under sub-paragraph (1) above, the Crown Court—

(a) shall take into account the extent to which the offender has complied with the requirements of the attendance centre order; and

(b) in the case of an offender who has willfully and persistently failed to comply with those requirements, may impose a custodial sentence notwithstanding anything in section 152(2) of the Criminal Justice Act 2003.

(4) In proceedings before the Crown Court under this paragraph any question whether there has been a failure to attend or a breach of the rules shall be determined by the court and not by the verdict of a jury.

Revocation of order with or without re-sentencing

4.—(1) Where an attendance centre order is in force in respect of an offender, an appropriate court may, on an application made by the offender or by the officer in charge of the relevant attendance centre, revoke the order. **5-343**

(2) In sub-paragraph (1) above "an appropriate court" means—

(a) where the court which made the order was the Crown Court and there is included in the order a direction that the power to revoke the order is reserved to that court, the Crown Court;

(b) in any other case, either of the following—

(i) a magistrates' court acting for the petty sessions area in which the relevant attendance centre is situated;

(ii) the court which made the order.

(3) Any power conferred by this paragraph—

(a)   on a magistrates' court to revoke an attendance centre order made by such a court, or

(b)   on the Crown Court to revoke an attendance centre order made by the Crown Court,

includes power to deal with the offender, for the offence in respect of which the order was made, in any way in which he could have been dealt with for that offence by the court which made the order if the order had not been made.

(4) A person sentenced by a magistrates' court under sub-paragraph (3) above for an offence may appeal to the Crown Court against the sentence.

(5) The proper officer of a court which makes an order under this paragraph revoking an attendance centre order shall—

(a)   deliver a copy of the revoking order to the offender or send a copy by registered post or the recorded delivery service addressed to the offender's last or usual place of abode; and

(b)   deliver or send a copy to the officer in charge of the relevant attendance centre.

(6) In this paragraph "the relevant attendance centre", in relation to an attendance centre order, means the attendance centre specified in the order or substituted for the attendance centre so specified by an order made by virtue of paragraph 5(1)(b) below.

(7) In this paragraph "proper officer" means—

(a)   in relation to a magistrates' court, the justices' chief executive for the court; and

(b)   in relation to the Crown Court, the appropriate officer.

Amendment of order

5-344   5.—(1) Where an attendance centre order is in force in respect of an offender, an appropriate magistrates' court may, on application made by the offender or by the officer in charge of the relevant attendance centre, by order—

(a)   vary the day or hour specified in the order for the offender's first attendance at the relevant attendance centre; or

(b)   substitute for the relevant attendance centre an attendance centre which the court is satisfied is reasonably accessible to the offender, having regard to his age, the means of access available to him and any other circumstances.

(2) In sub-paragraph (1) above "an appropriate magistrates' court" means—

(a)   a magistrates' court acting for the petty sessions area in which the relevant attendance centre is situated; or

(b)   (except where the attendance centre order was made by the Crown Court) the magistrates' court which made the order.

(3) The justices' chief executive for a court which makes an order under this paragraph shall—

(a)   deliver a copy to the offender or send a copy by registered post or the recorded delivery service addressed to the offender's last or usual place of abode; and

(b)   deliver or send a copy—

(i)   if the order is made by virtue of sub-paragraph (1)(a) above, to the officer in charge of the relevant attendance centre; and

(ii)   if it is made by virtue of sub-paragraph (1)(b) above, to the officer in charge of the attendance centre which the order as amended will require the offender to attend.

(4) In this paragraph "the relevant attendance centre" has the meaning given by paragraph 4(6) above.

Orders made on appeal

5-345   6.—(1) Where an attendance centre order has been made on appeal, for the purposes of this Schedule it shall be deemed—

(a)   if it was made on an appeal brought from a magistrates' court, to have been made by that magistrates' court;

(b)   if it was made on an appeal brought from the Crown Court or from the criminal division of the Court of Appeal, to have been made by the Crown Court.

(2) In relation to an attendance centre order made on appeal, paragraphs 2(1)(b) and 4(3) above shall each have effect as if the words "if the order had not been made" were omitted and paragraph 3(1) above shall have effect as if the words "if it had not made the order" were omitted.

Orders for defaulters

5-346   7.—(1) References in this Schedule to an "offender" include a person who has been ordered to attend at an attendance centre for such a default or failure as is mentioned in section 60(1)(b) or (c) of this Act.

(2) Where a person has been ordered to attend at an attendance centre for such a default or failure—

    (a) paragraphs 2(1)(b), 3(1) and 4(3) above shall each have effect in relation to the order as if the words ", for the offence in respect of which the order was made," and "for that offence" were omitted; and

    (b) paragraphs 2(5)(b) and 3(3)(b) above (which relate to custodial sentences for offences) do not apply.

[This schedule is printed as amended by the CJA 2003, s.304, and Sched. 32, paras 90 and 126; and the Domestic Violence, Crime and Victims Act 2004, s.29, and Sched. 5, para. 6. The whole schedule is repealed as from a day to be appointed (as to which, see §§ 5-1, 5-232, 5-233 in the main work) by the CJIA 2008, ss.6(1) and 149, and Sched. 28, Pt 1.]

When dealing with an offender under paragraph 3(1), the court must observe any limitations **5-347** related to his age which applied at the time when he was sentenced: he must be sentenced on the basis of his age when he was originally convicted of the offence for which the attendance centre order was made.

In a case coming within paragraph 4, the failure to attend the attendance centre, or breach of the rules, must be proved to the satisfaction of the Crown Court: the certificate of the magistrates' court is merely evidence.

VI. CUSTODIAL SENTENCES

A. MANDATORY LIFE SENTENCE

(2) Legislation

Fixing the minimum term

The whole life starting point

    The Grand Chamber of the European Court of Human Rights has upheld the chamber deci- **5-377** sion in *Hutchinson v. U.K.* (see the main work): *Hutchinson v. U.K. (No. 2), The Times*, January 27, 2017. It was decided (by a majority (14:3)) that the Court of Appeal in *Att.-Gen.'s Reference (No. 69 of 2013) (R. v. McLoughlin); R. v. Newell (ibid.)* had dispelled the lack of clarity identified in *Vinter v. U.K. (ibid.)*, and that a whole-life order could now be regarded as reducible, in keeping with Article 3 of the ECHR (*ibid.*, § 16-46).

A guilty plea

    As to a new sentencing guideline on reduction in sentence for a guilty plea, see *ante*, § 5-178; **★5-378** and *post*, Appendix S-28 *et seq.*

The 30-year starting point and deliberate arson

    In *R. v. Dunstan* [2017] 1 Cr.App.R.(S.) 24, CA, a case of a drunken attack by the defendant on **★5-380** the deceased, with whom he had been in a relationship for a month, in the course of which he poured white spirit on her which he set alight, causing her to suffer burns to 15 per cent of her body, the court distinguished what was said in *R. v. Jones* (as to which, see the main work) about cases involving a deliberately planned arson attack upon an occupied home. It was held that the appropriate starting point had been 15 years.

Criminal Justice Act 2003, Sched. 22, paras 1, 2, 9 and 10

Section 276   SCHEDULE 22

MANDATORY LIFE SENTENCES: TRANSITIONAL CASES

Interpretation

1. In this Schedule—   **5-405**
    "the commencement date" means the day on which section 269 comes into force;

"the early release provisions" means the provisions of section 28(5) to (8) of the Crime (Sentences) Act 1997;

"existing prisoner" means a person serving one or more mandatory life sentences passed before the commencement date (whether or not he is also serving any other sentence);

"life sentence" means a sentence of imprisonment for life or custody for life passed in England and Wales or by a court-martial outside England and Wales;

"mandatory life sentence" means a life sentence passed in circumstances where the sentence was fixed by law.

Existing prisoners notified by Secretary of State

5-406
2. Paragraph 3 applies in relation to any existing prisoner who, in respect of any mandatory life sentence, has before the commencement date been notified in writing by the Secretary of State (otherwise than in a notice that is expressed to be provisional) either—

(a) of a minimum period which in the view of the Secretary of State should be served before the prisoner's release on licence, or

(b) that the Secretary of State does not intend that the prisoner should ever be released on licence.

Sentences passed on or after commencement date in respect of offences committed before that date

5-407
9. Paragraph 10 applies where—

(a) on or after the commencement date a court passes a life sentence in circumstances where the sentence is fixed by law, and

(b) the offence to which the sentence relates was committed before the commencement date.

10. The court—

(a) may not make an order under subsection (2) of section 269 specifying a part of the sentence which in the opinion of the court is greater than that which, under the practice followed by the Secretary of State before December 2002, the Secretary of State would have been likely to notify as mentioned in paragraph 2(a), and

(b) may not make an order under subsection (4) of section 269 unless the court is of the opinion that, under the practice followed by the Secretary of State before December 2002, the Secretary of State would have been likely to give the prisoner a notification falling within paragraph 2(b).

(3) Practice

Offences committed before December 18, 2003

Criminal Practice Direction VII Sentencing N: Transitional Arrangements for Sentences Where the Offence was Committed before 18 December 2003

5-409
N.1 Where the court is passing a sentence of mandatory life imprisonment for an offence committed before 18 December 2003, the court should take a fourth step in determining the minimum term in accordance with section 276 and Schedule 22 ... .

N.2 The purpose of those provisions is to ensure that the sentence does not breach the principle of non-retroactivity by ensuring that a lower minimum term would not have been imposed for the offence when it was committed. Before setting the minimum term the court must check whether the proposed term is greater than that which the Secretary of State would probably have notified under the practice followed by the Secretary of State before December 2002.

N.3 The decision in *Sullivan* [*ante*] ... gives detailed guidance as to the correct approach to this practice and judges passing mandatory life sentences where the murder was committed prior to 18 December 2003 are well advised to read that judgment before proceeding.

N.4 The practical result of that judgment is that in sentences where the murder was committed before 31st May 2002, the best guide to what would have been the practice of the Secretary of State is the letter sent to judges by Lord Bingham C.J. on 10th February 1997, the relevant parts of which are set out below.

N.5 The practice of Lord Bingham, as set out in his letter ... was to take 14 years as the period actually to be served for the "average", "normal" or "unexceptional" murder. Examples of factors he outlined as capable, in appropriate cases, of mitigating the normal penalty were:

youth;

age (where relevant to physical capacity on release or the likelihood of the defendant dying in prison);

intellectual disability or mental disorder;

provocation (in a non-technical sense), or an excessive response to a personal threat;

the absence of an intention to kill;

spontaneity and lack of premeditation (beyond that necessary to constitute the offence: *e.g.* a sudden response to family pressure or to prolonged and eventually insupportable stress);

mercy killing;

a plea of guilty, or hard evidence of remorse or contrition.

N.6 Lord Bingham then listed the following factors as likely to call for a sentence more severe than the norm:

evidence of a planned, professional, revenge or contract killing;

the killing of a child or a very old or otherwise vulnerable victim;

evidence of sadism, gratuitous violence, or sexual maltreatment, humiliation or degradation before the killing;

killing for gain (in the course of burglary, robbery, blackmail, insurance fraud, etc.);

multiple killings;

the killing of a witness or potential witness to defeat the ends of justice;

the killing of those doing their public duty (policemen, prison officers, postmasters, firemen, judges, etc.);

terrorist or politically motivated killings;

the killing of those doing their public duty (policemen, prison officers, postmasters, firemen, judges, etc);

terrorist or politically motivated killings;

the use of firearms or other dangerous weapons, whether carried for defensive or offensive reasons;

a substantial record of serious violence;

macabre attempts to dismember or conceal the body.

N.7 Lord Bingham further stated that the fact that a defendant was under the influence of drink or drugs at the time of the killing is so common he would be inclined to treat as neutral. But in the not unfamiliar case in which a couple, inflamed by drink, indulge in a violent quarrel in which one dies, often against a background of long-standing drunken violence, then he would tend to recommend a term somewhat below the norm.

N.8 Lord Bingham went on to say that given the intent necessary for proof of murder, the consequences of taking life and the understandable reaction of relatives to the deceased, a substantial term will almost always be called for, save perhaps in a truly venial case of mercy killing. While a recommendation of a punitive term longer than, say, 30 years will be very rare indeed, there should not be any upper limit. Some crimes will certainly call for terms very well in excess of the norm.

N.9 For the purposes of sentences where the murder was committed after 31 May 2002 and before 18 December 2003, the judge should apply the practice statement handed down on 31 May 2002 reproduced at paras N.10 to N.20 below.

N.10 This statement replaces the previous single normal tariff of 14 years by substituting a higher and a normal starting point of respectively 16 (comparable to 32 years) and 12 years (comparable to 24 years). These starting points have then to be increased or reduced because of aggravating or mitigating factors such as those referred to below. It is emphasised that they are no more than starting points.

The normal starting point of 12 years

N.11 Cases falling within this starting point will normally involve the killing of an adult victim,   **5-410**
arising from a quarrel or loss of temper between two people known to each other. It will not have the characteristics referred to in paragraph N.13. Exceptionally, the starting point may be reduced because of the sort of circumstances described in the next paragraph.

N.12 The normal starting point can be reduced because the murder is one where the offender's culpability is significantly reduced, for example, because: (a) the case came close to the borderline between murder and manslaughter; or (b) the offender suffered from mental disorder, or from a mental disability which lowered the degree of his criminal responsibility for the killing, although not affording a defence of diminished responsibility; or (c) the offender was provoked (in a non-technical sense), such as by prolonged and eventually unsupportable stress; or (d) the case involved an over reaction in self-defence; or (e) the offence was a mercy killing. These factors could justify a reduction to 8/9 years (equivalent to 16/18 years).

The higher starting point of 15/16 years

N.13 The higher starting point will apply to cases where the offender's culpability was exception-   **5-411**

ally high or the victim was in a particularly vulnerable position. Such cases will be characterised by a feature which makes the crime especially serious, such as: (a) the killing was "professional" or a contract killing; (b) the killing was politically motivated; (c) the killing was done for gain (in the course of a burglary, robbery etc.); (d) the killing was intended to defeat the ends of justice (as in the killing of a witness or potential witness); (e) the victim was providing a public service; (f) the victim was a child or was otherwise vulnerable; (g) the killing was racially aggravated; (h) the victim was deliberately targeted because of his or her religion or sexual orientation; (i) there was evidence of sadism, gratuitous violence or sexual maltreatment, humiliation or degradation of the victim before the killing; (j) extensive and/or multiple injuries were inflicted on the victim before death; (k) the offender committed multiple murders.

Variation of the starting point

5-412   **N.14** Whichever starting point is selected in a particular case, it may be appropriate for the trial judge to vary the starting point upwards or downwards, to take account of aggravating or mitigating factors, which relate to either the offence or the offender, in the particular case.

N.15 Aggravating factors relating to the offence can include: (a) the fact that the killing was planned; (b) the use of a firearm; (c) arming with a weapon in advance; (d) concealment of the body, destruction of the crime scene and/or dismemberment of the body; (e) particularly in domestic violence cases, the fact that the murder was the culmination of cruel and violent behaviour by the offender over a period of time.

N.16 Aggravating factors relating to the offender will include the offender's previous record and failures to respond to previous sentences, to the extent that this is relevant to culpability rather than to risk.

N.17 Mitigating factors relating to the offence will include: (a) an intention to cause grievous bodily harm, rather than to kill; (b) spontaneity and lack of pre-meditation.

N.18 Mitigating factors relating to the offender may include: (a) the offender's age; (b) clear evidence of remorse or contrition; (c) a timely plea of guilt.

Very serious cases

5-413   **N.19** A substantial upward adjustment may be appropriate in the most serious cases, for example, those involving a substantial number of murders, or if there are several factors identified as attracting the higher starting point present. In suitable cases, the result might even be a minimum term of 30 years (equivalent to 60 years) which would offer little or no hope of the offender's eventual release. In cases of exceptional gravity, the judge, rather than setting a whole life minimum term, can state that there is no minimum period which could properly be set in that particular case.

N.20 Among the categories of case referred to in paragraph N.13 some offences may be especially grave. These include cases where the victim was performing his duties as a prison officer at the time of the crime or the offence was a terrorist or sexual or sadistic murder or involved a young child. In such a case, a term of 20 years and upwards could be appropriate.

N.21 In following this guidance, judges should bear in mind the conclusion of the court in *Sullivan* [*ante*] that the general effect of both these statements is the same. While Lord Bingham does not identify as many starting points, it is open to the judge to come to exactly the same decision irrespective of which was followed. Both pieces of guidance give the judge a considerable degree of discretion.

B. Automatic Life Sentences

Powers of Criminal Courts (Sentencing) Act 2000, s.109

Life sentence for second serious offence

5-415   **109.**–(1) This section applies where–

(a) a person is convicted of a serious offence committed after 30th September 1997; and

(b) at the time when that offence was committed, he was 18 or over and had been convicted in any part of the United Kingdom of another serious offence.

(2) The court shall impose a life sentence, that is to say—

(a) *where the offender is 21 or over when convicted of the offence mentioned in subsection (1)(a) above, a sentence of imprisonment for life,*

(b) where he is under 21 at that time, a sentence of custody for life under section 94 above,

[a sentence of imprisonment for life] unless the court is of the opinion that there are exceptional circumstances relating to either of the offences or to the offender which justify its not doing so.

(3) Where the court does not impose a life sentence, it shall state in open court that it is of that opinion and what the exceptional circumstances are.

(4) An offence the sentence for which is imposed under *subsection (2)* above shall not be regarded as an offence the sentence for which is fixed by law.

(5) An offence committed in England and Wales is a serious offence for the purposes of this section if it is any of the following, namely—

(a) an attempt to commit murder, a conspiracy to commit murder or an incitement to murder;

(b) an offence under section 4 of the Offences Against the Person Act 1861 (soliciting murder);

(c) manslaughter;

(d) an offence under section 18 of the Offences Against the Person Act 1861 (wounding, or causing grievous bodily harm, with intent);

(e) rape or an attempt to commit rape;

(f) an offence under section 5 of the Sexual Offences Act 1956 (intercourse with a girl under 13);

(g) an offence under section 16 (possession of a firearm with intent to injure), section 17 (use of a firearm to resist arrest) or section 18 (carrying a firearm with criminal intent) of the Firearms Act 1968; and

(h) robbery where, at some time during the commission of the offence, the offender had in his possession a firearm or imitation firearm within the meaning of that Act.

(6) An offence committed in Scotland is a serious offence for the purposes of this section if the conviction for it was obtained on indictment in the High Court of Justiciary and it is any of the following, namely—

(a) culpable homicide;

(b) attempted murder, incitement to commit murder or conspiracy to commit murder;

(c) rape or attempted rape;

(d) clandestine injury to women or an attempt to cause such injury;

(e) sodomy, or an attempt to commit sodomy, where the complainer, that is to say, the person against whom the offence was committed, did not consent;

(f) assault where the assault—

(i) is aggravated because it was carried out to the victim's severe injury or the danger of the victim's life; or

(ii) was carried out with an intention to rape or to ravish the victim;

(g) robbery where, at some time during the commission of the offence, the offender had in his possession a firearm or imitation firearm within the meaning of the Firearms Act 1968;

(h) an offence under section 16 (possession of a firearm with intent to injure), section 17 (use of a firearm to resist arrest) or section 18 (carrying a firearm with criminal intent) of that Act;

(i) lewd, libidinous or indecent behaviour or practices; and

(j) an offence under section 5(1) of the Criminal Law (Consolidation) (Scotland) Act 1995 (unlawful intercourse with a girl under 13).

(7) An offence committed in Northern Ireland is a serious offence for the purposes of this section if it is any of the following, namely—

(a) an offence falling within any of paragraphs (a) to (e) of subsection (5) above;

(b) an offence under section 4 of the Criminal Law Amendment Act 1885 (intercourse with a girl under 14);

(c) an offence under Article 17 (possession of a firearm with intent to injure), Article 18(1) (use of a firearm to resist arrest) or Article 19 (carrying a firearm with criminal intent) of the Firearms (Northern Ireland) Order 1981; and

(d) robbery where, at some time during the commission of the offence, the offender had in his possession a firearm or imitation firearm within the meaning of that Order.

[This section is printed as amended, as from a day to be appointed, by the CJCSA 2000, s.74, and Sched. 7, para. 189 (substitution of words in square brackets for paras (a) and (b) in subs. (2)). It is repealed, as from April 4, 2005 (Criminal Justice Act 2003 (Commencement No. 8 and Transitional and Saving Provisions) Order 2005 (S.I. 2005 No. 950), by the CJA 2003, s.332, and Sched. 37 Pt 7. For the saving provisions in relation to an offence committed before April 4, 2005, see § 5-2 in the main work.]

Serious offences

The only attempts which are serious offences are those specifically mentioned: *R. v. Buckland*; **5-416** *R. v. Newman* [2000] 1 Cr.App.R. 471, CA. Offences under the Firearms Act 1968, s.17(2) are serious offences: *ibid.*; as are offences under sections 16, 17 and 18 of that Act where the firearm was an imitation only: *ibid.*

An offence of robbery is a "serious offence" within section 109(2)(h) if the offence was committed as a joint enterprise where a firearm or imitation was used, even though the offender himself had never had possession of it, provided that there was joint possession of it; where, in relation to the alleged index offence, there is an issue as to whether this was established against the offender, the court must be satisfied that at the earlier hearing the offender admitted, or it was admitted on his behalf, that he was in joint possession of the firearm: *R. v. Flamson* [2002] 2 Cr.App.R.(S.) 48, CA. The court considered that *R. v. Eubank* [2002] 1 Cr.App.R.(S.) 4, CA (§ 24-49 in the main work) had no application to the facts of the case. In *R. v. Murphy* [2003] 1 Cr.App.R.(S.) 39, CA, however, it was held, without reference to *Flamson*, that where there was an issue as to whether the defendant had been in possession of a firearm, the proper way to resolve the issue was, in accordance with *Eubank*, for an appropriate count under the Firearms Act 1968 to be included in the indictment. Where this course had not been adopted, it was not open to the judge to conclude in relation to either the index offence or the fresh offence that it fell within section 109(1)(h); absent an unequivocal admission on the part of the defendant (see *R. v. Benfield*; *R. v. Sobers* [2004] 1 Cr.App.R.(S.) 52, CA).

R. v. Benfield; *R. v. Sobers* was followed in *R. v. Hylands* [2005] 2 Cr.App.R.(S.) 25, CA, where it was said that for an offence of robbery to fall within section 109(5)(h) of the 2000 Act, the qualifying condition relating to a firearm or imitation firearm had to be established either by means of an appropriate count under the Firearms Act 1968 being included in the indictment, or there had to be an unequivocal admission in relation thereto; and this applies where the only issue in relation to the robbery is identity (there being unchallenged evidence before the jury that the robber was in possession of a firearm at the time of the robbery); if there was any doubt about the matter, it was to be resolved in favour of the defendant.

As to whether a conviction at a court-martial in Germany for an offence of wounding with intent to cause grievous bodily harm committed whilst a serving member of the armed forces in Germany may qualify as a "serious offence" within the meaning of section 109(1)(a) of the PCC(S)A 2000, see *R. v. Sanders, post*, § 5-423.

"exceptional circumstances"

5-417   The meaning of "exceptional circumstances" (s.109(2)) was reconsidered in *R. v. Offen* [2001] 1 W.L.R. 253, CA. Lord Woolf C.J. said that quite apart from the impact of the Human Rights Act 1998, the rationale of the section should be highly relevant in deciding whether or not exceptional circumstances existed. The question whether circumstances were appropriately regarded as "exceptional" must be influenced by the context in which the question was being asked. The policy and intention of Parliament were to protect the public against a person who had committed two serious offences. It therefore could be assumed that the section was not intended to apply to someone in relation to whom it was established that there would be no need for protection in the future. In other words, if the facts showed the statutory assumption was misplaced, then this, in the statutory context, was not the normal situation and in consequence, for the purposes of the section, the position was exceptional. The time that elapsed between the two offences could, but would not necessarily, reflect on whether, after the second serious offence was committed, there was any danger against which the public would need protection. The same was true of two differing offences, and the age of the offender. These were all circumstances which could give rise to the conclusion that what could be normal and not exceptional in a different context was exceptional in this context. If this approach was not adopted, then in the case of the serious offences listed in the section, the gravity of which could vary greatly, the approach to "exceptional circumstances" could be unduly restrictive. The aim of section 2 was not to increase the time offenders spent in prison as a punishment for the offence they had committed, but to provide for an assessment to be made to see whether the offender posed a real risk to the public, in which event his release was deferred. Section 109 established a norm. The norm was that those who commit two serious offences were a danger or risk to the public. If in fact, taking into account all the circumstances relating to a particular offender, he did not create an unacceptable risk to the public, he was an exception to this norm.

Construing section 109 in accordance with the duty imposed on the court by section 3 of the 1998 Act, and taking into account the rationale of the section, gave content to "exceptional circumstances". In the court's judgment, section 109 would not contravene Convention rights if courts applied the section so that it did not result in offenders being sentenced to life imprisonment when they did not constitute a significant risk to the public. Whether there was a significant risk would depend on the evidence which was before the court. If the offender was a significant risk, the court could impose a life sentence under section 109 without contravening the Convention. It would be part of the responsibility of judges to assess the risk to the public that offenders constituted. In many cases the degree of risk that an offender constituted would be established by his record, with or without the assistance of assessments made in reports which were available to the court. If courts needed further assistance, they could call for it when deciding whether a discretionary life sentence should be imposed. There should be no undue difficulty in making a similar assessment when considering whether the court was required to impose an automatic life sentence, although the task would not be straightforward, because of the lack of information as to the first serious offence which will sometimes exist because of the passage of time. This did not mean that the court was approaching the passing of an automatic life sentence as if it was no different from the imposition of a discretionary life sentence. Notwithstanding the interpretation resulting from the application of section 3(1) of the 1998 Act suggested, section 109 would give effect to the intention of Parliament. It would do so, however, in a more just, less arbitrary and more proportionate manner. Section 109 would still mean that a judge was obliged to pass a life sentence in accordance with its terms unless, in all the circumstances, the offender posed no significant risk to the public. There was no such obligation in cases where section 109 did not apply. In addition, if the judge decided not to impose a life sentence under section 109, he would have to give reasons as required by section 109(3). Furthermore, the issue of dangerousness would have to be addressed in every case and a decision made as to whether or not to impose a life sentence.

Offen has since been applied in *R. v. McDonald* [2001] 2 Cr.App.R.(S.) 127, CA (having regard, in particular, to the length of time since the appellant's conviction for his previous "serious" offences (14 years) and to the fact that it was not the appellant but a co-defendant who had produced an imitation firearm in the course of the robbery, although it belonged to the appellant, it would be wrong to conclude that the appellant presented a serious risk of harm to the public so as to justify the imposition of an automatic life sentence); and in *R. v. Kelly (No. 2)* [2002] 1 Cr.App.R.(S.) 85, CA, it was held that the statutory presumption that arises under section 109(2), and which flows from the existence of two qualifying offences remains in place, and has to be displaced by the defendant in any given case; and such displacement may be achieved in a number of ways, including scrutiny of the offending and behaviour pattern, or by positive psychiatric or similar evidence, such evidence being likely to be required if the court is to be persuaded that the presumption cannot apply since the criterion to be established is that there is "no need to protect the public in the future" or "no significant risk to the public".

In *R. v. Baff* [2003] 2 Cr.App.R.(S.) 37, CA, it was said that the use of imitation firearms for the purpose of robbery caused as much fear and alarm to vulnerable members of the public as robbery with a real firearm; and that, if the court were to rule that section 109 did not as a matter of principle apply where the offender limited his offending to robberies with an imitation firearm, it would be creating an exception to an express provision flatly contradicting an aspect of sentencing policy laid down by Parliament.

In *R. v. Richards* [2002] 2 Cr.App.R.(S.) 26, CA, it was held that in considering whether a defendant who qualifies for an automatic life sentence under section 109 presents a significant risk to the public, the judge may take account of a significant risk of the commission of serious offences other than those listed as "serious" in the section itself, for example, burglaries of dwellings or a conspiracy to import hard drugs. For a criticism of this decision, see the commentary in the *Criminal Law Review*. It is inconsistent with the view of the court in *R. v. Fletcher; R. v. Smith* [2002] 1 Cr.App.R.(S.) 82, CA, to the effect that the "danger in point is that of violent or sexual offending."

Richards was not cited in *R. v. Stark* [2002] 2 Cr.App.R.(S.) 104, CA, where there was a high risk of further offences being committed by the appellant, but no significant risk of danger to the public by way of either violent or sexual offences; accordingly, it was held that the case was to be regarded as an exception to the norm, which was that those who committed two serious offences were a danger or risk to the public.

The approach in *R. v. Stark* and *R. v. Fletcher; R. v. Smith* was followed, and that in *Richards* expressly disapproved in *R. v. Magalhaes* [2005] 2 Cr.App.R.(S.) 13, CA.

In *R. v. Frost* [2001] 2 Cr.App.R.(S.) 26, CA, the appellant had been found guilty by a youth court in 1991 of wounding with intent to resist arrest. He was later convicted of wounding with intent to cause grievous bodily harm. The court held that the finding of guilt by the youth court amounted to a "conviction" for the purposes of PCC(S)A 2000, s.109(1), by virtue of the CYPA 1933, s.59. If the appellant had been older and had been subject to a probation order, the "conviction" would have been deemed not to be a conviction by virtue of the PCCA 1973, s.13(1) (*rep.*), but this provision did not apply to a supervision order. The anomaly which resulted from this amounted to an "exceptional circumstance" for the purposes of section 109, and the sentence of life imprisonment was quashed, even though it could not be said that the offender presented no significant risk to the public.

The fact that the offender is mentally ill and eligible for a hospital order does not in itself amount to an "exceptional circumstance" for this purpose: see *R. v. Newman* [2000] 2 Cr.App.R.(S.) 227, CA; *R. v. Drew* [2003] 2 Cr.App.R. 24, HL (where a submission that an automatic life sentence on conviction of wounding with intent constituted inhuman or degrading treatment was rejected; having been transferred administratively to hospital within a few days of the passing of sentence, the appellant was receiving the same treatment as he would have received had he been made subject to a hospital order, and he could not complain of the stigma attaching to the sentence as he had been convicted by a jury, who must therefore have been satisfied as to his intent).

On appeal, the issue is whether the offender created an unacceptable risk to the public at the time when he was sentenced, not at the time when the Court of Appeal is considering the matter: see *R. v. Watkins* [2003] 1 Cr.App.R.(S.) 16, CA; *R. v. Noorkoiv* [2002] 2 Cr.App.R.(S.) 91, CA.

C. Minimum Fixed Term Sentences

(1) Legislation

Powers of Criminal Courts (Sentencing) Act 2000, ss.112–115

Offences under service law

5-423   In *R. v. Sanders* [2007] 1 Cr.App.R.(S.) 74, CA, it was held that the effect of section 114 of the PCC(S)A 2000 was limited to deeming the conviction to have been in England and Wales; it did not deem the offence to have been committed in England and Wales; where, therefore, the appellant had previously been convicted of an offence under section 70 of the Army Act 1955 and the corresponding civil offence had been one of those listed in section 109(5), but the offence had been committed abroad, he was not to be regarded as having previously been convicted of a serious offence, since, under section 109(5), an offence would only be "serious" if committed in England and Wales; section 114 would bite only in relation to convictions under section 70 where the offence occurred in England and Wales. It should be noted that the repeal of the words "a serious offence" in section 114(1)(b) is of no effect where an offender is being dealt with for an offence committed prior to April 4, 2005.

(2) Practice

"exceptional circumstances" (1968 Act, s.51A(2))

5-432   In *Att.-Gen.'s Reference (No. 115 of 2015) (R. v. Greenfield)* [2016] 2 Cr.App.R.(S.) 23, CA, it was said that there has been a clear steer from the court in recent years to the effect that the word "exceptional" in section 51A(2) (§ 5-425 in the main work) of the 1968 Act is not to be diluted; sympathy for an offender is not enough to justify a judge failing to do his statutory duty; here, the offender had knowingly stored a potentially lethal weapon for a drug dealer in exchange for drugs, and must have known of its possible uses; the only conceivable "exceptional" feature might have been her willingness to name the drug dealer but, on the facts, that was not enough. The court went on to say that reliance on *R. v. Edwards (Michelle Marie)* (as to which, see the main work), was misplaced, given that it was very much based on its own facts, it set no precedent, and it should not be cited in future; rather, it is essential that judges do not lose sight of what was said in *Att.-Gen.'s Reference (No. 37 of 2013) (R. v. Culpeper)* (as to which, see also the main work).

Disputed issues of fact

5-434   *R. v. Rogers (Georgina)*; *R. v. Tapecrown Ltd*; *R. v. Beaman (Paul)* is now reported at [2016] 2 Cr.App.R.(S.) 36, *sub nom. R. v. Rogers*.

D. Discretionary Custodial Sentences

(1) General restrictions

(a) *Legislation*

Criminal Justice Act 2003, ss.152, 153

General restrictions on imposing discretionary custodial sentences

The Sentencing Council for England and Wales has issued a definitive guideline relating to the **5-438** imposition of community and custodial sentences: see *ante*, § 5-178; and *post*, Appendix S-27 *et seq.*

(b) *Authorities*

Deterrence/prevalence

R. v. Bondzie (Marco) (Practice Note) is now reported at [2016] 2 Cr.App.R.(S.) 28, *sub nom. R. v.* **5-447** *Bondzie*.

(c) *Legislation (offences committed before April 4, 2005)*

Powers of Criminal Courts (Sentencing) Act 2000, ss.79, 80

General restrictions on imposing discretionary custodial sentences

79.–(1) This section applies where a person is convicted of an offence punishable with a custodial **5-451** sentence other than one–

    (a)   fixed by law; or

    (b)   falling to be imposed under section 109(2), 110(2) or 111(2) below.

(2) Subject to subsection (3) below, the court shall not pass a custodial sentence on the offender unless it is of the opinion–

    (a)   that the offence, or the combination of the offence and one or more offences associated with it, was so serious that only such a sentence can be justified for the offence; or

    (b)   where the offence is a violent or sexual offence, that only such a sentence would be adequate to protect the public from serious harm from him.

(3) Nothing in subsection (2) above shall prevent the court from passing a custodial sentence on the offender if he fails to express his willingness to comply with–

    (a)   a requirement which is proposed by the court to be included in a community rehabilitation order or supervision order and which requires an expression of such willingness; or

    (b)   a requirement which is proposed by the court to be included in a drug treatment and testing order or an order under section 52(4) above (order to provide samples). In relation to an offence committed before 1st October 1997:

(4) Where a court passes a custodial sentence, it shall–

    (a)   in a case not falling within subsection (3) above, state in open court that it is of the opinion that either or both of paragraphs (a) and (b) of subsection (2) above apply and why it is of that opinion; and

    (b)   in any case, explain to the offender in open court and in ordinary language why it is passing a custodial sentence on him.

(5) A magistrates' court shall cause a reason stated by it under subsection (4) above to be specified in the warrant of commitment and to be entered in the register.

[This section is printed as amended by the CJCSA 2000, s.74 and Sched. 7, para. 1. It is repealed, as from April 4, 2005 (Criminal Justice Act 2003 (Commencement No. 8 and Transitional and Saving Provisions) Order 2005 (S.I. 2005 No. 950)), by the CJA 2003, s.332, and Sched. 37, Pt 7. As to the saving provision in relation to offences committed before April 4, 2005, see § 5-2 in the main work.]

In relation to an offence committed before October 1, 1997, see the transitional provision in Sched. 11, para. 4(d).

Length of discretionary custodial sentences: general provision

80.–(1) This section applies where a court passes a custodial sentence other than one fixed by law **5-452** or falling to be imposed under section 109(2) below.

(2) Subject to sections 110(2) and 111(2) below, the custodial sentence shall be–

(a) for such term (not exceeding the permitted maximum) as in the opinion of the court is commensurate with the seriousness of the offence, or the combination of the offence and one or more offences associated with it; or

(b) where the offence is a violent or sexual offence, for such longer term (not exceeding that maximum) as in the opinion of the court is necessary to protect the public from serious harm from the offender.

(3) Where the court passes a custodial sentence for a term longer than is commensurate with the seriousness of the offence, or the combination of the offence and one or more offences associated with it, the court shall–

(a) state in open court that it is of the opinion that subsection (2)(b) above applies and why it is of that opinion; and

(b) explain to the offender in open court and in ordinary language why the sentence is for such a term.

(4) A custodial sentence for an indeterminate period shall be regarded for the purposes of subsections (2) and (3) above as a custodial sentence for a term longer than any actual term.

(5) Subsection (3) above shall not apply in any case where the court passes a custodial sentence falling to be imposed under subsection (2) of section 110 or 111 below which is for the minimum term specified in that subsection.

[This section is repealed, as from April 4, 2005 (Criminal Justice Act 2003 (Commencement No. 8 and Transitional and Saving Provisions) Order 2005 (S.I. 2005 No. 950)), by the CJA 2003, s.332, and Sched. 37, Pt 7. As to the saving provision in relation to offences committed before April 4, 2005, see § 5-2 in the main work.]

Powers of Criminal Courts (Sentencing) Act 2000, s.161

Meaning of "associated offence", "sexual offence", "violent offence" and "protecting the public from serious harm"

5-453 **161.**–(1) [*See § 5-4 in the main work.*]

(2) In this Act, "sexual offence" means any of the following–

(f) an offence under the Protection of Children Act 1978;

(fa) an offence under section 3 of the Sexual Offences (Amendment) Act 2000;

(fa) an offence under any provision of Part 1 of the Sexual Offences Act 2003; except section 52, 53 or 71

(g) an offence under section 1 of the Criminal Law Act 1977; of conspiracy to commit any of the offences in paragraphs (a) to (f) above;

(h) an offence under section 1 of the Criminal Attempts Act 1981; of attempting to commit any of those offences;

(i) an offence of inciting another to commit any of those offences.

(3) In this Act, "violent offence" means an offence which leads, or is intended or likely to lead, to a person's death or to physical injury to a person, and includes an offence which is required to be charged as arson (whether or not it would otherwise fall within this definition).

(4) In this Act any reference, in relation to an offender convicted of a violent or sexual offence, to protecting the public from serious harm from him shall be construed as a reference to protecting members of the public from death or serious personal injury, whether physical or psychological, occasioned by further such offences committed by him.

[Subss. (2) to (4) are printed as amended and repealed in part, by the Sexual Offences (Amendment) Act 2000, s.6(1); and the SOA 2003, ss.139 and 140, and Sched. 6, para. 4 (insertion of second para. (fa) in subs. (2)), and Sched. 7 (repeal of subs. (2)(a)-(e), the failure to repeal the first para. (fa) being accounted for by the draftsman having overlooked the amendment made by the 2000 Act). The amendments effected by the 2003 Act took effect on May 1, 2004 (Sexual Offences Act 2003 (Commencement) Order 2004 (S.I. 2004 No. 874)). For the former provisions, which will continue to apply in relation to offences committed before that date (Interpretation Act 1978, s.16 (*post*, Appendix F-16)), see the 2004 edition of this work. Subss. (2) to (4) are repealed, as from April 4, 2005 (Criminal Justice Act 2003 (Commencement No. 8 and Transitional and Saving Provisions) Order 2005 (S.I. 2005 No. 950)), by the CJA 2003, s.332, and Sched. 7. As to the saving provision in relation to offences committed before April 4, 2005, see § 5-2 in the main work.]

"Violent" and "sexual" offences

5-454   Whether any particular offence is a violent offence depends on the facts of the individual offence. An offence which leads to or is intended to lead only to psychological injury is not a "violent offence" but it is not necessary that serious harm should have been caused (see *R. v. Robinson* [1994] 1 W.L.R. 168, CA). Nor does it have to be established that physical injury was a probability: *R. v. Szczerba* [2002] 2 Cr.App.R.(S.) 86, CA.

In *R. v. Cochrane*, 15 Cr.App.R.(S.) 708, CA, it was held that a robbery in which the victim was threatened with a knife was a "violent offence" as the incident could have resulted in injury, either accidentally or if the victim had resisted. See also *R. v. Bibby*, 16 Cr.App.R.(S.) 127, CA. For cases of robbery by persons armed with a firearm, see *R. v. Touriq Khan*, 16 Cr.App.R.(S.) 180, CA, *R. v. Palin*, 16 Cr.App.R.(S.) 888, CA, and *R. v. Baker* [2001] 1 Cr.App.R.(S.) 55, CA. An offence of threatening to kill which does not involve the infliction of physical injury will not normally be a "violent offence": see *R. v. Richart*, 16 Cr.App.R.(S.) 977, CA, *R. v. Ragg* [1996] 1 Cr.App.R.(S.) 176, CA and *R. v. Birch* [2002] 1 Cr.App.R.(S.) 129, CA; but see *R. v. Wilson* [1998] 1 Cr.App.R.(S.) 341, CA.

Attempted arson is "an offence which is required to be charged as arson" and is accordingly a "violent offence" within section 161(3): *R. v. Guirke* [1997] 1 Cr.App.R.(S.) 170, CA.

"Serious harm" (s.161(4) of the Act of 2000)

See § 5-473 in the main work. **5-455**

The criterion of seriousness

For discussion of the relevant authorities in relation to section 79(1), see § 5-445 in the main **5-456**
work.

Sentences commensurate with the seriousness of the offence

For relevant considerations where a court is deciding what term of custody is commensurate **5-457**
with an offence or group of offences, see § 5-446 in the main work.

Longer than normal sentences

For the definitions of "sexual offence" and "violent offence", see section 161(2) and (3) of the **5-458**
PCC(S)A 2000 (*ante*, § 5-453); and for the authorities in relation thereto, see *ante*, § 5-454. For the construction of references to "protecting the public from serious harm", see section 161(4) of the 2000 Act (*ante*, § 5-453); and the authorities referred to at §§ 5-473 *et seq.* in the main work.

An isolated offence, however serious, will rarely be sufficient to justify a longer than normal sentence under section 80(2)(b), whether the offence is violent or sexual, or both: *R. v. Walsh*, 16 Cr.App.R.(S.) 204, CA; *R. v. Mumtaz Ali*, 16 Cr.App.R.(S.) 692, CA. A longer than commensurate sentence may be passed on an offender with no previous convictions: *R. v. Thomas*, 16 Cr.App.R.(S.) 616, CA.

A court deciding whether to draw the inference that the offender is likely to commit further violent or sexual offences may need to examine the circumstances of the current offence in some detail, going beyond what would be necessary if only a commensurate sentence were in issue: *R. v. Oudkerk*, 16 Cr.App.R.(S.) 172, CA. Equally, if the inference is to be based on a previous conviction, the court may need to examine the circumstances of that offence in detail: *R. v. Samuels*, 16 Cr.App.R.(S.) 856, CA.

An offender may satisfy the requirements of section 80(2)(b) even though the members of the public who are at risk from him are a small group, or possibly an individual: *R. v. Hashi*, 16 Cr.App.R.(S.) 121, CA. Where the offender's behaviour is directed at a small group of people, who can be protected from him by other means, a longer than commensurate sentence may not be justified: *R. v. Nicholas*, 15 Cr.App.R.(S.) 381, CA; *R. v. Swain*, 15 Cr.App.R.(S.) 765, CA; *R. v. L.*, 15 Cr.App.R.(S.) 501, CA.

In many cases the inference of dangerousness will be based in part on psychiatric evidence: *R. v. Lyons*, 15 Cr.App.R.(S.) 460, CA; *R. v. Fawcett*, 16 Cr.App.R.(S.) 55, CA; *R. v. Etchells* [1996] 1 Cr.App.R.(S.) 163, CA.

The principles which should be applied in deciding the length of a longer than commensurate sentence were considered in *R. v. Mansell*, 15 Cr.App.R.(S.) 771, CA; and *R. v. Crow; R. v. Pennington*, 16 Cr.App.R.(S.) 409, CA. Lord Taylor C.J. said that some allowance should usually be made, even in the worst cases, for a plea of guilty. A sentence imposed under section 80(2)(b), whilst long enough to give necessary protection for the public, should still bear a reasonable relationship to the offence for which it was imposed.

This principle was not applied in *R. v. Chapman* [2000] 1 Cr.App.R. 77, CA, where it was said that there was no necessary ratio between the part of the sentence intended to punish and the part intended to protect. There was no objection in principle if the court regarded a sentence of two years as necessary to punish, but an additional term of six or eight years as necessary to protect, making a total term of eight or 10 years. *Chapman* was followed in *R. v. Wilson* [2000] 2 Cr.App.R.(S.) 323, CA, but not apparently in *R. v. De Silva* [2000] 2 Cr.App.R.(S.) 408, CA.

5-459   The question whether a longer than commensurate sentence may properly be imposed to run consecutively to a sentence of imprisonment was considered by the Court of Appeal in *R. v. Everleigh* [2002] 1 Cr.App.R.(S.) 32. The court considered *R. v. King*, 16 Cr.App.R.(S.) 987; *R. v. Walters* [1997] 2 Cr.App.R.(S.) 87; *R. v. Johnson* [1998] 1 Cr.App.R.(S.) 126; *R. v. Cuthbertson and Jenks* [2000] 1 Cr.App.R.(S.) 359; *R. v. Parsons* [2000] 1 Cr.App.R.(S.) 428; *R. v. Blades* [2000] 1 Cr.App.R.(S.) 463; *R. v. Sullivan* [2000] 2 Cr.App.R.(S.) 318; *R. v. Sowden* [2000] 2 Cr.App.R.(S.) 360; *R. v. Wilson* [2000] 2 Cr.App.R.(S.) 323; and *R. v. Ellis* [2001] 1 Cr.App.R.(S.) 43. Accepting that not all of these of authorities could be reconciled, the court held that they showed that it was inappropriate to pass a longer than the normal sentence to run consecutively to another sentence imposed on the same occasion, because a longer than normal sentence is intended in itself to protect the public from serious harm, without the need for any additional penalty in relation to other conduct punishable at the same time. Secondly, there was nothing inappropriate, but on the contrary it might be desirable, for a longer than normal sentence to be passed consecutively either to a sentence passed on an earlier occasion (*Wilson*) or to a period of return to custody ordered under the PCC(S)A 2000, s.116, which was a consequence of a sentence passed on an earlier occasion (*Blades*). As was pointed out in *Blades*, it was important that both the public and the defendant should know that a sentence once passed would have to be served (subject to any reduction which might be appropriate in accordance with *R. v. Taylor* [1998] 1 Cr.App.R.(S.) 312). It was desirable that the sentencing judge, if imposing a consecutive sentence, should make it plain what were the factors which he had taken into consideration in so passing the sentence under section 80(2)(b).

In *R. v. Christie*, 16 Cr.App.R.(S.) 469, CA, it was said to be wrong to add an additional period to the sentence under section 80(2)(b) if the commensurate sentence already incorporated an element for the protection of the public. In *R. v. Campbell* [1997] 1 Cr.App.R.(S.) 119, CA, it was held that if the sentencing guidelines for a particular offence included an element for the protection of the public, the sentencer should decide what was the appropriate sentence, leaving out of account any element for the protection of the public, and should then add the greater element needed for the protection of the public from serious harm under section 80(2)(b). This would avoid the risk of imposing an element of the sentence twice over. In *R. v. Gabbidon and Bramble* [1997] 2 Cr.App.R.(S.) 19, CA, this approach was described as too difficult an exercise in forensic archaeology; it was better that the sentencer simply applied the principle of balance stated by Lord Taylor C.J. in *R. v. Mansell*, 15 Cr.App.R.(S.) 771.

In a case where a longer than normal sentence is passed on one offender and a commensurate sentence on the other, it does not necessarily follow that there is any disparity of sentence, provided that there is evidence of continuing dangerousness on the part of one offender and not in the case of the other: *R. v. Bestwick and Huddlestone*, 16 Cr.App.R.(S.) 168, CA.

A longer than commensurate sentence may be imposed on an offender under section 80(2)(b) even though he does not qualify for a sentence of life imprisonment under the criteria established for that form of sentence: *R. v. Helm*, 16 Cr.App.R.(S.) 834, CA. The enactment of section 80(2)(b) has not reduced the requirements for a life sentence: *R. v. Roche*, 16 Cr.App.R.(S.) 849, CA.

Where a sentencer has in mind the possibility of passing a longer than commensurate sentence, he should warn counsel for the defendant of his intentions and invite submissions on the question: *R. v. Baverstock*, 96 Cr.App.R. 435, CA. This point has been repeated in many cases; it is particularly important when any question arises as to whether the offence is a "violent offence" for the purposes of the Act. Where a court passes a longer than commensurate sentence it is required by the PCC(S)A 2000, s.80(3) to state in open court that it is of the opinion that subsection (2)(b) applies and why it is of that opinion, and explain to the offender in open court and in ordinary language why the sentence is for such a term. Failure to comply with this obligation does not invalidate the sentence: *Baverstock, ante; R. v. Thomas*, 16 Cr.App.R.(S.) 616, CA. Even where the nature of the expected future harm is obvious, the sentencer should ensure that he has properly identified what the harm was before he proceeded to sentence, and should point out clearly and in straightforward terms what it was that he considered to be the serious harm in question: *R. v. Bacon*, 16 Cr.App.R.(S.) 1031, CA.

Where a court fails to pass a longer than commensurate sentence where such a sentence should be passed, the resulting sentence may be "unduly lenient" and may be the subject of a reference by the Attorney-General under the CJA 1988, s.36: *Att-Gen.'s Reference (No. 9 of 1994) (R. v. Groves)*, 16 Cr.App.R.(S.) 366, CA. Where a person sentenced to a longer than commensurate sentence persuades the Court of Appeal that the case is not one in which a longer than commensurate sentence should have been passed, the court is not bound to substitute a shorter sentence; its powers are at large, and it may approve the sentence passed as a commensurate sentence if it considers it appropriate to do so: *R. v. Palmer* [1996] 2 Cr.App.R.(S.) 68, CA; and see also *R. v. Henshaw* [1996] 2 Cr.App.R.(S.) 310, CA; and *R. v. Rai and Robinson* [2000] 2 Cr.App.R.(S.) 120, CA.

(2) Imprisonment

(b) *Maximum*

Powers of magistrates' courts

R. v. Chamberlain (as to which, see the main work) was approved and followed in *R. v. Hester-Wox* [2016] 2 Cr.App.R.(S.) 43, CA. **5-470**

(c) *Dangerous offenders*

Introduction

The Supreme Court has upheld the decision of the Court of Appeal (see the main work) in *R. v. Docherty*, and held that article 6 of the Legal Aid, Sentencing and Punishment of Offenders Act 2012 (Commencement No. 4 and Saving Provisions) Order 2012 (S.I. 2012 No. 2906) (*ibid.*, § 5-3) did not breach Article 7 of the ECHR (*ibid.*, § 16-130) and was lawful: *R. v. Docherty (Shaun)* [2017] 1 W.L.R. 181, SC (considering *Scoppola v. Italy (No. 2)* (as to which, see *post*, § 16-136)). **5-472**

Specified violent and sexual offences

With effect from April 3, 2017 (Serious Crime Act 2015 (Commencement No. 7) Regulations 2017 (S.I. 2017 No. 511)), paragraph 68(2) of Schedule 4 to the 2015 Act (see the main work) was brought into force. **★5-483**

Discretionary life sentences and extended sentences

(i) *General matters*

The words "members of the public" in the dangerousness provisions of the CJA 2003 (§§ 5-473 *et seq.* in the main work) (*viz.* "the court considers that there is a significant risk to members of the public of serious harm occasioned by the commission by the offender of further specified offences"), are intended to include the public in other countries; but it will only be relevant to consider the risk of harm to such persons where the further specified offences in contemplation are offences that, in view of their territorial scope, are capable of causing harm abroad, and are justiciable in England and Wales: *R. v. Abdallah; R. v. Khan (Junead); R. v. Shaukat* [2017] 1 W.L.R. 1699, CA. As to this case, see also *post*, § 25-192a. **★5-491**

(iv) *Assessment of significant risk*

Sentencers should exercise particular care before reaching a finding of dangerousness in relation to young people, especially where there is no pattern of offending; young people are more likely to act impulsively, more likely to be responsive to any sentence imposed, and more likely to effect change, especially when any sentence is likely to be long: *R. v. Chowdhury* [2016] 2 Cr.App.R.(S.) 41, CA. **5-493**

Application of principles

5-500   *R. v. Terrell* (as to which, see the main work) was applied in *R. v. Hayes* [2016] 2 Cr.App.R.(S.) 24, CA, where the court said that the link between offences of possession of indecent photographs of children (CJA 1988, s.160 (*ibid.*, § 31-115)) and any possible harm to children was too remote. In this context, the court also referred to its decision in *R. v. Guest*, unreported, July 1, 2011 ([2011] EWCA Crim. 1762), which had "built on" *Terrell*, in holding that it had not been open to a judge to find an offender involved in the sophisticated distribution of images dangerous.

(d) *Offenders of particular concern*

Criminal Justice Act 2003, s.236A

Special custodial sentence for certain offenders of particular concern
5-521   *R. v. L.F.; R. v. D.S.* is now reported at [2016] 2 Cr.App.R.(S.) 30, *sub nom. R. v. L.F.*

(e) *Suspended sentences*

Criminal Justice Act 2003, ss.189-192

Suspended sentences of imprisonment
5-524   The Sentencing Council for England and Wales has issued a definitive guideline relating to the imposition of community and custodial sentences: see *ante*, § 5-178; and *post*, Appendix S-27 *et seq*. This includes general guidance on the use of suspended sentences and the requirements to be attached thereto.

Imposition of requirements by suspended sentence order
5-527   As to the commencement of Part 4 of Schedule 16 (paras 11-21) to the Crime and Courts Act 2013, see *ante*, § 5-240.

★   As to the amendment of the Legal Aid, Sentencing and Punishment of Offenders Act 2012 (Alcohol Abstinence and Monitoring Requirements) Piloting Order 2016 (S.I. 2016 No. 286) (see the main work), see *ante*, § 5-240.

★   As to the further commencement of section 76 of the LASPOA 2012 (see the main work) to give effect to a second pilot scheme, see *ante*, § 5-240.

Periodic reviews of suspended sentence order
5-529   As to the commencement of Part 4 of Schedule 16 (paras 11-21) to the Crime and Courts Act 2013 (see the main work), see *ante*, § 5-240.

Criminal Justice Act 2003, Sched. 12

Supplementary
5-552   As to the commencement of Part 4 of Schedule 16 (paras 11-21) to the Crime and Courts Act 2013 (see the main work), see *ante*, § 5-240.

Authorities

The decision as to implementation
5-555   Where a judge decided to implement a suspended sentence to which community requirements had been attached, he had not been under an obligation to reduce the length of the sentence where the offender had substantially complied with those requirements, but where they had been therapeutic, rather than punitive, in nature and where it was evident that he had not put into practice anything that he had learnt on the courses that he had attended, see *R. v. Wolstenholme* [2016] 2 Cr.App.R.(S.) 19, CA.

(5) Detention of offenders under 18 convicted of certain serious offences

Use of the power in cases of dangerous young offenders

5-590   For a case considering the assessment of dangerousness in relation to young people, see *ante*, § 5-493.

E. Release on Licence

Modifications of Chapter 6 in certain transitional cases

As explained in the main work (see § 5-597), the effect of LASPOA 2012 is to apply Chapter 6 **5-631** of Part 12 of the CJA 2003 to all prisoners regardless of the date of their offence or the date of sentence. However, two new Schedules (20A and 20B) are inserted into the 2003 Act (by the 2012 Act, s.121(5) and (6), and Scheds 16, paras 1 and 3, and 17, paras 1 and 10) for the purpose of preserving the transitional provisions that existed prior to their commencement. These have the effect of modifying Chapter 6 where they apply. It is submitted that they now only have potential relevance to the release date of an offender sentenced after their commencement in one situation, *viz.* where an offender serving a "1991 Act sentence" who has never been released from that sentence (and theoretically also an offender serving a "1967 Act sentence" who has never been released) is sentenced to a consecutive term for a fresh offence (see paras 22 and 33, *post*).

As to the commencement of these provisions of the 2012 Act, see § 5-3 in the main work.

Criminal Justice Act 2003, Sched. 20B, paras 1–3, 7, 8, 18–20, 22, 23, 30, 33

Part 1

Introductory

Interpretation

1.–(1) The following provisions apply for the purposes of this Schedule. **5-632**

(2) "The commencement date" means the date on which section 121 of the Legal Aid, Sentencing and Punishment of Offenders Act 2012 comes into force.

(3) "The 1967 Act" means the Criminal Justice Act 1967.

(4) "The 1991 Act" means the Criminal Justice Act 1991.

(5) A "section 85 extended sentence" means an extended sentence under section 85 of the Sentencing Act and includes (in accordance with paragraph 1(3) of Schedule 11 to that Act) a sentence under section 58 of the Crime and Disorder Act 1998.

(6) In relation to a section 85 extended sentence, "the custodial term" and "the extension period" have the meaning given by that section.

(7) References to section 86 of the Sentencing Act include (in accordance with paragraph 1(3) of Schedule 11 to that Act) section 44 of the 1991 Act as originally enacted.

(8) A "1967 Act sentence" is a sentence imposed before 1 October 1992.

(9) A "1991 Act sentence" is a sentence which is—

  (a) imposed on or after 1 October 1992 but before 4 April 2005, or

  (b) imposed on or after 4 April 2005 but before the commencement date and is either—

    (i) imposed in respect of an offence committed before 4 April 2005, or

    (ii) for a term of less than 12 months.

(10) A "2003 Act sentence" is a sentence which is—

  (a) imposed on or after the commencement date, or

  (b) imposed on or after 4 April 2005 but before the commencement date and is both—

    (i) imposed in respect of an offence committed on or after 4 April 2005, and

    (ii) for a term of 12 months or more.

(11) Where an offence is found to have been committed over a period of two or more days, or at some time during a period of two or more days, it is to be taken for the purposes of this Schedule to have been committed on the last of those days.

Explanation of dates

2. The following dates (which are mentioned in this Schedule) are dateson which changes to the **5-633** law relating to the release and recall of prisoners came into force—

    1 October 1992 is the date on which Part 2 of the 1991 Act came into force;

    30 September 1998 is the date on which certain provisions of the Crime and Disorder Act 1998 came into force;

    4 April 2005 is the date on which this Chapter came into force;

    9 June 2008 is the date on which section 26 of the Criminal Justice and Immigration Act 2008 came into force;

    14 July 2008 is the date on which certain other provisions of that Act came into force;

2 August 2010 is the date on which section 145 of the Coroners and Justice Act 2009 came into force.

PART 2

Prisoners Serving 1991 Act Sentences, etc.

5-634   3.—(1) This Part applies to certain persons serving a 1991 Act sentence.

(2) This Part also applies to a person serving a 2003 Act sentence which is—

(b) an extended sentence imposed under section 227 or 228 before 14 July 2008.

(3) But this Part does not apply to a person who—

(a) has been released on licence under Part 2 of the 1991 Act,

(b) has been recalled to prison, and

(c) (whether or not having returned to custody in consequence of that recall) is unlawfully at large on the commencement date.

[Para. 3(2)(a) was repealed by the Criminal Justice and Courts Act 2015, s.15(8).]

Release on licence at one-half of sentence: section 85 extended sentence prisoners

5-635   7. This paragraph applies to a person if—

(a) the person has been convicted of an offence committed on or after 30 September 1998 but before 4 April 2005,

(b) the person is serving a section 85 extended sentence in respect of that offence,

(c) the person has not previously been released from prison on licence in respect of that sentence, and

(d) paragraph 4 does not apply to the person.

5-636   8.—(1) As soon as a person to whom paragraph 7 applies has served one-half of the custodial term, it is the duty of the Secretary of State to release the person on licence under this paragraph.

(2) Sub-paragraph (1) applies in place of section 243A or 244, as the case may be (release of prisoners serving less than 12 months, or serving 12 months or more).

It should be noted that paragraph 4 (see para. 7(d)) has no application to a person sentenced after "the commencement date".

Period for which licence to remain in force: section 85 extended sentence prisoners

5-637   18. This paragraph applies to a person who—

(a) has been convicted of an offence committed on or after 30 September 1998 but before 4 April 2005,

(b) is serving a section 85 extended sentence imposed in respect of that offence, and

(c) has not previously been released from prison on licence in respect of that sentence.

5-638   19.—(1) Where a person to whom paragraph 18 applies is released on licence and the custodial term is less than 12 months, the licence shall remain in force until the end of the period found by adding—

(a) one-half of the custodial term, and

(b) the extension period.

(2) Where a person to whom paragraph 18 applies is released on licence and the custodial term is 12 months or more, the licence shall remain in force until the end of the period found by adding—

(a) three-quarters of the custodial term, and

(b) the extension period.

(3) Sub-paragraphs (1) and (2) are subject to any revocation under section 254.

(4) Sub-paragraphs (1) to (3) apply in place of section 249 (duration of licence).

Concurrent or consecutive terms

5-639   20. Paragraphs 21 and 22 apply where a person ("P") is serving two or more sentences of imprisonment imposed on or after 1 October 1992 and—

(a) the sentences were passed on the same occasion, or

(b) where they were passed on different occasions, the person has not been released under Part 2 of the 1991 Act or under this Chapter at any time during the period beginning with the first and ending with the last of those occasions.

5-640   22.—(1) This paragraph applies where two or more sentences are to be served consecutively on each other and—

(a) one or more of those sentences is a 1991 Act sentence, and

(b) one or more of them is a 2003 Act sentence.

(2) Section 264 does not affect the length of the period which P must serve in prison in respect of the 1991 Act sentence or sentences.

(3) Nothing in this Chapter requires the Secretary of State to release P until P has served a period equal in length to the aggregate of the length of the periods which P must serve in relation to each of the sentences mentioned in sub-paragraph (1).

(3A) If P is subject to supervision requirements under section 256AA (by virtue of section 264(3C)(b)), section 256AA(4)(b) (end of supervision period) applies in relation to P as if the reference to the requisite custodial period were to the period described in sub-paragraph (3) of this paragraph.

(4) If P is also serving one or more 1967 Act sentences, paragraphs 32 and 33 apply instead of this paragraph.

[Sub-para. (3A) was inserted, as from February 1, 2015 (Offender Rehabilitation Act 2014 (Commencement No. 2) Order 2015 (S.I. 2015 No. 40)) by the Offender Rehabilitation Act 2014, s.5(1), (6) and (7). This amendment applies only in relation to any person who falls to be released under Chapter 6 of Part 12 of the 2003 Act on or after the day on which it came into force: 2014 Act, s.21, and Sched. 7, paras 1 and 2.]

PART 3

Prisoners Serving 1967 Act Sentences

23.–(1) This Part applies to certain persons serving a 1967 Act sentence.   **5-641**

(2) But this Part does not apply to a person who—

(a) has been released on licence,

(b) has been recalled to prison, and

(c) (whether or not having returned to custody in consequence of that recall) is unlawfully at large on the commencement date.

(3) In this Part, references to release under Part 2 of the 1991 Act include release under section 60 of the 1967 Act.

Concurrent or consecutive terms

30. Paragraphs 31 to 33 apply where a person ("P") is serving two or more sentences of imprison- **5-642** ment and—

(a) the sentences were passed on the same occasion, or

(b) where they were passed on different occasions, the person has not been released under Part 2 of the 1991 Act or under this Chapter at any time during the period beginning with the first and ending with the last of those occasions.

33.–(1) This paragraph applies where two or more sentences are to be served consecutively on **5-643** each other and—

(a) one or more of those sentences is a 1967 Act sentence, and

(b) one or more of them is a 2003 Act sentence.

(2) Section 264 does not affect the length of the period which P must serve in prison in respect of the 1967 Act sentence or sentences.

(3) Nothing in this Chapter requires the Secretary of State to release P until P has served a period equal in length to the aggregate of the length of the periods which P must serve in relation to each of the sentences mentioned in sub-paragraph (1).

(4) If P is subject to supervision requirements under section 256AA (by virtue of section 264(3C)(b)), section 256AA(4)(b) (end of supervision period) applies in relation to P as if the reference to the requisite custodial period were to the period described in sub-paragraph (3) of this paragraph.

[Sub-para. (4) was inserted, as from February 1, 2015 (Offender Rehabilitation Act 2014 (Commencement No. 2) Order 2015 (S.I. 2015 No. 40)) by the Offender Rehabilitation Act 2014, s.5(1), (6) and (8). This amendment applies only in relation to any person who falls to be released under Chapter 6 of Part 12 of the 2003 Act on or after the day on which it came into force: 2014 Act, s.21, and Sched. 7, paras 1 and 2.]

VII. FINES

Powers of Criminal Courts (Sentencing) Act 2000, ss.139, 140, 142

Enforcement of fines imposed and recognizances forfeited by Crown Court

5-651   *R. (Gibson) v. Secretary of State for Justice* is now reported at [2017] 1 W.L.R. 1115. The claimant has had permission to appeal to the Supreme Court.

The approach in *Gibson* was applied in *Emu v. Westminster Magistrates' Court* [2016] A.C.D. 122, DC ([2016] EWHC 2561 (Admin.)).

Criminal Practice Direction VII Sentencing Q: Financial, Etc. Information Required for Sentencing

★5-662   In *R. v. Thelwall* [2017] Crim.L.R. 240, CA, it was said that: (i) health and safety cases are no different to other criminal cases, and must be approached on that basis; and (ii) *R. v. Friskies Petcare (U.K.) Ltd* has been superseded by paragraphs 3 to 6 of Criminal Practice Direction VII Sentencing Q (as to both of which, see the main work). As to this case, see also *post*, §§ 6-35, 7-135.

IX. DEPRIVATION AND CONFISCATION

B. CONFISCATION UNDER THE DRUG TRAFFICKING ACT 1994

Assessment of benefit

5-716   When determining for the purposes of section 2 of the DTA 1994 (confiscation orders) whether an offender has benefited from an offence of drug trafficking in respect of which he has not been convicted at trial, the statutory assumptions provided for in section 4(3) are not the only way in which the Act permits the court to determine the fact (or extent) of such benefit; where those assumptions are not applicable, the court is entitled to rely on other evidence led at trial to show that one or more offences of drug trafficking (other than those charged) have been committed (and then to estimate the benefit that must have been obtained from those offences): *R. v. Briggs-Price* [2009] 1 A.C. 1026, HL. A majority of their Lordships held, however, that a judge should only rely on evidence of other offences not charged if he was satisfied to the criminal standard that they had been proved (the minority taking the view that the civil standard was the applicable standard).

Valuation of property

5-717   Where a judge assessed the value of the defendant's proceeds of drug trafficking at £3.2 million, he was correct in taking the view that he was required by the DTA 1994 to make a confiscation order in that amount, unless the defendant satisfied him (to the civil standard) that his realisable assets were less than that amount; and where the defendant had failed to do so, there was no obligation on the judge to assume that the defendant would have incurred some expenses to be set against that figure, and to make some discount in respect thereof; such approach was misconceived; his task under the statute was to assess the value of the proceeds in accord with the provisions of the statute (which was not the same as profit), and to make an order in that amount unless the value of the realisable assets was less than that amount, and the burden of proof in that regard was on the defendant: *R. v. Versluis* [2005] 2 Cr.App.R.(S.) 26, CA.

"drug trafficking offence"

5-718   Where the defendant was convicted of a conspiracy to convert the proceeds of drug trafficking "or" the proceeds of criminal conduct (the substantive offences being created by the DTA 1994, s.49, and the CJA 1988, s.93C, respectively), this was to be construed as a finding that the agreement was not restricted to the laundering of the proceeds of drug trafficking or to the proceeds of criminal conduct other than drug trafficking, but was an agreement to launder money, whatever its provenance; it was, in effect, an agreement to launder both the proceeds of drug trafficking and the proceeds of other criminal conduct; accordingly, the defendant was properly to be regarded as having been convicted of a "drug trafficking offence" for the purposes of the confiscation provisions of the 1994 Act as the definition of that expression extended to a conspiracy to commit an offence contrary to section 49; and the judge had, therefore, erred in declining to conduct confiscation proceedings under the 1994 Act: *R. v. Suchedina (Att.-Gen.'s Reference (No. 4 of 2003))* [2005] 1 Cr.App.R. 2, CA.

Increase in realisable property

In *Re Peacock (Secretary of State for the Home Department intervening)* [2012] 2 Cr.App.R.(S.) 81, **5-719** SC, it was held that the High Court has power, under section 16(2) of the 1994 Act, to certify that the amount that might be realised is greater than the amount taken into account at the time a confiscation order under that Act was made, and to do so by reference to assets honestly acquired since the date of the making of the order. As to the argument that increasing a confiscation order by reference to after-acquired assets would militate against a defendant's reform and rehabilitation, and be likely to discourage him from engaging in lawful and openly profitable employment, the court pointed out that section 16(4) confers a discretion on the Crown Court, rather than obliging it to order an increase in the amount of the confiscation order in parallel with the assessment of the amount of increase in the defendant's realisable property under section 16(2).

Certificate of inadequacy

It is unambiguously clear from the wording of sections 6 and 8(1) of the 1994 Act that the **5-720** value of a gift made by a defendant will be included in the amount of a confiscation order and will constitute "realisable property", even though it may not itself be realisable by the defendant because it is no longer in his power or control; and it is implicit in the statutory scheme that, where the value of a gift has been included in the amount of a confiscation order pursuant to section 6(1), it will not then be open to the defendant to seek a certificate of inadequacy under section 17(1) on the basis that he cannot realise or recover that gift; section 17 cannot be used as a device for upsetting an original finding that an item is "realisable property" within section 6(2), and thus to be included in the "amount that might be realised" under section 6(1), and thus within the amount of the confiscation order: *Re L.*, unreported, June 23, 2010, QBD (Hickinbottom J.) ([2010] EWHC 1531 (Admin.)).

Variation of realisable amount

Where, following the grant of a certificate of inadequacy by the High Court under section 17 **5-721** of the 1994 Act, the Crown Court had, pursuant to subsection (4) of that section, substituted a nil amount as the amount to be recovered, it was possible, if the defendant thereafter came into funds, for the amount to be varied upwards again if the High Court issued a certificate under section 16(2) that the amount that might be realised was now more than the amount that had been substituted for the original amount; but the Crown Court had a discretion as to whether to accede to an application for the amount to be increased following such certification, and one factor to be taken into account by it in deciding how to exercise its discretion would be whether the state had sat on its hands after significant and clear evidence about the defendant's change in financial circumstances had come to its attention or had unreasonably delayed in re-opening the issue: *R. v. Griffin* [2009] 2 Cr.App.R.(S.) 89, CA.

Restraint orders; payment of legal expenses out of restrained assets

See *Revenue and Customs Prosecution Office v. Briggs-Price and O'Reilly, post,* § 5-729.   **5-722**

C. Confiscation under the Criminal Justice Act 1988

Postponement of determinations

In *R. v. Haisman* [2004] 1 Cr.App.R.(S.) 63, CA, it was held that where prosecuting counsel had **5-724** invited the judge to postpone confiscation proceedings and to proceed to sentence, and the judge responded by saying, "If everyone agrees to that, I will do that" and there was no dissent from any counsel to that course, the judge had "manifestly reached a decision" (*R. v. Ross* [2001] 2 Cr.App.R.(S.) 109, CA) to postpone the confiscation proceedings under section 72A of the CJA

1988, with the consequence that the confiscation orders made subsequent to the imposition of sentence were lawful.

In *R. v. Paivarinta-Taylor* [2010] 2 Cr.App.R.(S.) 64, CA, the court said that whereas section 72A(1) of the CJA 1988 enables a court to postpone making a determination as to a defendant's benefit for the purpose of a confiscation order, or as to the amount to be recovered from him under such an order, for such period as it may specify in certain circumstances, and whereas section 72A(9) provides that, in sentencing the defendant at any time during the specified postponement period, the court shall not impose any fine on him, the decision in *R. v. Soneji* [2006] 1 A.C. 340, HL (that where there is a breach of a procedural requirement in a statute, a court should ask itself what Parliament intended should be the consequences and whether it fairly could be taken to have intended total invalidity), remains binding authority, as do *R. v. Ruddick* [2004] 1 Cr.App.R.(S.) 7, CA, *R. v. Simpson* [2003] 2 Cr.App.R. 36, CA, and *R. v. Donohoe* [2007] 1 Cr.App.R.(S.) 88, CA, in so far as they add to the principles identified in *Soneji* as to the correct approach to the consequences of a breach of the procedural provisions relating to confiscation orders under the 1988 Act. Cases such as *R. v. Threapleton* [2002] 2 Cr.App.R.(S.) 46, CA, were decided without reference to *Soneji*, and the Court of Appeal said that they should in future be disregarded when considering the consequences of such a breach. It was held that Parliament could not be taken to have intended that a breach of section 72A(9) would lead to total invalidity, that the imposition of a fine before making a confiscation order would render the fine itself invalid, that, having imposed such a fine, the court could then no longer proceed to consider the making of a confiscation order, or that any confiscation order so made would itself be rendered invalid.

Assessment of benefit/making of assumptions

5-725 The assumption provided for in section 72AA(4)(a) of the 1988 Act (*viz.* that any property transferred to the defendant since the beginning of the relevant period was received by him "in connection with the commission of offences to which this Part of this Act applies") includes within its scope offences committed by persons other than the defendant; thus it is not sufficient to rebut the presumption to show that the property was obtained by the defendant as a result of somebody else's criminal conduct; but the defendant's knowledge or lack of knowledge would be highly material in deciding whether to apply the safety valve in subsection (5) (assumption not to be made if court is satisfied that there would be a serious risk of injustice): *R. v. Ilyas* [2009] 1 Cr.App.R.(S.) 59, CA. See the commentary by David Thomas Q.C. in the *Criminal Law Review* ([2008] Crim.L.R. 908) for the suggestion that this decision will not carry across to the PCA 2002 regime; and see the commentary in CLW/08/39/9 as to the limitations of the actual decision, and, in particular, for the suggestion that it is out of kilter with the decision of the House of Lords in *R. v. May* (§ 5-1035 in the main work).

Whereas section 72AA of the 1988 Act provided that in certain cases it was to be assumed against the defendant that he had committed offences other than those of which he had been convicted or which he had asked to be taken into consideration, and that this assumed criminal conduct should be included within his "relevant criminal conduct" (the assessed benefit from which would form the basis of any confiscation order, subject only to his realisable assets being insufficient), there was nothing objectionable in imposing on the defendant the burden of showing in the particular case that the assumptions should not be made; the assumptions were founded on his holding of property or expenditure of money, and there was nothing unfair in requiring him to show that the source of his property was legitimate: *R. v. Bagnall and Sharma* [2013] 1 W.L.R. 204, CA.

As to the assessment of benefit under the 1988 Act, see also *R. v. Ahmad (Shakeel) and Ahmad (Syed Mubarak)* (§ 5-1056 in the main work).

Factual basis for making order

5-726 Where an agreement is reached as to the amount of a confiscation order, that agreement will be binding on the defendant unless there are the sort of exceptional circumstances referred to in *R. v. Hirani*, unreported, June 11, 2008, CA ([2008] EWCA Crim. 1463) (save in most exceptional circumstances, a confiscation order based on an agreed amount will not be set aside where the essence of complaint is that, in seeking to secure the best deal available, erroneous advice was given to a party to the agreement; without exhaustively identifying such circumstances, there would need to be a well-founded submission that the whole process was unfair): *R. v. Ayankoya*, unreported, May 24, 2011, CA ([2011] EWCA Crim. 1488). The circumstances had, however, been wholly exceptional where: (i) the defendant had agreed to the amount after being incorrectly informed by his counsel that the judge had ruled that an adjournment to await bank statements supporting his claims would be impossible and that he therefore had a choice of either agreeing the amount or giving evidence without the statements with the inherent risk that a higher amount would result, and (ii) where the bank statements had in fact shown that there was force in the defendant's claims; in these circumstances, the erroneous advice had been of a potentially fundamental nature: *ibid*.

Amount that might be realised

In *R. v. Blee* [2004] 1 Cr.App.R.(S.) 33, CA, it was held that whereas section 74(3) of the CJA   **5-727**
1988 provides that "the amount that might be realised at the time a confiscation order is made" includes "the total of the values at that time of all gifts caught by this Part of this Act" and whereas section 74(10) provides that a gift is caught by that part of the Act if "(a) it was made by the defendant at any time after the commission of the offence ...; and (b) the court considers it appropriate in all the circumstances to take the gift into account" it follows that the fact that the property held by the donee at the time of the confiscation order is less than the value of the gift does not *per se* preclude the court from taking the full value of the gift into account; the court is given a discretion by section 74(10) and the question for it to decide is whether it is "appropriate" to take the gift into account; if it considers it appropriate to take it into account (in whole or in part), then to the extent that it does so, the value of the gift is to be included in the computation of the amount that might be realised; in exercising the discretion, the court may have regard to the timing of the gift (here, made when the defendant, having been on the run, had decided to surrender), to the fact that it was made to a person from whom the defendant would be likely to be able to receive an equivalent benefit in return, if he wished, and to the fact that whilst the donee currently had assets worth considerably less than the value of the gift, he was in highly paid employment and would be likely again to hold substantial assets; and, where it is said that the gift has been dissipated prior to the confiscation order, this is a matter to be considered under section 74(10), rather than on a subsequent application for a certificate of inadequacy.

As to the approach to be taken where the prosecution allege that the defendant is the beneficial owner of property registered in the name of a third party, see *Revenue and Customs Prosecutions Office v. May* [2010] 3 All E.R. 1173, CA (Civ. Div.) (§ 5-1081 in the main work).

Valuation of property

In *R. v. Hedges* (2004) 148 S.J. 974, CA, it was held that in making a confiscation order against   **5-728**
a defendant whose only realisable asset was the house which he owned jointly with his wife, the correct approach to valuation of his interest in the property had been to determine the market value of the property, then deduct the outstanding mortgage and the reasonable costs of sale before making a confiscation order in respect of half the remaining amount; such an approach properly reflected the intention of section 74(4) of the CJA 1988 and was to be preferred to that of dividing the value of the house and then deducting the remaining mortgage and costs of sale from the defendant's half share, on the basis that he was responsible for payment of the mortgage; whilst it was true that the defendant was in theory liable to repay the whole mortgage, being jointly and severally liable, the reality was that the mortgage and the costs of sale would be discharged out of the proceeds of sale, the net effect of which would be to reduce his share in the value of the house by half the amount of the mortgage and costs of sale.

In *R. v. Ahmed* [2005] 1 All E.R. 128, CA, it was held that where a court concludes that an offender has benefited from relevant criminal conduct (CJA 1988, s.71(1A)), the court has no discretion, in valuing the realisable assets for the purposes of determining the amount of the confiscation order, to exclude from the computation, the value of the defendant's share in the matrimonial home, notwithstanding the probability that the home would have to be sold to meet the confiscation order; the words "the amount appearing to the court" in subsection (6)(b) ("... the sum which an order made by a court under this section requires an offender to pay shall be equal to (a) ...; or (b) the amount appearing to the court to be the amount that might be realised at the time the order is made, whichever is the less") did not give the court a discretion; it merely referred to the valuation process to be carried out under section 74, and section 3 of the Human Rights Act 1998 (§ 16-16 in the main work) did not require it to be read as construing such a discretion on the court on account of the possible interference with innocent third parties' rights under Article 8 of the ECHR (*ibid.*, § 16-137); the court is merely concerned with the arithmetic exercise of computing what is, in effect, a statutory debt; such process does not involve any assessment of the way in which the debt may ultimately be paid; different considerations would apply if the debt is not met and the prosecution determine to take enforcement action; if a court is asked to make an order for the sale of the matrimonial home then the third party's rights under Article 8 would clearly be engaged; and it would be at that stage that the court would have to consider whether or not it would be proportionate to make an order for the sale of the home. In connection with this case, see *Webber v. Webber (CPS intervening)*, § 5-1087 in the main work.

In the earlier case of *R. v. Goodenough* [2005] 1 Cr.App.R.(S.) 88, CA, it was held that where a defendant's only realisable asset was his equity in the matrimonial home, the making of a confiscation order in accordance with the requirements of the 1988 Act for the amount by which he had benefited from his offending (being an amount less than the value of his equity) did not infringe or interfere with his rights under Article 8 or under Article 1 of the First Protocol (right to peaceful enjoyment of possessions); the rights of the defendant's wife might be infringed if the house were to be sold in order to raise the money to pay the amount of the confiscation order, and it would be open to the wife to oppose any application to appoint a receiver to enforce the order.

Restraint orders; payment of legal expenses out of restrained assets

5-729   In *Revenue and Customs Prosecution Office v. Briggs-Price and O'Reilly* [2007] L.S. Gazette, June 28, 32, CA (Civ. Div.) ([2007] EWCA Civ. 568) it was held, in relation to the confiscation regimes under the CJA 1988 and the DTA 1994, that the principle in *Customs and Excise Commrs v. Norris* [1991] 2 Q.B. 293, CA (Civ. Div.) (defendant's legal expenses may be met from restrained assets), applies both to legal expenses incurred prior to conviction (and any appeal against conviction) and to legal expenses incurred in connection with the making of a confiscation order and an appeal against such order; there is a discretion in such cases, which will be exercised for a proper and legitimate purpose within the scope of the statutory regime where the released assets are to meet expenses for a prospective appeal which are neither excessive nor improperly incurred (such amount as is released being capable of control by assessment).

Restraint orders; appointment of receiver

5-730   See *Revenue and Customs Prosecutions Office v. Pigott (Lamb, interested party)* [2010] S.T.C. 1190, CA (Civ. Div.) (§ 5-846 in the main work).

Certificate of inadequacy

5-731   There is no rule of law that says that, on an application under section 83 of the 1988 Act for a certificate of inadequacy, the High Court could not be persuaded that a defendant was unable to pay the outstanding amount by reason of a worsening of his financial circumstances unless he gave full disclosure of what had happened in the meantime to all his assets, including previously unidentified assets (that the Crown Court had found to exist when making the confiscation order); any such rule would trammel the width of section 83 by imposing a restriction which was not in the statute; and it would also be capable of causing not merely hardship, but hardship amounting to injustice; in the case of previously unidentified assets, it is possible that a defendant may genuinely have no idea or only a dim recollection of what originally happened to them; he should be allowed to try to persuade the court, if this be the case, that his identified assets have shrunk in value and that as a result he is not able to pay the amount outstanding: *Glaves v. CPS* [2011] Costs L.R. 556, CA (Civ. Div.) (considering *Telli v. Revenue and Customs Prosecutions Office* (see § 5-1070 in the main work)).

It was held in *Escobar v. DPP* [2009] 1 W.L.R. 64, DC, that when making an order under section 83(4) of the CJA 1988 for the reduction of a sum payable under a confiscation order (following the issue of a certificate of inadequacy), the Crown Court has jurisdiction to fix a time for payment (by way of extension of the original date). The court said that although there is no express power to extend time in section 83, section 75(1) ("(1) Where the Crown Court orders the defendant to pay an amount under this Part ..., sections 139(1) to (4) ... of the Powers of Criminal Courts (Sentencing) Act 2000 (powers of Crown Court in relation to fines and enforcement of Crown Court fines) shall have effect as if that amount were a fine imposed on him by the Crown Court.") operates so as to incorporate section 139(1) of the 2000 Act (§ 5-650 in the main work), which in turn gives the court power to extend the time for payment when it substitutes a lesser sum under section 83. When read as a whole, section 75 is generally concerned to make provision for orders made under section 83 as well as those under other provisions in Part VI, and this is consistent with the natural and grammatical meaning of the relevant provisions, in that the Crown Court is making an order under section 83(4) and the effect of that order is that the defendant has to pay an amount due under Part VI. For the suggestion that the court's conclusion is out of kilter with the legislative structure, see CLW/09/02/5. For the relevant provisions of the PCA 2002, see sections 23 and 39 (§§ 5-783, 5-805 in the main work), neither of which contain any provision for an extension of the time allowed to pay.

Enforcement

See *Revenue and Customs Prosecutions Office v. May* [2010] 3 All E.R. 1173, CA (Civ. Div.) (§ 5-1081 in the main work). **5-732**

Presence of the accused

See *R. v. Spearing* (§ 3-225 in the main work). **5-733**

D. CONFISCATION UNDER THE PROCEEDS OF CRIME ACT 2002

(2) Legislation

(a) *Statute*

Proceeds of Crime Act 2002, ss.6-91

The Supreme Court has reversed the decision of the Court of Appeal (see the main work) in **5-772** *R. v. Guraj*. It was held that where section 14(11) of the 2002 Act (*ibid.*, § 5-770) is unavailable because subsection (12) applies (here, because the court had made forfeiture and deprivation orders prior to the confiscation order in contravention of s.15(2) (*ibid.*, § 5-773)), not every procedural defect (here, failure to apply for an extension of the postponement of confiscation proceedings before it expired pursuant to s.14(8)) will invalidate a confiscation order. The judge should apply the approach in *R. v. Soneji* (as to which, see *ibid.*, § 5-1027), and ask whether any injustice had been sustained by the defendant before deciding whether to proceed to make a confiscation order: *R. v. Guraj* [2017] 1 W.L.R. 22, SC (approving *R. v. Donohoe* (as to which, see *ibid.*, § 5-1027)).

Enforcement as fines
R. v. Malhi is now reported at [2017] 4 W.L.R. 27. **★5–801**

Restraint orders
Delay in making an application for a restraint order will not act as a bar to the making of an **★5-807** order *per se*: *Ready Rentals Ltd (In Liquidation) v. Ahmed; CPS v. Ahmed* [2017] Lloyd's Rep. F.C. 30, Ch D (Newey J.). As to this case, see also *post*, § 5-872.

Powers of court and receiver etc.
Given the provision in section 69(3) of the PCA 2002 (see the main work), the claimant company **★5-872** retained an interest in monies paid into court to cover the costs of a successful action it had brought against the defendant, and which had been awarded to the claimant in principle (subject only to a detailed assessment), where that sum later became subject to a restraint order; further, the claimant company enjoyed security for such further sums as proved to be due to it in respect of costs (in particular, by assessment); accordingly, the restraint order had to be framed in such a way as to make it clear that it took effect subject to that security: *Ready Rentals Ltd (In Liquidation) v. Ahmed; CPS v. Ahmed* [2017] Lloyd's Rep. F.C. 30, Ch D (Newey J.). As to this case, see also *ante*, § 5-807.

Value: the basic rule
As to the reference to "the market value" in section 79(2) of the PCA 2002, see *R. v. Gor, post*, § **★5-886** 5-1066.

Value of tainted gifts

5-889   *R. v. Johnson* is now reported at [2016] 2 Cr.App.R.(S.) 38.

Property: general provisions

5-892   With effect from November 30, 2016, section 84(2)(d) of the 2002 Act is amended by the Bankruptcy (Scotland) Act 2016 (Consequential Provisions and Modifications) Order 2016 (S.I. 2016 No. 1034), so as to substitute the words "or liquidator or in the trustee or interim trustee in the sequestration, under the Bankruptcy (Scotland) Act 2016), of his estate;" for the words from "permanent" to the end.

(b) *Subordinate legislation*

Commencement

Proceeds of Crime Act 2002 (Commencement No. 5, Transitional Provisions, Savings and Amendment) Order 2003 (S.I. 2003 No. 333)

Citation and interpretation

5-914   **1.**–(1) [*Citation.*]

(2) In this Order, "the Act" means the Proceeds of Crime Act 2002.

(3) Where an offence is found to have been committed over a period of two or more days, or at some time during a period of two or more days, it shall be taken for the purposes of this order to have been committed on the earliest of those days.

Commencement of provisions

5-915   **2.**–(1) The provisions of the Act listed in column 1 of the Schedule to this Order shall come into force on 24th March 2003, subject to the transitional provisions and savings contained in this order.

(2) But where a particular purpose is specified in relation to any such provision in column 2 of that Schedule, the provision concerned shall come into force only for that purpose.

Transitional provisions relating to confiscation orders–England and Wales

5-916   **3.**–(1) Section 6 of the Act (making of confiscation order) shall not have effect where the offence, or any of the offences, mentioned in section 6(2) was committed before 24th March 2003.

(2) Section 27 of the Act (defendant convicted or committed absconds) shall not have effect where the offence, or any of the offences, mentioned in section 27(2) was committed before 24th March 2003.

(3) Section 28 of the Act (defendant neither convicted nor acquitted absconds) shall not have effect where the offence, or any of the offences, in respect of which proceedings have been started but not concluded was committed before 24th March 2003.

4. [*Transitional provisions relating to confiscation orders–Northern Ireland.*]

It was held in *R. v. Moulden* [2009] 1 Cr.App.R. 27, CA, that where the respondent appeared before the Crown Court to be dealt with in respect of two indictments, one alleging offences committed before March 24, 2003, and the other alleging offences committed after that date, each indictment represented a separate set of "proceedings" for the purposes of section 6(2)(a) of the 2002 Act (see § 5-754 in the main work) and accordingly, by virtue of article 3(1), the 2002 Act had no application to the pre-March 24, 2003, indictment, but did apply to the post-March 24, 2003, indictment. The judge had, therefore, been correct to apply the confiscation provisions of the CJA 1988 to the one indictment and the confiscation provisions of the 2002 Act to the other indictment, and to reject the prosecution submission that the effect of these provisions was to disapply the 2002 Act in relation to both indictments, thereby triggering the assumptions provided for by section 72AA of the 1988 Act.

Where the defendant pleaded guilty to a count of conspiracy to make false instruments, the particulars of offence alleging that the offence took place "between the 1st day of January 2003 and the 16th day of May 2007", and where his written basis of plea was to the effect that his first admitted act in pursuance of the criminal agreement took place only on October 29, 2003, his offence had begun before March 24, 2003, for the purposes of article 3(1) (having regard to article 1(3)), such that the applicable confiscation provisions were those under Part VI of the CJA 1988, not Part 2 of the PCA 2002, see *R. v. Evwierhowa* [2011] 2 Cr.App.R.(S.) 77, CA.

As to whether, in principle, rental income from criminally-obtained properties could properly be regarded as benefit even though it was derived from properties obtained subject to offences, in respect of which there were convictions, that were committed before the commencement of Part 2 of the 2002 Act, see *R. v. Oyebola*, (§ 5-1045 in the main work).

By virtue of articles 3(1) and 10(1)(e) (*post*, § 5-919), section 16 of the DTA 1994 (increase in realisable property) continues to have effect where an offence mentioned in section 6(2) of the PCA Act 2002 (making of confiscation order (§ 5-754 in the main work)) was committed before March 24, 2003: *Re Peacock (Secretary of State for the Home Department intervening)* [2012] 2 Cr.App.R.(S.) 81, SC. For the suggestion that the court misconstrued the order (albeit reaching the correct result), see CLW/12/08/5.

Transitional provisions relating to restraint orders and enforcement abroad–England and Wales

5. Sections 41 (restraint orders) and 74 (enforcement abroad) of the Act shall not have effect where— **5-917**

    (a)   the powers in those sections would otherwise be exercisable by virtue of a condition in section 40(2) or (3) of the Act being satisfied; and

    (b)   the offence mentioned in section 40(2)(a) or 40(3)(a), as the case may be, was committed before 24th March 2003.

6. [*Transitional provisions relating to restraint orders and enforcement abroad–Northern Ireland.*]

Transitional provisions relating to criminal lifestyle–England and Wales

7.—(1) This article applies where the court is determining under section 6(4)(a) of the Act whether the defendant has a criminal lifestyle. **5-918**

(2) Conduct shall not form part of a course of criminal activity under section 75(3)(a) of the Act where any of the three or more offences mentioned in section 75(3)(a) was committed before 24th March 2003.

(3) Where the court is applying the rule in section 75(5) of the Act on the calculation of relevant benefit for the purposes of determining whether or not the test in section 75(2)(b) of the Act is satisfied by virtue of conduct forming part of a course of criminal activity under section 75(3)(a) of the Act, the court must not take into account benefit from conduct constituting an offence mentioned in section 75(5)(c) of the Act which was committed before 24th March 2003.

(4) Conduct shall form part of a course of criminal activity under section 75(3)(b) of the Act, notwithstanding that any of the offences of which the defendant was convicted on at least two separate occasions in the period mentioned in section 75(3)(b) were committed before 24th March 2003.

(5) Where the court is applying the rule in section 75(5) of the Act on the calculation of relevant benefit for the purposes of determining whether or not the test in section 75(2)(b) of the Act is satisfied by virtue of conduct forming part of a course of criminal activity under section 75(3)(b) of the Act, the court may take into account benefit from conduct constituting an offence committed before 24th March 2003.

(6) Where the court is applying the rule in section 75(6) of the Act on the calculation of relevant benefit for the purposes of determining whether or not the test in section 75(2)(c) of the Act is satisfied, the court must not take into account benefit from conduct constituting an offence mentioned in section 75(6)(b) of the Act which was committed before 24th March 2003.

[This article is printed as substituted by the Proceeds of Crime Act 2002 (Commencement No. 5) (Amendment of Transitional Provisions) Order 2003 (S.I. 2003 No. 531).]

8. [*Transitional provisions relating to criminal lifestyle–Northern Ireland.*]

Transitional provisions relating to particular criminal conduct

9. Conduct which constitutes an offence which was committed before 24th March 2003 is not particular criminal conduct under section 76(3) or 224(3) of the Act.

Savings for England and Wales

10.—(1) Where, under article 3 or 5, a provision of the Act does not have effect, the following provisions shall continue to have effect— **5-919**

    (a)   sections 71 to 89 (including Schedule 4) and 102 of the Criminal Justice Act 1988;

    (b)   paragraphs 83 and 84 of Schedule 17 to the Housing Act 1988;

    (c)   sections 21(3)(e) to (g), 27, 28 and 34 of the Criminal Justice Act 1993;

  (d) paragraph 36 of Schedule 9 to the Criminal Justice and Public Order Act 1994;

  (e) sections 1 to 36 and 41 of the Drug Trafficking Act 1994;

  (f) sections 1 to 10, 15(1) and (3) (including Schedule 1), 16(2), (5) and (6) of the Proceeds of Crime Act 1995;

  (g) section 4(3) of the Private International Law (Miscellaneous Provisions) Act 1995;

  (h) sections 35 to 38 of the Proceeds of Crime (Scotland) Act 1995;

  (i) the Proceeds of Crime (Enforcement of Confiscation Orders made in England and Wales or Scotland) Order (Northern Ireland) 1997 and the Proceeds of Crime (Northern Ireland) Order 1996, so far as necessary for the continued operation of the Proceeds of Crime (Enforcement of Confiscation Orders made in England and Wales or Scotland) Order (Northern Ireland) 1997;

  (j) paragraphs 23 and 36 of Schedule 5 to the Justices of the Peace Act 1997;

  (k) section 83 of, paragraph 114 of Schedule 8 to and paragraph 8 of Schedule 9 to the Crime and Disorder Act 1998;

  (l) paragraphs 139 and 172 of Schedule 13 to the Access to Justice Act 1999;

  (m) paragraphs 105 to 113 and 163 to 173 of Schedule 9 to the Powers of Criminal Courts (Sentencing) Act 2000;

  (n) paragraphs 6(1) to (3) and 10 of Schedule 15 to the Terrorism Act 2000.

(2) Where under article 3 or 5, a provision of the Act does not have effect, the following provisions shall continue to have effect as if they had not been amended by Schedule 11 to the Act—

  (a) section 13(6) of the Criminal Justice (International Co-operation) Act 1990;

  (b) paragraph 17(3) of Schedule 8 to the Terrorism Act 2000.

11. [*Savings for Northern Ireland.*]

12. [*Savings for enforcement of Scottish orders in England, Wales and Northern Ireland.*]

13. [*Savings in relation to external orders.*]

14. [*Amendment of arts 3 and 5 of S.I. 2003 No. 120, §§ 26-4, 26-5 in the main work.*]

Article 2   THE SCHEDULE

5-920

Column 1	Column 2
Part 2 (sections 6 to 91, including Schedule 2) (Confiscation: England and Wales).	So far as not already in force.
Part 4 (sections 156 to 239, including Schedule 5) (Confiscation: Northern Ireland).	
Part 9 (sections 417 to 434) (Insolvency etc.).	
Part 10 (sections 435 to 442) (Information).	So far as not already in force.
Section 444 (External requests and orders).	
Section 445 (External investigations).	
Section 447 (Interpretation).	
Section 456 (Amendments).	Commenced for the purposes of the provisions of Schedule 11 to the Act commenced by this Order.
Section 457 (Repeals).	Commenced for the purposes of the provisions of Schedule 12 to the Act commenced by this Order.
In Schedule 11, paragraphs 1, 4, 5, 7, 8, 9, 11, 14(2) and (3), 15, 16, 17(2), (4) and (6), 19(2) and (3), 20, 21, 25(2)(a) and (h) to (j), 26, 27, 28(1) and (2)(e) and (g), 31(2) and (3)(a) to (c), 32, 37 and 39.	Paragraphs 7, 11, 15, 16, 20, 21 and 39 are commenced except to the extent that they relate to Part 3 of the Act. Paragraph 17(2) is commenced so far as it repeals sections 71 to 89, 94 and 99 to 102 of the Criminal Justice Act 1988. Paragraph 25(2)(a) is commenced so far as it repeals sections 1 to 38 and 41 of the Drug Traficking Act 1994. Paragraph 27 is commenced so far as not already in force. Paragraph

Column 1

Column 2

In Schedule 12, the following entries; the entry relating to the Criminal Appeal (Northern Ireland) Act 1980; the entry relating to the Police and Criminal Evidence Act 1984; the entry relating to the Criminal Justice Act 1988; the entry relating to the Housing Act 1988; the entry relating to the Police and Criminal Evidence (Northern Ireland) Order 1989; in the entry relating to the Criminal Justice (International Co-operation) Act 1990, the entry in the second column concerning section 13 of that Act; the entry relating to the Criminal Justice (Confiscation) (Northern Ireland) Order 1990; the entry relating to the Criminal Justice Act 1993; the entry relating to the Drug Traficking Act 1994; the entry relating to the Proceeds of Crime Act 1995; in the entry relating to the Criminal Procedure (Consequential Provisions) (Scotland) Act 1995, the entry in the second column concerning Schedule 4 of that Act; the entry relating to the Private International Law (Miscellaneous Provisions) Act 1995; in the entry relating to the Proceeds of Crime (Scotland) Act 1995, the entry in the second column concerning sections 35 to 39 of that Act, the entry in the second column concerning section 40 of that Act and the entry in the second column concerning section 42 of that Act; the entry relating to the Proceeds of Crime (Northern Ireland) Order 1996; the entry relating to the Justices of the Peace Act 1997; in the entry relating to the Crime and Disorder Act 1998, the entry in the second column concerning section 83 of that Act, the entry in the second column concerning Schedule 8 of that Act and the entry in the second column concerning Schedule 9 of that Act; the entry relating to the Access to Justice Act 1999; the entry relating to the Powers of Criminal Courts (Sentencing) Act 2000; the entry relating to the Terrorism Act 2000; and the entry relating to the Criminal Justice and Police Act 2001.

31(2) is commenced so far as it repeals articles 4 to 41 of the Proceeds of Crime (Northern Ireland) Order 1996.

The entry relating to sections 71 to 102 of the Criminal Justice Act 1988 is commenced so far as it repeals sections 71 to 89, 94 and 99 to 102 of that Act. The entries relating to the Criminal Justice Act 1993, the Proceeds of Crime Act 1995 and the Access to Justice Act 1999 are commenced so far as not already in force. The entry relating to sections 1 to 54 of the Drug Traficking Act 1994 is commenced so far as it repeals sections 1 to 38 and 41 of that Act. The entry relating to Parts II and III of the Proceeds of Crime (Northern Ireland) Order 1996 is commenced so far as it repeals articles 4 to 41 of that Order. The entry relating to the Terrorism Act 2000 is commenced so far as it repeals paragraphs 6 and 10 of Schedule 15 to that Act.

Rules of court relating to confiscation, restraint and receivership proceedings

Criminal Procedure Rules 2015 (S.I. 2015 No. 1490), Pt 33

Application for reconsideration

With effect from April 3, 2017, rule 33.15 of the 2015 rules was amended by the Criminal Procedure (Amendment) Rules 2017 (S.I. 2017 No. 144), r.7(a), to substitute new paragraphs (2) to (5) for paragraphs (2) to (4), as follows— ★5-935

"(2) The application must—
(a) be in writing and give—
(i) the name of the defendant,
(ii) the date on which and the place where any relevant conviction occurred,
(iii) the date on which and the place where any relevant confiscation order was made or varied,
(iv) details of any slavery and trafficking reparation order made by virtue of any relevant confiscation order,
(v) the grounds for the application, and
(vi) an indication of the evidence available to support the application; and

(b) where the parties are agreed on the terms of the proposed order include, in one or more documents–
  (i) a draft order in the terms proposed, and
  (ii) evidence of the parties' agreement.
(3) The application must be served on–
  (a) the court officer; and
  (b) the defendant.
(4) The court–
  (a) may determine the application without a hearing where the parties are agreed on the terms of the proposed order;
  (b) must determine the application at a hearing in any other case.
(5) Where this rule or the court requires the application to be heard, the court officer must arrange for the court to hear it no sooner than the eighth day after it was served unless the court otherwise directs.".

Application for new calculation of available amount

★**5-936**   With effect from April 3, 2017, rule 33.16 of the 2015 rules was amended by the Criminal Procedure (Amendment) Rules 2017 (S.I. 2017 No. 144), r.7(b), so as: (i) to omit "and" at the end of paragraph (2)(a); (ii) to insert "and" at the end of paragraph (2)(b); (iii) to insert a new paragraph (2)(c), as follows–

"(c) where the parties are agreed on the terms of the proposed order, must include in one or more documents–
  (i) a draft order in the terms proposed, and
  (ii) evidence of the parties' agreement";

(iv) in paragraph (4), to omit the words "at least 7 days before the date fixed by the court for hearing the application, unless the court specifies a shorter period"; and (v) to insert new paragraphs (5) and (6), as follows–

"(5) The court–
  (a) may determine the application without a hearing where the parties are agreed on the terms of the proposed order;
  (b) must determine the application at a hearing in any other case.
(6) Where this rule or the court requires the application to be heard, the court officer must arrange for the court to hear it no sooner than the eighth day after it was served unless the court otherwise directs.".

Variation of confiscation order due to inadequacy of available amount

★**5-937**   With effect from April 3, 2017, rule 33.17 of the 2015 rules was amended by the Criminal Procedure (Amendment) Rules 2017 (S.I. 2017 No. 144), r.7(c). The amendments are identical to those made to rule 33.16 (*ante*).

(3) Authorities

Effect of postponement

5-1027   For the Supreme Court's decision in *R. v. Guraj* (see the main work), which approved *R. v. Donohoe* (*ibid.*), see *ante*, § 5-772.

Benefit

Property

5-1046   **Offences committed in connection with the running of a business through a company or otherwise.** In *R. v. Neuberg (Karen) (No. 2)* [2017] 4 W.L.R. 58, CA, the court expressly approved the original decision in *R. v. Neuberg* (as to which see the main work) (on a reference by the Criminal Cases Review Commission). It did not address the criticism of the original decision in *R. v. Seager; R. v. Blatch*, although it has to be assumed that this was present to the mind of the court as that decision was mentioned in the judgment. The suggestion by the commission that the decisions in *R. v. McDowell* (as to which, see § 5-1047 in the main work), and *Sumal & Sons (Properties) Ltd v. Newham LBC* (as to which, see *ibid.*, § 5-1049) would lead to a different conclusion in relation to benefit and/or the assessment of benefit was roundly rejected. The court merely pointed out that those cases were concerned with different legislation, and held that, in this case, where the appellant had been convicted of trading under a prohibited name (Insolvency Act 1986, s.216), it was clear that she had benefited, and that the extent of her benefit was the turnover of her business (not the profit) during the period of the unlawful trading.

"Lifting the veil". The second test propounded in *R. v. Seager; R. v. Blatch* (as to which, see the main work) (*viz.* "the corporate veil can be pierced ... where an offender does acts in the name of a company which (with the necessary *mens rea*) constitute a criminal offence which leads to the offender's conviction ...") should not be read literally and without regard to the context of the case: *R. v. Powell* [2016] Lloyd's Rep. F.C. 546, CA. Rather, it must be read in a way that is consistent with *Prest v. Petrodel Resources Ltd* (*ibid.*); first, regard should be had to the nature and extent of the criminality involved and the approach should be geared to the facts and circumstances of the particular case (*R. v. Boyle Transport (Northern Ireland) Ltd* (*ibid.*)); secondly, the distinction drawn in *R. v. King (Scott)* between cases in which goods or services are provided by way of a lawful contract (or when payment is properly paid for legitimate services), but the transaction is tainted by associated illegality, and cases in which an entire undertaking is unlawful, whilst not of itself determinative, is likely to be relevant; thirdly, whether the offenders were sole shareholders is also likely to be relevant. The instant case was not concerned with a company that was being run for an unlawful purpose, but rather a legitimate business that had broken the criminal law through its failure to observe the necessary regulations; it was relevant that the criminal liability of the respondents was parasitic upon proof that the company had committed an offence, and also that they were not the sole shareholders; there was no legal right against the person controlling the company that existed independently of the company's involvement and the company had not been interposed so that its separate legal personality would defeat or frustrate the enforcement of some rights. **5-1047**

Offences under regulatory legislation. *R. v. Palmer* is now reported at [2017] 4 W.L.R. 15, *sub nom. R. v. Palmer (Keith).* **5-1049**

Treatment of VAT element of invoice raised by fraudulent invoice. *R. v. Harvey (Jack)* is now reported at [2017] A.C. 105. **★5-1053**

Assumptions to be made in case of a criminal lifestyle

In a criminal lifestyle case, the statutory assumptions in section 10 of the 2002 Act (§ 5-761 in the main work) are not displaced where property held post-conviction was obtained in part at least by the defendant's particular criminal conduct: *R. v. Gor* [2017] Lloyds Rep. F.C. 73, CA (considering *R. v. Waya* (as to which, see *ibid.*, §§ 5-1030, 5-1067)). As to this case, see also *post*, § 5-1066. **★5-1064**

Valuation of benefit (ss.79, 80)

In *R. v. Gor* [2017] Lloyds Rep. F.C. 73, CA, it was held that the reference to "the market value" of property in section 79 of the 2002 Act (§ 5-886 in the main work) is to the open market rather than the forced sale value (considering *R. v. Islam* (as to which, see *ibid.*, § 5-1043)). As to this case, see also *ante*, § 5-1064. **★5-1066**

X. DISQUALIFICATION, RESTRICTION, EXCLUSION, ETC., ORDERS

C. DISQUALIFICATION FROM DRIVING

(4) Notes on disqualification from driving (ss.147A, 147B)

For a case considering the duty of the prosecution advocate when a court may be considering both imprisonment and a period of disqualification for the same or another offence, see *post*, § 32-271a. **5-1128**

H. SERIOUS CRIME PREVENTION ORDERS

(1) Summary

Serious Crime Act 2007, Pt 1

With effect from November 30, 2016, section 27 of the 2007 Act (see the main work) is **5-1149** amended by the Bankruptcy (Scotland) Act 2016 (Consequential Provisions and Modifications) Order 2016 (S.I. 2016 No. 1034).

Serious offences

★**5-1198**   With effect from April 1, 2017 (Policing and Crime Act 2017 (Commencement No. 2) Regulations 2017 (S.I. 2017 No. 482)), Part 1 of Schedule 1 to the SCA 2007 (see the main work) was amended by the Policing and Crime Act 2017, s.151(1) and (2), so as to add to the list of serious offences, an offence under an instrument made under the European Communities Act 1972, s.2(2), for the purpose of implementing, or otherwise in relation to, EU obligations created or arising by or under an EU financial sanctions regulation (as to which, see s.143 of the 2017 Act), an offence under an Act or under subordinate legislation where the offence was created for the purpose of implementing a United Nations financial sanctions resolution (as to which, see *ibid.*), an offence under the Anti-terrorism, Crime and Security Act 2001, Sched. 3, para. 7, an offence under the Counter-Terrorism Act 2008, Sched. 7, para. 30 or 30A, where the offence relates to a requirement of the kind mentioned in paragraph 13 of that schedule, and an offence under the 2008 Act, Sched. 7, para. 31.

I. Criminal Behaviour Orders

(3) Authorities

(b) *Criminal behaviour orders*

5-1226   Where the appellant was convicted of two offences of fraud for overcharging an elderly man £7,850 for work carried out at his home, a criminal behaviour order effectively prohibiting him from "touting for business" for a period of 10 years was not wrong in principle; whilst section 22 of the Anti-social Behaviour, Crime and Policing Act 2014 (§ 5-1206 in the main work) envisages that the order should not interfere with the times at which the offender normally works, and whilst that might imply that such orders should not prevent an offender from working so far as practicable, where the offence was committed in the very performance of work, there was no *a priori* reason not to make such an order; while anti-social behaviour orders were usually invoked to restrain the unruly behaviour of offenders, the 2014 legislation is not confined to behaviour of that character; however, the period was too long and would be reduced to three years: *R. v. Janes* [2016] 2 Cr.App.R.(S.) 27, CA.

The use of the word "such" in section 22(4) of the 2014 Act does not have the effect that any criminal behaviour order should be confined to preventing the offender from engaging in like behaviour in the same location: *R. v. Browne-Morgan* [2017] 1 Cr.App.R.(S.) 33, CA.

K. Procedure

Introduction

★**5-1228**   The notes to Part 31 of the Criminal Procedure Rules 2015 (S.I. 2015 No. 1490) (as to which, see the main work) have been amended to add labour market enforcement orders to the list of orders considered by the Criminal Procedure Rule Committee to be "civil orders" for the purposes of Part 31.

Criminal Procedure Rules 2015 (S.I. 2015 No. 1490), Pt 31

Application for behaviour order and notice of terms of proposed order: special rules

★**5-1231**   With effect from April 3, 2017, rule 31.3 of the 2015 rules was amended by the Criminal Procedure (Amendment) Rules 2017 (S.I. 2017 No. 144), r.6, so as: (i) to substitute a new paragraph (1), as follows–

"(1) This rule applies where–

    (a) a prosecutor wants the court to make one of the following orders if the defendant is convicted–

        (i) an anti-social behaviour order (but this rule does not apply to an application for an interim anti-social behaviour order),

        (ii) a serious crime prevention order,

    (iii) a criminal behaviour order, or

    (iv) a prohibition order;

  (b) a prosecutor proposes, on the prosecutor's initiative or at the court's request, a sexual harm prevention order if the defendant is convicted;

  (c) a prosecutor proposes a restraining order whether the defendant is convicted or acquitted.";

(ii) to insert, in paragraph (2), after the words "Where paragraph (1)(a) applies", the words "(order on application)"; (iii) to insert, in paragraph (5), after the words "Where paragraph (1)(b) applies", the words "(sexual harm prevention order proposed)"; (iv) to omit the words "in a case in which a sexual harm prevention order is proposed," from paragraph (5)(b); (v) to re-number paragraph (6) as (7); and (vi) to insert a new paragraph (6) as follows—

"(6) Where paragraph (1)(c) applies (restraining order proposed), the prosecutor must—

  (a) serve a draft order on the court officer and on the defendant as soon as practicable (without waiting for the verdict);

  (b) in the draft order specify—

    (i) those prohibitions which, if the defendant is convicted, the prosecutor proposes for the purpose of protecting a person from conduct which amounts to harassment or will cause fear of violence, or

    (ii) those prohibitions which, if the defendant is acquitted, the prosecutor proposes as necessary to protect a person from harassment by the defendant.".

XI. ORDERS UNDER THE MENTAL HEALTH ACT 1983

(1) Hospital and guardianship orders

Inter-relationship with custodial sentences generally

R. v. Vowles (as to which, see the main work) was considered in *R. v. Ahmed (Saber Mohammed Ali)* [2017] Crim.L.R. 150, CA, in which a hospital order under section 37 of the MHA 1983, with a restriction order under section 41 of that Act (§§ 5-1249, 5-1259 in the main work), was substituted for a sentence of life imprisonment for a person who had been convicted of manslaughter by reason of diminished responsibility. The court held that, even if the option of giving hospital and limitation directions under section 45A of the 1983 Act (*ibid.*, § 5-1268) had been available, such a disposal would not have been appropriate because it was imperative that the appellant should be subject to appropriate expert supervision on his release and thereafter, which was not possible under section 45A. The court expressly acknowledged that the release regime under the 1983 Act may well provide better protection for the public than that under the 2003 Act precisely because those responsible for monitoring a released patient in the community have a level of expertise and resources that is not matched by probation officers. **5-1251**

(3) Hospital and limitation directions

Mental Health Act 1983, ss.45A, 45B

Power of courts to direct hospital admission

As to section 45A of the 1983 Act (§ 5-1268 in the main work), and *R. v. Vowles* [2015] 2 Cr. App. R. (S.) 6 (cited in the main work), see *R. v. Ahmed (Saber Mohammed Ali), ante,* § 5-1251. **5-1269**

XII. RECOMMENDATION FOR DEPORTATION

Criteria for exercise of power to make recommendation

Automatic deportation (under the UK Borders Act 2007 (as to which, see the main work)) of an offender, who was a third-country national and the mother of a young child who was born in the United Kingdom and had always resided here, would violate her rights under European Union law where an expulsion decision would effectively deprive the child of the enjoyment of the substance of the rights conferred by virtue of his status as a citizen: *S. v. Secretary of State for the Home Department (Case C-304/14)* [2017] Q.B. 558, ECJ (Grand Chamber). **5-1286**

With effect from February 1, 2017, the Immigration (European Economic Area) Regulations **5-1289**

2016 (S.I. 2016 No. 1052) revoke and replace, so as to consolidate, the Immigration (European Economic Area) Regulations (S.I. 2006 No. 1003) (see the main work), and their amending instruments (*viz.*, *inter alia*, S.I. 2009 No. 1117, S.I. 2014 No. 1976, and S.I. 2015 No. 694 (*ibid.*)). Regulations 23 and 27 correspond to regulations 19 and 21 of the 2006 regulations.

5-1290   As to the revocation and replacement of S.I. 2006 No. 1003 (see the main work), see *ante*, § 5-1289.

★   *F.V. (Italy) v. Secretary of State for the Home Department* is now reported at [2017] 1 All E.R. 999, *sub nom. F.V. (Italy) v. Secretary of State for the Home Department (Note)*.

5-1292   As to the revocation and replacement of S.I. 2006 No. 1003 (see the main work), see *ante*, § 5-1289.

XIV. ORDERS AGAINST PARENTS OR GUARDIANS

(3) Parenting orders

Crime and Disorder Act 1998, ss.8–10

★5-1309   The Sentencing Council's new guideline on the sentencing of children and young persons (as to which, see *ante*, § 5-178; and *post*, Appendix S-29 *et seq.*) makes provision in relation to the decision whether to make a parenting order or an order binding over the offender's parent.

CHAPTER 6

COSTS AND LEGAL AID

I. COSTS

B. PROSECUTION OF OFFENCES ACT 1985

(1) Award of costs out of central funds

(a) *Defence costs*

Review of order

★6-21a   In *R. v. Patel (Hitendra)* [2017] Costs L.R. 77, CA, the court revoked the defendant's costs order made in *Re Patel (Hitendra) and a Defendant's Costs Order* (as to which, see the main work). What emerges from this litigation is that where a successful application for a defendant's costs order is shown to have been fraudulent, the court can revisit the order and set it aside on the basis that there are "exceptional circumstances" (within the principle espoused in *Taylor v. Lawrence* (as to which, see *ibid.*, § 7-222)).

(2) Award of costs against accused

Costs on abandonment/dismissal of appeal

★6-35   On an appeal against sentence in a health and safety case, the respondent could not justify the cost of attendance of a solicitor or of rates of payment for counsel that were vastly in excess of what would be paid to counsel instructed by the CPS: *R. v. Thelwall* [2017] Crim.L.R. 240, CA. As to this case, see also *ante*, § 5-662; and *post*, § 7-135.

C. COSTS IN CRIMINAL CASES (GENERAL) REGULATIONS 1986 (S.I. 1986 No. 1335)

Principles governing exercise of jurisdiction

★6-57   In *R. (Haigh) v. City of Westminster Magistrates' Court* [2017] Costs L.R. 175, DC, it was held that the principles set out in the main work apply equally to private prosecutors as to public prosecutors; a private prosecutor will not be liable for costs merely because the prosecution fails or is withdrawn, still less because it is a private prosecution. The court commented, however, that, while the private prosecutor must enjoy a wide measure of discretion and section 19 must not be abused so as to have a chilling effect, realistically there will likely be more room for questioning the initiation and conduct of a private prosecution; and this is, perhaps, especially so where individuals in effect seek to prosecute or turn the tables on their accusers, where the contrast with the independence and detachment of a public prosecutor is particularly noteworthy.

D. Miscellaneous Enactments

(1) Senior Courts Act 1981

High Court

In *Darroch v. Football Association Premier League Ltd* [2017] 4 W.L.R. 6, CA (Civ. Div.), the court **6-95** declined to entertain an appeal from the refusal of the Divisional Court in *Darroch v. Hull and Holderness Magistrates' Court, Media Protection Services Ltd and Football Association Premier League Ltd (Interested parties)* (see the main work) to make a civil third party costs order for want of jurisdiction. The underlying proceedings were criminal and the judicial review proceedings were in a "criminal cause or matter" from which no appeal lay to the Court of Appeal (Senior Courts Act 1981, s.18(1)(a)). The court did, however, express the *obiter* opinion that section 51(1) of the 1981 Act did not empower the High Court to make an order in respect of the costs of the proceedings in a magistrates' court or the Crown Court when disposing of an appeal by way of case stated or an application for judicial review; whilst section 51(1) provides that "... the costs of and incidental to all proceedings in ... the High Court ... shall be in the discretion of the court", the costs of the proceedings in the lower court are not "incidental to" the proceedings in the High Court (disapproving *Murphy v. Media Protection Services Ltd* (see the main work) on this point).

II. LEGAL AID

C. Secondary Legislation

Criminal Legal Aid (General) Regulations 2013 (S.I. 2013 No. 9), Pt 1

Interpretation
    With effect from April 1, 2017, the Criminal Legal Aid (Standard Crime Contract) (Amend- ★**6-233** ment) Regulations 2017 (S.I. 2017 No. 311) amended regulation 2 of S.I. 2013 No. 9 so as (i) in the definition of "Unit of Work", to substitute the words "paragraph 1.3 of" for the words "paragraph 1.5 of Part A of" and to substitute "2017" for "2010"; and (ii) in the final definition, to substitute "2017" for "2010".

Criminal Legal Aid (General) Regulations 2013 (S.I. 2013 No. 9), Pt 2

Applications
    With effect from April 1, 2017, the Criminal Legal Aid (Standard Crime Contract) (Amend- ★**6-239** ment) Regulations 2017 (S.I. 2017 No. 311) amended regulation 8(b) of S.I. 2013 No. 9 so as to substitute "2017" for "2010".

Criminal Legal Aid (General) Regulations 2013 (S.I. 2013 No. 9), Pt 3

Criminal proceedings
    Brown v. London Borough of Haringey is now reported at [2017] 1 W.L.R. 542, *sub nom. Haringey* **6-240** *L.B.C. v. Brown*

Criminal Legal Aid (General) Regulations 2013 (S.I. 2013 No. 9), Pt 4

General
    With effect from April 1, 2017, the Criminal Legal Aid (Standard Crime Contract) (Amend- ★**6-242** ment) Regulations 2017 (S.I. 2017 No. 311) amended regulation 11(3) of S.I. 2013 No. 9 so as to substitute "2017" for "2010".

Applications

★**6-245**   With effect from April 1, 2017, the Criminal Legal Aid (Standard Crime Contract) (Amendment) Regulations 2017 (S.I. 2017 No. 311) amended regulation 14 of S.I. 2013 No. 9 so as to substitute "2017" for "2010" in both places.

Determinations

★**6-246**   With effect from April 1, 2017, the Criminal Legal Aid (Standard Crime Contract) (Amendment) Regulations 2017 (S.I. 2017 No. 311) amended regulation 15(1)(b) of S.I. 2013 No. 9 so as to substitute "2017" for "2010".

Withdrawal

★**6-247**   With effect from April 1, 2017, the Criminal Legal Aid (Standard Crime Contract) (Amendment) Regulations 2017 (S.I. 2017 No. 311) amended regulation 16(e)(ii) of S.I. 2013 No. 9 so as to substitute "2017" for "2010".

Appeal

★**6-248**   With effect from April 1, 2017, the Criminal Legal Aid (Standard Crime Contract) (Amendment) Regulations 2017 (S.I. 2017 No. 311) amended regulation 17(b) of S.I. 2013 No. 9 so as to substitute "2017" for "2010".

CHAPTER 7

CRIMINAL APPEAL

II. HIGH COURT JURISDICTION IN CROWN COURT PROCEEDINGS

C. APPEAL FROM HIGH COURT

(2) Criminal cause or matter

7-23   Judicial review proceedings, and orders in relation to the costs of such proceedings, give rise to a judgment "in a criminal cause or mater" within section 18(1)(a) of the Senior Courts Act 1981 where they arise out of criminal proceedings, see *Darroch v. Football Association Premier League Ltd* [2017] 4 W.L.R. 6, CA (Civ. Div.). As to this case, see also *ante*, § 6-95.

IV. APPEAL TO COURT OF APPEAL BY THE DEFENDANT

A. APPEAL AGAINST CONVICTION ON INDICTMENT

(3) Determination of appeals

Conviction "unsafe"

Appeals following pleas of guilty

7-46   For a case considering the approach where the appellant's legal representatives failed to advise him in relation to a potential defence under section 31 of the Immigration and Asylum Act 1999 (§ 25-284 in the main work), see *post*, § 25-285.

(4) Grounds of appeal

Misdirection

★**7-55**   As to whether failure to give a written route to verdict to the jury is capable of rendering a conviction unsafe, see *ante*, § 4-418.

Miscellaneous

(ii) *Conduct of legal representatives at trial*

7-83   *R. v. McCook* is now reported at [2016] 2 Cr.App.R. 30, *sub nom. R. v. McCook (Practice Note)*.

(x) *Prosecution failure to comply with duty of disclosure*

When deciding upon the safety of a conviction, the approach should be the same in a case of ★**7-91** the non-disclosure of material that ought to have been disclosed by the prosecution as it is in a case of fresh evidence: *R. v. Garland* [2017] Crim.L.R. 402, CA (considering, in particular, *R. v. Pendleton* (as to which, see § 7-50 in the main work), and *McInnes (Paul) v. H.M. Advocate* (as to which, see *ibid.*, § 7-53)).

(xvi) *Irregularity in relation to jury trial*

R. v. Ul Hamid and Khan is now reported at [2016] 2 Cr.App.R. 29, *sub nom. R. v. Ul Hamid and* **7-97** *Khan (Gulbar)*.

B. Appeal Against Sentence

(1) Who can appeal

Criminal Appeal Act 1968, s.9

Appeal against sentence following conviction on indictment

Whilst section 9 of the 1968 Act (§ 7-119 in the main work) does not expressly limit any **7-120** prospective appellant to a single appeal in respect of two or more orders following the same conviction, it has long been recognised that, normally and in the interests of finality, successive appeals will not be entertained; cases where a second or subsequent order is only made after an appeal against an earlier order has been disposed of will continue to be capable in appropriate cases of providing an exception to the general rule against repeated applications; and there is a residual category of case in which the court enjoys a limited jurisdiction to avoid real injustice in exceptional circumstances by exercising an implicit power to reopen a concluded appeal where it is necessary to do so (considering *R. v. Yasain* (as to which, see *ibid.*, § 7-222)): *R. v. Geraghty* [2017] 1 Cr.App.R.(S.) 10, CA

Criminal Appeal Act 1968, s.50

Meaning of "sentence"

A financial reporting order is a "sentence" for the purposes of section 50(1) of the 1968 Act (§ **7-122** 7-121 in the main work): *R. v. Geraghty* [2017] 1 Cr.App.R.(S.) 10, CA.

(2) Notes on appeal against sentence

Principles on which court acts

In *R. v. Thelwall* [2017] Crim.L.R. 240, CA, it was said that, where an offence is the subject of ★**7-135** a guideline, whether issued by the Sentencing Council or contained in statute (as for murder (CJA 2003, Sched. 21 (§§ 5-402 *et seq.* in the main work)), the citation of decisions of the Court of Appeal on the application and interpretation of the guideline is generally of no assistance; there may be cases where the court is asked to say something about a guideline where, in wholly exceptional circumstances, the guideline may be unclear; in such circumstances, the court will make observations that may be cited to the court in the future; it is important that practitioners appreciate that the system now proceeds on the basis of guidelines, not case law; it will, therefore, be very rare, where there is an applicable guideline, for any party to cite to the court cases that seek to express how the guideline works; further, it is impermissible to refer the court to sources other than the sentencing guidelines (for example, as occurred here, to online articles from the websites of the Health and Safety Executive, the CPS, BBC News, and newspapers, as to sentencing ranges). As to this case, see also *ante*, §§ 5-662, 6-35.

(iii) *Matters improperly taken into account or fresh matters to be taken into account*

Where a defendant has been ordered in the Crown Court to pay an amount towards the ★**7-139** prosecution costs at a time when it was properly assessed that he had the assets to meet such a liability, it would not be appropriate for the Court of Appeal to interfere with the order or its enforcement on the grounds of a subsequent change in financial circumstances on the part of the defendant: *R. v. Coleman (John)* [2017] 4 W.L.R. 29, CA.

F. Reference of Cases to Court of Appeal

Criminal Appeal Act 1995, s.9

Cases dealt with on indictment in England and Wales

★**7-159**   Rules 47.53 to 47.57 of the Criminal Procedure Rules 2015 (S.I. 2015 No. 1490) (see the main work) have been re-numbered as rules 47.54 to 47.58: Criminal Procedure (Amendment) Rules 2017 (S.I. 2017 No. 144).

G. Procedure from Notice of Appeal to Hearing

(4) Drafting of grounds

★**7-168**   As to the drafting of grounds of appeal, see *R. v. James; R. v. Selby, post,* § 7-200.

★   Where, following the lodging of grounds of appeal against sentence, the sentencing judge adjusts the sentence downwards in exercise of his powers under section 155 of the PCC(S)A 2000 (§ 5-1312 in the main work), it is incumbent on the defendant and those advising him to lodge fresh grounds of appeal if he wishes to appeal the reduced sentence: *R. v. Egginton* [2017] 1 Cr.App.R.(S.) 20, CA.

(7) Extension of time

7-171   In approaching applications for leave to appeal out of time against convictions for murder that were secured prior to the decision in *R. v. Jogee; Ruddock v. The Queen* (as to which, see §§ 19-23 *et seq.* in the main work), (i) leave will only be granted if substantial injustice has been done (see *Jogee* at [100]); in determining whether that high threshold has been met, the court will primarily and ordinarily have regard to the strength of the case advanced that the change in the law would, in fact, have made a difference; the court will also have regard to other matters, including whether the applicant was guilty of other, though less serious, criminal conduct; if there has been a substantial injustice, it is not material to consider the length of time that has elapsed; the court should also not take into account the observations of the judge when sentencing in determining the factual basis for the conviction; its duty is to examine the matters before the jury and the jury's verdict (including the findings of fact that would have been essential to reach such a verdict); (ii) if exceptional leave is granted, the court will then, and only then, consider the question as to whether, in the light of the direction given to the jury, the conviction is unsafe; however, if the threshold required to justify exceptional leave to appeal is reached, it is likely to be difficult to conclude that the conviction remains safe; (iii) where an application for leave to appeal has been made within 28 days on non-*Jogee* grounds and either granted or refused, but renewed to the full court, and subsequently an application has been made to add grounds based on the decision in *Jogee*, exceptional leave to put forward the new grounds is required on the same principles as above; where the application was made within 28 days on non-*Jogee* grounds, but the issue of leave to appeal was not determined by either the single judge or the full court, as progress in the case was adjourned by the registrar pending the decision in *Jogee*, it is just to allow the issue to be argued; (iv) finally, where the appellant has appealed on *Jogee* grounds in time and a co-defendant (who did not) then seeks to appeal on similar grounds out of time, given that the appeal in time has to be determined in accordance with the usual principles (unhampered by the need to seek exceptional leave), the potential substantial injustice as between defendants is likely, depending on the circumstances, to require that a co-defendant who seeks leave should be permitted to argue his appeal: *R. v. Johnson; R. v. Burton; R. v. Moises; R. v. Hore; R. v. Miah; R. v. Hall (Practice Note)* [2017] 1 Cr.App.R. 12 CA (considering, *inter alia, R. v. R.* (as to which, see the main work)). As to this case, see also *post,* § 19-29.

★   In the context of a conviction (based on a guilty plea) properly returned under the law as it was understood at the time, but where that understanding of the law had since been declared to have been mistaken, it was for the defendant, on making an application for exceptional leave to appeal out of time, to demonstrate that a substantial injustice would be done if the application were to be refused (and not merely that the conviction was unsafe): *R. v. Ordu* [2017] 1 Cr.App.R. 21, CA (considering *R. v. Mitchell* (as to which, see the main work), *R. v. Jogee; Ruddock v. The Queen* (*ante*), *R. v. Johnson* (*ante*), *R. v. Asfaw* (*United Nations High Commr for Refugees intervening*) (as to which, see § 25-285 in the main work), *R. v. Mohamed* (*Abdalla*); *R. v. V. (M.);* *R. v. Mohamed*

(Rahma Abukar); R. v. Nofallah (as to which, see §§ 7-46, 25-285 in the main work) and *R. v. Mateta; R. v. Ghavami and Afshar; R. v. Bashir; R. v. Andukwa* (as to which, see § 25-285 in the main work)). Where there were no continuing consequences of the conviction, the applicant had failed to demonstrate that a substantial injustice would be done: *ibid.* For criticism of this decision, see CLW/17/13/2, and [2017] 3 *Archbold Review* 8 (*per* John Spencer Q.C.).

(12) Abandonment of appeal

Criminal Procedure Rules 2015 (S.I. 2015 No. 1490), rr.36.13, 36.14

Abandoning a ground of appeal or opposition

With effect from April 3, 2017, the Criminal Procedure (Amendment) Rules 2017 (S.I. 2017 No. 144), r.9, substituted rule 36.14 of the 2015 rules as follows— ★**7-186**

"**36.14.**–(1) If the court gives permission to appeal then unless the court otherwise directs the decision indicates that—
    (a) the appellant has permission to appeal on every ground identified by the appeal notice; and
    (b) the court finds reasonably arguable each ground on which the appellant has permission to appeal.
(2) If the court gives permission to appeal but not on every ground identified by the appeal notice the decision indicates that—
    (a) at the hearing of the appeal the court will not consider representations that address any ground thus excluded from argument; and
    (b) an appellant who wants to rely on such an excluded ground needs the court's permission to do so.
(3) An appellant who wants to rely at the hearing of an appeal on a ground of appeal excluded from argument by a judge of the Court of Appeal when giving permission to appeal must—
    (a) apply in writing, with reasons, and identify each such ground;
    (b) serve the application on—
      (i) the Registrar, and
      (ii) any respondent;
    (c) serve the application not more than 14 days after—
      (i) the giving of permission to appeal, or
      (ii) the Registrar serves notice of that decision on the applicant, if the applicant was not present in person or by live link when permission to appeal was given.
(4) Paragraph (5) applies where a party wants to abandon—
    (a) a ground of appeal on which that party has permission to appeal; or
    (b) a ground of opposition identified in a respondent's notice.
(5) Such a party must serve notice on—
    (a) the Registrar; and
    (b) each other party,
before any hearing at which that ground will be considered by the court.".

H. The Hearing

(1) Presence of appellant

Criminal Procedure Rules 2015 (S.I. 2015 No. 1490), rr.39.11, 39.12

Right to attend hearing

With effect from April 3, 2017, rule 39.11 of the 2015 rules was amended by the Criminal Procedure (Amendment) Rules 2017 (S.I. 2017 No. 144), r.10, so as (i) to omit "or" at the end of paragraph (a), (ii) to re-number paragraph (b) as paragraph (c), and (iii) to insert a new paragraph (b), as follows— ★**7-194**

    "(b) it is the hearing of an appeal and the court directs that—
      (i) the appeal involves a question of law alone, and
      (ii) for that reason the appellant has no permission to attend; or".

(5) Skeleton arguments and citation of authorities

Criminal Practice Direction IX Appeal 39F: Skeleton Arguments

Grounds of appeal in excess of 100 pages are not acceptable; legal documents of unnecessary ★**7-200** length offer little assistance to the court; no area of law is exempt from the requirement to produce careful and concise documents (see *Tchenguiz v. Director of the Serious Fraud Office (H.M. Procureur for Guernsey intervening)* (as to which, see the main work), and the Criminal Procedure Rules 2015 (S.I. 2015 No. 1490), r.39.3 (*ibid.*, § 7-382)); it is essential that this increasing difficulty should be controlled; various obvious risks, of which an applicant should be aware, arise, *viz.* the court might, if grounds are inexcusably prolix and not consolidated after a warning shot by the registrar, refuse an application on the basis that no ground was identifiable; adverse outcomes for the applicant could include a loss of time order or an order to bear the costs of the respondent's notice (those outcomes do not constitute an exhaustive list of dispositions open to the court); the practitioner should have the requirements of the rules at his fingertips; additionally, he should most assuredly react swiftly and, if necessary, apologetically when the registrar intervenes before a hearing to indicate non-compliance with them; the rules, and the practice directions, are explicit and easily accessed; they are to be followed; they are not an optional extra: *R. v. James; R. v. Selby* [2017] Crim. L.R. 228, CA.

(7) Leave to call additional evidence
Criminal Appeal Act 1968, s.23

7-206   *R. v. Ul Hamid and Khan* is now reported at [2016] 2 Cr.App.R. 29, *sub nom. R. v. Ul Hamid and Khan (Gulbar).*

Practical application

Sentence appeals

7-215   *R. v. Rogers (Georgina); R. v. Tapecrown Ltd; R. v. Beaman (Paul)* is now reported at [2016] 2 Cr.App.R.(S.) 36, *sub nom. R. v. Rogers.*

Procedure

★7-219   As to the amendment of rule 39.7 of the Criminal Procedure Rules 2015 (S.I. 2015 No. 1490) (see the main work), see *post*, § 7-386. Paragraph (1) now includes a reference to Part 16 (written witness statements).

I. NOTIFICATION OF RESULT OF APPEAL AND MATTERS DEPENDING THEREON

(2) Alteration of decision, relisting of cases

7-222   For a case considering *R. v. Yasain* (see the main work), see *ante*, § 7-122.

J. SUPPLEMENTARY PROVISIONS

(2) Powers exercisable by a single judge

Considerations in deciding whether to grant leave

7-237   *R. v. Hyde* is now reported at [2016] 2 Cr.App.R.(S.) 39.

K. APPELLANTS LIABLE TO AUTOMATIC DEPORTATION

7-244   For a case considering the compatibility of the automatic deportation provisions in the UK Borders Act 2007 (as to which, see the main work) with EU law, see *ante*, § 5-1286.

IX. APPEAL TO THE COURT OF APPEAL: PROCEDURE AND FORMS

A. PROCEDURAL RULES

Criminal Procedure Rules 2015 (S.I. 2015 No. 1490), Pt 39

Adaptation of rules about introducing evidence

★7-386   With effect from April 3, 2017, the Criminal Procedure (Amendment) Rules 2017 (S.I. 2017 No. 144), r.10, amended the 2015 rules so as to substitute a new rule 39.7, as follows—

"Introducing evidence

    39.7.–(1) The following Parts apply with such adaptations as the court or the Registrar may direct–

(a) Part 16 (written witness statements);

(b) Part 18 (measures to assist a witness or defendant to give evidence);

(c) Part 19 (expert evidence);

(d) Part 20 (hearsay evidence);

(e) Part 21 (evidence of bad character); and

(f) Part 22 (evidence of a complainant's previous sexual behaviour).

(2) But the general rule is that—

(a) a respondent who opposes an appellant's application or notice to which one of those Parts applies must do so in the respondent's notice, with reasons;

(b) an appellant who opposes a respondent's application or notice to which one of those Parts applies must serve notice, with reasons, on—
(i) the Registrar, and
(ii) the respondent
not more than 14 days after service of the respondent's notice; and

(c) the court or the Registrar may give directions with or without a hearing.

(3) A party who wants the court to order the production of a document, exhibit or other thing connected with the proceedings must—

(a) identify that item; and

(b) explain—
(i) how it is connected with the proceedings,
(ii) why its production is necessary for the determination of the case, and
(iii) to whom it should be produced (the court, appellant or respondent, or any two or more of them).

(4) A party who wants the court to order a witness to attend to be questioned must—

(a) identify the proposed witness; and

(b) explain—
(i) what evidence the proposed witness can give,
(ii) why that evidence is capable of belief,
(iii) if applicable, why that evidence may provide a ground for allowing the appeal,
(iv) on what basis that evidence would have been admissible in the case which is the subject of the application for permission to appeal or appeal, and
(v) why that evidence was not introduced in that case.

(5) Where the court orders a witness to attend to be questioned, the witness must attend the hearing of the application for permission to appeal or of the appeal, as applicable, unless the court otherwise directs.

(6) Where the court orders a witness to attend to be questioned before an examiner on the court's behalf, the court must identify the examiner and may give directions about—

(a) the time and place, or times and places, at which that questioning must be carried out;

(b) the manner in which that questioning must be carried out, in particular as to—
(i) the service of any report, statement or questionnaire in preparation for the questioning,
(ii) the sequence in which the parties may ask questions, and
(iii) if more than one witness is to be questioned, the sequence in which those witnesses may be questioned; and

(c) the manner in which, and when, a record of the questioning must be submitted to the court.

(7) Where the court orders the questioning of a witness before an examiner, the court may delegate to that examiner the giving of directions under paragraph (6)(a), (b) and (c).".

X. APPEAL TO THE SUPREME COURT FROM THE COURT OF APPEAL

A. THE APPEAL

(1) Right of appeal

Criminal Appeal Act 1968, s.33

In *R. v. Garwood* [2017] 3 *Archbold Review* 1, CA ([2017] EWCA Crim. 59), the court reaffirmed ★**7-396** that it has no jurisdiction to certify a point of law of general public importance where it refuses an application.

XIII. REFERENCES TO THE COURT OF APPEAL BY THE ATTORNEY-GENERAL

B. OF SENTENCES

Double jeopardy

★**7-449**   For a rare example of the Court of Appeal making an allowance for double jeopardy where a sentence was increased following an Attorney-General's reference, see *Att.-Gen.'s Reference (R. v. Ferizi)* [2017] 1 Cr.App.R.(S.) 26, CA. The respondents were both young (18 and 19). One had received a non-custodial sentence and the other was approaching his release date. In the circumstances, the court discounted the appropriate sentence by a third for double jeopardy.

★   In *Att.-Gen.'s Reference (R. v. Susorovs)* [2017] 1 Cr.App.R.(S.) 15, CA, it was held that some allowance ought to be made for double jeopardy when increasing a sentence pursuant to an Attorney-General's reference, where the offender had suffered some unfairness given the way the prosecution had conducted their case (the submissions of the Attorney-General on the reference had been inconsistent with those advanced by counsel for the prosecution in the Crown Court).

C. PROCEDURE

★**7-460**   Service of a notice of application for leave to refer a sentence as being unduly lenient under section 36 of the CJA 1988 (§ 7-442 in the main work) can be effected by electronic means: *Att.-Gen.'s Reference (R. v. Lindley)* [2017] 1 Cr.App.R.(S.) 39, CA.

CHAPTER 8

ORAL TESTIMONY OF WITNESSES

IV. RULES OF EVIDENCE AND PRACTICE RELATING TO THE QUESTIONING OF WITNESSES

A. GENERAL

(2) Special measures directions

Defendants

8-72   For a case considering *R. (C.) v. Sevenoaks Youth Court* (see the main work), see *post*, § 8-94.

Youth Justice and Criminal Evidence Act 1999, ss.23–30

Evidence by live link

8-85   For a new practice direction relating to the use of live link and supplementing the introduction of rules 3.2(4) and (5) and 3.3(2)(e) of the 2015 rules by the Criminal Procedure (Amendment No. 2) Rules 2016 (S.I. 2016 No. 705) (as to which, see § 4-115 in the main work), see *post*, Appendix B-72a *et seq.*

Transcript for jury

Video recorded cross-examination or re-examination

8-93   With effect from January 2, 2017 (Youth Justice and Criminal Evidence Act 1999 (Commencement No. 15) Order 2016 (S.I. 2016 No. 1201)), section 28 of the 1999 Act was brought into force in relation to "relevant proceedings". Proceedings are "relevant" if (a) they take place before the Crown Court sitting at Kingston-upon-Thames, Leeds, or Liverpool, and (b) the witness is eligible for assistance by virtue of section 16(1)(a) (witnesses eligible for assistance on grounds of age (§ 8-74 in the main work)), where the witness is aged 16 or 17 at the time of the hearing.

Examination of witness through intermediary

8-94   Since section 33BA (examination of accused through an intermediary (§ 8-101 in the main work)) of the YJCEA 1999 is not yet in force, the power of a judge to appoint an intermediary for a defendant derives from the common law (*R. (C.) v. Sevenoaks Youth Court* (as to which, see the main work)); in analysing a defendant's need for an intermediary at different stages of the trial (as he is required to do), a judge is entitled to determine the defendant's mental capacity on all the evidence, including the defendant's educational background and his own observations of the defendant; he is not bound to accept the conclusions of the experts, even if they are agreed; as stated in *R. (O.P.) v. Secretary of State for Justice* (*ibid.*), there are two distinct types of assistance that may be required (*viz.* (a) general support, reassurance and calm interpretation of unfolding events, and (b) skilled support and interpretation and possible intervention or suggestion to the bench, associated with the giving of evidence by the defendant); after determining the mental capacity of a defendant, courts must therefore distinguish between those two types in determining what is necessary for the particular defendant; in considering what is needed, the court must take into account the fact that, in all but the rarest cases, a competent advocate will be able to do what is needed so that a defendant is able fully to participate in his trial without an intermediary, at least until the point is reached when the defendant gives evidence; in the event that an advocate asks a question that is too complex or tagged, then the judge should intervene; cases in which the threshold of disability is crossed, such that an intermediary is required when the defendant gives evidence, will be rare; but cases in which an order will be made for an intermediary to be present for the whole trial will be very rare: *R. v. Rashid* [2017] 1 Cr.App.R. 25, CA (commenting that the approach taken by the judge in this case, based on the common law, is now reflected in *Criminal Practice Direction I (General Matters) 3F*, paras 3F.11 *et seq.* (*ibid.*, § 8-131j, Appendix B-42)).

Youth Justice and Criminal Evidence Act 1999, ss.33A–33C

Live link directions

For a new practice direction relating to the use of live link and supplementing the introduction **8-99**
of rules 3.2(4) and (5) and 3.3(2)(e) of the 2015 rules by the Criminal Procedure (Amendment No. 2) Rules 2016 (S.I. 2016 No. 705) (as to which, see § 4-115 in the main work), see *post*, Appendix B-72a *et seq.*

Examination of accused through intermediary

For a case considering the position of a defendant pending the commencement of section **8-101**
33BA of the 1999 Act, see *ante*, § 8-94.

Criminal Procedure Rules 2015 (S.I. 2015 No. 1490), Pt 18

Decisions and reasons

In connection with rule 18.4, see paragraph 2 of *Criminal Practice Direction (General matters) 3N* **8-113**
(use of live link and telephone facilities), *post*, Appendix B-72a.

Live link directions

For a new practice direction relating to the use of live link and supplementing the introduction **8-131a**
of rules 3.2(4) and (5) and 3.3(2)(e) of the 2015 rules by the Criminal Procedure (Amendment No. 2) Rules 2016 (S.I. 2016 No. 705) (as to which, see § 4-115 in the main work), see *post*, Appendix B-72a *et seq.*

(5) Evidence by live link
Criminal Justice Act 2003, ss.51–56

Live links in criminal proceedings

For a new practice direction relating to the use of live link and supplementing the introduction **8-139**
of rules 3.2(4) and (5) and 3.3(2)(e) of the 2015 rules by the Criminal Procedure (Amendment No. 2) Rules 2016 (S.I. 2016 No. 705) (as to which, see § 4-115 in the main work), see *post*, Appendix B-72a *et seq.*

Procedural provision

For procedural provision in relation to live link directions, see also a new practice direction **8-144**
supplementing the introduction of rules 3.2(4) and (5) and 3.3(2)(e) of the 2015 rules by the Criminal Procedure (Amendment No. 2) Rules 2016 (S.I. 2016 No. 705) (as to which, see § 4-115 in the main work), see *post*, Appendix B-72a *et seq.*

B. Examination-in-Chief

(2) Identifying the witness

(a) *Name*

Coroners and Justice Act 2009, ss.86–90

Conditions for making order

8-158   When a court makes a witness anonymity order under section 88 of the 2009 Act (as to which, see the main work), it has a continuing duty to review the order throughout the trial to ensure the fairness of the proceedings; if the original basis for making the order is displaced during the trial, such that the trial may potentially become unfair, the matter needs to be revisited; that approach would be consistent with general considerations under Article 6 (right to a fair trial (*ibid.*, § 16-72)) of the ECHR, and, in particular, the need to view the proceedings as a whole: *R. v. Calvert* [2016] 7 *Archbold Review* 1, CA.

Authorities

★8-172   *Disclosure*: it is not appropriate to read into section 87(3) of the Coroners and Justice Act 2009 (§ 8-157 in the main work) the words "unless to inform the prosecutor would deprive the defendant of a fair trial", so that the defence are not always under an obligation, when applying for a witness anonymity order, to disclose the identity of the witness to the prosecution as well as to the court: *R. v. Sardar* [2017] 1 Cr.App.R. 15, CA.

C. Cross-Examination

(3) Restrictions

(b) *In proceedings for sexual offences*

Compatibility with ECHR

8-242   *R. v. A. (No. 2)* was considered in *R. v. Evans, post*, § 8-243.

Section 41(3)(c)—similarity of behaviour

8-243   In *R. v. Evans (Chedwyn)* [2017] 1 Cr.App.R. 13, CA, it was held: (i) where a judge gives leave in relation to questions about a complainant's sexual history pursuant to section 41 of the YJCEA 1999 (§ 8-238 in the main work), the defence could not possibly be bound by the answers; if the proposed questioning, or the evidence the defence wish to adduce, goes solely or mainly (emphasis being placed on the latter two words) to the issue of the credibility of the complainant, it would be prohibited by subsection (4) and the judge would not give leave; whilst, to an extent, any challenge to a complainant's evidence involves an attack upon her credibility, to obtain leave under section 41, the defence must satisfy the court that the provisions of one or more of the other subsections apply and that, if leave is refused, any subsequent conviction would be unsafe; thus, it is only if the proposed questioning and evidence of specific instances of sexual behaviour relate to a relevant issue, and either do not go to the issue of consent under subsection (3)(a) or do go to the issue of consent, and the requirements of subsection (3)(b) or (c)(i) or (ii) are fulfilled, that a judge may give leave; and (ii) where, on appeal against conviction for rape, the appellant sought to adduce fresh evidence of two men who claimed to have had sexual intercourse with the complainant, where both the appellant and those men described specific instances of the complainant behaving in a very similar fashion in the days before the alleged rape and in the days that followed, where on each occasion she had been drinking, and was said to have instigated certain sexual activity, directed her partner into certain positions, and used specific words of encouragement, whilst acutely aware of the hurdle facing any defendant in persuading a judge that evidence of this kind from third parties is admissible, on these facts, the evidence of both witnesses would have been relevant and admissible at trial and was arguably sufficiently similar to come within the terms of section 41(3)(c)(i); it may also have been relevant and admissible under section 41(3)(a) on the issue of reasonable belief; the behaviour does not have to be unusual or bizarre; it has to be sufficiently similar that it cannot be explained reasonably as a coincidence; it may well be a rare case in which it would be appropriate to indulge in this kind of forensic examination of sexual behaviour with others, but this was potentially such a rare case where the requirements of section 41 necessarily gave way to the requirements of a fair trial: *R. v. Evans* [2016] 9 *Archbold Review* 3, CA (considering *R. v. A. (No. 2)* (as to which, see § 8-242 in the main work)). For the suggestion that the judgment is unclear as to the precise basis of the decision, see CLW/16/42/3.

Previous complaints and statements about sexual behaviour

For a decision of the Supreme Court of New Zealand that recognises that questions about false **8-246** allegations of rape are in certain circumstances questions about sexual behaviour as opposed to merely being questions about things said (where the falsity lies in the suggestion that the encounter was non-consensual), see *Best v. The Queen*, unreported, September 8, 2016 ([2016] NZSC 122) (considering *R. v. All-Hilly* (as to which, see the main work)).

CHAPTER 9

DOCUMENTARY AND REAL EVIDENCE

II. PUBLIC DOCUMENTS

D. CATEGORIES OF PUBLIC DOCUMENTS

(8) Judicial documents

(g) *Convictions and acquittals*

Police and Criminal Evidence Act 1984, ss.74, 75

Section 74(1), (2)

Discretionary exclusion

When considering the admission of evidence of the conviction of a co-accused under section **9-89** 74 (§ 9-82 in the main work) of the PACE Act 1984, and the operation of section 78 (*ibid.*, § 15-520) in respect thereof, such evidence should never be admitted simply because it is convenient for the jury "to have the whole picture"; where, however, there is no real question that the offence alleged was committed and the real issue is whether the defendant was party to it, such evidence is likely to be perfectly fair, save where it closes off (as opposed to "makes more difficult") an issue that the jury have to try; on appeal, if the judge's decision on the issue of fairness were one of pure discretion, this would unduly confine any possible challenge; it is an exercise of judgment, in which a balance has to be struck on the issue of fairness, which is either right or wrong, but such decisions are fact-sensitive and the trial judge will be in a particularly good position to assess the issue of fairness: *R. v. Denham and Stansfield* [2017] 1 Cr.App.R. 7, CA (considering, *inter alia*, *R. v. Curry* and *R. v. Kempster* (as to both of which, see the main work)).

CHAPTER 10

MISCELLANEOUS SOURCES OF EVIDENCE

VI. LETTERS OF REQUEST

Designation of prosecuting authorities

With effect from November 9, 2016, the Secretaries of State for Business, Energy and Industrial **10-28** Strategy, for International Trade and for Exiting the European Union and the Transfer of Functions (Education and Skills) Order 2016 (S.I. 2016 No. 992) amended the Crime (International Co-operation) Act 2003 (Designation of Prosecuting Authorities) Order 2004 (S.I. 2004 No. 1034) so as to substitute a reference to the Secretary of State for Business, Energy and Industrial Strategy for the reference to the Secretary of State for Business, Innovation and Skills.

VII. EXPERT EVIDENCE

A. LEGISLATION

Criminal Procedure Rules 2015 (S.I. 2015 No. 1490), Pt 19

Content of expert's report

10-42   As to new practice directions setting out the statement and declaration required by rule 19.4(j) and (k) (see the main work and Appendix B-265) and making provision for the bringing together of experts at an early stage, see *post*, Appendix B-271a, B-271b.

★   As to the subsequent amendment of the first of those new practice directions, see *post*, Appendix B-271a.

B. OPINION EVIDENCE

Test of admissibility

10-47   Whereas an expert for the prosecution had visually illustrated her opinions by the use of "animations" or cartoons, which were different from simulations, in that they were not a scientific model produced by a computer in accordance with set parameters, the judge's decision to admit the animations was well within the ambit of his discretion under section 78 of the PACE Act (§ 15-520 in the main work); by the terms of his ruling, his intervention during the expert's evidence and his directions to the jury, the judge understood and made clear that the animations were no more than an illustration of the expert's opinion and did not constitute any form of independent scientific evidence; there was no arguable basis for submitting that the animations were capable of having a subliminal effect that could undermine the jury's focus on the evidence, the defence's extensive criticisms of the expert, other alternative scenarios, or the clear directions of the judge: *R. v. Metcalfe* [2016] 2 Cr.App.R. 21, CA.

Scope

10-51   For a case considering *Pora v. The Queen* (as to which, see the main work) in relation to gross negligence manslaughter, see *post*, § 19-123.

CHAPTER 11

HEARSAY EVIDENCE

II. STATUTE

A. CRIMINAL JUSTICE ACT 2003

(1) The basic rules

Criminal Justice Act 2003, ss.114, 115, 133, 134

Hearsay and the right to a fair trial

11-3   The Grand Chamber decision of the European Court of Human Rights in *Al-Khawaja v. U.K.* (as to which, see the main work) was reconsidered by the Grand Chamber in *Schatschaschwili v.*

Germany (2016) 63 E.H.R.R. 14. The court referred to the fact that, in *Al-Khawaja* the court had said that there were three issues to be considered where the untested evidence of an absent witness was admitted against the defendant, *viz.* whether there was good reason for the absence of the witness, whether or not the evidence of the absent witness was the sole or decisive basis for the conviction, and what counter-balancing factors had been deployed to compensate for the handicap to the defence as a result of the admission of the untested evidence and to ensure that the trial, as a whole, was fair. It then said that (i) the absence of a good reason cannot of itself be conclusive of the unfairness of a trial; however, it is an important factor to be weighed in the balance, and one that may tip the balance in favour of a finding of a breach; (ii) the court must review the existence of sufficient counter-balancing factors not only where the evidence of the absent witness was the sole or the decisive basis for a conviction, but also where it was unclear whether that is the case, but the court is satisfied that it carried significant weight and that its admission may have handicapped the defence; the extent of the necessary counter-balancing factors will depend on the weight of the evidence of the absent witness; and (iii) as a rule, it will be appropriate to consider the three *Al-Khawaja* issues in the above order; however, they are interrelated and, taken together, serve to establish whether the proceedings, as a whole, were fair; it may therefore be appropriate, in a given case, to examine the steps in a different order, in particular if one of them proves conclusive one way or the other.

For a decision of the High Court of Australia considering the approach to the assessment of **11-3a**
the reliability of a representation of fact made by an absent witness, see *Sio v. The Queen*, 334 A.L.R. 57 ([2016] HCA 32).

III. COMMON LAW

(5) Res gestae

(a) *Possibility of concoction or distortion can be disregarded by reason of emotional involvement in events*

Practical considerations

As stated in *Barnaby v. DPP*, referring to *R. v. Andrews (D.)* (as to both of which, see the main **11-78**
work), the key question when deciding whether to admit evidence as *res gestae* (CJA 2003, s.118 (*ibid.*, § 11-70)) is whether the possibility of concoction or distortion can be disregarded; that must be answered by considering the circumstances in which the particular statement was made; the time between the event and the statement is obviously a factor; but there may be special features quite apart from the time lapse that relate to the possibility of concoction or distortion; while the doctrine should not be used as a device to avoid calling the maker of a statement and while the prosecution should not use it to avoid evidence that is potentially inconsistent with their case (*Att.-Gen.'s Reference (No. 1 of 2003)* (as to which, see the main work)), that situation must be distinguished from the situation where a victim of domestic violence refuses to co-operate out of fear: *R. (Ibrahim) v. CPS*, 181 J.P. 11, QBD (Cranston J.) (where the court took account not just of the apparent time lapse between an alleged assault and a 999 call, but also the hysterical tone of the call, the fact that the caller had received recent injuries that were still developing when the police arrived within a few minutes, the disturbance in the caller's flat that had not been remedied and her demeanour when they arrived (distressed, shaking and crying)).

For a decision of the Divisional Court to similar effect, see *Morgan v. DPP* [2017] A.C.D. 23, ★
DC ([2016] EWHC 3414 (Admin.)) (also a case of domestic violence, where the complainant's explanation for a delay of about an hour in calling 999 was that, the defendant having left the home, she was so terrified that he would return, that she hid outside in a state of undress).

CHAPTER 12

PRIVILEGE, PUBLIC INTEREST IMMUNITY AND DISCLOSURE

I. PRIVILEGE

B. Answers Which May Incriminate a Witness

Documents

12-2a   As from a day to be appointed, section 49 of the RIPA 2000 (see the main work) is amended by the Investigatory Powers Act 2016, s.271(1), and Sched. 10, paras 44, 46, 53 and 55. The amendments have no effect on the decision in *R. v. S. (F.) and A. (S.)* (as to which, see the main work).

C. Legal Professional Privilege

(1) The nature of legal professional privilege

Legal advice privilege

★**12-11**   Where interviews were conducted by or on behalf of lawyers instructed by RBS with RBS employees as part of internal investigations carried out in response to two US *subpoenas* and allegations made by a former employee, for the purpose of enabling RBS to seek legal advice, and where the interviewees were authorised to participate in the interviews but not to seek legal advice or give instructions to the lawyers, *Three Rivers D.C. v. Governor and Company of the Bank of England (No. 5)* (as to which, see the main work) was binding authority to the effect that the interview notes were not subject to legal advice privilege; the fact that an employee may be authorised to communicate with the corporation's lawyer did not make that employee the client or a recognised emanation of the client; nor were the notes subject to "lawyers' working papers" privilege in that they might give an indication as to legal advice given, there being no evidence in them of any analysis carried out by the lawyers, even in the most general terms: *RBS Rights Issue Litigation* [2017] Lloyd's Rep. F.C. 83, Ch D (Hildyard J.).

(3) Duration and waiver of privilege

Waiver

12-15   The decision of the High Court in *Eurasian Natural Resources Corpn Ltd v. Dechert LLP* (as to which see the main work) has been upheld on appeal: see *Eurasian Natural Resources Corpn Ltd v. Dechert LLP* [2016] 1 W.L.R. 5027, CA (Civ. Div.).

II. PUBLIC INTEREST IMMUNITY

B. Categories of Public Interest Immunity

Police complaints investigations

★**12-38**   As to the reference in the main work to a complaint against the police under Part IV of the Police Act 1996, it should be noted that Part IV was repealed by the Police Reform Act 2002, which contained its own regime for the regulation of complaints against the police. The authority of the decision in *ex p. Wiley* (as to which, see the main work) applies as much to complaints under the 2002 Act as it does to complaints under the 1996 Act.

III. DISCLOSURE

B. LEGISLATION

(1) Criminal Procedure and Investigations Act 1996

Criminal Procedure and Investigations Act 1996, ss.3, 4

Initial duty of prosecutor to disclose

As from a day to be appointed, section 3(7) of the 1996 Act is amended by the Investigatory **12-58**
Powers Act 2016, s.271(1), and Sched. 10, paras 39(1) and (2), so as to substitute the words "section 56 of the Investigatory Powers Act 2016" for the words "section 17 of the Regulation of Investigatory Powers Act 2000".

The disclosure regime under the 1996 Act applies to documentation created (or received) by an accused himself (and now in the possession of the prosecution), and it is not arguable that documents said to be required for memory refreshing purposes fall outside the regime; there is only one test to be applied, *viz.* that in section 3(1)(a) of the Act (see the main work): *R. v. Whale and West* [2016] 7 *Archbold Review* 1, CA ([2016] EWCA Crim. 246).

Criminal Procedure and Investigations Act 1996, ss.7–9

Continuing duty of prosecutor to disclose

As from a day to be appointed, section 7A(9) of the 1996 Act is amended by the Investigatory **12-74**
Powers Act 2016, s.271(1), and Sched. 10, paras 39(1) and (3), so as to substitute the words "section 56 of the Investigatory Powers Act 2016" for the words "section 17 of the Regulation of Investigatory Powers Act 2000".

Application by accused for disclosure

As from a day to be appointed, section 8(6) of the 1996 Act is amended by the Investigatory **12-76**
Powers Act 2016, s.271(1), and Sched. 10, paras 39(1) and (4), so as to substitute the words "section 56 of the Investigatory Powers Act 2016" for the words "section 17 of the Regulation of Investigatory Powers Act 2000".

Criminal Procedure and Investigations Act 1996, s.21A

Code of practice for police interviews of witnesses notified by accused

With effect from April 3, 2017 (Policing and Crime Act 2017 (Commencement No. 1 and **★12-95**
Transitional Provisions) Regulations 2017 (S.I. 2017 No. 399)), section 21A(4) of the 1996 Act was amended by the Policing and Crime Act 2017, s.51, and Sched. 14, para. 5(b).

(4) Sexual offences

Sexual Offences (Protected Material) Act 1997

Introductory

[Meaning of "protected material"

1.–(1) In this Act "protected material", in relation to proceedings for a sexual offence, means a **12-129**
copy (in whatever form) of any of the following material, namely—
    (a)   a statement relating to that or any other sexual offence made by any victim of the offence (whether the statement is recorded in writing or in any other form),
    (b)   a photograph or pseudo-photograph of any such victim, or
    (c)   a report of a medical examination of the physical condition of any such victim,
which is a copy given by the prosecutor to any person under this Act.

(2) For the purposes of subsection (1) a person is, in relation to any proceedings for a sexual offence, a victim of that offence if—
    (a)   the charge, summons or indictment by which the proceedings are instituted names that person as a person in relation to whom that offence was committed; or
    (b)   that offence can, in the prosecutor's opinion, be reasonably regarded as having been committed in relation to that person;
and a person is, in relation to any such proceedings, a victim of any other sexual offence if that offence can, in the prosecutor's opinion, be reasonably regarded as having been committed in relation to that person.

(3) In this Act, where the context so permits (and subject to subsection (4))–

    (a) references to any protected material include references to any part of any such material; and

    (b) references to a copy of any such material include references to any part of any such copy.

(4) Nothing in this Act–

    (a) so far as it refers to a defendant making any copy of–

      (i) any protected material, or

      (ii) a copy of any such material,

    applies to a manuscript copy which is not a verbatim copy of the whole of that material or copy; or

    (b) so far as it refers to a defendant having in his possession any copy of any protected material, applies to a manuscript copy made by him which is not a verbatim copy of the whole of that material.]

[Meaning of other expressions

12-130   **2.**–(1) In this Act–

    "contracted out prison" means a contracted out prison within the meaning of Part IV of the Criminal Justice Act 1991;

    "defendant", in relation to any proceedings for a sexual offence, means any person charged with that offence (whether or not he has been convicted);

    "governor", in relation to a contracted out prison, means the director of the prison;

    "inform" means inform in writing;

    "legal representative", in relation to a defendant, means a person who, for the purposes of the Legal Services Act 2007, is an authorised person in relation to an activity which constitutes the exercise of a right of audience or the conduct of litigation (within the meaning of that Act) and who is acting for the defendant in connection with any proceedings for the sexual offence in question;

    "photograph" and "pseudo-photograph" shall be construed in accordance with section 7(4) and (7) of the Protection of Children Act 1978;

    "prison" means any prison, young offender institution or remand centre which is under the general superintendence of, or is provided by, the Secretary of State under the Prison Act 1952, including a contracted out prison;

    "proceedings" means (subject to subsection (2)) criminal proceedings;

    "the prosecutor", in relation to any proceedings for a sexual offence, means any person acting as prosecutor (whether an individual or a body);

    "relevant proceedings", in relation to any material which has been disclosed by the prosecutor under this Act, means any proceedings for the purposes of which it has been so disclosed or any further proceedings for the sexual offence in question;

    "sexual offence" means one of the offences listed in the Schedule to this Act.

(2) For the purposes of this Act references to proceedings for a sexual offence include references to—

    (a) any appeal or application for leave to appeal brought or made by or in relation to a defendant in such proceedings;

    (b) any application made to the Criminal Cases Review Commission for the reference under section 9 or 11 of the Criminal Appeal Act 1995 of any conviction, verdict, finding or sentence recorded or imposed in relation to any such defendant; and

    (c) any petition to the Secretary of State requesting him to recommend the exercise of Her Majesty's prerogative of mercy in relation to any such defendant.

(3) In this Act, in the context of the prosecutor giving a copy of any material to any person–

    (a) references to the prosecutor include references to a person acting on behalf of the prosecutor; and

    (b) where any such copy falls to be given to the defendant's legal representative, references to the defendant's legal representative include references to a person acting on behalf of the defendant's legal representative.]

[The definition of "legal representative" is printed as amended by the Legal Services Act 2007, s.208(1), and Sched 21, para. 123.]

Regulation of disclosures to defendant

[Regulation of disclosures by prosecutor

12-131   **3.**–(1) Where, in connection with any proceedings for a sexual offence, any statement or other material falling within any of paragraphs (a) to (c) of section 1(1) would (apart from this section) fall to be disclosed by the prosecutor to the defendant—

(a) the prosecutor shall not disclose that material to the defendant; and

(b) it shall instead be disclosed under this Act in accordance with whichever of subsections (2) and (3) below is applicable.

(2) If—

(a) the defendant has a legal representative, and

(b) the defendant's legal representative gives the prosecutor the undertaking required by section 4 (disclosure to defendant's legal representative),

the prosecutor shall disclose the material in question by giving a copy of it to the defendant's legal representative.

(3) If subsection (2) is not applicable, the prosecutor shall disclose the material in question by giving a copy of it to the appropriate person for the purposes of section 5 (disclosure to unrepresented defendant) in order for that person to show that copy to the defendant under that section.

(4) Where under this Act a copy of any material falls to be given to any person by the prosecutor, any such copy—

(a) may be in such form as the prosecutor thinks fit, and

(b) where the material consists of information which has been recorded in any form, need not be in the same form as that in which the information has already been recorded.

(5) Once a copy of any material is given to any person under this Act by the prosecutor, the copy shall (in accordance with section 1(1)) be protected material for the purposes of this Act.]

[Disclosure to defendant's legal representative

4.–(1) For the purposes of this Act the undertaking which a defendant's legal representative is required to give in relation to any protected material given to him under this Act is an undertaking by him to discharge the obligations set out in subsections (2) to (7). **12-132**

(2) He must take reasonable steps to ensure—

(a) that the protected material, or any copy of it, is only shown to the defendant in circumstances where it is possible to exercise adequate supervision to prevent the defendant retaining possession of the material or copy or making a copy of it, and

(b) that the protected material is not shown and no copy of it is given, and its contents are not otherwise revealed, to any person other than the defendant, except so far as it appears to him necessary to show the material or give a copy of it to any such person—

(i) in connection with any relevant proceedings, or

(ii) for the purposes of any assessment or treatment of the defendant (whether before or after conviction).

(3) He must inform the defendant—

(a) that the protected material is such material for the purposes of this Act,

(b) that the defendant can only inspect that material, or any copy of it, in circumstances such as are described in subsection (2)(a), and

(c) that it would be an offence for the defendant—

(i) to have that material, or any copy of it, in his possession otherwise than while inspecting it or the copy in such circumstances, or

(ii) to give that material or any copy of it, or otherwise reveal its contents, to any other person.

(4) He must, where the protected material or a copy of it has been shown or given in accordance with subsection (2)(b)(i) or (ii) to a person other than the defendant, inform that person—

(a) that that person must not give any copy of that material, or otherwise reveal its contents—

(i) to any other person other than the defendant, or

(ii) to the defendant otherwise than in circumstances such as are described in subsection (2)(a); and

(b) that it would be an offence for that person to do so.

(5) He must, where he ceases to act as the defendant's legal representative at a time when any relevant proceedings are current or in contemplation—

(a) inform the prosecutor of that fact, and

(b) if he is informed by the prosecutor that the defendant has a new legal representative who has given the prosecutor the undertaking required by this section, give the protected material, and any copies of it in his possession, to the defendant's new legal representative.

(6) He must, at the time of giving the protected material to the new legal representative under subsection (5), inform that person—

(a) that that material is protected material for the purposes of this Act, and

(b) of the extent to which–

(i)   that material has been shown by him, and

(ii) any copies of it have been given by him,

to any other person (including the defendant).

(7) He must keep a record of every occasion on which the protected material was shown, or a copy of it was given, as mentioned in subsection (6)(b).]

[Disclosure to unrepresented defendant

12-133   **5.**–(1) This section applies where, in accordance with section 3(3), a copy of any material falls to be given by the prosecutor to the appropriate person for the purposes of this section in order for that person to show that copy to the defendant under this section.

(2) Subject to subsection (3), the appropriate person in such a case is–

(a) if the defendant is detained in a prison, the governor of the prison or any person nominated by the governor for the purposes of this section; and

(b) otherwise the officer in charge of such police station as appears to the prosecutor to be suitable for enabling the defendant to have access to the material in accordance with this section or any person nominated by that officer for the purposes of this section.

(3) The Secretary of State may by regulations provide that, in such circumstances as are specified in the regulations, the appropriate person for the purposes of this section shall be a person of any description so specified.

(4) The appropriate person shall take reasonable steps to ensure–

(a) that the protected material, or any copy of it, is only shown to the defendant in circumstances where it is possible to exercise adequate supervision to prevent the defendant retaining possession of the material or copy or making a copy of it,

(b) that, subject to paragraph (a), the defendant is given such access to that material, or a copy of it, as he reasonably requires in connection with any relevant proceedings, and

(c) that that material is not shown and no copy of it is given, and its contents are not otherwise revealed, to any person other than the defendant.

(5) The prosecutor shall, at the time of giving the protected material to the appropriate person, inform him–

(a) that that material is protected material for the purposes of this Act, and

(b) that he is required to discharge the obligations set out in subsection (4) in relation to that material.

(6) The prosecutor shall at that time also inform the defendant–

(a) that that material is protected material for the purposes of this Act,

(b) that the defendant can only inspect that material, or any copy of it, in circumstances such as are described in subsection (4)(a), and

(c) that it would be an offence for the defendant–

(i)   to have that material, or any copy of it, in his possession otherwise than while inspecting it or the copy in such circumstances, or

(ii) to give that material or any copy of it, or otherwise reveal its contents, to any other person,

as well as informing him of the effect of subsection (7).

(7) If–

(a) the defendant requests the prosecutor in writing to give a further copy of the material mentioned in subsection (1) to some other person, and

(b) it appears to the prosecutor to be necessary to do so–

(i)   in connection with any relevant proceedings, or

(ii) for the purposes of any assessment or treatment of the defendant (whether before or after conviction),

the prosecutor shall give such a copy to that other person.

(8) The prosecutor may give such a copy to some other person where no request has been made under subsection (7) but it appears to him that in the interests of the defendant it is necessary to do so as mentioned in paragraph (b) of that subsection.

(9) The prosecutor shall, at the time of giving such a copy to a person under subsection (7) or (8), inform that person–

(a) that the copy is protected material for the purposes of this Act,

(b) that he must not give any copy of the protected material or otherwise reveal its contents–

(i)   to any person other than the defendant, or

    (ii) to the defendant otherwise than in circumstances such as are described in subsection (4)(a); and

  (c) that it would be an offence for him to do so.

  (10) If the prosecutor—

    (a) receives a request from the defendant under subsection (7) to give a further copy of the material in question to another person, but

    (b) does not consider it to be necessary to do so as mentioned in paragraph (b) of that subsection and accordingly refuses the request,

he shall inform the defendant of his refusal.

  (11) [*Making of regulations under subs. (3).*]]

[*Further disclosures by prosecutor*

  6.—(1) Where— **12-134**

    (a) any material has been disclosed in accordance with section 3(2) to the defendant's legal representative, and

    (b) at a time when any relevant proceedings are current or in contemplation the legal representative either—

      (i) ceases to act as the defendant's legal representative in circumstances where section 4(5)(b) does not apply, or

      (ii) dies or becomes incapacitated,

that material shall be further disclosed under this Act in accordance with whichever of section 3(2) or (3) is for the time being applicable.

  (2) Where—

    (a) any material has been disclosed in accordance with section 3(3), and

    (b) at a time when any relevant proceedings are current or in contemplation the defendant acquires a legal representative who gives the prosecutor the undertaking required by section 4,

that material shall be further disclosed under this Act, in accordance with section 3(2), to the defendant's legal representative.]

  7. [*Regulation of disclosures by Criminal Cases Review Commission.*]] **12-135**

Supplementary

[*Offences*

  8.—(1) Where any material has been disclosed under this Act in connection with any proceedings **12-136** for a sexual offence, it is an offence for the defendant—

    (a) to have the protected material, or any copy of it, in his possession otherwise than while inspecting it or the copy in circumstances such as are described in section 4(2)(a) or 5(4)(a), or

    (b) to give that material or any copy of it, or otherwise reveal its contents, to any other person.

  (2) Where any protected material, or any copy of any such material, has been shown or given to any person in accordance with section 4(2)(b)(i) or (ii) or section 5(7) or (8), it is an offence for that person to give any copy of that material or otherwise reveal its contents—

    (a) to any person other than the defendant, or

    (b) to the defendant otherwise than in circumstances such as are described in section 4(2)(a) or 5(4)(a).

  (3) Subsections (1) and (2) apply whether or not any relevant proceedings are current or in contemplation (and references to the defendant shall be construed accordingly).

  (4) A person guilty of an offence under this section is liable—

    (a) on summary conviction, to imprisonment for a term not exceeding *six* [12] months or a fine not exceeding the statutory maximum or both;

    (b) on conviction on indictment, to imprisonment for a term not exceeding two years or a fine or both.

  (5) Where a person is charged with an offence under this section relating to any protected material or copy of any such material, it is a defence to prove that, at the time of the alleged offence, he was not aware, and neither suspected nor had reason to suspect, that the material or copy in question was protected material or (as the case may be) a copy of any such material.

  (6) The court before which a person is tried for an offence under this section may (whether or not he is convicted of that offence) make an order requiring him to return any protected material, or any copy of any such material, in his possession to the prosecutor.

(7) Nothing in subsection (1) or (2) shall be taken to apply to—

    (a) any disclosure made in the course of any proceedings before a court or in any report of any such proceedings, or

    (b) any disclosure made or copy given by a person when returning any protected material, or a copy of any such material, to the prosecutor or the defendant's legal representative;

and accordingly nothing in section 4, or 5 shall be read as precluding the making of any disclosure or the giving of any copy in circumstances falling within paragraph (a) or (as the case may be) paragraph (b) above.]

[In subs. (4)(a), "12" is substituted for "six", as from a day to be appointed, by the CJA 2003, s.282(2) and (3). The increase has no application to offences committed before the substitution takes effect: s.282(4).]

[Modification and amendment of other enactments

12-137   **9.**—(1) [*Repealed by CJA 2003, s.332, and Sched. 37, Pt 4.*]

(2) Despite section 20(1) of the Criminal Procedure and Investigations Act 1996 (disclosure provisions of the Act not affected by other statutory duties), section 3(3) to (5) of that Act (manner of disclosure) shall not apply in relation to any disclosure required by section 3, 7 or 9 of that Act if section 3(1) above applies in relation to that disclosure.

(3) [*See ss.17 and 18 of the Criminal Procedure and Investigations Act 1996, §§ 12-88 et seq. in the main work.*]

(4) [*Inserts subs. 1(6) into the Criminal Procedure and Investigations Act 1996, § 12-56 in the main work.*]

12-138   **10.** [*Financial provision.*]]

[Short title, commencement and extent

12-139   **11.**—(1) [*Short title.*]

(2) This Act shall come into force on such day as the Secretary of State may appoint by order made by statutory instrument.

(3) Nothing in this Act applies to any proceedings for a sexual offence where the defendant was charged with the offence before the commencement of this Act.

(4) This Act extends to England and Wales only.]

[Section 2   SCHEDULE

SEXUAL OFFENCES FOR PURPOSES OF THIS ACT

12-140   5. Any offence under section 1 of the Protection of Children Act 1978 or section 160 of the Criminal Justice Act 1988 (indecent photographs of children).

5A. Any offence under any provision of Part 1 of the Sexual Offences Act 2003 except section 64, 65, 69 or 71.

6. Any offence under section 1 of the Criminal Law Act 1977 of conspiracy to commit any of the offences mentioned in paragraphs 5 and 5A.

7. Any offence under section 1 of the Criminal Attempts Act 1981 of attempting to commit any of those offences.

8. Any offence of inciting another to commit any of those offences.]

[This schedule is printed as amended by the SOA 2003, ss.139 and 140, and Scheds 6, para. 36, and 7. The reference in para. 8 to inciting another to commit an offence has effect as a reference to the offences under Part 2 of the SCA 2007: 2007 Act, s.63(1), and Sched. 6, para. 34.]

(5) Miscellaneous

Criminal Procedure Rules 2015 (S.I. 2015 No. 1490), Pt 8

★**12-144**   With effect from April 3, 2017, the Criminal Procedure (Amendment) Rules 2017 (S.I. 2017 No. 144) inserted a new rule 8.4 into the 2015 rules, as follows—

"Use of initial details

    8.4.– (1) This rule applies where—

    (a) the prosecutor wants to introduce information contained in a document listed in rule 8.3; and

    (b) the prosecutor has not

       (i) served that document on the defendant, or

      (ii) made that information available to the defendant.

(2) The court must not allow the prosecutor to introduce that information unless the court first allows the defendant sufficient time to consider it.".

CHAPTER 13

EVIDENCE OF BAD CHARACTER

III. DEFENDANTS

A. ADMISSIBILITY

Criminal Justice Act 2003, ss.101, 108

Offences committed by defendant when a child
  R. v. D.M. is now reported at [2016] 2 Cr.App.R. 20, *sub nom. R. v. M. (D.).*   **13-26**

B. THE SEVEN GATEWAYS

(4) Important matter in issue between defendant and prosecution (ss.101(1)(d), 103)

(b) *Evidence that would have been admissible at common law*

Practical application

Accident, mistake, etc.
  R. v. Awoyemi (see the main work) is now reported at [2016] 2 Cr.App.R. 22.   **13-49**

(c) *Propensity evidence*

Establishing a propensity

In *R. v. G. (G.)* [2017] 1 Cr.App.R. 27, CA, it was said that propensity evidence under the CJA   **★13-67**
2003, ss.101(1)(d) and 103(1)(a) (§§ 13-25, 13-37 in the main work) was not limited to propensity
to commit offences of the "type" charged. However, it is submitted that this has to be seen in
context. First, section 103(1)(a) refers to the relevant propensity being a propensity to commit offences of the "kind" charged. Secondly, subsection (2) stipulates that such a propensity may be
proved by proof that the defendant has been convicted of an offence of the same category as the
one with which he is charged, subsection (4) provides that offences are in the same category as
each other if they are so specified in an order made by the Secretary of State, and subsection (5)
requires any such order to limit offences in any category to offences "of the same type." Thirdly,
the appellant was charged with a violent rape. He had convictions for offences of violence against
the person, albeit not in a sexual context. Rape, however, is an offence of violence against the
person (although typically categorised as a "sexual" offence), and thus, whilst the offences may
not have carried the same legal label, it is submitted that they were indeed offences of the same
"kind".

Where several non-conviction incidents are being relied on by the prosecution to establish a   **13-67a**
propensity to commit offences of the kind with which the defendant is charged (CJA 2003,
ss.101(1)(d), 103(1)(a) (§§ 13-25, 13-37 in the main work)), but where that evidence is disputed by
the defendant, it is not necessary (a) to prove beyond reasonable doubt that each incident happened in precisely the way that it is alleged to have occurred, and (b) that the facts of each
individual incident be considered by the jury in isolation from each other: *R. v. Mitchell* [2016] 3
W.L.R. 1405, SC (considering, *inter alia*, all the leading common law authorities (as to which, see
ibid., §§ 13-39 *et seq.*), *R. v. Ngyuen* (as to which, see *ibid.*, § 13-9), *R. v. McAllister* and *R. v.
O'Dowd* (as to both of which, see the main work), and *R. v. Lafayette* (as to which, see *ibid.*, § 13-
68)).

V. REHABILITATION OF OFFENDERS

(1) Introduction

With effect from March 1, 2017, the Rehabilitation of Offenders Act 1974 (Exceptions) Order   **★13-120**

1975 (S.I. 1975 No. 1023) was further amended by the Bank of England and Financial Services (Consequential Amendments) Regulations 2017 (S.I. 2017 No. 80).

(3) Statute

Pardons for convictions, etc., for certain abolished offences

★**13-138**   With effect from January 31, 2016, section 165 of the Policing and Crime Act 2017 provides for pardons for living persons convicted of, or cautioned for, certain offences where their conviction or caution has been, or becomes, disregarded under the Protection of Freedoms Act 2012 (as to which, see § 13-137 in the main work). Section 167 provides that a pardon under section 165 does not affect any conviction, caution or sentence.

CHAPTER 14

EVIDENCE OF IDENTIFICATION

I. VISUAL IDENTIFICATION

C. POLICE AND CRIMINAL EVIDENCE ACT 1984: CODE D

(1) Application of Code D

General

14-39   As to the replacement of Code D (see the main work), see *post*, § 15-7.

Revisions and modifications of the code

14-40   As to the replacement of Code D (see the main work), see *post*, § 15-7.

(2) Identification Procedure

Holding an identification procedure

14-45   As to the replacement of Code D (see the main work), particularly in relation to the eye-witness identification provisions, see *post*, § 15-7.

Selection of identification procedures

14-46   As to the replacement of Code D (see the main work), particularly in relation to the eye-witness identification provisions, see *post*, § 15-7.

The effect of a failure to hold an identification procedure

14-47   As to the replacement of Code D (see the main work), particularly in relation to the eye-witness identification provisions, see *post*, § 15-7.

(3) Video identification

14-50   As to the replacement of Code D (see the main work), particularly in relation to the eye-witness identification provisions, see *post*, § 15-7.

E. IDENTIFICATION AND THE USE OF VISUAL AIDS

(2) Identification of the defendant

14-65   As to the replacement of Code D (see the main work), particularly in relation to the eye-witness identification provisions, see *post*, § 15-7. The revisions take account of, in particular, the decisions of the Court of Appeal in *R. v. Deakin* and *R. v. Lariba* (as to both of which, see the main work).

II. IDENTIFICATION BY OTHER PERSONAL CHARACTERISTICS

C. Blood, Body Samples, Secretions, Scent and Odontology

DNA

The fact that DNA was on an article left at the scene of a crime can be sufficient without more ★**14-81b**
to raise a case to answer where the match probability was 1:1 billion or similar; whether it will do so depends on the facts of the particular case; relevant factors will include, (i) whether there is any evidence of some other explanation for the presence of the defendant's DNA other than involvement in the crime, (ii) whether the article was apparently associated with the offence itself, (iii) how readily movable the article in question was, (iv) whether there is evidence of some geographical association between the offence and the offender, (v) in the case of a mixed profile, whether the DNA profile which matches the defendant is the major contributor to the overall DNA profile, and (vi) whether it is more or less likely that the DNA profile attributable to the defendant was deposited by primary or secondary transfer: *R. v. Tsekiri* [2017] 2 *Archbold Review* 2, CA ([2017] EWCA Crim. 40) (following *R. v. F.N.C.*, and doubting the approach in *R. v. Byron* (as to both of which, see the main work)).

Chapter 15

INVESTIGATORY POWERS; CONFESSIONS; DISCRETION TO EXCLUDE EVIDENCE, ETC.

I. INVESTIGATORY POWERS

A. Police and Criminal Evidence Act 1984

(2) Codes of practice

(a) *Statute*

Police and Criminal Evidence Act 1984, ss.66, 67

Code of practice – supplementary

With effect from April 3, 2017 (Policing and Crime Act 2017 (Commencement No. 1 and ★**15-3**
Transitional Provisions) Regulations 2017 (S.I. 2017 No. 399)), section 67 of the 1984 Act was amended by the Policing and Crime Act 2017, s.78, so as to insert subsections (4A) to (4C) (modifying the duty to consult).

As from a day to be appointed, section 67(4) of the 1984 Act is amended by section 51 of, and ★
paragraphs 4 and 5 of Schedule 14 to, the 2017 Act, to substitute a reference to the National Police Chiefs' Council for the reference to the Association of Chief Police Officers.

As from a day to be appointed, section 67(9A)(a) of the 1984 Act is amended by section 45 of, ★
and paragraph 7(1) and (4) of Schedule 12 to, the 2017 Act, so as to insert the words "and volunteers" after the words "civilian staff".

(b) *Commencement*

With effect from February 23, 2017, the Police and Criminal Evidence Act 1984 (Codes of **15-7**
Practice) (Revision of Codes C, D and H) Order 2017 (S.I. 2017 No. 103) brought into force revised Codes of Practice C (Appendix A-39 *et seq.*), D (*ibid.*, Appendix A-113 *et seq.*)) and H (*ibid.*, Appendix A-214 *et seq.*)), which will supersede the corresponding existing codes of practice.

The principal revisions to Code C (i) allow for interpretation services for persons who are suspected of a criminal offence to be provided by interpreters who are not physically present in the suspect's location, by way of a "live-link" electronic communication system, (ii) implement amendments to the 1984 Act made by the CJCA 2015, which define a "juvenile" for the purpose of detention as a person who is under the age of 18, rather than under the age of 17, (iii) permit an appropriate adult to be removed from an interview if he prevents proper questioning, and (iv) reflect other minor changes in legislation and practice.

The principal revisions to Code D (i) update the eye-witness identification provisions to take account of developments in case law and police practice and address operational concerns raised by the police, (ii) reflect amendments to the 1984 Act concerning the retention of fingerprints, footwear impressions and DNA profiles and samples, made by the Anti-Social Behaviour, Crime and Policing Act 2014, and (iii) reflect other minor changes in legislation and practice.

The revisions to Code H correspond to the changes being made to Code C.

See Appendix A-38 *et seq.*, A-112 *et seq.*, A-213 *et seq.*, *post*, for the full text of the new codes.

(7) Application of Act to Armed Forces
Police and Criminal Evidence Act 1984, s.113

Application of Act to Armed Forces

★**15-22**   With effect from March 31, 2017, section 113 of the 1984 Act was amended by the Policing and Crime Act 2017, s.76(1) and (3), to substitute references to the "audio-recording" of interviews for the "tape-recording" of interviews.

(9) Application of Act to Revenue and Customs and immigration officers
Police and Criminal Evidence Act 1984, s.114

Application of Act to Revenue and Customs

15-31   With effect from December 25, 2016, the Crime and Courts Act 2013 (Application and Modification of Enactments) Order 2016 (S.I. 2016 No. 1143) modified the Police and Criminal Evidence Act 1984 (Application to Revenue and Customs) Order 2015 (S.I. 2015 No. 1783) (see the main work), in relation to its application to National Crime Agency officers designated as having the powers and privileges of an officer of Revenue and Customs. This was done by substituting different equivalent grades in Part 2 of Schedule 2 (*post*, § 15-51).

Equivalent grades

15-51   As to the modification of the Police and Criminal Evidence Act 1984 (Application to Revenue and Customs) Order 2015 (S.I. 2015 No. 1783), in relation to its application to National Crime Agency officers, see *ante*, § 15-31. "Designated person of at least grade 4" is substituted for "officer"; "designated person of at least grade 3" is substituted for "higher officer"; and "designated person of at least grade 2" is substituted for "senior officer".

(10) Application of Act to Department for Business, Innovation and Skills investigations
Police and Criminal Evidence Act 1984, s.114A

Power to apply Act to officers of the Secretary of State, etc.

15-80   With effect from November 9, 2016, the Secretaries of State for Business, Energy and Industrial Strategy, for International Trade and for Exiting the European Union and the Transfer of Functions (Education and Skills) Order 2016 (S.I. 2016 No. 992) amended section 114A(2)(a) of the 1984 Act, and the Police and Criminal Evidence Act 1984 (Department of Trade and Industry Investigations) Order 2002 (S.I. 2002 No. 2326) (as to both of which, see the main work). The effect of both amendments was to substitute "Business, Energy and Industrial Strategy" for "Business, Innovation and Skills".

(11) Application of Act to labour abuse prevention officers

★**15-80a**   With effect from April 30, 2017, the Police and Criminal Evidence Act 1984 (Application to Labour Abuse Prevention Officers) Regulations 2017 (S.I. 2017 No. 520) apply the following provisions of the 1984 Act to investigations undertaken by labour abuse prevention officers into labour market offences, subject to modifications: ss.1(1) to (3) and (6), 2(1) to (3), (8) and (9), 3(1), (2), (6), (6A), (7) and (9), 8(1) to (5); 9(1) and Schedule 1, 15, 16, 17(1)(a)(i) and (b), (2) and (4), 18, 19, 20, 21(1) to (9), 22(1), (2)(a), (3), (4) and (7), 24(1)(b) and (d), (2) to (4) and (5)(a), (b),

(c)(i) to (iii), (d), (e) and (f), 28, 29, 30(1)(a), (1A), (1B) and (7) to (11), 32(1) to (9), 43, 44, 77 and
117, and 10 to 14, 23, 82 and 118 (to the extent that they are relevant to the other provisions applied by these regulations).

B. STOP AND SEARCH

(2) Criminal Justice and Public Order Act 1994

Criminal Justice and Public Order Act 1994, s.60AA

Powers to require removal of disguises

With effect from April 3, 2017 (Policing and Crime Act 2017 (Commencement No. 1 and ★**15-95**
Transitional Provisions) Regulations 2017 (S.I. 2017 No. 399)), section 60AA of the 1994 Act was
amended by the Policing and Crime Act 2017, s.120, so as to substitute, for subsection (6), new
subsections (6) to (6B), as follows—

"(6) Subject to subsection (6A), an authorisation under subsection (3)—
(a) shall be in writing and signed by the officer giving it; and
(b) shall specify—
(i) the grounds on which it is given;
(ii) the locality in which the powers conferred by this section are exercisable; and
(iii) the period during which those powers are exercisable.
(6A) An authorisation under subsection (3) need not be given in writing where it is not practicable
to do so but any oral authorisation—
(a) must state the matters which would otherwise have to be specified under subsection (6);
and
(b) must be recorded in writing as soon as it is practicable to do so.
(6B) A direction under subsection (4) shall be given in writing or, where that is not practicable,
recorded in writing as soon as it is practicable to do so.".

C. ENTRY, SEARCH AND SEIZURE

(2) Statute

Police and Criminal Evidence Act 1984, s.8

Power of justice of the peace to authorise entry and search of premises

Where a warrant was sought in relation to the home and business premises of the claimant, in ★**15-106**
respect of whom there were reasonable grounds to suspect that he had been trading as a property
developer and professional landlord and had been involved in tax evasion, his mere involvement
in such business did not mean that there were therefore reasonable grounds for believing that it
was likely that privileged documents would be included in the transactional material sought: *R.
(Sharer) v. City of London Magistrates' Court and H.M. Revenue and Customs*, 181 J.P. 48, DC
(distinguishing *Bates v. Chief Constable of Avon and Somerset Police and Bristol Magistrates' Court* (see
the main work)).

R. (Haralambous) v. Crown Court at St Albans is now reported at [2016] 2 Cr.App.R. 7. An ap- ★
plication by the claimant for leave to appeal from the Divisional Court's decision has been
allowed: see [2017] 1 W.L.R. 490, SC.

Procedure

It has been pointed out to us that *The Times* report of *R. v. Central Criminal Court, ex p. Brown* **15-117**
(see the main work) was slightly misleading, and that the passage in the main work would more
accurately reflect the judgment if "a medical report" were replaced by "a patient's medical
records".

Police and Criminal Evidence Act 1984, s.17

Entry for purpose of arrest, etc.

With effect from April 3, 2017 (Policing and Crime Act 2017 (Commencement No. 1 and ★**15-144**
Transitional Provisions) Regulations 2017 (S.I. 2017 No. 399)), section 17(1) of the 1984 Act was
amended by the Policing and Crime Act 2017, s.72, so as to insert, after paragraph (caa), a new
paragraph (cab), as follows—

"(cab) of arresting a person under any of the following provisions—
    (i)   section 30D(1) or (2A) ;
    (ii) section 46A(1) or (1A);
    (iii) section 5B(7) of the Bail Act 1976 (arrest where a person fails to surrender to custody in accordance with a court order);
    (iv) section 7(3) of the Bail Act 1976 (arrest where a person is not likely to surrender to custody etc);
    (v) section 97(1) of the Legal Aid, Sentencing and Punishment of Offenders Act 2012 (arrest where a child is suspected of breaking conditions of remand);".

Police and Criminal Evidence Act 1984, s.18

Entry and search after arrest

★**15-147**   With effect from April 3, 2017 (Policing and Crime Act 2017 (Commencement No. 1 and Transitional Provisions) Regulations 2017 (S.I. 2017 No. 399)), section 18(5)(a) of the 1984 Act was amended by the Policing and Crime Act 2017, s.53(1) and (2), so as to omit the words "on bail". For related transitional provision, see *ante*, § 3-136.

Police and Criminal Evidence Act 1984, ss.20, 21

Access and copying

★**15-153**   With effect from April 3, 2017 (Policing and Crime Act 2017 (Commencement No. 1 and Transitional Provisions) Regulations 2017 (S.I. 2017 No. 399)), section 21 of the 1984 Act was amended by the Policing and Crime Act 2017, s.20(2), so as to insert, after subsection (9), a new subsection (10), as follows—

"(10) The references to a constable in subsections (1) and (2) do not include a constable who has seized a thing under paragraph 19ZE of Schedule 3 to the Police Reform Act 2002.".

★   Section 46B(2) of the UK Borders Act 2007 applies section 21 of the 1984 Act to nationality documents retained under section 46A. Sections 46A to 46C of the 2007 Act are inserted therein, as from a day to be appointed, by the Policing and Crime Act 2017, s.160. Section 46A enables an immigration officer or constable to give an individual who has been arrested on suspicion of the commission of an offence, but who has been released after arrest, a written notice requiring the production of a nationality document not later than 72 hours after the release, where the officer or constable suspects that the individual may not be a British citizen. Section 46B provides for the retention of that document while the officer or constable suspects that retention may facilitate the individual's removal in accordance with a provision of the Immigration Acts.

Powers of seizure (Schedule 1, Parts 1, 2 and 3)

Powers to which section 50 applies (list 1)

★**15-183**   As from a day to be appointed, Part 1 of Schedule 1 to the CJPA 2001 is amended by the Cultural Property (Armed Conflicts) Act 2017, s.23(9), so as to insert a new paragraph 73Q, referring to the Cultural Property (Armed Conflicts) Act 2017, s.23.

(3) Code of practice

15-187   As from a day to be appointed, section 29 of the Consumer Protection Act 1987 (see the main work) is amended by the Investigatory Powers Act 2016, s.12(1), and Sched. 2, para. 3. The amendment is not material to the discussion in the main work.

D. ARREST

(2) The Police and Criminal Evidence Act 1984

Police and Criminal Evidence Act 1984, s.24

Arrest without warrant: constables

★**15-194**   In considering whether a person's arrest is necessary under section 24(5)(e), the arresting officer would in principle be entitled to take into account that this would facilitate the imposition of bail conditions that would protect a witness from intimidation that would or might render an investigation substantially less effective: *R. (T.L.) v. Chief Constable of Surrey*, unreported, January 31, 2017, DC ([2017] EWHC 129 (Admin.)) (considering *Hayes v. Chief Constable of Merseyside Police* and *B. v. Chief Constable of Northern Ireland* (as to both of which, see the main work)).

"Recordable offences"

With effect from November 14, 2016, the National Police Records (Recordable Offences) **15-199**
(Amendment) Regulations 2016 (S.I. 2016 No. 1006) further amended the National Police
Records (Recordable Offences) Regulations 2000 (S.I. 2000 No. 1139) (see the main work).

Police and Criminal Evidence Act 1984, ss.29, 30

Arrest elsewhere than at police station

With effect from April 3, 2017 (Policing and Crime Act 2017 (Commencement No. 1 and ★**15-205**
Transitional Provisions) Regulations 2017 (S.I. 2017 No. 399)), section 30 of the 1984 Act was
amended by the Policing and Crime Act 2017, s.53(1) and (3), so as: (i) in subsection (1B), to
substitute, for the words "on bail", the words "of a person arrested elsewhere than at police station"; (ii) in subsection (7A), to omit the words from "or releasing" to the end; and (iii) in subsections (10) and (11), to substitute, for the words "on bail", the words "under section 30A". For
related transitional provision, see *ante*, § 3-136.

Police and Criminal Evidence Act 1984, ss.30A-30D

Bail elsewhere than at police station

With effect from April 3, 2017 (Policing and Crime Act 2017 (Commencement No. 1 and ★**15-208**
Transitional Provisions) Regulations 2017 (S.I. 2017 No. 399)), section 30A of the 1984 Act was
amended by the Policing and Crime Act 2017, ss.52 and 73(1) and (2), so as: (i) in the heading, to
substitute, for the word "Bail", the words "Release of a person arrested"; (ii) in subsection (1), to
omit the words "on bail", and to insert at the end:

"—
    (a) without bail unless subsection (1A) applies, or
    (b) on bail if subsection (1A) applies";

(iii) to insert, after subsection (1), a new subsection (1A), as follows—

"(1A) This subsection applies if—
    (a) the constable is satisfied that releasing the person on bail is necessary and proportionate in
        all the circumstances (having regard, in particular, to any conditions of bail which would
        be imposed), and
    (b) a police officer of the rank of inspector or above authorises the release on bail (having
        considered any representations made by the person).";

(iv) in subsection (2), to omit the words "on bail"; and (v) in subsection (3B)(d), to substitute, for
the words "under the age of 17", the words "under the age of 18". For related transitional provision in relation to the section 52 amendments (*viz.* (i)-(iv)), see *ante*, § 3-136.

Bail under section 30A: notices

With effect from April 3, 2017 (Policing and Crime Act 2017 (Commencement No. 1 and ★**15-209**
Transitional Provisions) Regulations 2017 (S.I. 2017 No. 399)), section 30B of the 1984 Act was
amended by the Policing and Crime Act 2017, ss.53(1) and (4) to (8), and 62(1) to (8), so as: (i) in
the heading, to omit the words "Bail under"; (ii) in subsection (1), to substitute, for the words
"grants bail to", the word "releases"; (iii) in subsection (2), to omit the word "and" before
paragraph (b), and to insert after that paragraph—

    "and
    (c) whether the person is being released without bail or on bail";

(iv) in subsection (3), to substitute, for the words "The notice", the words "A notice given to a
person who is released on bail"; (v) to substitute a new subsection (4), as follows—

"(4) The notice must also specify—
    (a) the police station which the person is required to attend, and
    (b) the time on the bail end date when the person is required to attend the police station.";

(vi) to omit subsection (4A)(c) and the word "and" before it; (vii) to omit subsection (5); (viii) in
subsection (6), to substitute, for the words from "(5)" to the end, the words "to attend at a different time or an additional time"; (ix) to insert, after subsection (6), a new subsection (6A), as follows—

"(6A) A person may not be required under subsection (6) to attend a police station at a time which is after the bail end date in relation to the person.";

and (x) to insert, after subsection (7), a new subsection (8), as follows—

"(8) In this section 'bail end date', in relation to a person, means the last day of the period of 28 days beginning with the day after the day on which the person was arrested for the offence in relation to which bail is granted under section 30A.".

For related transitional provision, see *ante*, § 3-136.

Bail under section 30A: supplemental

★**15-210** With effect from April 3, 2017 (Policing and Crime Act 2017 (Commencement No. 1 and Transitional Provisions) Regulations 2017 (S.I. 2017 No. 399)), section 30C of the 1984 Act was amended by the Policing and Crime Act 2017, ss.53(1) and (9), and 65(1) and (2), so as: (i) in the heading, to omit the words "Bail under"; (ii) in subsection (4), to omit the words "on bail"; and (iii) in subsection (4), to substitute, for the words from "new" to the end, the words ", since the person's release, new evidence has come to light or an examination or analysis of existing evidence has been made which could not reasonably have been made before the person's release". For related transitional provision, see *ante*, § 3-136.

Bail under section 30A: variation of conditions by police

★**15-211** With effect from April 3, 2017 (Policing and Crime Act 2017 (Commencement No. 1 and Transitional Provisions) Regulations 2017 (S.I. 2017 No. 399)), section 30CA of the 1984 Act was amended by the Policing and Crime Act 2017, s.62(1) and (9), so as to omit subsection (1)(b) and the word "or" before it. For related transitional provision, see *ante*, § 3-136.

Failure to answer bail under section 30A

★**15-214** With effect from April 3, 2017 (Policing and Crime Act 2017 (Commencement No. 1 and Transitional Provisions) Regulations 2017 (S.I. 2017 No. 399)), section 30D(3) of the 1984 Act was amended by the Policing and Crime Act 2017, s.62(1) and (10), so as to omit the words "or (5)". For related transitional provision, see *ante*, § 3-136.

(3) The Criminal Justice and Public Order Act 1994

★**15-219** As from a day to be appointed, new sections 137A to 137E are inserted in the 1994 Act by the Policing and Crime Act 2017, ss.116 and 117. They provide for cross-border enforcement within the United Kingdom and close a gap in the current legislation to ensure that a person who commits a specified offence in one jurisdiction can be arrested without a warrant by an officer from the jurisdiction in which the person is found in urgent cases. Schedules 15 (s.116(2)) and 16 (s.116(3)) set out new Schedules 7A and 7B to the 1994 Act. Schedule 7A lists the offences that are specified for the purposes of section 137A (in addition to any offence that carries 10 years' custody or more), and Schedule 7B sets out modifications of legislation that applies in relation to persons arrested under section 137A. In the case of persons arrested in Scotland or Northern Ireland for offences committed in England and Wales, the legislation that is applied comprises sections 28 (§ 15-200 in the main work), 56 and 58 of the PACE Act 1984 and sections 31 and 34 of the CYPA 1933, with sections 56 and 58 (*ibid.*, §§ 15-232, 15-236) of the 1984 Act, and section 34 of the 1933 Act (*ibid.*, § 15-234), being subject to modifications.

★ As from a day to be appointed, section 119 of, and Part 1 (paras 1-8) of Schedule 17 to, the 2017 Act make minor and consequential amendments to sections 136, 137, 139 and 140 of the 1994 Act (see the main work).

★ As from a day to be appointed, section 87 of the Finance Act 2007 (see the main work) is amended by the 2016 Act, ss.118 and 119, and Sched. 17, para. 9.

★ As from a day to be appointed, section 119 of, and paragraph 10 of Schedule 17 to, the 2017 Act amend the Crime and Courts Act 2013, Sched. 21, para. 41 (*ibid.*), and insert new paragraphs 42A to 42D.

E. Questioning and Treatment of Persons

(2) Searches of detained persons
Police and Criminal Evidence Act 1984, s.55

Intimate searches

★**15-229** As from a day to be appointed, section 55(17) of the 1984 Act is amended by the Policing and

Crime Act 2017, s.45, and Sched. 12, para. 7(1) and (2), so as to omit paragraph (b) in the definition of "appropriate officer".

(3) Right to have someone informed when arrested
Police and Criminal Evidence Act 1984, s.56

As to the further modified application of section 56 of the 1984 Act, see *ante*, § 15-219. ★15-233

(4) Additional rights of children and young persons
Children and Young Persons Act 1933, s.34

As to the modified application of section 34 of the 1933 Act, see *ante*, § 15-219. ★15-234

As to the revision of Code C (*post*, Appendix A-39 *et seq.*) on February 23, 2017, see *ante*, §
15-7.

(5) Access to legal advice
Police and Criminal Evidence Act 1984, s.58

As to the modified application of section 58 of the 1984 Act, see *ante*, § 15-219. ★15-236

(6) Tape-recording of interviews
Police and Criminal Evidence Act 1984, s.60

With effect from March 31, 2017, section 60 of the 1984 Act was amended by the Policing and ★15-244
Crime Act 2017, s.76(1) and (2), to substitute references to the "audio-recording" of interviews for
the "tape-recording" of interviews.

(7A) Notification of decisions not to prosecute

With effect from April 3, 2017 (Policing and Crime Act 2017 (Commencement No. 1 and ★15-247a
Transitional Provisions) Regulations 2017 (S.I. 2017 No. 399), a new section 60B was inserted
into the 1984 Act by the Policing and Crime Act 2017, s.77.

Police and Criminal Evidence Act 1984, s.60B

Notification of decisions not to prosecute
60B.—(1) This section applies where—
   (a) a person suspected of the commission of a criminal offence is interviewed by a police of-
      ficer but is not arrested for the offence, and
   (b) the police officer in charge of investigating the offence determines that—
      (i) there is not sufficient evidence to charge the person with an offence, or
      (ii) there is sufficient evidence to charge the person with an offence but the person
         should not be charged with an offence or given a caution in respect of an offence.
(2) A police officer must give the person notice in writing that the person is not to be prosecuted.
(3) Subsection (2) does not prevent the prosecution of the person for an offence if new evidence
comes to light after the notice was given.
(4) In this section "caution" includes—
   (a) a conditional caution within the meaning of Part 3 of the Criminal Justice Act 2003;
   (b) a youth conditional caution within the meaning of Chapter 1 of Part 4 of the Crime and
      Disorder Act 1998;
   (c) a youth caution under section 66ZA of that Act.

(8) Fingerprints, photographs, intimate and other samples
Police and Criminal Evidence Act 1984, s.61

Intimate searches

With effect from April 3, 2017 (Policing and Crime Act 2017 (Commencement No. 1 and ★15-248
Transitional Provisions) Regulations 2017 (S.I. 2017 No. 399), section 61(5A) of the 1984 Act was
amended by the Policing and Crime Act 2017, s.59(1) and (2), so as: (i) in paragraph (a), to omit
the words "in the case of a person who is on bail,"; and (ii) in paragraph (b), to omit the words "in
any case,".

Police and Criminal Evidence Act 1984, s.63

Other samples

With effect from April 3, 2017 (Policing and Crime Act 2017 (Commencement No. 1 and ★15-254

Transitional Provisions) Regulations 2017 (S.I. 2017 No. 399), section 63(3ZA) of the 1984 Act was amended by the Policing and Crime Act 2017, s.59(1) and (3), so as: (i) in paragraph (a), to omit the words "in the case of a person who is on bail,"; and (ii) in paragraph (b), to omit the words "in any case,".

National DNA database

★**15-262**   As to the amendment of sections 63F, 63H, 63J, 63K and 63N of the PACE Act 1984, see *post*, § 15-273.

Police and Criminal Evidence Act 1984, ss.63B, 63C

Testing for presence of Class A drugs

★**15-265**   With effect from April 3, 2017 (Policing and Crime Act 2017 (Commencement No. 1 and Transitional Provisions) Regulations 2017 (S.I. 2017 No. 399), section 63B of the 1984 Act was amended by the Policing and Crime Act 2017, ss.73(1) and (3), and 79, so as: (i) in subsections (5A) and (10), to substitute, for the words "has not attained the age of 17", the words "has not attained the age of 18"; and (ii) in subsection (10), in paragraph (c), in the definition of "appropriate adult", to substitute, for the words "a person employed by the police", the words "a person employed for, or engaged on, police purposes; and 'police purposes' has the meaning given by section 101(2) of the Police Act 1996".

Destruction, retention and use of fingerprints, etc.

★**15-273**   With effect from April 3, 2017 (Policing and Crime Act 2017 (Commencement No. 1 and Transitional Provisions) Regulations 2017 (S.I. 2017 No. 399), sections 63F, 63H, 63J, 63K and 63N of the PACE Act 1984 (as to which, see the main work) were amended, and new sections 63IA (retention of material: persons convicted of an offence outside England and Wales after taking of s.63D material) and 63KA (retention of s.63D material under s.63IA: exception for persons under 18 convicted of first minor offence outside England and Wales) were inserted, by the Policing and Crime Act 2017, s.70. The effect is to allow DNA profiles and fingerprints to be retained on the basis of convictions outside England and Wales in the same way as such material may currently be retained for persons convicted of a recordable offence in England and Wales, so long as the offence would constitute a recordable offence if committed in England and Wales. Regulation 6 of S.I. 2017 No. 399 provides that section 70 of the 2017 Act only applies to fingerprints and DNA profiles, to which section 63D of the 1984 Act applies taken, or (in the case of a DNA profile) derived from a sample taken, after April 2, 2017, except that the amendments made by section 70 to sections 63F, 63H, 63K and 63N apply for the purposes of section 63P(2) of the 1984 Act where the date mentioned in section 63P(2)(b) is April 3, 2017, or any subsequent date.

Police and Criminal Evidence Act 1984, s.64A

Photographing of suspects, etc.

★**15-277**   As from a day to be appointed, section 64A(1B) of the 1984 Act is amended by the Policing and Crime Act 2017, s.45, and Sched. 12, para. 7(1) and (3), so as: (i) in paragraph (c), to substitute, for the words "with a community support officer under paragraph 2(3) or (3B) of Schedule 4", the words "with a community support officer or a community support volunteer under paragraph 7 of Schedule 3B"; and (ii) to substitute a new paragraph (e), as follows—

> "(e) given a fixed penalty notice by a community support officer or community support volunteer who is authorised to give the notice by virtue of his or her designation under section 38 of the Police Reform Act 2002;".

(9) Definitions

Police and Criminal Evidence Act 1984, s.65

Part V: supplementary

★**15-279**   With effect from April 3, 2017 (Policing and Crime Act 2017 (Commencement No. 1 and Transitional Provisions) Regulations 2017 (S.I. 2017 No. 399), section 65(1) of the 1984 Act was amended by the Policing and Crime Act 2017, s.73(1) and (4), so as, in the definition of "appropriate consent", in paragraph (a), to substitute, for the words "has attained the age of 17 years", the words "has attained the age of 18 years".

(10) Codes of practice

As to the replacement of Codes C and H (see the main work), see *ante*, § 15-7. **15-283**

F. Police Act 1997 and Regulation of Investigatory Powers Act 2000

As from a day to be appointed, Part III of the 1997 Act and Part II of the 2000 Act are **15-284** amended in matters of detail by the Investigatory Powers Act 2016: see, in particular, ss.233 and 271(1), and Sched. 10; and, as from a further day to be appointed, section 29 of the 2000 Act is also amended by the Policing and Crime Act 2017, ss.44 and 157(5), and Sched. 19, paras 2 and 3.

With effect from February 13, 2017 (Investigatory Powers Act 2016 (Commencement No. 2 and **15-286** Transitory Provision) Regulations 2017 (S.I. 2017 No. 137)), section 5 of the Intelligence Services Act 1994 (see the main work) was amended in matters of detail by the Investigatory Powers Act 2016, s.251(1) and (3).

H. Proceeds of Crime Act 2002

(2) Statute

Proceeds of Crime Act 2002, ss.341–345

Investigations

With effect from February 1, 2017 (Crime and Courts Act 2013 (Commencement No. 16 and **15-310** Savings) Order 2017 (S.I. 2017 No. 4)), the amendments effected by section 49 of, and Schedule 19, paras 1 to 3, 24 to 27, 29 and 30 (as to which, see the main work, and *ibid.*, §§ 15-311, 15-315, 15-317, 15-323, 15-325, 15-330, 15-332, 15-337, 15-339, 15-345, 15-346, 15-352 and 15-356) to, the 2013 Act, are brought into force in Northern Ireland, so far as not already in force. There are saving provisions (art. 3).

Proceeds of Crime Act 2002, ss.346–369

Disclosure orders

In *Nuttall v. National Crime Agency* [2016] 4 W.L.R. 134, QBD (Collins J.), it was held: (i) **15-331** although a disclosure order once obtained should be acted upon as speedily as is reasonably possible, all will depend on whether any lapse of time and the investigators' actions are justified; the magnitude of the investigation and the need to avoid any action which targets might take to frustrate any claim will be relevant considerations; (ii) the statement in *National Crime Agency v. Simkus*; *Same v. Khan*; *Same v. Jardine* (see the main work, and now reported at [2016] 1 W.L.R. 3481), to the effect that a judge should give reasons for making a disclosure order, was "clearly wrong", because a judge making a disclosure order on paper will only do so if satisfied that the material put before him shows that the grounds for making it are established, thus making the giving of reasons otiose; (iii) an error in a disclosure order's penal notice (referring to a failure to comply as a contempt of court and not as an offence under s.359 of the 2002 Act (§ 15-333 in the main work)) was of no consequence, the important point being that the recipients of the order were on notice that they faced penal sanctions if they failed to comply; and (iv) a proposal by the respondent to make keyword searches of tablets and mobile phones, that would eliminate those that would not be of interest and identify those that would, sufficiently safeguarded the applicants' human rights where the information notices had sought disclosure of passwords and pin numbers.

Requirements for making of disclosure order

There is an error in section 358(2)(c) of the 2002 Act, as it appears in the main work, in that **15-332** the word "warrant" should read "order".

(3) Procedural rules

As to the amendment of Part 47 of the Criminal Procedure Rules 2015 (S.I. 2015 No. 1490), **★15-363** see *post*, § 15-401a.

Criminal Procedure Rules 2015 (S.I. 2015 No. 1490), Pt 47 (as substituted by the Criminal Procedure (Amendment) Rules 2016 (S.I. 2016 No. 120), r.15)

When this Part applies

As to the amendment of rule 47.1, see *post*, § 15-401a. **★15-364**

Application containing information withheld from another party

★**15-401a**   With effect from April 3, 2017, new rule 47.39 (application containing information withheld from another party) is inserted into the 2015 rules by the Criminal Procedure (Amendment) Rules 2017 (S.I. 2017 No. 144), r.11(c), to provide for the submission to the court of information not served on the other party to an application for the retention or return of property. In consequence, rule 47.1 (§ 15-364 in the main work) is amended (to substitute "47.42, 47.46, 47.51 and 47.54" for "47.41, 47.45, 47.50 and 47.53") and rules 47.39 to 47.57 (*ibid.*, §§ 2-106, 7-159, 15-402 *et seq.*, 25-401c *et seq.* (in the main work), and Appendix B-653 *et seq.* (*post*)) are renumbered as rules 47.40 to 47.58, respectively (and r.47.40 (representations in response) (see § 15-402 in the main work), as renumbered, is amended in consequence) (r.11(a), (b) and (e)).

Application containing information withheld from another party
47.39.–(1) This rule applies where–
  (a) an applicant serves an application to which rule 47.37 (application for an order under section 1 of the Police (Property) Act 1897) or rule 47.38 (application for an order under section 59 of the Criminal Justice and Police Act 2001) applies; and
  (b) the application includes information that the applicant thinks ought not be revealed to another party.
(2) The applicant must–
  (a) omit that information from the part of the application that is served on that other party;
  (b) mark the other part to show that, unless the court otherwise directs, it is only for the court; and
  (c) in that other part, explain why the applicant has withheld that information from that other party.
(3) If the court so directs, any hearing of an application to which this rule applies may be, wholly or in part, in the absence of a party from whom information has been withheld.
(4) At any hearing of an application to which this rule applies–
  (a) the general rule is that the court must consider, in the following sequence–
    (i) representations first by the applicant and then by each other party, in all the parties' presence, and then
    (ii) further representations by the applicant, in the absence of a party from whom information has been withheld; but
  (b) the court may direct other arrangements for the hearing.

Representations in response

★**15-402**   As to the renumbering of rule 47.39, see *ante*, § 15-401a. With effect from April 3, 2017, the renumbered rule 47.40 (previously rule 47.39) was amended by the Criminal Procedure (Amendment) Rules 2017 (S.I. 2017 No. 144), r.11(e), so as to insert a new paragraph (4), as follows–

"(4) Where representations include information that the person making them thinks ought not be revealed to another party, that person must–
  (a) omit that information from the representations served on that other party;
  (b) mark the information to show that, unless the court otherwise directs, it is only for the court; and
  (c) with that information include an explanation of why it has been withheld from that other party.".

Application to punish for contempt of court

★**15-403**   As to the renumbering of rule 47.40, see *ante*, § 15-401a.

When this Section applies

★**15-404**   As to the renumbering of rule 47.41, see *ante*, § 15-401a.

Exercise of court's powers

★**15-405**   As to the renumbering of rule 47.42, see *ante*, § 15-401a.

Application to extend retention period

★**15-406**   As to the renumbering of rule 47.43, see *ante*, § 15-401a.

Appeal

★**15-407**   As to the renumbering of rule 47.44, see *ante*, § 15-401a.

As to the renumbering of rules 47.45 to 47.57, see *ante*, § 15-401a. ★**15-408**

K. Policing and Crime Act 2017

Chapter 5 (ss.84-95) of Part 4 of the 2017 Act makes provision in relation to maritime enforce- ★**15-425a**
ment in England and Wales. Under section 84(1), a law enforcement officer (defined in subs. (3))
may exercise the powers set out in sections 88 to 90 (for the purpose of preventing, detecting,
investigating or prosecuting an offence under the law of England and Wales) in relation to a
United Kingdom ship in England and Wales waters, foreign waters or international waters, a ship
without nationality in England and Wales waters or international waters, a foreign ship in England
and Wales waters or international waters, or a ship, registered under the law of a relevant territory, in England and Wales waters or international waters. Section 86 provides for the exercise of
maritime enforcement powers following the hot pursuit of vessels into Scotland or Northern
Ireland waters. A person commits an offence where he intentionally obstructs a law enforcement
officer in the performance of functions under this chapter, or fails without reasonable excuse to
comply with a requirement made by a law enforcement officer in the performance of those functions (s.93(1)). A person who provides information in response to a requirement made by a law
enforcement officer in the performance of such functions commits an offence if the information
is false in a material particular, and the person either knows it is or is reckless as to whether it is,
or the person intentionally fails to disclose any material particular (s.93(2)). The offences are triable summarily and carry a fine (s.94(4)). Chapters 6 and 7 make equivalent provision for
Scotland and Northern Ireland.

II. CONFESSIONS AND RELATED TOPICS

A. Confessions

(1) Police and Criminal Evidence Act 1984

(b) *Words and phrases*

"likely...to render unreliable any confession which might be made by him in consequence thereof"

For an example of the prosecution failing to show that a confession had not been rendered **15-439**
unreliable, see *McPhee v. The Queen* [2017] 1 Cr.App.R.10 (failure to apprise appropriate adult of
the nature of his role, coupled with evidence suggesting unrecorded interviews with the juvenile
suspect prior to his confession).

The chamber decision in *Ibrahim v. U.K.* (see the main work) has been reversed in relation to **15-440**
the applicant Abdurahman: *Ibrahim v. U.K.*, *The Times*, December 19, 2016, ECHR (Grand
Chamber); the government had failed to demonstrate why the overall fairness of his trial was not
irretrievably prejudiced by the decision not to caution and to restrict the applicant's access to legal
advice and there had, therefore, been a violation of Article 6(1) and (3). As to this case, see also
post, §§ 15-542, 15-553, 16-116, 25-139.

(c) *Codes of practice*

As to the replacement of Code C (see the main work), see *ante*, § 15-7. **15-441**

III. DISCRETION TO EXCLUDE EVIDENCE

A. Under Statute

(5) Access to legal advice

For proceedings subsequent to the chamber decision in *Ibrahim v. U.K.* (see the main work), **15-542**
which, *inter alia*, expanded on the list of factors relevant to assessing the fairness of the admission
in evidence of a statement made by a defendant when he had been denied access to legal advice,
see *Ibrahim v. U.K.*, *The Times*, December 19, 2016, ECHR (Grand Chamber). These factors,

described as non-exhaustive, are: (a) whether the applicant was particularly vulnerable, (b) the legal framework governing pre-trial proceedings and the admissibility of evidence at trial, and whether it was complied with; where an exclusionary rule applied, it is particularly unlikely that the proceedings as a whole would be considered unfair, (c) whether the applicant had the opportunity to challenge the authenticity of the evidence and oppose its use, (d) the quality of the evidence and whether the circumstances in which it was obtained cast doubt on its reliability or accuracy, taking into account the degree and nature of any compulsion, (e) where evidence was obtained unlawfully, the unlawfulness in question and, where it stems from a violation of another article of the ECHR, the nature of the violation, (f) in the case of a statement, the nature of the statement and whether it was promptly retracted or modified, (g) the use to which the evidence was put, and, in particular, whether it formed an integral or significant part of the evidence upon which the conviction was based, and the strength of the other evidence in the case, (h) whether the assessment of guilt was performed by professional judges or lay jurors, and, in the case of the latter, the content of any jury directions, (i) the weight of the public interest in the investigation and punishment of the particular offence in issue, and (j) other relevant procedural safeguards afforded by domestic law and practice. As to this case, see also *ante*, § 15-440; and *post*, §§ 15-553, 16-116, 25-139.

(7) Codes C and H and section 78

(a) *Introduction*

15-545   As to the replacement of Codes C and H (see the main work), see *ante*, § 15-7.

(b) *Summary of the provisions of Code C*

15-546   As to the replacement of Codes C (see the main work), see *ante*, § 15-7.

(d) *Particular topics: authorities*

Information as to rights

15-548   As to the replacement of Code C (see the main work), see *ante*, § 15-7.

Incorrect form of caution

15-553   For proceedings subsequent to the chamber decision in *Ibrahim v. U.K.* (see the main work), which, *inter alia*, agreed with the aspects of the chamber's decision discussed in the main work, and which held that it was untenable to suggest that the giving of an incorrect caution (the applicants were wrongly told that failure to mention facts subsequently relied on could harm their defence) had compelled them to tell lies in their interviews, see *Ibrahim v. U.K.*, *The Times*, December 19, 2016, ECHR (Grand Chamber). As to this case, see also *ante*, §§ 15-440, 15-542; and *post*, §§ 16-116, 25-139.

Juveniles—"appropriate adult"

15-558   As to the replacement of Code C (see the main work) and, in particular, changes to the provisions relating to appropriate adults, see *ante*, § 15-7.

CHAPTER 16

HUMAN RIGHTS

II. THE HUMAN RIGHTS ACT 1998

B. The Interpretation of 'Convention Rights'

Human Rights Act 1998, s.2(1)-(3)

Interpretation of Convention rights

★**16-15**   The decision of the Court of Appeal in *R. (Hicks) v. Commr of Police of the Metropolis* (as to which, see the main work) has been upheld by the Supreme Court: see *R. (Hicks) v. Commr of Police of the Metropolis (Secretary of State for the Home Department intervening)* [2017] A.C. 256, SC, but on different grounds. Like the Court of Appeal, however, the Supreme Court said that, whilst there is a duty on domestic courts to take account of Strasbourg case law, when that law is not clear, the domestic court has a judicial choice to make. Accordingly, the Supreme Court felt free to follow the minority view in the Strasbourg decision in *Ostendorf v. Germany* (as to which, see § 16-60 in the main work, and *post*).

D. Application to Public Authorities

Human Rights Act 1998, ss.6, 7(1)-(9)

Where it is alleged that a decision to prosecute violated the defendant's Convention rights, time **16-26** runs from the date of conviction or acquittal for the purposes of the stipulation in section 7(5)(a) of the 1998 Act (§ 16-25 in the main work) that proceedings under subsection (1) must be brought before the end of "the period of one year beginning with the date on which the act complained of took place": *O'Connor v. Bar Standards Board* [2016] 1 W.L.R. 4085, CA (Civ. Div.).

Human Rights Act 1998, s.9

Judicial acts
  Hammerton v. U.K. is now reported at (2016) 63 E.H.R.R. 23.   **16-30**

IV. THE RIGHTS GUARANTEED

A. Right to Life

Article 2

Permissible exceptions

The decision of the Divisional Court in *R. (Duggan) v. H.M. Assistant Deputy Coroner for the* ★**16-43** *Northern District of Greater London* (as to which, see the main work) has been upheld on appeal: see *R. (Duggan) v. North London Assistant Deputy Coroner, The Times*, April 21, 2017, CA (Civ. Div.) ([2017] EWCA Civ. 142).

B. Prohibition of Torture

Article 3

Scope

In *Murray v. Netherlands* (2016) 64 E.H.R.R. 3, ECtHR (Grand Chamber), it was held that: (i) **16-47** the applicant's eventual pardon and release on health grounds had not deprived him of victim status in respect of his claim that a failure to provide him with a prospect of release during the 33 years he spent in prison violated Article 3; a decision or measure favourable to an applicant is not in principle sufficient to deprive him of his status as a "victim" unless the national authorities have acknowledged, either expressly or in substance, and then afforded redress for, the violation; (ii) applying the principles set out in European case law, principally *Kafkaris v. Cyprus* and *Vinter v. U.K.* (as to both of which, see the main work), as to the compatibility of a *de facto* or *de jure* irreducible life sentence with Article 3 to the specific issue of the reducibility of life sentences imposed on persons who have been diagnosed as suffering from a mental condition, and particularly the principle that life prisoners should be detained under such conditions, and be provided with such treatment as gives them a realistic opportunity to rehabilitate themselves in order to have a hope of release (a failure to do so rendering the life sentence *de facto* irreducible), the following approach is appropriate; it is first required that an assessment be made of those prisoners' needs as regards treatment, with a view to facilitating their rehabilitation and reducing the risk of their reoffending; this assessment should also address the likely chances of success of any identified forms of treatment and account should be taken of the life prisoner's individual situation and personality; that assessment should be conducted regardless of whether any request for treatment has been expressed by them; where the assessment leads to the conclusion that a particular treatment or therapy (medical, psychological or psychiatric) may indeed help the life prisoner to rehabilitate himself, he is to be enabled to receive that treatment to the extent possible within the constraints of the prison context; this is of particular importance where treatment in effect constitutes a pre-condition for the life prisoner's possible future eligibility for release and is thus a crucial aspect of *de facto* reducibility of the life sentence; in general it will be for the state to decide which facilities, measures or treatments are required in order to enable a life prisoner to rehabilitate himself in such a way as to become eligible for release; consequently, a state will have complied with its obligations under Article 3 when it has provided conditions of detention and facilities, measures or treatments that are capable of enabling a life prisoner to rehabilitate himself, even when that prisoner has not succeeded in making sufficient progress to allow the conclusion that the danger he poses to society has been alleviated to such an extent that he has become eligible for release.

For the decision of the Grand Chamber of the European Court of Human Rights upholding the chamber decision in *Hutchinson v. U.K.* (see the main work), see *ante*, § 5-377.

D. Right to Liberty and Security

Article 5

Detention following conviction

16-58 For a case distinguishing *M. v. Germany* (see the main work), see *post*, § 16-135.

Arrest on reasonable suspicion

★16-60 The Supreme Court has upheld the decision of the Court of Appeal in *R. (Hicks) v. Commr of Police of the Metropolis* (as to which, see the main work) on different grounds: see *R. (Hicks) v. Commr of Police of the Metropolis (Secretary of State for the Home Department intervening)* [2017] A.C. 256. The Supreme Court ruled that the view of the minority in *Ostendorf v. Germany* (*ibid.*) that Article 5(1)(c) of the ECHR (§ 16-53 in the main work) is capable of applying in a case of detention for preventive purposes followed by early release (that is, before the detainee could practicably be brought before a court), was correct. The court said that, in order to make coherent sense and achieve the fundamental purpose of Article 5, the qualification on the power of arrest or detention under Article 5(1)(c) contained in the words "for the purpose of bringing him before the competent legal authority" should be read as implicitly dependent on the cause for detention continuing long enough for the person to be brought before the court.

Detention of persons of unsound mind and alcoholics

16-60a As to detention of persons of unsound mind and alcoholics (as to which, see Art. 5(1)(e)), see *Bergmann v. Germany* (2016) 63 E.H.R.R. 21, in which it was held that the detention of an offender (convicted of two counts of attempted murder and a related count of attempted rape) at a time when it could no longer be justified under Article 5(1)(a), because it was no longer detention after conviction by a competent court, could, however, on the facts, be justified as the detention of a person of unsound mind under Article 5(1)(e) where he was housed in a purpose-built preventive detention centre, which was a separate building on the premises of a domestic prison, where the staffing levels were similar to a psychiatric hospital, and where he was offered appropriate treatment (some of which he refused), including anti-hormone medication to reduce his sadistic fantasies and libido.

E. Right to a Fair Trial

The presumption of innocence

★16-109 For a case considering the impact of security measures taken at trial on the presumption of innocence, see *ante*, § 4-331.

Article 6

The right to legal representation and legal aid

Pre-trial

16-116 For proceedings subsequent to the chamber decision in *Ibrahim v. U.K.* (see the main work) in the Grand Chamber of the European Court of Human Rights, where it was held, *inter alia*, that the court in *Salduz v. Turkey* (*ibid.*) did not intend to lay down a bright-line rule precluding any use at trial of statements made without legal advice, see *Ibrahim v. U.K.*, *The Times*, December 19, 2016. As to this case, see also *ante*, §§ 15-440, 15-542, 15-553; and *post*, § 25-139.

O'Neill and Lauchlan v. U.K. is now reported at (2017) 64 E.H.R.R. 16. ★16-117

F. No Punishment Without Law

Article 7

Retroactive penalties

M. v. Germany (as to which, see the main work) was distinguished in *Bergmann v. Germany* **16-135** (2016) 63 E.H.R.R. 21. Whilst the court reaffirmed that decision to the extent that it held that a period of preventive detention ordered by a criminal court on conviction of an offender is a "penalty" for the purposes of Article 7(1), it went on to hold that, in cases such as that of the applicant, where the original period of preventive detention was extended because of, and with a view to the need to treat, his mental disorder, both the nature and the purpose of his detention had substantially changed; the punitive element, and its connection to his criminal conviction, were eclipsed to such an extent that the measure was no longer to be classified as a penalty within the meaning of Article 7.

Legislative changes favourable to defendant

Scoppola v. Italy (No. 2) (as to which, see the main work) was considered in *R. v. Docherty (Shaun)* **16-136** [2017] 1 W.L.R. 181, SC. Having said that there were real difficulties in interpreting that decision, the Supreme Court held that English practice recognises *lex mitior* in its ordinary form, namely, the principle that an offender should be sentenced according to the law and practice prevailing at the time of his sentence, subject to not exceeding the limits (*i.e.* in England normally the maximum) provided for at the time the offence was committed; and that an extended concept of the principle, according to which a defendant would be entitled to insist on being sentenced according to any more favourable law or practice that has at any time obtained between the commission of the offence and the passing of sentence, has not been clearly adopted by the Strasbourg court, appears not to be within the stated rationale for the principle of *lex mitior*, and would entail unwarranted consequences. Thus, it should not be applied in this jurisdiction. As to this case, see also *ante*, § 5-472.

G. Right to Respect for Private and Family Life

Article 8

Scope

A decision by a public prosecutor to bring criminal proceedings against a person does not fall ★16-138 within the scope of Article 8 of the ECHR (§ 16-137 in the main work) where (a) the prosecutor has reasonable cause to believe the person to be guilty of the offence with which he is charged, and (b) the law relating to the offence is compatible with Article 8: *S.X.H. v. CPS (United Nations High Commr for Refugees intervening)* [2017] 1 W.L.R. 1401, SC (considering, *inter alia, G. v. U.K.* (as to which, see *ibid.*, §§ 16-107, 16-145)). Four of the Supreme Court justices left open the question whether the continuation of a prosecution may engage Article 8, but Lord Kerr opined that continuation of a prosecution may engage Article 8. As to this case, see also *post*, § 22-49.

Interference

As to the replacement of Code C (see the main work) and, in particular, the updating of the **16-141** definition of "juvenile", see *ante*, § 15-7.

Justification

Re JR38 (see the main work) is now reported at [2016] A.C. 1131. **16-142**

Intrusive surveillance, interception of communications, etc.

16-148   For a decision of the Grand Chamber of the European Court of Human Rights approving the
approach taken in *Kennedy v. U.K.* (see the main work) in relation to the need to ensure that the
secrecy of surveillance measures does not result in the measures being effectively unchallenge-
able, see *Zakharov v. Russia*, 63 E.H.R.R. 17.

CHAPTER 17

THE MENTAL ELEMENT IN CRIME

I. MENS REA

G. OFFENCES BY CORPORATIONS

17-30   There is a distinction between the principles governing the admissibility of the acts and
declarations of one joint venturer that are in furtherance of the common design against another
joint venturer (as to which, see § 33-66 in the main work), and those relating to the attribution of
the acts and mental state of the directing mind of a corporation to that corporation; where,
therefore, a company (A. Ltd), its chairman and an overseas manager were prosecuted for a
conspiracy to commit bribery, and where it was alleged that B., another director of the company,
who was beyond the jurisdiction of the court, was part of the controlling mind of the company,
the admissibility of evidence that tended to show his guilty participation in the offence was not
governed by the principles relating to the acts and declarations of joint venturers; once he was
shown to be part of the controlling mind, then evidence of his guilty participation went directly
to the issue of the guilt of the corporate defendant; and the fact that B. may have acquired his
guilty knowledge or formed his guilty intent when he had not been acting as a director of A. Ltd
was irrelevant; he brought to his actions on behalf of A. Ltd all the knowledge that he had by
then acquired, in whatever capacity; it would be absurd to suggest that, although he formed an
intention to pay a bribe when acting in a different role (for another company in the group), that
intention was to be ignored when, acting as a director of A. Ltd, he put that intention into
practice: *R. v. A. Ltd* [2017] 1 Cr.App.R. 1, CA (considering, *inter alia, Lennard's Carrying Co. v.
Asiatic Petroleum Co.*, and *Tesco Supermarkets Ltd v. Nattrass* (as to both of which, see the main work),
and *R. v. St Regis Paper Company Ltd* (as to which, see *ibid.*, § 17-32)).

VI. DURESS

A. AVAILABILITY

(1) Common law

★17-119   For a case considering *R. v. M. (L.), B. (M.) and G. (D.); R. v. Tabot; R. v. Tijani* and *R. v. van
Dao* (as to both of which, see the main work), see *post*, § 19-464.

B. PRINCIPLE

17-120   Having said that the defence of duress is to be narrowly confined, the Court of Appeal in *R. v.
Brandford* [2017] 1 Cr. App. R. 14, CA, said, in particular, (i) where no reasonable jury properly
directed could fail to find the defence of duress disproved, the judge is entitled to withdraw it
from the jury; however, that power is to be exercised with caution; (ii) whilst it is very likely that
the more directly a threat is conveyed, the more it will be capable of founding a defence of
duress, the mere fact that a threat was conveyed indirectly will not be a fatal bar to the defence;
and (iii) whereas duress does afford a defence, mere pressure based on the exploitation of a
relationship does not, but they are not necessarily irreconcilable, and there may be circumstances
in which they operate in a cumulative manner.

CHAPTER 19

OFFENCES AGAINST THE PERSON

I. HOMICIDE

A. MURDER

(2) Liability of secondary parties

Effect on prior convictions

In *R. v. Johnson; R. v. Burton; R. v. Moises; R. v. Hore; R. v. Miah; R. v. Hall (Practice Note)*   **19-29**
[2017] 1 Cr.App.R. 12, CA, it was held: (i) in approaching appeals in respect of convictions prior
to the decision in *R. v. Jogee; Ruddock v. The Queen* (see §§ 19-23 *et seq.* in the main work),
consideration has to be given to the extent to which the verdict could properly be interpreted in
accordance with the common law principles of joint enterprise (two or more people setting out to
commit an offence, crime A, or intending to encourage or assist in the commission of that offence), rather than parasitic accessory liability (the law as set out in *Chan Wing-Siu v. The Queen*
and *R. v. Powell; R. v. English* (as to which, see the main work), and reversed by *Jogee*); (ii) it is also
necessary to distinguish between appeals brought within the time limit of 28 days specified in section 18(2) of the CAA 1968 (*ibid.*, § 7-161) and those brought outside that time; in the former,
the only issue is whether the conviction is "unsafe" (1968 Act, s.2(1) (*ibid.*, § 7-41)); as to this, it is
not sufficient that there was some misdirection or error in the conduct of the trial; what is critical
is that the verdict is thereby rendered unsafe; even in relation to in-time appeals, the fact that the
jury were correctly directed in accordance with the then prevailing law does not automatically
render the verdict unsafe; and (iii) [as to out of time appeals, see *ante*, § 7-171].

Subsequent decisions

R. v. Anwar is now reported at [2016] 2 Cr.App.R. 23.   **19-30**

Jogee in Australia

Miller v. The Queen; Smith v. The Queen; Presley v. D.P.P. for the State of South Australia is now   **19-31**
reported at 334 A.L.R. 1.

Jogee in Hong Kong

For a decision of the Hong Kong Court of Final Appeal rejecting the criticism of *Chan Wing-*   **19-31a**
Siu v. The Queen by the Supreme Court and the Privy Council in *R. v. Jogee; Ruddock v. The Queen*
(as to which, see, *inter alia*, §§ 19-23 *et seq.* in the main work) ("largely in agreement" with the
views expressed by the majority of the High Court of Australia in *Miller v. The Queen; Smith v. The
Queen; Presley v. D.P.P. for the State of South Australia* (as to which, see § 19-31 in the main work and
ante)), see *H.K.S.A.R. v. Chan Kam-Shing*, unreported, December 16, 2016 (considering, *inter alia*,
R. v. Powell; R. v. English (as to which, see § 19-23 in the main work), and *Johns v. The Queen* (as to
which, see *ibid.*, § 19-31)). The court held: (i) as to the culpability of the secondary party, the liability of a party to a joint criminal enterprise is not derivative but arises independently by virtue
of his participation in the joint criminal enterprise; so viewed, there is nothing anomalous about
having different *mens rea* requirements for different individuals that depend on the manner of
their participation in the joint enterprise; in an "extended joint criminal enterprise" case, a
person who agrees to carry out a criminal venture with others, foreseeing that one or more of
them might, in certain contingencies, commit some further, more serious offence, and proceeds
with the venture nonetheless, should be treated as gravely culpable (it being impossible to regard

liability so imposed as verging on the constructive); the foresight required under this rule is not open-ended; it is foresight of the commission of the actual further offence as a possible incident of the execution of their planned enterprise, and of a real possibility of the offence being committed; it thus excludes a risk fleetingly foreseen and dismissed as negligible; culpability of the secondary party may therefore be seen to be based on implied authorisation of the actual perpetrator to act as the instrument of the other participants to deal with the foreseen exigencies of carrying their enterprise into effect (as stated in *Miller*); (ii) *Jogee's* abolition of the joint criminal enterprise doctrine, confining secondary liability to cases where the prosecution can prove intentional assistance or encouragement of a principal offender, creates a serious gap in the law of complicity in crime by depriving it of a valuable principle for dealing with dynamic situations involving evidential and situational uncertainties that traditional accessorial liability rules are ill-adapted to address; (iii) the concept of "conditional intent" introduced in *Jogee* causes conceptual and practical difficulties; first, given that it was central to *Jogee* that the doctrine of joint criminal enterprise should be abolished in favour of traditional accessorial liability, it was strikingly odd that the Supreme Court (at [92]-[94]) explained the conditional intent concept in the context of joint criminal enterprise (referring to acts pursuant to "prior joint criminal ventures", "common purpose" and "common intent") and gave no indication of how the concept was meant to fit in with the *actus reus* and *mens rea* of traditional accessorial offences; secondly, the Supreme Court's treatment of conditional intent gives rise to the question whether there is any practical difference between that concept and the principle of assigning liability on the basis of foresight of the possible commission of an offence in an extended joint criminal enterprise situation; the only suggested difference between conditional intent so explained and the foresight principle in the extended joint criminal enterprise doctrine appears to involve *Jogee's* proposition that foresight is only evidence upon which intent, including conditional intent, may be inferred; but that gives rise to a third difficulty, *viz.* foresight and conditional intent are both mental states and can only be found to exist by drawing inferences from the conduct of the participant in question; if the jury were to decide that the irresistible inference is that the defendant foresaw that one of them might, if necessary, commit the further offence, that would be the inferential conclusion reached; it would not be "evidence" upon which a further inference as to the existence of conditional intent might be drawn; the proposition that a finding of foresight is only evidence of conditional intent is therefore difficult to follow. The court added that the two post-*Jogee* decisions in the Court of Appeal (*R. v. Anwar* (as to which, see § 19-30 in the main work), and *R. v. Johnson; R. v. Burton; R. v. Moises; R. v. Hore; R. v. Miah; R. v. Hall (Practice Note)* (as to which, see *ante*, § 19-29)) indicate that difficulties regarding the conditional intent concept have already been encountered in practice.

(4) Defences

(a) *"Loss of control"*

Directing the jury

19-63   In *R. v Wilcocks* [2017] 1 Cr.App.R. 23, CA, it was held that, for a defendant's personality disorder to be relevant to the defence of loss of control under section 54 of the Coroners and Justice Act 2009 (§ 19-55 in the main work), it must go further than simply reducing his general capacity for tolerance and self-restraint (see subs. (3)). As to this case, see also *post*, § 19-91.

(b) *Provocation*

Common law

19-65   At common law, provocation reduced murder to manslaughter; and was available as a potential defence both for a principal and an accessory: *R. v. Marks* [1998] Crim.L.R. 676, CA. It was irrelevant on the issue of guilt in all other crimes.

The jury should be directed that before they have to consider the issue of provocation the Crown must have proved beyond reasonable doubt that all the other elements of murder were present, including the necessary intent: see *Lee Chun-Chuen v. R.* [1963] A.C. 220, PC; and *R. v. Martindale*, 50 Cr.App.R. 273, Ct-MAC.

The law as to provocation immediately prior to October 4, 2010 (as to which, see § 19-54 in the main work) was governed by a blend of common law and statute, *viz.* the Homicide Act 1957, s.3 (*post*, § 19-66).

Homicide Act 1957, s.3

Provocation

3. Where on a charge of murder there is evidence on which the jury can find that the person **19-66** charged was provoked (whether by things done or by things said or by both together) to lose his self-control, the question whether the provocation was enough to make a reasonable man do as he did shall be left to be determined by the jury; and in determining that question the jury shall take into account everything both done and said according to the effect which, in their opinion, it would have on a reasonable man.

This section altered as well as clarified the common law on this subject.

Duty of judge

Section 3 involves two questions: (a) is there any evidence of specific provoking conduct of the **19-67** accused, and (b) is there any evidence that the provocation caused him to lose his self-control? If both questions are answered in the affirmative, the issue of provocation should be left to the jury notwithstanding the fact that in the opinion of the judge no reasonable jury could conclude on the evidence that a reasonable person would have been provoked to lose his self-control: *R. v. Gilbert*, 66 Cr.App.R. 237, CA; *Franco v. R.*, *The Times*, October 11, 2001, PC; notwithstanding that there may be circumstances suggesting that the accused acted in revenge, rather than as a result of a sudden and temporary loss of self-control: *R. v. Baillie* [1995] 2 Cr.App.R. 31, CA; and notwithstanding that the issue has not been raised by the defence: *Bullard v. R.* [1957] A.C. 635, PC; *DPP v. Camplin* [1978] A.C. 705, HL; *R. v. Rossiter*, 95 Cr.App.R. 326, CA; and would prefer it not to be left to the jury: *R. v. Dhillon* [1997] 2 Cr.App.R. 104, CA.

Where, however, there is only a speculative possibility of the accused having acted as a result of provoking conduct, the issue should not be left to the jury: *R. v. Acott* [1997] 2 Cr.App.R. 94, HL (there must be some evidence of specific provoking conduct resulting in a loss of control by the accused; the source of such evidence is immaterial as is reliance thereon by the accused); and *R. v. Evans (John Derek)* [2010] Crim.L.R. 491, CA (§ 19-62 in the main work). Evidence of a loss of self-control is insufficient, for a loss of self-control might be brought on by fear, panic or sheer bad temper, as well as by provoking conduct: *ibid.* Questions put in cross-examination are not evidence: *ibid.* The observations in *Acott* are equally apt when considering whether there is sufficient evidence that a defendant was provoked, as they are when considering whether there was evidence of provoking conduct: *R. v. Miao*, *The Times*, November 26, 2003, CA. For the issue to be left to the jury, there has to be evidence from which a reasonable jury might conclude that the defendant was or may have been provoked: *R. v. Cambridge*, 99 Cr.App.R. 142, CA. See also *R. v. Jones (Robert James)* [2000] 3 *Archbold News* 2, CA (where the defence is self-defence, with no reliance by the defence on provocation, the judge should not leave provocation to the jury where the evidence of provoking conduct by the deceased, or the evidence that such conduct caused a loss of self-control by the defendant is minimal or fanciful).

In *Daniel v. State of Trinidad and Tobago* [2014] A.C. 1290, PC, it was held that while, in the event of dispute, it is for the judge to rule whether the issue of provocation arises on the evidence in relation to the first, subjective, limb of the test (namely, whether there was provocative behaviour and whether the defendant was in fact provoked by it to lose his self-control and kill in consequence), it is of great importance that judges respect the clear principle that the question as to whether the second, objective, limb of the test for provocation (namely, whether the provocation was such as might cause a reasonable man to act as the accused had) has been met, is a matter for the jury. Provocation has to be left to the jury, it was held, even if it is not the accused's primary case if, taking the evidence at its most favourable to the accused and remembering that the onus of proof is on the prosecution to rebut it, manslaughter by reason of provocation is a conclusion to which a jury might reasonably come. The board added that a judge could not withdraw the issue simply because he would decide the issue against the accused, nor even if he regarded the answer as obvious; but in a case where no jury, properly directed, could possibly find the test met, it is in the interests of a fair trial and of coherent law that an issue that does not arise ought not to be inserted into the jury's deliberations. As to this case, see also, § 19-56a; and *post*, § 19-75.

Where a judge is obliged to leave provocation to the jury, he should indicate to them, unless it is obvious, what evidence might support the conclusion that the defendant had lost his self-control; this is particularly important where the defence have not raised the issue: *R. v. Stewart* [1996] 1 Cr.App.R. 229, CA. See also *R. v. Humphreys* [1995] 4 All E.R. 1008, CA (similar duty where there is a complex history with several distinct strands of potentially provocative conduct, building up over time until the final encounter).

Where provocation is not left to the jury when it should have been, a conviction for manslaughter will be substituted unless the court is sure that the jury would inevitably have convicted: *R. v. Dhillon, ante*, but an appellate court should be cautious in drawing inferences or making findings about how the jury would have resolved issues which were never before them; and that is particularly so in the context of section 3, since Parliament had gone out of its way, unusually, to stipulate that resolution of the objective issue should be exclusively reserved to the jury; to the extent that an appellate court took it upon itself to decide that issue, it was doing what Parliament had said that the jury should do, and section 3 could not be read as applying only to the trial court: *Franco v. R., ante*.

In *R. v. Van Dongen and Van Dongen* [2005] 2 Cr.App.R. 38, CA, it was held that: (i) section 3 is concerned with provocative conduct, as opposed to merely causative conduct; yet a judgment that particular conduct was no more than causative risks straying into an evaluation of the objective element of the defence, which statute has left to the jury; accordingly, the prudent course for judges to take, in borderline cases, especially if the defence ask for a provocation direction to be given, is to leave the issue to the jury; (ii) where, therefore, in a case in which the defence had been self-defence and/or lack of intent and/or accident, but not provocation, there was evidence of conduct that was capable of being provoking conduct and there was evidence of a loss of self-control, the matter should have been left to the jury, more particularly as defence counsel had sought such a direction; but (iii) the failure to leave it did not mean that the conviction could not be upheld, notwithstanding that the Act specifically provides for the jury to determine the objective issue; *Franco v. R., ante*, was not authority for the proposition that a conviction could not be upheld in such circumstances; whilst it was necessary to be cautious in drawing inferences or making findings about how the jury would have resolved issues which were never before them, the court must not overlook the matter of justice for those concerned with the victim, nor the requirements of a proportionate appellate system, which included that those who were surely and fairly shown to be guilty of murder, and were so found by a jury, should not escape the consequences on gossamer grounds; where, therefore, the unavoidable facts of the case and the necessary logic of the jury's verdict ruled out any possibility of a miscarriage of justice, the conviction should be upheld.

Duty of counsel

19-68   See *R. v. Cox (A.M.)* [1995] 2 Cr.App.R. 513, CA (§ 19-61 in the main work).

Onus of proof

19-69   Once there is evidence from any source, sufficient to be left to the jury on the issue of provocation, the onus remains throughout upon the Crown to prove absence of provocation beyond reasonable doubt: *R. v. McPherson*, 41 Cr.App.R. 213, CCA. As to the necessity for a careful direction on onus of proof, see *R. v. Wheeler*, 52 Cr.App.R. 28, CA (§ 19-48 in the main work).

"Provoked ... to lose his self control"

(i) Meaning of "provocation"

19-70   In *R. v. Whitfield*, 63 Cr.App.R. 39 at 42, the Court of Appeal said that the meaning of provocation was still that given to it by Devlin J. in *R. v. Duffy* [1949] 1 All E.R. 932, as cited by Lord Goddard C.J. when giving the judgment of the Court of Criminal Appeal:

> "Provocation is some act, or series of acts, done [or words spoken] [by the dead man to the accused] which would cause in any reasonable person, and actually causes in the accused, a sudden and temporary loss of self-control, rendering the accused so subject to passion as to make him or her for the moment not master of his mind" (at p.932).

The words in the first pair of square brackets were not actually said by Devlin J. but appear in the quotation of him by Lord Lane C.J. as if spoken by him (presumably to take account of the express reference to "things said" in section 3 of the 1957 Act, *ante*, § 19-66); the words in the second pair of square brackets must be ignored in view of the wording of section 3. See also *post*, § 19-73.

(ii) *Loss of self-control must be associated with the act which causes death*

19-71 The point was considered in *R. v. Ibrams and Gregory*, 74 Cr.App.R. 154, CA. Provocation is available only in the case of a sudden and temporary loss of self-control of such a kind as to make the accused for the moment not master of his mind: see *R. v. Duffy* and *R. v. Whitfield*, *ante*. Circumstances which induce a desire for revenge are inconsistent with provocation, since the conscious formulation of a desire for revenge means that a person has had time to think, to reflect and that would negative a sudden temporary loss of self-control, which is the essence of provocation. But the mere existence of such circumstances does not mean that the judge should not leave the issue to the jury if there is evidence that the accused was in fact provoked; it is for the jury to decide: see *R. v. Baillie* [1995] 2 Cr.App.R. 31, CA.

(iii) *Cumulative provocation*

19-72 Although it is established that a temporary and sudden loss of self-control arising from an act of provocation is essential, it is less clear to what extent previous acts of provocation are admissible. Each case must be considered against the background of its own particular facts: *R. v. Thornton*, 96 Cr.App.R. 112, CA. In *R. v. Brown* [1972] 2 Q.B. 229, 56 Cr.App.R. 564, CA, a direction that the jury had to find provocation in something done on the morning of the killing was approved. In *R. v. Davies (P.)* [1975] Q.B. 691, 60 Cr.App.R. 253, the Court of Appeal described as "too generous" a direction that the jury could review the whole of the deceased's conduct throughout the years preceding death: and see *R. v. Ibrams and Gregory*, *ante*. In *R. v. Pearson* [1992] Crim.L.R. 193, the Court of Appeal substituted manslaughter for a conviction for murder on the grounds, *inter alia*, that the jury may have been left with the impression that an eight-year history of violent conduct by the deceased towards his younger son was not to be taken into account when considering the case of the elder son, who had spent much of that time away from home.

A general approach can, however, be discerned from the authorities, namely that evidence of previous provocative acts or past conduct, particularly in cases of domestic violence, is admissible in order to place in its appropriate context the reaction of the accused to the alleged provocation on the occasion of the killing: see *R. v. Thornton*, *ante*, at p. 118. For the proper approach in relation to a history of provocation leading to a post-traumatic stress syndrome or "battered woman syndrome", see *R. v. Ahluwalia*, 96 Cr.App.R. 133, CA, and *R. v. Thornton (No. 2)* [1996] 2 Cr.App.R. 108, CA (a jury might more easily find that there was a sudden loss of self-control triggered even by a minor incident if the defendant had endured abuse over a period, on a last-straw basis).

"Things done or said"

19-73 The things done or said may be done or said by the deceased or anyone else: *R. v. Davies (P.)*, *ante*; *R. v. Doughty (S.)*, 83 Cr.App.R. 319, CA.

"Reasonable man"

19-74 The "reasonable man" means "an ordinary person of either sex, not exceptionally excitable or pugnacious, but possessed of such powers of self-control as everyone is entitled to expect that his fellow citizens will exercise in society as it is today": *per* Lord Diplock in *DPP v. Camplin* [1978] A.C. 705 at 771, HL; means "a man of ordinary self-control": *ibid.*, *per* Lord Simon at p.726. Both formulations were approved by the majority in *Att.-Gen. for Jersey v. Holley* [2005] 2 A.C. 580, PC, in which an enlarged board of nine was assembled for the purpose of considering the conflict between *Camplin* and *Luc Thiet Thuan v. R.* [1997] A.C. 131, PC, on the one hand, and *R. v. Smith (Morgan)* [2001] 1 A.C. 146, HL, on the other, and to "clarify definitively the present state of English law". That it had done so was accepted by the Court of Appeal in *R. v. James; R. v. Karimi* [2006] 1 Cr.App.R. 29.

The majority opinion in *Holley* was that the jury, in deciding whether the defendant lost his self-control and, if he did, whether he did so as a result of provocation, should take the defendant exactly as they find him ("warts and all" (including that he had a violent temperament: see *R. v. Mohammed (Faqir)* [2005] 9 *Archbold News* 3, CA)); but, having assessed the gravity of the provocation to the defendant (for which purpose they must, for example, take account of the fact that he is a homosexual if taunted for his homosexuality, that he is disabled if taunted for being a "cripple", etc.), the standard of self-control by which his conduct is to be evaluated is the external standard of a person having and exercising the ordinary powers of self-control to be expected of a person of the defendant's age and sex. The majority ruling in *Smith* was held to be wrong in that section 3 of the 1957 Act adopted a uniform, objective standard; whether the provocative act or words and the defendant's response met the "ordinary person" standard prescribed by the statute is the question the jury must consider, not the altogether looser question (suggested by *Smith*) of whether, having regard to all the circumstances, the jury consider the loss of self-control was sufficiently excusable; the statute, it was said, does not leave each jury free to set whatever standard they consider appropriate. Accordingly, it was held to follow that if the defendant had been taunted by reference to his being an alcoholic or a drug addict, his alcoholism or addiction might be relevant to the jury's consideration of the gravity of the taunt to the defendant, but it would not be relevant to the question whether he exercised ordinary self-control.

Self-induced provocation

19-75   The mere fact that the defendant caused a reaction in others which in turn led him to lose his self-control does not preclude a successful defence of provocation: *R. v. Johnson (C.)*, 89 Cr.App.R. 148, CA.

In *Edwards v. R.* [1973] A.C. 648, PC, the appellant's case was that the man whom he was blackmailing attacked him with a knife and he thereupon lost his temper and killed him. The relevant ordinance in Hong Kong was in the same terms as section 3 of the Homicide Act 1957, *ante*. The Board said (at p. 658):

> "No authority has been cited with regard to what may be called 'self-induced provocation'. On principle it seems reasonable to say that: (1) a blackmailer cannot rely on the predictable results of his own blackmailing conduct as constituting provocation sufficient to reduce his killing of the victim from murder to manslaughter, and the predictable results may include a considerable degree of hostile reaction by the person sought to be blackmailed, for instance vituperous words and even some hostile action such as blows with a fist; (2) but, if the hostile reaction by the person sought to be blackmailed goes to extreme lengths, it might constitute sufficient provocation even for a blackmailer; (3) there would in many cases be a question of degree to be decided by the jury."

In *Daniel v. State of Trinidad and Tobago* [2014] A.C. 1290, PC, it was held that there is no room for any general rule of law that provocation cannot arise because the accused himself generated the provocative conduct in issue. Subject to the proper role of the judge, the issue is for the jury, and the jury should ordinarily be directed that, if they find conduct by the accused which generates the provocative behaviour in question, that conduct will be directly relevant to both the subjective and the objective limbs of provocation. As to the subjective limb, it will go to both (a) the question whether the accused killed as a result of the provocative behaviour relied upon and (b) whether he lost self-control as a result of that behaviour. Generally, the more he generates the reaction of the deceased, the less likely it will be that he lost control and killed as a result of it; he might have been out of control from the outset, but that is not loss of control as a result of the provocative behaviour of the deceased. As to the objective limb, it will go to whether the provocative behaviour was enough to make a reasonable man in the defendant's position do as he did. Generally, the more he has himself generated the provocative behaviour, the less likely it will be that a reasonable man would have killed in consequence of it, but there may be cases where the jury may judge that the provocative behaviour may have induced a similar reaction in a reasonable man, notwithstanding the origins of the dispute between the accused and the deceased. On both limbs of the test of provocation, the extent to which the provocative behaviour relied upon was or was not a predictable result of what the accused did, *i.e.* how far it was to be expected, is itself a jury question and clearly a relevant factor, which the jury should take into account along with all the other circumstances of the killing. As to this case, see also *ante*, §§ 19-56a, 19-67.

Provocation and lies

19-76   Lies and attempts to cover up a killing are not necessarily inconsistent with provocation. In directions about lies, when the issue was murder or manslaughter, the jury should be alerted to the fact that, before they could treat lies as proof of guilt of the offence charged, they had to be sure that there was not some possible explanation which destroyed their potentially probative effect. A failure to give such a direction, coupled with an indication that the jury might regard lies as probative of murder rather than manslaughter, amounted to a material misdirection: *R. v. Richens*, 98 Cr.App.R. 43, CA; *R. v. Taylor* [1998] 7 *Archbold News* 3, CA.

Provocation and good character

Where there is evidence of the defendant's good character, the judge should direct the jury as to the relevance of that both to credibility and propensity; and, in particular, should remind them that, as a man of good character, the defendant might have been unlikely to indulge in serious violence without first being provoked: *Paria v. R.* [2004] Crim.L.R. 228, PC. **19-77**

Sentence

See the guideline issued by the Sentencing Guidelines Council (*post*, K-71 *et seq.*). Of the pre-guideline authorities, see, in particular, *Att.-Gen.'s References (Nos 74, 95 and 118 of 2002) (R. v. Suratan; R. v. Humes; R. v. Wilkinson)* [2003] 2 Cr.App.R.(S.) 42, CA, which is summarised at paragraph 2.1 of the guideline (Appendix S-3.3). **19-78**

See also *R. v. Brook (Neil)*, § 5-502 in the main work.

(c) *Diminished responsibility*

Abnormality of "mind"/"mental functioning"—substantial impairment

(iv) "Substantially" (see (i)(c), ante).

The Supreme Court has upheld the decision of the Court of Appeal in *R. v. Golds* (see the main work) and held that, where diminished responsibility is in issue, the judge need not direct the jury beyond the terms of the statute and should not attempt to define the word "substantially" in section 2(1) of the Homicide Act 1957 (§ 19-79 in the main work). However, their Lordships went on to say that if the question whether any impairment beyond the merely trivial will suffice has been aired, or the concept of a spectrum between the greater than trivial and the total has been mentioned, the judge should explain that, whilst the impairment must indeed pass the merely trivial, it is not the law that any impairment beyond the trivial will suffice. The judge should likewise make this clear if there is a risk that the jury might misunderstand the import of the word: *R. v. Golds* [2017] 1 Cr.App.R. 18, SC (considering, *inter alia, R. v. Brown (Robert), R. v. Lloyd* and *R. v. Ramchurn* (as to all of which, see the main work)). As to this case, see also *post*, § 19-94. **19-86**

Direction to jury

(ii) Burden of proof

The amendment of section 2 of the Homicide Act 1957 (§ 19-79 in the main work) by the Coroners and Justice Act 2009 did not change the legal burden on the defence to prove diminished responsibility, and there was nothing arbitrary or unreasonable about that legal burden (to the civil standard of proof) being placed on a defendant: *R. v Wilcocks* [2017] 1 Cr.App.R. 23, CA (following *R. v. Foye* (as to which, see the main work)). As to this case, see also *ante*, § 19-63. **19-91**

Medical evidence

In *R. v. Golds* [2017] 1 Cr.App.R. 18, the Supreme Court, having considered the decision in *R. v. Brennan* (as to which, see the main work), observed *obiter* that, whilst, if it is clear that a defendant charged with murder was suffering from a recognised medical condition that substantially impaired him in one of the material respects, and that this condition was a significant cause of the killing, the prosecution are entitled to, and frequently do, accept a plea to manslaughter on the ground of diminished responsibility, and whilst the ordinary principles relating to submissions of "no case to answer" in *R. v. Galbraith* (§ 4-364 in the main work), are capable of applica- **19-94** tion in a trial in which the sole issue is diminished responsibility, a court ought to be cautious about doing so; first, a murder trial is a particularly sensitive event and it is of considerable importance that any verdict should be that of the jury; secondly, the onus of proof in relation to diminished responsibility is on the defendant and the *Galbraith* process is generally a conclusion that no jury, properly directed, could be satisfied that the prosecution have proved all the elements of the offence charged; in the context of diminished responsibility, murder should only be withdrawn from the jury if the judge is satisfied that no jury could fail to find that the defence had discharged the burden cast upon them; thirdly, causation in such cases is essentially a jury issue; where, however, the medical evidence supports the plea and is uncontradicted, the judge needs to ensure that the prosecution explain the basis on which they are inviting the jury to reject that evidence, and that the basis advanced is one that the jury can properly adopt; if the matter is then left to the jury, while the judge needs to make it clear to the jury that, if there is a proper basis for rejecting the expert evidence, the decision is theirs, it will also ordinarily be wise to advise them against attempting to make themselves amateur psychiatrists and that, if there is undisputed expert evidence, they will probably wish to accept it, unless there is some identified reason for not doing so. As to this case, see also *ante*, § 19-86.

Sentence

19-97   When sentencing for manslaughter on the basis of diminished responsibility, the serious aggravating factor of more than one killing with an intention to kill will have an impact upon sentence; where there are two deaths, not only the harm, but also the culpability, is likely to be significantly higher; to the extent that there is any inconsistency between *R. v. Dighton* and *Att.-Gen.'s Reference (No. 34 of 2014) (R. v. Jenkin)* (as to both of which, see the main work), the approach in *Jenkin* is to be preferred, *Dighton* being a decision very much on its own facts that may be explained by the court's conclusion that there was a low level of residual responsibility in that case: *R. v. Dantes* [2016] 2 Cr.App.R.(S.) 25, CA.

B. Manslaughter

(2) Involuntary manslaughter

(c) *Manslaughter by gross negligence*

The test

19-123   *R. v. Rudling* is now reported at [2016] 7 *Archbold Review* 1.
    Where the appellant (a consultant surgeon) appealed against his conviction for manslaughter by gross negligence on the grounds that, *inter alia*, the prosecution experts had been allowed (and indeed encouraged) to proffer an opinion at various stages as to whether, in the particular regard then being discussed, the appellant's conduct had been grossly negligent (thus, on the ultimate issue) and that the judge's directions to the jury were inadequate, the law has developed to the point where an expert has been permitted to give his opinion on what has been called the "ultimate issue", but, in such a case, the judge is required to make it clear to the jury that they are not bound by the expert's opinion; here, for the jury to reach an adverse conclusion in relation to negligence, they had to be sure that the appellant's standard of care fell below what should reasonably have been expected from a competent consultant surgeon; in order to consider that question, the jury were entitled to receive evidence from appropriate medical experts as to their opinion as to what should reasonably have been expected from a competent surgeon, and so to decide whether, on the facts as they found them to be, the appellant fell below the requisite standard; however, whether any such negligence was "gross" (which is not a medical term) involved an evaluation for the jury; medical opinion may be better informed on that point, but it is not and could not be determinative; experts might be able to place negligence on a spectrum (and examples can be given of that spectrum) but that assistance needs to be considered by the jury in the context of all the circumstances as they find them to be, rather than as evaluated by the experts; as to the directions to the jury, whilst no particular formulation is mandatory, what is mandatory is that the jury are assisted sufficiently to understand how to approach their task of identifying the line that separates even serious or very serious mistakes or lapses, from conduct that was truly exceptionally bad and was such a departure from the standard of a reasonably

116

competent doctor that it consequently amounted to being criminal; here, the way in which the issue of gross negligence was approached (and, in particular, the consequential direction to the jury) was inadequate (the judge did not identify where the line that the jury were seeking to identify should be drawn (in response to a question they asked) and had failed to emphasise that what was gross negligence was a matter for them and not the experts), and, accordingly, the conviction was unsafe and would be quashed: *R. v. Sellu* [2017] 1 Cr.App.R. 24, CA (considering, *inter alia, Pora v. The Queen* (as to which, see § 10-51 in the main work), and *R. v. Misra and Srivastava* (as to which, see the main work)).

(8) Sentence

Involuntary manslaughter

For further guidance as to how to sentence historic offences, see Appendix S-1053. **19-136**

Where a killing results from a campaign of domestic violence, this is a seriously aggravating ★ feature: *Att.-Gen.'s Reference (R. v. Maling)* [2017] 1 Cr.App.R.(S.) 14, CA.

Culpability in unlawful act manslaughter will be significantly influenced by the extent to which ★ the death could have been foreseen: *Att.-Gen.'s Reference (R. v. Huggins)* [2017] 1 Cr.App.R.(S.) 21, CA.

C. Corporate Manslaughter

(1) The offence

Corporate Manslaughter and Corporate Homicide Act 2007, s.1

The offence

With effect from November 9, 2016, the Secretaries of State for Business, Energy and Industrial **19-139** Strategy, for International Trade and for Exiting the European Union and the Transfer of Functions (Education and Skills) Order 2016 (S.I. 2016 No. 992) amended Schedule 1 to the Corporate Manslaughter and Corporate Homicide Act 2007 so as to insert, at the appropriate place, a reference to the Department for Business, Energy and Industrial Strategy and to omit the references to the Department for Business, Innovation and Skills and the Department of Energy and Climate Change.

F. Threats to Kill

(4) Sentence

As to a consultation guideline issued by the Sentencing Council for England and Wales on ★**19-179** intimidatory offences, covering threats to kill (Offences against the Person Act 1861, s.16 (see § 19-176 in the main work)), see *ante,* § 5-178.

IV. COMMON ASSAULT AND BATTERY

C. Defences

Lawful correction

It should be noted that the reference in the main work to "specified nursery education" should **19-237** be a reference to "specified early years education" as a result of an amendment of section 548 of the Education Act 1996 (as to which, see the main work) effected by the Childcare Act 2006, s.103(1), and Sched. 2, para. 27. Furthermore, the amendment of section 548 of the 1996 Act to extend its ambit to an "independent educational institution other than a school" effected by the Education and Skills Act 2008, Sched. 1, para. 9, is not yet in force.

With effect from January 9, 2017, the Childcare (Early Years Provision Free of Charge) (Extended Entitlement) Regulations 2016 (S.I. 2016 No. 1257) amended the definition of "specified early years education" in section 548(8) of the 1996 Act.

X. OFFENCES INVOLVING THE CAUSING OF ALARM OR DISTRESS TO ANOTHER OR AN INTENT TO DO SO

A. Harassment (Including By Stalking)

(2) The offences

Protection from Harassment Act 1997, ss.1, 2

Prohibition of harassment

★**19-339**   For harassment, contrary to section 1(1) of the 1997 Act (see the main work), to be established, the victim must actually be harassed, and he must suffer such harassment within the jurisdiction: *Shakil-Ur-Rahman v. ARY Network Ltd* [2017] 4 W.L.R. 22, QBD (Sir David Eady, sitting as a High Court judge).

Protection from Harassment Act 1997, ss.3–5

Putting people in fear of violence

★**19-347**   With effect from April 3, 2017 (Policing and Crime Act 2017 (Commencement No. 1 and Transitional Provisions) Regulations 2017 (S.I. 2017 No. 399)), section 4(4)(a) of the 1997 Act was amended by the Policing and Crime Act 2017, s.175(1)(a), so as to substitute "ten" for "five". This applies only to offences committed on or after April 3, 2017: s.175(3). Where the course of conduct constituting an offence is found to have occurred over a period of two or more days, or at some time during a period of two or more days, the offence must be taken for the purposes of subsection (3) to have been committed on the last of those days: s.175(4).

Stalking involving fear of violence or serious alarm or distress

★**19-349**   With effect from April 3, 2017 (Policing and Crime Act 2017 (Commencement No. 1 and Transitional Provisions) Regulations 2017 (S.I. 2017 No. 399)), section 4A(5)(a) of the 1997 Act was amended by the Policing and Crime Act 2017, s.175(1)(b), so as to substitute "ten" for "five". Section 175(3) and (4) (as to which, see *ante*, § 19-347) apply to this amendment as they apply to the amendment of section 4(4).

The offence in section 4A of the 1997 Act is wide enough to cover the case of a person who is, on a particular occasion, caused to fear that violence will (as opposed to "might") be used against him on some future, unknown occasion; and there is no requirement for there to be a specific threat of violence: *R. v. Qosja* [2017] 1 Cr.App.R. 17, CA.

(3) Racially or religiously aggravated harassment

Crime and Disorder Act 1998, s.32

Racially or religiously aggravated harassment etc.

★**19-350**   With effect from April 3, 2017 (Policing and Crime Act 2017 (Commencement No. 1 and Transitional Provisions) Regulations 2017 (S.I. 2017 No. 399)), section 32(4)(b) of the 1998 Act was amended by the Policing and Crime Act 2017, s.175(2), so as to substitute "14 years" for "seven years". Section 175(3) and (4) (as to which, see *ante*, § 19-347) apply to this amendment as they apply to the amendment of section 4(4) of the Protection from Harassment Act 1997.

(4) Sentence

Guideline

★**19-352**   As to a consultation guideline issued by the Sentencing Council for England and Wales on intimidatory offences, covering harassment and stalking (Protection from Harassment Act 1997, ss.2 (§ 19-341 in the main work), 2A (*ibid.*, § 19-343), 4 (*ibid.*, § 19-347) and 4A (*ibid.*, § 19-349)), and the racially or religiously aggravated forms of those offences (CDA 1998, s.32 (*ibid.*, § 19-350)), see *ante*, § 5-178.

C. Controlling or Coercive Behaviour

Serious Crime Act 2015, s.76

Controlling or coercive behaviour in an intimate or family relationship

★**19–358**   As to a consultation guideline issued by the Sentencing Council for England and Wales on intimidatory offences, covering controlling or coercive behaviour (2015 Act, s.76 (see the main work)), see *ante*, § 5-178.

D. RESTRAINING ORDERS

(1) On conviction

Protection from Harassment Act 1997, s.5

Restraining orders on conviction

In *R. v. Khellaf* [2017] 1 Cr.App.R.(S.) 1, CA, it was held that: (i) when deciding whether a **19-358b** restraining order should be made under section 5 (§ 19-358a in the main work) of the Protection from Harassment Act 1997, a court should take into account the views of the person to be protected by such an order; but there may be cases where such an order will be appropriate even though the subject of the order does not seek one; nor is it the case that a court must have direct evidence of the views of the victim, which may prove impossible; the court may be able to draw a proper inference as to those views, or may conclude that a restraining order should be made whatever the views of the victim, although clearly if a victim does not want an order to be made because he wants to have contact, that may make such an order impractical; in normal circumstances, however, the views of the victim should be obtained; and it is the responsibility of the prosecution to ensure that the necessary enquiries are made; (ii) an order should not be made unless the court concludes that this is necessary to protect the victim; (iii) the terms of the order should be proportionate to the harm that it is sought to prevent; and (iv) particular care should be taken when children are involved to ensure that the order does not make it impossible for contact to take place between a parent and child if that is otherwise inappropriate.

XIII. OFFENCES RELATING TO CHILDREN AND YOUNG PERSONS

A. OFFENCES RELATING TO THE TREATMENT, CONTROL AND MAINTENANCE OF CHILDREN AND YOUNG PERSONS

(2) Cruelty

(d) *Sentence*

For further guidance as to how to sentence historic offences, see Appendix S-1053. **19-379**

B. ABDUCTION OF CHILDREN

Child Abduction Act 1984, ss.3, 4

Penalties and prosecutions

In *R. v. R.H.* [2017] 1 Cr.App.R.(S.) 23, CA, it was said: (i) sentencers should assess the **19-401** seriousness of offences contrary to the 1984 Act, ss.1 (of child by parent, *etc.* (§ 19-395 in the main work)) and 2 (of child by other persons (*ibid.*, § 19-397)), by reference to culpability and harm caused as required by the CJA 2003, s.143 (*ibid.*, § 5-78)); but cases of this sort should normally incorporate a significant element of deterrence; (ii) a high level of harm will involve a very lengthy period of abduction or detention, a serious effect on the child (whether emotional or otherwise), or serious damage to, or severance of, a loving relationship with a parent, sibling, or other relevant person; high culpability may be exemplified by persistent non-disclosure or conceal-ment of the place of abduction, significant and sophisticated planning, breach of a court order or disregard of court process, an intention to sever the relationship between the child and another relevant person, or abduction for a criminal purpose (*e.g.* a sexual purpose, female genital mutila-tion, or forced marriage); where there is both a high level of harm and culpability, the bracket should be five to seven years' imprisonment; (iii) at the lower end of the spectrum of harm will be cases where there has been a brief period of abduction or detention, and minimal effect on the child or on the relationship between the child and other affected party; where the abduction or detention was impulsive or spontaneous, or where there has been prompt disclosure of the place of abduction, culpability will be less; such cases will be particularly fact-sensitive, and a range between a high level community order and a term of 18 months' imprisonment will be appropriate for cases of low level harm and culpability; (iv) any other case, including cases involving levels of harm or culpability that fall between "high" and "low" will fall between the two ranges; (v) in considering where to place a case within a range, the court will also need to have regard to aggravating and mitigating factors in the usual way; non-exhaustive offence-related aggravating factors include exposing the child to a risk of harm, abduction of an already vulnerable child, group action, the use of significant force, abduction to a non-Hague Convention country, abduction to a place with which the child has no prior links, and, in section 2 cases, removal from the jurisdiction; non-exhaustive mitigating factors include enabling prompt contact to take place with the adult deprived of custody or control, compliance with court orders, and cooperation with authorities; (vi) it is open to the court to take into account the effect of a sentence on a child where the offending person is the sole carer for the child abducted or other children; that is not a matter of mitigation personal to the offender, but rather, it arises from the need for the court to have regard to the interests of the child or children affected; careful consideration of the principles in *R. v. Petherick* (*ibid.*, § 5-173), is required so that the wider public interest and the interests of any children are dealt with proportionately (considering *R. v. Kayani; R. v. Solliman* (as to which, see the main work)).

XV. TORTURE, SLAVERY AND HUMAN TRAFFICKING

B. Slavery and Human Trafficking

(2) Prevention orders

(c) *Offences and supplementary provision*

Offences

19-459   With effect from December 17, 2016, the Human Trafficking and Exploitation (Scotland) Act 2015 (Consequential Provisions and Modifications) Order 2016 (S.I. 2016 No. 1031), amended section 30(1) of the Modern Slavery Act 2015, so as to omit the word "or" at the end of paragraph (e), and to insert new paragraphs (g) to (j), as follows—

"(g) a trafficking and exploitation prevention order under section 17 or 18 of the Human Trafficking and Exploitation (Scotland) Act 2015;
  (h) an interim trafficking and exploitation prevention order under section 24 of that Act;
  (i) a trafficking and exploitation risk order under section 26 of that Act; or
  (j) an interim trafficking and exploitation risk order under section 30 of that Act;".

Slavery and human trafficking offences

19-461   With effect from December 17, 2016, the Human Trafficking and Exploitation (Scotland) Act 2015 (Consequential Provisions and Modifications) Order 2016 (S.I. 2016 No. 1031) amended Schedule 1 to the Modern Slavery Act 2015 to include references to an offence under section 1 or 4 of the Human Trafficking and Exploitation (Scotland) Act 2015 and an offence aggravated by a connection with human trafficking activity in accordance with section 5 of that Act.

(d) *Defences to criminal proceedings*

Modern Slavery Act 2015, s.45

Defence for slavery or trafficking victims who commit an offence

★19-464   In *R. v. Joseph and conjoined appeals* [2017] 2 Archbold Review 2, CA, it was held that: (i) whereas section 45 of the 2015 Act provides a defence for slavery and trafficking victims charged with certain offences if certain conditions are met, as the Act was not drafted to provide retrospective protection, the regime that was developed by the courts prior to the coming into force of section 45 on July 31, 2015 (in *R. v. M. (L.), B. (M.) and G. (D.); R. v. Tabot; R. v. Tijani, R. v. N. (A.); R. v. Le,* and *R. v. L. (C.); R. v. N. (H.V.); R. v. N. (T.H.); R. v. T. (H.D.) (Children's Commr for England and Equality and Human Rights Commission Intervening)* (as to all of which, see *post,* E-12d)), continues to apply to those not within the scope of the Act who claim that there is a nexus between the crime with which they are charged and their status as victims of trafficking; accordingly, it is not necessary to develop the law of duress so that it matches section 45 of the 2015 Act for those not entitled to its protection; in particular, the defence of duress should not be expanded so that a threat of false imprisonment would suffice (agreeing with the provisional view to that effect expressed in *R. v. van Dao* (see § 17-119 in the main work)); further, the submission that it was no longer appropriate to rely on prosecutorial discretion and review by the court (pursuant to its abuse of process jurisdiction) and that it should be for the jury to decide whether the defendant was a victim, whether there was a nexus and whether there was compulsion, fell to be rejected as the principles developed in the case law ensure that the domestic law is in accordance with the United Kingdom's international obligations; (ii) when deciding whether to prosecute, whether to exercise the abuse jurisdiction or whether to allow an appeal against conviction where the claim to victim status was first made after conviction, three general points warranted restatement; first, the gravity of the alleged offence is relevant to the decision whether to prosecute; secondly, once it is established that a child is the victim of trafficking and there is a sufficient nexus between the trafficking for exploitation and the offence, there is no need for the child to have been coerced into commission of the offence; thirdly, the decision of the competent authority as to whether the defendant is a victim of trafficking does not bind the court, although a court will bear its conclusion very much in mind; it does not follow from the fact that an individual "fits the profile" of a victim of trafficking that he is necessarily such a victim.

CHAPTER 20

SEXUAL OFFENCES

I. INTRODUCTION

Sentencing guidelines

The Sentencing Council for England and Wales has issued a definitive guideline relating to the   ★**20-9c**
overarching principles for sentencing those aged under 18 at the date of conviction (Pt 1), and to the sentencing of such persons for, *inter alia*, sexual offences (Pt 2). It applies to all offenders who are sentenced after May 31, 2017, regardless of the date of the offence. For the details, see *post*, Appendix S-29 *et seq.*

II. OFFENCES

A. GENERAL INTERPRETATION

(2) "Sexual"

Sexual Offences Act 2003, s.78

"Sexual"

With effect from April 3, 2017 (Serious Crime Act 2015 (Commencement No. 7) Regulations   ★**20-17**
2017 (S.I. 2017 No. 511)), paragraph 63 of Schedule 4 to the 2015 Act (see the main work) was brought into force.

F. CHILD SEX OFFENCES

(8) Sexual communication with a child

(a) *Statute*

Sexual Offences Act 2003, s.15A

Sexual communication with a child

With effect from April 3, 2017 (Serious Crime Act 2015 (Commencement No. 6) Regulations   ★**20-95a**
2017 (S.I. 2017 No. 451)), section 67 of the SCA 2015 was brought into force.

L. Sexual Exploitation of Children

(2) Causing, inciting, facilitating, etc., child prostitution or pornography

(a) *Statute*

Sexual Offences Act 2003, ss.48, 50, 51

Sections 48 to 50: interpretation

★**20-162**   With effect from March 31, 2017, section 51(2) of the 2003 Act (see the main work) was amended by the Policing and Crime Act 2017, s.176, to provide that a child is also sexually exploited for the purposes of sections 48 to 50 (*ibid.*, §§ 20-160, 20-167, 20-161) of that Act if an indecent image of the child is streamed or otherwise transmitted (the words "or streamed or otherwise transmitted" being inserted at the end of subs. (2)(b)).

O. Preparatory Offences

(3) Trespass with intent

(e) *Elements of the offences*

20-201   *R. v. Pacurar* is now reported at [2016] 2 Cr.App.R. 26.

Q. Other Statutory Offences

(5) Sexual activity in a public lavatory

20-228   The Sentencing Council for England and Wales has issued new sentencing guidelines for magistrates' courts, which revise, in relation to, *inter alia*, the offence of sexual activity in a public lavatory, the Sentencing Guidelines Council's guidelines. The guidelines apply to all offenders aged 18 or over who are sentenced on or after April 24, 2017, regardless of the date of the offence. The format is the same as for other offence-specific guidelines issued by the council. At step 1, the court should determine which of three categories applies. Category 1 involves higher culpability and greater harm, category 2 involves one or the other, but not both, and category 3 involves neither. The sole indicators of higher culpability are: intimidating behaviour/ threats of violence to members of the public, and blatant behaviour. The sole indicators of greater harm are: distress suffered by members of the public, and children or young persons being present. Where none of these indicators are present, the case is one of lower culpability and/or lesser harm. For a category 1 case, the starting point is a low level community order and the range is a band C fine to a high level community order. For a category 2 offence, the starting point is a band C fine and the range is a band B fine to a low level community order. For a category 3 offence, the starting point is a band B fine, and the range is from a band A fine to a band C fine. Having identified a sentence within the range, the court should adjust this for any aggravating or mitigating factors (a non-exhaustive list being included in the guideline) and then go through the other standard steps required by any offence-specific guideline, *viz.* consider the SOCPA 2005, ss.73 and 74 (assistance by defendants: reduction or review of sentence (§§ 5-155, 5-156 in the main work)), credit for a guilty plea, the totality principle, the question of compensation and any appropriate ancillary orders, the need to give reasons and (where relevant) to make any appropriate allowance for time spent on bail (CJA 2003, s.240A (*ibid.*, § 5-604)).

(8) Disclosing a private sexual photograph or film

Criminal Justice and Courts Act 2015, ss.33–35

Disclosing private sexual photographs and films with intent to cause distress

★**20-237a**   As to a consultation guideline issued by the Sentencing Council for England and Wales on intimidatory offences, covering the offence of disclosure of private sexual images (2015 Act, s.33 (see the main work)), see *ante*, § 5-178.

IV. NOTIFICATION AND ORDERS

A. NOTIFICATION REQUIREMENTS

(3) Legislation

Sexual Offences Act 2003, ss.87–91

Method of notification and related matters

With effect from May 12, 2017, the Sexual Offences Act 2003 (Prescribed Police Stations) ★**20-272** Regulations 2017 (S.I. 2017 No. 573) revoke and replace the Sexual Offences Act 2003 (Prescribed Police Stations) (No. 2) Regulations 2015 (S.I. 2015 No. 1523) (see the main work).

Sexual Offences Act 2003, Sched. 3

With effect from April 3, 2017 (Serious Crime Act 2015 (Commencement No. 7) Regulations ★**20-320** 2017 (S.I. 2017 No. 511)), paragraph 66(2) of Schedule 4 to the 2015 Act (see the main work) was brought into force.

D. SEXUAL HARM PREVENTION ORDERS

(2) Legislation

Sexual Offences Act 2003, ss.103A-103K

Sexual harm prevention orders: applications and grounds

For a case considering *R. v. Terrell* (as to which, see the main work), see *ante*, § 5-500. **20-325**

A draft of a proposed order under the SOA, s.103A (§ 20-324 in the main work), that was only **20-328** produced to the judge and defence counsel shortly before the sentence hearing, on the day itself, was not good enough, especially where the judge was wrongly given the impression that he was merely approving an order that was in standard terms for a case of this nature; as stated in *R. v. Smith* (see the main work) (in relation to sexual "offences" prevention orders), a proposed order should be provided in electronic form at least two clear days before the hearing, and, if a judge has had insufficient time to consider its terms, he can adjourn the matter; the practice noted in that case of presenting judges with hastily and inadequately prepared drafts at a late stage is wholly unsatisfactory; as a consequence, there will not be the proper scrutiny which orders of this kind require, given that they interfere with personal liberty; either they will remain in force when they ought not to do so, or they will have to be remedied on appeal with the attendant waste of time and costs: *R. v. Lewis* [2017] 1 Cr.App.R.(S.) 2, CA. As was also pointed out in *Smith*, there is no reason why notification requirements and the duration of an order of this nature should be the same: *ibid.*

When considering whether to make an order under section 103A, a court should ask itself whether the order is necessary to protect the public from sexual harm through the commission of scheduled offences, and, if it is, whether the terms are oppressive and whether the order is proportionate overall (slightly adapting what was said in *R. v. Smith, ante*, in relation to sexual offences prevention orders): *Att.-Gen.'s Reference (R. v. N.C.)* [2017] 1 Cr.App.R.(S.) 13, CA (reiterating what was said in *Lewis, ante*, about timely service of a draft order). The court also said that the position with regard to internet use has developed since *Smith*; accordingly, it upheld a prohibition on the offender's internet use given that the internet figured in one of his offences (causing a child to watch a sexual act, the others being three counts of sexual assault on a child under 13). However, a prohibition on undertaking any activity likely to bring him into supervisory contact with a child under 16 would be deleted since it added nothing to the restrictions under the Safeguarding Vulnerable Groups Act 2006.

CHAPTER 21

OFFENCES UNDER THE THEFT AND FRAUD ACTS

II. THEFT

(2) Indictment

(a) *General*

Charge distinct takings

21-18   As to the replacement of *Criminal Practice Direction II (Preliminary Proceedings) 10A* (see the main work), see *post*, Appendix B-149.

III. ROBBERY AND ASSAULT WITH INTENT TO ROB

A. ROBBERY

(4) Sentence

Sentencing guidelines

★**21-90**   The Sentencing Council for England and Wales has issued a definitive guideline relating to the overarching principles for sentencing those aged under 18 at the date of conviction (Pt 1), and to the sentencing of such persons for, *inter alia*, robbery (Pt 3). It applies to all offenders who are sentenced after May 31, 2017, regardless of the date of the offence. For the details, see *post*, Appendix S-29 *et seq.*, S-31 *et seq.*

VI. TAKING CONVEYANCES WITHOUT AUTHORITY

A. THE SIMPLE OFFENCE

(5) Sentence

21-146   The Sentencing Council for England and Wales has issued new sentencing guidelines for magistrates' courts, which revise, in relation to, *inter alia*, the offence of vehicle-taking without consent (§ 21-141 in the main work), the Sentencing Guidelines Council's guidelines. The guidelines apply to all offenders aged 18 or over who are sentenced on or after April 24, 2017, regardless of the date of the offence. For further details, see *post*, Appendix S-11.110.

B. THE AGGRAVATED OFFENCE

(5) Sentence

Disqualification and endorsement

★**21-164**   In *R. v. Beech* [2017] R.T.R. 8, CA, it was said that the decision in *R. v. Bradshaw and Waters (Note – 1994)* (as to which, see the main work), turned on its particular facts (and was properly decided on those facts), but did not mean that a court should invariably exercise its discretion, under the RTOA 1988, s.36(4) (*ibid.*, § 32-273), not to disqualify someone who had been a passenger until an extended test had been passed; it is necessary to examine the facts of the case to see if the imposition of the requirement for an extended test is necessary for the proper protection of the public.

CHAPTER 22

FORGERY, PERSONATION AND CHEATING

I. FORGERY

B. MISCELLANEOUS OFFENCES AKIN TO FORGERY

(2) Identity documents

(a) *Offences*

Identity Documents Act 2010, ss.4–6

Possession of false identity documents etc. with improper intention

The decision of the Court of Appeal in *S.X.H. v. CPS* (see the main work) in relation to the ★**22-49**
original decision to prosecute the appellant has been unanimously upheld: see *S.X.H. v. CPS
(United Nations High Commr for Refugees intervening)* [2017] 1 W.L.R. 1401, SC. It was held that the
decision to prosecute for an offence that was convention-compliant did not engage Article 8 of the
ECHR (*ibid.*, § 16-137) where the prosecutor had reasonable cause to believe the defendant to be
guilty of the offence charged, and that, even if Article 8 was engaged, although things could have
been done better, there was no breach, which would have been the case even if the original decision to prosecute had been an error of judgment in good faith. As to this case, see also *ante*, § 16-
141.

(f) *Defences*

For a case considering *R. v. M. (L.), B. (M.) and G. (D.); R. v. Tabot; R. v. Tijani* (as to which, ★**22-59**
see the main work), see *ante*, § 19-464.

III. CHEATING

B. BY STATUTE

Gambling Act 2005, s.42

Cheating

In *Ivey v. Genting Casinos U.K. Ltd (trading as Crockfords Club)* [2017] 1 Cr.App.R. 16, CA (Civ. ★**22-80**
Div.), Arden L.J. was of the view that dishonesty was not an ingredient of the offence of cheating,
contrary to section 42 of the 2005 Act (§ 22-79 in the main work). Sharp L.J., however, was of the
opinion that a person could not be convicted of this offence without a finding of dishonesty.
Tomlinson L.J. agreed with Arden L.J. as to the result, but took the stance that it was not necessary to express an opinion about the ambit of the criminal offence, but did express the view that a
person could be guilty of a deception amounting to a cheat without being dishonest. An application by the claimant for permission to appeal has been allowed: [2017] 1 W.L.R. 1248, SC.

CHAPTER 24

FIREARMS AND OFFENSIVE WEAPONS

I. FIREARMS

A. FIREARMS ACT 1968

(2) Offences relating to firearms certificates

Firearms Act 1968, s.3

Dealing in firearms

With effect from April 10, 2017, the Air Weapons and Licensing (Scotland) Act 2015 ★**24-16**

(Consequential Provisions) Order 2017 (S.I. 2017 No. 452), *inter alia*, amended section 3 of the 1968 Act so as to add new subsections (7) and (8), thereby creating a new offence applicable only to Scotland in relation to air weapons.

(3) Conversion of weapons

★24-23a   With effect from May 2, 2017 (Policing and Crime Act 2017 (Commencement No. 1 and Transitional Provisions) Regulations 2017 (S.I. 2017 No. 399)), a new section 4A was inserted into the 1968 Act by the Policing and Crime Act 2017, s.127.

Firearms Act 1968, s.4A

Possession of articles for conversion of imitation firearms

4A.–(1) A person, other than a registered firearms dealer, commits an offence if–

(a) the person has in his or her possession or under his or her control an article that is capable of being used (whether by itself or with other articles) to convert an imitation firearm into a firearm, and

(b) the person intends to use the article (whether by itself or with other articles) to convert an imitation firearm into a firearm.

(2) A person guilty of an offence under this section is liable–

(a) on summary conviction–

(i) in England and Wales, to imprisonment for a term not exceeding 12 months (or, in relation to offences committed before section 154(1) of the Criminal Justice Act 2003 comes into force, 6 months) or to a fine, or to both;

(ii) [*Scotland*];

(b) on conviction on indictment, to imprisonment for a term not exceeding 5 years or to a fine, or to both.

(4) Prohibited weapons and ammunition

Firearms Act 1968, s.5

★24-24   With effect from May 2, 2017 (Policing and Crime Act 2017 (Commencement No. 1 and Transitional Provisions) Regulations 2017 (S.I. 2017 No. 399)), section 5(1A)(f) of the 1968 Act was substituted by the Policing and Crime Act 2017, s.129(1) and (2), as follows–

"(f) any ammunition which is designed to be used with a pistol and incorporates a missile designed or adapted to expand on impact;".

With effect from the same date, section 9 of the Firearms (Amendment) Act 1997 (see the main work) was repealed by the 2017 Act, s.129(4).

Firearms Act 1968, s.5A

Exemptions from requirement of authority under s.5

★24-40   With effect from May 2, 2017 (Policing and Crime Act 2017 (Commencement No. 1 and Transitional Provisions) Regulations 2017 (S.I. 2017 No. 399)), section 5A(8)(a) of the 1968 Act was amended by the Policing and Crime Act 2017, s.129(1) and (3), so as to insert the words "is designed to be used with a pistol and" after the first "which".

(5) Special exemptions from sections 1 to 5

Firearms Act 1968, ss.9–13

Sports, athletics and other approved activities

★24-47   With effect from May 2, 2017 (Policing and Crime Act 2017 (Commencement No. 1 and Transitional Provisions) Regulations 2017 (S.I. 2017 No. 399)), section 11(5) of the 1968 Act was repealed by the Policing and Crime Act 2017, s.130(2)(a).

★24-47a   With effect from May 2, 2017 (Policing and Crime Act 2017 (Commencement No. 1 and Transitional Provisions) Regulations 2017 (S.I. 2017 No. 399)), a new section 11A was inserted into the 1968 Act by the Policing and Crime Act 2017, s.130(1).

Firearms Act 1968, s.11A

Authorised lending and possession of firearms for hunting etc.

11A.–(1) A person ("the borrower") may, without holding a certificate under this Act, borrow a

rifle or shot gun from another person on private premises ("the lender") and have the rifle or shot
gun in his or her possession on those premises if—

(a) the four conditions set out in subsections (2) to (5) are met, and

(b) in the case of a rifle, the borrower is aged 17 or over.

(2) The first condition is that the borrowing and possession of the rifle or shot gun are for either
or both of the following purposes—

(a) hunting animals or shooting game or vermin;

(b) shooting at artificial targets.

(3) The second condition is that the lender—

(a) is aged 18 or over,

(b) holds a certificate under this Act in respect of the rifle or shot gun, and

(c) is either—

(i) a person who has a right to allow others to enter the premises for the purposes of
hunting animals or shooting game or vermin, or

(ii) a person who is authorised in writing by a person mentioned in sub-paragraph (i) to
lend the rifle or shot gun on the premises (whether generally or to persons specified
in the authorisation who include the borrower).

(4) The third condition is that the borrower's possession and use of the rifle or shot gun complies
with any conditions as to those matters specified in the lender's certificate under this Act.

(5) The fourth condition is that, during the period for which the rifle or shot gun is borrowed, the
borrower is in the presence of the lender or—

(a) where a rifle is borrowed, a person who, although not the lender, is aged 18 or over, holds
a certificate under this Act in respect of that rifle and is a person described in subsection
(3)(c)(i) or (ii);

(b) where a shot gun is borrowed, a person who, although not the lender, is aged 18 or over,
holds a certificate under this Act in respect of that shot gun or another shot gun and is a
person described in subsection (3)(c)(i) or (ii).

(6) Where a rifle is borrowed on any premises in reliance on subsection (1), the borrower may,
without holding a firearm certificate, purchase or acquire ammunition on the premises, and have the
ammunition in his or her possession on those premises for the period for which the firearm is borrowed, if—

(a) the ammunition is for use with the firearm,

(b) the lender's firearm certificate authorises the lender to have in his or her possession during
that period ammunition of a quantity not less than that purchased or acquired by, and in
the possession of, the borrower, and

(c) the borrower's possession and use of the ammunition complies with any conditions as to
those matters specified in the certificate.

(6) Prevention of crime and public safety

(d) *Carrying firearm with criminal intent*

"Have with him"

For the meaning of "have with him", in the context of a similarly worded provision of the CJA   **24-70**
1988, s.139 (§ 24-195 in the main work), see *R. v. Henderson (Christopher)*, *post*, § 24-170.

(8) Firearm and shot gun certificates
Firearms Act 1968, ss.28A, 28B

Section 28A was inserted into the 1968 Act by Schedule 2 to the Firearms (Amendment) Act   **★24-92a**
1997 and makes supplementary provision in relation to firearms and shot gun certificates. *Inter
alia*, it provides that it is an offence for a person knowingly or recklessly to make any statement,
which is false in any material particular for the purpose of procuring (whether for himself or
another) the grant or renewal of a certificate under the Act (s.28A(7)).

As from a day to be appointed, a new section 28B (certificates: limited extension) is inserted
into the 1968 Act by the Policing and Crime Act 2017, s.131(1), which provides that where an application for renewal of a firearm certificate is made at least eight weeks before the expiry of the
existing certificate, but the police have not completed the renewal process before the certificate
expires, there can be automatic extension of the current certificate's validity until the police reach
a decision, for a maximum of eight weeks after the expiry date of the current certificate. A
consequential amendment is made to section 28A (s.131(2)).

(12) Appeals

★**24-106**   With effect from April 3, 2017 (Policing and Crime Act 2017 (Commencement No. 1 and Transitional Provisions) Regulations 2017 (S.I. 2017 No. 399)), section 44 of the 1968 Act was amended by the Policing and Crime Act 2017, s.133(1) and (3), so as to insert subsection (3A), which provides that in hearing an appeal the court must have regard to any guidance issued under section 55A (*post*, § 24-119) that is relevant to the appeal.

(13) Law enforcement and punishment of offences
Firearms Act 1968, ss.49, 51, 51A, 52

Forfeiture and disposal of firearms and cancellation of certificate on conviction

★**24-118**   With effect from April 10, 2017, the Air Weapons and Licensing (Scotland) Act 2015 (Consequential Provisions) Order 2017 (S.I. 2017 No. 452), *inter alia*, amended section 52 of the 1968 Act so as to insert, after subsection (1), new subsections (1ZA) and (1ZB), as follows—

"(1ZA) Where—
>   (a) a person is convicted as mentioned in subsection (1)(a) by or before a court in England and Wales, or
>   (b) an order of the kind mentioned in subsection (1)(b) or (c) is made in relation to a person by a court in England and Wales,

the court may cancel any air weapon certificate granted to the person under section 5 of the Air Weapons and Licensing (Scotland) Act 2015 which has not expired or been revoked or cancelled.
>   (1ZB) [*Scotland.*]".

(14) General provisions

★**24-119**   As from a day to be appointed, section 54 of the 1968 Act (dealing with the application of the Act to Crown servants) is amended by the Policing and Crime Act 2017, s.39(1) and (2).

★   With effect from April 3, 2017 (Policing and Crime Act 2017 (Commencement No. 1 and Transitional Provisions) Regulations 2017 (S.I. 2017 No. 399)), a new section 55A (Secretary of State's power to issue guidance as to exercise of police functions) was inserted into the 1968 Act by the Policing and Crime Act 2017, s.133(1) and (2).

(15) Definitions
Firearms Act 1968, s.57

★**24-120**   With effect from May 2, 2017 (Policing and Crime Act 2017 (Commencement No. 1 and Transitional Provisions) Regulations 2017 (S.I. 2017 No. 399)), section 57 of the 1968 Act was amended by the Policing and Crime Act 2017, s.125(1) to (4), so as: (i) in subsection (1), to substitute the following text for the text from the beginning to the end of paragraph (c)—

"(1) In this Act, the expression 'firearm' means—
>   (a) a lethal barrelled weapon (see subsection (1B));
>   (b) a prohibited weapon;
>   (c) a relevant component part in relation to a lethal barrelled weapon or a prohibited weapon (see subsection (1D));
>   (d) an accessory to a lethal barrelled weapon or a prohibited weapon where the accessory is designed or adapted to diminish the noise or flash caused by firing the weapon;";

and (ii) to insert new subsections (1B) to (1D), as follows—

"(1B) In subsection (1)(a), "lethal barrelled weapon" means a barrelled weapon of any description from which a shot, bullet or other missile, with kinetic energy of more than one joule at the muzzle of the weapon, can be discharged.
>   (1C) Subsection (1) is subject to section 57A (exception for airsoft guns).
>   (1D) For the purposes of subsection (1)(c), each of the following items is a relevant component part in relation to a lethal barrelled weapon or a prohibited weapon—
>   (a) a barrel, chamber or cylinder,
>   (b) a frame, body or receiver,
>   (c) a breech block, bolt or other mechanism for containing the pressure of discharge at the rear of a chamber,

but only where the item is capable of being used as a part of a lethal barrelled weapon or a prohibited weapon.".

As from a day to be appointed, section 57 is further amended by the Policing and Crime Act ★
2017, s.39(1) and (3), by inserting, after the definition of "imitation firearm" in subsection (4),
the following definitions—

"'member of a police force' means—
  (a) as respects England and Wales, a constable who is a member of a police force or a special
      constable appointed under section 27 of the Police Act 1996;
  (b) [*Scotland*];
  'member of the British Transport Police Force' includes a special constable appointed under
    section 25 of the Railways and Transport Safety Act 2003;".

Firearms Act 1968, ss. 57A, 57B

With effect from May 2, 2017 (Policing and Crime Act 2017 (Commencement No. 1 and ★**24-120a**
Transitional Provisions) Regulations 2017 (S.I. 2017 No. 399), new sections 57A and 57B were
inserted into the 1968 Act by the Policing and Crime Act 2017, s.125(1), (5) and (6). Section 57A
provides that an "airsoft gun" is not to be regarded as a firearm for the purposes of the Act. An
"airsoft gun" is defined by subsection (2) as a barrelled weapon of any description that is designed
to discharge only a small plastic missile (as to which, see subs. (3)) (whether or not it is also
capable of discharging any other kind of missile), and is not capable of discharging a missile (of
any kind) with kinetic energy at the muzzle of the weapon that exceeds the permitted level (as to
which, see subs. (4)). Section 57B provides for a power to amend new section 57(1D) (as to which,
see *ante*, § 24-120).

"Firearm"
As to the amended definition of a firearm in section 57(1) of the 1968 Act, see *ante*, § 24-120.   ★**24-121**

"Lethal"
As to the amended definition of a firearm in section 57(1) of the 1968 Act, see *ante*, § 24-120.   ★**24-122**

"Barrelled"
As to the amended definition of a firearm in section 57(1) of the 1968 Act, see *ante*, § 24-120.   ★**24-123**

"From which any...missile can be discharged"
As to the amended definition of a firearm in section 57(1) of the 1968 Act, see *ante*, § 24-120.   ★**24-124**

"Accessory"
As to the amended definition of a firearm in section 57(1) of the 1968 Act, see *ante*, § 24-120.   ★**24-125**

(16) Particular savings
Firearms Act 1968, s.58

As from a day to be appointed, section 58 of the 1968 Act is amended by the Policing and ★**24-131**
Crime Act 2017, s.126(1) and (2), to insert, after subsection (2), new subsections (2A) to (2H), as
follows—

"(2A) For the purposes of subsection (2), a firearm is an 'antique firearm' if—
  (a) either the conditions in subsection (2B) are met or the condition in subsection (2C) is met,
      and
  (b) if an additional condition is specified in regulations under subsection (2D), that condition
      is also met.
(2B) The conditions in this subsection are that—
  (a) the firearm's chamber or, if the firearm has more than one chamber, each of its chambers
      is either—
    (i) a chamber that the firearm had when it was manufactured, or
    (ii) a replacement for such a chamber that is identical to it in all material respects;
  (b) the firearm's chamber or (as the case may be) each of the firearm's chambers is designed
      for use with a cartridge of a description specified in regulations made by statutory instru-
      ment by the Secretary of State (whether or not it is also capable of being used with other
      cartridges).
(2C) The condition in this subsection is that the firearm's propulsion system is of a description
specified in regulations made by statutory instrument by the Secretary of State.

(2D) [*Regulations under subs. (2A)(b).*]

(2E) [*Scotland.*]

(2F), (2G) *Regulations under subss. (2B) to (2D).*]

(2G) Subject to subsection (2H), a statutory instrument containing regulations under subsection (2B), (2C) or (2D) may not be made unless a draft of the instrument has been laid before and approved by a resolution of each House of Parliament.

(2H) [*Regulations under subss. (2B) or (2C).*]".

★ Section 126(1) and (3) of the 2017 Act apply sections 19 (§ 24-71 in the main work) and 20 (*ibid.*, § 24-77) of the 1968 Act to antique firearms. Section 126(4) to (7) (not yet in force) contain transitional provisions where, in consequence of regulations made under section 58(2B) to (2D), *ante*, a person has in his possession a firearm that ceases to be an antique firearm for those purposes.

Antiques

★24-132 As to the amendment of section 58 of the 1968 Act and the new definition of "antique firearm", see *ante*, § 24-131.

C. FIREARMS (AMENDMENT) ACT 1988

(2) Converted and de-activated weapons

★24-140a With effect from May 2, 2017 (Policing and Crime Act 2017 (Commencement No. 1 and Transitional Provisions) Regulations 2017 (S.I. 2017 No. 399)), a new section 8A was inserted into the 1988 Act by the Policing and Crime Act 2017, s.128.

Firearms (Amendment) Act 1988, s.8A

Controls on defectively deactivated weapons

8A.–(1) It is an offence for a person who owns or claims to own a defectively deactivated weapon—

(a) to make the weapon available for sale or as a gift to another person, or

(b) to sell it or give it (as a gift) to another person.

(2) Subsection (1)(a) does not apply if—

(a) the weapon is made available for sale or as a gift only to a person who is outside the EU (or to persons all of whom are outside the EU), and

(b) it is made so available on the basis that, if a sale or gift were to take place, the weapon would be transferred to a place outside the EU.

(3) Subsection (1)(b) does not apply if—

(a) the weapon is sold or given to a person who is outside the EU (or to persons all of whom are outside the EU), and

(b) in consequence of the sale or gift, it is (or is to be) transferred to a place outside the EU.

(4) For the purpose of this section, something is a "defectively deactivated weapon" if—

(a) it was at any time a firearm,

(b) it has been rendered incapable of discharging any shot, bullet or other missile (and, accordingly, has either ceased to be a firearm or is a firearm only by virtue of the Firearms Act 1982), but

(c) it has not been rendered so incapable in a way that meets the technical specifications for the deactivation of the weapon that apply at the time when the weapon is made available for sale or as a gift or (as the case may be) when it is sold or given as a gift.

(5) The Secretary of State must publish a document setting out the technical specifications that apply for the purposes of subsection (4)(c) ("the technical specifications document").

(6) The technical specifications document may set out different technical specifications for different kinds of weapon.

(7) The Secretary of State—

(a) may from time to time revise the technical specifications document, and

(b) where it is revised—

(i) must publish the document as revised, and

(ii) specify in it the date on which any changes to the technical specifications that apply for the purposes of subsection (4)(c) take effect.

(8) In the case of a weapon rendered incapable as mentioned in subsection (4)(b) before 8 April 2016, subsection (1)(a) or (b) does not apply if the weapon is made available for sale or as a gift, or

(as the case may be) sold or given, by or on behalf of a museum in respect of which a museum firearms licence is in force to another museum in respect of which such a licence is in force.

(9) References in this section to "sale" include exchange or barter (and references to sell are to be construed accordingly).

(10) In this section, "museum firearms licence" means a licence granted under the Schedule to the Firearms (Amendment) Act 1988.

(11) A person guilty of an offence under this section is liable—

  (a) on summary conviction—

  (i) in England and Wales, to imprisonment for a term not exceeding 12 months (or, in relation to offences committed before section 154(1) of the Criminal Justice Act 2003 comes into force, 6 months) or to a fine, or to both;

  (ii) [*Scotland*];

  (b) on conviction on indictment, to imprisonment for a term not exceeding 5 years or to a fine, or to both.

(4) Exemptions

Firearms (Amendment) Act 1988, s.15

Approved rifle clubs and muzzle-loading pistol clubs

With effect from May 2, 2017 (Policing and Crime Act 2017 (Commencement No. 1 and Transitional Provisions) Regulations 2017 (S.I. 2017 No. 399)), section 15(6) of the 1988 Act was repealed by the Policing and Crime Act 2017, s.130(5). ★**24-142**

Firearms (Amendment) Act 1988, ss.16, 16A, 16B

Borrowed rifles on private premises

With effect from May 2, 2017 (Policing and Crime Act 2017 (Commencement No. 1 and Transitional Provisions) Regulations 2017 (S.I. 2017 No. 399)), section 16 of the 1988 Act was repealed by the Policing and Crime Act 2017, s.130(2)(b). ★**24-144**

Firearms (Amendment) Act 1988, Sched., paras 1(1), (2), (4), 6

As from a day to be appointed, in the schedule to the 1988 Act, paragraph 3 is repealed and a new paragraph 3A is inserted by the Policing and Crime Act 2017, s.132(3) and (4). ★**24-153**

D. Firearms (Amendment) Act 1997

(3) Regulation of firearms and ammunition

Firearms (Amendment) Act 1997, ss.32-36

Permitted electronic means

With effect from April 3, 2017 (Policing and Crime Act 2017 (Commencement No. 1 and Transitional Provisions) Regulations 2017 (S.I. 2017 No. 399), section 35A(2) of the 1997 Act was amended by the Policing and Crime Act 2017, s.51, and Sched. 14, para. 7(d). ★**24-161**

II. OFFENSIVE WEAPONS, BLADED ARTICLES AND KNIVES

A. Having an Offensive Weapon In Public Place

(4) Sentence

As to a new consultation guideline on sentencing for offences involving bladed articles and offensive weapons, which covers the sentencing of offenders convicted of an offence contrary to section 1(1) of the Prevention of Crime Act 1953 (§ 24-165 in the main work), see *ante*, § 5-178. **24-168**

(5) Ingredients of the offences

(a) "*has with him*"

"Has with him" distinguished from possession

In *R. v. Henderson (Christopher)* [2017] 1 Cr.App.R. 4, CA, it was held on reviewing the authori- **24-170** ties (including *R. v. Kelt* and *R. v. Pawlicki and Swindell* (as to both of which, see § 24-70 in the main work)) that, in determining whether a person has a weapon "with him", relevant considerations include: (i) possession of a weapon is a wider concept than having it "with him"; (ii) having a weapon "with him" is a wider concept than carrying it; (iii) the propinquity between the person and the weapon; (iv) whether the weapon is immediately available to the person; (v) the accessibility of the weapon; (vi) the context of any criminal enterprise embarked upon; and (vii) the purpose of the applicable statute. On the facts, a knife had been found in the appellant's car in a bag containing baby-changing items, while he himself was in a second-floor flat, a considerable distance away; there was no evidence that he had shortly left or was shortly to return to the car, or that the knife in the car was linked in any way to his presence in the flat on that day or at all; accordingly, as a matter of law, the appellant did not have the knife "with him" for the purposes of section 139 of the CJA 1988 (§ 24-195 in the main work).

B. Threatening with Offensive Weapon In Public Place

(4) Sentence

24-190   As to a new consultation guideline on sentencing for offences involving bladed articles and offensive weapons, which covers the sentencing of offenders convicted of an offence contrary to section 1A(1) of the Prevention of Crime Act 1953 (§ 24-187 in the main work), see *ante*, § 5-178.

C. Having Article with Blade or Point In Public Place

Criminal Justice Act 1988, s.139

Sentence

24-197   As to a new consultation guideline on sentencing for offences involving bladed articles and offensive weapons, which covers the sentencing of offenders convicted of an offence contrary to section 139 of the 1988 Act (§ 24-195 in the main work), see *ante*, § 5-178.

D. Having Article with Blade or Point or Offensive Weapon on School Premises

Criminal Justice Act 1988, s.139A

Sentence

24-201   As to a new consultation guideline on sentencing for offences involving bladed articles and offensive weapons, which covers the sentencing of offenders convicted of an offence contrary to section 139A of the 1988 Act (§ 24-199 in the main work), see *ante*, § 5-178.

E. Threatening with Bladed or Pointed Article (in Public Place or on School Premises) or with Offensive Weapon (on School Premises)

Criminal Justice Act 1988, s.139AA

Sentence

24-204   As to a new consultation guideline on sentencing for offences involving bladed articles and offensive weapons, which covers the sentencing of offenders convicted of an offence contrary to section 139AA(1) of the 1988 Act (§ 24-203 in the main work), see *ante*, § 5-178.

Chapter 25

OFFENCES AGAINST THE CROWN AND GOVERNMENT

III. TERRORISM

A. Terrorism Act 2000

Terrorism Act 2000, s.1

Terrorism: interpretation

25-13   *R. v. Kahar; R. v. Ziamani; R. v. Eshati; R. v. Rashid; R. v. Ozcelik; R. v. Khan (Sana) (Practice*

Note) is now reported at [2016] 2 Cr.App.R.(S.) 32, *sub nom. Att.-Gen.'s Reference (R. v. Kahar)*; *R. v. Ziamani.*

Terrorism Act 2000, ss.11–13

Support

Under section 12(1) of the 2000 Act (support for proscribed organisation (see the main work)), **25-18** it is for the prosecution to show that (a) the organisation was proscribed, (b) the defendant used words that in fact invited support for that organisation, and (c) he knew at the time he did so that he was inviting such support; the words "invite" and "support" require no elaboration; the criminality lies in inviting support (from third parties) for the organisation, not in inviting those third parties to join with the defendant in providing it; the "support" in question may be practical or tangible, but it need not be; it can be "intellectual support", *i.e.* agreement with, and approval, approbation or endorsement of, that which is supported; but inviting support for a proscribed organisation is to be distinguished from a mere expression of personal beliefs, or an invitation to someone else to share an opinion or belief; (ii) in its ordinary meaning, section 12(1) is not uncertain or insufficiently precise; and, to the extent that it interferes with Article 9 (freedom of thought, conscience and religion (*ibid.*, § 16-153)) or 10 (freedom of expression (*ibid.*, § 16-157)) of the ECHR, that interference is fully justified; there is no "bright line" drawn, in the Strasbourg authorities, between speech that amounts to an incitement to violence and speech that does not: *R. v. Choudary*, unreported, March 22, 2016, CA ([2016] EWCA Crim. 61).

Terrorism Act 2000, ss.15–23B

With effect from March 1, 2017, Schedule 3A to the 2000 Act (see the main work) was further ★**25-26** amended by the Bank of England and Financial Services (Consequential Amendments) Regulations 2017 (S.I. 2017 No. 80).

Terrorism Act 2000, ss.47A–47AE

Effect of code

As from a day to be appointed, section 47AE(5) of the 2000 Act is amended by the Policing ★**25-58** and Crime Act 2017, s.45, and Sched. 12, para. 13, so as to omit the words "paragraph 15 of Schedule 4 to the Police Reform Act 2002 or".

Terrorism Act 2000, ss.54–58

Collection of information

R. v. G.; *R. v. J.* (as to which, see the main work) was considered in *R. v. Amjad* [2017] 1 **25-69** Cr.App.R 22, CA, in which it was held that, on a prosecution under section 58(1) of the 2000 Act (§ 25-68 in the main work), all the prosecution have to prove is that the information in question could be useful to a terrorist, and not that the information is true; and, for the purpose of proving that, where the material in question is innocuous on its face (here, a list of fitness exercises), it was open to the prosecution to put in evidence open source website material that consisted of very similar lists of exercises and that appeared on websites that were undoubtedly sympathetic to, or supportive of, terrorism, regardless of who the author of any such material was; the internet material was not being relied on to prove any facts; it was a question of perception; and, whilst there was no direct evidence to show that the appellant had ever visited any of the websites in question, the jury had been entitled to reject the suggestion that it was just coincidence that the exercise regimes in his possession were similar to those found on two websites that were supportive of terrorism.

Terrorism Act 2000, Sched. 2

With effect from December 9, 2016, the Proscribed Organisations (Name Change) Order 2016 **25-91** (S.I. 2016 No. 1187) provides that the name "Jabhat Fatah al-Sham", not being a name specified in Schedule 2 to the 2000 Act, is to be treated as an additional name for the organisation listed in that schedule as "Al-Qa'ida".

With effect from December 16, 2016, the Terrorism Act 2000 (Proscribed Organisations) (Amendment) (No.3) Order 2016 (S.I. 2016 No. 1238) added "National Action" to the list of proscribed organisations in Schedule 2 to the 2000 Act.

Terrorism Act 2000, Sched. 5

25-101   *Sher v. U.K.* is now reported at (2016) 63 E.H.R.R. 24.

Terrorism Act 2000, Sched. 8

25-139   In *Ibrahim v. U.K.*, *The Times*, December 19, 2016, the Grand Chamber of the European Court of Human Rights agreed with the aspects of the Court of Appeal and chamber decisions set out in the main work, and held that it was untenable to suggest that the giving of an incorrect caution (as to which, see the main work) had compelled the defendants to tell lies in their interviews. As to this case, see also *ante*, §§ 15-542, 15-553, 16-116.

Destruction and retention of fingerprints and samples etc.: United Kingdom

★**25-145b**   With effect from April 3, 2017 (Policing and Crime Act 2017 (Commencement No. 1 and Transitional Provisions) Regulations 2017 (S.I. 2017 No. 399)), paragraph 20B of Schedule 8 to the 2000 Act was amended by the Policing and Crime Act 2017, s.71(1) and (2), so as to insert a new sub-paragraph (2A), as follows—

> "(2A) In sub-paragraph (2) –
>> (a) the reference to a recordable offence includes an offence under the law of a country or territory outside the United Kingdom where the act constituting the offence would constitute—
>>> (i) a recordable offence under the law of England and Wales if done there, or
>>> (ii) a recordable offence under the law of Northern Ireland if done there,
>>> (and, in the application of sub-paragraph (2) where a person has previously been convicted, this applies whether or not the act constituted such an offence when the person was convicted);
>> (b) the reference to an offence in Scotland which is punishable by imprisonment includes an offence under the law of a country or territory outside the United Kingdom where the act constituting the offence would constitute an offence under the law of Scotland which is punishable by imprisonment if done there (and, in the application of sub-paragraph (2) where a person has previously been convicted, this applies whether or not the act constituted such an offence when the person was convicted).".

★**25-145c**   With effect from April 3, 2017 (Policing and Crime Act 2017 (Commencement No. 1 and Transitional Provisions) Regulations 2017 (S.I. 2017 No. 399)), paragraph 20C of Schedule 8 to the 2000 Act was amended by the Policing and Crime Act 2017, s.71(1) and (3), so as to insert a new sub-paragraph (2A) (in identical terms to the new para. (2A) of para. 20B (as to which, see *ante*, § 25-145b)).

★**25-145d**   With effect from April 3, 2017 (Policing and Crime Act 2017 (Commencement No. 1 and Transitional Provisions) Regulations 2017 (S.I. 2017 No. 399)), paragraph 20D of Schedule 8 to the 2000 Act was amended by the Policing and Crime Act 2017, s.71(1) and (4), so as to insert new sub-paragraphs (5A) and (5B), as follows—

> "(5A) For the purposes of sub-paragraph (4)–
>> (a) a person is to be treated as having previously been convicted in England and Wales of a recordable offence if –
>>> (i) the person has previously been convicted of an offence under the law of a country or territory outside the United Kingdom, and
>>> (ii) the act constituting the offence would constitute a recordable offence under the law of England and Wales if done there (whether or not it constituted such an offence when the person was convicted);
>> (b) a person is to be treated as having previously been convicted in Northern Ireland of a recordable offence if—
>>> (i) the person has previously been convicted of an offence under the law of a country or territory outside the United Kingdom, and
>>> (ii) the act constituting the offence would constitute a recordable offence under the law of Northern Ireland if done there (whether or not it constituted such an offence when the person was convicted);
>> (c) a person is to be treated as having previously been convicted in Scotland of an offence which is punishable by imprisonment if—
>>> (i) the person has previously been convicted of an offence under the law of a country or territory outside the United Kingdom, and
>>> (ii) the act constituting the offence would constitute an offence punishable by imprison-

ment under the law of Scotland if done there (whether or not it constituted such an offence when the person was convicted);

(d) the reference in sub-paragraph (4)(b) to a qualifying offence includes a reference to an offence under the law of a country or territory outside the United Kingdom where the act
constituting the offence would constitute a qualifying offence under the law of England
and Wales if done there or (as the case may be) under the law of Northern Ireland if done
there (whether or not it constituted such an offence when the person was convicted).

(5B) For the purposes of paragraphs 20B and 20C and this paragraph—

(a) offence, in relation to any country or territory outside the United Kingdom, includes an
act punishable under the law of that country or territory, however it is described;

(b) a person has in particular been convicted of an offence under the law of a country or territory outside the United Kingdom if—

(i) a court exercising jurisdiction under the law of that country or territory has made in
respect of such an offence a finding equivalent to a finding that the person is not
guilty by reason of insanity, or

(ii) such a court has made in respect of such an offence a finding equivalent to a finding
that the person is under a disability and did the act charged against the person in
respect of the offence.".

Sher v. U.K. is now reported at (2016) 63 E.H.R.R. 24.   **25-158**

C. Terrorism Act 2006

(2) Preparation of terrorist acts and training

Terrorism Act 2006, ss.5–8

R. v. Kahar; R. v. Ziamani; R. v. Eshati; R. v. Rashid; R. v. Ozcelik; R. v. Khan (Sana) (Practice   **25-192**
Note) is now reported at [2016] 2 Cr.App.R.(S.) 32, *sub nom. Att.-Gen.'s Reference (R. v. Kahar); R. v.
Ziamani.*

Sentence

In *R. v. Abdallah; R. v. Khan (Junead); R. v. Shaukat* [2017] 1 W.L.R. 1699, CA, it was said: (i)   **★25-192a**
the guidance on sentencing in *R. v. Kahar* (see the main work (and now reported at [2016] 2
Cr.App.R.(S.) 32, *sub nom. Att.-Gen.'s Reference (R. v. Kahar); R. v. Ziamani*) should continue to be
applied pending the issue of guidelines by the Sentencing Council, (ii) any argument that attempts to contrast the facts of another case with those of *Kahar*, as part of a submission that the
offending falls into a less serious category, is misconceived and should not be embarked on, and
(iii) the descriptions of the guideline levels in *Kahar* should not be applied mechanistically. As to
this case, see also *ante*, § 5-491.

F. Suppression of Terrorism Act 1978

Suppression of Terrorism Act 1978, s.8

Provisions as to interpretation and orders

To the list of orders set out in the main work should be added: the Suppression of Terrorism   **25-227**
Act 1978 (Designation of Countries) Order 2003 (S.I. 2003 No. 6) (Albania, Bulgaria, Estonia,
Georgia, Hungary, Latvia, Lithuania, Malta, Moldova, Poland, Romania, the Russian Federation,
San Marino, Slovenia and the Ukraine), and the Suppression of Terrorism Act 1978 (Designation
of Countries) (No. 2) Order 2003 (S.I. 2003 No. 1863) (Croatia and Serbia and Montenegro).

IV. IMMIGRATION

Immigration and Asylum Act 1999, s.31

Defences based on Article 31(1) of the Refugee Convention

On an appeal against conviction following a guilty plea to an offence for which the refugee   **25-285**
defence in section 31 of the Immigration and Asylum Act 1999 (§ 25-284 in the main work) is
available, the Court of Appeal will assess the prospects of the defence having been successfully
deployed where it is apparent that the appellant's legal representatives failed in their professional

duty to advise him as to the potential availability of the defence and its parameters; and, in doing so, it will have regard to any findings of the First-tier Tribunal (Immigration and Asylum Chamber); and, although the Crown could indicate their view as to the safety of the conviction, it was for the court alone to determine whether to allow the appeal; that would depend on whether the court concluded that the defence would "quite probably" have succeeded: *R. v. Zaredar* [2017] Crim.L.R. 57, CA (considering, *inter alia*, *R. v. Mateta*; *R. v. Ghavami and Afshar*; *R. v. Bashir*; *R. v. Andukwa* (as to which, see the main work)).

★   For a case considering *R. v. Asfaw (United Nations High Commr for Refugees intervening)*, *R. v. Mohamed (Abdalla)*; *R. v. V. (M.)*; *R. v. Mohamed (Rahma Abukar)*; *R. v. Nofallah*, and *R. v. Mateta*; *R. v. Ghavami and Afshar*; *R. v. Bashir*; *R. v. Andukwa* (as to all of which, see the main work), see *R. v. Ordu*, *ante*, § 7-171.

★   For the Supreme Court's decision in *S.X.H. v. CPS* (see the main work), see *S.X.H. v. CPS (United Nations High Commr for Refugees intervening)*, *ante*, § 22-49.

IX. DISCLOSURE, ETC., OF GOVERNMENT SECRETS

C. OFFICIAL SECRETS ACT 1989

Official Secrets Act 1989, s.1

Security and intelligence

25-357   An application by the claimant for permission to appeal from the decision of the civil division of the Court of Appeal in *R. (Bancoult) v. Secretary of State for Foreign and Commonwealth Affairs (No. 3)* (as to which, see the main work) has been allowed: see *R. (Bancoult) v. Secretary of State for Foreign and Commonwealth Affairs (No. 3)* [2016] 1 W.L.R. 3480, SC.

Official Secrets Act 1989, s.4

Crime and special investigation powers

25-360   As from a day to be appointed, section 4(3) of the 1989 Act is amended by the Investigatory Powers Act 2016, s.271(1), and Sched. 10, para. 37, so as to omit the word "and" at the end of paragraph (a), to insert the word "and" at the end of paragraph (b), and to insert a new paragraph (c), as follows—

> "(c) any information obtained under a warrant under Chapter 1 of Part 2 or Chapter 1 of Part 6 of the Investigatory Powers Act 2016, any information relating to the obtaining of information under such a warrant and any document or other article which is or has been used or held for use in, or has been obtained by reason of, the obtaining of information under such a warrant".

"Prescribed" bodies or persons

★**25-371**   As from a day to be appointed, the "Independent Police Complaints Commission" (see the main work) is to be renamed as the "Independent Office for Police Conduct": Policing and Crime Act 2017, s.33(1)(b).

XI. OFFENCES RELATING TO POSTS AND TELECOMMUNICATIONS

A. POSTAL SERVICES ACT 2000

Postal Services Act 2000, s.83

Interfering with the mail: postal operators

25-376   Where the Office of Communications served an information request on the claimant, an international door-to-door courier of goods, pursuant to its powers under section 55 of, and Schedule 8, para. 1, to, the Postal Services Act 2011, seeking information about the claimant's business on the basis that it was a "postal operator" within the meaning of section 27(3) of that Act ("(3) "Postal operator" means a person who provides— (a) the service of conveying postal packets from one place to another by post, or (b) any of the incidental services of receiving, collecting, sorting and delivering postal packets." (a definition adopted for the purposes of the 2000

Act by s.125(1) thereof)), and where the claimant sought judicial review of the decision to make the request on the ground that it was not a postal operator (arguing that there were five particular features of their business that distinguished it from a postal operator, *viz.* collection from customers' premises rather than delivery by customers to some form of collection point, the international conveyance of items, including by air, the requirement for full details of the consignor and items being consigned, and the absence of postage labels), the claimant was a postal operator within the meaning of section 27(3); for the purposes of the Act, collection from the sender's premises was part of the postal service and a parcel was treated as in course of transmission in the post from that moment; neither the features of the claimant's international courier business (including the fact that goods were carried by air), nor any of the other features of its service, individually or cumulatively, were inconsistent with the conclusion that the claimant was a postal operator; the regulator's request for information was not a nullity: *R. (DHL International (U.K.) Ltd) v. Office of Communications* [2016] 1 W.L.R. 4274, QBD (Soole J.).

C. Regulation of Investigatory Powers Act 2000

25-384 Chapters I and II of Part I of the 2000 Act (ss.1–25) (see the main work) are repealed and replaced as from a day to be appointed, as to which see *post*, §§ 25-386, 25-399.

As from a day to be appointed, section 49 of the 2000 Act (*ibid.*) is amended by the 2016 Act, s.271(1), and Sched. 10, paras 44, 46, 53 and 55.

As from a day to be appointed, section 71 of the 2000 Act (*ibid.*) is amended by the 2016 Act, s.271(1), and Sched. 10, paras 3, 5, 53, 56, 75 and 81.

As from a day to be appointed, section 83 of, and paragraph 18 of Schedule 4 to, the SCA 2015 (see the main work) are repealed by the 2016 Act, s.271(1) and Sched. 10, Pt 8.

As to the amendment of section 5 of the Intelligence Services Act 1994, see *ante*, § 15-286.

As from a day to be appointed, section 81 of the 2000 Act (*ibid.*) is amended by the 2016 Act, s.271(1), and Sched. 10, paras 3, 6, 53, 60, 75 and 83.

With effect from December 30, 2016 (S.I. 2016 No. 1233 (*post*, § 25-402b)), section 1 of the Data Retention and Investigatory Powers Act 2014 (see the main work) was repealed by the 2016 Act, s.271(1), and Sched. 10, para. 63. The Data Retention Regulations 2014 (S.I. 2014 No. 2042), which modified section 71 of the RIPA 2000 (reg. 15) (see the main work), no longer have effect because they are made under section 1 of the 2014 Act. However, the commencement of paragraph 5 of Schedule 9 to the 2016 Act (*post*, § 25-402b) saves regulation 15 of S.I. 2014 No. 2042 for a period of six months from December 30, 2016. It should be noted however, that the saving is subject to any further modification of regulations made under section 1 of the 2014 Act. Regulation 3 of S.I. 2016 No. 1233 modifies S.I. 2014 No. 2042 by omitting regulation 15(7), which effected the further modification of section 71 of the 2000 Act (as well as providing that reg. 15(5) is to have effect as if reg. 7 of those regulations continued to have effect).

As from a day to be appointed, section 102 of the Anti-terrorism, Crime and Security Act 2001 (*ibid.*) is repealed by the 2016 Act, s.271(1), and Sched. 10, para. 62.

As from a day to be appointed, section 72 of the 2000 Act (*ibid.*) is amended by the 2016 Act, s.271(1), and Sched. 10, paras 75 and 82.

As from a day to be appointed, the Regulation of Investigatory Powers (Monetary Penalty Notices and Consents for Interceptions) Regulations 2011 (S.I. 2011 No. 1340) (*ibid.*) are revoked by the 2016 Act, s.271(1), and Sched. 10, Pt 8.

Codes of practice

25-385 As to the repeal of Chapters I and II of Part I of the 2000 Act (ss.1–25) (see the main work), see *post*, §§ 25-386, 25-399; and as to the amendment of sections 71 and 72 of the 2000 Act, see *ante*, § 25-384.

Compatibility with ECHR

25-385a For a decision of the Grand Chamber of the European Court of Human Rights approving the approach taken in *Kennedy v. U.K.* (see the main work), see *ante*, § 16-148.

Regulation of Investigatory Powers Act 2000, ss.1–5

Unlawful interception

25-386 As from a day to be appointed, Chapter I of Part I of the 2000 Act (ss.1–20) (see the main work *et seq.*) is repealed by the Investigatory Powers Act 2016, s.271(1), and Sched. 10, paras 44 and 45.

As to the revocation of the Regulation of Investigatory Powers (Monetary Penalty Notices and Consents for Interceptions) Regulations 2011 (S.I. 2011 No. 1340) (see the main work), see *ante*, § 25-384.

Meaning and location of "interception" etc.

25-387   As to the repeal of section 2 of the 2000 Act (see the main work), see *ante*, § 25-386. As from a day to be appointed, section 5 of the Data Retention and Investigatory Powers Act 2014 (*ibid.*) is repealed by the Investigatory Powers Act 2016, s.271(1), and Sched. 10, Pt 8.

As to the amendments to the 2000 Act made by sections 3 to 6 of the 2014 Act, the effect of paragraph 9 of Schedule 9 to the 2016 Act should be noted. Section 270(1) gives effect to Schedule 9, and paragraph 9 (into force on December 30, 2016 (*post*, § 25-402b)) provides that the amendments to the 2000 Act effected by sections 3 to 6 of the 2014 Act (and those sections) continue to have effect despite section 8(3) of the Act of 2014 (sunset provision for that Act) until the provisions they amend (and those sections) are repealed by the 2016 Act in connection with the coming into force of provisions of the 2016 Act.

As from a day to be appointed, section 8 of the 2014 Act (*ibid.*) is repealed by the 2016 Act, s.271(1), and Sched. 10, para. 34.

Lawful interception without an interception warrant

25-388   As to the repeal of section 3 of the 2000 Act (see the main work), see *ante*, § 25-386.

As from a day to be appointed, section 100 of the Policing and Crime Act 2009, and paragraph 2 of Schedule 8 to the Counter-Terrorism and Security Act 2015 (see the main work) are repealed by the Investigatory Powers Act 2016, s. 271(1), and Sched. 10, Pt 8.

As to the revocation of the Regulation of Investigatory Powers (Monetary Penalty Notices and Consents for Interceptions) Regulations 2011 (S.I. 2011 No. 1340) (see the main work), see *ante*, § 25-384.

Power to provide for lawful interception

25-389   As to the repeal of sections 1 and 4 of the 2000 Act (see the main work), see *ante*, § 25-386.

As from a day to be appointed, paragraph 208 of Schedule 1 to the National Health Service (Consequential Provisions) Act 2006, and paragraph 98 of Schedule 5 to the Health and Social Care Act 2012 (see the main work) are repealed by the Investigatory Powers Act 2016, s.271(1), and Sched. 10, Pt 8.

Interception with a warrant

25-390   As to the repeal of section 5 of the 2000 Act (see the main work), see *ante*, § 25-386.

As to the repeal of section 8 of the Data Retention and Investigatory Powers Act 2014 (see the main work), see *ante*, § 25-387.

As from a day to be appointed, section 3(1) and (2) of the 2014 Act (see the main work) are repealed by the Investigatory Powers Act 2016, s.271(1), and Sched. 10, Pt 8. As to section 3 of the 2014 Act, note the effect of the transitional provision in paragraph 9 of Schedule 9 to the 2016 Act, *ante*, § 25-387.

Interception warrants

25-391   As to the repeal of sections 6 to 11 of the 2000 Act (see the main work), see *ante*, § 25-386.

As from a day to be appointed, section 32 of the Terrorism Act 2006, paragraph 6 of Schedule 12 to the SCA 2007, and paragraph 78 of Schedule 8 to the Crime and Courts Act 2013 (see the main work) are repealed by the Investigatory Powers Act 2016, s.271(1), and Sched. 10, Pt 8.

Regulation of Investigatory Powers Act 2000, s.11

Implementation of warrants

25-392   As to the repeal of section 11 of the 2000 Act (see the main work), see *ante*, § 25-386.

As from a day to be appointed, sections 4(1) and 8 of the Data Retention and Investigatory Powers Act 2014 (see the main work) are repealed by the Investigatory Powers Act 2016, s.271(1), and Sched. 10, para. 34.

As from a day to be appointed, section 4(2) to (4) of the 2014 Act (see the main work) are repealed by the 2016 Act, s.271(1), and Sched. 10, Pt 8.

As to section 4 of the 2014 Act, note the effect of the transitional provision in paragraph 9 of Schedule 9 to the 2016 Act, *ante,* § 25-387.

Regulation of Investigatory Powers Act 2000, ss.15–19

General safeguards

As to the repeal of section 15 of the 2000 Act (see the main work), see *ante,* § 25-386. **25-393**

Extra safeguards in the case of certificated warrants

As to the repeal of section 16 of the 2000 Act (see the main work), see *ante,* § 25-386; and as to **25-394** the repeal of section 32 of the Terrorism Act 2006 (*ibid.*), see *ante,* § 25-391.

Exclusion of matters from legal proceedings

As to the repeal of sections 1, 3 to 5 and 17 of the 2000 Act (see the main work), see *ante,* § **25-395** 25-386.

As from a day to be appointed, paragraph 20 of Schedule 2 to the Inquiries Act 2005, and section 100 of the Policing and Crime Act 2009 (see the main work), are repealed by the Investigatory Powers Act 2016, s.271(1), and Sched. 10, Pt 8.

Exceptions to section 17

As to the repeal of section 18 of the 2000 Act (see the main work), see *ante,* § 25-386. **25-396**

As from a day to be appointed, paragraph 21 of Schedule 2 to the Inquiries Act 2005, paragraph 169 of Schedule 16 to the AFA 2006, sections 69 and 74 of the Counter-Terrorism Act 2008, section 28 of the Terrorist Asset-Freezing etc. Act 2010, paragraph 4 of Schedule 7 to the Terrorism Prevention and Investigation Measures Act 2011, section 16 of, and paragraph 11 of Schedule 2 to, the Justice and Security Act 2013, and section 15 of the Counter-Terrorism and Security Act 2015 (see the main work) are repealed by the Investigatory Powers Act 2016, s.271(1), and Sched. 10, Pt 8.

Offence of unauthorised disclosures

As to the repeal of section 19 of the 2000 Act (see the main work), see *ante,* § 25-386. **25-397**

Regulation of Investigatory Powers Act 2000, s.20

Interpretation of Chapter 1

As to the repeal of section 20 of the 2000 Act (see the main work), see *ante,* § 25-386. **25-398**

Regulation of Investigatory Powers Act 2000, ss.21–23B

Lawful acquisition and disclosure of communications data

As from a day to be appointed, Chapter 2 of Part 1 of the 2000 Act (ss.21–25) (see the main **25-399** work *et seq.*) is repealed by the Investigatory Powers Act 2016, s.271(1), and Sched. 10, paras 53 and 54.

As from a day to be appointed, paragraph 7 of Schedule 12 to the SCA 2007 (see the main work) is repealed by the 2016 Act, s.271(1), and Sched. 10, Pt 8.

Obtaining and disclosing communications data

As to the repeal of section 22 of the 2000 Act (see the main work), see *ante,* § 25-399. **25-400**

As from a day to be appointed, section 7 of, and paragraph 13 of Schedule 7 to, the Policing and Crime Act 2009, paragraph 7 of Schedule 9 to the Protection of Freedoms Act 2012, and sections 3(3) and (4) and 4(8) and (9) of the Data Retention and Investigatory Powers Act 2014 (*ibid.*) are repealed, and the relevant part of S.I. 2013 No. 602 (*ibid.*) is revoked, by the Investigatory Powers Act 2016, s.271(1), and Sched. 10, Pt 8.

As from a day to be appointed, sections 4(1) and 8 of the 2014 Act (*ibid.*) are repealed by the 2016 Act, s.271(1), and Sched. 10, para. 34.

As to section 4 of the 2014 Act, note the effect of the transitional provision in paragraph 9 of Schedule 9 to the 2016 Act, *ante,* § 25-387.

R. (Davis) v. Secretary of State for the Home Department (Open Rights Group intervening) is now reported at [2017] 1 All E.R. 62, *sub nom. R. (Davis M.P.) v. Secretary of State for the Home Department (Open Rights Group intervening) (Note).*

The questions (set out in the main work) that were referred to the Court of Justice in the European Union in *R. (Davis M.P.) v. Secretary of State for the Home Department (Open Rights Group intervening) (Note)*, *ante*, were considered by that court, together with questions referred to it by a court in Sweden, in *Tele2 Sverige AB v. Post-och telestyrelsen*; *R. (Watson) v. Secretary of State for the Home Department (Open Rights Group intervening)*; *R. (Brice) v. Same (Same intervening)*; *R. (Lewis) v. Same (Same intervening) (Joined Cases C-203/15 and C-698/15)* [2017] 2 W.L.R. 1289, ECJ (Grand Chamber). It was held (considering *Digital Rights Ireland Ltd* (as to which, see the main work)): (i) European Union law precludes national legislation (a) that, for the purpose of fighting crime, provides for general and indiscriminate retention of all traffic and location data of all subscribers and registered users relating to all means of electronic communication, and (b) governing access of the competent national authorities to the retained data, where the objective pursued by that access, in the context of fighting crime, is not restricted solely to fighting serious crime (although access to data of individuals not themselves suspected of being implicated may also be granted in particular situations), where access is not subject to prior review by a court or an independent administrative authority (except in cases of validly established urgency), where persons affected are not notified as soon as notification is no longer liable to jeopardise investigations being undertaken by authorities, and where the integrity and confidentiality of that data is not guaranteed by a high level of protection and security, particularly where there is no requirement that the data concerned should be retained within the European Union; national legislation must lay down clear and precise rules governing the scope and application of such measures and imposing minimum safeguards, based on objective criteria; and accordingly (ii), section 1 of the Data Retention and Investigatory Powers Act 2014 (as to which, see the main work) was unlawful as failing to comply with (i)(b), *ante*.

Whilst section 1 of the 2014 Act was repealed with effect from December 30, 2016 (*ante*, § 25-384), by the Investigatory Powers Act 2016, s.271(1), and Sched. 10, para. 63, this decision has obvious relevance to the transitional provisions in the 2016 Act, Sched. 9, paras 3 to 5, which preserve the effect of things done under section 1 of the 2014 Act during the transitional period (or purport to do so); and it has potential relevance to Part 4 of the 2016 Act, which replaces section 1.

Form and duration of authorisations and notices

25-401   As to the repeal of section 23 of the 2000 Act (see the main work), see *ante*, § 25-399.

As from a day to be appointed, section 7 of, and paragraph 14 of Schedule 7 to, the Policing and Crime Act 2009, and paragraph 8 of Schedule 9 to the Protection of Freedoms Act 2012 (*ibid.*) are repealed, and the relevant part of S.I. 2013 No. 602 (*ibid.*) is revoked, by the Investigatory Powers Act 2016, s.271(1), and Sched. 10, Pt 8.

Authorisations requiring judicial approval

25-401a   As to the repeal of section 23A of the 2000 Act (see the main work), see *ante*, § 25-399.

As from a day to be appointed, the relevant part of S.I. 2013 No. 602 (see the main work) is revoked by the Investigatory Powers Act, s.271(1), and Sched. 10, Pt 8.

Procedure for judicial approval

25-401b   As to the repeal of section 23B of the 2000 Act (see the main work), see *ante*, § 25-399.

As from a day to be appointed, section 37 of the Protection of Freedoms Act 2012 (*ibid.*) is repealed by the Investigatory Powers Act 2016, s.271(1), and Sched. 10, Pt 8.

Criminal Procedure Rules 2015 (S.I. 2015 No. 1490), rr.47.50–47.52 (as substituted by the Criminal Procedure (Amendment) Rules 2016 (S.I. 2016 No. 120), r.15)

When this Section applies

★**25-401c**   Rule 47.50 of the Criminal Procedure Rules 2015 (S.I. 2015 No. 1490) has been renumbered as rule 47.51: Criminal Procedure (Amendment) Rules 2017 (S.I. 2017 No. 144), r.11.

Exercise of court's powers

★**25-401d**   Rules 47.51 of the Criminal Procedure Rules 2015 (S.I. 2015 No. 1490) has been renumbered as rule 47.52: Criminal Procedure (Amendment) Rules 2017 (S.I. 2017 No. 144), r.11.

Application for approval for authorisation or notice

★**25-401e**   Rule 47.52 of the Criminal Procedure Rules 2015 (S.I. 2015 No. 1490) has been renumbered as rule 47.53: Criminal Procedure (Amendment) Rules 2017 (S.I. 2017 No. 144), r.11.

As to the repeal of sections 23A and 23B of the 2000 Act (see the main work), see *ante*, § 25-399.

Interpretation of Part II

As to the repeal of section 25 of the 2000 Act (see the main work), see *ante*, § 25-399.

As from a day to be appointed, paragraph 135 of Schedule 4 to the SOCPA 2005, paragraph 8 of Schedule 12 to the SCA 2007, and paragraph 81 of Schedule 8 to the Crime and Courts Act 2013, are repealed, and the relevant parts of S.I. 2007 No. 1098 and S.I. 2013 No. 602 (*ibid.*) are revoked, by the Investigatory Powers Act 2016, s.271(1), and Sched. 10, Pt 8.

D. Investigatory Powers Act 2016

Introduction

The Investigatory Powers Act 2016 received Royal Assent on November 29, 2016. The long title   **25-402a**
proclaims it to be an Act to make provision "about the interception of communications, equipment interference and the acquisition and retention of communications data, bulk personal datasets and other information; ... about the treatment of material held as a result of such interception, equipment interference or acquisition or retention; to establish the Investigatory Powers Commissioner and other Judicial Commissioners and make provision about them and other oversight arrangements; to make further provision about investigatory powers and national security; to amend ... the Intelligence Services Act 1994; and for connected purposes." There are 272 sections (in nine parts) and 10 schedules.

Part 1 (ss.1–14) imposes certain duties in relation to privacy and contains other protections for privacy. Section 3 makes it an either-way offence intentionally to intercept a communication in the course of its transmission by means of a public telecommunication system, a private telecommunication system, or a public postal service (those terms being defined in ss.261 and 262), where the interception is carried out in the United Kingdom, and the person does not have lawful authority (as to which, see s.6) to carry out the interception. Section 4(1) makes provision as to what constitutes interception of a communication in the course of its transmission by means of a telecommunication system. Section 5 sets out conduct that does not constitute interception for the purposes of the Act. Section 6 sets out the circumstances in which a person has lawful authority to carry out an interception. Under section 11, a relevant person (a person who holds an office, rank or position with a relevant public authority (within the meaning of Pt 3)) who, without lawful authority, knowingly or recklessly obtains communications data from a telecommunications operator or a postal operator is guilty of an either-way offence.

Part 2 (ss.15–60) relates to the lawful interception of communications. In particular, section 56 provides that subject to the exceptions provided for in Schedule 3, no evidence may be adduced, question asked, assertion or disclosure made, or other thing done in, for the purposes of, or in connection with, any legal proceedings or proceedings under the Inquiries Act 2005 that (in any manner) discloses, in circumstances from which its origin in interception-related conduct (as to which, see subss. (2)–(4)) may be inferred, any content of an intercepted communication, or any secondary data obtained from a communication (subs. (1)(a)), or tends to suggest that any interception-related conduct has or may have occurred or may be going to occur (subs. (1)(b)). The exceptions in Schedule 3 include disclosures of certain lawfully intercepted communications (para. 2), disclosures of convictions for certain offences (s.56(1)(b) does not prohibit the doing of anything that discloses any conduct of a person for which that person has been convicted of specified offences under this Act, the RIPA 2000 or the Interception of Communications Act 1985 (para. 3)), specified proceedings including the prosecution of certain offences (para. 20), and disclosures to prosecutors and judges (para. 21).

Part 3 (ss.61–86) makes provision for obtaining communications data, and Part 4 (ss.87–98) for the retention of such data. Part 5 (ss.99–135) provides for equipment interference. Part 6 (ss.136–198) provides for bulk warrants, and section 156 applies section 56 (and Sched. 3) in relation to such warrants.

In Part 7 (bulk personal data set warrants (ss.199–226)), section 199 provides that, for the purposes of Part 7, an intelligence service retains a bulk personal dataset if it obtains a set of information that includes personal data (defined in sub. (2)) relating to a number of individuals, the nature of the set is such that the majority of the individuals are not, and are unlikely to become, of interest to the intelligence service in the exercise of its functions, after any initial examination of the contents, the intelligence service retains the set for the purpose of the exercise of its functions, and the set is held, or is to be held, electronically for analysis in the exercise of those functions. Under section 200, an intelligence service may not exercise a power to retain (subs. (1)) or examine (subs. (2)) a bulk personal dataset unless the retention thereof is authorised by a warrant under Part 7, of which there are two kinds, *viz.* a "class BPD warrant" and a "specific BPD warrant" (subs. (3)), or unless one of the exceptions in section 201 applies.

Part 8 (ss.227-247) provides for oversight arrangements. Part 9 (ss.248-272) contains miscellaneous and general provisions.

Commencement

25-402b
Section 272(1) provides for commencement of the Act (ss.260 to 269, 270(2), 271(2) to (4) and 272, Royal Assent: s.272(2); ss.227 and 228, January 29, 2017: s.272(3); otherwise on a date to be appointed).

The Investigatory Powers Act 2016 (Commencement No. 1 and Transitional Provisions) Regulations 2016 (S.I. 2016 No. 1233) brought into force on December 30, 2016, sections 2 (general duties in relation to privacy (so far as it applies to Pt 4 (retention of communications data))), 61(7)(a) to (j) (purposes for which communications data may be obtained (for the purpose of the operation of ss.87 (powers to require retention of certain data) and 94 (variation or revocation of notices))), 87 (except subs. (1)(b)), 88 (matters to be taken into account before giving retention notices), 90(13) (duty to keep retention notice under review), 92 (data integrity and security), 93 (disclosure of retained data), 94(1) to (3), (4)(a), (5), (7), (8) (except in so far as it applies to s.94(4)(b)), (9), (11) (so far as it applies to s.90(13)), and (13) to (16), 95 (enforcement of notices and certain other requirements and restrictions), 97 (extra-territorial application of Pt 4), 98 (Pt 4: interpretation), 244 (oversight by Information Commissioner in relation to Pt 4), and 249 (payments towards certain compliance costs (for the purposes of the payment of a contribution in respect of costs incurred, or likely to be incurred, in complying with Pt 4 and the purposes of para. 3 of Sched. 9 (transitional, transitory and saving provision) only)), and Schedule 9, paras 3 to 5, 8 and 9 (and s.270(1) so far as it relates to those paragraphs), and Schedule 10 (minor and consequential provisions), para. 63, and, in Part 8, the repeals relating to the Counter-Terrorism and Security Act 2015, ss.21 and 52(3)(a) (and s.271(1) so far as it relates to those provisions of Sched. 10). Regulation 3 provides for regulation 15 of the Data Retention Regulations 2014 (S.I. 2014 No. 2042), in its continued operation by virtue of paragraph 5(1) of Schedule 9 to the 2016 Act, to have effect with specified modifications.

★   With effect from February 13, 2017 (Investigatory Powers Act 2016 (Commencement No. 2 and Transitory Provision) Regulations 2017 (S.I. 2017 No. 137)), sections 1, 227, 228, 229(6) and (7), 229(9) (the definition of "police force", and s.60(1) for the purpose of that definition), 230, 232, 233(1), 234(1), (2)(g) to (i) and (3) to (9), 235(1) to (4) and (7), 237, 238 (other than subs. (6)(b) and (c)), 239, 241, 246, 247, 250, 251, and 253(3) to (6) of, and Schedule 7 to, the 2016 Act (as to which, see *ante* § 25-402a) came into force.

Investigatory Powers Act 2016, ss.1–6

Part 1

General Privacy Protections

Overview and general privacy duties

[Overview of Act
25-402c
1.–(1) This Act sets out the extent to which certain investigatory powers may be used to interfere with privacy.

(2) This Part imposes certain duties in relation to privacy and contains other protections for privacy.

(3) These other protections include offences and penalties in relation to—

    (a) the unlawful interception of communications, and

    (b) the unlawful obtaining of communications data.

(4) This Part also abolishes and restricts various general powers to obtain communications data and restricts the circumstances in which equipment interference, and certain requests about the interception of communications, can take place.

(5) Further protections for privacy—

    (a) can be found, in particular, in the regimes provided for by Parts 2 to 7 and in the oversight arrangements in Part 8, and

    (b) also exist—

       (i) by virtue of the Human Rights Act 1998,

      (ii) in section 55 of the Data Protection Act 1998 (unlawful obtaining etc. of personal data),

     (iii) in section 48 of the Wireless Telegraphy Act 2006 (offence of interception or disclosure of messages),

     (iv) in sections 1 to 3A of the Computer Misuse Act 1990 (computer misuse offences),

      (v) in the common law offence of misconduct in public office, and

     (vi) elsewhere in the law.

(6) The regimes provided for by Parts 2 to 7 are as follows—

    (a) Part 2 and Chapter 1 of Part 6 set out circumstances (including under a warrant) in which the interception of communications is lawful and make further provision about the interception of communications and the treatment of material obtained in connection with it,

    (b) Part 3 and Chapter 2 of Part 6 set out circumstances in which the obtaining of communications data is lawful in pursuance of an authorisation or under a warrant and make further provision about the obtaining and treatment of such data,

    (c) Part 4 makes provision for the retention of certain communications data in pursuance of a notice,

    (d) Part 5 and Chapter 3 of Part 6 deal with equipment interference warrants, and

    (e) Part 7 deals with bulk personal dataset warrants.

(7) As to the rest of the Act—

    (a) Part 8 deals with oversight arrangements for regimes in this Act and elsewhere, and

    (b) Part 9 contains miscellaneous and general provisions including amendments to sections 3 and 5 of the Intelligence Services Act 1994 and provisions about national security and combined warrants and authorisations.]

As to commencement, see *ante*, § 25-402b.

General duties in relation to privacy

2.—(1) Subsection (2) applies where a public authority is deciding whether—   **25-402d**

    (a) to issue, renew or cancel a warrant under Part 2, 5, 6 or 7,

    (b) to modify such a warrant,

    (c) to approve a decision to issue, renew or modify such a warrant,

    (d) to grant, approve or cancel an authorisation under Part 3,

    (e) to give a notice in pursuance of such an authorisation or under Part 4 or section 252, 253 or 257,

    (f) to vary or revoke such a notice,

    (g) to approve a decision to give or vary a notice under Part 4 or section 252, 253 or 257,

    (h) to approve the use of criteria under section 153, 194 or 222,

    (i) to give an authorisation under section 219(3)(b),

    (j) to approve a decision to give such an authorisation, or

    (k) to apply for or otherwise seek any issue, grant, giving, modification, variation or renewal of a kind falling within paragraph (a), (b), (d), (e), (f) or (i).

(2) The public authority must have regard to—

    (a) whether what is sought to be achieved by the warrant, authorisation or notice could reasonably be achieved by other less intrusive means,

    (b) whether the level of protection to be applied in relation to any obtaining of information by virtue of the warrant, authorisation or notice is higher because of the particular sensitivity of that information,

    (c) the public interest in the integrity and security of telecommunication systems and postal services, and

(d) any other aspects of the public interest in the protection of privacy.

(3) The duties under subsection (2)-

(a) apply so far as they are relevant in the particular context, and

(b) are subject to the need to have regard to other considerations that are also relevant in that context.

(4) The other considerations may, in particular, include–

(a) the interests of national security or of the economic well-being of the United Kingdom,

(b) the public interest in preventing or detecting serious crime,

(c) other considerations which are relevant to–

(i) whether the conduct authorised or required by the warrant, authorisation or notice is proportionate, or

(ii) whether it is necessary to act for a purpose provided for by this Act,

(d) the requirements of the Human Rights Act 1998, and

(e) other requirements of public law.

(5) For the purposes of subsection (2)(b), examples of sensitive information include–

(a) items subject to legal privilege,

(b) any information identifying or confirming a source of journalistic information, and

(c) relevant confidential information within the meaning given by paragraph 2(4) of Schedule 7 (certain information held in confidence and consisting of personal records, journalistic material or communications between Members of Parliament and their constituents).

(6) In this section "public authority" includes the relevant judicial authority (within the meaning of section 75) where the relevant judicial authority is deciding whether to approve under that section an authorisation under Part 3.

As to the limited commencement of this section, see *ante*, § 25-402b.

Prohibitions against unlawful interception

[*Offence of unlawful interception*

25-402e   **3.**–(1) A person commits an offence if–

(a) the person intentionally intercepts a communication in the course of its transmission by means of–

(i) a public telecommunication system,

(ii) a private telecommunication system, or

(iii) a public postal service,

(b) the interception is carried out in the United Kingdom, and

(c) the person does not have lawful authority to carry out the interception.

(2) But it is not an offence under subsection (1) for a person to intercept a communication in the course of its transmission by means of a private telecommunication system if the person–

(a) is a person with a right to control the operation or use of the system, or

(b) has the express or implied consent of such a person to carry out the interception.

(3) Sections 4 and 5 contain provision about–

(a) the meaning of "interception", and

(b) when interception is to be regarded as carried out in the United Kingdom.

(4) Section 6 contains provision about when a person has lawful authority to carry out an interception.

(5) For the meaning of the terms used in subsection (1)(a)(i) to (iii), see sections 261 and 262.

(6) A person who is guilty of an offence under subsection (1) is liable–

(a) on summary conviction in England and Wales, to a fine;

(b) [*Scotland, Northern Ireland*];

(c) on conviction on indictment, to imprisonment for a term not exceeding 2 years or to a fine, or to both.

(7) No proceedings for any offence which is an offence by virtue of this section may be instituted–

(a) in England and Wales, except by or with the consent of the Director of Public Prosecutions;

(b) [*Northern Ireland*].]

As to commencement, see *ante*, § 25-402b.

As to sections 261 and 262, see *post*, §§ 25-402l, 25-402m.

[*Definition of "interception" etc.*

4.– *Interception in relation to telecommunication systems*

(1) For the purposes of this Act, a person intercepts a communication in the course of its transmis-   **25-402f**
sion by means of a telecommunication system if, and only if—

  (a) the person does a relevant act in relation to the system, and

  (b) the effect of the relevant act is to make any content of the communication available, at a
       relevant time, to a person who is not the sender or intended recipient of the communication.

For the meaning of "content" in relation to a communication, see section 261(6).

(2) In this section "relevant act", in relation to a telecommunication system, means—

  (a) modifying, or interfering with, the system or its operation;

  (b) monitoring transmissions made by means of the system;

  (c) monitoring transmissions made by wireless telegraphy to or from apparatus that is part of
       the system.

(3) For the purposes of this section references to modifying a telecommunication system include
references to attaching any apparatus to, or otherwise modifying or interfering with—

  (a) any part of the system, or

  (b) any wireless telegraphy apparatus used for making transmissions to or from apparatus that
       is part of the system.

(4) In this section "relevant time", in relation to a communication transmitted by means of a
telecommunication system, means—

  (a) any time while the communication is being transmitted, and

  (b) any time when the communication is stored in or by the system (whether before or after its
       transmission).

(5) For the purposes of this section, the cases in which any content of a communication is to be
taken to be made available to a person at a relevant time include any case in which any of the communication is diverted or recorded at a relevant time so as to make any content of the communication
available to a person after that time.

(6) In this section "wireless telegraphy" and "wireless telegraphy apparatus" have the same meaning as in the Wireless Telegraphy Act 2006 (see sections 116 and 117 of that Act).

Interception in relation to postal services

(7) Section 125(3) of the Postal Services Act 2000 applies for the purposes of determining for the
purposes of this Act whether a postal item is in the course of its transmission by means of a postal
service as it applies for the purposes of determining for the purposes of that Act whether a postal
packet is in course of transmission by post.

Interception carried out in the United Kingdom

(8) For the purposes of this Act the interception of a communication is carried out in the United
Kingdom if, and only if—

  (a) the relevant act or, in the case of a postal item, the interception is carried out by conduct
       within the United Kingdom, and

  (b) the communication is intercepted—

      (i)   in the course of its transmission by means of a public telecommunication system or a
            public postal service, or

      (ii) in the course of its transmission by means of a private telecommunication system in a
            case where the sender or intended recipient of the communication is in the United
            Kingdom.]

As to commencement, see *ante*, § 25-402b.

As to section 261, see *post*, § 25-402l.

[Conduct that is not interception

5.—(1) References in this Act to the interception of a communication do not include references to   **25-402g**
the interception of any communication broadcast for general reception.

(2) References in this Act to the interception of a communication in the course of its transmission
by means of a postal service do not include references to—

  (a) any conduct that takes place in relation only to so much of the communication as consists
       of any postal data comprised in, included as part of, attached to, or logically associated with
       a communication (whether by the sender or otherwise) for the purposes of any postal
       service by means of which it is being or may be transmitted, or

  (b) any conduct, in connection with conduct falling within paragraph (a), that gives a person
       who is neither the sender nor the intended recipient only so much access to a communica-
       tion as is necessary for the purpose of identifying such postal data.

       For the meaning of "postal data", see section 262.]

As to commencement, see *ante*, § 25-402b.

As to section 262, see *post*, § 25-402m.

[Definition of "lawful authority"

25-402h   6.–(1) For the purposes of this Act, a person has lawful authority to carry out an interception if, and only if–

    (a) the interception is carried out in accordance with–

        (i) a targeted interception warrant or mutual assistance warrant under Chapter 1 of Part 2, or

        (ii) a bulk interception warrant under Chapter 1 of Part 6,

    (b) the interception is authorised by any of sections 44 to 52, or

    (c) in the case of a communication stored in or by a telecommunication system, the interception–

        (i) is carried out in accordance with a targeted equipment interference warrant under Part 5 or a bulk equipment interference warrant under Chapter 3 of Part 6,

        (ii) is in the exercise of any statutory power that is exercised for the purpose of obtaining information or taking possession of any document or other property, or

        (iii) is carried out in accordance with a court order made for that purpose.

    (2) Conduct which has lawful authority for the purposes of this Act by virtue of subsection (1)(a) or (b) is to be treated as lawful for all other purposes.

    (3) Any other conduct which–

    (a) is carried out in accordance with a warrant under Chapter 1 of Part 2 or a bulk interception warrant, or

    (b) is authorised by any of sections 44 to 52,

is to be treated as lawful for all purposes.]

As to commencement, see *ante*, § 25-402b.

Investigatory Powers Act 2016, s.11

Prohibition against unlawful obtaining of communications data

[Offence of unlawfully obtaining communications data

25-402i   11.–(1) A relevant person who, without lawful authority, knowingly or recklessly obtains communications data from a telecommunications operator or a postal operator is guilty of an offence.

    (2) In this section "relevant person" means a person who holds an office, rank or position with a relevant public authority (within the meaning of Part 3).

    (3) Subsection (1) does not apply to a relevant person who shows that the person acted in the reasonable belief that the person had lawful authority to obtain the communications data.

    (4) A person guilty of an offence under this section is liable–

    (a) on summary conviction in England and Wales–

        (i) to imprisonment for a term not exceeding 12 months (or 6 months, if the offence was committed before the commencement of section 154(1) of the Criminal Justice Act 2003), or

        (ii) to a fine,

        or to both;

    (b) [*Scotland*];

    (c) [*Northern Ireland*].]

As to commencement, see *ante*, § 25-402b.

As to section 154 of the CJA 2003, see § 5-441 in the main work.

Investigatory Powers Act 2016, s.56

[Exclusion of matters from legal proceedings etc.

25-402j   56.–(1) No evidence may be adduced, question asked, assertion or disclosure made or other thing done in, for the purposes of or in connection with any legal proceedings or Inquiries Act proceedings which (in any manner)–

    (a) discloses, in circumstances from which its origin in interception-related conduct may be inferred–

        (i) any content of an intercepted communication, or

        (ii) any secondary data obtained from a communication, or

    (b) tends to suggest that any interception-related conduct has or may have occurred or may be going to occur.

    This is subject to Schedule 3 (exceptions).

(2) "Interception-related conduct" means—

    (a) conduct by a person within subsection (3) that is, or in the absence of any lawful authority would be, an offence under section 3(1) (offence of unlawful interception);

    (b) a breach of the prohibition imposed by section 9 (restriction on requesting interception by overseas authorities);

    (c) a breach of the prohibition imposed by section 10 (restriction on requesting assistance under mutual assistance agreements etc.);

    (d) the making of an application by any person for a warrant, or the issue of a warrant, under Chapter 1 of this Part;

    (e) the imposition of any requirement on any person to provide assistance in giving effect to a targeted interception warrant or mutual assistance warrant.

(3) The persons referred to in subsection (2)(a) are—

    (a) any person who is an intercepting authority (see section 18);

    (b) any person holding office under the Crown;

    (c) any person deemed to be the proper officer of Revenue and Customs by virtue of section 8(2) of the Customs and Excise Management Act 1979;

    (d) any person employed by, or for the purposes of, a police force;

    (e) any postal operator or telecommunications operator;

    (f) any person employed or engaged for the purposes of the business of a postal operator or telecommunications operator.

(4) Any reference in subsection (1) to interception-related conduct also includes any conduct taking place before the coming into force of this section and consisting of—

    (a) conduct by a person within subsection (3) that—

        (i) was an offence under section 1(1) or (2) of the Regulation of Investigatory Powers Act 2000 ("RIPA"), or

        (ii) would have been such an offence in the absence of any lawful authority (within the meaning of section 1(5) of RIPA);

    (b) conduct by a person within subsection (3) that—

        (i) was an offence under section 1 of the Interception of Communications Act 1985, or

        (ii) would have been such an offence in the absence of subsections (2) and (3) of that section;

    (c) a breach by the Secretary of State of the duty under section 1(4) of RIPA (restriction on requesting assistance under mutual assistance agreements);

    (d) the making of an application by any person for a warrant, or the issue of a warrant, under—

        (i) Chapter 1 of Part 1 of RIPA, or

        (ii) the Interception of Communications Act 1985;

    (e) the imposition of any requirement on any person to provide assistance in giving effect to a warrant under Chapter 1 of Part 1 of RIPA.

(5) In this section—

    "Inquiries Act proceedings" means proceedings of an inquiry under the Inquiries Act 2005;

    "intercepted communication" means any communication intercepted in the course of its transmission by means of a postal service or telecommunication system.]

As to commencement, see *ante*, § 25-402b.

Section 156(1) stipulates that section 56 and Schedule 3 (*post*, §§ 25-402n *et seq.*) apply in rela- **25-402k** tion to bulk interception warrants (as to which, see *ante*, § 25-402a) as they apply in relation to targeted interception warrants.

Investigatory Powers Act 2016, ss.261, 262

Telecommunications definitions

    261.—(1) The definitions in this section have effect for the purposes of this Act. *Communication*   **25-402l**

    (2) "Communication", in relation to a telecommunications operator, telecommunications service or telecommunication system, includes—

    (a) anything comprising speech, music, sounds, visual images or data of any description, and

    (b) signals serving either for the impartation of anything between persons, between a person and a thing or between things or for the actuation or control of any apparatus.

Entity data

    (3) "Entity data" means any data which—

    (a) is about—

>   (i) an entity,
>   (ii) an association between a telecommunications service and an entity, or
>   (iii) an association between any part of a telecommunication system and an entity,
>   (b) consists of, or includes, data which identifies or describes the entity (whether or not by reference to the entity's location), and
>   (c) is not events data.

Events data

(4) "Events data" means any data which identifies or describes an event (whether or not by reference to its location) on, in or by means of a telecommunication system where the event consists of one or more entities engaging in a specific activity at a specific time.

Communications data

(5) "Communications data", in relation to a telecommunications operator, telecommunications service or telecommunication system, means entity data or events data—

>   (a) which is (or is to be or is capable of being) held or obtained by, or on behalf of, a telecommunications operator and—
>   (i) is about an entity to which a telecommunications service is provided and relates to the provision of the service,
>   (ii) is comprised in, included as part of, attached to or logically associated with a communication (whether by the sender or otherwise) for the purposes of a telecommunication system by means of which the communication is being or may be transmitted, or
>   (iii) does not fall within sub-paragraph (i) or (ii) but does relate to the use of a telecommunications service or a telecommunication system,
>   (b) which is available directly from a telecommunication system and falls within sub-paragraph (ii) of paragraph (a), or
>   (c) which—
>   (i) is (or is to be or is capable of being) held or obtained by, or on behalf of, a telecommunications operator,
>   (ii) is about the architecture of a telecommunication system, and
>   (iii) is not about a specific person,
>   but does not include any content of a communication or anything which, in the absence of subsection (6)(b), would be content of a communication.

Content of a communication

(6) "Content", in relation to a communication and a telecommunications operator, telecommunications service or telecommunication system, means any element of the communication, or any data attached to or logically associated with the communication, which reveals anything of what might reasonably be considered to be the meaning (if any) of the communication, but—

>   (a) any meaning arising from the fact of the communication or from any data relating to the transmission of the communication is to be disregarded, and
>   (b) anything which is systems data is not content.

Other definitions

(7) "Entity" means a person or thing.

(8) "Public telecommunications service" means any telecommunications service which is offered or provided to the public, or a substantial section of the public, in any one or more parts of the United Kingdom.

(9) "Public telecommunication system" means a telecommunication system located in the United Kingdom—

>   (a) by means of which any public telecommunications service is provided, or
>   (b) which consists of parts of any other telecommunication system by means of which any such service is provided.

(10) "Telecommunications operator" means a person who—

>   (a) offers or provides a telecommunications service to persons in the United Kingdom, or
>   (b) controls or provides a telecommunication system which is (wholly or partly)—
>   (i) in the United Kingdom, or
>   (ii) controlled from the United Kingdom.

(11) "Telecommunications service" means any service that consists in the provision of access to, and of facilities for making use of, any telecommunication system (whether or not one provided by the person providing the service).

(12) For the purposes of subsection (11), the cases in which a service is to be taken to consist in the provision of access to, and of facilities for making use of, a telecommunication system include any

case where a service consists in or includes facilitating the creation, management or storage of communications transmitted, or that may be transmitted, by means of such a system.

(13) "Telecommunication system" means a system (including the apparatus comprised in it) that exists (whether wholly or partly in the United Kingdom or elsewhere) for the purpose of facilitating the transmission of communications by any means involving the use of electrical or electromagnetic energy.

(14) "Private telecommunication system" means any telecommunication system which—

(a) is not a public telecommunication system,

(b) is attached, directly or indirectly, to a public telecommunication system (whether or not for the purposes of the communication in question), and

(c) includes apparatus which is both located in the United Kingdom and used (with or without other apparatus) for making the attachment to that public telecommunication system.

As to the commencement of this section on Royal Assent, see *ante*, § 25-402b.

Postal definitions

262.—(1) The definitions in this section have effect for the purposes of this Act. *Communication*   **25-402m**

(2) "Communication", in relation to a postal operator or postal service (but not in the definition of "postal service" in this section), includes anything transmitted by a postal service.

Communications data

(3) "Communications data", in relation to a postal operator or postal service, means—

(a) postal data comprised in, included as part of, attached to or logically associated with a communication (whether by the sender or otherwise) for the purposes of a postal service by means of which it is being or may be transmitted,

(b) information about the use made by any person of a postal service (but excluding any content of a communication (apart from information within paragraph (a)), or

(c) information not within paragraph (a) or (b) that is (or is to be or is capable of being) held or obtained by or on behalf of a person providing a postal service, is about those to whom the service is provided by that person and relates to the service so provided.

Postal data

(4) "Postal data" means data which—

(a) identifies, or purports to identify, any person, apparatus or location to or from which a communication is or may be transmitted,

(b) identifies or selects, or purports to identify or select, apparatus through which, or by means of which, a communication is or may be transmitted,

(c) identifies, or purports to identify, the time at which an event relating to a communication occurs, or

(d) identifies the data or other data as data comprised in, included as part of, attached to or logically associated with a particular communication.

For the purposes of this definition "data", in relation to a postal item, includes anything written on the outside of the item.

Other definitions

(5) "Postal item" means—

(a) any letter, postcard or other such thing in writing as may be used by the sender for imparting information to the recipient, or

(b) any packet or parcel.

(6) "Postal operator" means a person providing a postal service to persons in the United Kingdom.

(7) "Postal service" means a service that—

(a) consists in the following, or in any one or more of them, namely, the collection, sorting, conveyance, distribution and delivery (whether in the United Kingdom or elsewhere) of postal items, and

(b) has as its main purpose, or one of its main purposes, to make available, or to facilitate, a means of transmission from place to place of postal items containing communications.

(8) "Public postal service" means a postal service that is offered or provided to the public, or a substantial section of the public, in any one or more parts of the United Kingdom.

As to the commencement of this section on Royal Assent, see *ante*, § 25-402b.

Investigatory Powers Act 2016, Sched. 3, paras 3, 20, 21

[Disclosures of convictions for certain offences

3. Section 56(1)(b) does not prohibit the doing of anything that discloses any conduct of a person   **25-402n**
for which that person has been convicted of—

(a) an offence under section 3(1), 43(7), 59 or 155,

(b) an offence under section 1(1) or (2), 11(7) or 19 of the Regulation of Investigatory Powers Act 2000, or

(c) an offence under section 1 of the Interception of Communications Act 1985.

Proceedings for certain offences

25-402o   20.—(1) Section 56(1) does not apply in relation to any proceedings for a relevant offence.

(2) "Relevant offence" means—

(a) an offence under any provision of this Act;

(b) an offence under section 1 of the Interception of Communications Act 1985;

(c) an offence under any provision of the Regulation of Investigatory Powers Act 2000;

(d) an offence under section 47 or 48 of the Wireless Telegraphy Act 2006;

(e) an offence under section 83 or 84 of the Postal Services Act 2000;

(f) an offence under section 4 of the Official Secrets Act 1989 relating to any such information, document or article as is mentioned in subsection (3)(a) or (c) of that section;

(g) an offence under section 1 or 2 of the Official Secrets Act 1911 relating to any sketch, plan, model, article, note, document or information which—

(i) incorporates, or relates to, the content of any intercepted communication or any secondary data obtained from a communication, or

(ii) tends to suggest that any interception-related conduct has or may have occurred or may be going to occur;

(h) an offence of perjury committed in the course of any relevant proceedings;

(i) an offence of attempting or conspiring to commit an offence falling within any of paragraphs (a) to (h);

(j) an offence under Part 2 of the Serious Crime Act 2007 in relation to an offence falling within any of those paragraphs;

(k) an offence of aiding, abetting, counselling or procuring the commission of an offence falling within any of those paragraphs;

(l) contempt of court committed in the course of, or in relation to, any relevant proceedings.

(3) In this paragraph—

intercepted communication" and "interception-related conduct" have the same meaning as in section 56;

"relevant proceedings" means any proceedings mentioned in paragraphs 4 to 19.

Disclosures to prosecutors and judges

25-402p   21.—(1) Nothing in section 56(1) prohibits—

(a) a disclosure to a person ("P") conducting a criminal prosecution that is made for the purpose only of enabling P to determine what is required of P by P's duty to secure the fairness of the prosecution, or

(b) a disclosure to a relevant judge in a case in which the judge has ordered the disclosure to be made to the judge alone.

(2) A relevant judge may order a disclosure under sub-paragraph (1)(b) only if the judge considers that the exceptional circumstances of the case make the disclosure essential in the interests of justice.

(3) Where in any criminal proceedings—

(a) a relevant judge orders a disclosure under sub-paragraph (1)(b), and

(b) in consequence of that disclosure, the judge considers that there are exceptional circumstances requiring the judge to make a direction under this sub-paragraph,

the judge may direct the person conducting the prosecution to make for the purposes of the proceedings any admission of fact which the judge considers essential in the interests of justice.

(4) But nothing in any direction under sub-paragraph (3) may authorise or require anything to be done in contravention of section 56(1).

(5) In this paragraph "relevant judge" means—

(a) any judge of the High Court or of the Crown Court or any Circuit judge,

(b) any judge of the High Court of Justiciary or any sheriff,

(c) in relation to proceedings before the Court Martial, the judge advocate for those proceedings, or

(d) any person holding a judicial office that entitles the person to exercise the jurisdiction of a judge falling within paragraph (a) or (b).]

As to commencement, see *ante*, § 25-402b.

XII. MISCONDUCT IN JUDICIAL OR PUBLIC OFFICE

Misfeasance

Where the appellant, a prison officer, was convicted of one count of misconduct in public of- **25-403**
fice for receiving sums totalling £10,684 between 2006 and 2011 in return for information he
provided to a tabloid journalist about his prison, which formed the subject matter of numerous
published articles, and where, during a police investigation, the owners and publishers of the
newspaper concerned revealed his identity to the police, the judge had not erred (i) in failing to
stay the prosecution as an abuse of process on the ground that both the appellant's identity, and
the material upon which the prosecution against him was founded, were obtained from the
newspapers through improper pressure applied by the police and in violation of Article 10 of the
ECHR (§ 16-157 in the main work), and (ii) in rejecting a submission that the appellant's conduct
did not reach the high threshold of seriousness required for the offence: *R. v. Norman (Robert)* 1
Cr.App.R. 8, CA). As to (i), there was no evidential basis for suggesting that the police had
exerted any improper pressure upon the newspapers; they made no threat or promise, express or
implied, about the bringing of a prosecution against the company at the top of the newspaper's
management; they were seeking voluntary disclosure; the fact that it was made by a suspect, in the
sense that a corporate charge against the newspapers had not been ruled out, did nothing to
"taint" it; furthermore, the voluntary disclosure was not a breach of the appellant's Article 10
rights, as a journalistic source, to have his anonymity maintained; assuming (without deciding)
that Article 10(1) was engaged so as to provide him with a prima facie right to have his anonymity
as a source protected, there was little doubt that use of the material in his prosecution would fall
within the qualification provided for in Article 10(2); the expression for which the appellant was
claiming protection was itself serious criminal conduct. As to (ii), the prosecution evidence was
capable of meeting the high threshold of criminality because of the harm to the public interest
caused by the appellant's conduct; the extent of his corrupt activity could not be justified as
disclosure in the public interest, and was conduct that caused significant public harm, because
corruption of a prison officer on this scale undermined public confidence in the prison service,
and was capable of damaging the efficient and effective running of the prison and undermining
confidence in its management.

XIII. REVENUE AND CUSTOMS OFFENCES

B. Customs and Excise Management Act 1979

(4) Illegal importation

Customs and Excise Management Act 1979, s.50

Penalty for improper importation of goods

With effect from February 22, 2017, the Export Control (North Korea and Ivory Coast Sanc- ★**25-431**
tions and Syria Amendment) Order 2013 (S.I. 2013 No. 3182) (see the main work) was revoked by
the Export Control (North Korea Sanctions and Iran, Ivory Coast and Syria Amendment) Order
2017 (S.I. 2017 No. 83). Article 15(4) of the 2017 order provides that, in the case of an offence
under section 50(4)(b) (*ibid.*, § 25-430) or 170(3)(b) (*ibid.*, § 25-474) of the 1979 Act in connection
with the prohibitions on importation in Article 2(3), (4)(a) or (b), 2a(2), 4(1)(b) and 4a(1)(b) of
Council Regulation (EC) No. 329/2007, the maximum penalty on conviction on indictment is
increased to 10 years' imprisonment.

(5) Illegal exportation

Customs and Excise Management Act 1979, s.68

Offences in relation to exportation of prohibited or restricted goods

With effect from February 22, 2017, the Export Control (Syria Sanctions) Order 2013 (S.I. ★**25-436**
2013 No. 2012) (see the main work) was amended by the Export Control (North Korea Sanctions
and Iran, Ivory Coast and Syria Amendment) Order 2017 (S.I. 2017 No. 83), so as to continue
the amendments that were made to that order by the Export Control (North Korea and Ivory
Coast Sanctions and Syria Amendment) Order 2013 (S.I. 2013 No. 3182) (*ibid.*), which was

revoked by the 2017 order. Article 15(4) of the 2017 order provides that, in the case of an offence under sections 68(3)(b) (*ibid.*, § 25-435) or 170(3)(b) (*ibid.*, § 25-474) of the 1979 Act in connection with the prohibitions on exportation in Article 2(1)(a) or (b), 2a(1), 4(1)(a), 4a(1)(a) and 4b of Council Regulation (EC) No. 329/2007, the maximum penalty on conviction on indictment is increased to 10 years' imprisonment.

(10) General provisions as to legal proceedings
Customs and Excise Management Act 1979, s.146A

Time limits for proceedings

25-448   With effect from September 15, 2016, the Finance Act 2016, s.174(1) and (2), amended section 146A(7) of the 1979 Act, in relation to proceedings commenced on or after that date, so as (i) to substitute "prosecution" for "prosecuting", and (ii) to make changes relating to Scotland and Northern Ireland only. As to the first of these amendments, it should be noted that the Queen's Printer copy actually says that the word "prosecuting" should be substituted for the word "prosecution". It has been assumed that this is a drafting error as the Queen' Printer copy of the Finance Act 1989 which inserted the section into the 1979 Act uses the word "prosecuting". As to this, see also *post*, § 25-452.

Customs and Excise Management Act 1979, ss.150, 152

Incidental provisions as to legal proceedings

25-452   With effect from September 15, 2016, the Finance Act 2016, s.174(1) and (3), amended section 150(1) of the 1979 Act, in relation to proceedings commenced on or after that date, by substituting the words "prosecuting authority (within the meaning of section 146A)" for the words from "the Director" to "Ireland)". This naturally compounds the drafting error in relation to the amendment of section 146A (as to which, see *ante*, § 25-448).

(13) Fraudulent evasion offences
Customs and Excise Management Act 1979, s.170

Penalty for fraudulent evasion of duty, etc.

★25-475   As to the further modification of section 170 of the 1979 Act (§ 25-474 in the main work), and as to the further amendment of S.I. 2013 No. 2012 and the revocation of S.I. 2013 No. 3182 (as to both of which, see the main work), see *ante*, §§ 25-431, 25-436.

CHAPTER 26

MONEY LAUNDERING OFFENCES

I. PROCEEDS OF CRIME ACT 2002

B. OFFENCES

(4) Legislation

The regulated sector and supervisory authorities

★26-24   With effect from March 1, 2017, Schedule 9 to the 2002 Act (see the main work) was further amended by the Bank of England and Financial Services (Consequential Amendments) Regulations 2017 (S.I. 2017 No. 80).

II. MONEY LAUNDERING REGULATIONS 2007

26-58   With effect from September 22, 2016, the Al-Qaida (Asset-Freezing) (Amendment) Regulations 2016 (S.I. 2016 No. 937) further amended the Money Laundering Regulations 2007 (S.I. 2007 No. 2157).

CHAPTER 27

HARMFUL OR DANGEROUS DRUGS

I. CONTROLLED DRUGS

A. INTRODUCTION

(3) Definition of a "controlled drug"

Temporary class drug orders

With effect from November 27, 2016, the Misuse of Drugs Act 1971 (Temporary Class Drug) **27-5a** (No. 2) Order 2016 (S.I. 2016 No. 1126) replaced the Misuse of Drugs Act 1971 (Temporary Class Drug) (No. 3) Order 2015 (S.I. 2015 No. 1929) (see the main work), which expired at the end of November 26, 2016, so as to renew the controls on the substances and products that are the subject of that order. The order stipulates that the provisions of the Misuse of Drugs (Safe Custody) Regulations 1973 (S.I. 1973 No. 798) (see § 27-91 in the main work) apply to these substances and products (art. 3(1)), and that the Misuse of Drugs Regulations 2001 (S.I. 2001 No. 3998) (see § 27-83 in the main work) are to apply to them as if they were specified as controlled drugs to which Schedule 1 to those regulations applied (art. 3(2)). The specified substances and products will cease to be subject to temporary control after one year, or, if earlier, upon the coming into force of an order under section 2(2) listing them in Schedule 2 to the 1971 Act (s.2A(6) of the 1971 Act).

(4) Classification of controlled drugs

Misuse of Drugs Act 1971, Sched. 2

Class B drugs

With effect from December 14, 2016, the Misuse of Drugs Act 1971 (Amendment) Order 2016 **27-9** (S.I. 2016 No. 1109) amended Part II of Schedule 2 to the 1971 Act so as (i) to insert new paragraph 1(ca), as follows—

"(ca) any compound (not being clonitazene, etonitazene, acemetacin, atorvastatin, bazedoxifene, indometacin, losartan, olmesartan, proglumetacin, telmisartan, viminol, zafirlukast or a compound for the time being specified in sub-paragraph (c) above) structurally related to 1-pentyl-3-(1-naphthoyl)indole (JWH-018), in that the four sub-structures, that is to say the indole ring, the pentyl substituent, the methanone linking group and the naphthyl ring, are linked together in a similar manner, whether or not any of the sub-structures have been modified, and whether or not substituted in any of the linked sub-structures with one or more univalent substituents and, where any of the sub-structures have been modified, the modifications of the sub-structures are limited to any of the following, that is to say—
    (i) replacement of the indole ring with indane, indene, indazole, pyrrole, pyrazole, imidazole, benzimidazole, pyrrolo[2,3-b]pyridine, pyrrolo[3,2-c]pyridine or pyrazolo[3,4-b]pyridine;
    (ii) replacement of the pentyl substituent with alkyl, alkenyl, benzyl, cycloalkylmethyl, cycloalkylethyl, (*N*-methylpiperidin-2-yl)methyl, 2-(4-morpholinyl)ethyl or (tetrahydropyran-4-yl)methyl;
    (iii) replacement of the methanone linking group with an ethanone, carboxamide, carboxylate, methylene bridge or methine group;
    (iv) replacement of the 1-naphthyl ring with 2-naphthyl, phenyl, benzyl, adamantyl, cycloalkyl, cycloalkylmethyl, cycloalkylethyl, bicyclo[2.2.1]heptanyl, 1,2,3,4-tetrahydronaphthyl, quinolinyl, isoquinolinyl, 1-amino-1-oxopropan-2-yl, 1-hydroxy-1-oxopropan-2-yl, piperidinyl, morpholinyl, pyrrolidinyl, tetrahydropyranyl or piperazinyl.",

and (ii) to substitute "(c), (ca)" for "(c)" in paragraph 2A.

Class C drugs

27-10   With effect from December 14, 2016, the Misuse of Drugs Act 1971 (Amendment) Order 2016 (S.I. 2016 No. 1109) amended paragraph 1(b) of Part III of Schedule 2 to the 1971 Act so as to insert "Dienedione (estra-4, 9-diene-3,17-dione)" after "Desoxymethyltestosterone".

B. Restrictions Relating to Controlled Drugs, etc

(5) Authorisation of activities otherwise unlawful under sections 3 to 6

27-83   As to the application of the Misuse of Drugs Regulations 2001 (S.I. 2001 No. 3998) (as to which, see the main work) to an order replacing S.I. 2015 No. 1929 (*ibid.*), see *ante*, § 27-5a.

S.I. 2001 No. 3998 was further amended by the Misuse of Drugs (Amendment) (England, Wales and Scotland) Regulations 2016 (S.I. 2016 No. 1125), with effect from December 14, 2016.

The Misuse of Drugs (Designation) (England, Wales and Scotland) Order 2015 (S.I. 2015 No. 704) (as to which, see the main work) was amended by the Misuse of Drugs (Designation) (Amendment) (England, Wales and Scotland) Order 2016 (S.I. 2016 No. 1124), with effect from December 14, 2016.

D. Powers of Secretary of State for Preventing Misuse of Controlled Drugs

(1) Regulations for preventing misuse of controlled drugs

27-91   As to the application of the Misuse of Drugs (Safe Custody) Regulations 1973 (S.I. 1973 No. 798) (as to which, see the main work) to an order replacing S.I. 2015 No. 1929 (*ibid.*), see *ante*, § 27-5a.

Chapter 28

OFFENCES AGAINST PUBLIC JUSTICE

I. PERVERTING THE COURSE OF JUSTICE

A. The Elements of the Offence

★28-1   For a case considering *R. v. Clark* (see the main work), see *DPP v. S.K.*, *post*, § 28-18a.

B. Conduct Capable of Amounting to the Offence

(1) Introduction

★28-2   For a case considering *R. v. Kenny* and *R. v. Selvage and Morgan* (as to both of which, see the main work), see *DPP v. S.K.*, *post*, § 28-18a.

(11) Frustrating the enforcement of court orders

★28-18a   In *DPP v. S.K.* [2017] Crim.L.R. 226, DC, the defendant carried out unpaid work, purporting to be another male who had received a community sentence with an unpaid work requirement. The defendant was charged with conspiring to pervert the course of justice. In rejecting the submission that imposition of the community sentence concluded proceedings, and that no other proceedings were in being or imminent, it was held that, like cases involving restraint orders (*R. v. Kenny, ante,* § 28-2), there was a continuing criminal process; such conduct frustrates the course of justice; the other male was not performing the obligation placed upon him by the court and so would be liable to further criminal sanction; and the effect of the defendant's conduct would be to pervert the course of justice by delaying and potentially undermining the investigation of that failure.

III. CONTEMPT OF COURT

B. Common Law

(4) Mens rea

28-36   *Dallas v. U.K.* is now reported at (2016) 63 E.H.R.R. 13.

C. CONTEMPT OF COURT ACT 1981

(4) Protection of sources of information

Contempt of Court Act 1981, s.10

Sources of information

For a case considering the proper approach to determination of the issue whether a person is a   **★28-77**
"source" of information, within section 10 of the 1981 Act, see *Hourani v. Thomson* [2017] 1
W.L.R. 933, QBD (Warby J.) (considering, *inter alia, Re An Inquiry Under the Company Securities
(Insider Dealing) Act 1985* (as to which, see the main work)).

(5) Restriction of publication of matters exempted from disclosure

Contempt of Court Act 1981, s.11

Publication of matters exempted from disclosure in court

In *Re Times Newspapers Ltd* [2016] 2 Cr.App.R.28, CA, it was held that there was jurisdiction   **28-80**
under section 11 of the 1981 Act (§ 28-79 in the main work) to prohibit the publication of wording used in open court explaining the reasons for making an order that certain evidence in a jury
trial was to be heard *in camera*; the evidence to be heard *in camera* was a "matter" in the context of
section 11; the explanation of the court's order in relation to that evidence was part of the same
"matter"; and the fact that the explanation was given in open court did not deprive the court of
jurisdiction under section 11 to prohibit the explanation's publication (following *Re Times
Newspapers Ltd* [2008] 1 Cr.App.R. 16 (as to which, see the main work)).

VII. PRISON SECURITY

E. SMUGGLING AND UNAUTHORISED PHOTOGRAPHY, ETC.

Prison Act 1952, ss. 40A–40E

Unauthorised possession in prison of knife or offensive weapons

As to a new consultation guideline on sentencing for offences involving bladed articles and of-   **28-195a**
fensive weapons, which covers the sentencing of offenders convicted of an offence contrary to section 40CA of the Prison Act 1952, see *ante*, § 5-178.

CHAPTER 30

COMMERCE, FINANCIAL MARKETS AND INSOLVENCY

IV. OFFENCES BY BANKRUPTS, ETC

A. INSOLVENCY ACT 1986

(2) Investigation of a bankrupt's affairs

Insolvency Act 1986, ss.288-291

Statement of affairs

With effect from April 6, 2017 (Deregulation Act 2015 (Commencement No. 6 and Savings   **30-71**
Provision) Order 2016 (S.I. 2016 No. 1016)), section 19 of, and paragraph 15 of Schedule 6 to,
the 2015 Act (see the main work) are brought into force. There is a saving provision that the 1986
Act continues to apply without the amendments made by paragraph 15 of Schedule 6 where a
bankruptcy order is made before April 6, 2017, and the bankrupt is required to submit a statement of affairs: S.I. 2016 No. 1016, art. 3

Duties of bankrupt in relation to official receiver

With effect from April 6, 2017 (Small Business, Enterprise and Employment Act 2015 (Com-   **30-74** mencement No. 6 and Transitional and Savings Provisions) Regulations 2016 (S.I. 2016 No. 1020)), section 133 of, and Schedule 10 to, the 2015 Act (see the main work) are brought into force.

Evidence and procedure

30-79   As to the revocation and replacement of the Insolvency Rules 1986 (S.I. 1986 No. 1925), see *post*, § 30-82.

Statement of affairs

30-80   As to the revocation and replacement of the Insolvency Rules 1986 (S.I. 1986 No. 1925), see *post*, § 30-82.

Public examination

30-82   With effect from April 6, 2017, the Insolvency (England and Wales) Rules 2016 (S.I. 2016 No. 1024) revoke and replace the Insolvency Rules 1986 (S.I. 1986 No. 1925) (see the main work), along with 29 sets of amending rules. The new rules set out detailed procedures for the conduct of all company and personal insolvency proceedings in England and Wales under the Insolvency Act 1986 and otherwise give effect to that Act. *Inter alia*, the rules create a number of offences and rule 6 in the introductory rules gives effect to Schedule 3, which sets out a table detailing the mode of trial and maximum penalties for those offences. The new rules contain provisions that broadly correspond to the provisions specifically mentioned in the main work: thus, for rule 6.175 of the 1986 rules, see rule 10.103 of the 2016 rules, for rules 7.19 to 7.25 of the 1986 rules, see rules 12.51 to 12.57 of the 2016 rules, for rules 9.1 to 9.6 of the 1986 rules, see rules 12.17 to 12.22 of the 2016 rules, and for rule 12A.37 of the 1986 rules, see rule 1.14 of the 2016 rules.

(3) General provisions of the Act applying to investigations
Insolvency Act 1986, s.433

Admissibility in evidence of statements of affairs, etc

30-85   With effect from April 6, 2017 (Small Business, Enterprise and Employment Act 2015 (Commencement No. 6 and Transitional and Savings Provisions) Regulations 2016 (S.I. 2016 No. 1020), section 126 of, and Schedule 9 to, the 2015 Act (see the main work) are brought into force. There are transitional and savings provisions.

(5) Bankruptcy offences

(a) *General*

Insolvency Act 1986, ss.384, 385

Miscellaneous definitions

★**30-100**   With effect from April 6, 2017, section 385 of the 1986 Act was amended by the Insolvency (England and Wales) Rules 2016 (Consequential Amendments and Savings) Rules 2017 (S.I. 2017 No. 369), so as, in the definition of "the Rules", to substitute, for the words "Insolvency Rules 1986", the words "Insolvency (England and Wales) Rules 2016".

Insolvency Act 1986, ss.355–358

False statements

★**30-106**   With effect from April 6, 2017 (Small Business, Enterprise and Employment Act 2015 (Commencement No. 6 and Transitional and Savings Provisions) Regulations 2016 (S.I. 2016 No. 1020), section 126 of, and Schedule 9 to, the 2015 Act (see the main work) are brought into force. There are transitional and savings provisions, one of which has been amended by the Small Business, Enterprise and Employment Act 2015 (Commencement No. 6 and Transitional and Savings Provisions) Regulations 2016 (Amendment) Regulations 2017 (S.I. 2017 No. 363).

B. COMPANY DIRECTORS DISQUALIFICATION ACT 1986

Company Directors Disqualification Act 1986, s.11

Undischarged bankrupts

30-118   With effect from November 30, 2016, section 11(2)(b)(i) of the 1986 Act is amended by the

Bankruptcy (Scotland) Act 2016 (Consequential Provisions and Modifications) Order 2016 (S.I. 2016 No. 1034) so as to insert "or 2016" after "1985".

CHAPTER 31

OFFENCES AGAINST PUBLIC MORALS AND POLICY

I. OFFENCES RELATING TO MARRIAGE

A. BIGAMY

(5) Ingredients of the offence

Mens rea

For a further case to the effect that the crime of bigamy requires *mens rea* or intent, and that an ★**31-9** honest and reasonable belief by the defendant in a fact (namely, that she was validly divorced from her previous marriage) which, if true, would make a second marriage lawful is a good defence, see *Azizi v. Aghaty* [2017] 1 F.L.R. 351, Fam D (Holman J.).

B. FORCED MARRIAGE

(2) Offence of forced marriage

Anonymity of victims

With effect from March 31, 2017, the Policing and Crime Act 2017, s.173, inserted section ★**31-32e** 122A (anonymity of victims of forced marriage) into the Anti-social Behaviour, Crime and Policing Act 2014, giving effect to new Schedule 6A. Paragraph 1 imposes a prohibition on the publication of any matter likely to lead members of the public to identify a person against whom an offence of forced marriage is alleged to have been committed during that person's lifetime. The schedule is then almost identical to that in relation to the anonymity of victims of female genital mutilation in Schedule 1 to the Female Genital Mutilation Act 2003 (§§ 19-367b, 19-367c in the main work). The only significant difference is that there is no equivalent of paragraph 1(3) in Schedule 1 to the 2003 Act (*viz.* any consent is not to be taken as preventing that person from being regarded as a person against whom the alleged offence was committed).

III. OBSCENE OR INDECENT PLUBLICATIONS AND DISPLAYS, ETC

B. STATUTE

(4) Protection of Children Act 1978

Ingredients of the offences

It is not anomalous that there should be different approaches to the *mens rea* required for **31-108a** "making" and "taking" indecent photographs or pseudo-photographs of a child for the purposes of the 1978 Act; there is a distinction to be drawn between images "made" by being downloaded from the internet or via email, where there is a requirement of knowledge that the image was likely to be an indecent one of a child, and the "taking" of a photograph where there is no *mens rea* requirement beyond establishing that the defendant took the photograph deliberately and intentionally: *R. v. W. (P.)* [2016] 2 Cr.App.R. 27, CA. Involvement in the sexual activity depicted in an indecent image is at least capable of giving rise to an inference of participation in an offence contrary to section 1(1)(a): *ibid.* (commenting that it would be a matter for the trial judge to determine, as a matter of law, whether involvement as an accessory only would require the prosecution additionally to prove that the defendant knew that the person depicted in the image was under 18 years old).

(6) Criminal Justice and Immigration Act 2008

Criminal Justice and Immigration Act 2008, ss.63–68

Possession of extreme pornographic images

31-120   Where a defendant was charged with possession of extreme pornographic images sent to his phone in a series of WhatsApp messages addressed to a group of people, including himself, where the images had been opened and later deleted, where the messages had not been requested, responded to or forwarded, where the images appeared to be part of a collection of assumed humorous content, and where the defendant contended that the relevant purpose under section 63(3) of the 2008 Act had to be that of the person who sent the images to him, rather than that of the photographer who took the original images, the trial judge had been correct to reject that submission; section 63(2) and (3) of the Act identified what images it was an offence to possess; section 63(3) was concerned with defining what was a pornographic image and the question was simply whether it was produced solely or principally for the purpose of sexual arousal of anyone who came to have it; the circumstances in which the images were received were immaterial: *R. v. Baddiel* [2016] 2 Cr.App.R 25, CA.

CHAPTER 32

MOTOR VEHICLE OFFENCES

II. DRIVING OFFENCES

A. CAUSING DEATH BY DANGEROUS DRIVING

(6) Ingredients of the offence

"mechanically proprelled vehicle"

★**32-12**   *Croituru v. CPS* is now reported at [2017] 1 W.L.R. 1130, *sub nom. Croituru v. DPP.*

B. CAUSING SERIOUS INJURY BY DANGEROUS DRIVING

(5) Sentence

Guidelines

★**32-30**   Where an offender's dangerous driving causes serious injury to one person, thus making him guilty of an offence contrary to section 1A of the RTA 1988, it is legitimate, in assessing the seriousness of the offence, to take account of injuries not amounting to serious injuries caused to other persons by the same piece of bad driving: *R. v. Aziz* [2017] 1 Cr.App.R.(S.) 28, CA.

E. CARELESS AND INCONSIDERATE DRIVING

(3) Sentence

32-60   The Sentencing Council for England and Wales has issued new sentencing guidelines for magistrates' courts, which revise, in relation to, *inter alia*, the offence under section 3 of the RTA 1988 (§ 32-58 in the main work), the Sentencing Guidelines Council's guidelines. The guidelines apply to all offenders aged 18 or over who are sentenced on or after April 24, 2017, regardless of the date of the offence. For further details, see *post*, Appendix S-11.117.

F. CAUSING DEATH BY CARELESS DRIVING WHEN UNDER THE INFLUENCE

(6) Ingredients of the offence

32-68   *Croitoru v. CPS* (see the main work) is now reported at [2017] 1 W.L.R. 1130, *sub nom. Croituru v. DPP.*

I. Driving, Being in Charge, Whilst Unfit

(5) Sentence

The Sentencing Council for England and Wales has issued new sentencing guidelines for magistrates' courts, which revise, in relation to, *inter alia*, the offences under section 4 of the RTA 1988 (§ 32-77 in the main work), the Sentencing Guidelines Council's guidelines. The guidelines apply to all offenders aged 18 or over who are sentenced on or after April 24, 2017, regardless of the date of the offence. For further details, see *post*, Appendix S-11.134. **32-81**

J. Driving, Being in Charge, Whilst Above the Prescribed Limit

(4) Sentence

The Sentencing Council for England and Wales has issued new sentencing guidelines for magistrates' courts, which revise, in relation to, *inter alia*, the offences under section 5 of the RTA 1988 (§ 32-89 in the main work), the Sentencing Guidelines Council's guidelines. The guidelines apply to all offenders aged 18 or over who are sentenced on or after April 24, 2017, regardless of the date of the offence. For further details, see *post*, Appendix S-11.124, S-11.126. **32-92**

(7) Evidence

Specimen of breath, blood or urine

Whilst the specimens of breath that establish whether a person has committed an offence under section 5 of the RTA 1988 (§ 32-89 in the main work) are those provided at the police station pursuant to section 7 of that Act (*ibid.*, § 32-126), and not the preliminary roadside test (s.6 of the 1988 Act (*ibid.*, § 32-113)), a court is entitled to rely on a roadside test reading as one piece of evidence among others to support the reliability of the breath-testing device used in the police station procedure: *DPP v. Vince; Same v. Kang* [2017] 4 W.L.R. 3, DC (considering *Smith v. DPP* (as to which, see *ibid.*, § 32-122), and *Hussain v. DPP* (as to which, see *ibid.*, § 32-135)). **32-100**

It should be noted that section 8(2) of the RTA 1988 (option to have sample of breath replaced by sample of blood or urine) has now been repealed: Deregulation Act 2015, s.52, and Sched. 11, para 1(1). **32-101**

K. Driving, Being in Charge, with Concentration of Specified Controlled Drug above Specified Limit

(4) Sentence

The Sentencing Council issued guidance on November 17, 2016, to assist those sentencing the offence of driving, attempting to drive, or being in charge of, a motor vehicle with a specified controlled drug in the body above the specified limit (RTA 1988, s.5A (§ 32-105 in the main work)), pending the production of a definitive guideline. The guideline for driving or attempting to drive with excess alcohol (Appendix S-11.124) should not be relied on when sentencing for offences under section 5A. The guidance does not carry the same authority as a definitive guideline and sentencers are not obliged to follow it. However, "it is hoped that the majority of sentencers will find it useful in assisting them to deal with these cases." **32-108**

Driving or attempting to drive

Where there are no factors that increase seriousness (as to which, see *post*), the court should consider a starting point of a Band C fine, and a disqualification in the region of 12 to 22 months. Where there are factors that increase seriousness, it should consider increasing the sentence. The community order threshold is likely to be crossed where there is evidence of one or more factors that increase seriousness. The court should also consider imposing a disqualification in the region of 23 to 28 months. The custody threshold is likely to be crossed where there is evidence of one or more factors that increase seriousness and one or more aggravating factors (*post*). The court should also consider imposing a disqualification in the region of 29 to 36 months. Having determined a starting point, the court should consider additional factors that may make the offence more or less serious.

In charge

As for driving or attempting to drive, *ante*, except that, where there are no factors that increase seriousness, the court should consider a starting point of a Band B fine, and endorsing the licence with 10 penalty points. The community order threshold is likely to be crossed where there is evidence of one or more factors that increase seriousness and one or more aggravating factors (*post*), in which case the court should also consider imposing a disqualification. Where there is evidence of one or more factors that increase seriousness and a greater number of aggravating factors, the court may consider it appropriate to impose a short custodial sentence of up to 12 weeks, as well as considering whether to impose a disqualification.

Factors that increase seriousness (this is an exhaustive list)
- Evidence of another specified drug (cocaine and benzoylecgonine (BZE) should be treated as one drug, as they both occur in the body as a result of cocaine use rather than poly-drug use; similarly, for 6-monoacteylmorphine and morphine, which both occur in the body as a result of heroin use, and diazepam and temazepam, which both occur in the body as a result of temazepam use) or of alcohol in the body.
- Evidence of an unacceptable standard of driving.
- Driving (or in charge of) a large goods vehicle, heavy goods vehicle or public service vehicle.
- Driving (or in charge of) a vehicle driven for hire or reward.

Aggravating and mitigating factors (these are non-exhaustive lists)
Aggravating factors
- Previous convictions having regard to (a) the nature of the offence to which the conviction relates and its relevance to the current offence, and (b) the time that has elapsed since the conviction.
- Location, *e.g.* near school.
- Carrying passengers.
- High level of traffic or pedestrians in the vicinity.
- Poor road or weather conditions.

Mitigating factors
- No previous convictions or no relevant/ recent convictions.
- Remorse.
- Good character and/ or exemplary conduct.
- Age and/ or lack of maturity where it affects the responsibility of the offender.
- Mental disorder or learning disability.
- Sole or primary carer for dependent relatives.
- Very short distance driven.
- Genuine emergency established.

L. Failure to Co-operate with Preliminary Test

(5) Disclosure

32-122   For a case considering *Smith v. DPP* (as to which, see the main work), see *DPP v. Vince; Same v. Kang, ante,* § 32-100.

M. Failing to Provide Evidential Specimen

(4) Sentence

32-130   The Sentencing Council for England and Wales has issued new sentencing guidelines for magistrates' courts, which revise, in relation to, *inter alia*, the offence under section 7 of the RTA 1988 (§ 32-126 in the main work), the Sentencing Guidelines Council's guidelines. The guidelines apply to all offenders aged 18 or over who are sentenced on or after April 24, 2017, regardless of the date of the offence. For further details, see *post*, Appendix S-11.128, S-11.129.

(6) Ingredients of the offence

"without reasonable excuse"

Burden of proof
    R. *(Cuns) v. Hammersmith Magistrates' Court* is now reported at 181 J.P. 111.   **★32-143**

P. DRIVING WITHOUT A LICENCE

(5) Grant and form of licences

With effect from December 9, 2016, the Motor Vehicles (Driving Licences) Regulations 1999   **32-160**
(S.I. 1999 No. 2864) (see the main work) were further amended by the Driving and Motorcycle
Riding Instructors (Recognition of European Professional Qualifications) Regulations 2016 (S.I.
2016 No. 1089).

Q. OBTAINING A LICENCE, OR DRIVING, WHILE DISQUALIFIED

(3) Sentence

The Sentencing Council for England and Wales has issued new sentencing guidelines for   **32-166**
magistrates' courts, which revise, in relation to, *inter alia*, the offence under section 103 of the
RTA 1988 (§ 32-164 in the main work), the Sentencing Guidelines Council's guidelines. The
guidelines apply to all offenders aged 18 or over who are sentenced on or after April 24, 2017,
regardless of the date of the offence. For further details, see *post*, S-11.122.

R. NO INSURANCE

(3) Sentence

The Sentencing Council for England and Wales has issued new sentencing guidelines for   **32-172**
magistrates' courts, which revise, in relation to, *inter alia*, the offence under section 143 of the
RTA 1988 (§ 32-170 in the main work), the Sentencing Guidelines Council's guidelines. The
guidelines apply to all offenders aged 18 or over who are sentenced on or after April 24, 2017,
regardless of the date of the offence. The format is the same as for other offence-specific
guidelines issued by the council. At step 1, the court should determine which of three categories
applies. Category 1 involves higher culpability and greater harm, category 2 involves one or the
other, but not both, and category 3 involves neither. The sole indicators of higher culpability are:
"never passed test", "gave false details", "driving LGV, HGV, PSV *etc.*", "driving for hire or
reward", and "evidence of sustained uninsured use". The sole indicator of greater harm is being
involved in an accident where injury or damage was caused. Where none of these indicators are
present, the case is one of lower culpability and/or lesser harm. For all three categories the starting point is a band C fine, and the range is also a band C fine, save for a category 3 case where it
is a band B fine to a band C fine. For a category 1 case, disqualification for between six and 12
months is recommended, for a category 2 case, disqualification for up to six months should be
considered; if disqualification is not ordered, the offender's licence should be endorsed with
eight penalty points; for a category 3 case, endorsement of between six and eight penalty points
should be ordered. Having identified a sentence within the range, the court should adjust this for
any aggravating or mitigating factors (a non-exhaustive list being included in the guideline) and
then go through the other standard steps required by any offence-specific guideline, *viz.* consider
the SOCPA 2005, ss.73 and 74 (assistance by defendants: reduction or review of sentence (§§
5-155, 5-156 in the main work)), credit for a guilty plea, the totality principle, the question of
compensation and any appropriate ancillary orders, and the need to give reasons.

(4) Ingredients of the offence

"requirements of the Act"

Road Traffic Act 1988, s.145

Requirements in respect of policies of insurance
    With effect from December 31, 2016, the Motor Vehicles (Compulsory Insurance) Regulations   **32-175**

2016 (S.I. 2016 No. 1193) increased the minimum level of compulsory insurance required for motor vehicles in respect of property damage, as specified in sections 145(4)(b) (see the main work) and 151(6) of the RTA 1988, to £1,200,000. There is an error in the main work in that a previous amendment to section 145(4)(b) by the Motor Vehicles (Compulsory Insurance) Regulations 2007 (S.I. 2007 No. 1426), which increased the minimum level to £1,000,000, was not taken in. The 2007 regulations are revoked with effect from December 31, 2016.

S. Failing to Stop or Report

(3) Sentence

32-183   The Sentencing Council for England and Wales has issued new sentencing guidelines for magistrates' courts, which revise, in relation to, *inter alia*, the offence under section 170 of the RTA 1988 (§ 32-180 in the main work), the Sentencing Guidelines Council's guidelines. The guidelines apply to all offenders aged 18 or over who are sentenced on or after April 24, 2017, regardless of the date of the offence. The format is the same as for other offence-specific guidelines issued by the council. At step 1, the court should determine which of three categories applies. Category 1 involves higher culpability and greater harm, category 2 involves one or the other, but not both, and category 3 involves neither. The sole indicators of higher culpability are: "offence committed in circumstances where a request for a sample of breath, blood or urine would have been made had the offender stopped", "offence committed by offender seeking to avoid arrest for another offence", "offender knew or suspected that personal injury caused and/or left injured party at scene", and "giving false details". The sole indicator of greater harm is injury or significant damage being caused. Where none of these indicators are present, the case is one of lower culpability and/or lesser harm. For a category 1 case, the starting point is a high level community order and the range is a low level community order to 26 weeks' custody, with disqualification of between six and 12 months, or endorsement of nine or ten points. For a category 2 offence, the starting point is a band C fine and the range is a band B fine to a medium level community order, with disqualification of up to six months or endorsement of seven or eight points. For a category 3 offence, the starting point is a band B fine, and the range is from a band A fine to a band C fine, with endorsement of five or six points. Having identified a sentence within the range, the court should adjust this for any aggravating or mitigating factors (a non-exhaustive list being included in the guideline) and then go through the other standard steps required by any offence-specific guideline, *viz.* consider the SOCPA 2005, ss.73 and 74 (assistance by defendants: reduction or review of sentence (§§ 5-155, 5-156 in the main work)), credit for a guilty plea, the totality principle, the question of compensation and any appropriate ancillary orders, the need to give reasons and (where relevant) to make any appropriate allowance for time spent on bail (CJA 2003, s.240A (*ibid.*, § 5-604)).

W. Disqualification and Endorsement

(2) Disqualification

32-229   *R. v. Needham* is now reported at [2016] 2 Cr.App.R.(S.) 26.

(5) Statutory provisions – general

32-252   *R. v. Needham* is now reported at [2016] 2 Cr.App.R.(S.) 26.

(8) Extension of disqualification where custodial sentence also imposed

32-269   *R. v. Needham* is now reported at [2016] 2 Cr.App.R.(S.) 26.

32-271a   *R. v. Needham* is now reported at [2016] 2 Cr.App.R.(S.) 26. Prosecution counsel has a duty to refer the court to this case (and in particular, to the checklist at para. [31] of the judgment) when a court may be considering both imprisonment and a period of disqualification for the same or another offence: *R. v. Ellis* [2017] 1 Cr.App.R.(S.) 4, CA.

(10) Disqualification until test is passed

Road Traffic Offenders Act 1988, s.36

Disqualification until test is passed

★**32-274**   The decisions in *R. v. Wiggins* (see the main work) and *R. v. Bradshaw and Waters (Note)* (§ 21-

194 in the main work) turned on their own facts and were properly decided, but it is not an invariable rule that an order under section 36 should not be made against a passenger: *R. v. Beech* [2017] R.T.R. 8, CA. Where a car escapes at speed from the scene of a professional crime, the passengers can be taken to have participated in the escape, putting the public at significant risk of serious injury, if not loss of life; in such a case, an extended test will bring home the importance of having regard to the safety of others, and not driving at excessive speeds: *ibid.*

X. Prosecution and Punishment of Offences

Road Traffic Offenders Act 1988, Sched. 2

As from a day to be appointed, Part I of Schedule 2 to the 1988 Act is amended by the Policing and Crime Act 2017, s.46(10), and Sched. 13, para. 3, so as, in relation to the entry for section 35 of the RTA 1988 (failing to comply with traffic directions), in the fifth column, to substitute, for the words "traffic officer or traffic warden", the words "or traffic officer". ★**32-312**

With effect from March 1, 2017, the Road Traffic Offenders Act 1988 (Penalty Points) (Amendment) Order 2017 (S.I. 2017 No. 104) amended Part I of Schedule 2 to the 1988 Act to increase the number of penalty points attributable to the offence under section 41D(b) of the RTA 1988 (contravening or failing to comply with a construction and use requirement as to the use of hand-held mobile telephones, or other hand-held interactive devices, while driving) from three to six penalty points. This was achieved by inserting the following text in the final column in lieu of "3"— ★

"(a) 3, in the case of an offence under section 41D(a).
 (b) 6, in the case of an offence under section 41D(b)".

CHAPTER 33

CONSPIRACY, ENCOURAGEMENT AND ATTEMPT TO COMMIT CRIME

I. CONSPIRACY

D. Pleading, Evidence and Practice

(2) The indictment

Election by prosecution

As to the replacement of *Criminal Practice Direction II (Preliminary Proceedings) 10A* (see the main work), see *post*, Appendix B-149 *et seq.* Paragraph 4 of the replacement direction (*post*, Appendix B-150a) corresponds to paragraph 3 of the replaced direction. **33-59**

(5) Acts and declarations in furtherance of the common design

Determination of the issue

For a case distinguishing between the principles governing the admissibility of the acts and declarations of one joint venturer that are in furtherance of the common design against another joint venturer (as to which, see the main work), and those relating to the attribution of the acts and mental state of the directing mind of a corporation to that corporation, see *R. v. A. Ltd., ante,* § 17-30. **33-66**

V. ATTEMPT TO COMMIT CRIME

B. Statutory Offence of Attempt

"More than merely preparatory"

For a New Zealand case to the effect that the tribunal of fact may have regard to the defendant's proved intention when considering whether his act or acts were more than merely preparatory, **33-133** see *Johnston v. The Queen* [2016] 1 N.Z.L.R. 1134, Supreme Court of New Zealand ([2016] NZSC 83) (considering, in particular, *R. v. Geddes* (as to which, see the main work)); and for a submission that this case should constitute persuasive authority in England and Wales, see the commentary in CLW/16/46/32.

APPENDIX A
Codes of Practice and Attorney-General's Guidelines

I. CODES OF PRACTICE

A. UNDER THE POLICE AND CRIMINAL EVIDENCE ACT 1984

(1) Introduction

The Police and Criminal Evidence Act 1984 makes provision for the issuing by the Secretary of **A-1**
State of codes of practice in connection with the tape-recording of interviews (s.60, § 15-244 in
the main work), the visual recording of interviews (s.60A, § 15-247 in the main work), the
exercise by police officers of statutory powers of "stop and search" (s.66(1)(a)(i) and (ii), § 15-2 in
the main work), the exercise by police officers of statutory powers to arrest a person (s.66(1)(a)(iii),
§ 15-2 in the main work) the detention, treatment, questioning and identification of persons by
police officers (s.66(1)(b), § 15-2 in the main work), and searches of premises and seizure of
property (s.66(1)(c) and (d), § 15-2 in the main work).

There are eight extant codes: Code A (stop and search); Code B (search and seizure); Code C
(detention, treatment and questioning of persons), Code D (identification), Code E (audio-
recording of interviews), Code F (visual recording of interviews), Code G (arrest) and Code H
(detention, treatment and questioning of persons under section 41 of, and Schedule 8 to, the Terrorism Act 2000).

Code D came into force on March 7, 2011: Police and Criminal Evidence Act 1984 (Codes of
Practice) (Revision of Codes A, B and D) Order 2011 (S.I. 2011 No. 412). Code G came into force
on November 12, 2012: Police and Criminal Evidence Act 1984 (Codes of Practice) (Revision of
Codes C, G and H) Order 2012 (S.I. 2012 No. 1798).

The Police and Criminal Evidence Act 1984 (Codes of Practice) (Revisions to Codes A, B, C, E,
F and H) Order 2013 (S.I. 2013 No. 2685) brought revised Codes A, B, C, E, F and H into force
on October 27, 2013. The revisions were required in order to give effect to (i) the United
Kingdom's obligations under European Parliament and Council Directive 2010/64/EU on the
right to interpretation and translation in criminal proceedings, and (ii) the decision of the
Divisional Court in *R. (C.) v. Secretary of State for the Home Department* (as to which, see §§ 15-7, 15-
235, 16-141 in the main work).

The Police and Criminal Evidence Act 1984 (Codes of Practice) (Revisions to Codes C and H)
Order 2014 (S.I. 2014 No. 1237) brought revised Codes C and H into force on June 2, 2014. The
revisions implemented obligations under European Parliament and Council Directive 2012/13/
EU, in relation to the right to information in criminal proceedings. In particular, every detainee
must be given a revised written notice setting out his rights and entitlements whilst in custody,
which has been updated to reflect the new substantive rights conferred by the 2012 directive.

The Police and Criminal Evidence Act 1984 (Revision of Code A) Order 2015 (S.I. 2015 No.
418) brought a revised Code A into force on March 19, 2015. The main changes were intended to
make clear what constitutes "reasonable grounds for suspicion". The revised code also emphasises
that where officers are not using their powers properly they will be subject to formal performance
or disciplinary proceedings.

The Police and Criminal Evidence Act 1984 (Codes of Practice) (Revision of Code E) Order

2016 (S.I. 2016 No. 35) brought a revised Code E on the audio recording of interviews with suspects into force on February 2, 2016. The revisions exempt four offences from the requirement that the interviews of individuals regarding indictable offences must be audio-recorded. The conditions that must be met before the exemption can apply are set out in a new annex to the code.

As to the replacement of Codes C, D and H from February 23, 2017, see *ante*, § 15-7. For further details of the various versions of the codes and their revisions, see §§ 15-5 *et seq.* in the main work. For further details in relation to the codes generally, see the main work at §§ 15-2 *et seq.* (primary legislation), § 15-5 (commencement), § 15-8 (status of codes), § 15-9 (who is bound by the codes), § 15-11 (admissibility), and § 15-12 (breaches).

It should be noted that the original text of the codes has a series of errors. Only in the most obvious cases has any change been made to the wording, but the punctuation, use of case, use of number and paragraphing have been amended with a view to injecting consistency and intelligibility.

(2) Stop and search

A. CODE OF PRACTICE FOR THE EXERCISE BY: POLICE OFFICERS OF STATUTORY POWERS OF STOP AND SEARCH; POLICE OFFICERS AND POLICE STAFF OF REQUIREMENTS TO RECORD PUBLIC ENCOUNTERS

Commencement—transitional arrangements

This code applies to any search by a police officer and the recording of public encounters taking place after 00.00 on 19 March 2015.

A:1.0 General

A-2
A:1.01 This code of practice must be readily available at all police stations for consultation by police officers, police staff, detained persons and members of the public.

A:1.02 The notes for guidance included are not provisions of this code, but are guidance to police officers and others about its application and interpretation. Provisions in the annexes to the code are provisions of this code.

A:1.03 This code governs the exercise by police officers of statutory powers to search a person or a vehicle without first making an arrest. The main stop and search powers to which this code applies are set out in Annex A, but that list should not be regarded as definitive [see *Note 1*]. In addition, it covers requirements on police officers and police staff to record encounters not governed by statutory powers (see paras 2.11 and 4.12). This code does not apply to:

(a) the powers of stop and search under:
   (i) the Aviation Security Act 1982, s.27(2), and
   (ii) the Police and Criminal Evidence Act 1984, s.6(1) (which relates specifically to powers of constables employed by statutory undertakers on the premises of the statutory undertakers);
(b) searches carried out for the purposes of examination under Schedule 7 to the Terrorism Act 2000 and to which the code of practice issued under paragraph 6 of Schedule 14 to the Terrorism Act 2000 applies;
(c) the powers to search persons and vehicles and to stop and search in specified locations to which the code of practice issued under section 47AB of the Terrorism Act 2000 applies.

A:1 Principles governing stop and search

A-3
A:1.1 Powers to stop and search must be used fairly, responsibly, with respect for people being searched and without unlawful discrimination. Under the Equality Act 2010, s.149, when police officers are carrying out their functions, they also have a duty to have due regard to the need to eliminate unlawful discrimination, harassment and victimisation, to advance equality of opportunity between people who share a relevant protected characteristic and people who do not share it, and to take steps to foster good relations between those persons. [See *Notes 1* and *1A.*] The Children Act 2004, s.11, also requires chief police officers and other specified persons and bodies to ensure that in the discharge of their functions they have regard to the need to safeguard and promote the welfare of all persons under the age of 18.

A:1.2 The intrusion on the liberty of the person stopped or searched must be brief and detention for the purposes of a search must take place at or near the location of the stop.

A:1.3 If these fundamental principles are not observed the use of powers to stop and search may be drawn into question. Failure to use the powers in the proper manner reduces their effectiveness. Stop and search can play an important role in the detection and prevention of crime, and using the powers fairly makes them more effective.

A:1.4 The primary purpose of stop and search powers is to enable officers to allay or confirm suspicions about individuals without exercising their power of arrest. Officers may be required to justify the use or authorisation of such powers, in relation both to individual searches and the overall pattern of their activity in this regard, to their supervisory officers or in court. Any misuse of the powers is likely to be harmful to policing and lead to mistrust of the police. Officers must also be able to explain their actions to the member of the public searched. The misuse of these powers can lead to disciplinary action (see paras 5.5 and 5.6).

A:1.5 An officer must not search a person, even with his or her consent, where no power to search is applicable. Even where a person is prepared to submit to a search voluntarily, the person must not be searched unless the necessary legal power exists, and the search must be in accordance with the relevant power and the provisions of this code. The only exception, where an officer does not require a specific power, applies to searches of persons entering sports grounds or other premises carried out with their consent given as a condition of entry.

A:1.6 Evidence obtained from a search to which this code applies may be open to challenge if the provisions of this code are not observed.

A:2 Types of stop and search powers

A:2.1 This code applies, subject to paragraph 1.03, to powers of stop and search as follows: **A-4**
  (a) powers which require reasonable grounds for suspicion, before they may be exercised; that articles unlawfully obtained or possessed are being carried such as section 1 of PACE for stolen and prohibited articles and section 23 of the Misuse of Drugs Act 1971 for controlled drugs;
  (b) authorised under section 60 of the Criminal Justice and Public Order Act 1994, based upon a reasonable belief that incidents involving serious violence may take place or that people are carrying dangerous instruments or offensive weapons within any locality in the police area, or that it is expedient to use the powers to find such instruments or weapons that have been used in incidents of serious violence;
  (c) [*not used*];
  (d) the powers in Schedule 5 to the Terrorism Prevention and Investigation Measures (TPIM) Act 2011 to search an individual who has not been arrested, conferred by:
    (i) paragraph 6(2)(a) at the time of serving a TPIM notice;
    (ii) paragraph 8(2)(a) under a search warrant for compliance purposes; and
    (iii) paragraph 10 for public safety purposes;
    see paragraph 2.18A;
  (e) powers to search a person who has not been arrested in the exercise of a power to search premises (see Code B, para. 2.4).

  (a) Stop and search powers requiring reasonable grounds for suspicion - explanation

General

A:2.2 Reasonable grounds for suspicion is the legal test which a police officer must satisfy before **A-5**
they can stop and detain individuals or vehicles to search them under powers such as section 1 of PACE (to find stolen or prohibited articles) and section 23 of the Misuse of Drugs Act 1971 (to find controlled drugs). This test must be applied to the particular circumstances in each case and is in two parts:
  (i) firstly, the officer must have formed a genuine suspicion in their own mind that they will find the object for which the search power being exercised allows them to search (see Annex A, second column, for examples); and
  (ii) secondly, the suspicion that the object will be found must be reasonable. This means that there must be an objective basis for that suspicion based on facts, information and/or intelligence which are relevant to the likelihood that the object in question will be found, so that a reasonable person would be entitled to reach the same conclusion based on the same facts and information and/or intelligence.

Officers must therefore be able to explain the basis for their suspicion by reference to intelligence or information about, or some specific behaviour by, the person concerned (see paras 3.8(d), 4.6 and 5.5).

A:2.2A The exercise of these stop and search powers depends on the likelihood that the person searched is in possession of an item for which they may be searched; it does not depend on the person concerned being suspected of committing an offence in relation to the object of the search. A police officer who has reasonable grounds to suspect that a person is in innocent possession of a stolen or prohibited article, controlled drug or other item for which the officer is empowered to search, may stop and search the person even though there would be no power of arrest. This would apply when a child under the age of criminal responsibility (10 years) is suspected of carrying any such item, even if they knew they had it. (See *Notes 1B* and *1BA*.)

Personal factors can never support reasonable grounds for suspicion

A-5a

A:2.2B Reasonable suspicion can never be supported on the basis of personal factors. This means that unless the police have information or intelligence which provides a description of a person suspected of carrying an article for which there is a power to stop and search, the following cannot be used, alone or in combination with each other, or in combination with any other factor, as the reason for stopping and searching any individual, including any vehicle which they are driving or are being carried in:

> (a) a person's physical appearance with regard, for example, to any of the "relevant protected characteristics" set out in the Equality Act 2010, s.149, which are age, disability, gender reassignment, pregnancy and maternity, race, religion or belief, sex and sexual orientation (see para. 1.1 and *Note 1A*), or the fact that the person is known to have a previous conviction; and
>
> (b) generalisations or stereotypical images that certain groups or categories of people are more likely to be involved in criminal activity.

A:2.3 [*Not used.*]

Reasonable grounds for suspicion based on information and/or intelligence

A-5b

A:2.4 Reasonable grounds for suspicion should normally be linked to accurate and current intelligence or information, relating to articles for which there is a power to stop and search, being carried by individuals or being in vehicles in any locality. This would include reports from members of the public or other officers describing:

> • a person who has been seen carrying such an article or a vehicle in which such an article has been seen;
>
> • crimes committed in relation to which such an article would constitute relevant evidence, for example, property stolen in a theft or burglary, an offensive weapon or bladed or sharply pointed article used to assault or threaten someone or an article used to cause criminal damage to property.

A:2.4A Searches based on accurate and current intelligence or information are more likely to be effective. Targeting searches in a particular area at specified crime problems not only increases their effectiveness but also minimises inconvenience to law-abiding members of the public. It also helps in justifying the use of searches both to those who are searched and to the public. This does not, however, prevent stop and search powers being exercised in other locations where such powers may be exercised and reasonable suspicion exists.

A:2.5 [*Not used.*]

Reasonable grounds for suspicion and searching groups

A-5c

A:2.6 Where there is reliable information or intelligence that members of a group or gang habitually carry knives unlawfully or weapons or controlled drugs, and wear a distinctive item of clothing or other means of identification in order to identify themselves as members of that group or gang, that distinctive item of clothing or other means of identification may provide reasonable grounds to stop and search any person believed to be a member of that group or gang. [See *Note 9.*]

A:2.6A A similar approach would apply to particular organised protest groups where there is reliable information or intelligence:

> (a) that the group in question arranges meetings and marches to which one or more members bring articles intended to be used to cause criminal damage and/or injury to others in support of the group's aims;
>
> (b) that at one or more previous meetings or marches arranged by that group, such articles have been used and resulted in damage and/or injury; and
>
> (c) that on the subsequent occasion in question, one or more members of the group have brought with them such articles with similar intentions.

These circumstances may provide reasonable grounds to stop and search any members of the group to find such articles (see *Note 9A*). See also paragraphs 2.12 to 2.18, "Searches authorised under section 60 of the Criminal Justice and Public Order Act 1994", when serious violence is anticipated at meetings and marches.

Reasonable grounds for suspicion based on behaviour, time and location

A:2.6B Reasonable suspicion may also exist without specific information or intelligence and on **A-5d** the basis of the behaviour of a person. For example, if an officer encounters someone on the street at night who is obviously trying to hide something, the officer may (depending on the other surrounding circumstances) base such suspicion on the fact that this kind of behaviour is often linked to stolen or prohibited articles being carried. An officer who forms the opinion that a person is acting suspiciously or that they appear to be nervous must be able to explain, with reference to specific aspects of the person's behaviour or conduct which they have observed, why they formed that opinion (see paras 3.8(d) and 5.5). A hunch or instinct which cannot be explained or justified to an objective observer can never amount to reasonable grounds.

A:2.7 [*Not used.*]

A:2.8 [*Not used.*]

Securing public confidence and promoting community relations

A:2.8A All police officers must recognise that searches are more likely to be effective, legitimate **A-5e** and secure public confidence when their reasonable grounds for suspicion are based on a range of objective factors. The overall use of these powers is more likely to be effective when up-to-date and accurate intelligence or information is communicated to officers and they are well-informed about local crime patterns. Local senior officers have a duty to ensure that those under their command who exercise stop and search powers have access to such information, and the officers exercising the powers have a duty to acquaint themselves with that information (see paras 5.1 to 5.6).

Questioning to decide whether to carry out a search

A:2.9 An officer who has reasonable grounds for suspicion may detain the person concerned in **A-5f** order to carry out a search. Before carrying out the search the officer may ask questions about the person's behaviour or presence in circumstances which gave rise to the suspicion. As a result of questioning the detained person, the reasonable grounds for suspicion necessary to detain that person may be confirmed or, because of a satisfactory explanation, be dispelled. [See *Notes 2* and *3.*] Questioning may also reveal reasonable grounds to suspect the possession of a different kind of unlawful article from that originally suspected. Reasonable grounds for suspicion however cannot be provided retrospectively by such questioning during a person's detention or by refusal to answer any questions asked.

A:2.10 If, as a result of questioning before a search, or other circumstances which come to the attention of the officer, there cease to be reasonable grounds for suspecting that an article of a kind for which there is a power to stop and search is being carried, no search may take place. [See *Note 3.*] In the absence of any other lawful power to detain, the person is free to leave at will and must be so informed.

A:2.11 There is no power to stop or detain a person in order to find grounds for a search. Police officers have many encounters with members of the public which do not involve detaining people against their will and do not require any statutory power for an officer to speak to a person (see para. 4.12 and *Note 1*). However, if reasonable grounds for suspicion emerge during such an encounter, the officer may detain the person to search them, even though no grounds existed when the encounter began. As soon as detention begins, and before searching, the officer must inform the person that they are being detained for the purpose of a search and take action in accordance with paragraphs 3.8 to 3.11 under *"Steps to be taken prior to a search".*

(b) Searches authorised under section 60 of the Criminal Justice and Public Order Act 1994

A:2.12 Authority for a constable in uniform to stop and search under section 60 of the Criminal **A-5g** Justice and Public Order Act 1994 may be given if the authorising officer reasonably believes:

    (a) that incidents involving serious violence may take place in any locality in the officer's police area, and it is expedient to use these powers to prevent their occurrence;

    (b) that persons are carrying dangerous instruments or offensive weapons without good reason in any locality in the officer's police area; or

    (c) that an incident involving serious violence has taken place in the officer's police area, a dangerous instrument or offensive weapon used in the incident is being carried by a person in any locality in that police area, and it is expedient to use these powers to find that instrument or weapon.

A:2.13 An authorisation under section 60 may only be given by an officer of the rank of inspector or above and in writing, or orally if paragraph 2.12(c) applies and it is not practicable to give the authorisation in writing. The authorisation (whether written or oral) must specify the grounds on which it was given, the locality in which the powers may be exercised and the period of time for which they are in force. The period authorised shall be no longer than appears reasonably necessary to prevent, or seek to prevent incidents of serious violence, or to deal with the problem of carrying dangerous instruments or offensive weapons or to find a dangerous instrument or offensive weapon that has been used. It may not exceed 24 hours. An oral authorisation given where paragraph 2.12(c) applies must be recorded in writing as soon as practicable. [See *Notes 10-13.*]

A:2.14 An inspector who gives an authorisation must, as soon as practicable, inform an officer of or above the rank of superintendent. This officer may direct that the authorisation shall be extended for a further 24 hours, if violence or the carrying of dangerous instruments or offensive weapons has occurred, or is suspected to have occurred, and the continued use of the powers is considered necessary to prevent or deal with further such activity or to find a dangerous instrument or offensive weapon that has been used. That direction must be given in writing unless it is not practicable to do so, in which case it must be recorded in writing as soon as practicable afterwards. [See *Note 12.*]

A:2.14A The selection of persons and vehicles under section 60 to be stopped and, if appropriate, searched should reflect an objective assessment of the nature of the incident or weapon in question and the individuals and vehicles thought likely to be associated with that incident or those weapons [see *Notes 10* and *11*]. The powers must not be used to stop and search persons and vehicles for reasons unconnected with the purpose of the authorisation. When selecting persons and vehicles to be stopped in response to a specific threat or incident, officers must take care not to discriminate unlawfully against anyone on the grounds of any of the protected characteristics set out in the Equality Act 2010 (see paragraph 1.1).

A:2.14B The driver of a vehicle which is stopped under section 60 and any person who is searched under section 60 are entitled to a written statement to that effect if they apply within twelve months from the day the vehicle was stopped or the person was searched. This statement is a record which states that the vehicle was stopped or (as the case may be) that the person was searched under section 60 and it may form part of the search record or be supplied as a separate record.

Powers to require removal of face coverings

A-6 A:2.15 Section 60AA of the Criminal Justice and Public Order Act 1994 also provides a power to demand the removal of disguises. The officer exercising the power must reasonably believe that someone is wearing an item wholly or mainly for the purpose of concealing identity. There is also a power to seize such items where the officer believes that a person intends to wear them for this purpose. There is no power to stop and search for disguises. An officer may seize any such item which is discovered when exercising a power of search for something else, or which is being carried, and which the officer reasonably believes is intended to be used for concealing anyone's identity. This power can only be used if an authorisation given under section 60, or under section 60AA, is in force. [See *Note 4.*]

A:2.16 Authority under section 60AA for a constable in uniform to require the removal of disguises and to seize them may be given if the authorising officer reasonably believes that activities may take place in any locality in the officer's police area that are likely to involve the commission of offences and it is expedient to use these powers to prevent or control these activities.

A:2.17 An authorisation under section 60AA may only be given by an officer of the rank of inspector or above, in writing, specifying the grounds on which it was given, the locality in which the powers may be exercised and the period of time for which they are in force. The period authorised shall be no longer than appears reasonably necessary to prevent, or seek to prevent the commission of offences. It may not exceed 24 hours. [See *Notes 10-13.*]

A:2.18 An inspector who gives an authorisation must, as soon as practicable, inform an officer of or above the rank of superintendent. This officer may direct that the authorisation shall be extended for a further 24 hours, if crimes have been committed, or are suspected to have been committed, and the continued use of the powers is considered necessary to prevent or deal with further such activity. This direction must also be given in writing at the time or as soon as practicable afterwards. [See *Note 12.*]

(c) [Not used]

(d) Searches under Schedule 5 to the Terrorism Prevention and Investigation Measures Act 2011

A-7 A:2.18A Paragraph 3 of Schedule 5 to the TPIM Act 2011 allows a constable to detain an individual to be searched under the following powers:

(i) paragraph 6(2)(a) when a TPIM notice is being, or has just been, served on the individual for the purpose of ascertaining whether there is anything on the individual that contravenes measures specified in the notice;

(ii) paragraph 8(2)(a) in accordance with a warrant to search the individual issued by a justice of the peace in England and Wales, a sheriff in Scotland or a lay magistrate in Northern Ireland who is satisfied that a search is necessary for the purpose of determining whether an individual in respect of whom a TPIM notice is in force is complying with measures specified in the notice (see para. 2.20); and

(iii) paragraph 10 to ascertain whether an individual in respect of whom a TPIM notice is in force is in possession of anything that could be used to threaten or harm any person.

See paragraph 2.1(e).

A:2.19 The exercise of the powers mentioned in paragraph 2.18A does not require the constable to have reasonable grounds to suspect that the individual:

(a) has been, or is, contravening any of the measures specified in the TPIM notice; or

(b) has on them anything which:

• in the case of the power in sub-paragraph (i), contravenes measures specified in the TPIM notice;

• in the case of the power in sub-paragraph (ii) is not complying with measures specified in the TPIM notice; or

• in the case of the power in sub-paragraph (iii), could be used to threaten or harm any person.

A:2.20 A search of an individual on warrant under the power mentioned in paragraph 2.18A(ii) must carried [*sic*] out within 28 days of the issue of the warrant and:

• the individual may be searched on one occasion only within that period;

• the search must take place at a reasonable hour unless it appears that this would frustrate the purposes of the search.

A:2.21–2.25 [*Not used.*]

A:2.26 The powers under Schedule 5 allow a constable to conduct a search of an individual only for specified purposes relating to a TPIM notice as set out above. However, anything found may be seized and retained if there are reasonable grounds for believing that it is or it contains evidence of any offence for use at a trial for that offence or to prevent it being concealed, lost, damaged, altered, or destroyed. However, this would not prevent a search being carried out under other search powers if, in the course of exercising these powers, the officer formed reasonable grounds for suspicion.

(e) Powers to search persons in the exercise of a power to search premises

A:2.27 The following powers to search premises also authorise the search of a person, not under **A-8** arrest, who is found on the premises during the course of the search:

(a) section 139B of the Criminal Justice Act 1988 under which a constable may enter school premises and search the premises and any person on those premises for any bladed or pointed article or offensive weapon;

(b) under a warrant issued under section 23(3) of the Misuse of Drugs Act 1971 to search premises for drugs or documents but only if the warrant specifically authorises the search of persons found on the premises; and

(c) under a search warrant or order issued under paragraph 1, 3 or 11 of Schedule 5 to the Terrorism Act 2000 to search premises and any person found there for material likely to be of substantial value to a terrorist investigation.

A:2.28 Before the power under section 139B of the Criminal Justice Act 1988 may be exercised, the constable must have reasonable grounds to suspect that an offence under section 139A or 139AA of the Criminal Justice Act 1988 (having a bladed or pointed article or offensive weapon on school premises) has been or is being committed. A warrant to search premises and persons found therein may be issued under section 23(3) of the Misuse of Drugs Act 1971 if there are reasonable grounds to suspect that controlled drugs or certain documents are in the possession of a person on the premises.

A:2.29 The powers in paragraph 2.27 do not require prior specific grounds to suspect that the person to be searched is in possession of an item for which there is an existing power to search. However, it is still necessary to ensure that the selection and treatment of those searched under these powers is based upon objective factors connected with the search of the premises, and not upon personal prejudice.

A:3 Conduct of searches

A:3.1 All stops and searches must be carried out with courtesy, consideration and respect for the **A-9** person concerned. This has a significant impact on public confidence in the police. Every reasonable effort must be made to minimise the embarrassment that a person being searched may experience. [See *Note 4*.]

A:3.2 The co-operation of the person to be searched must be sought in every case, even if the person initially objects to the search. A forcible search may be made only if it has been established that the person is unwilling to co-operate or resists. Reasonable force may be used as a last resort if necessary to conduct a search or to detain a person or vehicle for the purposes of a search.

As to this paragraph, see *James v. DPP* (§ 15-87 in the main work).

A:3.3 The length of time for which a person or vehicle may be detained must be reasonable and kept to a minimum. Where the exercise of the power requires reasonable suspicion, the thoroughness and extent of a search must depend on what is suspected of being carried, and by whom. If the suspicion relates to a particular article which is seen to be slipped into a person's pocket, then, in the absence of other grounds for suspicion or an opportunity for the article to be moved elsewhere, the search must be confined to that pocket. In the case of a small article which can readily be concealed, such as a drug, and which might be concealed anywhere on the person, a more extensive search may be necessary. In the case of searches mentioned in paragraph 2.1(b) and (d), which do not require reasonable grounds for suspicion, officers may make any reasonable search to look for items for which they are empowered to search. [See *Note 5*.]

A:3.4 The search must be carried out at or near the place where the person or vehicle was first detained. [See *Note 6*.]

A:3.5 There is no power to require a person to remove any clothing in public other than an outer coat, jacket or gloves, except under section 60AA of the Criminal Justice and Public Order Act 1994 (which empowers a constable to require a person to remove any item worn to conceal identity). [See *Notes 4* and *6*.] A search in public of a person's clothing which has not been removed must be restricted to superficial examination of outer garments. This does not, however, prevent an officer from placing his or her hand inside the pockets of the outer clothing, or feeling round the inside of collars, socks and shoes if this is reasonably necessary in the circumstances to look for the object of the search or to remove and examine any item reasonably suspected to be the object of the search. For the same reasons, subject to the restrictions on the removal of headgear, a person's hair may also be searched in public (see paragraphs 3.1 and 3.3).

A:3.6 Where on reasonable grounds it is considered necessary to conduct a more thorough search (*e.g.* by requiring a person to take off a T-shirt), this must be done out of public view, for example, in a police van unless paragraph 3.7 applies, or police station if there is one nearby. [See *Note 6*.] Any search involving the removal of more than an outer coat, jacket, gloves, headgear or footwear, or any other item concealing identity, may only be made by an officer of the same sex as the person searched and may not be made in the presence of anyone of the opposite sex unless the person being searched specifically requests it. [See Code C, Annex L and *Notes 4* and *7*.]

A:3.7 Searches involving exposure of intimate parts of the body must not be conducted as a routine extension of a less thorough search, simply because nothing is found in the course of the initial search. Searches involving exposure of intimate parts of the body may be carried out only at a nearby police station or other nearby location which is out of public view (but not a police vehicle). These searches must be conducted in accordance with paragraph 11 of Annex A to Code C except that an intimate search mentioned in paragraph 11(f) of Annex A to Code C may not be authorised or carried out under any stop and search powers. The other provisions of Code C do not apply to the conduct and recording of searches of persons detained at police stations in the exercise of stop and search powers. [See *Note 7*.]

Steps to be taken prior to a search

A-10   A:3.8 Before any search of a detained person or attended vehicle takes place the officer must take reasonable steps, if not in uniform (see para. 3.9), to show their warrant card to the person to be searched or in charge of the vehicle to be searched and, whether or not in uniform, to give that person the following information:

    (a) that they are being detained for the purposes of a search;

    (b) the officer's name (except in the case of enquiries linked to the investigation of terrorism, or otherwise where the officer reasonably believes that giving their name might put them in danger, in which case a warrant or other identification number shall be given) and the name of the police station to which the officer is attached;

    (c) the legal search power which is being exercised; and

    (d) a clear explanation of:

        (i) the object of the search in terms of the article or articles for which there is a power to search; and

(ii) in the case of:

- the power under section 60 of the Criminal Justice and Public Order Act 1994 (see para. 2.1(b)), the nature of the power, the authorisation and the fact that it has been given;
- the powers under Schedule 5 to the Terrorism Prevention and Investigation Measures Act 2011 (see paras 2.1(e) and 2.18A):
  - the fact that a TPIM notice is in force or (in the case of para. 6(2)(a)) that a TPIM notice is being served;
  - the nature of the power being exercised (for a search under para. 8 of Schedule 5, the warrant must be produced and the person provided with a copy of it);
- all other powers requiring reasonable suspicion (see para. 2.1(a)), the grounds for that suspicion (this means explaining the basis for the suspicion by reference to information and/or intelligence about, or some specific behaviour by, the person concerned (see para. 2.2));

(e) that they are entitled to a copy of the record of the search if one is made (see section 4 below) if they ask within 3 months from the date of the search and:

(i) if they are not arrested and taken to a police station as a result of the search and it is practicable to make the record on the spot, that immediately after the search is completed they will be given, if they request, either:

- a copy of the record, or
- a receipt which explains how they can obtain a copy of the full record or access to an electronic copy of the record; or

(ii) if they are arrested and taken to a police station as a result of the search, that the record will be made at the station as part of their custody record and they will be given, if they request, a copy of their custody record which includes a record of the search as soon as practicable whilst they are at the station. [See *Note 16.*]

A:3.9 Stops and searches under the power mentioned in paragraph 2.1(b) may be undertaken only by a constable in uniform.

A:3.10 The person should also be given information about police powers to stop and search and the individual's rights in these circumstances.

A:3.11 If the person to be searched, or in charge of a vehicle to be searched, does not appear to understand what is being said, or there is any doubt about the person's ability to understand English, the officer must take reasonable steps to bring information regarding the person's rights and any relevant provisions of this code to his or her attention. If the person is deaf or cannot understand English and is accompanied by someone, then the officer must try to establish whether that person can interpret or otherwise help the officer to give the required information.

A:4 Recording requirements

(a) Searches which do not result in an arrest

A:4.1 When an officer carries out a search in the exercise of any power to which this code applies **A-11** and the search does not result in the person searched or person in charge of the vehicle searched being arrested and taken to a police station, a record must be made of it, electronically or on paper, unless there are exceptional circumstances which make this wholly impracticable (*e.g.* in situations involving public disorder or when the recording officer's presence is urgently required elsewhere). If a record is to be made, the officer carrying out the search must make the record on the spot unless this is not practicable, in which case the officer must make the record as soon as practicable after the search is completed. [See *Note 16.*]

A:4.2 If the record is made at the time, the person who has been searched or who is in charge of the vehicle that has been searched must be asked if they want a copy and if they do, they must be given immediately, either:

- a copy of the record, or
- a receipt which explains how they can obtain a copy of the full record or access to an electronic copy of the record.

A:4.2A An officer is not required to provide a copy of the full record or a receipt at the time if they are called to an incident of higher priority. [See *Note 21.*]

(b) Searches which result in an arrest

A:4.2B If a search in the exercise of any power to which this code applies results in a person being **A-11a** arrested and taken to a police station, the officer carrying out the search is responsible for ensuring that a record of the search is made as part of their custody record. The custody officer must then ensure that the person is asked if they want a copy of the record and if they do, that they are given a copy as soon as practicable. [See *Note 16.*]

(c) Record of search

A-11b   A:4.3 The record of a search must always include the following information:

(a) a note of the self-defined ethnicity, and if different, the ethnicity as perceived by the officer making the search, of the person searched or of the person in charge of the vehicle searched (as the case may be) [see *Note 18*];

(b) the date, time and place the person or vehicle was searched [see *Note 6*];

(c) the object of the search in terms of the article or articles for which there is a power to search;

(d) in the case of:

- the power under section 60 of the Criminal Justice and Public Order Act 1994 (see paragraph 2.1(b)), the nature of the power, the authorisation and the fact that it has been given [see *Note 17*];

- the powers under Schedule 5 to the Terrorism Prevention and Investigation Measures Act 2011 (see paras 2.1(e) and 2.18A):
  - the fact that a TPIM notice is in force or (in the case of para. 6(2)(a)) that a TPIM notice is being served;
  - the nature of the power, and
  - for a search under paragraph 8, the date the search warrant was issued, the fact that the warrant was produced and a copy of it provided and the warrant must also be endorsed by the constable executing it to state whether anything was found and whether anything was seized, and

- all other powers requiring reasonable suspicion (see para. 2.1(a)), the grounds for that suspicion;

(e) subject to paragraph 3.8(b), the identity of the officer carrying out the search. [See *Note 15.*]

A:4.3A For the purposes of completing the search record, there is no requirement to record the name, address and date of birth of the person searched or the person in charge of a vehicle which is searched. The person is under no obligation to provide this information and they should not be asked to provide it for the purpose of completing the record.

A:4.4 Nothing in paragraph 4.3 requires the names of police officers to be shown on the search record or any other record required to be made under this code in the case of enquiries linked to the investigation of terrorism or otherwise where an officer reasonably believes that recording names might endanger the officers. In such cases the record must show the officers' warrant or other identification number and duty station.

A:4.5 A record is required for each person and each vehicle searched. However, if a person is in a vehicle and both are searched, and the object and grounds of the search are the same, only one record need be completed. If more than one person in a vehicle is searched, separate records for each search of a person must be made. If only a vehicle is searched, the self-defined ethnic background of the person in charge of the vehicle must be recorded, unless the vehicle is unattended.

A:4.6 The record of the grounds for making a search must, briefly but informatively, explain the reason for suspecting the person concerned, by reference to information and/or intelligence about, or some specific behaviour by, the person concerned (see para. 2.2).

A:4.7 Where officers detain an individual with a view to performing a search, but the need to search is eliminated as a result of questioning the person detained, a search should not be carried out and a record is not required. [See paragraph 2.10, *Notes 3* and *22A.*]

A:4.8 After searching an unattended vehicle, or anything in or on it, an officer must leave a notice in it (or on it, if things on it have been searched without opening it) recording the fact that it has been searched.

A:4.9 The notice must include the name of the police station to which the officer concerned is attached and state where a copy of the record of the search may be obtained and how (if applicable) an electronic copy may be accessed and where any application for compensation should be directed.

A:4.10 The vehicle must if practicable be left secure.

Recording of encounters not governed by statutory powers

A:4.11 [*Not used.*]

A:4.12 There is no national requirement for an officer who requests a person in a public place to **A-11d** account for themselves, *i.e.* their actions, behaviour, presence in an area or possession of anything, to make any record of the encounter or to give the person a receipt. [See para. 2.11 and *Notes 22A* and *22B.*]

A:5 Monitoring and supervising the use of stop and search powers

General

A:5.1 Any misuse of stop and search powers is likely to be harmful to policing and lead to mistrust **A-12** of the police by the local community and by the public in general. Supervising officers must monitor the use of stop and search powers and should consider in particular whether there is any evidence that they are being exercised on the basis of stereotyped images or inappropriate generalisations. Supervising officers must satisfy themselves that the practice of officers under their supervision in stopping, searching and recording is fully in accordance with this code. Supervisors must also examine whether the records reveal any trends or patterns which give cause for concern, and if so take appropriate action to address this. (See para. 2.8A.)

A:5.2 Senior officers with area or force-wide responsibilities must also monitor the broader use of stop and search powers and, where necessary, take action at the relevant level.

A:5.3 Supervision and monitoring must be supported by the compilation of comprehensive statistical records of stops and searches at force, area and local level. Any apparently disproportionate use of the powers by particular officers or groups of officers or in relation to specific sections of the community should be identified and investigated.

A:5.4 In order to promote public confidence in the use of the powers, forces in consultation with police and crime commissioners must make arrangements for the records to be scrutinised by representatives of the community, and to explain the use of the powers at a local level. [See *Note 19.*]

Suspected misuse of powers by individual officers

A:5.5 Police supervisors must monitor the use of stop and search powers by individual officers to **A-12a** ensure that they are being applied appropriately and lawfully. Monitoring takes many forms, such as direct supervision of the exercise of the powers, examining stop and search records (particularly examining the officer's documented reasonable grounds for suspicion) and asking the officer to account for the way in which they conducted and recorded particular searches or through complaints about a stop and search that an officer has carried out.

A:5.6 Where a supervisor identifies issues with the way that an officer has used a stop and search power, the facts of the case will determine whether the standards of professional behaviour as set out in the Code of Ethics (see http://www.college.police.uk/en/20972.htm) have been breached and which formal action is pursued. Improper use might be a result of poor performance or a conduct matter, which will require the supervisor to take appropriate action such as performance or misconduct procedures. It is imperative that supervisors take both timely and appropriate action to deal with all such cases that come to their notice.

Notes for Guidance

Officers exercising stop and search powers

A:1 *This code does not affect the ability of an officer to speak to or question a person in the ordinary course of* **A-13** *the officer's duties without detaining the person or exercising any element of compulsion. It is not the purpose of the code to prohibit such encounters between the police and the community with the co-operation of the person concerned and neither does it affect the principle that all citizens have a duty to help police officers to prevent crime and discover offenders. This is a civic rather than a legal duty; but when a police officer is trying to discover whether, or by whom, an offence has been committed he or she may question any person from whom useful information might be obtained, subject to the restrictions imposed by Code C. A person's unwillingness to reply does not alter this entitlement, but in the absence of a power to arrest, or to detain in order to search, the person is free to leave at will and cannot be compelled to remain with the officer.*

A:1A *In paragraphs 1.1 and 2.2B(a), the "relevant protected characteristics" are: age, disability, gender reassignment, pregnancy and maternity, race, religion or belief, sex and sexual orientation.*

A:1B *Innocent possession means that the person does have* [sic] *the guilty knowledge that they are carrying an unlawful item which is required before an arrest on suspicion that the person has committed an offence in respect of the item sought (if arrest is necessary - see PACE Code G) and/or a criminal prosecution) can be considered. It is not uncommon for children under the age of criminal responsibility to be used by older children and adults to carry stolen property, drugs and weapons and, in some cases, firearms, for the criminal benefit of others, either:*

- *in the hope that police may not suspect they are being used for carrying the items; or*
- *knowing that if they are suspected of being couriers and are stopped and searched, they cannot be arrested or prosecuted for any criminal offence.*

Stop and search powers therefore allow the police to intervene effectively to break up criminal gangs and groups that use young children to further their criminal activities.

A:1BA *Whenever a child under 10 is suspected of carrying unlawful items for someone else, or is found in circumstances which suggest that their welfare and safety may be at risk, the facts should be reported and actioned in accordance with established force safeguarding procedures. This will be in addition to treating them as a potentially vulnerable or intimidated witness in respect of their status as a witness to the serious criminal offence(s) committed by those using them as couriers. Safeguarding considerations will also apply to other persons aged under 18 who are stopped and searched under any of the powers to which this code applies. See paragraph 1.1 with regard to the requirement under the Children Act 2004, s.11, for chief police officers and other specified persons and bodies, to ensure that in the discharge of their functions, they have regard to the need to safeguard and promote the welfare of all persons under the age of 18.*

A:2 *In some circumstances preparatory questioning may be unnecessary, but in general a brief conversation or exchange will be desirable not only as a means of avoiding unsuccessful searches, but to explain the grounds for the stop/search, to gain cooperation and reduce any tension there might be surrounding the stop/ search.*

A:3 *Where a person is lawfully detained for the purpose of a search, but no search in the event takes place, the detention will not thereby have been rendered unlawful.*

A:4 *Many people customarily cover their heads or faces for religious reasons–for example, Muslim women, Sikh men, Sikh or Hindu women, or Rastafarian men or women. A police officer cannot order the removal of a head or face covering except where there is reason to believe that the item is being worn by the individual wholly or mainly for the purpose of disguising identity, not simply because it disguises identity. Where there may be religious sensitivities about ordering the removal of such an item, the officer should permit the item to be removed out of public view. Where practicable, the item should be removed in the presence of an officer of the same sex as the person and out of sight of anyone of the opposite sex (see Code C, Annex L).*

A:5 *A search of a person in public should be completed as soon as possible.*

A:6 *A person may be detained under a stop and search power at a place other than where the person was first detained, only if that place, be it a police station or elsewhere, is nearby. Such a place should be located within a reasonable travelling distance using whatever mode of travel (on foot or by car) is appropriate. This applies to all searches under stop and search powers, whether or not they involve the removal of clothing or exposure of intimate parts of the body (see paragraphs 3.6 and 3.7) or take place in or out of public view. It means, for example, that a search under the stop and search power in section 23 of the Misuse of Drugs Act 1971 which involves the compulsory removal of more than a person's outer coat, jacket or gloves cannot be carried out unless a place which is both nearby the place they were first detained and out of public view, is available. If a search involves exposure of intimate parts of the body and a police station is not nearby, particular care must be taken to ensure that the location is suitable in that it enables the search to be conducted in accordance with the requirements of paragraph 11 of Annex A to Code C.*

A:7 *A search in the street itself should be regarded as being in public for the purposes of paragraphs 3.6 and 3.7 above, even though it may be empty at the time a search begins. Although there is no power to require a person to do so, there is nothing to prevent an officer from asking a person voluntarily to remove more than an outer coat, jacket or gloves in public.*

A:8 *[Not used.]*

A:9 *Other means of identification might include jewellery, insignias, tattoos or other features which are known to identify members of the particular gang or group.*

A:9A *A decision to search individuals believed to be members of a particular group or gang must be judged on a case by case basis according to the circumstances applicable at the time of the proposed searches and in particular, having regard to:*

(a) *the number of items suspected of being carried;*

(b) *the nature of those items and the risk they pose; and*

(c) *the number of individuals to be searched.*

A group search will only be justified if it is a necessary and proportionate approach based on the facts and having regard to the nature of the suspicion in these cases. The extent and thoroughness of the searches must not be excessive.

The size of the group and the number of individuals it is proposed to search will be a key factor and steps should be taken to identify those who are to be searched to avoid unnecessary inconvenience to unconnected members of the public who are also present.

The onus is on the police to be satisfied and to demonstrate that their approach to the decision to search is in pursuit of a legitimate aim, necessary and proportionate.

Authorising officers

A-14   **A:10** *The powers under section 60 are separate from and additional to the normal stop and search powers* which require reasonable grounds to suspect an individual of carrying an offensive weapon (or other article). Their overall purpose is to prevent serious violence and the widespread carrying of weapons which might lead to persons being seriously injured by disarming potential offenders or finding weapons that have been used in circumstances where other powers would not be sufficient. They should not therefore be used to replace or circumvent the normal powers for dealing with routine crime problems. A particular example might be an authorisation to prevent serious violence or the carrying of offensive weapons at a sports event by rival team supporters when the expected general appearance and age range of those likely to be responsible, alone, would not be sufficiently distinctive to support reasonable suspicion (see paragraph 2.6). The purpose of the powers under section 60AA is to prevent those involved in intimidatory or violent protests using face coverings to disguise identity.

A:11 *Authorisations under section 60 require a reasonable belief on the part of the authorising officer. This must have an objective basis, for example: intelligence or relevant information such as a history of antagonism and violence between particular groups; previous incidents of violence at, or connected with, particular events or locations; a significant increase in knife-point robberies in a limited area; reports that individuals are regularly carrying weapons in a particular locality; information following an incident in which weapons were used about where the weapons might be found or in the case of section 60AA previous incidents of crimes being committed while wearing face coverings to conceal identity.*

A:12 *It is for the authorising officer to determine the period of time during which the powers mentioned in paragraph 2.1(b) may be exercised. The officer should set the minimum period he or she considers necessary to deal with the risk of violence, the carrying of knives or offensive weapons, or to find dangerous instruments or weapons that have been used. A direction to extend the period authorised under the powers mentioned in paragraph 2.1(b) may be given only once. Thereafter further use of the powers requires a new authorisation.*

A:13 *It is for the authorising officer to determine the geographical area in which the use of the powers is to be authorised. In doing so the officer may wish to take into account factors such as the nature and venue of the anticipated incident or the incident which has taken place, the number of people who may be in the immediate area of that incident, their access to surrounding areas and the anticipated or actual level of violence. The officer should not set a geographical area which is wider than that he or she believes necessary for the purpose of preventing anticipated violence, the carrying of knives or offensive weapons, or for finding a dangerous instrument or weapon that has been used or, in the case of section 60AA, the prevention of commission of offences. It is particularly important to ensure that constables exercising such powers are fully aware of the locality within which they may be used. The officer giving the authorisation should therefore specify either the streets which form the boundary of the locality or a divisional boundary if appropriate within the force area. If the power is to be used in response to a threat or incident that straddles police force areas, an officer from each of the forces concerned will need to give an authorisation.*

A:14 [Not used.]

Recording

A:15 *Where a stop and search is conducted by more than one officer the identity of all the officers engaged in the search must be recorded on the record. Nothing prevents an officer who is present but not directly involved in searching from completing the record during the course of the encounter.* **A-15**

A:16 *When the search results in the person searched or in charge of a vehicle which is searched being arrested, the requirement to make the record of the search as part of the person's custody record does not apply if the person is granted "street bail" after arrest (see section 30A of PACE) to attend a police station and is not taken in custody to the police station. An arrested person's entitlement to a copy of the search record which is made as part of their custody record does not affect their entitlement to a copy of their custody record or any other provisions of PACE Code C section 2 (custody records).*

A:17 *It is important for monitoring purposes to specify when authority is given for exercising the stop and search power under section 60 of the Criminal Justice and Public Order Act 1994.*

A:18 *Officers should record the self-defined ethnicity of every person stopped according to the categories used in the 2001 census question listed in Annex B. The person should be asked to select one of the five main categories representing broad ethnic groups and then a more specific cultural background from within this group. The ethnic classification should be coded for recording purposes using the coding system in Annex B. An additional "Not stated" box is available but should not be offered to respondents explicitly. Officers should be aware and explain to members of the public, especially where concerns are raised, that this information is required to obtain a true picture of stop and search activity and to help improve ethnic monitoring, tackle discriminatory practice, and promote effective use of the powers. If the person gives what appears to the officer to be an "incorrect" answer (e.g. a person who appears to be white states that they are black), the officer should record the response that has been given and then record their own perception of the person's ethnic background by using the PNC classification system. If the "Not stated" category is used the reason for this must be recorded on the form.*

A:19 *Arrangements for public scrutiny of records should take account of the right to confidentiality of those stopped and searched. Anonymised forms and/or statistics generated from records should be the focus of the examinations by members of the public. The groups that are consulted should always include children and young persons.*

A:20 [Not used.]

A:21 *In situations where it is not practicable to provide a written copy of the record or immediate access to an electronic copy of the record or a receipt of the search at the time (see paragraph 4.2A above), the officer should consider giving the person details of the station which they may attend for a copy of the record. A receipt may take the form of a simple business card which includes sufficient information to locate the record should the person ask for copy [sic], for example, the date and place of the search, and a reference number or the name of the officer who carried out the search (unless paragraph 4.4 applies).*

A:22 [Not used.]

A:22A *Where there are concerns which make it necessary to monitor any local disproportionality, forces have discretion to direct officers to record the self-defined ethnicity of persons they request to account for themselves in a public place or who they detain with a view to searching but do not search. Guidance should be provided locally and efforts made to minimise the bureaucracy involved. Records should be closely monitored and supervised in line with paragraphs 5.1 to 5.6, and forces can suspend or re-instate recording of these encounters as appropriate.*

A:22B *A person who is asked to account for themselves should, if they request, be given information about how they can report their dissatisfaction about how they have been treated.*

Definition of offensive weapon

A:23 *"Offensive weapon" is defined as "any article made or adapted for use by him for causing injury to the person, or intended by the person having it with him for such use or by someone else". There are three categories of offensive weapons: those made for causing injury to the person; those adapted for such a purpose; and those not so made or adapted, but carried with the intention of causing injury to the person. A firearm, as defined by section 57 of the Firearms Act 1968, would fall within the definition of offensive weapon if any of the criteria above apply.*

ANNEX A

Summary of main stop and search powers to which Code A applies

A-16   This table relates to stop and search powers only. Individual statutes below may contain other police powers of entry, search and seizure.

Power	*Object of search*	*Extent of Search*	*Where Exercisable*
Unlawful articles general			
1. Public Stores Act 1875, s.6	HM Stores stolen or unlawfully obtained	Persons, vehicles and vessels	Anywhere where the constabulary powers are exercisable
2. Firearms Act 1968, s.47	Firearms	Persons and vehicles	A public place, or anywhere in the case of reasonable suspicion of offences of carrying rearms with criminal intent or trespassing with firearms
3. Misuse of Drugs Act 1971, s.23	Controlled drugs	Persons and vehicles	Anywhere
4. Customs and Excise Management Act 1979, s.163	Goods: (a) on which duty has not been paid; (b) being unlawfully removed, imported or exported; (c) otherwise liable to forfeiture to HM Revenue and Customs	Vehicles and vessels only	Anywhere
5. Aviation Security Act 1982, s.24B *Note: This power applies throughout the UK but the provisions of this code will apply only when the power is exercised at an aerodrome situated in England and Wales.*	Stolen articles or articles made, adapted or intended for use in the course of/in connection with conduct which constitutes an offence in the part of the UK where the aerodrome is situated or would do so, if it occurred there.	Persons, vehicles, aircraft Anything in or on a vehicle or aircraft	Any part of an aerodrome
6. Police and Criminal Evidence Act 1984, s.1	Stolen goods;	Persons and vehicles	Where there is public access
	Articles made, adapted or intended for use in the course of or in connection with, certain offences under the Theft Act 1968, Fraud Act and Criminal Damage Act 1971;	Persons and vehicles	Where there is public access
	Offensive weapons, bladed or sharply-pointed articles (except folding pocket knives with a blade cutting edge not exceeding 3 inches);	Persons and vehicles	Where there is public access
	Fireworks: category 4 (display grade) fireworks if possession prohibited, adult fireworks in possession of a person under 18 in a public place.	Persons and vehicles	Where there is public access

Power	Object of search	Extent of Search	Where Exercisable
7. Sporting Events (Control of Alcohol etc.) Act 1985, s.7	Intoxicating liquor	Persons, coaches and trains	Designated sports grounds or coaches and trains travelling to or from a designated sporting event.
8. Crossbows Act 1987, s.4	Crossbows or parts of crossbows (except crossbows with a draw weight of less than 1.4 kilograms)	Persons and vehicles	Anywhere except dwellings
9. Criminal Justice Act 1988 s.139B	Offensive weapons, bladed or sharply pointed article	Persons	School premises
Evidence of game and wildlife offences			
10. Poaching Prevention Act 1862, s.2	Game or poaching equipment	Persons and vehicles	A public place
11. Deer Act 1991, s.12	Evidence of offences under the Act	Persons and vehicles	Anywhere except dwellings
12. Conservation of Seals Act 1970, s.4	Seals or hunting equipment	Vehicles only	Anywhere
13. Protection of Badgers Act 1992, s.11	Evidence offences under the Act	Persons and vehicles	Anywhere
14. Wildlife and Countryside Act 1981, s.19	Evidence of wildlife offences	Persons and vehicles	Anywhere except dwellings
Other			
15. Paragraphs 6 & 8 of Schedule 5 to the Terrorism Prevention and Investigation Measures Act 2011	Anything that contravenes measures specied in a TPIM notice.	Persons in respect of whom a TPIM notice is being served or is in force	Anywhere
16. Paragraph 10 of Schedule 5 to the Terrorism Prevention and Investigation Measures Act 2011	Anything that could be used to threaten or harm any person.	Persons in respect of whom a TPIM notice is in force.	Anywhere
17. [*Not used.*]			
18. [*Not used.*]			
19. Section 60 Criminal Justice and Public Order Act 1994	Offensive weapons or dangerous instruments to prevent incidents of serious violence or to deal with the carrying of such items or nd such items which have been used in incidents of serious violence	Persons and vehicles	Anywhere within a locality authorised under subsection (1)

ANNEX B

Self-defined ethnic classification categories

White	**W**
A. White–British	W1
B. White–Irish	W2
C. Any other White background	W9
Mixed	**M**
D. White and Black Caribbean	M1
E. White and Black African	M2
F. White and Asian	M3
G. Any other Mixed background	M9
Asian/ Asian–British	**A**
H. Asian–Indian	A1
I. Asian–Pakistani	A2
J. Asian–Bangladeshi	A3
K. Any other Asian background	A9
Black / Black–British	**B**
L. Black–Caribbean	B1
M. Black African	B2
N. Any other Black background	B9
Other	**O**
O. Chinese	O1
P. Any other	O9
Not stated	**NS**

ANNEX C

Summary of powers of community support officers to search and seize

The following is a summary of the search and seizure powers that may be exercised by a community support officer (CSO) who has been designated with the relevant powers in accordance with Part 4 of the Police Reform Act 2002. **A-17a**

When exercising any of these powers, a CSO must have regard to any relevant provisions of this code, including section 3 governing the conduct of searches and the steps to be taken prior to a search.

1. [*Not used.*]

2. Powers to search requiring the consent of the person and seizure

A CSO may detain a person using reasonable force where necessary as set out in Part 1 of Schedule 4 to the Police Reform Act 2002. If the person has been lawfully detained, the CSO may search the person provided that person gives consent to such a search in relation to the following:

Designation	Powers conferred	Object of Search	Extent of Search	Where Exercisable
Police Reform Act 2002, Schedule 4, paragraphs 7 and 7A	(a) Criminal Justice and Police Act 2001, s.12(2)	(a) Alcohol or a container for alcohol	(a) Persons	(a) Designated public place
	(b) Confiscation of Alcohol (Young Persons) Act 1997, s.1	(b) Alcohol	(b) Persons under 18 years old	(b) Public place
	(c) Children and Young Persons Act 1933, s.7(3)	(c) Tobacco or cigarette papers	(c) Persons under 16 years old found smoking	(c) Public place

3. Powers to search not requiring the consent of the person and seizure

A CSO may detain a person using reasonable force where necessary as set out in Part 1 of Schedule 4 to the Police Reform Act 2002. If the person has been lawfully detained, the CSO may search the person without the need for that person's consent in relation to the following:

Designation	Power conferred	Object of Search	Extent of Search	Where Exercisable
Police Reform Act 2002, Schedule 4, paragraph 2A	Police and Criminal Evidence Act 1984, s.32	(a) Objects that might be used to cause physical injury to the person or the CSO. (b) Items that might be used to assist escape.	Persons made subject to a requirement to wait.	Any place where the requirement to wait has been made.

4. Powers to seize without consent

This power applies when drugs are found in the course of any search mentioned above.

Designation	Power conferred	Object of Seizure	Where Exercisable
Police Reform Act 2002, Schedule 4, paragraph 7B	Police Reform Act 2002, Schedule 4, paragraph 7B	Controlled drugs in a person's possession.	Any place where the person is in possession of the drug.

Annex D—Deleted
Annex E—Deleted

ANNEX F

Establishing gender of persons for the purpose of searching

See Code C, Annex L.   **A-17b**

(3) Search and seizure

The text that follows is of the version of the code that came into force on October 27, 2013: see   **A-18**
ante, Appendix A-1.

For authorities in relation to Code B, see, in particular, § 15-187 in the main work.

B. CODE OF PRACTICE FOR SEARCHES OF PREMISES BY POLICE OFFICERS AND THE SEIZURE OF PROPERTY FOUND BY POLICE OFFICERS ON PERSONS OR PREMISES

Commencement—transitional arrangements

This code applies to applications for warrants made after 00.00 on 27 October 2013 and to   **A-19**
searches and seizures taking place after 00.00 on 27 October 2013.

B:1 Introduction

B:1.1 This code of practice deals with police powers to: **A-20**
- search premises
- seize and retain property found on premises and persons.

B:1.1A These powers may be used to find:
- property and material relating to a crime
- wanted persons
- children who abscond from local authority accommodation where they have been remanded or committed by a court.

B:1.2 A justice of the peace may issue a search warrant granting powers of entry, search and seizure, *e.g.* warrants to search for stolen property, drugs, firearms and evidence of serious offences. Police also have powers without a search warrant. The main ones provided by the Police and Criminal Evidence Act 1984 (PACE) include powers to search premises:
- to make an arrest
- after an arrest.

B:1.3 The right to privacy and respect for personal property are key principles of the Human Rights Act 1998. Powers of entry, search and seizure should be fully and clearly justified before use because they may significantly interfere with the occupier's privacy. Officers should consider if the necessary objectives can be met by less intrusive means.

B:1.3A Powers to search and seize must be used fairly, responsibly, with respect for people who occupy premises being searched or are in charge of property being seized and without unlawful discrimination. Under the Equality Act 2010, s.149, when police officers are carrying out their functions, they also have a duty to have due regard to the need to eliminate unlawful discrimination, harassment and victimisation, to advance equality of opportunity between people who share a relevant protected characteristic and people who do not share it, and to take steps to foster good relations between those persons. [See *Note 1A*.]

B:1.4 In all cases, police should therefore:
- exercise their powers courteously and with respect for persons and property
- only use reasonable force when this is considered necessary and proportionate to the circumstances.

B:1.5 If the provisions of PACE and this code are not observed, evidence obtained from a search may be open to question.

Notes for guidance

B:1A *In paragraph 1.3A, "relevant protected characteristic" includes: age, disability, gender reassignment, pregnancy and maternity, race, religion/belief, sex and sexual orientation.*

B:2 General

B:2.1 This code must be readily available at all police stations for consultation by:

- police officers
- police staff
- detained persons
- members of the public.

B:2.2 The *Notes for Guidance* included are not provisions of this code.

B:2.3 This code applies to searches of premises:

    (a) by police for the purposes of an investigation into an alleged offence, with the occupier's consent, other than:

- routine scene of crime searches;
- calls to a fire or burglary made by or on behalf of an occupier or searches following the activation of fire or burglar alarms or discovery of insecure premises;
- searches when paragraph 5.4 applies;
- bomb threat calls;

    (b) under powers conferred on police officers by PACE, ss.17, 18 and 32;

    (c) undertaken in pursuance of search warrants issued to and executed by constables in accordance with PACE, ss.15 and 16 [see *Note 2A*];

    (d) subject to paragraph 2.6, under any other power given to police to enter premises with or without a search warrant for any purpose connected with the investigation into an alleged or suspected offence. [See *Note 2B.*]

For the purposes of this code, "premises" as defined in PACE, s.23, includes any place, vehicle, vessel, aircraft, hovercraft, tent or movable structure and any offshore installation as defined in the Mineral Workings (Offshore Installations) Act 1971, s.1. [See *Note 2D.*]

B:2.4 A person who has not been arrested but is searched during a search of premises should be searched in accordance with Code A. [See *Note 2C.*]

B:2.5 This code does not apply to the exercise of a statutory power to enter premises or to inspect goods, equipment or procedures if the exercise of that power is not dependent on the existence of grounds for suspecting that an offence may have been committed and the person exercising the power has no reasonable grounds for such suspicion.

B:2.6 This code does not affect any directions or requirements of a search warrant, order or other power to search and seize lawfully exercised in England or Wales that any item or evidence seized under that warrant, order or power be handed over to a police force, court, tribunal, or other authority outside England or Wales. For example, warrants and orders issued in Scotland or Northern Ireland [see *Note 2B(f)*] and search warrants and powers provided for in sections 14 to 17 of the Crime (International Co-operation) Act 2003.

B:2.7 When this code requires the prior authority or agreement of an officer of at least inspector or superintendent rank, that authority may be given by a sergeant or chief inspector authorised to perform the functions of the higher rank under PACE, s.107.

B:2.8 Written records required under this code not made in the search record shall, unless otherwise specified, be made:

- in the recording officer's pocket book ("pocket book" includes any official report book issued to police officers), or
- on forms provided for the purpose.

B:2.9 Nothing in this code requires the identity of officers, or anyone accompanying them during a search of premises, to be recorded or disclosed:

    (a) in the case of enquiries linked to the investigation of terrorism; or

    (b) if officers reasonably believe recording or disclosing their names might put them in danger.

In these cases officers should use warrant or other identification numbers and the name of their police station. Police staff should use any identification number provided to them by the police force. [See *Note 2E.*]

B:2.10 The "officer in charge of the search" means the officer assigned specific duties and responsibilities under this code. Whenever there is a search of premises to which this code applies one officer must act as the officer in charge of the search. [See *Note 2F.*]

B:2.11 In this code:

    (a) "designated person" means a person other than a police officer, designated under the Police Reform Act 2002, Pt 4 who has specified powers and duties of police officers conferred or imposed on them [see *Note 2G*];

    (b) any reference to a police officer includes a designated person acting in the exercise or performance of the powers and duties conferred or imposed on them by their designation;

    (c) a person authorised to accompany police officers or designated persons in the execution of a warrant has the same powers as a constable in the execution of the warrant and the search and seizure of anything related to the warrant. These powers must be exercised in the company and under the supervision of a police officer. [See *Note 3C.*]

B:2.12 If a power conferred on a designated person:

    (a) allows reasonable force to be used when exercised by a police officer, a designated person exercising that power has the same entitlement to use force;

    (b) includes power to use force to enter any premises, that power is not exercisable by that designated person except:

        (i) in the company and under the supervision of a police officer; or

        (ii) for the purpose of:

            • saving life or limb; or

            • preventing serious damage to property.

B:2.13 Designated persons must have regard to any relevant provisions of the codes of practice.

Notes for guidance

B:2A *PACE ss.15 and 16 apply to all search warrants issued to and executed by constables under any enact-* **A-22** *ment, e.g. search warrants issued by a:*

    (a) *justice of the peace under the:*

      • *Theft Act 1968, s.26–stolen property;*

      • *Misuse of Drugs Act 1971, s.23–controlled drugs;*

      • *PACE, s.8–evidence of an indictable offence;*

      • *Terrorism Act 2000, Sched. 5, para. 1;*

      • *Terrorism Prevention and Investigation Measures Act 2011, Sched. 5, para. 8(2)(b)– search of premises for compliance purposes (see para. 10.1);*

    (b) *circuit judge under:*

      • *PACE, Sched. 1;*

      • *Terrorism Act 2000, Sched. 5, para. 11.*

B:2B *Examples of the other powers in paragraph 2.3(d) include:*

    (a) *Road Traffic Act 1988, s.6E(1) giving police power to enter premises under section 6E(1) to:*

      • *require a person to provide a specimen of breath; or*

      • *arrest a person following:*

        - *a positive breath test;*

        - *failure to provide a specimen of breath;*

    (b) *Transport and Works Act 1992, s.30(4) giving police powers to enter premises mirroring the powers in (a) in relation to specified persons working on transport systems to which the Act applies;*

    (c) *Criminal Justice Act 1988, s.139B giving police power to enter and search school premises for offensive weapons, bladed or pointed articles;*

    (d) *Terrorism Act 2000, Sched. 5, paras 3 and 15 empowering a superintendent in urgent cases to give written authority for police to enter and search premises for the purposes of a terrorist investigation;*

    (e) *Explosives Act 1875, s.73(b) empowering a superintendent to give written authority for police to enter premises, examine and search them for explosives;*

    (f) *search warrants and production orders or the equivalent issued in Scotland or Northern Ireland endorsed under the Summary Jurisdiction (Process) Act 1881 or the Petty Sessions (Ireland) Act 1851 respectively for execution in England and Wales;*

    (g) *Terrorism Prevention and Investigation Measures Act 2011, Sched. 5, paras 5(1), 6(2)(b) and 7(2), searches relating to TPIM notices (see para. 10.1).*

B:2C *The Criminal Justice Act 1988, s.139B provides that a constable who has reasonable grounds to suspect an offence under the Criminal Justice Act 1988, s.139A or 139AA has or is being committed may enter school premises and search the premises and any persons on the premises for any bladed or pointed article or offensive weapon. Persons may be searched under a warrant issued under the Misuse of Drugs Act 1971, s.23(3) to search premises for drugs or documents only if the warrant specifically authorises the search of persons on the premises. Powers to search premises under certain terrorism provisions also authorise the search of persons on the premises, for example, under paragraphs 1, 2, 11 and 15 of Schedule 5 to the Terrorism Act 2000 and section 52 of the Anti-terrorism, Crime and Security Act 2001.*

B:2D *The Immigration Act 1971, Pt III and Sched. 2 gives immigration officers powers to enter and search premises, seize and retain property, with and without a search warrant. These are similar to the powers available to police under search warrants issued by a justice of the peace and without a warrant under PACE, ss.17, 18, 19 and 32 except they only apply to specified offences under the Immigration Act 1971 and immigration control powers. For certain types of investigations and enquiries these powers avoid the need for the Immigration Service to rely on police officers becoming directly involved. When exercising these powers, immigration officers are required by the Immigration and Asylum Act 1999, s.145 to have regard to this code's corresponding provisions. When immigration officers are dealing with persons or property at police stations, police officers should give appropriate assistance to help them discharge their specific duties and responsibilities.*

B:2E *The purpose of paragraph 2.9(b) is to protect those involved in serious organised crime investigations or arrests of particularly violent suspects when there is reliable information that those arrested or their associates may threaten or cause harm to the officers or anyone accompanying them during a search of premises. In cases of doubt, an officer of inspector rank or above should be consulted.*

B:2F *For the purposes of paragraph 2.10, the officer in charge of the search should normally be the most senior officer present. Some exceptions are:*

> (a) *a supervising officer who attends or assists at the scene of a premises search may appoint an officer of lower rank as officer in charge of the search if that officer is:*
>   • *more conversant with the facts;*
>   • *a more appropriate officer to be in charge of the search;*
> (b) *when all officers in a premises search are the same rank. The supervising officer if available, must make sure one of them is appointed officer in charge of the search, otherwise the officers themselves must nominate one of their number as the officer in charge;*
> (c) *a senior officer assisting in a specialist role. This officer need not be regarded as having a general supervisory role over the conduct of the search or be appointed or expected to act as the officer in charge of the search.*

Except in (c), nothing in this note diminishes the role and responsibilities of a supervisory officer who is present at the search or knows of a search taking place.

B:2G *An officer of the rank of inspector or above may direct a designated investigating officer not to wear a uniform for the purposes of a specific operation.*

B:3 Search warrants and production orders

(a) *Before making an application*

B:3.1 When information appears to justify an application, the officer must take reasonable steps to check the information is accurate, recent and not provided maliciously or irresponsibly. An application may not be made on the basis of information from an anonymous source if corroboration has not been sought. See *Note 3A.*

B:3.2 The officer shall ascertain as specifically as possible the nature of the articles concerned and their location.

B:3.3 The officer shall make reasonable enquiries to:
> (i) establish if:
>   • anything is known about the likely occupier of the premises and the nature of the premises themselves;
>   • the premises have been searched previously and how recently;
> (ii) obtain any other relevant information.

B:3.4 An application:
> (a) to a justice of the peace for a search warrant or to a circuit judge for a search warrant or production order under PACE, Sched. 1 must be supported by a signed written authority from an officer of inspector rank or above; [Note: if the case is an urgent application to a justice of the peace and an inspector or above is not readily available, the next most senior officer on duty can give the written authority];
> (b) to a circuit judge under the Terrorism Act 2000, Sched. 5 for:
>   • a production order;
>   • search warrant; or
>   • an order requiring an explanation of material seized or produced under such a warrant or production order,
> must be supported by a signed written authority from an officer of superintendent rank or above.

B:3.5 Except in a case of urgency, if there is reason to believe a search might have an adverse effect on relations between the police and the community, the officer in charge shall consult the local police/community liaison officer:

- before the search; or
- in urgent cases, as soon as practicable after the search.

(b) *Making an application*

B:3.6 A search warrant application must be supported in writing, specifying:
- (a) the enactment under which the application is made [see *Note 2A*];
- (b) (i) whether the warrant is to authorise entry and search of:
  - one set of premises; or
  - if the application is under PACE, s.8, or Sched. 1, para. 12, more than one set of specified premises or all premises occupied or controlled by a specified person, and
  - (ii) the premises to be searched;
- (c) the object of the search [see *Note 3B*];
- (d) the grounds for the application, including, when the purpose of the proposed search is to find evidence of an alleged offence, an indication of how the evidence relates to the investigation;
- (da) where the application is under PACE, s.8, or Sched. 1, para. 12 for a single warrant to enter and search:
  - (i) more than one set of specified premises, the officer must specify each set of premises which it is desired to enter and search;
  - (ii) all premises occupied or controlled by a specified person, the officer must specify:
    - as many sets of premises which it is desired to enter and search as it is reasonably practicable to specify;
    - the person who is in occupation or control of those premises and any others which it is desired to search;
    - why it is necessary to search more premises than those which can be specified;
    - why it is not reasonably practicable to specify all the premises which it is desired to enter and search;
- (db) whether an application under PACE, s.8 is for a warrant authorising entry and search on more than one occasion, and if so, the officer must state the grounds for this and whether the desired number of entries authorised is unlimited or a specified maximum;
- (e) that there are no reasonable grounds to believe the material to be sought, when making application to a:
  - (i) justice of the peace or a circuit judge consists of or includes items subject to legal privilege;
  - (ii) justice of the peace, consists of or includes excluded material or special procedure material;
  - [Note: this does not affect the additional powers of seizure in the Criminal Justice and Police Act 2001, Pt 2 covered in paragraph 7.7 [see *Note 3B*]];
- (f) if applicable, a request for the warrant to authorise a person or persons to accompany the officer who executes the warrant [see *Note 3C*].

B:3.7 A search warrant application under PACE, Sched. 1, para. 12(a), shall if appropriate indicate why it is believed service of notice of an application for a production order may seriously prejudice the investigation. Applications for search warrants under the Terrorism Act 2000, Schedule 5, paragraph 11 must indicate why a production order would not be appropriate.

B:3.8 If a search warrant application is refused, a further application may not be made for those premises unless supported by additional grounds.

Notes for guidance

B:3A *The identity of an informant need not be disclosed when making an application, but the officer should* **A-24** *be prepared to answer any questions the magistrate or judge may have about:*
- *the accuracy of previous information from that source, and*
- *any other related matters.*

B:3B *The information supporting a search warrant application should be as specific as possible, particularly in relation to the articles or persons being sought and where in the premises it is suspected they may be found. The meaning of "items subject to legal privilege", "excluded material" and "special procedure material" are defined by PACE, ss.10, 11 and 14 respectively.*

B:3C *Under PACE, s.16(2), a search warrant may authorise persons other than police officers to accompany the constable who executes the warrant. This includes, e.g. any suitably qualified or skilled person or an expert in a particular field whose presence is needed to help accurately identify the material sought or to advise where certain evidence is most likely to be found and how it should be dealt with. It does not give them any right to force entry, but it gives them the right to be on the premises during the search and to search for or seize property without the occupier's permission.*

B:4 Entry without warrant—particular powers

(a) *Making an arrest etc*

A-25   B:4.1 The conditions under which an officer may enter and search premises without a warrant are set out in PACE, s.17. It should be noted that this section does not create or confer any powers of arrest. See other powers in *Note 2B(a)*.

(b) *Search of premises where arrest takes place or the arrested person was immediately before arrest*

B:4.2 When a person has been arrested for an indictable offence, a police officer has power under PACE, s.32 to search the premises where the person was arrested or where the person was immediately before being arrested.

(c) *Search of premises occupied or controlled by the arrested person*

B:4.3 The specific powers to search premises which are occupied or controlled by a person arrested for an indictable offence are set out in PACE, s.18. They may not be exercised, except if section 18 (5) applies, unless an officer of inspector rank or above has given written authority. That authority should only be given when the authorising officer is satisfied that the premises are occupied or controlled by the arrested person and that the necessary grounds exist. If possible the authorising officer should record the authority on the Notice of Powers and Rights and, subject to paragraph 2.9, sign the notice. The record of the grounds for the search and the nature of the evidence sought as required by section 18(7) of the Act should be made in:

- the custody record if there is one, otherwise
- the officer's pocket book, or
- the search record.

B:5 Search with consent

A-26   B:5.1 Subject to paragraph 5.4, if it is proposed to search premises with the consent of a person entitled to grant entry the consent must, if practicable, be given in writing on the Notice of Powers and Rights before the search. The officer must make any necessary enquiries to be satisfied the person is in a position to give such consent. [See *Notes 5A* and *5B*.]

B:5.2 Before seeking consent the officer in charge of the search shall state the purpose of the proposed search and its extent. This information must be as specific as possible, particularly regarding the articles or persons being sought and the parts of the premises to be searched. The person concerned must be clearly informed they are not obliged to consent, that any consent given can be withdrawn at any time, including before the search starts or while it is under way and anything seized may be produced in evidence. If at the time the person is not suspected of an offence, the officer shall say this when stating the purpose of the search.

B:5.3 An officer cannot enter and search or continue to search premises under paragraph 5.1 if consent is given under duress or withdrawn before the search is completed.

B:5.4 It is unnecessary to seek consent under paragraphs 5.1 and 5.2 if this would cause disproportionate inconvenience to the person concerned. [See *Note 5C*.]

Notes for guidance

A-27   B:5A *In a lodging house, hostel or similar accommodation, every reasonable effort should be made to obtain the consent of the tenant, lodger or occupier. A search should not be made solely on the basis of the landlord's consent.*

B:5B *If the intention is to search premises under the authority of a warrant or a power of entry and search without warrant, and the occupier of the premises co-operates in accordance with paragraph 6.4, there is no need to obtain written consent.*

B:5C *Paragraph 5.4 is intended to apply when it is reasonable to assume innocent occupiers would agree to, and expect, police to take the proposed action, e.g. if:*

- *a suspect has fled the scene of a crime or to evade arrest and it is necessary quickly to check surrounding gardens and readily accessible places to see if the suspect is hiding, or*
- *police have arrested someone in the night after a pursuit and it is necessary to make a brief check of gardens along the pursuit route to see if stolen or incriminating articles have been discarded.*

B:6 Searching premises—general considerations

(a) *Time of searches*

B:6.1 Searches made under warrant must be made within three calendar months of the date the **A-28**
warrant is issued or within the period specified in the enactment under which the warrant is issued
if this is shorter.

B:6.2 Searches must be made at a reasonable hour unless this might frustrate the purpose of the
search.

B:6.3 When the extent or complexity of a search mean it is likely to take a long time, the officer in
charge of the search may consider using the seize and sift powers referred to in section 7.

B:6.3A A warrant under PACE, s.8 may authorise entry to and search of premises on more than
one occasion if, on the application, the justice of the peace is satisfied that it is necessary to authorise
multiple entries in order to achieve the purpose for which the warrant is issued. No premises may be
entered or searched on any subsequent occasions without the prior written authority of an officer of
the rank of inspector who is not involved in the investigation. All other warrants authorise entry on
one occasion only.

B:6.3B Where a warrant under PACE, s.8, or Sched. 1, para. 12 authorises entry to and search of
all premises occupied or controlled by a specified person, no premises which are not specified in the
warrant may be entered and searched without the prior written authority of an officer of the rank of
inspector who is not involved in the investigation.

(b) *Entry other than with consent*

B:6.4 The officer in charge of the search shall first try to communicate with the occupier, or any
other person entitled to grant access to the premises, explain the authority under which entry is
sought and ask the occupier to allow entry, unless:

    (i) the search premises are unoccupied;

    (ii) the occupier and any other person entitled to grant access are absent;

    (iii) there are reasonable grounds for believing that alerting the occupier or any other person
        entitled to grant access would frustrate the object of the search or endanger officers or
        other people.

B:6.5 Unless sub-paragraph 6.4(iii) applies, if the premises are occupied the officer, subject to
paragraph 2.9, shall, before the search begins:

    (i) identify him or herself, show their warrant card (if not in uniform) and state the purpose
        of, and grounds for, the search; and

    (ii) identify and introduce any person accompanying the officer on the search (such persons
        should carry identification for production on request) and briefly describe that person's
        role in the process.

B:6.6 Reasonable and proportionate force may be used if necessary to enter premises if the officer
in charge of the search is satisfied the premises are those specified in any warrant, or in exercise of
the powers described in paragraph 4.1 to 4.3, and if:

    (i) the occupier or any other person entitled to grant access has refused entry;

    (ii) it is impossible to communicate with the occupier or any other person entitled to grant ac-
        cess; or

    (iii) any of the provisions of paragraph 6.4 apply.

(c) *Notice of powers and rights*

B:6.7 If an officer conducts a search to which this code applies the officer shall, unless it is **A-29**
impracticable to do so, provide the occupier with a copy of a notice in a standard format:

    (i) specifying if the search is made under warrant, with consent, or in the exercise of the
        powers described in paragraphs 4.1 to 4.3. Note: the notice format shall provide for
        authority or consent to be indicated (see paragraphs 4.3 and 5.1);

    (ii) summarising the extent of the powers of search and seizure conferred by PACE and other
        relevant legislation as appropriate;

    (iii) explaining the rights of the occupier and the owner of the property seized;

    (iv) explaining compensation may be payable in appropriate cases for damages [*sic*] caused
        entering and searching premises, and giving the address to send a compensation applica-
        tion [see *Note 6A*]; and

    (v) stating this code is available at any police station.

B:6.8 If the occupier is:

    • present, copies of the notice and warrant shall, if practicable, be given to them before the

search begins, unless the officer in charge of the search reasonably believes this would frustrate the object of the search or endanger officers or other people;
- not present, copies of the notice and warrant shall be left in a prominent place on the premises or appropriate part of the premises and endorsed, subject to paragraph 2.9 with the name of the officer in charge of the search, the date and time of the search.

The warrant shall be endorsed to show this has been done.

(d) *Conduct of searches*

B:6.9 Premises may be searched only to the extent necessary to achieve the purpose of the search, having regard to the size and nature of whatever is sought.

B:6.9A A search may not continue under:
- a warrant's authority once all the things specified in that warrant have been found;
- any other power once the object of that search has been achieved.

B:6.9B No search may continue once the officer in charge of the search is satisfied whatever is being sought is not on the premises [see *Note 6B*]. This does not prevent a further search of the same premises if additional grounds come to light supporting a further application for a search warrant or exercise or further exercise of another power. For example, when, as a result of new information, it is believed articles previously not found or additional articles are on the premises.

B:6.10 Searches must be conducted with due consideration for the property and privacy of the occupier and with no more disturbance than necessary. Reasonable force may be used only when necessary and proportionate because the co-operation of the occupier cannot be obtained or is insufficient for the purpose. [See *Note 6C*.]

B:6.11 A friend, neighbour or other person must be allowed to witness the search if the occupier wishes unless the officer in charge of the search has reasonable grounds for believing the presence of the person asked for would seriously hinder the investigation or endanger officers or other people. A search need not be unreasonably delayed for this purpose. A record of the action taken should be made on the premises search record including the grounds for refusing the occupier's request.

B:6.12 A person is not required to be cautioned prior to being asked questions that are solely necessary for the purpose of furthering the proper and effective conduct of a search, see Code C, paragraph 10.1(c). For example, questions to discover the occupier of specified premises, to find a key to open a locked drawer or cupboard or to otherwise seek co-operation during the search or to determine if a particular item is liable to be seized.

B:6.12A If questioning goes beyond what is necessary for the purpose of the exemption in Code C, the exchange is likely to constitute an interview as defined by Code C, paragraph 11.1A and would require the associated safeguards included in Code C, section 10.

(e) *Leaving premises*

B:6.13 If premises have been entered by force, before leaving the officer in charge of the search must make sure they are secure by:
- arranging for the occupier or their agent to be present;
- any other appropriate means.

(f) *Searches under PACE, Schedule 1 or the Terrorism Act 2000, Schedule 5*

B:6.14 An officer shall be appointed as the officer in charge of the search (see paragraph 2.10), in respect of any search made under a warrant issued under PACE Act 1984, Sched. 1 or the Terrorism Act 2000, Sched. 5. They are responsible for making sure the search is conducted with discretion and in a manner that causes the least possible disruption to any business or other activities carried out on the premises.

B:6.15 Once the officer in charge of the search is satisfied material may not be taken from the premises without their knowledge, they shall ask for the documents or other records concerned. The officer in charge of the search may also ask to see the index to files held on the premises, and the officers conducting the search may inspect any files which, according to the index, appear to contain the material sought. A more extensive search of the premises may be made only if:
- the person responsible for them refuses to:
  - produce the material sought, or
  - allow access to the index;
- it appears the index is:
  - inaccurate, or
  - incomplete;

- for any other reason the officer in charge of the search has reasonable grounds for believing such a search is necessary in order to find the material sought.

Notes for guidance

B:6A *Whether compensation is appropriate depends on the circumstances in each case. Compensation for damage caused when effecting entry is unlikely to be appropriate if the search was lawful, and the force used can be shown to be reasonable, proportionate and necessary to effect entry. If the wrong premises are searched by mistake everything possible should be done at the earliest opportunity to allay any sense of grievance and there should normally be a strong presumption in favour of paying compensation.* **A-31**

B:6B *It is important that, when possible, all those involved in a search are fully briefed about any powers to be exercised and the extent and limits within which it should be conducted.*

B:6C *In all cases the number of officers and other persons involved in executing the warrant should be determined by what is reasonable and necessary according to the particular circumstances.*

B:7 Seizure and retention of property

(a) *Seizure*

B:7.1 Subject to paragraph 7.2, an officer who is searching any person or premises under any statutory power or with the consent of the occupier may seize anything: **A-32**
- (a) covered by a warrant;
- (b) the officer has reasonable grounds for believing is evidence of an offence or has been obtained in consequence of the commission of an offence but only if seizure is necessary to prevent the items being concealed, lost, disposed of, altered, damaged, destroyed or tampered with;
- (c) covered by the powers in the Criminal Justice and Police Act 2001, Pt 2 allowing an officer to seize property from persons or premises and retain it for sifting or examination elsewhere.

See *Note 7B.*

B:7.2 No item may be seized which an officer has reasonable grounds for believing to be subject to legal privilege, as defined in PACE, s.10, other than under the Criminal Justice and Police Act 2001, Pt 2.

B:7.3 Officers must be aware of the provisions in the Criminal Justice and Police Act 2001, s.59, allowing for applications to a judicial authority for the return of property seized and the subsequent duty to secure in section 60 (see paragraph 7.12(iii)).

B:7.4 An officer may decide it is not appropriate to seize property because of an explanation from the person holding it but may nevertheless have reasonable grounds for believing it was obtained in consequence of an offence by some person. In these circumstances, the officer should identify the property to the holder, inform the holder of their suspicions and explain the holder may be liable to civil or criminal proceedings if they dispose of, alter or destroy the property.

B:7.5 An officer may arrange to photograph, image or copy, any document or other article they have the power to seize in accordance with paragraph 7.1. This is subject to specific restrictions on the examination, imaging or copying of certain property seized under the Criminal Justice and Police Act 2001, Pt 2. An officer must have regard to their statutory obligation to retain an original document or other article only when a photograph or copy is not sufficient.

B:7.6 If an officer considers information stored in any electronic form and accessible from the premises could be used in evidence, they may require the information to be produced in a form:
- which can be taken away and in which it is visible and legible; or
- from which it can readily be produced in a visible and legible form.

(b) *Criminal Justice and Police Act 2001: specific procedures for seize and sift powers*

B:7.7 The Criminal Justice and Police Act 2001, Pt 2 gives officers limited powers to seize property from premises or persons so they can sift or examine it elsewhere. Officers must be careful they only exercise these powers when it is essential and they do not remove any more material than necessary. The removal of large volumes of material, much of which may not ultimately be retainable, may have serious implications for the owners, particularly when they are involved in business or activities such as journalism or the provision of medical services. Officers must carefully consider if removing copies or images of relevant material or data would be a satisfactory alternative to removing originals. When originals are taken, officers must be prepared to facilitate the provision of copies or images for the owners when reasonably practicable. [See *Note 7C.*] **A-33**

B:7.8 Property seized under the Criminal Justice and Police Act 2001, s.50 or 51 must be kept securely and separately from any material seized under other powers. An examination under section

53 to determine which elements may be retained must be carried out at the earliest practicable time, having due regard to the desirability of allowing the person from whom the property was seized, or a person with an interest in the property, an opportunity of being present or represented at the examination.

B:7.8A All reasonable steps should be taken to accommodate an interested person's request to be present, provided the request is reasonable and subject to the need to prevent harm to, interference with, or unreasonable delay to the investigatory process. If an examination proceeds in the absence of an interested person who asked to attend or their representative, the officer who exercised the relevant seizure power must give that person a written notice of why the examination was carried out in those circumstances. If it is necessary for security reasons or to maintain confidentiality officers may exclude interested persons from decryption or other processes which facilitate the examination but do not form part of it. [See *Note 7D.*]

B:7.9 It is the responsibility of the officer in charge of the investigation to make sure property is returned in accordance with sections 53 to 55. Material which there is no power to retain must be:

- separated from the rest of the seized property; and
- returned as soon as reasonably practicable after examination of all the seized property.

B:7.9A Delay is only warranted if very clear and compelling reasons exist, for example:

- the unavailability of the person to whom the material is to be returned; or
- the need to agree a convenient time to return a large volume of material.

B:7.9B Legally privileged, excluded or special procedure material which cannot be retained must be returned:

- as soon as reasonably practicable; and
- without waiting for the whole examination.

B:7.9C As set out in section 58, material must be returned to the person from whom it was seized, except when it is clear some other person has a better right to it. [See *Note 7E.*]

B:7.10 When an officer involved in the investigation has reasonable grounds to believe a person with a relevant interest in property seized under section 50 or 51 intends to make an application under section 59 for the return of any legally privileged, special procedure or excluded material, the officer in charge of the investigation should be informed as soon as practicable and the material seized should be kept secure in accordance with section 61. [See *Note 7C.*]

B:7.11 The officer in charge of the investigation is responsible for making sure property is properly secured. Securing involves making sure the property is not examined, copied, imaged or put to any other use except at the request, or with the consent, of the applicant or in accordance with the directions of the appropriate judicial authority. Any request, consent or directions must be recorded in writing and signed by both the initiator and the officer in charge of the investigation. [See *Notes 7F* and *7G.*]

B:7.12 When an officer exercises a power of seizure conferred by sections 50 or 51 they shall provide the occupier of the premises or the person from whom the property is being seized with a written notice:

(i) specifying what has been seized under the powers conferred by that section;
(ii) specifying the grounds for those powers;
(iii) setting out the effect of sections 59 to 61 covering the grounds for a person with a relevant interest in seized property to apply to a judicial authority for its return and the duty of officers to secure property in certain circumstances when an application is made; and
(iv) specifying the name and address of the person to whom:
- notice of an application to the appropriate judicial authority in respect of any of the seized property must be given;
- an application may be made to allow attendance at the initial examination of the property.

B:7.13 If the occupier is not present but there is someone in charge of the premises, the notice shall be given to them. If no suitable person is available, so the notice will easily be found it should either be:

- left in a prominent place on the premises; or
- attached to the exterior of the premises.

(c) *Retention*

B:7.14 Subject to paragraph 7.15, anything seized in accordance with the above provisions may be retained only for as long as is necessary. It may be retained, among other purposes: **A-34**

    (i) for use as evidence at a trial for an offence;

    (ii) to facilitate the use in any investigation or proceedings of anything to which it is inextricably linked [see *Note 7H*];

    (iii) for forensic examination or other investigation in connection with an offence;

    (iv) in order to establish its lawful owner when there are reasonable grounds for believing it has been stolen or obtained by the commission of an offence.

B:7.15 Property shall not be retained under paragraph 7.14(i), (ii) or (iii) if a copy or image would be sufficient.

(d) *Rights of owners etc*

B:7.16 If property is retained, the person who had custody or control of it immediately before seizure must, on request, be provided with a list or description of the property within a reasonable time.

B:7.17 That person or their representative must be allowed supervised access to the property to examine it or have it photographed or copied, or must be provided with a photograph or copy, in either case within a reasonable time of any request and at their own expense, unless the officer in charge of an investigation has reasonable grounds for believing this would:

    (i) prejudice the investigation of any offence or criminal proceedings; or

    (ii) lead to the commission of an offence by providing access to unlawful material such as pornography.

A record of the grounds shall be made when access is denied.

Notes for guidance

B:7A *Any person claiming property seized by the police may apply to a magistrates' court under the Police* **A-35** *(Property) Act 1897 for its possession and should, if appropriate, be advised of this procedure.*

B:7B *The powers of seizure conferred by PACE, ss.18(2) and 19(3) extend to the seizure of the whole premises when it is physically possible to seize and retain the premises in their totality and practical considerations make seizure desirable. For example, police may remove premises such as tents, vehicles or caravans to a police station for the purpose of preserving evidence.*

B:7C *Officers should consider reaching agreement with owners and/or other interested parties on the procedures for examining a specific set of property, rather than awaiting the judicial authority's determination. Agreement can sometimes give a quicker and more satisfactory route for all concerned and minimise costs and legal complexities.*

B:7D *What constitutes a relevant interest in specific material may depend on the nature of that material and the circumstances in which it is seized. Anyone with a reasonable claim to ownership of the material and anyone entrusted with its safe keeping by the owner should be considered.*

B:7E *Requirements to secure and return property apply equally to all copies, images or other material created because of seizure of the original property.*

B:7F *The mechanics of securing property vary according to the circumstances; "bagging up", i.e. placing material in sealed bags or containers and strict subsequent control of access is the appropriate procedure in many cases.*

B:7G *When material is seized under the powers of seizure conferred by PACE, the duty to retain it under the code of practice issued under the Criminal Procedure and Investigations Act 1996 is subject to the provisions on retention of seized material in PACE, s.22.*

B:7H *Paragraph 7.14(ii) applies if inextricably linked material is seized under the Criminal Justice and Police Act 2001, s.50 or 51. Inextricably linked material is material it is not reasonably practicable to separate from other linked material without prejudicing the use of that other material in any investigation or proceedings. For example, it may not be possible to separate items of data held on computer disk without damaging their evidential integrity. Inextricably linked material must not be examined, imaged, copied or used for any purpose other than for proving the source and/or integrity of the linked material.*

B:8 Action after searches

B:8.1 If premises are searched in circumstances where this code applies, unless the exceptions in paragraph 2.3(a) apply, on arrival at a police station the officer in charge of the search shall make or have made a record of the search, to include: **A-36**

    (i) the address of the searched premises;

    (ii) the date, time and duration of the search;

    (iii) the authority used for the search:
- if the search was made in exercise of a statutory power to search premises without warrant, the power which was used for the search:
- if the search was made under a warrant or with written consent;
   - a copy of the warrant and the written authority to apply for it, see paragraph 3.4; or
   - the written consent;

shall be appended to the record or the record shall show the location of the copy warrant or consent;
    (iv) subject to paragraph 2.9, the names of:
- the officer(s) in charge of the search;
- all other officers and any authorised persons who conducted the search;

    (v) the names of any people on the premises if they are known;
    (vi) any grounds for refusing the occupier's request to have someone present during the search, see paragraph 6.11;
    (vii) a list of any articles seized or the location of a list and, if not covered by a warrant, the grounds for their seizure;
    (viii) whether force was used, and the reason;
    (ix) details of any damage caused during the search, and the circumstances;
    (x) if applicable, the reason it was not practicable:
      (a) to give the occupier a copy of the notice of powers and rights, see paragraph 6.7;
      (b) before the search to give the occupier a copy of the notice, see paragraph 6.8;
    (xi) when the occupier was not present, the place where copies of the notice of powers and rights and search warrant were left on the premises, see paragraph 6.8.

B:8.2 On each occasion when premises are searched under warrant, the warrant authorising the search on that occasion shall be endorsed to show:
    (i) if any articles specified in the warrant were found and the address where found;
    (ii) if any other articles were seized;
    (iii) the date and time it was executed and if present, the name of the occupier or if the occupier is not present the name of the person in charge of the premises;
    (iv) subject to paragraph 2.9, the names of the officers who executed it and any authorised persons who accompanied them; and
    (v) if a copy, together with a copy of the notice of powers and rights was:
- handed to the occupier; or
- endorsed as required by paragraph 6.8; and left on the premises and where.

B:8.3 Any warrant shall be returned within three calendar months of its issue or sooner on completion of the search(es) authorised by that warrant, if it was issued by a:
- justice of the peace, to the designated officer for the local justice area in which the justice was acting when issuing the warrant; or
- judge, to the appropriate officer of the court concerned.

B:9 Search registers

A-37
    B:9.1 A search register will be maintained at each sub-divisional or equivalent police station. All search records required under paragraph 8.1 shall be made, copied, or referred to in the register. [*See Note 9A.*]

Note for guidance

    B:9A *Paragraph 9.1 also applies to search records made by immigration officers. In these cases, a search register must also be maintained at an immigration office.* [*See also Note 2D.*]

B:10 Searches under Schedule 5 to the Terrorism Prevention and Investigation Measures Act 2011

A-37a
    B:10.1 This code applies to the powers of constables under Schedule 5 to the Terrorism Prevention and Investigation Measures Act 2011 relating to TPIM notices to enter and search premises subject to the modifications in the following paragraphs.

    B:10.2 In paragraph 2.3(d), the reference to the investigation into an alleged or suspected offence include [*sic*] the enforcement of terrorism prevention and investigation measures which may be imposed on an individual by a TPIM notice in accordance with the Terrorism Prevention and Investigation Measures Act 2011.

    B:10.3 References to the purpose and object of the entry and search of premises, the nature of articles sought and what may be seized and retained include (as appropriate):

(a) in relation to the power to search without a search warrant in paragraph 5 (for purposes of serving TPIM notice), finding the individual on whom the notice is to be served;

(b) in relation to the power to search without a search warrant in paragraph 6 (at time of serving TPIM notice), ascertaining whether there is anything in the premises, that contravenes measures specified in the notice [see *Note 10A*];

(c) in relation to the power to search without a search warrant under paragraph 7 (suspected absconding), ascertaining whether a person has absconded or if there is anything on the premises which will assist in the pursuit or arrest of an individual in respect of whom a TPIM notice is force who is reasonably suspected of having absconded;

(d) in relation to the power to search under a search warrant issued under paragraph 8 (for compliance purposes), determining whether an individual in respect of whom a notice is in force is complying with measures specified in the notice [see *Note 10A*].

Note for guidance

B:10A *Searches of individuals under Schedule 5, paras 6(2)(a) (at time of serving TPIM notice) and 8(2)(a) (for compliance purposes) must be conducted and recorded in accordance with Code A. See Code A, para. 2.18A for details.*

(4) Detention, treatment and questioning of persons

The text that follows is of the version of the code that came into force on February 23, 2017: see *ante*, A-1. ★**A-38**

For authorities in relation to Code C, see, in particular, §§ 15-237 *et seq.* (right of access to solicitor), § 15-283 (general), § 15-427 (confessions), § 15-489 (sufficient evidence for prosecution to succeed), §§ 15-520 *et seq.* (discretionary exclusion of evidence) in the main work.

C. CODE OF PRACTICE FOR THE DETENTION, TREATMENT AND QUESTIONING OF PERSONS BY POLICE OFFICERS

Commencement—transitional arrangements

This code applies to people in police detention after 00.00 on February 23, 2017, notwithstanding that their period of detention may have commenced before that time. ★**A-39**

C:1 General

C:1.0 The powers and procedures in this code must be used fairly, responsibly, with respect for the people to whom they apply and without unlawful discrimination. Under the Equality Act 2010, section 149 (public sector equality duty), police forces must, in carrying out their functions, have due regard to the need to eliminate unlawful discrimination, harassment, victimisation and any other conduct which is prohibited by that Act, to advance equality of opportunity between people who share a relevant protected characteristic and people who do not share it, and to foster good relations between those persons. The Equality Act *also* makes it unlawful for police officers to discriminate against, harass or victimise any person on the grounds of the 'protected characteristics' of age, disability, gender reassignment, race, religion or belief, sex and sexual orientation, marriage and civil partnership, pregnancy and maternity, when using their powers. See *Notes 1A* and *1AA*. ★**A-40**

C:1.1 All persons in custody must be dealt with expeditiously, and released as soon as the need for detention no longer applies.

C:1.1A A custody officer must perform the functions in this code as soon as practicable. A custody officer will not be in breach of this code if delay is justifiable and reasonable steps are taken to prevent unnecessary delay. The custody record shall show when a delay has occurred and the reason. See *Note 1H*.

C:1.2 This code of practice must be readily available at all police stations for consultation by:

• police officers;
• police staff;
• detained persons;
• members of the public.

C:1.3 The provisions of this code:

• include the *Annexes*
• do not include the *Notes for Guidance.*

C:1.4 If an officer has any suspicion, or is told in good faith, that a person of any age may be mentally disordered or otherwise mentally vulnerable, in the absence of clear evidence to dispel that suspicion, the person shall be treated as such for the purposes of this code. See *Note 1G*.

C:1.5 Anyone who appears to be under 18, shall, in the absence of clear evidence that they are older and subject to paragraph 1.5A, be treated as a juvenile for the purposes of this Code and any other Code. *See Note 1L*

C:1.5A Paragraph 1.5 does not change the statutory provisions in section 65(1) of PACE (appropriate consent) which require the consent of a juvenile's parent or guardian.

In this Code, s.65(1) is relevant to Annex A, paras 2(b) and 2B (Intimate searches) and Annex K, paras 1(b) and 3 (X-Ray and ultrasound scan). In Code D (Identification), section 65(1) is relevant to para. 2.12 and *Note 2A*, which apply to identification procedures, to taking fingerprints, samples, footwear impressions, photographs and to evidential searches and examinations.

C:1.6 If a person appears to be blind, seriously visually impaired, deaf, unable to read or speak or has difficulty orally because of a speech impediment, they shall be treated as such for the purposes of this Code in the absence of clear evidence to the contrary.

★**A-41**

C:1.7 "The appropriate adult" means, in the case of a:

(a) juvenile:

    (i) the parent, guardian or, if the juvenile is in the care of a local authority or voluntary organisation, a person representing that authority or organisation (see *Note 1B*);

    (ii) a social worker of a local authority (see *Note 1C*);

    (iii) failing these, some other responsible adult aged 18 or over who is *not*:
- a police officer;
- employed by the police;
- under the direction or control of the chief officer of a police force; or
- a person who provides services under contractual arrangements (but without being employed by the chief officer of a police force), to assist that force in relation to the discharge of its chief officer's functions,

whether or not they are on duty at the time.

See *Note 1F*.

(b) person who is mentally disordered or mentally vulnerable: See *Note 1D*.

    (i) a relative, guardian or other person responsible for their care or custody;

    (ii) someone experienced in dealing with mentally disordered or mentally vulnerable people but who is not:
- a police officer;
- employed by the police;
- under the direction or control of the chief officer of a police force; or
- a person who provides services under contractual arrangements (but without being employed by the chief officer of a police force), to assist that force in relation to the discharge of its chief officer's functions,

whether or not they are on duty at the time;

    (iii) failing these, some other responsible adult aged 18 or over other than a person described in the bullet points in sub-paragraph (b)(ii) above.

See *Note 1F*.

C:1.8 If this code requires a person be given certain information, they do not have to be given it if at the time they are incapable of understanding what is said, are violent or may become violent or in urgent need of medical attention, but they must be given it as soon as practicable.

C:1.9 References to a custody officer include any police officer who, for the time being, is performing the functions of a custody officer.

C:1.9A When this code requires the prior authority or agreement of an officer of at least inspector or superintendent rank, that authority may be given by a sergeant or chief inspector authorised to perform the functions of the higher rank under the Police and Criminal Evidence Act 1984 (PACE), s.107.

C:1.10 Subject to paragraph 1.12, this code applies to people in custody at police stations in England and Wales, whether or not they have been arrested, and to those removed to a police station as a place of safety under the Mental Health Act 1983, ss.135 and 136, as a last resort (see para. 3.16). Section 15 applies solely to people in police detention, *e.g.* those brought to a police station under arrest or arrested at a police station for an offence after going there voluntarily.

C:1.11 No part of this code applies to a detained person:

(a) to whom PACE Code H applies because:
- they are detained following arrest under section 41 of the Terrorism Act 2000 (TACT) and not charged; or
- an authorisation has been given under section 22 of the Counter-Terrorism Act 2008 (CTACT) (post-charge questioning of terrorist suspects) to interview them.

(b) to whom the code of practice issued under paragraph 6 of Schedule 14 to TACT applies because they are detained for examination under Schedule 7 to TACT.

C:1.12 This code does not apply to people in custody:

  (i) arrested by officers under the Criminal Justice and Public Order Act 1994, s.136(2) on warrants issued in Scotland, or arrested or detained without warrant under section 137(2) by officers from a police force in Scotland. In these cases, police powers and duties and the person's rights and entitlements whilst at a police station in England or Wales are the same as those in Scotland;

  (ii) arrested under the Immigration and Asylum Act 1999, s.142(3) in order to have their fingerprints taken;

  (iii) whose detention has been authorised under Schedules 2 or 3 to the Immigration Act 1971 or section 62 of the Nationality, Immigration and Asylum Act 2002;

  (iv) who are convicted or remanded prisoners held in police cells on behalf of the Prison Service under the Imprisonment (Temporary Provisions) Act 1980;

  (v) [*not used;*]

  (vi) detained for searches under stop and search powers except as required by Code A.

The provisions on conditions of detention and treatment in sections 8 and 9 must be considered as the minimum standards of treatment for such detainees.

C:1.13 In this code:

  (a) "designated person" means a person other than a police officer, who has specified powers and duties conferred or imposed on them by designation under section 38 or 39 of the Police Reform Act 2002;

  (b) reference to a police officer includes a designated person acting in the exercise or performance of the powers and duties conferred or imposed on them by their designation;

  (c) where a search or other procedure to which this code applies may only be carried out or observed by a person of the same sex as the detainee, the gender of the detainee and other parties present should be established and recorded in line with Annex L of this Code.

C:1.14 Designated persons are entitled to use reasonable force as follows: ★**A-42**

  (a) when exercising a power conferred on them which allows a police officer exercising that power to use reasonable force, a designated person has the same entitlement to use force; and

  (b) at other times when carrying out duties conferred or imposed on them that also entitle them to use reasonable force, for example:

    • when at a police station carrying out the duty to keep detainees for whom they are responsible under control and to assist any police officer or designated person to keep any detainee under control and to prevent their escape;

    • when securing, or assisting any police officer or designated person in securing, the detention of a person at a police station;

    • when escorting, or assisting any police officer or designated person in escorting, a detainee within a police station;

    • for the purpose of saving life or limb; or

    • preventing serious damage to property.

C:1.15 Nothing in this code prevents the custody officer, or other police officer or designated person (see para. 1.13) given custody of the detainee by the custody officer, from allowing another person (see (a) and (b) below) to carry out individual procedures or tasks at the police station if the law allows. However, the officer or designated person given custody remains responsible for making sure the procedures and tasks are carried out correctly in accordance with the codes of practice (see para. 3.5 and *Note 3F*). The other person who is allowed to carry out the procedures or tasks must be someone who *at that time*, is:

  (a) under the direction and control of the chief officer of the force responsible for the police station in question; or

  (b) providing services under contractual arrangements (but without being employed by the chief officer the police force), to assist a police force in relation to the discharge of its chief officer's functions.

C:1.16 Designated persons and others mentioned in sub-paras (a) and (b) of para. 1.15, must have regard to any relevant provisions of the codes of practice.

C:1.17 In any provision of this or any other code which allows or requires police officers or police staff to make a record in their report book, the reference to report book shall include any official report book or electronic recording device issued to them that enables the record in question to be made and dealt with in accordance with that provision. References in this and any other code to written records, forms and signatures include electronic records and forms and electronic confirmation that identifies the person making the record or completing the form.

Chief officers must be satisfied as to the integrity and security of the devices, records and forms to which this paragraph applies and that use of those devices, records and forms satisfies relevant data protection legislation.

Notes for guidance

★**A-43**   C:1A *Although certain sections of this code apply specifically to people in custody at police stations, those there voluntarily to assist with an investigation should be treated with no less consideration, e.g. offered refreshments at appropriate times, and enjoy an absolute right to obtain legal advice or communicate with anyone outside the police station.*

C:1AA *In paragraph 1.0, under the Equality Act 2010, s.149, the 'relevant protected characteristics' are age, disability, gender reassignment, pregnancy and maternity, race, religion/belief and sex and sexual orientation. For further detailed guidance and advice on the Equality Act, see: https://www.gov.uk/guidance/eq uality-act-2010-guidance.*

C:1B *A person, including a parent or guardian, should not be an appropriate adult if they:*

- *are:*
    - ~ *suspected of involvement in the offence;*
    - ~ *the victim;*
    - ~ *a witness;*
    - ~ *involved in the investigation.*
- *received admissions prior to attending to act as the appropriate adult.*

Note: If a juvenile's parent is estranged from the juvenile, they should not be asked to act as the appropriate adult if the juvenile expressly and specifically objects to their presence.

C:1C *If a juvenile admits an offence to, or in the presence of, a social worker or member of a youth offending team other than during the time that person is acting as the juvenile's appropriate adult, another appropriate adult should be appointed in the interest of fairness.*

C:1D *In the case of people who are mentally disordered or otherwise mentally vulnerable, it may be more satisfactory if the appropriate adult is someone experienced or trained in their care rather than a relative lacking such qualifications. But if the detainee prefers a relative to a better qualified stranger or objects to a particular person their wishes should, if practicable, be respected.*

C:1E *A detainee should always be given an opportunity, when an appropriate adult is called to the police station, to consult privately with a solicitor in the appropriate adult's absence if they want. An appropriate adult is not subject to legal privilege.*

C:1F *A solicitor or independent custody visitor who is present at the police station and acting in that capacity, may not be the appropriate adult.*

C:1G *"Mentally vulnerable" applies to any detainee who, because of their mental state or capacity, may not understand the significance of what is said, of questions or of their replies. "Mental disorder" is defined in the Mental Health Act 1983, s.1(2) as "any disorder or disability of mind". When the custody officer has any doubt about the mental state or capacity of a detainee, that detainee should be treated as mentally vulnerable and an appropriate adult called.*

C:1H *Paragraph 1.1A is intended to cover delays which may occur in processing detainees e.g. if:*

- *a large number of suspects are brought into the station simultaneously to be placed in custody;*
- *interview rooms are all being used;*
- *there are difficulties contacting an appropriate adult, solicitor or interpreter.*

C:1I *The custody officer must remind the appropriate adult and detainee about the right to legal advice and record any reasons for waiving it in accordance with section 6.*

C:1J *[Not used.]*

C:1K *This Code does not affect the principle that all citizens have a duty to help police officers to prevent crime and discover offenders. This is a civic rather than a legal duty; but when police officers are trying to discover whether, or by whom, offences have been committed they are entitled to question any person from whom they think useful information can be obtained, subject to the restrictions imposed by this Code. A person's declaration that they are unwilling to reply does not alter this entitlement.*

C:1L *Paragraph 1.5 reflects the statutory definition of "arrested juvenile" in section 37(15) of PACE. This section was amended by section 42 of the Criminal Justice and Courts Act 2015 with effect from 26 October 2015, and includes anyone who appears to be under the age of 18. This definition applies for the purposes of the detention and bail provisions in sections 34 to 51 of PACE.*

C:2 Custody records

C:2.1A When a person:
- is brought to a police station under arrest
- is arrested at the police station having attended there voluntarily or
- attends a police station to answer bail

they must be brought before the custody officer as soon as practicable after their arrival at the station or if applicable, following their arrest after attending the police station voluntarily. This applies to both designated and non-designated police stations. A person is deemed to be "at a police station" for these purposes if they are within the boundary of any building or enclosed yard which forms part of that police station.

C:2.1 A separate custody record must be opened as soon as practicable for each person brought to a police station under arrest or arrested at the station having gone there voluntarily or attending a police station in answer to street bail. All information recorded under this Code must be recorded as soon as practicable in the custody record unless otherwise specified. Any audio or video recording made in the custody area is not part of the custody record.

C:2.2 If any action requires the authority of an officer of a specified rank, subject to paragraph 2.6A, their name and rank must be noted in the custody record.

C:2.3 The custody officer is responsible for the custody record's accuracy and completeness and for making sure the record or copy of the record accompanies a detainee if they are transferred to another police station. The record shall show the:
- time and reason for transfer;
- time a person is released from detention.

C:2.3A If a person is arrested and taken to a police station as a result of a search in the exercise of any stop and search power to which PACE Code A (stop and search) or the "search powers code" is-sued under TACT applies, the officer carrying out the search is responsible for ensuring that the record of that stop and search is made as part of the person's custody record. The custody officer must then ensure that the person is asked if they want a copy of the search record and if they do, that they are given a copy as soon as practicable. The person's entitlement to a copy of the search record which is made as part of their custody record is in addition to, and does not affect, their entitlement to a copy of their custody record or any other provisions of section 2 (custody records) of this code. (See Code A, para. 4.2B and the TACT search powers code, para. 5.3.5).

C:2.4 The detainee's solicitor and appropriate adult must be permitted to inspect the whole of the detainee's custody record as soon as practicable after their arrival at the station and at any other time on request, whilst the person is detained. This includes the following *specific* records relating to the reasons for the detainee's arrest and detention and the offence concerned to which paragraph 3.1(b) refers:

(a) The information about the circumstances and reasons for the detainee's arrest as recorded in the custody record in accordance with paragraph 4.3 of Code G. This applies to any further offences for which the detainee is arrested whilst in custody;

(b) The record of the grounds for each authorisation to keep the person in custody. The authorisations to which this applies are the same as those described at items (i)(a) to (d) in the table in paragraph 2 of Annex M [*sic*] of this Code.

Access to the records in sub-paragraphs (a) and (b) is *in addition* to the requirements in paragraphs 3.4(b), 11.1A, 15.0, 15,7A(c) and 16.7A to make certain documents and materials available and to provide information about the offence and the reasons for arrest and detention.

Access to the custody record for the purposes of this paragraph must be arranged and agreed with the custody officer and may not unreasonably interfere with the custody officer's duties. A record shall be made when access is allowed and whether it includes the records described in sub-paragraphs (a) and (b) above.

C:2.4A When a detainee leaves police detention or is taken before a court they, their legal representative or appropriate adult shall be given, on request, a copy of the custody record as soon as practicable. This entitlement lasts for 12 months after release.

C:2.5 The detainee, appropriate adult or legal representative shall be permitted to inspect the original custody record after the detainee has left police detention provided they give reasonable notice of their request. Any such inspection shall be noted in the custody record.

C:2.6 Subject to paragraph 2.6A, all entries in custody records must be timed and signed by the maker. Records entered on computer shall be timed and contain the operator's identification.

C:2.6A Nothing in this Code requires the identity of officers or other police staff to be recorded or disclosed:

(a) [*not used*];

(b) if the officer or police staff reasonably believe recording or disclosing their name might put them in danger.

In these cases, they shall use their warrant or other identification numbers and the name of their police station. See *Note 2A.*

C:2.7 The fact and time of any detainee's refusal to sign a custody record, when asked in accordance with this code, must be recorded.

Note for guidance

★A-45   C:2A *The purpose of paragraph 2.6A(b) is to protect those involved in serious organised crime investigations or arrests of particularly violent suspects when there is reliable information that those arrested or their associates may threaten or cause harm to those involved. In cases of doubt, an officer of inspector rank or above should be consulted.*

C:3 Initial action

(a) *Detained persons–normal procedure*

★A-46   C:3.1 When a person is brought to a police station under arrest or arrested at the station having gone there voluntarily, the custody officer must make sure the person is told clearly about:

   (a) the following continuing rights, which may be exercised at any stage during the period in custody:
   (i) their right to consult privately with a solicitor and that free independent legal advice is available as in section 6;
   (ii) their right to have someone informed of their arrest as in section 5;
   (iii) their right to consult the codes of practice (see *Note 3D*); and
   (iv) if applicable, their right to interpretation and translation (see para. 3.12) and their right to communicate with their High Commission, Embassy or Consulate (see para. 3.12A).
   (b) their right to be informed about the offence and (as the case may be) any further offences for which they are arrested whilst in custody and why they have been arrested and detained in accordance with paragraphs 2.4, 3.4(a) and 11.1A of this code and paragraph 3.3 of Code G.

C:3.2 The detainee must also be given a written notice, which contains information:

   (a) to allow them to exercise their rights by setting out:
   (i) their rights under paragraph 3.1, paragraph 3.12 and 3.12A;
   (ii) the arrangements for obtaining legal advice, see section 6;
   (iii) their right to a copy of the custody record as in paragraph 2.4A;
   (iv) their right to remain silent as set out in the caution in the terms prescribed in section 10;
   (v) their right to have access to materials and documents which are essential to effectively challenging the lawfulness of their arrest and detention for any offence and (as the case may be) any further offences for which they are arrested whilst in custody, in accordance with paragraphs 3.4(b), 15.0, 15.7A(c) and 16.7A of this code;
   (vi) the maximum period for which they may be kept in police detention without being charged, when detention must be reviewed and when release is required;
   (vii) their right to medical assistance in accordance with section 9 of this code;
   (viii) their right, if they are prosecuted, to have access to the evidence in the case before their trial in accordance with the Criminal Procedure and Investigations Act 1996, the Attorney General's Guidelines on Disclosure, the common law and the Criminal Procedure Rules; and
   (b) briefly setting out their other entitlements while in custody, by:
   (i) mentioning:
      – the provisions relating to the conduct of interviews;
      – the circumstances in which an appropriate adult should be available to assist the detainee and their statutory rights to make representations whenever the need for their detention is reviewed;
   (ii) listing the entitlements in this code, concerning;
      – reasonable standards of physical comfort;
      – adequate food and drink;
      – access to toilets and washing facilities, clothing, medical attention, and exercise

when practicable.

See *Note 3A.*

C:3.2A The detainee must be given an opportunity to read the notice and shall be asked to sign the custody record to acknowledge receipt of the notice. Any refusal to sign must be recorded on the custody record.

C:3.3 [*Not used.*]

C:3.3A An 'easy read' illustrated version should also be provided if available (see *Note 3A*).

C:3.4 (a) The custody officer shall:

- record the offence(s) that the detainee has been arrested for and the reason(s) for the arrest on the custody record. See paragraph 10.3 and Code G paragraphs 2.2 and 4.3;
- note on the custody record any comment the detainee makes in relation to the arresting officer's account but shall not invite comment. If the arresting officer is not physically present when the detainee is brought to a police station, the arresting officer's account must be made available to the custody officer remotely or by a third party on the arresting officer's behalf. If the custody officer authorises a person's detention, subject to paragraph 1.8, that officer must record the grounds for detention in the detainee's presence and at the same time, inform them of the grounds. The detainee must be informed of the grounds for their detention before they are questioned about any offence;
- note any comment the detainee makes in respect of the decision to detain them but shall not invite comment;
- not put specific questions to the detainee regarding their involvement in any offence, nor in respect of any comments they may make in response to the arresting officer's account or the decision to place them in detention. Such an exchange is likely to constitute an interview as in paragraph 11.1A and require the associated safeguards in section 11.

Note: This sub-paragraph also applies to any further offences and grounds for detention which come to light whilst the person is detained.

See paragraph 11.13 in respect of unsolicited comments.

(b) Documents and materials which are essential to effectively challenging the lawfulness of the detainee's arrest and detention must be made available to the detainee or their solicitor. Documents and materials will be "essential" for this purpose if they are capable of undermining the reasons and grounds which make the detainee's arrest and detention *necessary*. The decision about whether particular documents or materials must be made available for the purpose of this requirement therefore rests with the custody officer who determines whether detention is necessary, in consultation with the investigating officer who has the knowledge of the documents and materials in a particular case necessary to inform that decision. A note should be made in the detainee's custody record of the *fact* that documents or materials have been made available under this sub-paragraph and when. The investigating officer should make a separate note of what is made available and how it is made available in a particular case. This sub-paragraph also applies (with modifications) for the purposes of sections 15 (reviews and extensions of detention) and 16 (charging detained persons). See *Note 3ZA* and paragraphs 15.0 and 16.7A.

C:3.5 The custody officer or other custody staff as directed by the custody officer shall:

(a) ask the detainee whether at this time, they:

  (i) would like legal advice, see paragraph 6.5;

  (ii) want someone informed of their detention, see section 5;

(b) ask the detainee to sign the custody record to confirm their decisions in respect of (a);

(c) determine whether the detainee:

  (i) is, or might be, in need of medical treatment or attention, see section 9;

  (ii) requires:

- an appropriate adult (see paras 1.4, 1.5, 1.5A and 3.15);
- help to check documentation (see para. 3.20);
- an interpreter (see para. 3.12 and *Note 13B*).

(d) record the decision in respect of (c).

Where any duties under this paragraph have been carried out by custody staff at the direction of the custody officer, the outcomes shall, as soon as practicable, be reported to the custody officer who retains overall responsibility for the detainee's care and treatment and ensuring that it complies with this code. See *Note 3F.*

C:3.6 When the needs mentioned in paragraph 3.5(c) are being determined, the custody officer is responsible for initiating an assessment to consider whether the detainee is likely to present specific risks to custody staff, any individual who may have contact with detainee (*e.g.* legal advisers, medical staff) or themselves. This risk assessment must include the taking of reasonable steps to establish the detainee's identity and to obtain information about the detainee that is relevant to their safe custody, security and welfare and risks to others. Such assessments should therefore always include a check on the Police National Computer (PNC), to be carried out as soon as practicable, to identify any risks that have been highlighted in relation to the detainee. Although such assessments are primarily the custody officer's responsibility, it may be necessary for them to consult and involve others, *e.g.* the arresting officer or an appropriate healthcare professional, see paragraph 9.13. Other records held by or on behalf of the police and other UK law enforcement authorities that might provide information relevant to the detainee's safe custody, security and welfare and risk to others and to confirming their identity should also be checked. Reasons for delaying the initiation or completion of the assessment must be recorded.

C:3.7 Chief officers should ensure that arrangements for proper and effective risk assessments required by paragraph 3.6 are implemented in respect of all detainees at police stations in their area.

C:3.8 Risk assessments must follow a structured process which clearly defines the categories of risk to be considered and the results must be incorporated in the detainee's custody record. The custody officer is responsible for making sure those responsible for the detainee's custody are appropriately briefed about the risks. If no specific risks are identified by the assessment, that should be noted in the custody record. See *Note 3E* and paragraph 9.14.

C:3.8A The content of any risk assessment and any analysis of the level of risk relating to the person's detention is not required to be shown or provided to the detainee or any person acting on behalf of the detainee. But information should not be withheld from any person acting on the detainee's behalf, for example, an appropriate adult, solicitor or interpreter, if to do so might put that person at risk.

C:3.9 The custody officer is responsible for implementing the response to any specific risk assessment, *e.g.*:

- reducing opportunities for self harm;
- calling an appropriate healthcare professional;
- increasing levels of monitoring or observation;
- reducing the risk to those who come into contact with the detainee.

See *Note 3E.*

C:3.10 Risk assessment is an ongoing process and assessments must always be subject to review if circumstances change.

C:3.11 If video cameras are installed in the custody area, notices shall be prominently displayed showing cameras are in use. Any request to have video cameras switched off shall be refused.

(b) *Detained persons–special groups*

★**A-47**   C:3.12 If the detainee appears to be someone who does not speak or understand English or who has a hearing or speech impediment, the custody officer must ensure:

- (a) that without delay, arrangements (see para. 13.1ZA) are made for the detainee to have the assistance of an interpreter in the action under paragraphs 3.1 to 3.5. If the person appears to have a hearing or speech impediment, the reference to 'interpreter' includes appropriate assistance necessary to comply with paragraphs 3.1 to 3.5. See paragraph 13.1C if the detainee is in Wales. See section 13 and *Note 13B*;
- (b) that in addition to the continuing rights set out in paragraph 3.1(a)(i) to (iv), the detainee is told clearly about their right to interpretation and translation;
- (c) that the written notice given to the detainee in accordance with paragraph 3.2 is in a language the detainee understands and includes the right to interpretation and translation together with information about the provisions in section 13 and Annex M, which explain how the right applies (see *Note 3A*); and
- (d) that if the translation of the notice is not available, the information in the notice is given through an interpreter and a written translation provided without undue delay.

C:3.12A If the detainee is a citizen of an independent Commonwealth country or a national of a foreign country, including the Republic of Ireland, the custody officer must ensure that in addition to the continuing rights set out in paragraph 3.1(a)(i) to (iv), they are informed as soon as practicable about their rights of communication with their High Commission, Embassy or Consulate set out in section 7. This right must be included in the written notice given to the detainee in accordance with paragraph 3.2.

C:3.13 If the detainee is a juvenile, the custody officer must, if it is practicable, ascertain the identity of a person responsible for their welfare. That person:

- may be:
    - the parent or guardian;
    - if the juvenile is in local authority or voluntary organisation care, or is otherwise being looked after under the Children Act 1989, a person appointed by that authority or organisation to have responsibility for the juvenile's welfare;
    - any other person who has, for the time being, assumed responsibility for the juvenile's welfare.
- must be informed as soon as practicable that the juvenile has been arrested, why they have been arrested and where they are detained. This right is in addition to the juvenile's right in section 5 not to be held incommunicado. See *Note 3C*.

C:3.14 If a juvenile is known to be subject to a court order under which a person or organisation is given any degree of statutory responsibility to supervise or otherwise monitor them, reasonable steps must also be taken to notify that person or organisation (the "responsible officer"). The responsible officer will normally be a member of a Youth Offending Team, except for a curfew order which involves electronic monitoring when the contractor providing the monitoring will normally be the responsible officer.

C:3.15 If the detainee is a juvenile, mentally disordered or otherwise mentally vulnerable, the custody officer must, as soon as practicable:

- inform the appropriate adult, who in the case of a juvenile may or may not be a person responsible for their welfare, as in paragraph 3.13, of:
    - the grounds for their detention;
    - their whereabouts.
- ask the adult to come to the police station to see the detainee.

C:3.16 It is imperative that a mentally disordered or otherwise mentally vulnerable person, detained under the Mental Health Act 1983, s.136, be assessed as soon as possible. A police station should only be used as a place of safety as a last resort but if that assessment is to take place at the police station, an approved mental health professional and a registered medical practitioner shall be called to the station as soon as possible to carry it out. See *Note 9D*. The appropriate adult has no role in the assessment process and their presence is not required. Once the detainee has been assessed and suitable arrangements made for their treatment or care, they can no longer be detained under section 136. A detainee must be immediately discharged from detention under section 136 if a registered medical practitioner, having examined them, concludes they are not mentally disordered within the meaning of the Act.

C:3.17 If the appropriate adult is:

- already at the police station, the provisions of paragraphs 3.1 to 3.5 must be complied with in the appropriate adult's presence;
- not at the station when these provisions are complied with, they must be complied with again in the presence of the appropriate adult when they arrive,

and a copy of the notice given to the detainee in accordance with paragraph 3.2, shall also be given to the appropriate adult.

C:3.18 The detainee shall be advised that:

- the duties of the appropriate adult include giving advice and assistance;
- they can consult privately with the appropriate adult at any time.

C:3.19 If the detainee, or appropriate adult on the detainee's behalf, asks for a solicitor to be called to give legal advice, the provisions of section 6 apply.

C:3.20 If the detainee is blind, seriously visually impaired or unable to read, the custody officer shall make sure their solicitor, relative, appropriate adult or some other person likely to take an interest in them and not involved in the investigation is available to help check any documentation. When this Code requires written consent or signing the person assisting may be asked to sign instead, if the detainee prefers. This paragraph does not require an appropriate adult to be called solely to assist in checking and signing documentation for a person who is not a juvenile, or mentally disordered or otherwise mentally vulnerable (see para. 3.15 and *Note 13C*).

C:3.20A The Children and Young Persons Act 1933, s.31, requires that arrangements must be made for ensuring that a girl under the age of 18, while detained in a police station, is under the care of a woman. See *Note 3G*. It also requires that arrangements must be made for preventing any person under 18, while being detained in a police station, from associating with an adult charged with any offence, unless that adult is a relative or the adult is jointly charged with the same offence as the person under 18.

(c) *Persons attending a police station or elsewhere voluntarily*

★**A-48**   C:3.21 Anybody attending a police station or other location (see paragraph 3.22) voluntarily to assist police with the investigation of an offence may leave at will unless arrested. See *Note 1K*. The person may only be prevented from leaving at will if their arrest on suspicion of committing the offence is necessary in accordance with Code G. See Code G, *Note 2G*.

(a) If during an interview it is decided that their arrest is necessary, they must:

- be informed at once that they are under arrest and of the grounds and reasons as required by Code G, and

- be brought before the custody officer at the police station where they are arrested or, as the case may be, at the police station to which they are taken after being arrested elsewhere. The custody officer is then responsible for making sure that a custody record is opened and that they are notified of their rights in the same way as other detainees as required by this code.

(b) If they are not arrested but are cautioned as in section 10, the person who gives the caution must, at the same time, inform them they are not under arrest and they are not obliged to remain at the station or other location, but if they agree to remain, they may obtain free and independent legal advice if they want. They shall also be given a copy of the notice explaining the arrangements for obtaining legal advice and told that the right to legal advice includes the right to speak with a solicitor on the telephone and be asked if they want advice. If advice is requested, the interviewer is responsible for securing its provision without delay by contacting the Defence Solicitor Call Centre. The interviewer is responsible for confirming that the suspect has given their agreement to be interviewed voluntarily. In the case of a juvenile or mentally vulnerable suspect, this must be given in the presence of the appropriate adult and for a juvenile, the agreement of a parent or guardian of the juvenile is also required. The interviewer must ensure that other provisions of this code and Codes E and F concerning the conduct and recording of interviews of suspects and the rights and entitlements and safeguards for suspects who have been arrested and detained are followed insofar as they can be applied to suspects who are not under arrest. This includes:

- informing them of the offence and, as the case may be, any further offences, they are suspected of and the grounds and reasons for that suspicion and their right to be so informed (see para. 3.1(b));

- the caution as required in section 10;

- determining whether they require an appropriate adult and help to check documentation (see paragraph 3.5(c)(ii)); and

- determining whether they require an interpreter and the provision of interpretation and translation services and informing them of that right. See paragraphs 3.1(a)(iv), 3.5(c)(ii) and 3.12, *Note 6B* and section 13.

but does not include any requirement to provide a written notice in addition to that above which concerns the arrangements for obtaining legal advice.

C:3.22 If the other location mentioned in paragraph 3.21 is any place or premises for which the interviewer requires the person's informed consent to remain, for example, the person's home, then the references that the person is "not obliged to remain'" and that they "may leave at will" mean that the person may also withdraw their consent and require the interviewer to leave.

(d) *Documentation*

C:3.23 The grounds for a person's detention shall be recorded, in the person's presence if practicable. See paragraph 1.8.

C:3.24 Action taken under paragraphs 3.12 to 3.20 shall be recorded.

(e) *Persons answering street bail*

C:3.25 When a person is answering street bail, the custody officer should link any documentation held in relation to arrest with the custody record. Any further action shall be recorded on the custody record in accordance with paragraphs 3.23 and 3.24 above.

(f) *Requirements for suspects to be informed of certain rights*

C:3.26 The provisions of this section identify the information which must be given to suspects who have been cautioned in accordance with section 10 of this code according to whether or not they have been arrested and detained. It includes information required by EU Directive 2012/13 on the right to information in criminal proceedings. If a complaint is made by or on behalf of such a suspect that the information and (as the case may be) access to records and documents has not been provided as required, the matter shall be reported to an inspector to deal with as a complaint for the purposes of paragraph 9.2, or paragraph 12.9 if the challenge is made during an interview. This would include, for example:

(a) in the case of a detained suspect:
- not informing them of their rights (see paragraph 3.1);
- not giving them a copy of the notice (see paragraph 3.2(a));
- not providing an opportunity to read the notice (see paragraph 3.2A);
- not providing the required information (see paragraphs 3.2(a), 3.12(b) and, 3.12A;
- not allowing access to the custody record (see paragraph 2.4);
- not providing a translation of the notice (see paragraph 3.12(c) and (d)); and

(b) in the case of a suspect who is not detained:
- not informing them of their rights or providing the required information (see paragraph 3.21(b)).

Notes for guidance

C:3ZA *For the purposes of paragraphs 3.4(b) and 15.0:* ★**A-49**

(a) *Investigating officers are responsible for bringing to the attention of the officer who is responsible for authorising the suspect's detention or (as the case may be) continued detention (before or after charge), any documents and materials in their possession or control which appear to undermine the need to keep the suspect in custody. In accordance with Part IV of PACE, this officer will be either the custody officer, the officer reviewing the need for detention before or after charge (PACE, s.40), or the officer considering the need to extend detention without charge from 24 to 36 hours (PACE, s.42) who is then responsible for determining, which, if any, of those documents and materials are capable of undermining the need to detain the suspect and must therefore be made available to the suspect or their solicitor.*

(b) *the way in which documents and materials are "made available", is a matter for the investigating officer to determine on a case by case basis and having regard to the nature and volume of the documents and materials involved. For example, they may be made available by supplying a copy or allowing supervised access to view. However, for view only access, it will be necessary to demonstrate that sufficient time is allowed for the suspect and solicitor to view and consider the documents and materials in question.*

C:3A *For access to currently available notices, including "easy-read" versions, see https://www.gov.uk/guidance/notice-of-rights-and-entitlements-a-persons-rights-in-police-detention.*

C:3B [*Not used.*]

C:3C *If the juvenile is in local authority or voluntary organisation care but living with their parents or other adults responsible for their welfare, although there is no legal obligation to inform them, they should normally be contacted, as well as the authority or organisation unless they are suspected of involvement in the offence concerned. Even if the juvenile is not living with their parents, consideration should be given to informing them.*

C:3D *The right to consult the codes of practice does not entitle the person concerned to delay unreasonably any necessary investigative or administrative action whilst they do so. Examples of action which need not be delayed unreasonably include:*

- *procedures requiring the provision of breath, blood or urine specimens under the Road Traffic Act 1988 or the Transport and Works Act 1992;*
- *searching detainees at the police station;*
- *taking fingerprints, footwear impressions or non-intimate samples without consent for evidential purposes.*

C:3E *The Detention and Custody Authorised Professional Practice (APP) produced by the College of Policing (see http://www.app.college.police.uk) provides more detailed guidance on risk assessments and identifies key risk areas which should always be considered. See Home Office Circular 34/2007 (safety of solicitors and probationary representatives at police stations).*

C:3F *A custody officer or other officer who, in accordance with this code, allows or directs the carrying out of any task or action relating to a detainee's care, treatment, rights and entitlements to another officer or any other person, must be satisfied that the officer or person concerned is suitable, trained and competent to carry out the task or action in question.*

C:3G *Guidance for police officers and police staff on the operational application of section 31 of the Children and Young Persons Act 1933 has been published by the College of Policing and is available at: https://www.app.college.police.uk/app-content/detention-and-custody-2/detainee-care/children-and-young-persons/#girls.*

C:4 Detainee's property

(a) *Action*

★**A-50**   C:4.1 The custody officer is responsible for:
(a) ascertaining what property a detainee:
(i) has with them when they come to the police station, whether on:
- arrest or re-detention on answering to bail;
- commitment to prison custody on the order or sentence of a court;
- lodgement at the police station with a view to their production in court from prison custody;
- transfer from detention at another station or hospital;
- detention under the Mental Health Act 1983, section 135 or 136;
- remand into police custody on the authority of a court.
(ii) might have acquired for an unlawful or harmful purpose while in custody;
(b) the safekeeping of any property taken from a detainee which remains at the police station.

The custody officer may search the detainee or authorise their being searched to the extent they consider necessary, provided a search of intimate parts of the body or involving the removal of more than outer clothing is only made as in Annex A. A search may only be carried out by an officer of the same sex as the detainee. See *Note 4A* and Annex L.

C:4.2 Detainees may retain clothing and personal effects at their own risk unless the custody officer considers they may use them to cause harm to themselves or others, interfere with evidence, damage property, effect an escape or they are needed as evidence. In this event the custody officer may withhold such articles as they consider necessary and must tell the detainee why.

C:4.3 Personal effects are those items a detainee may lawfully need, use or refer to while in detention but do not include cash and other items of value.

(b) *Documentation*

C:4.4 It is a matter for the custody officer to determine whether a record should be made of the property a detained person has with him or had taken from him on arrest. Any record made is not required to be kept as part of the custody record but the custody record should be noted as to where such a record exists and that record shall be treated as being part of the custody record for the purpose of this and any other Code of Practice (see paragraphs 2.4, 2.4A and 2.5). Whenever a record is made the detainee shall be allowed to check and sign the record of property as correct. Any refusal to sign shall be recorded.

C:4.5 If a detainee is not allowed to keep any article of clothing or personal effects, the reason must be recorded.

Notes for guidance

★**A-51**   C:4A *PACE, s.54(1) and para. 4.1 require a detainee to be searched when it is clear the custody officer will have continuing duties in relation to that detainee or when that detainee's behaviour or offence makes an inventory appropriate. They do not require every detainee to be searched, e.g. if it is clear a person will only be detained for a short period and is not to be placed in a cell, the custody officer may decide not to search them. In such a case the custody record will be endorsed 'not searched', paragraph 4.4 will not apply, and the detainee will be invited to sign the entry. If the detainee refuses, the custody officer will be obliged to ascertain what property they have in accordance with paragraph 4.1.*

C:4B *Paragraph 4.4 does not require the custody officer to record on the custody record property in the detainee's possession on arrest if, by virtue of its nature, quantity or size, it is not practicable to remove it to the police station.*

C:4C *Paragraph 4.4 does not require items of clothing worn by the person to be recorded unless withheld by the custody officer as in paragraph 4.2.*

C:5 Right not to be held incommunicado

(a) *Action*

★**A-52**   C:5.1 Subject to paragraph 5.7B, any person arrested and held in custody at a police station or other premises may, on request, have one person known to them or likely to take an interest in their welfare informed at public expense of their whereabouts as soon as practicable. If the person cannot be contacted the detainee may choose up to two alternatives. If they cannot be contacted, the person in charge of detention or the investigation has discretion to allow further attempts until the information has been conveyed. See *Notes 5C* and *5D*.

C:5.2 The exercise of the above right in respect of each person nominated may be delayed only in accordance with Annex B.

C:5.3 The above right may be exercised each time a detainee is taken to another police station.

C:5.4 If the detainee agrees, they may at the custody officer's discretion, receive visits from friends, family or others likely to take an interest in their welfare, or in whose welfare the detainee has an interest. See *Note 5B*.

C:5.5 If a friend, relative or person with an interest in the detainee's welfare enquires about their whereabouts, this information shall be given if the suspect agrees and Annex B does not apply. See *Note 5D*.

C:5.6 The detainee shall be given writing materials, on request, and allowed to telephone one person for a reasonable time, see *Notes 5A* and *5E*. Either or both of these privileges may be denied or delayed if an officer of inspector rank or above considers sending a letter or making a telephone call may result in any of the consequences in:

> (a) Annex B paras 1 and 2 and the person is detained in connection with an indictable offence;
>
> (b) [*not used*].

Nothing in this paragraph permits the restriction or denial of the rights in paragraphs 5.1 and 6.1.

C:5.7 Before any letter or message is sent, or telephone call made, the detainee shall be informed that what they say in any letter, call or message (other than in a communication to a solicitor) may be read or listened to and may be given in evidence. A telephone call may be terminated if it is being abused. The costs can be at public expense at the custody officer's discretion.

C:5.7A Any delay or denial of the rights in this section should be proportionate and should last no longer than necessary.

C:5.7B In the case of a person in police custody for specific purposes and periods in accordance with a direction under the Crime (Sentences) Act 1997, Sched. 1 (productions from prison etc.), the exercise of the rights in this section shall be subject to any additional conditions specified in the direction for the purpose of regulating the detainee's contact and communication with others whilst in police custody. See *Note 5F*.

(b) *Documentation*

C:5.8 A record must be kept of any:

> (a) request made under this section and the action taken;
>
> (b) letters, messages or telephone calls made or received or visit received;
>
> (c) refusal by the detainee to have information about them given to an outside enquirer. The detainee must be asked to countersign the record accordingly and any refusal recorded.

Notes for guidance

C:5A *A person may request an interpreter to interpret a telephone call or translate a letter.* ★A-53

C:5B *At the custody officer's discretion and subject to the detainee's consent, visits should be allowed when possible, subject to having sufficient personnel to supervise a visit and any possible hindrance to the investigation.*

C:5C *If the detainee does not know anyone to contact for advice or support or cannot contact a friend or relative, the custody officer should bear in mind any local voluntary bodies or other organisations who might be able to help. Paragraph 6.1 applies if legal advice is required.*

C:5D *In some circumstances it may not be appropriate to use the telephone to disclose information under paragraphs 5.1 and 5.5.*

C:5E *The telephone call at paragraph 5.6 is in addition to any communication under paragraphs 5.1 and 6.1.*

C:5F *Prison Service Instruction 26/2012 (Production of Prisoners at the Request of Warranted Law Enforcement Agencies) provides detailed guidance and instructions for police officers and Governors and Directors of Prisons regarding applications for prisoners to be transferred to police custody and their safe custody and treatment while in police custody.*

C:6 Right to legal advice

(a) *Action*

C:6.1 Unless Annex B applies, all detainees must be informed that they may at any time consult ★A-54 and communicate privately with a solicitor, whether in person, in writing or by telephone, and that free independent legal advice is available. See paragraph 3.1, *Notes 11, 6B and 6J*

C:6.2 [*Not used.*]

C:6.3 A poster advertising the right to legal advice must be prominently displayed in the charging area of every police station. See *Note 6H*.

C:6.4 No police officer should, at any time, do or say anything with the intention of dissuading any person who is entitled to legal advice in accordance with this code, whether or not they have been arrested and are detained, from obtaining legal advice. See *Note 6ZA*.

C:6.5 The exercise of the right of access to legal advice may be delayed only as in Annex B. Whenever legal advice is requested, and unless Annex B applies, the custody officer must act without delay to secure the provision of such advice. If the detainee has the right to speak to a solicitor in person but declines to exercise the right the officer should point out that the right includes the right to speak with a solicitor on the telephone. If the detainee continues to waive this right, or a detainee whose right to free legal advice is limited to telephone advice from the Criminal Defence Service (CDS) Direct (see *Note 6B*) declines to exercise that right, the officer should ask them why and any reasons should be recorded on the custody record or the interview record as appropriate. Reminders of the right to legal advice must be given as in paragraphs 3.5, 11.2, 15.4, 16.4, 16.5, 2B of Annex A, 3 of Annex K and 5 of Annex M of this code and Code D, paras 3.17(ii) and 6.3. Once it is clear a detainee does not want to speak to a solicitor in person or by telephone they should cease to be asked their reasons. See *Note 6K*.

C:6.5A In the case of a person who is a juvenile or is mentally disordered or otherwise mentally vulnerable, an appropriate adult should consider whether legal advice from a solicitor is required. If such a detained person wants to exercise the right to legal advice, the appropriate action should be taken and should not be delayed until the appropriate adult arrives. If the person indicates that they do not want legal advice, the appropriate adult has the right to ask for a solicitor to attend if this would be in the best interests of the person. However, the person cannot be forced to see the solicitor if they are adamant that they do not wish to do so.

C:6.6 A detainee who wants legal advice may not be interviewed or continue to be interviewed until they have received such advice unless:

    (a) Annex B applies, when the restriction on drawing adverse inferences from silence in Annex C will apply because the detainee is not allowed an opportunity to consult a solicitor; or

    (b) an officer of superintendent rank or above has reasonable grounds for believing that:

        (i) the consequent delay might:

          • lead to interference with, or harm to, evidence connected with an offence;

          • lead to interference with, or physical harm to, other people;

          • lead to serious loss of, or damage to, property;

          • lead to alerting other people suspected of having committed an offence but not yet arrested for it;

          • hinder the recovery of property obtained in consequence of the commission of an offence.

        See *Note 6A*

        (ii) when a solicitor, including a duty solicitor, has been contacted and has agreed to attend, awaiting their arrival would cause unreasonable delay to the process of investigation.

        Note: In these cases the restriction on drawing adverse inferences from silence in Annex C will apply because the detainee is not allowed an opportunity to consult a solicitor.

    (c) the solicitor the detainee has nominated or selected from a list:

        (i) cannot be contacted;

        (ii) has previously indicated they do not wish to be contacted; or

        (iii) having been contacted, has declined to attend; and

          • the detainee has been advised of the Duty Solicitor Scheme but has declined to ask for the duty solicitor;

          • in these circumstances the interview may be started or continued without further delay provided an officer of inspector rank or above has agreed to the interview proceeding.

        Note: The restriction on drawing adverse inferences from silence in Annex C will not apply because the detainee is allowed an opportunity to consult the duty solicitor;

    (d) the detainee changes their mind about wanting legal advice or (as the case may be) about wanting a solicitor present at the interview and states that they no longer wish to speak to a solicitor. In these circumstances, the interview may be started or continued without delay provided that:

        (i) an officer of inspector rank or above:

- speaks to the detainee to enquire about the reasons for their change of mind (see *Note 6K*), and
- makes, or directs the making of, reasonable efforts to ascertain the solicitor's expected time of arrival and to inform the solicitor that the suspect has stated that they wish to change their mind and the reason (if given);

(ii) the detainee's reason for their change of mind (if given) and the outcome of the action in (i) are recorded in the custody record;

(iii) the detainee, after being informed of the outcome of the action in (i) above, confirms in writing that they want the interview to proceed without speaking or further speaking to a solicitor or (as the case may be) without a solicitor being present and do not wish to wait for a solicitor by signing an entry to this effect in the custody record;

(iv) an officer of inspector rank or above is satisfied that it is proper for the interview to proceed in these circumstances and:

- gives authority in writing for the interview to proceed and, if the authority is not recorded in the custody record, the officer must ensure that the custody record shows the date and time of the authority and where it is recorded, and
- takes, or directs the taking of, reasonable steps to inform the solicitor that the authority has been given and the time when the interview is expected to commence and records or causes to be recorded, the outcome of this action in the custody record;

(v) when the interview starts and the interviewer reminds the suspect of their right to legal advice (see para. 11.2, Code E, para. 4.5 and Code F, para. 4.5), the interviewer shall then ensure that the following is recorded in the written interview record or the interview record made in accordance with Code E or F:

- confirmation that the detainee has changed their mind about wanting legal advice or (as the case may be) about wanting a solicitor present and the reasons for it if given;
- the fact that authority for the interview to proceed has been given and, subject to paragraph 2.6A, the name of the authorising officer;
- that if the solicitor arrives at the station before the interview is completed, the detainee will be so informed without delay and *a break will be taken* to allow them to speak to the solicitor if they wish, unless paragraph 6.6(a) applies, and
- that at any time during the interview, the detainee may again ask for legal advice and that if they do, a break will be taken to allow them to speak to the solicitor, unless paragraph 6.6(a), (b), or (c) applies.

Note: In these circumstances, the restriction on drawing adverse inferences from silence in Annex C will not apply because the detainee is allowed an opportunity to consult a solicitor if they wish.

C:6.7 If paragraph 6.6(a) applies, where the reason for authorising the delay ceases to apply, there ★**A-55** may be no further delay in permitting the exercise of the right in the absence of a further authorisation unless paragraph 6.6(b), (c) or (d) applies. If paragraph 6.6(b)(i) applies, once sufficient information has been obtained to avert the risk, questioning must cease until the detainee has received legal advice unless paragraph 6.6(a), (b)(ii), (c) or (d) applies.

C:6.8 A detainee who has been permitted to consult a solicitor shall be entitled on request to have the solicitor present when they are interviewed unless one of the exceptions in paragraph 6.6 applies.

C:6.9 The solicitor may only be required to leave the interview if their conduct is such that the interviewer is unable properly to put questions to the suspect. See *Notes 6D* and *6E.*

C:6.10 If the interviewer considers a solicitor is acting in such a way, they will stop the interview and consult an officer not below superintendent rank, if one is readily available, and otherwise an officer not below inspector rank not connected with the investigation. After speaking to the solicitor, the officer consulted will decide if the interview should continue in the presence of that solicitor. If they decide it should not, the suspect will be given the opportunity to consult another solicitor before the interview continues and that solicitor given an opportunity to be present at the interview. *See Note 6E.*

C:6.11 The removal of a solicitor from an interview is a serious step and, if it occurs, the officer of superintendent rank or above who took the decision will consider if the incident should be reported to the Solicitors Regulatory Authority. If the decision to remove the solicitor has been taken by an officer below superintendent rank, the facts must be reported to an officer of superintendent rank or above, who will similarly consider whether a report to the Solicitors Regulatory Authority would be appropriate. When the solicitor concerned is a duty solicitor, the report should be both to the Solicitors Regulatory Authority and to the Legal Aid Agency.

C:6.12 "Solicitor" in this code means:
- a solicitor who holds a current practising certificate;
- an accredited or probationary representative included on the register of representatives maintained by the Legal Aid Agency.

C:6.12A An accredited or probationary representative sent to provide advice by, and on behalf of, a solicitor shall be admitted to the police station for this purpose unless an officer of inspector rank or above considers such a visit will hinder the investigation and directs otherwise. Hindering the investigation does not include giving proper legal advice to a detainee as in *Note 6D*. Once admitted to the police station, paragraphs 6.6 to 6.10 apply.

C:6.13 In exercising their discretion under paragraph 6.12A, the officer should take into account in particular:
- whether:
  - the identity and status of an accredited or probationary representative have been satisfactorily established;
  - they are of suitable character to provide legal advice, *e.g.* a person with a criminal record is unlikely to be suitable unless the conviction was for a minor offence and not recent.
- any other matters in any written letter of authorisation provided by the solicitor on whose behalf the person is attending the police station. See *Note 6F*.

C:6.14 If the inspector refuses access to an accredited or probationary representative or a decision is taken that such a person should not be permitted to remain at an interview, the inspector must notify the solicitor on whose behalf the representative was acting and give them an opportunity to make alternative arrangements. The detainee must be informed and the custody record noted.

C:6.15 If a solicitor arrives at the station to see a particular person, that person must, unless Annex B applies, be so informed whether or not they are being interviewed and asked if they would like to see the solicitor. This applies even if the detainee has declined legal advice or, having requested it, subsequently agreed to be interviewed without receiving advice. The solicitor's attendance and the detainee's decision must be noted in the custody record.

(b) *Documentation*

C:6.16 Any request for legal advice and the action taken shall be recorded.

C:6.17 A record shall be made in the interview record if a detainee asks for legal advice and an interview is begun either in the absence of a solicitor or their representative, or they have been required to leave an interview.

Notes for guidance

★A-56

C:6ZA *No police officer or police staff shall indicate to any suspect, except to answer a direct question, that the period for which they are liable to be detained, or if not detained, the time taken to complete the interview, might be reduced:*
- *if they do not ask for legal advice or do not want a solicitor present when they are interviewed; or*
- *if they have asked for legal advice or (as the case may be) asked for a solicitor to be present when they are interviewed but change their mind and agree to be interviewed without waiting for a solicitor.*

C:6A *In considering if paragraph 6.6(b) applies, the officer should, if practicable, ask the solicitor for an estimate of how long it will take to come to the station and relate this to the time detention is permitted, the time of day (i.e. whether the rest period under paragraph 12.2 is imminent) and the requirements of other investigations. If the solicitor is on their way or is to set off immediately, it will not normally be appropriate to begin an interview before they arrive. If it appears necessary to begin an interview before the solicitor's arrival, they should be given an indication of how long the police would be able to wait before 6.6(b) applies so there is an opportunity to make arrangements for someone else to provide legal advice.*

C:6B *A detainee has a right to free legal advice and to be represented by a solicitor. This note for guidance explains the arrangements which enable detainees to obtain legal advice. An outline of these arrangements is also included in the Notice of Rights and Entitlements given to detainees in accordance with paragraph 3.2. The arrangements also apply, with appropriate modifications, to persons attending a police station or other location voluntarily who are cautioned prior to being interviewed. See paragraph 3.21.*

When a detainee asks for free legal advice, the Defence Solicitor Call Centre (DSCC) must be informed of the request.

Free legal advice will be limited to telephone advice provided by CDS Direct if a detainee is:
- *detained for a non-imprisonable offence;*
- *arrested on a bench warrant for failing to appear and being held for production at court (except where the solicitor has clear documentary evidence available that would result in the client being released from custody);*

- arrested for drink driving (driving/in charge with excess alcohol, failing to provide a specimen, driving/in charge whilst unfit through drink), or
- detained in relation to breach of police or court bail conditions

unless one or more exceptions apply, in which case the DSCC should arrange for advice to be given by a solicitor at the police station, for example:

- the police want to interview the detainee or carry out an eye-witness identification procedure;
- the detainee needs an appropriate adult;
- the detainee is unable to communicate over the telephone;
- the detainee alleges serious misconduct by the police;
- the investigation includes another offence not included in the list,
- the solicitor to be assigned is already at the police station.

When free advice is not limited to telephone advice, a detainee can ask for free advice from a solicitor they know or if they do not know a solicitor or the solicitor they know cannot be contacted, from the duty solicitor.

To arrange free legal advice, the police should telephone the DSCC. The call centre will decide whether legal advice should be limited to telephone advice from CDS Direct, or whether a solicitor known to the detainee or the duty solicitor should speak to the detainee.

When a detainee wants to pay for legal advice themselves:

- the DSCC will contact a solicitor of their choice on their behalf;
- they may, when free advice is only available by telephone from CDS Direct, still speak to a solicitor of their choice on the telephone for advice, but the solicitor would not be paid by legal aid and may ask the person to pay for the advice;
- they should be given an opportunity to consult a specific solicitor or another solicitor from that solicitor's firm. If this solicitor is not available, they may choose up to two alternatives. If these alternatives are not available, the custody officer has discretion to allow further attempts until a solicitor has been contacted and agreed to provide advice;
- they are entitled to a private consultation with their chosen solicitor on the telephone or the solicitor may decide to come to the police station;
- If their chosen solicitor cannot be contacted, the DSCC may still be called to arrange free legal advice.

Apart from carrying out duties necessary to implement these arrangements, an officer must not advise the suspect about any particular firm of solicitors.

C:6C [*Not used.*]

C:6D *The solicitor's only role in the police station is to protect and advance the legal rights of their client. On occasions this may require the solicitor to give advice which has the effect of the client avoiding giving evidence which strengthens a prosecution case. The solicitor may intervene in order to seek clarification, challenge an improper question to their client or the manner in which it is put, advise their client not to reply to particular questions, or if they wish to give their client further legal advice. Paragraph 6.9 only applies if the solicitor's approach or conduct prevents or unreasonably obstructs proper questions being put to the suspect or the suspect's response being recorded. Examples of unacceptable conduct include answering questions on a suspect's behalf or providing written replies for the suspect to quote.*

C:6E *An officer who takes the decision to exclude a solicitor must be in a position to satisfy the court the decision was properly made. In order to do this they may need to witness what is happening.*

C:6F *If an officer of at least inspector rank considers a particular solicitor or firm of solicitors is persistently sending probationary representatives who are unsuited to provide legal advice, they should inform an officer of at least superintendent rank, who may wish to take the matter up with the Solicitors Regulation Authority.*

C:6G *Subject to the constraints of Annex B, a solicitor may advise more than one client in an investigation if they wish. Any question of a conflict of interest is for the solicitor under their professional code of conduct. If, however, waiting for a solicitor to give advice to one client may lead to unreasonable delay to the interview with another, the provisions of paragraph 6.6(b) may apply.* ★A-57

C:6H *In addition to a poster in English, a poster or posters containing translations into Welsh, the main minority ethnic languages and the principal European languages should be displayed wherever they are likely to be helpful and it is practicable to do so.*

C:6I [*Not used.*]

C:6J *Whenever a detainee exercises their right to legal advice by consulting or communicating with a solicitor, they must be allowed to do so in private. This right to consult or communicate in private is fundamental. If the requirement for privacy is compromised because what is said or written by the detainee or solicitor for the purpose of giving and receiving legal advice is overheard, listened to, or read by others without the informed consent of the detainee, the right will effectively have been denied. When a detainee speaks to a solicitor on the telephone, they should be allowed to do so in private unless this is impractical because of the design and layout of the custody area or the location of telephones. However, the normal expectation should be that facilities will be available, unless they are being used, at all police stations to enable detainees to speak in private to a solicitor either face to face or over the telephone.*

C:6K A detainee is not obliged to give reasons for declining legal advice and should not be pressed to do so.

C:7 Citizens of independent Commonwealth countries or foreign nationals

(a) *Action*

★**A-58**   C:7.1 A detainee who is a citizen of an independent Commonwealth country or a national of a foreign country, including the Republic of Ireland, has the right, upon request, to communicate at any time with the appropriate High Commission, Embassy or Consulate. That detainee must be informed as soon as practicable of this right and asked if they want to have their High Commission, Embassy or Consulate told of their whereabouts and the grounds for their detention. Such a request should be acted upon as soon as practicable. See *Note 7A.*

C:7.2 A detainee who is a citizen of a country with which a bilateral consular convention or agreement is in force requiring notification of arrest must also be informed that subject to paragraph 7.4, notification of their arrest will be sent to the appropriate High Commission, Embassy or Consulate as soon as practicable, whether or not they request it. A list of the countries to which this requirement currently applies and contact details for the relevant High Commissions, Embassies and Consulates can be obtained from the Consular Directorate of the Foreign and Commonwealth Office (FCO) as follows:

- from the FCO web pages:
  - https://gov.uk/government/publications/table-of-consular-conventions-and-mandatory-notification-obligations, and
  - https://www.gov.uk/government/publications/foreign-embassies-in-the-uk
- by telephone to 020 7008 3100,
- by email to fcocorrespondence@fco.gov.uk.
- by letter to the Foreign and Commonwealth Office, King Charles Street, London, SW1A 2AH.

C:7.3 Consular officers may, if the detainee agrees, visit one of their nationals in police detention to talk to them and, if required, to arrange for legal advice. Such visits shall take place out of the hearing of a police officer.

C:7.4 Notwithstanding the provisions of consular conventions, if the detainee claims that they are a refugee or have applied or intend to apply for asylum, the custody officer must ensure that UK Visas and Immigration (UKVI) (formerly the UK Border Agency) is informed as soon as practicable of the claim. UKVI will then determine whether compliance with relevant international obligations requires notification of the arrest to be sent and will inform the custody officer as to what action police need to take.

(b) *Documentation*

★**A-59**   C:7.5 A record shall be made:

- when a detainee is informed of their rights under this section and of any requirement in paragraph 7.2;
- of any communications with a High Commission, Embassy or Consulate, and
- of any communications with UKVI about a detainee's claim to be a refugee or to be seeking asylum and the resulting action taken by police.

Note for guidance

★**A-60**   *C:7A The exercise of the rights in this section may not be interfered with even though Annex B applies.*

C:8 Conditions of detention

(a) *Action*

★**A-61**   C:8.1 So far as it is practicable, not more than one detainee should be detained in each cell. See *Note 8C.*

C:8.2 Cells in use must be adequately heated, cleaned and ventilated. They must be adequately lit, subject to such dimming as is compatible with safety and security to allow people detained overnight to sleep. No additional restraints shall be used within a locked cell unless absolutely necessary and then only restraint equipment, approved for use in that force by the chief officer, which is reasonable and necessary in the circumstances having regard to the detainee's demeanour and with a view to ensuring their safety and the safety of others. If a detainee is deaf, mentally disordered or otherwise mentally vulnerable, particular care must be taken when deciding whether to use any form of approved restraints.

C:8.3 Blankets, mattresses, pillows and other bedding supplied shall be of a reasonable standard and in a clean and sanitary condition. See *Note 8A.*

C:8.4 Access to toilet and washing facilities must be provided.

C:8.5 If it is necessary to remove a detainee's clothes for the purposes of investigation, for hygiene, health reasons or cleaning, replacement clothing of a reasonable standard of comfort and cleanliness shall be provided. A detainee may not be interviewed unless adequate clothing has been offered.

C:8.6 At least two light meals and one main meal should be offered in any 24-hour period. See *Note 8B.* Drinks should be provided at meal times and upon reasonable request between meals. Whenever necessary, advice shall be sought from the appropriate healthcare professional, see *Note 9A*, on medical and dietary matters. As far as practicable, meals provided shall offer a varied diet and meet any specific dietary needs or religious beliefs the detainee may have. The detainee may, at the custody officer's discretion, have meals supplied by their family or friends at their expense. See *Note 8A.*

C:8.7 Brief outdoor exercise shall be offered daily if practicable.

C:8.8 A juvenile shall not be placed in a police cell unless no other secure accommodation is available and the custody officer considers it is not practicable to supervise them if they are not placed in a cell or that a cell provides more comfortable accommodation than other secure accommodation in the station. A juvenile may not be placed in a cell with a detained adult.

(b) *Documentation*

C:8.9 A record must be kept of replacement clothing and meals offered. ★**A-62**

C:8.10 If a juvenile is placed in a cell, the reason must be recorded.

C:8.11 The use of any restraints on a detainee whilst in a cell, the reasons for it and, if appropriate, the arrangements for enhanced supervision of the detainee whilst so restrained, shall be recorded. See paragraph 3.9.

Notes for guidance

C:8A *The provisions in paragraph 8.3 and 8.6 respectively are of particular importance in the case of a* ★**A-63** *person likely to be detained for an extended period. In deciding whether to allow meals to be supplied by family or friends, the custody officer is entitled to take account of the risk of items being concealed in any food or package and the officer's duties and responsibilities under food handling legislation.*

C:8B *Meals should, so far as practicable, be offered at recognised meal times, or at other times that take account of when the detainee last had a meal.*

C:8C *The Detention and Custody Authorised Professional Practice (APP) produced by the College of Policing (see http://www.app.college.police.uk) provides more detailed guidance on matters concerning detainee healthcare and treatment and associated forensic issues which should be read in conjunction with sections 8 and 9 of this Code.*

C:9 Care and treatment of detained persons

(a) *General*

C:9.1 Nothing in this section prevents the police from calling an appropriate healthcare profes- ★**A-64** sional to examine a detainee for the purposes of obtaining evidence relating to any offence in which the detainee is suspected of being involved. See *Notes 9A and 8C.*

C:9.2 If a complaint is made by, or on behalf of, a detainee about their treatment since their arrest, or it comes to notice that a detainee may have been treated improperly, a report must be made as soon as practicable to an officer of inspector rank or above not connected with the investigation. If the matter concerns a possible assault or the possibility of the unnecessary or unreasonable use of force, an appropriate healthcare professional must also be called as soon as practicable.

C:9.3 Detainees should be visited at least every hour. If no reasonably foreseeable risk was identified in a risk assessment, see paragraphs 3.6 to 3.10, there is no need to wake a sleeping detainee. Those suspected of being under the influence of drink or drugs or both or of having swallowed drugs, see *Note 9CA*, or whose level of consciousness causes concern must, subject to any clinical directions given by the appropriate healthcare professional, see paragraph 9.13:

- be visited and roused at least every half hour;
- have their condition assessed as in Annex H;
- and clinical treatment arranged if appropriate.

See *Notes 9B, 9C* and *9H*

C:9.4 When arrangements are made to secure clinical attention for a detainee, the custody officer must make sure all relevant information which might assist in the treatment of the detainee's condition is made available to the responsible healthcare professional. This applies whether or not the healthcare professional asks for such information. Any officer or police staff with relevant information must inform the custody officer as soon as practicable.

(b) *Clinical treatment and attention*

★**A-65**   C:9.5 The custody officer must make sure a detainee receives appropriate clinical attention as soon as reasonably practicable if the person:

(a) appears to be suffering from physical illness; or

(b) is injured; or

(c) appears to be suffering from a mental disorder; or

(d) appears to need clinical attention.

C:9.5A This applies even if the detainee makes no request for clinical attention and whether or not they have already received clinical attention elsewhere. If the need for attention appears urgent,*e.g.* when indicated as in Annex H, the nearest available healthcare professional or an ambulance must be called immediately.

C:9.5B The custody officer must also consider the need for clinical attention as set out in *Note 9C* in relation to those suffering the effects of alcohol or drugs.

C:9.6 Paragraph 9.5 is not meant to prevent or delay the transfer to a hospital if necessary of a person detained under the Mental Health Act 1983, s.136. See *Note 9D*. When an assessment under that Act is to take place at a police station (see para. 3.16) the custody officer must consider whether an appropriate healthcare professional should be called to conduct an initial clinical check on the detainee. This applies particularly when there is likely to be any significant delay in the arrival of a suitably qualified medical practitioner.

C:9.7 If it appears to the custody officer, or they are told, that a person brought to a station under arrest may be suffering from an infectious disease or condition, the custody officer must take reasonable steps to safeguard the health of the detainee and others at the station. In deciding what action to take, advice must be sought from an appropriate healthcare professional. See *Note 9E*. The custody officer has discretion to isolate the person and their property until clinical directions have been obtained.

★**A-66**   C:9.8 If a detainee requests a clinical examination, an appropriate healthcare professional must be called as soon as practicable to assess the detainee's clinical needs. If a safe and appropriate care plan cannot be provided, the appropriate healthcare professional's advice must be sought. The detainee may also be examined by a medical practitioner of their choice at their expense.

C:9.9 If a detainee is required to take or apply any medication in compliance with clinical directions prescribed before their detention, the custody officer must consult the appropriate healthcare professional before the use of the medication. Subject to the restrictions in paragraph 9.10, the custody officer is responsible for the safekeeping of any medication and for making sure the detainee is given the opportunity to take or apply prescribed or approved medication. Any such consultation and its outcome shall be noted in the custody record.

C:9.10 No police officer may administer or supervise the self-administration of medically prescribed controlled drugs of the types and forms listed in the Misuse of Drugs Regulations 2001, Sched. 2 or 3. A detainee may only self-administer such drugs under the personal supervision of the registered medical practitioner authorising their use or other appropriate healthcare professional. The custody officer may supervise the self-administration of, or authorise other custody staff to supervise the self-administration of, drugs listed in Schedule 4 or 5 if the officer has consulted the appropriate healthcare professional authorising their use and both are satisfied self-administration will not expose the detainee, police officers or anyone else to the risk of harm or injury.

C:9.11 When appropriate healthcare professionals administer drugs or authorise the use of other medications, supervise their self-administration or consult with the custody officer about allowing self-administration of drugs listed in Schedule 4 or 5, it must be within current medicines legislation and the scope of practice as determined by their relevant statutory regulatory body.

C:9.12 If a detainee has in their possession, or claims to need, medication relating to a heart condition, diabetes, epilepsy or a condition of comparable potential seriousness then, even though paragraph 9.5 may not apply, the advice of the appropriate healthcare professional must be obtained.

C:9.13 Whenever the appropriate healthcare professional is called in accordance with this section to examine or treat a detainee, the custody officer shall ask for their opinion about:

- any risks or problems which police need to take into account when making decisions about the detainee's continued detention;

- when to carry out an interview if applicable; and

- the need for safeguards.

C:9.14 When clinical directions are given by the appropriate healthcare professional, whether orally or in writing, and the custody officer has any doubts or is in any way uncertain about any aspect of the directions, the custody officer shall ask for clarification. It is particularly important that directions concerning the frequency of visits are clear, precise and capable of being implemented. See *Note 9F*.

(c) *Documentation*

C:9.15 A record must be made in the custody record of: ★**A-67**

(a) the arrangements made for an examination by an appropriate healthcare professional under paragraph 9.2 and of any complaint reported under that paragraph together with any relevant remarks by the custody officer;

(b) any arrangements made in accordance with paragraph 9.5;

(c) any request for a clinical examination under paragraph 9.8 and any arrangements made in response;

(d) the injury, ailment, condition or other reason which made it necessary to make the arrangements in (a) to (c); See *Note 9G*.

(e) any clinical directions and advice, including any further clarifications, given to police by a healthcare professional concerning the care and treatment of the detainee in connection with any of the arrangements made in (a) to (c); See *Notes 9E* and *9F*.

(f) if applicable, the responses received when attempting to rouse a person using the procedure in Annex H. See *Note 9H*.

C:9.16 If a healthcare professional does not record their clinical findings in the custody record, the record must show where they are recorded. See *Note 9G*. However, information which is necessary to custody staff to ensure the effective ongoing care and well being of the detainee must be recorded openly in the custody record, see paragraph 3.8 and Annex G, para. 7.

C:9.17 Subject to the requirements of Section 4, the custody record shall include:

- a record of all medication a detainee has in their possession on arrival at the police station;
- a note of any such medication they claim to need but do not have with them.

Notes for guidance

C:9A *A "healthcare professional" means a clinically qualified person working within the scope of practice as* ★**A-68** *determined by their relevant statutory regulatory body. Whether a healthcare professional is 'appropriate' depends on the circumstances of the duties they carry out at the time.*

C:9B *Whenever possible juveniles and mentally vulnerable detainees should be visited more frequently.*

C:9C *A detainee who appears drunk or behaves abnormally may be suffering from illness, the effects of drugs or may have sustained injury, particularly a head injury which is not apparent. A detainee needing or dependent on certain drugs, including alcohol, may experience harmful effects within a short time of being deprived of their supply. In these circumstances, when there is any doubt, police should always act urgently to call an appropriate healthcare professional or an ambulance. Paragraph 9.5 does not apply to minor ailments or injuries which do not need attention. However, all such ailments or injuries must be recorded in the custody record and any doubt must be resolved in favour of calling the appropriate healthcare professional.*

C:9CA *Paragraph 9.3 would apply to a person in police custody by order of a magistrates' court under the Criminal Justice Act 1988, s.152 (as amended by the Drugs Act 2005, s.8) to facilitate the recovery of evidence after being charged with drug possession or drug trafficking and suspected of having swallowed drugs. In the case of the healthcare needs of a person who has swallowed drugs, the custody officer, subject to any clinical directions, should consider the necessity for rousing every half hour. This does not negate the need for regular visiting of the suspect in the cell.*

C:9D *Whenever practicable, arrangements should be made for persons detained for assessment under the Mental Health Act 1983, s.136 to be taken to a hospital. Chapter 10 of the Mental Health Act 1983 Code of Practice (as revised) provides more detailed guidance about arranging assessments under section 136 and transferring detainees from police stations to other places of safety.*

C:9E *It is important to respect a person's right to privacy and information about their health must be kept confidential and only disclosed with their consent or in accordance with clinical advice when it is necessary to protect the detainee's health or that of others who come into contact with them.*

C:9F *The custody officer should always seek to clarify directions that the detainee requires constant observation or supervision and should ask the appropriate healthcare professional to explain precisely what action needs to be taken to implement such directions.*

C:9G *Paragraphs 9.15 and 9.16 do not require any information about the cause of any injury, ailment or condition to be recorded on the custody record if it appears capable of providing evidence of an offence.*

C:9H *The purpose of recording a person's responses when attempting to rouse them using the procedure in Annex H is to enable any change in the individual's consciousness level to be noted and clinical treatment arranged if appropriate.*

C:10 Cautions

(a) *When a caution must be given*

★**A-69** C:10.1 A person whom there are grounds to suspect of an offence, see *Note 10A*, must be cautioned before any questions about an offence, or further questions if the answers provide the grounds for suspicion, are put to them if either the suspect's answers or silence, (i.e. failure or refusal to answer or answer satisfactorily) may be given in evidence to a court in a prosecution. A person need not be cautioned if questions are for other necessary purposes, *e.g.*:

(a) solely to establish their identity or ownership of any vehicle;

(b) to obtain information in accordance with any relevant statutory requirement, see paragraph 10.9;

(c) in furtherance of the proper and effective conduct of a search, *e.g.* to determine the need to search in the exercise of powers of stop and search or to seek co-operation while carrying out a search; or

(d) to seek verification of a written record as in paragraph 11.13.

(e) [*Not used.*]

C:10.2 Whenever a person not under arrest is initially cautioned, or reminded that they are under caution, that person must at the same time be told they are not under arrest and must be informed of the provisions of paragraph 3.21 which explain that they need to agree to be interviewed, how they may obtain legal advice according to whether they are at a police station or elsewhere and the other rights and entitlements that apply to a voluntary interview. See *Note 10C*.

C:10.3 A person who is arrested, or further arrested, must be informed at the time if practicable or, if not, as soon as it becomes practicable thereafter, that they are under arrest and of the grounds and reasons for their arrest, see paragraph 3.4, *Note 10B* and Code G, paras 2.2 and 4.3.

C:10.4 As required by Code G, s. 3, a person who is arrested, or further arrested, must also be cautioned unless:

(a) it is impracticable to do so by reason of their condition or behaviour at the time;

(b) they have already been cautioned immediately prior to arrest as in paragraph 10.1.

(b) *Terms of the cautions*

C:10.5 The caution which must be given on:

(a) arrest; or

(b) all other occasions before a person is charged or informed they may be prosecuted; see section 16,

should, unless the restriction on drawing adverse inferences from silence applies, see Annex C, be in the following terms:

"You do not have to say anything. But it may harm your defence if you do not mention when questioned something which you later rely on in Court. Anything you do say may be given in evidence."

Where the use of the Welsh Language is appropriate, a constable may provide the caution directly in Welsh in the following terms:

"Does dim rhaid i chi ddweud dim byd. Ond gall niweidio eich amddiffyniad os na fyddwch chi'n sôn, wrth gael eich holi, am rywbeth y byddwch chi'n dibynnu arno nes ymlaen yn y Llys. Gall unrhyw beth yr ydych yn ei ddweud gael ei roi fel tystiolaeth."

See *Note 10G*

★**A-70** C:10.6 Annex C, para. 2 sets out the alternative terms of the caution to be used when the restriction on drawing adverse inferences from silence applies.

C:10.7 Minor deviations from the words of any caution given in accordance with this code do not constitute a breach of this code, provided the sense of the relevant caution is preserved. See *Note 10D*.

C:10.8 After any break in questioning under caution, the person being questioned must be made aware they remain under caution. If there is any doubt the relevant caution should be given again in full when the interview resumes. See *Note 10E*.

C:10.9 When, despite being cautioned, a person fails to co-operate or to answer particular questions which may affect their immediate treatment, the person should be informed of any relevant consequences and that those consequences are not affected by the caution. Examples are when a person's refusal to provide:

- their name and address when charged may make them liable to detention;
- particulars and information in accordance with a statutory requirement, *e.g.* under the Road Traffic Act 1988, may amount to an offence or may make the person liable to a further arrest.

(c) *Special warnings under the Criminal Justice and Public Order Act 1994, ss. 36 and 37*

★**A-71**

C:10.10 When a suspect interviewed at a police station or authorised place of detention after arrest fails or refuses to answer certain questions, or to answer satisfactorily, after due warning, see *Note 10F*, a court or jury may draw such inferences as appear proper under the Criminal Justice and Public Order Act 1994, ss.36 and 37. Such inferences may only be drawn when:

(a) the restriction on drawing adverse inferences from silence, see Annex C, does not apply; and

(b) the suspect is arrested by a constable and fails or refuses to account for any objects, marks or substances, or marks on such objects found:
- on their person;
- in or on their clothing or footwear;
- otherwise in their possession; or
- in the place they were arrested;

(c) the arrested suspect was found by a constable at a place at or about the time the offence for which that officer has arrested them is alleged to have been committed, and the suspect fails or refuses to account for their presence there.

When the restriction on drawing adverse inferences from silence applies, the suspect may still be asked to account for any of the matters in (b) or (c) but the special warning described in paragraph 10.11 will not apply and must not be given.

C:10.11 For an inference to be drawn when a suspect fails or refuses to answer a question about one of these matters or to answer it satisfactorily, the suspect must first be told in ordinary language:

(a) what offence is being investigated;

(b) what fact they are being asked to account for;

(c) this fact may be due to them taking part in the commission of the offence;

(d) a court may draw a proper inference if they fail or refuse to account for this fact; and

(e) a record is being made of the interview and it may be given in evidence if they are brought to trial.

(d) *Juveniles and persons who are mentally disordered or otherwise mentally vulnerable*

C:10.11A The information required in paragraph 10.11 must not be given to a suspect who is a juvenile or who is mentally disordered or otherwise mentally vulnerable unless the appropriate adult is present.

C:10.12 If a juvenile or a person who is mentally disordered or otherwise mentally vulnerable is cautioned in the absence of the appropriate adult, the caution must be repeated in the adult's presence.

(e) *Documentation*

C:10.13 A record shall be made when a caution is given under this section, either in the interviewer's report book or in the interview record.

Notes for guidance

C:10A *There must be some reasonable, objective grounds for the suspicion, based on known facts or informa-* ★**A-72** *tion which are relevant to the likelihood the offence has been committed and the person to be questioned committed it.*

C:10B *An arrested person must be given sufficient information to enable them to understand that they have been deprived of their liberty and the reason they have been arrested, e.g. when a person is arrested on suspicion of committing an offence they must be informed of the suspected offence's nature, when and where it was committed. The suspect must also be informed of the reason or reasons why the arrest is considered necessary. Vague or technical language should be avoided.*

C:10C *The restriction on drawing inferences from silence, see Annex C, para. 1, does not apply to a person who has not been detained and who therefore cannot be prevented from seeking legal advice if they want, see paragraph 3.21.*

C:10D *If it appears a person does not understand the caution, the person giving it should explain it in their own words.*

C:10E *It may be necessary to show to the court that nothing occurred during an interview break or between interviews which influenced the suspect's recorded evidence. After a break in an interview or at the beginning of a subsequent interview, the interviewer should summarise the reason for the break and confirm this with the suspect.*

C:10F *The Criminal Justice and Public Order Act 1994, ss.36 and 37 apply only to suspects who have been arrested by a constable or an officer of Revenue and Customs and are given the relevant warning by the police or Revenue and Customs officer who made the arrest or who is investigating the offence. They do not apply to any interviews with suspects who have not been arrested.*

C:10G *Nothing in this code requires a caution to be given or repeated when informing a person not under arrest they may be prosecuted for an offence. However, a court will not be able to draw any inferences under the Criminal Justice and Public Order Act 1994, s.34, if the person was not cautioned.*

C:11 Interviews—general

(a) *Action*

★**A-73**   C:11.1A An interview is the questioning of a person regarding their involvement or suspected involvement in a criminal offence or offences which, under paragraph 10.1, must be carried out under caution. Before a person is interviewed, they and, if they are represented, their solicitor must be given sufficient information to enable them to understand the nature of any such offence, and why they are suspected of committing it (see paras 3.4(a) and 10.3), in order to allow for the effective exercise of the rights of the defence. However, whilst the information must always be sufficient for the person to understand the nature of any offence (see *Note 11ZA*), this does not require the disclosure of details at a time which might prejudice the criminal investigation. The decision about what needs to be disclosed for the purpose of this requirement therefore rests with the investigating officer who has sufficient knowledge of the case to make that decision. The officer who discloses the information shall make a record of the information disclosed and when it was disclosed. This record may be made in the interview record, in the officer's report book or other form provided for this purpose. Procedures under the Road Traffic Act 1988, s.7 or the Transport and Works Act 1992, s. 31 do not constitute interviewing for the purpose of this Code.

C:11.1 Following a decision to arrest a suspect, they must not be interviewed about the relevant offence except at a police station or other authorised place of detention, unless the consequent delay would be likely to:

(a) lead to:
- interference with, or harm to, evidence connected with an offence;
- interference with, or physical harm to, other people; or
- serious loss of, or damage to, property;

(b) lead to alerting other people suspected of committing an offence but not yet arrested for it; or

(c) hinder the recovery of property obtained in consequence of the commission of an offence.

Interviewing in any of these circumstances shall cease once the relevant risk has been averted or the necessary questions have been put in order to attempt to avert that risk.

C:11.2 Immediately prior to the commencement or re-commencement of any interview at a police station or other authorised place of detention, the interviewer should remind the suspect of their entitlement to free legal advice and that the interview can be delayed for legal advice to be obtained, unless one of the exceptions in paragraph 6.6 applies. It is the interviewer's responsibility to make sure all reminders are recorded in the interview record.

C:11.3 [*Not used.*]

C:11.4 At the beginning of an interview the interviewer, after cautioning the suspect, see section 10, shall put to them any significant statement or silence which occurred in the presence and hearing of a police officer or other police staff before the start of the interview and which have not been put to the suspect in the course of a previous interview. See *Note 11A*. The interviewer shall ask the suspect whether they confirm or deny that earlier statement or silence and if they want to add anything.

C:11.4A A significant statement is one which appears capable of being used in evidence against the suspect, in particular a direct admission of guilt. A significant silence is a failure or refusal to answer a question or answer satisfactorily when under caution, which might, allowing for the restriction on drawing adverse inferences from silence, see Annex C, give rise to an inference under the Criminal Justice and Public Order Act 1994, Pt III.

C:11.5 No interviewer may try to obtain answers or elicit a statement by the use of oppression. Except as in paragraph 10.9, no interviewer shall indicate, except to answer a direct question, what action will be taken by the police if the person being questioned answers questions, makes a statement or refuses to do either. If the person asks directly what action will be taken if they answer questions, make a statement or refuse to do either, the interviewer may inform them what action the police propose to take provided that action is itself proper and warranted.

C:11.6 The interview or further interview of a person about an offence with which that person has not been charged or for which they have not been informed they may be prosecuted, must cease when:

- (a) the officer in charge of the investigation is satisfied all the questions they consider relevant to obtaining accurate and reliable information about the offence have been put to the suspect, this includes allowing the suspect an opportunity to give an innocent explanation and asking questions to test if the explanation is accurate and reliable, *e.g.* to clear up ambiguities or clarify what the suspect said;
- (b) the officer in charge of the investigation has taken account of any other available evidence; and
- (c) the officer in charge of the investigation, or in the case of a detained suspect, the custody officer, see paragraph 16.1, reasonably believes there is sufficient evidence to provide a realistic prospect of conviction for that offence. See *Note 11B.*

This paragraph does not prevent officers in revenue cases or acting under the confiscation provisions of the Criminal Justice Act 1988 or the Drug Trafficking Act 1994 from inviting suspects to complete a formal question and answer record after the interview is concluded.

(b) *Interview records*

C:11.7 (a) An accurate record must be made of each interview, whether or not the interview takes   ★**A-74**
place at a police station.
- (b) The record must state the place of interview, the time it begins and ends, any interview breaks and, subject to paragraph 2.6A, the names of all those present; and must be made on the forms provided for this purpose or in the interviewer's report book or in accordance with Codes of Practice E or F.
- (c) Any written record must be made and completed during the interview, unless this would not be practicable or would interfere with the conduct of the interview, and must constitute either a verbatim record of what has been said or, failing this, an account of the interview which adequately and accurately summarises it.

C:11.8 If a written record is not made during the interview it must be made as soon as practicable after its completion.

C:11.9 Written interview records must be timed and signed by the maker.

C:11.10 If a written record is not completed during the interview the reason must be recorded in the interview record.

C:11.11 Unless it is impracticable, the person interviewed shall be given the opportunity to read the interview record and to sign it as correct or to indicate how they consider it inaccurate. If the person interviewed cannot read or refuses to read the record or sign it, the senior interviewer present shall read it to them and ask whether they would like to sign it as correct or make their mark or to indicate how they consider it inaccurate. The interviewer shall certify on the interview record itself what has occurred. See *Note 11E.*

C:11.12 If the appropriate adult or the person's solicitor is present during the interview, they should also be given an opportunity to read and sign the interview record or any written statement taken down during the interview.

C:11.13 A record shall be made of any comments made by a suspect, including unsolicited comments, which are outside the context of an interview but which might be relevant to the offence. Any such record must be timed and signed by the maker. When practicable the suspect shall be given the opportunity to read that record and to sign it as correct or to indicate how they consider it inaccurate. See *Note 11E.*

C:11.14 Any refusal by a person to sign an interview record when asked in accordance with this Code must itself be recorded.

(c) *Juveniles and mentally disordered or otherwise mentally vulnerable people*

C:11.15 A juvenile or person who is mentally disordered or otherwise mentally vulnerable must   ★**A-75**
not be interviewed regarding their involvement or suspected involvement in a criminal offence or offences, or asked to provide or sign a written statement under caution or record of interview, in the absence of the appropriate adult unless paragraphs 11.1 or 11.18 to 11.20 apply. See *Note 11C.*

C:11.16 Juveniles may only be interviewed at their place of education in exceptional circumstances and only when the principal or their nominee agrees. Every effort should be made to notify the parent(s) or other person responsible for the juvenile's welfare and the appropriate adult, if this is a different person, that the police want to interview the juvenile and reasonable time should be allowed to enable the appropriate adult to be present at the interview. If awaiting the appropriate adult would cause unreasonable delay, and unless the juvenile is suspected of an offence against the educational establishment, the principal or their nominee can act as the appropriate adult for the purposes of the interview.

C:11.17 If an appropriate adult is present at an interview, they shall be informed:

- that they are not expected to act simply as an observer; and
- that the purpose of their presence is to:
  - advise the person being interviewed;
  - observe whether the interview is being conducted properly and fairly; and
  - facilitate communication with the person being interviewed.

C:11.17A The appropriate adult may be required to leave the interview if their conduct is such that the interviewer is unable properly to put questions to the suspect. This will include situations where the appropriate adult's approach or conduct prevents or unreasonably obstructs proper questions being put to the suspect or the suspect's responses being recorded (see *Note 11F*). If the interviewer considers an appropriate adult is acting in such a way, they will stop the interview and consult an officer not below superintendent rank, if one is readily available, and otherwise an officer not below inspector rank not connected with the investigation. After speaking to the appropriate adult, the officer consulted must remind the adult that their role under paragraph 11.17 does not allow them to obstruct proper questioning and give the adult an opportunity to respond. The officer consulted will then decide if the interview should continue without the attendance of that appropriate adult. If they decide it should, another appropriate adult must be obtained before the interview continues, unless the provisions of paragraph 11.18 below apply.

(d) Vulnerable suspects–urgent interviews at police stations

C:11.18 The following interviews may take place only if an officer of superintendent rank or above considers delaying the interview will lead to the consequences in paragraph 11.1(a) to (c), and is satisfied the interview would not significantly harm the person's physical or mental state (see Annex G):

(a) an interview of a detained juvenile or person who is mentally disordered or otherwise mentally vulnerable without the appropriate adult being present;

(b) an interview of anyone detained other than in (a) who appears unable to:
  - appreciate the significance of questions and their answers; or
  - understand what is happening because of the effects of drink, drugs or any illness, ailment or condition;

(c) an interview, without an interpreter having been arranged, of a detained person whom the custody officer has determined requires an interpreter (see para. 3.5(c)(ii) and 3.12) which is carried out by an interviewer speaking the suspect's own language or (as the case may be) otherwise establishing effective communication which is sufficient to enable the necessary questions to be asked and answered in order to avert the consequences. See paragraphs 13.2 and 13.5.

C:11.19 These interviews may not continue once sufficient information has been obtained to avert the consequences in paragraph 11.1(a) to (c).

C:11.20 A record shall be made of the grounds for any decision to interview a person under paragraph 11.18.

Notes for guidance

★**A-76**

C:11ZA *The requirement in paragraph 11.1A for a suspect to be given sufficient information about the offence applies prior to the interview and whether or not they are legally represented. What is sufficient will depend on the circumstances of the case, but it should normally include, as a minimum, a description of the facts relating to the suspected offence that are known to the officer, including the time and place in question. This aims to avoid suspects being confused or unclear about what they are supposed to have done and to help an innocent suspect to clear the matter up more quickly.*

C:11A *Paragraph 11.4 does not prevent the interviewer from putting significant statements and silences to a suspect again at a later stage or a further interview.*

C:11B *The Criminal Procedure and Investigations Act 1996 Code of Practice, para. 3.5 states "In conducting an investigation, the investigator should pursue all reasonable lines of enquiry, whether these point towards or away from the suspect. What is reasonable will depend on the particular circumstances." Interviewers should keep this in mind when deciding what questions to ask in an interview.*

C:11C *Although juveniles or people who are mentally disordered or otherwise mentally vulnerable are often capable of providing reliable evidence, they may, without knowing or wishing to do so, be particularly prone in certain circumstances to provide information that may be unreliable, misleading or self-incriminating. Special care should always be taken when questioning such a person, and the appropriate adult should be involved if there is any doubt about a person's age, mental state or capacity. Because of the risk of unreliable evidence it is also important to obtain corroboration of any facts admitted whenever possible.*

C:11D *Juveniles should not be arrested at their place of education unless this is unavoidable. When a juvenile is arrested at their place of education, the principal or their nominee must be informed.*

C:11E *Significant statements described in paragraph 11.4 will always be relevant to the offence and must be recorded. When a suspect agrees to read records of interviews and other comments and sign them as correct, they should be asked to endorse the record with, e.g. 'I agree that this is a correct record of what was said' and add their signature. If the suspect does not agree with the record, the interviewer should record the details of any disagreement and ask the suspect to read these details and sign them to the effect that they accurately reflect their disagreement. Any refusal to sign should be recorded.*

C:11F *The appropriate adult may intervene if they consider it is necessary to help the suspect understand any question asked and to help the suspect to answer any question. Paragraph 11.17A only applies if the appropriate adult's approach or conduct prevents or unreasonably obstructs proper questions being put to the suspect or the suspect's response being recorded. Examples of unacceptable conduct include answering questions on a suspect's behalf or providing written replies for the suspect to quote. An officer who takes the decision to exclude an appropriate adult must be in a position to satisfy the court the decision was properly made. In order to do this they may need to witness what is happening and give the suspect's solicitor (if they have one) who witnessed what happened, an opportunity to comment.*

C:12 Interviews in police stations

(a) *Action*

C:12.1 If a police officer wants to interview or conduct enquiries which require the presence of a ★A-77 detainee, the custody officer is responsible for deciding whether to deliver the detainee into the officer's custody. An investigating officer who is given custody of a detainee takes over responsibility for the detainee's care and safe custody for the purposes of this code until they return the detainee to the custody officer when they must report the manner in which they complied with the code whilst having custody of the detainee.

C:12.2 Except as below, in any period of 24 hours a detainee must be allowed a continuous period of at least 8 hours for rest, free from questioning, travel or any interruption in connection with the investigation concerned. This period should normally be at night or other appropriate time which takes account of when the detainee last slept or rested. If a detainee is arrested at a police station after going there voluntarily, the period of 24 hours runs from the time of their arrest and not the time of arrival at the police station. The period may not be interrupted or delayed, except:

    (a) when there are reasonable grounds for believing not delaying or interrupting the period would:

        (i) involve a risk of harm to people or serious loss of, or damage to, property;

        (ii) delay unnecessarily the person's release from custody; or

        (iii) otherwise prejudice the outcome of the investigation;

    (b) at the request of the detainee, their appropriate adult or legal representative;

    (c) when a delay or interruption is necessary in order to:

        (i) comply with the legal obligations and duties arising under section 15; or

        (ii) to take action required under section 9 or in accordance with medical advice.

If the period is interrupted in accordance with (a), a fresh period must be allowed. Interruptions under (b) and (c) do not require a fresh period to be allowed.

C:12.3 Before a detainee is interviewed, the custody officer, in consultation with the officer in charge of the investigation and appropriate healthcare professionals as necessary, shall assess whether the detainee is fit enough to be interviewed. This means determining and considering the risks to the detainee's physical and mental state if the interview took place and determining what safeguards are needed to allow the interview to take place. See Annex G. The custody officer shall not allow a detainee to be interviewed if the custody officer considers it would cause significant harm to the detainee's physical or mental state. Vulnerable suspects listed at paragraph 11.18 shall be treated as always being at some risk during an interview and these persons may not be interviewed except in accordance with paragraphs 11.18 to 11.20.

C:12.4 As far as practicable interviews shall take place in interview rooms which are adequately heated, lit and ventilated.

C:12.5 A suspect whose detention without charge has been authorised under PACE because the detention is necessary for an interview to obtain evidence of the offence for which they have been arrested may choose not to answer questions but police do not require the suspect's consent or agreement to interview them for this purpose. If a suspect takes steps to prevent themselves being questioned or further questioned, *e.g.* by refusing to leave their cell to go to a suitable interview room or by trying to leave the interview room, they shall be advised their consent or agreement to interview is not required. The suspect shall be cautioned as in section 10, and informed if they fail or refuse to co-operate, the interview may take place in the cell and that their failure or refusal to co-operate may be given in evidence. The suspect shall then be invited to co-operate and go into the interview room.

C:12.6 People being questioned or making statements shall not be required to stand.

★**A-78**   C:12.7 Before the interview commences each interviewer shall, subject to paragraph 2.6A, identify themselves and any other persons present to the interviewee.

C:12.8 Breaks from interviewing should be made at recognised meal times or at other times that take account of when an interviewee last had a meal. Short refreshment breaks shall be provided at approximately two hour intervals, subject to the interviewer's discretion to delay a break if there are reasonable grounds for believing it would:

    (i) involve a:
- risk of harm to people;
- serious loss of, or damage to, property;

    (ii) unnecessarily delay the detainee's release; or

    (iii) otherwise prejudice the outcome of the investigation.

See *Note 12B*

C:12.9 If during the interview a complaint is made by or on behalf of the interviewee concerning the provisions of any of the codes, or it comes to the interviewer's notice that the interviewee may have been treated improperly, the interviewer should:

    (i) record the matter in the interview record; and

    (ii) inform the custody officer, who is then responsible for dealing with it as in section 9.

(b) *Documentation*

★**A-79**   C:12.10 A record must be made of the:
- time a detainee is not in the custody of the custody officer, and why
- reason for any refusal to deliver the detainee out of that custody.

C:12.11 A record shall be made of:

    (a) the reasons it was not practicable to use an interview room; and

    (b) any action taken as in paragraph 12.5.

The record shall be made on the custody record or in the interview record for action taken whilst an interview record is being kept, with a brief reference to this effect in the custody record.

C:12.12 Any decision to delay a break in an interview must be recorded, with reasons, in the interview record.

C:12.13 All written statements made at police stations under caution shall be written on forms provided for the purpose.

C:12.14 All written statements made under caution shall be taken in accordance with Annex D. Before a person makes a written statement under caution at a police station, they shall be reminded about the right to legal advice. See *Note 12A*.

Notes for guidance

★**A-80**   C:12A *It is not normally necessary to ask for a written statement if the interview was recorded in writing and the record signed in accordance with paragraph 11.11 or audibly or visually recorded in accordance with Code E or F. Statements under caution should normally be taken in these circumstances only at the person's express wish. A person may however be asked if they want to make such a statement.*

C:12B *Meal breaks should normally last at least 45 minutes and shorter breaks after two hours should last at least 15 minutes. If the interviewer delays a break in accordance with paragraph 12.8 and prolongs the interview, a longer break should be provided. If there is a short interview and another short interview is contemplated, the length of the break may be reduced if there are reasonable grounds to believe this is necessary to avoid any of the consequences in paragraph 12.8(i) to (iii).*

C:13 Interpreters

(a) *General*

C:13.1 Chief officers are responsible for making arrangements (see para. 13.1ZA) to provide ap-   ★**A-81**
propriately qualified independent persons to act as interpreters and to provide translations of essential documents for:

(a) detained suspects who, in accordance with paragraph 3.5(c)(ii), the custody officer has determined require an interpreter, and

(b) suspects who are not under arrest but are cautioned as in section 10 who, in accordance with paragraph 3.21(b), the interviewer has determined require an interpreter. In these cases, the responsibilities of the custody officer are, if appropriate, assigned to the interviewer. An interviewer who has any doubts about whether and what arrangements for an interpreter must be made or about how the provisions of this section should be applied to a suspect who is not under arrest should seek advice from an officer of the rank of sergeant or above.

If the suspect has a hearing or speech impediment, references to "interpreter" and "interpretation" in this Code include arrangements for appropriate assistance necessary to establish effective communication with that person. See paragraph 13.1C below if the person is in Wales.

C:13.1ZA References in paragraph 13.1 above and elsewhere in this Code (see paras 3.12(a), 13.2, 13.2A, 13.5, 13.6, 13.9, 13.10, 13.10A, 13.10D and 13.11 below and in any other Code, to making arrangements for an interpreter to assist a suspect, mean making arrangements for the interpreter to be *physically* present in the same location as the suspect *unless* the provisions in paragraph 13.12 below, and Part 1 of Annex N, allow livelink interpretation to be used.

C:13.1A The arrangements *must* comply with the minimum requirements set out in Directive 2010/64/EU of the European Parliament and of the Council of 20 October 2010 on the right to interpretation and translation in criminal proceedings (see *Note 13A*). The provisions *of this* code implement the requirements for those to whom this code applies. These requirements include the following:

- That the arrangements made and the quality of interpretation and translation provided shall be sufficient to "*safeguard the fairness of the proceedings, in particular by ensuring that suspected or accused persons have knowledge of the cases against them and are able to exercise their right of defence*". This term which is used by the Directive means that the suspect must be able to understand their position and be able to communicate effectively with police officers, interviewers, solicitors and appropriate adults as provided for by this and any other Code in the same way as a suspect who can speak and understand English and who does not have a hearing or speech impediment and who would therefore not require an interpreter. See paragraphs 13.12 to 13.14 and Annex N for application to live-link interpretation.

- The provision of a written translation of all documents considered essential for the person to exercise their right of defence and to "*safeguard the fairness of the proceedings*" as described above. For the purposes of this Code, this includes any decision to authorise a person to be detained and details of any offence(s) with which the person has been charged or for which they have been told they may be prosecuted, see Annex M.

- Procedures to help determine:

 ˜ whether a suspect can speak and understand English and needs the assistance of an interpreter, see paragraph 13.1 and *Notes 13B* and *13C*; and

 ˜ whether another interpreter should be arranged or another translation should be provided when a suspect complains about the quality of either or both, see paragraphs 13.10A and 13.10C.

C:13.1B All reasonable attempts should be made to make the suspect understand that interpretation and translation will be provided at public expense.

C:13.1C With regard to persons in Wales, nothing in this or any other code affects the application of the Welsh Language Schemes produced by police and crime commissioners in Wales in accordance with the Welsh Language Act 1993. See paragraphs 3.12 and 13.1.

(b) *Interviewing suspects–foreign languages*

C:13.2 Unless paragraphs 11.1 or 11.18(c) apply, a suspect who for the purposes of this code requires an interpreter because they do not appear to speak or understand English (see paragraphs 3.5(c)(ii) and 3.12) must not be interviewed unless arrangements are made for a person capable of interpreting to assist the suspect to understand and communicate.

C:13.2A If a person who is a juvenile or is mentally disordered or mentally vulnerable is interviewed and the person acting as the appropriate adult does not appear to speak or understand English, arrangements must be made for an interpreter to assist communication between the person, the appropriate adult and the interviewer, unless the interview is urgent and paragraphs 11.1 or 11.18(c) apply.

C:13.3 When a written record of the interview is made (see paragraph 11.7), the interviewer shall make sure the interpreter makes a note of the interview at the time in the person's language for use in the event of the interpreter being called to give evidence, and certifies its accuracy. The interviewer should allow sufficient time for the interpreter to note each question and answer after each is put, given and interpreted. The person should be allowed to read the record or have it read to them and sign it as correct or indicate the respects in which they consider it inaccurate. If an audio or visual record of the interview is made, the arrangements in Code E or F shall apply. See paragraphs 13.12 to 13.14 and Annex N for application to live-link interpretation.

C:13.4 In the case of a person making a statement under caution (see Annex D) to a police officer or other police staff in a language other than English:

    (a) the interpreter shall record the statement in the language it is made;

    (b) the person shall be invited to sign it;

    (c) an official English translation shall be made in due course. See paragraphs 13.12 to 13.14 and Annex N for application to live-link interpretation.

(c) Interviewing suspects who have a hearing or speech impediment

★**A-82**   C:13.5 Unless paragraphs 11.1 or 11.18(c) (urgent interviews) apply, a suspect who for the purposes of this Code requires an interpreter or other appropriate assistance to enable effective communication with them because they appear to have a hearing or speech impediment (see paras 3.5(c)(ii) and 3.12) must not be interviewed without arrangements having been made to provide an independent person capable of interpreting or of providing other appropriate assistance.

C:13.6 An interpreter should also be arranged if a person who is a juvenile or who is mentally disordered or mentally vulnerable is interviewed and the person who is present as the appropriate adult, appears to have a hearing or speech impediment, unless the interview is urgent and paragraphs 11.1 or 11.18(c) apply.

C:13.7 If a written record of the interview is made, the interviewer shall make sure the interpreter is allowed to read the record and certify its accuracy in the event of the interpreter being called to give evidence. If an audio or visual recording is made, the arrangements in Code E or F apply.

See paragraphs 13.12 to 13.14 and Annex N for application to live-link interpretation.

(d) Additional rules for detained persons

C:13.8 [*Not used.*]

C:13.9 If paragraph 6.1 applies and the detainee cannot communicate with the solicitor because of language, hearing or speech difficulties, arrangements must be made for an interpreter to enable communication. A police officer or any other police staff may not be used for this purpose.

C:13.10 After the custody officer has determined that a detainee requires an interpreter (see paragraph 3.5(c)(ii)) and following the initial action in paragraphs 3.1 to 3.5, arrangements must also be made for an interpreter to:

    • explain the grounds and reasons for any authorisation for their *continued* detention, before or after charge and any information about the authorisation given to them by the authorising officer and which is recorded in the custody record. See paragraphs 15.3, 15.4 and 15.16(a) and (b);

    • to provide interpretation at the magistrates' court for the hearing of an application for a warrant of further detention or any extension or further extension of such warrant to explain any grounds and reasons for the application and any information about the authorisation of their further detention given to them by the court (see PACE, ss.43 and 44 and paras 15.2 and 15.16(c)); and

    • explain any offence with which the detainee is charged or for which they are informed they may be prosecuted and any other information about the offence given to them by or on behalf of the custody officer, see paragraphs 16.1 and 16.3.

C:13.10A If a detainee complains that they are not satisfied with the quality of interpretation, the custody officer or (as the case may be) the interviewer, is responsible for deciding whether to make arrangements for a different interpreter in accordance with the procedures set out in the arrangements made by the chief officer, see paragraph 13.1A.

(e) *Translations of essential documents*

C:13.10B Written translations, oral translations and oral summaries of essential documents in a language the detainee understands shall be provided in accordance with Annex M (translations of documents and records).

C:13.10C If a detainee complains that they are not satisfied with the quality of the translation, the custody officer or (as the case may be) the interviewer, is responsible for deciding whether a further translation should be provided in accordance with the procedures set out in the arrangements made by the chief officer, see paragraph 13.1A.

(f) *Decisions not to provide interpretation and translation.*

C:13.10D If a suspect challenges a decision:

- made by the custody officer or (as the case may be) by the interviewer, in accordance with this code (see paras 3.5(c)(ii) and 3.21(b)) that they do not require an interpreter, or
- made in accordance with paragraphs 13.10A, 13.10B or 13.10C not to make arrangements to provide a different interpreter or another translation or not to translate a requested document,

the matter shall be reported to an inspector to deal with as a complaint for the purposes of paragraph 9.2 or paragraph 12.9 if the challenge is made during an interview.

(g) *Documentation*

C:13.11 The following must be recorded in the custody record or, as applicable, the interview record:

(a) action taken to arrange for an interpreter, including the live-link requirements in Annex N as applicable;

(b) action taken when a detainee is not satisfied about the standard of interpretation or translation provided, see paragraphs 13.10A and 13.10C;

(c) when an urgent interview is carried out in accordance with paragraph 13.2 or 13.5 in the absence of an interpreter;

(d) when a detainee has been assisted by an interpreter for the purpose of providing or being given information or being interviewed;

(e) action taken in accordance with Annex M when:

- a written translation of an essential document is provided;
- an oral translation or oral summary of an essential document is provided instead of a written translation and the authorising officer's reason(s) why this would not prejudice the fairness of the proceedings (see Annex M, para. 3);
- a suspect waives their right to a translation of an essential document (see Annex M, para. 4);
- when representations that a document which is not included in the table is essential and that a translation should be provided are refused and the reason for the refusal (see Annex M, para. 8).

(h) *Live-link interpretation*

C:13.12 In this section and in Annex N, "live-link interpretation" means an arrangement to enable communication between the suspect and an interpreter who is not *physically* present with the suspect. The arrangement must ensure that anything said by any person in the suspect's presence and hearing can be interpreted in the same way as if the interpreter was physically present at that time. The communication must be by audio *and* visual means for the purpose of an interview, and for all other purposes it may be *either*, by audio and visual means, or by audio means *only*, as follows:

(a) Audio and visual communication

This applies for the purposes of an interview conducted and recorded in accordance with Code E (audio recording) or Code F (visual recording) and during that interview, live link interpretation must *enable*:

(i) the suspect, the interviewer, solicitor, appropriate adult and any other person *physically* present with the suspect at any time during the interview and an interpreter who is not *physically* present, to *see* and *hear* each other; and

(ii) the interview to be conducted and recorded in accordance with the provisions of Codes C, E and F, subject to the modifications in Part 2 of Annex N.

(b) Audio and visual or audio without visual communication.

This applies to communication for the purposes of any provision of this or any other code except as described in (a), which requires or permits information to be given to, sought from, or provided by a suspect, whether orally or in writing, which would include communication between the suspect and their solicitor and/or appropriate adult, and for these cases, live link interpretation must:

  (i) *enable* the suspect, the person giving or seeking that information, any other person *physically* present with the suspect at that time and an interpreter who is not so present, to either *see* and *hear* each other, or to *hear without seeing* each other (for example by using a telephone); and

  (ii) enable that information to be given to, sought from, or provided by, the suspect in accordance with the provisions of this or any other code that apply to that information, as modified for the purposes of the live-link, by Part 2 of Annex N.

C:13.12A The requirement in sub-paragraphs 13.12(a)(ii) and (b)(ii), that live-link interpretation must enable compliance with the relevant provisions of the Codes C, E and F, means that the arrangements must provide for any written or electronic record of what the suspect says in their own language which is made by the interpreter, to be securely transmitted without delay so that the suspect can be invited to read, check and if appropriate, sign or otherwise confirm that the record is correct or make corrections to the record.

C:13.13 Chief officers must be satisfied that live-link interpretation used in their force area for the purposes of paragraphs 3.12(a) and (b), provides for accurate and secure communication with the suspect. This includes ensuring that at any time during which live link interpretation is being used: a person cannot see, hear or otherwise obtain access to any communications between the suspect and interpreter or communicate with the suspect or interpreter unless so authorised or allowed by the custody officer or, in the case of an interview, the interviewer and that as applicable, the confidentiality of any private consultation between a suspect and their solicitor and appropriate adult (see paragraphs 13.2A, 13.6 and 13.9) is maintained.. See Annex N, para. 4.

Notes for guidance

C:13A *Chief officers have discretion when determining the individuals or organisations they use to provide interpretation and translation services for their forces provided that these are compatible with the requirements of the Directive. One example which chief officers may wish to consider is the Ministry of Justice commercial agreements for interpretation and translation services.*

C:13B *A procedure for determining whether a person needs an interpreter might involve a telephone interpreter service or using cue cards or similar visual aids which enable the detainee to indicate their ability to speak and understand English and their preferred language. This could be confirmed through an interpreter who could also assess the extent to which the person can speak and understand English.*

C:13C *There should also be a procedure for determining whether a suspect who requires an interpreter requires assistance in accordance with paragraph 3.20 to help them check and if applicable, sign any documentation.*

C:14 Questioning–special restrictions

★**A-83**   C:14.1 If a person is arrested by one police force on behalf of another and the lawful period of detention in respect of that offence has not yet commenced in accordance with PACE, s.41, no questions may be put to them about the offence while they are in transit between the forces except to clarify any voluntary statement they make.

C:14.2 If a person is in police detention at a hospital, they may not be questioned without the agreement of a responsible doctor. See *Note 14A.*

Note for guidance

★**A-84**   C:14A *If questioning takes place at a hospital under paragraph 14.2, or on the way to or from a hospital, the period of questioning concerned counts towards the total period of detention permitted.*

C:15 Reviews and extensions of detention

(a) *Persons detained under PACE*

★**A-85**   C:15.0 The requirement in paragraph 3.4(b) that documents and materials essential to challenging the lawfulness of the detainee's arrest and detention must be made available to the detainee or their solicitor, applies for the purposes of this section as follows:

  (a) The officer reviewing the need for detention without charge (PACE, s.40), or (as the case may be) the officer considering the need to extend detention without charge from 24 to 36 hours (PACE, s.42), is responsible, in consultation with the investigating officer, for deciding which documents and materials are essential and must be made available.

  (b) When paragraph 15.7A applies (application for a warrant of further detention or extension of such a warrant), the officer making the application is responsible for deciding which documents and materials are essential and must be made available *before* the hearing. See *Note 3ZA.*

C:15.1 The review officer is responsible under PACE, s.40 for periodically determining if a person's detention, before or after charge, continues to be necessary. This requirement continues throughout the detention period and, except as in paragraph 15.10, the review officer must be present at the police station holding the detainee. See *Notes 15A* and *15B.*

C:15.2 Under PACE, s.42, an officer of superintendent rank or above who is responsible for the station holding the detainee may give authority any time after the second review to extend the maximum period the person may be detained without charge by up to 12 hours. Further detention without charge may be authorised only by a magistrates' court in accordance with PACE, sections 43 and 44. See *Notes 15C, 15D* and *15E.*

C:15.2A An authorisation under section 42(1) of PACE extends the maximum period of detention permitted before charge for indictable offences from 24 hours to 36 hours. Detaining a juvenile or mentally vulnerable person for longer than 24 hours will be dependent on the circumstances of the case and with regard to the person's:

    (a) special vulnerability;

    (b) the legal obligation to provide an opportunity for representations to be made prior to a decision about extending detention;

    (c) the need to consult and consider the views of any appropriate adult; and

    (d) any alternatives to police custody.

C:15.3 Before deciding whether to authorise continued detention the officer responsible under paragraph 15.1 or 15.2 shall give an opportunity to make representations about the detention to:

    (a) the detainee, unless in the case of a review as in paragraph 15.1, the detainee is asleep;

    (b) the detainee's solicitor if available at the time; and

    (c) the appropriate adult if available at the time.

See *Note 15CA*

C:15.3A Other people having an interest in the detainee's welfare may also make representations at the authorising officer's discretion.

C:15.3B Subject to paragraph 15.10, the representations may be made orally in person or by telephone or in writing. The authorising officer may, however, refuse to hear oral representations from the detainee if the officer considers them unfit to make representations because of their condition or behaviour. See *Note 15C.*

C:15.3C The decision on whether the review takes place in person or by telephone or by video conferencing (see *Note 15G*) is a matter for the review officer. In determining the form the review may take, the review officer must always take full account of the needs of the person in custody. The benefits of carrying out a review in person should always be considered, based on the individual circumstances of each case with specific additional consideration if the person is:

    (a) a juvenile (and the age of the juvenile); or

    (b) suspected of being mentally vulnerable; or

    (c) in need of medical attention for other than routine minor ailments; or

    (d) subject to presentational or community issues around their detention.

C:15.4 Before conducting a review or determining whether to extend the maximum period of **★A-86** detention without charge, the officer responsible must make sure the detainee is reminded of their entitlement to free legal advice, see paragraph 6.5, unless in the case of a review the person is asleep.

C:15.5 If, after considering any representations, the review officer under paragraph 15.1 decides to keep the detainee in detention or the superintendent under paragraph 15.2 extends the maximum period for which they may be detained without charge, then any comment made by the detainee shall be recorded. If applicable, the officer shall be informed of the comment as soon as practicable. See also paragraphs 11.4 and 11.13.

C:15.6 No officer shall put specific questions to the detainee:

    • regarding their involvement in any offence; or

    • in respect of any comments they may make:

      – when given the opportunity to make representations; or

      – in response to a decision to keep them in detention or extend the maximum period of detention.

Such an exchange could constitute an interview as in paragraph 11.1A and would be subject to the associated safeguards in section 11 and, in respect of a person who has been charged, paragraph 16.5. See also paragraph 11.13.

C:15.7 A detainee who is asleep at a review, see paragraph 15.1, and whose continued detention is authorised must be informed about the decision and reason as soon as practicable after waking.

C:15.7A When an application is made to a magistrates' court under PACE, section 43 for a warrant of further detention to extend detention without charge of a person arrested for an *indictable offence*, or under section 44, to extend or further extend that warrant, the detainee:

(a) must be brought to court for the hearing of the application;

(b) is entitled to be legally represented if they wish, in which case, Annex B cannot apply; and

(c) must be given a copy of the information which supports the application and states:

(i) the nature of the offence for which the person to whom the application relates has been arrested;

(ii) the general nature of the evidence on which the person was arrested;

(iii) what inquiries about the offence have been made and what further inquiries are proposed;

(iv) the reasons for believing continued detention is necessary for the purposes of the further inquiries;

Note: A warrant of further detention can only be issued or extended if the court has reasonable grounds for believing that the person's further detention is necessary for the purpose of obtaining evidence of an indictable offence for which the person has been arrested and that the investigation is being conducted diligently and expeditiously.

See paragraph 15.0(b).

C:15.8 [*Not used.*]

(b) *Review of detention by telephone and video conferencing facilities*

★A-87   C:15.9 PACE, section 40A provides that the officer responsible under section 40 for reviewing the detention of a person who has not been charged, need not attend the police station holding the detainee and may carry out the review by telephone.

C:15.9A PACE, section 45A(2) provides that the officer responsible under section 40 for reviewing the detention of a person who has not been charged, need not attend the police station holding the detainee and may carry out the review by video conferencing facilities. See *Note 15G*.

C:15.9B A telephone review is not permitted where facilities for review by video conferencing exist and it is practicable to use them.

C:15.9C The review officer can decide at any stage that a telephone review or review by video conferencing should be terminated and that the review will be conducted in person. The reasons for doing so should be noted in the custody record.

See *Note 15F*.

C:15.10 When a review is carried out by telephone or by video conferencing facilities, an officer at the station holding the detainee shall be required by the review officer to fulfil that officer's obligations under PACE section 40 and this code by:

(a) making any record connected with the review in the detainee's custody record;

(b) if applicable, making the record in (*a*) in the presence of the detainee; and

(c) for a review by telephone, giving the detainee information about the review.

C:15.11 When a review is carried out by telephone or by video conferencing facilities, the requirement in paragraph 15.3 will be satisfied:

(a) if facilities exist for the immediate transmission of written representations to the review officer, *e.g.* fax or email message, by allowing those who are given the opportunity to make representations, to make their representations:

(i) orally by telephone or (as the case may be) by means of the video conferencing facilities; or

(ii) in writing using the facilities for the immediate transmission of written representations; and

(b) in all other cases, by allowing those who are given the opportunity to make representations, to make their representations orally by telephone or by means of the video conferencing facilities.

(c) *Documentation*

C:15.12 It is the officer's responsibility to make sure all reminders given under paragraph 15.4 are noted in the custody record.

C:15.13 The grounds for, and extent of, any delay in conducting a review shall be recorded.

C:15.14 When a review is carried out by telephone or video conferencing facilities, a record shall be made of:

(a) the reason the review officer did not attend the station holding the detainee;

(b) the place the review officer was;

(c) the method representations, oral or written, were made to the review officer, see paragraph 15.11.

C:15.15 Any written representations shall be retained.

C:15.16 A record shall be made as soon as practicable of:

(a) the outcome of each review of detention before or after charge, and if paragraph 15.7 applies, of when the person was informed and by whom;

(b) the outcome of any determination under PACE, s.42 by a superintendent whether to extend the maximum period of detention without charge beyond 24 hours from the relevant time. If an authorisation is given, the record shall state the number of hours and minutes by which the detention period is extended or further extended.

(c) the outcome of each application under PACE, s.43, for a warrant of further detention or under section 44, for an extension or further extension of that warrant. If a warrant for further detention is granted under section 43 or extended or further extended under 44, the record shall state the detention period authorised by the warrant and the date and time it was granted or (as the case may be) the period by which the warrant is extended or further extended.

Note: Any period during which a person is released on bail does not count towards the maximum period of detention without charge allowed under PACE, ss.41 to 44.

Notes for guidance

★**A-88**

C:15A *Review officer for the purposes of:*

- *PACE, ss.40, 40A and 45A means, in the case of a person arrested but not charged, an officer of at least inspector rank not directly involved in the investigation and, if a person has been arrested and charged, the custody officer.*

C:15B *The detention of persons in police custody not subject to the statutory review requirement in paragraph 15.1 should still be reviewed periodically as a matter of good practice. Such reviews can be carried out by an officer of the rank of sergeant or above. The purpose of such reviews is to check the particular power under which a detainee is held continues to apply, any associated conditions are complied with and to make sure appropriate action is taken to deal with any changes. This includes the detainee's prompt release when the power no longer applies, or their transfer if the power requires the detainee be taken elsewhere as soon as the necessary arrangements are made. Examples include persons:*

(a) *arrested on warrant because they failed to answer bail to appear at court;*

(b) *arrested under the Bail Act 1976, s.7(3) for breaching a condition of bail granted after charge;*

(c) *in police custody for specific purposes and periods under the Crime (Sentences) Act 1997, Sched.1;*

(d) *convicted, or remand prisoners, held in police stations on behalf of the Prison Service under the Imprisonment (Temporary Provisions) Act 1980, s.6;*

(e) *being detained to prevent them causing a breach of the peace;*

(f) *detained at police stations on behalf of Immigration Enforcement (formerly the UK Immigration Service);*

(g) *detained by order of a magistrates' court under the Criminal Justice Act 1988, s.152 (as amended by the Drugs Act 2005, s.8) to facilitate the recovery of evidence after being charged with drug possession or drug trafficking and suspected of having swallowed drugs.*

The detention of persons remanded into police detention by order of a court under the Magistrates' Courts Act 1980, s.128 is subject to a statutory requirement to review that detention. This is to make sure the detainee is taken back to court no later than the end of the period authorised by the court or when the need for their detention by police ceases, whichever is the sooner.

C:15C *In the case of a review of detention, but not an extension, the detainee need not be woken for the review. However, if the detainee is likely to be asleep, e.g. during a period of rest allowed as in paragraph 12.2, at the latest time a review or authorisation to extend detention may take place, the officer should, if the legal obligations and time constraints permit, bring forward the procedure to allow the detainee to make representations. A detainee not asleep during the review must be present when the grounds for their continued detention are recorded and must at the same time be informed of those grounds unless the review officer considers the person is incapable of understanding what is said, violent or likely to become violent or in urgent need of medical attention.*

C:15CA *In paragraph 15.3(b) and (c), "available" includes being contactable in time to enable them to make representations remotely by telephone or other electronic means or in person by attending the station. Reasonable efforts should therefore be made to give the solicitor and appropriate adult sufficient notice of the time the decision is expected to be made so that they can make themselves available.*

C:15D *An application to a magistrates' court under PACE, ss.43 or 44 for a warrant of further detention or its extension should be made between 10am and 9pm, and if possible during normal court hours. It will not usu-*

ally be practicable to arrange for a court to sit specially outside the hours of 10am to 9pm. If it appears a special sitting may be needed outside normal court hours but between 10am and 9pm, the clerk to the justices should be given notice and informed of this possibility, while the court is sitting if possible.

C:15E *In paragraph 15.2, the officer responsible for the station holding the detainee includes a superintendent or above who, in accordance with their force operational policy or police regulations, is given that responsibility on a temporary basis whilst the appointed long-term holder is off duty or otherwise unavailable.*

C:15F *The provisions of PACE, s.40A allowing telephone reviews do not apply to reviews of detention after charge by the custody officer. When video conferencing is not required, they allow the use of a telephone to carry out a review of detention before charge. The procedure under PACE, s.42 must be done in person.*

C:15G *Video conferencing facilities means any facilities (whether a live television link or other facilities) by means of which the review can be carried out with the review officer, the detainee concerned and the detainee's solicitor all being able to both see and to hear each other. The use of video conferencing facilities for decisions about detention under section 45A of PACE is subject to regulations made by the Secretary of State being in force.*

C:16 Charging detained persons

(a) *Action*

★A-89 C:16.1 When the officer in charge of the investigation reasonably believes there is sufficient evidence to provide a realistic prospect of conviction for the offence (see para. *11.6*), they shall without delay, and subject to the following qualification, inform the custody officer who will be responsible for considering whether the detainee should be charged. See *Notes 11B* and *16A*. When a person is detained in respect of more than one offence it is permissible to delay informing the custody officer until the above conditions are satisfied in respect of all the offences, but see para. *11.6*. If the detainee is a juvenile, mentally disordered or otherwise mentally vulnerable, any resulting action shall be taken in the presence of the appropriate adult if they are present at the time.

See *Notes 16B* and *16C*.

C:16.1A Where guidance issued by the Director of Public Prosecutions under PACE, section 37A is in force the custody officer must comply with that Guidance in deciding how to act in dealing with the detainee. See *Notes 16AA* and *16AB*.

C:16.1B Where in compliance with the DPP's Guidance the custody officer decides that the case should be immediately referred to the CPS to make the charging decision, consultation should take place with a Crown Prosecutor as soon as is reasonably practicable. Where the Crown Prosecutor is unable to make the charging decision on the information available at that time, the detainee may be released without charge and on bail (with conditions if necessary) under section 37(7)(a). In such circumstances, the detainee should be informed that they are being released to enable the Director of Public Prosecutions to make a decision under section 37B.

C:16.2 When a detainee is charged with or informed they may be prosecuted for an offence, see *Note 16B*, they shall, unless the restriction on drawing adverse inferences from silence applies, see Annex C, be cautioned as follows:

"You do not have to say anything. But it may harm your defence if you do not mention now something which you later rely on in court. Anything you do say may be given in evidence."

Where the use of the Welsh Language is appropriate, a constable may provide the caution directly in Welsh in the following terms:

"Does dim rhaid i chi ddweud dim byd. Ond gall niweidio eich amddiffyniad os na fyddwch chi'n sôn, yn awr, am rywbeth y byddwch chi'n dibynnu arno nes ymlaen yn y llys. Gall unrhyw beth yr ydych yn ei ddweud gael ei roi fel tystiolaeth."

Annex C, para. 2 sets out the alternative terms of the caution to be used when the restriction on drawing adverse inferences from silence applies.

C:16.3 When a detainee is charged they shall be given a written notice showing particulars of the offence and, subject to paragraph 2.6A, the officer's name and the case reference number. As far as possible the particulars of the charge shall be stated in simple terms, but they shall also show the precise offence in law with which the detainee is charged. The notice shall begin:

"You are charged with the offence(s) shown below." Followed by the caution.

If the detainee is a juvenile, mentally disordered or otherwise mentally vulnerable, a copy of the notice should also be given to the appropriate adult.

C:16.4 If, after a detainee has been charged with or informed they may be prosecuted for an offence, an officer wants to tell them about any written statement or interview with another person relating to such an offence, the detainee shall either be handed a true copy of the written statement or the content of the interview record brought to their attention. Nothing shall be done to invite any reply or comment except to:

  (a) caution the detainee, *"You do not have to say anything, but anything you do say may be given in evidence."*

  Where the use of the Welsh Language is appropriate, caution the detainee in the following terms:

    "Does dim rhaid i chi ddweud dim byd, ond gall unrhyw beth yr ydych yn ei ddweud gael ei roi fel tystiolaeth."

and

  (b) remind the detainee about their right to legal advice.

C:16.4A If the detainee:

  • cannot read, the document may be read to them;

  • is a juvenile, mentally disordered or otherwise mentally vulnerable, the appropriate adult shall also be given a copy, or the interview record shall be brought to their attention.

C:16.5 A detainee may not be interviewed about an offence after they have been charged with, or **★A-90** informed they may be prosecuted for it, unless the interview is necessary:

  • to prevent or minimise harm or loss to some other person, or the public

  • to clear up an ambiguity in a previous answer or statement

  • in the interests of justice for the detainee to have put to them, and have an opportunity to comment on, information concerning the offence which has come to light since they were charged or informed they might be prosecuted

Before any such interview, the interviewer shall:

  (a) caution the detainee, *"You do not have to say anything, but anything you do say may be given in evidence."*

  Where the use of the Welsh Language is appropriate, the interviewer shall caution the detainee: *"Does dim rhaid i chi ddweud dim byd, ond gall unrhyw beth yr ydych yn ei ddweud gael ei roi fel tystiolaeth."*

  (b) remind the detainee about their right to legal advice.

See *Note 16B*

C:16.6 The provisions of paragraphs 16.2 to 16.5 must be complied with in the appropriate adult's presence if they are already at the police station. If they are not at the police station then these provisions must be complied with again in their presence when they arrive unless the detainee has been released. See *Note 16C.*

C:16.7 When a juvenile is charged with an offence and the custody officer authorises their continued detention after charge, the custody officer must make arrangements for the juvenile to be taken into the care of a local authority to be detained pending appearance in court *unless* the custody officer certifies in accordance with PACE, section 38(6), that:

  (a) for any juvenile; it is impracticable to do so and the reasons why it is impracticable must be set out in the certificate that must be produced to the court; or,

  (b) in the case of a juvenile of at least 12 years old, no secure accommodation is available and other accommodation would not be adequate to protect the public from serious harm from that juvenile. See *Note 16D.*

Note: Chief officers should ensure that the operation of these provisions at police stations in their areas is subject to supervision and monitoring by an officer of the rank of inspector or above.

C:16.7A The requirement in paragraph 3.4(b) that documents and materials essential to effectively challenging the lawfulness of the detainee's arrest and detention must be made available to the detainee and, if they are represented, their solicitor, applies for the purposes of this section and a person's detention after charge. This means that the custody officer making the bail decision (PACE, s.38) or reviewing the need for detention after charge (PACE, s.40), is responsible for determining what, if any, documents or materials are essential and must be made available to the detainee or their solicitor. See *Note 3ZA.*

(b) *Documentation*

C:16.8 A record shall be made of anything a detainee says when charged.

C:16.9 Any questions put in an interview after charge and answers given relating to the offence shall be recorded in full during the interview on forms for that purpose and the record signed by the detainee or, if they refuse, by the interviewer and any third parties present. If the questions are audibly recorded or visually recorded the arrangements in Code E or F apply.

C:16.10 If arrangements for a juvenile's transfer into local authority care as in paragraph 16.7 are not made, the custody officer must record the reasons in a certificate which must be produced before the court with the juvenile. See *Note 16D.*

Notes for guidance

★**A-91**   C:16A *The custody officer must take into account alternatives to prosecution under the Crime and Disorder Act 1998 applicable to persons under 18, and in national guidance on the cautioning of offenders applicable to persons aged 18 and over.*

C:16AA *When a person is arrested under the provisions of the Criminal Justice Act 2003 which allow a person to be re-tried after being acquitted of a serious offence which is a qualifying offence specified in Schedule 5 to that Act and not precluded from further prosecution by virtue of section 75(3) of that Act the detention provisions of PACE are modified and make an officer of the rank of superintendent or above who has not been directly involved in the investigation responsible for determining whether the evidence is sufficient to charge.*

C:16AB *Where guidance issued by the Director of Public Prosecutions under section 37B is in force, a custody officer who determines in accordance with that guidance that there is sufficient evidence to charge the detainee, may detain that person for no longer than is reasonably necessary to decide how that person is to be dealt with under PACE, s.37(7)(a) to (d), including, where appropriate, consultation with the Duty Prosecutor. The period is subject to the maximum period of detention before charge determined by PACE, ss.41 to 44. Where in accordance with the guidance the case is referred to the CPS for decision, the custody officer should ensure that an officer involved in the investigation sends to the CPS such information as is specified in the guidance.*

C:16B *The giving of a warning or the service of the notice of intended prosecution required by the Road Traffic Offenders Act 1988, s.1 does not amount to informing a detainee they may be prosecuted for an offence and so does not preclude further questioning in relation to that offence.*

C:16C *There is no power under PACE to detain a person and delay action under paragraphs 16.2 to 16.5 solely to await the arrival of the appropriate adult. Reasonable efforts should therefore be made to give the appropriate adult sufficient notice of the time the decision (charge etc.) is to be implemented so that they can be present. If the appropriate adult is not, or cannot be, present at that time, the detainee should be released on bail to return for the decision to be implemented when the adult is present, unless the custody officer determines that the absence of the appropriate adult makes the detainee unsuitable for bail for this purpose. After charge, bail cannot be refused, or release on bail delayed, simply because an appropriate adult is not available, unless the absence of that adult provides the custody officer with the necessary grounds to authorise detention after charge under PACE, s.38.*

C:16D *Except as in paragraph 16.7, neither a juvenile's behaviour nor the nature of the offence provides grounds for the custody officer to decide it is impracticable to arrange the juvenile's transfer to local authority care. Impracticability concerns the transport and travel requirements and the lack of secure accommodation which is provided for the purposes of restricting liberty does not make it impracticable to transfer the juvenile. The availability of secure accommodation is only a factor in relation to a juvenile aged 12 or over when other local authority accommodation would not be adequate to protect the public from serious harm from them. The obligation to transfer a juvenile to local authority accommodation applies as much to a juvenile charged during the daytime as to a juvenile to be held overnight, subject to a requirement to bring the juvenile before a court under PACE, s.46.*

C:17 Testing persons for the presence of specified Class A drugs

(a) *Action*

★**A-91a**   C:17.1 This section of Code C applies only in selected police stations in police areas where the provisions for drug testing under s.63B of PACE (as amended by s.5 of the Criminal Justice Act 2003 and s.7 of the Drugs Act 2005) are in force and in respect of which the Secretary of State has given a notification to the relevant chief officer of police that arrangements for the taking of samples have been made. Such a notification will cover either a police area as a whole or particular stations within a police area. The notification indicates whether the testing applies to those arrested or charged or under the age of 18 as the case may be and testing can only take place in respect of the persons so indicated in the notification. Testing cannot be carried out unless the relevant notification has been given and has not been withdrawn. See *Note 17F.*

C:17.2 A sample of urine or a non-intimate sample may be taken from a person in police detention for the purpose of ascertaining whether they have any specified Class A drug in their body only where they have been brought before the custody officer and:

    (a) either the arrest condition, see paragraph 17.3, or the charge condition, see paragraph 17.4 is met;

    (b) the age condition see paragraph 17.5, is met;

    (c) the notification condition is met in relation to the arrest condition, the charge condition, or the age condition, as the case may be. (Testing on charge and/or arrest must be specifically provided for in the notification for the power to apply. In addition, the fact that testing of under 18s is authorised must be expressly provided for in the notification before the power to test such persons applies.). See paragraph 17.1; and

 (d) a police officer has requested the person concerned to give the sample (the request condition).

C:17.3 The arrest condition is met where the detainee:

 (a) has been arrested for a trigger offence, see *Note 17E*, but not charged with that offence; or

 (b) has been arrested for any other offence but not charged with that offence and a police officer of inspector rank or above, who has reasonable grounds for suspecting that their misuse of any specified Class A drug caused or contributed to the offence, has authorised the sample to be taken.

C:17.4 The charge condition is met where the detainee:

 (a) has been charged with a trigger offence, or

 (b) has been charged with any other offence and a police officer of inspector rank or above, who has reasonable grounds for suspecting that the detainee's misuse of any specified Class A drug caused or contributed to the offence, has authorised the sample to be taken.

C:17.5 The age condition is met where:

 (a) in the case of a detainee who has been arrested but not charged as in paragraph 17.3, they are aged 18 or over;

 (b) in the case of a detainee who has been charged as in paragraph 17.4, they are aged 14 or over.

C:17.6 Before requesting a sample from the person concerned, an officer must:

 (a) inform them that the purpose of taking the sample is for drug testing under PACE. This is to ascertain whether they have a specified Class A drug present in their body;

 (b) warn them that if, when so requested, they fail without good cause to provide a sample they may be liable to prosecution;

 (c) where the taking of the sample has been authorised by an inspector or above in accordance with paragraph 17.3(b) or 17.4(b) above, inform them that the authorisation has been given and the grounds for giving it;

 (d) remind them of the following rights, which may be exercised at any stage during the period in custody:

  (i) the right to have someone informed of their arrest [see section 5];

  (ii) the right to consult privately with a solicitor and that free independent legal advice is available [see section 6]; and

  (iii) the right to consult these Codes of Practice [see section 3].

C:17.7 In the case of a person who has not attained the age specified in section 63B(5A) of PACE—

 (a) the making of the request for a sample under paragraph 17.2(d) above;

 (b) the giving of the warning and the information under paragraph 17.6 above; and

 (c) the taking of the sample,

may not take place except in the presence of an appropriate adult. See *Note 17G*.

C:17.8 Authorisation by an officer of the rank of inspector or above within paragraph 17.3(b) or 17.4(b) may be given orally or in writing but, if it is given orally, it must be confirmed in writing as soon as practicable.

C:17.9 If a sample is taken from a detainee who has been arrested for an offence but not charged with that offence as in paragraph 17.3, no further sample may be taken during the same continuous period of detention. If during that same period the charge condition is also met in respect of that detainee, the sample which has been taken shall be treated as being taken by virtue of the charge condition, see paragraph 17.4, being met.

C:17.10 A detainee from whom a sample may be taken may be detained for up to six hours from the time of charge if the custody officer reasonably believes the detention is necessary to enable a sample to be taken. Where the arrest condition is met, a detainee whom the custody officer has decided to release on bail without charge may continue to be detained, but not beyond 24 hours from the relevant time (as defined in section 41(2) of PACE), to enable a sample to be taken.

C:17.11 A detainee in respect of whom the arrest condition is met, but not the charge condition, see paragraphs 17.3 and 17.4, and whose release would be required before a sample can be taken had they not continued to be detained as a result of being arrested for a further offence which does not satisfy the arrest condition, may have a sample taken at any time within 24 hours after the arrest for the offence that satisfies the arrest condition.

(b) *Documentation*

C:17.12 The following must be recorded in the custody record:

(a) if a sample is taken following authorisation by an officer of the rank of inspector or above, the authorisation and the grounds for suspicion;

(b) the giving of a warning of the consequences of failure to provide a sample;

(c) the time at which the sample was given; and

(d) the time of charge or, where the arrest condition is being relied upon, the time of arrest and, where applicable, the fact that a sample taken after arrest but before charge is to be treated as being taken by virtue of the charge condition, where that is met in the same period of continuous detention. See paragraph 17.9.

(c) *General*

C:17.13 A sample may only be taken by a prescribed person. See *Note 17C*.

C:17.14 Force may not be used to take any sample for the purpose of drug testing.

C:17.15 The terms "Class A drug" and "misuse" have the same meanings as in the Misuse of Drugs Act 1971. "Specified" (in relation to a Class A drug) and "trigger offence" have the same meanings as in Part III of the Criminal Justice and Court Services Act 2000.

C:17.16 Any sample taken:

(a) may not be used for any purpose other than to ascertain whether the person concerned has a specified Class A drug present in his body; and

(b) can be disposed of as clinical waste unless it is to be sent for further analysis in cases where the test result is disputed at the point when the result is known, including on the basis that medication has been taken, or for quality assurance purposes.

(d) *Assessment of misuse of drugs*

C:17.17 Under the provisions of Part 3 of the Drugs Act 2005, where a detainee has tested positive for a specified Class A drug under section 63B of PACE a police officer may, at any time before the person's release from the police station, impose a requirement on the detainee to attend an initial assessment of their drug misuse by a suitably qualified person and to remain for its duration. Where such a requirement is imposed, the officer must, at the same time, impose a second requirement on the detainee to attend and remain for a follow-up assessment. The officer must inform the detainee that the second requirement will cease to have effect if, at the initial assessment they are informed that a follow-up assessment is not necessary These requirements may only be imposed on a person if:

(a) they have reached the age of 18

(b) notification has been given by the Secretary of State to the relevant chief officer of police that arrangements for conducting initial and follow-up assessments have been made for those from whom samples for testing have been taken at the police station where the detainee is in custody.

C:17.18 When imposing a requirement to attend an initial assessment and a follow-up assessment the police officer must:

(a) inform the person of the time and place at which the initial assessment is to take place;

(b) explain that this information will be confirmed in writing; and

(c) warn the person that they may be liable to prosecution if they fail without good cause to attend the initial assessment and remain for its duration and if they fail to attend the follow-up assessment and remain for its duration (if so required).

C:17.19 Where a police officer has imposed a requirement to attend an initial assessment and a follow-up assessment in accordance with paragraph 17.17, he must, before the person is released from detention, give the person notice in writing which:

(a) confirms their requirement to attend and remain for the duration of the assessments; and

(b) confirms the information and repeats the warning referred to in paragraph 17.18.

C:17.20 The following must be recorded in the custody record:

(a) that the requirement to attend an initial assessment and a follow-up assessment has been imposed; and

(b) the information, explanation, warning and notice given in accordance with paragraphs 17.17 and 17.19.

C:17.21 Where a notice is given in accordance with paragraph 17.19, a police officer can give the person a further notice in writing which informs the person of any change to the time or place at which the initial assessment is to take place and which repeats the warning referred to in paragraph 17.18(c).

C:17.22 Part 3 of the Drugs Act 2005 also requires police officers to have regard to any guidance issued by the Secretary of State in respect of the assessment provisions.

Notes for guidance

C:17A *When warning a person who is asked to provide a urine or non-intimate sample in accordance with paragraph 17.6(b), the following form of words may be used:*

"You do not have to provide a sample, but I must warn you that if you fail or refuse without good cause to do so, you will commit an offence for which you may be imprisoned, or fined, or both".

Where the Welsh language is appropriate, the following form of words may be used:

"Does dim rhaid i chi roi sampl, ond mae'n rhaid i mi eich rhybuddio y byddwch chi'n cyflawni trosedd os byddwch chi'n methu neu yn gwrthod gwneud hynny heb reswm da, ac y gellir, oherwydd hynny, eich carcharu, eich dirwyo, neu'r ddau."

C:17B *A sample has to be sufficient and suitable. A sufficient sample is sufficient in quantity and quality to enable drug-testing analysis to take place. A suitable sample is one which by its nature, is suitable for a particular form of drug analysis.*

C:17C *A prescribed person in paragraph 17.13 is one who is prescribed in regulations made by the Secretary of State under section 63B(6) of the Police and Criminal Evidence Act 1984. [The regulations are currently contained in regulation S.I. 2001 No. 2645, the Police and Criminal Evidence Act 1984 (Drug Testing Persons in Police Detention) (Prescribed Persons) Regulations 2001.]*

C:17D *Samples, and the information derived from them, may not be subsequently used in the investigation of any offence or in evidence against the persons from whom they were taken.*

C:17E *Trigger offences are:*

1. *Offences under the following provisions of the Theft Act 1968:*

section 1	(theft)
section 8	(robbery)
section 9	(burglary)
section 10	(aggravated burglary)
section 12	(taking a motor vehicle or other conveyance without authority)
section 12A	(aggravated vehicle-taking)
section 22	(handling stolen goods)
section 25	(going equipped for stealing etc.)

2. *Offences under the following provisions of the Misuse of Drugs Act 1971, if committed in respect of a specified Class A drug:-*

section 4	(restriction on production and supply of controlled drugs)
section 5(2)	(possession of a controlled drug)
section 5(3)	(possession of a controlled drug with intent to supply)

3. *Offences under the following provisions of the Fraud Act 2006:*

section 1	(fraud)
section 6	(possession etc. of articles for use in frauds)
section 7	(making or supplying articles for use in frauds)

3A. *An offence under section 1(1) of the Criminal Attempts Act 1981 if committed in respect of an offence under*

(a) *any of the following provisions of the Theft Act 1968:*

section 1	(theft)
section 8	(robbery)
section 9	(burglary)
section 22	(handling stolen goods)

(b) *section 1 of the Fraud Act 2006 (fraud)*

4. *Offences under the following provisions of the Vagrancy Act 1824:*

section 3	(begging)
section 4	(persistent begging)

C:17F *The power to take samples is subject to notification by the Secretary of State that appropriate arrangements for the taking of samples have been made for the police area as a whole or for the particular police station concerned for whichever of the following is specified in the notification:*

> (a) *persons in respect of whom the arrest condition is met;*
>
> (b) *persons in respect of whom the charge condition is met;*
>
> (c) *persons who have not attained the age of 18.*

Note: Notification is treated as having been given for the purposes of the charge condition in relation to a police area, if testing (on charge) under section 63B(2) of PACE was in force immediately before section 7 of the Drugs Act 2005 was brought into force; and for the purposes of the age condition, in relation to a police area or police station, if immediately before that day, notification that arrangements had been made for the taking of samples from persons under the age of 18 (those aged 14-17) had been given and had not been withdrawn.

C:17G *Appropriate adult in paragraph 17.7 means the person's-*

> (a) *parent or guardian or, if they are in the care of a local authority or voluntary organisation, a person representing that authority or organisation; or*
>
> (b) *a social worker of a local authority; or*
>
> (c) *if no person falling within (a) or (b) above is available, any responsible person aged 18 or over who is not:*
>
> > - *a police officer;*
> > - *employed by the police;*
> > - *under the direction or control of the chief officer of police force; or*
> > - *a person who provides services under contractual arrangements (but without being employed by the chief officer of a police force), to assist that force in relation to the discharge of its chief officer's functions whether or not they are on duty at the time.*

Note: Paragraph 1.5 extends this note to the person called to fulfil the role of the appropriate adult for a 17-year old detainee for the purposes of paragraph 17.7.

ANNEX A

Intimate and strip searches

A Intimate search

★**A-92**   C:1. An intimate search consists of the physical examination of a person's body orifices other than the mouth. The intrusive nature of such searches means the actual and potential risks associated with intimate searches must never be underestimated.

(a) Action

★**A-93**   C:2. Body orifices other than the mouth may be searched only:

> (a) if authorised by an officer of inspector rank or above who has reasonable grounds for believing that the person may have concealed on themselves:
>
> > (i) anything which they could and might use to cause physical injury to themselves or others at the station; or
> >
> > (ii) a Class A drug which they intended to supply to another or to export;
> >
> > and the officer has reasonable grounds for believing that an intimate search is the only means of removing those items; and
>
> (b) if the search is under paragraph 2(a)(ii) (a drug offence search), the detainee's appropriate consent has been given in writing.

C:2A. Before the search begins, a police officer or designated detention officer, must tell the detainee:-

> (a) that the authority to carry out the search has been given;
>
> (b) the grounds for giving the authorisation and for believing that the article cannot be removed without an intimate search.

C:2B. Before a detainee is asked to give appropriate consent to a search under paragraph 2(a)(ii) (a drug offence search) they must be warned that if they refuse without good cause their refusal may harm their case if it comes to trial, see *Note A6.* This warning may be given by a police officer or member of police staff. In the case of juveniles, mentally vulnerable or mentally disordered suspects, the seeking and giving of consent must take place in the presence of the appropriate adult. A juvenile's consent is only valid if their parent's or guardian's consent is also obtained unless the juvenile is under 14, when their parent's or guardian's consent is sufficient in its own right. A detainee who is not legally represented must be reminded of their entitlement to have free legal advice, see Code C, paragraph 6.5, and the reminder noted in the custody record.

C:3. An intimate search may only be carried out by a registered medical practitioner or registered nurse, unless an officer of at least inspector rank considers this is not practicable and the search is to take place under paragraph 2(a)(i), in which case a police officer may carry out the search. See *Notes A1* to *A5.*

C:3A. Any proposal for a search under paragraph 2(a)(i) to be carried out by someone other than a registered medical practitioner or registered nurse must only be considered as a last resort and when the authorising officer is satisfied the risks associated with allowing the item to remain with the detainee outweigh the risks associated with removing it. See *Notes A1* to *A5.*

C:4. An intimate search under:

- paragraph 2(a)(i) may take place only at a hospital, surgery, other medical premises or police station;
- paragraph 2(a)(ii) may take place only at a hospital, surgery or other medical premises and must be carried out by a registered medical practitioner or a registered nurse.

C:5. An intimate search at a police station of a juvenile or mentally disordered or otherwise mentally vulnerable person may take place only in the presence of an appropriate adult of the same sex (see Annex L), unless the detainee specifically requests a particular adult of the opposite sex who is readily available. In the case of a juvenile, the search may take place in the absence of the appropriate adult only if the juvenile signifies in the presence of the appropriate adult they do not want the adult present during the search and the adult agrees. A record shall be made of the juvenile's decision and signed by the appropriate adult.

C:6. When an intimate search under paragraph 2(a)(i) is carried out by a police officer, the officer must be of the same sex as the detainee (see Annex L). A minimum of two people, other than the detainee, must be present during the search. Subject to paragraph 5, no person of the opposite sex who is not a medical practitioner or nurse shall be present, nor shall anyone whose presence is unnecessary. The search shall be conducted with proper regard to the sensitivity and vulnerability of the detainee.

(b) Documentation

C:7. In the case of an intimate search, the following shall be recorded as soon as practicable in the detainee's custody record: **★A-94**

(a) for searches under paragraphs 2(a)(i) and (ii);
- the authorisation to carry out the search;
- the grounds for giving the authorisation;
- the grounds for believing the article could not be removed without an intimate search;
- which parts of the detainee's body were searched;
- who carried out the search;
- who was present;
- the result.

(b) for searches under paragraph 2(a)(ii):
- the giving of the warning required by paragraph 2B;
- the fact that the appropriate consent was given or (as the case may be) refused, and if refused, the reason given for the refusal (if any).

C:8. If an intimate search is carried out by a police officer, the reason why it was impracticable for a registered medical practitioner or registered nurse to conduct it must be recorded.

B *Strip search*

C:9. A strip search is a search involving the removal of more than outer clothing. In this code, outer clothing includes shoes and socks. **★A-95**

(a) Action

C:10. A strip search may take place only if it is considered necessary to remove an article which a detainee would not be allowed to keep and the officer reasonably considers the detainee might have concealed such an article. Strip searches shall not be routinely carried out if there is no reason to consider that articles are concealed. **★A-96**

The conduct of strip searches

C:11. When strip searches are conducted:
(a) a police officer carrying out a strip search must be the same sex as the detainee (see *Annex L*);
(b) the search shall take place in an area where the detainee cannot be seen by anyone who

does not need to be present, nor by a member of the opposite sex (see Annex L) except an appropriate adult who has been specifically requested by the detainee;

(c) except in cases of urgency, where there is risk of serious harm to the detainee or to others, whenever a strip search involves exposure of intimate body parts, there must be at least two people present other than the detainee, and if the search is of a juvenile or mentally disordered or otherwise mentally vulnerable person, one of the people must be the appropriate adult. Except in urgent cases as above, a search of a juvenile may take place in the absence of the appropriate adult only if the juvenile signifies in the presence of the appropriate adult that they do not want the adult to be present during the search and the adult agrees. A record shall be made of the juvenile's decision and signed by the appropriate adult. The presence of more than two people, other than an appropriate adult, shall be permitted only in the most exceptional circumstances;

(d) the search shall be conducted with proper regard to the sensitivity and vulnerability of the detainee in these circumstances and every reasonable effort shall be made to secure the detainee's co-operation and minimise embarrassment. Detainees who are searched shall not normally be required to remove all their clothes at the same time, *e.g.* a person should be allowed to remove clothing above the waist and redress before removing further clothing;

(e) if necessary to assist the search, the detainee may be required to hold their arms in the air or to stand with their legs apart and bend forward so a visual examination may be made of the genital and anal areas provided no physical contact is made with any body orifice;

(f) if articles are found, the detainee shall be asked to hand them over. If articles are found within any body orifice other than the mouth, and the detainee refuses to hand them over, their removal would constitute an intimate search, which must be carried out as in Part A;

(g) a strip search shall be conducted as quickly as possible, and the detainee allowed to dress as soon as the procedure is complete.

(b) Documentation

★**A-97**   C:12. A record shall be made on the custody record of a strip search including the reason it was considered necessary, those present and any result.

Notes for guidance

★**A-98**   C:A1 *Before authorising any intimate search, the authorising officer must make every reasonable effort to persuade the detainee to hand the article over without a search. If the detainee agrees, a registered medical practitioner or registered nurse should whenever possible be asked to assess the risks involved and, if necessary, attend to assist the detainee.*

C:A2 *If the detainee does not agree to hand the article over without a search, the authorising officer must carefully review all the relevant factors before authorising an intimate search. In particular, the officer must consider whether the grounds for believing an article may be concealed are reasonable.*

C:A3 *If authority is given for a search under paragraph 2(a)(i), a registered medical practitioner or registered nurse shall be consulted whenever possible. The presumption should be that the search will be conducted by the registered medical practitioner or registered nurse and the authorising officer must make every reasonable effort to persuade the detainee to allow the medical practitioner or nurse to conduct the search.*

C:A4 *A constable should only be authorised to carry out a search as a last resort and when all other approaches have failed. In these circumstances, the authorising officer must be satisfied the detainee might use the article for one or more of the purposes in paragraph 2(a)(i) and the physical injury likely to be caused is sufficiently severe to justify authorising a constable to carry out the search.*

C:A5 *If an officer has any doubts whether to authorise an intimate search by a constable, the officer should seek advice from an officer of superintendent rank or above.*

C:A6 *In warning a detainee who is asked to consent to an intimate drug offence search, as in paragraph 2B, the following form of words may be used:*

"You do not have to allow yourself to be searched, but I must warn you that if you refuse without good cause, your refusal may harm your case if it comes to trial."

Where the use of the Welsh Language is appropriate, the following form of words may be used:

"Nid oes rhaid i chi roi caniatâd i gael eich archwilio, ond mae'n rhaid i mi eich rhybuddio os gwrthodwch heb reswm da, y gallai eich penderfyniad i wrthod wneud niwed i'ch achos pe bai'n dod gerbron llys."

ANNEX B

Delay in notifying arrest or allowing access to legal sdvice

A *Persons detained under PACE*

C:1. The exercise of the rights in section 5 or section 6, or both, may be delayed if the person is in   ★**A-99**
police detention, as in PACE, section 118(2), in connection with an indictable offence, has not yet
been charged with an offence and an officer of superintendent rank or above, or inspector rank or
above only for the rights in s.5, has reasonable grounds for believing their exercise will:
- (i) lead to:
  - interference with, or harm to, evidence connected with an indictable offence; or
  - interference with, or physical harm to, other people; or
- (ii) lead to alerting other people suspected of having committed an indictable offence but not yet arrested for it; or
- (iii) hinder the recovery of property obtained in consequence of the commission of such an offence.

C:2. These rights may also be delayed if the officer has reasonable grounds to believe that:
- (i) the person detained for an indictable offence has benefited from their criminal conduct (decided in accordance with Part 2 of the Proceeds of Crime Act 2002); and
- (ii) the recovery of the value of the property constituting that benefit will be hindered by the exercise of either right.

C:3. Authority to delay a detainee's right to consult privately with a solicitor may be given only if
the authorising officer has reasonable grounds to believe the solicitor the detainee wants to consult
will, inadvertently or otherwise, pass on a message from the detainee or act in some other way which
will have any of the consequences specified under paragraphs 1 or 2. In these circumstances, the
detainee must be allowed to choose another solicitor. See *Note B3.*

C:4. If the detainee wishes to see a solicitor, access to that solicitor may not be delayed on the
grounds they might advise the detainee not to answer questions or the solicitor was initially asked to
attend the police station by someone else. In the latter case, the detainee must be told the solicitor has
come to the police station at another person's request, and must be asked to sign the custody record
to signify whether they want to see the solicitor.

C:5. The fact the grounds for delaying notification of arrest may be satisfied does not automatically mean the grounds for delaying access to legal advice will also be satisfied.

C:6. These rights may be delayed only for as long as grounds exist and in no case beyond 36 hours
after the relevant time as in PACE, s.41. If the grounds cease to apply within this time, the detainee
must, as soon as practicable, be asked if they want to exercise either right, the custody record must be
noted accordingly, and action taken in accordance with the relevant section of the code.

C:7. A detained person must be permitted to consult a solicitor for a reasonable time before any
court hearing.

B [*Not used.*]

C *Documentation*

C:13. The grounds for action under this annex shall be recorded and the detainee informed of   ★**A-100**
them as soon as practicable.

C:14. Any reply given by a detainee under paragraphs 6 or 11 must be recorded and the detainee
asked to endorse the record in relation to whether they want to receive legal advice at this point.

D *Cautions and special warnings*

C:15. When a suspect detained at a police station is interviewed during any period for which access to legal advice has been delayed under this annex, the court or jury may not draw adverse inferences from their silence.

Notes for guidance

C:B1 *Even if Annex B applies in the case of a juvenile, or a person who is mentally disordered or otherwise*   ★**A-101**
*mentally vulnerable, action to inform the appropriate adult and the person responsible for a juvenile's welfare, if
that is a different person, must nevertheless be taken as in paragraph 3.13 and 3.15.*

C:B2 *In the case of Commonwealth citizens and foreign nationals, see Note 7A.*

C:B3 *A decision to delay access to a specific solicitor is likely to be a rare occurrence and only when it can be
shown the suspect is capable of misleading that particular solicitor and there is more than a substantial risk that*

the suspect will succeed in causing information to be conveyed which will lead to one or more of the specified consequences.

ANNEX C

Restriction on drawing adverse inferences from silence and terms of the caution when the restriction applies

(a) *The restriction on drawing adverse inferences from silence*

★**A-102**   C:1. The Criminal Justice and Public Order Act 1994, ss.34, 36 and 37 as amended by the Youth Justice and Criminal Evidence Act 1999, s.58 describe the conditions under which adverse inferences may be drawn from a person's failure or refusal to say anything about their involvement in the offence when interviewed, after being charged or informed they may be prosecuted. These provisions are subject to an overriding restriction on the ability of a court or jury to draw adverse inferences from a person's silence. This restriction applies:

    (a) to any detainee at a police station, see *Note 10C* who, before being interviewed, see section 11 or being charged or informed they may be prosecuted, see section 16, has:

        (i) asked for legal advice, see section 6, para. 6.1;

        (ii) not been allowed an opportunity to consult a solicitor, including the duty solicitor, as in this code; and

        (iii) not changed their mind about wanting legal advice, see section 6, para. 6.6(d).
        Note the condition in (ii) will:

          – apply when a detainee who has asked for legal advice is interviewed before speaking to a solicitor as in section 6, para. 6.6(a) or (b);

          – not apply if the detained person declines to ask for the duty solicitor, see section 6, paras 6.6(c) and (d).

    (b) to any person charged with, or informed they may be prosecuted for, an offence who:

        (i) has had brought to their notice a written statement made by another person or the content of an interview with another person which relates to that offence, see section 16, para. 16.4;

        (ii) is interviewed about that offence, see section 16, para. 16.5; or

        (iii) makes a written statement about that offence, see Annex D, paras 4 and 9.

(b) *Terms of the caution when the restriction applies*

    C:2. When a requirement to caution arises at a time when the restriction on drawing adverse inferences from silence applies, the caution shall be:

"You do not have to say anything, but anything you do say may be given in evidence."

Where the use of the Welsh Language is appropriate, the caution may be used directly in Welsh in the following terms:

"Does dim rhaid i chi ddweud dim byd, ond gall unrhyw beth yr ydych chi'n ei ddweud gael ei roi fel tystiolaeth."

    C:3. Whenever the restriction either begins to apply or ceases to apply after a caution has already been given, the person shall be re-cautioned in the appropriate terms. The changed position on drawing inferences and that the previous caution no longer applies shall also be explained to the detainee in ordinary language. See *Note C2.*

Notes for guidance

    C:C1 *The restriction on drawing inferences from silence does not apply to a person who has not been detained and who therefore cannot be prevented from seeking legal advice if they want to, see paragraphs 10.2 and 3.21.*

    C:C2 *The following is suggested as a framework to help explain changes in the position on drawing adverse inferences if the restriction on drawing adverse inferences from silence:*

        (a) begins to apply:

          "The caution you were previously given no longer applies. This is because after that caution:

            (i) you asked to speak to a solicitor but have not yet been allowed an opportunity to speak to a solicitor." See paragraph 1(a); or

          "(ii) you have been charged with/informed you may be prosecuted." See paragraph 1(b).

        "This means that from now on, adverse inferences cannot be drawn at court and your defence

will not be harmed just because you choose to say nothing. Please listen carefully to the caution I am about to give you because it will apply from now on. You will see that it does not say anything about your defence being harmed."

(b) ceases to apply before or at the time the person is charged or informed they may be prosecuted, see paragraph 1(a);

"The caution you were previously given no longer applies. This is because after that caution you have been allowed an opportunity to speak to a solicitor. Please listen carefully to the caution I am about to give you because it will apply from now on. It explains how your defence at court may be affected if you choose to say nothing."

ANNEX D

Written statements under caution

(a) *Written by a person under caution*

C:1. A person shall always be invited to write down what they want to say. **★A-103**

C:2. A person who has not been charged with, or informed they may be prosecuted for, any offence to which the statement they want to write relates, shall:

(a) unless the statement is made at a time when the restriction on drawing adverse inferences from silence applies, see Annex C, be asked to write out and sign the following before writing what they want to say:

"I make this statement of my own free will. I understand that I do not have to say anything but that it may harm my defence if I do not mention when questioned something which I later rely on in court. This statement may be given in evidence.";

(b) if the statement is made at a time when the restriction on drawing adverse inferences from silence applies, be asked to write out and sign the following before writing what they want to say;

"I make this statement of my own free will. I understand that I do not have to say anything. This statement may be given in evidence."

C:3. When a person, on the occasion of being charged with or informed they may be prosecuted for any offence, asks to make a statement which relates to any such offence and wants to write it they shall:

(a) unless the restriction on drawing adverse inferences from silence, see Annex C, applied when they were so charged or informed they may be prosecuted, be asked to write out and sign the following before writing what they want to say:

"I make this statement of my own free will. I understand that I do not have to say anything but that it may harm my defence if I do not mention when questioned something which I later rely on in court. This statement may be given in evidence."

(b) if the restriction on drawing adverse inferences from silence applied when they were so charged or informed they may be prosecuted, be asked to write out and sign the following before writing what they want to say:

"I make this statement of my own free will. I understand that I do not have to say anything. This statement may be given in evidence."

C:4. When a person who has already been charged with or informed they may be prosecuted for any offence asks to make a statement which relates to any such offence and wants to write it, they shall be asked to write out and sign the following before writing what they want to say:

"I make this statement of my own free will. I understand that I do not have to say anything. This statement may be given in evidence.";

C:5. Any person writing their own statement shall be allowed to do so without any prompting except a police officer or other police staff may indicate to them which matters are material or question any ambiguity in the statement.

(b) *Written by a police officer or other police staff*

C:6. If a person says they would like someone to write the statement for them, a police officer, or **★A-104** other police staff shall write the statement.

C:7. If the person has not been charged with, or informed they may be prosecuted for, any offence to which the statement they want to make relates they shall, before starting, be asked to sign, or make their mark, to the following:

(a) unless the statement is made at a time when the restriction on drawing adverse inferences from silence applies, see Annex C:

> *"I, ..., wish to make a statement. I want someone to write down what I say. I understand that I do not have to say anything but that it may harm my defence if I do not mention when questioned something which I later rely on in court. This statement may be given in evidence.";*

(b) if the statement is made at a time when the restriction on drawing adverse inferences from silence applies:

> *"I, ..., wish to make a statement. I want someone to write down what I say. I understand that I do not have to say anything. This statement may be given in evidence."*

C:8. If, on the occasion of being charged with or informed they may be prosecuted for any offence, the person asks to make a statement which relates to any such offence they shall before starting be asked to sign, or make their mark to, the following:

(a) unless the restriction on drawing adverse inferences from silence applied, see Annex C, when they were so charged or informed they may be prosecuted:

> *"I, ..., wish to make a statement. I want someone to write down what I say. I understand that I do not have to say anything but that it may harm my defence if I do not mention when questioned something which I later rely on in court. This statement may be given in evidence.";*

(b) if the restriction on drawing adverse inferences from silence applied when they were so charged or informed they may be prosecuted:

> *"I, ..., wish to make a statement. I want someone to write down what I say. I understand that I do not have to say anything. This statement may be given in evidence."*

C:9. If, having already been charged with or informed they may be prosecuted for any offence, a person asks to make a statement which relates to any such offence they shall before starting, be asked to sign, or make their mark to:

> *"I, ..., wish to make a statement. I want someone to write down what I say. I understand that I do not have to say anything. This statement may be given in evidence."*

C:10. The person writing the statement must take down the exact words spoken by the person making it and must not edit or paraphrase it. Any questions that are necessary, *e.g.* to make it more intelligible, and the answers given must be recorded at the same time on the statement form.

C:11. When the writing of a statement is finished the person making it shall be asked to read it and to make any corrections, alterations or additions they want. When they have finished reading they shall be asked to write and sign or make their mark on the following certificate at the end of the statement:

> *"I have read the above statement, and I have been able to correct, alter or add anything I wish. This statement is true. I have made it of my own free will."*

C:12. If the person making the statement cannot read, or refuses to read it, or to write the above mentioned certificate at the end of it or to sign it, the person taking the statement shall read it to them and ask them if they would like to correct, alter or add anything and to put their signature or make their mark at the end. The person taking the statement shall certify on the statement itself what has occurred.

ANNEX E

Summary of provisions relating to mentally disordered and otherwise mentally vulnerable people

★A-105

C:1. If an officer has any suspicion, or is told in good faith, that a person of any age may be mentally disordered or otherwise mentally vulnerable, or mentally incapable of understanding the significance of questions or their replies that person shall be treated as mentally disordered or otherwise mentally vulnerable for the purposes of this Code. See paragraph 1.4 and *Note E4*

C:2. In the case of a person who is mentally disordered or otherwise mentally vulnerable, "the appropriate adult" means:

(a) a relative, guardian or other person responsible for their care or custody;

(b) someone experienced in dealing with mentally disordered or mentally vulnerable people but who is not a police officer or employed by the police;

(c) failing these, some other responsible adult aged 18 or over who is not a police officer or employed by the police.

See paragraph 1.7(b) and *Note 1D.*

C:3. If the custody officer authorises the detention of a person who is mentally vulnerable or appears to be suffering from a mental disorder, the custody officer must as soon as practicable inform the appropriate adult of the grounds for detention and the person's whereabouts, and ask the adult to come to the police station to see them. If the appropriate adult:

- is already at the station when information is given as in paragraphs 3.1 to 3.5 the information must be given in their presence;
- is not at the station when the provisions of paragraph 3.1 to 3.5 are complied with these provisions must be complied with again in their presence once they arrive.

See paragraphs 3.15 to 3.17

C:4. If the appropriate adult, having been informed of the right to legal advice, considers legal advice should be taken, the provisions of section 6 apply as if the mentally disordered or otherwise mentally vulnerable person had requested access to legal advice. See paragraphs 3.19, 6.5A and *Note E1.*

C:5. The custody officer must make sure a person receives appropriate clinical attention as soon as reasonably practicable if the person appears to be suffering from a mental disorder or in urgent cases immediately call the nearest appropriate healthcare professional or an ambulance. It is not intended these provisions delay the transfer of a detainee to a place of safety under the Mental Health Act 1983, s.136 if that is applicable. If an assessment under that Act is to take place at a police station, the custody officer must consider whether an appropriate healthcare professional should be called to conduct an initial clinical check on the detainee. See paragraph 9.5 and 9.6

C:6. It is imperative a mentally disordered or otherwise mentally vulnerable person detained under the Mental Health Act 1983, s.136 be assessed as soon as possible. A police station should only be used as a place of safety as a last resort but if that assessment is to take place at the police station, an approved social worker and registered medical practitioner shall be called to the station as soon as possible to carry it out. Once the detainee has been assessed and suitable arrangements been made for their treatment or care, they can no longer be detained under s.136. A detainee should be immediately discharged from detention if a registered medical practitioner having examined them, concludes they are not mentally disordered within the meaning of the Act. See paragraph 3.16.

C:7. If a mentally disordered or otherwise mentally vulnerable person is cautioned in the absence of the appropriate adult, the caution must be repeated in the appropriate adult's presence. See paragraph 10.12.

C:8. A mentally disordered or otherwise mentally vulnerable person must not be interviewed or asked to provide or sign a written statement in the absence of the appropriate adult unless the provisions of paragraphs 11.1 or 11.18 to 11.20 apply. Questioning in these circumstances may not continue in the absence of the appropriate adult once sufficient information to avert the risk has been obtained. A record shall be made of the grounds for any decision to begin an interview in these circumstances. See paragraphs 11.1, 11.15 and 11.18 to 11.20.

C:9. If the appropriate adult is present at an interview, they shall be informed they are not expected to act simply as an observer and the purposes of their presence are to:

- advise the interviewee;
- observe whether or not the interview is being conducted properly and fairly;
- facilitate communication with the interviewee.

See paragraph 11.17

C:10. If the detention of a mentally disordered or otherwise mentally vulnerable person is reviewed by a review officer or a superintendent, the appropriate adult must, if available at the time, be given an opportunity to make representations to the officer about the need for continuing detention. See paragraph 15.3. ★**A-106**

C:11. If the custody officer charges a mentally disordered or otherwise mentally vulnerable person with an offence or takes such other action as is appropriate when there is sufficient evidence for a prosecution this must be carried out in the presence of the appropriate adult if they are at the police station. A copy of the written notice embodying any charge must also be given to the appropriate adult. See paragraphs 16.1 to 16.4A

C:12. An intimate or strip search of a mentally disordered or otherwise mentally vulnerable person may take place only in the presence of the appropriate adult of the same sex, unless the detainee specifically requests the presence of a particular adult of the opposite sex. A strip search may take place in the absence of an appropriate adult only in cases of urgency when there is a risk of serious harm to the detainee or others. See Annex A, paras 5 and 11(c).

C:13. Particular care must be taken when deciding whether to use any form of approved restraints on a mentally disordered or otherwise mentally vulnerable person in a locked cell. See paragraph 8.2.

Notes for guidance

★A-107   C:E1 *The purpose of the provisions at paragraphs 3.19 and 6.5A is to protect the rights of a mentally disordered or otherwise mentally vulnerable detained person who does not understand the significance of what is said to them. A mentally disordered or otherwise mentally vulnerable detained person should always be given an opportunity, when an appropriate adult is called to the police station, to consult privately with a solicitor in the absence of the appropriate adult if they want.*

C:E2 *Although people who are mentally disordered or otherwise mentally vulnerable are often capable of providing reliable evidence, they may, without knowing or wanting to do so, be particularly prone in certain circumstances to provide information that may be unreliable, misleading or self-incriminating. Special care should always be taken when questioning such a person, and the appropriate adult should be involved if there is any doubt about a person's mental state or capacity. Because of the risk of unreliable evidence, it is important to obtain corroboration of any facts admitted whenever possible.*

C:E3 *Because of the risks referred to in Note E2, which the presence of the appropriate adult is intended to minimise, officers of superintendent rank or above should exercise their discretion to authorise the commencement of an interview in the appropriate adult's absence only in exceptional cases, if it is necessary to avert an immediate risk of serious harm. See paragraphs 11.1 and 11.18 to 11.20.*

C:E4 *When a person is detained under section 136 of the Mental Health Act 1983 for assessment, the appropriate adult has no role in the assessment process and their presence is not required.*

ANNEX F

★A-108   [*Not used.*]

ANNEX G

Fitness to be interviewed

★A-109   C:1. This Annex contains general guidance to help police officers and healthcare professionals assess whether a detainee might be at risk in an interview.

C:2. A detainee may be at risk in a interview if it is considered that:

(a) conducting the interview could significantly harm the detainee's physical or mental state;

(b) anything the detainee says in the interview about their involvement or suspected involvement in the offence about which they are being interviewed *might* be considered unreliable in subsequent court proceedings because of their physical or mental state.

C:3. In assessing whether the detainee should be interviewed, the following must be considered:

(a) how the detainee's physical or mental state might affect their ability to understand the nature and purpose of the interview, to comprehend what is being asked and to appreciate the significance of any answers given and make rational decisions about whether they want to say anything;

(b) the extent to which the detainee's replies may be affected by their physical or mental condition rather than representing a rational and accurate explanation of their involvement in the offence;

(c) how the nature of the interview, which could include particularly probing questions, might affect the detainee.

★A-110   C:4. It is essential healthcare professionals who are consulted consider the functional ability of the detainee rather than simply relying on a medical diagnosis, *e.g.* it is possible for a person with severe mental illness to be fit for interview.

C:5. Healthcare professionals should advise on the need for an appropriate adult to be present, whether reassessment of the person's fitness for interview may be necessary if the interview lasts beyond a specified time, and whether a further specialist opinion may be required.

C:6. When healthcare professionals identify risks they should be asked to quantify the risks. They should inform the custody officer:

• whether the person's condition:

– is likely to improve;

– will require or be amenable to treatment; and

• indicate how long it may take for such improvement to take effect.

C:7. The role of the healthcare professional is to consider the risks and advise the custody officer of the outcome of that consideration. The healthcare professional's determination and any advice or recommendations should be made in writing and form part of the custody record.

C:8. Once the healthcare professional has provided that information, it is a matter for the custody officer to decide whether or not to allow the interview to go ahead and if the interview is to proceed, to determine what safeguards are needed. Nothing prevents safeguards being provided in addition to those required under the code. An example might be to have an appropriate healthcare professional present during the interview, in addition to an appropriate adult, in order constantly to monitor the person's condition and how it is being affected by the interview.

ANNEX H

Detained person: observation list

C:1. If any detainee fails to meet any of the following criteria, an appropriate healthcare professional or an ambulance must be called.   ★**A-111**

C:2. When assessing the level of rousability, consider:

> *Rousability* – can they be woken?
> - go into the cell
> - call their name
> - shake gently
>
> *Response to questions* – can they give appropriate answers to questions such as:
> - What's your name?
> - Where do you live?
> - Where do you think you are?
>
> *Response to commands* – can they respond appropriately to commands such as:
> - Open your eyes!
> - Lift one arm, now the other arm!

C:3. Remember to take into account the possibility or presence of other illnesses, injury, or mental condition; a person who is drowsy and smells of alcohol may also have the following:

- Diabetes
- Epilepsy
- Head injury
- Drug intoxication or overdose
- Stroke

ANNEX I

[*Not used.*]

ANNEX J

[*Not used.*]

ANNEX K

X-rays and ultrasound scans

(a) *Action*

C:1. PACE, s.55A allows a person who has been arrested and is in police detention to have an X-ray taken of them or an ultrasound scan to be carried out on them (or both) if: ★**A-111a**

> (a) authorised by an officer of inspector rank or above who has reasonable grounds for believing that the detainee:
> > (i) may have swallowed a Class A drug; and
> > (ii) was in possession of that Class A drug with the intention of supplying it to another or to export; and
> (b) the detainee's appropriate consent has been given in writing.

C:2. Before an x-ray is taken or an ultrasound scan carried out, a police officer or designated detention officer must tell the detainee:-

> (a) that the authority has been given; and
> (b) the grounds for giving the authorisation.

C:3. Before a detainee is asked to give appropriate consent to an x-ray or an ultrasound scan, they must be warned that if they refuse without good cause their refusal may harm their case if it comes to trial, see *Notes K1* and *K2*. This warning may be given by a police officer or member of police staff. In the case of juveniles, mentally vulnerable or mentally disordered suspects the seeking and giving of consent must take place in the presence of the appropriate adult. A juvenile's consent is only valid if their parent's or guardian's consent is also obtained unless the juvenile is under 14, when their parent's or guardian's consent is sufficient in its own right. A detainee who is not legally represented must be reminded of their entitlement to have free legal advice, see Code C, paragraph 6.5, and the reminder noted in the custody record.

C:4. An x-ray may be taken, or an ultrasound scan may be carried out, only by a registered medical practitioner or registered nurse, and only at a hospital, surgery or other medical premises.

(b) *Documentation*

C:5. The following shall be recorded as soon as practicable in the detainee's custody record:

(a) the authorisation to take the x-ray or carry out the ultrasound scan (or both);

(b) the grounds for giving the authorisation;

(c) the giving of the warning required by paragraph 3; and

(d) the fact that the appropriate consent was given or (as the case may be) refused, and if refused, the reason given for the refusal (if any); and

(e) if an x-ray is taken or an ultrasound scan carried out:

- where it was taken or carried out;
- who took it or carried it out;
- who was present;
- the result.

Notes for guidance

★A-111b

C:K1 *If authority is given for an x-ray to be taken or an ultrasound scan to be carried out (or both), consideration should be given to asking a registered medical practitioner or registered nurse to explain to the detainee what is involved and to allay any concerns the detainee might have about the effect which taking an x-ray or carrying out an ultrasound scan might have on them. If appropriate consent is not given, evidence of the explanation may, if the case comes to trial, be relevant to determining whether the detainee had a good cause for refusing.*

C:K2 *In warning a detainee who is asked to consent to an x-ray being taken or an ultrasound scan being carried out (or both), as in paragraph 3, the following form of words may be used:*

"You do not have to allow an x-ray of you to be taken or an ultrasound scan to be carried out on you, but I must warn you that if you refuse without good cause, your refusal may harm your case if it comes to trial."

Where the use of the Welsh Language is appropriate, the following form of words may be provided in Welsh:

"Does dim rhaid i chi ganiatáu cymryd sgan uwchsain neu belydr-x (neu'r ddau) arnoch, ond mae'n rhaid i mi eich rhybuddio os byddwch chi'n gwrthod gwneud hynny heb reswm da, fe allai hynny niweidio eich achos pe bai'n dod gerbron llys."

ANNEX L

Establishing gender of persons for the purpose of searching

★A-111c

C:1. Certain provisions of this and other PACE Codes explicitly state that searches and other procedures may only be carried out by, or in the presence of, persons of the same sex as the person subject to the search or other procedure. See *Note L1*.

C:2. All searches and procedures must be carried out with courtesy, consideration and respect for the person concerned. Police officers should show particular sensitivity when dealing with transgender individuals (including transsexual persons) and transvestite persons (see *Notes L2, L3* and *L4*).

(a) *Consideration*

★A-111d

C:3. In law, the gender (and accordingly the sex) of an individual is their gender as registered at birth unless they have been issued with a Gender Recognition Certificate (GRC) under the Gender Recognition Act 2004 (GRA), in which case the person's gender is their acquired gender. This means that if the acquired gender is the male gender, the person's sex becomes that of a man and, if it is the female gender, the person's sex becomes that of a woman and they must be treated as their acquired gender.

C:4. When establishing whether the person concerned should be treated as being male or female for the purposes of these searches and procedures, the following approach which is designed to minimise embarrassment and secure the person's co-operation should be followed:

(a) The person must not be asked whether they have a GRC (see paragraph 8);

(b) If there is no doubt as to as to whether the person concerned should be treated as being male or female, they should be dealt with as being of that sex.

(c) If at any time (including during the search or carrying out the procedure) there is doubt as to whether the person should be treated, or continue to be treated, as being male or female:

    (i) the person should be asked what gender they consider themselves to be. If they express a preference to be dealt with as a particular gender, they should be asked to indicate and confirm their preference by signing the custody record or, if a custody record has not been opened, the search record or the officer's notebook. Subject to (ii) below, the person should be treated according to their preference;

    (ii) if there are grounds to doubt that the preference in (i) accurately reflects the person's predominant lifestyle, for example, if they ask to be treated as a woman but documents and other information make it clear that they live predominantly as a man, or vice versa, they should be treated according to what appears to be their predominant lifestyle and not their stated preference;

    (iii) If the person is unwilling to express a preference as in (i) above, efforts should be made to determine their predominant lifestyle and they should be treated as such. For example, if they appear to live predominantly as a woman, they should be treated as being female; or

    (iv) if none of the above apply, the person should be dealt with according to what reasonably appears to have been their sex as registered at birth.

C:5. Once a decision has been made about which gender an individual is to be treated as, each officer responsible for the search or procedure should where possible be advised before the search or procedure starts of any doubts as to the person's gender and the person informed that the doubts have been disclosed. This is important so as to maintain the dignity of the person and any officers concerned.

(b) *Documentation*

C:6. The person's gender as established under paragraph 4(c)(i) to (iv) above must be recorded in the person's custody record or, if a custody record has not been opened, on the search record or in the officer's notebook.   ★**A-111e**

C:7. Where the person elects which gender they consider themselves to be under paragraph 4(b)(i) but, following 4(b)(ii) is not treated in accordance with their preference, the reason must be recorded in the search record, in the officer's notebook or, if applicable, in the person's custody record.

(c) *Disclosure of information*

C:8. Section 22 of the GRA defines any information relating to a person's application for a GRC or to a successful applicant's gender before it became their acquired gender as "protected information". Nothing in this annex is to be read as authorising or permitting any police officer or any police staff who has acquired such information when acting in their official capacity to disclose that information to any other person in contravention of the GRA. Disclosure includes making a record of "protected information" which is read by others.   ★**A-111f**

Notes for guidance

C:L1 *Provisions to which paragraph 1 applies include:*   ★**A-111g**

- *In Code C; paragraph 4.1 and Annex A, paras 5, 6, and 11 (searches, strip and intimate searches of detainees under sections 54 and 55 of PACE);*
- *In Code A; paragraphs 2.8 and 3.6 and Note 4;*
- *In Code D; paragraph 5.5 and Note 5F (searches, examinations and photographing of detainees under section 54A of PACE) and paragraph 6.9 (taking samples);*
- *In Code H; paragraph 4.1 and Annex A, paras 6, 7 and 12 (searches, strip and intimate searches under sections 54 and 55 of PACE of persons arrested under section 41 of the Terrorism Act 2000).*

C:L2 *While there is no agreed definition of transgender (or trans), it is generally used as an umbrella term to describe people whose gender identity (self-identification as being a woman, man, neither or both) differs from the sex they were registered as at birth. The term includes, but is not limited to, transsexual people.*

C:L3 *Transsexual means a person who is proposing to undergo, is undergoing or has undergone a process (or part of a process) for the purpose of gender reassignment, which is a protected characteristic under the Equality Act 2010 (see paragraph 1.0), by changing physiological or other attributes of their sex. This includes aspects of gender such as dress and title. It would apply to a woman making the transition to being a man and a man making the transition to being a woman, as well as to a person who has only just started out on the process of gender reassignment and to a person who has completed the process. Both would share the characteristic of gender reassignment with each having the characteristics of one sex, but with certain characteristics of the other sex.*

C:L4 *Transvestite means a person of one gender who dresses in the clothes of a person of the opposite gender. However, a transvestite does not live permanently in the gender opposite to their birth sex.*

C:L5 *Chief officers are responsible for providing corresponding operational guidance and instructions for the deployment of transgender officers and staff under their direction and control to duties which involve carrying out, or being present at, any of the searches and procedures described in paragraph 1. The guidance and instructions must comply with the Equality Act 2010 and should therefore complement the approach in this annex.*

ANNEX M

Documents and records to be translated

★**A-111h**   C:1. For the purposes of Directive 2010/64/EU of the European Parliament and of the Council of 20 October 2010 and this code, essential documents comprise records required to be made in accordance with this code which are relevant to decisions to deprive a person of their liberty, to any charge and to any record considered necessary to enable a detainee to defend themselves in criminal proceedings and to safeguard the fairness of the proceedings. Passages of essential documents which are not relevant need not be translated. See *Note M1*

C:2. The table below lists the documents considered essential for the purposes of this code and when (subject to paragraphs 3 to 7) written translations must be created and provided. See paragraphs 13.12 to 13.14 and Annex N for application to live-link interpretation.

Table of essential documents:

★**A-111i**

	Essential documents for the purposes of this code	When translation to be created	When translation to be provided.
(i)	The grounds for each of the following authorisations to keep the person in custody as they are described and referred to in the custody record: (a) Authorisation for detention before and after charge given by the custody officer and by the review officer, see Code C, paras 3.4 and 15.16(a). (b) Authorisation to extend detention without charge beyond 24 hours given by a superintendent, see Code C, para.15.16(b). (c) A warrant of further detention issued by a magistrates' court and any extension(s) of the warrant, see Code C, para.15.16(c). (d) An authority to detain in accordance with the directions in a warrant of arrest issued in connection with criminal proceedings including the court issuing the warrant.	As soon as practicable after each authorisation has been recorded in the custody record.	As soon as practicable after the translation has been created, whilst the person is detained or after they have been released (see *Note M3*).
(ii)	Written notice showing particulars of the offence charged required by Code C, para. 16.3 or the offence for which the suspect has been told they may be prosecuted.	As soon as practicable after the person has been charged or reported.	
(iii)	Written interview records: Code C:11.11, 13.3, 13.4 & Code E4.7 Written statement under caution: Code C, Annex D.	To be created contemporaneously by the interpreter for the person to check and sign.	As soon as practicable after the person has been charged or told they may be prosecuted.

C:3. The custody officer may authorise an oral translation or oral summary of documents (i) to

(ii) in the table (but not (iii)) to be provided (through an interpreter) instead of a written translation. Such an oral translation or summary may only be provided if it would not prejudice the fairness of the proceedings by in any way adversely affecting or otherwise undermining or limiting the ability of the suspect in question to understand their position and to communicate effectively with police officers, interviewers, solicitors and appropriate adults with regard to their detention and the investigation of the offence in question and to defend themselves in the event of criminal proceedings. The quantity and complexity of the information in the document should always be considered and specific additional consideration given if the suspect is mentally disordered or otherwise mentally vulnerable or is a juvenile (see Code C, para. 1.5). The reason for the decision must be recorded (see paragraph 13.11(e))

C:4. Subject to paragraphs 5 to 7 below, a suspect may waive their right to a written translation of the essential documents described in the table but only if they do so voluntarily after receiving legal advice or having full knowledge of the consequences and give their unconditional and fully informed consent in writing (see paragraph 9).

C:5. The suspect may be asked if they wish to waive their right to a written translation and before giving their consent, they must be reminded of their right to legal advice and asked whether they wish to speak to a solicitor.

C:6. No police officer or police staff should do or say anything with the intention of persuading a suspect who is entitled to a written translation of an essential document to waive that right. See *Notes M2* and *M3*.

C:7. For the purpose of the waiver:
    (a) the consent of a person who is mentally disordered or otherwise mentally vulnerable person is only valid if the information about the circumstances under which they can waive the right and the reminder about their right to legal advice mentioned in paragraphs 3 to 5 and their consent is given in the presence of the appropriate adult.
    (b) the consent of a juvenile is only valid if their parent's or guardian's consent is also obtained unless the juvenile is under 14, when their parent's or guardian's consent is sufficient in its own right and the information and reminder mentioned in subparagraph (a) above and their consent is also given in the presence of the appropriate adult (who may or may not be a parent or guardian).

C:8. The detainee, their solicitor or appropriate adult may make representations to the custody officer that a document which is not included in the table is essential and that a translation should be provided. The request may be refused if the officer is satisfied that the translation requested is not essential for the purposes described in paragraph 1 above.

C:9. If the custody officer has any doubts about
    • providing an oral translation or summary of an essential document instead of a written translation (see paragraph 3);
    • whether the suspect fully understands the consequences of waiving their right to a written translation of an essential document (see paragraph 4), or
    • about refusing to provide a translation of a requested document (see paragraph 7),
the officer should seek advice from an inspector or above.

Documentation

C:10. Action taken in accordance with this Annex shall be recorded in the detainee's custody record or interview record as appropriate (see Code C, paragraph 13.11(e)).   ★**A-111j**

Notes for guidance

C:M1 *It is not necessary to disclose information in any translation which is capable of undermining or otherwise adversely affecting any investigative processes, for example, by enabling the suspect to fabricate an innocent explanation or to conceal lies from the interviewer.*   ★**A-111k**

C:M2 *No police officer or police staff shall indicate to any suspect, except to answer a direct question, whether the period for which they are liable to be detained or if not detained, the time taken to complete the interview, might be reduced:*
    • *if they do not ask for legal advice before deciding whether they wish to waive their right to a written translation of an essential document; or*
    • *if they decide to waive their right to a written translation of an essential document.*

C:M3 *There is no power under PACE to detain a person or to delay their release solely to create and provide a written translation of any essential document.*

ANNEX N

Live-link interpretation (para. 13.12)

Part 1: When the physical presence of the interpreter is not required.

★**A-111l** C:1. EU Directive 2010/64 (see paragraph 13.1), Article 2(6) provides "Where appropriate, communication technology such as videoconferencing, telephone or the Internet may be used, unless the physical presence of the interpreter is required in order to safeguard the fairness of the proceedings." This Article permits, but does not require the use of a live-link, and the following provisions of this Annex determine whether the use of a live-link is appropriate in any particular case.

C:2. Decisions in accordance with this Annex that the physical presence of the interpreter is not required and to permit live-link interpretation, must be made on a case by case basis. Each decision must take account of the age, gender and vulnerability of the suspect, the nature and circumstances of the offence and the investigation and the impact on the suspect according to the particular purpose(s) for which the suspect requires the assistance of an interpreter and the time(s) when that assistance is required (see *Note N1*). For this reason, the custody officer in the case of a detained suspect, or in the case of a suspect who has not been arrested, the interviewer (subject to paragraph 13.1(b)), must consider whether the ability of the particular suspect, to communicate confidently and effectively for the purpose in question (see paragraph 3) is likely to be adversely affected or otherwise undermined or limited if the interpreter is not physically present and live-link interpretation is used. Although a suspect for whom an appropriate adult is required may be more likely to be adversely affected as described, it is important to note that a person who does not require an appropriate adult may also be adversely impacted by the use of live-link interpretation.

C:3. Examples of purposes referred to in paragraph 2 include:

  (a) understanding and appreciating their position having regard to any information given to them, or sought from them, in accordance with this or any other code of practice which, in particular, include:
  - the caution (see paragraphs C:10.1 and 10.12).
  - the special warning (see paragraphs 10.10 to 10.12).
  - information about the offence (see paragraphs 10.3, 11.1A and Note 11ZA).
  - the grounds and reasons for detention (see paragraphs 13.10 and 13.10A).
  - the translation of essential documents (see paragraph 13.10B and Annex M).
  - their rights and entitlements (see paragraph 3.12 and C3.21(b)).
  - intimate and non-intimate searches of detained persons at police stations.
  - provisions and procedures to which Code D (identification) applies concerning, for example, eye-witness identification, taking fingerprints, samples and photographs.

  (b) understanding and seeking clarification from the interviewer of questions asked during an interview conducted and recorded in accordance with Code E or Code F and of anything else that is said by the interviewer and answering the questions.

  (c) consulting privately with their solicitor and (if applicable) the appropriate adult (see paragraphs 3.18, 13.2A, 13.6 and 13.9):
  (i) to help decide whether to answer questions put to them during interview; and
  (ii) about any other matter concerning their detention and treatment whilst in custody.

  (d) communicating with practitioners and others who have some formal responsibility for, or an interest in, the health and welfare of the suspect. Particular examples include appropriate healthcare professionals (see section 9 of this code), Independent Custody Visitors and drug arrest referral workers.

C:4. If the custody officer or the interviewer (subject to paragraph 13.1(b)) is satisfied that for a particular purpose as described in paragraphs 2 and 3 above, the live-link interpretation *would not* adversely affect or otherwise undermine or limit the suspect's ability to communicate confidently and effectively for *that* purpose, they must so inform the suspect, their solicitor and (if applicable) the appropriate adult. At the same time, the operation of livelink interpretation must be explained and demonstrated to them, they must be advised of the chief officer's obligations concerning the security of live-link communications under paragraph 13.13 (see *Note N2*) and they must be asked if they wish to make representations that livelink interpretation should not be used or if they require more information about the operation of the arrangements. They must also be told that at any time live-link interpretation is in use, they may make representations to the custody officer or the interviewer that its operation should cease and that the physical presence of an interpreter should be arranged.

When the authority of an inspector is required

C:5. If representations are made that live-link interpretation should not be used, or that at any **A-111m** time live-link interpretation is in use, its operation should cease and the physical presence of an interpreter arranged, and the custody officer or interviewer (subject to paragraph 13.1(b)) is unable to allay the concerns raised, live-link interpretation may not be used, or (as the case may be) continue to be used, *unless* authorised in writing by an officer of the rank of inspector or above, in accordance with paragraph 6.

C:6. Authority may be given if the officer is satisfied that for the purpose(s) in question at the time an interpreter is required, live-link interpretation is necessary and justified. In making this decision, the officer must have regard to:

    (a) the circumstances of the suspect;

    (b) the nature and seriousness of the offence;

    (c) the requirements of the investigation, including its likely impact on both the suspect and any victim(s);

    (d) the representations made by the suspect, their solicitor and (if applicable) the appropriate adult that live-link interpretation should not be used (see paragraph 5)

    (e) the availability of a suitable interpreter to be *physically* present compared with the availability of a suitable interpreter for live-link interpretation (see *Note N3*); and

    (f) the risk if the interpreter is not *physically* present, evidence obtained using link interpretation might be excluded in subsequent criminal proceedings; and

    (g) the likely impact on the suspect and the investigation of any consequential delay to arrange for the interpreter to be *physically* present with the suspect.

C:7. For the purposes of Code E and live-link interpretation, there is no requirement to make a visual recording which shows the interpreter as viewed by the suspect and others present at the interview. The audio recording required by that Code is sufficient. However, the authorising officer, in consultation with the officer in charge of the investigation, may direct that the interview is conducted and recorded in accordance with Code F. This will require the visual record to show the live-link interpretation arrangements and the interpreter as seen and experienced by the suspect during the interview. This should be considered if it appears that the admissibility of interview evidence might be challenged because the interpreter was not *physically* present or if the suspect, solicitor or appropriate adult make representations that Code F should be applied.

Documentation

C:8. A record must be made of the actions, decisions, authorisations and outcomes arising from ★**A-111n** the requirements of this Annex. This includes representations made in accordance with paragraphs 4 and 7.

Part 2: Modifications for live-link interpretation

C:9. The following modification shall apply for the purposes of live-link interpretation: ★**A-111o**

(a) Code C, para. 13.3: For the third sentence, *substitute*: "A clear legible copy of the complete record shall be sent without delay via the live-link to the interviewer. The interviewer, after confirming with the suspect that the copy is legible and complete, shall allow the suspect to read the record, or have the record read to them by the interpreter and to sign the copy as correct or indicate the respects in which they consider it inaccurate. The interviewer is responsible for ensuring that that the signed copy and the original record made by the interpreter are retained with the case papers for use in evidence if required and must advise the interpreter of their obligation to keep the original record securely for that purpose.";

(b) Code C, para. 13.4: For sub-paragraph (b), *substitute*: "A clear legible copy of the complete statement shall be sent without delay via the live-link to the interviewer. The interviewer, after confirming with the suspect that the copy is legible and complete, shall invite the suspect to sign it. The interviewer is responsible for ensuring that that the signed copy and the original record made by the interpreter are retained with the case papers for use in evidence if required and must advise the interpreter of their obligation to keep the original record securely for that purpose.";

(c) Code C, para. 13.7: After the first sentence, *insert*: "A clear legible copy of the certified record must be sent without delay via the live-link to the interviewer. The interviewer is responsible for ensuring that the original certified record and the copy are retained with the case papers for use as evidence if required and must advise the interpreter of their obligation to keep the original record securely for that purpose."

(d) Code C, para. 11.2 and Codes E and F, para. 4.4 – interviews: At the beginning of each paragraph, *insert*: "Before the interview commences, the operation of live-link interpretation shall be explained and demonstrated to the suspect, their solicitor and appropriate adult, unless it has been previously explained and demonstrated (see Code C, Annex N, para. 4)."

(e) Codes E and F, para.4.18 (signing master recording label): After the *third sentence*, insert, "If live-link interpretation has been used, the interviewer should ask the interpreter to observe the removal and sealing of the master recording and to confirm in writing that they have seen it sealed and signed by the interviewer. A clear legible copy of the confirmation signed by the interpreter must be sent via the livelink to the interviewer. The interviewer is responsible for ensuring that the original confirmation and the copy are retained with the case papers for use in evidence if required and must advise the interpreter of their obligation to keep the original confirmation securely for that purpose."

Notes for guidance

★**A-111p**   C:N1 *For purposes other than an interview, audio-only live-link interpretation, for example by telephone (see Code C, para.13.12(b)) may provide an appropriate option until an interpreter is physically present or audio-visual live-link interpretation becomes available. A particular example would be the initial action required when a detained suspect arrives at a police station to inform them of, and to explain, the reasons for their arrest and detention and their various rights and entitlements. Another example would be to inform the suspect by telephone, that an interpreter they will be able to see and hear is being arranged. In these circumstances, telephone live-link interpretation may help to allay the suspect's concerns and contribute to the completion of the risk assessment (see Code C, para.3.6).*

C:N2 *The explanation and demonstration of live-link interpretation is intended to help the suspect, solicitor and appropriate adult make an informed decision and to allay any concerns they may have.*

C:N3 *Factors affecting availability of a suitable interpreter will include the location of the police station and the language and type of interpretation (oral or sign language) required.*

(5) Identification

★**A-112**   The text that follows is of the version of the code that came into force on February 23, 2017: see *ante* Appendix A-1.

In connection with Code D, see also §§ 14-39 *et seq.* (application of code), §§ 14-45 *et seq.* (identification procedures), § 14-54 (group identification, confrontation and video identification), §§ 14-57 *et seq.* (effect of breaches), §§ 14-60 *et seq.* (photographs), § 14-62 (video recordings), and § 15-277 (photographs) of the main work.

D. CODE OF PRACTICE FOR THE IDENTIFICATION OF PERSONS BY POLICE OFFICERS

Commencement—Transitional arrangements

★**A-113**   This code has effect in relation to any identification procedure carried out after midnight on 23 February 2017.

D:1 Introduction

★**A-114**   D:1.1 This code of practice concerns the principal methods used by police to identify people in connection with the investigation of offences and the keeping of accurate and reliable criminal records. The powers and procedures in this code must be used fairly, responsibly, with respect for the people to whom they apply and without unlawful discrimination. Under the Equality Act 2010, s.149 (public sector equality duty), police forces must, in carrying out their functions, have due regard to the need to eliminate unlawful discrimination, harassment, victimisation and any other conduct which is prohibited by that Act, to advance equality of opportunity between people who share a relevant "protected characteristic" and people who do not share it, and to foster good relations between those persons. The Equality Act also makes it unlawful for police officers to discriminate against, harass or victimise any person on the grounds of the 'protected characteristics' of age, disability, gender reassignment, race, religion or belief, sex and sexual orientation, marriage and civil partnership, pregnancy and maternity when using their powers. See *Note 1A.*

D:1.2 In this code, identification by an eye-witness arises when a witness who has seen the offender committing the crime and is given an opportunity to identify a person suspected of involvement in the offence in a video identification, identification parade or similar procedure. These eye-witness identification procedures which are in Part A of section 3 below, are designed to:

- test the eye-witness' ability to identify the suspect as the person they saw on a previous occasion
- provide safeguards against mistaken identification.

While this code concentrates on visual identification procedures, it does not prevent the police making use of aural identification procedures such as a "voice identification parade", where they judge that appropriate. See *Note 1B*.

D:1.2A In this code, separate provisions in Part B of section 3 below, apply when any person, including a police officer, is asked if they recognise anyone they see in an image as being someone who is known to them and to test their claim that they recognise that person. These separate provisions are not subject to the eye-witnesses identification procedures described in paragraph 1.2.

D:1.2B Part C applies when a film, photograph or image relating to the offence or any description of the suspect is broadcast or published in any national or local media or on any social networking site or on any local or national police communication systems.

D:1.3 Identification by fingerprints applies when a person's fingerprints are taken to:
- compare with fingerprints found at the scene of a crime
- check and prove convictions
- help to ascertain a person's identity.

D:1.3A Identification using footwear impressions applies when a person's footwear impressions are taken to compare with impressions found at the scene of a crime.

D:1.4 Identification by body samples and impressions includes taking samples such as a cheek swab, hair or blood to generate a DNA profile for comparison with material obtained from the scene of a crime, or a victim.

D:1.5 Taking photographs of arrested people applies to recording and checking identity and locating and tracing persons who:
- are wanted for offences
- fail to answer their bail.

D:1.6 Another method of identification involves searching and examining detained suspects to find, *e.g.*, marks such as tattoos or scars which may help establish their identity or whether they have been involved in committing an offence.

D:1.7 The provisions of the Police and Criminal Evidence Act 1984 (PACE) and this ode are designed to make sure fingerprints, samples, impressions and photographs are taken, used and retained, and identification procedures carried out, only when justified and necessary for preventing, detecting or investigating crime. If these provisions are not observed, the application of the relevant procedures in particular cases may be open to question.

D:1.8 The provisions of this code do not authorise, or otherwise permit, fingerprints or samples to be taken from a person detained solely for the purposes of assessment under section 136 of the Mental Health Act 1983.

Note for guidance

D:1A *In paragraph 1.1, under the Equality Act 1949, s.149, the "relevant protected characteristics" are: age, disability, gender reassignment, pregnancy and maternity, race, religion/belief, sex and sexual orientation. For further detailed guidance and advice on the Equality Act, see: https://www.gov.uk/guidance/equality-act-2010-guidance.*

D:1B *See Home Office Circular 57/2003 "Advice on the use of voice identification parades".*

D:2 General

D:2.1 This code must be readily available at all police stations for consultation by: ★A-115
- police officers and police staff
- detained persons
- members of the public

D:2.2 The provisions of this code:
- include the Annexes
- do not include the *Notes for guidance*.

D:2.3 Code C, para. 1.4 and the *Notes for guidance* applicable to those provisions apply to this code with regard to a suspected person who may be mentally disordered or otherwise mentally vulnerable.

D:2.4 Code C, paras 1.5 and 1.5A and the *Notes for guidance* applicable to those provisions apply to this Code with regard to a suspected person who appears to be under the age of 18.

D:2.5 Code C, para. 1.6 applies to this code with regard to a suspected person who appears to be blind, seriously visually impaired, deaf, unable to read or speak or has difficulty communicating orally because of a speech impediment.

D:2.6 In this code: ★A-116
- "appropriate adult" means the same as in Code C, para. 1.7
- "solicitor" means the same as in Code C, para. 6.12

and the *Notes for guidance* applicable to those provisions apply to this code.

- where a search or other procedure under this code may only be carried out or observed by a person of the same sex as the person to whom the search or procedure applies, the gender of the detainee and other persons present should be established and recorded in line with Annex L of Code C.

D:2.7 References to a custody officer include any police officer who, for the time being, is performing the functions of a custody officer, see paragraph 1.9 of Code C.

D:2.8 When a record of any action requiring the authority of an officer of a specified rank is made under this code, subject to paragraph 2.18, the officer's name and rank must be recorded.

D:2.9 When this code requires the prior authority or agreement of an officer of at least inspector or superintendent rank, that authority may be given by a sergeant or chief inspector who has been authorised to perform the functions of the higher rank under PACE, s.107.

D:2.10 Subject to paragraph 2.18, all records must be timed and signed by the maker.

★**A-117**   D:2.11 Records must be made in the custody record, unless otherwise specified. In any provision of this code which allows or requires police officers or police staff to make a record in their report book, the reference to "report book" shall include any official report book or electronic recording device issued to them that enables the record in question to be made and dealt with in accordance with that provision. References in this code to written records, forms and signatures include electronic records and forms and electronic confirmation that identifies the person completing the record or form.

Chief officers must be satisfied as to the integrity and security of the devices, records and forms to which this paragraph applies and that use of those devices, records and forms satisfies relevant data protection legislation.

D:2.12 If any procedure in this Code requires a person's consent, the consent of a:

- mentally disordered or otherwise mentally vulnerable person is only valid if given in the presence of the appropriate adult
- juvenile is only valid if their parent's or guardian's consent is also obtained unless the juvenile is under 14, when their parent's or guardian's consent is sufficient in its own right. If the only obstacle to an identification procedure in section 3 is that a juvenile's parent or guardian refuses consent or reasonable efforts to obtain it have failed, the identification officer may apply the provisions of paragraph 3.21 (suspect known but not available). See *Note 2A*.

D:2.13 If a person is blind, seriously visually impaired or unable to read, the custody officer or identification officer shall make sure their solicitor, relative, appropriate adult or some other person likely to take an interest in them and not involved in the investigation is available to help check any documentation. When this code requires written consent or signing, the person assisting may be asked to sign instead, if the detainee prefers. This paragraph does not require an appropriate adult to be called solely to assist in checking and signing documentation for a person who is not a juvenile, or mentally disordered or otherwise mentally vulnerable (see *Note 2B* and Code C, para. 3.15).

D:2.14 If any procedure in this code requires information to be given to or sought from a suspect, it must be given or sought in the appropriate adult's presence if the suspect is mentally disordered, otherwise mentally vulnerable or a juvenile. If the appropriate adult is not present when the information is first given or sought, the procedure must be repeated in the presence of the appropriate adult when they arrive. If the suspect appears deaf or there is doubt about their hearing or speaking ability or ability to understand English, the custody officer or identification officer must ensure that the necessary arrangements in accordance with Code C are made for an interpreter to assist the suspect.

D:2.15 Any procedure in this code involving the participation of a suspect who is mentally disordered, otherwise mentally vulnerable or a juvenile must take place in the presence of the appropriate adult. See Code C, para. 1.4.

D:2.15A Any procedure in this code involving the participation of a witness who is or appears to be mentally disordered, otherwise mentally vulnerable or a juvenile should take place in the presence of a pre-trial support person unless the witness states that they do not want a support person to be present. A support person must not be allowed to prompt any identification of a suspect by a witness. See *Note 2AB*.

D:2.16 References to:

- "taking a photograph", include the use of any process to produce a single, still or moving, visual image
- "photographing a person", should be construed accordingly
- "photographs", "films", "negatives" and "copies" include relevant visual images recorded, stored, or reproduced through any medium
- "destruction" includes the deletion of computer data relating to such images or making access to that data impossible

D:2.17 This code does not affect or apply to, the powers and procedures:

(i) for requiring and taking samples of breath, blood and urine in relation to driving offences, etc, when under the influence of drink, drugs or excess alcohol under the:

- Road Traffic Act 1988, ss.4 to 11
- Road Traffic Offenders Act 1988, ss.15 and 16
- Transport and Works Act 1992, ss.26 to 38;

(ii) under the Immigration Act 1971, Sched. 2, para.18, for taking photographs, measuring and identifying and taking biometric information (not including DNA) from persons detained or liable to be detained under that Act, Sched. 2, para. 16 (administrative provisions as to control on entry etc.); or for taking fingerprints in accordance with the Immigration and Asylum Act 1999, ss.141 and 142(4), or other methods for collecting information about a person's external physical characteristics provided for by regulations made under that Act, s.144;

(iii) under the Terrorism Act 2000, Sched. 8, for taking photographs, fingerprints, skin impressions, body samples or impressions from people:

- arrested under that Act, s.41,
- detained for the purposes of examination under that Act, Sched. 7, and to whom the code of practice issued under that Act, Sched.14, para. 6, applies ("the terrorism provisions")

(iv) for taking photographs, fingerprints, skin impressions, body samples or impressions from people who have been:

- arrested on warrants issued in Scotland, by officers exercising powers mentioned in Part X of the Criminal Justice and Public Order Act 1994;
- arrested or detained without warrant by officers from a police force in Scotland exercising their powers of arrest or detention mentioned in Part X of the Criminal Justice and Public Order Act 1994.

Note: In these cases, police powers and duties and the person's rights and entitlements whilst at a police station in England and Wales are the same as if the person had been arrested in Scotland by a Scottish police officer.

D:2.18 Nothing in this code requires the identity of officers or police staff to be recorded or disclosed:

(a) in the case of enquiries linked to the investigation of terrorism;

(b) if the officers or police staff reasonably believe recording or disclosing their names might put them in danger.

In these cases, they shall use their warrant or other identification numbers and the name of their police station. See *Note 2D.*

D:2.19 In this code: **★A-118**

(a) "designated person" means a person other than a police officer, who has specified powers and duties conferred or imposed on them by designation under section 38 or 39 of the Police Reform Act 2002;

(b) any reference to a police officer includes a designated person acting in the exercise or performance of the powers and duties conferred or imposed on them by their designation.

D:2.20 If a power conferred on a designated person:

(a) allows reasonable force to be used when exercised by a police officer, a designated person exercising that power has the same entitlement to use force;

(b) includes power to use force to enter any premises, that power is not exercisable by that designated person except:

(i) in the company, and under the supervision, of a police officer; or

(ii) for the purpose of:

- saving life or limb; or
- preventing serious damage to property.

D:2.21 In the case of a detained person, nothing in this code prevents the custody officer, or other police officer or designated person given custody of the detainee by the custody officer for the purposes of the investigation of an offence for which the person is detained, from allowing another person (see (a) and (b) below) to carry out individual procedures or tasks at the police station if the law allows. However, the officer or designated person given custody remains responsible for making sure the procedures and tasks are carried out correctly in accordance with the Codes of Practice. The other person who is allowed to carry out the procedures or tasks must be *someone who at that time* is:

(a) under the direction and control of the chief officer of the force responsible for the police station in question; or

(b) providing services under contractual arrangements (but without being employed by the chief officer the police force), to assist a police force in relation to the discharge of its chief officer's functions.

D:2.22 Designated persons and others mentioned in sub-paragraphs (a) and (b) of paragraph 2.21 must have regard to any relevant provisions of the codes of practice.

Notes for guidance

★A-119   D:2A *For the purposes of paragraph 2.12, the consent required from a parent or guardian may, for a juvenile in the care of a local authority or voluntary organisation, be given by that authority or organisation. In the case of a juvenile, nothing in paragraph 2.12 requires the parent, guardian or representative of a local authority or voluntary organisation to be present to give their consent, unless they are acting as the appropriate adult under paragraphs 2.14 or 2.15. However, it is important that a parent or guardian not present is fully informed before being asked to consent. They must be given the same information about the procedure and the juvenile's suspected involvement in the offence as the juvenile and appropriate adult. The parent or guardian must also be allowed to speak to the juvenile and the appropriate adult if they wish. Provided the consent is fully informed and is not withdrawn, it may be obtained at any time before the procedure takes place.*

D:2AB *The Youth Justice and Criminal Evidence Act 1999 guidance "Achieving Best Evidence in Criminal Proceedings" indicates that a pre-trial support person should accompany a vulnerable witness during any identification procedure unless the witness states that they do not want a support person to be present. It states that this support person should not be (or not be likely to be) a witness in the investigation.*

D:2B *People who are seriously visually impaired or unable to read may be unwilling to sign police documents. The alternative, i.e. their representative signing on their behalf, seeks to protect the interests of both police and suspects.*

D:2C [*Not used.*]

D:2D *The purpose of paragraph 2.18(b) is to protect those involved in serious organised crime investigations or arrests of particularly violent suspects when there is reliable information that those arrested or their associates may threaten or cause harm to the officers. In cases of doubt, an officer of inspector rank or above should be consulted.*

D:3 Identification and recognition of suspects

Part (A) Identification of a suspect by an eye-witness

★A-120   D:3.0 This part applies when an eye-witness has seen a person committing a crime or in any other circumstances which tend to prove or disprove the involvement of the person they saw in a crime, for example, close to the scene of the crime, immediately before or immediately after it was committed. It sets out the procedures to be used to test the ability of that eye-witness to identify a person suspected of involvement in the offence ("the suspect") as the person they saw on the previous occasion. This part does not apply to the procedure described in Part B (see *Note 3AA*) which is used to test the ability of someone who is not an eye-witness, to recognise anyone whose image they see.

D:3.1 A record shall be made of the description of the suspect as first given by the eye-witness . This record must:

(a) be made and kept in a form which enables details of that description to be accurately produced from it, in a visible and legible form, which can be given to the suspect or the suspect's solicitor in accordance with this Code; and

(b) unless otherwise specified, be made before the eye-witness takes part in any identification procedures under paragraphs 3.5 to 3.10, 3.21, 3.23 or Annex E (showing photographs to eye-witnesses).

A copy of the record shall where practicable, be given to the suspect or their solicitor before any procedures under paragraphs 3.5 to 3.10, 3.21 or 3.23 are carried out. See *Note 3E.*

D:3.1A References in this Part:

(a) to the identity of the suspect being "known" mean that there is sufficient information known to the police to establish, in accordance with Code G (arrest), that there are reasonable grounds to suspect a particular person of involvement in the offence;

(b) to the suspect being "available" mean that the suspect is immediately available, or will be available within a reasonably short time, in order that they can be invited to take part in at least one of the eye-witness identification procedures under paragraphs 3.5 to 3.10 and it is practicable to arrange an effective procedure under paragraphs 3.5 to 3.10; and

(c) to the eye-witness identification procedures under paragraphs 3.5 to 3.10 mean:
- video identification (paragraphs 3.5 and 3.6);
- identification parade (paragraphs 3.7 and 3.8); and

- group identification (paragraphs 3.9 and 3.10).

(a) Cases when the suspect's identity is not known

D:3.2 In cases when the suspect's identity is not known, an eye-witness may be taken to a particular neighbourhood or place to see whether they can identify the person they saw on a previous occasion. Although the number, age, sex, race, general description and style of clothing of other people present at the location and the way in which any identification is made cannot be controlled, the principles applicable to the formal procedures under paragraphs 3.5 to 3.10 shall be followed as far as practicable. For example:

(a) where it is practicable to do so, a record should be made of the eye-witness' description of the person they saw on the previous occasion, as in paragraph 3.1(a), before asking the eye-witness to make an identification;

(b) care must be taken not provide the eye-witness with any information concerning the description of the suspect (if such information is available) and not to direct the eyewitness' attention to any individual unless, taking into account all the circumstances, this cannot be avoided. However, this does not prevent an eye-witness being asked to look carefully at the people around at the time or to look towards a group or in a particular direction, if this appears necessary to make sure that the witness does not overlook a possible suspect simply because the eye-witness is looking in the opposite direction and also to enable the eye-witness to make comparisons between any suspect and others who are in the area;

(c) where there is more than one eye-witness, every effort should be made to keep them separate and eye-witnesses should be taken to see whether they can identify a person independently;

(d) once there is sufficient information to establish, in accordance with paragraph 3.1A(a), that the suspect is "known", *e.g.* after the eye-witness makes an identification, the provisions set out from paragraph 3.4 onwards shall apply for that and any other eyewitnesses in relation to that individual;

(e) the officer or police staff accompanying the eye-witness must record, in their report book, the action taken as soon as practicable and in as much detail, as possible. The record should include:

    (i) the date, time and place of the relevant occasion when the eye-witness claims to have previously seen the person committing the offence in question or in any other circumstances which tend to prove or disprove the involvement of the person they saw in a crime (see paragraph 3.0); and

    (ii) where any identification was made:

- how it was made and the conditions at the time (*e.g.*, the distance the eyewitness was from the suspect, the weather and light);
- if the eye-witness's attention was drawn to the suspect; the reason for this; and
- anything said by the eye-witness or the suspect about the identification or the conduct of the procedure.

See *Note 3F*

D:3.3 An eye-witness must not be shown photographs, computerised or artist's composite likenesses or similar likenesses or pictures (including "E-fit" images) if in accordance with paragraph 3.1A, the identity of the suspect is known and they are available to take part in one of the procedures under paragraphs 3.5 to 3.10. If the suspect's identity is not known, the showing of any such images to an eye-witness to see if they can identify a person whose image they are shown as the person they saw on a previous occasion must be done in accordance with Annex E.

(b) Cases when the suspect is known and available

D:3.4 If the suspect's identity is known to the police (see paragraph 3.1A(a)) and they are available (see paragraph 3.1A(b)), the identification procedures that may be used are set out in paragraphs 3.5 to 3.10 below as follows: ★**A-121**

   (i) video identification;

   (ii) identification parade; or

   (iii) group identification.

(i) Video identification

D:3.5 A "video identification" is when the eye-witness is shown images of a known suspect, together with similar images of others who resemble the suspect. *Moving* images must be used unless the conditions in sub-paragraph (a) or (b) below apply:

(a) this sub-paragraph applies if:

> (i) the identification officer, in consultation with the officer in charge of the investigation, is satisfied that because of aging, or other physical changes or differences, the appearance of the suspect has significantly changed since the previous occasion when the eye-witness claims to have seen the suspect (see paragraph 3.0 and *Note 3ZA*);
>
> (ii) an image (moving or still) is available which the identification officer and the officer in charge of the investigation reasonably believe shows the appearance of the suspect as it was at the time the suspect was seen by the eye-witness; and
>
> (iii) having regard to the extent of change and the purpose of eye-witness identification procedures (see paragraph 3.0), the identification officer believes that that such an image should be shown to the eye-witness.

In such a case, the identification officer may arrange a video identification procedure using the image described in (ii). In accordance with the "Notice to suspect" (see paragraph 3.17(vi)), the suspect must first be given an opportunity to provide their own image(s) for use in the procedure but it is for the identification officer and officer in charge of the investigation to decide whether, following (ii) and (iii), any image(s) provided by the suspect should be used.

A video identification using an image described above may, at the discretion of the identification officer be arranged in addition to, or as an alternative to, a video identification using *moving* images taken after the suspect has been given the information and notice described in paragraphs 3.17 and 3.18.

See paragraph 3.21 and *Note 3D* in any case where the suspect deliberately takes steps to frustrate the eye-witness identification arrangements and procedures.

(b) this sub-paragraph applies if, in accordance with paragraph 2A of Annex A of this code, the identification officer does not consider that replication of a physical feature or concealment of the location of the feature can be achieved using a moving image. In these cases, still images may be used.

D:3.6 Video identifications must be carried out in accordance with Annex A.

(ii) Identification parade

D:3.7 An "identification parade" is when the eye-witness sees the suspect in a line of others who resemble the suspect.

D:3.8 Identification parades must be carried out in accordance with Annex B.

(iii) Group identification

D:3.9 A "group identification" is when the eye-witness sees the suspect in an informal group of people.

D:3.10 Group identifications must be carried out in accordance with Annex C.

Arranging eye-witness identification procedures–duties of identification officer

D:3.11 Except as provided for in paragraph 3.19, the arrangements for, and conduct of, the eyewitness identification procedures in paragraphs 3.5 to 3.10 and circumstances in which any such identification procedure must be held shall be the responsibility of an officer not below inspector rank who is not involved with the investigation ("the identification officer"). The identification officer may direct another officer or police staff, see paragraph 2.21, to make arrangements for, and to conduct, any of these identification procedures and except as provided for in paragraph 7 of Annex A, any reference in this section to the identification officer includes the officer or police staff to whom the arrangements for, and/or conduct of, any of these procedure has been delegated. In delegating these arrangements and procedures, the identification officer must be able to supervise effectively and either intervene or be contacted for advice. Where any action referred to in this paragraph is taken by another officer or police staff at the direction of the identification officer, the outcome shall, as soon as practicable, be reported to the identification officer. For the purpose of these procedures, the identification officer retains overall responsibility for ensuring that the procedure complies with this code and in addition, in the case of detained suspect, their care and treatment until returned to the custody officer. Except as permitted by this code, no officer or any other person involved with the investigation of the case against the suspect may take any part in these procedures or act as the identification officer.

This paragraph does not prevent the identification officer from consulting the officer in charge of the investigation to determine which procedure to use. When an identification procedure is required, in the interest of fairness to suspects and eye-witnesses, it must be held as soon as practicable.

Circumstances in which an eye-witness identification procedure must be held

D:3.12 If, before any identification procedure set out in paragraphs 3.5 to 3.10 has been held   ★A-122
 (a) an eye-witness has identified a suspect or purported to have identified them; or
 (b) there is an eye-witness available who expresses an ability to identify the suspect; or
 (c) there is a reasonable chance of an eye-witness being able to identify the suspect,
and the eye-witness in (a) to (c) has not been given an opportunity to identify the suspect in any of the procedures set out in paragraphs 3.5 to 3.10, then an identification procedure shall be held if the suspect disputes being the person the eye-witness claims to have seen on a previous occasion (see paragraph 3.0), unless:
 (i) it is not practicable to hold any such procedure; or
 (ii) any such procedure would serve no useful purpose in proving or disproving whether the suspect was involved in committing the offence, for example
  • where the suspect admits being at the scene of the crime and gives an account of what took place and the eye-witness does not see anything which contradicts that; or
  • when it is not disputed that the suspect is already known to the eye-witness who claims to have recognised them when seeing them commit the crime.

D:3.13 An eye-witness identification procedure may also be held if the officer in charge of the investigation, after consultation with the identification officer, considers it would be useful.

Selecting an eye-witness identification procedure

D:3.14 If, because of paragraph 3.12, an identification procedure is to be held, the suspect shall initially be invited to take part in a video identification unless:
 (a) a video identification is not practicable; or
 (b) an identification parade is both practicable and more suitable than a video identification; or
 (c) paragraph 3.16 applies.
The identification officer and the officer in charge of the investigation shall consult each other to determine which option is to be offered. An identification parade may not be practicable because of factors relating to the witnesses, such as their number, state of health, availability and travelling requirements. A video identification would normally be more suitable if it could be arranged and completed sooner than an identification parade. Before an option is offered the suspect must also be reminded of their entitlement to have free legal advice, see Code C, para. 6.5.

D:3.15 A suspect who refuses the identification procedure in which the suspect is first invited to take part shall be asked to state their reason for refusing and may get advice from their solicitor and/or if present, their appropriate adult. The suspect, solicitor and/or appropriate adult shall be allowed to make representations about why another procedure should be used. A record should be made of the reasons for refusal and any representations made. After considering any reasons given, and representations made, the identification officer shall, if appropriate, arrange for the suspect to be invited to take part in an alternative which the officer considers suitable and practicable. If the officer decides it is not suitable and practicable to invite the suspect to take part in an alternative identification procedure, the reasons for that decision shall be recorded.

D:3.16 A suspect may initially be invited to take part in a group identification if the officer in charge of the investigation considers it is more suitable than a video identification or an identification parade and the identification officer considers it practicable to arrange.

Notice to suspect

D:3.17 Unless paragraph 3.20 applies, before any eye-witness identification procedure set out in   ★A-123
paragraphs 3.5 to 3.10 is arranged, the following shall be explained to the suspect:
 (i) the purpose of the procedure (see paragraph 3.0);
 (ii) their entitlement to free legal advice; see Code C, para. 6.5;
 (iii) the procedures for holding it, including their right, subject to Annex A para. 9, to have a solicitor or friend present;
 (iv) that they do not have to consent to or co-operate in the procedure;
 (v) that if they do not consent to, and co-operate in, a procedure, their refusal may be given in evidence in any subsequent trial and police may proceed covertly without their consent or make other arrangements to test whether an eye-witness can identify them, see paragraph 3.21;
 (vi) whether, for the purposes of a video identification procedure, images of them have previously been obtained either:

- in accordance with paragraph 3.20, and if so, that they may co-operate in providing further, suitable images to be used instead; or
- in accordance with paragraph 3.5(a), and if so, that they may provide their own images for the identification officer to consider using.

(vii) if appropriate, the special arrangements for juveniles;

(viii) if appropriate, the special arrangements for mentally disordered or otherwise mentally vulnerable people;

(ix) that if they significantly alter their appearance between being offered an identification procedure and any attempt to hold an identification procedure, this may be given in evidence if the case comes to trial, and the identification officer may then consider other forms of identification, see paragraph 3.21 and *Note 3C*;

(x) that a moving image or photograph may be taken of them when they attend for any identification procedure;

(xi) whether, before their identity became known, the eye-witness was shown photographs, a computerised or artist's composite likeness or similar likeness or image by the police, see *Note 3B*;

(xii) that if they change their appearance before an identification parade, it may not be practicable to arrange one on the day or subsequently and, because of the appearance change, the identification officer may consider alternative methods of identification, see *Note 3C*;

(xiii) that they or their solicitor will be provided with details of the description of the suspect as first given by any eye-witnesses who are to attend the procedure or confrontation, see paragraph 3.1.

D:3.18 This information must also be recorded in a written notice handed to the suspect. The suspect must be given a reasonable opportunity to read the notice, after which, they should be asked to sign a copy of the notice to indicate if they are willing to co-operate with the making of a video or take part in the identification parade or group identification. The signed copy shall be retained by the identification officer.

D:3.19 In the case of a detained suspect, the duties under paragraphs 3.17 and 3.18 may be performed by the custody officer or by another officer or police staff not involved in the investigation as directed by the custody officer, if:

(a) it is proposed to release the suspect in order that an identification procedure can be arranged and carried out and an inspector is not available to act as the identification officer, see paragraph 3.11, before the suspect leaves the station; or

(b) it is proposed to keep the suspect in police detention whilst the procedure is arranged and carried out and waiting for an inspector to act as the identification officer, see paragraph 3.11, would cause unreasonable delay to the investigation.

The officer concerned shall inform the identification officer of the action taken and give them the signed copy of the notice. See *Note 3C*.

D:3.20 If the identification officer and officer in charge of the investigation suspect, on reasonable grounds that if the suspect was given the information and notice as in paragraphs 3.17 and 3.18, they would then take steps to avoid being seen by a witness in any identification procedure, the identification officer may arrange for images of the suspect suitable for use in a video identification procedure to be obtained before giving the information and notice. If suspect's [*sic*] images are obtained in these circumstances, the suspect may, for the purposes of a video identification procedure, co-operate in providing new images which if suitable, would be used instead, see paragraph 3.17(vi).

(c) Cases when the suspect is known but not available

★**A-124**

D:3.21 When a known suspect is not available or has ceased to be available, see paragraph 3.1A, the identification officer may make arrangements for a video identification (see paragraph 3.5 and Annex A). If necessary, the identification officer may follow the video identification procedures using any suitable moving or still images and these may be obtained covertly if necessary. Alternatively, the identification officer may make arrangements for a group identification without the suspect's consent (see Annex C, para. 34). See *Note 3D*. These provisions may also be applied to juveniles where the consent of their parent or guardian is either refused or reasonable efforts to obtain that consent have failed (see paragraph 2.12).

D:3.22 Any covert activity should be strictly limited to that necessary to test the ability of the eyewitness to identify the suspect as the person they saw on the relevant previous occasion.

D:3.23 The identification officer may arrange for the suspect to be confronted by the eye-witness if none of the options referred to in paragraphs 3.5 to 3.10 or 3.21 are practicable. A "confrontation" is when the suspect is directly confronted by the eye-witness. A confrontation does not require the suspect's consent. Confrontations must be carried out in accordance with Annex D.

D:3.24 Requirements for information to be given to, or sought from, a suspect or for the suspect to be given an opportunity to view images before they are shown to an eye-witness, do not apply if the suspect's lack of co-operation prevents the necessary action.

(d) Documentation

D:3.25 A record shall be made of the video identification, identification parade, group identifica- **★A-125**
tion or confrontation on forms provided for the purpose.

D:3.26 If the identification officer considers it is not practicable to hold a video identification or identification parade requested by the suspect, the reasons shall be recorded and explained to the suspect.

D:3.27 A record shall be made of a person's failure or refusal to co-operate in a video identifica-
tion, identification parade or group identification and, if applicable, of the grounds for obtaining images in accordance with paragraph 3.20.

(e) Not used

D:3.28 [*Not used.*] **★A-126**
D:3.29 [*Not used.*]

(f) Destruction and retention of photographs taken or used in eye-witness identification procedures

D:3.30 PACE, s.64A, see paragraph 5.12, provides powers to take photographs of suspects and allows these photographs to be used or disclosed only for purposes related to the prevention or detec-
tion of crime, the investigation of offences or the conduct of prosecutions by, or on behalf of, police or other law enforcement and prosecuting authorities inside and outside the United Kingdom or the enforcement of a sentence. After being so used or disclosed, they may be retained but can only be used or disclosed for the same purposes.

D:3.31 Subject to paragraph 3.33, the photographs (and all negatives and copies), of suspects *not* taken in accordance with the provisions in paragraph 5.12 which are taken for the purposes of, or in connection with, the identification procedures in paragraphs 3.5 to 3.10, 3.21 or 3.23 must be destroyed unless the suspect:

    (a) is charged with, or informed they may be prosecuted for, a recordable offence;
    (b) is prosecuted for a recordable offence;
    (c) is cautioned for a recordable offence or given a warning or reprimand in accordance with
        the Crime and Disorder Act 1998 for a recordable offence; or
    (d) gives informed consent, in writing, for the photograph or images to be retained for
        purposes described in paragraph 3.30.

D:3.32 When paragraph 3.31 requires the destruction of any photograph, the person must be given an opportunity to witness the destruction or to have a certificate confirming the destruction if they request one within five days of being informed that the destruction is required.

D:3.33 Nothing in paragraph 3.31 affects any separate requirement under the Criminal Procedure and Investigations Act 1996 to retain material in connection with criminal investigations.

Part (B) Recognition by controlled showing of films, photographs and images

D:3.34 This Part of this section applies when, for the purposes of obtaining evidence of recogni- **★A-126a**
tion, arrangements are made for a person, including a police officer, who is *not* an eye-witness (see *Note 3AA*):

    (a) to view a film, photograph or any other visual medium; and
    (b) on the occasion of the viewing, to be asked whether they recognise anyone whose image is
        shown in the material as someone who is known to them.

The arrangements for such viewings may be made by the officer in charge of the relevant investigation. Although there is no requirement for the identification officer to make the arrangements or to be consulted about the arrangements, nothing prevents this. See *Notes 3AA* and *3G*.

D:3.35 To provide safeguards against mistaken recognition and to avoid any possibility of collusion, on the occasion of the viewing, the arrangements should ensure:

    (a) that the films, photographs and other images are shown on an individual basis;
    (b) that any person who views the material;
        (i) is unable to communicate with any other individual to whom the material has been, or
           is to be, shown;
        (ii) is not reminded of any photograph or description of any individual whose image is
           shown or given any other indication as to the identity of any such individual;

> (iii) is not be told whether a previous witness has recognised any one;
> (c) that immediately before a person views the material, they are told that:
>> (i) an individual who is known to them may, or may not, appear in the material they are shown and that if they do not recognise anyone, they should say so;
>> (ii) at any point, they may ask to see a particular part of the material frozen for them to study and there is no limit on how many times they can view the whole or any part or parts of the material; and
> (d) that the person who views the material is not asked to make any decision as to whether they recognise anyone whose image they have seen as someone known to them until they have seen the whole of the material at least twice, unless the officer in charge of the viewing decides that because of the number of images the person has been invited to view, it would not be reasonable to ask them to view the whole of the material for a second time. A record of this decision must be included in the record that is made in accordance with paragraph 3.36.

(see *Note 3G*).

D:3.36 A record of the circumstances and conditions under which the person is given an opportunity to recognise an individual must be made and the record must include:

> (a) whether the person knew or was given information concerning the name or identity of any suspect;
> (b) what the person has been told *before* the viewing about the offence, the person(s) depicted in the images or the offender and by whom;
> (c) how and by whom the witness was asked to view the image or look at the individual;
> (d) whether the viewing was alone or with others and if with others, the reason for it;
> (e) the arrangements under which the person viewed the film or saw the individual and by whom those arrangements were made;
> (f) subject to paragraph 2.18, the name and rank of the officer responsible for deciding that the viewing arrangements should be made in accordance with this Part;
> (g) the date time and place images were viewed or further viewed or the individual was seen;
> (h) the times between which the images were viewed or the individual was seen;
> (i) how the viewing of images or sighting of the individual was controlled and by whom;
> (j) whether the person was familiar with the location shown in any images or the place where they saw the individual and if so, why;
> (k) whether or not, on this occasion, the person claims to recognise any image shown, or any individual seen, as being someone known to them, and if they do:
>> (i) the reason;
>> (ii) the words of recognition;
>> (iii) any expressions of doubt; and
>> (iv) what features of the image or the individual triggered the recognition.

D:3.37 The record required under paragraph 3.36 may be made by the person who views the image or sees the individual and makes the recognition; and if applicable, by the officer or police staff in charge of showing the images to that person or in charge of the conditions under which that person sees the individual. The person must be asked to read and check the completed record and as applicable, confirm that it is correctly and accurately reflects the part they played in the viewing (see *Note 3H*).

Part (C) Recognition by uncontrolled viewing of films, photographs and images

★A-126b   D:3.38 This Part applies when, for the purpose of identifying and tracing suspects, films and photographs of incidents or other images are:

> (a) shown to the public (which may include police officers and police staff as well as members of the public) through the national or local media or any social media networking site; or
> (b) circulated through local or national police communication systems for viewing by police officers and police staff; and

the viewing is not formally controlled and supervised as set out in Part B.

D:3.39 A copy of the relevant material released to the national or local media for showing as described in sub-paragraph 3.38(a), shall be kept. The suspect or their solicitor shall be allowed to view such material before any eye-witness identification procedure under paragraphs 3.5 to 3.10, 3.21 or 3.23 of Part A are carried out, provided it is practicable and would not unreasonably delay the investigation. This paragraph does not affect any separate requirement under the Criminal Procedure and Investigations Act 1996 to retain material in connection with criminal investigations that might apply to sub-paragraphs 3.38(a) and (b).

D:3.40 Each eye-witness involved in any eye-witness identification procedure under paragraphs 3.5 to 3.10, 3.21 or 3.23 shall be asked, *after they have taken part*, whether they have seen any film, photograph or image relating to the offence or any description of the suspect which has been broadcast or published as described in paragraph 3.38(a) and their reply recorded. If they have, they should be asked to give details of the circumstances and subject to the eye-witness's recollection, the record described in paragraph 3.41 should be completed.

D:3.41 As soon as practicable after an individual (member of the public, police officer or police staff) indicates in response to a viewing that they may have information relating to the identity and whereabouts of anyone they have seen in that viewing, arrangements should be made to ensure that they are asked to give details of the circumstances and, subject to the individual's recollection, a record of the circumstances and conditions under which the viewing took place is made. This record shall be made in accordance with the provisions of paragraph 3.36 insofar as they can be applied to the viewing in question (see *Note 3H*).

Notes for guidance

D:3AA *The eye-witness identification procedures in Part A should not be used to test whether a witness can* ★A-127 *recognise a person as someone they know and would be able to give evidence of recognition along the lines that "On (describe date, time, location and circumstances) I saw an image of an individual who I recognised as AB." In these cases, the procedures in Part B shall apply if the viewing is controlled and the procedure in Part C shall apply if the viewing is not controlled.*

D:3ZA *In paragraph 3.5(a)(i), examples of physical changes or differences that the identification officer may wish to consider include hair style and colour, weight, facial hair, wearing or removal of spectacles and tinted contact lenses, facial injuries, tattoos and makeup.*

D:3A *Except for the provisions of Annex E, para.1, a police officer who is a witness for the purposes of this part of the Code is subject to the same principles and procedures as a civilian witness.*

D:3B *When an eye-witness attending an identification procedure has previously been shown photographs, or been shown or provided with computerised or artist's composite likenesses, or similar likenesses or pictures, it is the officer in charge of the investigation's responsibility to make the identification officer aware of this.*

D:3C *The purpose of paragraph 3.19 is to avoid or reduce delay in arranging identification procedures by enabling the required information and warnings, see sub-paragraphs 3.17(ix) and 3.17(xii), to be given at the earliest opportunity.*

D:3D *Paragraph 3.21 would apply when a known suspect becomes "unavailable" and thereby delays or frustrates arrangements for obtaining identification evidence. It also applies when a suspect refuses or fails to take part in a video identification, an identification parade or a group identification, or refuses or fails to take part in the only practicable options from that list. It enables any suitable images of the suspect, moving or still, which are available or can be obtained, to be used in an identification procedure. Examples include images from custody and other CCTV systems and from visually recorded interview records, see Code F, Note for Guidance 2D.*

D:3E *When it is proposed to show photographs to a witness in accordance with Annex E, it is the responsibility of the officer in charge of the investigation to confirm to the officer responsible for supervising and directing the showing, that the first description of the suspect given by that eye-witness has been recorded. If this description has not been recorded, the procedure under Annex E must be postponed, see Annex E, para. 2.*

D:3F *The admissibility and value of identification evidence obtained when carrying out the procedure under paragraph 3.2 may be compromised if:*

   (a) *before a person is identified, the eye-witness' attention is specifically drawn to that person; or*

   (b) *the suspect's identity becomes known before the procedure.*

D:3G *The admissibility and value of evidence of recognition obtained when carrying out the procedures in Part B may be compromised if, before the person is recognised, the witness who has claimed to know them is given or is made, or becomes aware of, information about the person which was not previously known to them personally but which they have purported to rely on to support their claim that the person is in fact known to them.*

D:3H *It is important that the record referred to in paragraphs 3.36 and 3.41 is made as soon as practicable after the viewing and whilst it is fresh in the mind of the individual who makes the recognition.*

D:4 Identification by fingerprints and footwear impressions

(a) *Taking fingerprints in connection with a criminal investigation*

(a) General

D:4.1 References to "fingerprints" means any record, produced by any method, of the skin pattern ★A-128 and other physical characteristics or features of a person's:

   (i) fingers; or

   (ii) palms.

(b) Action

D:4.2 A person's fingerprints may be taken in connection with the investigation of an offence only with their consent or if paragraph 4.3 applies. If the person is at a police station, consent must be in writing.

D:4.3 PACE, s.61, provides powers to take fingerprints without consent from any person aged ten or over as follows:

(a) under section 61(3), from a person detained at a police station in consequence of being arrested for a recordable offence, see *Note 4A*, if they have not had their fingerprints taken in the course of the investigation of the offence unless those previously taken fingerprints are not a complete set or some or all of those fingerprints are not of sufficient quality to allow satisfactory analysis, comparison or matching.

(b) under section 61(4), from a person detained at a police station who has been charged with a recordable offence, see *Note 4A*, or informed they will be reported for such an offence if they have not had their fingerprints taken in the course of the investigation of the offence unless those previously taken fingerprints are not a complete set or some or all of those fingerprints are not of sufficient quality to allow satisfactory analysis, comparison or matching.

(c) under section 61(4A), from a person who has been bailed to appear at a court or police station if the person:

  (i) has answered to bail for a person whose fingerprints were taken previously and there are reasonable grounds for believing they are not the same person; or

  (ii) who has answered to bail claims to be a different person from a person whose fingerprints were previously taken;

  and in either case, the court or an officer of inspector rank or above, authorises the fingerprints to be taken at the court or police station (an inspector's authority may be given in writing or orally and confirmed in writing, as soon as practicable);

(ca) under section 61(5A) from a person who has been arrested for a recordable offence and released if the person:

  (i) is on bail and has not had their fingerprints taken in the course of the investigation of the offence, or;

  (ii) has had their fingerprints taken in the course of the investigation of the offence, but they do not constitute a complete set or some, or all, of the fingerprints are not of sufficient quality to allow satisfactory analysis, comparison or matching.

(cb) under section 61(5B) from a person not detained at a police station who has been charged with a recordable offence or informed they will be reported for such an offence if:

  (i) they have not had their fingerprints taken in the course of the investigation; or

  (ii) their fingerprints have been taken in the course of the investigation of the offence but either:

    • they do not constitute a complete set or some, or all, of the fingerprints are not of sufficient quality to allow satisfactory analysis, comparison or matching; or

    • the investigation was discontinued but subsequently resumed and, before the resumption, their fingerprints were destroyed pursuant to section 63D(3).

(d) under section 61(6), from a person who has been:

  (i) convicted of a recordable offence; or

  (ii) given a caution in respect of a recordable offence (see *Note 4A*) which, at the time of the caution, the person admitted;

  if, since being convicted or cautioned:

    • their fingerprints have not been taken; or

    • their fingerprints which have been taken do not constitute a complete set or some, or all, of the fingerprints are not of sufficient quality to allow satisfactory analysis, comparison or matching;

  and in either case, an officer of inspector rank or above is satisfied that taking the fingerprints is necessary to assist in the prevention or detection of crime and authorises the taking;

(e) under section 61(6A) from a person a constable reasonably suspects is committing or attempting to commit, or has committed or attempted to commit, any offence if either:

  (i) the person's name is unknown to, and cannot be readily ascertained by, the constable; or

  (ii) the constable has reasonable grounds for doubting whether a name given by the person as their name is their real name.

Note: fingerprints taken under this power are not regarded as having been taken in the course of the investigation of an offence.

[See *Note 4C*]

(f) under section 61(6D) from a person who has been convicted outside England and Wales of an offence which if committed in England and Wales would be a qualifying offence as defined by PACE, section 65A (see *Note 4AB*) if:

(i) the person's fingerprints have not been taken previously under this power or their fingerprints have been so taken on a previous occasion but they do not constitute a complete set or some, or all, of the fingerprints are not of sufficient quality to allow satisfactory analysis, comparison or matching; and

(ii) a police officer of inspector rank or above is satisfied that taking fingerprints is necessary to assist in the prevention or detection of crime and authorises them to be taken.

D:4.4 PACE, s.63A(4) and Sched. 2A provide powers to:

(a) make a requirement (in accordance with Annex G) for a person to attend a police station to have their fingerprints taken in the exercise of one of the following powers (described in paragraph 4.3 above) within certain periods as follows:

(i) section 61(5A)—Persons arrested for a recordable offence and released, see paragraph 4.3(ca): In the case of a person whose fingerprints were taken in the course of the investigation but those fingerprints do not constitute a complete set or some, or all, of the fingerprints are not of sufficient quality, the requirement may not be made more than six months from the day the investigating officer was informed that the fingerprints previously taken were incomplete or below standard. In the case of a person whose fingerprints were destroyed prior to the resumption of the investigation, the requirement may not be made more than six months from the day on which the investigation resumed.

(ii) section 61(5B)—Persons not detained at a police station charged etc. with a recordable offence, see paragraph 4.3(cb): the requirement may not be made more than six months from:

- the day the person was charged or informed that they would be reported, if fingerprints have not been taken in the course of the investigation of the offence; or

- the day the investigating officer was informed that the fingerprints previously taken were incomplete or below standard, if fingerprints have been taken in the course of the investigation but those fingerprints do not constitute a complete set or some, or all, of the fingerprints are not of sufficient quality; or

- the day on which the investigation was resumed, in the case of a person whose fingerprints were destroyed prior to the resumption of the investigation.

(iii) section 61(6)—Persons convicted or cautioned for a recordable offence in England and Wales, see paragraph 4.3(d): where the offence for which the person was convicted or cautioned is a qualifying offence (see *Note 4AB*), there is no time limit for the exercise of this power. Where the conviction or caution is for a recordable offence which is not a qualifying offence, the requirement may *not* be made more than two years from:

- in the case of a person who has not had their fingerprints taken since the conviction or caution, the day on which the person was convicted or cautioned, or, if later, the day on which Schedule 2A came into force (March 7, 2011), ; or

- in the case of a person whose fingerprints have been taken in the course of the investigation but those fingerprints do not constitute a complete set or some, or all, of the fingerprints are not of sufficient quality, the day on which an officer from the force investigating the offence was informed that the fingerprints previously taken were incomplete or below standard, or, if later, the day on which Schedule 2A came into force (March 7, 2011).

(iv) section 61(6D)—A person who has been convicted of a qualifying offence (see *Note 4AB*) outside England and Wales, see paragraph 4.3(g): there is no time limit for making the requirement.

Note: A person who has had their fingerprints taken under any of the powers in section 61 mentioned in paragraph 4.3 on two occasions in relation to any offence may not be required under Schedule 2A to attend a police station for their fingerprints to be taken again under section 61 in relation to that offence, unless authorised by an officer of inspector rank or above. The fact of the authorisation and the reasons for giving it must be recorded as soon as practicable.

(b) arrest, without warrant, a person who fails to comply with the requirement.

D:4.5 A person's fingerprints may be taken, as above, electronically.

D:4.6 Reasonable force may be used, if necessary, to take a person's fingerprints without their consent under the powers as in paragraphs 4.3 and 4.4.

D:4.7 Before any fingerprints are taken:

- (a) without consent under any power mentioned in paragraphs 4.3 and 4.4 above, the person must be informed of:
  - (i) the reason their fingerprints are to be taken;
  - (ii) the power under which they are to be taken; and
  - (iii) the fact that the relevant authority has been given if any power mentioned in paragraph 4.3(c), (d) or (f) applies.
- (b) with or without consent at a police station or elsewhere, the person must be informed:
  - (i) that their fingerprints may be subject of a speculative search against other fingerprints, see *Note 4B*; and
  - (ii) that their fingerprints may be retained in accordance with Annex F, Part (a) unless they were taken under the power mentioned in paragraph 4.3(e) when they must be destroyed after they have being [*sic*] checked (see *Note 4C*).

(c) Documentation

D:4.8A A record must be made as soon as practicable after the fingerprints are taken, of:

- the matters in paragraph 4.7(a)(i) to (iii) and the fact that the person has been informed of those matters; and
- the fact that the person has been informed of the matters in paragraph 4.7(b)(i) and (ii).

The record must be made in the person's custody record if they are detained at a police station when the fingerprints are taken.

D:4.8 If force is used, a record shall be made of the circumstances and those present.

D:4.9 [*Not used.*]

(b) Not used.

D:4.10 [*Not used.*]
D:4.11 [*Not used.*]
D:4.12 [*Not used.*]
D:4.13 [*Not used.*]
D:4.14 [*Not used.*]
D:4.15 [*Not used.*]

(c) Taking footwear impressions in connection with a criminal investigation

(a) Action

★A-129   D:4.16 Impressions of a person's footwear may be taken in connection with the investigation of an offence only with their consent or if paragraph 4.17 applies. If the person is at a police station consent must be in writing.

D:4.17 PACE, s.61A, provides power for a police officer to take footwear impressions without consent from any person over the age of ten years who is detained at a police station:

- (a) in consequence of being arrested for a recordable offence, see *Note 4A*; or if the detainee has been charged with a recordable offence, or informed they will be reported for such an offence; and
- (b) the detainee has not had an impression of their footwear taken in the course of the investigation of the offence unless the previously taken impression is not complete or is not of sufficient quality to allow satisfactory analysis, comparison or matching (whether in the case in question or generally).

D:4.18 Reasonable force may be used, if necessary, to take a footwear impression from a detainee without consent under the power in paragraph 4.17.

D:4.19 Before any footwear impression is taken with, or without, consent as above, the person must be informed:

- (a) of the reason the impression is to be taken;
- (b) that the impression may be retained and may be subject of a speculative search against other impressions, see *Note 4B*, unless destruction of the impression is required in accordance with Annex F, Pt B.

(b) Documentation

D:4.20 A record must be made, as soon as possible, of the reason for taking a person's footwear impressions without consent. If force is used, a record shall be made of the circumstances and those present.

D:4.21 A record shall be made when a person has been informed under the terms of paragraph 4.19(b), of the possibility that their footwear impressions may be subject of a speculative search.

Notes for guidance

D:4A *References to "recordable offences" in this code relate to those offences for which convictions or cautions may be recorded in national police records. See PACE, s.27(4). The recordable offences current at the time when this Code was prepared, are any offences which carry a sentence of imprisonment on conviction (irrespective of the period, or the age of the offender or actual sentence passed) as well as the non-imprisonable offences under the Vagrancy Act 1824 ss.3 and 4 (begging and persistent begging), the Street Offences Act 1959, s.1 (loitering or soliciting for purposes of prostitution), the Road Traffic Act 1988, s.25 (tampering with motor vehicles), the Criminal Justice and Public Order Act 1994, s.167 (touting for hire car services) and others listed in the National Police Records (Recordable Offences) Regulations 2000 as amended.*

D:4AB *A qualifying offence is one of the offences specified in PACE, s.65A. These include offences which involve the use or threat of violence or unlawful force against persons, sexual offences, offences against children and other offences, for example:*

- *murder, false imprisonment, kidnapping contrary to Common law*
- *manslaughter, conspiracy to murder, threats to kill, wounding with intent to cause grievous bodily harm (GBH), causing GBH and assault occasioning actual bodily harm contrary to the Offences Against the Person Act 1861;*
- *criminal possession or use of firearms contrary to sections 16 to 18 of the Firearms Act 1968;*
- *robbery, burglary and aggravated burglary contrary to sections 8, 9 or 10 of the Theft Act 1968 or an offence under section 12A of that Act involving an accident which caused a person's death;*
- *criminal damage required to be charged as arson contrary to section 1 of the Criminal Damage Act 1971;*
- *taking, possessing and showing indecent photographs of children contrary to section 1 of the Protection of Children Act 1978;*
- *rape, sexual assault, child sex offences, exposure and other offences contrary to the Sexual Offences Act 2003.*

D:4B *Fingerprints, footwear impressions or a DNA sample (and the information derived from it) taken from a person arrested on suspicion of being involved in a recordable offence, or charged with such an offence, or informed they will be reported for such an offence, may be subject of a speculative search. This means the fingerprints, footwear impressions or DNA sample may be checked against other fingerprints, footwear impressions and DNA records held by, or on behalf of, the police and other law enforcement authorities in, or outside, the UK, or held in connection with, or as a result of, an investigation of an offence inside or outside the UK.*

D:4C *The power under section 61(6A) of PACE described in paragraph 4.3(e) allows fingerprints of a suspect who has not been arrested, and whose name is not known or cannot be ascertained, or who gave a doubtful name, to be taken in connection with any offence (whether recordable or not) using a mobile device and then checked on the street against the database containing the national fingerprint collection. Fingerprints taken under this power cannot be retained after they have been checked. The results may make an arrest for the suspected offence based on the name condition unnecessary (see Code G, para. 2.9(a)) and enable the offence to be disposed of without arrest, for example, by summons/charging by post, penalty notice or words of advice. If arrest for a non-recordable offence is necessary for any other reasons, this power may also be exercised at the station. Before the power is exercised, the officer should:*

- *inform the person of the nature of the suspected offence and why they are suspected of committing it.*
- *give them a reasonable opportunity to establish their real name before deciding that their name is unknown and cannot be readily ascertained or that there are reasonable grounds to doubt that a name they have given is their real name.*
- *as applicable, inform the person of the reason why their name is not known and cannot be readily ascertained or of the grounds for doubting that a name they have given is their real name, including, for example, the reason why a particular document the person has produced to verify their real name, is not sufficient.*

D:5 Examinations to establish identity and the taking of photographs

(a) *Detainees at police stations*

(a) Searching or examination of detainees at police stations

★A-130   D:5.1 PACE, s.54A(1), allows a detainee at a police station to be searched or examined or both, to establish:

(a) whether they have any marks, features or injuries that would tend to identify them as a person involved in the commission of an offence and to photograph any identifying marks, see paragraph 5.5; or

(b) their identity, see *Note 5A*.

A person detained at a police station to be searched under a stop and search power, see Code A, is not a detainee for the purposes of these powers.

D:5.2 A search and/or examination to find marks under s.54A(1)(a) may be carried out without the detainee's consent, see paragraph 2.12, only if authorised by an officer of at least inspector rank when consent has been withheld or it is not practicable to obtain consent, see *Note 5D*.

D:5.3 A search or examination to establish a suspect's identity under section 54A(1)(b) may be carried out without the detainee's consent, see paragraph 2.12, only if authorised by an officer of at least inspector rank when the detainee has refused to identify themselves or the authorising officer has reasonable grounds for suspecting the person is not who they claim to be.

D:5.4 Any marks that assist in establishing the detainee's identity, or their identification as a person involved in the commission of an offence, are identifying marks. Such marks may be photographed with the detainee's consent, see paragraph 2.12; or without their consent if it is withheld or it is not practicable to obtain it, see *Note 5D*.

D:5.5 A detainee may only be searched, examined and photographed under section 54A, by a police officer of the same sex.

D:5.6 Any photographs of identifying marks, taken under section 54A, may be used or disclosed only for purposes related to the prevention or detection of crime, the investigation of offences or the conduct of prosecutions by, or on behalf of, police or other law enforcement and prosecuting authorities inside, and outside, the UK. After being so used or disclosed, the photograph may be retained but must not be used or disclosed except for these purposes, see *Note 5B*.

D:5.7 The powers, as in paragraph 5.1, do not affect any separate requirement under the Criminal Procedure and Investigations Act 1996 to retain material in connection with criminal investigations.

D:5.8 Authority for the search and/or examination for the purposes of paragraphs 5.2 and 5.3 may be given orally or in writing. If given orally, the authorising officer must confirm it in writing as soon as practicable. A separate authority is required for each purpose which applies.

D:5.9 If it is established a person is unwilling to co-operate sufficiently to enable a search and/or examination to take place or a suitable photograph to be taken, an officer may use reasonable force to:

(a) search and/or examine a detainee without their consent; and

(b) photograph any identifying marks without their consent.

D:5.10 The thoroughness and extent of any search or examination carried out in accordance with the powers in section 54A must be no more than the officer considers necessary to achieve the required purpose. Any search or examination which involves the removal of more than the person's outer clothing shall be conducted in accordance with Code C, Annex A, para. 11.

D:5.11 An intimate search may not be carried out under the powers in s.54A.

(b) Photographing detainees at police stations and other persons elsewhere than at a police station

★A-131   D:5.12 Under PACE, s.64A, an officer may photograph:

(a) any person whilst they are detained at a police station; and

(b) any person who is elsewhere than at a police station and who has been:

(i) arrested by a constable for an offence;

(ii) taken into custody by a constable after being arrested for an offence by a person other than a constable;

(iii) made subject to a requirement to wait with a community support officer under paragraph 2(3) or (3B) of Schedule 4 to the Police Reform Act 2002;

(iiia) given a direction by a constable under section 27 of the Violent Crime Reduction Act 2006.

(iv) given a penalty notice by a constable in uniform under Chapter 1 of Part 1 of the Criminal Justice and Police Act 2001, a penalty notice by a constable under section

444A of the Education Act 1996, or a fixed penalty notice by a constable in uniform under section 54 of the Road Traffic Offenders Act 1988;

(v) given a notice in relation to a relevant fixed penalty offence (within the meaning of paragraph 1 of Schedule 4 to the Police Reform Act 2002) by a community support officer by virtue of a designation applying that paragraph to him;

(vi) given a notice in relation to a relevant fixed penalty offence (within the meaning of paragraph 1 of Schedule 5 to the Police Reform Act 2002) by an accredited person by virtue of accreditation specifying that that paragraph applies to him; or

(vii) given a direction to leave and not return to a specified location for up to 48 hours by a police constable (under section 27 of the Violent Crime Reduction Act 2006).

D:5.12A Photographs taken under PACE, s.64A:

(a) may be taken with the person's consent, or without their consent if consent is withheld or it is not practicable to obtain their consent, see *Note 5E*; and

(b) may be used or disclosed only for purposes related to the prevention or detection of crime, the investigation of offences or the conduct of prosecutions by, or on behalf of, police or other law enforcement and prosecuting authorities inside and outside the United Kingdom or the enforcement of any sentence or order made by a court when dealing with an offence. After being so used or disclosed, they may be retained but can only be used or disclosed for the same purposes. See *Note 5B*.

D:5.13 The officer proposing to take a detainee's photograph may, for this purpose, require the person to remove any item or substance worn on, or over, all, or any part of, their head or face. If they do not comply with such a requirement, the officer may remove the item or substance.

D:5.14 If it is established the detainee is unwilling to co-operate sufficiently to enable a suitable photograph to be taken and it is not reasonably practicable to take the photograph covertly, an officer may use reasonable force, see *Note 5F*.

(a) to take their photograph without their consent; and

(b) for the purpose of taking the photograph, remove any item or substance worn on, or over, all, or any part of, the person's head or face which they have failed to remove when asked.

D:5.15 For the purposes of this code, a photograph may be obtained without the person's consent by making a copy of an image of them taken at any time on a camera system installed anywhere in the police station.

(c) Information to be given

D:5.16 When a person is searched, examined or photographed under the provisions as in paragraph 5.1 and 5.12, or their photograph obtained as in paragraph 5.15, they must be informed of the: ★A-132

(a) purpose of the search, examination or photograph;

(b) grounds on which the relevant authority, if applicable, has been given; and

(c) purposes for which the photograph may be used, disclosed or retained.

This information must be given before the search or examination commences or the photograph is taken, except if the photograph is:

(i) to be taken covertly;

(ii) obtained as in paragraph 5.15, in which case the person must be informed as soon as practicable after the photograph is taken or obtained.

(d) Documentation

D:5.17 A record must be made when a detainee is searched, examined, or a photograph of the person, or any identifying marks found on them, are [*sic*] taken. The record must include the:

(a) identity, subject to paragraph 2.18, of the officer carrying out the search, examination or taking the photograph;

(b) purpose of the search, examination or photograph and the outcome;

(c) detainee's consent to the search, examination or photograph, or the reason the person was searched, examined or photographed without consent;

(d) giving of any authority as in paragraphs 5.2 and 5.3, the grounds for giving it and the authorising officer.

D:5.18 If force is used when searching, examining or taking a photograph in accordance with this section, a record shall be made of the circumstances and those present.

(b) *Persons at police stations not detained*

★**A-133**   D:5.19 When there are reasonable grounds for suspecting the involvement of a person in a criminal offence, but that person is at a police station *voluntarily* and not detained, the provisions of paragraphs 5.1 to 5.18 should apply, subject to the modifications in the following paragraphs.

D:5.20 References to the "person being detained" and to the powers mentioned in paragraph 5.1 which apply only to detainees at police stations shall be omitted.

D:5.21 Force may not be used to:

(a) search and/or examine the person to:

(i) discover whether they have any marks that would tend to identify them as a person involved in the commission of an offence; or

(ii) establish their identity, see *Note 5A*;

(b) take photographs of any identifying marks, see paragraph 5.4; or

(c) take a photograph of the person.

D:5.22 Subject to paragraph 5.24, the photographs of persons or of their identifying marks which are not taken in accordance with the provisions mentioned in paragraphs 5.1 or 5.12, must be destroyed (together with any negatives and copies) unless the person:

(a) is charged with, or informed they may be prosecuted for, a recordable offence;

(b) is prosecuted for a recordable offence;

(c) is cautioned for a recordable offence or given a warning or reprimand in accordance with the Crime and Disorder Act 1998 for a recordable offence; or

(d) gives informed consent, in writing, for the photograph or image to be retained as in paragraph 5.6.

D:5.23 When paragraph 5.22 requires the destruction of any photograph, the person must be given an opportunity to witness the destruction or to have a certificate confirming the destruction provided they so request the certificate within five days of being informed the destruction is required.

D:5.24 Nothing in paragraph 5.22 affects any separate requirement under the Criminal Procedure and Investigations Act 1996 to retain material in connection with criminal investigations.

Notes for guidance

★**A-134**   D:5A *The conditions under which fingerprints may be taken to assist in establishing a person's identity, are described in section 4.*

D:5B *Examples of purposes related to the prevention or detection of crime, the investigation of offences or the conduct of prosecutions include:*

(a) *checking the photograph against other photographs held in records or in connection with, or as a result of, an investigation of an offence to establish whether the person is liable to arrest for other offences;*

(b) *when the person is arrested at the same time as other people, or at a time when it is likely that other people will be arrested, using the photograph to help establish who was arrested, at what time and where;*

(c) *when the real identity of the person is not known and cannot be readily ascertained or there are reasonable grounds for doubting a name and other personal details given by the person, are their real name and personal details. In these circumstances, using or disclosing the photograph to help to establish or verify their real identity or determine whether they are liable to arrest for some other offence, e.g. by checking it against other photographs held in records or in connection with, or as a result of, an investigation of an offence;*

(d) *when it appears any identification procedure in section 3 may need to be arranged for which the person's photograph would assist;*

(e) *when the person's release without charge may be required, and if the release is:*

(i) *on bail to appear at a police station, using the photograph to help verify the person's identity when they answer their bail and if the person does not answer their bail, to assist in arresting them; or*

(ii) *without bail, using the photograph to help verify their identity or assist in locating them for the purposes of serving them with a summons to appear at court in criminal proceedings;*

(f) *when the person has answered to bail at a police station and there are reasonable grounds for doubting they are the person who was previously granted bail, using the photograph to help establish or verify their identity;*

(g) *when the person arrested on a warrant claims to be a different person from the person named on the warrant and a photograph would help to confirm or disprove their claim;*

(h) *when the person has been charged with, reported for, or convicted of, a recordable offence and their photograph is not already on record as a result of (a) to (f) or their photograph is on record but their appearance has changed since it was taken and the person has not yet been released or brought before a court.*

D:5C *There is no power to arrest a person convicted of a recordable offence solely to take their photograph. The power to take photographs in this section applies only where the person is in custody as a result of the exercise of another power, e.g. arrest for fingerprinting under PACE, Sched. 2A, para. 17.*

D:5D *Examples of when it would not be practicable to obtain a detainee's consent, see paragraph 2.12, to a search, examination or the taking of a photograph of an identifying mark include:*

    (a) *when the person is drunk or otherwise unfit to give consent;*

    (b) *when there are reasonable grounds to suspect that if the person became aware a search or examination was to take place or an identifying mark was to be photographed, they would take steps to prevent this happening, e.g. by violently resisting, covering or concealing the mark etc and it would not otherwise be possible to carry out the search or examination or to photograph any identifying mark;*

    (c) *in the case of a juvenile, if the parent or guardian cannot be contacted in sufficient time to allow the search or examination to be carried out or the photograph to be taken.*

D:5E *Examples of when it would not be practicable to obtain the person's consent, see paragraph 2.12, to a photograph being taken include:*

    (a) *when the person is drunk or otherwise unfit to give consent;*

    (b) *when there are reasonable grounds to suspect that if the person became aware a photograph, suitable to be used or disclosed for the use and disclosure described in paragraph 5.6, was to be taken, they would take steps to prevent it being taken, e.g. by violently resisting, covering or distorting their face etc, and it would not otherwise be possible to take a suitable photograph;*

    (c) *when, in order to obtain a suitable photograph, it is necessary to take it covertly; and*

    (d) *in the case of a juvenile, if the parent or guardian cannot be contacted in sufficient time to allow the photograph to be taken.*

D:5F *The use of reasonable force to take the photograph of a suspect elsewhere than at a police station must be carefully considered. In order to obtain a suspect's consent and cooperation to remove an item of religious headwear to take their photograph, a constable should consider whether in the circumstances of the situation the removal of the headwear and the taking of the photograph should be by an officer of the same sex as the person. It would be appropriate for these actions to be conducted out of public view (see paragraph 1.1 and Note 1A).*

D:6　Identification by body samples and impressions

(a)　*General*

D:6.1 References to:　　　　　　　　　　　　　　　　　　　　　　★A-135

    (a) an "intimate sample" mean a dental impression or sample of blood, semen or any other tissue fluid, urine, or pubic hair, or a swab taken from any part of a person's genitals or from a person's body orifice other than the mouth;

    (b) a "non-intimate sample" means:

        (i) a sample of hair, other than pubic hair, which includes hair plucked with the root, see *Note 6A*;

        (ii) a sample taken from a nail or from under a nail;

        (iii) a swab taken from any part of a person's body other than a part from which a swab taken would be an intimate sample;

        (iv) saliva;

        (v) a skin impression which means any record, other than a fingerprint, which is a record, in any form and produced by any method, of the skin pattern and other physical characteristics or features of the whole, or any part of, a person's foot or of any other part of their body.

(b)　*Action*

(a)　Intimate samples

D:6.2 PACE, s.62, provides that intimate samples may be taken under:　　★A-136

    (a) section 62(1), from a person in police detention only:

        (i) if a police officer of inspector rank or above has reasonable grounds to believe such an impression or sample will tend to confirm or disprove the suspect's involvement in a recordable offence, see *Note 4A*, and gives authorisation for a sample to be taken; and

      (ii) with the suspect's written consent;
- (b) section 62(1A), from a person not in police detention but from whom two or more nonintimate samples have been taken in the course of an investigation of an offence and the samples, though suitable, have proved insufficient if:
  - (i) a police officer of inspector rank or above authorises it to be taken; and
  - (ii) the person concerned gives their written consent. See *Notes 6B* and *6C*
- (c) section 62(2A), from a person convicted outside England and Wales of an offence which if committed in England and Wales would be qualifying offence [*sic*] as defined by PACE, s.65A (see *Note 4AB*) from whom two or more non-intimate samples taken under section 63(3E) (see paragraph 6.6(h)) have proved insufficient if:
  - (i) a police officer of inspector rank or above is satisfied that taking the sample is necessary to assist in the prevention or detection of crime and authorises it to be taken; and
  - (ii) the person concerned gives their written consent.

D:6.2A PACE, s.63A(4) and Sched. 2A provide powers to:
- (a) make a requirement (in accordance with Annex G) for a person to attend a police station to have an intimate sample taken in the exercise of one of the following powers (see paragraph 6.2) :
  - (i) section 62(1A)–Persons from whom two or more non-intimate samples have been taken and proved to be insufficient, see paragraph 6.2(b): There is no time limit for making the requirement.
  - (ii) section 62(2A)–Persons convicted outside England and Wales from whom two or more non-intimate samples taken under section 63(3E) (see paragraph 6.6(g)have proved insufficient, see paragraph 6.2(c): There is no time limit for making the requirement.
- (b) arrest without warrant a person who fails to comply with the requirement

D:6.3 Before a suspect is asked to provide an intimate sample, they must be:
- (a) informed:
  - (i) of the reason, including the nature of the suspected offence (except if taken under paragraph 6.2(c) from a person convicted outside England and Wales).
  - (ii) that authorisation has been given and the provisions under which given;
  - (iii) that a sample taken at a police station may be subject of a speculative search;
- (b) warned that if they refuse without good cause their refusal may harm their case if it comes to trial, see *Note 6D*. If the suspect is in police detention and not legally represented, they must also be reminded of their entitlement to have free legal advice, see Code C, para. 6.5, and the reminder noted in the custody record. If paragraph 6.2(b) applies and the person is attending a station voluntarily, their entitlement to free legal advice as in Code C, para. 3.21 shall be explained to them.

D:6.4 Dental impressions may only be taken by a registered dentist. Other intimate samples, except for samples of urine, may only be taken by a registered medical practitioner or registered nurse or registered paramedic.

(b) Non-intimate samples

★A-137   D:6.5 A non-intimate sample may be taken from a detainee only with their written consent or if paragraph 6.6 applies.

    D:6.6 A non-intimate sample may be taken from a person without the appropriate consent in the following circumstances:
- (a) under section 63(2A) from a person who is in police detention as a consequence of being arrested for a recordable offence and who has not had a non-intimate sample of the same type and from the same part of the body taken in the course of the investigation of the offence by the police or they have had such a sample taken but it proved insufficient;
- (b) under section 63(3) from a person who is being held in custody by the police on the authority of a court if an officer of at least the rank of inspector authorises it to be taken. An authorisation may be given:
  - (i) if the authorising officer has reasonable grounds for suspecting the person of involvement in a recordable offence and for believing that the sample will tend to confirm or disprove that involvement, and
  - (ii) in writing or orally and confirmed in writing, as soon as practicable;

  but an authorisation may not be given to take from the same part of the body a further non-intimate sample consisting of a skin impression unless the previously taken impression proved insufficient;

(c) under section 63(3ZA) from a person who has been arrested for a recordable offence and released if:

(i) in the case of a person who is on bail, they have not had a sample of the same type and from the same part of the body taken in the course of the investigation of the offence, or;

(ii) in any case, the person has had such a sample taken in the course of the investigation of the offence, but either:

- it was not suitable or proved insufficient; or
- the investigation was discontinued but subsequently resumed and before the resumption, any DNA profile derived from the sample was destroyed and the sample itself was destroyed pursuant to section 63R(4), (5) or (12);

(d) under section 63(3A), from a person (whether or not in police detention or held in custody by the police on the authority of a court) who has been charged with a recordable offence or informed they will be reported for such an offence if the person:

(i) has not had a non-intimate sample taken from them in the course of the investigation of the offence; or

(ii) has had a sample so taken, but it was not suitable or proved insufficient, see *Note 6B*; or

(iii) has had a sample taken in the course of the investigation of the offence and the sample has been destroyed and in proceedings relating to that offence there is a dispute as to whether a DNA profile relevant to the proceedings was derived from the destroyed sample;

(e) under section 63(3B), from a person who has been:

(i) convicted of a recordable offence; or

(ii) given a caution in respect of a recordable offence which, at the time of the caution, the person admitted;

if, since their conviction or caution a non-intimate sample has not been taken from them or a sample which has been taken since then was not suitable or proved insufficient and in either case, an officer of inspector rank or above, is satisfied that taking the fingerprints is necessary to assist in the prevention or detection of crime and authorises the taking;

(f) under section 63(3C) from a person to whom section 2 of the Criminal Evidence (Amendment) Act 1997 applies (persons detained following acquittal on grounds of insanity or finding of unfitness to plead);

(g) under section 63(3E) from a person who has been convicted outside England and Wales of an offence which if committed in England and Wales would be a qualifying offence as defined by PACE, section 65A (see *Note 4AB*) if:

(i) a non-intimate sample has not been taken previously under this power or unless a sample was so taken but was not suitable or proved insufficient; and

(ii) a police officer of inspector rank or above is satisfied that taking a sample is necessary to assist in the prevention or detection of crime and authorises it to be taken.

D:6.6A PACE, s.63A(4) and Sched. 2A provide powers to:

(a) make a requirement (in accordance with Annex G) for a person to attend a police station to have a non-intimate sample taken in the exercise of one of the following powers (see paragraph 6.6 above) within certain time limits as follows:

(i) section 63(3ZA)—Persons arrested for a recordable offence and released, see paragraph 6.6(c): In the case of a person from whom a non-intimate sample was taken in the course of the investigation but that sample was not suitable or proved insufficient, the requirement may not be made more than six months from the day the investigating officer was informed that the sample previously taken was not suitable or proved insufficient. In the case of a person whose DNA profile and sample was destroyed prior to the resumption of the investigation, the requirement may not be made more than six months from the day on which the investigation resumed.

(ii) section 63(3A)—Persons charged etc. with a recordable offence, see paragraph 6.6(d): The requirement may not be made more than six months from:

- the day the person was charged or informed that they would be reported, if a sample has not been taken in the course of the investigation;
- the day the investigating officer was informed that the sample previously taken was not suitable or proved insufficient, if a sample has been taken in the course of the investigation but the sample was not suitable or proved insufficient; or
- the day on which the investigation was resumed, in the case of a person whose DNA profile and sample were destroyed prior to the resumption of the investigation.

(iii) section 63(3B)—Person convicted or cautioned for a recordable offence in England and Wales, see paragraph 6.6(e): Where the offence for which the person was convicted etc is also a qualifying offence (see *Note 4AB*), there is no time limit for the exercise of this power. Where the conviction etc was for a recordable offence that is *not* a qualifying offence, the requirement may not be made more than two years from:

- in the case of a person whose sample has not been taken since they were convicted or cautioned, the day the person was convicted or cautioned, or, if later, the day Schedule 2A came into force (March 7, 2011); or
- in the case of a person whose sample has been taken but was not suitable or proved insufficient, the day an officer from the force investigating the offence was informed that the sample previously taken was not suitable or proved insufficient or, if later, the day Schedule 2A came into force (March 7, 2011).

(iv) section 63(3E)—A person who has been convicted of qualifying offence (see *Note 4AB*) outside England and Wales, see paragraph 6.6(h): there is no time limit for making the requirement.

Note: A person who has had a non-intimate sample taken under any of the powers in section 63 mentioned in paragraph 6.6 on two occasions in relation to any offence may not be required under Schedule 2A to attend a police station for a sample to be taken again under section 63 in relation to that offence, unless authorised by an officer of inspector rank or above. The fact of the authorisation and the reasons for giving it must be recorded as soon as practicable.

(b) arrest, without warrant, a person who fails to comply with the requirement.

D:6.7 Reasonable force may be used, if necessary, to take a non-intimate sample from a person without their consent under the powers mentioned in paragraph 6.6.

D:6.8 Before any non-intimate sample is taken:

(a) without consent under any power mentioned in paragraphs 6.6 and 6.6A, the person must be informed of:

(i) the reason for taking the sample;

(ii) the power under which the sample is to be taken;

(iii) the fact that the relevant authority has been given if any power mentioned in paragraph 6.6(b), (e) or (g) applies, including the nature of the suspected offence (except if taken under paragraph 6.6(e) from a person convicted or cautioned, or under paragraph 6.6(g) if taken from a person convicted outside England and Wales;

(b) with or without consent at a police station or elsewhere, the person must be informed:

(i) that their sample or information derived from it may be subject of a speculative search against other samples and information derived from them, see *Note 6E* and

(ii) that their sample and the information derived from it may be retained in accordance with Annex F, Part (a).

(c) Removal of clothing

D:6.9 When clothing needs to be removed in circumstances likely to cause embarrassment to the person, no person of the opposite sex who is not a registered medical practitioner or registered health care professional shall be present, (unless in the case of a juvenile, mentally disordered or mentally vulnerable person, that person specifically requests the presence of an appropriate adult of the opposite sex who is readily available) nor shall anyone whose presence is unnecessary. However, in the case of a juvenile, this is subject to the overriding proviso that such a removal of clothing may take place in the absence of the appropriate adult only if the juvenile signifies in their presence, that they prefer the adult's absence and they agree.

(c) Documentation

D:6.10 A record must be made as soon as practicable after the sample is taken of:

- The matters in paragraph 6.8(a)(i) to (iii) and the fact that the person has been informed of those matters; and
- The fact that the person has been informed of the matters in paragraph 6.8(b)(i) and (ii).

D:6.10A If force is used, a record shall be made of the circumstances and those present.

D:6.11 A record must be made of a warning given as required by paragraph 6.3.

Notes for guidance

D:6A *When hair samples are taken for the purpose of DNA analysis (rather than for other purposes such as* ★**A-138** *making a visual match), the suspect should be permitted a reasonable choice as to what part of the body the hairs are taken from. When hairs are plucked, they should be plucked individually, unless the suspect prefers otherwise and no more should be plucked than the person taking them reasonably considers necessary for a sufficient sample.*

D:6B *(a) An insufficient sample is one which is not sufficient either in quantity or quality to provide information for a particular form of analysis, such as DNA analysis. A sample may also be insufficient if enough information cannot be obtained from it by analysis because of loss, destruction, damage or contamination of the sample or as a result of an earlier, unsuccessful attempt at analysis.*

(b) An unsuitable sample is one which, by its nature, is not suitable for a particular form of analysis.

D:6C *Nothing in paragraph 6.2 prevents intimate samples being taken for elimination purposes with the consent of the person concerned but the provisions of paragraph 2.12 relating to the role of the appropriate adult, should be applied. Paragraph 6.2(b) does not, however, apply where the non-intimate samples were previously taken under the Terrorism Act 2000, Sched. 8, para. 10.*

D:6D *In warning a person who is asked to provide an intimate sample as in paragraph 6.3, the following form of words may be used:*

"You do not have to provide this sample/allow this swab or impression to be taken, but I must warn you that if you refuse without good cause, your refusal may harm your case if it comes to trial."

D:6E *Fingerprints or a DNA sample and the information derived from it taken from a person arrested on suspicion of being involved in a recordable offence, or charged with such an offence, or informed they will be reported for such an offence, may be subject of a speculative search. This means they may be checked against other fingerprints and DNA records held by, or on behalf of, the police and other law enforcement authorities in or outside the UK or held in connection with, or as a result of, an investigation of an offence inside or outside the UK.*

See Annex F regarding the retention and use of fingerprints and samples taken with consent for elimination purposes.

D:6F *Samples of urine and non-intimate samples taken in accordance with sections 63B and 63C of PACE may not be used for identification purposes in accordance with this Code. See Code C, Note for guidance 17D.*

ANNEX A

Video Identification

(a) *General*

D:1. The arrangements for obtaining and ensuring the availability of a suitable set of images to be ★**A-139** used in a video identification must be the responsibility of an identification officer (see paragraph 3.11 of this code) who has no direct involvement with the case.

D:2. The set of images must include the suspect and at least eight other people who, so far as possible, and subject to paragraph 7, resemble the suspect in age, general appearance and position in life. Only one suspect shall appear in any set unless there are two suspects of roughly similar appearance, in which case they may be shown together with at least twelve other people.

D:2A If the suspect has an unusual physical feature, *e.g.*, a facial scar, tattoo or distinctive hairstyle or hair colour which does not appear on the images of the other people that are available to be used, steps may be taken to:

(a) conceal the location of the feature on the images of the suspect and the other people; or

(b) replicate that feature on the images of the other people.

For these purposes, the feature may be concealed or replicated electronically or by any other method which it is practicable to use to ensure that the images of the suspect and other people resemble each other. The identification officer has discretion to choose whether to conceal or replicate the feature and the method to be used.

D:2B If the identification officer decides that a feature should be concealed or replicated, the reason for the decision and whether the feature was concealed or replicated in the images shown to any eye-witness shall be recorded.

D:2C If the eye-witness requests to view any image where an unusual physical feature has been concealed or replicated without the feature being concealed or replicated, the identification officer has discretion to allow the eye-witness to view such image(s) if they are available.

D:3. The images used to conduct a video identification shall, as far as possible, show the suspect and other people in the same positions or carrying out the same sequence of movements. They shall also show the suspect and other people under identical conditions unless the identification officer reasonably believes:

    (a) because of the suspect's failure or refusal to co-operate or other reasons, it is not practicable for the conditions to be identical; and

    (b) any difference in the conditions would not direct an eye-witness' attention to any individual image.

D:4. The reasons identical conditions are not practicable shall be recorded on forms provided for the purpose.

D:5. Provision must be made for each person shown to be identified by number.

D:6. If police officers are shown, any numerals or other identifying badges must be concealed. If a prison inmate is shown, either as a suspect or not, then either all, or none of, the people shown should be in prison clothing.

★**A-140**
D:7. The suspect or their solicitor, friend, or appropriate adult must be given a reasonable opportunity to see the complete set of images before it is shown to any eye-witness. If the suspect has a reasonable objection to the set of images or any of the participants, the suspect shall be asked to state the reasons for the objection. Steps shall, if practicable, be taken to remove the grounds for objection. If this is not practicable, the suspect and/or their representative shall be told why their objections cannot be met and the objection, the reason given for it and why it cannot be met shall be recorded on forms provided for the purpose. The requirement in paragraph 2 that the images of the other people 'resemble' the suspect does not require the images to be identical or extremely similar (see *Note A1*).

D:8. Before the images are shown in accordance with paragraph 7, the suspect or their solicitor shall be provided with details of the first description of the suspect by any eye-witnesses who are to attend the video identification. When a broadcast or publication is made, as in paragraph 3.38(a), the suspect or their solicitor must also be allowed to view any material released to the media by the police for the purpose of recognising or tracing the suspect, provided it is practicable and would not unreasonably delay the investigation.

D:9. No unauthorised people may be present when the video identification is conducted. The suspect's solicitor, if practicable, shall be given reasonable notification of the time and place the video identification is to be conducted. The suspect's solicitor may only be present at the video identification on request and with the prior agreement of the identification officer, if the officer is satisfied that the solicitor's presence will not deter or distract any eye-witness from viewing the images and making an identification. If the identification officer is not satisfied and does not agree to the request, the reason must be recorded. The solicitor must be informed of the decision and the reason for it. and that they may then make representations about why they should be allowed to be present. The representations may be made orally or in writing, in person or remotely by electronic communication and must be recorded. These representations must be considered by an officer of at least the rank of inspector who is not involved with the investigation and responsibility for this may not be delegated under paragraph 3.11. If, after considering the representations, the officer is satisfied that the solicitor's presence will deter or distract the eye-witness, the officer shall inform the solicitor of the decision and reason for it and ensure that any response by the solicitor is also recorded. If allowed to be present, the solicitor is not entitled to communicate in any way with an eye-witness during the procedure but this does not prevent the solicitor from communicating with the identification officer. The suspect may not be present when the images are shown to any eye-witness and is not entitled to be informed of the time and place the video identification procedure is to be conducted. The video identification procedure itself shall be recorded on video with sound. The recording must show all persons present within the sight or hearing of the eye-witness whilst the images are being viewed and must include what the eye-witness says and what is said to them by the identification officer and by any other person present at the video identification procedure. A supervised viewing of the recording of the video identification procedure by the suspect and/or their solicitor may be arranged on request, at the discretion of the investigating officer. Where the recording of the video identification procedure is to be shown to the suspect and/or their solicitor, the investigating officer may arrange for anything in the recording that might allow the eye-witness to be identified to be concealed if the investigating officer considers that this is justified (see *Note A2*). In accordance with paragraph 2.18, the investigating officer may also arrange for anything in that recording that might allow any police officers or police staff to be identified to be concealed.

(b) *Conducting the video identification*

★**A-141**
D:10. The identification officer is responsible for making the appropriate arrangements to make sure, before they see the set of images, eye-witnesses are not able to communicate with each other about the case, see any of the images which are to be shown, see, or be reminded of, any photograph or description of the suspect or be given any other indication as to the suspect's identity, or overhear an eye-witness who has already seen the material. There must be no discussion with the eye-witness about the composition of the set of images and they must not be told whether a previous eye-witness has made any identification.

D:11. Only one eye-witness may see the set of images at a time. Immediately before the images are shown, the eye-witness shall be told that the person they saw on a specified earlier occasion may, or may not, appear in the images they are shown and that if they cannot make an identification, they should say so. The eye-witness shall be advised that at any point, they may ask to see a particular part of the set of images or to have a particular image frozen for them to study. Furthermore, it should be pointed out to the eye-witness that there is no limit on how many times they can view the whole set of images or any part of them. However, they should be asked not to make any decision as to whether the person they saw is on the set of images until they have seen the whole set at least twice.

D:12. Once the eye-witness has seen the whole set of images at least twice and has indicated that they do not want to view the images, or any part of them, again, the eye-witness shall be asked to say whether the individual they saw in person on a specified earlier occasion has been shown and, if so, to identify them by number of the image. The eye-witness will then be shown that image to confirm the identification, see paragraph 17.

D:13. Care must be taken not to direct the eye-witness' attention to any one individual image or give any indication of the suspect's identity. Where an eye-witness has previously made an identification by photographs, or a computerised or artist's composite or similar likeness, they must not be reminded of such a photograph or composite likeness once a suspect is available for identification by other means in accordance with this code. Nor must the eyewitness be reminded of any description of the suspect.

D:13A. If after the video identification procedure has ended, the eye-witness informs any police officer or police staff involved in the post-viewing arrangements that they wish to change their decision about their identification, or they have not made an identification when in fact they could have made one, an accurate record of the words used by the eye-witness and of the circumstances immediately after the procedure ended, shall be made. If the eyewitness has not had an opportunity to communicate with other people about the procedure, the identification officer has the discretion to allow the eye-witness a second opportunity to make an identification by repeating the video identification procedure using the same images but in different positions.

D:14. After the procedure, action required in accordance with paragraph 3.40 applies.

(c) *Image security and destruction*

D:15. Arrangements shall be made for all relevant material containing sets of images used for specific identification procedures to be kept securely and their movements accounted for. In particular, no-one involved in the investigation shall be permitted to view the material prior to it being shown to any witness.

D:16. As appropriate, paragraph 3.30 or 3.31 applies to the destruction or retention of relevant sets of images.

(d) *Documentation*

D:17. A record must be made of all those participating in, or seeing, the set of images whose names are known to the police.

D:18. A record of the conduct of the video identification must be made on forms provided for the purpose. This shall include anything said by the witness about any identifications or the conduct of the procedure and any reasons it was not practicable to comply with any of the provisions of this Code governing the conduct of video identifications. This record is in addition to any statement that is taken from any eye-witness after the procedure.

Note for guidance

D:A1 *The purpose of the video identification is to test the eye-witness' ability to distinguish the suspect from others and it would not be a fair test if all the images shown were identical or extremely similar to each other. The identification officer is responsible for ensuring that the images shown are suitable for the purpose of this test.*

D:A2 *The purpose of allowing the identity of the eye-witness to be concealed is to protect them in cases when there is information that suspects or their associates, may threaten the witness or cause them harm or when the investigating officer considers that special measures may be required to protect their identity during the criminal process.*

ANNEX B

Identification parades

(a) *General*

★**A-142**   D:1. A suspect must be given a reasonable opportunity to have a solicitor or friend present, and the suspect shall be asked to indicate on a second copy of the notice whether or not they wish to do so.

D:2. An identification parade may take place either in a normal room or one equipped with a screen permitting witnesses to see members of the identification parade without being seen. The procedures for the composition and conduct of the identification parade are the same in both cases, subject to paragraph 8 (except that an identification parade involving a screen may take place only when the suspect's solicitor, friend or appropriate adult is present or the identification parade is recorded on video).

D:3. Before the identification parade takes place, the suspect or their solicitor shall be provided with details of the first description of the suspect by any witnesses who are attending the identification parade. When a broadcast or publication is made as in paragraph 3.38(a), the suspect or their solicitor should also be allowed to view any material released to the media by the police for the purpose of identifying and tracing the suspect, provided it is practicable to do so and would not unreasonably delay the investigation.

(b) *Identification parades involving prison inmates*

D:4. If a prison inmate is required for identification, and there are no security problems about the person leaving the establishment, they may be asked to participate in an identification parade or video identification.

D:5. An identification parade may be held in a Prison Department establishment but shall be conducted, as far as practicable under normal identification parade rules. Members of the public shall make up the identification parade unless there are serious security, or control, objections to their admission to the establishment. In such cases, or if a group or video identification is arranged within the establishment, other inmates may participate. If an inmate is the suspect, they are not required to wear prison clothing for the identification parade unless the other people taking part are other inmates in similar clothing, or are members of the public who are prepared to wear prison clothing for the occasion.

(c) *Conduct of the identification parade*

★**A-143**   D:6. Immediately before the identification parade, the suspect must be reminded of the procedures governing its conduct and cautioned in the terms of Code C, paras 10.5 or 10.6, as appropriate.

D:7. All unauthorised people must be excluded from the place where the identification parade is held.

D:8. Once the identification parade has been formed, everything afterwards, in respect of it, shall take place in the presence and hearing of the suspect and any interpreter, solicitor, friend or appropriate adult who is present (unless the identification parade involves a screen, in which case everything said to, or by, any witness at the place where the identification parade is held, must be said in the hearing and presence of the suspect's solicitor, friend or appropriate adult or be recorded on video).

D:9. The identification parade shall consist of at least eight people (in addition to the suspect) who, so far as possible, resemble the suspect in age, height, general appearance and position in life. Only one suspect shall be included in an identification parade unless there are two suspects of roughly similar appearance, in which case they may be paraded together with at least twelve other people. In no circumstances shall more than two suspects be included in one identification parade and where there are separate identification parades, they shall be made up of different people.

D:10. If the suspect has an unusual physical feature, *e.g.*, a facial scar, tattoo or distinctive hairstyle or hair colour which cannot be replicated on other members of the identification parade, steps may be taken to conceal the location of that feature on the suspect and the other members of the identification parade if the suspect and their solicitor, or appropriate adult, agree. For example, by use of a plaster or a hat, so that all members of the identification parade resemble each other in general appearance.

D:11. When all members of a similar group are possible suspects, separate identification parades shall be held for each unless there are two suspects of similar appearance when they may appear on the same identification parade with at least twelve other members of the group who are not suspects. When police officers in uniform form an identification parade any numerals or other identifying badges shall be concealed.

D:12. When the suspect is brought to the place where the identification parade is to be held, they shall be asked if they have any objection to the arrangements for the identification parade or to any of the other participants in it and to state the reasons for the objection. The suspect may obtain advice from their solicitor or friend, if present, before the identification parade proceeds. If the suspect has a reasonable objection to the arrangements or any of the participants, steps shall, if practicable, be taken to remove the grounds for objection. When it is not practicable to do so, the suspect shall be told why their objections cannot be met and the objection, the reason given for it and why it cannot be met, shall be recorded on forms provided for the purpose.

D:13. The suspect may select their own position in the line, but may not otherwise interfere with the order of the people forming the line. When there is more than one witness, the suspect must be told, after each witness has left the room, that they can, if they wish, change position in the line. Each position in the line must be clearly numbered, whether by means of a number laid on the floor in front of each identification parade member or by other means.

D:14. Appropriate arrangements must be made to make sure, before witnesses attend the identification parade, they are not able to: ★**A-144**

 (i) communicate with each other about the case or overhear a witness who has already seen the identification parade;
 (ii) see any member of the identification parade;
 (iii) see, or be reminded of, any photograph or description of the suspect or be given any other indication as to the suspect's identity; or
 (iv) see the suspect before or after the identification parade.

D:15. The person conducting a witness to an identification parade must not discuss with them the composition of the identification parade and, in particular, must not disclose whether a previous witness has made any identification.

D:16. Witnesses shall be brought in one at a time. Immediately before the witness inspects the identification parade, they shall be told the person they saw on a specified earlier occasion may, or may not, be present and if they cannot make an identification, they should say so. The witness must also be told they should not make any decision about whether the person they saw is on the identification parade until they have looked at each member at least twice.

D:17. When the officer or police staff (see paragraph 3.11) conducting the identification procedure is satisfied the witness has properly looked at each member of the identification parade, they shall ask the witness whether the person they saw on a specified earlier occasion is on the identification parade and, if so, to indicate the number of the person concerned, see paragraph 28.

D:18. If the witness wishes to hear any identification parade member speak, adopt any specified posture or move, they shall first be asked whether they can identify any person(s) on the identification parade on the basis of appearance only. When the request is to hear members of the identification parade speak, the witness shall be reminded that the participants in the identification parade have been chosen on the basis of physical appearance only. Members of the identification parade may then be asked to comply with the witness' request to hear them speak, see them move or adopt any specified posture.

D:19. If the witness requests that the person they have indicated remove anything used for the purposes of paragraph 10 to conceal the location of an unusual physical feature, that person may be asked to remove it. ★**A-145**

D:20. If the witness makes an identification after the identification parade has ended, the suspect and, if present, their solicitor, interpreter or friend shall be informed. When this occurs, consideration should be given to allowing the witness a second opportunity to identify the suspect.

D:21 After the procedure, action required in accordance with paragraph 3.40 applies.

D:22. When the last witness has left, the suspect shall be asked whether they wish to make any comments on the conduct of the identification parade.

(d) *Documentation*

D:23. A video recording must normally be taken of the identification parade. If that is impracticable, a colour photograph must be taken. A copy of the video recording or photograph shall be supplied, on request, to the suspect or their solicitor within a reasonable time.

D:24. As appropriate, paragraph 3.30 or 3.31, should apply to any photograph or video taken as in paragraph 23.

D:25. If any person is asked to leave an identification parade because they are interfering with its conduct, the circumstances shall be recorded.

D:26. A record must be made of all those present at an identification parade whose names are known to the police.

D:27. If prison inmates make up an identification parade, the circumstances must be recorded.

D:28. A record of the conduct of any identification parade must be made on forms provided for the purpose. This shall include anything said by the witness or the suspect about any identifications or the conduct of the procedure, and any reasons it was not practicable to comply with any of this Code's provisions.

ANNEX C

Group identification

(a) *General*

★A-146   D:1. The purpose of this annex is to make sure, as far as possible, group identifications follow the principles and procedures for identification parades so the conditions are fair to the suspect in the way they test the witness' ability to make an identification.

D:2. Group identifications may take place either with the suspect's consent and co-operation or covertly without their consent.

D:3. The location of the group identification is a matter for the identification officer, although the officer may take into account any representations made by the suspect, appropriate adult, their solicitor or friend.

D:4. The place where the group identification is held should be one where other people are either passing by or waiting around informally, in groups such that the suspect is able to join them and be capable of being seen by the witness at the same time as others in the group. For example people leaving an escalator, pedestrians walking through a shopping centre, passengers on railway and bus stations, waiting in queues or groups or where people are standing or sitting in groups in other public places.

D:5. If the group identification is to be held covertly, the choice of locations will be limited by the places where the suspect can be found and the number of other people present at that time. In these cases, suitable locations might be along regular routes travelled by the suspect, including buses or trains or public places frequented by the suspect.

★A-147   D:6. Although the number, age, sex, race and general description and style of clothing of other people present at the location cannot be controlled by the identification officer, in selecting the location the officer must consider the general appearance and numbers of people likely to be present. In particular, the officer must reasonably expect that over the period the witness observes the group, they will be able to see, from time to time, a number of others whose appearance is broadly similar to that of the suspect.

D:7. A group identification need not be held if the identification officer believes, because of the unusual appearance of the suspect, none of the locations it would be practicable to use, satisfy the requirements of paragraph 6 necessary to make the identification fair.

D:8. Immediately after a group identification procedure has taken place (with or without the suspect's consent), a colour photograph or video should be taken of the general scene, if practicable, to give a general impression of the scene and the number of people present. Alternatively, if it is practicable, the group identification may be video recorded.

D:9. If it is not practicable to take the photograph or video in accordance with paragraph 8, a photograph or film of the scene should be taken later at a time determined by the identification officer if the officer considers it practicable to do so.

D:10. An identification carried out in accordance with this code remains a group identification even though, at the time of being seen by the witness, the suspect was on their own rather than in a group.

D:11. Before the group identification takes place, the suspect or their solicitor shall be provided with details of the first description of the suspect by any witnesses who are to attend the identification. When a broadcast or publication is made, as in paragraph 3.38(a), the suspect or their solicitor should also be allowed to view any material released by the police to the media for the purposes of identifying and tracing the suspect, provided that it is practicable and would not unreasonably delay the investigation.

D:12. After the procedure, action required in accordance with paragraph 3.40 applies.

(b) *Identification with the consent of the suspect*

★A-148   D:13. A suspect must be given a reasonable opportunity to have a solicitor or friend present. They shall be asked to indicate on a second copy of the notice whether or not they wish to do so.

D:14. The witness, the person carrying out the procedure and the suspect's solicitor, appropriate adult, friend or any interpreter for the witness, may be concealed from the sight of the individuals in the group they are observing, if the person carrying out the procedure considers this assists the conduct of the identification.

D:15. The person conducting a witness to a group identification must not discuss with them the forthcoming group identification and, in particular, must not disclose whether a previous witness has made any identification.

D:16. Anything said to, or by, the witness during the procedure about the identification should be said in the presence and hearing of those present at the procedure.

D:17. Appropriate arrangements must be made to make sure, before witnesses attend the group identification, they are not able to:

    (i) communicate with each other about the case or overhear a witness who has already been given an opportunity to see the suspect in the group;

    (ii) see the suspect; or

    (iii) see, or be reminded of, any photographs or description of the suspect or be given any other indication of the suspect's identity.

D:18. Witnesses shall be brought one at a time to the place where they are to observe the group. Immediately before the witness is asked to look at the group, the person conducting the procedure shall tell them that the person they saw on a specified earlier occasion may, or may not, be in the group and that if they cannot make an identification, they should say so. The witness shall be asked to observe the group in which the suspect is to appear. The way in which the witness should do this will depend on whether the group is moving or stationary.

Moving group

D:19. When the group in which the suspect is to appear is moving, *e.g.* leaving an escalator, the provisions of paragraphs 20 to 24 should be followed.   ★**A-149**

D:20. If two or more suspects consent to a group identification, each should be the subject of separate identification procedures. These may be conducted consecutively on the same occasion.

D:21. The person conducting the procedure shall tell the witness to observe the group and ask them to point out any person they think they saw on the specified earlier occasion.

D:22. Once the witness has been informed as in paragraph 21 the suspect should be allowed to take whatever position in the group they wish.

D:23. When the witness points out a person as in paragraph 21 they shall, if practicable, be asked to take a closer look at the person to confirm the identification. If this is not practicable, or they cannot confirm the identification, they shall be asked how sure they are that the person they have indicated is the relevant person.

D:24. The witness should continue to observe the group for the period which the person conducting the procedure reasonably believes is necessary in the circumstances for them to be able to make comparisons between the suspect and other individuals of broadly similar appearance to the suspect as in paragraph 6.

Stationary groups

D:25. When the group in which the suspect is to appear is stationary, *e.g.* people waiting in a queue, the provisions of paragraphs 26 to 29 should be followed.   ★**A-150**

D:26. If two or more suspects consent to a group identification, each should be subject to separate identification procedures unless they are of broadly similar appearance when they may appear in the same group. When separate group identifications are held, the groups must be made up of different people.

D:27. The suspect may take whatever position in the group they wish. If there is more than one witness, the suspect must be told, out of the sight and hearing of any witness, that they can, if they wish, change their position in the group.

D:28. The witness shall be asked to pass along, or amongst, the group and to look at each person in the group at least twice, taking as much care and time as possible according to the circumstances, before making an identification. Once the witness has done this, they shall be asked whether the person they saw on the specified earlier occasion is in the group and to indicate any such person by whatever means the person conducting the procedure considers appropriate in the circumstances. If this is not practicable, the witness shall be asked to point out any person they think they saw on the earlier occasion.

D:29. When the witness makes an indication as in paragraph 28, arrangements shall be made, if practicable, for the witness to take a closer look at the person to confirm the identification. If this is not practicable, or the witness is unable to confirm the identification, they shall be asked how sure they are that the person they have indicated is the relevant person.

All cases

★**A-151**   D:30. If the suspect unreasonably delays joining the group, or having joined the group, deliberately conceals themselves [*sic*] from the sight of the witness, this may be treated as a refusal to co-operate in a group identification.

D:31. If the witness identifies a person other than the suspect, that person should be informed what has happened and asked if they are prepared to give their name and address. There is no obligation upon any member of the public to give these details. There shall be no duty to record any details of any other member of the public present in the group or at the place where the procedure is conducted.

D:32. When the group identification has been completed, the suspect shall be asked whether they wish to make any comments on the conduct of the procedure.

D:33. If the suspect has not been previously informed, they shall be told of any identifications made by the witnesses.

(c) Group Identification without the suspect's consent

★**A-152**   D:34. Group identifications held covertly without the suspect's consent should, as far as practicable, follow the rules for conduct of group identification by consent.

D:35. A suspect has no right to have a solicitor, appropriate adult or friend present as the identification will take place without the knowledge of the suspect.

D:36. Any number of suspects may be identified at the same time.

(d) Identifications in police stations

D:37. Group identifications should only take place in police stations for reasons of safety, security or because it is not practicable to hold them elsewhere.

D:38. The group identification may take place either in a room equipped with a screen permitting witnesses to see members of the group without being seen, or anywhere else in the police station that the identification officer considers appropriate.

D:39. Any of the additional safeguards applicable to identification parades should be followed if the identification officer considers it is practicable to do so in the circumstances.

(e) Identifications involving prison inmates

★**A-153**   D:40. A group identification involving a prison inmate may only be arranged in the prison or at a police station.

D:41. When a group identification takes place involving a prison inmate, whether in a prison or in a police station, the arrangements should follow those in paragraphs 37 to 39. If a group identification takes place within a prison, other inmates may participate. If an inmate is the suspect, they do not have to wear prison clothing for the group identification unless the other participants are wearing the same clothing.

(f) Documentation

D:42 When a photograph or video is taken as in paragraph 8 or 9, a copy of the photograph or video shall be supplied on request to the suspect or their solicitor within a reasonable time.

D:43. Paragraph 3.30 or 3.31, as appropriate, shall apply when the photograph or film taken in accordance with paragraph 8 or 9 includes the suspect.

D:44. A record of the conduct of any group identification must be made on forms provided for the purpose. This shall include anything said by the witness or suspect about any identifications or the conduct of the procedure and any reasons why it was not practicable to comply with any of the provisions of this Code governing the conduct of group identifications.

ANNEX D

Confrontation by an eye-witness

★**A-154**   D:1. Before the confrontation takes place, the eye-witness must be told that the person they saw on a specified earlier occasion may, or may not, be the person they are to confront and that if they are not that person, then the witness should say so.

D:2. Before the confrontation takes place the suspect or their solicitor shall be provided with details of the first description of the suspect given by any eye-witness who is to attend. When a broadcast or publication is made, as in paragraph 3.38(a), the suspect or their solicitor should also be allowed to view any material released to the media for the purposes of recognising or tracing the suspect, provided it is practicable to do so and would not unreasonably delay the investigation.

D:3. Force may not be used to make the suspect's face visible to the eye-witness.

D:4. Confrontation must take place in the presence of the suspect's solicitor, interpreter or friend unless this would cause unreasonable delay.

D:5. The suspect shall be confronted independently by each eye-witness, who shall be asked "Is this the person?". If the eye-witness identifies the person but is unable to confirm the identification, they shall be asked how sure they are that the person is the one they saw on the earlier occasion.

D:6. The confrontation should normally take place in the police station, either in a normal room or one equipped with a screen permitting the eye-witness to see the suspect without being seen. In both cases, the procedures are the same except that a room equipped with a screen may be used only when the suspect's solicitor, friend or appropriate adult is present or the confrontation is recorded on video.

D:7. After the procedure, action required in accordance with paragraph 3.40 applies.

ANNEX E

Showing photographs to eye-witnesses

D:1. An officer of sergeant rank or above shall be responsible for supervising and directing the showing of photographs. The actual showing may be done by another officer or police staff, see paragraph 3.11. **★A-155**

D:2. The supervising officer must confirm the first description of the suspect given by the eyewitness has been recorded before they are shown the photographs. If the supervising officer is unable to confirm the description has been recorded they shall postpone showing the photographs.

D:3. Only one eye-witness shall be shown photographs at any one time. Each witness shall be given as much privacy as practicable and shall not be allowed to communicate with any other eye-witness in the case.

D:4. The eye-witness shall be shown not less than twelve photographs at a time, which shall, as far as possible, all be of a similar type.

D:5. When the eye-witness is shown the photographs, they shall be told the photograph of the person they saw on a specified earlier occasion may, or may not, be amongst them and if they cannot make an identification, they should say so. The eye-witness shall also be told they should not make a decision until they have viewed at least twelve photographs. The eye-witness shall not be prompted or guided in any way but shall be left to make any selection without help.

D:6. If an eye-witness makes an identification from photographs, unless the person identified is otherwise eliminated from enquiries or is not available, other eye-witnesses shall not be shown photographs. But both they, and the eye-witness who has made the identification, shall be asked to attend a video identification, an identification parade or group identification unless there is no dispute about the suspect's identification.

D:7. If the eye-witness makes a selection but is unable to confirm the identification, the person showing the photographs shall ask them how sure they are that the photograph they have indicated is the person they saw on the specified earlier occasion. **★A-156**

D:8. When the use of a computerised or artist's composite or similar likeness has led to there being a known suspect who can be asked to participate in a video identification, appear on an identification parade or participate in a group identification, that likeness shall not be shown to other potential eye-witnesses.

D:9. When an eye-witness attending a video identification, an identification parade or group identification has previously been shown photographs or computerised or artist's composite or similar likeness (and it is the responsibility of the officer in charge of the investigation to make the identification officer aware that this is the case), the suspect and their solicitor must be informed of this fact before the identification procedure takes place.

D:10. None of the photographs shown shall be destroyed, whether or not an identification is made, since they may be required for production in court. The photographs shall be numbered and a separate photograph taken of the frame or part of the album from which the eye-witness made an identification as an aid to reconstituting it.

(b) *Documentation*

D:11. Whether or not an identification is made, a record shall be kept of the showing of photographs on forms provided for the purpose. This shall include anything said by the eye-witness about any identification or the conduct of the procedure, any reasons it was not practicable to comply with any of the provisions of this Code governing the showing of photographs and the name and rank of the supervising officer. **★A-157**

D:12. The supervising officer shall inspect and sign the record as soon as practicable.

ANNEX F

Fingerprints, Samples and Footwear Impressions—Destruction and Speculative Searches

Part A: Fingerprints and samples

★A-158   Paragraphs 1 to 12 summarise and update information which is available at:

https://www.gov.uk/government/publications/protection-of-freedoms-act-2012-dna-and-fingerpri
ntprovisions/protection-of-freedoms-act-2012-how-dna-and-fingerprint-evidence-is-protected-in-law

DNA samples

D:1. A DNA sample is an individual's biological material, containing all of their genetic information. The Act requires all DNA samples to be destroyed within 6 months of being taken. This allows sufficient time for the sample to be analysed and a DNA profile to be produced for use on the database.

D:2. The only exception to this is if the sample is or may be required for disclosure as evidence, in which case it may be retained for as long as this need exists under the Criminal Procedure and Investigations Act 1996.

DNA profiles and fingerprints

D:3. A DNA profile consists of a string of 16 pairs of numbers and 2 letters (XX for women, XY for men) to indicate gender. This number string is stored on the National DNA Database (NDNAD). It allows the person to be identified if they leave their DNA at a crime scene.

D:4. Fingerprints are usually scanned electronically from the individual in custody and the images stored on IDENT1, the national fingerprint database.

Retention Periods: Fingerprints and DNA profiles

D:5. The retention period depends on the outcome of the investigation of the recordable offence in connection with which the fingerprints and DNA samples was taken, the age of the person at the time the offence was committed and whether the *recordable* offence is a qualifying offence and whether it is an excluded offence (See Table Notes (a) to (c)) , as follows:

Table - Retention periods

(a) Convictions

Age when offence committed	Outcome	Retention Period
Any age	Convicted or given a caution or youth caution for a recordable offence which is also a qualifying offence	Indefinite
18 or over	Convicted or given a caution for a recordable offence which is NOT a qualifying offence	Indefinite
Under 18	Convicted or given a youth caution for a recordable offence which is NOT a qualifying offence.	1st conviction or youth caution – 5 years plus length of any prison sentence. Indefinite if prison sentence 5 years or more 2nd conviction or youth caution: indefinite

(b) Non-convictions

Age when offence committed	Outcome	Retention Period
Any age	Charged but not convicted of a recordable qualifying offence.	3 years plus a 2-year extension if granted by a District Judge (or indefinite if the individual has a previous conviction for a

Age when offence committed	Outcome	Retention Period
		recordable offence which is not excluded)
Any age	Arrested for, but not charged with, a recordable qualifying offence	3 years if granted by the Biometrics Commissioner plus a 2-year extension if granted by a District Judge (or indefinite if the individual has a previous conviction for a recordable offence which is not excluded)
Any age	Arrested for or charged with a recordable offence which is not a qualifying offence.	Indefinite if the person has a previous conviction for a recordable offence which is not excluded otherwise NO RETENTION)
18 or over	Given Penalty Notice for Disorder for recordable offence	2 years

Table notes:

(a) A "recordable" offence is one for which the police are required to keep a record. Generally speaking, these are imprisonable offences; however, it also includes a number of nonimprisonable offences such as begging and taxi touting. The police are not able to take or retain the DNA or fingerprints of an individual who is arrested for an offence which is not recordable.

(b) A "qualifying" offence is one listed under section 65A of the Police and Criminal Evidence Act 1984 (the list comprises sexual, violent, terrorism and burglary offences).

(c) An "excluded" offence is a recordable offence which is not a qualifying offence, was committed when the individual was under 18, for which they received a sentence of fewer than 5 years imprisonment and is the only recordable offence for which the person has been convicted

Speculative searches

D:6. Where the retention framework above requires the deletion of a person's DNA profile and fingerprints, the Act first allows a *speculative search* of their DNA and fingerprints against DNA and fingerprints obtained from crime scenes which are stored on NDNAD and IDENT1. Once the speculative search has been completed, the profile and fingerprints are deleted unless there is a match, in which case they will be retained for the duration of any investigation and thereafter in accordance with the retention framework (*e.g.* if that investigation led to a conviction for a qualifying offence, they would be retained indefinitely).

Extensions of retention period

D:7. For qualifying offences, PACE allows chief constables to apply for extensions to the given retention periods for DNA profiles and fingerprints if considered necessary for prevention or detection of crime.

D:8. Section 20 of the Protection of Freedoms Act 2012 established the independent office of Commissioner for the Retention and Use of Biometric Material ("the 'Biometrics Commissioner'). For details, see https://www.gov.uk/government/organisations/biometricscommissioner.

D:9. Where an individual is arrested for, but not charged with, a qualifying offence, their DNA profile and fingerprint record will normally be deleted. However, the police can apply to the Biometrics Commissioner for permission to retain their DNA profile and fingerprint record for a period of 3 years. The application must be made within 28 days of the decision not to proceed with a prosecution.

D:10. If the police make such an application, the Biometrics Commissioner would first give both them and the arrested individual an opportunity to make written representations and then, taking into account factors including the age and vulnerability of the victim(s) of the alleged offences, and their relationship to the suspect, make a decision on whether or not retention is appropriate.

D:11. If after considering the application, the Biometrics Commissioner decides that retention is not appropriate, the DNA profile and fingerprint record in question must be destroyed.

D:12. If the Biometrics Commissioner agrees to allow retention, the police will be able to retain that individual's DNA profile and fingerprint record for a period of 3 years from the date the samples were taken. At the end of that period, the police will be able to apply to a District Judge (magistrates' courts) for a single 2 year extension to the retention period. If the application is rejected, the force must then destroy the DNA profile and fingerprint record.

Part B: Footwear impressions

D:13. Footwear impressions taken in accordance with section 61A of PACE (see paragraphs 4.16 to 4.21) may be retained for as long as is necessary for purposes related to the prevention or detection of crime, the investigation of an offence or the conduct of a prosecution.

Part C: Fingerprints, samples and footwear impressions taken in connection with a criminal investigation from a person not suspected of committing the offence under investigation for elimination purposes.

★**A-159**   D:14. When fingerprints, footwear impressions or DNA samples are taken from a person in connection with an investigation and the person is *not suspected of having committed the offence*, see *Note F1*, they must be destroyed as soon as they have fulfilled the purpose for which they were taken unless:

    (a) they were taken for the purposes of an investigation of an offence for which a person has been convicted; and

    (b) fingerprints, footwear impressions or samples were also taken from the convicted person for the purposes of that investigation.

However, subject to paragraph 14, the fingerprints, footwear impressions and samples, and the information derived from samples, may not be used in the investigation of any offence or in evidence against the person who is, or would be, entitled to the destruction of the fingerprints, footwear impressions and samples, see *Note F2*.

D:15. The requirement to destroy fingerprints, footwear impressions and DNA samples, and information derived from samples and restrictions on their retention and use in paragraph 14 do not apply if the person gives their written consent for their fingerprints, footwear impressions or sample to be retained and used after they have fulfilled the purpose for which they were taken, see *Note F1*.

This consent can be withdrawn at any time.

D:16. When a person's fingerprints, footwear impressions or sample are to be destroyed:

    (a) any copies of the fingerprints and footwear impressions must also be destroyed; and

    (b) neither the fingerprints, footwear impressions, the sample, or any information derived from the sample, may be used in the investigation of any offence or in evidence against the person who is, or would be, entitled to its destruction.

Notes for guidance

★**A-160**   D:F1 *Fingerprints, footwear impressions and samples given voluntarily for the purposes of elimination play an important part in many police investigations. It is, therefore, important to make sure innocent volunteers are not deterred from participating and their consent to their fingerprints, footwear impressions and DNA being used for the purposes of a specific investigation is fully informed and voluntary. If the police or volunteer seek to have the fingerprints, footwear impressions or samples retained for use after the specific investigation ends, it is important the volunteer's consent to this is also fully informed and voluntary. The volunteer must be told that they may withdraw their consent at any time.*

The consent must be obtained in writing using current nationally agreed forms provided for police use according to the purpose for which the consent is given. This purpose may be either:

    • *DNA/fingerprints/footwear impressions - to be used only for the purposes of a specific investigation; or*

    • *DNA/fingerprints/footwear impressions - to be used in the specific investigation and retained by the police for future use.*

To minimise the risk of confusion:

    • *if a police officer or member of police staff has any doubt about:*

        - *how the consent forms should be completed and signed, or*

        - *whether a consent form they propose to use and refer to is fully compliant with the current nationally agreed form,*

    the relevant national police helpdesk (for DNA or fingerprints) should be contacted.

    • *in each case, the meaning of consent should be explained orally and care taken to ensure the oral explanation accurately reflects the contents of the written form the person is to be asked to sign.*

★**A-161**   D:F2 *The provisions for the retention of fingerprints, footwear impressions and samples in paragraph 15 allow for all fingerprints, footwear impressions and samples in a case to be available for any subsequent miscarriage of justice investigation.*

ANNEX G

Requirement for a person to attend a police station for fingerprints and samples (paragraphs 4.4, 6.2a and 6.6a).

D:1. A requirement under Schedule 2A for a person to attend a police station to have fingerprints or samples taken:　★**A-161a**

    (a) must give the person a period of at least seven days within which to attend the police station; and

    (b) may direct them to attend at a specified time of day or between specified times of day.

D:2. When specifying the period and times of attendance, the officer making the requirements must consider whether the fingerprints or samples could reasonably be taken at a time when the person is required to attend the police station for any other reason. See *Note G1*.

D:3. An officer of the rank of inspector or above may authorise a period shorter than 7 days if there is an urgent need for person's fingerprints or sample for the purposes of the investigation of an offence. The fact of the authorisation and the reasons for giving it must be recorded as soon as practicable.

D:4. The constable making a requirement and the person to whom it applies may agree to vary it so as to specify any period within which, or date or time at which, the person is to attend. However, variation shall not have effect for the purposes of enforcement, unless it is confirmed by the constable in writing.

Notes for guidance

D:G1 *The specified period within which the person is to attend need not fall within the period allowed (if applicable) for making the requirement.*　★**A-161b**

D:G2 *To justify the arrest without warrant of a person who fails to comply with a requirement, (see paragraphs 4.4(b) and 6.7(b) above), the officer making the requirement, or confirming a variation, should be prepared to explain how, when and where the requirement was made or the variation was confirmed and what steps were taken to ensure the person understood what to do and the consequences of not complying with the requirement.*

(6) Tape-recording of interviews

The text that follows is of the version of the code that came into force on February 2, 2016: see **A-162** *ante*, Appendix A-1.

For further details of the application of the code, and as to the commencement of the governing legislation, see § 15-245 of the main work.

E. CODE OF PRACTICE ON AUDIO RECORDING INTERVIEWS WITH SUSPECTS

Commencement—transitional arrangements

This code applies to interviews carried out after 00.00 on [on February 2, 2016] notwithstanding that the interview may have commenced before that time.　**A-162a**

E:1 General

E:1.0 The procedures in this code must be used fairly, responsibly, with respect for the people to whom they apply and without unlawful discrimination. Under the Equality Act 2010, s.149, when police officers are carrying out their functions, they also have a duty to have due regard to the need to eliminate unlawful discrimination, harassment and victimisation, to advance equality of opportunity between people who share a relevant protected characteristic and people who do not share it, and to take steps to foster good relations between those persons. See *Note 1B*.　**A-163**

E:1.1 This code of practice must be readily available for consultation by:

    • police officers;

    • police staff;

    • detained persons;

    • members of the public.

E:1.2 The *Notes for Guidance* included are not provisions of this code.

E:1.3 Nothing in this code shall detract from the requirements of Code C, the code of practice for the detention, treatment and questioning of persons by police officers.

E:1.4 The interviews to which this code applies are described in section 3.

E:1.5 The term:

    • "appropriate adult" has the same meaning as in Code C, para. 1.7, and in the case of a

17-year-old suspect, includes the person called to fulfil that role in accordance with paragraph 1.5A of Code C;

- "solicitor" has the same meaning as in Code C, para. 6.12;
- "interview" has the same meaning as in Code C, para. 11.1A.

E:1.5A Recording of interviews shall be carried out openly to instil confidence in its reliability as an impartial and accurate record of the interview.

A-164

E:1.6 In this code:

(aa) "recording media" means any removable, physical audio recording medium (such as magnetic tape, optical disc or solid state memory) which can be played and copied;

(a) "designated person" means a person other than a police officer, designated under the Police Reform Act 2002, Pt 4, who has specified powers and duties of police officers conferred or imposed on them;

(b) any reference to a police officer includes a designated person acting in the exercise or performance of the powers and duties conferred or imposed on them by their designation; and

(c) "secure digital network" is a computer network system which enables an original interview recording to be stored as a digital multi media file or a series of such files, on a secure file server which is accredited by the National Accreditor for Police Information Systems in accordance with the UK Government Protective Marking Scheme. (See section 7 of this code.).

E:1.7 Sections 2 to 6 of this code set out the procedures and requirements which apply to all audio recorded interviews which are audio together with the provisions which apply only to interviews which are audio recorded using removable media. Section 7 sets out the provisions which apply to interviews which are audio recorded using a secure digital network and specifies the provisions in sections 2 to 6 which do not apply to secure digital network recording. The annex to this code sets out the terms and conditions of the exemption from the requirement to audio record interviews about indictable offences referred to in paragraph 3.1(a)(iii).

A-165

E:1.8 Nothing in this code prevents the custody officer, or other officer given custody of the detainee, from allowing police staff who are not designated persons to carry out individual procedures or tasks at the police station if the law allows. However, the officer remains responsible for making sure the procedures and tasks are carried out correctly in accordance with this code. Any such police staff must be:

(a) a person employed by a police force and under the control and direction of the chief officer of that force; or

(b) employed by a person with whom a police force has a contract for the provision of services relating to persons arrested or otherwise in custody.

E:1.9 Designated persons and other police staff must have regard to any relevant provisions of the codes of practice.

E:1.10 References to pocket book [*sic*] include any official report book issued to police officers or police staff.

E:1.11 References to a custody officer include those performing the functions of a custody officer as in paragraph 1.9 of Code C.

E:1.12 In the application of this code to the conduct and recording of an interview of a suspect who has not been arrested:

(a) references to the "custody officer" include references to an officer of the rank of sergeant or above who is not directly involved in the investigation of the offence(s);

(b) if the interview takes place elsewhere than at a police station, references to "interview room" include any place or location which the interviewer is satisfied will enable the interview to be conducted and recorded in accordance with this code and where the suspect is present voluntarily (see Note 1A); and

(c) provisions in addition to those which expressly apply to these interviews shall be followed insofar as they are relevant and can be applied in practice.

Notes for guidance

E:1A *An interviewer who is not sure, or has any doubt, about the suitability of a place or location of an interview to be carried out elsewhere than at a police station, should consult an officer of the rank of sergeant or above for advice.*

E:1B *In paragraph 1.0, the "relevant protected characteristics" are: age, disability, gender reassignment, pregnancy and maternity, race, religion/belief, sex and sexual orientation.*

E:2 Recording and sealing master recordings

E:2.1 [*Not used.*]

E:2.2 One recording, the master recording, will be sealed in the suspect's presence. A second recording will be used as a working copy. The master recording is any of the recordings made by a multi-deck/drive machine or the only recording made by a single deck/drive machine. The working copy is one of the other recordings made by a multi-deck/drive machine or a copy of the master recording made by a single deck/drive machine. (See *Note 2A.*)

[This paragraph does not apply to interviews recorded using a secure digital network, see paras 7.4 to 7.6.]

E:2.3 Nothing in this code requires the identity of officers or police staff conducting interviews to be recorded or disclosed:

    (a) [*not used*];

    (b) if the interviewer reasonably believes recording or disclosing their name might put them in danger.

In these cases interviewers should use warrant or other identification numbers and the name of their police station. Such instances and the reasons for them shall be recorded in the custody record or the interviewer's pocket book. See *Note 2C.*

Notes for guidance

E:2A *The purpose of sealing the master recording before it leaves the suspect's presence is to establish their* *confidence that the integrity of the recording is preserved. If a single deck/drive machine is used the working copy of the master recording must be made in the suspect's presence and without the master recording leaving their sight. The working copy shall be used for making further copies if needed.*

E:2B [*Not used.*]

E:2C *The purpose of paragraph 2.3(b) is to protect those involved in serious organised crime investigations or arrests of particularly violent suspects when there is reliable information that those arrested or their associates may threaten or cause harm to those involved. In cases of doubt, an officer of inspector rank or above should be consulted.*

E:3 Interviews to be audio recorded

E:3.1 Subject to paragraph 3.4, audio recording shall be used for any interview:

    (a) with a person cautioned under Code C, section 10 in respect of any indictable offence, which includes any offence triable either way, except when:

        (i) that person has been arrested and the interview takes place elsewhere than at a police station in accordance with Code C, paragraph 11.1 for which a written record would be required;

        (ii) the conditions in paragraph 3.3A are satisfied and authority not to audio record the interview is given by:

            • the custody officer in the case of a detained suspect, or

            • an officer of the rank of sergeant or above in the case of a suspect who has not been arrested and to whom paragraphs 3.21 and 3.22 of Code C (persons attending a police station or elsewhere voluntarily) apply; or

        (iii) the conditions in Part 1 of the annex to this code are satisfied, in which case the interview must be conducted and recorded in writing, in accordance with section 11 of Code C (see *Note 3A*);

    (b) which takes place as a result of an interviewer exceptionally putting further questions to a suspect about an indictable offence after they have been charged with, or told they may be prosecuted for, that offence, see Code C, para. 16.5 and *Note 3E*;

    (c) when an interviewer wants to tell a person, after they have been charged with, or informed they may be prosecuted for, an indictable offence, about any written statement or interview with another person, see Code C, para. 16.4 and *Note 3F*.

See *Note 3D.*

E:3.2 The Terrorism Act 2000 and the Counter-Terrorism Act 2008 make separate provisions for a code of practice for the video recording with sound of:

    • interviews of persons detained under section 41 of, or Schedule 7 to, the 2000 Act; and

    • post-charge questioning of persons authorised under section 22 or 23 of the 2008 Act.

The provisions of this code do not apply to such interviews. (See *Note 3C.*)

E:3.3 [*Not used.*]

E:3.3A The conditions referred to in paragraph 3.1(a)(ii) are:

(a) it is not reasonably practicable to audio record, or as the case may be, continue to audio record, the interview because of equipment failure or the unavailability of a suitable interview room or recording equipment; and

(b) the authorising officer considers, on reasonable grounds, that the interview or continuation of the interview should not be delayed until the failure has been rectified or until a suitable room or recording equipment becomes available.

In these cases:

- the interview must be recorded or continue to be recorded in writing in accordance with Code C, section 11; and
- the authorising officer shall record the specific reasons for not audio recording and the interviewer is responsible for ensuring that the written interview record shows the date and time of the authority, the authorising officer and where the authority is recorded. (See *Note 3B*.)

E:3.4 If a detainee refuses to go into or remain in a suitable interview room, see Code C, paragraph 12.5, and the custody officer considers, on reasonable grounds, that the interview should not be delayed the interview may, at the custody officer's discretion, be conducted in a cell using portable recording equipment or, if none is available, recorded in writing as in Code C, section 11. The reasons for this shall be recorded in accordance with Code C, para. 12.11.

E:3.5 The whole of each interview shall be audio recorded, including the taking and reading back of any statement.

E:3.6 A sign or indicator which is visible to the suspect must show when the recording equipment is recording.

Notes for guidance

A-169   E:3A *Nothing in this code is intended to preclude audio recording at police discretion of interviews at police stations or elsewhere with people cautioned in respect of offences not covered by paragraph 3.1, or responses made by persons after they have been charged with, or told they may be prosecuted for, an offence, provided this code is complied with.*

E:3B *A decision made in accordance with paragraphs 3.1(a)(ii) and 3.3A not to audio record an interview for any reason may be the subject of comment in court. The authorising offcer should be prepared to justify that decision.*

E:3C *If, during the course of an interview under this code, it becomes apparent that the interview should be conducted under the terrorism code for the video recording with sound of interviews, the interview should only continue in accordance with that code.*

E:3D *Attention is drawn to the provisions set out in Code C about the matters to be considered when deciding whether a detained person is fit to be interviewed.*

E:3E *Code C sets out the circumstances in which a suspect may be questioned about an offence after being charged with it.*

E:3F *Code C sets out the procedures to be followed when a person's attention is drawn after charge, to a statement made by another person. One method of bringing the content of an interview with another person to the notice of a suspect may be to play them a recording of that interview.*

E:4 The interview

(a) *General*

A-170   E:4.1 The provisions of Code C:

- sections 10 and 11, and the applicable *Notes for Guidance* apply to the conduct of interviews to which this code applies;
- paragraphs 11.7 to 11.14 apply only when a written record is needed.

E:4.2 Code C, paragraphs 10.10, 10.11 and Annex C describe the restriction on drawing adverse inferences from an arrested suspect's failure or refusal to say anything about their involvement in the offence when interviewed or after being charged or informed they may be prosecuted, and how it affects the terms of the caution and determines if and by whom a special warning under sections 36 and 37 of the Criminal Justice and Public Order Act 1994 can be given.

(b) *Commencement of interviews*

E:4.3 When the suspect is brought into the interview room the interviewer shall, without delay but in the suspect's sight, load the recorder with new recording media and set it to record. The recording media must be unwrapped or opened in the suspect's presence.

[This paragraph does not apply to interviews recorded using a secure digital network, see paras 7.4 and 7.5.]

E:4.4 The interviewer should tell the suspect about the recording process and point out the sign or indicator which shows that the recording equipment is activated and recording. See paragraph 3.6. The interviewer shall:

(a) explain that the interview is being audibly recorded;

(b) subject to paragraph 2.3, give their name and rank and that of any other interviewer present;

(c) ask the suspect and any other party present, *e.g.* the appropriate adult, a solicitor or interpreter, to identify themselves;

(d) state the date, time of commencement and place of the interview; and

(e) state the suspect will be given a notice about what will happen to the recording. [This subparagraph does not apply to interviews recorded using a secure digital network, see paras 7.4 and 7.6 to 7.7.]

See *Note 4A.*

E:4.4A Any person entering the interview room after the interview has commenced shall be invited by the interviewer to identify themselves for the purpose of the audio recording and state the reason why they have entered the interview room.

E:4.5 The interviewer shall:

• caution the suspect, see Code C, section 10; and

• if they are detained, remind them of their entitlement to free legal advice, see Code C, para. 11.2; or

• if they are not detained under arrest, explain this and their entitlement to free legal advice, see Code C, para. 3.21.

E:4.6 The interviewer shall put to the suspect any significant statement or silence, see Code C, paragraph 11.4.

(c) *Interviews with suspects who appear to have a hearing impediment*

E:4.7 If the suspect appears to have a hearing impediment, the interviewer shall make a written **A-171** note of the interview in accordance with Code C, at the same time as audio recording it in accordance with this code. (See *Notes 4B* and *4C.*)

(d) *Objections and complaints by the suspect*

E:4.8 If the suspect or an appropriate adult on their behalf objects to the interview being audibly recorded either at the outset, during the interview or during a break, the interviewer shall explain that the interview is being audibly recorded and that this code requires the objections to be recorded on the audio recording. When any objections have been audibly recorded or the suspect or appropriate adult have refused to have their objections recorded, the interviewer shall say they are turning off the recorder, give their reasons and turn it off. The interviewer shall then make a written record of the interview as in Code C, section 11. If, however, the interviewer reasonably considers they may proceed to question the suspect with the audio recording still on, the interviewer may do so. This procedure also applies in cases where the suspect has previously objected to the interview being visually recorded, see Code F, para. 4.8, and the investigating officer has decided to audibly record the interview. (See *Note 4D.*)

E:4.9 If in the course of an interview a complaint is made by or on behalf of the person being questioned concerning the provisions of this or any other codes, or it comes to the interviewer's notice that the person may have been treated improperly, the interviewer shall act as in Code C, para. 12.9. (See *Notes 4E* and *4F.*)

E:4.10 If the suspect indicates they want to tell the interviewer about matters not directly connected with the offence of which they are suspected and they are unwilling for these matters to be audio recorded, the suspect should be given the opportunity to tell the interviewer about these matter [*sic*] after the conclusion of the formal interview.

(e) *Changing recording media*

E:4.11 When the recorder shows the recording media only has a short time left to run, the interviewer shall so inform the person being interviewed and round off that part of the interview. If the interviewer leaves the room for a second set of recording media, the suspect shall not be left unattended. The interviewer will remove the recording media from the recorder and insert the new recording media which shall be unwrapped or opened in the suspect's presence. The recorder should be set to record on the new media. To avoid confusion between the recording media, the interviewer shall mark the media with an identification number immediately after it is removed from the recorder.

[This paragraph does not apply to interviews recorded using a secure digital network as this does not use removable media, see paras 1.6(c), 7.4 and 7.14 to 7.15.]

(f) Taking a break during interview

A-172

E:4.12 When a break is taken, the fact that a break is to be taken, the reason for it and the time shall be recorded on the audio recording.

E:4.12A When the break is taken and the interview room vacated by the suspect, the recording media shall be removed from the recorder and the procedures for the conclusion of an interview followed, see paragraph 4.18.

E:4.13 When a break is a short one and both the suspect and an interviewer remain in the interview room, the recording may be stopped. There is no need to remove the recording media and when the interview recommences the recording should continue on the same recording media. The time the interview recommences shall be recorded on the audio recording.

E:4.14 After any break in the interview the interviewer must, before resuming the interview, remind the person being questioned of their right to legal advice if they have not exercised it and that they remain under caution or, if there is any doubt, give the caution in full again. (See *Note 4G.*)

[Paragraphs 4.12 to 4.14 do not apply to interviews recorded using a secure digital network, see paras 7.4 and 7.8 to 7.10.]

(g) Failure of recording equipment

E:4.15 If there is an equipment failure which can be rectified quickly, *e.g.* by inserting new recording media, the interviewer shall follow the appropriate procedures as in paragraph 4.11. When the recording is resumed the interviewer shall explain what happened and record the time the interview recommences. If, however, it will not be possible to continue recording on that recorder and no replacement recorder is readily available, the interview may continue without being audibly recorded. If this happens, the interviewer shall seek the authority as in paragraph 3.3 of the custody officer, or as applicable, a sergeant or above. (See *Note 4H.*)

[This paragraph does not apply to interviews recorded using a secure digital network, see paras 7.4 and 7.11.]

(h) Removing recording media from the recorder

E:4.16 Recording media which is removed from the recorder during the interview shall be retained and the procedures in paragraph 4.18 followed.

[This paragraph does not apply to interviews recorded using a secure digital network as this does not use removable media, see 1.6(c), 7.4 and 7.14 to 7.15.]

(i) Conclusion of interview

E:4.17 At the conclusion of the interview, the suspect shall be offered the opportunity to clarify anything they have said and asked if there is anything they want to add.

E:4.18 At the conclusion of the interview, including the taking and reading back of any written statement, the time shall be recorded and the recording shall be stopped. The interviewer shall seal the master recording with a master recording label and treat it as an exhibit in accordance with force standing orders. The interviewer shall sign the label and ask the suspect and any third party present during the interview to sign it. If the suspect or third party refuse to sign the label an officer of at least the rank of inspector, or if not available the custody officer, or if the suspect has not been arrested, a sergeant, shall be called into the interview room and asked, subject to paragraph 2.3, to sign it.

E:4.19 The suspect shall be handed a notice which explains:
- how the audio recording will be used;
- the arrangements for access to it;
- that if they are charged or informed they will be prosecuted, a copy of the audio recording will be supplied as soon as practicable or as otherwise agreed between the suspect and the police or on the order of the court.

[Paragraphs 4.17 to 4.19 do not apply to interviews recorded using a secure digital network, see paras 7.4 and 7.12 to 7.13.]

Notes for guidance

E:4A *For the purpose of voice identification the interviewer should ask the suspect and any other people* **A-173**
present to identify themselves.

E:4B *This provision is to give a person who is deaf or has impaired hearing equivalent rights of access to the
full interview record as far as this is possible using audio recording.*

E:4C *The provisions of Code C on interpreters for suspects who do not appear to speak or understand English,
or who appear to have a hearing or speech impediment, continue to apply.*

E:4D *The interviewer should remember that a decision to continue recording against the wishes of the suspect
may be the subject of comment in court.*

E:4E *If the custody officer, or in the case of a person who has not been arrested, a sergeant, is called to deal
with the complaint, the recorder should, if possible, be left on until the officer has entered the room and spoken to
the person being interviewed. Continuation or termination of the interview should be at the interviewer's discretion pending action by an inspector under Code C, para. 9.2.*

E:4F *If the complaint is about a matter not connected with this code or Code C, the decision to continue is at* **A-174**
*the interviewer's discretion. When the interviewer decides to continue the interview, they shall tell the suspect that
at the conclusion of the interview, the complaint will be brought to the attention of the custody officer, or in the
case of a person who has not been arrested, a sergeant. When the interview is concluded the interviewer must, as
soon as practicable, inform the custody officer or, as the case may be, the sergeant, about the existence and nature
of the complaint made.*

E:4G *In considering whether to caution again after a break, the interviewer should bear in mind that they
may have to satisfy a court that the person understood that they were still under caution when the interview
resumed. The interviewer should also remember that it may be necessary to show to the court that nothing occurred during a break or between interviews which influenced the suspect's recorded evidence. After a break or at
the beginning of a subsequent interview, the interviewer should consider summarising on the record the reason for
the break and confirming this with the suspect.*

E:4H *Where the interview is being recorded and the media or the recording equipment fails, the interviewer
should stop the interview immediately. Where part of the interview is unaffected by the error and is still accessible
on the media, that part shall be copied and sealed in the suspect's presence as a master copy and the interview
recommenced using new equipment/media as required. Where the content of the interview has been lost in its
entirety, the media should be sealed in the suspect's presence and the interview begun again. If the recording
equipment cannot be fixed or no replacement is immediately available, the interview should be recorded in accordance with Code C, section 11.*

E:5 After the interview

E:5.1 The interviewer shall make a note in their pocket book that the interview has taken place **A-175**
and that it was audibly recorded, the time it commenced, its duration and date and identification
number of the master recording.

E:5.2 If no proceedings follow in respect of the person whose interview was recorded, the recording media must be kept securely as in paragraph 6.1 and *Note 6A*.

[This section (paras 5.1, 5.2 and Note 5A) does not apply to interviews recorded using a secure
digital network, see paras 7.4 and 7.14 to 7.15.]

Note for guidance

E:5A *Any written record of an audio recorded interview should be made in accordance with current national* **A-176**
*guidelines for police officers, police staff and CPS prosecutors concerned with the preparation, processing and
submission of prosecution files.*

E:6 Master recording security

(a) *General*

E:6.1 The officer in charge of each police station at which interviews with suspects are recorded or **A-177**
as the case may be, where recordings of interviews carried out elsewhere than at a police station are
held, shall make arrangements for master recordings to be kept securely and their movements accounted for on the same basis as material which may be used for evidential purposes, in accordance
with force standing orders. (See *Note 6A*.)

(b) *Breaking master recording seal for criminal proceedings*

E:6.2 A police officer has no authority to break the seal on a master recording which is required for criminal trial or appeal proceedings. If it is necessary to gain access to the master recording, the police officer shall arrange for its seal to be broken in the presence of a representative of the Crown Prosecution Service. The defendant or their legal adviser should be informed and given a reasonable opportunity to be present. If the defendant or their legal representative is present they shall be invited to re-seal and sign the master recording. If either refuses or neither is present this should be done by the representative of the Crown Prosecution Service. (See *Notes 6B* and *6C.*)

(c) *Breaking master recording seal: other cases*

E:6.3 The chief officer of police is responsible for establishing arrangements for breaking the seal of the master copy where no criminal proceedings result, or the criminal proceedings to which the interview relates have been concluded and it becomes necessary to break the seal. These arrangements should be those which the chief officer considers are reasonably necessary to demonstrate to the person interviewed and any other party who may wish to use or refer to the interview record that the master copy has not been tampered with and that the interview record remains accurate. (See *Note 6D.*)

E:6.3A Subject to paragraph 6.3C, a representative of each party must be given a reasonable opportunity to be present when the seal is broken and the master recording copied and resealed.

E:6.3B If one or more of the parties is not present when the master copy seal is broken because they cannot be contacted or refuse to attend or paragraph 6.6 applies, arrangements should be made for an independent person such as a custody visitor, to be present. Alternatively, or as an additional safeguard, arrangement should be made for a film or photographs to be taken of the procedure.

E:6.3C Paragraph 6.3A does not require a person to be given an opportunity to be present when:

(a) it is necessary to break the master copy seal for the proper and effective further investigation of the original offence or the investigation of some other offence; and

(b) the officer in charge of the investigation has reasonable grounds to suspect that allowing an opportunity might prejudice any such an investigation or criminal proceedings which may be brought as a result or endanger any person. (See *Note 6E.*)

(d) *Documentation*

E:6.4 When the master recording seal is broken, a record must be made of the procedure followed, including the date, time, place and persons present.

[This section (paras 6.1 to 6.4 and *Notes 6A* to *6E*) does not apply to interviews recorded using a secure digital network, see paras 7.4 and 7.14 to 7.15.]

Notes for guidance

A-178 E:6A *This section is concerned with the security of the master recording sealed at the conclusion of the interview. Care must be taken of working recordings because their loss or destruction may lead unnecessarily to the need to access master recordings.*

E:6B *If the master recording has been delivered to the Crown Court for their keeping after committal for trial the crown prosecutor will apply to the chief clerk of the Crown Court centre for the release of the recording for unsealing by the crown prosecutor.*

A-179 E:6C *Reference to the Crown Prosecution Service or to the crown prosecutor in this part of the code should be taken to include any other body or person with a statutory responsibility for the proceedings for which the police recorded interview is required.*

E:6D *The most common reasons for needing access to master copies that are not required for criminal proceedings arise from civil actions and complaints against police and civil actions between individuals arising out of allegations of crime investigated by police.*

E:6E *Paragraph 6.3C could apply, for example, when one or more of the outcomes or likely outcomes of the investigation might be: (i) the prosecution of one or more of the original suspects; (ii) the prosecution of someone previously not suspected, including someone who was originally a witness; and (iii) any original suspect being treated as a prosecution witness and when premature disclosure of any police action, particularly through contact with any parties involved, could lead to a real risk of compromising the investigation and endangering witnesses.*

E:7 Recording of interviews by secure digital network

E:7.1 A secure digital network does not use removable media and this section specifies the provisions which will apply when a secure digital network is used.   **A-179a**

E:7.2 [*Not used.*]

E:7.3 The following requirements are solely applicable to the use of a secure digital network for the recording of interviews.

(a) *Application of sections 1 to 6 of Code E*

E:7.4 Sections 1 to 6 of Code E above apply except for the following paragraphs: **A-179b**
- paragraph 2.2 under "Recording and sealing of master recordings";
- paragraph 4.3 under "(b) Commencement of interviews";
- paragraph 4.4 (e) under "(b) Commencement of interviews";
- paragraphs 4.11 to 4.19 under "(e) Changing recording media", "(f) Taking a break during interview", "(g) Failure of recording equipment", "(h) Removing recording media from the recorder" and (i) "Conclusion of the interview"; and
- paragraphs 6.1 to 6.4 and *Notes 6A to 6C* under "Media security".

(b) *Commencement of interviews*

E:7.5 When the suspect is brought into the interview room, the interviewer shall without delay and in the sight of the suspect, switch on the recording equipment and enter the information necessary to log on to the secure network and start recording.   **A-179c**

E:7.6 The interviewer must then inform the suspect that the interview is being recorded using a secure digital network and that recording has commenced.

E:7.7 In addition to the requirements of paragraph 4.4(a) to (d) above, the interviewer must inform the person that:
- they will be given access to the recording of the interview in the event that they are charged or informed that they will be prosecuted but if they are not charged or informed that they will be prosecuted they will only be given access as agreed with the police or on the order of a court; and
- they will be given a written notice at the end of the interview setting out their rights to access the recording and what will happen to the recording.

(c) *Taking a break during interview*

E:7.8 When a break is taken, the fact that a break is to be taken, the reason for it and the time shall be recorded on the audio recording. The recording shall be stopped and the procedures in paragraphs 7.12 and 7.13 for the conclusion of an interview followed.   **A-179d**

E:7.9 When the interview recommences the procedures in paragraphs 7.5 to 7.7 for commencing an interview shall be followed to create a new file to record the continuation of the interview. The time the interview recommences shall be recorded on the audio recording.

E:7.10 After any break in the interview the interviewer must, before resuming the interview, remind the person being questioned that they remain under caution or, if there is any doubt, give the caution in full again. (See *Note 4G.*)

(d) *Failure of recording equipment*

E:7.11 If there is an equipment failure which can be rectified quickly, *e.g.* by commencing a new secure digital network recording, the interviewer shall follow the appropriate procedures as in paragraphs 7.8 to 7.10. When the recording is resumed the interviewer shall explain what happened and record the time the interview recommences. If, however, it is not possible to continue recording on the secure digital network the interview should be recorded on removable media as in paragraph 4.3 unless the necessary equipment is not available. If this happens the interview may continue without being audibly recorded and the interviewer shall seek the authority of the custody officer or a sergeant as in paragraph 3.3(a) or (b). (See *Note 4H.*)   **A-179e**

(e) *Conclusion of interview*

E:7.12 At the conclusion of the interview, the suspect shall be offered the opportunity to clarify anything he or she has said and asked if there is anything they want to add.   **A-179f**

E:7.13 At the conclusion of the interview, including the taking and reading back of any written statement:
(a) the time shall be orally recorded;

(b) the suspect shall be handed a notice (see *Note 7A*) which explains:
  • how the audio recording will be used,
  • the arrangements for access to it,
  • that if they are charged or informed that they will be prosecuted, they will be given access to the recording of the interview either electronically or by being given a copy on removable recording media, but if they are not charged or informed that they will prosecuted, they will only be given access as agreed with the police or on the order of a court;

(c) the suspect must be asked to confirm that he or she has received a copy of the notice at sub-paragraph (b) above; if the suspect fails to accept or to acknowledge receipt of the notice, the interviewer will state for the recording that a copy of the notice has been provided to the suspect and that he or she has refused to take a copy of the notice or has refused to acknowledge receipt;

(d) the time shall be recorded and the interviewer shall notify the suspect that the recording is being saved to the secure network. The interviewer must save the recording in the presence of the suspect. The suspect should then be informed that the interview is terminated.

(f) *After the interview*

E:7.14 The interviewer shall make a note in their pocket book that the interview has taken place and that it was audibly recorded, the time it commenced, its duration and date and the identification number of the original recording.

E:7.15 If no proceedings follow in respect of the person whose interview was recorded, the recordings must be kept securely as in paragraphs 7.16 and 7.17. (See *Note 5A*.)

(g) *Security of secure digital network interview records*

E:7.16 Interview record files are stored in read only format on non-removable storage devices, for example, hard disk drives, to ensure their integrity. The recordings are first saved locally to a secure non-removable device before being transferred to the remote network device. If for any reason the network connection fails, the recording remains on the local device and will be transferred when the network connections are restored.

E:7.17 Access to interview recordings, including copying to removable media, must be strictly controlled and monitored to ensure that access is restricted to those who have been given specific permission to access for specified purposes when this is necessary. For example, police officers and CPS lawyers involved in the preparation of any prosecution case, persons interviewed if they have been charged or informed they may be prosecuted and their legal representatives.

Note for guidance

A-179g   E:7A *The notice at paragraph 7.13 above should provide a brief explanation of the secure digital network and how access to the recording is strictly limited. The notice should also explain the access rights of the suspect, his or her legal representative, the police and the prosecutor to the recording of the interview. Space should be provided on the form to insert the date and the file reference number for the interview.*

ANNEX

Paragraph 3.1(a)(iii) - exemption from the requirement to audio record interviews for indictable offences - conditions

[See *Notes A1, A2* and *A3*.]

Part 1: Four specified indictable offence types - four conditions

A-179h   E:1. The first condition is that the person has not been arrested.

E:2. The second condition is that the interview takes place elsewhere than at a police station (see *Note A4*).

E:3. The third condition is that the indictable offence in respect of which the person has been cautioned is one of the following:
  (a) possession of a controlled drug, contrary to section 5(2) of the Misuse of Drugs Act 1971 if the drug is cannabis as defined by that Act but it is not cannabis oil (see *Note A5*);
  (b) possession of a controlled drug, contrary to section 5(2) of the Misuse of Drugs Act 1971 if the drug is khat as defined by that Act (see *Note A5*);
  (c) retail theft (shoplifting), contrary to section 1 of the Theft Act 1968 (see *Note A6*); and
  (d) criminal damage to property, contrary to section 1(1) of the Criminal Damage Act 1971

(see *Note A6*),

and in this paragraph, the reference to each of the above offences applies to an attempt to commit that offence, as defined by section 1 of the Criminal Attempts Act 1981.

E:4. The fourth condition is that:

(a) where the person has been cautioned in respect of an offence described in paragraph 3(a) (possession of cannabis) or paragraph 3(b) (possession of khat), the requirements of paragraphs 5 and 6 are satisfied; or

(b) where the person has been cautioned in respect of an offence described in paragraph 3(c) (retail theft), the requirements of paragraphs 5 and 7 are satisfied; or

(c) where the person has been cautioned in respect of an offence described in paragraph 3(d) (criminal damage), the requirements of paragraphs 5 and 8 are satisfied.

E:5. The requirements of this paragraph that apply to all four offences described in paragraph 3 are that:

(i) the person suspected of committing the offence:
- appears to be aged 18 or over;
- does not require an appropriate adult (see paragraph 1.5 of this code);
- appears to be able to appreciate the significance of questions and their answers;
- does not appear to be unable to understand what is happening because of the effects of drink, drugs or illness, ailment or condition; and
- does not require an interpreter in accordance with Code C, section 13;

(ii) it appears that the commission of the offence:
- has not resulted in any injury to any person;
- has not involved any realistic threat or risk of injury to any person; and
- has not caused any substantial financial or material loss to the private property of any individual;

(iii) in accordance with Code G (arrest), the person's arrest is not necessary in order to investigate the offence; and

(iv) the person is not being interviewed about any other offence.

See *Notes A3* and *A8*.

E:6. The requirements of this paragraph that apply to the offences described in paragraph 3(a) (possession of cannabis) and paragraph 3(b) (possession of khat) are that a police officer who is experienced in the recognition of the physical appearance, texture and smell of cannabis or (as the case may be) khat, is able to say that the substance which has been found in the suspect's possession by that officer or, as the case may be, by any other officer not so experienced and trained:

(i) is a controlled drug being either cannabis which is not cannabis oil or khat; and

(ii) the quantity of the substance found is consistent with personal use by the suspect and does not provide any grounds to suspect an intention to supply others.

See *Note A5*.

E:7. The requirements of this paragraph that apply to the offence described in paragraph 3(c) (retail theft), are that it appears to the officer:

(i) that the value of the property stolen does not exceed £100 inclusive of VAT;

(ii) that the stolen property has been recovered and remains fit for sale unless the items stolen comprised drink or food and have been consumed; and

(iii) that the person suspected of stealing the property is not employed (whether paid or not) by the person, company or organisation to which the property belongs.

See *Note A3*.

E:8. The requirements of this paragraph that apply to the offence described in paragraph 3(d) (criminal damage), are that it appears to the officer:

(i) that the value of the criminal damage does not exceed £300; and

(ii) that the person suspected of damaging the property is not employed (whether paid or not) by the person, company or organisation to which the property belongs.

See *Note A3*.

Part 2: Other provisions applicable to all interviews to which this annex applies

E:9. Subject to paragraph 10, the provisions of paragraphs 3.21 and 3.22 of Code C (persons at-   **A-179i** tending a police station or elsewhere voluntarily) regarding the suspect's right to free legal advice and the other rights and entitlements that apply to all voluntary interviews, irrespective of where they take place, will apply to any interview to which this annex applies. See *Note A7*.

E:10. If it appears to the interviewing officer that before the conclusion of an interview, any of the requirements in paragraphs 5 to 8 of Part 1 that apply to the offence in question described in paragraph 3 of Part 1 have ceased to apply, this annex shall cease to apply. The person being interviewed must be so informed and a break in the interview must be taken. The reason must be recorded in the interview record and the continuation of the interview shall be audio recorded in accordance with sections 1 to 7 of this code. For the purpose of the continuation, the provisions of paragraphs 4.3 and 7.5 (commencement of interviews) shall apply. See *Note A8.*

Notes for guidance

A-179j

E:A1 *This annex sets out conditions and requirements of the limited exemption referred to in paragraph 3.1(a)(iii), from the requirement to make an audio recording of an interview about an indictable offence, including offences triable either way.*

E:A2 *The purpose of the exemption is to support the policy which gives police in England and Wales options for dealing with low-level offences quickly and non-bureaucratically in a proportionate manner. Guidance for police about these options is available at: https://www.app.college.police.uk/app-content/prosecution-and-case-management/justiceoutcomes/.*

E:A3 *A decision in relation to a particular offence that the conditions and requirements in this annex for an audio-recording exemption are satisfied is an operational matter for the interviewing officer according to all the particular circumstances of the case. These circumstances include the outcome of the officer's investigation at that time and any other matters that are relevant to the officer's consideration as to how to deal with the matter.*

E:A4 *An interviewer who is not sure, or has any doubt, about the suitability of a place or location for carrying out an interview elsewhere than at a police station, should consult an officer of the rank of sergeant or above for advice. (Repeated from Note 1A).*

E:A5 *Under the Misuse of Drugs Act 1971 as at the date this code comes into force:*

    (a) *cannabis includes any part of the cannabis plant but not mature stalks and seeds separated from the plant, cannabis resin and cannabis oil, but paragraph 3(a) does not apply to the possession of cannabis oil; and*

    (b) *khat includes the leaves, stems and shoots of the plant.*

E:A6 *The power to issue a penalty notice for disorder (PND) for an offence contrary to section 1 of the Theft Act 1968 applies when the value of the goods stolen does not exceed £100 inclusive of VAT. The power to issue a PND for an offence contrary to section 1(1) of the Criminal Damage Act 1971 applies when the value of the damage does not exceed £300.*

E:A7 *The interviewing officer is responsible for ensuring compliance with the provisions of Code C applicable to the conduct and recording of voluntary interviews to which this annex applies. These include the right to free legal advice and the provision of a notice explaining the arrangements (see Code C, para. 3.21 and section 6), the provision of information about the offence before the interview (see Code C, para. 11.1A) and the right to interpretation and translation (see Code C, section 13).*

E:A8 *The requirements in paragraph 5 of Part 1 will cease to apply if, for example during the course of an interview, as a result of what the suspect says or other information which comes to the interviewing officer's notice:*

- *it appears that the suspect:*
  - ~ *is aged under 18;*
  - ~ *does require an appropriate adult;*
  - ~ *is unable to appreciate the significance of questions and their answers;*
  - ~ *is unable to understand what is happening because of the effects of drink, drugs or illness, ailment or condition; or*
  - ~ *requires an interpreter; or*
- *the police officer decides that the suspect's arrest is now necessary (see Code G).*

(7) Visual recording of interviews

A-180

The text that follows is of the version of the code that came into force on October 27, 2013: see *ante,* Appendix A-1.

As at May 26, 2017, there was no requirement on any police force to make visual recordings of interviews, but police officers who choose to make such recordings will still be required to have regard to the provisions of this code.

F. CODE OF PRACTICE ON VISUAL RECORDINGS WITH SOUND OF INTERVIEWS WITH SUSPECTS

Commencement—transitional arrangements

The contents of this code should be considered if an interviewer decides to make a visual record-   **A-180a**
ing with sound of an interview with a suspect after 00.00 on 27 October 2013. There is no statutory
requirement under *PACE* to visually record interviews.

F:1 General

F:1.0 The procedures in this code must be used fairly, responsibly, with respect for the people to   **A-181**
whom they apply and without unlawful discrimination. Under the Equality Act 2010, section 149,
when police officers are carrying out their functions, they also have a duty to have due regard to the
need to eliminate unlawful discrimination, harassment and victimisation, to advance equality of opportunity between people who share a relevant protected characteristic and people who do not share
it, and to take steps to foster good relations between those persons. [See *Note 1C.*]

F:1.1 This code of practice must be readily available for consultation by police officers and other
police staff, detained persons and members of the public.

F:1.2 The notes for guidance included are not provisions of this code. They form guidance to
police officers and others about its application and interpretation.

F:1.3 Nothing in this code shall be taken as detracting in any way from the requirements of the
Code of Practice for the Detention, Treatment and Questioning of Persons by Police Officers (Code
C). [See *Note 1A.*]

F:1.4 The interviews to which this code applies are described in section 3.

F:1.5 In this code, the term "appropriate adult", "solicitor" and "interview" have the same meaning as those set out in Code C and in the case of a 17-year-old suspect, "appropriate adult" includes
the person called to fulfil that role in accordance with paragraph 1.5A of Code C. The corresponding provisions and *Notes for Guidance* in Code C applicable to those terms shall also apply where
appropriate.

F:1.5A The visual recording of interviews shall be carried out openly to instil confidence in its
reliability as an impartial and accurate record of the interview.

F:1.6 Any reference in this code to visual recording shall be taken to mean visual recording with
sound and in this code:

    (aa) "recording media" means any removable, physical audio recording medium (such as
         magnetic tape, optical disc or solid state memory) which can be played and copied;

    (a) "designated person" means a person other than a police officer, designated under the
        Police Reform Act 2002, Pt 4, who has specified powers and duties of police officers
        conferred or imposed on them;

    (b) any reference to a police officer includes a designated person acting in the exercise or
        performance of the powers and duties conferred or imposed on them by their designa-
        tion;

    (c) "secure digital network" is a computer network system which enables an original interview
        recording to be stored as a digital multi media file or a series of such files, on a secure
        file server which is accredited by the National Accreditor for Police Information Systems
        in accordance with the UK Government Protective Marking Scheme. See paragraph 1.6A
        and section 7 of this code.

F:1.6A Section 7 below sets out the provisions which apply to interviews visually recorded using a
secure digital network by reference to Code E and by excluding provisions of sections 1 to 6 of this
code which relate or apply only to removable media.

F:1.7 References to "pocket book" in this code include any official report book issued to police
officers.

F:1.8 In the application of this code to the conduct and visual recording of an interview of a
suspect who has not been arrested:

    (a) references to the "custody officer" include references to an officer of the rank of sergeant
        or above who is not directly involved in the investigation of the offence(s);

    (b) if the interview takes place elsewhere than at a police station, references to "interview
        room" include any place or location which the interviewer is satisfied will enable the
        interview to be conducted and recorded in accordance with this code and where the
        suspect is present voluntarily [see *Note 1B*]; and

    (c) provisions in addition to those which expressly apply to these interviews shall be followed
        insofar as they are relevant and can be applied in practice.

Notes for guidance

F:1A *As in paragraph 1.9 of Code C, references to custody officers include those carrying out the functions of a custody officer.*

F:1B *An interviewer who is not sure, or has any doubt, about the suitability of a place or location of an interview to be carried out elsewhere than at a police station, should consult an officer of the rank of sergeant or above for advice.*

F:1C *In paragraph 1.0, "relevant protected characteristic" includes: age, disability, gender reassignment, pregnancy and maternity, race, religion/belief, sex and sexual orientation.*

F:2 Recording and sealing of master recordings

A-182

F:2.1 [*Not used.*]

F:2.2 The camera(s) shall be placed in the interview room so as to ensure coverage of as much of the room as is practicably possible whilst the interviews are taking place. [See *Note 2A.*]

F:2.3 When the recording medium is placed in the recorder and it is switched on to record, the correct date and time, in hours, minutes and seconds will be superimposed automatically, second by second, during the whole recording, see *Note 2B.* See section 7 regarding the use of a secure digital network to record the interview.

F:2.4 One recording, referred to in this code as the master recording copy, will be sealed before it leaves the presence of the suspect. A second recording will be used as a working copy. [See *Notes 2C* and *2D.*]

F:2.5 Nothing in this code requires the identity of an officer or police staff to be recorded or disclosed:

    (a) [*not used*];

    (b) if the interviewer reasonably believes that recording or disclosing their name might put them in danger.

In these cases, the interviewer will have their back to the camera and shall use their warrant or other identification number and the name of the police station to which they are attached. Such instances and the reasons for them shall be recorded in the custody record or the interviewer's pocket book. [See *Note 2E.*]

Notes for guidance

A-183

F:2A *Interviewers will wish to arrange that, as far as possible, visual recording arrangements are unobtrusive. It must be clear to the suspect, however, that there is no opportunity to interfere with the recording equipment or the recording media.*

F:2B *In this context, the recording medium should be capable of having an image of the date and time superimposed as the interview is recorded.*

F:2C *The purpose of sealing the master recording before it leaves the presence of the suspect is to establish their confidence that the integrity of the recording is preserved.*

F:2D *The visual recording of the interview may be used for identification procedures in accordance with paragraph 3.21 or Annex E of Code D.*

F:2E *The purpose of the [sic] paragraph 2.5(b) is to protect police officers and others involved in the investigation of serious organised crime or the arrest of particularly violent suspects when there is reliable information that those arrested or their associates may threaten or cause harm to the officers, their families or their personal property. In cases of doubt, an officer of inspector rank should be consulted.*

F:3 Interviews to be visually recorded

A-184

F:3.1 Subject to paragraph 3.2 below, when an interviewer is deciding whether to make a visual recording, these are the areas where it might be appropriate:

    (a) with a suspect in respect of an indictable offence (including an offence triable either way) [see *Notes 3A* and *3B*];

    (b) which takes place as a result of an interviewer exceptionally putting further questions to a suspect about an offence described in sub-paragraph (a) above after they have been charged with, or informed they may be prosecuted for, that offence [see *Note 3C*];

    (c) in which an interviewer wishes to bring to the notice of a person, after that person has been charged with, or informed they may be prosecuted for an offence described in subparagraph (a) above, any written statement made by another person, or the content of an interview with another person [see *Note 3D*];

    (d) with, or in the presence of, a deaf or deaf/blind or speech impaired person who uses sign language to communicate;

    (e) with, or in the presence of anyone who requires an "appropriate adult"; or

    (f) in any case where the suspect or their representative requests that the interview be recorded visually.

F:3.2 The Terrorism Act 2000 and the Counter-Terrorism Act 2008 make separate provisions for a **A-185** code of practice for the video recording with sound of:

    • interviews of persons detained under section 41 of, or Schedule 7 to, the 2000 Act; and

    • post-charge questioning of persons authorised under section 22 or 23 of the 2008 Act.

The provisions of this code do not therefore apply to such interviews. [See *Note 3E.*]

F:3.3 Following a decision by an interviewer to visually record any interview mentioned in paragraph 3.1 above, the custody officer in the case of a detained person, or a sergeant in the case of a suspect who has not been arrested, may authorise the interviewer not to make a visual record and for the purpose of this code (F), the provisions of Code E, paras 3.1, 3.2, 3.3, 3.3A and 3.4 shall apply as appropriate. However, authority not to make a visual recording does not detract in any way from the requirement for audio recording. This would require a further authorisation not to make in accordance with Code E. [See *Note 3F.*]

F:3.4 [*Not used.*]

F:3.5 The whole of each interview shall be recorded visually, including the taking and reading back of any statement.

F:3.6 A sign or indicator which is visible to the suspect must show when the visual recording equipment is recording.

Notes for guidance

F:3A *Nothing in the code is intended to preclude visual recording at police discretion of interviews at police* **A-186** *stations or elsewhere with people cautioned in respect of offences not covered by paragraph 3.1, or responses made by persons after they have been charged with or informed they may be prosecuted for, an offence, provided that this code is complied with.*

F:3B *Attention is drawn to the provisions set out in Code C about the matters to be considered when deciding whether a detained person is fit to be interviewed.*

F:3C *Code C sets out the circumstances in which a suspect may be questioned about an offence after being charged with it.*

F:3D *Code C sets out the procedures to be followed when a person's attention is drawn after charge, to a statement made by another person. One method of bringing the content of an interview with another person to the notice of a suspect may be to play them a recording of that interview.*

F:3E *If during the course of an interview under this code, it becomes apparent that the interview should be conducted under the terrorism code for the video recording with sound of interviews, the interview should only continue in accordance with that code.*

F:3F *A decision not to record an interview visually for any reason may be the subject of comment in court. The authorising officer should therefore be prepared to justify their decision in each case.*

F:4 The interview

(a) *General*

F:4.1 The provisions of Code C in relation to cautions and interviews and the Notes for Guidance **A-187** applicable to those provisions shall apply to the conduct of interviews to which this code applies.

F:4.2 Particular attention is drawn to those parts of Code C that describe the restrictions on drawing adverse inferences from an arrested suspect's failure or refusal to say anything about their involvement in the offence when interviewed, or after being charged or informed they may be prosecuted and how those restrictions affect the terms of the caution and determine whether a special warning under sections 36 and 37 of the Criminal Justice and Public Order Act 1994 can be given.

(b) *Commencement of interviews*

F:4.3 When the suspect is brought into the interview room the interviewer shall without delay, but **A-188** in sight of the suspect, load the recording equipment and set it to record. The recording media must be unwrapped or otherwise opened in the presence of the suspect. [See *Note 4A.*]

F:4.4 The interviewer shall then tell the suspect formally about the visual recording and point out the sign or indicator which shows that the recording equipment is activated and recording. See paragraph 3.6. The interviewer shall:

    (a) explain that the interview is being visually recorded;

    (b) subject to paragraph 2.5, give their name and rank, and that of any other interviewer present;

(c) ask the suspect and any other party present (*e.g.* the appropriate adult, a solicitor or interpreter) to identify themselves;

(d) state the date, time of commencement and place of the interview; and

(e) state that the suspect will be given a notice about what will happen to the recording.

[See *Note 4AA.*]

F:4.4A Any person entering the interview room after the interview has commenced shall be invited by the interviewer to identify themselves for the purpose of the recording and state the reason why they have entered the interview room.

F:4.5 The interviewer shall then caution the suspect, see Code C, section 10, and:

- if they are detained, remind them of their entitlement to free legal advice, see Code C, para. 11.2, or
- if they are not detained under arrest, explain this and their entitlement to free legal advice, see Code C, para. 3.21.

F:4.6 The interviewer shall then put to the suspect any significant statement or silence, see Code C, para. 11.4.

(c) *Interviews with suspects who appear to require an interpreter*

A-189

F:4.7 The provisions of Code C on interpreters for suspects who do not appear to speak or understand English, or who appear to have a hearing or speech impediment, continue to apply.

(d) *Objections and complaints by the suspect*

A-190

F:4.8 If the suspect or an appropriate adult on their behalf, objects to the interview being visually recorded either at the outset or during the interview or during a break in the interview, the interviewer shall explain that the interview is being visually recorded and that this code requires the objections to be recorded on the visual recording. When any objections have been recorded or the suspect or the appropriate adult have refused to have their objections recorded, the interviewer shall say that they are turning off the visual recording, give their reasons and turn it off. If a separate audio recording is being maintained, the interviewer shall ask the person to record the reasons for refusing to agree to the interview being visually recorded. Paragraph 4.8 of Code E will apply if the person also objects to the interview being audio recorded. If the interviewer reasonably considers they may proceed to question the suspect with the visual recording still on, the interviewer may do so. [See *Note 4G.*]

F:4.9 If in the course of an interview a complaint is made by the person being questioned, or on their behalf, concerning the provisions of this or any other code, or it comes to the interviewer's notice that the person may have been treated improperly, then the interviewer shall act as in Code C, para. 12.9. [See *Notes 4B* and *4C.*]

F:4.10 If the suspect indicates that they wish to tell the interviewer about matters not directly connected with the offence of which they are suspected and that they are unwilling for these matters to be visually recorded, the suspect should be given the opportunity to tell the interviewer about these matters after the conclusion of the formal interview.

(e) *Changing the recording media*

A-191

F:4.11 In instances where the recording medium is not of sufficient length to record all of the interview with the suspect, further certified recording medium will be used. When the recording equipment indicates that the recording medium has only a short time left to run, the interviewer shall advise the suspect and round off that part of the interview. If the interviewer wishes to continue the interview but does not already have further certified recording media with him, they shall obtain a set. The suspect should not be left unattended in the interview room. The interviewer will remove the recording media from the recording equipment and insert the new ones which have been unwrapped or otherwise opened in the suspect's presence. The recording equipment shall then be set to record. Care must be taken, particularly when a number of sets of recording media have been used, to ensure that there is no confusion between them. This could be achieved by marking the sets of recording media with consecutive identification numbers.

(f) *Taking a break during the interview*

A-192

F:4.12 When a break is taken, the fact that a break is to be taken, the reason for it and the time shall be recorded on the visual record.

F:4.12A When the break is taken and the interview room vacated by the suspect, the recording media shall be removed from the recorder and the procedures for the conclusion of an interview followed. (See para. 4.18.)

F:4.13 When a break is a short one and both the suspect and an interviewer remain in the interview room, the recording may be stopped. There is no need to remove the recording media and when the interview recommences the recording should continue on the same recording media. The time at which the interview recommences shall be recorded.

F:4.14 After any break in the interview the interviewer must, before resuming the interview, remind the person being questioned of their right to legal advice if they have not exercised it and that they remain under caution or, if there is any doubt, give the caution in full again. [See *Notes 4D* and *4E.*]

(g) *Failure of recording equipment*

F:4.15 If there is a failure of equipment which can be rectified quickly, the appropriate procedures **A-193** set out in paragraph 4.12 shall be followed. When the recording is resumed the interviewer shall explain what has happened and record the time the interview recommences. If, however, it is not possible to continue recording on that particular recorder and no alternative equipment is readily available, the interview may continue without being recorded visually. In such circumstances, the procedures set out in paragraph 3.3 of this code for seeking the authority of the custody officer or a sergeant will be followed. [See *Note 4F.*]

(h) *Removing used recording media from recording equipment*

F:4.16 Where used recording media are removed from the recording equipment during the course **A-194** of an interview, they shall be retained and the procedures set out in paragraph 4.18 below followed.

(i) *Conclusion of interview*

F:4.17 Before the conclusion of the interview, the suspect shall be offered the opportunity to **A-195** clarify anything he or she has said and asked if there is anything that they wish to add.

F:4.18 At the conclusion of the interview, including the taking and reading back of any written statement, the time shall be recorded and the recording equipment switched off. The master recording shall be removed from the recording equipment, sealed with a master recording label and treated as an exhibit in accordance with the force standing orders. The interviewer shall sign the label and also ask the suspect and any third party present during the interview to sign it. If the suspect or third party refuses to sign the label, an officer of at least the rank of inspector, or if one is not available, the custody officer or, if the suspect has not been arrested, a sergeant, shall be called into the interview room and asked, subject to paragraph 2.5, to sign it.

F:4.19 The suspect shall be handed a notice which explains the use which will be made of the recording and the arrangements for access to it. The notice will also advise the suspect that a copy of the tape shall be supplied as soon as practicable if the person is charged or informed that he will be prosecuted.

Notes for guidance

F:4AA *For the purpose of voice identification the interviewer should ask the suspect and any other people* **A-196** *present to identify themselves.*

F:4A *The interviewer should attempt to estimate the likely length of the interview and ensure that an appropriate quantity of certified recording media and labels with which to seal the master copies are available in the interview room.*

F:4B *Where the custody offcer, or in the case of a person who has not been arrested, a sergeant, is called to deal with the complaint, wherever possible the recorder should be left to run until the offcer has entered the interview room and spoken to the person being interviewed. Continuation or termination of the interview should be at the discretion of the interviewer pending action by an inspector under Code C, para. 9.2.*

F:4C *Where the complaint is about a matter not connected with this code or Code C, the decision to continue with the interview is at the interviewer's discretion. Where the interviewer decides to continue with the interview, the person being interviewed shall be told that at the conclusion of the interview, the complaint will be brought to the attention of the custody officer, or in the case of a person who has not been arrested, a sergeant. When the interview is concluded, the interviewer must, as soon as practicable, inform the custody officer or the sergeant of the existence and nature of the complaint made.*

F:4D *In considering whether to caution again after a break, the interviewer should bear in mind that they may have to satisfy a court that the person understood that they were still under caution when the interview resumed.*

F:4E *The officer should bear in mind that it may be necessary to satisfy the court that nothing occurred during a break in an interview or between interviews which influenced the suspect's recorded evidence. On the recommencement of an interview, the interviewer should consider summarising on the record the reason for the break and confirming this with the suspect.*

F:4F *Where the interview is being recorded and the media or the recording equipment fails, the interviewer should stop the interview immediately. Where part of the interview is unaffected by the error and is still accessible on the media, that part shall be copied and sealed in the suspect's presence as a master copy and the interview recommenced using new equipment/media as required. Where the content of the interview has been lost in its entirety, the media should be sealed in the suspect's presence and the interview begun again. If the recording equipment cannot be fixed or no replacement is immediately available, the interview should be audio recorded in accordance with Code E.*

F:4G *The interviewer should be aware that a decision to continue recording against the wishes of the suspect may be the subject of comment in court.*

F:5 After the interview

A-197
F:5.1 The interviewer shall make a note in his or her pocket book of the fact that the interview has taken place and has been recorded, its time, duration and date and the identification number of the master copy of the recording media.

F:5.2 Where no proceedings follow in respect of the person whose interview was recorded, the recording media must nevertheless be kept securely in accordance with paragraph 6.1 and *Note 6A.*

Note for guidance

F:5A *Any written record of a recorded interview shall be made in accordance with current national guidelines for police offcers, police staff and CPS prosecutors concerned with the preparation, processing and submission of files.*

F:6 Master recording security

(a) *General*

A-198
F:6.1 The officer in charge of the police station at which interviews with suspects are recorded or as the case may be, where recordings of interviews carried out elsewhere than at a police station are held, shall make arrangements for the master copies to be kept securely and their movements accounted for on the same basis as other material which may be used for evidential purposes, in accordance with force standing orders. [See *Note 6A.*]

(b) *Breaking master recording seal for criminal proceedings*

A-199
F:6.2 A police officer has no authority to break the seal on a master copy which is required for criminal trial or appeal proceedings. If it is necessary to gain access to the master copy, the police officer shall arrange for its seal to be broken in the presence of a representative of the Crown Prosecution Service. The defendant or their legal adviser shall be informed and given a reasonable opportunity to be present. If the defendant or their legal representative is present they shall be invited to reseal and sign the master copy. If either refuses or neither is present, this shall be done by the representative of the Crown Prosecution Service. [See *Notes 6B* and *6C.*]

(c) *Breaking master recording seal: other cases*

A-200
F:6.3 The chief officer of police is responsible for establishing arrangements for breaking the seal of the master copy where no criminal proceedings result, or the criminal proceedings, to which the interview relates, have been concluded and it becomes necessary to break the seal. These arrangements should be those which the chief officer considers are reasonably necessary to demonstrate to the person interviewed and any other party who may wish to use or refer to the interview record that the master copy has not been tampered with and that the interview record remains accurate. [See *Note 6D.*]

F:6.4 Subject to paragraph 6.6, a representative of each party must be given a reasonable opportunity to be present when the seal is broken and the master recording copied and re-sealed.

F:6.5 If one or more of the parties is not present when the master copy seal is broken because they cannot be contacted or refuse to attend or paragraph 6.6 applies, arrangements should be made for an independent person such as a custody visitor, to be present. Alternatively, or as an additional safeguard, arrangement should be made for a film or photographs to be taken of the procedure.

F:6.6 Paragraph 6.4 does not require a person to be given an opportunity to be present when:

    (a) it is necessary to break the master copy seal for the proper and effective further investigation of the original offence or the investigation of some other offence; and

    (b) the officer in charge of the investigation has reasonable grounds to suspect that allowing an opportunity might prejudice any such an investigation or criminal proceedings which may be brought as a result or endanger any person. [See *Note 6E.*]

(d) Documentation

F:6.7 When the master copy seal is broken, copied and re-sealed, a record must be made of the **A-201** procedure followed, including the date time and place and persons present.

Notes for guidance

F:6A *This section is concerned with the security of the master recordings which will have been sealed at the* **A-202** *conclusion of the interview. Care should, however, be taken of working recordings since their loss or destruction may lead unnecessarily to the need to have access to master copies.*

F:6B *If the master recording has been delivered to the Crown Court for their keeping after committal for trial the crown prosecutor will apply to the chief clerk of the Crown Court centre for its release for unsealing by the crown prosecutor.*

F:6C *Reference to the Crown Prosecution Service or to the crown prosecutor in this part of the code shall be taken to include any other body or person with a statutory responsibility for prosecution for whom the police conduct any recorded interviews.*

F:6D *The most common reasons for needing access to master recordings that are not required for criminal proceedings arise from civil actions and complaints against police and civil actions between individuals arising out of allegations of crime investigated by police.*

F:6E *Paragraph 6.6 could apply, for example, when one or more of the outcomes or likely outcomes of the investigation might be: (i) the prosecution of one or more of the original suspects; (ii) the prosecution of someone previously not suspected, including someone who was originally a witness; and (iii) any original suspect being treated as a prosecution witness and when premature disclosure of any police action, particularly through contact with any parties involved, could lead to a real risk of compromising the investigation and endangering witnesses.*

F:7 Visual recording of interviews by secure digital network

F:7.1 This section applies if an officer wishes to make a visual recording with sound of an **A-202a** interview mentioned in section 3 of this code using a secure digital network which does not use removable media (see paragraph 1.6(c) above).

F:7.3 [*sic*] The provisions of sections 1 to 6 of this code which relate or apply only to removable media will not apply to a secure digital network recording.

F:7.4 The statutory requirement and provisions for the audio recording of interviews using a secure digital network set out in section 7 of Code E should be applied to the visual recording with sound of interviews mentioned in section 3 of this code as if references to audio recordings of interviews include visual recordings with sound.

(8) Statutory power of arrest

The first version of Code G came into force on January 1, 2006, to coincide with the com- **A-203** mencement of the substantial changes to the provisions of the PACE Act 1984 relating to the powers of arrest of police constables. As from that date, all offences became arrestable offences, but the lawfulness of an arrest by a constable for an offence became dependent on the constable having "reasonable grounds for believing that for any of the reasons mentioned in subsection (5) [of section 24] it is necessary to arrest the person in question". For the substituted section 24, see § 15-192 in the main work.

A revised code G came into force on November 12, 2012 (see *ante*, A-1).

G. CODE OF PRACTICE FOR THE STATUTORY POWER OF ARREST BY POLICE OFFICERS

Commencement

This code applies to any arrest made by a police officer after 00.00 on 12 November 2012. **A-203a**

G:1 Introduction

G:1.1 This code of practice deals with statutory power of police to arrest a person who is involved, **A-204** or suspected of being involved, in a criminal offence. The power of arrest must be used fairly, responsibly, with respect for people suspected of committing offences and without unlawful discrimination. The Equality Act 2010 makes it unlawful for police officers to discriminate against, harass or victimise any person on the grounds of the "protected characteristics" of age, disability, gender reassignment, race, religion or belief, sex and sexual orientation, marriage and civil partnership, pregnancy and maternity when using their powers. When police forces are carrying out their functions they also have a duty to have regard to the need to eliminate unlawful discrimination, harassment and victimisation and to take steps to foster good relations.

G:1.2 The exercise of the power of arrest represents an obvious and significant interference with the right to liberty and security under Article 5 of the European Convention on Human Rights set out in Part I of Schedule 1 to the Human Rights Act 1998.

G:1.3 The use of the power must be fully justified and officers exercising the power should consider if the necessary objectives can be met by other, less intrusive means. Absence of justification for exercising the power of arrest may lead to challenges should the case proceed to court. It could also lead to civil claims against police for unlawful arrest and false imprisonment. When the power of arrest is exercised it is essential that it is exercised in a non-discriminatory and proportionate manner which is compatible with the right to liberty under Article 5. See *Note 1B.*

G:1.4 Section 24 of the Police and Criminal Evidence Act 1984 (as substituted by section 110 of the Serious Organised Crime and Police Act 2005) provides the statutory power for a constable to arrest without warrant for all offences. If the provisions of the Act and this code are not observed, both the arrest and the conduct of any subsequent investigation may be open to question.

G:1.5 This code of practice must be readily available at all police stations for consultation by police officers and police staff, detained persons and members of the public.

G:1.6 The notes for guidance are not provisions of this code.

G:2 Elements of arrest under section 24 PACE

A-205   G:2.1 A lawful arrest requires two elements:

> a person's involvement or suspected involvement or attempted involvement in the commission of a criminal offence; and
>
> reasonable grounds for believing that the person's arrest is necessary.

Both elements must be satisfied, and it can never be necessary to arrest a person unless there are reasonable grounds to suspect them of committing an offence.

G:2.2 The arrested person must be informed that they have been arrested, even if this fact is obvious, and of the relevant circumstances of the arrest in relation to both the above elements. The custody officer must be informed of these matters on arrival at the police station. See paragraphs 2.9, 3.3 and *Note 3* and Code C, para. 3.4.

(a) *"Involvement in the commission of an offence"*

A-206   G:2.3 A constable may arrest without warrant in relation to any offence (see *Notes 1* and *1A*) anyone:

- who is about to commit an offence or is in the act of committing an offence;
- whom the officer has reasonable grounds for suspecting is about to commit an offence or to be committing an offence;
- whom the officer has reasonable grounds to suspect of being guilty of an offence which he or she has reasonable grounds for suspecting has been committed;
- anyone [*sic*] who is guilty of an offence which has been committed or anyone whom the officer has reasonable grounds for suspecting to be guilty of that offence.

G:2.3A There must be some reasonable, objective grounds for the suspicion, based on known facts and information which are relevant to the likelihood the offence has been committed and the person liable to arrest committed it. See *Notes 2* and *2A.*

(b) *Necessity criteria*

A-207   G:2.4 The power of arrest is only exercisable if the constable has reasonable grounds for believing that it is necessary to arrest the person. The statutory criteria for what may constitute necessity are set out in paragraph 2.9 and it remains an operational decision at the discretion of the constable to decide:

- which one or more of the necessity criteria (if any) applies to the individual; and
- if any of the criteria do apply, whether to arrest, grant street bail after arrest, report for summons or for charging by post, issue a penalty notice or take any other action that is open to the officer.

G:2.5 In applying the criteria, the arresting officer has to be satisfied that at least one of the reasons supporting the need for arrest is satisfied.

G:2.6 Extending the power of arrest to all offences provides a constable with the ability to use that power to deal with any situation. However, applying the necessity criteria requires the constable to examine and justify the reason or reasons why a person needs to be arrested or (as the case may be) further arrested, for an offence for the custody officer to decide whether to authorise their detention for that offence. See *Note 2C.*

G:2.7 The criteria in paragraph 2.9 below which are set out in section 24 of PACE, as substituted by section 110 of the Serious Organised Crime and Police Act 2005, are exhaustive. However, the circumstances that may satisfy those criteria remain a matter for the operational discretion of individual officers. Some examples are given to illustrate what those circumstances might be and what officers might consider when deciding whether arrest is necessary.

G:2.8 In considering the individual circumstances, the constable must take into account the situation of the victim, the nature of the offence, the circumstances of the suspect and the needs of the investigative process.

G:2.9 When it is practicable to tell a person why their arrest is necessary (as required by paragraphs **A-208** 2.2, 3.3 and *Note 3*), the constable should outline the facts, information and other circumstances which provide the grounds for believing that their arrest is necessary and which the officer considers satisfy one or more of the statutory criteria in sub-paragraphs (a) to (f), namely:

(a) to enable the name of the person in question to be ascertained (in the case where the constable does not know, and cannot readily ascertain, the person's name, or has reasonable grounds for doubting whether a name given by the person as his name is his real name):

an officer might decide that a person's name cannot be readily ascertained if they fail or refuse to give it when asked, particularly after being warned that failure or refusal is likely to make their arrest necessary (see *Note 2D*); grounds to doubt a name given may arise if the person appears reluctant or hesitant when asked to give their name or to verify the name they have given;

where mobile fingerprinting is available and the suspect's name cannot be ascertained or is doubted, the officer should consider using the power under section 61(6A) of PACE (see Code D, para. 4.3(e)) to take and check the fingerprints of a suspect as this may avoid the need to arrest solely to enable their name to be ascertained;

(b) correspondingly as regards the person's address:

an officer might decide that a person's address cannot be readily ascertained if they fail or refuse to give it when asked, particularly after being warned that such a failure or refusal is likely to make their arrest necessary (see *Note 2D*); grounds to doubt an address given may arise if the person appears reluctant or hesitant when asked to give their address or is unable to provide verifiable details of the locality they claim to live in;

when considering reporting to consider summons or charging by post as alternatives to arrest, an address would be satisfactory if the person will be at it for a sufficiently long period for it to be possible to serve them with the summons or requisition and charge; or, that some other person at that address specified by the person will accept service on their behalf; when considering issuing a penalty notice, the address should be one where the person will be in the event of enforcement action if the person does not pay the penalty or is convicted and fined after a court hearing;

(c) to prevent the person in question:

(i) causing physical injury to himself or any other person; this might apply where the suspect has already used or threatened violence against others and it is thought likely that they may assault others if they are not arrested (see *Note 2D*);

(ii) suffering physical injury; this might apply where the suspect's behaviour and actions are believed likely to provoke, or have provoked, others to want to assault the suspect unless the suspect is arrested for their own protection (see *Note 2D*);

(iii) causing loss or damage to property; this might apply where the suspect is a known persistent offender with a history of serial offending against property (theft and criminal damage) and it is thought likely that they may continue offending if they are not arrested;

(iv) committing an offence against public decency (only applies where members of the public going about their normal business cannot reasonably be expected to avoid the person in question); this might apply when an offence against public decency is being committed in a place to which the public have access and is likely to be repeated in that or some other public place at a time when the public are likely to encounter the suspect (see *Note 2D*);

(v) causing an unlawful obstruction of the highway; this might apply to any offence where its commission causes an unlawful obstruction which it is believed may continue or be repeated if the person is not arrested, particularly if the person has been warned that they are causing an obstruction (see *Note 2D*);

(d) to protect a child or other vulnerable person from the person in question; this might apply when the health (physical or mental) or welfare of a child or vulnerable person is likely to be harmed or is at risk of being harmed, if the person is not arrested in cases where it is not practicable and appropriate to make alternative arrangements to prevent the suspect from having any harmful or potentially harmful contact with the child or vulnerable person;

(e) to allow the prompt and effective investigation of the offence or of the conduct of the person in question (see *Note 2E*); this may arise when it is thought likely that unless the person is arrested and then either taken in custody to the police station or granted "street bail" to attend the station later (see *Note 2J*), further action considered necessary to properly investigate their involvement in the offence would be frustrated, unreasonably delayed or otherwise hindered and therefore be impracticable; examples of such actions include:

(i) interviewing the suspect on occasions when the person's voluntary attendance is not considered to be a practicable alternative to arrest, because for example:

- it is thought unlikely that the person would attend the police station voluntarily to be interviewed;
- it is necessary to interview the suspect about the outcome of other investigative action for which their arrest is necessary, see (ii) to (v) below;
- arrest would enable the special warning to be given in accordance with Code C, paras 10.10 and 10.11 when the suspect is found:
  - in possession of incriminating objects, or at a place where such objects are found;
  - at or near the scene of the crime at or about the time it was committed;
- the person has made false statements and/or presented false evidence;
- it is thought likely that the person:
  - may steal or destroy evidence;
  - may collude or make contact with, co-suspects or conspirators;
  - may intimidate or threaten or make contact with, witnesses;

(see *Notes 2F* and *2G*);

(ii) when considering arrest in connection with the investigation of an indictable offence (see *Note 6*), there is a need:

- to enter and search without a search warrant any premises occupied or controlled by the arrested person or where the person was when arrested or immediately before arrest;
- to prevent the arrested person from having contact with others;
- to detain the arrested person for more than 24 hours before charge;

(iii) when considering arrest in connection with any recordable offence and it is necessary to secure or preserve evidence of that offence by taking fingerprints, footwear impressions or samples from the suspect for evidential comparison or matching with other material relating to that offence, for example, from the crime scene (see *Note 2H*);

(iv) when considering arrest in connection with any offence and it is necessary to search, examine or photograph the person to obtain evidence (see *Note 2H*);

(v) when considering arrest in connection with an offence to which the statutory Class A drug testing requirements in Code C, section 17, apply, to enable testing when it is thought that drug misuse might have caused or contributed to the offence (see *Note 2I*);

(f) to prevent any prosecution for the offence from being hindered by the disappearance of the person in question; this may arise when it is thought that:

- if the person is not arrested they are unlikely to attend court if they are prosecuted;
- the address given is not a satisfactory address for service of a summons or a written charge and requisition to appear at court because the person will not be at it for a sufficiently long period for the summons or charge and requisition to be served and no other person at that specified address will accept service on their behalf.

G:3 Information to be given on arrest

(a) *Cautions–when a caution must be given*

A-209   G:3.1 Code C, paras 10.1 and 10.2, set out the requirement for a person whom there are grounds to suspect of an offence (see *Note 2*) to be cautioned before being questioned or further questioned about an offence.

G:3.2 [*Not used.*]

G:3.3 A person who is arrested, or further arrested, must be informed at the time if practicable, or if not, as soon as it becomes practicable thereafter, that they are under arrest and of the grounds and reasons for their arrest (see paragraphs [*sic*] 2.2 and *Note 3*).

G:3.4 A person who is arrested, or further arrested, must be cautioned unless:
   (a) it is impracticable to do so by reason of their condition or behaviour at the time;
   (b) they have already been cautioned immediately prior to arrest as in paragraph 3.1.

(b) *Terms of the caution (taken from Code C, section 10)*

G:3.5 The caution, which must be given on arrest, should be in the following terms: **A-210**

"*You do not have to say anything. But it may harm your defence if you do not mention when questioned something which you later rely on in court. Anything you do say may be given in evidence.*".

Where the use of the Welsh language is appropriate, a constable may provide the caution directly in Welsh in the following terms:

"*Does dim rhaid i chi ddweud dim byd. Ond gall niweidio eich amddiffyniad os na fyddwch chi'n sôn, wrth gael eich holi, am rywbeth y byddwch chi'n dibynnu arno nes ymlaen yn y Llys. Gall unrhyw beth yr ydych yn ei ddweud gael ei roi fel tystiolaeth.*".

See *Note 4.*

G:3.6 Minor deviations from the words of any caution given in accordance with this code do not constitute a breach of this code, provided the sense of the relevant caution is preserved. See *Note 5*.

G:3.7 *Not used.*

G:4 Records of arrest

(a) *General*

G:4.1 The arresting officer is required to record in his pocket book or by other methods used for **A-211** recording information:
   • the nature and circumstances of the offence leading to the arrest;
   • the reason or reasons why arrest was necessary;
   • the giving of the caution; and
   • anything said by the person at the time of arrest.

G:4.2 Such a record should be made at the time of the arrest unless impracticable to do. If not made at that time, the record should then be completed as soon as possible thereafter.

G:4.3 On arrival at the police station or after being first arrested at the police station, the arrested person must be brought before the custody officer as soon as practicable and a custody record must be opened in accordance with section 2 of Code C. The information given by the arresting officer on the circumstances and reason or reasons for arrest shall be recorded as part of the custody record. Alternatively, a copy of the record made by the officer in accordance with paragraph 4.1 above shall be attached as part of the custody record. See paragraph 2.2 and Code C, paras 3.4 and 10.3.

G:4.4 The custody record will serve as a record of the arrest. Copies of the custody record will be provided in accordance with paragraphs 2.4 and 2.4A of Code C and access for inspection of the original record in accordance with paragraph 2.5 of Code C.

(b) *Interviews and arrests*

G:4.5 Records of interviews, significant statements or silences will be treated in the same way as set out in sections 10 and 11 of Code C and in Codes E and F (audio and visual recording of interviews).

Notes for guidance

G:1 *For the purposes of this code, "offence" means any statutory or common law offence for which a person* **A-212** *may be tried by a magistrates' court or the Crown Court and punished if convicted.* [The note then gives examples of statutory and common law offences.]

G:1A *This code does not apply to powers of arrest conferred on constables under any arrest warrant, for example, a warrant issued under the Magistrates' Courts Act 1980, ss.1 or 13, or the Bail Act 1976, s.7(1), or to the powers of constables to arrest without warrant other than under section 24 of PACE for an offence. These other powers to arrest without warrant do not depend on the arrested person committing any specific offence and include:*
   • *PACE, s.46A, arrest of person who fails to answer police bail to attend police station or is suspected of breaching any condition of that bail for the custody officer to decide whether they should be kept in*

police detention which applies whether or not the person commits an offence under section 6 of the Bail Act 1976 (e.g. failing without reasonable cause to surrender to custody);

- *Bail Act 1976, s.7(3), arrest of person bailed to attend court who is suspected of breaching, or is believed likely to breach, any condition of bail to take them to court for bail to be re-considered;*
- *Children and Young Persons Act 1969, s.32(1A) (absconding) - arrest to return the person to the place where they are required to reside;*
- *Immigration Act 1971, Sched. 2, to arrest a person liable to examination to determine their right to remain in the U.K.;*
- *Mental Health Act 1983, s.136 to remove person suffering from mental disorder to place of safety for assessment;*
- *Prison Act 1952, s.49, arrest to return person unlawfully at large to the prison, etc., where they are liable to be detained;*
- *Road Traffic Act 1988, s.6D, arrest of driver following the outcome of a preliminary roadside test requirement to enable the driver to be required to provide an evidential sample;*
- *common law power to stop or prevent a breach of the peace–after arrest a person aged 18 or over may be brought before a justice of the peace court to show cause why they should not be bound over to keep the peace - not criminal proceedings.*

G:1B *Juveniles should not be arrested at their place of education unless this is unavoidable. When a juvenile is arrested at their place of education, the principal or their nominee must be informed (from Code C, Note 11D).*

G:2 *Facts and information relevant to a person's suspected involvement in an offence should not be confined to those which tend to indicate the person has committed or attempted to commit the offence. Before making a decision to arrest, a constable should take account of any facts and information that are available, including claims of innocence made by the person, that might dispel the suspicion.*

G:2A *Particular examples of facts and information which might point to a person's innocence and may tend to dispel suspicion include those which relate to the statutory defence provided by the Criminal Law Act 1967, s.3(1) which allows the use of reasonable force in the prevention of crime or making an arrest and the common law of self-defence. This may be relevant when a person appears, or claims, to have been acting reasonably in defence of themselves or others or to prevent their property or the property of others from being stolen, destroyed or damaged, particularly if the offence alleged is based on the use of unlawful force, e.g. a criminal assault. When investigating allegations involving the use of force by school staff, the power given to all school staff under the Education and Inspections Act 2006, s.93, to use reasonable force to prevent their pupils from committing any offence, injuring persons, damaging property or prejudicing the maintenance of good order and discipline may be similarly relevant. The Association of Chief Police Officers and the Crown Prosecution Service have published joint guidance to help the public understand the meaning of reasonable force and what to expect from the police and CPS in cases which involve claims of self-defence. Separate advice for school staff on their powers to use reasonable force is available from the Department for Education.*

G:2B *If a constable who is dealing with an allegation of crime and considering the need to arrest becomes an investigator for the purposes of the Code of Practice under the Criminal Procedure and Investigations Act 1996, the officer should, in accordance with paragraph 3.5 of that code, "pursue all reasonable lines of inquiry, whether these point towards or away from the suspect. What is reasonable in each case will depend on the particular circumstances."*

G:2C *For a constable to have reasonable grounds for believing it necessary to arrest, he or she is not required to be satisfied that there is no viable alternative to arrest. However, it does mean that in all cases, the officer should consider that arrest is the practical, sensible and proportionate option in all the circumstances at the time the decision is made. This applies equally to a person in police detention after being arrested for an offence who is suspected of involvement in a further offence and the necessity to arrest them for that further offence is being considered.*

G:2D *Although a warning is not expressly required, officers should if practicable, consider whether a warning which points out their offending behaviour, and explains why, if they do not stop, the resulting consequences may make their arrest necessary. Such a warning might:*

- *if heeded, avoid the need to arrest, or*
- *if it is ignored, support the need to arrest and also help prove the mental element of certain offences, for example, the person's intent or awareness, or help to rebut a defence that they were acting reasonably.*

A person who is warned that they may be liable to arrest if their real name and address cannot be ascertained, should be given a reasonable opportunity to establish their real name and address before deciding that either or both are unknown and cannot be readily ascertained or that there are reasonable grounds to doubt that a name and address they have given is their real name and address. They should be told why their name is not known and cannot be readily ascertained and (as the case may be) of the grounds for doubting that a name and address they have given is their real name and address, including, for example, the reason why a particular document the person has produced to verify their real name and/or address, is not sufficient.

G:2E *The meaning of "prompt" should be considered on a case by case basis taking account of all the circumstances. It indicates that the progress of the investigation should not be delayed to the extent that it would adversely affect the effectiveness of the investigation. The arresting officer also has discretion to release the arrested person on "street bail" as an alternative to taking the person directly to the station (see Note 2J).*

G:2F *An officer who believes that it is necessary to interview the person suspected of committing the offence must then consider whether their arrest is necessary in order to carry out the interview. The officer is not required to interrogate the suspect to determine whether they will attend a police station voluntarily to be interviewed but they must consider whether the suspect's voluntary attendance is a practicable alternative for carrying out the interview. If it is, then arrest would not be necessary. Conversely, an officer who considers this option but is not satisfied that it is a practicable alternative, may have reasonable grounds for deciding that the arrest is necessary at the outset "on the street". Without such considerations, the officer would not be able to establish that arrest was necessary in order to interview.*

Circumstances which suggest that a person's arrest "on the street" would not be necessary to interview them might be where the officer:

- *is satisfied as to their identity and address and that they will attend the police station voluntarily to be interviewed, either immediately or by arrangement at a future date and time; and*
- *is not aware of any other circumstances which indicate that voluntary attendance would not be a practicable alternative (see paragraph 2.9(e)(i) to (v)).*

When making arrangements for the person's voluntary attendance, the officer should tell the person:

- *that to properly investigate their suspected involvement in the offence they must be interviewed under caution at the police station, but in the circumstances their arrest for this purpose will not be necessary if they attend the police station voluntarily to be interviewed;*
- *that if they attend voluntarily, they will be entitled to free legal advice before, and to have a solicitor present at, the interview;*
- *that the date and time of the interview will take account of their circumstances and the needs of the investigation; and*
- *that if they do not agree to attend voluntarily at a time which meets the needs of the investigation, or having so agreed, fail to attend, or having attended, fail to remain for the interview to be completed, their arrest will be necessary to enable them to be interviewed.*

G:2G *When the person attends the police station voluntarily for interview by arrangement as in Note 2F above, their arrest on arrival at the station prior to interview would only be justified if:*

- *new information coming to light after the arrangements were made indicates that from that time, voluntary attendance ceased to be a practicable alternative and the person's arrest became necessary; and*
- *it was not reasonably practicable for the person to be arrested before they attended the station.*

If a person who attends the police station voluntarily to be interviewed decides to leave before the interview is complete, the police would at that point be entitled to consider whether their arrest was necessary to carry out the interview. The possibility that the person might decide to leave during the interview is therefore not a valid reason for arresting them before the interview has commenced (see Code C, para. 3.21).

G:2H *The necessity criteria do not permit arrest solely to enable the routine taking, checking (speculative searching) and retention of fingerprints, samples, footwear impressions and photographs when there are no prior grounds to believe that checking and comparing the fingerprints, etc., or taking a photograph would provide relevant evidence of the person's involvement in the offence concerned or would help to ascertain or verify their real identity.*

G:2I *The necessity criteria do not permit arrest for an offence solely because it happens to be one of the statutory drug testing "trigger offences" (see Code C, Note 17E) when there is no suspicion that Class A drug misuse might have caused or contributed to the offence.*

G:2J *Having determined that the necessity criteria have been met and having made the arrest, the officer can then consider the use of street bail on the basis of the effective and efficient progress of the investigation of the offence in question. It gives the officer discretion to compel the person to attend a police station at a date/ time that best suits the overall needs of the particular investigation. Its use is not confined to dealing with child care issues or allowing officers to attend to more urgent operational duties and granting street bail does not retrospectively negate the need to arrest.*

G:3 *An arrested person must be given sufficient information to enable them to understand they have been deprived of their liberty and the reason they have been arrested, as soon as practicable after the arrest, e.g. when a person is arrested on suspicion of committing an offence they must be informed of the nature of the suspected offence and when and where it was committed. The suspect must also be informed of the reason or reasons why arrest is considered necessary. Vague or technical language should be avoided. When explaining why one or more of the arrest criteria apply, it is not necessary to disclose any specific details that might undermine or otherwise adversely affect any investigative processes. An example might be the conduct of a formal interview when prior disclosure of such details might give the suspect an opportunity to fabricate an innocent explanation or to otherwise conceal lies from the interviewer.*

G:4 *Nothing in this code requires a caution to be given or repeated when informing a person not under arrest they may be prosecuted for an offence. However, a court will not be able to draw any inferences under the Criminal Justice and Public Order Act 1994, s.34, if the person was not cautioned.*

G:5 *If it appears a person does not understand the caution, the person giving it should explain it in their own words.*

G:6 *Certain powers available as the result of an arrest - for example, entry and search of premises, detention without charge beyond 24 hours, holding a person incommunicado and delaying access to legal advice - only apply in respect of indictable offences and are subject to the specific requirements on authorisation as set out in PACE and the relevant code of practice.*

(9) Detention, treatment and questioning of terrorist suspects

★**A-213**   The Police and Criminal Evidence Act 1984 (Code of Practice C and Code of Practice H) Order 2006 (S.I. 2006 No. 1938) provided for a revised Code C, and for a new Code H (on detention, treatment and questioning by police officers of persons under section 41 of, and Schedule 8 to, the Terrorism Act 2000), to come into operation on July 25, 2006. The new codes were consequential upon the commencement of the provisions of the Terrorism Act 2006, which were concerned with the 28-day detention of those arrested under section 41 of the 2000 Act. Whereas Code C had previously regulated the detention, treatment and questioning of those detained following arrest under section 41, from that date onwards these matters were regulated by Code H. Code C was revised so as to remove references to detention under the 2000 Act. The new Code H largely mirrored the provisions of Code C, but with various differences.

A revised Code H came into force on July 10, 2012, and further revisions came into force on October 27, 2013 and June 2, 2014.

The text that follows is that of a further revision that came into force on February 23, 2017 (as to which, see *ante*, § 15-7).

H. CODE OF PRACTICE IN CONNECTION WITH THE DETENTION, TREATMENT AND QUESTIONING BY POLICE OFFICERS OF PERSONS UNDER SECTION 41 OF, AND SCHEDULE 8 TO, THE TERRORISM ACT 2000

Commencement—transitional arrangements

★**A-214**   This code applies to people in police detention after 00.00 on 27 February 2017.

H:1 General

★**A-214a**   H:1.0 [*Identical to C:1.0.*]

H:1.1 This code of practice applies to, and *only* to:

(a) persons in police detention after being arrested under section 41 of the Terrorism Act 2000 (TACT) and detained under section 41 of, or Schedule 8 to that Act and *not charged*, and

(b) detained persons in respect of whom an authorisation has been given under section 22 of the Counter-Terrorism Act 2008 (post-charge questioning of terrorist suspects) to interview them in which case, section 15 of this Code will apply.

H:1.2 The provisions in PACE Code C apply when a person:

(a) is in custody *otherwise* than as a result of being arrested under section 41 of TACT or detained for examination under Schedule 7 to TACT (see paragraph 1.4);

(b) is charged with an offence, or

(c) is being questioned about any offence after being charged with that offence *without* an authorisation being given under section 22 of the Counter-Terrorism Act 2008.

See *Note 1N.*

H:1.3 In this code references to an offence and to a person's involvement or suspected involvement in an offence where the person has not been charged with an offence, include being concerned, or suspected of being concerned, in the commission, preparation or instigation of acts of terrorism.

H:1.4 The code of practice issued under paragraph 6 of Schedule 14 to TACT applies to persons detained for examination under Schedule 7 to TACT. See *Note 1N.*

H:1.5 [*Identical to C:1.1.*]

H:1.6 There is no provision for bail under TACT before or after charge. See *Note 1N.*

H:1.7 An officer must perform the assigned duties in this code as soon as practicable. An officer will not be in breach of this code if delay is justifiable and reasonable steps are taken to prevent unnecessary delay. The custody record shall show when a delay has occurred and the reason. See *Note 1H*.

H:1.8, 1.9, 1.10 [*Identical to C:1.2 to C:1.4, respectively.*]

H:1.11 Anyone who appears to be under 18 shall, in the absence of clear evidence that they are older, be treated as a juvenile for the purposes of this code.

H:1.11A Paragraph 1.11 does not change the statutory provisions in section 65(1) of PACE (appropriate consent) which require the consent of a juvenile's parent or guardian. By virtue of paragraph 15 of Schedule 8 to the Terrorism Act 2000, this is applied to the powers in paragraphs 10 to 14 of that Schedule to take fingerprints, intimate and non-intimate samples.

H:1.12 [*Identical to C:1.6.*]

H:1.13 [*Effectively identical to C:1.7.*]

H:1.14 [*Identical to C:1.8.*]

H:1.15 [*Identical to C:1.9.*]

H:1.16 When this Code requires the prior authority or agreement of an officer of at least inspector or superintendent rank, that authority may be given by a sergeant or chief inspector authorised by section 107 of PACE to perform the functions of the higher rank under TACT.

H:1.17 [*Identical to C:1.13, save for reference to "Annex I" in lieu of reference to "Annex L".*]

H1.18 Designated persons are entitled to use reasonable force as follows:

(a) when exercising a power conferred on them which allows a police officer exercising that power to use reasonable force, a designated person has the same entitlement to use force; and

(b) at other times when carrying out duties conferred or imposed on them that also entitle them to use reasonable force, for example:

- when at a police station carrying out the duty to keep detainees for whom they are responsible under control and to assist any other police officer or designated person to keep any detainee under control and to prevent their escape.
- when securing, or assisting any other police officer or designated person in securing, the detention of a person at a police station.
- when escorting, or assisting any other police officer or designated person in escorting, a detainee within a police station.
- for the purpose of saving life or limb; or
- preventing serious damage to property.

H:1.19 [*Identical to C:1.15, save for reference to "paragraph 1.17" in lieu of reference to "paragraph 1.13".*]

H:1.20 Designated persons and others mentioned in sub-paragraphs (a) and (b) of paragraph 1.19 must have regard to any relevant provisions of this code.

H:1.21 [*Identical to C:1.17.*]

Notes for guidance

H:1A, 1AA [*Identical to C:1A and C:1AA, respectively.*]   ★**A-214b**

H:1B *A person, including a parent or guardian, should not be an appropriate adult if they:*
- *are:*
  - *suspected of involvement in the offence or involvement in the commission, preparation or instigation of acts of terrorism;*
  - *the victim;*
  - *a witness;*
  - *involved in the investigation;*
- *received admissions prior to attending to act as the appropriate adult.*

Note: if a juvenile's parent is estranged from the juvenile, they should not be asked to act as the appropriate adult if the juvenile expressly and specifically objects to their presence.

H:1C–H:1K [*Identical to C:1C-1K, respectively, save for reference to "Paragraph 1.17" In H:1H in lieu of reference to "Paragraph 1.1A" in C:1H.*]

H:1L *If a person is moved from a police station to receive medical treatment, or for any other reason, the period of detention is still calculated from the time of arrest under section 41 of TACT (or, if a person was being detained under TACT, Sched. 7 when arrested, from the time at which the examination under Schedule 7 began).*

H:1M *Under Paragraph 1 of Schedule 8 to TACT, all police stations are designated for detention of persons arrested under section 41 of TACT. Paragraph 4 of Schedule 8 requires that the constable who arrests a person under section 41 takes them as soon as practicable to the police station which the officer considers is "most appropriate".*

H:1N *The powers under Part IV of PACE to detain and release on bail (before or after charge) a person arrested under section 24 of PACE for any offence (see PACE Code G (arrest)) do not apply to persons whilst they are detained under the terrorism powers following their arrest/detention under section 41 of, or Schedule 7 to, TACT. If when the grounds for detention under these powers cease the person is arrested under section 24 of PACE for a specific offence, the detention and bail provisions of PACE will apply and must be considered from the time of that arrest.*

H:1O [*Not used.*]

H:1P [*Not used.*]

H:2 Custody Records

★**A-215**

H:2.1 When a person is:

- brought to a police station following arrest under TACT, s.41,
- arrested under TACT, s.41 at a police station having attended there voluntarily,
- brought to a police station and there detained to be questioned in accordance with an authorisation under section 22 of the Counter-Terrorism Act 2008 (post-charge questioning) (see *Notes 15A* and *15B*), or
- at a police station and there detained when authority for post-charge questioning is given under section 22 of the Counter-Terrorism Act 2008 (see *Notes 15A* and *15B*),

they should be brought before the custody officer as soon as practicable after their arrival at the station or, if appropriate, following the authorisation of post-charge questioning or following arrest after attending the police station voluntarily see *Note 3H*. A person is deemed to be "at a police station" for these purposes if they are within the boundary of any building or enclosed yard which forms part of that police station.

H:2.2 A separate custody record must be opened as soon as practicable for each person described in paragraph 2.1. All information recorded under this code must be recorded as soon as practicable in the custody record unless otherwise specified. Any audio or video recording made in the custody area is not part of the custody record.

H:2.3 If any action requires the authority of an officer of a specified rank, this must be noted in the custody record, subject to paragraph 2.8.

H:2.3A If a person is arrested under TACT, s.41 and taken to a police station as a result of a search in the exercise of any stop and search power to which PACE Code A (stop and search) or the "search powers code" issued under TACT applies, the officer carrying out the search is responsible for ensuring that the record of that stop and search is made as part of the person's custody record. The custody officer must then ensure that the person is asked if they want a copy of the search record and if they do, that they are given a copy as soon as practicable. The person's entitlement to a copy of the search record which is made as part of their custody record is in addition to, and does not affect, their entitlement to a copy of their custody record or any other provisions of section 2 (custody records) of this code. See Code A, para. 4.2B and the TACT search powers code paragraph 5.3.5).

H:2.4 [*Identical to C:2.3.*]

H:2.5 The detainee's solicitor and appropriate adult must be permitted to inspect the detainee's custody record as soon as practicable after their arrival at the station and at any other time whilst the person is detained.

On request, the detainee, their solicitor and appropriate adult must be allowed to inspect the following records, as promptly as is practicable at any time whilst the person is detained:

- (a) The information about the circumstances and reasons for the detainee's arrest as recorded in the custody record in accordance with paragraph 3.4. This applies to any further reasons which come to light and are recorded whilst the detainee is detained;
- (b) The record of the grounds for each authorisation to keep the person in custody. The authorisations to which this applies are the same as those described in paragraph 2 of Annex M of this code.

Access to the custody record for the purposes of this paragraph must be arranged and agreed with the custody officer and may not unreasonably interfere with the custody officer's duties or the justifiable needs of the investigation. A record shall be made when access is allowed. This access is in addition to the requirements in paragraphs 3.4(b), 11.1 and 14.0 to provide information about the reasons for arrest and detention and in 14.4A to give the detainee written information about the grounds for continued detention when an application for a warrant of further detention (or for an extension of such a warrant) is made.

H:2.6 [*Identical to C:2.4A.*]

H:2.7 The detainee, appropriate adult or legal representative shall be permitted to inspect the original custody record once the detained person is no longer being held under the provisions of

TACT, s.41 and Sched. 8 or being questioned after charge as authorised under section 22 of the Counter-Terrorism Act 2008 (see section 15), provided they give reasonable notice of their request. Any such inspection shall be noted in the custody record.

H:2.8 All entries in custody records must be timed and identified by the maker. Nothing in this code requires the identity of officers or other police staff to be recorded or disclosed in the case of enquiries linked to the investigation of terrorism. In these cases, they shall use their warrant or other identification numbers and the name of their police station, see *Note 2A*. Records entered on computer shall be timed and contain the operator's identification.

H:2.9 [*Identical to C:2.7.*]

Note for guidance

H:2A *The purpose of paragraph 2.8 is to protect those involved in terrorist investigations or arrests of terrorist suspects from the possibility that those arrested, their associates or other individuals or groups may threaten or cause harm to those involved.* ★**A-215a**

H:3 Initial action

(a) *Detained persons–normal procedure*

H:3.1 When a person to whom paragraph 2.1 applies is at a police station, the custody officer must make sure the person is told clearly about: ★**A-215b**
- (a) the following continuing rights which may be exercised at any stage during the period in custody:
    - (i) their right to consult privately with a solicitor and that free independent legal advice is available as in section 6;
    - (ii) their right to have someone informed of their arrest as in section 5;
    - (iii) their right to consult this code of practice (see *Note 3D*);
    - (iv) their right to medical help as in section 9;
    - (v) their right to remain silent as set out in the caution (see section 10); and
    - (vi) if applicable, their right to interpretation and translation (see paragraph 3.14) and the right to communication with their High Commission, Embassy or Consulate (see paragraph 3.14A).
- (b) their right to be informed about why they have been arrested and detained on suspicion of being involved in the commission, preparation or instigation of acts of terrorism in accordance with paragraphs 2.5, 3.4 and 11.1A of this code.

H:3.2 The detainee must also be given a written notice, which contains information:
- (a) to allow them to exercise their rights by setting out:
    - (i) their rights under paragraph 3.1 (subject to paragraphs 3.14 and 3.14A);
    - (ii) the arrangements for obtaining legal advice, see section 6;
    - (iii) their right to a copy of the custody record as in paragraph 2.6;
    - (iv) the caution in the terms prescribed in section 10;
    - (v) their rights to:
        - information about the reasons and grounds for their arrest and detention and (as the case may be) any further grounds and reasons that come to light whilst they are in custody;
        - to have access to records and documents which are essential to effectively challenging the lawfulness of their arrest and detention;
        as required in accordance with paragraphs 2.4, 2.4A, 2.5, 3.4, 11.1, 14.0 and 15.7A(c) of this code and paragraph 3.3 of Code G;
    - (vi) the maximum period for which they may be kept in police detention without being charged, when detention must be reviewed and when release is required.
    - (vii) their right to communicate with their High Commission Embassy or Consulate in accordance with section 7 of this code, see paragraph 3.14A;
    - (xiii) their right to medical assistance in accordance with section 9 of this code
    - (xi) their right, if they are prosecuted, to have access to the evidence in the case in accordance with the Criminal Procedure and Investigations Act 1996, the Attorney General's Guidelines on Disclosure and the common law and the Criminal Procedure Rules; and
- (b) briefly setting out their entitlements while in custody, by:
    - (i) mentioning:
        - the provisions relating to the conduct of interviews;

> – the circumstances in which an appropriate adult should be available to assist the detainee and their statutory rights to make representations whenever the need for their detention is reviewed.
>
> (ii) listing the entitlements in this code, concerning
>
> – reasonable standards of physical comfort;
>
> – adequate food and drink;
>
> – access to toilets and washing facilities, clothing, medical attention, and exercise when practicable.

See *Note 3A*

H:3.2A The detainee must be given an opportunity to read the notice and shall be asked to sign the custody record to acknowledge receipt of the notices. Any refusal must be recorded on the custody record.

H:3.3 [*Not used.*]

H:3.3A An audio version of the notice and an "easy read" illustrated version should also be provided if they are available (see *Note 3A*).

H:3.4 (a) The custody officer shall:

- record that the person was arrested under s.41 of TACT and the reason(s) for the arrest on the custody record. See paragraph 10.2 and *Note 3G*
- note on the custody record any comment the detainee makes in relation to the arresting officer's account but shall not invite comment. If the arresting officer is not physically present when the detainee is brought to a police station, the arresting officer's account must be made available to the custody officer remotely or by a third party on the arresting officer's behalf;
- note any comment the detainee makes in respect of the decision to detain them but shall not invite comment;
- not put specific questions to the detainee regarding their involvement in any offence (see paragraph 1.3), nor in respect of any comments they may make in response to the arresting officer's account or the decision to place them in detention. See paragraphs 14.1 and 14.2 and Notes 3H, 14A and 14B. Such an exchange is likely to constitute an interview as in paragraph 11.1 and require the associated safeguards in section 11.

Note: This sub-paragraph also applies to any further reasons and grounds for detention which come to light whilst the person is detained.

See paragraph 11.8A in respect of unsolicited comments.

If the first review of detention is carried out at this time, see paragraphs 14.1 and 14.2, and Part II of Schedule 8 to the Terrorism Act 2000 in respect of action by the review officer.

(b) Documents and materials which are essential to effectively challenging the lawfulness the detainee's arrest and detention must be made available to the detainee or their solicitor. Documents and material will be "essential" for this purpose if they are capable of undermining the reasons and grounds which make the detainee's arrest and detention necessary. The decision about what needs to be disclosed for the purpose of this requirement rests with the custody officer in consultation with the investigating officer who has the knowledge of the documents and materials in a particular case necessary to inform that decision (see *Note 3G*). A note should be made in the detainee's custody record of the fact that action has been taken under this sub-paragraph and when. The investigating officer should make a separate note of what has been made available in a particular case. This also applies for the purposes of section 14, see paragraph 14.0.

H:3.5 The custody officer or other custody staff as directed by the custody officer shall:

(a) ask the detainee, whether at this time, they:

(i) would like legal advice, see paragraph 6.4;

(ii) want someone informed of their detention, see section 5;

(b) ask the detainee to sign the custody record to confirm their decisions in respect of (*a*);

(c) determine whether the detainee:

(i) is, or might be, in need of medical treatment or attention, see section 9;

(ii) requires:

- an appropriate adult (see paragraphs 1.10, 1.11A, and 3.15);
- help to check documentation (see paragraph 3.21);
- an interpreter (see paragraph 3.14 and *Note 13B*).

(d) record the decision in respect of (*c*).

Where any duties under this paragraph have been carried out by custody staff at the direction of the custody officer, the outcomes shall, as soon as practicable, be reported to the custody officer who retains overall responsibility for the detainee's care and safe custody and ensuring it complies with this Code. See *Note 3I.*

H:3.6 When the needs mentioned in paragraph 3.5(c) are being determined, the custody officer is responsible for initiating an assessment to consider whether the detainee is likely to present specific risks to custody staff, any individual who may have contact with detainee (*e.g.* legal advisers, medical staff), or themselves. This risk assessment must include the taking of reasonable steps to establish the detainee's identity and to obtain information about the detainee that is relevant to their safe custody, security and welfare and risks to others. Such assessments should therefore always include a check on the Police National Computer (PNC), to be carried out as soon as practicable, to identify any risks that have been highlighted in relation to the detainee. Although such assessments are primarily the custody officer's responsibility, it will be necessary to obtain information from other sources, especially the investigation team *see Note 3E,* the arresting officer or an appropriate healthcare professional, see paragraph 9.15. Other records held by or on behalf of the police and other UK law enforcement authorities that might provide information relevant to the detainee's safe custody, security and welfare and risk to others and to confirming their identity should also be checked. Reasons for delaying the initiation or completion of the assessment must be recorded.

H:3.7 [*Identical to C:3.7.*]

H:3.8 Risk assessments must follow a structured process which clearly defines the categories of risk to be considered and the results must be incorporated in the detainee's custody record. The custody officer is responsible for making sure those responsible for the detainee's custody are appropriately briefed about the risks. The content of any risk assessment and any analysis of the level of risk relating to the person's detention is not required to be shown or provided to the detainee or any person acting on behalf of the detainee. If no specific risks are identified by the assessment, that should be noted in the custody record. See *Note 3F* and paragraph 9.15.

H:3.8A [*Identical to C:3.8A.*]

H:3.9 Custody officers are responsible for implementing the response to any specific risk assessment, which should include for example:

- reducing opportunities for self harm;
- calling an appropriate healthcare professional;
- increasing levels of monitoring or observation;
- reducing the risk to those who come into contact with the detainee.

See *Note 3F*

H:3.10, 3.11 [*Identical to C:3.10 and C:3.11, respectively.*]

H:3.12 A constable, prison officer or other person authorised by the Secretary of State may take any steps which are reasonably necessary for:

(a) photographing the detained person;

(b) measuring the person, or

(c) identifying the person.

H:3.13 Paragraph 3.12 concerns the power in TACT, Sched. 8, para.2. The power in TACT, Sched. 8, para.2 does not cover the taking of fingerprints, intimate samples or nonintimate samples, which is covered in TACT, Sched. 8, paras 10 to 15.

(b) *Detained persons–special groups*

H:3.14 [*Identical to C:3.12, save for references to "paragraph 3.1(i) to (iii)" in sub-paragraph (b), and "Annex K" in sub-paragraph (c), in lieu of references to "3.1(a)(i) to (iv)" and "Annex M" respectively.*]

H:3.14A [*Identical to C:3.12A, save for reference to "paragraph 3.1(i) to (v)" in lieu of reference to "paragraph 3.1(a)(i) to (iv)".*]

H:3.15, 3.16 [*Identical to C:3.13 and C:3.14, respectively.*]

H:3.17 [*Identical to C:3.15, save for reference to "paragraph 3.15" in lieu of reference to "paragraph 3.13".*]

H:3.18 If the appropriate adult is:

- already at the police station, the provisions of *paragraphs 3.1* to *3.5* must be complied with in the appropriate adult's presence;
- not at the station when these provisions are complied with, they must be complied with again in the presence of the appropriate adult when they arrive, and a copy of the notice given to the detainee in accordance with paragraph 3.2, shall also be given to the appropriate adult if they wish to have a copy.

H:3.19, 3.20 [*Identical to C:3.18 and C:3.19, respectively.*]

H:3.21 [*Identical to C:3.20, save for reference to "paragraph 3.17" in lieu of reference to "paragraph 3.15".*]

H:3.21A The Children and Young Persons Act 1933, s.31, requires that arrangements must be made for ensuring that a girl under the age of 18, while detained in a police station, is under the care of a woman. See *Note 3J.* It also requires that arrangements must be made to prevent any person under 18 while being detained in a police station, from associating with an adult charged with any offence, unless that adult is a relative or the adult is jointly charged with the same offence as the person under 18.

(c) *Documentation*

H:3.22 The grounds for a person's detention shall be recorded, in the person's presence if practicable.

H:3.23 Action taken under paragraphs 3.14 to 3.22 shall be recorded.

(d) *Requirements for suspects to be informed of certain rights*

H:3.24 The provisions of this section identify the information which must be given to suspects who have been arrested under section 41 of the Terrorism Act and cautioned in accordance with section 10 of this code. It includes information required by EU Directive 2012/13 on the right to information in criminal proceedings. If a complaint is made by or on behalf of such a suspect that the information and (as the case may be) access to records and documents has not been provided as required, the matter shall be reported to an inspector to deal with as a complaint for the purposes of paragraph 9.3, or paragraph 12.10 if the challenge is made during an interview. This would include, for example:

- not informing them of their rights (see paragraph 3.1);
- not giving them a copy of the notice (see paragraph 3.2(a))
- not providing an opportunity to read the notice (see paragraph 3.2A)
- not providing the required information (see paragraphs 3.2(a), 3.14(b) and, 3.14A);
- not allowing access to the custody record (see paragraph 2.5);
- not providing a translation of the notice (see paragraph 3.14(c) and (d));

Notes for guidance

★A-216   H:3A–3C [*Identical to C:3A to 3C, respectively.*]

H:3D *The right to consult this or other relevant codes of practice does not entitle the person concerned to delay unreasonably any necessary investigative or administrative action whilst they do so. Examples of action which need not be delayed unreasonably include:*

- *searching detainees at the police station;*
- *taking fingerprints or non-intimate samples without consent for evidential purposes.*

H:3E *The investigation team will include any officer involved in questioning a suspect, gathering or analysing evidence in relation to the offences of which the detainee is suspected of having committed. Should a custody officer require information from the investigation team, the first point of contact should be the officer in charge of the investigation.*

H:3F *The Detention and Custody Authorised Professional Practice (APP) produced by the College of Policing (see http://www.app.college.police.uk) provides more detailed guidance on risk assessments and identifies key risk areas which should always be considered.*

H:3G *Arrests under TACT, s.41 can only be made where an officer has reasonable grounds to suspect that the individual concerned is a "terrorist". This differs from the constable's power of arrest for all offences under PACE, s.24, in that it need not be linked to a specific offence. There may also be circumstances where an arrest under TACT is made on the grounds of sensitive information which can not be disclosed. In such circumstances, the grounds for arrest may be given in terms of the interpretation of a "terrorist" set out in TACT, s.40(1)(a) or (b).*

H:3H *For the purpose of arrests under TACT, s.41, the review officer is responsible for authorising detention (see paragraphs 14.1 and 14.2, and Notes 14A and 14B). The review officer's role is explained in TACT, Sched. 8 Pt II. A person may be detained after arrest pending the first review, which must take place as soon as practicable after the person's arrest.*

H:3I [*Effectively identical to C:3F.*]

H:3J [*Identical to C:3G.*]

H:4 Detainee's property

(a) Action

H:4.1 The custody officer is responsible for:
    (a) ascertaining what property a detainee:
        (i) has with them when they come to the police station, either on first arrival at the police station or any subsequent arrivals at a police station in connection with that detention;
        (ii) might have acquired for an unlawful or harmful purpose while in custody.
    (b) the safekeeping of any property taken from a detainee which remains at the police station.

The custody officer may search the detainee or authorise their being searched to the extent they consider necessary, provided a search of intimate parts of the body or involving the removal of more than outer clothing is only made as in Annex A. A search may only be carried out by an officer of the same sex as the detainee. See *Note 4A* and Annex I.

H:4.2, 4.3 [*Identical to C:4.2 and C:4.3, respectively.*]

(b) Documentation

H:4.4 It is a matter for the custody officer to determine whether a record should be made of the property a detained person has with him or had taken from him on arrest (see *Note 4D*). Any record made is not required to be kept as part of the custody record but the custody record should be noted as to where such a record exists and that record shall be treated as being part of the custody record for the purpose of this Code of Practice (see paragraphs 2.4, 2.5 and 2.7). Whenever a record is made the detainee shall be allowed to check and sign the record of property as correct. Any refusal to sign shall be recorded.

H:4.5 [*Identical to C:4.5.*]

Notes for guidance

H:4A–4C [*Identical to C:4A to C:4C, respectively.*]

H:4D *Section 43(2) of TACT allows a constable to search a person who has been arrested under section 41 to discover whether they have anything in their possession that may constitute evidence that they are a terrorist.*

H:5 Right not to be held incommunicado

(a) Action

H:5.1 Any person to whom this code applies who is held in custody at a police station or other premises may, on request, have one named person who is a friend, relative or a person known to them who is likely to take an interest in their welfare informed at public expense of their whereabouts as soon as practicable. If the person cannot be contacted the detainee may choose up to two alternatives. If they cannot be contacted, the person in charge of detention or the investigation has discretion to allow further attempts until the information has been conveyed. See *Notes 5D* and *5E.*

H:5.2 [*Identical to C:5.2.*]

H:5.3 The above right may be exercised each time a detainee is taken to another police station or returned to a police station having been previously transferred to prison. This code does not afford such a right to a person on transfer to a prison, where a detainee's rights will be governed by Prison Rules, see Annex J, para.4.

H:5.4 If the detainee agrees, they may at the custody officer's discretion, receive visits from friends, family or others likely to take an interest in their welfare, or in whose welfare the detainee has an interest. Custody Officers should liaise closely with the investigation team (see *Note 3E*) to allow risk assessments to be made where particular visitors have been requested by the detainee or identified themselves to police. In circumstances where the nature of the investigation means that such requests can not be met, consideration should be given, in conjunction with a representative of the relevant scheme, to increasing the frequency of visits from independent visitor schemes. See *Notes 5B* and *5C.*

H:5.5 If a friend, relative or person with an interest in the detainee's welfare enquires about their whereabouts, this information shall be given if the suspect agrees and Annex B does not apply. See *Note 5E.*

H:5.6 The detainee shall be given writing materials, on request, and allowed to telephone one person for a reasonable time, see *Notes 5A* and *5F.* Either or both these privileges may be denied or delayed if an officer of inspector rank or above considers sending a letter or making a telephone call may result in any of the consequences in Annex B, paras 1 and 2, particularly in relation to the making of a telephone call in a language which an officer listening to the call (see paragraph 5.7) does not understand. See *Note 5G*.

Nothing in this paragraph permits the restriction or denial of the rights in paragraphs 5.1 and 6.1.

H:5.7 Before any letter or message is sent, or telephone call made, the detainee shall be informed that what they say in any letter, call or message (other than in a communication to a solicitor) may be read or listened to and may be given in evidence. A telephone call may be terminated if it is being abused see *Note 5G*. The costs can be at public expense at the custody officer's discretion.

H:5.8 [*Identical to C:5.7A.*]

(b) *Documentation*

H:5.9 A record must be kept of any:

(a) request made under this section and the action taken;

(b) letters, messages or telephone calls made or received or visit received;

(c) refusal by the detainee to have information about them given to an outside enquirer, or any refusal to see a visitor. The detainee must be asked to countersign the record accordingly and any refusal recorded.

Notes for guidance

★A-217a   H:5A [*Identical to C:5A.*]

H:5B *At the custody officer's discretion and subject to the detainee's consent, visits should be allowed when possible, subject to sufficient personnel being available to supervise a visit and any possible hindrance to the investigation. Custody Officers should bear in mind the exceptional nature of prolonged TACT detention and consider the potential benefits that visits may bring to the health and welfare of detainees who are held for extended periods.*

H:5C *Official visitors should be given access following consultation with the officer who has overall responsibility for the investigation provided the detainee consents, and they do not compromise safety or security or unduly delay or interfere with the progress of an investigation. Official visitors should still be required to provide appropriate identification and subject to any screening process in place at the place of detention. Official visitors may include:*

- *an accredited faith representative;*
- *Members of either House of Parliament;*
- *public officials needing to interview the prisoner in the course of their duties;*
- *other persons visiting with the approval of the officer who has overall responsibility for the investigation;*
- *consular officials visiting a detainee who is a national of the country they represent subject to section 7 of this code.*

Visits from appropriate members of the Independent Custody Visitors Scheme should be dealt with in accordance with the separate Code of Practice on Independent Custody Visiting.

H:5D, 5E [*Identical to C:5C and 5D, respectively.*]

H:5F *The telephone call at paragraph 5.6 is in addition to any communication under paragraphs 5.1 and 6.1. Further calls may be made at the custody officer's discretion.*

H:5G *The nature of terrorism investigations means that officers should have particular regard to the possibility of suspects attempting to pass information which may be detrimental to public safety, or to an investigation.*

H:6   Right to legal advice

(a) *Action*

★A-217b   H:6.1 Unless Annex B applies, all detainees must be informed that they may at any time consult and communicate privately with a solicitor, whether in person, in writing or by telephone, and that free independent legal advice is available from the duty solicitor. Where an appropriate adult is in attendance, they must also be informed of this right. See paragraph 3.1, *Note 1I*, *Notes 6B* and *6J*

H:6.2 [*Identical to C:6.3, save for the reference to "Note 6G" in lieu of the reference to "Note 6H".*]

H:6.3 No police officer should, at any time, do or say anything with the intention of dissuading any person who is entitled to legal advice in accordance with this code, from obtaining legal advice. See *Note 6ZA*.

H:6.4 The exercise of the right of access to legal advice may be delayed exceptionally only as in Annex B. Whenever legal advice is requested, and unless Annex B applies, the custody officer must act without delay to secure the provision of such advice. If, on being informed or reminded of this right, the detainee declines to speak to a solicitor in person, the officer should point out that the right includes the right to speak with a solicitor on the telephone (see paragraph 5.6). If the detainee continues to waive this right the officer should ask them why and any reasons should be recorded on the custody record or the interview record as appropriate. Reminders of the right to legal advice must be given as in paragraphs 3.5, 11.3 and 5 of Annex K of this Code and PACE Code D on the Identification of Persons by Police Officers, paragraphs 3.17(ii) and 6.3. Once it is clear a detainee does not want to speak to a solicitor in person or by telephone they should cease to be asked their reasons. See *Note 6J.*

H:6.5 An officer of the rank of Commander or Assistant Chief Constable or above may give a direction under TACT Sched.8, para.9 that a detainee may only consult a solicitor within the sight and hearing of a qualified officer. Such a direction may only be given if the officer has reasonable grounds to believe that if it were not, it may result in one of the consequences set out in TACT Sched.8, para.8(4) or (5)(c). See Annex B, para.3 and *Note 6I.* A "qualified officer" means a police officer who:

    (a) is at least the rank of inspector;

    (b) is of the uniformed branch of the force of which the officer giving the direction is a member, and

    (c) in the opinion of the officer giving the direction, has no connection with the detained person's case.

Officers considering the use of this power should first refer to Home Office *Circular 40/2003.*

H:6.6 [*Identical to C:6.5A.*]

H:6.7 A detainee who wants legal advice may not be interviewed or continue to be interviewed until they have received such advice unless:

    (a) [*identical to C:6.6(a)*];

    (b) [*identical to C:6.6(b)*];

    (c) [*identical to C:6.6(c)*];

    (d) the detainee changes their mind, about wanting legal advice or (as the case may be) about wanting a solicitor present at the interview, and states that they no longer wish to speak to a solicitor. In these circumstances the interview may be started or continued without delay provided that:

        (i) an officer of inspector rank or above:

            • speaks to the detainee to enquire about the reasons for their change of mind (see *Note 6J*); and

            • makes, or directs the making of, reasonable efforts to ascertain the solicitor's expected time of arrival and to inform the solicitor that the suspect has stated that they wish to change their mind and the reason (if given);

        (ii) the detainee's reason for their change of mind (if given) and the outcome of the action in (i) are recorded in the custody record;

        (iii) the detainee, after being informed of the outcome of the action in (i) above, confirms in writing that they want the interview to proceed without speaking or further speaking to a solicitor or (as the case may be) without a solicitor being present and do not wish to wait for a solicitor by signing an entry to this effect in the custody record;

        (iv) an officer of inspector rank or above is satisfied that it is proper for the interview to proceed in these circumstances and:

            • gives authority in writing for the interview to proceed and if the authority is not recorded in the custody record, the officer must ensure that the custody record shows the date and time of authority and where it is recorded; and

            • takes or directs the taking of, reasonable steps to inform the solicitor that the authority has been given and the time when the interview is expected to commence and records or causes to be recorded, the outcome of this action in the custody record;

        (v) when the interview starts and the interviewer reminds the suspect of their right to legal advice (see paragraph 11.3) and the code of practice issued under paragraph 3 of Schedule 8 to the Terrorism Act 2000 for the video recording with sound of interviews, the interviewer shall then ensure that the following is recorded in the interview record made in accordance with that code:

            • confirmation that the detainee has changed their mind about wanting legal advice or (as the case may be) about wanting a solicitor present and the reasons for it if given;

            • the fact that authority for the interview to proceed has been given and, subject to paragraph 2.8, the name of the authorising officer;

- that if the solicitor arrives at the station before the interview is completed, the detainee will be so informed without delay and a break will be taken to allow them to speak to the solicitor if they wish, unless paragraph 6.7(a) applies; and
- that at any time during the interview, the detainee may again ask for legal advice and that if they do, a break will be taken to allow them to speak to the solicitor, unless paragraph 6.7(a), (b) or (c) applies.

Note: in these circumstances the restriction on drawing adverse inferences from silence in Annex C will not apply because the detainee is allowed an opportunity to consult a solicitor if they wish.

H:6.8, 6.9 [*Identical to C:6.7 and C:6.8 respectively, save for references to "paragraph 6.7" in lieu of references to "paragraph 6.6".*]

H:6.10 [*Identical to C:6.9, save for reference to "Notes 6C and 6D" in lieu of reference to "Notes 6D and 6E".*]

H:6.11 [*Identical to C:6.10, save for reference to "Note 6D" in lieu of reference to "Note 6E".*]

H:6.12, 6.13 [*Identical to C:6.11 and C:6.12, respectively.*]

H:6.14 [*Identical to C:6.12A, save for references to "Note 6C" and to "paragraphs 6.7 to 6.11" in lieu of references to "Note 6D" and "paragraphs 6.6 to 6.10".*]

H:6.15 In exercising their discretion under paragraph 6.14, the officer should take into account in particular:

- whether:
  - the identity and status of an accredited or probationary representative have been satisfactorily established;
  - they are of suitable character to provide legal advice,
- any other matters in any written letter of authorisation provided by the solicitor on whose behalf the person is attending the police station. See *Note 6E.*

H:6.16, 6.17 [*Identical to C:6.14 and C:6.15, respectively.*]

(b) *Documentation*

H:6.18, 6.19 [*Identical to C:6.16, 6.17, respectively.*]

Notes for guidance

★**A-218**   H:6ZA *No police officer or police staff shall indicate to any suspect, except to answer a direct question, that the period for which they are liable to be detained, or the time taken to complete the interview, might be reduced:*

- *if they do not ask for legal advice or do not want a solicitor present when they are interviewed; or*
- *if after asking for legal advice, they change their mind about wanting it or (as the case may be) wanting a solicitor present when they are interviewed and agree to be interviewed without waiting for a solicitor.*

H:6A *In considering if paragraph 6.7(b) applies, the officer should, if practicable, ask the solicitor for an estimate of how long it will take to come to the station and relate this to the time detention is permitted, the time of day (i.e. whether the rest period under paragraph 12.2 is imminent) and the requirements of other investigations. If the solicitor is on their way or is to set off immediately, it will not normally be appropriate to begin an interview before they arrive. If it appears necessary to begin an interview before the solicitor's arrival, they should be given an indication of how long the police would be able to wait so there is an opportunity to make arrangements for someone else to provide legal advice. Nothing within this section is intended to prevent police from ascertaining immediately after the arrest of an individual whether a threat to public safety exists (see paragraph 11.2).*

H:6B *A detainee has a right to free legal advice and to be represented by a solicitor. This note for guidance explains the arrangements which enable detainees to whom this code applies to obtain legal advice. An outline of these arrangements is also included in the Notice of Rights and Entitlements given to detainees in accordance with paragraph 3.2.*

The detainee can ask for free advice from a solicitor they know or if they do not know a solicitor or the solicitor they know cannot be contacted, from the duty solicitor.

To arrange free legal advice, the police should telephone the Defence Solicitor Call Centre (DSCC). The call centre will contact either the duty solicitor or the solicitor requested by the detainee as appropriate.

When a detainee wants to pay for legal advice themselves:

- *the DSCC will contact a solicitor of their choice on their behalf;*
- *they should be given an opportunity to consult a specific solicitor or another solicitor from that solicitor's firm. If this solicitor is not available, they may choose up to two alternatives. If these alternatives are not available, the custody officer has discretion to allow further attempts until a solicitor has been contacted and agreed to provide advice;*

- *they are entitled to a private consultation with their chosen solicitor on the telephone or the solicitor may decide to come to the police station;*
- *if their chosen solicitor cannot be contacted, the DSCC may still be called to arrange free legal advice.*

Apart from carrying out duties necessary to implement these arrangements, an officer must not advise the suspect about any particular firm of solicitors.

H:6C, 6G [*Identical to C:6D to C:6H, respectively, save for the reference to "paragraph 6.7(b)" in C:6F in lieu of the reference to "paragraph 6.6(b)" in C:6G.*]

H:6H [*Not used.*]

H:6I *Whenever a detainee exercises their right to legal advice by consulting or communicating with a solicitor, they must be allowed to do so in private. This right to consult or communicate in private is fundamental. Except as allowed by the Terrorism Act 2000, Sched. 8, para. 9, if the requirement for privacy is compromised because what is said or written by the detainee or solicitor for the purpose of giving and receiving legal advice is overheard, listened to, or read by others without the informed consent of the detainee, the right will effectively have been denied. When a detainee speaks to a solicitor on the telephone, they should be allowed to do so in private unless a direction under Sched. 8, para. 9 of the Terrorism Act 2000 has been given or this is impractical because of the design and layout of the custody area, or the location of telephones. However, the normal expectation should be that facilities will be available, unless they are being used, at all police stations to enable detainees to speak in private to a solicitor either face to face or over the telephone.*

H:6J [*Identical to C:6K.*]

H:7 Citizens of independent Commonwealth countries or foreign nationals

(a) *Action*

H:7 [*Identical to C:7 (apart from use of "are" instead of "is" in paragraph 7.4).*]   ★**A-218a**

Note for guidance

H:7A *The exercise of the rights in this section may not be interfered with even though Annex B applies.*

H:8 Conditions of detention

(a) *Action*

H:8.1 [*Identical to C:8.1, save for the the reference to "Note 8E" in lieu of the reference to "Note 8C".*]   ★**A-218b**

H:8.2 [*Identical to C:8.2.*]

H:8.3 [*Identical to C:8.3, save for omission of reference to Note 8A.*]

H:8.4, 8.5 [*Identical to C:8.4 and C:8.5, respectively.*]

H:8.6 At least two light meals and one main meal should be offered in any 24-hour period. See *Note 8B*. Drinks should be provided at meal times and upon reasonable request between meals. Whenever necessary, advice shall be sought from the appropriate healthcare professional, see *Note 9A*, on medical and dietary matters. As far as practicable, meals provided shall offer a varied diet and meet any specific dietary needs or religious beliefs the detainee may have. Detainees should also be made aware that the meals offered meet such needs. The detainee may, at the custody officer's discretion, have meals supplied by their family or friends at their expense. See *Note 8A*.

H:8.7 Brief outdoor exercise shall be offered daily if practicable. Where facilities exist, indoor exercise shall be offered as an alternative if outside conditions are such that a detainee can not be reasonably expected to take outdoor exercise (*e.g.*, in cold or wet weather) or if requested by the detainee or for reasons of security. See *Note 8C*.

H:8.8 Where practicable, provision should be made for detainees to practice religious observance. Consideration should be given to providing a separate room which can be used as a prayer room. The supply of appropriate food and clothing, and suitable provision for prayer facilities, such as uncontaminated copies of religious books, should also be considered. See *Note 8D*.

H:8.9 A juvenile shall not be placed in a cell unless no other secure accommodation is available and the custody officer considers it is not practicable to supervise them if they are not placed in a cell or that a cell provides more comfortable accommodation than other secure accommodation in the station. A juvenile may not be placed in a cell with a detained adult.

H:8.10 Police stations should keep a reasonable supply of reading material available for detainees, including but not limited to, the main religious texts. See *Note 8D*. Detainees should be made aware that such material is available and reasonable requests for such material should be met as soon as practicable unless to do so would:

(i) interfere with the investigation; or

(ii) prevent or delay an officer from discharging his statutory duties, or those in this code.

If such a request is refused on the grounds of (i) or (ii) above, this should be noted in the custody record and met as soon as possible after those grounds cease to apply.

(b) *Documentation*

H:8.11, 8.11A, 8.12 [*Identical to C:8.9 to C:8.11, respectively.*]

Notes for guidance

★**A-219**   H:8A *In deciding whether to allow meals to be supplied by family or friends, the custody officer is entitled to take account of the risk of items being concealed in any food or package and the officer's duties and responsibilities under food handling legislation. If an officer needs to examine food or other items supplied by family and friends before deciding whether they can be given to the detainee, he should inform the person who has brought the item to the police station of this and the reasons for doing so.*

H:8B [*Identical to C:8B.*]

H:8C *In light of the potential for detaining individuals for extended periods of time, the overriding principle should be to accommodate a period of exercise, except where to do so would hinder the investigation, delay the detainee's release or charge, or it is declined by the detainee.*

H:8D *Police forces should consult with representatives of the main religious communities to ensure the provision for religious observance is adequate, and to seek advice on the appropriate storage and handling of religious texts or other religious items.*

H:8E [*Identical to C:8C.*]

H:9 Care and treatment of detained persons

(a) *General*

H:9.1 Notwithstanding other requirements for medical attention as set out in this section, detainees who are held for more than 96 hours must be visited by an appropriate healthcare professional at least once every 24 hours.

H:9.2 [*Identical to C:9.1, save for the omission of the reference to Note "8C".*]

H:9.3 [*Identical to C:9.2.*]

H:9.4 [*Identical to C:9.3, save for references to "Note 9C", "paragraph 9.15" and "Note 9G" in lieu of references to "Note 9CA", "paragraph 9.13" and "Note 9H", respectively.*]

H:9.5 [*Identical to C:9.4.*]

(b) *Clinical treatment and attention*

H:9.6, 9.7, 9.8 [*Identical to C:9.5, C:9.5A and C:9.5B, respectively.*]

H:9.9 [*Identical to C:9.7, save for reference to "Note 9D" in lieu of reference to "Note 9E".*]

H:9.10 [*Identical to C:9.8.*]

H:9.11 [*Identical to C:9.9, save for reference to "paragraph 9.12" in lieu of reference to "paragraph 9.10".*]

H:9.12 [*Identical to C:9.10.*]

H:9.13 When appropriate healthcare professionals administer drugs or authorise the use of other medications, or consult with the custody officer about allowing self administration of drugs listed in Schedule 4 or 5, it must be within current medicines legislation and the scope of practice as determined by their relevant regulatory body.

H:9.14 [*Identical to C:9.12, save for reference to "paragraph 9.6" in lieu of reference to "paragraph 9.5".*]

H:9.15 [*Identical to C:9.13.*]

H:9.16 [*Identical to C:9.14, save for reference to "Note 9E" in lieu of reference to "Note 9F".*]

(c) *Documentation*

H:9.17 [*Identical to C:9.15, save for references to "paragraph 9.3", "paragraph 9.6", "paragraph 9.10", "Note 9F", "Notes 9D and 9E" and "Note 9G" in lieu of references to "paragraph 9.2", "paragraph 9.5", "paragraph 9.8", "Note 9G", "Notes 9E and 9F" and "Note 9H", respectively.*]

H:9.18 [*Identical to C:9.16, save for reference to "Note 9F" in lieu of reference to "Note 9G".*]

H:9.19 [*Identical to C:9.17.*]

Notes for guidance

H:9A, 9B [*Identical to C:9A and C:9B, respectively.*]

H:9C [*Identical to C:9C, save for reference to "Paragraph 9.6" in lieu of reference to "Paragraph 9.5."*]

H:9D, 9E [*Identical to C:9E and C:9F, respectively.*]

H:9F [*Identical to C:9G, save for reference to "Paragraphs 9.17 and 9.18" in lieu of reference to "Paragraphs 9.15 and 9.16".*]

H:9G [*Identical to C:9H.*]

H:10 Cautions

(a) *When a caution must be given*

H:10.1 A person whom there are grounds to suspect of an offence, see *Note 10A*, must be cautioned before any questions about an offence, or further questions if the answers provide the grounds for suspicion, are put to them if either the suspect's answers or silence, (i.e. failure or refusal to answer or answer satisfactorily) may be given in evidence to a court in a prosecution.

H:10.2 [*Identical to C:10.3, save for reference to "Note 3G" in lieu of reference to "Code G, paras 2.2 and 4.3".*]

H:10.3 [*Effectively identical to C:10.4.*]

(b) *Terms of the cautions*

H:10.4 The caution which must be given:
(a) on arrest;
(b) on all other occasions before a person is charged or informed they may be prosecuted; see PACE Code C, s.16, and
(c) before post-charge questioning under section 22 of the Counter-Terrorism Act 2008 (see section 15.9),

should, unless the restriction on drawing adverse inferences from silence applies, see *Annex C*, be in the following terms:

"You do not have to say anything. But it may harm your defence if you do not mention when questioned something which you later rely on in Court. Anything you do say may be given in evidence."

Where the use of the Welsh Language is appropriate, a constable may provide the caution directly in Welsh in the following terms:

"Does dim rhaid i chi ddweud dim byd. Ond gall niweidio eich amddiffyniad os na fyddwch chi'n sôn, wrth gael eich holi, am rywbeth y byddwch chi'n dibynnu arno nes ymlaen yn y Llys. Gall unrhyw beth yr ydych yn ei ddweud gael ei roi fel tystiolaeth."

See *Note 10F*

H:10.5 [*Identical to C:10.6.*]

H:10.6 [*Identical to C:10.7, save for reference to "Note 10C" in lieu of reference to "Note 10D".*]

H:10.7 [*Identical to C:10.8, save for reference to "Note 10D" in lieu of reference to "Note 10E".*]

H:10.8 [*Identical to C:10.9, but the words following "statutory requirement" have been omitted.*]

(c) *Special warnings under the Criminal Justice and Public Order Act 1994, ss.36 and 37*

H:10.9 [*Identical to C:10.10, save for references to "Note 10E" and "paragraph 10.10" in lieu of references to "Note 10F" and "paragraph 10.11", respectively.*]

H:10.10 [*Identical to C:10.11.*]

(d) *Juveniles and persons who are mentally disordered or otherwise mentally vulnerable*

H:10.10A [*Identical to C:10.11A, save for reference to "paragraph 10.10" in lieu of reference to "paragraph 10.11".*]

H:10.11 [*Identical to C:10.12.*]

H:10.11A [*Not used.*]

(e) *Documentation*

H:10.12 [*Identical to C:10.13, save for reference to "pocket" in lieu of reference to "report".*]

Notes for guidance

★**A-220a**   H:10A [*Identical to C:10A.*]

H:10B [*Identical to C:10B, save for inclusion of reference to "Note 3G" after the word "committed".*]

H:10C, 10F [*Identical to C:10D to C:10G, respectively.*]

H:11 Interviews—general

(a) *Action*

★**A-220b**   H:11.1 An interview in this code is the questioning of a person arrested on suspicion of being a terrorist which, under paragraph 10.1, must be carried out under caution. Whenever a person is interviewed they and their solicitor must be informed of the grounds for arrest, and given sufficient information to enable them to understand the nature of their suspected involvement in the commission, preparation or instigation of acts of terrorism (see paragraph 3.4(a)) in order to allow for the effective exercise of the rights of the defence. However, whilst the information must always be sufficient information for the person to understand the nature of their suspected involvement in the commission, preparation or instigation of acts of terrorism, this does not require the disclosure of details at a time which might prejudice the terrorism investigation (see *Note 3G*). The decision about what needs to be disclosed for the purpose of this requirement therefore rests with the investigating officer who has sufficient knowledge of the case to make that decision. The officer who discloses the information shall make a record of the information disclosed and when it was disclosed. This record may be made in the interview record, in the officer's report book or other form provided for this purpose. See *Note 11ZA*.

H:11.2 Following the arrest of a person under section 41 TACT, that person must not be interviewed about the relevant offence except at a place designated for detention under Schedule 8 para. 1 of the Terrorism Act 2000, unless the consequent delay would be likely to:

> (a) lead to:
> > • interference with, or harm to, evidence connected with an offence;
> > • interference with, or physical harm to, other people; or
> > • serious loss of, or damage to, property;
> (b) lead to alerting other people suspected of committing an offence but not yet arrested for it; or
> (c) hinder the recovery of property obtained in consequence of the commission of an offence.

Interviewing in any of these circumstances shall cease once the relevant risk has been averted or the necessary questions have been put in order to attempt to avert that risk.

H:11.3 Immediately prior to the commencement or re-commencement of any interview at a designated place of detention, the interviewer should remind the suspect of their entitlement to free legal advice and that the interview can be delayed for legal advice to be obtained, unless one of the exceptions in paragraph 6.7 applies. It is the interviewer's responsibility to make sure all reminders are recorded in the interview record.

H:11.4, 11.5 [*Identical to C:11.4 and C:11.4A, respectively.*]

H:11.6 [*Identical to C:11.5, save for reference to "paragraph 10.8" in lieu of reference to "paragraph 10.9".*]

H:11.7 [*Identical to C:11.6, save for the addition of the words "PACE Code C" before "paragraph 16.1", and with the omission of the final sub-paragraph of that paragraph.*]

(b) *Interview records*

H:11.8 Interviews of a person detained under section 41 of, or Schedule 8 to, TACT must be video recorded with sound in accordance with the code of practice issued under paragraph 3 of Schedule 8 to the Terrorism Act 2000, or in the case of post-charge questioning authorised under section 22 of the Counter-Terrorism Act 2008, the code of practice issued under section 25 of that Act.

H:11.8A [*Identical to C:11.13, save for addition of word "written" between the words "A" and "record" in the first line.*]

(c) *Juveniles and mentally disordered or otherwise mentally vulnerable people*

H:11.9 [*Identical to C:11.15, save for reference to "paragraphs 11.2 or 11.11 to 11.13" in lieu of reference to "paragraphs 11.1 or 11.18 to 11.20".*]

H:11.10 [*Identical to C:11.17.*]

H:11.10A [*Identical to C:11.17A, save for references to "paragraph 11.10" and "paragraph 11.11" in lieu of references to "paragraph 11.17" and "paragraph 11.18", respectively.*]

(d) *Vulnerable suspects–urgent interviews at police station*

H:11.11 [*Identical to C:11.18, save for references to "paragraph 11.2(a) to (c) and "3.14" in lieu of "paragraph 11.1(a) to (c)" and "3.12", respectively.*]

H:11.12 [*Identical to C:11.19, save for reference to "paragraph 11.2(a) to (c)" in lieu of reference to "paragraph 11.1(a) to (c)".*]

H:11.13 [*Identical to C:11.20, save for reference to "paragraph 11.11" in lieu of reference to "paragraph 11.18".*]

Notes for guidance

H:11ZA *The requirement in paragraph 11.1 for a suspect to be given sufficient information about the nature of their suspected involvement in the commission, preparation or instigation of acts of terrorism offence applies prior to the interview and whether or not they are legally represented. What is sufficient will depend on the circumstances of the case, but it should normally include, as a minimum, a description of the facts relating to the suspected involvement that are known to the officer, including the time and place in question. This aims to avoid suspects being confused or unclear about what they are supposed to have done and to help an innocent suspect to clear the matter up more quickly.* ★A-221

H:11A, 11B, 11C [*Identical to C:11A (save for an erroneous reference to para. 3.4 of code of practice under 1996 Act) to C:11C, respectively.*]

H:11D *Consideration should be given to the effect of extended detention on a detainee and any subsequent information they provide, especially if it relates to information on matters that they have failed to provide previously in response to similar questioning (see Annex G).*

H:11E [*Identical to C:11E.*]

H:11F [*Identical to C:11F, save for reference to "Paragraph 11.10A" in lieu of reference to "Paragraph 11.17A".*]

H:12 Interviews in police stations

(a) *Action*

H:12.1 [*Identical to C:12.1, save for reference to "treatment" in lieu of reference to "safe custody".*] ★A-221a

H:12.2 Except as below, in any period of 24 hours a detainee must be allowed a continuous period of at least 8 hours for rest, free from questioning, travel or any interruption in connection with the investigation concerned. This period should normally be at night or other appropriate time which takes account of when the detainee last slept or rested. If a detainee is arrested at a police station after going there voluntarily, the period of 24 hours runs from the time of their arrest (or, if a person was being detained under TACT, Sched. 7 when arrested, from the time at which the examination under Sched. 7 began) and not the time of arrival at the police station. The period may not be interrupted or delayed, except:

   (a) when there are reasonable grounds for believing not delaying or interrupting the period would:

   (i) involve a risk of harm to people or serious loss of, or damage to, property;

   (ii) delay unnecessarily the person's release from custody; or

   (iii) otherwise prejudice the outcome of the investigation;

   (b) at the request of the detainee, their appropriate adult or legal representative;

   (c) when a delay or interruption is necessary in order to:

   (i) comply with the legal obligations and duties arising under section 14; or

   (ii) to take action required under section 9 or in accordance with medical advice.

If the period is interrupted in accordance with (a), a fresh period must be allowed. Interruptions under (b) and (c) do not require a fresh period to be allowed.

H:12.3 [*Identical to C:12.3, save that there is no reference to "Annex G" and the references to "paragraph 11.18" and "paragraphs 11.18 to 11.20" are replaced by references to "paragraphs 11.11" and "paragraphs 11.11 to 11.13".*]

H:12.4 [*Identical to C:12.4.*]

H:12.5 [*Identical to C:12.5, save for reference to "TACT Schedule 8" in lieu of reference to "PACE".*]

H:12.6 [*Identical to C:12.6.*]

H:12.7 Before the interview commences each interviewer shall, subject to the qualification at paragraph 2.8, identify themselves and any other persons present to the interviewee.

H:12.8 [*Effectively identical to C:12.8.*]

H:12.9 During extended periods where no interviews take place, because of the need to gather further evidence or analyse existing evidence, detainees and their legal representative shall be informed that the investigation into the relevant offence remains ongoing. If practicable, the detainee and legal representative should also be made aware in general terms of any reasons for long gaps between interviews. Consideration should be given to allowing visits, more frequent exercise, or for reading or writing materials to be offered see paragraph 5.4, section 8 and *Note 12C.*

H:12.10 [*Identical to C:12.9.*]

(b) *Documentation*

H:12.11–12.15 [*Identical to C:12.10 to C:12.14, respectively, save that the letters "(a)" and "(b)" in 12.11 are replaced with bullet points.*]

Notes for guidance

H:12A *It is not normally necessary to ask for a written statement if the interview was recorded in accordance with the Code of Practice issued under TACT, Sched. 8, para. 3. Statements under caution should normally be taken in these circumstances only at the person's express wish. A person may however be asked if they want to make such a statement.*

H:12B [*Identical to C:12B.*]

H:12C *Consideration should be given to the matters referred to in paragraph 12.9 after a period of over 24 hours without questioning. This is to ensure that extended periods of detention without an indication that the investigation remains ongoing do not contribute to a deterioration of the detainee's well-being.*

H:13 Interpreters

(a) *General*

H:13.1 Chief officers are responsible for making arrangements (see paragraph 13.1ZA) to provide appropriately qualified independent persons to act as interpreters and to provide translations of essential documents for detained suspects who, in accordance with paragraph 3.5(c)(ii), the custody officer has determined require an interpreter.

If the suspect has a hearing or speech impediment, references to "interpreter" and "interpretation" in this code include appropriate assistance necessary to establish effective communication with that person. See paragraph 13.1C if the detainee is in Wales.

H:13.1ZA [*Identical to C:13.1ZA, save for references to "13.2A" and "13.10" being omitted, and for reference to "Annex L" in lieu of reference to "Annex N".*]

H:13.1A [*Effectively identical to C:13.1A, save for references to "Annex L" and "Annex K" in lieu of references to "Annex N" and "Annex M".*]

H:13.1B [*Identical to C:13.1B.*]

H:13.1C [*Identical to C:13.1C, save for reference to paragraph "3.14" in lieu of reference to paragraph "3.12".*]

(b) *Interviewing suspects–foreign languages*

H:13.2 [*Identical to C:13.2, save for reference to "paragraphs 11.2 or 11.11(c)" and "3.14" in lieu of reference to "paragraphs 11.1 or 11.18(c)" and "3.12", respectively.*]

H:13.3 [*Identical to C:13.2A, save for reference to "paragraphs 11.2 or 11.11(c)" in lieu of reference to "paragraphs 11.1 or 11.18(c)".*]

H:13.4 In the case of a person making a statement under caution to a police officer or other police staff other than in English:

(a) the interpreter shall record the statement in the language it is made;

(b) the person shall be invited to sign it;

(c) an official English translation shall be made in due course.

See paragraphs 13.12 to 13.14 and Annex L for application to live-link interpretation.

(c) *Interviewing suspects who have a hearing or speech impediment*

H:13.5 [*Identical to C:13.5, save for reference to paragraph "3.14" in lieu of reference to paragraph "3.12".*]

H:13.6 [*Identical to C:13.6, save for reference to paragraphs "11.2 or 11.11(c)" in lieu or reference to paragraphs "11.1 or 11.18(c)".*]

H:13.7 [*Not used.*]

(d) *Additional rules for detained persons*

H:13.8 [*Not used.*]

H:13.9 [*Identical to C:13.9.*]

H:13.10 After the custody officer has determined that a detainee requires an interpreter (see paragraph 3.5(c)(ii)) and following the initial action in paragraphs 3.1 to 3.5, arrangements must also be made for an interpreter to explain:

- the grounds and reasons for any authorisation of their detention under the provisions of the Terrorism Act 2000 or the Counter Terrorism Act 2008 (post-charge questioning) to which this code applies; and
- any information about the authorisation given to them by the authorising officer or (as the case may be) the court and which is recorded in the custody record.

See sections 14 and 15 of this code.

H:13.10A [*Identical to C:13.10A.*]

(e) *Translations of essential documents*

H:13.10B [*Identical to C.13.10B, save for reference to "Annex K" in lieu of reference to "Annex M".*]

H:13.10C [*Identical to C:13.10C.*]

(f) *Decisions not to provide interpretation and translation*

H:13.10D If a suspect challenges a decision:

- made by the custody officer in accordance with this code (see paragraph 3.5(c)(ii)) that they do not require an interpreter, or
- made in accordance with paragraphs 13.10A, 13.10B or 13.10C not to make arrange-ments to provide a different interpreter or another translation or not to translate a requested document,

the matter shall be reported to an inspector to deal with as a complaint for the purposes of paragraph 9.3 or 12.10 if the challenge is made during an interview.

(g) *Documentation*

H:13.11 [*Effectively identical to C:13.11, save for reference to "Annex L" and "Annex K" in lieu of reference to "Annex N" and "Annex M", respectively.*]

(h) *Live-link interpretation*

H:13.12 In this section and in Annex L, 'live-link interpretation' means an arrangement to enable communication between the suspect and an interpreter who is not *physically* present with the suspect. The arrangement must ensure that anything said by any person in the suspect's presence and hearing can be interpreted in the same way as if the interpreter was physically present at that time. The com-munication must be by audio *and* visual means for the purpose of an interview, and for all other purposes it may be *either*, by audio and visual means, or by audio means *only*, as follows:

- (a) *Audio and visual communication.* This is required for interviews conducted and recorded in accordance with the Code of Practice for the video recording with sound, of interviews of persons detained under section 41 of the Terrorism Act 2000 and of persons for whom an authorisation to question after charge has been given under section 22 of the Counter-Terrorism Act 2008 (see *Note 13D*). In each of these cases, the interview must be video recorded with sound and during that interview, live link interpretation must *enable*:
    - (i) the suspect, the interviewer, solicitor, appropriate adult and any other person *physically* present with the suspect at any time during the interview and an interpreter who is not *physically* present, to *see* and *hear* each other; and
    - (ii) the interview to be conducted and recorded in accordance with the relevant provisions of the code, subject to the modifications in Part 2 of Annex L.
- (b) *Audio and visual or audio without visual communication.* This applies to communication for the purposes of any provision of this code except as described in (a), which requires or permits information to be given to, sought from, or provided by a suspect, whether orally or in writing, which would include communication between the suspect and their solicitor and/or appropriate adult, and for these cases, live link interpretation must:
    - (i) *enable* the suspect, the person giving or seeking that information, any other person *physically* present with the suspect at that time and an interpreter who is not so present, to either *see* and *hear* each other, or to *hear without seeing* each other (for example by us-ing a telephone); and

      (ii) enable that information to be given to, sought from, or provided by, the suspect in ac-
cordance with the provisions of this Code that apply to that information, as modified
for the purposes of the live-link, by Part 2 of Annex L.

H:13.12A [*Identical to C:13.12A, save for reference to "specified Codes" in lieu of reference to "Codes C, E
and F".*]

H:13.13 [*Identical to C:13.13, save for reference to "Annex L" in lieu of reference to "Annex N".*]

Notes for guidance

H:13A, 13B, 13C [*Identical to C:13A, 13B, 13C, respectively.*]

H:13D *The code of practice referred to in paragraph 13.12, is available here:*
https://www.gov.uk/government/publications/terrorism-act-2000-video-recording-code-of-practice.

H:14 Reviews and extensions of detention under the Terrorism Act 2000

(a) *General*

★A-222   H:14.0 The requirement in paragraph 3.4(b) that documents and materials essential to challenging the lawfulness the detainee's arrest and detention must be made available to the detainee or their
solicitor, applies for the purposes of this section.

H:14.1 The powers and duties of the review officer are in the Terrorism Act 2000, Sched. 8, Pt II.
See *Notes 14A* and *14B*. A review officer should carry out their duties at the police station where the
detainee is held and be allowed such access to the detainee as is necessary to exercise those duties.

H:14.2 For the purposes of reviewing a person's detention, no officer shall put specific questions
to the detainee:

    • regarding their involvement in any offence; or
    • in respect of any comments they may make:
      – when given the opportunity to make representations; or
      – in response to a decision to keep them in detention or extend the maximum period of
        detention.

Such an exchange could constitute an interview as in paragraph 11.1 and would be subject to the associated safeguards in section 11.

H:14.3 If detention is necessary for longer than 48 hours from the time of arrest or, if a person
was being detained under TACT, Sched. 7, from the time at which the examination under Sched. 7
began, a police officer of at least superintendent rank, or a Crown Prosecutor may apply for a warrant of further detention or for an extension or further extension of such a warrant under paragraph
29 or (as the case may be) 36 of Part III of Schedule 8 to the Terrorism Act 2000. See *Note 14C*.

H:14.4 When an application is made for a warrant as described in paragraph 14.3, the detained
person and their representative must be informed of their rights in respect of the application. These
include:

    (i) the right to a written notice of the application (see paragraph 14.4);
    (ii) the right to make oral or written representations to the judicial authority/High Court
       judge about the application;
    (iii) the right to be present and legally represented at the hearing of the application, unless
       specifically excluded by the judicial authority/High Court judge;
    (iv) their right to free legal advice (see section 6 of this code).

H:14.4A TACT, Sched. 8, para. 31 requires the notice of the application for a warrant of further
detention to be provided before the judicial hearing of the application for that warrant and that the
notice must include:

    (a) notification that the application for a warrant has been made;
    (b) the time at which the application was made;
    (c) the time at which the application is to be heard;
    (d) the grounds on which further detention is sought.

A notice must also be provided each time an application is made to extend or further extend an existing warrant.

(b) *Transfer of persons detained for more than 14 days to prison*

H:14.5 If the Detention of Terrorists Suspects (Temporary Extension) Bill is enacted and in force,
a High Court judge may extend or further extend a warrant of further detention to authorise a
person to be detained beyond a period of 14 days from the time of their arrest (or if they were being
detained under TACT, Sched. 7, from the time at which their examination under Sched. 7 began).
The provisions of Annex J will apply when a warrant of further detention is so extended or further
extended.

H:14.6–14.10 [*Not used.*]

(c) *Documentation*

H:14.11 It is the responsibility of the officer who gives any reminders as at paragraph 14.4, to ensure that these are noted in the custody record, as well any comments made by the detained person upon being told of those rights.

H:14.12 The grounds for, and extent of, any delay in conducting a review shall be recorded.

H:14.13 Any written representations shall be retained.

H:14.14 A record shall be made as soon as practicable about the outcome of each review and, if applicable, the grounds on which the review officer authorises continued detention. A record shall also be made as soon as practicable about the outcome of an application for a warrant of further detention or its extension.

H:14.15 [*Not used.*]

Notes for guidance

H:14A *TACT, Sched. 8, Pt II sets out the procedures for review of detention up to 48 hours from the time of arrest under TACT, s.41 (or if a person was being detained under TACT, Sched. 7, from the time at which the examination under Schedule 7 began). These include provisions for the requirement to review detention, postponing a review, grounds for continued detention, designating a review officer, representations, rights of the detained person and keeping a record. The review officer's role ends after a warrant has been issued for extension of detention under Part III of Schedule 8.* ★**A-222a**

H:14B *A review officer may authorise a person's continued detention if satisfied that detention is necessary:*

   (a) *to obtain relevant evidence whether by questioning the person or otherwise;*

   (b) *to preserve relevant evidence;*

   (c) *while awaiting the result of an examination or analysis of relevant evidence;*

   (d) *for the examination or analysis of anything with a view to obtaining relevant evidence;*

   (e) *pending a decision to apply to the Secretary of State for a deportation notice to be served on the detainee, the making of any such application, or the consideration of any such application by the Secretary of State;*

   (f) *pending a decision to charge the detainee with an offence.*

H:14C *Applications for warrants to extend detention beyond 48 hours, may be made for periods of 7 days at a time (initially under TACT, Sched. 8, para. 29, and extensions thereafter under TACT, Sched. 8, para. 36), up to a maximum period of 14 days (or 28 days if the Detention of Terrorists Suspects (Temporary Extension) Bill is enacted and in force) from the time of their arrest (or if they were being detained under TACT, Sched. 7, from the time at which their examination under Sched. 7 began). Applications may be made for shorter periods than 7 days, which must be specified. The judicial authority or High Court judge may also substitute a shorter period if they feel a period of 7 days is inappropriate.*

H:14D *Unless Note 14F applies, applications for warrants that would take the total period of detention up to 14 days or less should be made to a judicial authority, meaning a District Judge (Magistrates' Court) designated by the Lord Chief Justice to hear such applications.*

H:14E *If by virtue of the relevant provisions described in Note 14C being enacted the maximum period of detention is extended to 28 days, any application for a warrant which would take the period of detention beyond 14 days from the time of arrest (or if a person was being detained under TACT, Sched. 7, from the time at which the examination under Sched. 7 began), must be made to a High Court Judge.*

H:14F *If, when the Detention of Terrorists Suspects (Temporary Extension) Bill is enacted and in force, an application is made to a High Court judge for a warrant which would take detention beyond 14 days and the High Court judge instead issues a warrant for a period of time which would not take detention beyond 14 days, further applications for extension of detention must also be made to a High Court judge, regardless of the period of time to which they refer.*

H:14G [*Not used.*]

H:14H *An officer applying for an order under TACT, Sched. 8, para. 34 to withhold specified information on which they intend to rely when applying for a warrant of further detention or the extension or further extension of such a warrant, may make the application for the order orally or in writing. The most appropriate method of application will depend on the circumstances of the case and the need to ensure fairness to the detainee.*

H:14I *After hearing any representations by or on behalf of the detainee and the applicant, the judicial authority or High Court judge may direct that the hearing relating to the extension of detention under Pt III of Sched. 8 is to take place using video conferencing facilities. However, if the judicial authority requires the detained person to be physically present at any hearing, this should be complied with as soon as practicable. Paragraph 33(4) to (9) of TACT, Sched. 8 govern the hearing of applications via video-link or other means.*

H:15 Charging and post-charge questioning in terrorism cases

(a) *Charging*

★A-222b H:15.1 Charging of detained persons is covered by PACE and guidance issued under PACE by the Director of Public Prosecutions. Decisions to charge persons to whom this Code (H) applies, the charging process and related matters are subject to section 16 of PACE Code C.

(b) *Post-charge questioning*

★A-222c H:15.2 Under section 22 of the Counter-Terrorism Act 2008, a judge of the Crown Court may authorise the questioning of a person about an offence for which they have been charged, informed that they may be prosecuted or sent for trial, if the offence:

- is a terrorism offence as set out in section 27 of the Counter-Terrorism Act 2008; or
- is an offence which appears to the judge to have a terrorist connection. See *Note 15C.*

The decision on whether to apply for such questioning will be based on the needs of the investigation. There is no power to detain a person solely for the purposes of post-charge questioning. A person can only be detained whilst being so questioned (whether at a police station or in prison) if they are already there in lawful custody under some existing power. If at a police station the contents of sections 8 and 9 of this code must be considered the minimum standards of treatment for such detainees.

H:15.3 The Crown Court judge may authorise the questioning if they are satisfied that:

- further questioning is necessary in the interests of justice;
- the investigation for the purposes of which the further questioning is being proposed is being conducted diligently and expeditiously; and
- the questioning would not interfere unduly with the preparation of the person's defence to the charge or any other criminal charge that they may be facing.

See *Note 15E*

H:15.4 The judge authorising questioning may specify the location of the questioning.

H:15.5 The judge may only authorise a period up to a maximum of 48 hours before further authorisation must be sought. The 48 hour period would run continuously from the commencement of questioning. This period must include breaks in questioning in accordance with paragraphs 8.6 and 12.2 of this code (see *Note 15B*).

H:15.6 Nothing in this code shall be taken to prevent a suspect seeking a voluntary interview with the police at any time.

H:15.7 For the purposes of this section, any reference in sections 6, 10, 11, 12 and 13 of this code to:

- "suspect" means the person in respect of whom an authorisation has been given under section 22 of the Counter-Terrorism Act 2008 (post-charge questioning of terrorist suspects) to interview them;
- "interview" means post-charge questioning authorised under section 22 of the Counter-Terrorism Act 2008;
- "offence" means an offence for which the person has been charged, informed that they may be prosecuted or sent for trial and about which the person is being questioned; and
- "place of detention" means the location of the questioning specified by the judge (see paragraph 15.4),

and the provisions of those sections apply (as appropriate), to such questioning (whether at a police station or in prison) subject to the further modifications in the following paragraphs:

Right to legal advice

H:15.8 In section 6 of this code, for the purposes of post-charge questioning:

- access to a solicitor may not be delayed under Annex B; and
- paragraph 6.5 (direction that a detainee may only consult a solicitor within the sight and hearing of a qualified officer) does not apply.

Cautions

H:15.9 In section 10 of this code, unless the restriction on drawing adverse inferences from silence applies (see paragraph 15.10), for the purposes of post-charge questioning, the caution must be given in the following terms before any such questions are asked:

"*You do not have to say anything. But it may harm your defence if you do not mention when questioned something which you later rely on in court. Anything you do say may be given in evidence.*"

Where the use of the Welsh Language is appropriate, a constable may provide the caution directly in Welsh in the following terms:

"*Does dim rhaid i chi ddweud dim byd. Ond gall niweidio eich amddiffyniad os na fyddwch chi'n sôn, wrth gael eich holi, am rywbeth y byddwch chi'n dibynnu arno nes ymlaen yn y Llys. Gall unrhyw beth yr ydych yn ei ddweud gael ei roi fel tystiolaeth.*"

H:15.10 The only restriction on drawing adverse inferences from silence, see Annex C, applies in those situations where a person has asked for legal advice and is questioned before receiving such advice in accordance with paragraph 6.7(b).

Interviews

H:15.11 In section 11, for the purposes of post-charge questioning, whenever a person is questioned, they must be informed of the offence for which they have been charged or informed that they may be prosecuted, or that they have been sent for trial and about which they are being questioned.

H:15.12 Paragraph 11.2 (place where questioning may take place) does not apply to post-charge questioning.

Recording post-charge questioning

H:15.13 All interviews must be video recorded with sound in accordance with the separate Code of Practice issued under section 25 of the Counter-Terrorism Act 2008 for the video recording with sound of post-charge questioning authorised under section 22 of the Counter-Terrorism Act 2008 (see paragraph 11.8).

Notes for guidance

H:15A *If a person is detained at a police station for the purposes of post-charge questioning, a custody record*   ★**A-222d** *must be opened in accordance with section 2 of this code. The custody record must note the power under which the person is being detained, the time at which the person was transferred into police custody, their time of arrival at the police station and their time of being presented to the custody officer.*

H:15B *The custody record must note the time at which the interview process commences. This shall be regarded as the relevant time for any period of questioning in accordance with paragraph 15.5 of this code.*

H:15C *Where reference is made to "terrorist connection" in paragraph 15.2, this is determined in accordance with section 30 of the Counter-Terrorism Act 2008. Under section 30 of that Act a court must in certain circumstances determine whether an offence has a terrorist connection. These are offences under general criminal law which may be prosecuted in terrorism cases (for example explosives-related offences and conspiracy to murder). An offence has a terrorist connection if the offence is, or takes place in the course of, an act of terrorism or is committed for the purposes of terrorism (section 98 of the Act). Normally the court will make the determination during the sentencing process, however for the purposes of post-charge questioning, a Crown Court judge must determine whether the offence could have a terrorist connection.*

H:15D *The powers under section 22 of the Counter-Terrorism Act 2008 are separate from and additional to the normal questioning procedures within this code. Their overall purpose is to enable the further questioning of a terrorist suspect after charge. They should not therefore be used to replace or circumvent the normal powers for dealing with routine questioning.*

H:15E *Post-charge questioning has been created because it is acknowledged that terrorist investigations can be large and complex and that a great deal of evidence can come to light following the charge of a terrorism suspect. This can occur, for instance, from the translation of material or as the result of additional investigation. When considering an application for post-charge questioning, the police must "satisfy" the judge on all three points under paragraph 15.3. This means that the judge will either authorise or refuse an application on the balance of whether the conditions in paragraph 15.3 are all met. It is important therefore, that when making the application, to consider the following questions:*

- *What further evidence is the questioning expected to provide?*
- *Why was it not possible to obtain this evidence before charge?*
- *How and why was the need to question after charge first recognised?*
- *How is the questioning expected to contribute further to the case?*
- *To what extent could the time and place for further questioning interfere with the preparation of the person's defence (for example if authorisation is sought close to the time of a trial)?*
- *What steps will be taken to minimise any risk that questioning might interfere with the preparation of the person's defence?*

This list is not exhaustive but outlines the type of questions that could be relevant to any asked by a judge in considering an application.

H:16 Testing persons for the presence of specified Class A drugs

★**A-223**   H:16.1 The provisions for drug testing under section 63B of PACE (as amended by section 5 of the Criminal Justice Act 2003 and section 7 of the Drugs Act 2005), do not apply to persons to whom this code applies. Guidance on these provisions can be found in section 17 of PACE Code C.

ANNEX A

Intimate and strip searches

A *Intimate search*

★**A-223a**   H:1. [*Identical to Code C, Annex A, para. 1.*]

(a) Action

H:2. Body orifices other than the mouth may be searched if authorised by an officer of inspector rank or above who has reasonable grounds for believing that the person may have concealed on themselves anything which they could and might use to cause physical injury to themselves or others at the station and the officer has reasonable grounds for believing that an intimate search is the only means of removing those items.

H:3. Before the search begins, a police officer or designated detention officer, must tell the detainee:

  (a) that the authority to carry out the search has been given;
  (b) the grounds for giving the authorisation and for believing that the article cannot be removed without an intimate search.

Note: Paragraph 1.11A of this code requires someone to fulfil the role of the appropriate adult to be present when a 17-year-old is told about the authority and grounds for an intimate search.

H:4. An intimate search may only be carried out by a registered medical practitioner or registered nurse, unless an officer of at least inspector rank considers this is not practicable, in which case a police officer may carry out the search. See *Notes A1 to A5.*

H:5. [*Identical to Code C, Annex A, para. 3A, save for reference to paragraph "2" in lieu of reference to paragraph "2(a)(i)".*]

H:6. [*Identical to Code C, Annex A, para. 5, save for reference to "Annex I" in lieu of reference to "Annex L".*]

H:7. [*Identical to Code C, Annex A, para. 6, save for references to "paragraph 2", "Annex I" and "paragraph 6" in lieu of references to "paragraph 2(a)(i)", "Annex L" and "paragraph 5", respectively.*]

(b) Documentation

H:8. In the case of an intimate search under paragraph 2, the following shall be recorded as soon as practicable, in the detainee's custody record:

  • the authorisation to carry out the search;
  • the grounds for giving the authorisation;
  • the grounds for believing the article could not be removed without an intimate search;
  • which parts of the detainee's body were searched;
  • who carried out the search;
  • who was present;
  • the result.

H:9. [*Identical to Code C, Annex A, para. 8.*]

B *Strip search*

H:10. [*Identical to Code C, Annex A, para. 9.*]

(a) Action

H:11. [*Identical to Code C, Annex A, para. 10.*]

The conduct of strip searches

H:12. [*Identical to Code C, Annex A, para. 11, save for references to "Annex I" in lieu of references to "Annex L".*]

(b) Documentation

H:13. [*Identical to Code C, Annex A, para. 12.*]

Notes for guidance

H:A1, A2 [*Identical to Code C, Annex A, A1 and A2, respectively.*]   **★A-223b**

H:A3 [*Identical to Code C, Annex A, A3, save for reference to "paragraph 2" in lieu of reference to "paragraph 2(a)(i)".*]

H:A4 [*Identical to Code C, Annex A, A4, save for reference to "paragraph 2" in lieu of reference to "paragraph 2(a)(i)".*]

H:A5 [*Identical to Code C, Annex A, A5.*]

ANNEX B

Delay in notifying arrest or allowing access to legal advice for persons detained under the Terrorism Act 2000.

A Delays under TACT, Sched. 8

H:1. The rights as in sections 5 or 6, may be delayed if the person is detained under the Terrorism   **★A-224**
Act 2000, s.41, has not yet been charged with an offence and an officer of superintendent rank or
above has reasonable grounds for believing the exercise of either right will have one of the following
consequences:

  (a) interference with or harm to evidence of a serious offence,
  (b) interference with or physical injury to any person,
  (c) the alerting of persons who are suspected of having committed a serious offence but who
      have not been arrested for it,
  (d) the hindering of the recovery of property obtained as a result of a serious offence or in
      respect of which a forfeiture order could be made under section 23,
  (e) interference with the gathering of information about the commission, preparation or
      instigation of acts of terrorism,
  (f) the alerting of a person and thereby making it more difficult to prevent an act of terrorism, or
  (g) the alerting of a person and thereby making it more difficult to secure a person's apprehension, prosecution or conviction in connection with the commission, preparation or
      instigation of an act of terrorism.

H:2. These rights may also be delayed if the officer has reasonable grounds for believing that:

  (a) the detained person has benefited from his criminal conduct (to be decided in accordance with Part 2 of the Proceeds of Crime Act 2002), and
  (b) the recovery of the value of the property constituting the benefit will be hindered by—
      (i) informing the named person of the detained person's detention (in the case of an
          authorisation under paragraph 8(1)(a) of Schedule 8 to TACT), or
      (ii) the exercise of the right under paragraph 7 (in the case of an authorisation under
          paragraph 8(1)(b) of Schedule 8 to TACT).

H:3. Authority to delay a detainee's right to consult privately with a solicitor may be given only if
the authorising officer has reasonable grounds to believe the solicitor the detainee wants to consult
will, inadvertently or otherwise, pass on a message from the detainee or act in some other way which
will have any of the consequences specified under paragraph 8 of Schedule 8 to the Terrorism Act
2000. In these circumstances, the detainee must be allowed to choose another solicitor. See *Note B3*.

H:4. [*Identical to Code C, Annex B, para. 4.*]

H:5. [*Identical to Code C, Annex B, para. 5.*]

H:6. These rights may be delayed only for as long as is necessary but not beyond 48 hours from
the time of arrest (or if a person was being detained under TACT, Sched. 7, from the time at which
the examination under Sched. 7 began). If the above grounds cease to apply within this time the
detainee must as soon as practicable be asked if they wish to exercise either right, the custody record
noted accordingly, and action taken in accordance with the relevant section of this code.

H:7. A person must be allowed to consult a solicitor for a reasonable time before any court
hearing.

B *Documentation*

H:8. [*Identical to Code C, Annex B, para. 13.*]

H:9. [*Identical to Code C, Annex B, para. 14, save for reference to "paragraph 6" in lieu of reference to "paragraphs 6 or 11".*]

C *Cautions and special warnings*

H:10. [*Identical to Code C, Annex B, para. 15.*]

Notes for Guidance

★A-224a

H:B1 [*Identical to Code C, Annex B, B1, save for reference to "paragraph 3.15 and 3.17" in lieu of reference to "paragraph 3.13 and 3.15".*]

H:B2, B3 [*Identical to Code C, Annex B, B2 and B3, respectively.*]

ANNEX C

Restriction on drawing adverse inferences from silence and terms of the caution when the restriction applies

(a) *The restriction on drawing adverse inferences from silence*

★A-224b

H:1. The Criminal Justice and Public Orders Act 1994, ss.34, 36 and 37 as amended by the Youth Justice and Criminal Evidence Act 1999, s.58 describe the conditions under which adverse inferences may be drawn from a person's failure or refusal to say anything about their involvement in the offence when interviewed, after being charged or informed they may be prosecuted. These provisions are subject to an overriding restriction on the ability of a court or jury to draw adverse inferences from a person's silence. This restriction applies:

(a) to any detainee at a police station who, before being interviewed, see section 11 or being charged or informed they may be prosecuted, see section 15, has:

(i) asked for legal advice, see section 6, para. 6.1;

(ii) not been allowed an opportunity to consult a solicitor, including the duty solicitor, as in this code; and

(iii) not changed their mind about wanting legal advice, see section 6, para. 6.7(d).
Note the condition in (ii) will:

– apply when a detainee who has asked for legal advice is interviewed before speaking to a solicitor as in section 6, para. 6.6(a) or (b);

– not apply if the detained person declines to ask for the duty solicitor, see section 6, para. 6.7(b) and (c).

(b) to any person who has been charged with, or informed they may be prosecuted for, an offence who:

(i) has had brought to their notice a written statement made by another person or the content of an interview with another person which relates to that offence, see PACE Code C s.16, para. 16.4;

(ii) is interviewed about that offence, see PACE Code C s.16, para. 16.5; or

(iii) makes a written statement about that offence, see Annex D paragraphs 4 and 9, unless post-charge questioning has been authorised in accordance with section 22 of the Counter-Terrorism Act 2008, in which case the restriction will apply only if the person has asked for legal advice, see section 6, para.6.1, and is questioned before receiving such advice in accordance with paragraph 6.7(b). See paragraph 15.11.

(b) *Terms of the caution when the restriction applies*

H:2. [*Identical to Code C, Annex C, para. 2.*]

H:3. [*Identical to Code C, Annex C, para. 3, save for reference to "Note C1" in lieu of reference to "Note C2".*]

Notes for Guidance

★A-225

H:C1 [*Identical to Code C, Annex C, C2.*]

ANNEX D

Written statements under caution

[*Identical to Annex D to Code C.*]   ★**A-225a**

ANNEX E

Summary of provisions relating to mentally disordered and otherwise mentally vulnerable people

H:1. [*Identical to Code C, Annex E, para. 1, save for reference to "paragraph 1.10" in lieu of reference to*   ★**A-225b**
"paragraph 1.4" and absence of any reference to Note E4.]

H:2. [*Identical to Code C, Annex E, para. 2, save for reference to "paragraph 1.13(b)" in lieu of reference to*
"paragraph 1.7(b)".]

H:3. If the detention of a person who is mentally vulnerable or appears to be suffering from a
mental disorder is authorised by the review officer (see paragraphs 14.1 and 14.2 and *Notes 14A* and
14B), the custody officer must as soon as practicable inform the appropriate adult of the grounds for
detention and the person's whereabouts, and ask the adult to come to the police station to see them.
If the appropriate adult:

- is already at the station when information is given as in paragraphs 3.1 to 3.5 the information must be given in their presence;
- is not at the station when the provisions of paragraph 3.1 to 3.5 are complied with these
  provisions must be complied with again in their presence once they arrive.

See paragraphs 3.15 to 3.16

H:4. [*Identical to Code C, Annex E, para. 4, save for references to paragraphs "3.20" and "6.6" in lieu of*
references to paragraphs "3.19" and "6.5A", respectively.]

H:5. [*Identical to Code C, Annex E, para. 5, save for reference to "paragraph 9.6 and 9.8" in lieu of refer-*
ence to "paragraph 9.5 and 9.6".]

H:6. [*Identical to Code C, Annex E, para. 7, save for reference to "paragraph 10.11" in lieu of reference to*
"paragraph 10.12".]

H:7. [*Identical to Code C, Annex E, para. 8, save for reference to "paragraphs 11.2 or 11.11 or 11.13"*
and "paragraphs 11.2, 11.9 and 11.11 to 11.13" in lieu of reference to "paragraphs 11.1 or 11.18 or 11.20"
and "paragraphs 11.1, 11.15 and 11.18 to 11.20", respectively.]

H:8. [*Identical to Code C, Annex E, para. 9, save for reference to "paragraph 11.10" in lieu of reference to*
"paragraph 11.17".]

H:9. [*Identical to Code C, Annex E, para. 11, save for reference to "PACE Code C Section 16" in lieu of*
reference to "paragraphs 16.1 to 16.4A".]

H:10. [*Identical to Code C, Annex E, para. 12, save for reference to "paragraphs 6 and 12(c)" in lieu of*
reference to "paragraphs 5 and 11(c)".]

H:11. [*Identical to Code C, Annex E, para. 13.*]

Notes for guidance

H:E1 [*Effectively identical to Code C, Annex E, E1, save for reference to "paragraphs 3.20 and 6.6" in lieu*   ★**A-226**
of reference to "paragraphs 3.19 and 6.5A".]

H:E2 [*Identical to Code C, Annex E, E2.*]

H:E3 [*Identical to Code C, Annex E, E3, save for reference to "paragraphs 11.2 and 11.11 to 11.13" in*
lieu of reference to "paragraphs 11.1 and 11.18 to 11.20".]

ANNEX F

[*Not used.*]   ★**A-226a**

ANNEX G

Fitness to be interviewed

[*Identical to Annex G to Code C.*]   ★**A-226b**

ANNEX H

Detained person: observation list

★A-227   [*Identical to Annex H to Code C.*]

ANNEX I

Establishing gender of persons for the purpose of searching

★A-228   [*Identical to Annex L to Code C, save that the references to notes are to Note I1, I2 and so on, rather than to Note L1, L2 and so on, and that the reference to paragraph "12" of Annex A is included in the first bullet point of Note I1.*]

ANNEX J

Transfer of persons detained for more than 14 days to prison

★A-229   H:1. When a warrant of further detention is extended or further extended by a High Court judge to authorise a person's detention beyond a period of 14 days from the time of their arrest (or if they were being detained under TACT, Sched. 7, from the time at which their examination under Schedule 7 began), the person must be transferred from detention in a police station to detention in a designated prison as soon as is practicable after the warrant is issued, unless:

    (a) the detainee specifically requests to remain in detention at a police station and that request can be accommodated, or

    (b) there are reasonable grounds to believe that transferring the detainee to a prison would:

        (i) significantly hinder a terrorism investigation;

        (ii) delay charging of the detainee or their release from custody, or

        (iii) otherwise prevent the investigation from being conducted diligently and expeditiously.

Any grounds in (b)(i) to (iii) above which are relied upon for not transferring the detainee to prison must be presented to the senior judge as part of the application for the extension or further extension of the warrant. See *Note J1.*

H:2. If at any time during which a person remains in detention at a police station under the warrant, the grounds at (b)(i) to (iii) cease to apply, the person must be transferred to a prison as soon as practicable.

H:3. Police should maintain an agreement with the National Offender Management Service (NOMS) that stipulates named prisons to which individuals may be transferred under this paragraph. This should be made with regard to ensuring detainees are moved to the most suitable prison for the purposes of the investigation and their welfare, and should include provision for the transfer of male, female and juvenile detainees. Police should ensure that the Governor of a prison to which they intend to transfer a detainee is given reasonable notice of this. Where practicable, this should be no later than the point at which a warrant is applied for that would take the period of detention beyond 14 days.

H:4. Following a detainee's transfer to a designated prison, their detention will be governed by the terms of Schedule 8 to TACT 2000 and the Prison Rules and this code of practice will not apply during any period that the person remains in prison detention. The code will once more apply if the person is transferred back from prison detention to police detention. In order to enable the Governor to arrange for the production of the detainee back into police custody, police should give notice to the Governor of the relevant prison as soon as possible of any decision to transfer a detainee from prison back to a police station. Any transfer between a prison and a police station should be conducted by police and this code will be applicable during the period of transit. See *Note 2J.* A detainee should only remain in police custody having been transferred back from a prison, for as long as is necessary for the purpose of the investigation.

H:5. The investigating team and custody officer should provide as much information as necessary to enable the relevant prison authorities to provide appropriate facilities to detain an individual. This should include, but not be limited to:

    (i) medical assessments

    (ii) security and risk assessments

    (iii) details of the detained person's legal representatives

    (iv) details of any individuals from whom the detained person has requested visits, or who have requested to visit the detained person.

H:6. Where a detainee is to be transferred to prison, the custody officer should inform the detainee's legal adviser beforehand that the transfer is to take place (including the name of the prison). The custody officer should also make all reasonable attempts to inform:

- family or friends who have been informed previously of the detainee's detention; and
- the person who was initially informed of the detainee's detention in accordance with paragraph 5.1.

H:7. Any decision not to transfer a detained person to a designated prison under paragraph 1, must be recorded, along with the reasons for this decision. If a request under paragraph 1(a) is not accommodated, the reasons for this should also be recorded.

Notes for Guidance

H:J1 *Transfer to prison is intended to ensure that individuals who are detained for extended periods of time*   **★A-230**
are held in a place designed for longer periods of detention than police stations. Prison will provide detainees with a greater range of facilities more appropriate to longer detention periods.

H:J2 *This code will only apply as is appropriate to the conditions of detention during the period of transit. There is obviously no requirement to provide such things as bed linen or reading materials for the journey between prison and police station.*

ANNEX K

Documents and records to be translated

H:1. [*Identical to Code C, Annex M, para. 1, save for reference to "Note K1" in lieu of reference to "Note*   **★A-230a**
M1".]

H:2. The documents considered essential for the purposes of this Code and for which (subject to paragraphs 3 to 7) written translations must be created are the records made in accordance with this Code of the grounds and reasons for any authorisation of a suspects detention under the provisions of the Terrorism Act 2000 or the Counter Terrorism Act 2008 (post-charge questioning) to which this Code applies as they are described and referred to in the suspect's custody record. Translations should be created as soon as practicable after the authorisation has been recorded and provided as soon as practicable thereafter, whilst the person is detained or after they have been released (see *Note K3*). See paragraphs 13.12 to 13.14 and Annex L for application to live-link interpretation.

H:3. The custody officer may authorise an oral translation or oral summary of the documents to be provided (through an interpreter) instead of a written translation. Such an oral translation or summary may only be provided if it would not prejudice the fairness of the proceedings by in any way adversely affecting or otherwise undermining or limiting the ability of the suspect in question to understand their position and to communicate effectively with police officers, interviewers, solicitors and appropriate adults with regard to their detention and the investigation of the offence in question and to defend themselves in the event of criminal proceedings. The quantity and complexity of the information in the document should always be considered and specific additional consideration given if the suspect is mentally disordered or otherwise mentally vulnerable or is a juvenile or a 17-year-old (see Code H para.1.11A). The reason for the decision must be recorded (see paragraph 13.11(e)).

H:4. [*Identical to Code C, Annex M, para. 4 (but note that there is no table in Annex K, unlike Annex M to Code C)).*]

H:5. [*Identical to Code C, Annex M, para. 5.*]

H:6. [*Identical to Code C, Annex M, para. 6, save for reference to "Note K2 and K3" in lieu of reference to "Notes M2 and M3".*]

H:7. For the purpose of the waiver:
- (a) the consent of a person who is mentally disordered or otherwise mentally vulnerable person is only valid if the information about the circumstances under which they can waive the right and the reminder about their right to legal advice mentioned in paragraphs 3 to 5 and their consent is given in the presence of the appropriate adult, and the appropriate adult also agrees.
- (b) the consent of a juvenile is only valid if their parent's or guardian's consent is also obtained unless the juvenile is under 14, when their parent's or guardian's consent is sufficient in its own right and the information and reminder mentioned in sub-paragraph (a) above and their consent is also given in the presence of the appropriate adult (who may or may not be a parent or guardian).

H:8. [*Identical to Code C, Annex M, para. 8 (but note that there is no table in Annex K, unlike Annex M to Code C)).*]

H:9. [*Identical to Code C, Annex M, para. 9.*]

Documentation

H:10. [*Identical to Code C, Annex M, para. 10, save for reference to "Code H" in lieu of reference to "Code C".*]

Note for guidance

H:K1, H:K2, H:K3 [*Identical to Code C, Annex M, M1-M3, save for reference to 2000 Act in lieu of reference to 1984 Act.*]

ANNEX L

Live-link interpretation (para. 13.12)

Part 1: When the physical presence of the interpreter is not required.

★**A-230b**   H:1. [*Identical to Code C, Annex N, para. 1.*]

H:2. Decisions in accordance with this Annex that the physical presence of the interpreter is not required and to permit live-link interpretation, must be made on a case by case basis. Each decision must take account of the age, gender and vulnerability of the suspect, the nature and circumstances of the terrorism investigation and the impact on the suspect according to the particular purpose(s) for which the suspect requires the assistance of an interpreter and the time(s) when that assistance is required (see *Note L1*). For this reason, the custody officer must consider whether the ability of the particular suspect, to communicate confidently and effectively for the purpose in question (see paragraph 3) is likely to be adversely affected or otherwise undermined or limited if the interpreter is not physically present and live-link interpretation is used. Although a suspect for whom an appropriate adult is required may be more likely to be adversely affected as described, it is important to note that a person who does not require an appropriate adult may also be adversely impacted by the use of live-link interpretation.

H:3. Examples of purposes referred to in paragraph 2 include:

(a) understanding and appreciating their position having regard to any information given to them, or sought from them, in accordance with this or any other code of practice which, in particular, include:

- the caution (see paragraphs C10.1 and 10.12).
- the special warning (see paragraphs 10.9 to 10.11).
- information about their suspected involvement in the commission, preparation or instigation of acts of terrorism offence (see paragraphs 10.3, 11.1 and *Note 11ZA*).
- the grounds and reasons for detention (see paragraphs 13.10 and 13.10A).
- the translation of essential documents (see paragraph 13.10B and Annex L).
- their rights and entitlements (see paragraph 3.14).
- intimate and non-intimate searches of detained persons at police stations.
- provisions and procedures that apply to taking fingerprints, samples and photographs from persons detained for the purposes of a terrorism investigation.

(b) understanding and seeking clarification from the interviewer of questions asked during an interview that must be video recorded with sound (see paragraph 7) and of anything else that is said by the interviewer and answering the questions.

(c) consulting privately with their solicitor and (if applicable) the appropriate adult (see paragraphs 3.18, 13.3, 13.6 and 13.9):

(i) to help decide whether to answer questions put to them during interview; and

(ii) about any other matter concerning their detention and treatment whilst in custody.

(d) communicating with practitioners and others who have some formal responsibility for, or an interest in, the health and welfare of the suspect. Particular examples include appropriate healthcare professionals (see section 9 of this code) and Independent Custody Visitors.

H:4. [*Identical to Code C, Annex N, para. 4, save for reference to "Note L2" in lieu of reference to "Note N2".*]

When the authority of an inspector is required

★**A-230c**   H:5. [*Identical to Code C, Annex N, para. 5, save for the words "or interviewer (subject to paragraph 13.1(b))" being omitted.*]

H:6. [*Effectively identical to Code C, Annex N, para. 6, save for reference to "Note L3" in lieu of reference to "Note N3".*]

H:7. The separate code of practice that governs the conduct and recording of interviews of persons detained at a police station under section 41 of the Terrorism Act 2000 (TACT) and of persons in respect of whom an authorisation to question after charge has been given under section 22 of the Counter-Terrorism Act 2008 requires those interviews to be video recorded with sound. This will require the visual record to show the live-link interpretation arrangements and the interpreter as seen and experienced by the suspect during the interview (see *Note L4*).

Documentation

H:8. [*Identical to Code C, Annex N, para. 8.*] ★**A-230d**

Part 2: Modifications for live-link interpretation

H:9. The following modification shall apply for the purposes of live-link interpretation:

(a) Code H paragraph 13.4:

For sub-paragraph (b), *substitute*: "A clear legible copy of the complete statement shall be ★**A-230e** sent without delay via the live-link to the interviewer. The interviewer, after confirming with the suspect that the copy is legible and complete, shall invite the suspect to sign it. The interviewer is responsible for ensuring that that the signed copy and the original record made by the interpreter are retained with the case papers for use in evidence if required and must advise the interpreter of their obligation to keep the original record securely for that purpose.";

(b) Code of Practice for video recording interviews with sound—paragraph 4.4

At the beginning of the paragraph *insert*: "Before the interview commences, the operation ★**A-230f** of live-link interpretation shall be explained and demonstrated to the suspect, their solicitor and appropriate adult, unless it has been previously explained and demonstrated (see Code H Annex L para.4)."

(c) Code for video recording interviews with sound—paragraph 4.22 (signing master recording label)

After the *third sentence*, insert: "If live-link interpretation has been used, the interviewer ★**A-230g** should ask the interpreter to observe the removal and sealing of the master recording and to confirm in writing that they have seen it sealed and signed by the interviewer. A clear legible copy of the confirmation signed by the interpreter must be sent via the livelink to the interviewer. The interviewer is responsible for ensuring that the original confirmation and the copy are retained with the case papers for use in evidence if required, and must advise the interpreter of their obligation to keep the original confirmation securely for that purpose."

Notes for guidance

H:L1 [*Identical to Code C, Annex N, N1, save for reference to "Code H" in lieu of reference to "Code C".*] ★**A-230h**
H:L2 *The explanation and demonstration of live-link interpretation is intended to help the suspect, solicitor and appropriate adult make an informed decision on whether to agree to its use and to allay any concerns they may have.*
H:L3 [*Identical to Code C, Annex N, N3.*]
H:L4 *The Code of Practice referred to in paragraphs 7 and 9, is available here:*
https://www.gov.uk/government/publications/terrorism-act-2000-video-recording-code-of-practice.

B. Under the Criminal Procedure and Investigations Act 1996

(1) As to the recording and retention by the police of material obtained during an investigation and its supply to the prosecutor

Introduction

Pursuant to sections 23 and 25 of the 1996 Act (§§ 12-97, 12-98 in the main work), the Secretary **A-231** of State has prepared and published three codes of practice governing the action the police must take in recording and retaining material obtained in the course of a criminal investigation and regulating its supply to the prosecutor for a decision on disclosure.

The first code came into force on the day appointed for the purpose of Part I of the 1996 Act, namely April 1, 1997 (S.I. 1997 No. 1033). A second code came into force on April 4, 2005: Criminal Procedure and Investigations Act 1996 (Code of Practice) Order 2005 (S.I. 2005 No. 985). The third code (set out *post*) came into force on March 19, 2015: Criminal Procedure and Investigations Act 1996 (Code of Practice) Order 2015 (S.I. 2015 No. 861).

In connection with this code, see also § 12-96 in the main work (meaning of "investigation").

As to the significance of the code of practice in relation to material held overseas, outside the European Union, by entities not subject to the jurisdiction of the United Kingdom, see *R. v. Flook* [2010] 1 Cr.App.R. 30, CA (§ 12-53 in the main work).

CRIMINAL PROCEDURE AND INVESTIGATIONS ACT 1996 CODE OF PRACTICE UNDER PART II

Preamble

A-232   This code of practice is issued under Part II of the Criminal Procedure and Investigations Act 1996 ("the Act"). It sets out the manner in which police officers are to record, retain and reveal to the prosecutor material obtained in a criminal investigation and which may be relevant to the investigation, and related matters.

1. Introduction

A-232a   1.1 This code of practice applies in respect of criminal investigations conducted by police officers which begin on or after the day on which this code comes into effect. Persons other than police officers who are charged with the duty of conducting an investigation as defined in the Act are to have regard to the relevant provisions of the code, and should take these into account in applying their own operating procedures.

1.2 This code does not apply to persons who are not charged with the duty of conducting an investigation as defined in the Act.

1.3 Nothing in this code applies to material intercepted in obedience to a warrant issued under section 2 of the Interception of Communications Act 1985 or section 5 of the Regulation of Investigatory Powers Act 2000, or to any copy of that material as defined in section 10 of the 1985 Act or section 15 of the 2000 Act.

1.4 This code extends only to England and Wales.

2. Definitions

A-233   2.1 In this code:
- a criminal investigation is an investigation conducted by police officers with a view to it being ascertained whether a person should be charged with an offence, or whether a person charged with an offence is guilty of it. This will include:
  - investigations into crimes that have been committed;
  - investigations whose purpose is to ascertain whether a crime has been committed, with a view to the possible institution of criminal proceedings; and
  - investigations which begin in the belief that a crime may be committed, for example when the police keep premises or individuals under observation for a period of time, with a view to the possible institution of criminal proceedings;
- charging a person with an offence includes prosecution by way of summons or postal requisition;
- an investigator is any police officer involved in the conduct of a criminal investigation. All investigators have a responsibility for carrying out the duties imposed on them under this code, including in particular recording information, and retaining records of information and other material;
- the officer in charge of an investigation is the police officer responsible for directing a criminal investigation. He is also responsible for ensuring that proper procedures are in place for recording information, and retaining records of information and other material, in the investigation;
- the disclosure officer is the person responsible for examining material retained by the police during the investigation; revealing material to the prosecutor during the investigation and any criminal proceedings resulting from it, and certifying that he has done this; and disclosing material to the accused at the request of the prosecutor;
- the prosecutor is the authority responsible for the conduct, on behalf of the Crown, of criminal proceedings resulting from a specific criminal investigation;

- material is material of any kind, including information and objects, which is obtained or inspected in the course of a criminal investigation and which may be relevant to the investigation. This includes not only material coming into the possession of the investigator (such as documents seized in the course of searching premises) but also material generated by him (such as interview records);
- material may be relevant to the investigation if it appears to an investigator, or to the officer in charge of an investigation, or to the disclosure officer, that it has some bearing on any offence under investigation or any person being investigated, or on the surrounding circumstances of the case, unless it is incapable of having any impact on the case;
- sensitive material is material, the disclosure of which, the disclosure officer believes, would give rise to a real risk of serious prejudice to an important public interest;
- references to prosecution disclosure are to the duty of the prosecutor under sections 3 and 7A of the Act to disclose material which is in his possession or which he has inspected in pursuance of this code, and which might reasonably be considered capable of undermining the case against the accused, or of assisting the case for the accused;
- references to the disclosure of material to a person accused of an offence include references to the disclosure of material to his legal representative;
- references to police officers and to the chief officer of police include those employed in a police force as defined in section 3(3) of the Prosecution of Offences Act 1985.

As to the meaning of "criminal investigation", see *DPP v. Metten*, unreported, January 22, 1999, DC (§ 12-96 in the main work).

3. General responsibilities

3.1 The functions of the investigator, the officer in charge of an investigation and the disclosure officer are separate. Whether they are undertaken by one, two or more persons will depend on the complexity of the case and the administrative arrangements within each police force. Where they are undertaken by more than one person, close consultation between them is essential to the effective performance of the duties imposed by this code. **A-234**

3.2 In any criminal investigation, one or more deputy disclosure officers may be appointed to assist the disclosure officer, and a deputy disclosure officer may perform any function of a disclosure officer as defined in paragraph 2.1.

3.3 The chief officer of police for each police force is responsible for putting in place arrangements to ensure that in every investigation the identity of the officer in charge of an investigation and the disclosure officer is recorded. The chief officer of police for each police force shall ensure that disclosure officers and deputy disclosure officers have sufficient skills and authority, commensurate with the complexity of the investigation, to discharge their functions effectively. An individual must not be appointed as disclosure officer, or continue in that role, if that is likely to result in a conflict of interest, for instance, if the disclosure officer is the victim of the alleged crime which is the subject of the investigation. The advice of a more senior officer must always be sought if there is doubt as to whether a conflict of interest precludes an individual acting as disclosure officer. If thereafter the doubt remains, the advice of a prosecutor should be sought.

3.4 The officer in charge of an investigation may delegate tasks to another investigator, to civilians employed by the police force, or to other persons participating in the investigation under arrangements for joint investigations, but he remains responsible for ensuring that these have been carried out and for accounting for any general policies followed in the investigation. In particular, it is an essential part of his duties to ensure that all material which may be relevant to an investigation is retained, and either made available to the disclosure officer or (in exceptional circumstances) revealed directly to the prosecutor.

3.5 In conducting an investigation, the investigator should pursue all reasonable lines of inquiry, whether these point towards or away from the suspect. What is reasonable in each case will depend on the particular circumstances. For example, where material is held on computer, it is a matter for the investigator to decide which material on the computer it is reasonable to inquire into, and in what manner.

3.6 If the officer in charge of an investigation believes that other persons may be in possession of material that may be relevant to the investigation, and if this has not been obtained under paragraph 3.5 above, he should ask the disclosure officer to inform them of the existence of the investigation and to invite them to retain the material in case they receive a request for its disclosure. The disclosure officer should inform the prosecutor that they may have such material. However, the officer in charge of an investigation is not required to make speculative enquiries of other persons; there must be some reason to believe that they may have relevant material. That reason may come from information provided to the police by the accused or from other inquiries made or from some other source.

3.7 If, during a criminal investigation, the officer in charge of an investigation or disclosure officer for any reason no longer has responsibility for the functions falling to him, either his supervisor or the police officer in charge of criminal investigations for the police force concerned must assign someone else to assume that responsibility. That person's identity must be recorded, as with those initially responsible for these functions in each investigation.

As to the meaning of "criminal investigation", see *DPP v. Metten*, unreported, January 22, 1999, DC (§ 12-96 in the main work).

Where, in the run-up to an election, there was an arrangement that a local electoral office would notify the police of any suspected fraudulent applications for postal votes, where that office submitted 1,600 suspected fraudulent applications to the police (out of a total of 10,000 applications), where the criminal investigation that ensued resulted in the prosecution of the appellants for conspiracy to defraud the electoral officer, and where complaint was made about the non-disclosure of the 8,400 postal vote applications that had been examined by the electoral office, but had not been submitted to the police, there was no duty of disclosure on the electoral office as either a delegate of the investigator or as a joint investigator within paragraph 3.4; the role of the electoral office was in the nature of an examination by a complainant of suspicious documents subsequently handed to the police, comparable to that of a bank handing over suspicious cheques to the police: *R. v. Khan* [2011] L.S. Gazette, October 20, 23, CA ([2011] EWCA Crim. 2240).

4. Recording of information

A-235   4.1 If material which may be relevant to the investigation consists of information which is not recorded in any form, the officer in charge of an investigation must ensure that it is recorded in a durable or retrievable form (whether in writing, on video or audio tape, or on computer disk).

4.2 Where it is not practicable to retain the initial record of information because it forms part of a larger record which is to be destroyed, its contents should be transferred as a true record to a durable and more easily-stored form before that happens.

4.3 Negative information is often relevant to an investigation. If it may be relevant it must be recorded. An example might be a number of people present in a particular place at a particular time who state that they saw nothing unusual.

4.4 Where information which may be relevant is obtained, it must be recorded at the time it is obtained or as soon as practicable after that time. This includes, for example, information obtained in house-to-house enquiries, although the requirement to record information promptly does not require an investigator to take a statement from a potential witness where it would not otherwise be taken.

5. Retention of material

(a) Duty to retain material

A-236   5.1 The investigator must retain material obtained in a criminal investigation which may be relevant to the investigation. Material may be photographed, video-recorded, captured digitally or otherwise retained in the form of a copy rather than the original at any time, if the original is perishable; the original was supplied to the investigator rather than generated by him and is to be returned to its owner; or the retention of a copy rather than the original is reasonable in all the circumstances.

5.2 Where material has been seized in the exercise of the powers of seizure conferred by the Police and Criminal Evidence Act 1984, the duty to retain it under this code is subject to the provisions on the retention of seized material in section 22 of that Act.

5.3 If the officer in charge of an investigation becomes aware as a result of developments in the case that material previously examined but not retained (because it was not thought to be relevant) may now be relevant to the investigation, he should, wherever practicable, take steps to obtain it or ensure that it is retained for further inspection or for production in court if required.

5.4 The duty to retain material includes in particular the duty to retain material falling into the following categories, where it may be relevant to the investigation:

- crime reports (including crime report forms, relevant parts of incident report books or police officer's notebooks);
- custody records;
- records which are derived from tapes of telephone messages (for example, 999 calls) containing descriptions of an alleged offence or offender;
- final versions of witness statements (and draft versions where their content differs from

the final version), including any exhibits mentioned (unless these have been returned to their owner on the understanding that they will be produced in court if required);

- interview records (written records, or audio or video tapes, of interviews with actual or potential witnesses or suspects);
- communications between the police and experts such as forensic scientists, reports of work carried out by experts, and schedules of scientific material prepared by the expert for the investigator, for the purposes of criminal proceedings;
- records of the first description of a suspect by each potential witness who purports to identify or describe the suspect, whether or not the description differs from that of subsequent descriptions by that or other witnesses;
- any material casting doubt on the reliability of a witness.

5.5 The duty to retain material, where it may be relevant to the investigation, also includes in particular the duty to retain material which may satisfy the test for prosecution disclosure in the Act, such as:

- information provided by an accused person which indicates an explanation for the offence with which he has been charged;
- any material casting doubt on the reliability of a confession;
- any material casting doubt on the reliability of a prosecution witness.

5.6 The duty to retain material falling into these categories does not extend to items which are purely ancillary to such material and possess no independent significance (for example, duplicate copies of records or reports).

(b) Length of time for which material is to be retained

5.7 All material which may be relevant to the investigation must be retained until a decision is **A-236a** taken whether to institute proceedings against a person for an offence.

5.8 If a criminal investigation results in proceedings being instituted, all material which may be relevant must be retained at least until the accused is acquitted or convicted or the prosecutor decides not to proceed with the case.

5.9 Where the accused is convicted, all material which may be relevant must be retained at least until:

- the convicted person is released from custody, or discharged from hospital, in cases where the court imposes a custodial sentence or a hospital order;
- six months from the date of conviction, in all other cases.

If the court imposes a custodial sentence or hospital order and the convicted person is released from custody or discharged from hospital earlier than six months from the date of conviction, all material which may be relevant must be retained at least until six months from the date of conviction.

5.10 If an appeal against conviction is in progress when the release or discharge occurs, or at the end of the period of six months specified in paragraph 5.9, all material which may be relevant must be retained until the appeal is determined. Similarly, if the Criminal Cases Review Commission is considering an application at that point in time, all material which may be relevant must be retained at least until the Commission decides not to refer the case to the court.

6. Preparation of material for prosecutor

(a) Introduction

6.1 The officer in charge of the investigation, the disclosure officer or an investigator may seek **A-237** advice from the prosecutor about whether any particular item of material may be relevant to the investigation.

6.2 Material which may be relevant to an investigation, which has been retained in accordance with this code, and which the disclosure officer believes will not form part of the prosecution case, must be listed on a schedule. This process will differ depending on whether the case is likely to be heard in the magistrates' court or the Crown Court.

(b) Magistrates' Court

Anticipated guilty pleas

6.3 If the accused is charged with a summary offence or an either-way offence that is likely to **A-237a** remain in the magistrates' court, and it is considered that he is likely to plead guilty (*e.g.* because he has admitted the offence), a schedule or streamlined disclosure certificate is not required. However, the common law duty to disclose material which may assist the defence at bail hearings or in the early preparation of their case remains, and where there is such material the certification on the Police Report (MG5/SDF) must be completed. Where there is no such material, a certificate to that effect must be completed in like form to that attached at the Annex.

6.4 If, contrary to the expectation of a guilty plea being entered, the accused pleads not guilty at the first hearing, the disclosure officer must ensure that the streamlined disclosure certificate is prepared and submitted as soon as is reasonably practicable after that happens.

Anticipated not guilty pleas

A-237b   6.5 If the accused is charged with a summary offence or an either-way offence that is likely to remain in the magistrates' court, and it is considered that he is likely to plead not guilty, a streamlined disclosure certificate must be completed in like form to that attached at the Annex.

Material which may assist the defence

A-237c   6.6 In every case, irrespective of the anticipated plea, if there is material known to the disclosure officer that might assist the defence with the early preparation of their case or at a bail hearing (for example, a key prosecution witness has relevant previous convictions or a witness has withdrawn his or her statement), a note must be made on the MG5 (or other format agreed under the National File Standards). The material must be disclosed to the prosecutor who will disclose it to the defence if he thinks it meets this common law test.

No undermining or assisting material and sensitive material - magistrates' court cases

A-237d   6.7 If there is no material which might fall to be disclosed as undermining the prosecution case or assisting the defence, the officer should complete the appropriate entry on the streamlined disclosure certificate. If there is any sensitive unused material the officer should complete a sensitive material schedule (MG6D or similar) and attach it to the prosecution file. In exceptional circumstances, when its existence is so sensitive that it cannot be listed, it should be revealed to the prosecutor separately.

(c) Crown Court

A-237e   6.8 For cases to be held in the Crown Court, the unused material schedules (MG6 series) are used.

6.9 The disclosure officer must ensure that a schedule is prepared in the following circumstances:

- the accused is charged with an offence which is triable only on indictment;
- the accused is charged with an offence which is triable either way, and it is considered that the case is likely to be tried on indictment.

6.10 Material which the disclosure officer does not believe is sensitive must be listed on a schedule of non-sensitive material. The schedule must include a statement that the disclosure officer does not believe the material is sensitive.

Way in which material is to be listed on schedule

A-237f   6.11 For indictable only cases or either-way cases sent to the Crown Court, schedules MG6 C, D and E should be completed to facilitate service of the MG6C with the prosecution case, wherever possible. The disclosure officer should ensure that each item of material is listed separately on the schedule, and is numbered consecutively. The description of each item should make clear the nature of the item and should contain sufficient detail to enable the prosecutor to decide whether he needs to inspect the material before deciding whether or not it should be disclosed.

6.12 In some enquiries it may not be practicable to list each item of material separately. For example, there may be many items of a similar or repetitive nature. These may be listed in a block and described by quantity and generic title.

6.13 Even if some material is listed in a block, the disclosure officer must ensure that any items among that material which might satisfy the test for prosecution disclosure are listed and described individually.

(d) Sensitive material - Crown Court

A-237g   6.14 Any material which is believed to be sensitive either must be listed on a schedule of sensitive material or, in exceptional circumstances where its existence is so sensitive that it cannot be listed, it should be revealed to the prosecutor separately. If there is no sensitive material, the disclosure officer must record this fact on a schedule of sensitive material, or otherwise so indicate.

6.15 Subject to paragraph 6.16 below, the disclosure officer must list on a sensitive schedule any material the disclosure of which he believes would give rise to a real risk of serious prejudice to an important public interest, and the reason for that belief. The schedule must include a statement that the disclosure officer believes the material is sensitive. Depending on the circumstances, examples of such material may include the following among others:

- material relating to national security;
- material received from the intelligence and security agencies;
- material relating to intelligence from foreign sources which reveals sensitive intelligence gathering methods;
- material given in confidence;
- material relating to the identity or activities of informants, or undercover police officers, or witnesses, or other persons supplying information to the police who may be in danger if their identities are revealed;
- material revealing the location of any premises or other place used for police surveillance, or the identity of any person allowing a police officer to use them for surveillance;
- material revealing, either directly or indirectly, techniques and methods relied upon by a police officer in the course of a criminal investigation, for example covert surveillance techniques, or other methods of detecting crime;
- material whose disclosure might facilitate the commission of other offences or hinder the prevention and detection of crime;
- material upon the strength of which search warrants were obtained;
- material containing details of persons taking part in identification parades;
- material supplied to an investigator during a criminal investigation which has been generated by an official of a body concerned with the regulation or supervision of bodies corporate or of persons engaged in financial activities, or which has been generated by a person retained by such a body;
- material supplied to an investigator during a criminal investigation which relates to a child or young person and which has been generated by a local authority social services department, an Area Child Protection Committee or other party contacted by an investigator during the investigation;
- material relating to the private life of a witness.

6.16 In exceptional circumstances, where an investigator considers that material is so sensitive that its revelation to the prosecutor by means of an entry on the sensitive schedule is inappropriate, the existence of the material must be revealed to the prosecutor separately. This will apply only where compromising the material would be likely to lead directly to the loss of life, or directly threaten national security.

6.17 In such circumstances, the responsibility for informing the prosecutor lies with the investigator who knows the detail of the sensitive material. The investigator should act as soon as is reasonably practicable after the file containing the prosecution case is sent to the prosecutor. The investigator must also ensure that the prosecutor is able to inspect the material so that he can assess whether it is disclosable and, if so, whether it needs to be brought before a court for a ruling on disclosure.

7. Revelation of material to prosecutor

7.1 Certain unused material must be disclosed to the accused at common law if it would assist the   **A-238** defence with the early preparation of their case or at a bail hearing. This material may consist of items such as a previous relevant conviction of a key prosecution witness or the withdrawal of support for the prosecution by a witness. This material must be revealed to the prosecutor for service on the defence with the initial details of the prosecution case.

7.1A In anticipated not guilty plea cases for hearing in the magistrates' court the disclosure officer must give the streamlined disclosure certificate to the prosecutor at the same time as he gives the prosecutor the file containing the material for the prosecution case.

7.1B In cases sent to the Crown Court, wherever possible, the disclosure officer should give the schedules concerning unused material to the prosecutor at the same time as the prosecution file in preparation for the first hearing and any case management that the judge may wish to conduct at that stage.

7.2 The disclosure officer should draw the attention of the prosecutor to any material an investigator has retained (including material to which paragraph 6.13 applies) which may satisfy the test for prosecution disclosure in the Act, and should explain why he has come to that view.

N.B. The reference to paragraph 6.13 (a leftover from the previous version of the code) should have been updated to refer to paragraph 6.16.

7.3 At the same time as complying with the duties in paragraphs 7.1 and 7.2, the disclosure officer must give the prosecutor a copy of any material which falls into the following categories (unless such material has already been given to the prosecutor as part of the file containing the material for the prosecution case):

- information provided by an accused person which indicates an explanation for the offence with which he has been charged;
- any material casting doubt on the reliability of a confession;
- any material casting doubt on the reliability of a prosecution witness;
- any other material which the investigator believes may satisfy the test for prosecution disclosure in the Act;

7.4 If the prosecutor asks to inspect material which has not already been copied to him, the disclosure officer must allow him to inspect it. If the prosecutor asks for a copy of material which has not already been copied to him, the disclosure officer must give him a copy. However, this does not apply where the disclosure officer believes, having consulted the officer in charge of the investigation, that the material is too sensitive to be copied and can only be inspected.

7.5 If material consists of information which is recorded other than in writing, whether it should be given to the prosecutor in its original form as a whole, or by way of relevant extracts recorded in the same form, or in the form of a transcript, is a matter for agreement between the disclosure officer and the prosecutor.

8. Subsequent action by disclosure officer

A-239

8.1 At the time when a streamlined disclosure certificate is prepared for magistrates' court cases, or a schedule of non-sensitive material is prepared for Crown Court cases, the disclosure officer may not know exactly what material will form the case against the accused. In addition, the prosecutor may not have given advice about the likely relevance of particular items of material. Once these matters have been determined, the disclosure officer must give the prosecutor, where necessary, an amended certificate or schedule listing any additional material:

- which may be relevant to the investigation;
- which does not form part of the case against the accused;
- which is not already listed on the schedule; and
- which he believes is not sensitive,

unless he is informed in writing by the prosecutor that the prosecutor intends to disclose the material to the defence.

8.2 Section 7A of the Act imposes a continuing duty on the prosecutor, for the duration of criminal proceedings against the accused, to disclose material which satisfies the test for disclosure (subject to public interest considerations). To enable him to do this, any new material coming to light should be treated in the same way as the earlier material.

8.3 In particular, after a defence statement has been given, or details of the issues in dispute have been recorded on the effective trial preparation form, the disclosure officer must look again at the material which has been retained and must draw the attention of the prosecutor to any material which might reasonably be considered capable of undermining the case for the prosecution against the accused or of assisting the case for the accused; and he must reveal it to him in accordance with paragraphs 7.4 and 7.5 above.

9. Certification by disclosure officer

A-240

9.1 The disclosure officer must certify to the prosecutor that, to the best of his knowledge and belief, all relevant material which has been retained and made available to him has been revealed to the prosecutor in accordance with this code. He must sign and date the certificate. It will be necessary to certify not only at the time when the schedule and accompanying material is submitted to the prosecutor, and when relevant material which has been retained is reconsidered after the accused has given a defence statement, but also whenever a schedule is otherwise given or material is otherwise revealed to the prosecutor.

10. Disclosure of material to accused

A-240a

10.1 Other than early disclosure under common law, in the magistrates' court the streamlined certificate at the Annex (and any relevant unused material to be disclosed under it) must be disclosed to the accused either:

- at the hearing where a not guilty plea is entered, or
- as soon as possible following a formal indication from the accused or representative that a not guilty plea will be entered at the hearing.

10.1A If material has not already been copied to the prosecutor, and he requests its disclosure to the accused on the ground that:

- it satisfies the test for prosecution disclosure, or
    - the court has ordered its disclosure after considering an application from the accused,
the disclosure officer must disclose it to the accused.

10.2 If material has been copied to the prosecutor, and it is to be disclosed, whether it is disclosed by the prosecutor or the disclosure officer is a matter of agreement between the two of them.

10.3 The disclosure officer must disclose material to the accused either by giving him a copy or by allowing him to inspect it. If the accused person asks for a copy of any material which he has been allowed to inspect, the disclosure officer must give it to him, unless in the opinion of the disclosure officer that is either not practicable (for example because the material consists of an object which cannot be copied, or because the volume of material is so great), or not desirable (for example because the material is a statement by a child witness in relation to a sexual offence).

10.4 If material which the accused has been allowed to inspect consists of information which is recorded other than in writing, whether it should be given to the accused in its original form or in the form of a transcript is a matter for the discretion of the disclosure officer. If the material is transcribed, the disclosure officer must ensure that the transcript is certified to the accused as a true record of the material which has been transcribed.

10.5 If a court concludes that an item of sensitive material satisfies the prosecution disclosure test and that the interests of the defence outweigh the public interest in withholding disclosure, it will be necessary to disclose the material if the case is to proceed. This does not mean that sensitive documents must always be disclosed in their original form: for example, the court may agree that sensitive details still requiring protection should be blocked out, or that documents may be summarised, or that the prosecutor may make an admission about the substance of the material under section 10 of the Criminal Justice Act 1967.

ANNEX

The annex to the code is not set out in this work.   **A-241**

(2) As to the practice for arranging and conducting interviews of witnesses notified by the accused

Introduction

As from May 1, 2010, a new code of practice entitled "Code of Practice for Arranging and   **A-241a**
Conducting Interviews of Witnesses Notified by the Accused", which was prepared under section 21A of the CPIA 1996, was brought into force by the Criminal Procedure and Investigations Act 1996 (Code of Practice for Interviews of Witnesses Notified by Accused) Order 2010 (S.I. 2010 No. 1223).

CODE OF PRACTICE FOR ARRANGING AND CONDUCTING INTERVIEWS OF WITNESSES NOTIFIED BY THE ACCUSED

Preamble

This code of practice is issued under section 21A of the Criminal Procedure and Investigations   **A-241b**
Act 1996 ("the Act"). It sets out guidance that police officers and other persons charged with investigating offences must follow if they arrange or conduct interviews of proposed witnesses whose details are disclosed to the prosecution by an accused person pursuant to the disclosure provisions in Part I of the Act.

Introduction

1.1 Part I of the Act sets out rules governing disclosure of information in the course of criminal   **A-241c**
proceedings by both the prosecution and persons accused of offences to which that Part of the Act applies.

1.2. Sections 5 and 6 of the Act provide for accused persons to give defence statements to the prosecution and to the court and section 6A sets out what those defence statements must contain. Section 6A(2) requires that any defence statement that discloses an alibi must give particulars of it, including prescribed details of any witness who the accused believes is able to give evidence in support of the alibi and any information the accused has which may assist in identifying or finding such a witness.

1.3. Section 6C of the Act requires the accused to give to the prosecutor and the court a notice indicating whether he intends to call any witnesses at trial and giving details of those witnesses.

1.4. This code of practice sets out guidance that police officers and other persons charged with investigating offences must have regard to when they are arranging and conducting interviews of proposed witnesses identified in a defence statement given under section 6A(2) of the Act or a notice given under section 6C of the Act.

Definitions

A-241d   2. In this code:—

– *the accused* means a person mentioned in section 1(1) or (2) of the Act;

– "an appropriate person" means:

    (a) in the case of a witness under the age of 18:

        (i) the parent, guardian or, if the witness is in local authority or voluntary organisation care, or is otherwise being looked after under the Children Act 1989, a person representing that authority or organisation; or

        (ii) a social worker of a local authority; or

        (iii) failing these, some other responsible person aged 18 or over who is not a police officer or employed by the police; and

    (b) in the case of a witness who is mentally disordered or mentally vulnerable:

        (i) a relative, guardian or other person responsible for the witness's care or custody; or

        (ii) someone experienced in dealing with mentally disordered or mentally vulnerable people but who is not a police officer or employed by the police; or

        (iii) failing these, some other responsible person aged 18 or over who is not a police officer or employed by the police.

– *an investigator* is a police officer or any other person charged with the duty of investigating offences.

– *a witness* is a potential witness identified by an accused person either:

    – in a defence statement under section 6A(2) of the Act as being a witness that he believes is able to give evidence in support of an alibi disclosed in the statement; or

    – in a notice given to the court and the prosecutor under section 6C of the Act as being a person that he intends to call as a witness at his trial.

Arrangement of the interview

Information to be provided to the witness before any interview may take place

A-241e   3.1. If an investigator wishes to interview a witness, the witness must be asked whether he consents to being interviewed and informed that:

• an interview is being requested following his identification by the accused as a proposed witness under section 6A(2) or section 6C of the Act;

• he is not obliged to attend the proposed interview;

• he is entitled to be accompanied by a solicitor at the interview (but nothing in this code of practice creates any duty on the part of the Legal Services Commission to provide funding for any such attendance); and

• a record will be made of the interview and he will subsequently be sent a copy of the record.

3.2. If the witness consents to being interviewed, the witness must be asked:

• whether he wishes to have a solicitor present at the interview;

• whether he consents to a solicitor attending the interview on behalf of the accused, as an observer; and

• whether he consents to a copy of the record being sent to the accused. If he does not consent, the witness must be informed that the effect of disclosure requirements in criminal proceedings may nevertheless require the prosecution to disclose the record to the accused (and any co-accused) in the course of the proceedings.

Information to be provided to the accused before any interview may take place

A-241f   4.1. The investigator must notify the accused or, if the accused is legally represented in the proceedings, the accused's representatives:

• that the investigator requested an interview with the witness;

• whether the witness consented to the interview; and

• if the witness consented to the interview, whether the witness also consented to a solicitor attending the interview on behalf of the accused, as an observer.

4.2. If the accused is not legally represented in the proceedings, and if the witness consents to a solicitor attending the interview on behalf of the accused, the accused must be offered the opportunity, a reasonable time before the interview is held, to appoint a solicitor to attend it.

Identification of the date, time and venue for the interview

5. The investigator must nominate a reasonable date, time and venue for the interview and notify the witness of them and any subsequent changes to them.   **A-241g**

Notification to the accused's solicitor of the date, time and venue of the interview

6. If the witness has consented to the presence of the accused's solicitor, the accused's solicitor must be notified that the interview is taking place, invited to observe, and provided with reasonable notice of the date, time and venue of the interview and any subsequent changes.   **A-241h**

Conduct of the interview

The investigator conducting the interview

7. The identity of the investigator conducting the interview must be recorded. That person must have sufficient skills and authority, commensurate with the complexity of the investigation, to discharge his functions effectively. That person must not conduct the interview if that is likely to result in a conflict of interest, for instance, if that person is the victim of the alleged crime which is the subject of the proceedings. The advice of a more senior officer must always be sought if there is doubt as to whether a conflict of interest precludes an individual conducting the interview. If thereafter the doubt remains, the advice of a prosecutor must be sought.   **A-241i**

Attendance of the accused's solicitor

8.1. The accused's solicitor may only attend the interview if the witness has consented to his presence as an observer. Provided that the accused's solicitor was given reasonable notice of the date, time and place of the interview, the fact that the accused's solicitor is not present will not prevent the interview from being conducted. If the witness at any time withdraws consent to the accused's solicitor being present at the interview, the interview may continue without the presence of the accused's solicitor.   **A-241j**

8.2. The accused's solicitor may attend only as an observer.

Attendance of the witness's solicitor

9. Where a witness has indicated that he wishes to appoint a solicitor to be present, that solicitor must be permitted to attend the interview.   **A-241k**

Attendance of any other appropriate person

10. A witness under the age of 18 or a witness who is mentally disordered or otherwise mentally vulnerable must be interviewed in the presence of an appropriate person.   **A-241l**

Recording of the interview

11.1. An accurate record must be made of the interview, whether it takes place at a police station or elsewhere. The record must be made, where practicable, by audio recording or by visual recording with sound, or otherwise in writing. Any written record must be made and completed during the interview, unless this would not be practicable or would interfere with the conduct of the interview, and must constitute either a verbatim record of what has been said or, failing this, an account of the interview which adequately and accurately summarises it. If a written record is not made during the interview it must be made as soon as practicable after its completion. Written interview records must be timed and signed by the maker.   **A-241m**

11.2 A copy of the record must be given, within a reasonable time of the interview, to:
- (a) the witness; and
- (b) if the witness consents, to the accused or the accused's solicitor.

II. ATTORNEY-GENERAL'S GUIDELINES

A. DISCLOSURE

Introduction

On December 3, 2013, the Attorney-General published revised guidelines on disclosure, replac-   **A-242** ing the 2005 guidelines, and also the supplementary guidelines on digital material issued in 2011, which are now annexed to the new guidelines. The new guidelines should be read together with the revised protocol on the disclosure of unused material in criminal cases (*post*, Appendix N-52 *et seq.*), and are not designed to be a substitute for a thorough understanding of the relevant legislation, codes of practice, case law and procedure. They have immediate effect (para. 73).

Paragraphs 1 to 3 emphasise the importance of disclosure and a "timely dialogue between the prosecution, defence and the court", and are a shortened version of the introductory section to the 2005 guidelines. Paragraphs 4 to 14 relate to general principles and incorporate most of the corresponding section in the 2005 guidelines, but also stress the role the defence have to play in ensuring that the prosecution are directed towards appropriate material, the importance of communication within the prosecution team and the role of the reviewing lawyer. Paragraphs 15 to 27 relate to the duties on investigators and disclosure officers, incorporating a shortened version of the corresponding section in the 2005 guidelines. They underline that thought must be given to defining and limiting the scope of investigations under the guidance of the reviewing lawyer and prosecutor where appropriate, the need to keep full records of meetings and decisions taken and that, whilst there will be some cases where detailed examination of all material seized will be necessary, there will be others where this is impossible. Paragraphs 28 to 34 set out the disclosure duties on prosecutors, again incorporating a shortened version of the corresponding section in the 2005 guidelines, and also highlighting that prosecutors should challenge the lack of, or inadequate, defence statements in writing, copying the document to the court. Paragraphs 35 to 37 set out the disclosure duties on prosecution advocates, incorporating a shortened version of the corresponding section in the 2005 guidelines, and make clear the duty to keep disclosure under review, whenever possible in consultation with the reviewing prosecutor. Paragraphs 39 to 43 deal with the defence, and emphasise the importance of early and meaningful defence engagement and defence statements, including in the magistrates' courts.

Paragraphs 44 to 47 relate to disclosure obligations in magistrates' courts where a not guilty plea is entered. Paragraphs 48 and 49 relate to the Crown Court, particularly cases which involve digital material. Paragraphs 50 to 52 deal with large and complex cases in the Crown Court. Paragraphs 53 to 55 relate to material held by government departments and third parties and paragraphs 56 and 57 to material held by other domestic bodies. Both largely replicate the corresponding sections in the 2005 guidelines. Paragraphs 59 to 64 concern material held overseas (and correspond to paras 58-63 of the 2011 supplementary guidelines on digital material). Paragraphs 65 to 69 deal with applications for non-disclosure in the public interest and largely reproduce the corresponding section in the 2005 guidelines. Finally, paragraphs 70 to 72 ("other disclosure", "material relevant to sentence" and "post-conviction") correspond to the sections relating to material relevant to sentence and the post-conviction period in the 2005 guidelines.

As to the significance of the guidelines in relation to material held overseas, outside the European Union, by entities not subject to the jurisdiction of the United Kingdom, see *R. v. Flook* [2010] 1 Cr.App.R. 30, CA (§§ 12-53, 12-101 in the main work).

The 2013 guidelines (including the annex (*post*, A-262 *et seq.*)) were given extensive consideration in *R. v. R. (Practice Note)* (*ante*, § 12-59).

Foreword

A-242a   We are pleased to publish a revised judicial protocol and revised guidance on the disclosure of unused material in criminal cases. Proper disclosure of unused material, made through a rigorous and carefully considered application of the law, remains a crucial part of a fair trial, and essential to avoiding miscarriages of justice. These new documents are intended to clarify the procedures to be followed and to encourage the active participation of all parties.

They have been prepared following the recommendations of Lord Justice Gross in his September 2011 "Review of Disclosure in Criminal Proceedings" and take account of Lord Justice Gross and Lord Justice Treacy's "Further review of disclosure in criminal proceedings: sanctions for disclosure failure", published in November 2012.

There are important roles for the prosecution, the defence and the court in ensuring that disclosure is conducted properly, including on the part of the investigating, case progression and disclosure officers, as well as the lawyers and advocates. Lord Justice Gross particularly recommended that the guidance on disclosure of unused material in criminal cases should be consolidated and abbreviated. Given all of those involved in this process have separate constitutional roles, the judiciary and the

Attorney-General have worked together to produce complementary guidance that is shorter than the previous iterations, but remains comprehensive. The two documents are similarly structured for ease of reference and should be read together.

The Rt. Hon. Dominic Grieve Q.C. M.P., Attorney General

The Rt. Hon. The Lord Thomas, Lord Chief Justice of England and Wales

Introduction

These guidelines are issued by the Attorney General for investigators, prosecutors and defence **A-243** practitioners on the application of the disclosure regime contained in the Criminal Procedure and Investigations Act 1996 ("CPIA"). The guidelines emphasise the importance of prosecution-led disclosure and the importance of applying the CPIA regime in a "thinking manner", tailored, where appropriate, to the type of investigation or prosecution in question.

The guidelines do not contain the detail of the disclosure regime; they outline the high level principles which should be followed when the disclosure regime is applied.

These guidelines replace the existing Attorney General's Guidelines on Disclosure issued in 2005 and the Supplementary Guidelines on Digital Material issued in 2011, which is an annex to the general guidelines.

The guidelines are intended to operate alongside the Judicial Protocol on the Disclosure of Unused Material in Criminal Cases. They are not designed to be an unequivocal statement of the law at any one time, nor are they a substitute for a thorough understanding of the relevant legislation, codes of practice, case law and procedure.

Readers should note that a review of disclosure in the magistrates' courts is currently being undertaken by H.H.J. Kinch Q.C. and the Chief Magistrate, on behalf of Lord Justice Gross, the Senior Presiding Judge. Amendments may therefore be made to these documents following the recommendations of that review, and in accordance with other forthcoming changes to the criminal justice system.

The importance of disclosure

1. The statutory framework for criminal investigations and disclosure is contained in the Criminal **A-244** Procedure and Investigations Act 1996 (the CPIA) and the *CPIA Code of Practice*. The CPIA aims to ensure that criminal investigations are conducted in a fair, objective and thorough manner, and requires prosecutors to disclose to the defence material which has not previously been disclosed to the accused and which might reasonably be considered capable of undermining the case for the prosecution against the accused or of assisting the case for the accused. The CPIA requires a timely dialogue between the prosecution, defence and the court to enable the prosecution properly to identify such material.

2. Every accused person has a right to a fair trial, a right long embodied in our law and guaranteed by Article 6 of the European Convention on Human Rights (ECHR). A fair trial is the proper object and expectation of all participants in the trial process. Fair disclosure to the accused is an inseparable part of a fair trial. A fair trial should not require consideration of irrelevant material and should not involve spurious applications or arguments which serve to divert the trial process from examining the real issues before the court.

3. Properly applied, the CPIA should ensure that material is not disclosed which overburdens the participants in the trial process, diverts attention from the relevant issues, leads to unjustifiable delay, and is wasteful of resources. Consideration of disclosure issues should be an integral part of a good investigation and not something that exists separately.

Disclosure: general principles

4. Disclosure refers to providing the defence with copies of, or access to, any prosecution material **A-245** which might reasonably be considered capable of undermining the case for the prosecution against the accused, or of assisting the case for the accused, and which has not previously been disclosed (s.3 CPIA).

5. Prosecutors will only be expected to anticipate what material might undermine their case or strengthen the defence in the light of information available at the time of the disclosure decision, and they may take into account information revealed during questioning.

6. In deciding whether material satisfies the disclosure test, consideration should be given amongst other things to:

    a. the use that might be made of it in cross-examination;

    b. its capacity to support submissions that could lead to:

        (i) the exclusion of evidence;

        (ii) a stay of proceedings, where the material is required to allow a proper application to be made;

        (iii) a court or tribunal finding that any public authority had acted incompatibly with the accused's rights under the ECHR;

    c. its capacity to suggest an explanation or partial explanation of the accused's actions;

    d. the capacity of the material to have a bearing on scientific or medical evidence in the case.

7. It should also be borne in mind that while items of material viewed in isolation may not be reasonably considered to be capable of undermining the prosecution case or assisting the accused, several items together can have that effect.

8. Material relating to the accused's mental or physical health, intellectual capacity, or to any ill treatment which the accused may have suffered when in the investigator's custody is likely to fall within the test for disclosure set out in paragraph 4 above.

9. Disclosure must not be an open-ended trawl of unused material. A critical element to fair and proper disclosure is that the defence play their role to ensure that the prosecution are directed to material which might reasonably be considered capable of undermining the prosecution case or assisting the case for the accused. This process is key to ensuring prosecutors make informed determinations about disclosure of unused material. The defence statement is important in identifying the issues in the case and why it is suggested that the material meets the test for disclosure.

10. Disclosure should be conducted in a thinking manner and never be reduced to a box-ticking exercise[1]; at all stages of the process, there should be consideration of **why** the CPIA disclosure regime requires a particular course of action and what should be done to achieve that aim.

11. There will always be a number of participants in prosecutions and investigations: senior investigation officers, disclosure officers, investigation officers, reviewing prosecutors, leading counsel, junior counsel, and sometimes disclosure counsel. Communication within the "prosecution team" is vital to ensure that all matters which could have a bearing on disclosure issues are given sufficient attention by the right person. This is especially so given many reviewing lawyers will be unable to sit behind the trial advocate throughout the trial. In practice, this is likely to mean that a full log of disclosure decisions (with reasons) must be kept on the file and made available as appropriate to the prosecution team.

12. The role of the reviewing lawyer will be central to ensuring all members of the prosecution team are aware of, and carry out, their duties and role(s). Where this involves counsel or more than one reviewing lawyer, this should be done by giving clear written instructions and record keeping.

13. The centrality of the reviewing lawyer does not mean that he or she has to do all the work personally; on the contrary, it will often mean effective delegation. Where the conduct of a prosecution is assigned to more than one prosecutor, steps must be taken to ensure that all involved in the case properly record their decisions. Subsequent prosecutors must be able to see and understand previous disclosure decisions before carrying out their continuous review function.

14. Investigators must always be alive to the potential need to reveal and prosecutors to the potential need to disclose material, in the interests of justice and fairness in the particular circumstances of any case, after the commencement of proceedings but before their duty arises under the Act. For instance, disclosure ought to be made of significant information that might affect a bail decision. This is likely to depend on what the defence chooses to reveal at that stage.

Investigators and disclosure officers

A-246

15. Investigators and disclosure officers must be fair and objective and must work together with prosecutors to ensure that disclosure obligations are met. Investigators and disclosure officers should be familiar with the CPIA Code of Practice, in particular their obligations to **retain** and **record** relevant material, to **review** it and to **reveal** it to the prosecutor.

16. Whether a case is a summary only matter or a long and complex trial on indictment, it is important that investigators and disclosure officers should approach their duties in a "thinking manner" and not as a box ticking exercise. Where necessary, the reviewing lawyer should be consulted. It is important that investigators and disclosure officers are deployed on cases which are commensurate with their training, skills and experience. The conduct of an investigation provides the foundation for the entire case, and may even impact the conduct of linked cases. It is vital that there is always consideration of disclosure matters at the outset of an investigation, regardless of its size.

17. A fair investigation involves the pursuit of material following all reasonable lines of enquiry, whether they point towards or away from the suspect. What is "reasonable" will depend on the context of the case. A fair investigation does not mean an endless investigation: investigators and

---

[1] *R. v. Olu, Wilson and Brooks* [2010] EWCA Crim. 2975, [2011] 1 Cr.App.R. 33, CA (at [42]).

disclosure officers must give thought to defining, and thereby limiting, the scope of their investigations, seeking the guidance of the prosecutor where appropriate.

18. Where there are a number of disclosure officers assigned to a case, there should be a lead disclosure officer who is the focus for enquiries and whose responsibility it is to ensure that the investigator's disclosure obligations are complied with. Where appropriate, regular case conferences and other meetings should be held to ensure prosecutors are apprised of all relevant developments in investigations. Full records should be kept of such meetings.

19. The *CPIA Code of Practice* encourages investigators and disclosure officers to seek advice from prosecutors about whether any particular item of material may be relevant to the investigation, and if so, how. Investigators and disclosure officers should record key decisions taken on these matters and be prepared to account for their actions later. An identical approach is not called for in each and every case.

20. Investigators are to approach their task seeking to establish what actually happened. They are to be fair and objective.

21. Disclosure officers (or their deputies) must inspect, view, listen to or search all relevant material that has been retained by the investigator and the disclosure officer must provide a personal declaration to the effect that this task has been undertaken. In some cases, a detailed examination of all material seized may be required. In others, however, a detailed examination of every item of material seized would be virtually impossible: see the **Annex**.

22. Prosecutors only have knowledge of matters which are revealed to them by investigators and disclosure officers, and the schedules are the written means by which that revelation takes place. Whatever the approach taken by investigators or disclosure officers to examining the material gathered or generated in the course of an investigation, it is crucial that disclosure officers record their reasons for a particular approach in writing.

23. In meeting the obligations in paragraph 6.9 and 8.1 of the code, schedules must be completed in a form which not only reveals sufficient information to the prosecutor, but which demonstrates a transparent and thinking approach to the disclosure exercise, to command the confidence of the defence and the court. Descriptions on non-sensitive schedules must be clear and accurate, and must contain sufficient detail to enable the prosecutor to make an informed decision on disclosure. The use of abbreviations and acronyms can be problematic and lead to difficulties in appreciating the significance of the material.

24. Sensitive schedules must contain sufficiently clear descriptions to enable the prosecutor to make an informed decision as to whether or not the material itself should be viewed, to the extent possible without compromising the confidentiality of the information.

25. It may become apparent to an investigator that some material obtained in the course of an investigation, either because it was considered to be potentially relevant, or because it was inextricably linked to material that was relevant, is, in fact, incapable of impact. It is not necessary to retain such material, although the investigator should err on the side of caution in reaching that conclusion and should be particularly mindful of the fact that some investigations continue over some time and that what is incapable of impact may change over time. The advice of the prosecutor should be sought where appropriate.

26. Disclosure officers must specifically draw material to the attention of the prosecutor for consideration where they have any doubt as to whether it might reasonably be considered capable of undermining the prosecution case or of assisting the case for the accused.

27. Disclosure officers must seek the advice and assistance of prosecutors when in doubt as to their responsibility as early as possible. They must deal expeditiously with requests by the prosecutor for further information on material, which may lead to disclosure.

Prosecutors

28. Prosecutors are responsible for making proper disclosure in consultation with the disclosure **A-247** officer. The duty of disclosure is a continuing one and disclosure should be kept under review. In addition, prosecutors should ensure that advocates in court are properly instructed as to disclosure issues. Prosecutors must also be alert to the need to provide advice to, and where necessary probe actions taken by, disclosure officers to ensure that disclosure obligations are met. There should be no aspects of an investigation about which prosecutors are unable to ask probing questions.

29. Prosecutors must review schedules prepared by disclosure officers thoroughly and must be alert to the possibility that relevant material may exist which has not been revealed to them or material included which should not have been. If no schedules have been provided, or there are apparent omissions from the schedules, or documents or other items are inadequately described or are unclear, the prosecutor must at once take action to obtain properly completed schedules. Likewise schedules should be returned for amendment if irrelevant items are included. If prosecutors remain

dissatisfied with the quality or content of the schedules they must raise the matter with a senior investigator to resolve the matter satisfactorily.

30. Where prosecutors have reason to believe that the disclosure officer has not discharged the obligation in paragraph 21 to inspect, view, listen to or search relevant material, they must at once raise the matter with the disclosure officer and request that it be done. Where appropriate the matter should be raised with the officer in the case or a senior officer.

31. Prosecutors should copy the defence statement to the disclosure officer and investigator as soon as reasonably practicable and prosecutors should advise the investigator if, in their view, reasonable and relevant lines of further enquiry should be pursued. If the defence statement does point to other reasonable lines of enquiry, further investigation is required and evidence obtained as a result of these enquiries may be used as part of the prosecution case or to rebut the defence.

32. It is vital that prosecutors consider defence statements thoroughly. Prosecutors cannot comment upon, or invite inferences to be drawn from, failures in defence disclosure otherwise than in accordance with section 11 of the CPIA. Prosecutors may cross-examine the accused on differences between the defence case put at trial and that set out in his or her defence statement. In doing so, it may be appropriate to apply to the judge under section 6E of the CPIA for copies of the statement to be given to a jury, edited if necessary to remove inadmissible material. Prosecutors should examine the defence statement to see whether it points to other lines of enquiry.

33. Prosecutors should challenge the lack of, or inadequate, defence statements in writing, copying the document to the court and the defence and seeking directions from the court to require the provision of an adequate statement from the defence.

34. If the material does not fulfil the disclosure test there is no requirement to disclose it. For this purpose, the parties' respective cases should not be restrictively analysed but must be carefully analysed to ascertain the specific facts the prosecution seek to establish and the specific grounds on which the charges are resisted.

Prosecution advocates

35. Prosecution advocates should ensure that all material which ought to be disclosed under the Act is disclosed to the defence. However, prosecution advocates cannot be expected to disclose material if they are not aware of its existence. As far as is possible, prosecution advocates must place themselves in a fully informed position to enable them to make decisions on disclosure.

36. Upon receipt of instructions, prosecution advocates should consider as a priority all the information provided regarding disclosure of material. Prosecution advocates should consider, in every case, whether they can be satisfied that they are in possession of all relevant documentation and that they have been fully instructed regarding disclosure matters. If as a result the advocate considers that further information or action is required, written advice should promptly be provided setting out the aspects that need clarification or action.

37. The prosecution advocate must keep decisions regarding disclosure under review until the conclusion of the trial, whenever possible in consultation with the reviewing prosecutor. The prosecution advocate must in every case specifically consider whether he or she can satisfactorily discharge the duty of continuing review on the basis of the material supplied already, or whether it is necessary to inspect further material or to reconsider material already inspected. Prosecution advocates must not abrogate their responsibility under the CPIA by disclosing material which does not pass the test for disclosure, set out in paragraph 4, above.

38. There remains no basis in practice or law for counsel to counsel disclosure.

Defence

39. Defence engagement must be early and meaningful for the CPIA regime to function as intended. Defence statements are an integral part of this and are intended to help focus the attention of the prosecutor, court and co-defendants on the relevant issues in order to identify exculpatory unused material. Defence statements should be drafted in accordance with the relevant provisions of the CPIA.

40. Defence requests for further disclosure should ordinarily only be answered by the prosecution if the request is relevant to and directed to an issue identified in the defence statement. If it is not, then a further or amended defence statement should be sought by the prosecutor and obtained before considering the request for further disclosure.

41. In some cases that involve extensive unused material that is within the knowledge of a defendant, the defence will be expected to provide the prosecution and the court with assistance in identifying material which is suggested to pass the test for disclosure.

42. The prosecution's continuing duty to keep disclosure under review is crucial, and particular attention must be paid to understanding the significance of developments in the case on the unused

material and earlier disclosure decisions. Meaningful defence engagement will help the prosecution to keep disclosure under review. The continuing duty of review for prosecutors is less likely to require the disclosure of further material to the defence if the defence have clarified and articulated their case, as required by the CPIA.

43. In the magistrates' courts, where the provision of a defence statement is not mandatory, early identification of the material issues by the defence, whether through a defence statement, case management form or otherwise, will help the prosecution to focus its preparation of the case and allow any defence disclosure queries to be dealt with promptly and accurately.

Magistrates' courts (including the youth court)

44. The majority of criminal cases are heard in the magistrates' court. The requirement for the prosecution to provide initial disclosure only arises after a not guilty plea has been entered but prosecutors should be alert to the possibility that material may exist which should be disclosed to the defendant prior to the CPIA requirements applying to the case.[2]   **A-250**

45. Where a not guilty plea is entered in the magistrates' court, prosecutors should ensure that any issues of dispute which are raised are noted on the file. They should also seek to obtain a copy of any Magistrates' Court Trial Preparation Form. Consideration of the issues raised in court and on the trial preparation form will assist in deciding what material undermines the prosecution case or assists the defendant.

46. Where a matter is set down for trial in the magistrates' court, prosecutors should ensure that the investigator is requested to supply any outstanding disclosure schedules as a matter of urgency. Prosecutors should serve initial disclosure in sufficient time to ensure that the trial date is effective.

47. There is no requirement for a defence statement to be served in the magistrates' court but it should be noted that if none is given the court has no power to hear an application for further prosecution disclosure under section 8 of the CPIA and the Criminal Procedure Rules.

Cases in the Crown Court

48. The exponential increase in the use of technology in society means that many routine Crown Court cases are increasingly likely to have to engage with digital material of some form. It is not only in large and complex cases that there may be large quantities of such material. Where such investigations involve digital material, it will be virtually impossible for investigators (or prosecutors) to examine every item of such material individually and there should be no expectation that such material will be so examined. Having consulted with the prosecution as appropriate, disclosure officers should determine what their approach should be to the examination of the material. Investigators or disclosure officers should decide how best to pursue a reasonable line of enquiry in relation to the relevant digital material, and ensure that the extent and manner of the examination are commensurate with the issues in the case.   **A-251**

49. Consideration should be given to any local or national agreements in relation to disclosure in "Early Guilty Plea Scheme" cases.

Large and complex cases in the Crown Court

50. The particular challenges presented by large and complex criminal prosecutions require an approach to disclosure which is specifically tailored to the needs of such cases. In these cases more than any other is the need for careful thought to be given to prosecution-led disclosure matters from the very earliest stage. It is essential that the prosecution takes a grip on the case and its disclosure requirements from the very outset of the investigation, which must continue throughout all aspects of the case preparation.   **A-252**

Disclosure management documents

51. Accordingly, investigations and prosecutions of large and complex cases should be carefully defined and accompanied by a clear investigation and prosecution strategy. The approach to disclosure in such cases should be outlined in a document which should be served on the defence and the court at an early stage. Such documents, sometimes known as disclosure management documents, will require careful preparation and presentation, tailored to the individual case. They may include: **A-253**

    a. where prosecutors and investigators operate in an integrated office, an explanation as to how the disclosure responsibilities have been managed;

    b. a brief summary of the prosecution case and a statement outlining how the prosecutor's

---

[2] See for example *R. v. DPP, ex p. Lee* [1999] 2 Cr.App.R. 304, DC.

general approach will comply with the CPIA regime, these guidelines and the Judicial Protocol on the Disclosure of Unused Material in Criminal Cases;

c. the prosecutor's understanding of the defence case, including information revealed during interview;

d. an outline of the prosecution's general approach to disclosure, which may include detail relating to:

(i) digital material: explaining the method and extent of examination, in accordance with the **Annex** to these guidelines;

(ii) video footage;

(iii) linked investigations: explaining the nexus between investigations, any memoranda of understanding or disclosure agreements between investigators;

(iv) third party and foreign material, including steps taken to obtain the material;

(v) reasonable lines of enquiry: a summary of the lines pursued, particularly those that point away from the suspect, or which may assist the defence;

(vi) credibility of a witness: confirmation that witness checks, including those of professional witnesses have, or will be, carried out.

52. Thereafter the prosecution should follow the disclosure management document. They are living documents and should be amended in light of developments in the case; they should be kept up to date as the case progresses. Their use will assist the court in its own case management and will enable the defence to engage from an early stage with the prosecution's proposed approach to disclosure.

Material not held by the prosecution

Involvement of other agencies: material held by other government departments and third parties

A-254
53. Where it appears to an investigator, disclosure officer or prosecutor that a government department or other Crown body has material that may be relevant to an issue in the case, reasonable steps should be taken to identify and consider such material. Although what is reasonable will vary from case to case, the prosecution should inform the department or other body of the nature of its case and of relevant issues in the case in respect of which the department or body might possess material, and ask whether it has any such material.

54. It should be remembered that investigators, disclosure officers and prosecutors cannot be regarded to be in constructive possession of material held by government departments or Crown bodies simply by virtue of their status as government departments or Crown bodies.

55. Where, after reasonable steps have been taken to secure access to such material, access is denied, the investigator, disclosure officer or prosecutor should consider what if any further steps might be taken to obtain the material or inform the defence. The final decision on any further steps will be for the prosecutor.

Third party material: other domestic bodies

A-255
56. There may be cases where the investigator, disclosure officer or prosecutor believes that a third party (for example, a local authority, a social services department, a hospital, a doctor, a school, a provider of forensic services) has material or information which might be relevant to the prosecution case. In such cases, investigators, disclosure officers and prosecutors should take reasonable steps to identify, secure and consider material held by any third party where it appears to the investigator, disclosure officer or prosecutor that (a) such material exists and (b) that it may be relevant to an issue in the case.

57. If the investigator, disclosure officer or prosecutor seeks access to the material or information but the third party declines or refuses to allow access to it, the matter should not be left. If despite any reasons offered by the third party it is still believed that it is reasonable to seek production of the material or information, and the requirements of section 2 of the Criminal Procedure (Attendance of Witnesses) Act 1965 or as appropriate section 97 of the Magistrates' Courts Act 1980 are satisfied (or any other relevant power), then the prosecutor or investigator should apply for a witness summons causing a representative of the third party to produce the material to the court.

58. Sometimes, for example through multi-agency working arrangements, investigators, disclosure officers or prosecutors may become aware of the content or nature of material held by a third party. Consultation with the relevant third party must always take place before disclosure is made; there may be public interest reasons to apply to the court for an order for non-disclosure in the public interest, in accordance with the procedure outlined in paragraph 65 and following.

International matters

A-256
59. The obligations under the CPIA Code to pursue all reasonable lines of enquiry apply to material held overseas.

60. Where it appears that there is relevant material, the prosecutor must take reasonable steps to obtain it, either informally or making use of the powers contained in the Crime (International Co-operation) Act 2003 and any EU and international conventions. See CPS Guidance "Obtaining Evidence and Information from Abroad".

61. There may be cases where a foreign state or a foreign court refuses to make the material available to the investigator or prosecutor. There may be other cases where the foreign state, though willing to show the material to investigators, will not allow the material to be copied or otherwise made available and the courts of the foreign state will not order its provision.

62. It is for these reasons that there is no absolute duty on the prosecutor to disclose relevant material held overseas by entities not subject to the jurisdiction of the courts in England and Wales. However consideration should be given to whether the type of material believed to be held can be provided to the defence.

63. The obligation on the investigator and prosecutor under the CPIA is to take reasonable steps. Where investigators are allowed to examine files of a foreign state but are not allowed to take copies or notes or list the documents held, there is no breach by the prosecution in its duty of disclosure by reason of its failure to obtain such material, provided reasonable steps have been taken to try and obtain the material. Prosecutors have a margin of consideration as to what steps are appropriate in the particular case but prosecutors must be alive to their duties and there may be some circumstances where these duties cannot be met. Whether the prosecutor has taken reasonable steps is for the court to determine in each case if the matter is raised.

64. In these circumstances it is important that the position is clearly set out in writing so that the court and the defence know what the position is. Investigators and prosecutors must record and explain the situation and set out, insofar as they are permitted by the foreign state, such information as they can and the steps they have taken.

Applications for non-disclosure in the public interest

65. The CPIA allows prosecutors to apply to the court for an order to withhold material which   **A-257** would otherwise fall to be disclosed if disclosure would give rise to a real risk of serious prejudice to an important public interest. Before making such an application, prosecutors should aim to disclose as much of the material as they properly can (for example, by giving the defence redacted or edited copies or summaries). Neutral material or material damaging to the defendant need not be disclosed and there is no need to bring it to the attention of the court. Only in truly borderline cases should the prosecution seek a judicial ruling on whether material in its possession should be disclosed.

66. Prior to the hearing, the prosecutor and the prosecution advocate must examine all material which is the subject matter of the application and make any necessary enquiries of the investigator. The investigator must be frank with the prosecutor about the full extent of the sensitive material. Prior to or at the hearing, the court must be provided with full and accurate information about the material.

67. The prosecutor (or representative) and/or investigator should attend such applications. Section 16 of the CPIA allows a person claiming to have an interest in the sensitive material to apply to the court for the opportunity to be heard at the application.

68. The principles set out at paragraph 36 of *R. v. H.* [2004] 2 A.C. 134, [2004] UKHL 3, should be applied rigorously, firstly by the prosecutor and then by the court considering the material. It is essential that these principles are scrupulously adhered to, to ensure that the procedure for examination of material in the absence of the accused is compliant with Article 6.

69. If prosecutors conclude that a fair trial cannot take place because material which satisfies the test for disclosure cannot be disclosed, and that this cannot be remedied by the above procedure; how the case is presented; or by any other means, they should not continue with the case.

Other disclosure

70. Disclosure of any material that is made outside the ambit of CPIA will attract confidentiality   **A-258** by virtue of *Taylor v. Serious Fraud Office* [1999] 2 A.C. 177, HL.

Material relevant to sentence

71. In all cases the prosecutor must consider disclosing in the interests of justice any material   **A-259** which is relevant to sentence (*e.g.* information which might mitigate the seriousness of the offence or assist the accused to lay blame in part upon a co-accused or another person).

Post-conviction

72. Where, after the conclusion of the proceedings, material comes to light, that might cast doubt   **A-260**

upon the safety of the conviction, the prosecutor must consider disclosure of such material.

Applicability of these guidelines

A-261   73. These guidelines shall have immediate effect.

Annex: Attorney General's Guidelines on Disclosure: Supplementary Guidelines on Digitally Stored Material (2011)

A-262   A1. The guidelines are intended to supplement the Attorney General's Guidelines on Disclosure.

A2. As a result of the number of cases now involving digitally stored material and the scale of the digital material that may be involved, more detailed guidance is considered to be needed. The objective of these guidelines is to set out how material satisfying the tests for disclosure can best be identified and disclosed to the defence without imposing unrealistic or disproportionate demands on the investigator and prosecutor.

A3. The approach set out in these guidelines is in line with existing best practice, in that:

> a. investigating and prosecuting agencies, especially in large and complex cases, will apply their respective case management and disclosure strategies and policies and be transparent with the defence and the courts about how the prosecution has approached complying with its disclosure obligations in the context of the individual case; and,
>
> b. the defence will be expected to play their part in defining the real issues in the case. In this context, the defence will be invited to participate in defining the scope of the reasonable searches that may be made of digitally stored material by the investigator to identify material that might reasonably be expected to undermine the prosecution case or assist the defence.

A4. Only if this approach is followed can the courts be in a position to use their case management powers effectively and to determine applications for disclosure fairly.

A5. The Attorney General's Guidelines are not detailed operational guidelines. They are intended to set out a common approach to be adopted in the context of digitally stored material.

Types of digital material

A-263   A6. Digital material falls into two categories: the first category is material which is created natively within an electronic environment (*e.g.* email, office files, system files, digital photographs, audio, etc.); the second category is material which has been digitised from an analogue form (*e.g.* scanned copy of a document, scanned photograph, a faxed document). Irrespective of the way in which technology changes, the categorisation of digital material will remain the same.

A7. Digital material is usually held on one of the three types of media. Optical media (*e.g.* CD, DVD, Blu-ray) and solid-state media (*e.g.* removable memory cards, solid-state music players or mobile devices, etc.) cater for usually lower volume storage. Magnetic media (*e.g.* disk drives and back up tapes) usually cater for high volume storage.

General principles for investigators

A-264   A8. The general principles[3] to be followed by investigators in handling and examining digital material are:

> a. no action taken by investigators or their agents should change data held on a computer or storage media which may subsequently be relied upon in court;
>
> b. in circumstances where a person finds it necessary to access original data held on computer or storage media, that person must be competent to do so and be able to give evidence explaining the relevance and implications of their actions;
>
> c. an audit trail or other record of all processes applied to computer-based electronic evidence should be created and preserved; an independent third party should be able to examine those processes (see further the sections headed "Record keeping" and "Scheduling" below); and
>
> d. the person in charge of the investigation has overall responsibility for ensuring that the law and these principles are followed.

A9. Where an investigator has reasonable grounds for believing that digital material may contain material subject to legal professional privilege, very strong legal constraints apply. No digital material may be seized which an investigator has reasonable grounds for believing to be subject to legal privilege, other than where the provisions of the Criminal Justice and Police Act 2001 apply. Strict

---

[3] Based on: Association of Chief Police Officers: Good Practice Guide for Computer Based Electronic Evidence Version 0.1.4.

controls need to be applied where privileged material is seized. See the more detailed section on legal professional privilege starting at paragraph A28, below.

Seizure, relevance and retention

A10. The legal obligations are to be found in a combination of the Police and Criminal Evidence **A-265** Act 1984 (PACE), the Criminal Justice and Police Act 2001 (CJPA 2001) and the Criminal Procedure and Investigations Act 1996 (the CPIA 1996).

A11. These guidelines also apply to digital material seized or imaged under other statutory provisions. For example, the Serious Fraud Office has distinct powers of seizure under warrant obtained under section 2(4) of the Criminal Justice Act 1987. In cases concerning indecent images of children and obscene material, special provisions apply to the handling, storage and copying of such material. Practitioners should refer to specific guidance on the application of those provisions.

Seizure

A12. Before searching a suspect's premises where digital evidence is likely to be found, considera- **A-266** tion must be given to what sort of evidence is likely to be found and in what volume, whether it is likely to be possible to view and copy, if relevant, the material at the location (it is not uncommon with the advent of cloud computing for digital material to be hosted by a third party) and to what should be seized. Business and commercial premises will often have very substantial amounts of digital material stored on computers and other media. Investigators will need to consider the practicalities of seizing computer hard drives and other media, the effect this may have on the business and, where it is not feasible to obtain an image of digital material, the likely timescale for returning seized items.

A13. In deciding whether to seize and retain digital material it is important that the investigator either complies with the procedure under the relevant statutory authority, relying either on statutory powers or a search warrant, or obtains the owner's consent. In particular, investigators need to be aware of the constraints applying to legally privileged material.

A14. A computer hard drive or single item of media, such as a back up tape, is a single storage entity. This means that if any digital material found on the hard drive or other media can lawfully be seized the computer hard drive or single item of media may, if appropriate, be seized or imaged. In some circumstances investigators may wish to image specific folders, files or categories of data where it is feasible to do so without seizing the hard drive or other media, or instead of taking an image of all data on the hard drive or other media. In practice, the configuration of most systems means that data may be contained across a number of hard drives and more than one hard drive or item of media may be required in order to access the information sought.

A15. Digital material must not be seized if an investigator has reasonable grounds for believing it is subject to legal professional privilege, other than where sections 50 or 51 of the CJPA 2001 apply. If such material is seized it must be isolated from other seized material and any other investigation material in the possession of the investigating authority.

The Police and Criminal Evidence Act 1984

A16. PACE 1984 provides powers to seize and retain anything for which the search has been **A-267** authorised or after arrest, other than items attracting legal professional privilege.[4] In addition, there is a general power to seize anything which is on the premises if there are reasonable grounds to believe that it has been obtained in the commission of an offence, or that it is evidence and that it is necessary to seize it to prevent it being concealed, lost, altered or destroyed.[5] There is another related power to require information which is stored in any electronic form and is accessible from the premises to be produced in a form in which it can be taken away and in which it is visible and legible or from which it can readily be produced in a visible and legible form.[6]

A17. An image (a forensically sound copy) of the digital material may be taken at the location of the search. Where the investigator makes an image of the digital material at the location, the original need not be seized. Alternatively, when originals are taken, investigators must be prepared to copy or image the material for the owners when reasonably practicable in accordance with PACE 1984, Code B 7.17.

A18. Where it is not possible or reasonably practicable to image the computer or hard drive, it will need to be removed from the location or premises for examination elsewhere. This allows the

---

[4] By warrant under s.8, and Sched. 1 and s.18.
[5] S.19.
[6] S.20.

investigator to seize and sift material for the purpose of identifying that which meets the tests for retention in accordance with the 1984 PACE.[7]

The Criminal Justice and Police Act 2001

A-268

A19. The additional powers of seizure in sections 50 and 51 of the CJPA 2001 Act [*sic*] only extend the scope of existing powers of search and seizure under the PACE and other specified statutory authorities[8] where the relevant conditions and circumstances apply.

A20. Investigators must be careful only to exercise powers under the CJPA 2001 when it is necessary and not to remove any more material than is justified. The removal of large volumes of material, much of which may not ultimately be retainable, may have serious consequences for the owner of the material, particularly when they are involved in business or other commercial activities.

A21. A written notice must be given to the occupier of the premises where items are seized under sections 50 and 51.[9]

A22. Until material seized under the CJPA 2001 has been examined, it must be kept securely and separately from any material seized under other powers. Any such material must be examined as soon as reasonably practicable to determine which elements may be retained and which should be returned. Regard must be had to the desirability of allowing the person from whom the property was seized – or a person with an interest in the property – an opportunity of being present or represented at the examination.

Retention

A-269

A23. Where material is seized under the powers conferred by PACE the duty to retain it under the code of practice issued under the CPIA is subject to the provisions on retention under section 22 of PACE. Material seized under sections 50 and 51 of the CJPA 2001 may be retained or returned in accordance with sections 53–58 of that Act.

A24. Retention is limited to evidence and relevant material (as defined in the code of practice issued under the CPIA). Where either evidence or relevant material is inextricably linked to nonrelevant material which is not reasonably practicable to separate, that material can also be retained. Inextricably linked material is material that is not reasonably practicable to separate from other linked material without prejudicing the use of that other material in any investigation or proceedings.

A25. However, inextricably linked material must not be examined, imaged, copied or used for any purpose other than for providing the source of or the integrity of the linked material.

A26. There are four categories of material that may be retained:

 a. material that is evidence or potential evidence in the case; where material is retained for evidential purposes there will be a strong argument that the whole thing (or an authenticated image or copy) should be retained for the purpose of proving provenance and continuity;

 b. where evidential material has been retained, inextricably linked non-relevant material which is not reasonably practicable to separate can also be retained (PACE, Code B, para. 7);

 c. an investigator should retain material that is relevant to the investigation and required to be scheduled as unused material; this is broader than but includes the duty to retain material which may satisfy the test for prosecution disclosure; the general duty to retain relevant material is set out in the CPIA code at paragraph 5; or

 d. material which is inextricably linked to relevant unused material which of itself may not be relevant material; such material should be retained (PACE, Code B, para. 7).

A27. The balance of any digital material should be returned in accordance with sections 53–55 of the CJPA 2001 if seized under that Act.

Legal professional privilege (LPP)

A-270

A28. No digital material may be seized which an investigator has reasonable grounds for believing to be subject to LPP, other than under the additional powers of seizure in the CJPA 2001.

A29. The CJPA 2001 enables an investigator to seize relevant items which contain LPP material where it is not reasonably practicable on the search premises to separate LPP material from non-LPP material.

---

[7] Special provision exists for investigations conducted by Her Majesty's Revenue and Customs in the application of their powers under PACE – see s.114(2)(b) – and the CJPA 2001.
[8] Sched. 1 to the CJPA 2001.
[9] S.52.

A30. Where LPP material or material suspected of containing LPP is seized, it must be isolated from the other material which has been seized in the investigation. The mechanics of securing property vary according to the circumstances; "bagging up", *i.e.* placing materials in sealed bags or containers, and strict subsequent control of access, is the appropriate procedure in many cases.

A31. Where material has been identified as potentially containing LPP it must be reviewed by a lawyer independent of the prosecuting authority. No member of the investigative or prosecution team involved in either the current investigation or, if the LPP material relates to other criminal proceedings, in those proceedings should have sight of or access to the LPP material.

A32. If the material is voluminous, search terms or other filters may have to be used to identify the LPP material. If so this will also have to be done by someone independent and not connected with the investigation.

A33. It is essential that anyone dealing with LPP material maintains proper records showing the way in which the material has been handled and those who have had access to it as well as decisions taken in relation to that material.

A34. LPP material can only be retained in specific circumstances in accordance with section 54 of the CJPA 2001, *i.e.* where the property which comprises the LPP material has been lawfully seized and it is not reasonably practicable for the item to be separated from the rest of the property without prejudicing the use of the rest of the property. LPP material which cannot be retained must be returned as soon as practicable after the seizure without waiting for the whole examination of the seized material.

Excluded and special procedure material

A35. Similar principles to those that apply to LPP material apply to excluded or special procedure **A-271** material, as set out in section 55 of the CJPA 2001.[10]

Encryption

A36. Part III of the Regulation of Investigatory Powers Act 2000 (RIPA) and the *Investigation of* **A-272** *Protected Electronic Information Code of Practice* govern encryption. See the CPS's Guidance RIPA, Part III.

A37. RIPA enables specified law enforcement agencies to compel individuals or companies to provide passwords or encryption keys for the purpose of rendering protected material readable. Failure to comply with RIPA, Part III orders is a criminal offence. The code of practice provides guidance when exercising powers under RIPA, to require disclosure of protected electronic data in an intelligible form or to acquire the means by which protected electronic data may be accessed or put in an intelligible form.

Sifting/examination

A38. In complying with its duty of disclosure, the prosecution should follow the procedure as **A-273** outlined below.

A39. Where digital material is examined, the extent and manner of inspecting, viewing or listening will depend on the nature of the material and its form.

A40. It is important for investigators and prosecutors to remember that the duty under the CPIA code of practice is to "pursue all reasonable lines of enquiry including those that point away from the suspect". Lines of enquiry, of whatever kind, should be pursued only if they are reasonable in the context of the individual case. It is not the duty of the prosecution to comb through all the material in its possession - *e.g.* every word or byte of computer material - on the look out for anything which might conceivably or speculatively assist the defence. The duty of the prosecution is to disclose material which might reasonably be considered capable of undermining its case or assisting the case for the accused which they become aware of, or to which their attention is drawn.

A41. In some cases the sift may be conducted by an investigator/disclosure officer manually assessing the content of the computer or other digital material from its directory and determining which files are relevant and should be retained for evidence or unused material.

A42. In other cases such an approach may not be feasible. Where there is an enormous volume of material it is perfectly proper for the investigator/disclosure officer to search it by sample, key words, or other appropriate search tools or analytical techniques to locate relevant passages, phrases and identifiers.

A43. In cases involving very large quantities of data, the person in charge of the investigation will develop a strategy setting out how the material should be analysed or searched to identify categories

---

[10] Special provision exists for investigations conducted by Her Majesty's Revenue and Customs in the application of their powers under PACE − see s.114(2)(b) − and the CJPA.

of data. Where search tools are used to examine digital material it will usually be appropriate to provide the accused and his or her legal representative with a copy of reasonable search terms used, or to be used, and invite them to suggest any further reasonable search terms. If search terms are suggested which the investigator or prosecutor believes will not be productive – for example because of the use of common words that are likely to identify a mass of irrelevant material, the investigator or prosecutor is entitled to open a dialogue with the defence representative with a view to agreeing sensible refinements. The purpose of this dialogue is to ensure that reasonable and proportionate searches can be carried out.

A44. It may be necessary to carry out sampling and searches on more than one occasion, especially as there is a duty on the prosecutor to keep duties of disclosure under review. To comply with this duty it may be appropriate (and should be considered) where further evidence or unused material is obtained in the course of the investigation; the defence statement is served on the prosecutor; the defendant makes an application under section 8 of the CPIA for disclosure; or the defendant requests that further sampling or searches be carried out (provided it is a reasonable line of enquiry).

Record keeping

A-274

A45. A record or log must be made of all digital material seized or imaged and subsequently retained as relevant to the investigation.

A46. In cases involving very large quantities of data where the person in charge of the investigation has developed a strategy setting out how the material should be analysed or searched to identify categories of data, a record should be made of the strategy and the analytical techniques used to search the data. The record should include details of the person who has carried out the process and the date and time it was carried out. In such cases the strategy should record the reasons why certain categories have been searched for (such as names, companies, dates, etc).

A47. In any case it is important that any searching or analytical processing of digital material, as well as the data identified by that process, is properly recorded. So far as practicable, what is required is a record of the terms of the searches or processing that has been carried out. This means that in principle the following details may be recorded:

 a. a record of all searches carried out, including the date of each search and the person(s) who conducted it;

 b. a record of all search words or terms used on each search; however where it is impracticable to record each word or terms (such as where Boolean searches or search strings or conceptual searches are used) it will usually be sufficient to record each broad category of search;

 c. a log of the key judgements made while refining the search strategy in the light of what is found, or deciding not to carry out further searches; and

 d. where material relating to a "hit" is not examined, the decision not to examine should be explained in the record of examination or in a statement; for instance, a large number of "hits" may be obtained in relation to a particular search word or term, but material relating to the "hits" is not examined because they do not appear to be relevant to the investigation; any subsequent refinement of the search terms and further hits should also be noted and explained as above.

A48. Just as it is not necessary for the investigator or prosecutor to produce records of every search made of hard copy material, it is not necessary to produce records of what may be many hundreds of searches or analyses that have been carried out on digitally stored material, simply to demonstrate that these have been done. It should be sufficient for the prosecution to explain how the disclosure exercise has been approached and to give the accused or suspect's legal representative an opportunity to participate in defining the reasonable searches to be made, as described in the section on sifting/examination.

Scheduling

A-275

A49. The disclosure officer should ensure that scheduling of relevant material is carried out in accordance with the CPIA code of practice. This requires each item of unused material to be listed separately on the unused material schedule and numbered consecutively. The description of each item should make clear the nature of the item and should contain sufficient detail to enable the prosecutor to decide whether he needs to inspect the material before deciding whether or not it should be disclosed (see para. A24).

A50. In some enquiries it may not be practicable to list each item of material separately. If so, these may be listed in a block and described by quantity and generic title. Even if the material is listed in a block, the search terms used and any items of material which might satisfy the disclosure test are listed and described separately. In practical terms this will mean, where appropriate, cross referencing the schedules to your disclosure management document.

A51. The remainder of any computer hard drive/media containing material which is not responsive to search terms or other analytical technique or not identified by any "hits", and material identified by "hits" but not examined, is unused material and should be recorded (if appropriate by a generic description) and retained.

A52. Where continuation sheets of the unused material schedule are used, or additional schedules are sent subsequently, the item numbering must be, where possible, sequential to all other items on earlier schedules.

Third party material

A53. Third party material is material held by a person, organisation, or government department   **A-275a**
other than the investigator and prosecutor within the UK or outside the UK.

Within the UK

A54. The CPIA code and the AG's Guidelines make clear the obligation on the prosecution to   **A-275b**
pursue all reasonable lines of enquiry in relation to material held by third parties within the UK.

A55. If as a result of the duty to pursue all reasonable lines of enquiry, the investigator or prosecutor obtains or receives the material from the third party, then it must be dealt with in accordance with the CPIA, *i.e.* the prosecutor must disclose material if it meets the disclosure tests, subject to any public interest immunity claim. The person who has an interest in the material (the third party) may make representations to the court concerning public interest immunity (see s.16 of the CPIA 1996).

A56. Material not in the possession of an investigator or prosecutor falls outside the CPIA. In such cases the Attorney General's Guidelines on Disclosure prescribe the approach to be taken to disclosure of material held by third parties as does the judicial disclosure protocol.

B. Acceptance of Pleas

Introduction

The Attorney-General issued revised guidelines on the acceptance of pleas, which came into   **A-276**
force on December 1, 2009. The principal changes were to Part C (basis of plea). Paragraph C.1 now makes it clear that in multi-handed cases, any bases of plea must be factually consistent with each other. Paragraph C.2 now states that a defence advocate must reduce an acceptable basis of plea to writing in all cases save for those in which the defendant has indicated that the guilty plea has been or will be tendered on the basis of the prosecution case (previously this was not necessary in cases where the issue was "simple"). Paragraph C.4 now additionally provides that, where the basis of plea differs in its implications for sentencing or the making of ancillary orders from the case originally outlined by the prosecution, the prosecution advocate must ensure that such differences are accurately reflected in the written record prior to showing it to the prosecuting authority. New paragraph C.6 provides that in all cases where it is likely to assist the court where the sentencing issues are complex or unfamiliar, the prosecution must add to the written outline of the case served upon the court a summary of the key considerations, taking the form of brief notes on (a) any statutory limitations, (b) any relevant sentencing authorities or guidelines, (c) the scope for any ancillary orders, and (d) the age of the defendant and information regarding any outstanding offences. Paragraph C.7 was new and clarifies that the prosecution are able to provide further written information where they think that it is likely to assist the judge or where the judge requests it. Old paragraph C.7 became new paragraph C.8, and was amended to ensure that the procedure to be followed where the prosecution advocate takes issue with all or part of the written basis of plea is in line with the then consolidated criminal practice direction. Old paragraph C.8 is now paragraph C.11. For the relevant provisions of *Criminal Practice Direction VII (Sentence) B*, see § 4-175 in the main work; and *post*, Appendix B-149 *et seq.*

ATTORNEY-GENERAL'S GUIDELINES ON THE ACCEPTANCE OF PLEAS AND THE PROSECUTOR'S ROLE IN THE SENTENCING EXERCISE

A. Foreword

A:1. Prosecutors have an important role in protecting the victim's interests in the criminal justice process, not least in the acceptance of pleas and the sentencing exercise. The basis of plea, particularly in a case that is not contested, is the vehicle through which the victim's voice is heard. Factual inaccuracies in pleas in mitigation cause distress and offence to victims, the families of victims and witnesses. This can take many forms but may be most acutely felt when the victim is dead and the family hears inaccurate assertions about the victim's character or lifestyle. Prosecution advocates are reminded that they are required to adhere to the standards set out in the Victim's Charter, which places the needs of the victim at the heart of the criminal justice process, and that they are subject to a similar obligation in respect of the Code of Practice for Victims of Crime.

A:2. The principle of fairness is central to the administration of justice. The implementation of Human Rights Act 1998 [*sic*] in October 2000 incorporated into domestic law the principle of fairness to the accused articulated in the European Convention on Human Rights. Accuracy and reasonableness of plea plays an important part in ensuring fairness both to the accused and to the victim.

A:3. The Attorney General's Guidelines on the Acceptance of Pleas issued on December 7, 2000 highlighted the importance of transparency in the conduct of justice. The basis of plea agreed by the parties in a criminal trial is central to the sentencing process. An illogical or unsupported basis of plea can lead to an unduly lenient sentence being passed and has a consequential effect where consideration arises as to whether to refer the sentence to the Court of Appeal under section 36 of the Criminal Justice Act 1988.

A:4. These Guidelines, which replace the Guidelines issued in October 2005, give guidance on how prosecutors should meet these objectives of protection of victims' interests and of securing fairness and transparency in the process. They take into account paragraphs IV.45.4 and following of the consolidated criminal practice direction, amended May 2009, and the guidance issued by the Court of Appeal (Criminal) Division [*sic*] in *R. v. Beswick* [1996] 1 Cr.App.R. 343, *R. v. Tolera* [1999] 1 Cr.App.R. 25 and *R. v. Underwood* [2005] 1 Cr.App.R 13. They complement the Bar Council Guidance on Written Standards for the Conduct of Professional Work issued with the 7th edition of the Code of Conduct for the Bar of England and Wales and the Law Society's Professional Conduct Rules. When considering the acceptance of a guilty plea prosecution advocates are also reminded of the need to apply "The Farquharson Guidelines on The Role and Responsibilities of the Prosecution Advocate".

A:5. The Guidelines should be followed by all prosecutors and those persons designated under section 7 of the Prosecution of Offences Act 1985 (designated caseworkers) and apply to prosecutions conducted in England and Wales.

B. General Principles

B:1. Justice in this jurisdiction, save in the most exceptional circumstances, is conducted in public. This includes the acceptance of pleas by the prosecution and sentencing.

B:2. The Code for Crown Prosecutors governs the prosecutor's decision-making prior to the commencement of the trial hearing and sets out the circumstances in which pleas to a reduced number of charges, or less serious charges, can be accepted.

B:3. When a case is listed for trial and the prosecution form the view that the appropriate course is to accept a plea before the proceedings commence or continue, or to offer no evidence on the indictment or any part of it, the prosecution should whenever practicable speak to the victim or the victim's family, so that the position can be explained. The views of the victim or the family may assist in informing the prosecutor's decision as to whether it is the [*sic*] public interest, as defined by the Code for Crown Prosecutors, to accept or reject the plea. The victim or victim's family should then be kept informed and decisions explained once they are made at court.

B:4. The appropriate disposal of a criminal case after conviction is as much a part of the criminal justice process as the trial of guilt or innocence. The prosecution advocate represents the public interest, and should be ready to assist the court to reach its decision as to the appropriate sentence. This will include drawing the court's attention to:

- any victim personal statement or other information available to the prosecution advocate as to the impact of the offence on the victim;
- where appropriate, to any evidence of the impact of the offending on a community;
- any statutory provisions relevant to the offender and the offences under consideration;
- any relevant sentencing guidelines and guideline cases; and
- the aggravating and mitigating factors of the offence under consideration.

The prosecution advocate may also offer assistance to the court by making submissions, in the light of all these factors, as to the appropriate sentencing range.

In all cases, it is the prosecution advocate's duty to apply for appropriate ancillary orders, such as anti-social behaviour orders and confiscation orders. When considering which ancillary orders to apply for, prosecution advocates must always have regard to the victim's needs, including the question of his or her future protection.

C. The Basis of Plea

C:1. The basis of a guilty plea must not be agreed on a misleading or untrue set of facts and must **A-279** take proper account of the victim's interests. An illogical or insupportable basis of plea will inevitably result in the imposition of an inappropriate sentence and is capable of damaging public confidence in the criminal justice system. In cases involving multiple defendants the bases of plea for each defendant must be factually consistent with each other.

C:2. When the defendant indicates an acceptable plea, the defence advocate should reduce the basis of the plea to writing. This must be done in all cases save for those in which the defendant has indicated that the guilty plea has been or will be tendered on the basis of the prosecution case.

C:3. The written basis of plea must be considered with great care, taking account of the position of any other relevant defendant where appropriate. The prosecution should not lend itself to any agreement whereby a case is presented to the sentencing judge on a misleading or untrue set of facts or on a basis that is detrimental to the victim's interests. There will be cases where a defendant seeks to mitigate on the basis of assertions of fact which are outside the scope of the prosecution's knowledge. A typical example concerns the defendant's state of mind. If a defendant wishes to be sentenced on this basis, the prosecution advocate should invite the judge not to accept the defendant's version unless he or she gives evidence on oath to be tested in cross-examination. Paragraph IV.45.14 of the consolidated criminal practice direction states that in such circumstances the defence advocate should be prepared to call the defendant and, if the defendant is not willing to testify, subject to any explanation that may be given, the judge may draw such inferences as appear appropriate.

C:4. The prosecution advocate should show the prosecuting authority any written record relating to the plea and agree with them the basis on which the case will be opened to the court. If, as may well be the case, the basis of plea differs in its implications for sentencing or the making of ancillary orders from the case originally outlined by the prosecution, the prosecution advocate must ensure that such differences are accurately reflected in the written record prior to showing it to the prosecuting authority.

C:5. It is the responsibility of the prosecution advocate thereafter to ensure that the defence advocate is aware of the basis on which the plea is accepted by the prosecution and the way in which the prosecution case will be opened to the court.

C:6. In all cases where it is likely to assist the court where the sentencing issues are complex or unfamiliar the prosecution must add to the written outline of the case which is served upon the court a summary of the key considerations. This should take the form of very brief notes on:

— any relevant statutory limitations;
— the names of any relevant sentencing authorities or guidelines;
— the scope for any ancillary orders (*e.g.* concerning anti-social behaviour, confiscation or deportation will need to be considered).

The outline should also include the age of the defendant and information regarding any outstanding offences.

C:7. It remains open to the prosecutor to provide further written information (for example to supplement and update the analysis at later stages of the case) where he or she thought that likely to assist the court, or if the judge requests it.

C:8. When the prosecution advocate has agreed the written basis of plea submitted by the defence advocate, he or she should endorse the document accordingly. If the prosecution advocate takes issue with all or part of the written basis of plea, the procedure set out in the consolidated criminal practice direction (and in Part 37.10(5) of the Criminal Procedure Rules) should be followed. The defendant's basis of plea must be set out in writing identifying what is in dispute; the court may invite the parties to make representations about whether the dispute is material to sentence; and if the court decides that it is a material dispute, the court will invite further representations or evidence as it may require and decide the dispute in accordance with the principles set out in *R. v. Newton*, 77 Cr.App.R.13, CA. The signed original document setting out the disputed factual matters should be made available to the trial judge and thereafter lodged with the court papers, as it will form part of the record of the hearing.

C:9. Where the basis of plea cannot be agreed and the discrepancy between the two accounts is such as to have a potentially significant effect on the level of sentence, it is the duty of the defence advocate so to inform the court before the sentencing process begins. There remains an overriding duty on the prosecution advocate to ensure that the sentencing judge is made aware of the discrepancy and of the consideration which must be given to holding a *Newton* hearing to resolve the issue. The court should be told where a derogatory reference to a victim, witness or third party is not accepted, even though there may be no effect on sentence.

C:10. As emphasised in paragraph IV.45.10 of the consolidated criminal practice direction, whenever an agreement as to the basis of plea is made between the prosecution and defence, any such agreement will be subject to the approval of the trial judge, who may of his or her own motion disregard the agreement and direct that a *Newton* hearing should be held to determine the proper basis on which sentence should be passed.

C:11. Where a defendant declines to admit an offence that he or she previously indicated should be taken into consideration, the prosecution advocate should indicate to the defence advocate and the court that, subject to further review, the offence may now form the basis of a new prosecution.

D. Sentence Indications

A-280

D:1. Only in the Crown Court may sentence indications be sought. Advocates there are reminded that indications as to sentence should not be sought from the trial judge unless issues between the prosecution and defence have been addressed and resolved. Therefore, in difficult or complicated cases, no less than seven days notice in writing of an intention to seek an indication should normally be given to the prosecution and the court. When deciding whether the circumstances of a case require such notice to be given, defence advocates are reminded that prosecutors should not agree a basis of plea unless and until the necessary consultation has taken place first with the victim and/or the victim's family and second, in the case of an independent prosecution advocate, with the prosecuting authority.

D:2. If there is no final agreement about the plea to the indictment, or the basis of plea, and the defence nevertheless proceeds to seek an indication of sentence, which the judge appears minded to give, the prosecution advocate should remind him or her of the guidance given in *R. v. Goodyear (Karl)* [2005] EWCA 888 [*sic*] that normally speaking an indication of sentence should not be given until the basis of the plea has been agreed or the judge has concluded that he or she can properly deal with the case without the need for a trial of the issue.

D:3. If an indication is sought, the prosecution advocate should normally enquire whether the judge is in possession of or has access to all the evidence relied on by the prosecution, including any victim personal statement, as well as any information about relevant previous convictions recorded against the defendant.

D:4. Before the judge gives the indication, the prosecution advocate should draw the judge's attention to any minimum or mandatory statutory sentencing requirements. Where the prosecution advocate would be expected to offer the judge assistance with relevant guideline cases or the views of the Sentencing Guidelines Council, he or she should invite the judge to allow them to do so. Where it applies, the prosecution advocate should remind the judge that the position [*sic*] of the Attorney General to refer any sentencing decision as unduly lenient is unaffected. In any event, the prosecution advocate should not say anything which may create the impression that the sentence indication has the support or approval of the Crown.

E. Pleas in Mitigation

A-281

E:1. The prosecution advocate must challenge any assertion by the defence in mitigation which is derogatory to a person's character (for instance, because it suggests that his or her conduct is or has been criminal, immoral or improper) and which is either false or irrelevant to proper sentencing considerations. If the defence advocate persists in that assertion, the prosecution advocate should invite the court to consider holding a *Newton* hearing to determine the issue.

E:2. The defence advocate must not submit in mitigation anything that is derogatory to a person's character without giving advance notice in writing so as to afford the prosecution advocate the opportunity to consider their position under paragraph E:1. When the prosecution advocate is so notified they must take all reasonable steps to establish whether the assertions are true. Reasonable steps will include seeking the views of the victim. This will involve seeking the views of the victim's family if the victim is deceased, and the victim's parents or legal guardian where the victim is a child. Reasonable steps may also include seeking the views of the police or other law enforcement authority, as appropriate. An assertion which is derogatory to a person's character will rarely amount to mitigation unless it has a causal connection to the circumstances of the offence or is otherwise relevant to proper sentencing considerations.

E:3. Where notice has not been given in accordance with paragraph E:2, the prosecution advocate must not acquiesce in permitting mitigation which is derogatory to a person's character. In such circumstances, the prosecution advocate should draw the attention of the court to the failure to give advance notice and seek time, and if necessary, an adjournment to investigate the assertion in the same way as if proper notice had been given. Where, in the opinion of the prosecution advocate, there are substantial grounds for believing that such an assertion is false or irrelevant to sentence, he or she should inform the court of their opinion and invite the court to consider making an order under section 58(8) of the Criminal Procedure and Investigations Act 1996, preventing publication of the assertion.

E:4. Where the prosecution advocate considers that the assertion is, if true, relevant to sentence, or the court has so indicated, he or she should seek time, and if necessary an adjournment, to establish whether the assertion is true. If the matter cannot be resolved to the satisfaction of the parties, the prosecution advocate should invite the court to consider holding a *Newton* hearing to determine the issue.

C. Jury Checks

Introduction

For the background to these guidelines, see § 4-275 in the main work. They were updated in   **A-282**
November 2012.

Attorney-General's Guidelines: Jury checks, unreported, November 27, 2012

1. The principles which are generally to be observed are: **A-283**
   (a) that members of a jury should be selected at random from the panel,
   (b) the Juries Act 1974 identifies those classes of persons who alone are either disqualified from or ineligible for service on a jury; no other class of person may be treated as disqualified or ineligible,
   (c) the correct way for the Crown to seek to exclude a member of the panel from sitting as a juror is by the exercise in open court of the right to request a stand by or, if necessary, to challenge for cause.

2. Parliament has provided safeguards against jurors who may be corrupt or biased. In addition to the provision for majority verdicts, there is the sanction of a criminal offence for a disqualified person to serve on a jury. The omission of a disqualified person from the panel is a matter for court officials—they will check criminal records for the purpose of ascertaining whether or not a potential juror is a disqualified person.

3. There are, however, certain exceptional types of case of public importance for which the provi-   **A-284**
sions as to majority verdicts and the disqualification of jurors may not be sufficient to ensure the proper administration of justice. In such cases it is in the interests of both justice and the public that there should be further safeguards against the possibility of bias and in such cases checks which go beyond the investigation of criminal records may be necessary.

4. These classes of case may be defined broadly as (a) cases in which national security is involved and part of the evidence is likely to be heard *in camera*, and (b) security and terrorist cases in which a juror's extreme beliefs could prevent a fair trial.

5. The particular aspects of these cases which may make it desirable to seek extra precautions are:
   (a) in security cases a danger that a juror, either voluntarily or under pressure, may make an improper use of evidence which, because of its sensitivity, has been given in camera,
   (b) in both security and terrorist cases the danger that a juror's personal beliefs are so biased as to go beyond normally reflecting the broad spectrum of views and interests in the community to reflect the extreme views of sectarian interest or pressure group to a degree which might interfere with his fair assessment of the facts of the case or lead him to exert improper pressure on his fellow jurors.

6. In order to ascertain whether in exceptional circumstances of the above nature either of these   **A-285**
factors might seriously influence a potential juror's impartial performance of his duties or his respecting the secrecy of evidence given *in camera*, it may be necessary to conduct a limited investigation of the panel. In general, such further investigation beyond one of criminal records made for disqualifications may only be made with the records of the police. However, a check may, additionally, be made against the records of the Security Service. No checks other than on these sources and no general inquiries are to be made save to the limited extent that they may be needed to confirm the identity of a juror about whom the initial check has raised serious doubts.

7. No further investigation, as described in paragraph 6 above, should be made save with the personal authority of the Attorney-General on the application of the Director of Public Prosecutions and such checks are hereafter referred to as "authorised checks". When a chief officer of police or the prosecutor has reason to believe that it is likely that an authorised check may be desirable and proper in accordance with these guidelines, he should refer the matter to the Director of Public

Prosecutions. In those cases in which the Director of Public Prosecutions believes authorised checks are both proportionate and necessary, the Director will make an application to the Attorney-General.

8. The Director of Public Prosecutions will provide the Attorney-General with all relevant information in support of the requested authorised checks. The Attorney-General will consider personally the request and, if appropriate, authorise the check.

9. The result of any authorised check will be sent to the Director of Public Prosecutions. The Director will then decide, having regard to the matters set out in paragraph 5 above, what information ought to be brought to the attention of prosecuting counsel. The Director will also provide the Attorney-General with the result of the authorised check.

A-286   **10.** Although the right of stand by and the decision to authorise checks are wholly within the discretion of the Attorney-General, when the Attorney-General has agreed to an authorised check being conducted, the Director of Public Prosecutions will write to the presiding judge for the area to advise him that this is being done.

11. No right of stand by should be exercised by counsel for the Crown on the basis of information obtained as a result of an authorised check save with the personal authority of the Attorney-General and unless the information is such as, having regard to the facts of the case and the offences charged, to afford strong reason for believing that a particular juror might be a security risk, be susceptible to improper approaches or be influenced in arriving at a verdict for the reasons given above.

12. Information revealed in the course of an authorised check must be considered in line with the normal rules on disclosure.

13. A record is to be kept by the Director of Public Prosecutions of the use made by counsel of the information passed to him and of the jurors stood by or challenged by the parties to the proceedings. A copy of this record is to be forwarded to the Attorney-General for the sole purpose of enabling him to monitor the operation of these guidelines.

A-287   **14.** No use of the information obtained as a result of an authorised check is to be made except as may be necessary in direct relation to or arising out of the trial for which the check was authorised. The information may, however, be used for the prevention of crime or as evidence in a future criminal prosecution, save that material obtained from the Security Service may only be used in those circumstances with the authority of the Security Service.

D. Prosecution's Right of Stand By

A-288   For the background to these guidelines, see §§ 4-304, 4-305 in the main work. They were updated in November, 2012.

Attorney-General's Guidelines on the Exercise by the Crown of its Right of Stand By, unreported, November 27, 2012

A-289   **1.** Although the law has long recognised the right of the Crown to exclude a member of a jury panel from sitting as a juror by the exercise in open court of the right to request a stand by or, if necessary, by challenge for cause, it has been customary for those instructed to prosecute on behalf of the Crown to assert that right only sparingly and in exceptional circumstances. It is generally accepted that the prosecution should not use its right in order to influence the overall composition of a jury or with a view to tactical advantage.

2. The approach outlined above is founded on the principles that:

(a) the members of a jury should be selected at random from the panel subject to any rule of law as to right of challenge by the defence, and

(b) the Juries Act 1974 identifies those classes of persons who alone are disqualified from or ineligible for service on a jury. No other class of person may be treated as disqualified or ineligible.

3. The enactment by Parliament of section 118 of the Criminal Justice Act 1988 abolishing the right of defendants to remove jurors by means of peremptory challenge makes it appropriate that the Crown should assert its right to stand by only on the basis of clearly defined and restrictive criteria. Derogation from the principle that members of a jury should be selected at random should be permitted only where it is essential.

4. Primary responsibility for ensuring that an individual does not serve on a jury if he is not competent to discharge properly the duties of a juror rests with the appropriate court officer and, ultimately the trial judge. Current legislation provides, in sections 9 to 10 of the Juries Act 1974, fairly wide discretion to excuse, defer or discharge jurors.

5. The circumstances in which it would be proper for the Crown to exercise its right to stand by a member of a jury panel are:

(a) where a jury check authorised in accordance with the Attorney-General's guidelines on jury checks reveals information justifying exercise of the right to stand by in accordance with paragraph 11 of the guidelines ... and the Attorney-General personally authorises the exercise of the right to stand by; or

(b) where a person is about to be sworn as a juror who is manifestly unsuitable and the defence agree that, accordingly, the exercise by the prosecution of the right to stand by would be appropriate. An example of the sort of exceptional circumstances which might justify stand by is where it becomes apparent that, despite the provisions mentioned in paragraph 4 above, a juror selected for service to try a complex case is in fact illiterate.

E. Conspiracy to Defraud

The Attorney-General has issued guidance to prosecuting authorities in relation to charging a common law conspiracy to defraud instead of a substantive offence, contrary to the Fraud Act 2006, or a statutory conspiracy to commit a substantive offence, contrary to section 1 of the CLA 1977 (§ 33-2 in the main work); the prosecutor should consider (i) whether the conduct alleged falls within the ambit of a statutory offence, and (ii) whether such a charge or charges would adequately reflect the gravity of the alleged offending; as to (i), non-exhaustive examples of circumstances falling outside of the range of statutory offences, but within the ambit of the common law offence, are: (a) the dishonest obtaining of land or other property which cannot be stolen; (b) the dishonest infringement of another's right (*e.g.* the dishonest exploitation of another's patent); (c) an agreement involving an intention that the final offence be committed by someone outside the conspiracy; and (d) an agreement where the conspirators cannot be proved to have had the necessary degree of knowledge for the substantive offence to be perpetrated; as to (ii), prosecution for the common law offence may be more effective where the interests of justice can only be served by presenting an overall picture which could not be achieved by charging a series of substantive offences or statutory conspiracies (because of a large number of counts and/or the possibility of severed trials and evidence on one count being deemed inadmissible on another); where a case lawyer proposes to charge the common law offence, he must consider, and set out in the review note, how much such a charge would add to the amount of evidence likely to be called by the parties, the justification for using the charge, and why specific statutory offences are inadequate or otherwise inappropriate; a supervising lawyer experienced in fraud cases must also specifically approve the charge: *Attorney-General's guidance on the use of the common law offence of conspiracy to defraud*, unreported, January 9, 2007.

F. Prosecutor's Role in Applications for Witness Anonymity Orders

On July 21, 2008, the Attorney-General issued guidelines on the overarching principles which a prosecutor must consider when deciding whether to apply for witness anonymity orders under the Criminal Evidence (Witness Anonymity) Act 2008 (now the Coroners and Justice Act 2009, ss.86–97 (§§ 8-151 *et seq.* in the main work)).

The guidance is in four parts (Part A (foreword), Part B (prosecutor's duties), Part C (applications by defendants) and Part D (appointment and role of special counsel)), and, to a large extent, highlights various provisions of the Act and restates elementary aspects of fairness at trial. Paragraph A2 makes clear that, given that the defendant's right to confront and challenge those who accuse him is an important aspect of a fair trial, making a witness anonymity order is a serious step which must only be taken where there are genuine grounds to believe that the conditions set out in the Act have been satisfied, which must be evaluated with care on the facts of each case. Paragraph B3 sets out the prosecutor's role, which prosecutors must approach in light of their overriding duties to be fair, independent and objective, and which includes a duty: (a) to examine with care and probe where appropriate, the material provided in support of the application and the evidential basis for it, and (b) to put before the court and to disclose to the defendant all material relevant to the application and the defence, including material which may undermine or qualify the prosecution case. Any such material is particularly relevant if credibility is in issue, for example, if there is a known link between the witness and defendant or a co-accused. Paragraph B4 explains that applications should only be authorised by prosecutors of an appropriately senior level. Paragraph D5 explains that a prosecutor making an application for an order must always be prepared to assist the court to consider whether the circumstances are such that exceptionally the appointment of special counsel may be called for, and, where appropriate, should draw to the attention of the court any aspect of the application which may be relevant to such appointment. Where the court decides to invite the Attorney-General to appoint special counsel, the prosecutor should (regardless of any steps taken by the court or any defendant) ensure that the Attorney-General's office is promptly notified and receives all information needed to take a decision as to whether to make such appointment. If special counsel is appointed, the prosecutor should then provide special counsel with open material made available to the accused regarding the application, and any other open material requested by special counsel. Closed or unredacted material which has been provided to the court should only be given to special counsel after open material has been provided and after special counsel has subsequently sought instructions from the defendant and his legal representative.

G. Plea Discussions in Cases of Serious or Complex Fraud

(1) Guidelines

A-292   On March 18, 2009, the Attorney-General issued guidelines setting out the process by which a prosecutor may discuss allegations of serious or complex fraud with a person whom he is prosecuting or expecting to prosecute.

ATTORNEY GENERAL'S GUIDELINES ON PLEA DISCUSSIONS IN CASES OF SERIOUS OR COMPLEX FRAUD

A. Foreword

A-293   A:1 These guidelines set out a process by which a prosecutor may discuss an allegation of serious or complex fraud with a person who he or she is prosecuting or expects to prosecute, or with that person's legal representative. They come into force on the 5th day of May 2009 and apply to plea discussions initiated on or after that date.

A:2 The guidelines will be followed by all prosecutors in England and Wales when conducting plea discussions in cases of serious or complex fraud. For the purposes of the guidelines, fraud means any financial, fiscal or commercial misconduct or corruption which is contrary to the criminal law. Fraud may be serious or complex if at least two of the following factors are present:

- the amount obtained or intended to be obtained is alleged to exceed £500,000;
- there is a significant international dimension;
- the case requires specialised knowledge of financial, commercial, fiscal or regulatory matters such as the operation of markets, banking systems, trusts or tax regimes;
- the case involves allegations of fraudulent activity against numerous victims;
- the case involves an allegation of substantial and significant fraud on a public body;
- the case is likely to be of widespread public concern;
- the alleged misconduct endangered the economic well-being of the United Kingdom, for example by undermining confidence in financial markets.

Taking account of these matters, it is for the prosecutor to decide whether or not a case is one of fraud, and whether or not it is serious or complex.

A:3 The decision whether a person should be charged with a criminal offence rests with the prosecutor. In selecting the appropriate charge or charges, the prosecutor applies principles set out in the Code for Crown Prosecutors ("the code"). Charges should reflect the seriousness and extent of the offending, give the court adequate sentencing powers and enable the case to be presented in a clear and simple way. The code also states that prosecutors should not go ahead with more charges to encourage a defendant to plead guilty to a few; equally, prosecutors should not charge a more serious offence to encourage a defendant to plead to a less serious one.

A:4 Once proceedings are instituted, the accused may plead guilty to all of the charges selected. If the defendant will plead guilty to some, but not all, of the charges or to a different, possibly less serious charge, the code states that a prosecutor is entitled to accept such pleas if he or she assesses that the court could still pass an adequate sentence. In taking these decisions the prosecutor also applies the Attorney General's Guidelines on the Acceptance of Pleas and the Prosecutor's Role in the Sentencing Exercise ("the acceptance of pleas guidelines") [*ante*, A-259 *et seq.*].

A:5 The purpose of plea discussions is to narrow the issues in the case with a view to reaching a just outcome at the earliest possible time, including the possibility of reaching an agreement about acceptable pleas of guilty and preparing a joint submission as to sentence.

A:6 The potential benefits of plea discussions are that:

- early resolution of the case may reduce the anxiety and uncertainty for victims and witnesses, and provide earlier clarity for accused persons who admit their guilt (subject to the court's power to reject the agreement);

- the issues in dispute may be narrowed so that even if the case proceeds to trial, it can be managed more efficiently in accordance with rule 3.2 of the Criminal Procedure Rules 2005. If pleas are agreed, litigation can be kept to a minimum.

A:7 Where plea discussions take place prior to the commencement of proceedings, the charges brought by the prosecutor will reflect those agreed, rather than those that the prosecutor would necessarily have preferred if no agreement had been reached. Also, any criminal investigation may not be complete when these discussions take place. For these reasons it is important that the procedures followed should command public and judicial confidence; that any agreement reached is reasonable, fair and just; that there are safeguards to ensure that defendants are not under improper pressure to make admissions; and that there are proper records of discussions that have taken place.

A:8 The guidelines are not intended to prevent or discourage existing practices by which prosecutors and prosecuting advocates discuss cases with defence legal representatives after charge, in order to narrow the issues or to agree a basis of plea. Neither do they affect the existing practice of judicial sentence indications at the plea and case management hearing or later in accordance with the guidance in *R. v. Goodyear* [2005] 2 Cr.App.R. 20 (§ 5-125 in the main work) (see also the acceptance of pleas guidelines). They complement, and do not detract from or replace, the code and the acceptance of pleas guidelines, or any other relevant guidance such as the Prosecutor's Pledge, the Victim's Charter and the Code of Practice for Victims of Crime.

A:9 Where a plea agreement is reached, it remains entirely a matter for the court to decide how to deal with the case.

B. General Principles

B:1 In conducting plea discussions and presenting a plea agreement to the court, the prosecutor **A-294** must act openly, fairly and in the interests of justice.

B:2 Acting in the interests of justice means ensuring that the plea agreement reflects the seriousness and extent of the offending, gives the court adequate sentencing powers, and enables the court, the public and the victims to have confidence in the outcome. The prosecutor must consider carefully the impact of a proposed plea or basis of plea on the community and the victim, and on the prospects of successfully prosecuting any other person implicated in the offending. The prosecutor must not agree to a reduced basis of plea which is misleading, untrue or illogical.

B:3 Acting fairly means respecting the rights of the defendant and of any other person who is being or may be prosecuted in relation to the offending. The prosecutor must not put improper pressure on a defendant in the course of plea discussions, for example by exaggerating the strength of the case in order to persuade the defendant to plead guilty, or to plead guilty on a particular basis.

B:4 Acting openly means being transparent with the defendant, the victim and the court. The prosecutor must:

- ensure that a full and accurate record of the plea discussions is prepared and retained;
- ensure that the defendant has sufficient information to enable him or her to play an informed part in the plea discussions;
- communicate with the victim before accepting a reduced basis of plea, wherever it is practicable to do so, so that the position can be explained; and
- ensure that the plea agreement placed before the court fully and fairly reflects the matters agreed. The prosecutor must not agree additional matters with the defendant which are not recorded in the plea agreement and made known to the court.

C. Initiating Plea Discussions

When and with whom discussions should be initiated and conducted

C:1 Where he or she believes it advantageous to do so, the prosecutor may initiate plea discussions **A-295** with any person who is being prosecuted or investigated with a view to prosecution in connection with a serious or complex fraud, and who is legally represented. The prosecutor will not initiate plea discussions with a defendant who is not legally represented. If the prosecutor receives an approach from such a defendant, he or she may enter into discussions if satisfied that it is appropriate to do so.

C:2 Where proceedings have not yet been instituted, the prosecutor should not initiate plea discussions until he or she and the investigating officer are satisfied that the suspect's criminality is known. This will not usually be the case until after the suspect has been interviewed under caution.

C:3 The prosecutor should be alert to any attempt by the defendant to use plea discussions as a means of delaying the investigation or prosecution, and should not initiate or continue discussions where the defendant's commitment to the process is in doubt. The prosecutor should ensure that the position is preserved during plea discussions by, for example, restraining assets in anticipation of the making of a confiscation order. Where a defendant declines to take part in plea discussions, the prosecutor should not make a second approach unless there is a material change in circumstances.

Invitation letter

C:4 In order to initiate the plea discussions, the prosecutor will send the defendant's representatives a letter which:

- asks whether the defence wish to enter into discussions in accordance with these guidelines; and
- sets a deadline for a response from the defence.

Terms and conditions letter

C:5 Where the defence agree to engage in plea discussions, the prosecutor should send them a letter setting out the way in which the discussions will be conducted. This letter should deal with:

- the confidentiality of information provided by the prosecutor and defendant in the course of the plea discussions;
- the use which may be made by the prosecutor of information provided by the defendant; and
- the practical means by which the discussions will be conducted.

Confidentiality and use of information

C:6 In relation to confidentiality, the prosecutor will indicate that he or she intends to provide an undertaking to the effect that the fact that the defendant has taken part in the plea discussions, and any information provided by the defence in the course of the plea discussions will be treated as confidential and will not be disclosed to any other party other than for the purposes of the plea discussions and plea agreement (applying these guidelines), or as required by law. The undertaking will make it clear that the law in relation to the disclosure of unused material may require the prosecutor to provide information about the plea discussions to another defendant in criminal proceedings.

C:7 The prosecutor will require the defendant's legal representative to provide an undertaking to the effect that information provided by the prosecutor in the course of the plea discussions will be treated as confidential and will not be disclosed to any other party, other than for the purposes of the plea discussion and plea agreement or as required by law.

C:8 In relation to the use of information, the prosecutor will indicate that he or she intends to undertake not to rely upon the fact that the defendant has taken part in the plea discussions, or any information provided by the defendant in the course of the discussions, as evidence in any prosecution of that defendant for the offences under investigation, should the discussions fail. However, this undertaking will make it clear that the prosecutor is not prevented from:

- relying upon a concluded and signed plea agreement as confession evidence or as admissions;
- relying upon any evidence obtained from enquiries made as a result of the provision of information by the defendant;
- relying upon information provided by the defendant as evidence against him or her in any prosecution for an offence other than the fraud which is the subject of the plea discussion and any offence which is consequent upon it, such as money laundering; and
- relying upon information provided by the defendant in a prosecution of any other person for any offence (so far as the rules of evidence allow).

C:9 In exceptional circumstances the prosecutor may agree to different terms regarding the confidentiality and use of information. However, the prosecutor must not surrender the ability to rely upon a concluded and signed plea agreement as evidence against the defendant. The prosecutor may reserve the right to bring other charges (additional to those to which the defendant has indicated a willingness to plead guilty) in specific circumstances, for example if substantial new information comes to light at a later stage, the plea agreement is rejected by the court, or the defendant fails to honour the agreement.

C:10 Until the issues of confidentiality and use of information have been agreed to the satisfaction of both parties, and the agreement reflected in signed undertakings, the prosecutor must not continue with the substantive plea discussions.

D. Conducting Plea Discussions

Statement of case

D:1 Where plea discussions take place prior to proceedings being instituted, the prosecutor will **A-296** provide a statement of case to the defence. This is a written summary of the nature of the allegation against the suspect and the evidence which has been obtained, or is expected to be obtained, to support it. The statement of case should include a list of the proposed charges. Material in support of the statement of case may also be provided, whether or not in the form of admissible evidence. However, the prosecutor is not obliged to reveal to the suspect all of the information or evidence supporting his case, provided that this does not mislead the suspect to his or her prejudice.

D:2 Where plea discussions are initiated after proceedings have been commenced, but before the prosecutor has provided the defence with a case summary or opening note, the prosecutor may provide a statement of case to assist the defendant in understanding the evidence and identifying the issues.

Unused material

D:3 These guidelines do not affect the prosecutor's existing duties in relation to the disclosure of unused material. Where plea discussions take place prior to the institution of proceedings, the prosecutor should ensure that the suspect is not misled as to the strength of the prosecution case. It will not usually be necessary to provide copies of unused material in order to do this.

Conducting and recording the discussions

D:4 Having provided the defence with the statement of case and supporting material, the parties will then be in a position to conduct the plea discussion proper. Whether this is done by correspondence, by face-to-face meetings or by a combination of the two is a matter for the parties to decide in the individual case.

D:5 It is essential that a full written record is kept of every key action and event in the discussion process, including details of every offer or concession made by each party, and the reasons for every decision taken by the prosecutor. Meetings between the parties should be minuted and the minutes agreed and signed. Particular care should be taken where the defendant is not legally represented. The prosecutor should only meet with a defendant who is not legally represented if the defendant agrees to the meeting being recorded, or to the presence of an independent third party.

Queen's evidence

D:6 If the defendant offers at any stage to provide information, or to give evidence about the criminal activities of others, any such offer will be dealt with in accordance with sections 71 to 75 of the Serious Organised Crime and Police Act 2005 ("SOCPA"), the judgment of the Court of Appeal in *R. v. P.*; *R. v. Blackburn* [2008] 2 Cr.App.R.(S.) 5 (§ 5-162 in the main work) and the guidance agreed and issued by the Director of Public Prosecutions, the Director of the Serious Fraud Office and the Director of Revenue and Customs Prosecutions.

Discussion of pleas

D:7 In deciding whether or not to accept an offer by the defendant to plead guilty, the prosecutor will follow sections 7 and 10 of the code relating to the selection of charges and the acceptance of guilty pleas. The prosecutor should ensure that:
- the charges reflect the seriousness and extent of the offending;
- they give the court adequate powers to sentence and impose appropriate post-conviction orders;
- they enable the case to be presented in a clear and simple way (bearing in mind that many cases of fraud are necessarily complex);
- the basis of plea enables the court to pass a sentence that matches the seriousness of the offending, particularly if there are aggravating features;
- the interests of the victim, and where possible any views expressed by the victim, are taken into account when deciding whether it is in the public interest to accept the plea; and
- the investigating officer is fully appraised of developments in the plea discussions and his or her views are taken into account.

D:8 In reaching an agreement on pleas, the parties should resolve any factual issues necessary to allow the court to sentence the defendant on a clear, fair and accurate basis. Before agreeing to proposed pleas, the prosecutor should satisfy him or herself that the full code test as set out in the code will be made out in respect of each charge. In considering whether the evidential stage of the test will be met, the prosecutor should assume that the offender will sign a plea agreement amounting to an admission to the charge.

Discussion of sentence

D:9 Where agreement is reached as to pleas, the parties should discuss the appropriate sentence with a view to presenting a joint written submission to the court. This document should list the aggravating and mitigating features arising from the agreed facts, set out any personal mitigation available to the defendant, and refer to any relevant sentencing guidelines or authorities. In the light of all of these factors, it should make submissions as to the applicable sentencing range in the relevant guideline. The prosecutor must ensure that the submissions are realistic, taking full account of all relevant material and considerations.

D:10 The prosecutor should bear in mind all of the powers of the court, and seek to include in the joint submission any relevant ancillary orders. It is particularly desirable that measures should be included that achieve redress for victims (such as compensation orders) and protection for the public (such as directors' disqualification orders, serious crime prevention orders or financial reporting orders).

D:11 Due regard should be had to the court's asset recovery powers and the desirability of using these powers both as a deterrent to others and as a means of preventing the defendant from benefiting from the proceeds of crime or funding future offending. The Proceeds of Crime Act 2002 requires the Crown Court to proceed to the making of a confiscation order against a convicted defendant who has benefited from his criminal conduct where the prosecutor asks the court to do so, or the court believes that it is appropriate to do so. Fraud is an acquisitive crime, and the expectation in a fraud case should be that a confiscation order will be sought by the prosecutor reflecting the full benefit to the defendant. However, in doing so it is open to the prosecutor to take a realistic view of the likely approach of the court to the determination of any points in dispute (such as the interest of a third party in any property).

D:12 In the course of the plea discussions the prosecutor must make it clear to the defence that the joint submission as to sentence (including confiscation) is not binding on the court.

Liaison with another prosecutor or regulator

D:13 The prosecutor may become aware that another prosecuting authority or regulatory body (either in England and Wales or elsewhere) has an interest in the defendant. The prosecutor should liaise with the other agency, in accordance with the Prosecutors' Convention and any other relevant agreement or guidance. The other agency may wish to take part in the plea discussions, or they may authorise the prosecutor to discuss with the defendant the matters which they are interested in, with a view to resolving all matters in one plea agreement. The prosecutor should warn the defendant that a plea agreement will not bind any other agency which is not a party to it.

E. The Written Plea Agreement

A-297   E:1 All matters agreed between the prosecutor and the defence must be reduced to writing as a plea agreement and signed by both parties. The plea agreement will include:

- a list of the charges;
- a statement of the facts; and
- a declaration, signed by the defendant personally, to the effect that he or she accepts the stated facts and admits he or she is guilty of the agreed charges.

E:2 Any agreement under the SOCPA regarding the giving of assistance to the prosecutor by the defendant should be in a separate document accompanying the plea agreement.

E:3 Once a plea agreement is signed in a case where proceedings have not yet been commenced, the prosecutor will review the case in accordance with the code and, assuming the evidential stage of the full code test is satisfied on the basis of the signed plea agreement and the other available evidence, will arrange for proceedings to be instituted by summons or charge.

E:4 In advance of the defendant's first appearance in the Crown Court, the prosecutor should send the court sufficient material to allow the judge to understand the facts of the case and the history of the plea discussions, to assess whether the plea agreement is fair and in the interests of justice, and to decide the appropriate sentence. This will include:

- the signed plea agreement;
- a joint submission as to sentence and sentencing considerations;
- any relevant sentencing guidelines or authorities;
- all of the material provided by the prosecution to the defendant in the course of the plea discussions;

- any material provided by the defendant to the prosecution, such as documents relating to personal mitigation; and
- the minutes of any meetings between the parties and any correspondence generated in the plea discussions.

E:5 It will then be for the court to decide how to deal with the plea agreement. In particular, the court retains an absolute discretion as to whether or not it sentences in accordance with the joint submission from the parties.

F. Failure of Plea Discussions

F:1 There are several circumstances in which plea discussions may result in an outcome other **A-298** than the defendant pleading guilty in accordance with a plea agreement. The prosecutor or the defendant may break off the discussions. They may be unable to reach an agreement. They may reach an agreement, but intervening events may lead the prosecutor to decide that proceedings should not be instituted. Proceedings may be instituted but the court may reject the plea agreement. The defendant may decline to plead guilty in accordance with the plea agreement, either as a result of a sentence indication given under the procedure set out in *R. v. Goodyear*, or for some other reason.

F:2 If any of these situations arises, the prosecutor may wish for further enquiries to be made with a view to bringing or completing proceedings against the defendant. If proceedings have already been instituted, the prosecutor will use the appropriate means to delay them - either discontinuing under section 23 or 23A of the Prosecution of Offences Act 1985 or (if the indictment has already been preferred) applying for an adjournment or stay of the proceedings. The prosecutor and the defendant's representatives will continue to be bound by the preliminary undertakings made in relation to the confidentiality and use of information provided in the course of the plea discussions.

F:3 Where plea discussions have broken down for any reason, it will be rare that the prosecutor will wish to re-open them, but he or she may do so if there is a material change in circumstances which warrants it.

(2) Practice

See paragraphs 15 to 27 of *Criminal Practice Direction VII (Sentencing) B, post*, Appendix B-154 *et* **A-299** *seq.*

(3) Authorities

As to the limitations on prosecuting authorities' power to enter into agreements (with overseas **A-300** authorities or a potential accused) as to how a case should be disposed of, see *R. v. Innospec Ltd*, § 1-467 in the main work. As to this case, see also § 5-753 in the main work.

In *R. v. Dougall* [2011] 1 Cr.App.R.(S.) 37, CA, it was said that a joint submission as to sentence pursuant to the Attorney-General's Guidelines on Plea Discussions in Cases of Serious or Complex Fraud, *ante*, should recognise that it is the court alone that decides on sentence, should avoid advocacy of a particular outcome, and should confine itself to the appropriate range within which it is said the sentence should fall. As to this case, see also § 5-164 in the main work.

H. ASSET RECOVERY POWERS OF PROSECUTING AUTHORITIES

The Attorney-General and the Home Secretary have issued joint guidance under section 2A of **A-301** the PCA 2002 to the National Crime Agency, the DPP, the Director of Revenue and Customs Prosecutions, the Director of the Serious Fraud Office and the DPP for Northern Ireland directing them to consider using their civil asset recovery powers under the 2002 Act wherever proceeds of crime have been identified but it is not feasible to secure a conviction, or a conviction has been secured but no confiscation order made (para. 2). They must also consider whether the public interest might be better served by using these powers, rather than by instituting a criminal investigation or prosecution, whilst applying the principle that a criminal disposal will generally make the best contribution to the reduction of crime (para. 3). Paragraph 4 states that the factors listed in the Code for Crown Prosecutors (*post*, Appendix E-6) as being relevant to the question whether a prosecution would be in the public interest might also be relevant when considering at any stage whether or not the civil recovery powers should be used; but it is emphasised that a potential defendant should not be able to escape an appropriate prosecution by the simple device of agreeing to a civil recovery order. Paragraph 5 contains a non-exhaustive list of circumstances in which use of the powers might be appropriate because it is not feasible to secure a conviction and paragraph 6 contains an equivalent list for where a conviction is feasible but where the public interest might be better served by use of these powers. Paragraph 8 sets out the ways in which the relevant authorities should seek to minimise any potential prejudice to a related or potential criminal investigation or proceedings, including through the disclosure of relevant information. Paragraph 9 confirms that the guidance does not prohibit (i) a criminal investigation being carried out by a law enforcement authority at the same time as a civil recovery and/or a tax investigation; (ii) civil recovery and/or tax proceedings being instituted where a criminal investigation by a law enforcement authority is being carried out at the same time into unrelated criminality (subject to the duty set out in para. 8, *ante*); or (iii) criminal proceedings being instituted or carried on by a prosecuting authority at the same time as a civil recovery and/or tax investigation is being carried out. However, paragraph 10 prohibits in all circumstances criminal and civil/tax proceedings being carried on at the same time in relation to the same criminality. Where criminal proceedings have been stayed by a court, or cannot progress (*e.g.* because the defendant has absconded), they are not being "carried on" for the purposes of this prohibition. Paragraph 11 sets out the circumstances in which a relevant authority may agree to accept a reduced sum in satisfaction of a civil recovery claim. For the full text of the guidance, see http://www.attorneygen eral.gov.uk/Publications/Pages/AttorneyGeneralsGuidelines.aspx.

APPENDIX B
Criminal Procedure Rules and Criminal Practice Directions

Criminal Procedure Rules 2015 (as amended); Criminal Practice Directions (2015) (as amended) and Criminal Costs Practice Directions (2015)

(Appendix B and main work paragraph numbers are set out below. Main work paragraphs are shown in brackets. An italicised paragraph number is given where a procedure rule is summarised rather than set out in full.)

CRIMINAL PROCEDURE RULE	PARAGRAPH NUMBERS
Part 1 (The overriding objective)	
rr.1.1–1.3	B-1 (4-114)
Part 2 (Understanding and applying the rules)	
r.2.1	B-4 (2-159)
r.2.2	B-5 (2-160)
r.2.3	B-6 (2-161)
Part 3 (Case management)	
rr.3.1-3.4	B-7 (4-115)
rr.3.5-3.8	B-8 (4-116)
rr.3.9, 3.10	B-9 (4-117)
r.3.11	B-10 (4-118)
r.3.12	B-11 (4-119)
r.3.13	B-12 (4-120c)
rr.3.14, 3.15	B-13 (4-139)
rr.3.16-3.18	B-14 (4-140)
r.3.19	B-15 (4-120d)
r.3.20	B-16 (4-101a)
rr.3.21, 3.22	B-17 (4-120f)
r.3.23	B-18 (4-120g)
r.3.24	B-19 (4-121)
r.3.25	B-20 (4-122)
r.3.26	B-21 (4-64)
Part 4 (Service of documents)	
r.4.1	B-73 (2-162)
r.4.2	B-74 (2-163)
r.4.3	B-75 (2-164)
r.4.4	B-76 (2-165)
r.4.5	B-77 (2-166)
r.4.6	B-78 (2-167)
r.4.7	B-79 (2-168)
r.4.8	B-80 (2-169)
r.4.9	B-81 (2-170)
r.4.10	B-82 (2-171)
r.4.11	B-83 (2-172)
r.4.12	B-84 (2-173)
r.4.13	B-85 (2-174)
Part 5 (Forms and court records)	
r.5.1	B-86 (2-176)

CRIMINAL PROCEDURE RULE	PARAGRAPH NUMBERS
r.5.2	B-87 (2-178)
r.5.3	B-88 (2-179)
r.5.4	B-89 (2-180)
r.5.5	B-90 (2-181)
r.5.6	B-91 (2-182)
r.5.7	B-92 (2-183)
r.5.8	B-93 (2-184)
r.5.9	B-94 (2-186)
Part 6 (Reporting, etc., restrictions)	
rr.6.1-6.3	B-107 (4-47)
rr.6.4-6.8	B-108 (4-48)
r.6.9	B-109 (4-49)
r.6.10	B-110 (28-76)
Part 7 (Starting a prosecution in a magistrates' court)	*[Not set out in this work]*
Part 8 (Initial details of the prosecution case)	
r.8.1	B-118 (12-142)
r.8.2	B-119 (12-143)
r.8.3	B-120 (12-144)
r.8.4	B-120a (12-144, *ante*)
Part 9 (Allocation and sending for trial)	
r.9.1	B-123 (1-97)
r.9.2	B-124 (1-98)
r.9.3	B-125 (1-99)
r.9.4	B-126 (1-100)
r.9.5	B-127 (1-101)
r.9.6	B-128 (1-102)
r.9.7	B-129 (1-103)
r.9.8	B-130 (1-104)
r.9.9	B-131 (1-105)
r.9.10	B-132 (1-106)
r.9.11	B-133 (1-107)
r.9.12	B-134 (1-108)
r.9.13	B-135 (1-109)
r.9.14	B-136 (1-110)
r.9.15	B-137 (1-111)
r.9.16	B-138 (1-112)
Part 10 (The indictment)	
r.10.1	B-140 (1-182)
r.10.2	B-141 (1-183)
r.10.3	B-142 (1-184)
r.10.4	B-143 (1-185)
r.10.5	B-144 (1-186)

CRIMINAL PROCEDURE RULE	PARAGRAPH NUMBERS
r.10.6	B-145 (1-187)
r.10.7	B-146 (1-188)
r.10.8	B-147 (1-189)
r.10.9	B-148 (1-190)
Part 11 (Deferred prosecution agreements)	
r.11.1	B-153 (1-383)
r.11.2	B-154 (1-384)
r.11.3	B-155 (1-385)
r.11.4	B-156 (1-386)
r.11.5	B-157 (1-387)
r.11.6	B-158 (1-388)
r.11.7	B-159 (1-389)
r.11.8	B-160 (1-390)
r.11.9	B-161 (1-391)
rr.11.10, 11.11	B-162 (1-392, 1-393)
Part 12 (Discontinuing a prosecution)	
rr.12.1-12.3	B-163 (1-455, 1-456, 1-457)
Part 13 (Warrants for arrest, detention or imprisonment)	*[Not set out in this work]*
Part 14 (Bail and custody time limits)	
r.14.1	B-165 (3-118)
r.14.2	B-166 (3-119)
r.14.3	B-167 (3-120)
r.14.4	B-168 (3-121)
r.14.5	B-169 (3-122)
r.14.6	B-170 (3-123)
r.14.7	B-171 (3-124)
r.14.8	B-172 (3-125)
r.14.9	B-173 (3-126)
r.14.10	B-174 (3-127)
r.14.11	B-175 (3-128)
r.14.12	B-176 (3-129)
r.14.13	B-177 (3-130)
r.14.14	B-178 (3-131)
r.14.15	B-179 (3-132)
r.14.16	B-180 (3-132a)
r.14.17	B-181 (3-132b)
r.14.18	B-182 (3-133)
r.14.19	B-183 (3-134)
r.14.20	B-183a (§ 3-134a, *ante*)
r.14.21	B-183b (§ 3-134b, *ante*)
r.14.22	B-183c (§ 3-134c, *ante*)
Part 15 (Disclosure)	

CRIMINAL PROCEDURE RULE	PARAGRAPH NUMBERS
r.15.1	B-196 (12-103)
r.15.2	B-197 (12-104)
r.15.3	B-198 (12-105)
r.15.4	B-199 (12-112)
r.15.5	B-200 (12-113)
r.15.6	B-201 (12-114)
r.15.7	B-202 (12-115)
r.15.8	B-203 (12-116)
r.15.9	B-204 (12-117)
Part 16 (Written witness statements)	
r.16.1	B-206 (10-16)
r.16.2	B-207 (10-17)
r.16.3	B-208 (10-18)
r.16.4	B-209 (10-19)
Part 17 (Witness summonses, warrants and orders)	
r.17.1	B-215 (8-15)
r.17.2	B-216 (8-16)
r.17.3	B-217 (8-17)
r.17.4	B-218 (8-18)
r.17.5	B-219 (8-19)
r.17.6	B-220 (8-20)
r.17.7	B-221 (8-21)
r.17.8	B-222 (8-22)
Part 18 (Measures to assist a witness or defendant to give evidence)	
r.18.1	B-224 (8-110)
r.18.2	B-225 (8-111)
r.18.3	B-226 (8-112)
r.18.4	B-227 (8-113)
r.18.5	B-228 (8-114)
r.18.6	B-229 (8-115)
r.18.7	B-230 (8-116)
r.18.8	B-231 (8-117)
r.18.9	B-232 (8-118)
r.18.10	B-233 (8-119)
r.18.11	B-234 (8-120)
r.18.12	B-235 (8-121)
r.18.13	B-236 (8-122)
r.18.14	B-237 (8-123)
r.18.15	B-238 (8-124)
r.18.16	B-239 (8-125)
r.18.17	B-240 (8-126)

CRIMINAL PROCEDURE RULE	PARAGRAPH NUMBERS
r.18.18	B-241 (8-127)
r.18.19	B-242 (8-128)
r.18.20	B-243 (8-129)
r.18.21	B-244 (8-130)
r.18.22	B-245 (8-131)
r.18.23	B-246 (8-131a)
r.18.24	B-247 (8-131b)
r.18.25	B-248 (8-131c)
r.18.26	B-249 (8-131d)
Part 19 (Expert evidence)	
r.19.1	B-262 (10-39)
r.19.2	B-263 (10-40)
r.19.3	B-264 (10-41)
r.19.4	B-265 (10-42)
r.19.5	B-266 (10-43)
r.19.6	B-267 (10-44)
r.19.7	B-268 (10-45)
r.19.8	B-269 (10-46)
r.19.9	B-270 (10-46a)
Part 20 (Hearsay evidence)	
r.20.1	B-272 (11-52)
r.20.2	B-273 (11-53)
r.20.3	B-274 (11-54)
r.20.4	B-275 (11-55)
r.20.5	B-276 (11-56)
Part 21 (Evidence of bad character)	
r.21.1	B-277 (13-111)
r.21.2	B-278 (13-112)
r.21.3	B-279 (13-113)
r.21.4	B-280 (13-114)
r.21.5	B-281 (13-115)
r.21.6	B-282 (13-116)
Part 22 (Evidence of a complainant's previous sexual behaviour)	
r.22.1	B-284 (8-254)
r.22.2	B-285 (8-255)
r.22.3	B-286 (8-256)
r.22.4	B-287 (8-257)
r.22.5	B-288 (8-258)
r.22.6	B-289 (8-259)
r.22.7	B-290 (8-260)
Part 23 (Restriction on cross-examination by a defendant)	

CRIMINAL PROCEDURE RULE	PARAGRAPH NUMBERS
r.23.1	B-291 (8-232)
r.23.2	B-292 (8-233)
r.23.3	B-293 (8-234)
r.23.4	B-294 (8-235)
r.23.5	B-295 (8-235a)
r.23.6	B-296 (8-235b)
r.23.7	B-297 (8-235c)
r.23.8	B-298 (8-235d)
Part 24 (Trial and sentence in a magistrates' court)	
r.24.1	B-299
r.24.2	B-300
r.24.3	B-301
r.24.4	B-302
r.24.5	B-303
r.24.6	B-304
r.24.7	B-305
r.24.8	B-306
r.24.9	B-307
r.24.10	B-308
r.24.11	B-309
r.24.12	B-310
r.24.13	B-311
r.24.14	B-312
r.24.15	B-313
r.24.16	B-314
r.24.17	B-315
r.24.18	B-316
Part 25 (Trial and sentence in the Crown Court)	
rr.25.1, 25.2	B-319 (4-265a)
r.25.3	B-320 (4-265b)
r.25.4	B-321 (4-265c)
r.25.5	B-322 (4-254)
r.25.6	B-323 (4-265d)
rr.25.7, 25.8	B-324 (4-265e)
r.25.9	B-325 (4-265f)
r.25.10	B-326 (4-232a)
r.25.11	B-327 (8-70a)
r.25.12	B-328 (*10-19a, 10-46b and 11-56a*)
r.25.13	B-329 (*10-8*)
r.25.14	B-330 (4-265g)
r.25.15	B-331 (4-265h)

CRIMINAL PROCEDURE RULE	PARAGRAPH NUMBERS
r.25.16	B-332 (5-13)
r.25.17	B-333 (4-265j)
r.25.18	B-334 (2-16)
Part 26 (Jurors)	
r.26.1	B-336 (4-289)
r.26.2	B-337 (4-291)
r.26.3	B-338 (4-291b)
r.26.4	B-339 (4-291c)
r.26.5	B-340 (4-325c)
Part 27 (Retrial after acquittal)	
r.27.1	B-377 (4-199, 7-307a)
r.27.2	B-378 (4-200)
r.27.3	B-379 (7-307c)
r.27.4	B-380 (7-307d)
r.27.5	B-381 (7-307e)
r.27.6	B-382 (7-307f)
r.27.7	B-383 (7-307g)
Part 28 (Sentencing procedures in special cases)	
r.28.1	B-384
r.28.2	B-385 (5-274)
r.28.3	B-386
r.28.4	B-387 (5-1313)
r.28.5	B-388
r.28.6	B-389
r.28.7	B-390 (5-692)
r.28.8	B-391 (5-1272)
r.28.9	B-392 (5-1273)
r.28.10	B-393 (5-46)
r.28.11	B-394 (5-160)
Part 29 (Road traffic penalties)	
r.29.1	B-395
r.29.2	B-396 (32-308)
r.29.3	B-397 (32-309)
r.29.4	B-398
r.29.5	B-399 (32-310)
r.29.6	B-400
Part 30 (Enforcement of fines and other penalties)	*[Not set out in this work]*
Part 31 (Behaviour orders)	
r.31.1	B-402 (5-1229)
r.31.2	B-403 (5-1230)
r.31.3	B-404 (5-1231)

CRIMINAL PROCEDURE RULE	PARAGRAPH NUMBERS
r.31.4	B-405 (5-1232)
r.31.5	B-406 (5-1233)
r.31.6	B-407 (5-1234)
r.31.7	B-408 (5-1235)
r.31.8	B-409 (5-1236)
r.31.9	B-410 (5-1237)
r.31.10	B-411 (5-1238)
r.31.11	B-412 (5-1239)
Part 32 (Breach, revocation and amendment of community and other orders)	
r.32.1	B-413 (5-366)
r.32.2	B-414 (5-367)
r.32.3	B-415 (5-368)
r.32.4	B-416 (5-369)
Part 33 (Confiscation and related proceedings)	
r.33.1	B-418 (5-921)
r.33.2	B-419 (5-922)
r.33.3	B-420 (5-923)
r.33.4	B-421 (5-924)
r.33.5	B-422 (5-925)
r.33.6	B-423 (5-926)
r.33.7	B-424 (5-927)
r.33.8	B-425 (5-928)
r.33.9	B-426 (5-929)
r.33.10	B-427 (5-930)
r.33.11	B-428 (5-931)
r.33.12	B-429 (5-932)
r.33.13	B-430 (5-933)
r.33.14	B-431 (5-934)
r.33.15	B-432 (5-935)
r.33.16	B-433 (5-936)
r.33.17	B-434 (5-937)
r.33.18	B-435 (5-938)
r.33.19	B-436 (5-939)
r.33.20	B-437 (5-940)
r.33.21	B-438 (5-941)
r.33.22	B-439 (5-942)
r.33.23	B-440 (5-943)
r.33.24	B-441 (5-944)
r.33.25	B-442 (5-945)
r.33.26	B-443 (5-946)
r.33.27	B-444 (5-947)

CRIMINAL PROCEDURE RULE	PARAGRAPH NUMBERS
r.33.28	B-445 (5-948)
r.33.29	B-446 (5-949)
r.33.30	B-447 (5-950)
r.33.31	B-448 (5-951)
r.33.32	B-449 (5-952)
rr.33.33-33.35	B-450 (5-953)
r.33.36	B-451 (5-954)
rr.33.37, 33.38	B-452 (5-955, 5-956)
r.33.39	B-453 (5-957)
r.33.40	B-454 (5-958)
r.33.41	B-455 (5-959)
r.33.42	B-456 (5-960)
rr.33.43, 33.44	B-457 (5-961, 5-962)
r.33.45	B-458 (5-963)
r.33.46	B-459 (5-964)
r.33.47	B-460 (5-965)
r.33.48	B-461 (5-966)
rr.33.49, 33.50	B-462 (5-967, 5-968)
r.33.51	B-463 (5-969)
r.33.52	B-464 (5-970)
r.33.53	B-465 (5-971)
r.33.54	B-466 (5-972)
r.33.55	B-467 (5-973)
r.33.56	B-468 (5-974)
r.33.57	B-469 (5-975)
r.33.58	B-470 (5-976)
r.33.59	B-471 (5-977)
r.33.60	B-472 (5-978)
r.33.61	B-473 (5-979)
r.33.62	B-474 (5-980)
r.33.63	B-475 (5-981)
r.33.64	B-476
r.33.65	B-477
r.33.66	B-478
r.33.67	B-479
r.33.68	B-480
r.33.69	B-481
r.33.70	B-482 (5-988)
Part 34 (Appeal to the Crown Court)	
r.34.1	B-483 (2-117)
r.34.2	B-484 (2-118)
r.34.3	B-485 (2-119)
r.34.4	B-486 (2-120)

CRIMINAL PROCEDURE RULE	PARAGRAPH NUMBERS
r.34.5	B-487 (2-121)
r.34.6	B-488 (2-122)
r.34.7	B-489 (2-123)
r.34.8	B-490 (2-124)
r.34.9	B-491 (2-111)
r.34.10	B-492 (2-126)
r.34.11	B-493 (2-8)
Part 35 (Appeal to the High Court by case stated)	
r.35.1	B-495
rr.35.2, 35.3	B-496 (7-18)
r.35.4	B-497
r.35.5	B-498
Part 36 (Appeal to the Court of Appeal: general rules)	
r.36.1	B-499 (7-366)
r.36.2	B-500 (7-367)
r.36.3	B-501 (7-368)
r.36.4	B-502 (7-369)
r.36.5	B-503 (7-370)
r.36.6	B-504 (7-371)
r.36.7	B-505 (7-372)
r.36.8	B-506 (7-373)
r.36.9	B-507 (7-374)
r.36.10	B-508 (7-375)
r.36.11	B-509 (7-376)
r.36.12	B-510 (7-377)
r.36.13	B-511 (7-185)
r.36.14	B-512 (7-186)
Part 37 (Appeal to the Court of Appeal against ruling at a preparatory hearing)	
r.37.1	B-513 (7-315)
r.37.2	B-514 (7-316)
r.37.3	B-515 (7-317)
r.37.4	B-516 (7-318)
r.37.5	B-517 (7-319)
r.37.6	B-518 (7-320)
r.37.7	B-519 (7-321)
r.37.8	B-520 (7-322)
Part 38 (Appeal to the Court of Appeal against ruling adverse to the prosecution)	
r.38.1	B-521 (7-265)
r.38.2	B-522 (7-266)
r.38.3	B-523 (7-267)

CRIMINAL PROCEDURE RULE	PARAGRAPH NUMBERS
r.38.4	B-524 (7-268)
r.38.5	B-525 (7-269)
r.38.6	B-526 (7-270)
r.38.7	B-527 (7-271)
r.38.8	B-528 (7-272)
r.38.9	B-529 (7-273)
r.38.10	B-530 (7-274)
r.38.11	B-531 (7-275)
Part 39 (Appeal to the Court of Appeal about conviction or sentence)	
r.39.1	B-532 (7-380)
r.39.2	B-533 (7-381)
r.39.3	B-534 (7-382)
r.39.4	B-535 (7-383)
r.39.5	B-536 (*7-159*)
r.39.6	B-537 (7-203)
r.39.7	B-538 (7-386)
r.39.8	B-539 (7-177)
r.39.9	B-540 (7-178)
r.39.10	B-541 (7-179)
r.39.11	B-542 (7-194)
r.39.12	B-543 (7-195)
r.39.13	B-544 (7-150)
r.39.14	B-545 (7-115)
Part 40 (Appeal to the Court of Appeal about reporting or public access restriction)	
r.40.1	B-553 (7-326)
r.40.2	B-554 (7-327)
r.40.3	B-555 (7-328)
r.40.4	B-556 (7-329)
r.40.5	B-557 (7-330)
r.40.6	B-558 (7-331)
r.40.7	B-559 (7-332)
r.40.8	B-560 (7-333)
r.40.9	B-561 (7-334)
Part 41 (Reference to the Court of Appeal of point of law or unduly lenient sentencing)	
r.41.1	B-562 (7-453)
r.41.2	B-563 (7-454)
r.41.3	B-564 (7-455)
r.41.4	B-565 (7-456)
r.41.5	B-566 (7-457)
r.41.6	B-567 (7-458)

CRIMINAL PROCEDURE RULE	PARAGRAPH NUMBERS
r.41.7	B-568 (7-459)
r.41.8	B-569 (7-460)
Part 42 (Appeal to the Court of Appeal in confiscation and related proceedings)	
r.42.1	B-570 (5-1005)
r.42.2	B-571 (5-1006)
r.42.3	B-572 (5-1007)
r.42.4	B-573 (5-1008)
r.42.5	B-574 (5-1009)
r.42.6	B-575 (5-1010)
r.42.7	B-576 (5-1011)
r.42.8	B-577 (5-1012)
r.42.9	B-578 (5-1013)
r.42.10	B-579 (5-1014)
r.42.11	B-580 (5-1015)
r.42.12	B-581 (5-1016)
r.42.13	B-582 (5-1017)
r.42.14	B-583 (5-1018)
r.42.15	B-584 (5-1019)
r.42.16	B-585 (5-1020)
r.42.17	B-586 (5-1021)
r.42.18	B-587 (5-1022)
r.42.19	B-588 (5-1023)
r.42.20	B-589 (5-1024)
Part 43 (Appeal or reference to the Supreme Court)	
r.43.1	B-590 (7-400)
r.43.2	B-591 (7-401)
r.43.3	B-592 (7-402)
r.43.4	B-593 (7-403)
Part 44 (Request to the European Court for a preliminary ruling)	
r.44.1	B-594 (7-464)
r.44.2	B-595 (7-465)
r.44.3	B-596 (7-466)
Part 45 (Costs)	
r.45.1	B-598 (6-109)
r.45.2	B-599 (6-110)
r.45.3	B-600 (6-111)
r.45.4	B-601 (6-112)
r.45.5	B-602 (6-113)
r.45.6	B-603 (6-114)
r.45.7	B-604 (6-115)

CRIMINAL PROCEDURE RULE	PARAGRAPH NUMBERS
r.45.8	B-605 (6-116)
r.45.9	B-606 (6-117)
r.45.10	B-607 (6-118)
r.45.11	B-608 (6-119)
r.45.12	B-609 (6-120)
r.45.13	B-610 (6-121)
r.45.14	B-611 (6-122)
Part 46 (Representatives)	
r.46.1	B-612 (2-187)
r.46.2	B-613 (4-68a)
r.46.3	B-614 (6-286a)
Part 47 (Investigation orders and warrants)	
r.47.1	B-615 (15-364)
r.47.2	B-616 (15-365)
r.47.3	B-617 (15-366)
r.47.4	B-618 (15-367)
r.47.5	B-619 (15-368)
r.47.6	B-620 (15-369)
r.47.7	B-621 (15-370)
r.47.8	B-622 (15-371)
r.47.9	B-623 (15-372)
r.47.10	B-624 (15-373)
r.47.11	B-625 (15-374)
r.47.12	B-626 (15-375)
r.47.13	B-627 (15-376)
r.47.14	B-628 (15-377)
r.47.15	B-629 (15-378)
r.47.16	B-630 (15-379)
r.47.17	B-631 (15-380)
r.47.18	B-632 (15-381)
r.47.19	B-633 (15-382)
r.47.20	B-634 (15-383)
r.47.21	B-635 (15-384)
r.47.22	B-636 (15-385)
r.47.23	*[Not set out in this work]*
r.47.24	B-638 (15-387)
r.47.25	B-639 (15-388)
r.47.26	B-640 (15-389)
r.47.27	B-641 (15-390)
r.47.28	B-642 (15-391)
r.47.29	B-643 (15-392)
r.47.30	B-644 (15-393)
r.47.31	B-645 (15-394)

CRIMINAL PROCEDURE RULE	PARAGRAPH NUMBERS
r.47.32	B-646 (15-395)
r.47.33	B-647
r.47.34	B-648 (15-397)
r.47.35	B-649 (15-398)
r.47.36	B-650 (15-399)
r.47.37	B-651
r.47.38	B-652 (15-401)
r.47.39	B-652a (15-401a, *ante*)
r.47.40	B-653 (15-402)
r.47.41	B-654 (15-403)
r.47.42	B-655 (15-404)
r.47.43	B-656 (15-405)
r.47.44	B-657 (15-406)
r.47.45	B-658 (15-407)
r.47.46	B-659
r.47.47	B-660
r.47.48	B-661
r.47.49	B-662
r.47.50	B-663 (*2-106*)
r.47.51	B-664 (25-401c)
r.47.52	B-665 (25-401d)
r.47.53	B-666 (25-401e)
r.47.54	B-667
r.47.55	B-668
r.47.56	B-669
r.47.57	B-670
r.47.58	B-671
Part 48 (Contempt of court)	
r.48.1	B-673 (28-101)
r.48.2	B-674 (28-102)
r.48.3	B-675 (28-103)
r.48.4	B-676 (28-104)
r.48.5	B-677 (28-105)
r.48.6	B-678 (28-106)
r.48.7	B-679 (28-107)
r.48.8	B-680 (28-108)
r.48.9	B-681 (28-109)
r.48.10	B-682 (28-110)
r.48.11	B-683 (28-111)
r.48.12	B-684 (28-112)
r.48.13	B-685 (28-113)
r.48.14	B-686 (28-114)
r.48.15	B-687 (28-115)

CRIMINAL PROCEDURE RULE	PARAGRAPH NUMBERS
r.48.16	B-688 (28-116)
r.48.17	B-689 (28-117)
Part 49 (International co-operation)	*[Not set out in this work]*
Part 50 (Extradition)	*[Not set out in this work]*

Criminal Practice Directions (2015) (as amended) and Criminal Costs Practice Directions (2015)

(Appendix B and main work paragraph numbers are set out below. Main work paragraphs are shown in brackets. An italicised paragraph number is given where a practice direction is summarised rather than set out in full.)

CRIMINAL PRACTICE DIRECTION	PARAGRAPH NUMBERS
CPD I (General matters) A	B-2
CPD I (General matters) 1A (The overriding objective)	
1A.1, 1A.2	B-3 (4-114a)
CPD I (General matters) 3A (Case management)	
3A.1–3A.3	B-22 (4-120)
3A.4	B-23
3A.5, 3A.6	B-24
3A.7	B-25
3A.8	B-26
3A.9, 3A.10	B-27
3A.11	B-28
3A.12–3A.14	B-29 (12-144a)
3A.15	B-30
3A.16–3A.20	B-31 (4-123)
3A.21, 3A.22	B-32 (4-123a)
3A.23–3A.28	B-33 (4-120a)
Note to the Practice Direction	B-34 (4-123b)
CPD I (General matters) 3B (Pagination and indexing of served evidence)	
3B.1–3B.5	B-35
CPD I (General matters) 3C (Abuse of process stay applications)	
3C.1–3C.5	B-36 (4-101b)
CPD I (General matters) 3D (Vulnerable people in the courts)	
3D.1–3D.8	B-37 (8-131e)
CPD I (General matters) 3E (Ground rules hearings to plan the questioning of a vulnerable witness or defendant)	
3E.1–3E.6	B-38 (8-131f)
CPD I (General matters) 3F (Intermediaries)	
3F.1–3F.3	B-39 (8-131g)

CRIMINAL PRACTICE DIRECTION	PARAGRAPH NUMBERS
3F.4, 3F.5	B-40 (8-131h)
3F.6–3F.10	B-41 (8-131i)
3F.11–3F.18	B-42 (8-131j)
3F.19–3F.23	B-43 (8-131k)
3F.24–3F.26	B-44 (8-131l)
3F.27	B-45 (8-131m)
3F.28	B-46 (8-131n)
3F.29	B-47 (8-131o)
CPD I (General matters) 3G (Vulnerable defendants)	
3G.1–3G.6	B-48 (4-161a)
3G.7–3G.14	B-49 (4-161b)
CPD I (General matters) 3H (Wales and the Welsh language: devolution issues)	*[Not set out in this work]*
CPD I (General matters) 3J (Wales and the Welsh language: applications for evidence to be given in Welsh)	
3J.1	B-51
CPD I (General matters) 3K (Wales and the Welsh language: use of the Welsh language in courts in Wales)	
3K.1	B-52
3K.2–3K.6	B-53
3K.7	B-54
3K.8	B-55
3K.9	B-56
3K.10–3K.13	B-57
3K.14	B-58
3K.15	B-59
3K.16	B-60
CPD I (General matters) (Security of prisoners at court)	
3L.1–3L.4	B-61 (3-232a)
3L.5, 3L.6	B-62 (3-232b)
3L.7–3L.10	B-63 (3-232c)
3L.11	B-64 (3-232d)
CPD I (General matters) 3M (Procedure for application for armed police presence in Crown Court and magistrates' court buildings)	
3M.1–3M.3	B-65
3M.4	B-66
3M.5–3M.7	B-67
3M.8, 3M.9	B-68
3M.10–3M.14	B-68a

CRIMINAL PRACTICE DIRECTION	PARAGRAPH NUMBERS
3M.15–3M.19	B-69
3M.20, 3M.21	B-70
3M.22, 3M.23	B-71
3M.24, 3M.25	B-72
CPD I (General matters) 3N (Use of live link and telephone facilities)	
3N.1–3N.12	B-72a
3N.13–3N.15	B-72b
3N.16	B-72c
3N.17	B-72d
CPD I (General Matters) Annex (Guidance on establishing and using live link and telephone facilities for criminal court hearings)	
Paras 1, 2	B-72e
Paras 3, 4	B-72f
Paras 5, 6	B-72g
Para. 7	B-72h
Paras 8-10	B-72i
Para. 11	B-72j
Paras 12-14	B-72k
CPD I (General matters) 5A (Forms)	
5A.1–5A.4	B-95
CPD I (General matters) 5B (Access to information held by the court)	
5B.1–5B.9	B-96
5B.10, 5B.11	B-97
5B.12, 5B.13	B-98
5B.14–5B.16	B-99
5B.17	B-100
5B.18	B-101
5B.19, 5B.20	B-102
5B.21–5B.24	B-103
5B.25	B-104
5B.26–5B.30	B-105
CPD I (General matters) 5C (Issue of medical certificates)	
5C.1–5C.6	B-106 (4-71a)
CPD I (General matters) 6A (Unofficial sound recording of proceedings)	
6A.1–6A.6	B-111 (28-74a)
CPD I (General matters) 6B (Restrictions on reporting proceedings)	
6B.1–6B.7	B-112 (4-49)

CRIMINAL PRACTICE DIRECTION	PARAGRAPH NUMBERS
CPD I (General matters) 6C (Use of live text-based forms of communication (including Twitter) from court for the purposes of fair and accurate reporting)	
6C.1	B-113
6C.2–6C.5	B-114
6C.6–6C.14	B-115
CPD I (General matters) 6D (Taking notes in court)	
6D.1–6D.3	B-116 (4-5b)
CPD II (Preliminary proceedings) 8A (Defendant's record)	
8A.1–8A.5	B-121 (12-145)
8A.6–8A.8	B-122 (12-146)
CPD II (Preliminary proceedings) 9A (Allocation (mode of trial))	
9A.1–9A.3	B-139 (1-114)
CPD II (Preliminary proceedings) 10A (Preparation and content of the indictment)	
10A.1	B-149
10A.2	B-150
10A.3-10A.5	B-150a
10A.6, 10A.7	B-150b
10A.8, 10A.9	B-150c
10A.9	B-150d
10A.11-10A.14	B-151
10A.15-10A.20	B-151a
CPD II (Preliminary proceedings) 10B (Voluntary bills of indictment)	
10B.1-10B.6	B-152
CPD III (Custody and bail) 14A (Bail before sending for trial)	
14A.1	B-184 (3-206a)
14A.2	B-185 (3-206b)
CPD III (Custody and bail) 14B (Bail: failure to surrender and trials in absence)	
14B.1–14B.4	B-186 (3-39)
CPD III (Custody and bail) 14C (Penalties for failure to surrender)	
14C.1, 14C.2	B-187 (3-40)
14C.3, 14C.4	B-188 (3-41)
14C.5, 14C.6	B-189 (3-42)
14C.7-14C.10	B-190 (Appendix S-9)

CRIMINAL PRACTICE DIRECTION	PARAGRAPH NUMBERS
CPD III (Custody and bail) 14D (Relationship between the Bail Act offence and further remands on bail or in custody)	
14D.1–14D.4	B-191 (3-44)
CPD III (Custody and bail) 14E (Trials in absence)	
14E.1–14E.4	B-192 (3-225a, *3-225b*)
CPD III (Custody and bail) 14F (Forfeiture of monies lodged as security or pledged by a surety / estreatment of recognizances)	
14F.1–14F.5	B-193 (3-53a)
CPD III (Custody and bail) 14G (Bail during trial)	
14G.1–14G.4	B-194 (3-204)
CPD III (Custody and bail) 14H (Crown Court judge's certification of fitness to appeal and applications to the Crown Court for bail pending appeal)	
14H.1–14H.6	B-195 (7-38a)
CPD IV Disclosure 15A (Disclosure of unused material)	
15A.1, 15A.2	B-205
CPD V (Evidence) 16A (Evidence by written statement)	
16.A.1	B-210 (10-19a)
16A.2	B-211 (10-19b)
16A.3–16A.6	B-212 (10-19c)
CPD V (Evidence) 16B (Video recorded evidence in chief)	
16B.1–16B.4	B-213 (8-131p)
CPD V (Evidence) 16C (Evidence of audio and video recorded interviews)	
16C.1–16C.16	B-214 (15-246)
CPD V (Evidence) 17A (Wards of court and children subject to current family proceedings)	
17A.1–17A.8	B-223 (8-60)
CPD V (Evidence) 18A (Measures to assist a witness or defendant to give evidence)	
18A.1, 18A.2	B-250 (8-131q)
CPD V (Evidence) 18B (Witnesses giving evidence by live link)	
18B.1–18B.5	B-251 (8-131r)
CPD V (Evidence) 18C (Visually recorded interviews: memory refreshing and watching a different time from the jury)	
18C.1–18C.4	B-252 (8-131s)

CRIMINAL PRACTICE DIRECTION	PARAGRAPH NUMBERS
CPD V (Evidence) 18D (Witness anonymity orders)	
18D.1, 18D.2	B-253 (8-167)
18D.3	B-254 (8-168)
18D.4	B-255 (8-169)
18D.5	B-256 (8-169a)
18D.6, 18D.7	B-257 (8-169b)
18D.8–18D.16	B-258 (8-169c)
18D.17, 18D.18	B-259 (8-169d)
18D.19–18D.21	B-260 (8-169e)
18D.22	B-261 (8-169f)
CPD V (Evidence) 19A (Expert evidence)	
19.A.1–19A.6	B-271 (10-46c)
CPD V (Evidence) 19B (Statements of understanding and declarations of truth in expert reports)	
19B.1	B-271a
CPD V (Evidence) 19C (Pre-hearing discussion of expert evidence)	
19C.1-19C.8	B-271b
CPD V (Evidence) 21A (Spent convictions)	
21A.1–21A.3	B-283 (13-121)
CPD VI (Trial) 24A (Role of the justices' clerk/legal adviser)	
24A.1–24A.18	B-317
CPD VI (Trial) 24B (Identification for the court of the issues in the case)	
24B.1–24B.4	B-318
CPD VI (Trial) 25A (Identification for the jury of the issues in the case)	
25A.1–25A.6	B-335 (4-342, 4-343a)
CPD VI (Trial) 26A (Juries: introduction)	
26A.1, 26A.2	B-341
CPD VI (Trial) 26B (Juries: preliminary matters arising before jury service commences)	
26B.1–26B.4	B-342
CPD VI (Trial) 26C (Juries: eligibility)	
26C.1–26C.10	B-343 (4-291a)
CPD VI (Trial) 26D (Juries: precautionary measures before swearing)	
26D.1–26D.4	B-344 (4-291e)
CPD VI (Trial) 26E (Juries: swearing in jurors)	
26E.1–26E.3	B-345 (4-306)

CRIMINAL PRACTICE DIRECTION	PARAGRAPH NUMBERS
CPD VI (Trial) 26F (Juries: ensuring an effective jury panel)	
26F.1	B-345
CPD VI (Trial) 26G (Juries: preliminary instructions to jurors)	
26G.1–26G.4	B-346 (4-325)
CPD VI (Trial) 26H (Juries: discharge of a juror for personal reasons)	
26H.1–26H.3	B-347 (4-307a)
CPD VI (Trial) 26J) (Juries: views)	
26J.1	B-348 (4-111a)
CPD VI (Trial) 26K (Juries: directions, written materials and summing up)	
26K.1	B-349
26K.2–26K.7	B-350
26K.8–26K.10	B-351
26K.11–26K.15	B-352 (4-418a)
26K.16–26K.18	B-353 (4-418c)
26K.19–26K.22	B-354 (4-430a)
CPD VI (Trial) 26L (Juries: jury access to exhibits and evidence in retirement)	
26L.1–26L.3	B-355 (4-495a)
CPD VI (Trial) 26M (Juries: jury irregularities)	
26M.1–26M.4	B-356 (4-308)
26M.5–26M.7	B-357 (4-308a)
26M.8, 26M.9	B-358 (4-308b)
26M.10–26M.13	B-359 (4-308c)
26M.14–26M.19	B-360 (4-308d)
26M.20, 26M.21	B-361 (4-308e)
26M.22, 26M.23	B-362 (4-308f)
26M.24–26M.26	B-363 (4-308g)
26M.27–26M.34	B-364 (4-308h)
26M.35–26M.40	B-365 (4-308i)
26M.41, 26M.42	B-366
26M.43–26M.46	B-367
26M.47–26M.51	B-368
26M.52	B-369
26M.53	B-370
26M.54–26M.56	B-371
26M.57, 26M.58	B-372
Contact details	B-373
CPD VI (Trial) 26N (Open justice)	
26N.1	B-374 (4-107)

CRIMINAL PRACTICE DIRECTION	PARAGRAPH NUMBERS
CPD VI (Trial) 26P (Defendant's right to give or not to give evidence)	
26P.1–26P.5	B-375 (4-380)
CPD VI (Trial) 26Q (Majority verdicts)	
26Q.1–26Q.9	B-376 (4-510)
CPD VII (Sentencing) A (Pleas of guilty in the Crown Court)	*(4-175)*
CPD VII (Sentencing) B (Determining the factual basis of sentence)	
B.1–B.5	(5-99)
B.6	(5-100)
B.7–B.10	(5-101)
B.11–B.13	(5-102)
B.14	(5-103)
B.15–B.17	(5-104)
B.18–B.21	(5-105)
B.22–B.27	(5-106)
CPD VII (Sentencing) C (Indications of sentence: R. v. Goodyear)	
C.1–C.8	(5-127)
CPD VII (Sentencing) D (Facts to be stated on pleas of guilty)	
D.1	(5-123)
CPD VII (Sentencing) E (Concurrent and consecutive sentences)	
E.1–E.3	(5-558)
CPD VII (Sentencing) F (Victim personal statements)	
F.1–F.3	(5-117)
CPD VII (Sentencing) G (Families bereaved by homicide and other criminal conduct)	
G.1–G.3	(5-118)
CPD VII (Sentencing) H (Community impact statements)	
H.1–H.6	(5-448)
CPD VII (Sentencing) I (Impact statements for businesses)	
I.1–I.10	(5-121)
CPD VII (Sentencing) J (Binding over orders and conditional discharges)	
J.1	*(5-221)*
J.2, J.3	(5-222)
J.4	(5-223)
J.5–J.7	(5-224)
J.8, J.9	(5-225)

CRIMINAL PRACTICE DIRECTION	PARAGRAPH NUMBERS
J.10–J.12	(5-226)
J.13–J.15	(5-227)
J.16	(5-228)
J.17, J.18	(5-229)
J.19	(5-1305)
J.20	(5-209)
CPD VII (Sentencing) K (Committal for sentence)	
K.1	(5-48)
CPD VII (Sentencing) L (Imposition of life sentences)	
L.1–L.5	(5-515)
CPD VII (Sentencing) M (Mandatory life sentences)	
M.1–M.14	(5-408)
CPD VII (Sentencing) N (Transitional arrangements for sentences where the offence was committed before 18 December 2003)	
N.1–N.10	(5-409 in this supplement)
N.11, N.12	(5-410 in this supplement)
N.13	(5-411 in this supplement)
N.14–N.18	(5-412 in this supplement)
N.19–N.21	(5-413 in this supplement)
CPD VII (Sentencing) P (Procedure for announcing the minimum term in open court)	
P.1–P.3	(5-414)
CPD VII (Sentencing) Q (Financial, etc. information required for sentencing)	
Q.1–Q.6	(5-662)
CPD IX (Appeal) 34A (Appeals to the Crown Court)	
34A.1–34A.3	B-494 (2-128a)
CPD IX (Appeal) 39A (Appeals Against conviction and sentence – the provision of notice to the prosecution)	
39A.1–39A.6	B-546 (7-202)
CPD IX (Appeal) 39B (Listing of appeals against conviction and sentence in the Court of Appeal Criminal Division (CACD))	
39B.1–39B.5	B-547 (7-190)
CPD IX (Appeal) 39C (Appeal notices containing grounds of appeal)	
39C.1–39C.3	B-548 (7-168a)
CPD IX (Appeal) 39D (Respondents' notices)	

CRIMINAL PRACTICE DIRECTION	PARAGRAPH NUMBERS
39D.1	B-549 (*7-204*)
CPD IX (Appeal) 39E (Loss of time)	
39E.1, 39E.2	B-550 (7-226)
CPD IX (Appeal) 39F (Skeleton arguments)	
39F.1–39F.3	B-551 (7-200)
CPD IX (Appeal) 39G (Criminal Appeal Office summaries)	
39G.1–39G.7	B-552 (7-189)
CPD IX (Appeal) 44A (References to the European Court of Justice)	
44A.1–44A.7	B-597 (7-467)
CPD XI (Other Proceedings) 47A (Investigation orders and warrants)	
47A.1–47A.5	B-672 (15-409)
CPD XI (Other Proceedings) 48A (Contempt in the face of the magistrates' court)	
48A.1–48A.3	B-690 (*28-118a*)
CPD XI (Other proceedings) 50A to 50F (Extradition)	*[Not set out in this work]*
CPD XII (General application) A (Court dress)	
A.1, A.2	(2-29)
CPD XII (General application) B (Modes of address and titles of judges and magistrates)	
B.1, B.2	(2-14)
B.3	*[Not set out in this work (cause lists only)]*
CPD XII (General application) C (Availability of judgments given in the Court of Appeal and High Court)	*[Not set out in this work (but see § 7-33)]*
CPD XII (General application) D (Citation of authority and provision of copies of judgments to the court)	
D.1	(7-200a)
D.2–D.7	(7-200b)
D.8–D.10	(7-200c)
D.11–D.13	(7-200d)
D.14–D.16	(7-200e)
CPD XII (General application) E (Preparation of judgments: neutral citation)	*[Not set out in this work]*
CPD XII (General application) F (Citation of Hansard)	
F.1, F.2	(9-38)
CPD XIII (Listing) A (Judicial responsibility for listing and key principles)	
A.1, A.2	(2-22)
A.3, A.4	(2-22a)

CRIMINAL PRACTICE DIRECTION	PARAGRAPH NUMBERS
A.5, A.6	(2-22b)
CPD XIII (Listing) B (Classification)	
B.1	(2-22c)
B.2	(2-22d)
B.3	(2-22e)
CPD XIII (Listing) C (Referral of cases in the Crown Court to the resident judge and to the presiding judges)	
C.1–C.3	(2-22f)
C.4–C.6	(2-22g)
C.7–C.10	(2-22h)
CPD XIII (Listing) D (Authorisation of judges)	
D.1–D.4	(2-22i)
CPD XIII (Listing) E (Allocation of business within the Crown Court)	
E.1–E.13	(2-22j)
CPD XIII (Listing) F (Listing of trials, custody time limits and transfer of cases)	
F.1, F.2	(2-22k)
F.3	(2-22l)
F.4, F.5	(2-22m)
F.6, F.7	(2-22n)
F.8–F.10	(2-22o)
F.11–F.13	(2-22p)
CPD XIII (Listing) G (Listing of hearings other than trials)	
G.1–G.5	(2-22q)
G.6, G.7	(2-22r)
G.8	(2-22s)
G.9, G.10	(2-22t)
G.11	(2-22u)
CPD XIII (Listing) Annex 1 (General principles for the deployment of the kudiciary in the magistrates' court)	
Introduction	B-695
Paragraphs 1–4	B-696
CPD XIII (Listing) Annex 2 (Sexual offences in the youth court)	
Paragraphs 1–5	B-697
Paragraphs 6–10	B-698
Paragraph 11	B-699
CPD XIII (Listing) Annex 3 (Cases involving very large fines in the magistrates' court)	
Paragraphs 1–7	B-700

CRIMINAL PRACTICE DIRECTION	PARAGRAPH NUMBERS
CPD XIII (Listing) Annex 4 (The management of terrorism cases)	
Paragraph 1	B-701
Paragraphs 2, 3	B-702
Paragraphs 4-8	B-703
Paragraphs 9–11	B-704
Paragraphs 12, 13	B-705
Paragraphs 14, 15	B-706
Paragraph 16	B-707
Paragraph 17	B-708
CPD XIII (Listing) Annex 5 (Management of cases from the organised crime division of the Crown Prosecution Service)	
Paragraphs 1, 2	B-709
Paragraph 3	B-710
Paragraphs 4–6	B-711
Paragraph 7	B-712
Paragraph 8	B-713
Paragraph 9–11	B-714
Criminal Costs Practice Direction (2015)	(6-124 *et seq.*)

Criminal Procedure Rules 2015 (S.I. 2015 No. 1490), Pt 1

THE OVERRIDING OBJECTIVE

The overriding objective

B-1   **1.1.**–(1) The overriding objective of this procedural code is that criminal cases be dealt with justly.

(2) Dealing with a criminal case justly includes–

  (a) acquitting the innocent and convicting the guilty;

  (b) dealing with the prosecution and the defence fairly;

  (c) recognising the rights of a defendant, particularly those under Article 6 of the European Convention on Human Rights;

  (d) respecting the interests of witnesses, victims and jurors and keeping them informed of the progress of the case;

  (e) dealing with the case efficiently and expeditiously;

  (f) ensuring that appropriate information is available to the court when bail and sentence are considered; and

  (g) dealing with the case in ways that take into account–

    (i) the gravity of the offence alleged,

    (ii) the complexity of what is in issue,

    (iii) the severity of the consequences for the defendant and others affected, and

    (iv) the needs of other cases.

The duty of the participants in a criminal case

1.2.–(1) Each participant, in the conduct of each case, must–

  (a) prepare and conduct the case in accordance with the overriding objective;

  (b) comply with these Rules, practice directions and directions made by the court; and

  (c) at once inform the court and all parties of any significant failure (whether or not that participant is responsible for that failure) to take any procedural step required by these Rules, any practice direction or any direction of the court. A failure is significant if it might hinder the court in furthering the overriding objective.

(2) Anyone involved in any way with a criminal case is a participant in its conduct for the purposes of this rule.

The application by the court of the overriding objective

1.3. The court must further the overriding objective in particular when—

    (a) exercising any power given to it by legislation (including these rules);

    (b) applying any practice direction; or

    (c) interpreting any rule or practice direction.

CPD I General Matters A

A.1 The Lord Chief Justice has power, including power under section 74 of the Courts Act 2003 **B-2** and Part 1 of Schedule 2 to the Constitutional Reform Act 2005, to give directions as to the practice and procedure of the criminal courts. The following directions are given accordingly.

A.2 These practice directions replace the *Criminal Practice Directions* given on 7th October, 2013 [2013] EWCA Crim. 1631; [2013] 1 W.L.R. 3164 as amended by the directions given on (i) 10th December, 2013 [2013] EWCA Crim. 2328; [2014] 1 W.L.R. 35, (ii) 23rd July, 2014 [2014] EWCA Crim. 1569; [2014] 1 W.L.R. 3001, (iii) 18th March, 2015 [2015] EWCA Crim. 430; [2015] 1 W.L.R. 1643 and (iv) 16th July, 2015 [2015] EWCA Crim. 1253; [2015] 1 W.L.R. 3582.

A.3 Annexes D and E to the *Consolidated Criminal Practice Direction* of 8th July, 2002, [2002] 1 W.L.R. 2870; [2002] 2 Cr.App.R. 35, as amended, which set out forms for use in connection with the Criminal Procedure Rules, remain in force. See also para. I 5A of these practice directions.

A.4 These practice directions supplement many, but not all, parts of the Criminal Procedure Rules, and include other directions about practice and procedure in the courts to which they apply. They are to be known as the *Criminal Practice Directions* 2015. They come into force on 5th October, 2015. They apply to all cases in all the criminal courts of England and Wales from that date.

A.5 Consequent on the rearrangement of the Criminal Procedure Rules in the Criminal Procedure Rules 2015, S.I. 2015/1490:

    (a) the content of these practice directions is arranged to correspond; within each division of these directions the paragraphs are numbered to correspond with the associated part of the *Criminal Procedure Rules* 2015; compared with the criminal practice directions given in 2013, as amended, the numbering and content of some divisions is amended consequentially, as shown in this table:

Derivations	
Divisions of 2015 Directions	*Divisions of 2013 Directions*
I General matters	I General matters; II Preliminary proceedings 16A - C
II Preliminary proceedings	II Preliminary proceedings 9A, 10A, 14A - B
III Custody and bail	III Custody and bail
IV Disclosure	IV Disclosure
V Evidence	V Evidence
VI Trial	VI Trial
VII Sentencing	VII Sentencing
VIII Confiscation and related proceedings [empty]	VIII Confiscation and related proceedings [empty]
IX Appeal	X Appeal
X Costs [Criminal Costs Practice Direction]	XI Costs [Criminal Costs Practice Direction]
XI Other proceedings	II Preliminary proceedings 6A, 17A - F; IX Contempt of court
XII General application	XII General application
XIII Listing	XIII Listing

    (b) the text of these practice directions is amended:

        (i) to bring up to date the cross-references to the Criminal Procedure Rules and to other paragraphs of these directions which that text contains, and

        (ii) to adopt the abbreviation of references to the Criminal Procedure Rules ("CrimPR") for which rule 2.3(2) of the Criminal Procedure Rules 2015 provides.

A.6 In all other respects, the content of the *Criminal Practice Directions* 2015 reproduces that of the *Criminal Practice Directions* 2013, as amended.

CPD I General Matters 1A: The Overriding Objective

B-3

1A.1 The presumption of innocence and an adversarial process are essential features of English and Welsh legal tradition and of the defendant's right to a fair trial. But it is no part of a fair trial that questions of guilt and innocence should be determined by procedural manoeuvres. On the contrary, fairness is best served when the issues between the parties are identified as early and as clearly as possible. As Lord Justice Auld noted, a criminal trial is not a game under which a guilty defendant should be provided with a sporting chance. It is a search for truth in accordance with the twin principles that the prosecution must prove its case and that a defendant is not obliged to inculpate himself, the object being to convict the guilty and acquit the innocent.

1A.2 Further, it is not just for a party to obstruct or delay the preparation of a case for trial in order to secure some perceived procedural advantage, or to take unfair advantage of a mistake by someone else. If courts allow that to happen it damages public confidence in criminal justice. The rules and the practice directions, taken together, make it clear that courts must not allow it to happen.

Criminal Procedure Rules 2015 (S.I. 2015 No. 1490), Pt 2

Understanding and Applying the Rules

When the Rules apply

B-4

2.1.–(1) In general, Criminal Procedure Rules apply—

(a) in all criminal cases in magistrates' courts and in the Crown Court;

(b) in extradition cases in the High Court; and

(c) in all cases in the criminal division of the Court of Appeal.

(2) If a rule applies only in one or some of those courts, the rule makes that clear.

(3) These rules apply on and after 5th October, 2015, but—

(a) unless the court otherwise directs, they do not affect a right or duty existing under the Criminal Procedure Rules 2014; and

(b) unless the High Court otherwise directs, Section 3 of Part 50 (extradition – appeal to the High Court) does not apply to a case in which notice of an appeal was given before 6th October, 2014.

(4) In a case in which a request for extradition was received by a relevant authority in the United Kingdom on or before 31st December, 2003—

(a) the rules in Part 50 (extradition) do not apply; and

(b) the rules in Part 17 of the Criminal Procedure Rules 2012 continue to apply as if those rules had not been revoked.

Definitions

B-5

2.2.–(1) In these rules, unless the context makes it clear that something different is meant:

"advocate" means a person who is entitled to exercise a right of audience in the court under section 13 of the Legal Services Act 2007;

"business day" means any day except Saturday, Sunday, Christmas Day, Boxing Day, Good Friday, Easter Monday or a bank holiday;

"court" means a tribunal with jurisdiction over criminal cases. It includes a judge, recorder, District Judge (Magistrates' Court), lay justice and, when exercising their judicial powers, the Registrar of Criminal Appeals, a justices' clerk or assistant clerk;

"court officer" means the appropriate member of the staff of a court;

"justices' legal adviser" means a justices' clerk or an assistant to a justices' clerk;

"legal representative" means:

(i) the person for the time being named as a party's representative in any legal aid representation order made under section 16 of the Legal Aid, Sentencing and Punishment Offenders Act 2012 [§ 6-212 in the main work], or

(ii) subject to that, the person named as a party's representative in any notice for the time being given under rule 46.2 (notice of appointment or change of legal representative), provided that person is entitled to conduct litigation in the court under section 13 of the Legal Services Act 2007;

"live link" means an arrangement by which a person can see and hear, and be seen and heard by, the court when that person is not in the courtroom;

410

"Practice Direction" means the Lord Chief Justice's Criminal Practice Directions, as amended, and "Criminal Costs Practice Direction" means the Lord Chief Justice's Practice Direction (Costs in Criminal Proceedings), as amended;

"public interest ruling" means a ruling about whether it is in the public interest to disclose prosecution material under sections 3(6), 7A(8) or 8(5) of the Criminal Procedure and Investigations Act 1996 [*ibid.*, §§ 12-58, 12-74, 12-76]; and

"Registrar" means the Registrar of Criminal Appeals or a court officer acting with the Registrar's authority.

(2) Definitions of some other expressions are in the rules in which they apply.

[This rule is printed as amended by the Criminal Procedure (Amendment) Rules 2016 (S.I. 2016 No. 120).]

References to legislation, including these rules

2.3.–(1) In these rules, where a rule refers to an Act of Parliament or to subordinate legislation by **B-6** title and year, subsequent references to that Act or to that legislation in the rule are shortened: so, for example, after a reference to the Criminal Procedure and Investigations Act 1996 that Act is called "the 1996 Act"; and after a reference to the Criminal Procedure and Investigations Act 1996 (Defence Disclosure Time Limits) Regulations 2011 those Regulations are called "the 2011 Regulations".

(2) In the courts to which these rules apply–

(a) unless the context makes it clear that something different is meant, a reference to the Criminal Procedure Rules, without reference to a year, is a reference to the Criminal Procedure Rules in force at the date on which the event concerned occurs or occurred;

(b) a reference to the Criminal Procedure Rules may be abbreviated to "CrimPR"; and

(c) a reference to a Part or rule in the Criminal Procedure Rules may be abbreviated to, for example, "CrimPR Part 3" or "CrimPR 3.5".

Criminal Procedure Rules 2015 (S.I. 2015 No. 1490), Pt 3

CASE MANAGEMENT

General rules

When this Part applies

3.1.–(1) Rules 3.1 to 3.12 apply to the management of each case in a magistrates' court and in the **B-7** Crown Court (including an appeal to the Crown Court) until the conclusion of that case.

(2) Rules 3.13 to 3.26 apply where–

(a) the defendant is sent to the Crown Court for trial;

(b) a High Court or Crown Court judge gives permission to serve a draft indictment; or

(c) the Court of Appeal orders a retrial.

The duty of the court

3.2.–(1) The court must further the overriding objective by actively managing the case.

(2) Active case management includes–

(a) the early identification of the real issues;

(b) the early identification of the needs of witnesses;

(c) achieving certainty as to what must be done, by whom, and when, in particular by the early setting of a timetable for the progress of the case;

(d) monitoring the progress of the case and compliance with directions;

(e) ensuring that evidence, whether disputed or not, is presented in the shortest and clearest way;

(f) discouraging delay, dealing with as many aspects of the case as possible on the same occasion, and avoiding unnecessary hearings;

(g) encouraging the participants to co-operate in the progression of the case; and

(h) making use of technology.

(3) The court must actively manage the case by giving any direction appropriate to the needs of that case as early as possible.

(4) Where appropriate live links are available, making use of technology for the purposes of this rule includes directing the use of such facilities, whether an application for such a direction is made or not–

(a) for the conduct of a pre-trial hearing, including a pre-trial case management hearing;

(b) for the defendant's attendance at such a hearing–

(i) where the defendant is in custody, or where the defendant is not in custody and wants to attend by live link, but

    (ii)   only if the court is satisfied that the defendant can participate effectively by such means, having regard to all the circumstances including whether the defendant is represented or not; and

  (c) for receiving evidence under one of the powers to which the rules in Part 18 apply (measures to assist a witness or defendant to give evidence).

(5) Where appropriate telephone facilities are available, making use of technology for the purposes of this rule includes directing the use of such facilities, whether an application for such a direction is made or not, for the conduct of a pre-trial case management hearing—

  (a) if telephone facilities are more convenient for that purpose than live links;

  (b) unless at that hearing the court expects to take the defendant's plea; and

  (c) only if—

    (i)   the defendant is represented, or

    (ii) exceptionally, the court is satisfied that the defendant can participate effectively by such means without a representative.

[This rule is printed as amended by the Criminal Procedure (Amendment No. 2) Rules 2016 (S.I. 2016 No. 705).]

The duty of the parties

3.3.–(1) Each party must—

  (a) actively assist the court in fulfilling its duty under rule 3.2, without or if necessary with a direction; and

  (b) apply for a direction if needed to further the overriding objective.

(2) Active assistance for the purposes of this rule includes—

  (a) at the beginning of the case, communication between the prosecutor and the defendant at the first available opportunity and in any event no later than the beginning of the day of the first hearing;

  (b) after that, communication between the parties and with the court officer until the conclusion of the case;

  (c) by such communication establishing, among other things—

    (i)   whether the defendant is likely to plead guilty or not guilty,

    (ii) what is agreed and what is likely to be disputed,

    (iii) what information, or other material, is required by one party of another, and why, and

    (iv) what is to be done, by whom, and when (without or if necessary with a direction);

  (d) reporting on that communication to the court—

    (i)   at the first hearing, and

    (ii) after that, as directed by the court; and

  (e) alerting the court to any reason why—

    (i)   a direction should not be made in any of the circumstances listed in rule 3.2(4) or (5) (the duty of the court: use of live link or telephone facilities), or

    (ii) such a direction should be varied or revoked.

[This rule is printed as amended by S.I. 2016 No. 705 (*ante*).]

Case progression officers and their duties

3.4.–(1) At the beginning of the case each party must, unless the court otherwise directs—

  (a) nominate someone responsible for progressing that case; and

  (b) tell other parties and the court who that is and how to contact that person.

(2) In fulfilling its duty under rule 3.2, the court must where appropriate—

  (a) nominate a court officer responsible for progressing the case; and

  (b) make sure the parties know who that is and how to contact that court officer.

(3) In this Part a person nominated under this rule is called a case progression officer.

(4) A case progression officer must—

  (a) monitor compliance with directions;

  (b) make sure that the court is kept informed of events that may affect the progress of that case;

  (c) make sure that he or she can be contacted promptly about the case during ordinary business hours;

  (d) act promptly and reasonably in response to communications about the case; and

(e)   if he or she will be unavailable, appoint a substitute to fulfil his or her duties and inform the other case progression officers.

The court's case management powers

3.5.–(1) In fulfilling its duty under rule 3.2 the court may give any direction and take any step **B-8** actively to manage a case unless that direction or step would be inconsistent with legislation, including these rules.

(2) In particular, the court may—

(a)   nominate a judge, magistrate or justices' legal adviser to manage the case;

(b)   give a direction on its own initiative or on application by a party;

(c)   ask or allow a party to propose a direction;

(d)   receive applications, notices, representations and information by letter, by telephone, by live link, by email or by any other means of electronic communication, and conduct a hearing by live link, telephone or other such electronic means;

(e)   give a direction—

(i)   at a hearing, in public or in private, or

(ii)   without a hearing;

(f)   fix, postpone, bring forward, extend, cancel or adjourn a hearing;

(g)   shorten or extend (even after it has expired) a time limit fixed by a direction;

(h)   require that issues in the case should be—

(i)   identified in writing,

(ii)   determined separately, and decide in what order they will be determined; and

(i)   specify the consequences of failing to comply with a direction.

(3) A magistrates' court may give a direction that will apply in the Crown Court if the case is to continue there.

(4) The Crown Court may give a direction that will apply in a magistrates' court if the case is to continue there.

(5) Any power to give a direction under this Part includes a power to vary or revoke that direction.

(6) If a party fails to comply with a rule or a direction, the court may—

(a)   fix, postpone, bring forward, extend, cancel or adjourn a hearing;

(b)   exercise its powers to make a costs order; and

(c)   impose such other sanction as may be appropriate.

[This rule is printed as amended by the Criminal Procedure (Amendment No. 2) Rules 2016 (S.I. 2016 No. 705).]

Application to vary a direction

3.6.–(1) A party may apply to vary a direction if—

(a)   the court gave it without a hearing;

(b)   the court gave it at a hearing in that party's absence; or

(c)   circumstances have changed.

(2) A party who applies to vary a direction must—

(a)   apply as soon as practicable after becoming aware of the grounds for doing so; and

(b)   give as much notice to the other parties as the nature and urgency of the application permits.

Agreement to vary a time limit fixed by a direction

3.7.–(1) The parties may agree to vary a time limit fixed by a direction, but only if—

(a)   the variation will not—

(i)   affect the date of any hearing that has been fixed, or

(ii)   significantly affect the progress of the case in any other way;

(b)   the court has not prohibited variation by agreement; and

(c)   the court's case progression officer is promptly informed.

(2) The court's case progression officer must refer the agreement to the court if in doubt that the condition in paragraph (1)(a) is satisfied.

Court's power to vary requirements under this Part

3.8.–(1) The court may—

(a)   shorten or extend (even after it has expired) a time limit set by this Part; and

    (b) allow an application or representations to be made orally.

   (2) A person who wants an extension of time must–

    (a) apply when serving the application or representations for which it is needed; and

    (b) explain the delay.

Case preparation and progression

B-9
    3.9.–(1) At every hearing, if a case cannot be concluded there and then the court must give directions so that it can be concluded at the next hearing or as soon as possible after that.

   (2) At every hearing the court must, where relevant–

    (a) if the defendant is absent, decide whether to proceed nonetheless;

    (b) take the defendant's plea (unless already done) or if no plea can be taken then find out whether the defendant is likely to plead guilty or not guilty;

    (c) set, follow or revise a timetable for the progress of the case, which may include a timetable for any hearing including the trial or (in the Crown Court) the appeal;

    (d) in giving directions, ensure continuity in relation to the court and to the parties' representatives where that is appropriate and practicable; and

    (e) where a direction has not been complied with, find out why, identify who was responsible, and take appropriate action.

   (3) In order to prepare for the trial, the court must take every reasonable step–

    (a) to encourage and to facilitate the attendance of witnesses when they are needed; and

    (b) to facilitate the participation of any person, including the defendant.

   (4) Facilitating the participation of the defendant includes finding out whether the defendant needs interpretation because–

    (a) the defendant does not speak or understand English; or

    (b) the defendant has a hearing or speech impediment.

   (5) Where the defendant needs interpretation–

    (a) the court officer must arrange for interpretation to be provided at every hearing which the defendant is due to attend;

    (b) interpretation may be by an intermediary where the defendant has a speech impediment, without the need for a defendant's evidence direction;

    (c) on application or on its own initiative, the court may require a written translation to be provided for the defendant of any document or part of a document, unless–

     (i) translation of that document, or part, is not needed to explain the case against the defendant, or

     (ii) the defendant agrees to do without and the court is satisfied that the agreement is clear and voluntary and that the defendant has had legal advice or otherwise understands the consequences;

    (d) on application by the defendant, the court must give any direction which the court thinks appropriate, including a direction for interpretation by a different interpreter, where–

     (i) no interpretation is provided,

     (ii) no translation is ordered or provided in response to a previous application by the defendant, or

     (iii) the defendant complains about the quality of interpretation or of any translation.

   (6) Facilitating the participation of any person includes giving directions for the appropriate treatment and questioning of a witness or the defendant, especially where the court directs that such questioning is to be conducted through an intermediary.

   (7) Where directions for appropriate treatment and questioning are required, the court must–

    (a) invite representations by the parties and by any intermediary; and

    (b) set ground rules for the conduct of the questioning, which rules may include–

     (i) a direction relieving a party of any duty to put that party's case to a witness or a defendant in its entirety,

     (ii) directions about the manner of questioning,

     (iii) directions about the duration of questioning,

     (iv) if necessary, directions about the questions that may or may not be asked,

     (v) where there is more than one defendant, the allocation among them of the topics about which a witness may be asked, and

     (vi) directions about the use of models, plans, body maps or similar aids to help communicate a question or an answer.

Readiness for trial or appeal

3.10.–(1) This rule applies to a party's preparation for trial or appeal, and in this rule and rule 3.11 "trial" includes any hearing at which evidence will be introduced.

(2) In fulfilling the duty under rule 3.3, each party must—

(a) comply with directions given by the court;

(b) take every reasonable step to make sure that party's witnesses will attend when they are needed;

(c) make appropriate arrangements to present any written or other material; and

(d) promptly inform the court and the other parties of anything that may—

  (i) affect the date or duration of the trial or appeal, or

  (ii) significantly affect the progress of the case in any other way.

(3) The court may require a party to give a certificate of readiness.

Conduct of a trial or an appeal

3.11. In order to manage a trial or an appeal, the court— **B-10**

(a) must establish, with the active assistance of the parties, what are the disputed issues;

(b) must consider setting a timetable that—

  (i) takes account of those issues and of any timetable proposed by a party, and

  (ii) may limit the duration of any stage of the hearing;

(c) may require a party to identify—

  (i) which witnesses that party wants to give evidence in person,

  (ii) the order in which that party wants those witnesses to give their evidence,

  (iii) whether that party requires an order compelling the attendance of a witness,

  (iv) what arrangements are desirable to facilitate the giving of evidence by a witness,

  (v) what arrangements are desirable to facilitate the participation of any other person, including the defendant,

  (vi) what written evidence that party intends to introduce,

  (vii) what other material, if any, that person intends to make available to the court in the presentation of the case, and

  (viii) whether that party intends to raise any point of law that could affect the conduct of the trial or appeal; and

(d) may limit—

  (i) the examination, cross-examination or re-examination of a witness, and

  (ii) the duration of any stage of the hearing.

Duty of court officer

3.12. The court officer must— **B-11**

(a) where a person is entitled or required to attend a hearing, give as much notice as reasonably practicable to—

  (i) that person, and

  (ii) that person's custodian (if any);

(b) where the court gives directions, promptly make a record available to the parties.

Preparation for trial in the Crown Court

Pre-trial hearings: general rules

3.13.–(1) The Crown Court— **B-12**

(a) may, and in some cases must, conduct a preparatory hearing where rule 3.14 applies;

(b) must conduct a plea and trial preparation hearing;

(c) may conduct a further pre-trial case management hearing (and if necessary more than one such hearing) only where—

  (i) the court anticipates a guilty plea,

  (ii) it is necessary to conduct such a hearing in order to give directions for an effective trial, or

  (iii) such a hearing is required to set ground rules for the conduct of the questioning of a witness or defendant.

(2) A pre-trial case management hearing—

(a) must be in public, as a general rule, but all or part of the hearing may be in private if the court so directs; and

(b) must be recorded, in accordance with rule 5.5 (recording and transcription of proceedings in the Crown Court).

(3) Where the court determines a pre-trial application in private, it must announce its decision in public.

Preparatory hearing

B-13   **3.14.**–(1) This rule applies where the Crown Court—

(a) can order a preparatory hearing, under—

(i)   section 7 of the Criminal Justice Act 1987 (cases of serious or complex fraud [§ 4-125 in the main work]), or

(ii) section 29 of the Criminal Procedure and Investigations Act 1996 (other complex, serious or lengthy cases [*ibid.*, § 4-131]);

(b) must order such a hearing, to determine an application for a trial without a jury, under—

(i)   section 44 of the Criminal Justice Act 2003 (danger of jury tampering [*ibid.*, § 4-330]), or

(ii) section 17 of the Domestic Violence, Crime and Victims Act 2004 (trial of sample counts by jury, and others by judge alone [*ibid.*, § 4-338]);

(c) must order such a hearing, under section 29 of the 1996 Act, where section 29(1B) or (1C) applies (cases in which a terrorism offence is charged, or other serious cases with a terrorist connection).

(2) The court may decide whether to order a preparatory hearing—

(a) on an application or on its own initiative;

(b) at a hearing (in public or in private), or without a hearing;

(c) in a party's absence, if that party—

(i)   applied for the order, or

(ii) has had at least 14 days in which to make representations.

Application for preparatory hearing

3.15–(1) A party who wants the court to order a preparatory hearing must—

(a) apply in writing—

(i)   as soon as reasonably practicable, and in any event

(ii) not more than 14 days after the defendant pleads not guilty;

(b) serve the application on—

(i)   the court officer, and

(ii) each other party.

(2) The applicant must—

(a) if relevant, explain what legislation requires the court to order a preparatory hearing;

(b) otherwise, explain—

(i)   what makes the case complex or serious, or makes the trial likely to be long,

(ii) why a substantial benefit will accrue from a preparatory hearing, and

(iii) why the court's ordinary powers of case management are not adequate.

(3) A prosecutor who wants the court to order a trial without a jury must explain—

(a) where the prosecutor alleges a danger of jury tampering—

(i)   what evidence there is of a real and present danger that jury tampering would take place,

(ii) what steps, if any, reasonably might be taken to prevent jury tampering, and

(iii) why, notwithstanding such steps, the likelihood of jury tampering is so substantial as to make it necessary in the interests of justice to order such a trial;

(b) where the prosecutor proposes trial without a jury on some counts on the indictment—

(i)   why a trial by jury involving all the counts would be impracticable,

(ii) how the counts proposed for jury trial can be regarded as samples of the others, and

(iii) why it would be in the interests of justice to order such a trial.

Application for non-jury trial containing information withheld from a defendant

B-14   **3.16**–(1) This rule applies where—

(a) the prosecutor applies for an order for a trial without a jury because of a danger of jury tampering; and

(b) the application includes information that the prosecutor thinks ought not be revealed to a defendant.

(2) The prosecutor must—

   (a) omit that information from the part of the application that is served on that defendant;

   (b) mark the other part to show that, unless the court otherwise directs, it is only for the court; and

   (c) in that other part, explain why the prosecutor has withheld that information from that defendant.

(3) The hearing of an application to which this rule applies—

   (a) must be in private, unless the court otherwise directs; and

   (b) if the court so directs, may be, wholly or in part, in the absence of a defendant from whom information has been withheld.

(4) At the hearing of an application to which this rule applies—

   (a) the general rule is that the court must consider, in the following sequence—

      (i) representations first by the prosecutor and then by each defendant, in all the parties' presence, and then

      (ii) further representations by the prosecutor, in the absence of a defendant from whom information has been withheld; but

   (b) the court may direct other arrangements for the hearing.

(5) Where, on an application to which this rule applies, the court orders a trial without a jury—

   (a) the general rule is that the trial must be before a judge other than the judge who made the order; but

   (b) the court may direct other arrangements.

Representations in response to application for preparatory hearing

3.17.—(1) This rule applies where a party wants to make representations about—

   (a) an application for a preparatory hearing;

   (b) an application for a trial without a jury.

(2) Such a party must—

   (a) serve the representations on—

      (i) the court officer, and

      (ii) each other party;

   (b) do so not more than 14 days after service of the application;

   (c) ask for a hearing, if that party wants one, and explain why it is needed.

(3) Where representations include information that the person making them thinks ought not be revealed to another party, that person must—

   (a) omit that information from the representations served on that other party;

   (b) mark the information to show that, unless the court otherwise directs, it is only for the court; and

   (c) with that information include an explanation of why it has been withheld from that other party.

(4) Representations against an application for an order must explain why the conditions for making it are not met.

Commencement of preparatory hearing

3.18. At the beginning of a preparatory hearing, the court must—

   (a) announce that it is such a hearing; and

   (b) take the defendant's plea under rule 3.24 (arraigning the defendant on the indictment), unless already done.

Defence trial advocate

3.19.—(1) The defendant must notify the court officer of the identity of the intended defence trial **B-15** advocate—

   (a) as soon as practicable, and in any event no later than the day of the plea and trial preparation hearing;

   (b) in writing, or orally at that hearing.

(2) The defendant must notify the court officer in writing of any change in the identity of the intended defence trial advocate as soon as practicable, and in any event not more than 5 business days after that change.

Application to stay case for abuse of process

3.20.—(1) This rule applies where a defendant wants the Crown Court to stay the case on the **B-16** grounds that the proceedings are an abuse of the court, or otherwise unfair.

(2) Such a defendant must—
    (a) apply in writing—
        (i) as soon as practicable after becoming aware of the grounds for doing so,
        (ii) at a pre-trial hearing, unless the grounds for the application do not arise until trial, and
        (iii) in any event, before the defendant pleads guilty or the jury (if there is one) retires to consider its verdict at trial;
    (b) serve the application on—
        (i) the court officer, and
        (ii) each other party; and
    (c) in the application—
        (i) explain the grounds on which it is made,
        (ii) include, attach or identify all supporting material,
        (iii) specify relevant events, dates and propositions of law, and
        (iv) identify any witness the applicant wants to call to give evidence in person.
(3) A party who wants to make representations in response to the application must serve the representations on—
    (a) the court officer; and
    (b) each other party,
not more than 14 days after service of the application.

Application for joint or separate trials, etc.

B-17   **3.21.**–(1) This rule applies where a party wants the Crown Court to order—
    (a) the joint trial of—
        (i) offences charged by separate indictments, or
        (ii) defendants charged in separate indictments;
    (b) separate trials of offences charged by the same indictment;
    (c) separate trials of defendants charged in the same indictment; or
    (d) the deletion of a count from an indictment.
(2) Such a party must—
    (a) apply in writing—
        (i) as soon as practicable after becoming aware of the grounds for doing so, and
        (ii) before the trial begins, unless the grounds for the application do not arise until trial;
    (b) serve the application on—
        (i) the court officer, and
        (ii) each other party; and
    (c) in the application—
        (i) specify the order proposed, and
        (ii) explain why it should be made.
(3) A party who wants to make representations in response to the application must serve the representations on—
    (a) the court officer; and
    (b) each other party,
not more than 14 days after service of the application.
(4) Where the same indictment charges more than one offence, the court—
    (a) must exercise its power to order separate trials of those offences unless the offences to be tried together—
        (i) are founded on the same facts, or
        (ii) form or are part of a series of offences of the same or a similar character;
    (b) may exercise its power to order separate trials of those offences if of the opinion that—
        (i) the defendant otherwise may be prejudiced or embarrassed in his or her defence, or
        (ii) for any other reason it is desirable that the defendant should be tried separately for any one or more of those offences.

[This rule is printed as amended by the Criminal Procedure (Amendment No. 2) Rules 2016 (S.I. 2016 No. 705).]

Order for joint or separate trials, or amendment of the indictment
    3.22.–(1) This rule applies where the Crown Court makes an order—
    (a) on an application under rule 3.21 applies [*sic.*] (application for joint or separate trials, etc.); or

(b) amending an indictment in any other respect.

(2) Unless the court otherwise directs, the court officer must endorse any paper copy of each affected indictment made for the court with—

(a) a note of the court's order; and

(b) the date of that order.

Application for indication of sentence

3.23.—(1) This rule applies where a defendant wants the Crown Court to give an indication of the maximum sentence that would be passed if a guilty plea were entered when the indication is sought. **B-18**

(2) Such a defendant must—

(a) apply in writing as soon as practicable; and

(b) serve the application on—

(i) the court officer, and

(ii) the prosecutor.

(3) The application must—

(a) specify—

(i) the offence or offences to which it would be a guilty plea, and

(ii) the facts on the basis of which that plea would be entered; and

(b) include the prosecutor's agreement to, or representations on, that proposed basis of plea.

(4) The prosecutor must—

(a) provide information relevant to sentence, including—

(i) any previous conviction of the defendant, and the circumstances where relevant,

(ii) any statement of the effect of the offence on the victim, the victim's family or others; and

(b) identify any other matter relevant to sentence, including—

(i) the legislation applicable,

(ii) any sentencing guidelines, or guideline cases, and

(iii) aggravating and mitigating factors.

(5) The hearing of the application—

(a) may take place in the absence of any other defendant;

(b) must be attended by—

(i) the applicant defendant's legal representatives (if any), and

(ii) the prosecution advocate.

Arraigning the defendant on the indictment

3.24.—(1) In order to take the defendant's plea, the Crown Court must— **B-19**

(a) obtain the prosecutor's confirmation, in writing or orally—

(i) that the indictment (or draft indictment, as the case may be) sets out a statement of each offence that the prosecutor wants the court to try and such particulars of the conduct constituting the commission of each such offence as the prosecutor relies upon to make clear what is alleged, and

(ii) of the order in which the prosecutor wants the defendants' names to be listed in the indictment, if the prosecutor proposes that more than one defendant should be tried at the same time;

(b) ensure that the defendant is correctly identified by the indictment or draft indictment;

(c) in respect of each count—

(i) read the count aloud to the defendant, or arrange for it to be read aloud or placed before the defendant in writing,

(ii) ask whether the defendant pleads guilty or not guilty to the offence charged by that count, and

(iii) take the defendant's plea.

(2) Where a count is read which is substantially the same as one already read aloud, then only the materially different details need be read aloud.

(3) Where a count is placed before the defendant in writing, the court must summarise its gist aloud.

(4) In respect of each count in the indictment—

(a) if the defendant declines to enter a plea, the court must treat that as a not guilty plea unless rule 25.11 applies (defendant unfit to plead);

(b) if the defendant pleads not guilty to the offence charged by that count but guilty to another offence of which the court could convict on that count—

(i)   if the prosecutor and the court accept that plea, the court must treat the plea as one of guilty of that other offence, but

(ii)   otherwise, the court must treat the plea as one of not guilty;

(c)   if the defendant pleads a previous acquittal or conviction of the offence charged by that count—

(i)   the defendant must identify that acquittal or conviction in writing, explaining the basis of that plea, and

(ii)   the court must exercise its power to decide whether that plea disposes of that count.

(5) In a case in which a magistrates' court sends the defendant for trial, the Crown Court must take the defendant's plea—

(a)   not less than 2 weeks after the date on which that sending takes place, unless the parties otherwise agree; and

(b)   not more than 16 weeks after that date, unless the court otherwise directs (either before or after that period expires).

[This rule is printed as amended by the Criminal Procedure (Amendment) Rules 2016 (S.I. 2016 No. 120); and the Criminal Procedure (Amendment No. 2) Rules 2016 (S.I. 2016 No. 705).]

Place of trial

B-20   **3.25.**–(1) Unless the court otherwise directs, the court officer must arrange for the trial to take place in a courtroom provided by the Lord Chancellor.

(2) The court officer must arrange for the court and the jury (if there is one) to view any place required by the court.

Use of Welsh language at trial

B-21   **3.26.** Where the trial will take place in Wales and a participant wishes to use the Welsh language—

(a)   that participant must serve notice on the court officer, or arrange for such a notice to be served on that participant's behalf—

(i)   at or before the plea and trial preparation hearing, or

(ii)   in accordance with any direction given by the court; and

(b)   if such a notice is served, the court officer must arrange for an interpreter to attend.

CPD I General Matters 3A: Case Management

B-22   **3A.1** CrimPR 1.1(2)(e) requires that cases be dealt with efficiently and expeditiously. CrimPR 3.2 requires the court to further the overriding objective by actively managing the case, for example:

a)   when dealing with an offence which is triable only on indictment the court must ask the defendant whether he or she intends to plead guilty at the Crown Court (CrimPR 9.7(5));

b)   on a guilty plea, the court must pass sentence at the earliest opportunity, in accordance with CrimPR 24.11(9)(a) (magistrates' courts) and 25.16(7)(a) (the Crown Court).

3A.2 Given these duties, magistrates' courts and the Crown Court therefore will proceed as described in paragraphs 3A.3 to 3A.28 below. The parties will be expected to have prepared in accordance with CrimPR 3.3(1) to avoid unnecessary and wasted hearings. They will be expected to have communicated with each other by the time of the first hearing; to report to the court on that communication at the first hearing; and to continue thereafter to communicate with each other and with the court officer, in accordance with CrimPR 3.3(2).

3A.3 There is a Preparation for Effective Trial form for use in the magistrates' courts, and a Plea and Trial Preparation Hearing form for use in the Crown Court, each of which must be used as appropriate in connection with CrimPR, Pt 3: see para. 5A.2 .... Versions of those forms in pdf and Word, together with guidance notes, are available on the Criminal Procedure Rules pages of the Ministry of Justice website.

<small>Case Progression and Trial Preparation in Magistrates' Courts</small>

B-23   **3A.4** CrimPR 8.3 applies in all cases and requires the prosecutor to serve:

i.   a summary of the circumstances of the offence;

ii.   any account given by the defendant in interview, whether contained in that summary or in another document;

iii.   any written witness statement or exhibit that the prosecutor then has available and considers material to plea or to the allocation of the case for trial or sentence;

iv.   a list of the defendant's criminal record, if any; and

    v. any available statement of the effect of the offence on a victim, a victim's family or
        others.
The details must include sufficient information to allow the defendant and the court at the first
hearing to take an informed view:

    i. on plea;

    ii. on venue for trial (if applicable);

    iii. for the purposes of case management; or

    iv. for the purposes of sentencing (including committal for sentence, if applicable).

Defendant in custody

3A.5 If the defendant has been detained in custody after being charged with an offence which is   **B-24**
indictable only or triable either way, at the first hearing a magistrates' court will proceed at once with
the allocation of the case for trial, where appropriate, and, if so required, with the sending of the
defendant to the Crown Court for trial. The court will be expected to ask for and record any indication of plea and issues for trial to assist the Crown Court.

3A.6 If the offence charged is triable only summarily, or if at that hearing the case is allocated for
summary trial, the court will forthwith give such directions as are necessary, either (on a guilty plea)
to prepare for sentencing, or for a trial.

Defendant on bail

3A.7 If the defendant has been released on bail after being charged, the case must be listed for the   **B-25**
first hearing 14 days after charge, or the next available court date thereafter when the prosecutor
anticipates a guilty plea which is likely to be sentenced in the magistrates' court. In cases where there
is an anticipated not guilty plea or the case is likely to be sent or committed to the Crown Court for
either trial or sentence, then it must be listed for the first hearing 28 days after charge or the next
available court date thereafter.

Guilty plea in the magistrates' courts

3A.8 Where a defendant pleads guilty or indicates a guilty plea in a magistrates' court the court   **B-26**
should consider whether a pre-sentence report – a stand down report if possible – is necessary.

Guilty plea in the Crown Court

3A.9 Where a magistrates' court is considering committal for sentence or the defendant has   **B-27**
indicated an intention to plead guilty in a matter which is to be sent to the Crown Court, the
magistrates' court should request the preparation of a pre-sentence report for the Crown Court's use
if the magistrates' court considers that:

    (a) there is a realistic alternative to a custodial sentence; or

    (b) the defendant may satisfy the criteria for classification as a dangerous offender; or

    (c) there is some other appropriate reason for doing so.

3A.10 When a magistrates' court sends a case to the Crown Court for trial and the defendant indicates
an intention to plead guilty at the Crown Court, then that magistrates' court must set a date
for a Plea and Trial Preparation Hearing at the Crown Court, in accordance with CrimPR 9.7(5)(a)(i).

Case sent for Crown Court trial: no indication of guilty plea

3A.11 In any case sent to the Crown Court for trial, other than one in which the defendant   **B-28**
indicates an intention to plead guilty, the magistrates' court must set a date for a Plea and Trial
Preparation Hearing, in accordance with CrimPR 9.7(5)(a)(ii). The Plea and Trial Preparation Hearing must be held within 28 days of sending, unless the standard directions of the presiding judges of
the circuit direct otherwise. Paragraph 3A.16 below additionally applies to the arrangements for such
hearings. A magistrates' court may give other directions appropriate to the needs of the case, in accordance with CrimPR 3.5(3), and in accordance with any standard directions issued by the presiding
judges of the circuit.

Defendant on bail: anticipated not guilty plea

3A.12 Where the defendant has been released on bail after being charged, and where the prosecu-   **B-29**
tor does not anticipate a guilty plea at the first hearing in a magistrates' court, then it is essential that
the initial details of the prosecution case that are provided for that first hearing are sufficient to assist the court, in order to identify the real issues and to give appropriate directions for an effective
trial (regardless of whether the trial is to be heard in the magistrates' court or the Crown Court). In
these circumstances, unless there is good reason not to do so, the prosecution should make available
the following material in advance of the first hearing in the magistrates' court:

    (a) a summary of the circumstances of the offence(s) including a summary of any account
        given by the defendant in interview;

(b) statements and exhibits that the prosecution has identified as being of importance for the purpose of plea or initial case management, including any relevant CCTV that would be relied upon at trial and any streamlined forensic report;

(c) details of witness availability, as far as they are known at that hearing;

(d) defendant's criminal record;

(e) victim personal statements if provided;

(f) an indication of any medical or other expert evidence that the prosecution is likely to adduce in relation to a victim or the defendant;

(g) any information as to special measures, bad character or hearsay, where applicable.

3A.13 In addition to the material required by CrimPR, Pt 8, the information required by the Preparation for Effective Trial form must be available to be submitted at the first hearing, and the parties must complete that form, in accordance with the guidance published with it. Where there is to be a contested trial in a magistrates' court, that form includes directions and a timetable that will apply in every case unless the court otherwise orders.

3A.14 Nothing in paragraph 3A.12-3A.13 shall preclude the court from taking a plea pursuant to CrimPR 3.9(2)(b) at the first hearing and for the court to case manage as far as practicable under Part 3 CrimPR.

Exercise of magistrates' court's powers

B-30   **3A.15** In accordance with CrimPR 9.1, sections 49, 51(13) and 51A(11) of the CDA 1998[§§ 1-24, 1-25 in the main work], and sections 17E, 18(5) and 24D of the MCA 1980[*ibid.*, §§ 1-62, 1-64, 1-87 in the main work] a single justice can:

a) allocate and send for trial;

b) take an indication of a guilty plea (but not pass sentence);

c) take a not guilty plea and give directions for the preparation of trial including:
   i. timetable for the proceedings;
   ii. the attendance of the parties;
   iii. the service of documents;
   iv. the manner in which evidence is to be given.

CASE PROGRESSION AND TRIAL PREPARATION IN THE CROWN COURT

Plea and Trial Preparation Hearing

B-31   **3A.16** In a case in which a magistrates' court has directed a Plea and Trial Preparation Hearing, the period which elapses between sending for trial and the date of that hearing must be consistent within each circuit. In every case, the time allowed for the conduct of the Plea and Trial Preparation Hearing must be sufficient for effective trial preparation. It is expected in every case that an indictment will be lodged at least 7 days in advance of the hearing. Please see the Note to the Practice Direction.

3A.17 In a case in which the defendant, not having done so before, indicates an intention to plead guilty to his representative after being sent for trial but before the Plea and Trial Preparation Hearing, the defence representative will notify the Crown Court and the prosecution forthwith. The court will ensure there is sufficient time at the Plea and Trial Preparation Hearing for sentence and a judge should at once request the preparation of a pre-sentence report if it appears to the court that either:

(a) there is a realistic alternative to a custodial sentence; or

(b) the defendant may satisfy the criteria for classification as a dangerous offender; or

(c) there is some other appropriate reason for doing so.

3A.18 If at the Plea and Trial Preparation Hearing the defendant pleads guilty and no presentence report has been prepared, if possible the court should obtain a stand down report.

3A.19 Where the defendant was remanded in custody after being charged and was sent for trial without initial details of the prosecution case having been served, then at least 7 days before the Plea and Trial Preparation Hearing the prosecutor should serve, as a minimum, the material identified in paragraph 3A.12 above. If at the Plea and Trial Preparation Hearing the defendant does not plead guilty, the court will be expected to identify the issues in the case and give appropriate directions for an effective trial. Please see the Note to the Practice Direction.

3A.20 At the Plea and Trial Preparation Hearing, in addition to the material required by paragraph 3A.12 above, the prosecutor must serve sufficient evidence to enable the court to case manage effectively without the need for a further case management hearing, unless the case falls within paragraph 3A.21. In addition, the information required by the Plea and Trial Preparation Hearing form must be available to the court at that hearing, and it must have been discussed between the parties in advance. The prosecutor must provide details of the availability of likely prosecution witnesses so that a trial date can immediately be arranged if the defendant does not plead guilty.

Further case management hearing

3A.21 In accordance with CrimPR 3.13(1)(c), after the Plea and Trial Preparation Hearing there **B-32** will be no further case management hearing before the trial unless:

(i) a condition listed in that rule is met; and

(ii) the court so directs, in order to further the overriding objective.

The directions to be given at the Plea and Trial Preparation Hearing therefore may include a direction for a further case management hearing, but usually will do so only in one of the following cases:

(a) Class 1 cases;

(b) Class 2 cases which carry a maximum penalty of 10 years or more;

(c) cases involving death by driving (whether dangerous or careless), or death in the workplace;

(d) cases involving a vulnerable witness;

(e) cases in which the defendant is a child or otherwise under a disability, or requires special assistance;

(f) cases in which there is a corporate or unrepresented defendant;

(g) cases in which the expected trial length is such that a further case management hearing is desirable and any case in which the trial is likely to last longer than four weeks;

(h) cases in which expert evidence is to be introduced;

(i) cases in which a party requests a hearing to enter a plea;

(j) cases in which an application to dismiss or stay has been made;

(k) cases in which arraignment has not taken place, whether because of an issue relating to fitness to plead, or abuse of process or sufficiency of evidence, or for any other reason;

(l) cases in which there are likely to be linked criminal and care directions in accordance with the 2013 Protocol.

3A.22 If a further case management hearing is directed, a defendant in custody will not usually be expected to attend in person, unless the court otherwise directs.

Compliance hearing

3A.23 If a party fails to comply with a case management direction, that party may be required to **B-33** attend the court to explain the failure. Unless the court otherwise directs a defendant in custody will not usually be expected to attend. See paras 3A.26-3A.28 below.

Conduct of case progression hearings

3A.24 As far as possible, case progression should be managed without a hearing in the courtroom, using electronic communication in accordance with CrimPR 3.5(2)(d). Court staff should be nominated to conduct case progression as part of their role, in accordance with CrimPR 3.4(2). To aid effective communication the prosecution and defence representative should notify the court and provide details of who shall be dealing with the case at the earliest opportunity.

COMPLETION OF EFFECTIVE TRIAL MONITORING FORM

3A.25 It is imperative that the Effective Trial Monitoring form (as devised and issued by Her Majesty's Courts and Tribunals Service) is accurately completed by the parties for all cases that have been listed for trial. Advocates must engage with the process by providing the relevant details and completing the form.

COMPLIANCE COURTS

3A.26 To ensure effective compliance with directions of the courts made in accordance with the Criminal Procedure Rules and the overriding objective, courts should maintain a record whenever a party to the proceedings has failed to comply with a direction made by the court. The parties may have to attend a hearing to explain any lack of compliance.

3A.27 These hearings may be conducted by live link facilities or via other electronic means, as the court may direct.

3A.28 It will be for the presiding judges, resident judge and justices' clerks to decide locally how often compliance courts should be held, depending on the scale and nature of the problem at each court centre.

NOTE TO THE PRACTICE DIRECTION

B-34   In 3A.16 and 3A.19 the reference to "at least 7 days" in advance of the hearing is necessitated by
the fact that, for the time being, different circuits have different timescales for the Plea and Trial
Preparation Hearing. Had this not been so, the paragraphs would have been drafted forward from
the date of sending rather than backwards from the date of the Plea and Trial Preparation Hearing.

CPD I General Matters 3B: Pagination and Indexing of Served Evidence

B-35   **3B.1** The following directions apply to matters before the Crown Court, where–

(a) there is an application to prefer a bill of indictment in relation to the case;

(b) a person is sent for trial under section 51 of the CDA 1998 [§ 1-24 in the main work] ...,
to the service of copies of the documents containing the evidence on which the charge or
charges are based under paragraph 1 of Schedule 3 to that Act [*ibid.*, § 1-36]; or

(c) a defendant wishes to serve evidence.

3B.2 A party who serves documentary evidence in the Crown Court should:

(a) paginate each page in any bundle of statements and exhibits sequentially;

(b) provide an index to each bundle of statements produced including the following
information:

(i) the name of the case;

(ii) the author of each statement;

(iii) the start page number of the witness statement;

(iv) the end page number of the witness statement;

(c) provide an index to each bundle of documentary and pictorial exhibits produced, including the following information:

(i) the name of the case;

(ii) the exhibit reference;

(iii) a short description of the exhibit;

(iv) the start page number of the exhibit;

(v) the end page number of the exhibit;

(vi) where possible, the name of the person producing the exhibit should be added.

3B.3 Where additional documentary evidence is served, a party should paginate following on
from the last page of the previous bundle or in a logical and sequential manner. A party should also
provide notification of service of any amended index.

3B.4 The prosecution must ensure that the running total of the pages of prosecution evidence is
easily identifiable on the most recent served bundle of prosecution evidence.

3B.5 For the purposes of these directions, the number of pages of prosecution evidence served on
the court includes all (a) witness statements; (b) documentary and pictorial exhibits; (c) records of
interviews with the defendant; and (d) records of interviews with other defendants which form part
of the served prosecution documents or which are included in any notice of additional evidence, but
does not include any document provided on CD-ROM or by other means of electronic communication.

CPD I General Matters 3C: Abuse of Process Stay Applications

B-36   **3C.1** In all cases where a defendant in the Crown Court proposes to make an application to stay an
indictment on the ground of abuse of process, written notice of such application must be given to the
prosecuting authority and to any co-defendant as soon as practicable after the defendant becomes
aware of the grounds for doing so and not later than 14 days before the date fixed or warned for
trial ("the relevant date"). Such notice must (a) give the name of the case and the indictment number;
(b) state the fixed date or the warned date as appropriate; (c) specify the nature of the application; (d)
set out in numbered sub-paragraphs the grounds on which the application is to be made; (e) be
copied to the chief listing officer at the court centre where the case is due to be heard.

3C.2 Any co-defendant who wishes to make a like application must give a like notice not later than
seven days before the relevant date, setting out any additional grounds relied upon.

3C.3 In relation to such applications, the following automatic directions shall apply: (a) the
advocate for the applicant(s) must lodge with the court and serve on all other parties a skeleton argument in support of the application, at least five clear working days before the relevant date; if reference is to be made to any document not in the existing trial documents, a paginated and indexed
bundle of such documents is to be provided with the skeleton argument; (b) the advocate for the
prosecution must lodge with the court and serve on all other parties a responsive skeleton argument
at least two clear working days before the relevant date, together with a supplementary bundle if
appropriate.

3C.4 All skeleton arguments must specify any propositions of law to be advanced (together with the authorities relied on in support, with paragraph references to passages relied upon), and, where appropriate, include a chronology of events and a list of dramatis personae. In all instances where reference is made to a document, the reference in the trial documents or supplementary bundle is to be given.

3C.5 The above time limits are minimum time limits. In appropriate cases the court will order longer lead times. To this end in all cases where defence advocates are, at the time of the preliminary hearing or as soon as practicable after the case has been sent, considering the possibility of an abuse of process application, this must be raised with the judge dealing with the matter, who will order a different timetable if appropriate, and may wish, in any event, to give additional directions about the conduct of the application. If the trial judge has not been identified, the matter should be raised with the resident judge.

CPD I General Matters 3D: Vulnerable People in the Courts

3D.1 In respect of eligibility for special measures, "vulnerable" and "intimidated" witnesses are **B-37** defined in sections 16 and 17 of the YJCEA 1999 ...; "vulnerable" includes those under 18 years of age and people with a mental disorder or learning disability; a physical disorder or disability; or who are likely to suffer fear or distress in giving evidence because of their own circumstances or those relating to the case.

3D.2 However, many other people giving evidence in a criminal case, whether as a witness or defendant, may require assistance: the court is required to take "every reasonable step" to encourage and facilitate the attendance of witnesses and to facilitate the participation of any person, including the defendant (r.3.9(3)(a) and (b)). This includes enabling a witness or defendant to give their best evidence, and enabling a defendant to comprehend the proceedings and engage fully with his defence. The pre-trial and trial process should, so far as necessary, be adapted to meet those ends. Regard should be had to the welfare of a young defendant as required by section 44 of the CYPA 1933 [§ 5-74 in the main work], and generally to Parts 1 and 3 of the Criminal Procedure Rules ....

3D.3 Under Part 3 of the rules, the court must identify the needs of witnesses at an early stage (r.3.2(2)(b)) and may require the parties to identify arrangements to facilitate the giving of evidence and participation in the trial (r.3.11(c)(iv) and (v). There are various statutory special measures that the court may utilise to assist a witness in giving evidence. Part 18 of the rules gives the procedures to be followed. Courts should note the "primary rule" which requires the court to give a direction for a special measure to assist a child witness or qualifying witness and that in such cases an application to the court is not required (r.18.9).

3D.4 Court of Appeal decisions on this subject include ... *R. v. Cox*[§ 4-86 in the main work], *R. v. Wills*[§ 8-217a in the main work], and *R. v. E.* [§ 8-217a in the main work].

3D.5 In *R. v. Wills*, the court endorsed the approach taken by the report of the *Advocacy Training Council (ATC) "Raising the Bar: the Handling of Vulnerable Witnesses, Victims and Defendants in Court" (2011).* The report includes and recommends the use of "toolkits" to assist advocates as they prepare to question vulnerable people at court: http://advocacytrainingcouncil.org/images/word/raisingtheb ar.pdf.

3D.6 Further toolkits are available through the advocate's gateway which is managed by the ATC's management committee: http://www.theadvocatesgateway.org/.

3D.7 These toolkits represent best practice. Advocates should consult and follow the relevant guidance whenever they prepare to question a young or otherwise vulnerable witness or defendant. Judges may find it helpful to refer advocates to this material and to use the toolkits in case management.

3D.8 "Achieving Best Evidence in Criminal Proceedings" (Ministry of Justice 2011) [§ 8-91 in the main work] describes best practice in preparation for the investigative interview and trial: http://ww w.cps.gov.uk/publications/docs/best_evidence_in_criminal_proceedings.pdf.

CPD I General Matters 3E: Ground Rules Hearings to Plan the Questioning of a Vulnerable Witness or Defendant

3E.1 The judiciary is responsible for controlling questioning. Over-rigorous or repetitive cros- **B-38** sexamination of a child or vulnerable witness should be stopped. Intervention by the judge, magistrates or intermediary (if any) is minimised if questioning, taking account of the individual's communication needs, is discussed in advance and ground rules are agreed and adhered to.

3E.2 Discussion of ground rules is required in all intermediary trials where they must be discussed between the judge or magistrates, advocates and intermediary before the witness gives evidence. The intermediary must be present but is not required to take the oath (the intermediary's declaration is made just before the witness gives evidence).

3E.3 Discussion of ground rules is good practice, even if no intermediary is used, in all young witness cases and in other cases where a witness or defendant has communication needs. Discussion before the day of trial is preferable to give advocates time to adapt their questions to the witness's needs. It may be helpful for a trial practice note of boundaries to be created at the end of the discussion. The judge may use such a document in ensuring that the agreed ground rules are complied with.

3E.4 All witnesses, including the defendant and defence witnesses, should be enabled to give the best evidence they can. In relation to young and/or vulnerable people, this may mean departing radically from traditional cross-examination. The form and extent of appropriate cross-examination will vary from case to case. For adult non-vulnerable witnesses an advocate will usually put his case so that the witness will have the opportunity of commenting upon it and/or answering it. When the witness is young or otherwise vulnerable, the court may dispense with the normal practice and impose restrictions on the advocate "putting his case" where there is a risk of a young or otherwise vulnerable witness failing to understand, becoming distressed or acquiescing to leading questions. Where limitations on questioning are necessary and appropriate, they must be clearly defined. The judge has a duty to ensure that they are complied with and should explain them to the jury and the reasons for them. If the advocate fails to comply with the limitations, the judge should give relevant directions to the jury when that occurs and prevent further questioning that does not comply with the ground rules settled upon in advance. Instead of commenting on inconsistencies during cross-examination, following discussion between the judge and the advocates, the advocate or judge may point out important inconsistencies after (instead of during) the witness's evidence. The judge should also remind the jury of these during summing up. The judge should be alert to alleged inconsistencies that are not in fact inconsistent, or are trivial.

3E.5 If there is more than one defendant, the judge should not permit each advocate to repeat the questioning of a vulnerable witness. In advance of the trial, the advocates should divide the topics between them, with the advocate for the first defendant leading the questioning, and the advocate(s) for the other defendant(s) asking only ancillary questions relevant to their client's case, without repeating the questioning that has already taken place on behalf of the other defendant(s).

3E.6 In particular in a trial of a sexual offence, "body maps" should be provided for the witness's use. If the witness needs to indicate a part of the body, the advocate should ask the witness to point to the relevant part on the body map. In sex cases, judges should not permit advocates to ask the witness to point to a part of the witness's own body. Similarly, photographs of the witness's body should not be shown around the court while the witness is giving evidence.

CPD I General Matters 3F: Intermediaries (as substituted by Criminal Practice Directions 2015 (Amendment No. 1), unreported, March 23, 2016, Lord Thomas C.J.)

Role and functions of intermediaries in criminal courts

B-39

3F.1 Intermediaries facilitate communication with witnesses and defendants who have communication needs. Their primary function is to improve the quality of evidence and aid understanding between the court, the advocates and the witness or defendant. For example, they commonly advise on the formulation of questions so as to avoid misunderstanding. On occasion, they actively assist and intervene during questioning. The extent to which they do so (if at all) depends on factors such as the communication needs of the witness or defendant, and the skills of the advocates in adapting their language and questioning style to meet those needs.

3F.2 Intermediaries are independent of parties and owe their duty to the court. The court and parties should be vigilant to ensure they act impartially and their assistance to witnesses and defendants is transparent. It is however permissible for an advocate to have a private consultation with an intermediary when formulating questions (although control of questioning remains the overall responsibility of the court).

3F.3 Further information is in Intermediaries: Step by Step (Toolkit 16; The Advocate's Gateway, 2015) and chapter 5 of the Equal Treatment Bench Book (Judicial College, 2013).

Links to publications

- http://www.theadvocatesgateway.org/images/toolkits/16intermediariesstepbystep 060315.pdf
- http://www.judiciary.gov.uk/wp-content/uploads/2013/11/5-children-and-vulnera ble-adults.pdf

Assessment

B-40

3F.4 The process of appointment should begin with assessment by an intermediary and a report. The report will make recommendations to address the communication needs of the witness or defendant during trial.

3F.5 In light of the scarcity of intermediaries, the appropriateness of assessment must be decided with care to ensure their availability for those witnesses and defendants who are most in need. The decision should be made on an individual basis, in the context of the circumstances of the particular case.

Intermediaries for prosecution and defence witnesses

3F.6 Intermediaries are one of the special measures available to witnesses under the YJCEA 1999. **B-41** Witnesses deemed vulnerable in accordance with the criteria in [section 16] are eligible for the assistance of an intermediary when giving evidence pursuant to [section 29]. These provisions do not apply to defendants.

3F.7 An application for an intermediary to assist a witness when giving evidence must be made in accordance with Part 18 of the Criminal Procedure Rules. In addition, where an intermediary report is available (see 3F.4 above), it should be provided with the application

3F.8 The Witness Intermediary Scheme (WIS) operated by the National Crime Agency identifies intermediaries for witnesses and may be used by the prosecution and defence. The WIS is contactable at wit@nca.x.gsi.gov.uk / 0845 000 5463. An intermediary appointed through the WIS is defined as a "registered intermediary" and matched to the particular witness based on expertise, location and availability. Registered intermediaries are accredited by the WIS and bound by Codes of Practice and Ethics issued by the Ministry of Justice (which oversees the WIS).

3F.9 Having identified a registered intermediary, the WIS does not provide funding. The party appointing the registered intermediary is responsible for payment at rates specified by the Ministry of Justice.

3F.10 Further information is in the Registered Intermediaries Procedural Guidance Manual (Ministry of Justice, 2015) and Intermediaries: Step by Step (see 3F.3 above).

Link to publication

- http://www.theadvocatesgateway.org/images/procedures/registered-intermediarypr ocedural-guidance-manual.pdf

Intermediaries for defendants

3F.11 Statutory provisions providing for defendants to be assisted by an intermediary when giving **B-42** evidence (where necessary to ensure a fair trial) are not in force (because s.104 [of the] Coroners and Justice Act 2009, which would insert ss.33BA and 33BB into the YJCEA 1999[§§ 8-101, 8-102 in the main work], has yet to be commenced).

3F.12 The court may direct the appointment of an intermediary to assist a defendant in reliance on its inherent powers ([*R. (C.) v. Sevenoaks Youth Court* [2010] 1 All E.R. 735, DC] [*ibid.*, §§ 4-162, 8-72]). There is however no presumption that a defendant will be so assisted and, even where an intermediary would improve the trial process, appointment is not mandatory (*R. v. Cox (Practice Note)* [§ 4-86 in the main work]). The court should adapt the trial process to address a defendant's communication needs (*R. v. Cox*) and will rarely exercise its inherent powers to direct appointment of an intermediary.

3F.13 The court may exercise its inherent powers to direct appointment of an intermediary to assist a defendant giving evidence or for the entire trial. Terms of appointment are for the court and there is no illogicality in restricting the appointment to the defendant's evidence (*R. v. R.* [2015] EWCA Crim 1870), when the "most pressing need" arises ([*R. (O.P.) v. Secretary of State for Justice* [2015] 1 Cr.App.R. 7, DC]). Directions to appoint an intermediary for a defendant's evidence will thus be rare, but for the entire trial extremely rare.

3F.14 An application for an intermediary to assist a defendant must be made in accordance with Part 18 of the Criminal Procedure Rules. In addition, where an intermediary report is available (see 3F.4 above), it should be provided with the application.

3F.15 The WIS is not presently available to identify intermediaries for defendants (although in [*R. (O.P.) v. Secretary of State for Justice*], the Ministry of Justice was ordered to consider carefully whether it were justifiable to refuse equal provision to witnesses and defendants with respect to their evidence). "Non-registered intermediaries" (intermediaries appointed other than through the WIS) must therefore be appointed for defendants. Although training is available, there is no accreditation process for non-registered intermediaries and rates of payment are unregulated.

3F.16 Arrangements for funding of intermediaries for defendants depend on the stage of the appointment process. Where the defendant is publicly funded, an application should be made to the Legal Aid Agency for prior authority to fund a pre-trial assessment. If the application is refused, an application may be made to the court to use its inherent powers to direct a pre-trial assessment and funding thereof. Where the court uses its inherent powers to direct assistance by an intermediary at trial (during evidence or for the entire trial), court staff are responsible for arranging payment from central funds. Internal guidance for court staff is in Guidance for HMCTS Staff: Registered and Non-Registered Intermediaries for Vulnerable Defendants and Non-Vulnerable Defence and Prosecution Witnesses (Her Majesty's Courts and Tribunals Service, 2014).

3F.17 The court should be satisfied that a non-registered intermediary has expertise suitable to meet the defendant's communication needs.

3F.18 Further information is in Intermediaries: Step by Step (see 3F.3 above).

Ineffective directions for intermediaries to assist defendants

3F.19 Directions for intermediaries to help defendants may be ineffective due to general unavailability, lack of suitable expertise, or non-availability for the purpose directed (for example, where the direction is for assistance during evidence, but an intermediary will only accept appointment for the entire trial).

3F.20 Intermediaries may contribute to the administration of justice by facilitating communication with appropriate defendants during the trial process. A trial will not be rendered unfair because a direction to appoint an intermediary for the defendant is ineffective. "It would, in fact, be a most unusual case for a defendant who is fit to plead to be so disadvantaged by his condition that a properly brought prosecution would have to be stayed" because an intermediary with suitable expertise is not available for the purpose directed by the court (*R. v. Cox*).

3F.21 Faced with an ineffective direction, it remains the court's responsibility to adapt the trial process to address the defendant's communication needs, as was the case prior to the existence of intermediaries (*R. v. Cox*). In such a case, a ground rules hearing should be convened to ensure every reasonable step is taken to facilitate the defendant's participation in accordance with [rule 3.9 of the Criminal Procedure Rules]. At the hearing, the court should make new, further and / or alternative directions. This includes setting ground rules to help the defendant follow proceedings and (where applicable) to give evidence.

3F.22 For example, to help the defendant follow proceedings the court may require evidence to be adduced by simple questions, with witnesses being asked to answer in short sentences. Regular breaks may assist the defendant's concentration and enable the defence advocate to summarise the evidence and take further instructions.

3F.23 Further guidance is available in publications such as Ground Rules Hearings and the Fair Treatment of Vulnerable People in Court (Toolkit 1; The Advocate's Gateway, 2015) and General Principles from Research – Planning to Question a Vulnerable Person or Someone with Communication Needs (Toolkit 2(a); The Advocate's Gateway, 2015). In the absence of an intermediary, these publications include information on planning how to manage the participation and questioning of the defendant, and the formulation of questions to avert misunderstanding (for example, by avoiding "long and complicated questions...posed in a leading or 'tagged' manner" (*R. v. Wills* [2012] 1 Cr.App.R. 2, CA [§ 8-217a in the main work])).

Links to publications

- http://www.theadvocatesgateway.org/images/toolkits/1groundruleshearingsandthe fairtreatmentofvulnerablepeopleincourt060315.pdf
- http://www.theadvocatesgateway.org/images/toolkits/2generalprinciplesfromresear chpolicyandguidance-planningtoquestionavulnerablepersonorsomeonewithcommu nicationneeds141215.pdf

Intermediaries for witnesses and defendants under 18

3F.24 Communication needs (such as short attention span, suggestibility and reticence in relation to authority figures) are common to many witnesses and defendants under 18. Consideration should therefore be given to the communication needs of all children and young people appearing in the criminal courts and to adapting the trial process to address any such needs. Guidance is available in publications such as Planning to Question a Child or Young Person (Toolkit 6; The Advocate's Gateway, 2015) and Effective Participation of Young Defendants (Toolkit 8; The Advocate's Gateway, 2013).

Links to publications

- http://www.theadvocatesgateway.org/images/toolkits/6planningtoquestionachildoryoungp erson141215.pdf
- http://www.theadvocatesgateway.org/images/toolkits/8YoungDefendants211013.pdf

3F.25 For the reasons set out in 3F.5 above, the appropriateness of an intermediary assessment for witnesses and defendants under 18 must be decided with care. Whilst there is no presumption that they will be assessed by an intermediary (to evaluate their communication needs prior to trial) or assisted by an intermediary at court (for example, if / when giving evidence), the decision should be made on an individual basis in the context of the circumstances of the particular case.

3F.26 Assessment by an intermediary should be considered for witnesses and defendants under 18 who seem liable to misunderstand questions or to experience difficulty expressing answers, including those who seem unlikely to be able to recognise a problematic question (such as one that is misleading or not readily understood), and those who may be reluctant to tell a questioner in a position of authority if they do not understand.

Attendance at ground rules hearing

3F.27 Where the court directs questioning will be conducted through an intermediary, [rule 3.9 of **B-45** the Criminal Procedure Rules] requires the court to set ground rules. The intermediary should be present at the ground rules hearing to make representations in accordance with [rule] 3.9(7)(a).

Listing

3F.28 Where the court directs an intermediary will attend the trial, their dates of availability **B-46** should be provided to the court. It is preferable that such trials are fixed rather than placed in warned lists.

Photographs of court facilities

3F.29 Resident judges in the Crown Court or the chief clerk or other responsible person in the **B-47** magistrates' courts should, in consultation with HMCTS managers responsible for court security matters, develop a policy to govern under what circumstances photographs or other visual recordings may be made of court facilities, such as a live link room, to assist vulnerable or child witnesses to familiarise themselves with the setting, so as to be enabled to give their best evidence. For example, a photograph may provide a helpful reminder to a witness whose court visit has taken place sometime earlier. Resident judges should tend to permit photographs to be taken for this purpose by intermediaries or supporters, subject to whatever restrictions the resident judge or responsible person considers to be appropriate, having regard to the security requirements of the court.

CPD I General Matters 3G: Vulnerable Defendants

Before the trial, sentencing or appeal

3G.1 If a vulnerable defendant, especially one who is young, is to be tried jointly with one who is **B-48** not, the court should consider at the plea and case management hearing, or at a case management hearing in a magistrates' court, whether the vulnerable defendant should be tried on his own, but should only so order if satisfied that a fair trial cannot be achieved by use of appropriate special measures or other support for the defendant. If a vulnerable defendant is tried jointly with one who is not, the court should consider whether any of the modifications set out in this direction should apply in the circumstances of the joint trial and, so far as practicable, make orders to give effect to any such modifications.

3G.2 It may be appropriate to arrange that a vulnerable defendant should visit, out of court hours and before the trial, sentencing or appeal hearing, the courtroom in which that hearing is to take place so that he can familiarise him or herself with it.

3G.3 Where an intermediary is being used to help the defendant to communicate at court, the intermediary should accompany the defendant on his or her pre-trial visit. The visit will enable the defendant to familiarise him or herself with the layout of the court, and may include matters such as: where the defendant will sit, either in the dock or otherwise; court officials (what their roles are and where they sit); who else might be in the court, for example those in the public gallery and press box; the location of the witness box; basic court procedure; and the facilities available in the court.

3G.4 If the defendant's use of the live link is being considered, he or she should have an opportunity to have a practice session.

3G.5 If any case against a vulnerable defendant has attracted or may attract widespread public or media interest, the assistance of the police should be enlisted to try and ensure that the defendant is not, when attending the court, exposed to intimidation, vilification or abuse. Section 41 of the CJA 1925 prohibits the taking of photographs of defendants and witnesses (among others) in the court building or in its precincts, or when entering or leaving those precincts. A direction reminding media representatives of the prohibition may be appropriate. The court should also be ready at this stage, if it has not already done so, where relevant to make a reporting restriction under section 39 of the CYPA 1933 [*repealed (see now s.45 of the YJCEA 1999 (§ 4·27 in the main work))*] or, on an appeal to the Crown Court from a youth court, to remind media representatives of the application of section 49 of that Act.

3G.6 The provisions of the practice direction accompanying Part 6 should be followed.

The trial, sentencing or appeal hearing

3G.7 Subject to the need for appropriate security arrangements, the proceedings should, if **B-49**

practicable, be held in a courtroom in which all the participants are on the same or almost the same level.

3G.8 Subject again to the need for appropriate security arrangements, a vulnerable defendant, especially if he is young, should normally, if he wishes, be free to sit with members of his family or others in a like relationship, and with some other suitable supporting adult such as a social worker, and in a place which permits easy, informal communication with his legal representatives. The court should ensure that a suitable supporting adult is available throughout the course of the proceedings.

3G.9 It is essential that at the beginning of the proceedings, the court should ensure that what is to take place has been explained to a vulnerable defendant in terms he or she can understand and, at trial in the Crown Court, it should ensure in particular that the role of the jury has been explained. It should remind those representing the vulnerable defendant and the supporting adult of their responsibility to explain each step as it takes place and, at trial, explain the possible consequences of a guilty verdict and credit for a guilty plea. The court should also remind any intermediary of the responsibility to ensure that the vulnerable defendant has understood the explanations given to him/her. Throughout the trial the court should continue to ensure, by any appropriate means, that the defendant understands what is happening and what has been said by those on the bench, the advocates and witnesses.

3G.10 A trial should be conducted according to a timetable which takes full account of a vulnerable defendant's ability to concentrate. Frequent and regular breaks will often be appropriate. The court should ensure, so far as practicable, that the whole trial is conducted in clear language that the defendant can understand and that evidence in chief and cross-examination are conducted using questions that are short and clear. The conclusions of the "ground rules" hearing should be followed, and advocates should use and follow the "toolkits" as discussed above (*Criminal Practice Direction I (General matters) 3D*).

3G.11 A vulnerable defendant who wishes to give evidence by live link, in accordance with section 33A of the YJCEA 1999 [§ 8-99 in the main work], may apply for a direction to that effect; the procedure in rules 18.14 to 18.17 should be followed. Before making such a direction, the court must be satisfied that it is in the interests of justice to do so and that the use of a live link would enable the defendant to participate more effectively as a witness in the proceedings. The direction will need to deal with the practical arrangements to be made, including the identity of the person or persons who will accompany him or her.

3G.12 In the Crown Court, the judge should consider whether robes and wigs should be worn, and should take account of the wishes of both a vulnerable defendant and any vulnerable witness. It is generally desirable that those responsible for the security of a vulnerable defendant who is in custody, especially if he or she is young, should not be in uniform, and that there should be no recognisable police presence in the courtroom save for good reason.

3G.13 The court should be prepared to restrict attendance by members of the public in the courtroom to a small number, perhaps limited to those with an immediate and direct interest in the outcome. The court should rule on any challenged claim to attend. However, facilities for reporting the proceedings (subject to any restrictions under s.39 or 49 of the CYPA 1933) must be provided. The court may restrict the number of reporters attending in the courtroom to such number as is judged practicable and desirable. In ruling on any challenged claim to attend in the courtroom for the purpose of reporting, the court should be mindful of the public's general right to be informed about the administration of justice.

3G.14 Where it has been decided to limit access to the courtroom, whether by reporters or generally, arrangements should be made for the proceedings to be relayed, audibly and if possible visually, to another room in the same court complex to which the media and the public have access if it appears that there will be a need for such additional facilities. Those making use of such a facility should be reminded that it is to be treated as an extension of the courtroom and that they are required to conduct themselves accordingly.

CPD I General Matters 3H: Wales and the Welsh Language: Devolution Issues

B-50   [*Not set out in this work.*]

CPD I General Matters 3J: Wales and the Welsh Language: Applications for Evidence to be Given in Welsh

B-51   **3J.1** If a defendant in a court in England asks to give or call evidence in the Welsh language, the case should not be transferred to Wales. In ordinary circumstances, interpreters can be provided on request.

CPD I General Matters 3K: Wales and the Welsh Language: Use of the Welsh Language in Courts in Wales

B-52   **3K.1** The purpose of this direction is to reflect the principle of the Welsh Language Act 1993 that, in the administration of justice in Wales, the English and Welsh languages should be treated on a basis of equality.

GENERAL

3K.2 It is the responsibility of the legal representatives in every case in which the Welsh language **B-53** may be used by any witness or party, or in any document which may be placed before the court, to inform the court of that fact, so that appropriate arrangements can be made for the listing of the case.

3K.3 Any party or witness is entitled to use Welsh in a magistrates' court in Wales without giving prior notice. Arrangements will be made for hearing such cases in accordance with the "Magistrates' Courts' Protocol for Listing Cases where the Welsh Language is used" (January 2008) which is available on the judiciary's website: http://www.judiciary.gov.uk/NR/exeres/57AD4763-F265-47B9-8A35-0442E08160E6. See also r.24.14.

3K.4 If the possible use of the Welsh language is known at the time of sending or appeal to the Crown Court, the court should be informed immediately after sending or when the notice of appeal is lodged. Otherwise, the court should be informed as soon as the possible use of the Welsh language becomes known.

3K.5 If costs are incurred as a result of failure to comply with these directions, a wasted costs order may be made against the defaulting party and / or his legal representatives.

3K.6 The law does not permit the selection of jurors in a manner which enables the court to discover whether a juror does or does not speak Welsh, or to secure a jury whose members are bilingual, to try a case in which the Welsh language may be used.

PRELIMINARY AND PLEA AND CASE MANAGEMENT HEARINGS

3K.7 An advocate in a case in which the Welsh language may be used must raise that matter at the **B-54** preliminary and/or the plea and case management hearing and endorse details of it on the advocates' questionnaire, so that appropriate directions may be given for the progress of the case.

LISTING

3K.8 The listing officer, in consultation with the resident judge, should ensure that a case in **B-55** which the Welsh language may be used is listed—

    (a) wherever practicable before a Welsh speaking judge, and

    (b) in a court in Wales with simultaneous translation facilities.

INTERPRETERS

3K.9 Whenever an interpreter is needed to translate evidence from English into Welsh or from **B-56** Welsh into English, the court listing officer in whose court the case is to be heard shall contact the Welsh Language Unit who will ensure the attendance of an accredited interpreter.

JURORS

3K.10 The jury bailiff, when addressing the jurors at the start of their period of jury service, shall **B-57** inform them that each juror may take an oath or affirm in Welsh or English as he wishes.

3K.11 After the jury has been selected to try a case, and before it is sworn, the court officer swearing in the jury shall inform the jurors in open court that each juror may take an oath or affirm in Welsh or English as he wishes. A juror who takes the oath or affirms in Welsh should not be asked to repeat it in English.

3K.12 Where Welsh is used by any party or witness in a trial, an accredited interpreter will provide simultaneous translation from Welsh to English for the jurors who do not speak Welsh. There is no provision for the translation of evidence from English to Welsh for a Welsh speaking juror.

3K.13 The jury's deliberations must be conducted in private with no other person present and therefore no interpreter may be provided to translate the discussion for the benefit of one or more of the jurors.

WITNESSES

3K.14 When each witness is called, the court officer administering the oath or affirmation shall **B-58** inform the witness that he may be sworn or affirm in Welsh or English, as he wishes. A witness who takes the oath or affirms in Welsh should not be asked to repeat it in English.

OPENING / CLOSING OF CROWN COURTS

3K.15 Unless it is not reasonably practicable to do so, the opening and closing of the court should **B-59** be performed in Welsh and English.

Role of liaison judge

3K.16 If any question or problem arises concerning the implementation of these directions, contact should in the first place be made with the liaison judge for the Welsh language through the Wales Circuit Office: HMCTS WALES / GLITEM CYMRU, 3rd Floor, Churchill House / 3ydd Llawr Ty Churchill, Churchill Way / Ffordd Churchill, Cardiff / Caerdydd, CF10 2HH029 2067 8300.

CPD I General Matters 3L: Security of Prisoners at Court

B-61

3L.1 High-risk prisoners identified to the court as presenting a significant risk of escape, violence in court or danger to those in the court and its environs, and to the public at large, will as far as possible, have administrative and remand appearances listed for disposal by way of live link. They will have priority for the use of video equipment.

3L.2 In all other proceedings that require the appearance in person of a high-risk prisoner, the proceedings will be listed at an appropriately secure court building and in a court with a secure (enclosed or ceiling-high) dock.

3L.3 Where a secure dock or live link is not available the court will be asked to consider an application for additional security measures, which may include: (a) the use of approved restraints (but see below at para. 3L.6); (b) the deployment of additional escort staff; (c) securing the court room for all or part of the proceedings; (d) in exceptional circumstances, moving the hearing to a prison.

3L.4 National Offender Management Service ("NOMS") will be responsible for providing the assessment of the prisoner and it is accepted that this may change at short notice. NOMS must provide notification to the listing officer of all Category A prisoners, those on the escape list and restricted status prisoners or other prisoners who have otherwise been assessed as presenting a significant risk of violence or harm. There is a presumption that all prisoners notified as high-risk will be allocated a hearing by live link and/or secure dock facilities. Where the court cannot provide a secure listing, the reasons should be provided to the establishment so that alternative arrangements can be considered.

Applications for use of approved restraints

B-62

3L.5 It is the duty of the court to decide whether a prisoner who appears before them should appear in restraints or not. Their decision must comply with the requirements of the ECHR, particularly Article 3, which prohibits degrading treatment: see *Raninen v. Finland*, 26 E.H.R.R. 563.

3L.6 No prisoner should be handcuffed in court unless there are reasonable grounds for apprehending that he will be violent or will attempt to escape. If an application is made, it must be entertained by the court and a ruling must be given. The defence should be given the opportunity to respond to the application: proceeding in the absence of the defendant or his representative may give rise to an issue under Article 6.1 of the Convention [§ 16-72 in the main work]: *R. v. Rollinson*, 161 J.P. 107. If an application is to be made *ex parte* then that application should be made *inter partes* and the defence should be given an opportunity to respond.

Additional security measures

B-63

3L.7 It may be in some cases that additional dock officers are deployed to mitigate the risk that a prisoner presents. When the nature of the risk is so serious that increased deployment will be insufficient or would in itself be so obtrusive as to prejudice a fair trial, then the court may be required to consider the following measures: (a) reconsider the case for a live link hearing, including transferring the case to a court where the live link is available; (b) transfer the case to an appropriately secure court; (c) the use of approved restraints on the prisoner for all or part of the proceedings; (d) securing the court room for all or part of the proceedings; and (e) the use of (armed) police in the court building.

3L.8 The establishment seeking the additional security measures will submit a court management directions form setting out the evidence of the prisoner's identified risk of escape or violence and requesting the court's approval of security measures to mitigate that risk. This must be sent to the listing officer along with current, specific and credible evidence that the security measures are both necessary and proportionate to the identified risk and that the risk cannot be managed in any other way.

3L.9 If the court is asked to consider transfer of the case, then this must be in accordance with *Criminal Practice Direction XIII (Listing) F*, paras 11-13[§ 2-22p in the main work]. The listing officer will liaise with the establishment, prosecution and the defence to ensure the needs of the witnesses are taken into account.

3L.10 The judge who has conduct of the case must deal with any application for the use of restraints or any other security measure and will hear representations from the Crown Prosecution Service and the defence before proceeding. The application will only be granted if: (a) there are good grounds for believing that the prisoner poses a significant risk of trying to escape from the court (beyond the assumed motivation of all prisoners to escape) and/or risk of serious harm towards those persons in court or the public generally should an escape attempt be successful; and (b) where there is no other viable means of preventing escape or serious harm.

High-risk prisoners giving evidence from the witness box

3L.11 High-risk prisoners giving evidence from the witness box may pose a significant security **B-64** risk. In circumstances where such prisoners are required to move from a secure dock to an insecure witness box, an application may be made for the court to consider the use of additional security measures including: (a) the use of approved restraints; (b) the deployment of additional escort staff or police in the courtroom or armed police in the building (the decision to deploy an armed escort is for the chief inspector of the relevant borough: the decision to allow the armed escort in or around the court room is for the senior presiding judge [see Criminal Practice Direction I (General matters) 3M]); (c) securing the courtroom for all or part of the proceedings; (d) giving evidence from the secure dock; and (e) use of live link if the prisoner is not the defendant.

CPD I General Matters 3M: Procedure for Applications for Armed Police Presence in Crown Courts and Magistrates' Court Buildings (as substituted by Criminal Practice Directions 2015 (Amendment No. 2), unreported, November 16, 2016, Lord Thomas C.J.)

3M.1 This practice direction sets out the procedure for the making and handling of applications **B-65** for authorisation for the presence of armed police officers within the precincts of any Crown Court and magistrates' court buildings at any time. It applies to an application to authorise the carriage of firearms or tasers in court. It does not apply to officers who are carrying CS spray or PAVA incapacitant spray, which is included in the standard equipment issued to officers in some forces and therefore no separate authorisation is required for its carriage in court.

3M.2 This practice direction applies to all cases in England and Wales in which a police unit intends to request authorisation for the presence of armed police officers in the Crown Court or in the magistrates' court buildings at any time and including during the delivery of prisoners to court.

3M.3 This practice direction allows applications to be made for armed police presence in the Royal Courts of Justice.

Emergency situations

3M.4 This practice direction does not apply in an emergency situation. In such circumstances, the **B-66** police must be able to respond in a way in which their professional judgment deems most appropriate.

Designated court centres

3M.5 Applications may only be made for armed police presence in the designated Crown Court **B-67** and magistrates' court centres (see below). This list may be revised from time to time in consultation with the Association of Chief Police Officers (ACPO) and HMCTS. It will be reviewed at least every five years in consultation with ACPO armed police secretariat and the presiding judges.

3M.6 The Crown Court centres designated for firearms deployment are:

(a) Northern Circuit: Carlisle, Chester, Liverpool, Preston, Manchester Crown Square & Manchester Minshull Street.

(b) North Eastern Circuit: Bradford, Leeds, Newcastle upon Tyne, Sheffield, Teesside and Kingston-upon-Hull.

(c) Western Circuit: Bristol, Winchester and Exeter.

(d) South Eastern Circuit (not including London): Canterbury, Chelmsford, Ipswich, Luton, Maidstone, Norwich, Reading and St Albans.

(e) South Eastern Circuit (London only): Central Criminal Court, Woolwich, Kingston and Snaresbrook.

(f) Midland Circuit: Birmingham, Northampton, Nottingham and Leicester.

(g) Wales Circuit: Cardiff, Swansea and Caernarfon.

3M.7 The magistrates' courts designated for firearms deployment are: South Eastern Circuit (London only): Westminster Magistrates' Court and Belmarsh Magistrates' Court.

Preparatory work prior to applications in all cases

3M.8 Prior to the making of any application for armed transport of prisoners or the presence of **B-68** armed police officers in the court building, consideration must be given to making use of prison video link equipment to avoid the necessity of prisoners' attendance at court for the hearing in respect of which the application is to be made.

3M.9 Notwithstanding their designation, each requesting officer will attend the relevant court before an application is made to ensure that there have been no changes to the premises and that there are no circumstances that might affect security arrangements.

Applying in the Royal Courts of Justice

B-68a   **3M.10** All applications should be sent to the listing office of the division in which the case is due to appear. The application should be sent by email if possible and must be on the standard form.

3M.11 The listing office will notify the head of division, providing a copy of the email and any supporting evidence. The head of division may ask to see the senior police office [*sic*] concerned.

3M.12 The head of division will consider the application. If it is refused, the application fails and the police must be notified.

3M.13 In the absence of the head of division, the application should be considered by the vice-president of the division.

3M.14 The relevant court office will be notified of the decision and that office will immediately inform the police by telephone. The decision must then be confirmed in writing to the police.

Applying to the Crown Court

B-69   **3M.15** All applications should be sent to the cluster manager and should be sent by email if possible and must be on the standard form.

3M.16 The cluster manager will notify the presiding judge on the circuit and the resident judge by email, providing a copy of the form and any supporting evidence. The presiding judge may ask to see the senior police officer concerned.

3M.17 The presiding judge will consider the application. If it is refused the application fails and the police must be informed.

3M.18 If the presiding judge approves the application it should be forwarded to the secretary in the senior presiding judge's office. The senior presiding judge will make the final decision. The presiding judge will receive written confirmation of that decision.

3M.19 The presiding judge will notify the cluster manager and the resident judge of the decision. the cluster manager will immediately inform the police of the decision by telephone. The decision must then be confirmed in writing to the police.

Urgent applications to the Crown Court

B-70   **3M.20** If the temporary deployment of armed police arises as an urgent issue and a case would otherwise have to be adjourned; or if the trial judge is satisfied that there is a serious risk to public safety, then the resident judge will have a discretion to agree such deployment without having obtained the consent of a presiding judge or the senior presiding judge. In such a case:

   (a) the resident judge should assess the facts and agree the proposed solution with a police officer of at least superintendent level; that officer should agree the approach with the firearms division of the police;

   (b) if the proposed solution involves the use of armed police officers, the resident judge must try to contact the presiding judge and/or the senior presiding judge by email and telephone; the cluster manager should be informed of the situation;

   (c) if the resident judge cannot obtain a response from the presiding judge or the senior presiding judge, the resident judge may grant the application if satisfied:

       (i) that the application is necessary;

       (ii) that without such deployment there would be a significant risk to public safety; and

       (iii) that the case would have to be adjourned at significant difficulty or inconvenience.

3M.21 The resident judge must keep the position under continual review, to ensure that it remains appropriate and necessary. The resident judge must make continued efforts to contact the presiding judge and the senior presiding judge to notify them of the full circumstances of the authorisation.

Applying to the magistrates' courts

B-71   **3M.22** All applications should be directed, by email if possible, to the office of the Chief Magistrate, at Westminster Magistrates' Court and must be on the standard form.

3M.23 The Chief Magistrate should consider the application and, if approved, it should be forwarded to the senior presiding judge's office. The senior presiding judge will make the final decision. The Chief Magistrate will receive written confirmation of that decision and will then notify the requesting police officer and, where authorisation is given, the affected magistrates' court of the decision.

Urgent applications in the magistrates' courts

B-72   **3M.24** If the temporary deployment of armed police arises as an urgent issue and a case would otherwise have to be adjourned; or if the Chief Magistrate is satisfied that there is a serious risk to public safety, then the Chief Magistrate will have a discretion to agree such deployment without having obtained the consent of the senior presiding judge. In such a case:

(a) the Chief Magistrate should assess the facts and agree the proposed solution with a police officer of at least superintendent level; that officer should agree the approach with the firearms division of the police;

(b) if the proposed solution involves the use of armed police officers, the Chief Magistrate must try to contact the senior presiding judge by email and telephone; the cluster manager should be informed of the situation;

(c) if the Chief Magistrate cannot obtain a response from the senior presiding judge, the Chief Magistrate may grant the application if satisfied:

(i) that the application is necessary;

(ii) that without such deployment there would be a significant risk to public safety; and

(iii) that the case would have to be adjourned at significant difficulty or inconvenience.

3M.25 The Chief Magistrate must keep the position under continual review, to ensure that it remains appropriate and necessary. The Chief Magistrate must make continued efforts to contact the senior presiding judge to notify him of the full circumstances of the authorisation.

CPD I General matters 3N: Use of Live Link and Telephone Facilities (as inserted by Criminal Practice Directions 2015 (Amendment No. 3), unreported, January 31, 2017, Lord Thomas C.J.)

3N.1 Where it is lawful and in the interests of justice to do so, courts should exercise their statutory and other powers to conduct hearings by live link or telephone. This is consistent with the Criminal Procedure Rules and with the recommendations of the President of the Queen's Bench Division's *Review of Efficiency in Criminal Proceedings* published in January 2015. Save where legislation circumscribes the court's jurisdiction, the breadth of that jurisdiction is acknowledged by CrimPR 3.5(1), (2)(d). **B-72a**

3N.2 It is the duty of the court to make use of technology actively to manage the case: CrimPR 3.2(1), (2)(h). That duty includes an obligation to give directions for the use of live links and telephone facilities in the circumstances listed in CrimPR 3.2(4) and (5) (pre-trial hearings, including pre-trial case management hearings). Where the court directs that evidence is to be given by live link, and especially where such a direction is given on the court's own initiative, it is essential that the decision is communicated promptly to the witness: CrimPR 18.4. Contrary to a practice adopted by some courts, none of those rules or other provisions require the renewal of a live link direction merely because a trial has had to be postponed or adjourned. Once made, such a direction applies until it is discharged by the court, having regard to the relevant statutory criteria.

3N.3 It is the duty of the parties to alert the court to any reason why live links or telephones should not be used where CrimPR 3.2 otherwise would oblige the court to do so; and, where a direction for the use of such facilities has been made, it is the duty of the parties as soon as practicable to alert the court to any reason why that direction should be varied (CrimPR 3.3(2)(e) and 3.6).

3N.4 The word "appropriate" in CrimPR 3.2(4) and (5) is not a term of art. It has the ordinary English meaning of "fitting", or "suitable". Whether the facilities available to the court in any particular case can be considered appropriate is a matter for the court, but plainly to be appropriate such facilities must work, at the time at which they are required; all participants must be able to hear and, in the case of a live link, see each other clearly; and there must be no extraneous noise, movement or other distraction suffered by a participant, or transmitted by a participant to others. What degree of protection from accidental or deliberate interception should be considered appropriate will depend upon the purpose for which a live link or telephone is to be used. If it is to participate in a hearing which is open to the public anyway, then what is communicated by such means is by definition public and the use of links such as Skype or Facetime, which are not generally considered secure from interception, may not be objectionable. If it is to participate in a hearing in private, and especially one at which sensitive information will be discussed – for example, on an application for a search warrant – then a more secure service is likely to be required.

3N.5 There may be circumstances in which the court should not require the use of live link or telephone facilities despite their being otherwise appropriate at a pre-trial hearing. In every case, in deciding whether any such circumstances apply, the court will keep in mind that, for the purposes of what may be an essentially administrative hearing, it may be compatible with the overriding objective to proceed in the defendant's absence altogether, especially if he or she is represented, unless, exceptionally, a rule otherwise requires. The principle that the court always must consider proceeding in a defendant's absence is articulated in CrimPR 3.9(2)(a). Where at a pre-trial hearing bail may be under consideration, the provisions of CrimPR 14.2 will be relevant.

3N.6 Such circumstances will include any case in which the defendant's effective participation cannot be achieved by his or her attendance by such means, and CrimPR 3.2(4) and (5) except such cases from the scope of the obligation which that rule otherwise imposes on the court. That exception may apply where (this list is not exhaustive) the defendant has a disorder or disability, including a hearing, speech or sight impediment, or has communication needs to which the use of a live link or telephone is inimical (whether or not those needs are such as to require the appointment of an intermediary); or where the defendant requires interpretation and effective interpretation cannot be provided by live link or telephone, as the case may be.

3N.7 Finally, that exception sometimes may apply where the defendant's attendance in person at a pre-trial hearing will facilitate communication with his or her legal representatives. The court should not make such an exception merely to allow client and representatives to meet if that meeting can and should be held elsewhere. However, there will be cases in which defence representatives reasonably need to meet with a defendant, to take his or her instructions or to explain events to him or her, either shortly before or immediately after a pre-trial hearing and in circumstances in which that meeting cannot take place effectively by live link.

3N.8 Nothing prohibits the member or members of a court from conducting a pre-trial hearing by attending by live link or telephone from a location distant from all the other participants. Despite the conventional view that the venue for a court hearing is the court room in which that hearing has been arranged to take place, the Criminal Procedure Rules define "court" as "a tribunal with jurisdiction over criminal cases. It includes a judge, recorder, District Judge (Magistrates' Court), lay justice and, when exercising their judicial powers, the Registrar of Criminal Appeals, a justices' clerk or assistant clerk." Neither CrimPR 3.25 (place of trial), which applies in the Crown Court, nor CrimPR 24.14 (place of trial), which applies in magistrates' courts, each of which requires proceedings to take place in a courtroom provided by the Lord Chancellor, applies for the purposes of a pre-trial hearing. Thus for the purposes of such a hearing there is no legal obstacle to the judge, magistrate or magistrates conducting it from elsewhere, with other participants assembled in a courtroom from which the member or members of the court are physically absent. In principle, nothing prohibits the conduct of a pre-trial hearing by live link or telephone with each participant, including the member or members of the court, in a different location (an arrangement sometimes described as a "virtual hearing"). This is dependent upon there being means by which that hearing can be witnessed by the public – for example, by public attendance at a courtroom or other venue from which the participants all can be seen and heard (if by live link), or heard (if by telephone). The principle of open justice to which paragraph 3N.17 refers is relevant.

3N.9 Sections 57A to 57F of the CDA 1998 [§§ 3-226 *et seq.* in the main work] allow a defendant who is in custody to enter a plea by live link, and allow for such a defendant who attends by live link to be sentenced. In appropriate circumstances, the court may allow a defendant who is not in custody to enter a plea by live link; but the same considerations as apply to sentencing in such a case will apply: see para. 3N.13 beneath.

3N.10 The CDA 1998 does not allow for the attendance by live link at a contested trial of a defendant who is in custody. The court may allow a defendant who wishes to do so to observe all or part of his or her trial by live link, whether she or he is in custody or not, but (a) such a defendant cannot lawfully give evidence by such means unless he or she satisfies the criteria prescribed by section 33A of the YJCEA 1999 [*ibid.*, § 8-99] and the court so orders under that section (see also CrimPR 18.14 – 18.17); (b) a defendant who is in custody and who observes the trial by live link is not present, as a matter of law, and the trial must be treated as taking place in his or her absence, she or he having waived the right to attend; and (c) a defendant who has refused to attend his or her trial when required to do so, or who has absconded, must not be permitted to observe the proceedings by live link.

3N.11 Paragraphs I 3D to 3G inclusive of these practice directions (vulnerable people in the courts; ground rules hearings to plan the questioning of a vulnerable witness or defendant; intermediaries; vulnerable defendants) contain directions relevant to the use of a live link as a special measure for a young or otherwise vulnerable witness, or to facilitate the giving of evidence by a defendant who is likewise young or otherwise vulnerable, within the scope of the YJCEA 1999. Defence representatives and the court must keep in mind that special measures under the 1999 Act and CrimPR, Pt 18, including the use of a live link, are available to defence as well as to prosecution witnesses who meet the statutory criteria. Defence representatives should always consider whether their witnesses would benefit from giving evidence by live link and should apply for a direction if appropriate, either at the case management hearing or as soon as possible thereafter. A defence witness should be afforded the same facilities and treatment as a prosecution witness, including the same opportunity to make a pre-trial visit to the court building in order to familiarise himself or herself with it. Where a live link is sought as a special measure for a young or vulnerable witness or defendant, CrimPR 18.10 and 18.15 respectively require, among other things, that the applicant must identify someone to accompany that witness or defendant while they give evidence; must name the person, if possible; and must explain why that person would be an appropriate companion for that witness. The court must ensure that directions are given accordingly when ordering such a live link. Witness Service volunteers are available to support all witnesses, prosecution and defence, if required.

3N.12 Under sections 57A and 57D or 57E of the CDA 1998 [*ibid.*, §§ 3-226, 3-229, 3-230] the court may pass sentence on a defendant in custody who attends by live link. The court may allow a defendant who is not in custody and who wishes to attend his or her sentencing by live link to do so, and may receive representations (but not evidence) from her or him by such means. Factors of which the court will wish to take account in exercising its discretion include, in particular, the penalty likely to be imposed; the importance of ensuring that the explanations of sentence required by CrimPR 24.11(9), in magistrates' courts, and in the Crown Court by CrimPR 25.16(7), can be given satisfactorily, for the defendant, for other participants and for the public, including reporters; and the preferences of the maker of any victim personal statement which is to be read aloud or played pursuant to paragraph VII F.3(c) of these practice directions.

Youth defendants
3N.13 In the youth court or when a youth is appearing in the magistrates' court or the Crown Court, it will usually be appropriate for the youth to be produced in person at court. This is to ensure that the court can engage properly with the youth and that the necessary level of engagement can be facilitated with the youth offending team worker, defence representative and/or appropriate adult. The court should deal with any application for use of a live-link on a case-by-case basis, after consultation with the parties and the youth offending team. Such hearings that may be appropriate, include, onward remand hearings at which there is no bail application or case management hearings, particularly if the youth is already serving a custodial sentence. **B-72b**

3N.14 It rarely will be appropriate for a youth to be sentenced over a live link. However, notwithstanding the court's duties of engagement with a youth, the overriding welfare principle and the statutory responsibility of the youth offending worker to explain the sentence to the youth, after consultation with the parties and the youth offending team, there may be circumstances in which it may be appropriate to sentence a youth over the live-link:

(a) if the youth is already serving a custodial sentence and the sentence to be imposed by the court is bound to be a further custodial sentence, whether concurrent or consecutive;

(b) if the youth is already serving a custodial sentence and the court is minded to impose a non-custodial sentence which will have no material impact on the sentence being served;

(c) the youth is being detained in a secure establishment at such a distance from the court that the travelling time from one to the other will be significant so as to materially affect the welfare of the youth;

(d) the youth's condition - whether mental or otherwise - is so disturbed that his or her production would be a significant detriment to his or her welfare.

3N.15 Arrangements must be made in advance of any live link hearing to enable the youth offending worker to be at the secure establishment where the youth is in custody. In the event that such arrangements are not practicable, the youth offending worker must have sufficient access to the youth via the live link booth before and after the hearing.

Conduct of participants
3N.16 Where a live link is used, the immediate vicinity of the device by which a person attends becomes, temporarily, part of the courtroom for the purposes of that person's participation. That person, and any advocate or legal representative, custodian, court officer, intermediary or other companion, whether immediately visible to the court or not, becomes a participant for the purposes of CrimPR 1.2(2) and is subject to the court's jurisdiction to regulate behaviour in the courtroom. The substance and effect of this direction must be drawn to the attention of all such participants. **B-72c**

Open justice and records of proceedings
3N.17 The principle of open justice to which CrimPR 6.2(1) gives effect applies as strongly where electronic means of communication are used to conduct a hearing as it applies in other circumstances. Open justice is the principal means by which courts are kept under scrutiny by the public. It follows that where a participant attends a hearing in public by live link or telephone then that person's participation must be, as nearly as may be, equally audible and, if applicable, equally visible to the public as it would be were he or she physically present. Where electronic means of communication are used to conduct a hearing, records of the event must be maintained in the usual way: CrimPR 5.4. In the Crown Court, this includes the recording of the proceedings: CrimPR 5.5. **B-72d**

CPD I General matters: Annex: Guidance on Establishing and Using Live Link and Telephone Facilities for Criminal Court Hearings (as inserted by Criminal Practice Directions 2015 (Amendment No. 3), unreported, January 31, 2017, Lord Thomas C.J.)

1 This guidance supplements paragraph I 3N of these practice directions on the use of live link and telephone facilities to conduct a hearing or receive evidence in a criminal court. **B-72e**

2 This guidance deals with many of the practical considerations that arise in connection with setting up and using live link and telephone facilities. However, it does not contain detailed instructions about how to use particular live link or telephone equipment at particular locations (how to turn the equipment on; how, and exactly when, to establish a connection between the courtroom and the other location; *etc.*) because details vary from place to place and cannot practicably all be contained in general guidance. Those details will be made available locally to those who need them. Nor does this guidance contain detailed instructions about the individual responsibilities of court staff, police officers and prison staff because those are matters for court managers, chief constables and H.M. prison governors.

Installation of live link and telephone facilities in the courtroom

B-72f   **3** Everyone in the courtroom must be able to hear and, in the case of a live link, see clearly those who attend by live link or telephone; and the equipment in the courtroom must allow those who attend by live link or telephone to hear, and in the case of a live link see, all the participants in the courtroom. If more than one person is to attend by live link or telephone simultaneously then the equipment must be capable of accommodating them all. (These requirements of course are subject to any special or other measures which a court in an individual case may direct to prevent a witness seeing, or being seen by, the defendant or another participant, or members of the public.)

4 Some of the considerations that apply to the installation and use of equipment in other locations will apply in a courtroom, too. They are set out in the following paragraphs. In the case of a live link, attention will need to be given to lighting and to making sure that those attending by live link can see and hear clearly what takes place in the courtroom without being distracted by the movement of court staff, legal representatives or members of the public, or by noise inside the courtroom. The sensitivity and positioning of the courtroom microphones may mean that even the movement of papers, or the operation of keyboards, while barely audible inside the courtroom itself, is clearly audible and distracting to a witness or defendant attending by live link or telephone.

Installation and use of live link and telephone facilities in a live link room

B-72g   **5** Paragraph 6 applies to the installation and use of equipment in a building or in a vehicle which is to be used regularly for giving evidence by live link. It applies to a room within the court building, but separated from the courtroom itself, from which a witness can give evidence by live link; it applies to such a room at a police station or elsewhere which has been set aside for regular use for such a purpose; and it applies to a van or other vehicle which has been adapted for use as a mobile live link room. However, that paragraph does not apply to the courtroom itself; it does not apply to a place from which a witness gives evidence, or a participant takes part in the proceedings, by live link or telephone, if that place is not regularly used for such a purpose (but see para. 7 beneath); and it does not apply in a prison or other place of detention (as to which, see para. 12 beneath). The objective is to ensure that anyone who participates by live link or telephone is conscious of the gravity of the occasion and of the authority of the court, and realises that they are required to conduct themselves in the same respectful manner as if they were physically present in a courtroom.

6 A live link room should have the following features:

    (a) the room should be an appropriate size, neither too small nor too large;

    (b) the room should have suitable lighting, whether natural or electric; any windows may need blinds or curtains fitted that can be adjusted in accordance with the weather conditions outside and to ensure privacy;

    (c) there should be a sign or other means of making clear to those outside the room when the room is in use;

    (d) arrangements should be made to ensure that nobody in the vicinity of the room is able to hear the evidence being given inside, unless the court otherwise directs (for example, to allow a witness's family to watch the witness's evidence on a supplementary screen in a nearby waiting room, as if they were seeing and hearing that evidence by live link in the courtroom);

    (e) arrangements should be made to minimise the risk of disruption to the proceedings by noise outside the room; such noise will distract the witness and may be audible and distracting to the court;

    (f) the room should be provided with appropriate and comfortable seating for the witness and, where the witness is a civilian witness, seating for a Witness Service or other companion; a waiting area/room adjacent to the live link room may be required for any other persons attending with the witness; there must be adequate accommodation, support and, where appropriate, security within the premises for witnesses; if both prosecution and defence witnesses attend the same facility, they should wait in separate rooms; it may be inappropriate for defence witnesses to give evidence in police premises (for example in a trial for assaulting a police officer) and in that case parties and the court should identify an alternative venue such as a court building (not necessarily the location of the hearing), or arrange for evidence to be given from elsewhere by Skype, *etc*; care must be taken to ensure that all witnesses, whether prosecution or defence, are afforded the same assistance, respect and security;

(g) the equipment installed (monitor, microphone and camera, or cameras) in the room must be good enough to ensure that both the picture and sound quality from the room to the court, and from the court to the room, is fit for purpose; the link must enable all in the courtroom to see and hear the witness clearly and it must enable the witness to see and hear clearly all participants in the courtroom;

(h) unless the court otherwise directs, the witness usually will sit to take the oath or affirm and to give evidence; the camera(s) must be positioned to ensure that the witness's face and demeanour can be seen whether he or she sits or stands;

(i) the wall behind the witness, and thus in view of the camera, should be a pale neutral colour (beige and light green/blue are most suitable) and there should be no pictures or notices displayed on that wall;

(j) the royal coat of arms may be displayed to remind witnesses and others that when in use the room is part of the courtroom;

(k) a notice should be displayed that reminds users of the live link to conduct themselves in the same manner as if they were present in person in the courtroom, and to remind them that while using the live link they are subject to the court's jurisdiction to regulate behaviour in the courtroom;

(l) the room should be supplied with the same oath and affirmation cards and holy books as are available in a courtroom; the guidance for the taking of oaths and the making of affirmations which applies in a courtroom applies equally in a live link room; holy books must be treated with the utmost respect and stored with appropriate care;

(m) unless court or other staff are on hand to operate the live link or telephone equipment, clear instructions for users must be in the live link room explaining how, and when, to establish a connection to the courtroom.

Provision and use of live link and telephone facilities elsewhere

7 Where a witness gives evidence by live link, or a participant takes part in proceedings by live link **B-72h** or telephone, otherwise than from an established live link room, the objective remains the same as explained in paragraph 5 above. In accordance with that objective, the spirit of the requirements for a live link room should be followed as far as is reasonably practicable; but of course the court will not expect adherence to the letter of those requirements where, for example, a witness who is seriously ill but still able to testify is willing to do so from his or her sick bed, or a doctor or other expert witness is to testify by live link from her or his office. In any such case it is essential that the parties anticipate the arrangements and directions that may be required. Of particular and obvious importance is the need for arrangements that will exclude audible and visible interruptions during the proceedings, and the need for adequate clarity of communication between the remote location and the courtroom.

Conduct of hearings by live link or telephone

8 Before live link or telephone equipment is to be used to conduct a hearing, court staff must **B-72i** make sure that the equipment is in working order and that the essential criteria listed in paragraph I 3N.4 of the practice directions ("appropriate" facilities) are met.

9 If a witness who gives evidence by live link produces exhibits, the court must be asked to give appropriate directions during preparation for trial. In most cases the parties can be expected to agree the identity of the exhibit, whatever else is in dispute. In the absence of agreement, documentary exhibits, copies of which have been provided under CrimPR 24.13 (magistrates' court trial) or CrimPR 25.17 (Crown Court trial), and other exhibits which are clearly identifiable by reference to their features and which have been delivered by someone else to the court, may be capable of production by a witness who is using a live link.

10 Where a witness who gives evidence by live link is likely to be referred to exhibits or other material while he or she does so, whether or not as the producer of an exhibit, the court must be asked to give directions during preparation for trial to facilitate such a reference: for example, by requiring the preparation of a paginated and indexed trial bundle which will be readily accessible to the witness, on paper or in electronic form, as well as available to those who are in the courtroom. It is particularly important to make sure that documents and images which are to be displayed by electronic means in the courtroom will be accessible to the witness too. It is unlikely that the live link equipment will be capable of displaying sufficiently clearly to the witness images displayed only on a screen in the courtroom; and likely to be necessary to arrange for those images to be displayed also at the location from which the witness gives evidence, or made available to him or her by some other means. It is likewise important that there should be readily accessible to the witness, on paper or in electronic form, a copy of his or her witness statement (to which she or he may be referred under CrimPR 24.4(5), in a magistrates' court, or under CrimPR 25.11(5), in the Crown Court) and transcript of his or her ABE interview, if applicable.

Conduct of those attending by live link or telephone: practical considerations

B-72j

11 A person who gives evidence by live link, or who participates by live link or telephone, must behave exactly as if he or she were in the courtroom, addressing the court and the other participants in the proper manner and observing the appropriate social conventions, remembering that she or he will be heard, and if using a live link seen, as if physically present. A practical application of the rules and social conventions governing a participant's behaviour requires, among other things, the following:

    (i) in the case of a professional participant, including a police officer, lawyer or expert witness:

        (a) a participant should prepare themselves to communicate with the court with adequate time in hand, and especially where it will be necessary first to establish the live link or telephone connection with the court;

        (b) on entering a live link room a participant should ensure that those outside are made aware that the room is in use, to avoid being interrupted while in communication with the court

        (c) a participant should ensure that they have the means to communicate with court staff by some means other than the proposed live link or telephone equipment, in case the equipment they plan to use should fail; they should have to hand an alternative contact number for the court and, if using a mobile phone for the purpose, they should ensure that it is fully charged;

        (d) immediately before using the live link or telephone equipment to communicate with the court the person using that equipment and any other person in the live link room must as a general rule switch off any mobile telephone or other device which might interfere with that equipment or interrupt the proceedings; if the device is essential to giving evidence (for example, an electronic notebook), or if it is the only available means of communication with court staff should the other equipment fail, then every effort must be made to minimise the risk of interference, for example by switching a mobile telephone to silent and by placing electronic devices at a distance from the microphone;

        (e) a person who gives evidence by live link, or who takes part in the proceedings for some other purpose by live link, must dress as they would if attending by physical presence in the courtroom;

        (f) each person in a live link room, whether he or she can be seen by the court or not, and each person present where a telephone conference or loudspeaker facility is in use, must identify themselves clearly to the court;

        (g) a person who participates by telephone otherwise than from a room specially equipped for that purpose must take care to ensure that they cannot be interrupted while in communication with the court and that no extraneous noise will be audible so as to distract that participant or the court;

        (h) a person who participates by telephone in a call to which he or she, the court and others all contribute must take care to speak clearly and to avoid interrupting in such a way as to prevent any other participant hearing what is said; particular care is required where a participant uses a hands-free or other loudspeaker phone;

        (i) a witness who gives evidence by live link may take with him or her into the live link room a copy of her or his written witness statement and (if a police officer) his or her notebook; while giving evidence the witness must place the statement or notes face down, or otherwise out of sight, unless the court gives permission to refer to it; the witness must take the statement or notes away when leaving the live link room;

        (j) where successive witnesses are due to give evidence about the same events by live link, and especially where they are due to do so from the same live link room; where the events in question are controversial; or where there is any suggestion that arrangements are required to guard against the accidental or deliberate contamination of a witness's evidence by communication with one who has already given evidence, then the court must be asked to give directions accordingly; subject to those directions, the usual arrangement should be that a witness who has been released should remain in sight of the court, by means of the live link, in the live link room while the next witness enters, and then should leave, so that the court will be able to see that no inappropriate communication between the two has occurred;

(ii) in the case of any other participant:

    (a) the preparation of any live link room and the use of the equipment will be the responsibility of court staff, or of the staff present at that live link room if it is outside the court building; where the participant is a witness giving evidence pursuant to a special measures direction, detailed arrangements will have been made accordingly;

    (b) mobile telephones and other devices that might interfere with the live link or telephone equipment must be switched off;

    (c) a witness or other participant should take care to speak clearly and to avoid interrupting or making a sound which prevents another participant hearing what is said, especially where a hands-free or other loudspeaker phone is in use;

    (d) the party who calls a witness, or the witness supporter, or court or other staff, as the case may be, must supply the witness with all he or she may need for the purpose of giving evidence, in accordance with the relevant rules and practice directions; this may, and usually will, include a copy of the witness's statement, in case it becomes necessary to ask him or her to refer to it, and copies of any exhibits or other material to which he or she may be asked to refer: see also para. 10 above.

Prison to court video links

12 The objective of the guidance in the preceding paragraphs applies. It is essential that the authority and gravity of the proceedings is respected, by defendants and by their custodians. Detailed instructions are contained in the information issued jointly by the National Offender Management Service and by H.M. Courts and Tribunals Service, with which prison and court staff must familiarise themselves. The principles set out in that guidance correspond with those of the criminal practice directions, as elaborated in this guidance.   **B-72k**

13 Where a defendant in custody attends court by live link it is likely that he or she will need to communicate with his or her representatives before and after the hearing, using the live link or by telephone. Arrangements will be required to allow that to take place.

14 Court staff are reminded that a live link to a prison establishment is a means of communication with the defendant. It does not provide an alternative means of formal communication with that establishment and it may not be used in substitution for service on that establishment of those notices and orders required to be served by the Criminal Procedure Rules.

Criminal Procedure Rules 2015 (S.I. 2015 No. 1490), Pt 4

When this Part applies

4.1.–(1) The rules in this Part apply—   **B-73**

    (a) to the service of every document in a case to which these rules apply; and

    (b) for the purposes of section 12 of the Road Traffic Offenders Act 1988, to the service of a requirement to which that section applies.

(2) The rules apply subject to any special rules in other legislation (including other parts of these rules) or in the Practice Direction.

Methods of service

4.2.–(1) A document may be served by any of the methods described in rules 4.3 to 4.6 (subject to rules 4.7 and 4.10), or in rule 4.8.   **B-74**

(2) Where a document may be served by electronic means under rule 4.6, the general rule is that the person serving it must use that method.

Service by handing over a document

4.3.–(1) A document may be served on—   **B-75**

    (a) an individual by handing it to him or her;

    (b) a corporation by handing it to a person holding a senior position in that corporation;

    (c) an individual or corporation who is legally represented in the case by handing it to that legal representative;

    (d) the prosecution by handing it to the prosecutor or to the prosecution representative;

    (e) the court officer by handing it to a court officer with authority to accept it at the relevant court office; and

    (f) the Registrar of Criminal Appeals by handing it to a court officer with authority to accept it at the Criminal Appeal Office.

(2) If an individual is under 18, a copy of a document served under paragraph (1)(a) must be handed to his or her parent, or another appropriate adult, unless no such person is readily available.

(3) Unless the court otherwise directs, for the purposes of paragraph (1)(c) or (d) (service by handing a document to a party's representative) "representative" includes an advocate appearing for that party at a hearing.

(4) In this rule, "the relevant court office" means—

    (a) in relation to a case in a magistrates' court or in the Crown Court, the office at which that court's business is administered by court staff;

    (b) in relation to an application to a High Court judge for permission to serve a draft indictment

        (i) in London, the Listing Officer of the Queen's Bench Division of the High Court, and

        (ii) elsewhere, the office at which court staff administer the business of any court then constituted of a High Court judge;

    (c) in relation to an extradition appeal case in the High Court, the Administrative Court Office of the Queen's Bench Division of the High Court.

[This rule is printed as amended by the Criminal Procedure (Amendment) Rules 2016 (S.I. 2016 No. 120).]

Service by leaving or posting a document

B-76   **4.4.**–(1) A document may be served by addressing it to the person to be served and leaving it at the appropriate address for service under this rule, or by sending it to that address by first class post or by the equivalent of first class post.

(2) The address for service under this rule on—

    (a) an individual is an address where it is reasonably believed that he or she will receive it;

    (b) a corporation is its principal office, and if there is no readily identifiable principal office then any place where it carries on its activities or business;

    (c) an individual or corporation who is legally represented in the case is that legal representative's office;

    (d) the prosecution is the prosecutor's office;

    (e) the court officer is the relevant court office; and

    (f) the Registrar of Criminal Appeals is the Criminal Appeal Office, Royal Courts of Justice, Strand, London WC2A 2LL.

(3) In this rule, "the relevant court office" means—

    (a) in relation to a case in a magistrates' court or in the Crown Court, the office at which that court's business is administered by court staff;

    (b) in relation to an application to a High Court judge for permission to serve a draft indictment—

        (i) in London, the Queen's Bench Listing Office, Royal Courts of Justice, Strand, London WC2A 2LL, and

        (ii) elsewhere, the office at which court staff administer the business of any court then constituted of a High Court judge;

    (c) in relation to an extradition appeal case in the High Court, the Administrative Court Office, Royal Courts of Justice, Strand, London WC2A 2LL.

[This rule is printed as amended by the Criminal Procedure (Amendment) Rules 2016 (S.I. 2016 No. 120).]

Service by document exchange

B-77   **4.5.**–(1) This rule applies where—

    (a) the person to be served—

        (i) has given a document exchange (DX) box number, and

        (ii) has not refused to accept service by DX; or

    (b) the person to be served is legally represented in the case and the legal representative has given a DX box number.

(2) A document may be served by—

    (a) addressing it to that person or legal representative, as appropriate, at that DX box number; and

    (b) leaving it at—

        (i)   the document exchange at which the addressee has that DX box number, or

        (ii) a document exchange at which the person serving it has a DX box number.

Service by electronic means

B-78

    4.6.–(1) This rule applies where—

    (a) the person to be served—

        (i)   has given an electronic address and has not refused to accept service at that address, or

        (ii) is given access to an electronic address at which a document may be deposited and has not refused to accept service by the deposit of a document at that address; or

    (b) the person to be served is legally represented in the case and the legal representative—

        (i)   has given an electronic address, or

        (ii) is given access to an electronic address at which a document may be deposited.

    (2) A document may be served—

    (a) by sending it by electronic means to the address which the recipient has given; or

    (b) by depositing it at an address to which the recipient has been given access and—

        (i)   in every case, making it possible for the recipient to read the document, or view or listen to its content, as the case may be,

        (ii) unless the court otherwise directs, making it possible for the recipient to make and keep an electronic copy of the document, and

        (iii) notifying the recipient of the deposit of the document (which notice may be given by electronic means).

    (3) Where a document is served under this rule the person serving it need not provide a paper copy as well.

Documents that must be served by specified methods

B-79

    4.7.–(1) An application or written statement, and notice, under rule 48.9 alleging contempt of court may be served—

    (a) on an individual, only under rule 4.3(1)(a) (by handing it to him or her);

    (b) on a corporation, only under rule 4.3(1)(b) (by handing it to a person holding a senior position in that corporation).

    (2) For the purposes of section 12 of the Road Traffic Offenders Act 1988, a notice of a requirement under section 172 of the Road Traffic Act 1988 [§ 32-185 in the main work] or under section 112 of the Road Traffic Regulation Act 1984 to identify the driver of a vehicle may be served—

    (a) on an individual, only by post under rule 4.4(1) and (2)(a);

    (b) on a corporation, only by post under rule 4.4(1) and (2)(b).

Service by person in custody

B-80

    4.8.–(1) A person in custody may serve a document by handing it to the custodian addressed to the person to be served.

    (2) The custodian must—

    (a) endorse it with the time and date of receipt;

    (b) record its receipt; and

    (c) forward it promptly to the addressee.

Service by another method

B-81

    4.9.–(1) The court may allow service of a document by a method—

    (a) other than those described in rules 4.3 to 4.6 and in rule 4.8;

    (b) other than one specified by rule 4.7, where that rule applies.

    (2) An order allowing service by another method must specify—

    (a) the method to be used; and

    (b) the date on which the document will be served.

Documents that may not be served on a legal representative

B-82

    4.10. Unless the court otherwise directs, service on a party's legal representative of any of the following documents is not service of that document on that party—

(a) a summons, requisition, single justice procedure notice or witness summons;

(b) notice of an order under section 25 of the Road Traffic Offenders Act 1988;

(c) a notice of registration under section 71(6) of that Act;

(d) notice of a hearing to review the postponement of the issue of a warrant of detention or imprisonment under section 77(6) of the Magistrates' Courts Act 1980;

(e) notice under section 86 of that Act of a revised date to attend a means inquiry;

(f) any notice or document served under Part 14 (bail and custody time limits);

(g) notice under rule 24.16(a) of when and where an adjourned hearing will resume;

(h) notice under rule 28.5(3) of an application to vary or discharge a compensation order;

(i) notice under rule 28.10(2)(c) of the location of the sentencing or enforcing court;

(j) a collection order, or notice requiring payment, served under rule 30.2(a); or

(k) an application or written statement, and notice, under rule 48.9 alleging contempt of court.

Date of service

B-83   **4.11.**–(1) A document served under rule 4.3 or rule 4.8 is served on the day it is handed over.

(2) Unless something different is shown, a document served on a person by any other method is served–

(a) in the case of a document left at an address, on the next business day after the day on which it was left;

(b) in the case of a document sent by first class post or by the equivalent of first class post, on the second business day after the day on which it was posted or despatched;

(c) in the case of a document served by document exchange, on the second business day after the day on which it was left at a document exchange allowed by rule 4.5;

(d) in the case of a document served by electronic means–

(i) on the day on which it is sent under rule 4.6(2)(a), if that day is a business day and if it is sent by no later than 2.30 p.m. that day,

(ii) on the day on which notice of its deposit is given under rule 4.6(2)(b), if that day is a business day and if that notice is given by no later than 2.30pm that day, or

(iii) otherwise, on the next business day after it was sent or such notice was given; and

(e) in any case, on the day on which the addressee responds to it, if that is earlier.

(3) Unless something different is shown, a document produced by a computer system for dispatch by post is to be taken as having been sent by first class post, or by the equivalent of first class post, to the addressee on the business day after the day on which it was produced.

(4) Where a document is served on or by the court officer, "business day" does not include a day on which the court offce is closed.

Proof of service

B-84   **4.12.** The person who serves a document may prove that by signing a certificate explaining how and when it was served.

Court's power to give directions about service

B-85   **4.13.**–(1) The court may specify the time as well as the date by which a document must be–

(a) served under rule 4.3 (service by handing over a document) or rule 4.8 (service by person in custody); or

(b) sent or deposited by electronic means, if it is served under rule 4.6.

(2) The court may treat a document as served if the addressee responds to it even if it was not served in accordance with the rules in this Part.

Criminal Procedure Rules 2015 (S.I. 2015 No. 1490), Pt 5

FORMS AND COURT RECORDS

Forms

Applications, etc. by forms or electronic means

B-86   **5.1.**–(1) This rule applies where a rule, a practice direction or the court requires a person to–

(a) make an application or give a notice;

(b) supply information for the purposes of case management by the court; or

(c) supply information needed for other purposes by the court.

(2) Unless the court otherwise directs, such a person must—

    (a) use such electronic arrangements as the court officer may make for that purpose, in accordance with those arrangements; or

    (b) if no such arrangements have been made, use the appropriate form set out in the Practice Direction or the Criminal Costs Practice Direction, in accordance with those directions.

Forms in Welsh

5.2.—(1) Any Welsh language form set out in the Practice Direction, or in the Criminal Costs   **B-87** Practice Direction, is for use in connection with proceedings in courts in Wales.

(2) Both a Welsh form and an English form may be contained in the same document.

(3) Where only a Welsh form, or only the corresponding English form, is served—

    (a) the following words in Welsh and English must be added: "Darperir y ddogfen hon yn Gymraeg / Saesneg os bydd arnoch ei heisiau. Dylech wneud cais yn ddi-oed i (swyddog y llys) (rhodder yma'r cyfeiriad) This document will be provided in Welsh / English if you require it. You should apply immediately to (the court officer) (address)"; and

    (b) the court officer, or the person who served the form, must, on request, supply the corresponding form in the other language to the person served.

Signature of forms

5.3.—(1) This rule applies where a form provides for its signature.   **B-88**

(2) Unless other legislation otherwise requires, or the court otherwise directs, signature may be by any written or electronic authentication of the form by, or with the authority of, the signatory.

Court records

Duty to make records

5.4.—(1) For each case, as appropriate, the court officer must record, by such means as the Lord   **B-89** Chancellor directs—

    (a) each charge or indictment against the defendant;

    (b) the defendant's plea to each charge or count;

    (c) each acquittal, conviction, sentence, determination, direction or order;

    (d) each decision about bail;

    (e) the power exercised where the court commits or adjourns the case to another court—

        (i) for sentence, or

        (ii) for the defendant to be dealt with for breach of a community order, a deferred sentence, a conditional discharge, or a suspended sentence of imprisonment, imposed by that other court;

    (f) the court's reasons for a decision, where legislation requires those reasons to be recorded;

    (g) any appeal;

    (h) each party's presence or absence at each hearing;

    (i) any consent that legislation requires before the court can proceed with the case, or proceed to a decision;

    (j) in a magistrates' court—

        (i) any indication of sentence given in connection with the allocation of a case for trial, and

        (ii) the registration of a fixed penalty notice for enforcement as a fine, and any related endorsement on a driving record;

    (k) in the Crown Court, any request for assistance or other communication about the case received from a juror;

    (l) the identity of—

        (i) the prosecutor,

        (ii) the defendant,

        (iii) any other applicant to whom these rules apply,

        (iv) any interpreter or intermediary,

        (v) the parties' legal representatives, if any, and

        (vi) the judge, magistrate or magistrates, justices' legal adviser or other person who made each recorded decision;

    (m) where a defendant is entitled to attend a hearing, any agreement by the defendant to waive that right; and

(n) where interpretation is required for a defendant, any agreement by that defendant to do without the written translation of a document.

(2) Such records must include—

(a) each party's and representative's address, including any electronic address and telephone number available;

(b) the defendant's date of birth, if available; and

(c) the date of each event and decision recorded.

Recording and transcription of proceedings in the Crown Court

B-90   5.5.–(1) Where someone may appeal to the Court of Appeal, the court officer must—

(a) arrange for the recording of the proceedings in the Crown Court, unless the court otherwise directs; and

(b) arrange for the transcription of such a recording if—

   (i) the Registrar wants such a transcript, or

   (ii) anyone else wants such a transcript (but that is subject to the restrictions in paragraph (2)).

(2) Unless the court otherwise directs, a person who transcribes a recording of proceedings under such arrangements—

(a) must not supply anyone other than the Registrar with a transcript of a recording of—

   (i) a hearing in private, or

   (ii) information to which reporting restrictions apply;

(b) subject to that, must supply any person with any transcript for which that person asks—

   (i) in accordance with the transcription arrangements made by the court officer, and

   (ii) on payment by that person of any fee prescribed.

(3) A party who wants to hear a recording of proceedings must—

(a) apply—

   (i) in writing to the Registrar, if an appeal notice has been served where Part 36 applies (appeal to the Court of Appeal: general rules), or

   (ii) orally or in writing to the Crown Court officer;

(b) explain the reasons for the request; and

(c) pay any fee prescribed.

(4) If the Crown Court or the Registrar so directs, the Crown Court officer must allow that party to hear a recording of—

(a) a hearing in public;

(b) a hearing in private, if the applicant was present at that hearing.

Custody of case materials

B-91   5.6. Unless the court otherwise directs, in respect of each case the court officer may—

(a) keep any evidence, application, representation or other material served by the parties; or

(b) arrange for the whole or any part to be kept by some other appropriate person, subject to—

   (i) any condition imposed by the court, and

   (ii) the rules in Part 34 (appeal to the Crown Court) and Part 36 (appeal to the Court of Appeal: general rules) about keeping exhibits pending any appeal.

Supply to a party of information or documents from records or case materials

B-92   5.7.–(1) This rule applies where—

(a) a party wants information, or a copy of a document, from records or case materials kept by the court officer (for example, in case of loss, or to establish what is retained); or

(b) a person affected by an order made, or warrant issued, by the court wants such information or such a copy.

(2) Such a party must—

(a) apply to the court officer;

(b) specify the information or document required; and

(c) pay any fee prescribed.

(3) The application—

(a) may be made orally, giving no reasons, if paragraph (4) requires the court officer to supply the information or document requested;

(b) must be in writing, unless the court otherwise permits, and must explain for what purpose the information is required, in any other case.

(4) The court officer must supply to the applicant party or person—

  (a) a copy of any document served by, or on, that party or person (but not of any document not so served);

  (b) by word of mouth, or in writing, as requested—

    (i) information that was received from that party or person in the first place,

    (ii) information about the terms of any direction or order directed to that party or person, or made on an application by that party or person, or at a hearing in public,

    (iii) information about the outcome of the case.

(5) If the court so permits, the court officer must supply to the applicant party or person, by word of mouth or in writing, as requested, information that paragraph (4) does not require the court officer to supply.

(6) Where the information requested is about the grounds on which an order was made, or a warrant was issued, in the absence of the party or person applying for that information—

  (a) that party or person must also serve the request on the person who applied for the order or warrant;

  (b) if the person who applied for the order or warrant objects to the supply of the information requested, that objector must—

    (i) give notice of the objection not more than 14 days after service of the request (or within any longer period allowed by the court),

    (ii) serve that notice on the court officer and on the party or person requesting the information, and

    (iii) if the objector wants a hearing, explain why one is needed;

  (c) the court may determine the application for information at a hearing (which must be in private unless the court otherwise directs), or without a hearing;

  (d) the court must not permit the information requested to be supplied unless the person who applied for the order or warrant has had at least 14 days (or any longer period allowed by the court) in which to make representations.

(7) A notice of objection under paragraph (6) must explain—

  (a) whether the objection is to the supply of any part of the information requested, or only to the supply of a specified part, or parts, of it;

  (b) whether the objection is to the supply of the information at any time, or only to its supply before a date or event specified by the objector; and

  (c) the grounds of the objection.

(8) Where a notice of objection under paragraph (6) includes material that the objector thinks ought not be revealed to the party or person applying for information, the objector must—

  (a) omit that material from the notice served on that party or person;

  (b) mark the material to show that it is only for the court; and

  (c) with that material include an explanation of why it has been withheld.

(9) Where paragraph (8) applies—

  (a) a hearing of the application may take place, wholly or in part, in the absence of the party or person applying for information;

  (b) at any such hearing, the general rule is that the court must consider, in the following sequence—

    (i) representations first by the party or person applying for information and then by the objector, in the presence of both, and then

    (ii) further representations by the objector, in the absence of that party or person but the court may direct other arrangements for the hearing.

Supply to the public, including reporters, of information about cases

  5.8.—(1) This rule—   **B-93**

  (a) applies where a member of the public, including a reporter, wants information about a case from the court officer;

  (b) requires the court officer to publish information about cases due to be heard.

(2) A person who wants information about a case from the court officer must—

  (a) apply to the court officer;

  (b) specify the information requested; and

  (c) pay any fee prescribed.

(3) [*Identical to r.5.7(3), ante, § B-92.*]

(4) The court officer must supply to the applicant—

    (a) any information listed in paragraph (6), if—

        (i) the information is available to the court officer,

        (ii) the supply of the information is not prohibited by a reporting restriction, and

        (iii) the trial has not yet concluded, or the verdict was not more than 6 months ago; and

    (b) details of any reporting or access restriction ordered by the court.

(5) The court officer must supply that information—

    (a) by word of mouth; or

    (b) by such other arrangements as the Lord Chancellor directs.

(6) The information that paragraph (4) requires the court officer to supply is—

    (a) the date of any hearing in public, unless any party has yet to be notified of that date;

    (b) each alleged offence and any plea entered;

    (c) the court's decision at any hearing in public, including any decision about—

        (i) bail, or

        (ii) the committal, sending or transfer of the case to another court;

    (d) whether the case is under appeal;

    (e) the outcome of any trial and any appeal; and

    (f) the identity of—

        (i) the prosecutor,

        (ii) the defendant,

        (iii) the parties' representatives, including their addresses, and

        (iv) the judge, magistrate or magistrates, or justices' legal adviser by whom a decision at a hearing in public was made.

(7) If the court so directs, the court officer must—

    (a) supply to the applicant, by word of mouth, other information about the case; or

    (b) allow the applicant to inspect or copy a document, or part of a document, containing information about the case.

(8) The court may determine an application to which paragraph (7) applies—

    (a) at a hearing, in public or in private; or

    (b) without a hearing.

(9) The court officer must publish the information listed in paragraph (11) if—

    (a) the information is available to the court officer;

    (b) the hearing to which the information relates is due to take place in public; and

    (c) the publication of the information is not prohibited by a reporting restriction.

(10) The court officer must publish that information—

    (a) by notice displayed somewhere prominent in the vicinity of the court room in which the hearing is due to take place;

    (b) by such other arrangements as the Lord Chancellor directs, including arrangements for publication by electronic means; and

    (c) for no longer than 2 business days.

(11) The information that paragraph (9) requires the court officer to publish is—

    (a) the date, time and place of the hearing;

    (b) the identity of the defendant; and

    (c) such other information as it may be practicable to publish concerning—

        (i) the type of hearing,

        (ii) the identity of the court,

        (iii) the offence or offences alleged, and

        (iv) whether any reporting restriction applies.

Supply of written certificate or extract from records

B-94   **5.9.**–(1) This rule applies where legislation—

    (a) allows a certificate of conviction or acquittal, or an extract from records kept by the court officer, to be introduced in evidence in criminal proceedings; or

    (b) requires such a certificate or extract to be supplied by the court officer to a specified person for a specified purpose.

(2) A person who wants such a certificate or extract must—

    (a) apply in writing to the court officer;

    (b) specify the certificate or extract required;

    (c) explain under what legislation and for what purpose it is required; and

(d) pay any fee prescribed.

(3) If the application satisfies the requirements of that legislation, the court officer must supply the certificate or extract requested—

(a) to a party;

(b) unless the court otherwise directs, to any other applicant.

CPD I General Matters 5A: Forms

5A.1 The forms at Annex D to the *Consolidated Criminal Practice Direction* [2002] 1 W.L.R. 2870, or **B-95** forms to that effect, are to be used in the criminal courts, in accordance with rule 5.1.

5A.2 The forms at Annex E to that practice direction, the case management forms, must be used in the criminal courts, in accordance with that rule.

5A.3 The table at the beginning of each of those annexes lists the forms and:

(a) shows the rule in connection with which each applies;

(b) describes each form.

5A.4 The forms may be amended or withdrawn from time to time, or new forms added, under the authority of the Lord Chief Justice.

CPD I General Matters 5B: Access to Information Held by the Court

5B.1 Open justice, as Toulson L.J. ... reiterated in ... *R. (Guardian News and Media Ltd) v. City of* **B-96** *Westminster Magistrates' Court (Article 19 intervening); Guardian News and Media Ltd v. Government of the United States of America* [§ 2-185 in the main work], is a "principle at the heart of our system of justice and vital to the rule of law." There are exceptions but these "have to be justified by some even more important principle." However, the practical application of that undisputed principle, and the proper balancing of conflicting rights and principles, call for careful judgments to be made. The following is intended to provide some assistance to courts making decisions when asked to provide the public, including journalists, with access to or copies of information and documents held by the court. It is not a prescriptive list, as the court will have to consider all the circumstances of each individual case.

5B.2 It remains the responsibility of the recipient of information or documents to ensure that they comply with any and all restrictions such as reporting restrictions (see Pt 16 and the accompanying practice direction).

5B.3 For the purposes of this direction, the word document includes images in photographic, digital including DVD format, video, CCTV or any other form.

5B.4 Certain information can and should be provided to the public on request, unless there are restrictions, such as reporting restrictions, imposed in that particular case. Rule 5.8(4) and (6) read together specify the information that the court officer will supply to the public; an oral application is acceptable and no reason need be given for the request. There is no requirement for the court officer to consider the non-disclosure provisions of the Data Protection Act 1998 as the exemption under section 35 applies to all disclosure made under "any enactment ... or by the order of a court", which includes under the Criminal Procedure Rules.

5B.5 If the information sought is not listed at rule 5.8(6), rule 5.8(7) will apply, and the provision of information is at the discretion of the court. The following guidance is intended to assist the court in exercising that discretion.

5B.6 A request for access to documents used in a criminal case should first be addressed to the party who presented them to the court. Prosecuting authorities are subject to the Freedom of Information Act 2000 and the Data Protection Act 1998 and their decisions are susceptible to review.

5B.7 If the request is from a journalist or media organisation, note that there is a protocol between ACPO, the CPS and the media entitled "Publicity and the Criminal Justice System": http://www.cps. gov.uk/publications/agencies/mediaprotocol.html. There is additionally a protocol made under rule 5.8(5)(b) between the media and HMCTS: http://www.newspapersoc.org.uk/sites/default/files/Doc s/Protocol-for-Sharing-Court-Registers-and-Court-Lists-with-Local-Newspapers_September-2011.doc. This practice direction does not affect the operation of those protocols. Material should generally be sought under the relevant protocol before an application is made to the court.

5B.8 An application to which rule 5.8(7) applies must be made in accordance with rule 5.8; it must be in writing, unless the court permits otherwise, and "must explain for what purpose the information is required." A clear, detailed application, specifying the name and contact details of the applicant, whether or not he ... represents a media organisation, and setting out the reasons for the application and to what use the information will be put, will be of most assistance to the court. Applicants should state if they have requested the information under a protocol and include any reasons given for the refusal. Before considering such an application, the court will expect the applicant to have given notice of the request to the parties.

5B.9 The court will consider each application on its own merits. The burden of justifying a request for access rests on the applicant. Considerations to be taken into account will include: (i) whether or not the request is for the purpose of contemporaneous reporting; a request after the conclusion of the proceedings will require careful scrutiny by the court; (ii) the nature of the information or documents being sought; (iii) the purpose for which they are required; (iv) the stage of the proceedings at the time when the application is made; (v) the value of the documents in advancing the open justice principle, including enabling the media to discharge its role, which has been described as a "public watchdog", by reporting the proceedings effectively; (vi) any risk of harm which access to them may cause to the legitimate interests of others; and (vii) any reasons given by the parties for refusing to provide the material requested and any other representations received from the parties. Further, all of the principles below are subject to any specific restrictions in the case. Courts should be aware that the risk of providing a document may reduce after a particular point in the proceedings, and when the material requested may be made available.

Documents read aloud in their entirety

B-97

5B.10 If a document has been read aloud to the court in its entirety, it should usually be provided on request, unless to do so would be disruptive to the court proceedings or place an undue burden on the court, the advocates or others. It may be appropriate and convenient for material to be provided electronically, if this can be done securely.

5B.11 Documents likely to fall into this category are: (i) opening notes; (ii) statements agreed under section 9 of the CJA 1967 [§ 10-14 in the main work], including experts' reports, if read in their entirety; (iii) admissions made under section 10 of the CJA 1967 [§ 10-7 in the main work].

Documents treated as read aloud in their entirety

B-98

5B.12 A document treated by the court as if it had been read aloud in public, though in fact it has been neither read nor summarised aloud, should generally be made available on request. The burden on the court, the advocates or others in providing the material should be considered, but the presumption in favour of providing the material is greater when the material has only been treated as having been read aloud. Again, subject to security considerations, it may be convenient for the material to be provided electronically.

5B.13 Documents likely to fall into this category include: (i) skeleton arguments; (ii) written submissions.

Documents read aloud in part or summarised aloud

B-99

5B.14 Open justice requires only access to the part of the document that has been read aloud. If a member of the public requests a copy of such a document, the court should consider whether it is proportionate to order one of the parties to produce a suitably redacted version. If not, access to the document is unlikely to be granted; however, open justice will generally have been satisfied by the document having been read out in court.

5B.15 If the request comes from an accredited member of the press (see "Access by reporters" below), there may be circumstances in which the court orders that a copy of the whole document be shown to the reporter, or provided, subject to the condition that those matters that had not been read out to the court may not be used or reported. A breach of such an order would be treated as a contempt of court.

5B.16 Documents in this category are likely to include section 9 statements that are edited.

Jury bundles and exhibits (including video footage shown to the jury)

B-100

5B.17 The court should consider:

    (i) whether access to the specific document is necessary to understand or effectively to report the case;

    (ii) the privacy of third parties, such as the victim (in some cases, the reporting restriction imposed by s.1 of the Judicial Proceedings (Regulation of Reports) Act 1926 will apply (indecent or medical matter));

    (iii) whether the reporting of anything in the document may be prejudicial to a fair trial in this or another case, in which case whether it may be necessary to make an order under section 4(2) of the Contempt of Court Act 1981 [§ 28-65 in the main work].

The court may order one of the parties to provide a copy of certain pages (or parts of the footage), but these should not be provided electronically.

Statements of witnesses who give oral evidence

B-101

5B.18 A witness statement does not become evidence unless it is agreed under section 9 of the CJA 1967 [§ 10-14 in the main work] and presented to the court. Therefore the statements of witnesses who give oral evidence, including ABE interview and transcripts and experts' reports, should not usually be provided. Open justice is generally satisfied by public access to the court.

Confidential documents

5B.19 A document the content of which, though relied upon by the court, has not been com- **B-102** municated to the public or reporters, nor treated as if it had been, is likely to have been supplied in confidence and should be treated accordingly. This will apply even if the court has made reference to the document or quoted from the document. There is most unlikely to be a sufficient reason to displace the expectation of confidentiality ordinarily attaching to a document in this category, and it would be exceptional to permit the inspection or copying by a member of the public or of the media of such a document. The rights and legitimate interests of others are likely to outweigh the interests of open justice with respect these documents.

5B.20 Documents in this category are likely to include: (i) pre-sentence reports; (ii) medical reports; (iii) victim personal statements; (iv) reports and summaries for confiscation.

Prohibitions against the provision of information

5B.21 Statutory provisions may impose specific prohibitions against the provision of information. **B-103** Those most likely to be encountered are listed in the note to rule 5.8 and include the Rehabilitation of Offenders Act 1974 [§§ 13-120 *et seq.* in the main work], section 18 of the CPIA 1996 ("unused material" disclosed by the prosecution) [§ 12-91 in the main work], sections 33, 34 and 35 of the LASPOA 2012 (privileged information furnished to the Legal Aid Agency) and reporting restrictions generally.

5B.22 Reports of allocation or sending proceedings are restricted by section 52A of the CDA 1998 [§ 1-33 in the main work], so that only limited information, as specified in the statute, may be reported, whether it is referred to in the courtroom or not. The magistrates' court has power to order that the restriction shall not apply; if any defendant objects the court must apply the interests of justice test as specified in section 52A. The restriction ceases to apply either after all defendants indicate a plea of guilty, or after the conclusion of the trial of the last defendant to be tried. If the case does not result in a guilty plea, a finding of guilt or an acquittal, the restriction does not lift automatically and an application must be made to the court.

5B.23 Extradition proceedings have some features in common with committal proceedings, but no automatic reporting restrictions apply.

5B.24 Public interest immunity and the rights of a defendant, witnesses and victims under Article 6 and 8 of the ECHR [§§ 16-72, 16-137 in the main work] may also restrict the power to release material to third parties.

Other documents

5B.25 The following table indicates the considerations likely to arise on an application to inspect **B-104** or copy other documents.

Document	Considerations
Charge sheet/ Indictment	The alleged offence(s) will have been read aloud in court, and their terms must be supplied under rule 5.8(4).
Material disclosed under CPIA 1996	To the extent that the content is deployed at trial, it becomes public at that hearing. Otherwise, it is a criminal offence for it to be disclosed: s.18 of the 1996 Act[*ibid.*, § 12-91].
Written notices, applications, replies (including any application for representation)	To the extent that evidence is introduced, or measures taken, at trial, the content becomes public at that hearing. A statutory prohibition against disclosure applies to an application for representation: ss.33, 34 and 35 of the LASPOA 2012
Sentencing remarks	Sentencing remarks should usually be provided to the accredited press, if the judge was reading from a prepared script which was handed out immediately afterwards; if not, then permission for a member of the accredited press to obtain a transcript should usually be given (see also paras 26 and 29 below).
Official recordings/transcript	Rule 5.5

Access by reporters

B-105

5B.26 Under Part 5 of the rules, the same procedure applies for applications for access to information by reporters as to other members of the public. However, if the application is made by legal representatives instructed by the media, or by an accredited member of the media, who is able to produce in support of the application a valid press card (http://www.ukpresscardauthority.co.uk/) then there is a greater presumption in favour of providing the requested material, in recognition of the press' role as "public watchdog" in a democratic society (*Observer and Guardian v. U.K.*, 14 E.H.R.R. 153). The general principle in those circumstances is that the court should supply documents and information unless there is a good reason not to in order to protect the rights or legitimate interests of others and the request will not place an undue burden on the court (*R. (Guardian News and Media Ltd) v. City of Westminster Magistrates' Court (Article 19 intervening), ante* (at [87])). Subject to that, the paragraphs above relating to types of documents should be followed.

5B.27 Court staff should usually verify the authenticity of cards, checking the expiry date on the card and where necessary may consider telephoning the number on the reverse of the card to verify the card holder. Court staff may additionally request sight of other identification if necessary to ensure that the card holder has been correctly identified. The supply of information under rule 5.8(7) is at the discretion of the court, and court staff must ensure that they have received a clear direction from the court before providing any information or material under rule 5.8(7) to a member of the public, including to the accredited media or their legal representatives.

5B.28 Opening notes and skeleton arguments or written submissions, once they have been placed before the court, should usually be provided to the media. If there is no opening note, permission for the media to obtain a transcript of the prosecution opening should usually be given (see *post*). It may be convenient for copies to be provided electronically by counsel, provided that the documents are kept suitably secure. The media are expected to be aware of the limitations on the use to which such material can be put, for example that legal argument held in the absence of the jury must not be reported before the conclusion of the trial.

5B.29 The media should also be able to obtain transcripts of hearings held in open court directly from the transcription service provider, on payment of any required fee. The service providers commonly require the judge's authorisation before they will provide a transcript, as an additional verification to ensure that the correct material is released and reporting restrictions are noted. However, responsibility for compliance with any restriction always rests with the person receiving the information or material: see *Criminal Practice Direction I (General Matters) 6B*.

5B.30 It is not for the judge to exercise an editorial judgment about "the adequacy of the material already available to the paper for its journalistic purpose" (*R. (Guardian News and Media Ltd) v. City of Westminster Magistrates' Court (Article 19 intervening), ante* (at [82])), but the responsibility for complying with the Contempt of Court Act 1981 and any and all restrictions on the use of the material rests with the recipient.

CPD I General Matters: 5C Issue of Medical Certificates

B-106

5C.1 Doctors will be aware that medical notes are normally submitted by defendants in criminal proceedings as justification for not answering bail. Medical notes may also be submitted by witnesses who are due to give evidence and jurors.

5C.2 If a medical certificate is accepted by the court, this will result in cases (including contested hearings and trials) being adjourned rather than the court issuing a warrant for the defendant's arrest without bail. Medical certificates will also provide the defendant with sufficient evidence to defend a charge of failure to surrender to bail.

5C.3 However, a court is not absolutely bound by a medical certificate. The medical practitioner providing the certificate may be required by the court to give evidence. Alternatively the court may exercise its discretion to disregard a certificate which it finds unsatisfactory: *R. v. Ealing Magistrates' Court, ex p. Burgess*, 165 J.P. 82, DC.

5C.4 Circumstances where the court may find a medical certificate unsatisfactory include:

    (a) where the certificate indicates that the defendant is unfit to attend work (rather than to attend court);

    (b) where the nature of the defendant's ailment (e.g. a broken arm) does not appear to be capable of preventing his attendance at court;

    (c) where the defendant is certified as suffering from stress/anxiety/depression and there is no indication of the defendant recovering within a realistic timescale.

5C.5 It therefore follows that the minimum standards a medical certificate should set out are:

    (a) the date on which the medical practitioner examined the defendant;

   (b) the exact nature of the defendant's ailments

   (c) if it is not self-evident, why the ailment prevents the defendant attending court;

   (d) an indication as to when the defendant is likely to be able to attend court, or a date when the current certificate expires.

5C.6 Medical practitioners should be aware that when issuing a certificate to a defendant in criminal proceedings they make themselves liable to being summonsed to court to give evidence about the content of the certificate, and they may be asked to justify their statements.

Criminal Procedure Rules 2015 (S.I. 2015 No. 1490), Pt 6

Reporting, Etc. Restrictions

General rules

When this Part applies

   6.1.–(1) This Part applies where the court can—

   (a) impose a restriction on—

     (i) reporting what takes place at a public hearing, or

     (ii) public access to what otherwise would be a public hearing;

   (b) vary or remove a reporting or access restriction that is imposed by legislation;

   (c) withhold information from the public during a public hearing;

   (d) order a trial in private;

   (e) allow there to take place during a hearing—

     (i) sound recording, or

     (ii) communication by electronic means.

   (2) This Part does not apply to arrangements required by legislation, or directed by the court, in connection with—

   (a) sound recording during a hearing, or the transcription of such a recording; or

   (b) measures to assist a witness or defendant to give evidence.

B-107

Exercise of court's powers to which this Part applies

   6.2.–(1) When exercising a power to which this Part applies, as well as furthering the overriding objective, in accordance with rule 1.3, the court must have regard to the importance of—

   (a) dealing with criminal cases in public; and

   (b) allowing a public hearing to be reported to the public.

   (2) The court may determine an application or appeal under this Part—

   (a) at a hearing, in public or in private; or

   (b) without a hearing.

   (3) But the court must not exercise a power to which this Part applies unless each party and any other person directly affected—

   (a) is present; or

   (b) has had an opportunity—

     (i) to attend, or

     (ii) to make representations.

Court's power to vary requirements under this Part

   6.3.–(1) The court may—

   (a) shorten or extend (even after it has expired) a time limit under this Part;

   (b) require an application to be made in writing instead of orally;

   (c) consider an application or representations made orally instead of in writing;

   (d) dispense with a requirement to—

     (i) give notice, or

     (ii) serve an application.

   (2) Someone who wants an extension of time must—

   (a) apply when making the application or representations for which it is needed; and

   (b) explain the delay.

[This rule is printed as amended by the Criminal Procedure (Amendment No. 2) Rules 2016 (S.I. 2016 No. 705).]

Reporting and access restrictions

6.4.–(1) This rule applies where the court can–

   (a) impose a restriction on–

      (i) reporting what takes place at a public hearing, or

      (ii) public access to what otherwise would be a public hearing;

   (b) withhold information from the public during a public hearing.

(2) Unless other legislation otherwise provides, the court may do so–

   (a) on application by a party; or

   (b) on its own initiative.

(3) A party who wants the court to do so must–

   (a) apply as soon as reasonably practicable;

   (b) notify–

      (i) each other party, and

      (ii) such other person (if any) as the court directs;

   (c) specify the proposed terms of the order, and for how long it should last;

   (d) explain–

      (i) what power the court has to make the order, and

      (ii) why an order in the terms proposed is necessary;

   (e) where the application is for a reporting direction under section 45A of the Youth Justice and Criminal Evidence Act 1999 (power to restrict reporting of criminal proceedings for lifetime of witnesses and victims under 18 [§ 4-28 in the main work]), explain–

      (i) how the circumstances of the person whose identity is concerned meet the conditions prescribed by that section, having regard to the factors which that section lists; and

      (ii) why such a reporting direction would be likely to improve the quality of any evidence given by that person, or the level of co-operation given by that person to any party in connection with the preparation of that party's case, taking into account the factors listed in that section;

   (f) where the application is for a reporting direction under section 46 of the Youth Justice and Criminal Evidence Act 1999 (power to restrict reports about certain adult witnesses in criminal proceedings [*ibid.*, § 4-33]), explain–

      (i) how the witness is eligible for assistance, having regard to the factors listed in that section, and

      (ii) why such a reporting direction would be likely to improve the quality of the witness' evidence, or the level of co-operation given by the witness to the applicant in connection with the preparation of the applicant's case, taking into account the factors which that section lists.

Varying or removing restrictions

6.5.–(1) This rule applies where the court can vary or remove a reporting or access restriction.

(2) Unless other legislation otherwise provides, the court may do so–

   (a) on application by a party or person directly affected; or

   (b) on its own initiative.

(3) A party or person who wants the court to do so must–

   (a) apply as soon as reasonably practicable;

   (b) notify–

      (i) each other party, and

      (ii) such other person (if any) as the court directs;

   (c) specify the restriction;

   (d) explain, as appropriate, why it should be varied or removed.

(4), (5) [*Appeals from magistrates' courts under the Education Act 2002, s.141F(7) (relating to restrictions on reporting alleged offences by teachers).*]

Trial in private

6.6.–(1) This rule applies where the court can order a trial in private.

(2) A party who wants the court to do so must–

   (a) apply in writing not less than 5 business days before the trial is due to begin; and

   (b) serve the application on–

    (i)   the court officer, and

    (ii) each other party.

(3) The applicant must explain—

  (a) the reasons for the application;

  (b) how much of the trial the applicant proposes should be in private; and

  (c) why no measures other than trial in private will suffice, such as—

    (i)   reporting restrictions,

    (ii) an admission of facts,

    (iii) the introduction of hearsay evidence,

    (iv) a direction for a special measure under section 19 of the Youth Justice and Criminal Evidence Act 1999 [*ibid.*, § 8-78],

    (v) a witness anonymity order under section 86 of the Coroners and Justice Act 2009 [*ibid.*, § 8-156], or

    (vi) arrangements for the protection of a witness.

(4) Where the application includes information that the applicant thinks ought not be revealed to another party, the applicant must—

  (a) omit that information from the part of the application that is served on that other party;

  (b) mark the other part to show that, unless the court otherwise directs, it is only for the court; and

  (c) in that other part, explain why the applicant has withheld that information from that other party.

(5) The court officer must at once—

  (a) display notice of the application somewhere prominent in the vicinity of the courtroom; and

  (b) give notice of the application to reporters by such other arrangements as the Lord Chancellor directs.

(6) The application must be determined at a hearing which—

  (a) must be in private, unless the court otherwise directs;

  (b) if the court so directs, may be, wholly or in part, in the absence of a party from whom information has been withheld; and

  (c) in the Crown Court, must be after the defendant is arraigned but before the jury is sworn.

(7) At the hearing of the application—

  (a) the general rule is that the court must consider, in the following sequence—

    (i)   representations first by the applicant and then by each other party, in all the parties' presence, and then

    (ii) further representations by the applicant, in the absence of a party from whom information has been withheld; but

  (b) the court may direct other arrangements for the hearing.

(8) The court must not hear a trial in private until—

  (a) the business day after the day on which it orders such a trial, or

  (b) the disposal of any appeal against, or review of, any such order, if later.

Representations in response

6.7.—(1) This rule applies where a party, or person directly affected, wants to make representations about an application or appeal.

(2) Such a party or person must—

  (a) serve the representations on—

    (i)   the court officer,

    (ii) the applicant,

    (iii) each other party, and

    (iv) such other person (if any) as the court directs;

  (b) do so as soon as reasonably practicable after notice of the application; and

  (c) ask for a hearing, if that party or person wants one, and explain why it is needed.

(3) Representations must—

  (a) explain the reasons for any objection;

  (b) specify any alternative terms proposed.

Order about restriction or trial in private

6.8.—(1) This rule applies where the court—

  (a) orders, varies or removes a reporting or access restriction; or

(b)   orders a trial in private.
(2) The court officer must—
    (a)   record the court's reasons for the decision; and
    (b)   as soon as reasonably practicable, arrange for notice of the decision to be—
        (i)   displayed somewhere prominent in the vicinity of the courtroom, and
        (ii)   communicated to reporters by such other arrangements as the Lord Chancellor directs.

Sound recording and electronic communication
    6.9.–(1) This rule applies where the court can give permission to—
    (a)   bring into a hearing for use, or use during a hearing, a device for—
        (i)   recording sound, or
        (ii)   communicating by electronic means; or
    (b)   publish a sound recording made during a hearing.
(2) The court may give such permission—
    (a)   on application; or
    (b)   on its own initiative.
(3) A person who wants the court to give such permission must—
    (a)   apply as soon as reasonably practicable;
    (b)   notify—
        (i)   each party, and
        (ii)   such other person (if any) as the court directs; and
    (c)   explain why the court should permit the use or publication proposed.
(4) As a condition of the applicant using such a device, the court may direct arrangements to minimise the risk of its use—
    (a)   contravening a reporting restriction;
    (b)   disrupting the hearing; or
    (c)   compromising the fairness of the hearing, for example by affecting—
        (i)   the evidence to be given by a witness, or
        (ii)   the verdict of a jury.
(5) Such a direction may require that the device is used only—
    (a)   in a specified part of the courtroom;
    (b)   for a specified purpose;
    (c)   for a purpose connected with the applicant's activity as a member of a specified group, for example representatives of news-gathering or reporting organisations;
    (d)   at a specified time, or in a specified way.

Forfeiture of unauthorised sound recording
B-110   **6.10.**–(1) This rule applies where someone without the court's permission—
    (a)   uses a device for recording sound during a hearing; or
    (b)   publishes a sound recording made during a hearing.
(2) The court may exercise its power to forfeit the device or recording—
    (a)   on application by a party, or on its own initiative;
    (b)   provisionally, despite rule 6.2(3), to allow time for representations.
(3) A party who wants the court to forfeit a device or recording must—
    (a)   apply as soon as reasonably practicable;
    (b)   notify—
        (i)   as appropriate, the person who used the device, or who published the recording, and
        (ii)   each other party; and
    (c)   explain why the court should exercise that power.

CPD I General Matters 6A: Unofficial Sound Recording of Proceedings

B-111   **6A.1** [Summarises s.9(1)(a)-(c) and (4) of the Contempt of Court Act 1981 (§ 28-74 in the main work).]

    6A.2 The discretion given to the court to grant, withhold or withdraw leave to use equipment for recording sound or to impose conditions as to the use of the recording is unlimited, but the following factors may be relevant to its exercise:
    (a) the existence of any reasonable need on the part of the applicant for leave, whether a

litigant or a person connected with the press or broadcasting, for the recording to be made;

(b) the risk that the recording could be used for the purpose of briefing witnesses out of court;

(c) any possibility that the use of the recorder would disturb the proceedings or distract or worry any witnesses or other participants.

6A.3 Consideration should always be given whether conditions as to the use of a recording made pursuant to leave should be imposed. The identity and role of the applicant for leave and the nature of the subject-matter of the proceedings may be relevant to this.

6A.4 The particular restriction imposed by section 9(1)(b) applies in every case, but may not be present to the mind of every applicant to whom leave is given. It may, therefore, be desirable on occasion for this provision to be drawn to the attention of those to whom leave is given.

6A.5 The transcript of a permitted recording is intended for the use of the person given leave to make it and is not intended to be used as, or to compete with, the official transcript mentioned in section 9(4).

6A.6 Where a contravention of section 9(1) is alleged, the procedure in section 2 of Part 48 of the Rules should be followed. Section 9(3) of the 1981 Act[§ 28-74 in the main work] permits the court to "order the instrument, or any recording made with it, or both, to be forfeited". The procedure at CrimPR 6.10 should be followed.

CPD I General Matters 6B: Restrictions on Reporting Proceedings

6B.1 Open justice is an essential principle in the criminal courts but the principle is subject to **B-112** some statutory restrictions. These restrictions are either automatic or discretionary. Guidance is provided in the joint publication, Reporting Restrictions in the Criminal Courts issued by the Judicial College, the Newspaper Society, the Society of Editors and the Media Lawyers Association. The current version is the fourth edition and has been updated to be effective from May 2015. [*Editorial note: a revised version was issued in May, 2016.*]

6B.2 Where a restriction is automatic no order can or should be made in relation to matters falling within the relevant provisions. However, the court may, if it considers it appropriate to do so, give a reminder of the existence of the automatic restriction. The court may also discuss the scope of the restriction and any particular risks in the specific case in open court with representatives of the press present. Such judicial observations cannot constitute an order binding on the editor or the reporter although it is anticipated that a responsible editor would consider them carefully before deciding what should be published. It remains the responsibility of those reporting a case to ensure that restrictions are not breached.

6B.3 Before exercising its discretion to impose a restriction the court must follow precisely the statutory provisions under which the order is to be made, paying particular regard to what has to be established, by whom and to what standard.

6B.4 Without prejudice to the above paragraph, certain general principles apply to the exercise of the court's discretion:

(a) the court must have regard to Parts 6 and 18 of the Criminal Procedure Rules;

(b) the court must keep in mind the fact that every order is a departure from the general principle that proceedings shall be open and freely reported;

(c) before making any order the court must be satisfied that the purpose of the proposed order cannot be achieved by some lesser measure, e.g. the grant of special measures, screens or the clearing of the public gallery (usually subject to a representative/s of the media remaining);

(d) the terms of the order must be proportionate so as to comply with Article 10 [of the] ECHR (freedom of expression) [§ 16-157 in the main work];

(e) no order should be made without giving other parties to the proceedings and any other interested party, including any representative of the media, an opportunity to make representations;

(f) any order should provide for any interested party who has not been present or represented at the time of the making of the order to have permission to apply within a limited period, e.g. 24 hours;

(g) the wording of the order is the responsibility of the judge or bench making the order; it must be in precise terms and, if practicable, agreed with the advocates.

(h) the order must be in writing and must state:

(i) the power under which it is made;

      (ii) its precise scope and purpose; and

      (iii) the time at which it shall cease to have effect, if appropriate;

   (i) the order must specify, in every case, whether or not the making or terms of the order may be reported or whether this itself is prohibited; such a report could cause the very mischief which the order was intended to prevent.

6B.5 A series of template orders have been prepared by the Judicial College and are available as an appendix to the Crown Court Bench Book Companion; these template orders should generally be used.

6B.6 A copy of the order should be provided to any person known to have an interest in reporting the proceedings and to any local or national media who regularly report proceedings in the court.

6B.7 Court staff should be prepared to answer any enquiry about a specific case; but it is and will remain the responsibility of anyone reporting a case to ensure that no breach of any order occurs and the onus rests on such person to make enquiry in case of doubt.

CPD I General Matters 6C: Use of Live Text-based Forms of Communication (including Twitter) from Court for the Purposes of Fair and Accurate Reporting

B-113

6C.1 This part clarifies the use which may be made of live text-based communications, such as mobile email, social media (including Twitter) and internet-enabled laptops in and from courts throughout England and Wales. For the purpose of this part these means of communication are referred to, compendiously, as "live text-based communications". It is consistent with the legislative structure which:

   (a) prohibits:

      (i) the taking of photographs in court (s.41 of the CJA 1925);

      (ii) the use of sound recording equipment in court unless the leave of the judge has first been obtained (s.9 of the Contempt of Court Act 1981 [§ 28-74 in the main work]); and

   (b) requires compliance with the strict prohibition rules created by sections 1, 2 and 4 of the Contempt of Court Act 1981 [§§ 28-55, 28-65 in the main work] in relation to the reporting of court proceedings.

GENERAL PRINCIPLES

B-114

6C.2 The judge has an overriding responsibility to ensure that proceedings are conducted consistently, with the proper administration of justice, and to avoid any improper interference with its processes.

6C.3 A fundamental aspect of the proper administration of justice is the principle of open justice. Fair and accurate reporting of court proceedings forms part of that principle. The principle is, however, subject to well-known statutory and discretionary exceptions. Two such exceptions are the prohibitions, set out in paragraph 6C.1(a), on photography in court and on making sound recordings of court proceedings.

6C.4 The statutory prohibition on photography in court, by any means, is absolute. There is no judicial discretion to suspend or dispense with it. Any equipment which has photographic capability must not have that function activated.

6C.5 Sound recordings are also prohibited unless, in the exercise of its discretion, the court permits such equipment to be used. In criminal proceedings, some of the factors relevant to the exercise of that discretion are contained in paragraph 6A.2. The same factors are likely to be relevant when consideration is being given to the exercise of this discretion in civil or family proceedings.

USE OF LIVE TEXT-BASED COMMUNICATIONS: GENERAL CONSIDERATIONS

B-115

6C.6 The normal, indeed almost invariable, rule has been that mobile phones must be turned off in court. There is however no statutory prohibition on the use of live text-based communications in open court.

6C.7 Where a member of the public, who is in court, wishes to use live text-based communications during court proceedings an application for permission to activate and use, in silent mode, a mobile phone, small laptop or similar piece of equipment, solely in order to make live text-based communications of the proceedings will need to be made. The application may be made formally or informally (for instance by communicating a request to the judge through court staff).

6C.8 It is presumed that a representative of the media or a legal commentator using live textbased communications from court does not pose a danger of interference to the proper administration of justice in the individual case. This is because the most obvious purpose of permitting the use of live text-based communications would be to enable the media to produce fair and accurate reports of the proceedings. As such, a representative of the media or a legal commentator who wishes to use live text-based communications from court may do so without making an application to the court.

6C.9 When considering, either generally on its own motion, or following a formal application or informal request by a member of the public, whether to permit live text-based communications, and if so by whom, the paramount question for the judge will be whether the application may interfere with the proper administration of justice.

6C.10 In considering the question of permission, the factors listed in paragraph 6A.2 are likely to be relevant.

6C.11 Without being exhaustive, the danger to the administration of justice is likely to be at its most acute in the context of criminal trials e.g., where witnesses who are out of court may be informed of what has already happened in court and so coached or briefed before they then give evidence, or where information posted on, for instance, Twitter about inadmissible evidence may influence members of the jury. However, the danger is not confined to criminal proceedings; in civil and sometimes family proceedings, simultaneous reporting from the courtroom may create pressure on witnesses, by distracting or worrying them.

6C.12 It may be necessary for the judge to limit live text-based communications to representatives of the media for journalistic purposes but to disallow its use by the wider public in court. That may arise if it is necessary, for example, to limit the number of mobile electronic devices in use at any given time because of the potential for electronic interference with the court's own sound recording equipment, or because the widespread use of such devices in court may cause a distraction in the proceedings.

6C.13 Subject to these considerations, the use of an unobtrusive, hand-held, silent piece of modern equipment, for the purposes of simultaneous reporting of proceedings to the outside world as they unfold in court, is generally unlikely to interfere with the proper administration of justice.

6C.14 Permission to use live text-based communications from court may be withdrawn by the court at any time.

CPD I General matters 6D: Taking Notes in Court (as inserted by Criminal Practice Directions 2015 (Amendment No. 1), unreported, March 23, 2016, Lord Thomas C.J.)

6D.1 As long as it does not interfere with the proper administration of justice, anyone who attends **B-116** a court hearing may quietly take notes, on paper or by silent electronic means. If that person is a participant, including an expert witness who is in the courtroom under CrimPR 24.4(2)(a)(ii) or 25.11(2)(a)(ii), note taking may be an essential aid to that person's own or (if they are a representative) to their client's effective participation. If that person is a reporter or a member of the public, attending a hearing to which, by definition, they have been admitted, note taking is a feature of the principle of open justice. The permission of the court is not required, and the distinctions between members of the public and others which are drawn at paragraphs 6C.7 and 6C.8 of these practice directions do not apply.

6D.2 However, where there is reason to suspect that the taking of notes may be for an unlawful purpose, or that it may disrupt the proceedings, then it is entirely proper for court staff to make appropriate enquiries, and ultimately it is within the power of the court to prohibit note taking by a specified individual or individuals in the court room if that is necessary and proportionate to prevent unlawful conduct. If, for example, there is reason to believe that notes are being taken in order to influence the testimony of a witness who is due to give evidence, perhaps by briefing that witness on what another witness has said, then because such conduct is unlawful (it is likely to be in contempt of court, and it may constitute a perversion of the course of justice) it is within the court's power to prohibit such note taking. If there is reason to believe that what purports to be taking notes with an electronic device is in fact the transmission of live text-based communications from court without the permission required by paragraph 6C.7 of these practice directions, or where permission to transmit such communications has been withdrawn under paragraph 6C.14, then that, too, would constitute grounds for prohibiting the taking of such notes.

6D.3 The existence of a reporting restriction, without more, is not a sufficient reason to prohibit note taking (though it may need to be made clear to those who take notes that the reporting restriction affects how much, if any, of what they have noted may be communicated to anyone else). However, if there is reason to believe that notes are being taken in order to facilitate the contravention of a reporting restriction then that, too, would constitute grounds for prohibiting such note taking.

Criminal Procedure Rules 2015 (S.I. 2015 No. 1490), Pt 7

<small>STARTING A PROSECUTION IN A MAGISTRATES' COURT</small>

B-117   [*Not set out in this work.*]

Criminal Procedure Rules 2015 (S.I. 2015 No. 1490), Pt 8

<small>INITIAL DETAILS OF THE PROSECUTION CASE</small>

When this part applies

B-118   **8.1.** This Part applies in a magistrates' court.

Providing initial details of the prosecution case

B-119   **8.2.**–(1) The prosecutor must serve initial details of the prosecution case on the court officer–

(a) as soon as practicable; and

(b) in any event, no later than the beginning of the day of the first hearing.

(2) Where a defendant requests those details, the prosecutor must serve them on the defendant–

(a) as soon as practicable; and

(b) in any event, no later than the beginning of the day of the first hearing.

(3) Where a defendant does not request those details, the prosecutor must make them available to the defendant at, or before, the beginning of the day of the first hearing.

Content of initial details

B-120   **8.3.** Initial details of the prosecution case must include–

(a) where, immediately before the first hearing in the magistrates' court, the defendant was in police custody for the offence charged–

(i)   a summary of the circumstances of the offence, and

(ii) the defendant's criminal record, if any;

(b) where paragraph (a) does not apply–

(i)   a summary of the circumstances of the offence,

(ii) any account given by the defendant in interview, whether contained in that summary or in another document,

(iii) any written witness statement or exhibit that the prosecutor then has available and considers material to plea, or to the allocation of the case for trial, or to sentence,

(iv) the defendant's criminal record, if any, and

(v)   any available statement of the effect of the offence on a victim, a victim's family or others.

Use of initial details

★B-120a   **8.4.**–(1) This rule applies where-

(a) the prosecutor wants to introduce information contained in a document listed in rule 8.3; and

(b) the prosecutor has not

(i)   served that document on the defendant, or

(ii) made that information available to the defendant.

(2) The court must not allow the prosecutor to introduce that information unless the court first allows the defendant sufficient time to consider it.

[This rule was inserted by the Criminal Procedure (Amendment) Rules 2017 (S.I. 2017 No. 144).]

CPD II Preliminary Proceedings 8A: Defendant's Record

Copies of record

B-121   **8A.1** The defendant's record (previous convictions, cautions, reprimands, etc) may be taken into account when the court decides not only on sentence but also, for example, about bail, or when allocating a case for trial. It is therefore important that up to date and accurate information is available.

Previous convictions must be provided as part of the initial details of the prosecution case under Part 8 of the rules.

8A.2 The record should usually be provided in the following format:

Personal details and summary of convictions and cautions – Police National Computer ["PNC"] Court / Defence / Probation Summary Sheet;

Previous convictions — PNC Court / Defence / Probation printout, supplemented by
Form MG16 if the police force holds convictions not shown on PNC;

Recorded cautions — PNC Court / Defence / Probation printout, supplemented by Form
MG17 if the police force holds cautions not shown on PNC.

8A.3 The defence representative should take instructions on the defendant's record and if the
defence wish to raise any objection to the record, this should be made known to the prosecutor
immediately.

8A.4 It is the responsibility of the prosecutor to ensure that a copy of the defendant's record has
been provided to the probation service.

8A.5 Where following conviction a custodial order is made, the court must ensure that a copy is
attached to the order sent to the prison.

Additional information

8A.6 In the Crown Court, the police should also provide brief details of the circumstances of the **B-122**
last three similar convictions and / or of convictions likely to be of interest to the court, the latter being judged on a case-by-case basis.

8A.7 Where the current alleged offence could constitute a breach of an existing sentence such as a
suspended sentence, community order or conditional discharge, and it is known that that sentence is
still in force then details of the circumstances of the offence leading to the sentence should be
included in the antecedents. The detail should be brief and include the date of the offence.

8A.8 On occasions the PNC printout provided may not be fully up to date. It is the responsibility
of the prosecutor to ensure that all of the necessary information is available to the court and the
probation service and provided to the defence. Oral updates at the hearing will sometimes be necessary, but it is preferable if this information is available in advance.

Criminal Procedure Rules 2015 (S.I. 2015 No. 1490), Pt 9

Allocation and Sending for Trial

General rules

When this Part applies

9.1.–(1) This Part applies to the allocation and sending of cases for trial under– **B-123**

(a) sections 17A to 26 of the Magistrates' Courts Act 1980; [§§ 1-57 *et seq.* in the main work]
and

(b) sections 50A to 52 of the Crime and Disorder Act 1998 [*ibid.*, §§ 1-23 *et seq.*] .

(2) Rules 9.6 and 9.7 apply in a magistrates' court where the court must, or can, send a defendant
to the Crown Court for trial, without allocating the case for trial there.

(3) Rules 9.8 and 9.14 apply in a magistrates' court where the court must allocate the case to a
magistrates' court or to the Crown Court for trial.

(4) Rules 9.15 and 9.16 apply in the Crown Court, where a defendant is sent for trial there.

Exercise of magistrates' court's powers

9.2.–(1) This rule applies to the exercise of the powers to which rules 9.6 to 9.14 apply. **B-124**

(2) The general rule is that the court must exercise its powers at a hearing in public, but it may
exercise any power it has to–

(a) withhold information from the public; or

(b) order a hearing in private.

(3) The general rule is that the court must exercise its powers in the defendant's presence, but it
may exercise the powers to which the following rules apply in the defendant's absence on the conditions specified–

(a) where rule 9.8 (adult defendant: request for plea), rule 9.9 (adult defendant: guilty plea) or
rule 9.13 (young defendant) applies, if–

(i) the defendant is represented, and

(ii) the defendant's disorderly conduct makes his or her presence in the courtroom
impracticable;

(b) where rule 9.10 (adult defendant: not guilty plea) or rule 9.11 (adult defendant: allocation
for magistrates' court trial) applies, if–

(i) the defendant is represented and waives the right to be present, or

(ii) the defendant's disorderly conduct makes his or her presence in the courtroom
impracticable.

(4) The court may exercise its power to adjourn—

(a) if either party asks; or

(b) on its own initiative.

(5) Where the court on the same occasion deals with two or more offences alleged against the same defendant, the court must deal with those offences in the following sequence—

(a) any to which rule 9.6 applies (prosecutor's notice requiring Crown Court trial);

(b) any to which rule 9.7 applies (sending for Crown Court trial, without allocation there), in this sequence—

(i) any the court must send for trial, then

(ii) any the court can send for trial; and

(c) any to which rule 9.14 applies (allocation for Crown Court trial).

(6) Where the court on the same occasion deals with two or more defendants charged jointly with an offence that can be tried in the Crown Court then in the following sequence—

(a) the court must explain, in terms each defendant can understand (with help, if necessary), that if the court sends one of them to the Crown Court for trial then the court must send for trial in the Crown Court, too, any other of them—

(i) who is charged with the same offence as the defendant sent for trial, or with an offence which the court decides is related to that offence,

(ii) who does not wish to plead guilty to each offence with which he or she is charged, and

(iii) (if that other defendant is under 18, and the court would not otherwise have sent him or her for Crown Court trial) where the court decides that sending is necessary in the interests of justice even if the court by then has decided to allocate that other defendant for magistrates' court trial; and

(b) the court may ask the defendants questions to help it decide in what order to deal with them.

(7) After following paragraph (5), if it applies, where the court on the same occasion—

(a) deals with two or more defendants charged jointly with an offence that can be tried in the Crown Court;

(b) allocates any of them to a magistrates' court for trial; and

(c) then sends another one of them to the Crown Court for trial,

the court must deal again with each one whom, on that occasion, it has allocated for magistrates' court trial.

Matters to be specified on sending for trial

B-125

9.3.—(1) Where the court sends a defendant to the Crown Court for trial, it must specify—

(a) each offence to be tried;

(b) in respect of each, the power exercised to send the defendant for trial for that offence; and

(c) the Crown Court centre at which the trial will take place.

(2) In a case in which the prosecutor serves a notice to which rule 9.6(1)(a) applies (notice requiring Crown Court trial in a case of serious or complex fraud), the court must specify the Crown Court centre identified by that notice.

(3) In any other case, in deciding the Crown Court centre at which the trial will take place, the court must take into account—

(a) the convenience of the parties and witnesses;

(b) how soon a suitable courtroom will be available; and

(c) the directions on the allocation of Crown Court business contained in the Practice Direction.

Duty of justices' legal adviser

B-126

9.4.—(1) This rule applies—

(a) only in a magistrates' court; and

(b) unless the court—

(i) includes a District Judge (Magistrates' Courts), and

(ii) otherwise directs.

(2) On the court's behalf, a justices' legal adviser may—

(a) read the allegation of the offence to the defendant;

(b) give any explanation and ask any question required by the rules in this Part;

(c) make any announcement required by the rules in this Part, other than an announcement of—

    (i)   the court's decisions about allocation and sending,

    (ii) any indication by the court of likely sentence, or

    (iii) sentence.

  (3) A justices' legal adviser must—

   (a) assist an unrepresented defendant;

   (b) give the court such advice as is required to enable it to exercise its powers;

   (c) if required, attend the members of the court outside the courtroom to give such advice, but inform the parties of any advice so given.

Duty of magistrates' court officer

9.5.—(1) The magistrates' court officer must—   **B-127**

   (a) serve notice of a sending for Crown Court trial on—

     (i)   the Crown Court officer, and

     (ii) the parties;

   (b) in that notice record—

     (i)   the matters specified by the court under rule 9.3 (matters to be specified on sending for trial),

     (ii) any indication of intended guilty plea given by the defendant under rule 9.7 (sending for Crown Court trial),

     (iii) any decision by the defendant to decline magistrates' court trial under rule 9.11 (adult defendant: allocation to magistrates' court for trial), and

     (iv) the date on which any custody time limit will expire;

   (c) record any indication of likely sentence to which rule 9.11 applies; and

   (d) give the court such other assistance as it requires.

  (2) The magistrates' court officer must include with the notice served on the Crown Court officer—

   (a) the initial details of the prosecution case served by the prosecutor under rule 8.2;

   (b) a record of any—

     (i)   listing or case management direction affecting the Crown Court,

     (ii) direction about reporting restrictions,

     (iii) decision about bail, for the purposes of section 5 of the Bail Act 1976 [§ 3-28 in the main work],

     (iv) recognizance given by a surety, or

     (v) representation order; and

   (c) if relevant, any available details of any—

     (i)   interpreter,

     (ii) intermediary, or

     (iii) other supporting adult, where the defendant is assisted by such a person.

Sending without allocation for Crown Court trial

Prosecutor's notice requiring Crown Court trial

9.6.—(1) This rule applies where a prosecutor with power to do so requires a magistrates' court to **B-128** send for trial in the Crown Court—

   (a) a case of serious or complex fraud; or

   (b) a case which will involve a child witness.

  (2) The prosecutor must serve notice of that requirement—

   (a) on the magistrates' court officer and on the defendant; and

   (b) before trial in a magistrates' court begins under Part 24 (trial and sentence in a magistrates' court).

  (3) The notice must identify—

   (a) the power on which the prosecutor relies; and

   (b) the Crown Court centre at which the prosecutor wants the trial to take place.

  (4) The prosecutor—

   (a) must, when choosing a Crown Court centre, take into account the matters listed in rule 9.3(3) (court deciding to which Crown Court centre to send a case); and

   (b) may change the centre identified before the case is sent for trial.

[This rule is printed as amended by the Criminal Procedure (Amendment No. 2) Rules 2016 (S.I. 2016 No. 705).]

Sending for Crown Court trial

B-129   **9.7.**–(1) This rule applies where a magistrates' court must, or can, send a defendant to the Crown Court for trial without first allocating the case for trial there.

(2) The court must read the allegation of the offence to the defendant.

(3) The court must explain, in terms the defendant can understand (with help, if necessary)–

    (a) the allegation, unless it is self-explanatory;

    (b) that the offence is one for which the court, as appropriate–

        (i) must send the defendant to the Crown Court for trial because the offence is one which can only be tried there or because the court for some other reason is required to send that offence for trial,

        (ii) may send the defendant to the Crown Court for trial if the magistrates' court decides that the offence is related to one already sent for trial there, or

        (iii) (where the offence is low-value shoplifting and the defendant is 18 or over) must send the defendant to the Crown Court for trial if the defendant wants to be tried there;

    (c) that reporting restrictions apply, which the defendant may ask the court to vary or remove.

(4) In the following sequence, the court must then–

    (a) invite the prosecutor to–

        (i) identify the court's power to send the defendant to the Crown Court for trial for the offence, and

        (ii) make representations about any ancillary matters, including bail and directions for the management of the case in the Crown Court;

    (b) invite the defendant to make representations about–

        (i) the court's power to send the defendant to the Crown Court, and

        (ii) any ancillary matters;

    (c) (where the offence is low-value shoplifting and the defendant is 18 or over) offer the defendant the opportunity to require trial in the Crown Court; and

    (d) decide whether or not to send the defendant to the Crown Court for trial.

(5) If the court sends the defendant to the Crown Court for trial, it must–

    (a) ask whether the defendant intends to plead guilty in the Crown Court and–

        (i) if the answer is "yes", make arrangements for the Crown Court to take the defendant's plea as soon as possible, or

        (ii) if the defendant does not answer, or the answer is "no", make arrangements for a case management hearing in the Crown Court; and

    (b) give any other ancillary directions.

Allocation for magistrates' court or Crown Court trial

Adult defendant: request for plea

B-130   **9.8.**–(1) This rule applies where–

    (a) the defendant is 18 or over; and

    (b) the court must decide whether a case is more suitable for trial in a magistrates' court or in the Crown Court.

(2) The court must read the allegation of the offence to the defendant.

(3) The court must explain, in terms the defendant can understand (with help, if necessary)–

    (a) the allegation, unless it is self-explanatory;

    (b) that the offence is one which can be tried in a magistrates' court or in the Crown Court;

    (c) that the court is about to ask whether the defendant intends to plead guilty;

    (d) that if the answer is "yes", then the court must treat that as a guilty plea and must sentence the defendant, or commit the defendant to the Crown Court for sentence;

    (e) that if the defendant does not answer, or the answer is "no", then–

        (i) the court must decide whether to allocate the case to a magistrates' court or to the Crown Court for trial,

        (ii) the value involved may require the court to order trial in a magistrates' court (where the offence is one to which section 22 of the Magistrates' Courts Act 1980 applies [§ 1-77 in the main work]), and

        (iii) if the court allocates the case to a magistrates' court for trial, the defendant can nonetheless require trial in the Crown Court (unless the offence is one to which section 22 of the Magistrates' Courts Act 1980 applies and the value involved requires magistrates' court trial); and

464

(f) that reporting restrictions apply, which the defendant may ask the court to vary or remove.

(4) The court must then ask whether the defendant intends to plead guilty.

Adult defendant: guilty plea

9.9.–(1) This rule applies where–

(a) rule 9.8 applies; and

(b) the defendant indicates an intention to plead guilty.

(2) The court must exercise its power to deal with the case–

(a) as if the defendant had just pleaded guilty at trial in a magistrates' court; and

(b) in accordance with rule 24.11 (procedure if the court convicts).

B-131

Adult defendant: not guilty plea

9.10.–(1) This rule applies where–

(a) rule 9.8 applies; and

(b) the defendant–

(i) indicates an intention to plead not guilty, or

(ii) gives no indication of intended plea.

(2) In the following sequence, the court must then–

(a) where the offence is one to which section 22 of the Magistrates' Courts Act 1980 applies, explain in terms the defendant can understand (with help, if necessary) that–

(i) if the court decides that the value involved clearly is less than £5,000, the court must order trial in a magistrates' court,

(ii) if the court decides that it is not clear whether that value is more or less than £5,000, then the court will ask whether the defendant agrees to be tried in a magistrates' court, and

(iii) if the answer to that question is "yes", then the court must order such a trial and if the defendant is convicted then the maximum sentence is limited;

(b) invite the prosecutor to–

(i) identify any previous convictions of which it can take account, and

(ii) make representations about how the court should allocate the case for trial, including representations about the value involved, if relevant;

(c) invite the defendant to make such representations;

(d) where the offence is one to which section 22 of the Magistrates' Courts Act 1980 applies–

(i) if it is not clear whether the value involved is more or less than £5,000, ask whether the defendant agrees to be tried in a magistrates' court,

(ii) if the defendant's answer to that question is "yes", or if that value clearly is less than £5,000, order a trial in a magistrates' court,

(iii) if the defendant does not answer that question, or the answer is "no", or if that value clearly is more than £5,000, apply paragraph (2)(e);

(e) exercise its power to allocate the case for trial, taking into account–

(i) the adequacy of a magistrates' court's sentencing powers,

(ii) any representations by the parties, and

(iii) any allocation guidelines issued by the Sentencing Council.

B-132

Adult defendant: allocation for magistrates' court trial

9.11.–(1) This rule applies where–

(a) rule 9.10 applies; and

(b) the court allocates the case to a magistrates' court for trial.

(2) The court must explain, in terms the defendant can understand (with help, if necessary) that–

(a) the court considers the case more suitable for trial in a magistrates' court than in the Crown Court;

(b) if the defendant is convicted at a magistrates' court trial, then in some circumstances the court may commit the defendant to the Crown Court for sentence;

(c) if the defendant does not agree to a magistrates' court trial, then the court must send the defendant to the Crown Court for trial; and

(d) before deciding whether to accept magistrates' court trial, the defendant may ask the court for an indication of whether a custodial or non-custodial sentence is more likely in the event of a guilty plea at such a trial, but the court need not give such an indication.

(3) If the defendant asks for such an indication of sentence and the court gives such an indication–

B-133

    (a) the court must then ask again whether the defendant intends to plead guilty;

    (b) if, in answer to that question, the defendant indicates an intention to plead guilty, then the court must exercise its power to deal with the case–

        (i) as if the defendant had just pleaded guilty to an offence that can be tried only in a magistrates' court, and

        (ii) in accordance with rule 24.11 (procedure if the court convicts);

    (c) if, in answer to that question, the defendant indicates an intention to plead not guilty, or gives no indication of intended plea, in the following sequence the court must then–

        (i) ask whether the defendant agrees to trial in a magistrates' court,

        (ii) if the defendant's answer to that question is "yes", order such a trial,

        (iii) if the defendant does not answer that question, or the answer is "no", apply rule 9.14.

    (4) If the defendant asks for an indication of sentence but the court gives none, or if the defendant does not ask for such an indication, in the following sequence the court must then–

    (a) ask whether the defendant agrees to trial in a magistrates' court;

    (b) if the defendant's answer to that question is "yes", order such a trial;

    (c) if the defendant does not answer that question, or the answer is "no", apply rule 9.14.

Adult defendant: prosecutor's application for Crown Court trial

B-134   **9.12.**–(1) This rule applies where–

    (a) rule 9.11 applies;

    (b) the defendant agrees to trial in a magistrates' court; but

    (c) the prosecutor wants the court to exercise its power to send the defendant to the Crown Court for trial instead.

    (2) The prosecutor must–

    (a) apply before trial in a magistrates' court begins under Part 24 (trial and sentence in a magistrates' court); and

    (b) notify–

        (i) the defendant, and

        (ii) the magistrates' court officer.

    (3) The court must determine an application to which this rule applies before it deals with any other pre-trial application.

Young defendant

B-135   **9.13.**–(1) This rule applies where–

    (a) the defendant is under 18; and

    (b) the court must decide whether to send the defendant for Crown Court trial instead of ordering trial in a youth court.

    (2) The court must read the allegation of the offence to the defendant.

    (3) The court must explain, in terms the defendant can understand (with help, if necessary)–

    (a) the allegation, unless it is self-explanatory;

    (b) that the offence is one which can be tried in the Crown Court instead of in a youth court;

    (c) that the court is about to ask whether the defendant intends to plead guilty;

    (d) that if the answer is "yes", then the court must treat that as a guilty plea and must sentence the defendant, or commit the defendant to the Crown Court for sentence;

    (e) that if the defendant does not answer, or the answer is "no", then the court must decide whether to send the defendant for Crown Court trial instead of ordering trial in a youth court; and

    (f) that reporting restrictions apply, which the defendant may ask the court to vary or remove.

    (4) The court must then ask whether the defendant intends to plead guilty.

    (5) If the defendant's answer to that question is "yes", the court must exercise its power to deal with the case–

    (a) as if the defendant had just pleaded guilty at a trial in a youth court; and

    (b) in accordance with rule 24.11 (procedure if the court convicts).

    (6) If the defendant does not answer that question, or the answer is "no", in the following sequence the court must then–

    (a) invite the prosecutor to make representations about whether Crown Court or youth court trial is more appropriate;

    (b) invite the defendant to make such representations;

    (c) exercise its power to allocate the case for trial, taking into account–

    (i)   the offence and the circumstances of the offence,

    (ii)   the suitability of a youth court's sentencing powers,

    (iii)   where the defendant is jointly charged with an adult, whether it is necessary in the interests of justice for them to be tried together in the Crown Court, and

    (iv)   any representations by the parties.

Allocation and sending for Crown Court trial

9.14.–(1) This rule applies where—   **B-136**

    (a)   under rule 9.10 or rule 9.13, the court allocates the case to the Crown Court for trial;

    (b)   under rule 9.11, the defendant does not agree to trial in a magistrates' court; or

    (c)   under rule 9.12, the court grants the prosecutor's application for Crown Court trial.

(2) In the following sequence, the court must—

    (a)   invite the prosecutor to make representations about any ancillary matters, including bail and directions for the management of the case in the Crown Court;

    (b)   invite the defendant to make any such representations; and

    (c)   exercise its powers to—

        (i)   send the defendant to the Crown Court for trial, and

        (ii)   give any ancillary directions.

Crown Court initial procedure after sending for trial

Service of prosecution evidence

9.15.–(1) This rule applies where—   **B-137**

    (a)   a magistrates' court sends the defendant to the Crown Court for trial; and

    (b)   the prosecutor serves on the defendant copies of the documents containing the evidence on which the prosecution case relies.

(2) The prosecutor must at the same time serve copies of those documents on the Crown Court officer.

Application to dismiss offence sent for Crown Court trial

9.16.–(1) This rule applies where a defendant wants the Crown Court to dismiss an offence sent   **B-138** for trial there.

(2) The defendant must—

    (a)   apply in writing—

        (i)   not more than 28 days after service of the prosecution evidence, and

        (ii)   before the defendant's arraignment;

    (b)   serve the application on—

        (i)   the Crown Court officer, and

        (ii)   each other party;

    (c)   in the application—

        (i)   explain why the prosecution evidence would not be sufficient for the defendant to be properly convicted,

        (ii)   ask for a hearing, if the defendant wants one, and explain why it is needed,

        (iii)   identify any witness whom the defendant wants to call to give evidence in person, with an indication of what evidence the witness can give,

        (iv)   identify any material already served that the defendant thinks the court will need to determine the application, and

        (v)   include any material not already served on which the defendant relies.

(3) A prosecutor who opposes the application must—

    (a)   serve notice of opposition, not more than 14 days after service of the defendant's notice, on—

        (i)   the Crown Court officer, and

        (ii)   each other party;

    (b)   in the notice of opposition—

        (i)   explain the grounds of opposition,

        (ii)   ask for a hearing, if the prosecutor wants one, and explain why it is needed,

        (iii)   identify any witness whom the prosecutor wants to call to give evidence in person, with an indication of what evidence the witness can give,

      (iv)   identify any material already served that the prosecutor thinks the court will need to determine the application, and

      (v)   include any material not already served on which the prosecutor relies.

  (4) The court may determine an application under this rule—

    (a) at a hearing, in public or in private, or without a hearing;

    (b) in the absence of—

      (i)   the defendant who made the application,

      (ii) the prosecutor, if the prosecutor has had at least 14 days in which to serve notice opposing the application.

  (5) The court may—

    (a) shorten or extend (even after it has expired) a time limit under this rule;

    (b) allow a witness to give evidence in person even if that witness was not identified in the defendant's application or in the prosecutor's notice.

CPD II Preliminary Proceedings 9A: Allocation (Mode of Trial) (as substituted by Criminal Practice Directions 2015 (Amendment No. 2), unreported, November 16, 2016, Lord Thomas C.J.)

B-139   9A.1 Courts must follow the Sentencing Council's guideline on allocation (mode of trial) when deciding whether or not to send defendants charged with "either-way" offences for trial in the Crown Court under section 51(1) of the CDA 1998 [§ 1-24 in the main work].

Criminal Procedure Rules 2015 (S.I. 2015 No. 1490), Pt 10 (as substituted by the Criminal Procedure (Amendment No. 2) Rules 2016 (S.I. 2016 No. 705)

THE INDICTMENT

When this Part applies

    10.1. This Part applies where—

B-140   (a) a magistrates' court sends a defendant to the Crown Court for trial under section 51 or section 51A of the Crime and Disorder Act 1998 [§§ 1-24, 1-25 in the main work];

    (b) a prosecutor wants a High Court judge's permission to serve a draft indictment;

    (c) the Crown Court approves a proposed indictment under paragraph 2 of Schedule 17 to the Crime and Courts Act 2013 [*ibid.*, § 1-371] and rule 11.4 (deferred prosecution agreements: application to approve the terms of an agreement);

    (d) a prosecutor wants to re-institute proceedings in the Crown Court under section 22B of the Prosecution of Offences Act 1985 [*ibid.*, § 1-427];

    (e) the Court of Appeal orders a retrial, under section 8 of the Criminal Appeal Act 1968 [*ibid.*, § 7-113] or under section 77 of the Criminal Justice Act 2003 [*ibid.*, § 7-280].

The indictment: general rules

B-141   **10.2.**–(1) The indictment on which the defendant is arraigned under rule 3.24 (arraigning the defendant on the indictment) must be in writing and must contain, in a paragraph called a "count"—

    (a) a statement of the offence charged that—

      (i)   describes the offence in ordinary language, and

      (ii) identifies any legislation that creates it; and

    (b) such particulars of the conduct constituting the commission of the offence as to make clear what the prosecutor alleges against the defendant.

  (2) More than one incident of the commission of the offence may be included in a count if those incidents taken together amount to a course of conduct having regard to the time, place or purpose of commission.

  (3) The counts must be numbered consecutively.

  (4) An indictment may contain—

    (a) any count charging substantially the same offence as one for which the defendant was sent for trial;

    (b) any count contained in a draft indictment served with the permission of a High Court judge or at the direction of the Court of Appeal; and

    (c) any other count charging an offence that the Crown Court can try and which is based on the prosecution evidence that has been served.

  (5) For the purposes of section 2 of the Administration of Justice (Miscellaneous Provisions) Act 1933 [§§ 1-328, 1-348 in the main work]—

(a) a draft indictment constitutes a bill of indictment;

(b) the draft, or bill, is preferred before the Crown Court and becomes the indictment—

    (i) where rule 10.3 applies (draft indictment generated electronically on sending for trial), immediately before the first count (or the only count, if there is only one) is read to or placed before the defendant to take the defendant's plea under rule 3.24(1)(c),

    (ii) when the prosecutor serves the draft indictment on the Crown Court officer, where rule 10.4 (draft indictment served by the prosecutor after sending for trial), rule 10.5 (draft indictment served by the prosecutor with a High Court judge's permission), rule 10.7 (draft indictment served by the prosecutor on re-instituting proceedings) or rule 10.8 (draft indictment served by the prosecutor at the direction of the Court of Appeal) applies,

    (iii) when the Crown Court approves the proposed indictment, where rule 10.6 applies (draft indictment approved by the Crown Court with deferred prosecution agreement).

(6) An indictment must be in one of the forms set out in the Practice Direction unless—

(a) rule 10.3 applies; or

(b) the Crown Court otherwise directs.

(7) Unless the Crown Court otherwise directs, the court officer must—

(a) endorse any paper copy of the indictment made for the court with—

    (i) a note to identify it as a copy of the indictment, and

    (ii) the date on which the draft indictment became the indictment under paragraph (5); and

(b) where rule 10.4, 10.5, 10.7 or 10.8 applies, serve a copy of the indictment on all parties.

(8) The Crown Court may extend the time limit under rule 10.4, 10.5, 10.7 or 10.8, even after it has expired.

Draft indictment generated electronically on sending for trial

10.3.—(1) Unless the Crown Court otherwise directs before the defendant is arraigned, this rule **B-142** applies where—

(a) a magistrates' court sends a defendant to the Crown Court for trial;

(b) the magistrates' court officer serves on the Crown Court officer the notice required by rule 9.5 (duty of magistrates' court officer); and

(c) by means of such electronic arrangements as the court officer may make for the purpose, there is presented to the Crown Court as a count—

    (i) each allegation of an indictable offence specified in the notice, and

    (ii) each allegation specified in the notice to which section 40 of the Criminal Justice Act 1988 applies (specified summary offences founded on the prosecution evidence [*ibid.*, § 1-128]).

(2) Where this rule applies—

(a) each such allegation constitutes a count;

(b) the allegation or allegations so specified together constitute a draft indictment;

(c) before the draft indictment so constituted is preferred before the Crown Court under rule 10.2(5)(b)(i) the prosecutor may substitute for any count an amended count to the same effect and charging the same offence;

(d) if under rule 9.15 (service of prosecution evidence) the prosecutor has served copies of the documents containing the evidence on which the prosecution case relies then, before the draft indictment is preferred before the Crown Court under rule 10.2(5)(b)(i), the prosecutor may substitute or add—

    (i) any count charging substantially the same offence as one specified in the notice, and

    (ii) any other count charging an offence which the Crown Court can try and which is based on the prosecution evidence so served; and

(e) a prosecutor who substitutes or adds a count under paragraph (2)(c) or (d) must serve that count on the Crown Court officer and the defendant.

Draft indictment served by the prosecutor after sending for trial

10.4.—(1) This rule applies where— **B-143**

(a) a magistrates' court sends a defendant to the Crown Court for trial; and

(b) rule 10.3 (draft indictment generated electronically on sending for trial) does not apply

(2) The prosecutor must serve a draft indictment on the Crown Court officer not more than 28

days after serving under rule 9.15 (service of prosecution evidence) copies of the documents containing the evidence on which the prosecution case relies.

Draft indictment served by the prosecutor with a High Court judge's permission

B-144   **10.5.**–(1) This rule applies where–
    (a) the prosecutor applies to a High Court judge under rule 10.9 (application to a High Court judge for permission to serve a draft indictment); and
    (b) the judge gives permission to serve a proposed indictment.
  (2) Where this rule applies–
    (a) that proposed indictment constitutes the draft indictment; and
    (b) the prosecutor must serve the draft indictment on the Crown Court officer not more than 28 days after the High Court judge's decision.

Draft indictment approved with deferred prosecution agreement

B-145   **10.6.**–(1) This rule applies where–
    (a) the prosecutor applies to the Crown Court under rule 11.4 (deferred prosecution agreements: application to approve the terms of an agreement); and
    (b) the Crown Court approves the proposed indictment served with that application.
  (2) Where this rule applies, that proposed indictment constitutes the draft indictment.

Draft indictment served by the prosecutor on re-instituting proceedings

B-146   **10.7.**–(1) This rule applies where the prosecutor wants to re-institute proceedings in the Crown Court under section 22B of the Prosecution of Offences Act 1985 [*ibid.*, § 1-427].
  (2) The prosecutor must serve a draft indictment on the Crown Court officer not more than 3 months after the proceedings were stayed under section 22(4) of that Act.

Draft indictment served by the prosecutor at the direction of the Court of Appeal

B-147   **10.8.**–(1) This rule applies where the Court of Appeal orders a retrial.
  (2) The prosecutor must serve a draft indictment on the Crown Court officer not more than 28 days after that order.

Application to a High Court judge for permission to serve a draft indictment

B-148   **10.9.**–(1) This rule applies where a prosecutor wants a High Court judge's permission to serve a draft indictment.
  (2) Such a prosecutor must–
    (a) apply in writing;
    (b) serve the application on–
      (i)   the court officer, and
      (ii) the proposed defendant, unless the judge otherwise directs; and
    (c) ask for a hearing, if the prosecutor wants one, and explain why it is needed.
  (3) The application must–
    (a) attach–
      (i)   the proposed indictment,
      (ii)   copies of the documents containing the evidence on which the prosecutor relies, including any written witness statement or statements complying with rule 16.2 (content of written witness statement) and any documentary exhibit to any such statement,
      (iii) a copy of any indictment on which the defendant already has been arraigned, and
      (iv)   if not contained in such an indictment, a list of any offence or offences for which the defendant already has been sent for trial;
    (b) include–
      (i)   a concise statement of the circumstances in which, and the reasons why, the application is made, and
      (ii)   a concise summary of the evidence contained in the documents accompanying the application, identifying each passage in those documents said to evidence each offence alleged by the prosecutor and relating that evidence to each count in the proposed indictment; and
    (c) contain a statement that, to the best of the prosecutor's knowledge, information and belief–
      (i)   the evidence on which the prosecutor relies will be available at the trial, and
      (ii)   the allegations contained in the application are substantially true

unless the application is made by or on behalf of the Director of Public Prosecutions or the Director of the Serious Fraud Office.

(4) A proposed defendant served with an application who wants to make representations to the judge must—

   (a) serve the representations on the court officer and on the prosecutor;

   (b) do so as soon as practicable, and in any event with in such period as the judge directs; and

   (c) ask for a hearing, if the proposed defendant wants one, and explain why it is needed.

(5) The judge may determine the application—

   (a) without a hearing, or at a hearing in public or in private;

   (b) with or without receiving the oral evidence of any proposed witness.

(6) At any hearing, if the judge so directs a statement required by paragraph (3)(c) must be repeated on oath or affirmation.

(7) If the judge gives permission to serve a draft indictment, the decision must be recorded in writing and endorsed on, or annexed to, the proposed indictment.

CPD II Preliminary Proceedings 10A: Preparation and Content of the Indictment (as substituted by Criminal Practice Directions 2015 (Amendment No. 2), unreported, November 16, 2016, Lord Thomas C.J.)

Preferring the indictment

10A.1 Section 2 of the Administration of Justice (Miscellaneous Provisions) Act 1933 [§§ 1-328, **B-149** 1-348 in the main work] allows Criminal Procedure Rules to "make provision ... as to the manner in which and the time at which bills of indictment are to be preferred". CrimPR 10.2(5) lists the events which constitute preferment for the purposes of that Act. Where a defendant is contemplating an application to the Crown Court to dismiss an offence sent for trial, under the provisions to which CrimPR 9.16 applies, or where the prosecutor is contemplating discontinuance, under the provisions to which CrimPR, Pt 12, applies, the parties and the court must be astute to the effect of the occurrence of those events: the right to apply for dismissal is lost if the defendant is arraigned, and the right to discontinue is lost if the indictment is preferred.

Printing and signature of indictment

10A.2 Neither section 2 of the Administration of Justice (Miscellaneous Provisions) Act 1933 nor **B-150** the Criminal Procedure Rules require an indictment to be printed or signed. Section 2(1) of the Act was amended by section 116 of the Coroners and Justice Act 2009 to remove the requirement for signature. For the potential benefit of the Criminal Appeal Office, CrimPR 10.2(7) requires only that any paper copy of the indictment which for any reason in fact is made for the court must be endorsed with a note to identify it as a copy of the indictment, and with the date on which the indictment came into being. For the same reason, CrimPR 3.22 requires only that any paper copy of an indictment which in fact has been made must be endorsed with a note of the order and of its date where the court makes an order for joint or separate trials affecting that indictment or makes an order for the amendment of that indictment in any respect.

Content of indictment; joint and separate trials

10A.3 The rule has been abolished which formerly required an indictment containing more than **B-150a** one count to include only offences founded on the same facts, or offences which constitute all or part of a series of the same or a similar character. However, if an indictment charges more than one offence, and if at least one of those offences does not meet those criteria, then CrimPR 3.21(4)(a) requires the court to order separate trials; thus maintaining the effect of the long-standing principle. Subject to that, it is for the court to decide which allegations, against whom, should be tried at the same time, having regard to the prosecutor's proposals, the parties' representations, the court's powers under section 5(3) of the Indictments Act 1915 [§ 1-249 in the main work] (see also CrimPR 3.21(4)(b)) and the overriding objective. Where necessary the court should be invited to exercise those powers. It is generally undesirable for a large number of counts to be tried at the same time and the prosecutor may be required to identify a selection of counts on which the trial should proceed, leaving a decision to be taken later whether to try any of the remainder.

10A.4 Where an indictment contains substantive counts and one or more related conspiracy counts, the court will expect the prosecutor to justify their joint trial. Failing justification, the prosecutor should be required to choose whether to proceed on the substantive counts or on the conspiracy counts. In any event, if there is a conviction on any counts that are tried, then those that have not been proceeded with can remain on the file marked "not to be proceeded with without the leave of the court or the Court of Appeal". In the event that a conviction is later quashed on appeal, the remaining counts can be tried.

10A.5 There is no rule of law or practice which prohibits two indictments being in existence at the same time for the same offence against the same person and on the same facts. However, the court will not allow the prosecutor to proceed on both indictments. They cannot be tried together and the court will require the prosecutor to elect the one on which the trial will proceed. Where different defendants have been separately sent for trial for offences which properly may be tried together then it is permissible to join in one indictment counts based on the separate sendings for trial even if an indictment based on one of them already exists.

Draft indictment generated electronically on sending for trial

10A.6 CrimPR 10.3 applies where court staff have introduced arrangements for the charges sent for trial to be presented in the Crown Court as the counts of a draft indictment without the need for those charges to be rewritten and served a second time on the defendant and on the court office. Where such arrangements are introduced, court users will be informed (and the fact will become apparent on the sending for trial).

10A.7 Now that there is no restriction on the counts that an indictment may contain (see para. 10A.3 above), and given the Crown Court's power, and in some cases obligation, to order separate trials, few circumstances will arise in which the court will wish to exercise the discretion conferred by rule 10.3(1) to direct that the rule will not apply, thus discarding such an electronically generated draft indictment. The most likely such circumstance to arise would be in a case in which prosecution evidence emerging soon after sending requires such a comprehensive amendment of the counts as to make it more convenient to all participants for the prosecutor to prepare and serve under CrimPR 10.4 a complete new draft indictment than to amend the electronically generated draft.

Draft indictment served by the prosecutor

10A.8 CrimPR 10.4 applies after sending for trial wherever CrimPR 10.3 does not. It requires the prosecutor to prepare a draft indictment and serve it on the Crown Court officer, who by CrimPR 10.2(7)(b) then must serve it on the defendant. In most instances service will be by electronic means, usually by making use of the Crown Court digital case system to which the prosecutor will upload the draft (which at once then becomes the indictment, under s.2 of the Administration of Justice (Miscellaneous Provisions) Act 1933 and CrimPR 10.2(5)(b)(ii)).

10A.9 The prosecutor's time limit for service of the draft indictment under CrimPR 10.4 is 28 days after serving under CrimPR 9.15 the evidence on which the prosecution case relies. The Crown Court may extend that time limit, under CrimPR 10.2(8). However, under paragraph CrimPD I 3A.16 of these practice directions the court will expect that in every case a draft indictment will be served at least 7 days before the plea and trial preparation hearing, whether the time prescribed by the rule will have expired or not.

Amending the content of the indictment

10A.10 Where the prosecutor wishes to substitute or add counts to a draft indictment, or to invite the court to allow an indictment to be amended, so that the draft indictment, or indictment, will charge offences which differ from those with which the defendant first was charged, the defendant should be given as much notice as possible of what is proposed. It is likely that the defendant will need time to consider his or her position and advance notice will help to avoid delaying the proceedings.

Multiple offending: count charging more than one incident

10A.11 CrimPR 10.2(2) allows a single count to allege more than one incident of the commission of an offence in certain circumstances. Each incident must be of the same offence. The circumstances in which such a count may be appropriate include, but are not limited to, the following:

    (a) the victim on each occasion was the same, or there was no identifiable individual victim as, for example, in a case of the unlawful importation of controlled drugs or of money laundering;

    (b) the alleged incidents involved a marked degree of repetition in the method employed or in their location, or both;

    (c) the alleged incidents took place over a clearly defined period, typically (but not necessarily) no more than about a year;

    (d) in any event, the defence is such as to apply to every alleged incident. Where what is in issue differs between different incidents, a single "multiple incidents" count will not be appropriate (though it may be appropriate to use two or more such counts according to the circumstances and to the issues raised by the defence).

10A.12 Even in circumstances such as those set out above, there may be occasions on which a prosecutor chooses not to use such a count, in order to bring the case within section 75(3)(a) of the

PCA 2002 (criminal lifestyle established by conviction of three or more offences in the same proceedings [§ 5-880 in the main work]): for example, because section 75(2)(c) of that Act does not apply (criminal lifestyle established by an offence committed over a period of at least six months). Where the prosecutor proposes such a course, it is unlikely that CrimPR, Pt 1 (the overriding objective) will require an indictment to contain a single "multiple incidents" count in place of a larger number of counts, subject to the general principles set out at paragraph 10A.3.

10A.13 For some offences, particularly sexual offences, the penalty for the offence may have changed during the period over which the alleged incidents took place. In such a case, additional "multiple incidents" counts should be used so that each count only alleges incidents to which the same maximum penalty applies.

10A.14 In other cases, such as sexual or physical abuse, a complainant may be in a position only to give evidence of a series of similar incidents without being able to specify when or the precise circumstances in which they occurred. In these cases, a "multiple incidents" count may be desirable. If on the other hand, the complainant is able to identify particular incidents of the offence by reference to a date or other specific event, but alleges that in addition there were other incidents which the complainant is unable to specify, then it may be desirable to include separate counts for the identified incidents and a "multiple incidents" count or counts alleging that incidents of the same offence occurred "many" times. Using a "multiple incidents" count may be an appropriate alternative to using "specimen" counts in some cases where repeated sexual or physical abuse is alleged. The choice of count will depend on the particular circumstances of the case and should be determined bearing in mind the implications for sentencing set out in *R. v. Canavan; R. v. Kidd; R. v. Shaw* [1998] 1 Cr.App.R. 79, CA. In *R. v A.* [2015] 2 Cr.App.R.(S.) 12, the Court of Appeal reviewed the circumstances in which a mixture of multiple incident and single incident counts might be appropriate where the prosecutor alleged sustained sexual abuse.

Multiple offending: trial by jury and then by judge alone

10A.15 Under sections 17 to 21 of the Domestic Violence, Crime and Victims Act 2004 [§§ 4-338   **B-151a**
et seq. in the main work], the court may order that the trial of certain counts will be by jury in the usual way and, if the jury convicts, that other associated counts will be tried by judge alone. The use of this power is likely to be appropriate where justice cannot be done without charging a large number of separate offences and the allegations against the defendant appear to fall into distinct groups by reference to the identity of the victim, by reference to the dates of the offences, or by some other distinction in the nature of the offending conduct alleged.

10A.16 In such a case, it is essential to make clear from the outset the association asserted by the prosecutor between those counts to be tried by a jury and those counts which it is proposed should be tried by judge alone, if the jury convict on the former. A special form of indictment is prescribed for this purpose.

10A.17 An order for such a trial may be made only at a preparatory hearing. It follows that where the prosecutor intends to invite the court to order such a trial it will normally be appropriate to proceed as follows. A draft indictment in the form appropriate to such a trial should be served with an application under CrimPR 3.15 for a preparatory hearing. This will ensure that the defendant is aware at the earliest possible opportunity of what the prosecutor proposes and of the proposed association of counts in the indictment.

10A.18 At the start of the preparatory hearing, the defendant should be arraigned on all counts in Part One of the indictment. Arraignment on Part Two need not take place until after there has been either a guilty plea to, or finding of guilt on, an associated count in Part One of the indictment.

10A.19 If the prosecutor's application is successful, the prosecutor should prepare an abstract of the indictment, containing the counts from Part One only, for use in the jury trial. Preparation of such an abstract does not involve "amendment" of the indictment. It is akin to where a defendant pleads guilty to certain counts in an indictment and is put in the charge of the jury on the remaining counts only.

10A.20 If the prosecutor's application for a two stage trial is unsuccessful, the prosecutor may apply to amend the indictment to remove from it any counts in Part Two which would make jury trial on the whole indictment impracticable and to revert to a standard form of indictment. It will be a matter for the court whether arraignment on outstanding counts takes place at the preparatory hearing, or at a future date.

CPD II Preliminary Proceedings 10B: Voluntary Bills of Indictment (as substituted by Criminal Practice Directions 2015 (Amendment No. 1), unreported, March 23, 2016, Lord Thomas C.J.)

10B.1 Section 2(2)(b) of the Administration of Justice (Miscellaneous Provisions) Act 1933 [§   **B-152**
1-328 in the main work] and paragraph 2(6) of Schedule 3 to the CDA 1998 [*ibid.*, § 1-36 *et seq.*] allow the preferment of a bill of indictment by the direction or with the consent of a judge of the High Court. Bills so preferred are known as "voluntary bills".

10B.2 Applications for such consent must comply with CrimPR 10.3.

10B.3 Those requirements should be complied with in relation to each defendant named in the indictment for which consent is sought, whether or not it is proposed to prefer any new count against him or her.

10B.4 The preferment of a voluntary bill is an exceptional procedure. Consent should only be granted where good reason to depart from the normal procedure is clearly shown and only where the interests of justice, rather than considerations of administrative convenience, require it.

10B.5 Prosecutors must follow the procedures prescribed by the rule unless there are good reasons for not doing so, in which case prosecutors must inform the judge that the procedures have not been followed and seek leave to dispense with all or any of them. Judges should not give leave to dispense unless good reasons are shown.

10B.6 A judge to whom application for consent to the preferment of a documents [sic] submitted by the prosecutor and any written submissions made by the prospective defendant, and may properly seek any necessary amplification [*sic*]. CrimPR 10.3(4)(b) allows the judge to set a timetable for representations. The judge may invite oral submissions from either party, or accede to a request for an opportunity to make oral submissions, if the judge considers it necessary or desirable to receive oral submissions in order to make a sound and fair decision on the application. Any such oral submissions should be made on notice to the other party and in open court unless the judge otherwise directs.

Criminal Procedure Rules 2015 (S.I. 2015 No. 1490), Pt 11

DEFERRED PROSECUTION AGREEMENTS

When this Part applies

B-153   **11.1.**–(1) This Part applies to proceedings in the Crown Court under Schedule 17 to the Crime and Courts Act 2013 [§§ 1-370 *et seq.* in the main work].

(2) In this Part—

    (a) "agreement" means a deferred prosecution agreement under paragraph 1 of that Schedule;

    (b) "prosecutor" means a prosecutor designated by or under paragraph 3 of that Schedule; and

    (c) "defendant" means the corporation, partnership or association with whom the prosecutor proposes to enter, or enters, an agreement.

Exercise of court's powers

B-154   **11.2.**–(1) The court must determine an application to which this Part applies at a hearing, which—

    (a) must be in private, under rule 11.3 (application to approve a proposal to enter an agreement);

    (b) may be in public or private, under rule 11.4 (application to approve the terms of an agreement), rule 11.6 (application to approve a variation of the terms of an agreement) or rule 11.9 (application to postpone the publication of information by the prosecutor);

    (c) must be in public, under rule 11.5 (application on breach of agreement) or rule 11.7 (application to lift suspension of prosecution), unless the court otherwise directs.

(2) If at a hearing in private to which rule 11.4 or rule 11.6 applies the court approves the agreement or the variation proposed, the court must announce its decision and reasons at a hearing in public.

(3) The court must not determine an application under rule 11.3, rule 11.4 or rule 11.6 unless—

    (a) both parties are present;

    (b) the prosecutor provides the court with a written declaration that, for the purposes of the application—

        (i) the investigator enquiring into the alleged offence or offences has certified that no information has been supplied which the investigator knows to be inaccurate, misleading or incomplete, and

        (ii) the prosecutor has complied with the prosecution obligation to disclose material to the defendant; and

    (c) the defendant provides the court with a written declaration that, for the purposes of the application—

        (i) the defendant has not supplied any information which the defendant knows to be inaccurate, misleading or incomplete, and

        (ii) the individual through whom the defendant makes the declaration has made reasonable enquiries and believes the defendant's declaration to be true.

(4) The court must not determine an application under rule 11.5 or rule 11.7–

    (a) in the prosecutor's absence; or

    (b) in the absence of the defendant, unless the defendant has had at least 28 days in which to make representations.

(5) If the court approves a proposal to enter an agreement–

    (a) the general rule is that any further application to which this Part applies must be made to the same judge; but

    (b) the court may direct other arrangements.

(6) The court may adjourn a hearing–

    (a) if either party asks, or on its own initiative;

    (b) in particular, if the court requires more information about–

        (i) the facts of an alleged offence,

        (ii) the terms of a proposal to enter an agreement, or of a proposed agreement or variation of an agreement, or

        (iii) the circumstances in which the prosecutor wants the court to decide whether the defendant has failed to comply with the terms of an agreement.

(7) The court may–

    (a) hear an application under rule 11.4 immediately after an application under rule 11.3, if the court approves a proposal to enter an agreement;

    (b) hear an application under rule 11.7 immediately after an application under rule 11.5, if the court terminates an agreement.

Application to approve a proposal to enter an agreement

11.3.–(1) This rule applies where a prosecutor wants the court to approve a proposal to enter an   **B-155**
agreement.

    (2) The prosecutor must–

    (a) apply in writing after the commencement of negotiations between the parties but before the terms of agreement have been settled; and

    (b) serve the application on–

        (i) the court officer, and

        (ii) the defendant.

    (3) The application must–

    (a) identify the parties to the proposed agreement;

    (b) attach a proposed indictment setting out such of the offences listed in Part 2 of Schedule 17 to the Crime and Courts Act 2013 as the prosecutor is considering;

    (c) include or attach a statement of facts proposed for inclusion in the agreement, which must give full particulars of each alleged offence, including details of any alleged financial gain or loss;

    (d) include any information about the defendant that would be relevant to sentence in the event of conviction for the offence or offences;

    (e) specify the proposed expiry date of the agreement;

    (f) describe the proposed terms of the agreement, including details of any–

        (i) monetary penalty to be paid by the defendant, and the time within which any such penalty is to be paid,

        (ii) compensation, reparation or donation to be made by the defendant, the identity of the recipient of any such payment and the time within which any such payment is to be made,

        (iii) surrender of profits or other financial benefit by the defendant, and the time within which any such sum is to be surrendered,

        (iv) arrangement to be made in relation to the management or conduct of the defendant's business,

        (v) co-operation required of the defendant in any investigation related to the offence or offences,

        (vi) other action required of the defendant,

        (vii) arrangement to monitor the defendant's compliance with a term,

        (viii) consequence of the defendant's failure to comply with a term, and

        (ix) prosecution costs to be paid by the defendant, and the time within which any such costs are to be paid;

    (g) in relation to those terms, explain how they comply with–

(i) the requirements of the code issued under paragraph 6 of Schedule 17 to the Crime and Courts Act 2013, and

(ii) any sentencing guidelines or guideline cases which apply;

(h) contain or attach the defendant's written consent to the proposal; and

(i) explain why—

(i) entering into an agreement is likely to be in the interests of justice, and

(ii) the proposed terms of the agreement are fair, reasonable and proportionate.

(4) If the proposed statement of facts includes assertions that the defendant does not admit, the application must—

(a) specify the facts that are not admitted; and

(b) explain why that is immaterial for the purposes of the proposal to enter an agreement.

Application to approve the terms of an agreement

B-156   **11.4.**–(1) This rule applies where—

(a) the court has approved a proposal to enter an agreement on an application under rule 11.3; and

(b) the prosecutor wants the court to approve the terms of the agreement.

(2) The prosecutor must—

(a) apply in writing as soon as practicable after the parties have settled the terms; and

(b) serve the application on—

(i) the court officer, and

(ii) the defendant.

(3) The application must—

(a) attach the agreement;

(b) indicate in what respect, if any, the terms of the agreement differ from those proposed in the application under rule 11.3;

(c) contain or attach the defendant's written consent to the agreement;

(d) explain why—

(i) the agreement is in the interests of justice, and

(ii) the terms of the agreement are fair, reasonable and proportionate;

(e) attach a draft indictment, charging the defendant with the offence or offences the subject of the agreement; and

(f) include any application for the hearing to be in private.

(4) If the court approves the agreement and the draft indictment, the court officer must—

(a) endorse any paper copy of the indictment made for the court with—

(i) a note to identify it as the indictment approved by the court, and

(ii) the date of the court's approval; and

(b) treat the case as if it had been suspended by order of the court.

Application on breach of agreement

B-157   **11.5.**–(1) This rule applies where—

(a) the prosecutor believes that the defendant has failed to comply with the terms of an agreement; and

(b) the prosecutor wants the court to decide—

(i) whether the defendant has failed to comply, and

(ii) if so, whether to terminate the agreement, or to invite the parties to agree proposals to remedy that failure.

(2) The prosecutor must—

(a) apply in writing, as soon as practicable after becoming aware of the grounds for doing so; and

(b) serve the application on—

(i) the court officer, and

(ii) the defendant.

(3) The application must—

(a) specify each respect in which the prosecutor believes the defendant has failed to comply with the terms of the agreement, and explain the reasons for the prosecutor's belief; and

(b) attach a copy of any document containing evidence on which the prosecutor relies.

(4) A defendant who wants to make representations in response to the application must serve the representations on—

(a) the court officer; and

(b) the prosecutor,

not more than 28 days after service of the application.

Application to approve a variation of the terms of an agreement

11.6.—(1) This rule applies where the parties have agreed to vary the terms of an agreement **B-158** because—

  (a) on an application under rule 11.5 (application on breach of agreement), the court has invited them to do so; or

  (b) variation of the agreement is necessary to avoid a failure by the defendant to comply with its terms in circumstances that were not, and could not have been, foreseen by either party at the time the agreement was made.

(2) The prosecutor must—

  (a) apply in writing, as soon as practicable after the parties have settled the terms of the variation; and

  (b) serve the application on—

    (i) the court officer, and

    (ii) the defendant.

(3) The application must—

  (a) specify each variation proposed;

  (b) contain or attach the defendant's written consent to the variation;

  (c) explain why—

    (i) the variation is in the interests of justice, and

    (ii) the terms of the agreement as varied are fair, reasonable and proportionate; and

  (d) include any application for the hearing to be in private.

Application to lift suspension of prosecution

11.7.—(1) This rule applies where— **B-159**

  (a) the court terminates an agreement before its expiry date; and

  (b) the prosecutor wants the court to lift the suspension of the prosecution that applied when the court approved the terms of the agreement.

(2) The prosecutor must—

  (a) apply in writing, as soon as practicable after the termination of the agreement; and

  (b) serve the application on—

    (i) the court officer, and

    (ii) the defendant.

(3) [*Identical to r.11.5(4)*, ante, § *B-157*.]

Notice to discontinue prosecution

11.8.—(1) This rule applies where an agreement expires— **B-160**

  (a) on its expiry date, or on a date treated as its expiry date; and

  (b) without having been terminated by the court.

(2) The prosecutor must—

  (a) as soon as practicable give notice in writing discontinuing the prosecution on the indictment approved by the court under rule 11.4 (application to approve the terms of an agreement); and

  (b) serve the notice on—

    (i) the court officer, and

    (ii) the defendant.

Application to postpone the publication of information by the prosecutor

11.9.—(1) This rule applies where the prosecutor— **B-161**

  (a) makes an application under rule 11.4 (application to approve the terms of an agreement), rule 11.5 (application on breach of agreement) or rule 11.6 (application to approve a variation of the terms of an agreement);

  (b) decides not to make an application under rule 11.5, despite believing that the defendant has failed to comply with the terms of the agreement; or

  (c) gives a notice under rule 11.8 (notice to discontinue prosecution).

(2) A party who wants the court to order that the publication of information by the prosecutor about the court's or the prosecutor's decision should be postponed must—

   (a) apply in writing, as soon as practicable and in any event before such publication occurs;

   (b) serve the application on—

      (i) the court officer, and

      (ii) the other party; and

   (c) in the application—

      (i) specify the proposed terms of the order, and for how long it should last, and

      (ii) explain why an order in the terms proposed is necessary.

Duty of court officer, etc.

B-162   **11.10.**—(1) Unless the court otherwise directs, the court officer must—

   (a) arrange for the recording of proceedings on an application to which this Part applies;

   (b) arrange for the transcription of such a recording if—

      (i) a party wants such a transcript, or

      (ii) anyone else wants such a transcript (but that is subject to the restrictions in paragraph (2)).

  (2) Unless the court otherwise directs, a person who transcribes a recording of proceedings under such arrangements—

   (a) must not supply anyone other than a party with a transcript of a recording of—

      (i) a hearing in private, or

      (ii) a hearing in public to which reporting restrictions apply;

   (b) subject to that, must supply any person with any transcript for which that person asks—

      (i) in accordance with the transcription arrangements made by the court officer, and

      (ii) on payment by that person of any fee prescribed.

  (3) The court officer must not identify either party to a hearing in private under rule 11.3 (application to approve a proposal to enter an agreement) or rule 11.4 (application to approve the terms of an agreement)—

   (a) in any notice displayed in the vicinity of the courtroom; or

   (b) in any other information published by the court officer.

Court's power to vary requirements under this Part

     11.11.—(1) The court may—

   (a) shorten or extend (even after it has expired) a time limit under this Part;

   (b) allow there to be made orally—

      (i) an application under rule 11.4 (application to approve the terms of an agreement), or

      (ii) an application under rule 11.7 (application to lift suspension of prosecution)

      where the court exercises its power under rule 11.2(7) to hear one application immediately after another.

  (2) A party who wants an extension of time must—

   (a) apply when serving the application or notice for which it is needed; and

   (b) explain the delay.

Criminal Procedure Rules 2015 (S.I. 2015 No. 1490), Pt 12

<small>DISCONTINUING A PROSECUTION</small>

When this Part applies

B-163   **12.1**—(1) This Part applies where—

   (a) the Director of Public Prosecutions can discontinue a case in a magistrates' court, under section 23 of the Prosecution of Offences Act 1985 [§ 1-454 in the main work];

   (b) the Director of Public Prosecutions, or another public prosecutor, can discontinue a case sent for trial in the Crown Court, under section 23A of the Prosecution of Offences Act 1985 [*ibid.*, § 1-459].

  (2) In this Part, "prosecutor" means one of those authorities.

Discontinuing a case

     12.2—(1) A prosecutor exercising a power to which this Part applies must serve notice on—

   (a) the court officer;

   (b) the defendant; and

   (c) any custodian of the defendant.

(2) Such a notice must—
  (a) identify—
    (i) the defendant and each offence to which the notice relates,
    (ii) the person serving the notice, and
    (iii) the power that that person is exercising;
  (b) explain—
    (i) in the copy of the notice served on the court officer, the reasons for discontinuing the case,
    (ii) that the notice brings the case to an end,
    (iii) if the defendant is in custody for any offence to which the notice relates, that the defendant must be released from that custody, and
    (iv) if the notice is under section 23 of the 1985 Act, that the defendant has a right to require the case to continue.
(3) Where the defendant is on bail, the court officer must notify—
  (a) any surety; and
  (b) any person responsible for monitoring or securing the defendant's compliance with a condition of bail.

Defendant's notice to continue
12.3–(1) This rule applies where a prosecutor serves a notice to discontinue under section 23 of the 1985 Act.
(2) A defendant who wants the case to continue must serve notice—
  (a) on the court officer; and
  (b) not more than 35 days after service of the notice to discontinue.
(3) If the defendant serves such a notice, the court officer must—
  (a) notify the prosecutor; and
  (b) refer the case to the court.

Criminal Procedure Rules 2015 (S.I. 2015 No. 1490), Pt 13

WARRANTS FOR ARREST, DETENTION OR IMPRISONMENT
[*Not set out in this work*].
B-164

Criminal Procedure Rules 2015 (S.I. 2015 No. 1490), Pt 14

BAIL AND CUSTODY TIME LIMITS

General rules

When this Part applies
14.1.–(1) This Part applies where—
  (a) a magistrates' court or the Crown Court can—
    (i) grant or withhold bail, or impose or vary a condition of bail, and
    (ii) where bail has been withheld, extend a custody time limit;
  (b) a magistrates' court can monitor and enforce compliance with a supervision measure imposed in another European Union member State.
(2) Rules 14.20, 14.21 and 14.22 apply where a magistrates' court can authorise an extension of the period for which a defendant is released on bail before being charged with an offence.
(3) In this part, "defendant" includes a person who has been granted bail by a police officer.
★**B-165**

[This rule is printed as amended by the Criminal Procedure (Amendment No. 2) Rules 2017 (S.I. 2017 No. 282).]

Exercise of court's powers: general
14.2.–(1) The court must not make a decision to which this Part applies unless—
  (a) each party to the decision and any surety directly affected by the decision—
    (i) is present, or
    (ii) has had an opportunity to make representations;
  (b) on an application for bail by a defendant who is absent and in custody, the court is satisfied that the defendant—
★**B-166**

      (i)   has waived the right to attend, or

     (ii)   was present when a court withheld bail in the case on a previous occasion and has been in custody continuously since then;

  (c) on a prosecutor's appeal against a grant of bail, application to extend a custody time limit or appeal against a refusal to extend such a time limit–

      (i)   the court is satisfied that a defendant who is absent has waived the right to attend, or

     (ii)   the court is satisfied that it would be just to proceed even though the defendant is absent;

  (d) the court is satisfied that sufficient time has been allowed–

      (i)   for the defendant to consider the information provided by the prosecutor under rule 14.5(2), and

     (ii)   for the court to consider the partie' representations and make the decision required.

(2) The court may make a decision to which this Part applies at a hearing, in public or in private.

(3) The court may determine without a hearing an application to vary a condition of bail if–

  (a) the parties to the application have agreed the terms of the variation proposed; or

  (b) on an application by a defendant, the court determines the application no sooner than the fifth business day after the application was served.

(4) The court may adjourn a determination to which this Part applies, if that is necessary to obtain information sufficient to allow the court to make the decision required.

(5) At any hearing at which the court makes one of the following decisions, the court must announce in terms the defendant can understand (with help, if necessary), and by reference to the circumstances of the defendant and the case, its reasons for–

  (a) withholding bail, or imposing or varying a bail condition;

  (b) granting bail, where the prosecutor opposed the grant; or

  (c) where the defendant is under 18–

      (i)   imposing or varying a bail condition when ordering the defendant to be detained in local authority accommodation, or

     (ii)   ordering the defendant to be detained in youth detention accommodation.

(6) At any hearing at which the court grants bail, the court must–

  (a) tell the defendant where and when to surrender to custody; or

  (b) arrange for the court officer to give the defendant, as soon as practicable, notice of where and when to surrender to custody.

(7) This rule does not apply on an application to a magistrates' court to authorise an extension of pre-charge bail.

[This rule is printed as amended by the Criminal Procedure (Amendment) Rules 2017 (S.I. 2017 No. 144); and the Criminal Procedure (Amendment No. 2) Rules 2017 (S.I. 2017 No. 282).]

Duty of justices' legal adviser

B-167   **14.3.**–(1) This rule applies–

  (a) only in a magistrates' court; and

  (b) unless the court–

      (i)   includes a District Judge (Magistrates' Courts), and

     (ii)   otherwise directs.

(2) A justices' legal adviser must–

  (a) assist an unrepresented defendant;

  (b) give the court such advice as is required to enable it to exercise its powers;

  (c) if required, attend the members of the court outside the courtroom to give such advice, but inform the parties of any advice so given.

General duties of court officer

★B-168   **14.4.**–(1) The court officer must arrange for a note or other record to be made of–

  (a) the parties' representations about bail; and

  (b) the court's reasons for a decision–

      (i)   to withhold bail, or to impose or vary a bail condition,

     (ii)   to grant bail, where the prosecutor opposed the grant, or

    (iii)   on an application to which rule 14.21 applies (application to authorise extension of pre-charge bail).

(2) The court officer must serve notice of a decision about bail on–

(a) the defendant (but, in the Crown Court, only where the defendant's legal representative asks for such a notice, or where the defendant has no legal representative);

(b) the prosecutor (but only where the court granted bail, the prosecutor opposed the grant, and the prosecutor asks for such a notice);

(c) a party to the decision who was absent when it was made;

(d) a surety who is directly affected by the decision;

(e) the defendant's custodian, where the defendant is in custody and the decision requires the custodian—

    (i) to release the defendant (or will do so, if a requirement ordered by the court is met), or

    (ii) to transfer the defendant to the custody of another custodian;

(f) the court officer for any other court at which the defendant is required by that decision to surrender to custody.

(3) Where the court postpones the date on which a defendant who is on bail must surrender to custody, the court officer must serve notice of the postponed date on—

(a) the defendant; and

(b) any surety.

(4) Where a magistrates' court withholds bail in a case to which section 5(6A) of the Bail Act 1976 [§ 3-28 in the main work] applies (remand in custody after hearing full argument on an application for bail), the court officer must serve on the defendant a certificate that the court heard full argument.

(5) Where the court determines without a hearing an application to which rule 14.21 applies (application to authorise extension of pre-charge bail), the court officer must—

(a) if the court allows the application, notify the applicant;

(b) if the court refuses the application, notify the applicant and the defendant.

[This rule is printed as amended by the Criminal Procedure (Amendment No. 2) Rules 2017 (S.I. 2017 No. 282).]

Bail

Prosecutor's representations about bail

14.5.—(1) This rule applies whenever the court can grant or withhold bail.

★**B-169**

(2) The prosecutor must as soon as practicable—

(a) provide the defendant with all the information in the prosecutor's possession which is material to what the court must decide; and

(b) provide the court with the same information.

(3) A prosecutor who opposes the grant of bail must specify—

(a) each exception to the general right to bail on which the prosecutor relies; and

(b) each consideration that the prosecutor thinks relevant.

(4) A prosecutor who wants the court to impose a condition on any grant of bail must—

(a) specify each condition proposed; and

(b) explain what purpose would be served by such a condition.

[This rule is printed as amended by the Criminal Procedure (Amendment) Rules 2017 (S.I. 2017 No. 144).]

Reconsideration of police bail by magistrates' court

14.6.—(1) This rule applies where—

★**B-170**

(a) a party wants a magistrates' court to reconsider a bail decision by a police officer after the defendant is charged with an offence;

(b) a defendant wants a magistrates' court to reconsider a bail condition imposed by a police officer before the defendant is charged with an offence.

(2) An application under this rule must be made to—

(a) the magistrates' court to whose custody the defendant is under a duty to surrender, if any; or

(b) any magistrates' court acting for the police officer's local justice area, in any other case.

(3) The applicant party must—

(a) apply in writing; and

(b) serve the application on—

    (i)   the court officer,

    (ii) the other party, and

    (iii) any surety affected or proposed.

(4) The application must—

  (a) specify—

    (i)   the decision that the applicant wants the court to make,

    (ii) each offence charged, or for which the defendant was arrested, and

    (iii) the police bail decision to be reconsidered and the reasons given for it;

  (b) explain, as appropriate—

    (i)   why the court should grant bail itself, or withdraw it, or impose or vary a condition, and

    (ii) if the applicant is the prosecutor, what material information has become available since the police bail decision was made;

  (c) propose the terms of any suggested condition of bail; and

  (d) if the applicant wants an earlier hearing than paragraph (7) requires, ask for that, and explain why it is needed.

(5) A prosecutor who applies under this rule must serve on the defendant, with the application, notice that the court has power to withdraw bail and, if the defendant is absent when the court makes its decision, order the defendant's arrest.

(6) A party who opposes an application must—

  (a) so notify the court officer and the applicant at once; and

  (b) serve on each notice of the reasons for opposition.

(7) Unless the court otherwise directs, the court officer must arrange for the court to hear the application as soon as practicable and in any event—

  (a) if it is an application to withdraw bail, no later than the second business day after it was served;

  (b) in any other case, no later than the fifth business day after it was served.

(8) The court may—

  (a) vary or waive a time limit under this rule;

  (b) allow an application to be in a different form to one set out in the Practice Direction;

  (c) if rule 14.2 allows, determine without a hearing an application to vary a condition.

[This rule is printed as amended by the Criminal Procedure (Amendment No. 2) Rules 2017 (S.I. 2017 No. 282).]

Notice of application to consider bail

B-171   **14.7.**—(1) This rule applies where—

  (a) in a magistrates' court—

    (i)   a prosecutor wants the court to withdraw bail granted by the court, or to impose or vary a condition of such bail, or

    (ii) a defendant wants the court to reconsider such bail before the next hearing in the case;

  (b) in the Crown Court—

    (i)   a party wants the court to grant bail that has been withheld, or to withdraw bail that has been granted, or to impose a new bail condition or to vary a present one, or

    (ii) a prosecutor wants the court to consider whether to grant or withhold bail, or impose or vary a condition of bail, under section 88 or section 89 of the Criminal Justice Act 2003 (bail and custody in connection with an intended application to the Court of Appeal to which Part 27 (retrial after acquittal) applies) [§§ 3-175, 7-294 in the main work].

(2) Such a party must—

  (a) apply in writing;

  (b) serve the application on—

    (i)   the court officer,

    (ii) the other party, and

    (iii) any surety affected or proposed; and

  (c) serve the application not less than 2 business days before any hearing in the case at which the applicant wants the court to consider it, if such a hearing is already due.

(3) The application must—

(a) specify—
  (i)   the decision that the applicant wants the court to make,
  (ii) each offence charged, and
  (iii) each relevant previous bail decision and the reasons given for each;
(b) if the applicant is a defendant, explain—
  (i)   as appropriate, why the court should not withhold bail, or why it should vary a condition, and
  (ii) what further information or legal argument, if any, has become available since the most recent previous bail decision was made;
(c) if the applicant is the prosecutor, explain—
  (i)   as appropriate, why the court should withdraw bail, or impose or vary a condition, and
  (ii) what material information has become available since the most recent previous bail decision was made;
(d) propose the terms of any suggested condition of bail; and
(e) if the applicant wants an earlier hearing than paragraph (6) requires, ask for that, and explain why it is needed.
(4), (5) [*Identical to r.14.6(5) and (6), ante, § B-170.*]
(6) Unless the court otherwise directs, the court officer must arrange for the court to hear the application as soon as practicable and in any event—
(a) if it is an application to grant or withdraw bail, no later than the second business day after it was served;
(b) if it is an application to impose or vary a condition, no later than the fifth business day after it was served.
(7) The court may—
(a) vary or waive a time limit under this rule;
(b) allow an application to be in a different form to one set out in the Practice Direction, or to be made orally;
(c) if rule 14.2 allows, determine without a hearing an application to vary a condition.

Defendant's application or appeal to the Crown Court after magistrates' court bail decision
14.8.—(1) This rule applies where a defendant wants to—   **B-172**
(a) apply to the Crown Court for bail after a magistrates' court has withheld bail; or
(b) appeal to the Crown Court after a magistrates' court has refused to vary a bail condition as the defendant wants.
(2) The defendant must—
(a) apply to the Crown Court in writing as soon as practicable after the magistrates' court's decision; and
(b) serve the application on—
  (i)   the Crown Court officer,
  (ii) the magistrates' court officer,
  (iii) the prosecutor, and
  (iv) any surety affected or proposed.
(3) The application must—
(a) specify—
  (i)   the decision that the applicant wants the Crown Court to make, and
  (ii) each offence charged;
(b) explain—
  (i)   as appropriate, why the Crown Court should not withhold bail, or why it should vary the condition under appeal, and
  (ii) what further information or legal argument, if any, has become available since the magistrates' court's decision;
(c) propose the terms of any suggested condition of bail; and
(d) if the applicant wants an earlier hearing than paragraph (6) requires, ask for that, and explain why it is needed; and
(e) on an application for bail, attach a copy of the certificate of full argument served on the defendant under rule 14.4(4).
(4) The magistrates' court officer must as soon as practicable serve on the Crown Court officer—
(a) a copy of the note or record made under rule 14.4(1) in connection with the magistrates' court's decision; and

(b)   the date of the next hearing, if any, in the magistrates' court.

(5) A prosecutor who opposes the application must—

(a)   so notify the Crown Court officer and the defendant at once; and

(b)   serve on each notice of the reasons for opposition.

(6) Unless the Crown Court otherwise directs, the court officer must arrange for the court to hear the application or appeal as soon as practicable and in any event no later than the business day after it was served.

(7) The Crown Court may vary a time limit under this rule.

Prosecutor's appeal against grant of bail

B-173   **14.9.**—(1) This rule applies where a prosecutor wants to appeal—

(a)   to the Crown Court against a grant of bail by a magistrates' court, in a case in which the defendant has been charged with, or convicted of, an offence punishable with imprisonment; or

(b)   to the High Court against a grant of bail—

(i)   by a magistrates' court, in an extradition case, or

(ii)   by the Crown Court, in a case in which the defendant has been charged with, or convicted of, an offence punishable with imprisonment (but not in a case in which the Crown Court granted bail on an appeal to which paragraph (1)(a) applies).

(2) The prosecutor must tell the court which has granted bail of the decision to appeal—

(a)   at the end of the hearing during which the court granted bail; and

(b)   before the defendant is released on bail.

(3) The court which has granted bail must exercise its power to remand the defendant in custody pending determination of the appeal.

(4) The prosecutor must serve an appeal notice—

(a)   on the court officer for the court which has granted bail and on the defendant;

(b)   not more than 2 hours after telling that court of the decision to appeal.

(5) The appeal notice must specify—

(a)   each offence with which the defendant is charged;

(b)   the decision under appeal;

(c)   the reasons given for the grant of bail; and

(d)   the grounds of appeal.

(6) On an appeal to the Crown Court, the magistrates' court officer must, as soon as practicable, serve on the Crown Court officer—

(a)   the appeal notice;

(b)   a copy of the note or record made under rule 14.4(1) (record of bail decision); and

(c)   notice of the date of the next hearing in the court which has granted bail.

(7) If the Crown Court so directs, the Crown Court officer must arrange for the defendant to be assisted by the Official Solicitor in a case in which the defendant—

(a)   has no legal representative; and

(b)   asks for such assistance.

(8) On an appeal to the Crown Court, the Crown Court officer must arrange for the court to hear the appeal as soon as practicable and in any event no later than the second business day after the appeal notice was served.

(9) The prosecutor—

(a)   may abandon an appeal to the Crown Court without the court's permission, by serving a notice of abandonment, signed by or on behalf of the prosecutor, on—

(i)   the defendant,

(ii)   the Crown Court officer, and

(iii)   the magistrates' court officer

before the hearing of the appeal begins; but

(b)   after the hearing of the appeal begins, may only abandon the appeal with the Crown Court's permission.

(10) The court officer for the court which has granted bail must instruct the defendant's custodian to release the defendant on the bail granted by that court, subject to any condition or conditions of bail imposed, if—

(a)   the prosecutor fails to serve an appeal notice within the time to which paragraph (4) refers; or

(b)   the prosecutor serves a notice of abandonment under paragraph (9).

Consideration of bail in a murder case

14.10.—(1) This rule applies in a case in which— **B-174**

    (a) the defendant is charged with murder; and

    (b) the Crown Court has not yet considered bail.

(2) The magistrates' court officer must arrange with the Crown Court officer for the Crown Court to consider bail as soon as practicable and in any event no later than the second business day after—

    (a) a magistrates' court sends the defendant to the Crown Court for trial; or

    (b) the first hearing in the magistrates' court, if the defendant is not at once sent for trial.

Condition of residence

14.11.—(1) The defendant must notify the prosecutor of the address at which the defendant will **B-175** live and sleep if released on bail with a condition of residence—

    (a) as soon as practicable after the institution of proceedings, unless already done; and

    (b) as soon as practicable after any change of that address.

(2) The prosecutor must help the court to assess the suitability of an address proposed as a condition of residence.

Electronic monitoring requirements

14.12.—(1) This rule applies where the court imposes electronic monitoring requirements, where **B-176** available, as a condition of bail.

(2) The court officer must—

    (a) inform the person responsible for the monitoring ("the monitor") of—

        (i) the defendant's name, and telephone number if available,

        (ii) each offence with which the defendant is charged,

      (iii) details of the place at which the defendant's presence must be monitored,

      (iv) the period or periods during which the defendant's presence at that place must be monitored, and

        (v) if fixed, the date on which the defendant must surrender to custody;

    (b) inform the defendant and, where the defendant is under 16, an appropriate adult, of the monitor's identity and the means by which the monitor may be contacted; and

    (c) notify the monitor of any subsequent—

        (i) variation or termination of the electronic monitoring requirements, or

        (ii) fixing or variation of the date on which the defendant must surrender to custody.

Accommodation or support requirements

14.13.—(1) This rule applies where the court imposes as a condition of bail a requirement, where **B-177** available, that the defendant must—

    (a) reside in accommodation provided for that purpose by, or on behalf of, a public authority;

    (b) receive bail support provided by, or on behalf of, a public authority.

(2) The court officer must—

    (a) inform the person responsible for the provision of any such accommodation or support ("the service provider") of—

        (i) the defendant's name, and telephone number if available,

        (ii) each offence with which the defendant is charged,

      (iii) details of the requirement,

      (iv) any other bail condition, and

        (v) if fixed, the date on which the defendant must surrender to custody;

    (b) inform the defendant and, where the defendant is under 16, an appropriate adult, of—

        (i) the service provider's identity and the means by which the service provider may be contacted, and

        (ii) the address of any accommodation in which the defendant must live and sleep; and

    (c) notify the service provider of any subsequent—

        (i) variation or termination of the requirement,

        (ii) variation or termination of any other bail condition, and

      (iii) fixing or variation of the date on which the defendant must surrender to custody.

Requirement for a surety or payment, etc.

14.14.—(1) This rule applies where the court imposes as a condition of bail a requirement for— **B-178**

　　(a)　a surety;
　　(b)　a payment;
　　(c)　the surrender of a document or thing.
　(2) The court may direct how such a condition must be met.
　(3) Unless the court otherwise directs, if any such condition or direction requires a surety to enter into a recognizance–
　　(a)　the recognizance must specify–
　　　　(i)　the amount that the surety will be required to pay if the purpose for which the recognizance is entered is not fulfilled, and
　　　　(ii)　the date, or the event, upon which the recognizance will expire;
　　(b)　the surety must enter into the recognizance in the presence of–
　　　　(i)　the court officer,
　　　　(ii)　the defendant's custodian, where the defendant is in custody, or
　　　　(iii)　someone acting with the authority of either; and
　　(c)　the person before whom the surety enters into the recognizance must at once serve a copy on–
　　　　(i)　the surety, and
　　　　(ii)　as appropriate, the court officer and the defendant's custodian.
　(4) Unless the court otherwise directs, if any such condition or direction requires someone to make a payment, or surrender a document or thing–
　　(a)　that payment, document or thing must be made or surrendered to–
　　　　(i)　the court officer,
　　　　(ii)　the defendant's custodian, where the defendant is in custody, or
　　　　(iii)　someone acting with the authority of either; and
　　(b)　the court officer or the custodian, as appropriate, must serve immediately on the other a statement that the payment, document or thing has been made or surrendered.
　(5) The custodian must release the defendant when each requirement ordered by the court has been met.

Forfeiture of a recognizance given by a surety

B-179　　　　**14.15.**–(1) This rule applies where the court imposes as a condition of bail a requirement that a surety enter into a recognizance and, after the defendant is released on bail–
　　(a)　the defendant fails to surrender to custody as required, or
　　(b)　it appears to the court that the surety has failed to comply with a condition or direction.
　(2) The court officer must serve notice on–
　　(a)　the surety; and
　　(b)　each party to the decision to grant bail,
of the hearing at which the court will consider the forfeiture of the recognizance.
　(3) The court must not forfeit the recognizance less than 5 business days after service of notice under paragraph (2).

Bail condition to be enforced in another European Union member State

B-180　　　　**14.16.**–(1) This rule applies where the court can impose as a condition of bail pending trial a requirement–
　　(a)　with which the defendant must comply while in another European Union member State; and
　　(b)　which that other member State can monitor and enforce.
　(2) The court–
　　(a)　must not exercise its power to impose such a requirement until the court has decided what, if any, condition or conditions of bail to impose while the defendant is in England and Wales;
　　(b)　subject to that, may exercise its power to make a request for the other member State to monitor and enforce that requirement.
　(3) Where the court makes such a request, the court officer must–
　　(a)　issue a certificate requesting the monitoring and enforcement of the defendant's compliance with that requirement, in the form required by EU Council Framework Decision 2009/829/JHA;
　　(b)　serve on the relevant authority of the other member State–
　　　　(i)　the court's decision or a certified copy of that decision,

  (ii)   the certificate, and
  (iii) a copy of the certificate translated into an official language of the other member
         State, unless English is such a language or the other member State has declared that it
         will accept a certificate in English; and
(c) report to the court—
  (i)   any request for further information returned by the competent authority in the other
         member State, and
  (ii)   that authority's decision.

(4) Where the competent authority in the other member State agrees to monitor and enforce the
requirement—
(a) the court—
  (i)   may exercise its power to withdraw the request (where it can), but
  (ii)   whether or not it does so, must continue to exercise the powers to which this Part ap-
         plies in accordance with the rules in this Part;
(b) the court officer must immediately serve notice on that authority if—
  (i)   legal proceedings are brought in relation to the requirement being monitored and
         enforced, or
  (ii)   the court decides to vary or revoke that requirement, or to issue a warrant for the
         defendant's arrest; and
(c) the court officer must promptly report to the court any information and any request
     received from that authority.

(5) A party who wants the court to exercise the power to which this rule applies must serve with an
application under rule 14.7 (notice of application to consider bail)—
(a) a draft order; and
(b) a draft certificate in the form required by EU Council Framework Decision 2009/829/JHA.

[This rule is printed as amended by the Criminal Procedure (Amendment No. 2) Rules 2016
(S.I. 2016 No. 705).]

Enforcement of measure imposed in another European Union member State

14.17.–(1) This rule applies where the Lord Chancellor serves on the court officer a certificate   **B-181**
requesting the monitoring and enforcement of a defendant's compliance with a supervision measure
imposed by an authority in another European Union member State.

(2) The court officer must arrange for the court to consider the request—
(a) as a general rule—
  (i)   within 20 business days of the date on which the Lord Chancellor received it from the
         requesting authority, or
  (ii)   within 40 business days of that date, if legal proceedings in relation to the supervision
         measure are brought within the first 20 business days;
(b) exceptionally, later than that, but in such a case the court officer must immediately serve on
     the requesting authority—
  (i)   an explanation for the delay, and
  (ii)   an indication of when the court's decision is expected.

(3) On consideration of the request by the court, the court officer must—
(a) without delay serve on the requesting authority—
  (i)   notice of any further information required by the court, and
  (ii)   subject to any such requirement and any response, notice of the court's decision; and
(b) where the court agrees to monitor the supervision measure, serve notice of the court's deci-
     sion on any supervisor specified by the court.

(4) Where the court agrees to monitor the supervision measure—
(a) the court officer must immediately serve notice on the requesting authority if there is
     reported to the court—
  (i)   a breach of the measure, or
  (ii)   any other event that might cause the requesting authority to review its decision;
(b) the court officer must without delay serve notice on the requesting authority if—
  (i)   legal proceedings are brought in relation to the decision to monitor compliance with
         the bail condition,
  (ii)   there is reported to the court a change of the defendant's residence, or
  (iii) the court decides (where it can) to stop monitoring the defendant's compliance with
         the measure.

Application to extend a custody time limit

B-182   **14.18.**—(1) This rule applies where the prosecutor gives notice of application to extend a custody
time limit.

(2) The court officer must arrange for the court to hear that application as soon as practicable
after the expiry of—

(a) 5 days from the giving of notice, in the Crown Court; or

(b) 2 days from the giving of notice, in a magistrates' court.

(3) The court may shorten a time limit under this rule.

Appeal against custody time limit decision

B-183   **14.19.**—(1) This rule applies where—

(a) a defendant wants to appeal to the Crown Court against a decision by a magistrates' court
to extend a custody time limit;

(b) a prosecutor wants to appeal to the Crown Court against a decision by a magistrates' court
to refuse to extend a custody time limit.

(2) The appellant must serve an appeal notice—

(a) on—

(i)   the other party to the decision,

(ii) the Crown Court officer, and

(iii) the magistrates' court officer;

(b) in a defendant's appeal, as soon as practicable after the decision under appeal;

(c) in a prosecutor's appeal—

(i)   as soon as practicable after the decision under appeal, and

(ii) before the relevant custody time limit expires.

(3) The appeal notice must specify—

(a) each offence with which the defendant is charged;

(b) the decision under appeal;

(c) the date on which the relevant custody time limit will expire;

(d) on a defendant's appeal, the date on which the relevant custody time limit would have
expired but for the decision under appeal; and

(e) the grounds of appeal.

(4) The Crown Court officer must arrange for the Crown Court to hear the appeal as soon as
practicable and in any event no later than the second business day after the appeal notice was served.

(5) The appellant—

(a) may abandon an appeal without the Crown Court's permission, by serving a notice of
abandonment, signed by or on behalf of the appellant, on—

(i)   the other party,

(ii) the Crown Court officer, and

(iii) the magistrates' court officer

before the hearing of the appeal begins; but

(b) after the hearing of the appeal begins, may only abandon the appeal with the Crown
Court's permission.

Extension of Bail before Charge

Exercise of court's powers: extension of pre-charge bail

★B-183a   **14.20.**—(1) The court must determine an application to which rule 14.21 (application to authorise
extension of pre-charge bail) applies—

(a) without a hearing, subject to paragraph (2); and

(b) as soon as practicable, but as a general rule no sooner than the fifth business day after the
application was served.

(2) The court must determine an application at a hearing where—

(a) if the application succeeds, its effect will be to extend the period for which the defendant is
on bail to less than 12 months from the day after the defendant's arrest for the offence and
the court considers that the interests of justice require a hearing;

(b) if the application succeeds, its effect will be to extend that period to more than 12 months
from that day and the applicant or the defendant asks for a hearing;

(c) it is an application to withhold information from the defendant and the court considers
that the interests of justice require a hearing.

(3) Any hearing must be in private.

(4) Subject to rule 14.22 (application to withhold information from the defendant), at a hearing the court may determine an application in the absence of—

(a) the applicant;

(b) the defendant, if the defendant has had at least 5 business days in which to make representations.

(5) If the court so directs, a party to an application may attend a hearing by live link or telephone.

(6) The court must not authorise an extension of the period for which a defendant is on bail before being charged unless—

(a) the applicant states, in writing or orally, that to the best of the applicant's knowledge and belief—

(i) the application discloses all the information that is material to what the court must decide, and

(ii) the content of the application is true; or

(b) the application includes a statement by an investigator of the suspected offence that to the best of that investigator's knowledge and belief those requirements are met.

(7) Where the statement required by paragraph (6) is made orally—

(a) the statement must be on oath or affirmation, unless the court otherwise directs; and

(b) the court must arrange for a record of the making of the statement.

(8) The court may shorten or extend (even after it has expired) a time limit imposed by this rule or by rule 14.21 (application to authorise extension of pre-charge bail).

[This rule was inserted by the Criminal Procedure (Amendment No. 2) Rules 2017 (S.I. 2017 No. 282).]

Application to authorise extension of pre-charge bail

14.21.—(1) This rule applies where an applicant wants the court to authorise an extension of the ★**B-183b** period for which a defendant is released on bail before being charged with an offence.

(2) The applicant must—

(a) apply in writing before the date on which the defendant's pre-charge bail is due to end;

(b) demonstrate that the applicant is entitled to apply as a constable, a member of staff of the Financial Conduct Authority, a member of the Serious Fraud Office or a Crown Prosecutor;

(c) serve the application on—

(i) the court officer, and

(ii) the defendant; and

(d) serve on the defendant, with the application, a form of response notice for the defendant's use.

(3) The application must specify—

(a) the offence or offences for which the defendant was arrested;

(b) the date on which the defendant's pre-charge bail began;

(c) the date and period of any previous extension of that bail;

(d) the date on which that bail is due to end;

(e) the conditions of that bail; and

(f) if different, the bail conditions which are to be imposed if the court authorises an extension, or further extension, of the period for which the defendant is released on pre-charge bail.

(4) The application must explain—

(a) the grounds for believing that, as applicable—

(i) further investigation is needed of any matter in connection with the offence or offences for which the defendant was released on bail, or

(ii) further time is needed for making a decision as to whether to charge the defendant with that offence or those offences;

(b) the grounds for believing that, as applicable—

(i) the investigation into the offence or offences for which the defendant was released on bail is being conducted diligently and expeditiously, or

(ii) the decision as to whether to charge the defendant with that offence or those offences is being made diligently and expeditiously; and

(c) the grounds for believing that the defendant's further release on bail is necessary and proportionate in all the circumstances having regard, in particular, to any conditions of bail imposed.

(5) The application must—

  (a) indicate whether the applicant wants the court to authorise an extension of the defendant's bail for 3 months or for 6 months; and

  (b) if for 6 months, explain why the investigation is unlikely to be completed or the charging decision made, as the case may be, within 3 months.

(6) The application must explain why it was not made earlier where—

  (a) the application is made before the date on which the defendant's bail is due to end; but

  (b) it is not likely to be practicable for the court to determine the application before that date.

(7) A defendant who objects to the application must—

  (a) serve notice on—

    (i) the court officer, and

    (ii) the applicant,

  not more than 5 business days after service of the application; and

  (b) in the notice explain the grounds of the objection.

[This rule was inserted by the Criminal Procedure (Amendment No. 2) Rules 2017 (S.I. 2017 No. 282).]

Application to withhold information from the defendant

★B-183c
    14.22.—(1) This rule applies where an application to authorise an extension of pre-charge bail includes an application to withhold information from the defendant.

(2) The applicant must—

  (a) omit that information from the part of the application that is served on the defendant;

  (b) mark the other part to show that, unless the court otherwise directs, it is only for the court; and

  (c) in that other part, explain the grounds for believing that the disclosure of that information would have one or more of the following results—

    (i) evidence connected with an indictable offence would be interfered with or harmed,

    (ii) a person would be interfered with or physically injured,

    (iii) a person suspected of having committed an indictable offence but not yet arrested for the offence would be alerted, or

    (iv) the recovery of property obtained as a result of an indictable offence would be hindered.

(3) At any hearing of an application to which this rule applies—

  (a) the court must first determine the application to withhold information, in the defendant's absence and that of any legal representative of the defendant;

  (b) if the court allows the application to withhold information, then in the following sequence—

    (i) the court must consider representations first by the applicant and then by the defendant, in the presence of both, and

    (ii) the court may consider further representations by the applicant in the defendant's absence and that of any legal representative of the defendant, if satisfied that there are reasonable grounds for believing that information withheld from the defendant would be disclosed during those further representations.

(4) If the court refuses an application to withhold information from the defendant, the applicant may withdraw the application to authorise an extension of pre-charge bail.

[This rule was inserted by the Criminal Procedure (Amendment No. 2) Rules 2017 (S.I. 2017 No. 282).]

CPD III Custody and Bail 14A: Bail before Sending for Trial

B-184
    14A.1 Before the Crown Court can deal with an application under rule 14.8 by a defendant after a magistrates' court has withheld bail, it must be satisfied that the magistrates' court has issued a certificate, under section 5(6A) of the Bail Act 1976 [§ 3-28 in the main work], that it heard full argument on the application for bail before it refused the application.

    The certificate of full argument is produced by the magistrates' court's computer system, Libra, as part of the GENORD (General Form of Order). Two hard copies are produced, one for the defence and one for the prosecution. Some magistrates' courts may also produce a manual certificate which will usually be available from the justices' legal adviser at the conclusion of the hearing; the GENORD may not be produced until the following day. Under rule 14.4(4), the magistrates' court officer will provide the defendant with a certificate that the court heard full argument. However, it is the responsibility of the defence, as the applicant in the Crown Court, to ensure that a copy of the certificate ... is provided to the Crown Court as part of the application (r.14.8(3)(e)). The applicant's solicitors should attach a copy of the certificate to the bail application form. If the certificate is not enclosed with the application form, it will be difficult to avoid some delay in listing.

Venue

14A.2 Applications should be made to the court to which the defendant will be, or would have **B-185** been, sent for trial. In the event of an application in a purely summary case, it should be made to the Crown Court centre which normally receives class 3 work. The hearing will be listed as a chambers matter unless a judge has directed otherwise.

CPD III Custody and Bail 14B: Bail: Failure to Surrender and Trials in Absence

14B.1 The failure of defendants to comply with the terms of their bail by not surrendering, or not **B-186** doing so at the appointed time, undermines the administration of justice and disrupts proceedings. The resulting delays impact on victims, witnesses and other court users and also waste costs. A defendant's failure to surrender affects not only the case with which he ... is concerned, but also the court's ability to administer justice more generally, by damaging the confidence of victims, witnesses and the public in the effectiveness of the court system and the judiciary. It is, therefore, most important that defendants who are granted bail appreciate the significance of the obligation to surrender to custody in accordance with the terms of their bail and that courts take appropriate action, if they fail to do so.

14B.2 A defendant who will be unable for medical reasons to attend court in accordance with his ... bail must obtain a certificate from his ... general practitioner or another appropriate medical practitioner such as the doctor with care of the defendant at a hospital. This should be obtained in advance of the hearing and conveyed to the court through the defendant's legal representative. In order to minimise the disruption to the court and to others, particularly witnesses if the case is listed for trial, the defendant should notify the court through his legal representative as soon as his inability to attend court becomes known.

14B.3 Guidance has been produced by the British Medical Association and the CPS on the roles and responsibilities of medical practitioners when issuing medical certificates in criminal proceedings. Judges and magistrates should seek to ensure that this guidance is followed. However, it is a matter for each individual court to decide whether, in any particular case, the issued certificate should be accepted. Without a medical certificate or if an unsatisfactory certificate is provided, the court is likely to consider that the defendant has failed to surrender to bail.

14B.4 If a defendant fails to surrender ...there are at least four courses of action for the courts to consider taking:—

    (a) imposing penalties for the failure to surrender [see the definitive sentencing guideline, Appendix S-9 *et seq.*];

    (b) revoking bail or imposing more stringent conditions;

    (c) conducting trials in the absence of the defendant; and

    (d) ordering that some or all of any sums of money lodged with the court as a security or pledged by a surety as a condition on the grant of bail be forfeit.

CPD III Custody and Bail 14C: Penalties for Failure to Surrender

Initiating proceedings–bail granted by a police officer

14C.1 When a person has been granted bail by a police officer to attend court and subsequently **B-187** fails to surrender ..., the decision whether to initiate proceedings for a section 6(1) or ... (2) [§ 3-31 in the main work] offence will be for the police/prosecutor and proceedings are commenced in the usual way.

14C.2 The offence in this form is a summary offence .... The offence should be dealt with on the first appearance after arrest, unless an adjournment is necessary, as it will be relevant in considering whether to grant bail again.

Initiating proceedings–bail granted by a court

14C.3 Where a person has been granted bail by a court and subsequently fails to surrender on ar- **B-188** rest that person should normally be brought as soon as appropriate before the court at which the proceedings in respect of which bail was granted are to be heard. (There is no requirement to lay an information within the time limit for a Bail Act offence where bail was granted by the court.)

14C.4 Given that bail was granted by a court, it is more appropriate that the court itself should initiate the proceedings by its own motion although the prosecutor may invite the court to take proceedings, if the prosecutor considers proceedings are appropriate.

Archbold paragraph numbers

B-189

Archbold's Criminal Pleading–2017 ed.

B-189   **14C.5** Courts should not, without good reason, adjourn the disposal of a section 6(1) or ... (2) ... offence ... until the conclusion of the proceedings in respect of which bail was granted but should deal with defendants as soon as is practicable. In deciding what is practicable, the court must take into account when the proceedings in respect of which bail was granted are expected to conclude, the seriousness of the offence for which the defendant is already being prosecuted, the type of penalty that might be imposed for the Bail Act offence and the original offence, as well as any other relevant circumstances.

14C.6 If the Bail Act offence is adjourned alongside the substantive proceedings, then it is still necessary to consider imposing a separate penalty at the trial. In addition, bail should usually be revoked in the meantime. Trial in the absence of the defendant is not a penalty for the Bail Act offence and a separate penalty may be imposed for the Bail Act offence.

Conduct of proceedings

B-190   **14C.7** Proceedings under section 6 ... may be conducted either as a summary offence or as a criminal contempt of court. Where proceedings are commenced by the police or prosecutor, the prosecutor will conduct the proceedings and, if the matter is contested, call the evidence. Where the court initiates proceedings, with or without an invitation from the prosecutor, the court may expect the assistance of the prosecutor, such as in cross-examining the defendant, if required.

14C.8 The burden of proof is on the defendant to prove that he had reasonable cause for his failure to surrender ... (s.6(3)).

14C.9, 14C.10 [Sentencing for a Bail Act offence: see Appendix S-9 *et seq.*]

CPD III Custody and Bail 14D: Relationship between the Bail Act Offence and Further Remands on Bail or in Custody

B-191   **14D.1** The court at which the defendant is produced should, where practicable and legally permissible, arrange to have all outstanding cases brought before it (including those from different courts) for the purpose of progressing matters and dealing with the question of bail. This is likely to be practicable in the magistrates' court where cases can easily be transferred from one magistrates' court to another. Practice is likely to vary in the Crown Court. If the defendant appears before a different court, for example because he is charged with offences committed in another area, and it is not practicable for all matters to be concluded by that court then the defendant may be remanded on bail or in custody, if appropriate, to appear before the first court for the outstanding offences to be dealt with.

14D.2 When a defendant has been convicted of a Bail Act offence, the court should review the remand status of the defendant, including the conditions of that bail, in respect of all outstanding proceedings against the defendant.

14D.3 Failure by the defendant to surrender or a conviction for failing to surrender to bail in connection with the main proceedings will be significant factors weighing against the re-granting of bail.

14D.4 Whether or not an immediate custodial sentence has been imposed for the Bail Act offence, the court may, having reviewed the defendant's remand status, also remand the defendant in custody in the main proceedings.

CPD III Custody and Bail 14E: Trials in Absence

B-192   **14E.1** A defendant has a right, in general, to be present and to be represented at his trial. However, a defendant may choose not to exercise those rights, such as by voluntarily absenting himself and failing to instruct his lawyers adequately so that they can represent him.

14E.2 The court has a discretion as to whether a trial should take place or continue in the defendant's absence and must exercise its discretion with due regard for the interests of justice. The overriding concern must be to ensure that such a trial is as fair as circumstances permit and leads to a just outcome. If the defendant's absence is due to involuntary illness or incapacity it would very rarely, if ever, be right to exercise the discretion in favour of commencing or continuing the trial.

Trials on indictment

14E.3 Proceeding in the absence of a defendant is a step which ought normally to be taken only if it is unavoidable. The court must exercise its discretion as to whether a trial should take place or continue in the defendant's absence with the utmost care and caution. Due regard should be had to the judgment of Lord Bingham in *R. v. Jones* [2003] 1 A.C. 1, HL[§ 3-222 in the main work]. Circumstances to be taken into account before proceeding include:

    i) the conduct of the defendant,
    ii) the disadvantage to the defendant,

iii) the public interest, taking account of the inconvenience and hardship to witnesses, and especially to any complainant, of a delay; if the witnesses have attended court and are ready to give evidence, that will weigh in favour of continuing with the trial,

iv) the effect of any delay,

v) whether the attendance of the defendant could be secured at a later hearing, and

vi) the likely outcome if the defendant is found guilty.

Even if the defendant is voluntarily absent, it is still generally desirable that he or she is represented.

Trials in the magistrates' courts

14E.4 Section 11 of the MCA 1980 applies. If either party is absent, the court should follow the procedure at Criminal Procedure Rule 24.12. Subject to the provisions of the statute, the principles outlined above are applicable. Benches and legal advisers will note that the presumption at rule 24.12(3)(a) does not apply if the defendant is under 18 years of age.

CPD III Custody and Bail 14F: Forfeiture of Monies Lodged as Security or Pledged by a Surety/ Estreatment of Recognizances

14F.1 A surety undertakes to forfeit a sum of money if the defendant fails to surrender as required. **B-193** Considerable care must be taken to explain that obligation and the consequences before a surety is taken. This system ... has great antiquity. It is immensely valuable. A court concerned that a defendant will fail to surrender will not normally know that defendant personally, nor indeed much about him. When members of the community who do know the defendant say they trust him to surrender and are prepared to stake their own money on that trust, that can have a powerful influence on the decision of the court as to whether or not to grant bail. There are two important side-effects. The first is that the surety will keep an eye on the defendant, and report to the authorities if there is a concern that he will abscond. In those circumstances, the surety can withdraw. The second is that a defendant will be deterred from absconding by the knowledge that if he does so then his family or friends who provided the surety will lose their money. In the experience of the courts, it is comparatively rare for a defendant to fail to surrender when meaningful sureties are in place.

14F.2 Any surety should have the opportunity to make representations to the defendant to surrender himself, in accordance with their obligations.

14F.3 The court should not wait or adjourn a decision on estreatment of sureties or securities until such time, if any, that the bailed defendant appears before the court. It is possible that any defendant who apparently absconds may have a defence of reasonable cause to the allegation of failure to surrender. If that happens, then any surety or security estreated would be returned. The reason for proceeding is that the defendant may never surrender, or may not surrender for many years. The court should still consider the sureties' obligations if that happens. Moreover, the longer the matter is delayed the more probable it is that the personal circumstances of the sureties will change.

14F.4 The court should follow the procedure at rule 14.15 of the Criminal Procedure Rules. Before the court makes a decision, it should give the sureties the opportunity to make representations, either in person, through counsel or by statement.

14F.5 The court has discretion to forfeit the whole sum, part only of the sum, or to remit the sum. The starting point is that the surety is forfeited in full. It would be unfortunate if this valuable method of allowing a defendant to remain at liberty were undermined. Courts would have less confidence in the efficacy of sureties. It is also important to note that a defendant who absconds without in any way forewarning his sureties does not thereby release them from any or all of their responsibilities. Even if a surety does his best, he remains liable for the full amount, except at the discretion of the court. However, all factors should be taken into account and the following are noted for guidance only:

(i) the presence or absence of culpability is a factor, but is not in itself a reason to reduce or set aside the obligations entered into by the surety;

(ii) the means of a surety, and in particular changed means, are relevant;

(iii) the court should forfeit no more than is necessary, in public policy, to maintain the integrity and confidence of the system of taking sureties.

CPD III Custody and Bail 14G: Bail during Trial

14G.1 The following should be read subject to the Bail Act 1976. **B-194**

14G.2 Once a trial has begun the further grant of bail, whether during the short adjournment or overnight, is in the discretion of the trial judge or trial bench. It may be a proper exercise of this discretion to refuse bail during the short adjournment if the accused cannot otherwise be segregated from witnesses and jurors.

14G.3 An accused who was on bail while on remand should not be refused bail during the trial unless, in the opinion of the court, there are positive reasons to justify this refusal. Such reasons might include:

(a) that a point has been reached where there is a real danger that the accused will abscond, either because the case is going badly for him, or for any other reason;

(b) that there is a real danger that he may interfere with witnesses, jurors or co-defendants.

14G.4 Once the jury has returned a guilty verdict or a finding of guilt has been made, a further renewal of bail should be decided in the light of the gravity of the offence, any friction between codefendants and the likely sentence to be passed in all the circumstances of the case.

CPD III Custody and Bail 14H: Crown Court Judge's Certificaton of Fitness to Appeal and Applications to the Crown Court for Bail Pending Appeal

B-195

14H.1 The trial or sentencing judge may grant a certificate of fitness for appeal (see, e.g., ss.1(2)(b) and 11(1A) of the CAA 1968 [§§ 7-37, 7-125 in the main work]); the judge ... should only certify cases in exceptional circumstances. The ... judge should use the Criminal Appeal Office Form C (Crown Court Judge's Certificate of fitness for appeal) which is available to court staff on the HMCTS intranet.

14H.2 The judge may well think it right to encourage the defendant's advocate to submit to the court, and serve on the prosecutor, before the hearing of the application, a draft of the grounds of appeal which he will ask the judge to certify on Form C.

14H.3 The first question for the judge is then whether there exists a particular and cogent ground of appeal. If there is no such ground, there can be no certificate; and if there is no certificate there can be no bail. A judge should not grant a certificate with regard to sentence merely in the light of mitigation to which he has, in his opinion, given due weight, nor in regard to conviction on a ground where he considers the chance of a successful appeal is not substantial. The judge should bear in mind that, where a certificate is refused, application may be made to the Court of Appeal for leave to appeal and for bail; it is expected that certificates will only be granted in exceptional circumstances.

14H.4 Defence advocates should note that the effect of a grant of a certificate is to remove the need for leave to appeal to be granted by the Court of Appeal. It does not in itself commence the appeal. The completed Form C will be sent by the Crown Court to the Criminal Appeal Office; it is not copied to the parties. The procedures in Part 39 of the Criminal Procedure Rules should be followed.

14H.5 Bail pending appeal ... may be granted by the ... judge if they have certified the case as fit for appeal (see s.81(1)(f) and (1B) of the Senior Courts Act 1981 [§ 7-175 in the main work]). Bail can only be granted in the Crown Court within 28 days of the conviction or sentence which is to be the subject of the appeal and may not be granted if an application for bail has already been made to the Court of Appeal. The procedure for bail to be granted by a judge of the Crown Court pending an appeal is governed by Part 14 of the Criminal Procedure Rules. The ... judge should use the Criminal Appeal Office Form BC (Crown Court Judge's Order granting bail) which is available to court staff on the HMCTS intranet.

14H.6 The length of the period which might elapse before the hearing of any appeal is not relevant to the grant of a certificate; but, if the judge does decide to grant a certificate, it may be one factor in the decision whether or not to grant bail. If bail is granted, the judge should consider imposing a condition of residence in line with the practice in the Court of Appeal.

Criminal Procedure Rules 2015 (S.I. 2015 No. 1490), Pt 15

DISCLOSURE

When this Part applies

B-196

15.1. This Part applies—

(a) in a magistrates' court and in the Crown Court;

(b) where Parts I and II of the Criminal Procedure and Investigations Act 1996 apply.

Prosecution disclosure

B-197

15.2.–(1) This rule applies in the Crown Court where, under section 3 of the Criminal Procedure and Investigations Act 1996 [§ 12-58 in the main work], the prosecutor—

(a) discloses prosecution material to the defendant; or

(b) serves on the defendant a written statement that there is no such material to disclose.

(2) The prosecutor must at the same time so inform the court officer.

Prosecutor's application for public interest ruling

15.3.—(1) This rule applies where—

(a)   without a court order, the prosecutor would have to disclose material; and

(b)   the prosecutor wants the court to decide whether it would be in the public interest to disclose it.

(2) The prosecutor must—

(a)   apply in writing for such a decision; and

(b)   serve the application on—

(i)   the court officer,

(ii)   any person who the prosecutor thinks would be directly affected by disclosure of the material, and

(iii) the defendant, but only to the extent that serving it on the defendant would not disclose what the prosecutor thinks ought not be disclosed.

(3) The application must—

(a)   describe the material, and explain why the prosecutor thinks that—

(i)   it is material that the prosecutor would have to disclose,

(ii)   it would not be in the public interest to disclose that material, and

(iii) no measure such as the prosecutor's admission of any fact, or disclosure by summary, extract or edited copy, adequately would protect both the public interest and the defendant's right to a fair trial;

(b)   omit from any part of the application that is served on the defendant anything that would disclose what the prosecutor thinks ought not be disclosed (in which case, paragraph (4) of this rule applies); and

(c)   explain why, if no part of the application is served on the defendant.

(4) Where the prosecutor serves only part of the application on the defendant, the prosecutor must—

(a)   mark the other part, to show that it is only for the court; and

(b)   in that other part, explain why the prosecutor has withheld it from the defendant.

(5) Unless already done, the court may direct the prosecutor to serve an application on—

(a)   the defendant;

(b)   any other person who the court considers would be directly affected by the disclosure of the material.

(6) The court must determine the application at a hearing which—

(a)   must be in private, unless the court otherwise directs; and

(b)   if the court so directs, may take place, wholly or in part, in the defendant's absence.

(7) At a hearing at which the defendant is present—

(a)   the general rule is that the court must consider, in the following sequence—

(i)   representations first by the prosecutor and any other person served with the application, and then by the defendant, in the presence of them all, and then

(ii)   further representations by the prosecutor and any such other person in the defendant's absence; but

(b)   the court may direct other arrangements for the hearing.

(8) The court may only determine the application if satisfied that it has been able to take adequate account of—

(a)   such rights of confidentiality as apply to the material; and

(b)   the defendant's right to a fair trial.

(9) Unless the court otherwise directs, the court officer—

(a)   must not give notice to anyone other than the prosecutor—

(i)   of the hearing of an application under this rule, unless the prosecutor served the application on that person, or

(ii)   of the court's decision on the application;

(b)   may—

(i)   keep a written application or representations, or

(ii)   arrange for the whole or any part to be kept by some other appropriate person, subject to any conditions that the court may impose.

Defence disclosure

15.4.—(1) This rule applies where—

(a)   under section 5 or 6 of the Criminal Procedure and Investigations Act 1996 [§§ 12-62, 12-63 in the main work], the defendant gives a defence statement;

(b) under section 6C of the 1996 Act [*ibid.*, § 12-68], the defendant gives a defence witness notice.

(2) The defendant must serve such a statement or notice on—

    (a) the court officer; and

    (b) the prosecutor.

Defendant's application for prosecution disclosure

B-200

15.5.—(1) This rule applies where the defendant—

    (a) has served a defence statement given under the Criminal Procedure and Investigations Act 1996; and

    (b) wants the court to require the prosecutor to disclose material.

(2) The defendant must serve an application on—

    (a) the court officer; and

    (b) the prosecutor.

(3) The application must—

    (a) describe the material that the defendant wants the prosecutor to disclose;

    (b) explain why the defendant thinks there is reasonable cause to believe that—

        (i) the prosecutor has that material, and

        (ii) it is material that the Criminal Procedure and Investigations Act 1996 requires the prosecutor to disclose; and

    (c) ask for a hearing, if the defendant wants one, and explain why it is needed.

(4) The court may determine an application under this rule—

    (a) at a hearing, in public or in private; or

    (b) without a hearing.

(5) The court must not require the prosecutor to disclose material unless the prosecutor—

    (a) is present; or

    (b) has had at least 14 days in which to make representations.

Review of public interest ruling

B-201

15.6.—(1) This rule applies where the court has ordered that it is not in the public interest to disclose material that the prosecutor otherwise would have to disclose, and—

    (a) the defendant wants the court to review that decision; or

    (b) the Crown Court reviews that decision on its own initiative.

(2) Where the defendant wants the court to review that decision, the defendant must—

    (a) serve an application on—

        (i) the court officer, and

        (ii) the prosecutor; and

    (b) in the application—

        (i) describe the material that the defendant wants the prosecutor to disclose, and

        (ii) explain why the defendant thinks it is no longer in the public interest for the prosecutor not to disclose it.

(3) The prosecutor must serve any such application on any person who the prosecutor thinks would be directly affected if that material were disclosed.

(4) The prosecutor, and any such person, must serve any representations on—

    (a) the court officer; and

    (b) the defendant, unless to do so would in effect reveal something that either thinks ought not be disclosed.

(5) The court may direct—

    (a) the prosecutor to serve any such application on any person who the court considers would be directly affected if that material were disclosed;

    (b) the prosecutor and any such person to serve any representations on the defendant.

(6) The court must review a decision to which this rule applies at a hearing which—

    (a) must be in private, unless the court otherwise directs; and

    (b) if the court so directs, may take place, wholly or in part, in the defendant's absence.

(7) At a hearing at which the defendant is present—

    (a) the general rule is that the court must consider, in the following sequence—

        (i) representations first by the defendant, and then by the prosecutor and any other person served with the application, in the presence of them all, and then

        (ii) further representations by the prosecutor and any such other person in the defendant's absence; but

(b) the court may direct other arrangements for the hearing.

(8) The court may only conclude a review if satisfied that it has been able to take adequate account of—

    (a) such rights of confidentiality as apply to the material; and

    (b) the defendant's right to a fair trial.

Defendant's application to use disclosed material

15.7.—(1) This rule applies where a defendant wants the court's permission to use disclosed   **B-202** prosecution material—

    (a) otherwise than in connection with the case in which it was disclosed; or

    (b) beyond the extent to which it was displayed or communicated publicly at a hearing.

(2) The defendant must serve an application on—

    (a) the court officer; and

    (b) the prosecutor.

(3) The application must—

    (a) specify what the defendant wants to use or disclose; and

    (b) explain why.

(4) The court may determine an application under this rule—

    (a) at a hearing, in public or in private; or

    (b) without a hearing.

(5) The court must not permit the use of such material unless—

    (a) the prosecutor has had at least 28 days in which to make representations; and

    (b) the court is satisfied that it has been able to take adequate account of any rights of confidentiality that may apply to the material.

Unauthorised use of disclosed material

15.8.—(1) This rule applies where a person is accused of using disclosed prosecution material in   **B-203** contravention of section 17 of the Criminal Procedure and Investigations Act 1996 [§ 12-88 in the main work].

(2) A party who wants the court to exercise its power to punish that person for contempt of court must comply with the rules in Part 48 (contempt of court).

(3) The court must not exercise its power to forfeit material used in contempt of court unless—

    (a) the prosecutor; and

    (b) any other person directly affected by the disclosure of the material, is present, or has had at least 14 days in which to make representations.

Court's power to vary requirements under this Part

15.9. The court may—   **B-204**

    (a) shorten or extend (even after it has expired) a time limit under this Part;

    (b) allow a defence statement or a defence witness notice to be in a different written form to one set out in the Practice Direction, as long as it contains what the Criminal Procedure and Investigations Act 1996 requires;

    (c) allow an application under this Part to be in a different form to one set out in the Practice Direction, or to be presented orally; and

    (d) specify the period within which—

        (i) any application under this Part must be made, or

        (ii) any material must be disclosed, on an application to which rule 15.5 applies (defendant's application for prosecution disclosure).

CPD IV Disclosure 15A: Disclosure of Unused Material

15A.1 Disclosure is a vital part of the preparation for trial, both in the magistrates' courts and in   **B-205** the Crown Court. All parties must be familiar with their obligations, in particular under the Criminal Procedure and Investigations Act 1996 as amended and the Code issued under that Act, and must comply with the relevant judicial protocol and guidelines from the Attorney-General. These documents have recently been revised and the new guidance will be issued shortly as Judicial Protocol on the Disclosure of Unused Material in Criminal Cases [*post*, Appendix N-52 *et seq.*] and the Attorney-General's Guidelines on Disclosure [*ante*, Appendix A-242a *et seq.*]. The new documents should be read together as complementary, comprehensive guidance. They will be available electronically on the respective websites.

15A.2 In addition, certain procedures are prescribed under CrimPR Part 15 and these should be followed. The notes to Part 15 contain a useful summary of the requirements of the CPIA 1996 as amended.

Criminal Procedure Rules 2015 (S.I. 2015 No. 1490), Pt 16

WRITTEN WITNESS STATEMENTS

When this Part applies

B-206   **16.1.**–(1) This Part applies where a party wants to introduce a written statement in evidence under section 9 of the Criminal Justice Act 1967 [§ 10-14 in the main work].

Content of written statement

B-207   **16.2.** The statement must contain–

    (a) at the beginning–
        (i) the witness' name, and
        (ii) the witness' age, if under 18;
    (b) a declaration by the witness that–
        (i) it is true to the best of the witness' knowledge and belief, and
        (ii) the witness knows that if it is introduced in evidence, then it would be an offence wilfully to have stated in it anything that the witness knew to be false or did not believe to be true;
    (c) if the witness cannot read the statement, a signed declaration by someone else that that person read it to the witness; and
    (d) the witness' signature.

Reference to exhibit

B-208   **16.3** Where the statement refers to a document or object as an exhibit, it must identify that document or object clearly.

[This rule is printed as amended by the Criminal Procedure (Amendment No. 2) Rules 2016 (S.I. 2016 No. 705).]

Written witness statement in evidence

B-209   **16.4.**–(1) A party who wants to introduce in evidence a written statement must–

    (a) before the hearing at which that party wants to introduce it, serve a copy of the statement on–
        (i) the court officer, and
        (ii) each other party; and
    (b) at or before that hearing, serve on the court officer the statement or an authenticated copy.

    (2) If that party relies on only part of the statement, that party must mark the copy in such a way as to make that clear.

    (3) A prosecutor must serve on a defendant, with the copy of the statement, a notice–

    (a) of the right to object to the introduction of the statement in evidence instead of the witness giving evidence in person;
    (b) of the time limit for objecting under this rule; and
    (c) that if the defendant does not object in time, the court–
        (i) can nonetheless require the witness to give evidence in person, but
        (ii) may decide not to do so.

    (4) A party served with a written witness statement who objects to its introduction in evidence must–

    (a) serve notice of the objection on–
        (i) the party who served it, and
        (ii) the court officer; and
    (b) serve the notice of objection not more than 7 days after service of the statement unless–
        (i) the court extends that time limit, before or after the statement was served,
        (ii) rule 24.8 (written guilty plea: special rules) applies, in which case the time limit is the later of 7 days after service of the statement or 7 days before the hearing date, or
        (iii) rule 24.9 (single justice procedure: special rules) applies, in which case the time limit is 21 days after service of the statement.

(5) The court may exercise its power to require the witness to give evidence in person—
  (a) on application by any party; or
  (b) on its own initiative.
(6) A party entitled to receive a copy of a statement may waive that entitlement by so informing—
  (a) the party who would have served it; and
  (b) the court.

CPD V Evidence 16A: Evidence by Written Statement

16A.1 Where the prosecution proposes to tender written statements in evidence under section 9 of **B-210** the CJA 1967 [§ 10-14 in the main work], it will frequently be necessary for certain statements to be edited. This will occur either because a witness has made more than one statement whose contents should conveniently be reduced into a single, comprehensive statement, or where a statement contains inadmissible, prejudicial or irrelevant material. Editing of statements must be done by a crown prosecutor (or by a legal representative, if any, of the prosecutor if the case is not being conducted by the CPS) and not by a police officer.

Composite statements
  16A.2 A composite statement giving the combined effect of two or more earlier statements must be **B-211** prepared in compliance with the requirements of section 9 of the 1967 Act and must then be signed by the witness.

Editing single statements
  16A.3 There are two acceptable methods of editing single statements. They are: **B-212**
  (a) by marking copies of the statement in a way which indicates the passages on which the prosecution will not rely; this merely indicates that the prosecution will not seek to adduce the evidence so marked; the original signed statement to be tendered to the court is not marked in any way; the marking on the copy statement is done by lightly striking out the passages to be edited, so that what appears beneath can still be read, or by bracketing, or by a combination of both; it is not permissible to produce a photocopy with the deleted material obliterated, since this would be contrary to the requirement that the defence and the court should be served with copies of the signed original statement; whenever the striking out / bracketing method is used, it will assist if the following words appear at the foot of the frontispiece or index to any bundle of copy statements to be tendered: *"The prosecution does not propose to adduce evidence of those passages of the attached copy statements which have been struck out and / or bracketed (nor will it seek to do so at the trial unless a notice of further evidence is served)."*;
  (b) by obtaining a fresh statement, signed by the witness, which omits the offending material, applying the procedure for composite statements above.
  16A.4 In most cases where a single statement is to be edited, the striking out/bracketing method will be the more appropriate, but the taking of a fresh statement is preferable in the following circumstances. (a) When a police (or other investigating) officer's statement contains details of interviews with more suspects than are eventually charged, a fresh statement should be prepared and signed omitting all details of interview with those not charged except, in so far as it is relevant, for the bald fact that a certain named person was interviewed at a particular time, date and place. (b) When a suspect is interviewed about more offences than are eventually made the subject of charges, a fresh statement should be prepared and signed, omitting all questions and answers about the uncharged offences unless either they might appropriately be taken into consideration, or evidence about those offences is admissible on the charges preferred. It may, however, be desirable to replace the omitted questions and answers with a phrase such as: "After referring to some other matters, I then said ... ", so as to make it clear that part of the interview has been omitted. (c) A fresh statement should normally be prepared and signed if the only part of the original on which the prosecution is relying is only a small proportion of the whole, although it remains desirable to use the alternative method if there is reason to believe that the defence might itself wish to rely, in mitigation or for any other purpose, on at least some of those parts which the prosecution does not propose to adduce. (d) When the passages contain material which the prosecution is entitled to withhold from disclosure to the defence.
  16A.5 Prosecutors should also be aware that, where statements are to be tendered under section 9 of the 1967 Act in the course of summary proceedings, there will be a need to prepare fresh statements excluding inadmissible or prejudicial material, rather than using the striking out or bracketing method.
  16A.6 Whenever a fresh statement is taken from a witness and served in evidence, the earlier,

unedited statement(s) becomes unused material and should be scheduled and reviewed for disclosure to the defence in the usual way.

CPD V Evidence 16B: Video Recorded Evidence in Chief

B-213

16B.1 [Recites the relevant provisions (s.27 of the 1999 Act (§ 8-89 in the main work) and Pt 18 of the 2014 rules).]

16B.2 Where a court, on application by a party to the proceedings or of its own motion, grants leave to admit a video recording in evidence under section 27(1) ..., it may direct that any part of the recording be excluded (s.27(2) and (3)). When such direction is given, the party who made the application to admit the video recording must edit the recording in accordance with the judge's directions and send a copy of the edited recording to the appropriate officer of the Crown Court and to every other party to the proceedings.

16B.3 Where a video recording is to be adduced during proceedings before the Crown Court, it should be produced and proved by the interviewer, or any other person who was present at the interview with the witness at which the recording was made. The applicant should ensure that such a person will be available for this purpose, unless the parties have agreed to accept a written statement in lieu of attendance by that person.

16B.4 Once a trial has begun, if, by reason of faulty or inadequate preparation or for some other cause, the procedures set out above have not been properly complied with and an application is made to edit the video recording, thereby necessitating an adjournment for the work to be carried out, the court may, at its discretion, make an appropriate award of costs.

CPD V Evidence 16C: Evidence of Audio and Video Recorded Interviews

B-214

16C.1 The interrogation of suspects is primarily governed by Code C [*ante*, Appendix A-39 *et seq.*] ... Under that code, interviews must normally be contemporaneously recorded. Under ... Code E [*ante*, Appendix A-162 *et seq.*], interviews conducted at a police station concerning an indictable offence must normally be audio-recorded. In practice, most interviews are audio-recorded under Code E, or video-recorded under Code F, and it is best practice to do so. The questioning of terrorism suspects is governed ... by Code H [*ante*, Appendix A-213 *et seq.*].

16C.2 Where a record of the interview is to be prepared, this should be in accordance with the current national guidelines, as envisaged by Note 5A of Code E.

16C.3 If the prosecution wishes to rely on the defendant's interview in evidence, the prosecution should seek to agree the record with the defence. Both parties should have received a copy of the audio or video recording, and can check the record against the recording. The record should be edited (see below) if inadmissible matters are included within it and, in particular if the interview is lengthy, the prosecution should seek to shorten it by editing or summary.

16C.4 If the record is agreed there is usually no need for the audio or video recording to be played in court. It is a matter for the discretion of the ... judge, but usual practice is for edited copies of the record to be provided to the court, and to the jury if there is one, and for the prosecution advocate to read the interview with the interviewing officer or the officer in the case, as part of the officer's evidence in chief, the officer reading the interviewer and the advocate reading the defendant and defence representative. In the magistrates' court, the Bench sometimes retire to read the interview themselves, and the document is treated as if it had been read aloud in court. This is permissible, but rule 24.5 should be followed.

16C.5 Where the prosecution intends to adduce the interview in evidence, and agreement between the parties has not been reached about the record, sufficient notice must be given to allow consideration of any amendment to the record, or the preparation of any transcript of the interview, or any editing of a recording for the purpose of playing it in court. To that end, the following practice should be followed:

    (a) where the defence is unable to agree a record of interview or transcript (where one is already available) the prosecution should be notified at latest at the Plea and Case Management Hearing ("PCMH"), with a view to securing agreement to amend; the notice should specify the part to which objection is taken, or the part omitted which the defence consider should be included; a copy of the notice should be supplied to the court within the period specified above; the PCMH form inquires about the admissibility of the defendant's interview and shortening by editing or summarising for trial;

    (b) if agreement is not reached and it is proposed that the audio or video recording or part of it be played in court, notice should be given to the prosecution by the defence as ordered at the PCMH, in order that the advocates for the parties may agree those parts of the audio or video recording that should not be adduced and that arrangements may be made, by editing or in some other way, to exclude that material; a copy of the notice should be supplied to the court;

(c) notice of any agreement reached should be supplied to the court by the prosecution, as soon as is practicable.

16C.6 Alternatively, if, the prosecution advocate proposes to play the audio or video recording or part of it, the prosecution should at latest at the PCMH, notify the defence and the court. The defence should notify the prosecution and the court within 14 days of receiving the notice, if they object to the production of the audio or video recording on the basis that a part of it should be excluded. If the objections raised by the defence are accepted, the prosecution should prepare an edited recording, or make other arrangements to exclude the material part; and should notify the court of the arrangements made.

16C.7 If the defendant wishes to have the audio or video recording or any part of it played to the court, the defence should provide notice to the prosecution and the court at latest at the PCMH. The defence should also, at that time, notify the prosecution of any proposals to edit the recording and seek the prosecution's agreement to those amendments.

16C.8 Whenever editing or amendment of a record of interview or of an audio or video recording or of a transcript takes place, the following general principles should be followed:

(i) where a defendant has made a statement which includes an admission of one or more other offences, the portion relating to other offences should be omitted unless it is or becomes admissible in evidence;

(ii) where the statement of one defendant contains a portion which exculpates him ... and partly implicates a co-defendant in the trial, the defendant making the statement has the right to insist that everything relevant which is exculpatory goes before the jury; in such a case the judge must be consulted about how best to protect the position of the co-defendant.

16C.9 If it becomes necessary for either party to access the master copy of the audio or video recording, they should give notice to the other party and follow the procedure in ... Code E at section 6.

16C.10 If there is a challenge to the integrity of the master recording, notice and particulars should be given to the court and to the prosecution by the defence as soon as is practicable. The court may then, at its discretion, order a case management hearing or give such other directions as may be appropriate.

16C.11 If an audio or video recording is to be adduced during proceedings before the Crown Court, it should be produced and proved in a witness statement by the interviewing officer or any other officer who was present at the interview at which the recording was made. The prosecution should ensure that the witness is available to attend court if required by the defence in the usual way.

16C.12 It is the responsibility of the prosecution to ensure that there is a person available to operate any audio or video equipment needed during the course of the proceedings. Subject to their other responsibilities, the court staff may be able to assist.

16C.13 If either party wishes to present audio or video evidence, that party must ensure, in advance of the hearing, that the evidence is in a format that is compatible with the court's equipment, and that the material to be used does in fact function properly in the relevant court room.

16C.14 In order to avoid the necessity for the court to listen to or watch lengthy or irrelevant material before the relevant part of a recording is reached, counsel shall indicate to the equipment operator those parts of a recording which it may be necessary to play. Such an indication should, so far as possible, be expressed in terms of the time track or other identifying process used by the interviewing police force and should be given in time for the operator to have located those parts by the appropriate point in the trial.

16C.15 Once a trial has begun, if, by reason of faulty preparation or for some other cause, the procedures above have not been properly complied with, and an application is made to amend the record of interview or transcript or to edit the recording, as the case may be, thereby making necessary an adjournment for the work to be carried out, the court may make at its discretion an appropriate award of costs.

16C.16 Where a case is listed for hearing on a date which falls within the time limits set out above, it is the responsibility of the parties to ensure that all the necessary steps are taken to comply with this Practice Direction within such shorter period as is available.

Criminal Procedure Rules 2015 (S.I. 2015 No. 1490), Pt 17

WITNESS SUMMONSES, WARRANTS AND ORDERS

When this Part applies

17.1.–(1) This Part applies in magistrates' courts and in the Crown Court where– **B-215**

(a) a party wants the court to issue a witness summons, warrant or order under–

    (i)   section 97 of the Magistrates' Courts Act 1980,

    (ii) paragraph 4 of Schedule 3 to the Crime and Disorder Act 1998 [§§ 1-36 *et seq.* in the main work],

    (iii) section 2 of the Criminal Procedure (Attendance of Witnesses) Act 1965 [*ibid.*, § 8-1], or

    (iv) section 7 of the Bankers' Books Evidence Act 1879 [*ibid.*, § 11-63];

  (b) the court considers the issue of such a summons, warrant or order on its own initiative as if a party had applied; or

  (c) one of those listed in rule 17.7 wants the court to withdraw such a summons, warrant or order.

(2) A reference to a "witness" in this Part is a reference to a person to whom such a summons, warrant or order is directed.

Issue etc. of summons, warrant or order with or without a hearing

B-216   **17.2.**–(1) The court may issue or withdraw a witness summons, warrant or order with or without a hearing.

(2) A hearing under this Part must be in private unless the court otherwise directs.

Application for summons, warrant or order: general rules

B-217   **17.3.**–(1) A party who wants the court to issue a witness summons, warrant or order must apply as soon as practicable after becoming aware of the grounds for doing so.

(2) A party applying for a witness summons or order must—

  (a) identify the proposed witness;

  (b) explain—

    (i)   what evidence the proposed witness can give or produce,

    (ii) why it is likely to be material evidence, and

    (iii) why it would be in the interests of justice to issue a summons, order or warrant as appropriate.

(3) A party applying for an order to be allowed to inspect and copy an entry in bank records must—

  (a) identify the entry;

  (b) explain the purpose for which the entry is required; and

  (c) propose—

    (i)   the terms of the order, and

    (ii) the period within which the order should take effect, if 3 days from the date of service of the order would not be appropriate.

(4) The application may be made orally unless—

  (a) rule 17.5 applies; or

  (b) the court otherwise directs.

(5) The applicant must serve any order made on the witness to whom, or the bank to which, it is directed.

[This rule is printed as amended by the Criminal Procedure (Amendment) Rules 2016 (S.I. 2016 No. 120).]

Written application: form and service

B-218   **17.4.**–(1) An application in writing under rule 17.3 must be in the form set out in the Practice Direction, containing the same declaration of truth as a witness statement.

(2) The party applying must serve the application—

  (a) in every case, on the court officer and as directed by the court; and

  (b) as required by rule 17.5, if that rule applies.

Application for summons to produce a document, etc.: special rules

B-219   **17.5.**–(1) This rule applies to an application under rule 17.3 for a witness summons requiring the proposed witness—

  (a) to produce in evidence a document or thing; or

  (b) to give evidence about information apparently held in confidence,

that relates to another person.

(2) The application must be in writing in the form required by rule 17.4.

(3) The party applying must serve the application—

(a) on the proposed witness, unless the court otherwise directs; and

(b) on one or more of the following, if the court so directs—

    (i) a person to whom the proposed evidence relates,

    (ii) another party.

(4) The court must not issue a witness summons where this rule applies unless—

(a) everyone served with the application has had at least 14 days in which to make representations, including representations about whether there should be a hearing of the application before the summons is issued; and

(b) the court is satisfied that it has been able to take adequate account of the duties and rights, including rights of confidentiality, of the proposed witness and of any person to whom the proposed evidence relates.

(5) This rule does not apply to an application for an order to produce in evidence a copy of an entry in bank records.

[This rule is printed as amended by S.I. 2016 No. 120 (*ante*, B-217).]

Application for summons to produce a document, etc.: court's assessment of relevance and confidentiality

17.6.—(1) This rule applies where a person served with an application for a witness summons **B-220** requiring the proposed witness to produce in evidence a document or thing objects to its production on the ground that—

(a) it is not likely to be material evidence; or

(b) even if it is likely to be material evidence, the duties or rights, including rights of confidentiality, of the proposed witness or of any person to whom the document or thing relates outweigh the reasons for issuing a summons.

(2) The court may require the proposed witness to make the document or thing available for the objection to be assessed.

(3) The court may invite—

(a) the proposed witness or any representative of the proposed witness; or

(b) a person to whom the document or thing relates or any representative of such a person,

to help the court assess the objection.

Application to withdraw a summons, warrant or order

17.7.—(1) The court may withdraw a witness summons, warrant or order if one of the following **B-221** applies for it to be withdrawn—

(a) the party who applied for it, on the ground that it is no longer is needed;

(b) the witness, on the grounds that—

    (i) he was not aware of any application for it, and

    (ii) he cannot give or produce evidence likely to be material evidence, or

    (iii) even if he can, his duties or rights, including rights of confidentiality, or those of any person to whom the evidence relates outweigh the reasons for the issue of the summons, warrant or order; or

(c) any person to whom the proposed evidence relates, on the grounds that—

    (i) he was not aware of any application for it, and

    (ii) that evidence is not likely to be material evidence, or

    (iii) even if it is, his duties or rights, including rights of confidentiality, or those of the witness outweigh the reasons for the issue of the summons, warrant or order.

(2) A person applying under the rule must—

(a) apply in writing as soon as practicable after becoming aware of the grounds for doing so, explaining why he wants the summons, warrant or order to be withdrawn; and

(b) serve the application on the court officer and as appropriate on—

    (i) the witness,

    (ii) the party who applied for the summons, warrant or order, and

    (iii) any other person who he knows was served with the application for the summons, warrant or order.

(3) Rule 17.6 applies to an application under this rule that concerns a document or thing to be produced in evidence.

Court's power to vary requirements under this Part

17.8.—(1) The court may— **B-222**

   (a) shorten or extend (even after it has expired) a time limit under this Part; and

   (b) where a rule or direction requires an application under this Part to be in writing, allow that application to be made orally instead.

(2) Someone who wants the court to allow an application to be made orally under paragraph (1)(b) of this rule must—

   (a) give as much notice as the urgency of his application permits to those on whom he would otherwise have served an application in writing; and

   (b) in doing so explain the reasons for the application and for wanting the court to consider it orally.

CPD V Evidence 17A: Wards of Court and Children Subject to Current Family Proceedings

B-223

17A.1 Where police wish to interview a child who is subject to current family proceedings, leave of the Family Court is only required where such an interview may lead to a child disclosing information confidential to those proceedings and not otherwise available to the police under Working Together to Safeguard Children (March 2013), a guide to inter-agency working to safeguard and promote the welfare of children: www.workingtogetheronline.co.uk/chapters/contents.html.

17A.2 Where exceptionally the child to be interviewed or called as a witness in criminal proceedings is a ward of court then the leave of the court which made the wardship order will be required.

17A.3 Any application for leave in respect of any such child must be made to the court in which the relevant family proceedings are continuing and must be made on notice to the parents, any actual carer (*e.g.* relative or foster parent) and, in care proceedings, to the local authority and the guardian. In private proceedings the family court reporter (if appointed) should be notified.

17A.4 If the police need to interview the child without the knowledge of another party (usually a parent or carer), they may make the application for leave without giving notice to that party.

17A.5 Where leave is given the order should ordinarily give leave for any number of interviews that may be required. However, anything beyond that actually authorised will require a further application.

17A.6 Exceptionally the police may have to deal with complaints by or allegations against such a child immediately without obtaining the leave of the court as, for example:

   (a) a serious offence against a child (like rape) where immediate medical examination and collection of evidence is required; or

   (b) where the child is to be interviewed as a suspect.

When any such action is necessary, the police should, in respect of each and every interview, notify the parents and other carer (if any) and the family court reporter (if appointed). In care proceedings the local authority and guardian should be notified. The police must comply with all relevant codes of practice when conducting any such interview.

17A.7 The Family Court should be appraised of the position at the earliest reasonable opportunity by one of the notified parties and should thereafter be kept informed of any criminal proceedings.

17A.8 No evidence or document in the family proceedings or information about the proceedings should be disclosed into criminal proceedings without the leave of the Family Court.

Criminal Procedure Rules 2015 (S.I. 2015 No. 1490), Pt 18

MEASURES TO ASSIST A WITNESS OR DEFENDANT TO GIVE EVIDENCE

General rules

When this Part applies

B-224

18.1. This Part applies—

   (a) where the court can give a direction (a "special measures direction"), under section 19 of the Youth Justice and Criminal Evidence Act 1999 [§ 8-78 in the main work], on an application or on its own initiative, for any of the following measures—

      (i) preventing a witness from seeing the defendant (section 23 of the 1999 Act [*ibid.*, § 8-83]),

     (ii) allowing a witness to give evidence by live link (section 24 of the 1999 Act [*ibid.*, § 8-85]),

    (iii) hearing a witness' evidence in private (section 25 of the 1999 Act [*ibid.*, § 8-86]),

    (iv) dispensing with the wearing of wigs and gowns (section 26 of the 1999 Act [*ibid.*, § 8-88]),

   (v)   admitting video recorded evidence (sections 27 and 28 of the 1999 Act [*ibid.*, §§ 8-88, 8-93]),

   (vi)   questioning a witness through an intermediary (section 29 of the 1999 Act *ibid.*, § 8-94),

   (vii)   using a device to help a witness communicate (section 30 of the 1999 Act [*ibid.*, § 8-95]);

  (b)   where the court can vary or discharge such a direction, under section 20 of the 1999 Act [*ibid.*, § 8-79];

  (c)   where the court can give, vary or discharge a direction (a "defendant's evidence direction") for a defendant to give evidence—

   (i)   by live link, under section 33A of the 1999 Act [*ibid.*, § 8-99], or

   (ii)   through an intermediary, under sections 33BA and 33BB of the 1999 Act [*ibid.*, §§ 8-101, 8-102];

  (d)   where the court can—

   (i)   make a witness anonymity order, under section 86 of the Coroners and Justice Act 2009 [*ibid.*, § 8-156], or

   (ii)   vary or discharge such an order, under section 91, 92 or 93 of the 2009 Act [*ibid.*, §§ 8-161 *et seq.*];

  (e)   where the court can give or discharge a direction (a "live link direction"), on an application or on its own initiative, for a witness to give evidence by live link under—

   (i)   section 32 of the Criminal Justice Act 1988 [*ibid.*, § 8-132], or

   (ii)   sections 51 and 52 of the Criminal Justice Act 2003 [*ibid.*, §§ 8-139, 8-140];

  (f)   where the court can exercise any other power it has to give, vary or discharge a direction for a measure to help a witness give evidence.

Meaning of "witness"

18.2. In this Part, "witness" means anyone (other than a defendant) for whose benefit an application, direction or order is made. **B-225**

Making an application for a direction or order

18.3. A party who wants the court to exercise its power to give or make a direction or order must— **B-226**

  (a)   apply in writing as soon as reasonably practicable, and in any event, not more than—

   (i)   28 days after the defendant pleads not guilty, in a magistrates' court, or

   (ii)   14 days after the defendant pleads not guilty, in the Crown Court; and

  (b)   serve the application on—

   (i)   the court officer, and

   (ii)   each other party.

Decisions and reasons

18.4.–(1) A party who wants to introduce the evidence of a witness who is the subject of an application, direction or order must— **B-227**

  (a)   inform the witness of the court's decision as soon as reasonably practicable; and

  (b)   explain to the witness the arrangements that as a result will be made for him or her to give evidence.

(2) The court must—

  (a)   promptly determine an application; and

  (b)   allow a party sufficient time to comply with the requirements of—

   (i)   paragraph (1), and

   (ii)   the code of practice issued under section 32 of the Domestic Violence, Crime and Victims Act 2004.

(3) The court must announce, at a hearing in public before the witness gives evidence, the reasons for a decision—

  (a)   to give, make, vary or discharge a direction or order; or

  (b)   to refuse to do so.

[This rule is printed as amended by the Criminal Procedure (Amendment No. 2) Rules 2016 (S.I. 2016 No. 705).]

Court's power to vary requirements under this Part

18.5.–(1) The court may— **B-228**

  (a)   shorten or extend (even after it has expired) a time limit under this Part; and

(b) allow an application or representations to be made in a different form to one set out in the Practice Direction, or to be made orally.

(2) A person who wants an extension of time must—

(a) apply when serving the application or representations for which it is needed; and

(b) explain the delay.

Custody of documents

B-229
18.6. Unless the court otherwise directs, the court officer may—

(a) keep a written application or representations; or

(b) arrange for the whole or any part to be kept by some other appropriate person, subject to any conditions that the court may impose.

Declaration by intermediary

B-230
18.7.–(1) This rule applies where—

(a) a video recorded interview with a witness is conducted through an intermediary;

(b) the court directs the examination of a witness or defendant through an intermediary.

(2) An intermediary must make a declaration—

(a) before such an interview begins;

(b) before the examination begins (even if such an interview with the witness was conducted through the same intermediary).

(3) The declaration must be in these terms—

"I solemnly, sincerely and truly declare [or I swear by Almighty God] that I will well and faithfully communicate questions and answers and make true explanation of all matters and things as shall be required of me according to the best of my skill and understanding."

Special measures directions

Exercise of court's powers

B-231
18.8. The court may decide whether to give, vary or discharge a special measures direction—

(a) at a hearing, in public or in private, or without a hearing;

(b) in a party's absence, if that party—

(i) applied for the direction, variation or discharge, or

(ii) has had at least 14 days in which to make representations.

Special measures direction for a young witness

B-232
18.9.–(1) This rule applies where, under section 21 or section 22 of the Youth Justice and Criminal Evidence Act 1999 [§§ 8-80, 8-81 in the main work], the primary rule requires the court to give a direction for a special measure to assist a child witness or a qualifying witness—

(a) on an application, if one is made; or

(b) on the court's own initiative, in any other case.

(2) A party who wants to introduce the evidence of such a witness must as soon as reasonably practicable—

(a) notify the court that the witness is eligible for assistance;

(b) provide the court with any information that the court may need to assess the witness' views, if the witness does not want the primary rule to apply; and

(c) serve any video recorded evidence on—

(i) the court officer, and

(ii) each other party.

Content of application for a special measures direction

B-233
18.10. An applicant for a special measures direction must—

(a) explain how the witness is eligible for assistance;

(b) explain why special measures would be likely to improve the quality of the witness' evidence;

(c) propose the measure or measures that in the applicant's opinion would be likely to maximise so far as practicable the quality of that evidence;

(d) report any views that the witness has expressed about—

(i) his or her eligibility for assistance,

(ii) the likelihood that special measures would improve the quality of his or her evidence, and

    (iii)   the measure or measures proposed by the applicant;

(e) in a case in which a child witness or a qualifying witness does not want the primary rule to apply, provide any information that the court may need to assess the witness' views;

(f) in a case in which the applicant proposes that the witness should give evidence by live link—

    (i)   identify someone to accompany the witness while the witness gives evidence,

    (ii) name that person, if possible, and

    (iii) explain why that person would be an appropriate companion for the witness, including the witness' own views;

(g) in a case in which the applicant proposes the admission of video recorded evidence, identify—

    (i)   the date and duration of the recording,

    (ii) which part the applicant wants the court to admit as evidence, if the applicant does not want the court to admit all of it;

(h) attach any other material on which the applicant relies; and

(i) if the applicant wants a hearing, ask for one, and explain why it is needed.

Application to vary or discharge a special measures direction

18.11.—(1) A party who wants the court to vary or discharge a special measures direction must—   **B-234**

(a) apply in writing, as soon as reasonably practicable after becoming aware of the grounds for doing so; and

(b) serve the application on—

    (i)   the court officer, and

    (ii) each other party.

(2) The applicant must—

(a) explain what material circumstances have changed since the direction was given (or last varied, if applicable);

(b) explain why the direction should be varied or discharged; and

(c) ask for a hearing, if the applicant wants one, and explain why it is needed.

Application containing information withheld from another party

18.12.—(1) This rule applies where—   **B-235**

(a) an applicant serves an application for a special measures direction, or for its variation or discharge; and

(b) the application includes information that the applicant thinks ought not be revealed to another party.

(2) The applicant must—

(a) omit that information from the part of the application that is served on that other party;

(b) mark the other part to show that, unless the court otherwise directs, it is only for the court; and

(c) in that other part, explain why the applicant has withheld that information from that other party.

(3) Any hearing of an application to which this rule applies—

(a) must be in private, unless the court otherwise directs; and

(b) if the court so directs, may be, wholly or in part, in the absence of a party from whom information has been withheld.

(4) At any hearing of an application to which this rule applies—

(a) the general rule is that the court must consider, in the following sequence—

    (i)   representations first by the applicant and then by each other party, in all the parties' presence, and then

    (ii) further representations by the applicant, in the absence of a party from whom information has been withheld; but

(b) the court may direct other arrangements for the hearing.

Representations in response

18.13.—(1) This rule applies where a party wants to make representations about—   **B-236**

(a) an application for a special measures direction;

(b) an application for the variation or discharge of such a direction; or

(c) a direction, variation or discharge that the court proposes on its own initiative.

(2) Such a party must—
   (a) serve the representations on—
     (i) the court officer, and
     (ii) each other party;
   (b) do so not more than 14 days after, as applicable—
     (i) service of the application, or
     (ii) notice of the direction, variation or discharge that the court proposes; and
   (c) ask for a hearing, if that party wants one, and explain why it is needed.
(3) Where representations include information that the person making them thinks ought not be revealed to another party, that person must—
   (a) omit that information from the representations served on that other party;
   (b) mark the information to show that, unless the court otherwise directs, it is only for the court; and
   (c) with that information include an explanation of why it has been withheld from that other party.
(4) Representations against a special measures direction must explain, as appropiate—
   (a) why the witness is not eligible for assistance; or
   (b) if the witness is eligible for assistance, why—
     (i) no special measure would be likely to improve the quality of the witness' evidence,
     (ii) the proposed measure or measures would not be likely to maximise so far as practicable the quality of the witness' evidence, or
     (iii) the proposed measure or measures might tend to inhibit the effective testing of that evidence;
   (c) in a case in which the admission of video recorded evidence is proposed, why it would not be in the interests of justice for the recording, or part of it, to be admitted as evidence.
(5) Representations against the variation or discharge of a special measures direction must explain why it should not be varied or discharged.

Defendant's evidence directions

Exercise of court's powers

B-237
   18.14. The court may decide whether to give, vary or discharge a defendant's evidence direction—
   (a) at a hearing, in public or in private, or without a hearing;
   (b) in a party's absence, if that party—
     (i) applied for the direction, variation or discharge, or
     (ii) has had at least 14 days in which to make representations.

Content of application for a defendant's evidence direction

B-238
   18.15. An applicant for a defendant's evidence direction must—
   (a) explain how the proposed direction meets the conditions prescribed by the Youth Justice and Criminal Evidence Act 1999;
   (b) in a case in which the applicant proposes that the defendant give evidence by live link—
     (i) identify a person to accompany the defendant while the defendant gives evidence, and
     (ii) explain why that person is appropriate;
   (c) ask for a hearing, if the applicant wants one, and explain why it is needed.

Application to vary or discharge a defendant's evidence direction

B-239
   18.16.—(1) A party who wants the court to vary or discharge a defendant's evidence direction must—
   (a) apply in writing, as soon as reasonably practicable after becoming aware of the grounds for doing so; and
   (b) serve the application on—
     (i) the court officer, and
     (ii) each other party.
(2) The applicant must—
   (a) on an application to discharge a live link direction, explain why it is in the interests of justice to do so;
   (b) on an application to discharge a direction for an intermediary, explain why it is no longer necessary in order to ensure that the defendant receives a fair trial;

(c) on an application to vary a direction for an intermediary, explain why it is necessary for the direction to be varied in order to ensure that the defendant receives a fair trial; and

(d) ask for a hearing, if the applicant wants one, and explain why it is needed.

Representations in response

18.17.–(1) This rule applies where a party wants to make representations about— **B-240**

(a) an application for a defendant's evidence direction;

(b) an application for the variation or discharge of such a direction; or

(c) a direction, variation or discharge that the court proposes on its own initiative.

(2) [*Identical to r.18.13(2), ante, § B-236.*]

(3) Representations against a direction, variation or discharge must explain why the conditions prescribed by the Youth Justice and Criminal Evidence Act 1999 are not met.

Witness anonymity orders

Exercise of court's powers

18.18.–(1) The court may decide whether to make, vary or discharge a witness anonymity order— **B-241**

(a) at a hearing (which must be in private, unless the court otherwise directs), or without a hearing (unless any party asks for one);

(b) in the absence of a defendant.

(2) The court must not exercise its power to make, vary or discharge a witness anonymity order, or to refuse to do so—

(a) before or during the trial, unless each party has had an opportunity to make representations;

(b) on an appeal by the defendant to which applies Part 34 (appeal to the Crown Court) or Part 39 (appeal to the Court of Appeal about conviction or sentence), unless in each party's case—

   (i) that party has had an opportunity to make representations, or

   (ii) the appeal court is satisfied that it is not reasonably practicable to communicate with that party;

(c) after the trial and any such appeal are over, unless in the case of each party and the witness—

   (i) each has had an opportunity to make representations, or

   (ii) the court is satisfied that it is not reasonably practicable to communicate with that party or witness.

Content and conduct of application for a witness anonymity order

18.19.–(1) An applicant for a witness anonymity order must— **B-242**

(a) include in the application nothing that might reveal the witness' identity;

(b) describe the measures proposed by the applicant;

(c) explain how the proposed order meets the conditions prescribed by section 88 of the Coroners and Justice Act 2009 [§ 8-158 in the main work];

(d) explain why no measures other than those proposed will suffice, such as—

   (i) an admission of the facts that would be proved by the witness,

   (ii) an order restricting public access to the trial,

   (iii) reporting restrictions, in particular under section 46 of the Youth Justice and Criminal Evidence Act 1999 [*ibid.*, § 4-33] or under section 39 of the Children and Young Persons Act 1933,

   (iv) a direction for a special measure under section 19 of the Youth Justice and Criminal Evidence Act 1999 [*ibid.*, § 8-78],

   (v) introduction of the witness' written statement as hearsay evidence, under section 116 of the Criminal Justice Act 2003 [*ibid.*, § 11-15], or

   (vi) arrangements for the protection of the witness;

(e) attach to the application—

   (i) a witness statement setting out the proposed evidence, edited in such a way as not to reveal the witness' identity,

   (ii) where the prosecutor is the applicant, any further prosecution evidence to be served, and any further prosecution material to be disclosed under the Criminal Procedure and Investigations Act 1996, similarly edited, and

   (iii) any defence statement that has been served, or as much information as may be available to the applicant that gives particulars of the defence; and

   (f)   ask for a hearing, if the applicant wants one.

  (2) At any hearing of the application, the applicant must—

    (a)   identify the witness to the court, unless at the prosecutor's request the court otherwise directs; and

    (b)   present to the court, unless it otherwise directs—

       (i)   the unedited witness statement from which the edited version has been prepared,

      (ii)   where the prosecutor is the applicant, the unedited version of any further prosecution evidence or material from which an edited version has been prepared, and

     (iii)   such further material as the applicant relies on to establish that the proposed order meets the conditions prescribed by section 88 of the 2009 Act.

  (3) At any such hearing—

    (a)   the general rule is that the court must consider, in the following sequence—

       (i)   representations dirst by the applicant and then by each other party, in all the parties' presence, and then

      (ii)   information withheld from a defendant, and further representations by the applicant, in the absence of any (or any other) defendant; but

    (b)   the court may direct other arrangements for the hearing.

  (4) Before the witness gives evidence, the applicant must identify the witness to the court—

    (a)   if not already done;

    (b)   without revealing the witness' identity to any other party or person; and

    (c)   unless at the prosecutor's request the court otherwise directs.

Duty of court officer to notify the Director of Public Prosecutions

B-243   **18.20.** The court officer must notify the Director of Public Prosecutions of an application, unless the prosecutor is, or acts on behalf of, a public authority.

Application to vary or discharge a witness anonymity order

B-244   **18.21.**–(1) A party who wants the court to vary or discharge a witness anonymity order, or a witness who wants the court to do so when the case is over, must—

    (a)   apply in writing, as soon as reasonably practicable after becoming aware of the grounds for doing so; and

    (b)   serve the application on—

       (i)   the court officer, and

      (ii)   each other party.

  (2) The applicant must—

    (a)   explain what material circumstances have changed since the order was made (or last varied, if applicable);

    (b)   explain why the order should be varied or discharged, taking account of the conditions for making an order; and

    (c)   ask for a hearing, if the applicant wants one.

  (3) Where an application includes information that the applicant thinks might reveal the witness' identity, the applicant must—

    (a)   omit that information from the application that is served on a defendant;

    (b)   mark the information to show that it is only for the court and the prosecutor (if the prosecutor is not the applicant); and

    (c)   with that information include an explanation of why it has been withheld.

  (4) Where a party applies to vary or discharge a witness anonymity order after the trial and any appeal are over, the party who introduced the witness' evidence must serve the application on the witness.

Representations in response

B-245   **18.22.**–(1) This rule applies where a party or, where the case is over, a witness, wants to make representations about—

    (a)   an application for a witness anonymity order;

    (b)   an application for the variation or discharge of such an order; or

    (c)   a variation or discharge that the court proposes on its own initiative.

  (2) Such a party or witness must—

    (a)   serve the representations on—

       (i)   the court officer, and

      (ii)   each other party;

   (b) do so not more than 14 days after, as applicable—

      (i)   service of the application, or

      (ii) notice of the variation or discharge that the court proposes; and

   (c) ask for a hearing, if that party or witness wants one.

(3) Where representations include information that the person making them thinks might reveal the witness' identity, that person must—

   (a) omit that information from the representations served on a defendant;

   (b) mark the information to show that it is only for the court (and for the prosecutor, if relevant); and

   (c) with that information include an explanation of why it has been withheld.

(4) Representations against a witness anonymity order must explain why the conditions for making the order are not met.

(5) Representations against the variation or discharge of such an order must explain why it would not be appropriate to vary or discharge it, taking account of the conditions for making an order.

(6) A prosecutor's representations in response to an application by a defendant must include all information available to the prosecutor that is relevant to the conditions and considerations specified by sections 88 and 89 of the Coroners and Justice Act 2009 [§§ 8-158, 8-159 in the main work].

Live link directions

Exercise of court's powers

18.23. The court may decide whether to give or discharge a live link direction—   **B-246**

   (a) at a hearing, in public or in private, or without a hearing;

   (b) in a party's absence, if that party—

      (i)   applied for the direction or discharge, or

      (ii) has had at least 14 days in which to make representations in response to an application by another party.

Content of application for a live link direction

18.24. An applicant for a live link direction must—   **B-247**

   (a) unless the court otherwise directs, identify the place from which the witness will give evidence;

   (b) if that place is in the United Kingdom, explain why it would be in the interests of the efficient or effective administration of justice for the witness to give evidence by live link;

   (c) if the applicant wants the witness to be accompanied by another person while giving evidence—

      (i)   name that person, if possible, and

      (ii) explain why it is appropriate for the witness to be accompanied;

   (d) ask for a hearing, if the applicant wants one, and explain why it is needed.

Application to discharge a live link direction

18.25.—(1) A party who wants the court to discharge a live link direction must—   **B-248**

   (a) apply in writing, as soon as reasonably practicable after becoming aware of the grounds for doing so; and

   (b) serve the application on—

      (i)   the court officer, and

      (ii) each other party.

(2) The applicant must—

   (a) explain what material circumstances have changed since the direction was given;

   (b) explain why it is in the interests of justice to discharge the direction; and

   (c) ask for a hearing, if the applicant wants one, and explain why it is needed.

Representations in response

18.26.—(1) This rule applies where a party wants to make representations about an application for   **B-249** a live link direction or for the discharge of such a direction.

(2) Such a party must—

   (a) serve the representations on—

      (i)   the court officer, and

      (ii) each other party;
   (b) do so not more than 14 days after service of the application; and
   (c) ask for a hearing, if that party wants one, and explain why it is needed.

(3) Representations against a direction or discharge must explain, as applicable, why the conditions prescribed by the Criminal Justice Act 1988 or the Criminal Justice Act 2003 are not met.

CPD V Evidence 18A: Measures to Assist a Witness or Defendant to Give Evidence

B-250

18A.1 For special measures applications, the procedures at Part 18 should be followed. However, assisting a vulnerable witness to give evidence is not merely a matter of ordering the appropriate measure. Further directions about vulnerable people in the courts, ground rules hearings and intermediaries are given in the practice direction accompanying Part 3.

18A.2 Special measures need not be considered or ordered in isolation. The needs of the individual witness should be ascertained, and a combination of special measures may be appropriate. For example, if a witness who is to give evidence by live link wishes, screens can be used to shield the live link screen from the defendant and the public, as would occur if screens were being used for a witness giving evidence in the court room.

CPD V Evidence 18B: Witnesses Giving Evidence by Live Link

B-251

18B.1 A special measures direction for the witness to give evidence by live link may also provide for a specified person to accompany the witness (r.18.10(f)). In determining who this should be, the court must have regard to the wishes of the witness. The presence of a supporter is designed to provide emotional support to the witness, helping reduce the witness's anxiety and stress and contributing to the ability to give best evidence. It is preferable for the direction to be made well before the trial begins and to ensure that the designated person is available on the day of the witness's testimony so as to provide certainty for the witness.

18B.2 An increased degree of flexibility is appropriate as to who can act as supporter. This can be anyone known to and trusted by the witness who is not a party to the proceedings and has no detailed knowledge of the evidence in the case. The supporter may be a member of the witness service but need not be an usher or court official. Someone else may be appropriate.

18B.3 The usher should continue to be available both to assist the witness and the witness supporter, and to ensure that the court's requirements are properly complied with in the live link room.

18B.4 In order to be able to express an informed view about special measures, the witness is entitled to practise speaking using the live link (and to see screens in place). Simply being shown the room and equipment is inadequate for this purpose.

18B.5 If, with the agreement of the court, the witness has chosen not to give evidence by live link but to do so in the court room, it may still be appropriate for a witness supporter to be selected in the same way, and for the supporter to sit alongside the witness while the witness is giving evidence.

CPD V Evidence 18C: Visually Recorded Interviews: Memory Refreshing and Watching at a Different Time from the Jury

B-252

18C.1 Witnesses are entitled to refresh their memory from their statement or visually recorded interview. The court should enquire at the PCMH or other case management hearing about arrangements for memory refreshing. The witness's first viewing of the visually recorded interview can be distressing or distracting. It should not be seen for the first time immediately before giving evidence. Depending upon the age and vulnerability of the witness several competing issues have to be considered and it may be that the assistance of the intermediary is needed to establish exactly how memory refreshing should be managed.

18C.2 If the interview is ruled inadmissible, the court must decide what constitutes an acceptable alternative method of memory refreshing.

18C.3 Decisions about how, when and where refreshing should take place should be court-led and made on a case-by-case basis in respect of each witness. General principles to be addressed include:

    (i) the venue for viewing; the delicate balance between combining the court familiarisation visit and watching the DVD, and having them on two separate occasions, needs to be considered in respect of each witness as combining the two may lead to "information overload"; refreshing need not necessarily take place within the court building but may be done, for example, at the police ABE suite;

    (ii) requiring that any viewing is monitored by a person (usually the officer in the case) who will report to the court about anything said by the witness;

    (iii) whether it is necessary for the witness to see the DVD more than once for the purpose of refreshing; the court will need to ask the advice of the intermediary, if any, with respect to this;

(iv) arrangements, if the witness will not watch the DVD at the same time as the trial bench or judge and jury, for the witness to watch it before attending to be cross-examined (depending upon their ability to retain information this may be the day before).

18C.4 There is no legal requirement that the witness should watch the interview at the same time as the trial bench or jury. Increasingly, this is arranged to occur at a different time, with the advantages that breaks can be taken as needed without disrupting the trial, and cross-examination starts while the witness is fresh. An intermediary may be present to facilitate communication but should not act as the independent person designated to take a note and report to the court if anything is said. Where the viewing takes place at a different time from that of the jury, the witness is sworn just before cross-examination, asked if he or she has watched the interview and if its contents are "true" (or other words tailored to the witness's understanding).

CPD V Evidence 18D: Witness Anonymity Orders

18D.1 [*Recites that this direction supplements the Coroners and Justice Act 2009, s.87 (§ 8-157 in the main* **B-253**
work) and rr.18.18-18.22.]

18D.2 As the Court of Appeal stated in *R. v. Mayers* [§§ 8-170 *et seq.* in the main work] and emphasised again in *R. v. Donovan and Kafunda* [§ 8-172 in the main work], "a witness anonymity order is to be regarded as a special measure of the last practicable resort". In making such an application, the prosecution's obligations of disclosure "go much further than the ordinary duties of disclosure" (*R. v. Mayers*); reference should be made to the Judicial Protocol on Disclosure (*post*, Appendix N-52 *et seq.*): see the practice direction accompanying Part 15.

CASE MANAGEMENT

18D.3 Where such an application is proposed, with the parties' active assistance the court should **B-254**
set a realistic timetable, in accordance with the duties imposed by rules 3.2 and 3.3. Where possible, the trial judge should determine the application, and any hearing should be attended by the parties' trial advocates.

SERVICE OF EVIDENCE AND DISCLOSURE OF PROSECUTION MATERIAL PENDING AN APPLICATION

18D.4 Where the prosecutor proposes an application for a witness anonymity order it is not neces- **B-255**
sary for that application to have been determined before the proposed evidence is served. In most cases an early indication of what that evidence will be if an order is made will be consistent with a party's duties under rules 1.2 and 3.3. The prosecutor should serve with the other prosecution evidence a witness statement setting out the proposed evidence, redacted in such a way as to prevent disclosure of the witness' identity, as permitted by section 87(4) ... . Likewise the prosecutor should serve with other prosecution material disclosed under the CPIA 1996 any such material appertaining to the witness, similarly redacted.

THE APPLICATION

18D.5 An application for a witness anonymity order should be made as early as possible and **B-256**
within the period for which rule 18.3 provides. The application, and any hearing of it, must comply with the requirements of that rule and with those of rule 18.19. In accordance with rules 1.2 and 3.3, the applicant must provide the court with all available information relevant to the considerations to which the Act requires a court to have regard.

RESPONSE TO THE APPLICATION

18D.6 A party upon whom an application for a witness anonymity order is served must serve a **B-257**
response in accordance with rule 18.22. That period may be extended or shortened in the court's discretion: r.18.5.

18D.7 To avoid the risk of injustice, a respondent, whether the prosecution or a defendant, must actively assist the court. If not already done, a respondent defendant should serve a defence statement under section 5 or 6 of the CPIA 1996 [§§ 12-62, 12-63 in the main work], so that the court is fully informed of what is in issue. When a defendant makes an application for a witness anonymity order the prosecutor should consider the continuing duty to disclose material under section 7A of the CPIA 1996 [§ 12-74 in the main work]; therefore a prosecutor's response should include confirmation that that duty has been considered. Great care should be taken to ensure that nothing disclosed contains anything that might reveal the witness' identity. A respondent prosecutor should provide the court with all available information relevant to the considerations to which the Act requires a court to have regard, whether or not that information falls to be disclosed under the 1996 Act.

DETERMINATION OF THE APPLICATION

B-258

18D.8 All parties must have an opportunity to make oral representations to the court on an application for a witness anonymity order: s.87(6) ... . However, a hearing may not be needed if none is sought: r.18.18(1)(a). Where, for example, the witness is an investigator who is recognisable by the defendant but known only by an assumed name, and there is no likelihood that the witness' credibility will be in issue, then the court may indicate a provisional decision and invite representations within a defined period, usually 14 days, including representations about whether there should be a hearing. In such a case, where the parties do not object the court may make an order without a hearing. Or where the court provisionally considers an application to be misconceived, an applicant may choose to withdraw it without requiring a hearing. Where the court directs a hearing of the application then it should allow adequate time for service of the representations in response.

18D.9 The hearing of an application for a witness anonymity order usually should be in private: r.18.18(1)(a). The court has power to hear a party in the absence of a defendant and that defendant's representatives: s.87(7) ... and r.18.18(1)(b). In the Crown Court, a recording of the proceedings will be made, in accordance with rule 5.5. The Crown Court officer must treat such a recording in the same way as the recording of an application for a public interest ruling. It must be kept in secure conditions, and the arrangements made by the Crown Court officer for any transcription must impose restrictions that correspond with those under rule 5.5(2).

18D.10 Where confidential supporting information is presented to the court before the last stage of the hearing, the court may prefer not to read that information until that last stage.

18D.11 The court may adjourn the hearing at any stage, and should do so if its duty under rule 3.2 so requires.

18D.12 On a prosecutor's application, the court is likely to be assisted by the attendance of a senior investigator or other person of comparable authority who is familiar with the case.

18D.13 During the last stage of the hearing it is essential that the court test thoroughly the information supplied in confidence in order to satisfy itself that the conditions prescribed by the Act are met. At that stage, if the court concludes that this is the only way in which it can satisfy itself as to a relevant condition or consideration, exceptionally it may invite the applicant to present the proposed witness to be questioned by the court. Any such questioning should be carried out at such a time, and the witness brought to the court in such a way, as to prevent disclosure of his ... identity.

18D.14 The court may ask the Attorney-General to appoint special counsel to assist. However, it must be kept in mind that, "Such an appointment will always be exceptional, never automatic; a course of last and never first resort. It should not be ordered unless and until the trial judge is satisfied that no other course will adequately meet the overriding requirement of fairness to the defendant": *R. v. H.* [§ 12-109 in the main work]. Whether to accede to such a request is a matter for the Attorney-General, and adequate time should be allowed for the consideration of such a request.

18D.15 The Court of Appeal in *R. v. Mayers* emphasised that all three conditions, A, B and C, must be met before the jurisdiction to make a witness anonymity order arises. Each is mandatory. Each is distinct. The court also noted that if there is more than one anonymous witness in a case any link, and the nature of any link, between the witnesses should be investigated: "questions of possible improper collusion between them, or cross-contamination of one another, should be addressed."

18D.16 Following a hearing the court should announce its decision ... in the parties' presence and in public: r.18.4(2). The court should give such reasons as it is possible to give without revealing the witness' identity. In the Crown Court, the court will be conscious that reasons given in public may be reported and reach the jury. Consequently, the court should ensure that nothing in its decision or its reasons could undermine any warning it may give jurors under section 90(2) [§ 8-160 in the main work] ... . A record of the reasons must be kept. In the Crown Court, the announcement of those reasons will be recorded.

ORDER

B-259

18D.17 Where the court makes a witness anonymity order, it is essential that the measures to be taken are clearly specified in a written record of that order approved by the court and issued on its behalf. An order made in a magistrates' court must be recorded in the court register, in accordance with rule 5.4.

18D.18 Self-evidently, the written record of the order must not disclose the identity of the witness to whom it applies. However, it is essential that there be maintained some means of establishing a clear correlation between witness and order, and especially where in the same proceedings witness anonymity orders are made in respect of more than one witness, specifying different measures in respect of each. Careful preservation of the application for the order, including the confidential part, ordinarily will suffice for this purpose.

DISCHARGE OR VARIATION OF THE ORDER

18D.19 Section 91 [§ 8-161 in the main work] ... allows the court to discharge or vary a witness **B-260** anonymity order: on application, if there has been a material change of circumstances since the order was made or since any previous variation of it; or on its own initiative. Rule 18.21 allows the parties to apply for the variation of a pre-trial direction where circumstances have changed.

18D.20 The court should keep under review the question of whether the conditions for making an order are met. In addition, consistently with the parties' duties under rules 1.2 and 3.3, it is incumbent on each, and in particular on the applicant for the order, to keep the need for it under review.

18D.21 Where the court considers the discharge or variation of an order, the procedure that it adopts should be appropriate to the circumstances. As a general rule, that procedure should approximate to the procedure for determining an application for an order. The court may need to hear further representations by the applicant for the order in the absence of a respondent defendant and that defendant's representatives.

RETENTION OF CONFIDENTIAL MATERIAL

18D.22 If retained by the court, confidential material must be stored in secure conditions by the **B-261** court officer. Alternatively, subject to such directions as the court may give, such material may be committed to the safe-keeping of the applicant or any other appropriate person in exercise of the powers conferred by rule 18.6. If the material is released to any such person, the court should ensure that it will be available to the court at trial.

Criminal Procedure Rules 2015 (S.I. 2015 No. 1490), Pt 19

EXPERT EVIDENCE

When this Part applies
19.1.–(1) This Part applies where a party wants to introduce expert opinion evidence.   **B-262**
(2) A reference to an "expert" in this part is a reference to a person who is required to give or prepare expert evidence for the purpose of criminal proceedings, including evidence required to determine fitness to plead or for the purpose of sentencing.

Expert's duty to the court
19.2.–(1) An expert must help the court to achieve the overriding objective—   **B-263**
  (a) by giving opinion which is—
     (i)   objective and unbiased, and
     (ii) within the expert's area or areas of expertise; and
  (b) by actively assisting the court in fulfilling its duty of case management under rule 3.2, in particular by—
     (i)   complying with directions made by the court, and
     (ii) at once informing the court of any significant failure (by the expert or another) to take any step required by such a direction.
(2) This duty overrides any obligation to the person from whom the expert receives instructions or by whom the expert is paid.
(3) This duty includes obligations—
  (a) to define the expert's area or areas of expertise—
     (i)   in the expert's report, and
     (ii) when giving evidence in person;
  (b) when giving evidence in person, to draw the court's attention to any question to which the answer would be outside the expert's area or areas of expertise; and
  (c) to inform all parties and the court if the expert's opinion changes from that contained in a report served as evidence or given in a statement.

Introduction of expert evidence
19.3.–(1) A party who wants another party to admit as fact a summary of an expert's conclusions **B-264** must serve that summary—
  (a) on the court officer and on each party from whom that admission is sought;

(b) as soon as practicable after the defendant whom it affects pleads not guilty.

(2) A party on whom such a summary is served must—

    (a) serve a response stating—

        (i) which, if any, of the expert's conclusions are admitted as fact, and

        (ii) where a conclusion is not admitted, what are the disputed issues concerning that conclusion; and

    (b) serve the response—

        (i) on the court officer and on the party who served the summary,

        (ii) as soon as practicable, and in any event not more than 14 days after service of the summary.

(3) A party who wants to introduce expert evidence otherwise than as admitted fact must—

    (a) serve a report by the expert which complies with rule 19.4 on—

        (i) the court officer, and

        (ii) each other party;

    (b) serve the report as soon as practicable, and in any event with any application in support of which that party relies on that evidence;

    (c) serve with the report notice of anything of which the party serving it is aware which might reasonably be thought capable of detracting substantially from the credibility of that expert;

    (d) if another party so requires, give that party a copy of, or a reasonable opportunity to inspect—

        (i) a record of any examination, measurement, test or experiment on which the expert's findings and opinion are based, or that were carried out in the course of reaching those findings and opinion, and

        (ii) anything on which any such examination, measurement, test or experiment was carried out.

(4) Unless the parties otherwise agree or the court directs, a party may not—

    (a) introduce expert evidence if that party has not complied with paragraph (3);

    (b) introduce in evidence an expert report if the expert does not give evidence in person.

Content of expert's report

B-265

19.4. Where rule 19.3(3) applies, an expert's report must—

    (a) give details of the expert's qualifications, relevant experience and accreditation;

    (b) give details of any literature or other information which the expert has relied on in making the report;

    (c) contain a statement setting out the substance of all facts given to the expert which are material to the opinions expressed in the report, or upon which those opinions are based;

    (d) make clear which of the facts stated in the report are within the expert's own knowledge;

    (e) say who carried out any examination, measurement, test or experiment which the expert has used for the report and—

        (i) give the qualifications, relevant experience and accreditation of that person,

        (ii) say whether or not the examination, measurement, test or experiment was carried out under the expert's supervision, and

        (iii) summarise the findings on which the expert relies;

    (f) where there is a range of opinion on the matters dealt with in the report—

        (i) summarise the range of opinion, and

        (ii) give reasons for the expert's own opinion;

    (g) if the expert is not able to give an opinion without qualification, state the qualification;

    (h) include such information as the court may need to decide whether the expert's opinion is sufficiently reliable to be admissible as evidence;

    (i) contain a summary of the conclusions reached;

    (j) contain a statement that the expert understands an expert's duty to the court, and has complied and will continue to comply with that duty; and

    (k) contain the same declaration of truth as a witness statement.

Expert to be informed of service of report

B-266

19.5. A party who serves on another party or on the court a report by an expert must, at once, inform that expert of that fact.

Pre-hearing discussion of expert evidence

B-267

19.6.—(1) This rule applies where more than one party wants to introduce expert evidence.

(2) The court may direct the experts to—

    (a)   discuss the expert issues in the proceedings; and

    (b)   prepare a statement for the court of the matters on which they agree and disagree, giving
their reasons.

(3) Except for that statement, the content of that discussion must not be referred to without the
court's permission.

(4) A party may not introduce expert evidence without the court's permission if the expert has not
complied with a direction under this rule.

Court's power to direct that evidence is to be given by a single joint expert

19.7.–(1) Where more than one defendant wants to introduce expert evidence on an issue at trial,   **B-268**
the court may direct that the evidence on that issue is to be given by one expert only.

(2) Where the co-defendants cannot agree who should be the expert, the court may–

    (a)   select the expert from a list prepared or identified by them; or

    (b)   direct that the expert be selected in another way.

Instructions to a single joint expert

19.8.–(1) Where the court gives a direction under rule 19.7 for a single joint expert to be used,   **B-269**
each of the co-defendants may give instructions to the expert.

(2) A co-defendant who gives instructions to the expert must, at the same time, send a copy of the
instructions to each other co-defendant.

(3) The court may give directions about–

    (a)   the payment of the expert's fees and expenses; and

    (b)   any examination, measurement, test or experiment which the expert wishes to carry out.

(4) The court may, before an expert is instructed, limit the amount that can be paid by way of fees
and expenses to the expert.

(5) Unless the court otherwise directs, the instructing co-defendants are jointly and severally liable
for the payment of the expert's fees and expenses.

Court's power to vary requirements under this Part

19.9–(1) The court may extend (even after it has expired) a time limit under this Part.   **B-270**

(2) A party who wants an extension of time must–

    (a)   apply when serving the report, summary or notice for which it is required; and

    (b)   explain the delay.

CPD V Evidence 19A: Expert Evidence

19A.1 Expert opinion evidence is admissible in criminal proceedings at common law if, in sum-   **B-271**
mary, (i) it is relevant to a matter in issue in the proceedings; (ii) it is needed to provide the court
with information likely to be outside the court's own knowledge and experience; and (iii) the witness
is competent to give that opinion.

19A.2 [*Summarises the CJA 1988, s.30 [§ 10-35 in the main work], and the Criminal Procedure Rules
2015, Pt 19.*]

19A.3 [*Refers to the non-implementation of a Law Commission proposal for the enactment of a statutory test
for admissibility.*] The common law, therefore, remains the source of the criteria by reference to which
the court must assess the admissibility and weight of such evidence; and rule 19.4 ... lists those matters with which an expert's report must deal, so that the court can conduct an adequate such
assessment.

19A.4 In ... [*R. v. Dlugosz; R. v. Pickering; R. v. S. (M.D.)* [2013] 1 Cr.App.R. 32], the Court of
Appeal observed (at [11]): "It is essential to recall the principle which is applicable, namely in
determining the issue of admissibility, the court must be satisfied that there is a sufficiently reliable
scientific basis for the evidence to be admitted. If there is then the court leaves the opposing views to
be tested before the jury." Nothing at common law precludes assessment by the court of the reliability
of anexpert opinion by reference to substantially similar factors to those the Law Commission recommended as conditions of admissibility, and courts are encouraged actively to enquire into such
factors.

19A.5 Therefore factors which the court may take into account in determining the reliability of
expert opinion, and especially of expert scientific opinion, include:

    (a) the extent and quality of the data on which the expert's opinion is based, and the validity
of the methods by which they were obtained;

    (b) if the expert's opinion relies on an inference from any findings, whether the opinion
properly explains how safe or unsafe the inference is (whether by reference to statistical
significance or in other appropriate terms);

(c) if the expert's opinion relies on the results of the use of any method (for instance, a test, measurement or survey), whether the opinion takes proper account of matters, such as the degree of precision or margin of uncertainty, affecting the accuracy or reliability of those results;

(d) the extent to which any material upon which the expert's opinion is based has been reviewed by others with relevant expertise (for instance, in peer-reviewed publications), and the views of those others on that material;

(e) the extent to which the expert's opinion is based on material falling outside the expert's own field of expertise;

(f) the completeness of the information which was available to the expert, and whether the expert took account of all relevant information in arriving at the opinion (including information as to the context of any facts to which the opinion relates);

(g) if there is a range of expert opinion on the matter in question, where in the range the expert's own opinion lies and whether the expert's preference has been properly explained; and

(h) whether the expert's methods followed established practice in the field and, if they did not, whether the reason for the divergence has been properly explained.

19A.6 In addition, in considering reliability, and especially the reliability of expert scientific opinion, the court should be astute to identify potential flaws in such opinion which detract from its reliability, such as:

(a) being based on a hypothesis which has not been subjected to sufficient scrutiny (including, where appropriate, experimental or other testing), or which has failed to stand up to scrutiny;

(b) being based on an unjustifiable assumption;

(c) being based on flawed data;

(d) relying on an examination, technique, method or process which was not properly carried out or applied, or was not appropriate for use in the particular case; or

(e) relying on an inference or conclusion which has not been properly reached.

CPD V Evidence 19B: Statements of Understanding and Declarations of Truth in Expert Reports (as inserted by Criminal Practice Directions 2015 (Amendment No. 2), unreported, November 16, 2016, Lord Thomas C.J., and as amended by Criminal Practice Directions 2015 (Amendment No. 4), unreported, March 28, 2017, Lord Thomas C.J.)

★**B-271a**

19B.1 The statement and declaration required by CrimPR 19.4(j), (k) should be in the following terms, or in terms substantially the same as these:

"I (name) DECLARE THAT:

1. I understand that my duty is to help the court to achieve the overriding objective by giving independent assistance by way of objective, unbiased opinion on matters within my expertise, both in preparing reports and giving oral evidence. I understand that this duty overrides any obligation to the party by whom I am engaged or the person who has paid or is liable to pay me. I confirm that I have complied with and will continue to comply with that duty.

2. I confirm that I have not entered into any arrangement where the amount or payment of my fees is in any way dependent on the outcome of the case.

3. I know of no conflict of interest of any kind, other than any which I have disclosed in my report.

4. I do not consider that any interest which I have disclosed affects my suitability as an expert witness on any issues on which I have given evidence.

5. I will advise the party by whom I am instructed if, between the date of my report and the trial, there is any change in circumstances which affect my answers to points 3 and 4 above.

6. I have shown the sources of all information I have used.

7. I have exercised reasonable care and skill in order to be accurate and complete in preparing this report.

8. I have endeavoured to include in my report those matters, of which I have knowledge or of which I have been made aware, that might adversely affect the validity of my opinion. I have clearly stated any qualifications to my opinion.

9. I have not, without forming an independent view, included or excluded anything which has been suggested to me by others including my instructing lawyers.

10. I will notify those instructing me immediately and confirm in writing if for any reason my existing report requires any correction or qualification.
11. I understand that:
    (a) my report will form the evidence to be given under oath or affirmation;
    (b) the court may at any stage direct a discussion to take place between experts;
    (c) the court may direct that, following a discussion between the experts, a statement should be prepared showing those issues which are agreed and those issues which are not agreed, together with the reasons;
    (d) I may be required to attend court to be cross-examined on my report by a cross-examiner assisted by an expert;
    (e) I am likely to be the subject of public adverse criticism by the judge if the court concludes that I have not taken reasonable care in trying to meet the standards set out above.
12. I have read Part 19 of the Criminal Procedure Rules and I have complied with its requirements.
13. I confirm that I have acted in accordance with the the code of practice or conduct for experts of my discipline, namely [*identify the code*].
14. [For experts instructed by the prosecution only] I confirm that I have read guidance contained in a booklet known as *Disclosure: Experts' Evidence and Unused Material* which details my role and documents my responsibilities, in relation to revelation as an expert witness. I have followed the guidance and recognise the continuing nature of my responsibilities of disclosure. In accordance with my duties of disclosure, as documented in the guidance booklet, I confirm that:
    (a) I have complied with my duties to record, retain and reveal material in accordance with the CPIA 1996, as amended;
    (b) I have compiled an index of all material; I will ensure that the index is updated in the event I am provided with or generate additional material;
    (c) in the event my opinion changes on any material issue, I will inform the investigating officer, as soon as reasonably practicable and give reasons.

I confirm that the contents of this report are true to the best of my knowledge and belief and that I make this report knowing that, if it is tendered in evidence, I would be liable to prosecution if I have wilfully stated anything which I know to be false or that I do not believe to be true."

CPD V Evidence 19C: Pre-hearing Discussion of Expert Evidence (as inserted by Criminal Practice Directions 2015 (Amendment No. 2), unreported, November 16, 2016, Lord Thomas C.J.)

19C.1 To assist the court in the preparation of the case for trial, parties must consider, with their **B-271b** experts, at an early stage, whether there is likely to be any useful purpose in holding an experts' discussion and, if so, when. Under CrimPR 19.6 such pre-trial discussions are not compulsory unless directed by the court. However, such a direction is listed in the magistrates' courts' Preparation for Effective Trial form and in the Crown Court Plea and Trial Preparation Hearing form as one to be given by default, and therefore the court can be expected to give such a direction in every case unless persuaded otherwise. Those standard directions include a timetable to which the parties must adhere unless it is varied.

19C.2 The purpose of discussions between experts is to agree and narrow issues and in particular to identify:
    (a) the extent of the agreement between them;
    (b) the points of and short reasons for any disagreement;
    (c) action, if any, which may be taken to resolve any outstanding points of disagreement; and
    (d) any further material issues not raised and the extent to which these issues are agreed.

19C.3 Where the experts are to meet, that meeting conveniently may be conducted by telephone conference or live link; and experts' meetings always should be conducted by those means where that will avoid unnecessary delay and expense.

19C.4 Where the experts are to meet, the parties must discuss and if possible agree whether an agenda is necessary, and if so attempt to agree one that helps the experts to focus on the issues which need to be discussed. The agenda must not be in the form of leading questions or hostile in tone. The experts may not be required to avoid reaching agreement, or to defer reaching agreement, on any matter within the experts' competence.

19C.5 If the legal representatives do attend:
    (a) they should not normally intervene in the discussion, except to answer questions put to them by the experts or to advise on the law; and

(b) the experts may if they so wish hold part of their discussions in the absence of the legal representatives.

19C.6 A statement must be prepared by the experts dealing with paragraphs 19C.2(a)-(d) above. Individual copies of the statements must be signed or otherwise authenticated by the experts, in manuscript or by electronic means, at the conclusion of the discussion, or as soon thereafter as practicable, and in any event within 5 business days. Copies of the statements must be provided to the parties no later than 10 business days after signing.

19C.7 Experts must give their own opinions to assist the court and do not require the authority of the parties to sign a joint statement. The joint statement should include a brief re-statement that the experts recognise their duties, which should be in the following terms, or in terms substantially the same as these:

"We each DECLARE THAT:

    1. We individually here re-state the expert's declaration contained in our respective reports that we understand our overriding duties to the court, have complied with them and will continue to do so.

    2. We have neither jointly nor individually been instructed to, nor has it been suggested that we should, avoid reaching agreement, or defer reaching agreement, on any matter within our competence."

19C.8 If an expert significantly alters an opinion, the joint statement must include a note or addendum by that expert explaining the change of opinion.

Criminal Procedure Rules 2015 (S.I. 2015 No. 1490), Pt 20

HEARSAY EVIDENCE

When this part applies

B-272
    20.1. This part applies—

    (a) in a magistrates' court and in the Crown Court;

    (b) where a party wants to introduce hearsay evidence, within the meaning of section 114 of the Criminal Justice Act 2003 [§ 11-2 in the main work].

Notice to introduce hearsay evidence

B-273
    20.2.–(1) This rule applies where a party wants to introduce hearsay evidence for admission under any of the following sections of the Criminal Justice Act 2003—

    (a) section 114(1)(d) (evidence admissible in the interests of justice);

    (b) section 116 (evidence where a witness is unavailable [*ibid.*, § 11-15]);

    (c) section 117(1)(c) (evidence in a statement prepared for the purposes of criminal proceedings [*ibid.*, § 11-26]);

    (d) section 121 (multiple hearsay [*ibid.*, § 11-41]).

    (2) That party must—

    (a) serve notice on—

        (i) the court officer, and

        (ii) each other party;

    (b) in the notice—

        (i) identify the evidence that is hearsay,

        (ii) set out any facts on which that party relies to make the evidence admissible,

        (iii) explain how that party will prove those facts if another party disputes them, and

        (iv) explain why the evidence is admissible; and

    (c) attach to the notice any statement or other document containing the evidence that has not already been served.

    (3) A prosecutor who wants to introduce such evidence must serve the notice not more than—

    (a) 28 days after the defendant pleads not guilty, in a magistrates' court; or

    (b) 14 days after the defendant pleads not guilty, in the Crown Court.

    (4) A defendant who wants to introduce such evidence must serve the notice as soon as reasonably practicable.

    (5) A party entitled to receive a notice under this rule may waive that entitlement by so informing—

    (a) the party who would have served it; and

    (b) the court.

Opposing the introduction of hearsay evidence
20.3.–(1) This rule applies where a party objects to the introduction of hearsay evidence.   **B-274**
(2) That party must—
  (a) apply to the court to determine the objection;
  (b) serve the application on—
    (i) the court officer, and
    (ii) each other party;
  (c) serve the application as soon as reasonably practicable, and in any event not more than 14 days after—
    (i) service of notice to introduce the evidence under rule 20.2,
    (ii) service of the evidence to which that party objects, if no notice is required by that rule, or
    (iii) the defendant pleads not guilty
    whichever of those events happens last; and
  (d) in the application, explain—
    (i) which, if any, facts set out in a notice under rule 20.2 that party disputes,
    (ii) why the evidence is not admissible,
    (iii) any other objection to the evidence.
(3) The court—
  (a) may determine an application—
    (i) at a hearing, in public or in private, or
    (ii) without a hearing;
  (b) must not determine the application unless the party who served the notice—
    (i) is present, or
    (ii) has had a reasonable opportunity to respond;
  (c) may adjourn the application; and
  (d) may discharge or vary a determination where it can do so under—
    (i) section 8B of the Magistrates' Courts Act 1980 (ruling at pre-trial hearing in a magistrates' court), or
    (ii) section 9 of the Criminal Justice Act 1987 [§ 10-14 in the main work], or section 31 or 40 of the Criminal Procedure and Investigations Act 1996 (ruling at preparatory or other pre-trial hearing in the Crown Court [*ibid.*, §§ 4-133, 4-153]).

Unopposed hearsay evidence
20.4.–(1) This rule applies where—   **B-275**
  (a) a party has served notice to introduce hearsay evidence under rule 20.2; and
  (b) no other party has applied to the court to determine an objection to the introduction of the evidence.
(2) The court must treat the evidence as if it were admissible by agreement.

Court's power to vary requirements under this part
20.5.–(1) The court may—   **B-276**
  (a) shorten or extend (even after it has expired) a time limit under this part;
  (b) allow an application or notice to be in a different form to one set out in the Practice Direction, or to be made or given orally;
  (c) dispense with the requirement for notice to introduce hearsay evidence.
(2) A party who wants an extension of time must—
  (a) apply when serving the application or notice for which it is needed; and
  (b) explain the delay.

Criminal Procedure Rules 2015 (S.I. 2015 No. 1490), Pt 21

EVIDENCE OF BAD CHARACTER

When this Part applies
21.1. This Part applies—   **B-277**
  (a) in a magistrates' court and in the Crown Court;
  (b) where a party wants to introduce evidence of bad character, within the meaning of section 98 of the Criminal Justice Act 2003 [§ 13-15 in the main work].

Content of application or notice

B-278   **21.2.**–(1) A party who wants to introduce evidence of bad character must–

    (a) make an application under rule 21.3, where it is evidence of a non-defendant's bad character;

    (b) give notice under rule 21.4, where it is evidence of a defendant's bad character.

  (2) An application or notice must–

    (a) set out the facts of the misconduct on which that party relies,

    (b) explain how that party will prove those facts (whether by certificate of conviction, other official record, or other evidence), if another party disputes them, and

    (c) explain why the evidence is admissible.

Application to introduce evidence of a non-defendant's bad character

B-279   **21.3.**–(1) This rule applies where a party wants to introduce evidence of the bad character of a person other than the defendant.

  (2) That party must serve an application to do so on–

    (a) the court officer; and

    (b) each other party.

  (3) The applicant must serve the application–

    (a) as soon as reasonably practicable; and in any event

    (b) not more than 14 days after the prosecutor discloses material on which the application is based (if the prosecutor is not the applicant).

  (4) A party who objects to the introduction of the evidence must–

    (a) serve notice on–

      (i) the court officer, and

      (ii) each other party

    not more than 14 days after service of the application; and

    (b) in the notice explain, as applicable–

      (i) which, if any, facts of the misconduct set out in the application that party disputes,

      (ii) what, if any, facts of the misconduct that party admits instead,

      (iii) why the evidence is not admissible, and

      (iv) any other objection to the application.

  (5) The court–

    (a) may determine an application–

      (i) at a hearing, in public or in private, or

      (ii) without a hearing;

    (b) must not determine the application unless each party other than the applicant–

      (i) is present, or

      (ii) has had at least 14 days in which to serve a notice of objection;

    (c) may adjourn the application; and

    (d) may discharge or vary a determination where it can do so under–

      (i) section 8B of the Magistrates' Courts Act 1980 (ruling at pre-trial hearing in a magistrates' court), or

      (ii) section 9 of the Criminal Justice Act 1987 [§ 10-14 in the main work], or section 31 or 40 of the Criminal Procedure and Investigations Act 1996) (ruling at preparatory or other pre-trial hearing in the Crown Court [*ibid.*, §§ 4-133, 4-153]).

Notice to introduce evidence of a defendant's bad character

B-280   **21.4.**–(1) This rule applies where a party wants to introduce evidence of a defendant's bad character.

  (2) A prosecutor or co-defendant who wants to introduce such evidence must serve notice on–

    (a) the court officer; and

    (b) each other party.

  (3) A prosecutor must serve any such notice not more than–

    (a) 28 days after the defendant pleads not guilty, in a magistrates' court; or

    (b) 14 days after the defendant pleads not guilty, in the Crown Court.

  (4) A co-defendant must serve any such notice–

    (a) as soon as reasonably practicable; and in any event

    (b) not more than 14 days after the prosecutor discloses material on which the notice is based.

  (5) A party who objects to the introduction of the evidence identified by such a notice must–

   (a) apply to the court to determine the objection;

   (b) serve the application on—

      (i) the court officer, and

      (ii) each other party

     not more than 14 days after service of the notice; and

   (c) in the application explain, as applicable—

      (i) which, if any, facts of the misconduct set out in the notice that party disputes,

      (ii) what, if any, facts of the misconduct that party admits instead,

      (iii) why the evidence is not admissible,

      (iv) why it would be unfair to admit the evidence, and

      (v) any other objection to the notice.

(6) The court—

   (a) may determine such an application—

      (i) at a hearing, in public or in private, or

      (ii) without a hearing;

   (b) must not determine the application unless the party who served the notice—

      (i) is present, or

      (ii) has had a reasonable opportunity to respond;

   (c) may adjourn the application; and

   (d) may discharge or vary a determination where it can do so under—

      (i) section 8B of the Magistrates' Courts Act 1980 (ruling at pre-trial hearing in a magistrates' court), or

      (ii) section 9 of the Criminal Justice Act 1987 [§ 10-14 in the main work], or section 31 or 40 of the Criminal Procedure and Investigations Act 1996 (ruling at preparatory or other pre-trial hearing in the Crown Court) [*ibid.*, §§ 8-133, 8-153].

(7) A party entitled to receive such a notice may waive that entitlement by so informing—

   (a) the party who would have served it; and

   (b) the court.

(8) A defendant who wants to introduce evidence of his or her own bad character must—

   (a) give notice, in writing or orally—

      (i) as soon as reasonably practicable, and in any event

      (ii) before the evidence is introduced, either by the defendant or in reply to a question asked by the defendant of another party's witness in order to obtain that evidence; and

   (b) in the Crown Court, at the same time give notice (in writing, or orally) of any direction about the defendant's character that the defendant wants the court to give the jury under rule 25.14 (directions to the jury and taking the verdict).

[This rule is printed as amended by the Criminal Procedure (Amendment) Rules 2016 (S.I. 2016 No. 120).]

Reasons for decisions

21.5. The court must announce at a hearing in public (but in the absence of the jury, if there is   **B-281** one) the reasons for a decision—

   (a) to admit evidence as evidence of bad character, or to refuse to do so; or

   (b) to direct an acquittal or a retrial under section 107 of the Criminal Justice Act 2003 [§ 13-105 in the main work].

Court's power to vary requirements under this Part

21.6.—(1) The court may—   **B-282**

   (a) shorten or extend (even after it has expired) a time limit under this Part;

   (b) allow an application or notice to be in a different form to one set out in the Practice Direction, or to be made or given orally;

   (c) dispense with a requirement for notice to introduce evidence of a defendant's bad character.

(2) A party who wants an extension of time must—

   (a) apply when serving the application or notice for which it is needed; and

   (b) explain the delay.

CPD V Evidence 21A: Spent Convictions

21A.1 The effect of section 4(1) of the Rehabilitation of Offenders Act 1974 [§ 13-125 in the main   **B-283**

work] is that a person who has become a rehabilitated person for the purpose of the Act in respect of a conviction ... shall be treated for all purposes in law as a person who has not committed, or been charged with or prosecuted for, or convicted of or sentenced for, the offence or offences which were the subject of that conviction.

21A.2 Section 4(1) ... does not apply, however, to evidence given in criminal proceedings: s.7(2)(a) [§ 13-133 in the main work]. During the trial of a criminal charge, reference to previous convictions (and therefore to spent convictions) can arise in a number of ways. The most common is when a bad character application is made under the CJA 2003. When considering bad character applications ...regard should always be had to the general principles of the [1974 Act].

21A.3 On conviction, the court must be provided with a statement of the defendant's record for the purposes of sentence. The record supplied should contain all previous convictions, but those which are spent should, so far as practicable, be marked as such. No one should refer in open court to a spent conviction without the authority of the judge, which authority should not be given unless the interests of justice so require. When passing sentence the judge should make no reference to a spent conviction unless it is necessary to do so for the purpose of explaining the sentence to be passed.

Criminal Procedure Rules 2015 (S.I. 2015 No. 1490), Pt 22

EVIDENCE OF A COMPLAINANT'S PREVIOUS SEXUAL BEHAVIOUR

When this Part applies

B-284   **22.1.** This Part applies in magistrates' courts and in the Crown Court where a defendant wants to—

    (a) introduce evidence; or

    (b) cross-examine a witness

about a complainant's sexual behaviour despite the prohibition in section 41 of the Youth Justice and Criminal Evidence Act 1999 [§ 8-238 in the main work].

Application for permission to introduce evidence or cross-examine

B-285   **22.2.** The defendant must apply for permission to do so—

    (a) in writing; and

    (b) not more than 28 days after the prosecutor has complied or purported to comply with section 3 of the Criminal Procedure and Investigations Act 1996 (disclosure by prosecutor [*ibid.*, § 12-58]).

Content of application

B-286   **22.3.** The application must—

    (a) identify the issue to which the defendant says the complainant's sexual behaviour is relevant;

    (b) give particulars of—

        (i) any evidence that the defendant wants to introduce, and

        (ii) any questions that the defendant wants to ask;

    (c) identify the exception to the prohibition in section 41 of the Youth Justice and Criminal Evidence Act 1999 on which the defendant relies; and

    (d) give the name and date of birth of any witness whose evidence about the complainant's sexual behaviour the defendant wants to introduce.

Service of application

B-287   **22.4.** The defendant must serve the application on the court officer and all other parties.

Reply to application

B-288   **22.5.** A party who wants to make representations about an application under rule 22.2 must—

    (a) do so in writing not more than 14 days after receiving it; and

    (b) serve those representations on the court officer and all other parties.

Application for special measures

B-289   **22.6.** If the court allows an application under rule 22.2 then—

    (a) a party may apply not more than 14 days later for a special measures direction or for the variation of an existing special measures direction; and

    (b) the court may shorten the time for opposing that application.

Court's power to vary requirements under this Part

B-290   **22.7.** The court may shorten or extend (even after it has expired) a time limit under this Part.

Criminal Procedure Rules 2015 (S.I. 2015 No. 1490), Pt 23

RESTRICTION ON CROSS-EXAMINATION BY A DEFENDANT

General rules

When this Part applies
23.1. This Part applies where—
  (a) a defendant may not cross-examine in person a witness because of section 34 or section 35 of the Youth Justice and Criminal Evidence Act 1999 (complainants in proceedings for sexual offences; child complainants and other child witnesses [§§ 8-226, 8-227 in the main work]);
  (b) the court can prohibit a defendant from cross-examining in person a witness under section 36 of that Act (direction prohibiting accused from cross-examining particular witness [*ibid.*, § 8-228]).

B-291

Appointment of advocate to cross-examine witness
23.2.—(1) This rule applies where a defendant may not cross-examine in person a witness in consequence of—
  (a) the prohibition imposed by section 34 or section 35 of the Youth Justice and Criminal Evidence Act 1999; or
  (b) a prohibition imposed by the court under section 36 of the 1999 Act.
(2) The court must, as soon as practicable, explain in terms the defendant can understand (with help, if necessary)—
  (a) the prohibition and its effect;
  (b) that the defendant is entitled to arrange for a lawyer with a right of audience in the court to cross-examine the witness on his or her behalf;
  (c) that the defendant must notify the court officer of the identity of any such lawyer, with details of how to contact that person, by no later than a date set by the court;
  (d) that if the defendant does not want to make such arrangements, or if the defendant gives no such notice by that date, then—
    (i) the court must decide whether it is necessary in the interests of justice to appoint such a lawyer to cross-examine the witness for the defendant, and
    (ii) if the court decides that that is necessary, the court will appoint a lawyer chosen by the court.
(3) Having given those explanations, the court must—
  (a) ask whether the defendant wants to arrange for a lawyer to cross-examine the witness, and set a date by when the defendant must notify the court officer of the identity of that lawyer if the answer to that question is "yes";
  (b) if the answer to that question is "no", or if by the date set the defendant has given no such notice—
    (i) decide whether it is necessary in the interests of justice for the witness to be cros-sexamined by an advocate appointed to represent the defendant's interests, and
    (ii) if the court decides that that is necessary, give directions for the appointment of such an advocate.
(4) Where an advocate is appointed by the court—
  (a) the directions that the court gives under paragraph (3)(b)(ii) must provide for the material to be supplied to that advocate, including by whom and when it must be supplied; and
  (b) the appointment terminates at the conclusion of the cross-examination of the witness.
(5) The court may give the explanations and ask the questions required by this rule—
  (a) at a hearing, in public or in private; or
  (b) without a hearing, by written notice to the defendant.
(6) The court may extend (even after it has expired) the time limit that it sets under paragraph (3)(a)—
  (a) on application by the defendant; or
  (b) on its own initiative.

B-292

Application to prohibit cross-examination

Exercise of court's powers
23.3.—(1) The court may decide whether to impose or discharge a prohibition against cros-sexamination under section 36 of the Youth Justice and Criminal Evidence Act 1999—

B-293

(a) at a hearing, in public or in private, or without a hearing;
(b) in a party's absence, if that party—
  (i) applied for the prohibition or discharge, or
  (ii) has had at least 14 days in which to make representations.

(2) The court must announce, at a hearing in public before the witness gives evidence, the reasons for a decision—
(a) to impose or discharge such a prohibition; or
(b) to refuse to do so.

Application to prohibit cross-examination

B-294   **23.4.**—(1) This rule applies where under section 36 of the Youth Justice and Criminal Evidence Act 1999 the prosecutor wants the court to prohibit the cross-examination of a witness by a defendant in person.

(2) The prosecutor must—
(a) apply in writing, as soon as reasonably practicable after becoming aware of the grounds for doing so; and
(b) serve the application on—
  (i) the court officer,
  (ii) the defendant who is the subject of the application, and
  (iii) any other defendant, unless the court otherwise directs.

(3) The application must—
(a) report any views that the witness has expressed about whether he or she is content to be cross-examined by the defendant in person;
(b) identify—
  (i) the nature of the questions likely to be asked, having regard to the issues in the case,
  (ii) any relevant behaviour of the defendant at any stage of the case, generally and in relation to the witness,
  (iii) any relationship, of any nature, between the witness and the defendant,
  (iv) any other defendant in the case who is subject to such a prohibition in respect of the witness, and
  (v) any special measures direction made in respect of the witness, or for which an application has been made;
(c) explain why the quality of evidence given by the witness on cross-examination—
  (i) is likely to be diminished if no such prohibition is imposed, and
  (ii) would be likely to be improved if it were imposed; and
(d) explain why it would not be contrary to the interests of justice to impose the prohibition.

Application to discharge prohibition imposed by the court

B-295   **23.5.**—(1) A party who wants the court to discharge a prohibition against cross-examination which the court imposed under section 36 of the Youth Justice and Criminal Evidence Act 1999 must—
(a) apply in writing, as soon as reasonably practicable after becoming aware of the grounds for doing so; and
(b) serve the application on—
  (i) the court officer, and
  (ii) each other party.

(2) The applicant must—
(a) explain what material circumstances have changed since the prohibition was imposed; and
(b) ask for a hearing, if the applicant wants one, and explain why it is needed.

Application containing information withheld from another party

B-296   **23.6.**—(1) This rule applies where—
(a) an applicant serves an application for the court to impose a prohibition against cross-sexamination, or for the discharge of such a prohibition; and
(b) the application includes information that the applicant thinks ought not be revealed to another party.

(2) The applicant must—
(a) omit that information from the part of the application that is served on that other party;
(b) mark the other part to show that, unless the court otherwise directs, it is only for the court; and

(c) in that other part, explain why the applicant has withheld that information from that other party.

(3) Any hearing of an application to which this rule applies—

(a) must be in private, unless the court otherwise directs; and

(b) if the court so directs, may be, wholly or in part, in the absence of a party from whom information has been withheld.

(4) At any hearing of an application to which this rule applies—

(a) the general rule is that the court must consider, in the following sequence—

    (i) representations first by the applicant and then by each other party, in all the parties' presence, and then

    (ii) further representations by the applicant, in the absence of a party from whom information has been withheld; but

(b) the court may direct other arrangements for the hearing.

Representations in response

23.7.–(1) This rule applies where a party wants to make representations about—   **B-297**

(a) an application under rule 23.4 for a prohibition against cross-examination;

(b) an application under rule 23.5 for the discharge of such a prohibition; or

(c) a prohibition or discharge that the court proposes on its own initiative.

(2) Such a party must—

(a) serve the representations on—

    (i) the court officer, and

    (ii) each other party;

(b) do so not more than 14 days after, as applicable—

    (i) service of the application, or

    (ii) notice of the prohibition or discharge that the court proposes; and

(c) ask for a hearing, if that party wants one, and explain why it is needed.

(3) Representations against a prohibition must explain in what respect the conditions for imposing it are not met.

(4) Representations against the discharge of a prohibition must explain why it should not be discharged.

(5) Where representations include information that the person making them thinks ought not be revealed to another party, that person must—

(a) omit that information from the representations served on that other party;

(b) mark the information to show that, unless the court otherwise directs, it is only for the court; and

(c) with that information include an explanation of why it has been withheld from that other party.

Court's power to vary requirements

23.8.–(1) The court may—   **B-298**

(a) shorten or extend (even after it has expired) a time limit under rule 23.4 (application to prohibit cross-examination), rule 23.5 (application to discharge prohibition imposed by the court) or rule 23.7 (representations in response); and

(b) allow an application or representations required by any of those rules to be made in a different form to one set out in the Practice Direction, or to be made orally.

(2) A person who wants an extension of time must—

(a) apply when serving the application or representations for which it is needed; and

(b) explain the delay.

Criminal Procedure Rules 2015 (S.I. 2015 No. 1490), Pt 24

TRIAL AND SENTENCE IN A MAGISTRATES' COURT

When this Part applies

24.1.–(1) This Part applies in a magistrates' court where—   **B-299**

(a) the court tries a case;

(b) the defendant pleads guilty;

(c) under section 14 or section 16E of the Magistrates' Courts Act 1980, the defendant makes a statutory declaration of not having found out about the case until after the trial began;

(d)   under section 142 of the 1980 Act, the court can–

    (i)   set aside a conviction, or

    (ii)   vary or rescind a costs order, or an order to which Part 31 applies (Behaviour orders).

(2) Where the defendant is under 18, in this Part–

(a)   a reference to convicting the defendant includes a reference to finding the defendant guilty of an offence; and

(b)   a reference to sentence includes a reference to an order made on a finding of guilt.

General rules

B-300   **24.2.**–(1) Where this Part applies–

(a)   the general rule is that the hearing must be in public; but

(b)   the court may exercise any power it has to

    (i)   impose reporting restrictions,

    (ii)   withhold information from the public, or

    (iii)   order a hearing in private; and

(c)   unless the court otherwise directs, only the following may attend a hearing in a youth court–

    (i)   the parties and their legal representatives,

    (ii)   a defendant's parents, guardian or other supporting adult,

    (iii)   a witness,

    (iv)   anyone else directly concerned in the case, and

    (v)   a representative of a news-gathering or reporting organisation.

(2) Unless already done, the justices' legal adviser or the court must–

(a)   read the allegation of the offence to the defendant;

(b)   explain, in terms the defendant can understand (with help, if necessary)–

    (i)   the allegation, and

    (ii)   what the procedure at the hearing will be;

(c)   ask whether the defendant has been advised about the potential effect on sentence of a guilty plea;

(d)   ask whether the defendant pleads guilty or not guilty; and

(e)   take the defendant's plea.

(3) The court may adjourn the hearing

(a)   at any stage, to the same or to another magistrates' court; or

(b)   to a youth court, where the court is not itself a youth court and the defendant is under 18.

(4) Paragraphs (1) and (2) of this rule do not apply where the court tries a case under rule 24.9 (single justice procedure: special rules)

Procedure on plea of not guilty

B-301   **24.3.**–(1) This rule applies–

(a)   if the defendant has–

    (i)   entered a plea of not guilty, or

    (ii)   not entered a plea; or

(b)   if, in either case, it appears to the court that there may be grounds for making a hospital order without convicting the defendant.

(2) If a not guilty plea was taken on a previous occasion, the justices' legal adviser or the court must ask the defendant to confirm that plea.

(3) In the following sequence–

(a)   the prosecutor may summarise the prosecution case, concisely identifying the relevant law, outlining the facts and indicating the matters likely to be in dispute;

(b)   to help the members of the court to understand the case and resolve any issue in it, the court may invite the defendant concisely to identify what is in issue;

(c)   the prosecutor must introduce the evidence on which the prosecution case relies;

(d)   at the conclusion of the prosecution case, on the defendant's application or on its own initiative, the court–

    (i)   may acquit on the ground that the prosecution evidence is insufficient for any reasonable court properly to convict, but

    (ii)   must not do so unless the prosecutor has had an opportunity to make representations;

(e)   the justices' legal adviser or the court must explain, in terms the defendant can understand (with help, if necessary)–

    (i) the right to give evidence, and

    (ii) the potential effect of not doing so at all, or of refusing to answer a question while doing so;

  (f) the defendant may introduce evidence;

  (g) a party may introduce further evidence if it is then admissible (for example, because it is in rebuttal of evidence already introduced);

  (h) the prosecutor may make final representations in support of the prosecution case, where—

    (i) the defendant is represented by a legal representative, or

    (ii) whether represented or not, the defendant has introduced evidence other than his or her own; and

  (i) the defendant may make final representations in support of the defence case.

(4) Where a party wants to introduce evidence or make representations after that party's opportunity to do so under paragraph (3), the court—

  (a) may refuse to receive any such evidence or representations; and

  (b) must not receive any such evidence or representations after it has announced its verdict.

(5) If the court—

  (a) convicts the defendant; or

  (b) makes a hospital order instead of doing so,

it must give sufficient reasons to explain its decision.

(6) If the court acquits the defendant, it may—

  (a) give an explanation of its decision; and

  (b) exercise any power it has to make—

    (i) a behaviour order.

    (ii) a costs order.

[This rule is printed as amended by the Criminal Procedure (Amendment) Rules 2016 (S.I. 2016 No. 120).]

Evidence of a witness in person

24.4.—(1) This rule applies where a party wants to introduce evidence by calling a witness to give **B-302** that evidence in person.

(2) Unless the court otherwise directs—

  (a) a witness waiting to give evidence must not wait inside the courtroom, unless that witness is—

    (i) a party, or

    (ii) an expert witness;

  (b) a witness who gives evidence in the courtroom must do so from the place provided for that purpose; and

  (c) a witness' address must not be announced unless it is relevant to an issue in the case.

(3) Unless other legislation otherwise provides, before giving evidence a witness must take an oath or affirm.

(4) In the following sequence—

  (a) the party who calls a witness must ask questions in examination-in-chief;

  (b) every other party may ask questions in cross-examination;

  (c) the party who called the witness may ask questions in re-examination.

(5) If other legislation so permits, at any time while giving evidence a witness may refer to a record of that witness' recollection of events.

(6) The justices' legal adviser or the court may—

  (a) ask a witness questions; and in particular

  (b) where the defendant is not represented, ask any question necessary in the defendant's interests.

Evidence of a witness in writing

24.5.—(1) This rule applies where a party wants to introduce in evidence the written statement of a **B-303** witness to which applies—

  (a) Part 16 (written witness statements);

  (b) Part 19 (expert evidence); or

  (c) Part 20 (hearsay evidence).

(2) If the court admits such evidence—

    (a) the court must read the statement; and

    (b) unless the court otherwise directs, if any member of the public, including any reporter, is present, each relevant part of the statement must be read or summarised aloud.

Evidence by admission

B-304   **24.6.** (1) This rule applies where—

    (a) a party introduces in evidence a fact admitted by another party; or

    (b) parties jointly admit a fact.

(2) Unless the court otherwise directs, a written record must be made of the admission.

Procedure on plea of guilty

B-305   **24.7.**–(1) This rule applies if—

    (a) the defendant pleads guilty; and

    (b) the court is satisfied that the plea represents a clear acknowledgement of guilt.

(2) The court may convict the defendant without receiving evidence.

Written guilty plea: special rules

B-306   **24.8.**–(1) This rule applies where—

    (a) the offence alleged—

        (i) can be tried only in a magistrates' court, and

        (ii) is not one specified under section 12(1)(a) of the Magistrates' Courts Act 1980.

    (b) the defendant is at least 16 years old;

    (c) the prosecutor has served on the defendant—

        (i) the summons or requisition.

        (ii) the material listed in paragraph (2) on which the prosecutor relies to set out the facts of the offence,

        (iii) the material listed in paragraph (3) on which the prosecutor relies to provide the court with information relevant to sentence,

        (iv) a notice that the procedure set out in this rule applies, and

        (v) a notice for the defendant's use if the defendant wants to plead guilty without attending court; and

    (d) the prosecutor has served on the court officer—

        (i) copies of those documents, and

        (ii) a certificate of service of those documents on the defendant.

(2) The material that the prosecutor must serve to set out the facts of the offence is—

    (a) a summary of the evidence on which the prosecution case is based;

    (b) any—

        (i) written witness statement to which Part 16 (written witness statements) applies, or

        (ii) document or extract setting out facts; or

    (c) any combination of such a summary, statement, document or extract.

(3) The material that the prosecutor must serve to provide information relevant to sentence is—

    (a) details of any previous conviction of the defendant which the prosecutor considers relevant, other than any conviction listed in the defendant's driving record;

    (b) if applicable, a notice that the defendant's driving record will be made available to the court;

    (c) a notice containing or describing any other information about the defendant, relevant to sentence. which will be made available to the court.

(4) A defendant who wants to plead guilty without attending court must, before the hearing date specified in the summons or requisition—

    (a) serve a notice of guilty plea on the court officer; and

    (b) include with that notice—

        (i) any representations that the defendant wants the court to consider, and

        (ii) a statement of the defendant's assets and other financial circumstances.

(5) A defendant who wants to withdraw such a notice must notify the court officer in writing before the hearing date.

(6) If the defendant does not withdraw the notice before the hearing date, then on or after that date—

    (a) to establish the facts of the offence and other information about the defendant relevant to sentence, the court may take account only of—

      (i)   information contained in a document served by the prosecutor under paragraph (1),

     (ii)   any previous conviction listed in the defendant's driving record, where the offence is under the Road Traffic Regulation Act 1984, the Road Traffic Act 1988, the Road Traffic (Consequential Provisions) Act 1988 or the Road Traffic (Driver Licensing and Information Systems) Act 1989,

    (iii)   any other information about the defendant, relevant to sentence, of which the prosecutor served notice under paragraph (1), and

    (iv)   any representations and any other information served by the defendant under paragraph (4)

and rule 24.11(3) to (9) inclusive must be read accordingly;

  (b) unless the court otherwise directs, the prosecutor need not attend; and

  (c) the court may accept such a guilty plea and pass sentence in the defendant's absence.

(7) With the defendant's agreement, the court may deal with the case in the same way as under paragraph (6) where the defendant is present and

  (a) has served a notice of guilty plea under paragraph (4); or

  (b) pleads guilty there and then.

Single justice procedure: special rules

24.9.–(1) This rule applies where–   **B-307**

  (a) the offence alleged–

      (i)   can be tried only in a magistrates' court, and

     (ii)   is not one punishable with imprisonment;

  (b) the defendant is at least 18 years old;

  (c) the prosecutor has served on the defendant–

      (i)   a written charge,

     (ii)   the material listed in paragraph (2) on which the prosecutor relies to set out the facts of the offence,

    (iii)   the material listed in paragraph (3) on which the prosecutor relies to provide the court with information relevant to sentence,

    (iv)   a notice that the procedure set out in this rule applies,

     (v)   a notice for the defendant's use if the defendant wants to plead guilty,

    (vi)   a notice for the defendant's use if the defendant wants to plead guilty but wants the case dealt with at a hearing by a court comprising more than one justice, and

   (vii)   a notice for the defendant's use if the defendant wants to plead not guilty; and

  (d) the prosecutor has served on the court officer–

      (i)   copies of those documents, and

     (ii)   a certificate of service of those documents on the defendant.

(2) The material that the prosecutor must serve to set out the facts of the offence is–

  (a) a summary of the evidence on which the prosecution case is based;

  (b) any–

      (i)   written witness statement to which Part 16 (written witness statements) applies, or

     (ii)   document or extract setting out facts; or

  (c) any combination of such a summary, statement, document or extract.

(3) The material that the prosecutor must serve to provide information relevant to sentence is–

  (a) details of any previous conviction of the defendant which the prosecutor considers relevant, other than any conviction listed in the defendant's driving record;

  (b) if applicable, a notice that the defendant's driving record will be made available to the court;

  (c) a notice containing or describing any other information about the defendant, relevant to sentence, which will be made available to the court.

(4) Not more than 21 days after service on the defendant of the documents listed in paragraph (1)(c)–

  (a) a defendant who wants to plead guilty must serve a notice to that effect on the court officer and include with that notice–

      (i)   any representations that the defendant wants the court to consider, and

     (ii)   a statement of the defendant's assets and other financial circumstances;

  (b) a defendant who wants to plead guilty but wants the case dealt with at a hearing by a court comprising more than one justice must serve a notice to that effect on the court officer;

  (c) a defendant who wants to plead not guilty must serve a notice to that effect on the court officer.

(5) If within 21 days of service on the defendant of the documents listed in paragraph (l)(c) the defendant serves a notice to plead guilty under paragraph (4)(a)–

    (a)   the court officer must arrange for the court to deal with the case in accordance with that notice; and

    (b)   the time for service of any other notice under paragraph (4) expires at once.

(6) If within 21 days of service on the defendant of the documents listed in paragraph (l)(c) the defendant wants to withdraw a notice which he or she has served under paragraph (4)(b) (notice to plead guilty at a hearing) or under paragraph (4)(c) (notice to plead not guilty), the defendant must–

    (a)   serve notice of that withdrawal on the court officer; and

    (b)   serve any substitute notice under paragraph (4).

(7) Paragraph (8) applies where by the date of trial the defendant has not–

    (a)   served notice under paragraph (4)(b) or (c) of wanting to plead guilty at a hearing, or wanting to plead not guilty; or

    (b)   given notice to that effect under section 16B(2) of the Magistrates' Courts Act 1980.

(8) Where this paragraph applies–

    (a)   the court may try the case in the parties' absence and without a hearing;

    (b)   the court may accept any guilty plea of which the defendant has given notice under paragraph (4)(a);

    (c)   [*identical to r.24.8(6)(a), ante, B-306*].

(9) Paragraph (10) applies where–

    (a)   the defendant serves on the court officer a notice under paragraph (4)(b) or (c); or

    (b)   the court which tries the defendant under paragraph (8) adjourns the trial for the defendant to attend a hearing by a court comprising more than one justice.

(10) Where this paragraph applies, the court must exercise its power to issue a summons and–

    (a)   the rules in Part 7 apply (starting a prosecution in a magistrates' court) as if the prosecutor had just served an information in the same terms as the written charge;

    (b)   the rules in Part 8 (initial details of the prosecution case) apply as if the documents served by the prosecutor under paragraph (1) had been served under that Part;

    (c)   except for rule 24.8 (written guilty plea: special rules) and this rule, the rules in this Part apply.

Application to withdraw a guilty plea

B-308   **24.10.**–(1) This rule applies where the defendant wants to withdraw a guilty plea.

(2) The defendant must apply to do so–

    (a)   as soon as practicable after becoming aware of the reasons for doing so; and

    (b)   before sentence.

(3) Unless the court otherwise directs, the application must be in writing and the defendant must serve it on–

    (a)   the court officer; and

    (b)   the prosecutor.

(4) The application must–

    (a)   explain why it would be unjust not to allow the defendant to withdraw the guilty plea,

    (b)   identify–

        (i)   any witness that the defendant wants to call, and

        (ii)   any other proposed evidence; and

    (c)   say whether the defendant waives legal professional privilege, giving any relevant name and date.

Procedure if the court convicts

B-309   **24.11.**–(1) This rule applies if the court convicts the defendant.

(2) The court–

    (a)   may exercise its power to require–

        (i)   a statement of the defendant's assets and other financial circumstances,

        (ii)   a pre-sentence report; and

    (b)   may (and in some circumstances must) remit the defendant to a youth court for sentence where–

        (i)   the defendant is under 18, and

        (ii)   the convicting court is not itself a youth court.

(3) The prosecutor must–

(a) summarise the prosecution case, if the sentencing court has not heard evidence;

(b) identify any offence to be taken into consideration in sentencing;

(c) provide information relevant to sentence, including any statement of the effect of the offence on the victim, the victim's family or others; and

(d) where it is likely to assist the court, identify any other matter relevant to sentence including–

    (i) the legislation applicable,

    (ii) any sentencing guidelines, or guideline cases,

    (iii) aggravating and mitigating features affecting the defendant's culpability and the harm which the offence caused, was intended to cause or might forseeably have caused, and

    (iv) the effect of such of the information listed in paragraph (2)(a) as the court may need to take into account.

(4) The defendant must provide details of financial circumstances–

(a) in any form required by the court officer,

(b) by any date directed by the court or by the court officer.

(5) Where the defendant pleads guilty but wants to be sentenced on a different basis to that disclosed by the prosecution case–

(a) the defendant must set out that basis in writing, identifying what is in dispute;

(b) the court may invite the parties to make representations about whether the dispute is material to sentence; and

(c) if the court decides that it is a material dispute, the court must–

    (i) invite such further representations or evidence as it may require, and

    (ii) decide the dispute.

(6) Where the court has power to order the endorsement of the defendant's driving record, or power to order the defendant to be disqualified from driving–

(a) if other legislation so permits, a defendant who wants the court not to exercise that power must introduce the evidence or information on which the defendant relies;

(b) the prosecutor may introduce evidence; and

(c) the parties may make representations about that evidence or information.

(7) Before the court passes sentence–

(a) the court must–

    (i) give the defendant an opportunity to make representations and introduce evidence relevant to sentence, and

    (ii) where the defendant is under 18, give the defendant's parents, guardian or other supporting adult, if present, such an opportunity as well; and

(b) the justices' legal adviser or the court must elicit any further information relevant to sentence that the court may require.

(8) If the court requires more information, it may exercise its power to adjourn the hearing for not more than–

(a) 3 weeks at a time, if the defendant will be in custody; or

(b) 4 weeks at a time.

(9) When the court has taken into account all the evidence, information and any report available, the court must–

(a) as a general rule, pass sentence there and then;

(b) when passing sentence, explain the reasons for deciding on that sentence, unless neither the defendant nor any member of the public, including any reporter, is present;

(c) when passing sentence, explain to the defendant its effect, the consequences of failing to comply with any order or pay any fine, and any power that the court has to vary or review the sentence, unless–

    (i) the defendant is absent, or

    (ii) the defendant's ill-health or disorderly conduct makes such an explanation impracticable;

(d) give any such explanation in terms the defendant, if present, can understand (with help, if necessary); and

(e) consider exercising any power it has to make a costs or other order.

(10) Despite the general rule–

(a) the court must adjourn the hearing if the defendant is absent, the case started with a summons, requisition or single justice procedure notice, and either–

    (i) the court considers passing a custodial sentence (where it can do so), or

    (ii) the court considers imposing a disqualification (unless it has already adjourned the hearing to give the defendant an opportunity to attend);

    (b) the court may exercise any power it has to—

        (i) commit the defendant to the Crown Court for sentence (and in some cases it must do so), or

        (ii) defer sentence for up to 6 months.

Procedure where a party is absent

B-310   **24.12.**—(1) This rule—

    (a) applies where a party is absent; but

    (b) does not apply where—

        (i) the defendant has served a notice of guilty plea under rule 24.8 (written guilty plea: special rules), or

        (ii) the court tries a case under rule 24.9 (single justice procedure: special rules).

(2) Where the prosecutor is absent, the court may—

    (a) if it has received evidence, deal with the case as if the prosecutor were present; and

    (b) in any other case—

        (i) enquire into the reasons for the prosecutor's absence, and

        (ii) if satisfied there is no good reason, exercise its power to dismiss the allegation.

(3) Where the defendant is absent—

    (a) the general rule is that the court must proceed as if the defendant—

        (i) were present, and

        (ii) had pleaded not guilty (unless a plea already has been taken)

    and the court must give reasons if it does not do so; but

    (b) the general rule does not apply if the defendant is under 18;

    (c) the general rule is subject to the court being satisfied that—

        (i) any summons or requisition was served on the defendant a reasonable time before the hearing, or

        (ii) in a case in which the hearing has been adjourned, the defendant had reasonable notice of where and when it would resume;

    (d) the general rule is subject also to rule 24.11(10)(a) (restrictions on passing sentence in the defendant's absence).

(4) Where the defendant is absent, the court—

    (a) must exercise its power to issue a warrant for the defendant's arrest, if it passes a custodial sentence; and

    (b) may exercise its power to do so in any other case, if it does not apply the general rule in paragraph (3)(a) of this rule about proceeding in the defendant's absence.

Provision of documents for the court

B-311   **24.13.**—(1) A party who introduces a document in evidence, or who otherwise uses a document in presenting that party's case, must provide a copy for—

    (a) each other party;

    (b) any witness that party wants to refer to that document;

    (c) the court; and

    (d) the justices' legal adviser.

(2) Unless the court otherwise directs, on application or on its own initiative, the court officer must provide for the court—

    (a) any copy received under paragraph (1) before the hearing begins; and

    (b) a copy of the court officer's record of—

        (i) information supplied by each party for the purposes of case management, including any revision of information previously supplied,

        (ii) each pre-trial direction for the management of the case,

        (iii) any pre-trial decision to admit evidence,

        (iv) any pre-trial direction about the giving of evidence, and

        (v) any admission to which rule 24.6 applies.

(3) Where rule 24.8 (written guilty plea: special rules) applies, the court officer must provide for the court—

    (a) each document served by the prosecutor under rule 24.8(1)(d);

    (b) the defendant's driving record, where the offence is under the Road Traffic Regulation Act 1984, the Road Traffic Act 1988 the Road Traffic (Consequential Provisions) Act 1988 or the Road Traffic (Driver Licensing and Information Systems) Act 1989;

(c) any other information about the defendant, relevant to sentence, of which the prosecutor served notice under rule 24.8(1); and

(d) the notice of guilty plea and any representations and other information served by the defendant under rule 24.8(4).

(4) Where the court tries a case under rule 24.9 (single justice procedure: special rules), the court officer must provide for the court—

(a) each document served by the prosecutor under rule 24.9(l)(d);

(b) the defendant's driving record, where the offence is under the Road Traffic Regulation Act 1984, the Road Traffic Act 1988, the Road Traffic (Consequential Provisions) Act 1988 or the Road Traffic (Driver Licensing and Information Systems) Act 1989;

(c) any other information about the defendant, relevant to sentence, of which the prosecutor served notice under rule 24.9(1); and

(d) any notice, representations and other information served by the defendant under rule 24.9(4)(a).

Place of trial

24.14.–(1) The hearing must take place in a courtroom provided by the Lord Chancellor, unless— **B-312**

(a) the court otherwise directs; or

(b) the court tries a case under rule 24.9 (single justice procedure: special rules).

(2) Where the hearing takes place in Wales—

(a) any party or witness may use the Welsh language; and

(b) if practicable, at least one member of the court must be Welsh-speaking.

Duty of justices' legal adviser

24.15.–(1) A justices' legal adviser must attend the court and carry out the duties listed in this **B-313** rule, as applicable, unless the court—

(a) includes a District Judge (magistrates' courts); and

(b) otherwise directs.

(2) A justices' legal adviser must—

(a) before the hearing begins, by reference to what is provided for the court under rule 24.13 (provision of documents for the court) draw the court's attention to—

(i) what the prosecutor alleges,

(ii) what the parties say is agreed,

(iii) what the parties say is in dispute, and

(iv) what the parties say about how each expects to present the case, especially where that may affect its duration and timetabling;

(b) whenever necessary, give the court legal advice and—

(i) if necessary, attend the members of the court outside the courtroom to give such advice, but

(ii) inform the parties (if present) of any such advice given outside the courtroom; and

(c) assist the court, where appropriate, in the formulation of its reasons and the recording of those reasons.

(3) A justices' legal adviser must—

(a) assist an unrepresented defendant;

(b) assist the court by—

(i) making a note of the substance of any oral evidence or representations, to help the court recall that information,

(ii) if the court rules inadmissible part of a written statement introduced in evidence, marking that statement in such a way as to make that clear,

(iii) ensuring that an adequate record is kept of the court's decisions and the reasons for them, and

(iv) making any announcement, other than of the verdict or sentence.

(4) Where the defendant has served a notice of guilty plea to which rule 24.8 (written guilty plea: special rules) applies, a justices' legal adviser must—

(a) unless the court otherwise directs, if any member of the public, including any reporter, is present, read aloud to the court—

(i) the material on which the prosecutor relies to set out the facts of the offence and to provide information relevant to sentence (or summarise any written statement included in that material, if the court so directs), and

      (ii)   any written representations by the defendant;

    (b) otherwise, draw the court's attention to—

      (i)   what the prosecutor alleges, and any significant features of the material listed in paragraph (4)(a)(i), and

      (ii)   any written representations by the defendant.

(5) Where the court tries a case under rule 24.9 (single justice procedure: special rules), a justices' legal adviser must draw the court's attention to—

    (a) what the prosecutor alleges, and any significant features of the material on which the prosecutor relies to prove the alleged offence and to provide information relevant to sentence; and

    (b) any representations served by the defendant.

Duty of court officer

B-314   **24.16.** The court officer must—

    (a) serve on each party notice of where and when an adjourned hearing will resume, unless—

      (i)   the party was present when that was arranged,

      (ii)   the defendant has served a notice of guilty plea to which rule 24.8 (written guilty plea: special rules) applies, and the adjournment is for not more than 4 weeks, or

      (iii)   the court tries a case under rule 24.9 (single justice procedure: special rules), and the adjourned trial will resume under that rule;

    (b) if the reason for the adjournment was to postpone sentence, include that reason in any such notice to the defendant;

    (c) unless the court otherwise directs, make available to the parties any written report to which rule 24.11 (procedure if the court convicts) applies;

    (d) where the court has ordered a defendant to provide information under section 25 of the Road Traffic Offenders Act 1988, serve on the defendant notice of that order unless the defendant was present when it was made;

    (e) serve on the prosecutor—

      (i)   any notice of guilty plea to which rule 24.8 (written guilty plea: special rules) applies,

      (ii)   any declaration served under rule 24.17 (statutory declaration of ignorance of proceedings) that the defendant did not know about the case;

    (f) serve on the prosecutor notice of any hearing date arranged in consequence of such a declaration, unless—

      (i)   the prosecutor was present when that was arranged, or

      (ii)   the court otherwise directs;

    (g) serve on the prosecutor—

      (i)   notice of any hearing date arranged in consequence of the issue of a summons under rule 37.9 (single justice procedure: special rules), and in that event

      (ii)   any notice served by the defendant under rule 37.9(2)(b) or (c);

    (h) record the court's reasons for not proceeding in the defendant's absence where rule 24.12(3)(a) applies; and

    (i) give the court such other assistance as it requires.

Statutory declaration of ignorance of proceedings

B-315   **24.17.**—(1) This rule applies where—

    (a) the case started with—

      (i)   an information and summons,

      (ii)   a written charge and requisition, or

      (iii)   a written charge and single justice procedure notice; and

    (b) under section 14 or section 16E of the Magistrates' Courts Act 1980, the defendant makes a statutory declaration of not having found out about the case until after the trial began.

(2) The defendant must—

    (a) serve such a declaration on the court officer—

      (i)   not more than 21 days after the date of finding out about the case, or

      (ii)   with an explanation for the delay, if serving it more than 21 days after that date;

    (b) serve with the declaration one of the following, as appropriate, if the case began with a written charge and single justice procedure notice—

      (i)   a notice under rule 24.9(4)(a) (notice of guilty plea), with any representations that the defendant wants the court to consider and a statement of the defendant's assets and other financial circumstances, as required by that rule,

     (ii)   a notice under rule 24.9(4)(b) (notice of intention to plead guilty at a hearing before a court comprising more than one justice), or

    (iii)   a notice under rule 24.9(4)(c) (notice of intention to plead not guilty).

(3) The court may extend that time limit, even after it has expired—

    (a)   at a hearing, in public or in private; or

    (b)   without a hearing.

(4) Where the defendant serves such a declaration, in time or with an extension of time in which to do so, and the case began with a summons or requisition—

    (a)   the court must treat the summons or requisition and all subsequent proceedings as void (but not the information or written charge with which the case began);

    (b)   if the defendant is present when the declaration is served, the rules in this Part apply as if the defendant had been required to attend the court on that occasion;

    (c)   if the defendant is absent when the declaration is served—

     (i)   the rules in Part 7 apply (starting a prosecution in a magistrates' court) as if the prosecutor had just served an information in the same terms as the original information or written charge;

     (ii)   the court may exercise its power to issue a summons in accordance with those rules; and

    (iii)   except for rule 24.8 (written guilty plea: special rules), the rules in this Part then apply.

(5) Where the defendant serves such a declaration, in time or with an extension of time in which to do so, and the case began with a single justice procedure notice—

    (a)   the court must treat the single justice procedure notice and all subsequent proceedings as void (but not the written charge with which the case began);

    (b)   rule 24.9 (single justice procedure: special rules) applies as if the defendant had served the notice required by paragraph (2)(b) of this rule within the time allowed by rule 24.9(4); and

    (c)   where that notice is under rule 24.9(4)(b) (notice of intention to plead guilty at a hearing before a court comprising more than one justice) or under rule 24.9(4)(c) (notice of intention to plead not guilty), then—

     (i)   if the defendant is present when the declaration is served, the rules in this Part apply as if the defendant had been required to attend the court on that occasion,

     (ii)   if the defendant is absent when the declaration is served, paragraph (6) of this rule applies.

(6) Where this paragraph applies, the court must exercise its power to issue a summons and—

    (a)   the rules in Part 7 apply (starting a prosecution in a magistrates' court) as if the prosecutor had just served an information in the same terms as the written charge:

    (b)   except for rule 24.8 (written guilty plea: special rules) and rule 24.9 (Single justice procedure: special rules), the rules in this Part apply.

Setting aside a conviction or varying a costs etc. order

24.18.—(1) This rule applies where under section 142 of the Magistrates' Courts Act 1980 the   **B-316** court can—

    (a)   set aside a conviction, or

    (b)   vary or rescind—

     (i)   a costs order, or

     (ii)   an order to which Part 31 applies (behaviour orders).

(2) The court may exercise its power—

    (a)   on application by a party, or on its own initiative;

    (b)   at a hearing, in public or in private, or without a hearing.

(3) The court must not exercise its power in a party's absence unless—

    (a)   the court makes a decision proposed by that party;

    (b)   the court makes a decision to which that party has agreed in writing; or

    (c)   that party has had an opportunity to make representations at a hearing (whether or not that party in fact attends).

(4) A party who wants the court to exercise its power must—

    (a)   apply in writing as soon as reasonably practicable after the conviction or order that that party wants the court to set aside, vary or rescind;

    (b)   serve the application on—

      (i)   the court officer, and

      (ii) each other party; and

  (c) in the application—

      (i)   explain why, as appropriate, the conviction should be set aside, or the order varied or rescinded,

      (ii) specify any variation of the order that the applicant proposes,

      (iii) identify any witness that the defendant wants to call, and any other proposed evidence,

      (iv) say whether the defendant waives legal professional privilege, giving any relevant name and date, and

      (v) if the application is late, explain why.

(5) The court may—

  (a) extend (even after it has expired) the time limit under paragraph (4), unless the court's power to set aside the conviction, or vary the order, can no longer be exercised,

  (b) allow an application to be made orally.

CPD VI Trial 24A: Role of the Justices' Clerk/Legal Adviser

B-317   **24A.1** The role of the justices' clerk/legal adviser is a unique one, which carries with it independence from direction when undertaking a judicial function and when advising magistrates. These functions must be carried out in accordance with the Bangalore Principles of Judicial Conduct (judicial independence, impartiality, integrity, propriety, ensuring fair treatment and competence and diligence). More specifically, duties must be discharged in accordance with the relevant professional Code of Conduct and the Legal Adviser Competence Framework.

      24A.2 A justices' clerk is responsible for:

  (a) the legal advice tendered to the justices within the area;

  (b) the performance of any of the functions set out below by any member of his staff acting as justices' legal adviser;

  (c) ensuring that competent advice is available to justices when the justices' clerk is not personally present in court; and

  (d) ensuring that advice given at all stages of proceedings and powers exercised (including those delegated to justices' legal advisers) take into account the court's duty to deal with cases justly and actively to manage the case.

      24A.3 Where a person other than the justices' clerk (a justices' legal adviser), who is authorised to do so, performs any of the functions referred to in this direction, he or she will have the same duties, powers and responsibilities as the justices' clerk. The justices' legal adviser may consult the justices' clerk, or other person authorised by the justices' clerk for that purpose, before tendering advice to the bench. If the justices' clerk or that person gives any advice directly to the bench, he or she should give the parties or their advocates an opportunity of repeating any relevant submissions, prior to the advice being given.

      24A.4 When exercising judicial powers, a justices' clerk or legal adviser is acting in exactly the same capacity as a magistrate. The justices' clerk may delegate powers to a justices' legal adviser in accordance with the relevant statutory authority. The scheme of delegation must be clear and in writing, so that all justices' legal advisers are certain of the extent of their powers. Once a power is delegated, judicial discretion in an individual case lies with the justices' legal adviser exercising the power. When exercise of a power does not require the consent of the parties, a justices' clerk or legal adviser may deal with and decide a contested issue or may refer that issue to the court

      24A.5 It shall be the responsibility of the justices' clerk or legal adviser to provide the justices with any advice they require to perform their functions justly, whether or not the advice has been requested, on:

  (a) questions of law;

  (b) questions of mixed law and fact;

  (c) matters of practice and procedure;

  (d) the process to be followed at sentence and the matters to be taken into account, together with the range of penalties and ancillary orders available, in accordance with the relevant sentencing guidelines;

  (e) any relevant decisions of the superior courts or other guidelines;

  (f) the appropriate decision-making structure to be applied in any given case; and

  (g) other issues relevant to the matter before the court.

      24A.6 In addition to advising the justices, it shall be the justices' legal adviser's responsibility to assist the court, where appropriate, as to the formulation of reasons and the recording of those reasons.

24A.7 The justices' legal adviser has a duty to assist an unrepresented defendant, see CrimPR 9.4(3)(a), 14.3(2)(a) and 24.15(3)(a), in particular when the court is making a decision on allocation, bail, at trial and on sentence.

24A.8 Where the court must determine allocation, the legal adviser may deal with any aspect of the allocation hearing save for the decision on allocation, indication of sentence and sentence.

24A.9 When a defendant acting in person indicates a guilty plea, the legal adviser must explain the procedure and inform the defendant of their right to address the court on the facts and to provide details of their personal circumstances in order that the court can decide the appropriate sentence.

24A.10 When a defendant indicates a not guilty plea but has not completed the relevant sections of the Magistrates' Courts Trial Preparation Form, the legal adviser must either ensure that the Form is completed or, in appropriate cases, assist the court to obtain and record the essential information on the form.

24A.11 Immediately prior to the commencement of a trial, the legal adviser must summarise for the court the agreed and disputed issues, together with the way in which the parties propose to present their cases. If this is done by way of pre-court briefing, it should be confirmed in court or agreed with the parties.

24A.12 A justices' clerk or legal adviser must not play any part in making findings of fact, but may assist the bench by reminding them of the evidence, using any notes of the proceedings for this purpose, and clarifying the issues which are agreed and those which are to be determined.

24A.13 A justices' clerk or legal adviser may ask questions of witnesses and the parties in order to clarify the evidence and any issues in the case. A legal adviser has a duty to ensure that every case is conducted justly.

24A.14 When advising the justices, the justices' clerk or legal adviser, whether or not previously in court, should:

(a) ensure that he is aware of the relevant facts; and

(b) provide the parties with an opportunity to respond to any advice given.

24A.15 At any time, justices are entitled to receive advice to assist them in discharging their responsibilities. If they are in any doubt as to the evidence which has been given, they should seek the aid of their legal adviser, referring to his notes as appropriate. This should ordinarily be done in open court Where the justices request their adviser to join them in the retiring room, this request should be made in the presence of the parties in court Any legal advice given to the justices other than in open court should be clearly stated to be provisional; and the adviser should subsequently repeat the substance of the advice in open court and give the parties the opportunity to make any representations they wish on that provisional advice. The legal adviser should then state in open court whether the provisional advice is confirmed or, if it is varied, the nature of the variation.

24A.16 The legal adviser is under a duty to assist unrepresented parties, whether defendants or not to present their case, but must do so without appearing to become an advocate for the party concerned. The legal adviser should also ensure that members of the court are aware of obligations under the Victims' Code.

24A.17 The role of legal advisers in fine default proceedings, or any other proceedings for the enforcement of financial orders, obligations or penalties, is to assist the court They must not act in an adversarial or partisan manner, such as by attempting to establish wilful refusal or neglect or any other type of culpable behaviour, to offer an opinion on the facts, or to urge a particular course of action upon the justices. The expectation is that a legal adviser will ask questions of the defaulter to elicit information which the justices will require to make an adjudication, such as the explanation for the default A legal adviser may also advise the justices as to the options open to them in dealing with the case.

24A.18 The performance of a legal adviser is subject to regular appraisal. For that purpose the appraiser may be present in the justices' retiring room. The content of the appraisal is confidential, but the fact that an appraisal has taken place, and the presence of the appraiser in the retiring room, should be briefly explained in open court

CPD VI Trial 24B: Identification for the Court of the Issues in the Case (as inserted by Criminal Practice Directions 2015 (Amendment No. 1) unreported, March 23, 2016, Lord Thomas C.J.)

24B.1 CrimPR 3.11(a) requires the court with the active assistance of the parties, to establish what **B-318** are the disputed issues in order to manage the trial. To that end, the purpose of the prosecutor's summary of the prosecution case is to explain briefly, in the prosecutor's own terms, what the case is about. It will not usually be necessary, or helpful, to present a detailed account of all the prosecution evidence due to be introduced.

24B.2 CrimPR 24.3(3)(b) provides for a defendant, or his or her advocate, immediately after the prosecution opening to set out the issues in the defendant's own terms, if invited to do so by the court The purpose of any such identification of issues is to provide the court with focus as to what it is likely to be called upon to decide, so that the members of the court will be alert to those issues from the outset and can evaluate the prosecution evidence that they hear accordingly.

24B.3 The parties should keep in mind that in most cases, the members of the court already will be aware of what has been declared to be in issue. The court will have access to any written admissions and to information supplied for the purposes of case management: CrimPR 24.13(2). The court's legal adviser will have drawn the court's attention to what is alleged and to what is understood to be in dispute: CrimPR 24.15(2). If a party has nothing of substance to add to that then he or she should say so. The requirement to be concise will be enforced and the exchange with the court properly may be confined to enquiry and confirmation that the court's understanding of those allegations and issues is correct. Nevertheless, for the defendant to be offered an opportunity to identify issues at this stage may assist even if all he or she wishes to announce, or confirm, is that the prosecution is being put to proof.

24B.4 The identification of issues at the case management stage will have been made without the risk that they would be used at trial as statements of the defendant admissible in evidence against the defendant provided the advocate follows the letter and the spirit of the Criminal Procedure Rules. The court may take the view that a party is not acting in the spirit of the Criminal Procedure Rules in seeking to ambush the other party or raising late and technical legal arguments that were not previously raised as issues. No party that seeks to ambush the other at trial should derive an advantage from such a course of action. The court may also take the view that a defendant is not acting in the spirit of the Criminal Procedure Rules if he or she refuses to identify the issues and puts the prosecutor to proof at the case management stage. In both such circumstances the court may limit the proceedings on the day of trial in accordance with CrimPR 3.11(d). In addition any significant divergence from the issues identified at case management at this late stage may well result in the exercise of the court's powers under CrimPR 3.5(6), the powers to impose sanctions.

Criminal Procedure Rules 2015 (S.I. 2015 No. 1490), Pt 25

TRIAL AND SENTENCE IN THE CROWN COURT

When this Part applies

B-319

25.1. This Part applies in the Crown Court where—
    (a) the court tries a case; or
    (b) the defendant pleads guilty.

General powers and requirements

25.2.—(1) Where this Part applies, the general rule is that—
    (a) the trial must be in public, but that is subject to the court's power to—
        (i) impose a restriction on reporting what takes place at a public hearing, or public access to what otherwise would be a public hearing,
        (ii) withhold information from the public during a public hearing, or
        (iii) order a trial in private;
    (b) the court must not proceed if the defendant is absent, unless the court is satisfied that—
        (i) the defendant has waived the right to attend, and
        (ii) the trial will be fair despite the defendant's absence;
    (c) the court must not sentence the defendant to imprisonment or detention unless—
        (i) the defendant has a legal representative,
        (ii) the defendant has been sentenced to imprisonment or detention on a previous occasion in the United Kingdom, or
        (iii) the defendant could have been represented under legal aid but is not because section 83(3) of the Powers of Criminal Courts (Sentencing) Act 2000 applies to him or her [§ 5-15 in the main work].
    (2) The court may adjourn the trial at any stage

Application for ruling on procedure, evidence or other question of law

B-320

25.3.—(1) This rule applies to an application—
    (a) about—
        (i) case management, or any other question of procedure, or
        (ii) the introduction or admissibility of evidence, or any other question of law;

(b) that has not been determined before the trial begins.

(2) The application is subject to any other rule that applies to it (for example, as to the time and form in which the application must be made).

(3) Unless the court otherwise directs, the application must be made, and the court's decision announced, in the absence of the jury (if there is one).

Procedure on plea of guilty

25.4.–(1) This rule applies if–   **B-321**

  (a) the defendant pleads guilty to an offence; and

  (b) the court is satisfied that the plea represents a clear acknowledgement of guilt.

(2) The court need not receive evidence unless rule 25.16(4) applies (determination of facts for sentencing).

Application to vacate a guilty plea

25.5.–(1) This rule applies where a party wants the court to vacate a guilty plea.   **B-322**

(2) Such a party must–

  (a) apply in writing–

    (i) as soon as practicable after becoming aware of the grounds for doing so, and

    (ii) in any event, before the final disposal of the case, by sentence or otherwise; and

  (b) serve the application on–

    (i) the court officer, and

    (ii) the prosecutor.

(3) Unless the court otherwise directs, the application must–

  (a) explain why it would be unjust for the guilty plea to remain unchanged;

  (b) indicate what, if any, evidence the applicant wishes to call;

  (c) identify any proposed witness; and

  (d) indicate whether legal professional privilege is waived, specifying any material name and date.

Selecting the jury

25.6.–(1) This rule–   **B-323**

  (a) applies where–

    (i) the defendant pleads not guilty, or

    (ii) the defendant declines to enter a plea and the court treats that as a not guilty plea,

    (iii) the court determines that the defendant is not fit to be tried;

  (b) does not apply where–

    (i) the court orders a trial without a jury because of a danger of jury tampering or where jury tampering appears to have taken place, or

    (ii) the court tries without a jury counts on an indictment after a trial of sample counts with a jury.

(2) The court must select a jury to try the case from the panel, or part of the panel, of jurors summoned by the Lord Chancellor to attend at that time and place.

(3) Where it appears that too few jurors to constitute a jury will be available from among those so summoned, the court–

  (a) may exercise its own power to summon others in the court room, or in the vicinity, up to the number likely to be required, and add their names to the panel summoned by the Lord Chancellor; but

  (b) must inform the parties, if they are absent when the court exercises that power.

(4) The court must select the jury by drawing at random each juror's name from among those so summoned and–

  (a) announcing each name so drawn; or

  (b) announcing an identifying number assigned by the court officer to that person, where the court is satisfied that that is necessary.

(5) If too few jurors to constitute a jury are available from the panel after all their names have been drawn, the court may–

  (a) exercise its own power to summon others in the court room, or in the vicinity, up to the number required; and

  (b) announce–

    (i) the name of each person so summoned, or

(ii)   an identifying number assigned by the court officer to that person, where the court is satisfied that that is necessary.

(6) The jury the court selects—

(a)   must comprise no fewer than 12 jurors;

(b)   may comprise as many as 14 jurors to begin with, where the court expects the trial to last for more than 4 weeks.

(7) Where the court selects a jury comprising more than 12 jurors, the court must explain to them that—

(a)   the purpose of selecting more than 12 jurors to begin with is to fill any vacancy or vacancies caused by the discharge of any of the first 12 before the prosecution evidence begins;

(b)   any such vacancy or vacancies will be filled by the extra jurors in order of their selection from the panel;

(c)   the court will discharge any extra juror or jurors remaining by no later than the beginning of the prosecution evidence; and

(d)   any juror who is discharged for that reason then will be available to be selected for service on another jury, during the period for which that juror has been summoned.

(8) Each of the 12 or more jurors the court selects—

(a)   must take an oath or affirm; and

(b)   becomes a full jury member until discharged.

(9) The oath or affirmation must be in these terms, or in any corresponding terms that the juror declares to be binding on him or her—

"I swear by Almighty God [*or* I do solemnly, sincerely and truly declare and affirm] that I will faithfully try the defendant and give a true verdict according to the evidence.".

Discharging jurors

B-324   **25.7.**–(1) The court may exercise its power to discharge a juror at any time—

(a)   after the juror completes the oath or affirmation; and

(b)   before the court discharges the jury.

(2) No later than the beginning of the prosecution evidence, if the jury then comprises more than 12 jurors the court must discharge any in excess of 12 in reverse order of their selection from the panel.

(3) The court may exercise its power to discharge the jury at any time—

(a)   after each juror has completed the oath or affirmation; and

(b)   before the jury has delivered its verdict on each offence charged in the indictment.

(4) The court must exercise its power to discharge the jury when, in respect of each offence charged in the indictment, either—

(a)   the jury has delivered its verdict on that offence; or

(b)   the court has discharged the jury from reaching a verdict.

Objecting to jurors

25.8.–(1) A party who objects to the panel of jurors must serve notice explaining the objection on the court officer and on the other party before the first juror's name or number is drawn.

(2) A party who objects to the selection of an individual juror must—

(a)   tell the court of the objection—

(i)   after the juror's name or number is announced, and

(ii)   before the juror completes the oath or affirmation; and

(b)   explain the objection.

(3) A prosecutor who exercises the prosecution right without giving reasons to prevent the court selecting an individual juror must announce the exercise of that right before the juror completes the oath or affirmation.

(4) The court must determine an objection under paragraph (1) or (2)—

(a)   at a hearing, in public or in private; and

(b)   in the absence of the jurors, unless the court otherwise directs.

Procedure on plea of not guilty

B-325   **25.9.**–(1) This rule applies where—

(a)   the defendant pleads not guilty; or

(b)   the defendant declines to enter a plea and the court treats that as a not guilty plea.

(2) In the following sequence—

(a) where there is a jury, the court must—
- (i) inform the jurors of each offence charged in the indictment to which the defendant pleads not guilty, and
- (ii) explain to the jurors that it is their duty, after hearing the evidence, to decide whether the defendant is guilty or not guilty of each offence;

(b) the prosecutor may summarise the prosecution case, concisely outlining the facts and the matters likely to be in dispute;

(c) where there is a jury, to help the jurors to understand the case and resolve any issue in it the court may—
- (i) invite the defendant concisely to identify what is in issue, if necessary in terms approved by the court,
- (ii) if the defendant declines to do so, direct that the jurors be given a copy of any defence statement served under rule 15.4 (defence disclosure), edited if necessary to exclude any reference to inappropriate matters or to matters evidence of which would not be admissible;

(d) the prosecutor must introduce the evidence on which the prosecution case relies;

(e) subject to paragraph (3), at the end of the prosecution evidence, on the defendant's application or on its own initiative, the court—
- (i) may direct the jury (if there is one) to acquit on the ground that the prosecution evidence is insufficient for any reasonable court properly to convict, but
- (ii) must not do so unless the prosecutor has had an opportunity to make representations;

(f) subject to paragraph (4), at the end of the prosecution evidence, the court must ask whether the defendant intends to give evidence in person and, if the answer is "no", then the court must satisfy itself that there has been explained to the defendant, in terms the defendant can understand (with help, if necessary)—
- (i) the right to give evidence in person, and
- (ii) that if the defendant does not give evidence in person, or refuses to answer a question while giving evidence, the court may draw such inferences as seem proper;

(g) the defendant may summarise the defence case, if he or she intends to call at least one witness other than him or herself to give evidence in person about the facts of the case;

(h) in this order (or in a different order, if the court so directs) the defendant may—
- (i) give evidence in person,
- (ii) call another witness, or witnesses, to give evidence in person, and
- (iii) introduce any other evidence;

(i) a party may introduce further evidence if it is then admissible (for example, because it is in rebuttal of evidence already introduced);

(j) the prosecutor may make final representations, where—
- (i) the defendant has a legal representative,
- (ii) the defendant has called at least one witness, other than the defendant him or herself, to give evidence in person about the facts of the case, or
- (iii) the court so permits; and

(k) the defendant may make final representations.

(3) Paragraph (2)(e) does not apply in relation to a charge of murder, manslaughter, attempted murder, or causing harm contrary to section 18 or 20 of the Offences against the Person Act 1861 until the court has heard all the evidence (including any defence evidence), where the defendant is charged with—

(a) any of those offences; and

(b) an offence of causing or allowing a child or vulnerable adult to die or to suffer serious physical harm, contrary to section 5 of the Domestic Violence, Crime and Victims Act 2004 [§ 19-163 in the main work].

(4) Paragraph (2)(f) does not apply where it appears to the court that, taking account of all the circumstances, the defendant's physical or mental condition makes it undesirable for the defendant to give evidence in person.

(5) Where there is more than one defendant, this rule applies to each in the order their names appear in the indictment, or in an order directed by the court.

(6) Unless the jury (if there is one) has retired to consider its verdict, the court may allow a party to introduce evidence, or make representations, after that party's opportunity to do so under paragraph (2).

(7) Unless the jury has already reached a verdict on a count, the court may exercise its power to—

(a) discharge the jury from reaching a verdict on that count;

(b) direct the jury to acquit the defendant on that count; or

(c) invite the jury to convict the defendant, if the defendant pleads guilty to the offence charged by that count.

[This rule is printed as amended by the Criminal Procedure (Amendment) Rules 2016 (S.I. 2016 No. 120).]

Defendant unfit to plead

B-326   **25.10.**—(1) This rule applies where—

(a) it appears to the court, on application or on its own initiative, that the defendant may not be fit to be tried; and

(b) the defendant has not by then been acquitted of each offence charged by the indictment.

(2) The court—

(a) must exercise its power to decide, without a jury, whether the defendant is fit to be tried;

(b) may postpone the exercise of that power until immediately before the opening of the defence case.

(3) Where the court determines that the defendant is not fit to be tried—

(a) the court must exercise its power to appoint a person to put the case for the defence, taking account of all the circumstances and in particular—

(i) the willingness and suitability (including the qualifications and experience) of that person,

(ii) the nature and complexity of the case,

(iii) any advantage of continuity of representation, and

(iv) the defendant's wishes and needs;

(b) the court must select a jury, if none has been selected yet; and

(c) rule 25.9 (procedure on plea of not guilty) applies, if the steps it lists have not already been taken, except that—

(i) everything which that rule requires to be done by the defendant may be done instead by the person appointed to put the case for the defence,

(ii) under rule 25.9(2)(a), the court must explain to the jurors that their duty is to decide whether or not the defendant did the act or made the omission charged as an offence, not whether the defendant is guilty of that offence, and

(iii) rule 25.9(2)(e) does not apply (warning of consequences of defendant not giving evidence).

Evidence of a witness in person

B-327   **25.11**—(1) This rule applies where a party wants to introduce evidence by calling a witness to give that evidence in person.

(2) Unless the court otherwise directs—

(a) a witness waiting to give evidence must not wait inside the courtroom, unless that witness is—

(i) a party, or

(ii) an expert witness;

(b) a witness who gives evidence in the courtroom must do so from the place provided for that purpose; and

(c) a witness' address—

(i) must not be given in public unless the address is relevant to an issue in the case,

(ii) may be given in writing to the court, parties and jury.

(3) Unless other legislation otherwise provides, before giving evidence a witness must take an oath or affirm.

(4) In the following sequence—

(a) the party who calls a witness may ask questions in examination-in-chief;

(b) if the witness gives evidence for the prosecution—

(i) the defendant, if there is only one, may ask questions in cross-examination, or

(ii) subject to the court's directions, each defendant, if there is more than one, may ask such questions, in the order their names appear in the indictment or as directed by the court;

(c) if the witness gives evidence for a defendant—

    (i)   subject to the court's directions, each other defendant, if there is more than one, may ask questions in cross-examination, in the order their names appear in the indictment or as directed by the court, and

    (ii)   the prosecutor may ask such questions;

  (d) the party who called the witness may ask questions in re-examination arising out of any cross-examination.

(5) If other legislation so permits, at any time while giving evidence a witness may refer to a record of that witness' recollection of events.

(6) The court may—

  (a) ask a witness questions; and in particular

  (b) where the defendant is not represented, ask a witness any question necessary in the defendant's interests.

Evidence of witness in writing

25.12.—(1) This rule applies where a party wants to introduce in evidence the written statement of **B-328** a witness to which applies—

  (a) Part 16 (written witness statements);

  (b) Part 19 (expert evidence); or

  (c) Part 20 (hearsay evidence).

(2) If the court admits such evidence each relevant part of the statement must be read or summarised aloud, unless the court otherwise directs.

[This rule is printed as amended by the Criminal Procedure (Amendment) Rules 2016 (S.I. 2016 No. 120).]

Evidence by admission

25.13.—(1) This rule applies where—   **B-329**

  (a) a party introduces in evidence a fact admitted by another party; or

  (b) parties jointly admit a fact.

(2) Unless the court otherwise directs, a written record must be made of the admission.

Directions to the jury and taking the verdict

25.14.—(1) This rule applies where there is a jury.   **B-330**

(2) The court must give the jury directions about the relevant law at any time at which to do so will assist jurors to evaluate the evidence.

(3) After following the sequence in rule 25.9 (procedure on plea of not guilty), the court must—

  (a) summarise for the jury, to such extent as is necessary, the evidence relevant to the issues they must decide;

  (b) give the jury such questions, if any, as the court invites jurors to answer in coming to a verdict;

  (c) direct the jury to retire to consider its verdict;

  (d) if necessary, recall the jury to answer jurors' questions;

  (e) if appropriate, recall the jury to give directions for a verdict by a majority; and

  (f) recall the jury when it informs the court that it has reached a verdict.

(4) The court may give the jury directions, questions or other assistance in writing.

(5) When the court recalls the jury to deliver its verdict, the court must ask the foreman chosen by the jury, in respect of each count—

  (a) whether the jury has reached a verdict on which all the jurors agree;

  (b) if so, whether that verdict is guilty or not guilty;

  (c) if not, where the jury has deliberated for at least 2 hours and if the court decides to invite a majority verdict, then—

    (i)   whether at least 10 (of 11 or 12 jurors), or 9 (of 10 jurors), agreed on a verdict,

    (ii) if so, is that verdict guilty or not guilty, and

    (iii) if (and only if) such a verdict is guilty, how many jurors agreed to that verdict and how many disagreed.

(6) Where evidence has been given that the defendant was insane, so as not to be responsible for the act or omission charged as the offence, then under paragraph (5)(b) the court must ask whether the jury's verdict is guilty, not guilty, or not guilty by reason of insanity.

[This rule is printed as amended by S.I. 2016 No. 120 (*ante*, § B-328).]

Conviction or acquittal without a jury

B-331   **25.15.**–(1) This rule applies where–

    (a) the court tries the case without a jury; and

    (b) after following the sequence in rule 25.9 (procedure on plea of not guilty).

(2) In respect of each count, the court must give reasons for its decision to convict or acquit.

Procedure if the court convicts

B-332   **25.16.**–(1) This rule applies where, in respect of any count in the indictment–

    (a) the defendant pleads guilty; or

    (b) the court convicts the defendant.

(2) The court may exercise its power–

    (a) if the defendant is an individual–

        (i) to require a pre-sentence report,

        (ii) to request a medical report,

        (iii) to require a statement of the defendant's assets and other financial circumstances;

    (b) if the defendant is a corporation, to require such information as the court directs about the defendant's corporate structure and financial resources;

    (c) to adjourn sentence pending–

        (i) receipt of any such report, statement or information,

        (ii) the verdict in a related case.

(3) The prosecutor must–

    (a) summarise the prosecution case, if the sentencing court has not heard evidence;

    (b) identify in writing any offence that the prosecutor proposes should be taken into consideration in sentencing;

    (c) provide information relevant to sentence, including–

        (i) any previous conviction of the defendant, and the circumstances where relevant,

        (ii) any statement of the effect of the offence on the victim, the victim's family or others; and

    (d) identify any other matter relevant to sentence, including–

        (i) the legislation applicable,

        (ii) any sentencing guidelines, or guideline cases,

        (iii) aggravating and mitigating features affecting the defendant's culpability and the harm which the offence caused, was intended to cause or might forseeably have caused, and

        (iv) the effect of such of the information listed in paragraph (2) as the court may need to take into account.

(4) Where the defendant pleads guilty, the court may give directions for determining the facts on the basis of which sentence must be passed if–

    (a) the defendant wants to be sentenced on a basis agreed with the prosecutor; or

    (b) in the absence of such agreement, the defendant wants to be sentenced on the basis of different facts to those disclosed by the prosecution case.

(5) Where the court has power to order the endorsement of the defendant's driving record, or power to order the defendant to be disqualified from driving–

    (a) if other legislation so permits, a defendant who wants the court not to exercise that power must introduce the evidence or information on which the defendant relies;

    (b) the prosecutor may introduce evidence; and

    (c) the parties may make representations about that evidence or information.

(6) Before passing sentence–

    (a) the court must give the defendant an opportunity to make representations and introduce evidence relevant to sentence;

    (b) where the defendant is under 18, the court may give the defendant's parents, guardian or other supporting adult, if present, such an opportunity as well; and

    (c) if the court requires more information, it may exercise its power to adjourn the hearing.

(7) When the court has taken into account all the evidence, information and any report available, the court must–

    (a) as a general rule, pass sentence at the earliest opportunity;

    (b) when passing sentence–

        (i) explain the reasons,

        (ii) explain to the defendant its effect, the consequences of failing to comply with any order or pay any fine, and any power that the court has to vary or review the sentence, unless the defendant is absent or the defendant's ill-health or disorderly conduct makes such an explanation impracticable, and

   (iii) give any such explanation in terms the defendant, if present, can understand (with help, if necessary); and

 (c) deal with confiscation, costs and any civil behaviour order.

(8) The general rule is subject to the court's power to defer sentence for up to 6 months.

Provision of documents for the court

25.17.–(1) Unless the court otherwise directs, a party who introduces a document in evidence, or **B-333** who otherwise uses a document in presenting that party's case, must provide a copy for—

  (a) each other party;

  (b) any witness that party wants to refer to the document; and

  (c) the court.

(2) If the court so directs, a party who introduces or uses a document for such a purpose must provide a copy for the jury.

(3) Unless the court otherwise directs, on application or on its own initiative, the court officer must provide for the court—

  (a) any copy received under paragraph (1) before the trial begins; and

  (b) a copy of the court officer's record of—

    (i) information supplied by each party for the purposes of case management, including any revision of information previously supplied,

    (ii) each pre-trial direction for the management of the case,

    (iii) any pre-trial decision to admit evidence,

    (iv) any pre-trial direction about the giving of evidence, and

    (v) any admission to which rule 25.13 (evidence by admission) applies; and

  (c) any other document served on the court officer for the use of the court.

Duty of court officer

25.18. The court officer must—

  (a) serve on each party notice of where and when an adjourned hearing will resume, unless **B-334** that party was present when that was arranged;

  (b) if the reason for the adjournment was to postpone sentence, include that reason in any such notice to the defendant;

  (c) unless the court otherwise directs, make available to the parties any written report to which rule 25.16(2) applies (pre-sentence and medical reports);

  (d) where the court has ordered a defendant to provide information under section 25 of the Road Traffic Offenders Act 1988, serve on the defendant notice of that order unless the defendant was present when it was made;

  (e) give the court such other assistance as it requires, including—

    (i) selecting jurors from the panel summoned by the Lord Chancellor, under rule 25.6 (selecting the jury),

    (ii) taking the oaths or affirmations of jurors and witnesses, under rules 25.6 and 25.11 (evidence of a witness in person),

    (iii) informing the jurors of the offence or offences charged in the indictment, and of their duty, under rule 25.9 (procedure on plea of not guilty),

    (iv) recording the date and time at which the court gives the jury oral directions under rule 25.14(2) (directions about the law),

    (v) recording the date and time at which the court gives the jury any written directions, questions or other assistance under rule 25.14(4), and

    (vi) asking the jury foreman to deliver the verdict under rule 25.14(5).

CPD VI Trial 25A: Identification for the Jury of the Issues in the Case (as inserted by Criminal Practice Directions 2015 (Amendment No. 1), unreported, March 23, 2016, Lord Thomas C.J.)

25A.1 CrimPR 3.11(a) requires the court, with the active assistance of the parties, to establish what **B-335** are the disputed issues in order to manage the trial. To that end, prosecution opening speeches are invaluable. They set out for the jury the principal issues in the trial, and the evidence which is to be introduced in support of the prosecution case. They should clarify, not obfuscate. The purpose of the prosecution opening is to help the jury understand what the case concerns, not necessarily to present a detailed account of all the prosecution evidence due to be introduced.

25A.2 CrimPR 25.9(2)(c) provides for a defendant, or his or her advocate, to set out the issues in the defendant's own terms (subject to superintendence by the court), immediately after the prosecution opening. Any such identification of issues at this stage is not to be treated as a substitute for or extension of the summary of the defence case which can be given later, under CrimPR 25.9(2)(g). Its purpose is to provide the jury with focus as to the issues that they are likely to be called upon to decide, so that jurors will be alert to those issues from the outset and can evaluate the prosecution evidence that they hear accordingly. For that purpose, the defendant is not confined to what is included in the defence statement (though any divergence from the defence statement will expose the defendant to adverse comment or inference), and for the defendant to take the opportunity at this stage to identify the issues may assist even if all he or she wishes to announce is that the prosecution is being put to proof.

25A.3 To identify the issues for the jury at this stage also provides an opportunity for the judge to give appropriate directions about the law; for example, as to what features of the prosecution evidence they should look out for in a case in which what is in issue is the identification of the defendant by an eye witness. Giving such directions at the outset is another means by which the jury can be helped to focus on the significant features of the evidence, in the interests of a fair and effective trial.

25A.4 A defendant is not entitled to identify issues at this stage by addressing the jury unless the court invites him or her to do so. Given the advantages described above, usually the court should extend such an invitation but there may be circumstances in which, in the court's judgment, it furthers the overriding objective not to do so. Potential reasons for denying the defendant the opportunity at this stage to address the jury about the issues include (i) that the case is such that the issues are apparent; (ii) that the prosecutor has given a fair, accurate and comprehensive account of the issues in opening, rendering repetition superfluous; and (iii) where the defendant is not represented, that there is a risk of the defendant, at this early stage, inflicting injustice on him or herself by making assertions to the jury to such an extent, or in such a manner, as is unfairly detrimental to his or her subsequent standing.

25A.5 Whether or not there is to be a defence identification of issues, and, if there is, in what manner and in what terms it is to be presented to the jury, are questions that must be resolved in the absence of the jury and that should be addressed at the opening of the trial.

25A.6 Even if invited to identify the issues by addressing the jury, the defendant is not obliged to accept the invitation. However, where the court decides that it is important for the jury to be made aware of what the defendant has declared to be in issue in the defence statement then the court may require the jury to be supplied with copies of the defence statement, edited at the court's direction if necessary, in accordance with section 6E(4) of the CPIA 1996 [§ 12-71 in the main work].

Criminal Procedure Rules 2015 (S.I. 2015 No. 1490), Pt 26

Jurors

Appeal against officer's refusal to excuse or postpone jury service

B-336
26.1.–(1) This rule applies where a person summoned for jury service in the Crown Court, the High Court or the County Court wants to appeal against a refusal by an officer on the Lord Chancellor's behalf—

    (a) to excuse that person from such service; or

    (b) to postpone the date on which that person is required to attend for such service.

(2) The appellant must appeal to the court to which the appellant has been summoned.

(3) The appellant must—

    (a) apply in writing, as soon as reasonably practicable; and

    (b) serve the application on the court officer.

(4) The application must—

    (a) attach a copy of—

        (i)   the jury summons, and

        (ii) the refusal to excuse or postpone which is under appeal; and

    (b) explain why the court should excuse the appellant from jury service, or postpone its date, as appropriate.

(5) The court to which the appeal is made—

    (a) may extend the time for appealing, and may allow the appeal to be made orally;

    (b) may determine the appeal at a hearing in public or in private, or without a hearing;

    (c) may adjourn any hearing of the appeal;

    (d) must not determine an appeal unless the appellant has had a reasonable opportunity to make representations in person.

Excusal from jury service by court

26.2. At any time before a juror completes the oath or affirmation, the court may exercise its   **B-337** power to excuse him or her from jury service for lack of capacity to act effectively as a juror because of an insufficient understanding of English—

(a) on the court's own initiative, or where the court officer refers the juror to the court; and

(b) after enquiry of the juror.

Provision of information for jurors

26.3. The court officer must arrange for each juror to receive—   **B-338**

(a) by such means as the Lord Chancellor directs, general information about jury service and about a juror's responsibilities;

(b) written notice of the prohibitions against—

    (i) research by a juror into the case,

    (ii) disclosure by a juror of any such research to another juror during the trial,

    (iii) conduct by a juror which suggests that that juror intends to try the case otherwise than on the evidence,

    (iv) disclosure by a juror of the deliberations of the jury;

(c) written warning that breach of those prohibitions is an offence, for which the penalty is imprisonment or a fine or both, and may be a contempt of court.

Assessment of juror's availability for long trial, etc.

26.4.—(1) The court may invite each member of a panel of jurors to provide such information, by   **B-339** such means and at such a time as the court directs, about—

(a) that juror's availability to try a case expected to last for longer than the juror had expected to serve;

(b) any association of that juror with, or any knowledge by that juror of—

    (i) a party or witness, or

    (ii) any other person, or any place, of significance to the case.

(2) Where jurors provide information under this rule, the court may postpone the selection of the jury to try a case to allow each juror an opportunity to review and amend that information before that selection.

(3) Using that information, the court may exercise its power to excuse a juror from selection as a member of the jury to try a case, but the court must not—

(a) excuse a juror without allowing the parties an opportunity to make representations; or

(b) refuse to excuse a juror without allowing that juror such an opportunity.

Surrender of electronic communication devices by jurors

26.5.—(1) This rule applies where the court can order the members of a jury to surrender for a   **B-340** specified period any electronic communication devices that they possess.

(2) The court may make such an order—

(a) on application; or

(b) on its own initiative.

(3) A party who wants the court to make such an order must—

(a) apply as soon as reasonably practicable;

(b) notify each other party;

(c) specify for what period any device should be surrendered; and

(d) explain why—

    (i) the proposed order is necessary or expedient in the interest of justice, and

    (ii) the terms of the proposed order are a proportionate means of safeguarding those interests.

CPD VI Trial 26A: Juries: Introduction

26A.1 Jury service is an important public duty which individual members of the public are chosen   **B-341** at random to undertake. As the Court has acknowledged: "Jury service is not easy; it never has been. It involves a major civic responsibility" (*R. v. Thompson* [2010] 2 Cr. App. R. 27, CA (*per* Lord Judge C.J. (at [9]))).

Provision of information to prospective jurors

26A.2 HMCTS provide every person summoned as a juror with information about the role and responsibilities of a juror. Prospective jurors are provided with a pamphlet, "Your Guide to Jury Service", and may also view the film "Your Role as a Juror" online at anytime on the Ministry of Justice YouTube site www.youtube.com/watch?v=JP7slp-X9Pc. There is also information at https://www.gov.uk/jury-service/overview.

CPD VI Trial 26B: Juries: Preliminary Matters Arising before Jury Service Commences

26B.1 The effect of section 321 of the CJA 2003 was to remove certain categories of persons from those previously ineligible for jury service (the judiciary and others concerned with the administration of justice) and certain other categories ceased to be eligible for excusal as of right (such as Members of Parliament and medical professionals). The normal presumption is that everyone, unless ineligible or disqualified, will be required to serve when summoned to do so.

Excusal and deferral
26B.2 The jury summoning officer is empowered to defer or excuse individuals in appropriate circumstances and in accordance with the HMCTS Guidance for summoning officers when considering deferral and excusal applications (2009): http://www.official-documents.gov.uk/document/other/9780108508400/9780108508400.pdf

Appeals from officer's refusal to excuse or postpone jury service
26B.3 CrimPR 26.1 governs the procedure for a person's appeal against a summoning officer's decision in relation to excusal or deferral of jury service.

Provision of information at court
26B.4 The court officer is expected to provide relevant further information to jurors on their arrival in the court centre.

CPD VI Trial 26C: Juries: Eligibility

English language ability

26C.1 Under the Juries Act 1974, s.10 [§ 4-291 in the main work], a person summoned for jury service who applies for excusal on the grounds of insufficient understanding of English may, where necessary, be brought before the judge.

26C.2 The court may exercise its power to excuse any person from jury service for lack of capacity to act effectively as a juror because of an insufficient understanding of English.

26C.3 The judge has the discretion to stand down jurors who are not competent to serve by reason of a personal disability: *R. v. Mason* [§ 4-275 in the main work]; *R. v. Jalil* [§ 4-292 in the main work].

Jurors with professional and public service commitments
26C.4 The legislative change in the CJA 2003 means that more individuals are eligible to serve as jurors, including those previously excused as of right or ineligible. Judges need to be vigilant to the need to exercise their discretion to adjourn a trial, excuse or discharge a juror should the need arise.

26C.5 Whether or not an application has already been made to the jury summoning officer for deferral or excusal, it is also open to the person summoned to apply to the court to be excused. Such applications must be considered with common sense and according to the interests of justice. An explanation should be required for an application being much later than necessary.

Serving police officers, prison officers or employees of prosecuting agencies
26C.6 A judge should always be made aware at the stage of jury selection if any juror in waiting is in these categories. The juror summons warns jurors in these categories that they will need to alert court staff.

26C.7 In the case of police officers an inquiry by the judge will have to be made to assess whether a police officer may serve as a juror. Regard should be had to: whether evidence from the police is in dispute in the case and the extent to which that dispute involves allegations made against the police; whether the potential juror knows or has worked with the officers involved in the case; whether the potential juror has served or continues to serve in the same police units within the force as those dealing with the investigation of the case or is likely to have a shared local service background with police witnesses in a trial.

26C.8 In the case of a serving prison officer summoned to a court, the judge will need to inquire whether the individual is employed at a prison linked to that court or is likely to have special knowledge of any person involved in a trial.

26C.9 The judge will need to ensure that employees of prosecuting authorities do not serve on a trial prosecuted by the prosecuting authority by which they are employed. They can serve on a trial prosecuted by another prosecuting authority: *R. v. Abdroikov* [§ 4-293 in the main work]; *Hanif v. U.K.* [§ 7-89 in the main work]; *R. v. L. (L.)* [§ 4-293 in the main work]. Similarly, a serving police officer can serve where there is no particular link between the court and the station where the police officer serves.

26C.10 Potential jurors falling into these categories should be excused from jury service unless there is a suitable alternative court/trial to which they can be transferred.

CPD VI Trial 26D: Juries: Precautionary Measures before Swearing

26D.1 There should be a consultation with the advocates as to the questions, if any, it may be appropriate to ask potential jurors. Topics to be considered include: (a) the availability of jurors for the duration of a trial that is likely to run beyond the usual period for which jurors are summoned; (b) whether any juror knows the defendant or parties to the case; (c) whether potential jurors are so familiar with any locations that feature in the case that they may have, or come to have, access to information not in evidence; (d) in cases where there has been any significant local or national publicity, whether any questions should be asked of potential jurors. **B-344**

26D.2 Judges should however exercise caution. At common law a judge has a residual discretion to discharge a particular juror who ought not to be serving, but this discretion can only be exercised to prevent an individual juror who is not competent from serving. It does not include a discretion to discharge a jury drawn from particular sections of the community or otherwise to influence the overall composition of the jury. However, if there is a risk that there is widespread local knowledge of the defendant or a witness in a particular case, the judge may, after hearing submissions from the advocates, decide to exclude jurors from particular areas to avoid the risk of jurors having or acquiring personal knowledge of the defendant or a witness.

Length of trial

26D.3 Where the length of the trial is estimated to be significantly longer than the normal period of jury service, it is good practice for the trial judge to enquire whether the potential jurors on the jury panel foresee any difficulties with the length and if the judge is satisfied that the jurors' concerns are justified, he may say that they are not required for that particular jury. This does not mean that the judge must excuse the juror from sitting at that court altogether, as it may well be possible for the juror to sit on a shorter trial at the same court.

Juror with potential connection to the case or parties

26D.4 Where a juror appears on a jury panel, it will be appropriate for a judge to excuse the juror from that particular case where the potential juror is personally concerned with the facts of the particular case, or is closely connected with a prospective witness. Judges need to exercise due caution as noted above.

CPD VI Trial 26E: Juries: Swearing in Jurors

Swearing jury for trial

26E.1 All jurors shall be sworn or affirm. All jurors shall take the oath or affirmation in open court in the presence of one another. If, as a result of the juror's delivery of the oath or affirmation, a judge has concerns that a juror has such difficulties with language comprehension or reading ability that might affect that juror's capacity to undertake his or her duties, bearing in mind the likely evidence in the trial, the judge should make appropriate inquiry of that juror. **B-345**

Form of oath or affirmation

26E.2 Each juror should have the opportunity to indicate to the court the Holy Book on which he or she wishes to swear. The precise wording will depend on his or her faith as indicated to the court.

26E.3 Any person who prefers to affirm shall be permitted to make a solemn affirmation instead. The wording of the affirmation is: "I do solemnly, sincerely and truly declare and affirm that I will faithfully try the defendant and give a true verdict according to the evidence."

CPD VI Trial 26F: Juries: Ensuring an Effective Jury Panel

Adequacy of numbers

26F.1 [*Merely summarises the Juries Act 1974, s.6(1) (§ 4-276 in the main work).*]

CPD VI Trial 26G: Juries: Preliminary Instructions to Jurors

26G.1 After the jury has been sworn and the defendant has been put in charge the judge will want to give directions to the jury on a number of matters. **B-346**

26G.2 Jurors can be expected to follow the instructions diligently. As the Privy Council stated in *Taylor (Bonnett) v. The Queen* [2013] 2 Cr.App.R. 18:

"The assumption must be that the jury understood and followed the direction that they were given: ... the experience of trial judges is that juries perform their duty according to law. ... [T]he law proceeds on the footing that the jury, acting in accordance with the instructions given to them by the trial judge, will render a true verdict in accordance with the evidence. To conclude otherwise would be to underrate the integrity of the system of trial by jury and the effect on the jury of the instructions by the trial judge."

At the start of the trial
26G.3 Trial judges should instruct the jury on general matters which will include the time estimate for the trial and normal sitting hours. The jury will always need clear guidance on the following:

   (i) the need to try the case only on the evidence and remain faithful to their oath or affirmation;

   (ii) the prohibition on internet searches for matters related to the trial, issues arising or the parties;

   (iii) the importance of not discussing any aspect of the case with anyone outside their own number or allowing anyone to talk to them about it, whether directly, by telephone, through internet facilities such as Facebook or Twitter or in any other way;

   (iv) the importance of taking no account of any media reports about the case;

   (v) the collective responsibility of the jury; as Lord Judge C.J. made clear in *R. v. Thompson* [2010] 2 Cr.App.R. 27: "[T]here is a collective responsibility for ensuring that the conduct of each member is consistent with the jury oath and that the directions of the trial judge about the discharge of their responsibilities are followed. The collective responsibility of the jury for its own conduct must be regarded as an integral part of the trial itself.";

   (vi) the need to bring any concerns, including concerns about the conduct of other jurors, to the attention of the judge at the time, and not to wait until the case is concluded; the point should be made that, unless that is done while the case is continuing, it may not be possible to deal with the problem at all.

Subsequent reminder of the jury instructions
26G.4 Judges should consider reminding jurors of these instructions as appropriate at the end of each day and in particular when they separate after retirement.

CPD VI Trial 26H: Juries: Discharge of a Juror for Personal Reasons

B-347

26H.1 Where a juror unexpectedly finds him or herself in difficult professional or personal circumstances during the course of the trial, the juror should be encouraged to raise such problems with the trial judge. This might apply, for example, to a parent whose childcare arrangements unexpectedly fail, or a worker who is engaged in the provision of services the need for which can be critical, or a Member of Parliament who has deferred their jury service to an apparently more convenient time, but is unexpectedly called back to work for a very important reason. Such difficulties would normally be raised through a jury note in the normal manner.

26H.2 In such circumstances, the judge must exercise his or her discretion according to the interests of justice and the requirements of each individual case. The judge must decide for him or herself whether the juror has presented a sufficient reason to interfere with the course of the trial. If the juror has presented a sufficient reason, in longer trials it may well be possible to adjourn for a short period in order to allow the juror to overcome the difficulty.

26H.3 In shorter cases, it may be more appropriate to discharge the juror and to continue the trial with a reduced number of jurors. The power to do this is implicit in section 16(1) of the Juries Act 1974 [§ 4-311 in the main work]. In unusual cases (such as an unexpected emergency arising overnight) a juror need not be discharged in open court. The good administration of justice depends on the cooperation of jurors, who perform an essential public service. All such applications should be dealt with sensitively and sympathetically and the trial judge should always seek to meet the interests of justice without unduly inconveniencing any juror.

CPD VI Trial 26J: Juries: Views

B-348

26J.1 In each case in which it is necessary for the jury to view a location, the judge should produce ground rules for the view, after discussion with the advocates. The rules should contain details of what the jury will be shown and in what order and who, if anyone, will be permitted to speak and what will be said. The rules should also make provision for the jury to ask questions and receive a response from the judge, following submissions from the advocates, while the view is taking place.

CPD VI Trial 26K: Juries: Directions, Written Materials and Summing Up (as inserted by Criminal Practice Directions 2015 (Amendment No. 1), unreported, March 23, 2016, Lord Thomas C.J.)

Overview

26K.1 Sir Brian Leveson's Review of Efficiency in Criminal Proceedings 2015 contained recom- **B-349** mendations to improve the efficiency of jury trials including:

- early provision of appropriate directions;
- provision of a written route to verdict;
- provision of a split summing up (a summing up delivered in two parts – the first part prior to the closing speeches and the second part afterwards); and
- streamlining the summing up to help the jury focus on the issues.

The purpose of this practice direction, and the associated criminal procedure rules, is to give effect to these recommendations.

Record-keeping

26K.2 Full and accurate record-keeping is essential to enable the Registrar of Criminal Appeals to **B-350** obtain transcripts in the event of an application or appeal to the Court of Appeal ....

26K.3 A court officer is required to record the date and time at which the court provides directions and written materials (CrimPR 25.18(e)(iv)-(v)).

26K.4 The judge should ensure that a court officer (such as a court clerk or usher) is present in court to record the information listed in paragraph 26K.5.

26K.5 A court officer should clearly record the:

- date, time and subject of submissions and rulings relating to directions and written materials;
- date, time and subject of directions and written materials provided prior to the summing up; and
- date and time of the summing up, including both parts of a split summing up.

26K.6 A court officer should retain a copy of written materials on the court file or database.

26K.7 The parties should also record the information listed in paragraph 26K.5 and retain a copy of written materials. Where relevant to a subsequent application or appeal to the Court of Appeal ..., the information listed in paragraph 26K.5 should be provided in the notice of appeal, and any written materials should be identified.

Early provision of appropriate directions

26K.8 The court is required to provide directions about the relevant law at any time that will assist **B-351** the jury to evaluate the evidence (CrimPR 25.14(2)). The judge may provide an early direction prior to any evidence being called, prior to the evidence to which it relates or shortly thereafter.

26K.9 Where the judge decides it will assist the jury in their approach to the evidence and/ or evaluating the evidence as they hear it, an early direction should be provided.

26K.10 For example:

- where identification is in issue, an early *Turnbull* direction is [see §§ 14-2 *et seq.* in the main work] likely to assist the jury in approaching the evidence with the requisite caution; and by having the relevant considerations in mind when listening to the evidence;
- where special measures are to be used and/ or ground rules will restrict the manner and scope of questioning, an early explanation may assist the jury in their approach to the evidence;
- an early direction may also assist the jury, by having the relevant approach, considerations and/ or test in mind, when listening to—
  - expert witnesses; and
  - evidence of bad character;
  - hearsay;
  - interviews of co-defendants; and
  - evidence involving legal concepts such as knowledge, dishonesty, consent, recklessness, conspiracy, joint enterprise, attempt, self-defence, excessive force, voluntary intoxication and duress.

Written route to verdict

26K.11 A route to verdict, which poses a series of questions that lead the jury to the appropriate **B-352**

verdict, may be provided by the court (CrimPR 25.14(3)(b)). Each question should tailor the law to the issues and evidence in the case.

26K.12 Save where the case is so straightforward that it would be superfluous to do so, the judge should provide a written route to verdict. It may be presented (on paper or digitally) in the form of text, bullet points, a flowchart or other graphic.

Other written materials

26K.13 Where the judge decides it will assist the jury, written materials should be provided. They may be presented (on paper or digitally) in the form of text, bullet points, a table, a flowchart or other graphic.

26K.14 For example, written materials may assist the jury in relation to a complex direction or where the case involves a complex chronology, competing expert evidence or differing descriptions of a suspect.

26K.15 Such written materials may be prepared by the judge or the parties at the direction of the judge. Where prepared by the parties at the direction of the judge, they will be subject to the judge's approval.

Split summing up and provision of appropriate directions prior to closing speeches

B-353   **26K.16** Where the judge decides it will assist the jury when listening to the closing speeches, a split summing up should be provided. For example, the provision of appropriate directions prior to the closing speeches may avoid repetitious explanations of the law by the advocates.

26K.17 By way of illustration, such directions may include:
- functions of the judge and jury;
- burden and standard of proof;
- separate consideration of counts;
- separate consideration of defendants;
- elements of offence(s);
- defence(s);
- route to verdict;
- circumstantial evidence; and
- inferences from silence.

Closing speeches

26K.18 The advocates closing speeches should be consistent with any directions and route to verdict already provided by the judge.

Summing up

B-354   **26K.19** Prior to beginning or resuming the summing up at the conclusion of the closing speeches, the judge should briefly list (without repeating) any directions provided earlier in the trial. The purpose of this requirement is to provide a definitive account of all directions for the benefit of the Registrar of Criminal Appeals and the Court of Appeal (...), in the event of an application or appeal.

26K.20 The court is required to summarise the evidence relevant to the issues to such extent as is necessary (CrimPR 25.14(3)(a))).

26K.21 To assist the jury to focus on the issues during retirement, save where the case is so straightforward that it would be superfluous to do so, the judge should provide:
- a reminder of the issues;
- a summary of the nature of the evidence relating to each issue;
- a balanced account of the points raised by the parties; and
- any outstanding directions.

It is not necessary for the judge to recount all relevant evidence or to rehearse all of the significant points raised by the parties.

26K.22 At the conclusion of the summing up, the judge should provide final directions to the jury on the need:
- for unanimity (in respect of each count and defendant, where relevant);
- to dismiss any thoughts of majority verdicts until further direction; and
- to select a juror to chair their discussions and speak on their behalf to the court.

CPD VI Trial 26L: Juries: Jury Access to Exhibits and Evidence in Retirement

B-355   **26L.1** At the end of the summing up it is also important that the judge informs the jury that any exhibits they wish to have will be made available to them.

26L.2 Judges should invite submissions from the advocates as to what material the jury should retire with and what material before them should be removed, such as the transcript of an ABE interview (which should usually be removed from the jury as soon as the recording has been played.)

26L.3 Judges will also need to inform the jury of the opportunity to view certain audio, DVD or CCTV evidence that has been played (excluding, for example ABE interviews). If possible, it may be appropriate for the jury to be able to view any such material in the jury room alone, such as on a sterile laptop, so that they can discuss it freely; this will be a matter for the judge's discretion, following discussion with counsel.

CPD VI Trial 26M: Juries: Jury Irregularities

26M.1 This practice direction replaces the protocol regarding jury irregularities issued by the   **B-356**
President of the Queen's Bench Division in November 2012, and the subsequent practice direction, in light of sections 20A to 20D of the Juries Act 1974 [§§ 28-41a *et seq.* in the main work] and the associated repeal of section 8 of the Contempt of Court Act 1981 (confidentiality of jury's deliberations) [*ibid.*, § 28-73].

26M.2 A jury irregularity is anything that may prevent one or more jurors from remaining faithful to their oath or affirmation to "faithfully try the defendant and give a true verdict according to the evidence." Jury irregularities take many forms. Some are clear-cut such as a juror conducting research about the case or an attempt to suborn or intimidate a juror. Others are less clear-cut – for example, when there is potential bias or friction between jurors.

26M.3 A jury irregularity may involve contempt of court and / or the commission of an offence by or in relation to a juror.

26M.4 Under the previous version of this practice direction, the Crown Court required approval from the Vice-President of the Court of Appeal (Criminal Division) (CACD) prior to providing a juror's details to the police for the purposes of an investigation into a jury irregularity. Such approval is no longer required. Provision of a juror's details to the police is now a matter for the Crown Court.

Jury Irregularity During Trial

26M.5 A jury irregularity that comes to light during a trial may impact on the conduct of the trial.   **B-357**
It may also involve contempt of court and / or the commission of an offence by or in relation to a juror. The primary concern of the judge should be the impact on the trial.

26M.6 A jury irregularity should be drawn to the attention of the judge in the absence of the jury as soon as it becomes known.

26M.7 When the judge becomes aware of a jury irregularity, the judge should follow the procedure set out below:

       STEP 1: Consider isolating juror(s)

       STEP 2: Consult with advocates

       STEP 3: Consider appropriate provisional measures (which may include surrender / seizure of electronic communications devices and taking defendant into custody)

       STEP 4: Seek to establish basic facts of jury irregularity

       STEP 5: Further consult with advocates

       STEP 6: Decide what to do in relation to conduct of trial

       STEP 7: Consider ancillary matters (contempt in face of court and / or commission of criminal offence)

STEP 1: Consider isolating juror(s)
26M.8 The judge should consider whether the juror(s) concerned should be isolated from the rest   **B-358**
of the jury, particularly if the juror(s) may have conducted research about the case.

26M.9 If two or more jurors are concerned, the judge should consider whether they should also be isolated from each other, particularly if one juror has made an accusation against another.

STEP 2: Consult with advocates
26M.10 The judge should consult with the advocates and invite submissions about appropriate   **B-359**
provisional measures (Step 3) and how to go about establishing the basic facts of the jury irregularity (Step 4).

26M.11 The consultation should be conducted

     – in open court;

     – in the presence of the defendant; and

     – with all parties represented

unless there is good reason not to do so.

26M.12 If the jury irregularity involves a suspicion about the conduct of the defendant or another party, there may be good reason for the consultation to take place in the absence of the defendant or the other party. There may also be good reason for it to take place in private. If so, the proper location is in the court room, with DARTS recording, rather than in the judge's room.

26M.13 If the jury irregularity relates to the jury's deliberations, the judge should warn all those present that it is an offence to disclose, solicit or obtain information about a jury's deliberations (s.20D(1) of the Juries Act 1974 [§ 28-41d in the main work] – see paras 26M.35 to 26M.38 regarding the offence and exceptions). This would include disclosing information about the jury's deliberations divulged in court during consultation with the advocates (Step 2 and Step 5) or when seeking to establish the basic facts of the jury irregularity (Step 4). The judge should emphasise that the advocates, court staff and those in the public gallery would commit the offence by explaining to another what is said in court about the jury's deliberations.

STEP 3: Consider appropriate provisional measures

B-360   **26M.14** The judge should consider appropriate provisional measures which may include surrender / seizure of electronic communications devices and taking the defendant into custody.

Surrender / seizure of electronic communications devices

26M.15 The judge should consider whether to make an order under section 15A(1) of the Juries Act 1974 [§ 4-325b in the main work] requiring the juror(s) concerned to surrender electronic communications devices, such as mobile telephones or smart phones.

26M.16 Having made an order for surrender, the judge may require a court security officer to search a juror to determine whether the juror has complied with the order. Section 54A of the Courts Act 2003 contains the court security officer's powers of search and seizure.

26M.17 Section 15A(5) of the Juries Act 1974 provides that it is contempt of court for a juror to fail to surrender an electronic communications device in accordance with an order for surrender (see paras 26M.29 to 26M.30 regarding the procedure for dealing with such a contempt).

26M.18 Any electronic communications device surrendered or seized under these provisions should be kept safe by the court until returned to the juror or handed to the police as evidence.

Taking defendant into custody

26M.19 If the defendant is on bail, and the jury irregularity involves a suspicion about the defendant's conduct, the judge should consider taking the defendant into custody. If that suspicion involves an attempt to suborn or intimidate a juror, the defendant should be taken into custody.

STEP 4: Seek to establish basic facts of jury irregularity

B-361   **26M.20** The judge should seek to establish the basic facts of the jury irregularity for the purpose of determining how to proceed in relation to the conduct of the trial. The judge's enquiries may involve having the juror(s) concerned write a note of explanation and / or questioning the juror(s). The judge may enquire whether the juror(s) feel able to continue and remain faithful to their oath or affirmation. If there is questioning, each juror should be questioned separately, in the absence of the rest of the jury, unless there is good reason not to do so.

26M.21 In accordance with paragraphs 26M.10 to 26M.13, the enquiries should be conducted in open court; in the presence of the defendant; and with all parties represented unless there is good reason not to do so.

STEP 5: Further consult with advocates

B-362   **26M.22** The judge should further consult with the advocates and invite submissions about how to proceed in relation to the conduct of the trial and what should be said to the jury (Step 6).

26M.23 In accordance with paragraphs 26M.10 to 26M.13, the consultation should be conducted in open court; in the presence of the defendant; and with all parties represented unless there is good reason not to do so.

STEP 6: Decide what to do in relation to conduct of trial

B-363   **26M.24** When deciding how to proceed, the judge may take time to reflect.

26M.25 Considerations may include the stage the trial has reached. The judge should be alert to attempts by the defendant or others to thwart the trial. In cases of potential bias, the judge should consider whether a fair minded and informed observer would conclude that there was a real possibility that the juror(s) or jury would be biased (*Porter v. Magill* [2002] 2 A.C. 357, HL).

26M.26 In relation to the conduct of the trial, there are three possibilities:

    1. Take no action and continue with the trial

        If so, the judge should consider what, if anything, to say to the jury. For example, the judge may reassure the jury nothing untoward has happened or remind them their verdict is a decision of the whole jury and that they should try to work together. Anything said should be tailored to the circumstances of the case.

2. Discharge the juror(s) concerned and continue with the trial

If so, the judge should consider what to say to the discharged juror(s) and the jurors who remain. All jurors should be warned not to discuss what has happened.

3. Discharge the whole jury

If so, the judge should consider what to say to the jury and they should be warned not to discuss what has happened.

If the judge is satisfied that jury tampering has taken place, depending on the circumstances, the judge may continue the trial without a jury (s.46(3) of the CJA 2003 [§ 4-333 in the main work]) or order a new trial without a jury (s.46(5) of the CJA 2003). Alternatively, the judge may re-list the trial. If there is a real and present danger of jury tampering in the new trial, the prosecution may apply for a trial without a jury (s.44 of the CJA 2003 [§ 4-330 in the main work]).

STEP 7: Consider ancillary matters

26M.27 A jury irregularity may also involve contempt in the face of the court and / or the com-   **B-364**
mission of a criminal offence. The possibilities include the following:

- contempt in the face of the court by a juror;
- an offence by a juror or a non-juror under the Juries Act 1974 (ss.20-20D [§§ 28-41 *et seq.* in the main work]);
- an offence by juror or a non-juror other than under the Juries Act 1974 (examples are given).

Contempt in the face of the court by a juror

26M.28 If a juror commits contempt in the face of the court, the juror's conduct may also constitute an offence. If so, the judge should decide whether to deal with the juror summarily under the procedure for contempt in the face of the court or refer the matter to the Attorney-General's office or the police (see paras 26M.31 and 26M.33).

26M.29 In the case of a minor and clear contempt in the face of the court, the judge may deal with the juror summarily. The judge should follow the procedure in CrimPR 48.5 to 48.8. The judge should also have regard to the practice direction regarding contempt of court issued in March 2015 (Practice Direction: Committal for Contempt of Court – Open Court) [§ 28-129a in the main work], which emphasises the principle of open justice in relation to proceedings for contempt before all courts.

26M.30 If a juror fails to comply with an order for surrender of an electronic communications device (see paras 26M.15 to 26M.18), the judge should deal with the juror summarily following the procedure for contempt in the face of the court.

Offence by a juror or non-juror under the Juries Act 1974

26M.31 If it appears that an offence under the Juries Act 1974 may have been committed by a juror or non-juror (and the matter has not been dealt with summarily under the procedure for contempt in the face of the court), the judge should contact the Attorney-General's office to consider a police investigation, setting out the position neutrally. The officer in the case should not be asked to investigate. Contact details for the Attorney-General's office are set out at the end of this practice direction.

26M.32 If relevant to an investigation, any electronic communications device surrendered or seized pursuant to an order for surrender should be passed to the police as soon as practicable.

Offence by a juror or non-juror other than under the Juries Act 1974

26M.33 If it appears that an offence, other than an offence under the Juries Act 1974, may have been committed by a juror or non-juror (and the matter has not been dealt with summarily under the procedure for contempt in the face of the court), the judge or a member of court staff should contact the police setting out the position neutrally. The officer in the case should not be asked to investigate.

26M.34 If relevant to an investigation, any electronic communications device surrendered or seized pursuant to an order for surrender should be passed to the police as soon as practicable.

OTHER MATTERS TO CONSIDER

- *Jury deliberations*

26M.35 In light of the offence of disclosing, soliciting or obtaining information about a jury's   **B-365**

deliberations (s.20D(1) of the Juries Act 1974 [§ 28-41 in the main work]), great care is required if a jury irregularity relates to the jury's deliberations.

26M.36 During the trial, there are exceptions to this offence that enable the judge (and only the judge) to:

- seek to establish the basic facts of a jury irregularity involving the jury's deliberations (Step 4); and
- disclose information about the jury's deliberations to the Attorney-General's office if it appears that an offence may have been committed (Step 7).

26M.37 With regard to seeking to establish the basic facts of a jury irregularity involving the jury's deliberations (Step 4), it is to be noted that during the trial it is not an offence for the judge to disclose, solicit or obtain information about the jury's deliberations for the purposes of dealing with the case (ss.20E(2)(a) and 20G(1) of the Juries Act 1974 [§§ 28-41e, 28-41g in the main work]).

26M.38 With regard to disclosing information about the jury's deliberations to the Attorney-General's office if it appears that an offence may have been committed (Step 7), it is to be noted that during the trial:

- it is not an offence for the judge to disclose information about the jury's deliberations for the purposes of an investigation by a relevant investigator into whether an offence or contempt of court has been committed by or in relation to a juror (s.20E(2)(b) of the Juries Act 1974); and
- a relevant investigator means a police force or the Attorney-General (s.20E(5) of the Juries Act 1974).

• *Minimum number of jurors*

26M.39 If it is decided to discharge one or more jurors (Step 6), a minimum of nine jurors must remain if the trial is to continue (s.16(1) of the Juries Act 1974 [§ 4-311 in the main work]).

• *Preparation of statement by judge*

26M.40 If a jury irregularity occurs, and the trial continues, the judge should have regard to the remarks of Lord Hope in *R. v. Connors and Mirza* [2004] 1 A.C. 1118, HL (at [127], [128]), and consider whether to prepare a statement that could be used in an application for leave to appeal or an appeal relating to the jury irregularity.

JURY IRREGULARITY AFTER JURY DISCHARGED

B-366

26M.41 A jury irregularity that comes to light after the jury has been discharged may involve the commission of an offence by or in relation to a juror. It may also provide a ground of appeal.

26M.42 A jury irregularity after the jury has been discharged may come to the attention of the:

- trial judge or court
- Registrar of Criminal Appeals (the Registrar)
- prosecution
- defence.

• *Role of the trial judge or court*

B-367

26M.43 The judge has no jurisdiction in relation to a jury irregularity that comes to light after the jury has been discharged (*R. v. Thompson* [2010] 2 Cr.App.R. 27, CA). The jury will be deemed to have been discharged when all verdicts on all defendants have been delivered or when the jury has been discharged from giving all verdicts on all defendants.

26M.44 The judge will be functus officio in relation to a jury irregularity that comes to light during an adjournment between verdict and sentence. The judge should proceed to sentence unless there is good reason not to do so.

26M.45 In practice, a jury irregularity often comes to light when the judge or court receives a communication from a former juror.

26M.46 If a jury irregularity comes to the attention of a judge or court after the jury has been discharged, and regardless of the result of the trial, the judge or a member of court staff should contact the Registrar setting out the position neutrally. Any communication from a former juror should be forwarded to the Registrar.

Contact details for the Registrar are set out at the end of this practice direction.

• *Role of the Registrar*

B-368

26M.47 If a jury irregularity comes to the attention of the Registrar after the jury has been discharged, and regardless of the result of the trial, the Registrar should consider if it appears that an offence may have been committed by or in relation to a juror. The Registrar should also consider if there may be a ground of appeal.

26M.48 When deciding how to proceed, particularly in relation to a communication from a former juror, the Registrar may seek the direction of the Vice-President of the Court of Appeal (Criminal Division) (CACD) or another judge of the CACD in accordance with instructions from the Vice-President.

26M.49 If it appears that an offence may have been committed by or in relation to a juror, the Registrar should contact the private offence of the Director of Public Prosecutions to consider a police investigation.

26M.50 If there may be a ground of appeal, the Registrar should inform the defence.

26M.51 If a communication from a former juror is not of legal significance, the Registrar should respond explaining that no action is required. An example of such a communication is if it is restricted to a general complaint about the verdict from a dissenting juror or an expression of doubt or second thoughts.

• *Role of the prosecution*
26M.52 If a jury irregularity comes to the attention of the prosecution after the jury has been discharged, which may provide a ground of appeal, they should notify the defence in accordance with their duties to act fairly and assist in the administration of justice (*R. v. Makin* [2004] EWCA Crim. 1607, (2004) 148 S.J. 821). **B-369**

• *Role of the defence*
26M.53 If a jury irregularity comes to the attention of the defence after the jury has been discharged, which provides an arguable ground of appeal, an application for leave to appeal may be made. **B-370**

• *Jury deliberations*
26M.54 In light of the offence of disclosing, soliciting or obtaining information about a jury's deliberations (s.20D(1) of the Juries Act 1974 [§ 28-41d in the main work]), great care is required if a jury irregularity relates to the jury's deliberations. **B-371**

26M.55 After the jury has been discharged, there are exceptions to this offence that enable a judge, a member of court staff, the Registrar, the prosecution and the defence to disclose information about the jury's deliberations if it appears that an offence may have been committed by or in relation to a juror or if there may be a ground of appeal.

26M.56 For example, it is to be noted that:

– after the jury has been discharged, it is not an offence for a person to disclose information about the jury's deliberations to defined persons if the person reasonably believes that an offence or contempt of court may have been committed by or in relation to a juror or the conduct of a juror may provide grounds of appeal (s.20F(1), (2) of the Juries Act 1974 [§ 28-41f in the main work]);

– the defined persons to whom such information may be disclosed are a member of a police force, a judge of the CACD, the Registrar, a judge where the trial took place or a member of court staff where the trial took place who would reasonably be expected to disclose the information only to one of the aforementioned defined persons (s.20F(2) of the Juries Act 1974);

– after the jury has been discharged, it is not an offence for a judge of the CACD or the Registrar to disclose information about the jury's deliberations for the purposes of an investigation by a relevant investigator into whether an offence or contempt of court has been committed by or in relation to a juror or the conduct of a juror may provide grounds of appeal (s.20F(4) of the Juries Act 1974);

– a relevant investigator means a police force, the Attorney-General, the Criminal Cases Review Commission (CCRC) or the CPS (s.20F(10) of the Juries Act 1974).

• *Investigation by the Criminal Cases Review Commission (CCRC)*
26M.57 If an application for leave to appeal, or an appeal, includes a ground of appeal relating to a jury irregularity, the Registrar may refer the case to the full court to decide whether to direct the CCRC to conduct an investigation under section 23A of the CAA 1968. **B-372**

26M.58 If the court directs the CCRC to conduct an investigation, directions should be given as to the scope of the investigation.

CONTACT DETAILS

Attorney General's Office **B-373**

Contempt.SharedMailbox@attorneygeneral.gsi.gov.uk

Telephone: 020 7271 2492

The Registrar

penny.donnelly@hmcts.x.gsi.gov.uk (Secretary) or

criminalappealoffice.generaloffice@hmcts.gsi.gov.uk

Telephone: 020 7947 6103 (Secretary) or 020 7947 6011

CPD VI Trial 26N: Open Justice

B-374

26N.1 There must be freedom of access between advocate and judge. Any discussion must, however, be between the judge and the advocates on both sides. If an advocate is instructed by a solicitor who is in court, he or she, too, should be allowed to attend the discussion. This freedom of access is important because there may be matters calling for communication or discussion of such a nature that the advocate cannot, in the client's interest, mention them in open court, *e.g.* the advocate, by way of mitigation, may wish to tell the judge that reliable medical evidence shows that the defendant is suffering from a terminal illness and may not have long to live. It is imperative that, so far as possible, justice must be administered in open court. Advocates should, therefore, only ask to see the judge when it is felt to be really necessary. The judge must be careful only to treat such communications as private where, in the interests of justice, this is necessary. Where any such discussion takes place it should be recorded, preferably by audio recording.

CPD VI Trial 26P: Defendant's Right to Give or not to Give Evidence

B-375

26P.1 At the conclusion of the evidence for the prosecution, section 35(2) of the CJPOA 1994 [§ 4-377 in the main work] requires the court to satisfy itself that the defendant is aware that the stage has been reached at which evidence can be given for the defence and that the defendant's failure to give evidence, or if he does so his failure to answer questions, without a good reason, may lead to inferences being drawn against him.

If the accused is legally represented

26P.2 After the close of the prosecution case, if the defendant's representative requests a brief adjournment to advise his client on this issue the request should, ordinarily, be granted. When appropriate the judge should, in the presence of the jury, inquire of the representative in these terms:

"Have you advised your client that the stage has now been reached at which he may give evidence and, if he chooses not to do so or, having been sworn, without good cause refuses to answer any question, the jury may draw such inferences as appear proper from his failure to do so?"

26P.3 If the representative replies to the judge that the defendant has been so advised, then the case shall proceed. If counsel replies that the defendant has not been so advised, then the judge shall direct the representative to advise his client of the consequences and should adjourn briefly for this purpose, before proceeding further.

If the defendant is not legally represented

26P.4 If the defendant is not represented, the judge shall, at the conclusion of the evidence for the prosecution, in the absence of the jury, indicate what he will say to him in the presence of the jury and ask if he understands and whether he would like a brief adjournment to consider his position.

26P.5 When appropriate, and in the presence of the jury, the judge should say to the defendant:

"You have heard the evidence against you. Now is the time for you to make your defence. You may give evidence on oath, and be cross-examined like any other witness. If you do not give evidence or, having been sworn, without good cause refuse to answer any question the jury may draw such inferences as appear proper. That means they may hold it against you. You may also call any witness or witnesses whom you have arranged to attend court or lead any agreed evidence. Afterwards you may also, if you wish, address the jury. But you cannot at that stage give evidence. Do you now intend to give evidence?"

CPD VI Trial 26Q: Majority Verdicts

B-376

26Q.1 It is very important that all those trying indictable offences should, so far as possible, adopt a uniform practice when complying with section 17 of the Juries Act 1974 [§ 4-509 in the main work], both in directing the jury in summing-up and also in receiving the verdict or giving further directions after retirement. So far as the summing-up is concerned, it is inadvisable for the judge, and indeed for advocates, to attempt an explanation of the section for fear that the jury will be confused. Before the jury retires, however, the judge should direct the jury in some such words as the following:

"As you may know, the law permits me, in certain circumstances, to accept a verdict which is not the verdict of you all. Those circumstances have not as yet arisen, so that when you retire I must ask you to reach a verdict upon which each one of you is agreed. Should, however, the time come when it is possible for me to accept a majority verdict, I will give you a further direction."

26Q.2 Thereafter the practice should be as follows. Should the jury return before two hours and ten minutes since the last member of the jury left the jury box to go to the jury room (or such longer time as the judge thinks reasonable) has elapsed (see s.17(4)), they should be asked: (a) "Have you reached a verdict upon which you are all agreed? Please answer Yes or No"; (b) (i) if unanimous, "What is your verdict?"; (ii) if not unanimous, the jury should be sent out again for further deliberation with a further direction to arrive if possible at a unanimous verdict.

26Q.3 Should the jury return (whether for the first time or subsequently) or be sent for after the two hours and ten minutes (or the longer period) has elapsed, questions (a) and (b)(i) in the paragraph above should be put to them and, if it appears that they are not unanimous, they should be asked to retire once more and told that they should continue to endeavour to reach a unanimous verdict but that, if they cannot, the judge will accept a majority verdict as in section 17(1).

26Q.4 When the jury finally return, they should be asked: (a) "Have at least ten (or nine as the case may be) of you agreed upon your verdict?"; (b) if "Yes", "What is your verdict? Please answer only Guilty or Not Guilty"; (c) (i) if "Not Guilty", accept the verdict without more ado; (ii) if "Guilty", "Is that the verdict of you all or by a majority?"; (d) if "Guilty" by a majority, "How many of you agreed to the verdict and how many dissented?"

26Q.5 At whatever stage the jury return, before question (a) is asked, the senior officer of the court present shall state in open court, for each period when the jury was out of court for the purpose of considering their verdict(s), the time at which the last member of the jury left the jury box to go to the jury room and the time of their return to the jury box; and will additionally state in open court the total of such periods.

26Q.6 The reason why section 17(3) is confined to a majority verdict of guilty, and for the somewhat complicated procedure set out above, is to prevent it being known that a verdict of "Not Guilty" is a majority verdict. If the final direction continues to require the jury to arrive, if possible, at a unanimous verdict and the verdict is received as specified, it will not be known for certain that the acquittal is not unanimous.

26Q.7 Where there are several counts (or alternative verdicts) left to the jury the above practice will, of course, need to be adapted to the circumstances. The procedure will have to be repeated in respect of each count (or alternative verdict), the verdict being accepted in those cases where the jury are unanimous and the further direction being given in cases in which they are not unanimous.

26Q.8 Should the jury in the end be unable to agree on a verdict by the required majority, the judge in his discretion will either ask them to deliberate further, or discharge them.

26Q.9 Section 17 will, of course, apply also to verdicts other than "Guilty" or "Not Guilty", *e.g.* to special verdicts under the Criminal Procedure (Insanity) Act 1964[§§ 4-231 *et seq.* in the main work], following a finding by the judge that the defendant is unfit to be tried, and special verdicts on findings of fact. Accordingly in such cases the questions to jurors will have to be suitably adjusted.

Criminal Procedure Rules 2015 (S.I. 2015 No. 1490), Pt 27

RETRIAL AFTER ACQUITTAL

General

When this Part applies
27.1.–(1) Rule 27.2 applies where, under section 54 of the Criminal Procedure and Investigations **B-377** Act 1996 [§ 4-196 in the main work], the Crown Court or a magistrates' court can certify for the High Court that interference or intimidation has been involved in proceedings leading to an acquittal.

(2) Rules 27.3 to 27.7 apply where, under section 77 of the Criminal Justice Act 2003 [*ibid.*, § 7-280], the Court of Appeal can–
    (a) quash an acquittal for a serious offence and order a defendant to be retried; or
    (b) order that an acquittal outside the United Kingdom is no bar to the defendant being tried in England and Wales,
if there is new and compelling evidence and it is in the interests of justice to make the order.

Application for certificate to allow order for retrial

Application for certificate
27.2.–(1) This rule applies where– **B-378**
    (a) a defendant has been acquitted of an offence;

    (b) a person has been convicted of one of the following offences involving interference with or intimidation of a juror or a witness (or potential witness) in any proceedings which led to the defendant's acquittal—

        (i) perverting the course of justice,

       (ii) intimidation etc. of witnesses, jurors and others under section 51(1) of the Criminal Justice and Public Order Act 1994 [*ibid.*, § 28-132], or

      (iii) aiding, abetting, counselling, procuring, suborning or inciting another person to commit an offence under section 1 of the Perjury Act 1911 [*ibid.*, § 28-138]; and

    (c) the prosecutor wants the court by which that person was convicted to certify for the High Court that there is a real possibility that, but for the interference or intimidation, the defendant would not have been acquitted.

(2) The prosecutor must—

    (a) apply in writing as soon as practicable after that person's conviction; and

    (b) serve the application on—

        (i) the court officer, and

       (ii) the defendant who was acquitted, if the court so directs.

(3) The application must—

    (a) give details, with relevant facts and dates, of—

        (i) the conviction for interference or intimidation, and

       (ii) the defendant's acquittal; and

    (b) explain—

        (i) why there is a real possibility that, but for the interference or intimidation, the defendant would not have been acquitted, and

       (ii) why it would not be contrary to the interests of justice to prosecute the defendant again for the offence of which he or she was acquitted, despite any lapse of time or other reason.

(4) The court may—

    (a) extend the time limit under paragraph (2);

    (b) allow an application to be in a different form to one set out in the Practice Direction, or to be made orally;

    (c) determine an application under this rule—

        (i) at a hearing, in private or in public; or

       (ii) without a hearing.

(5) If the court gives a certificate, the court officer must serve it on—

    (a) the prosecutor; and

    (b) the defendant who was acquitted.

Application to Court of Appeal to quash acquittal and order retrial

Application for reporting restriction pending application for order for retrial

B-379   27.3.—(1) This rule applies where—

    (a) no application has been made under rule 27.4 (application for order for retrial);

    (b) an investigation by officers has begun into an offence with a view to an application under that rule; and

    (c) the Director of Public Prosecutions wants the Court of Appeal to make, vary or remove an order for a reporting restriction under section 82 of the Criminal Justice Act 2003 (restrictions on publication in the interests of justice) *ibid.*, § 7-287.

(2) The Director must—

    (a) apply in writing;

    (b) serve the application on—

        (i) the Registrar, and

       (ii) the defendant, unless the court otherwise directs.

(3) The application must, as appropriate—

    (a) explain why the Director wants the court to direct that it need not be served on the defendant until the application under rule 27.4 is served;

    (b) specify the proposed terms of the order, and for how long it should last;

    (c) explain why an order in the terms proposed is necessary;

    (d) explain why an order should be varied or removed.

Application for order for retrial

B-380

27.4.—(1) This rule applies where—

    (a) a defendant has been acquitted—

        (i) in the Crown Court, or on appeal from the Crown Court, of an offence listed in Part 1 of Schedule 5 to the Criminal Justice Act 2003 (qualifying offences), [*ibid.*, § 7-278]

        (ii) in proceedings elsewhere than in the United Kingdom of an offence under the law of that place, if what was alleged would have amounted to or included one of those listed offences;

    (b) with the Director of Public Prosecutions' written consent, a prosecutor wants the Court of Appeal to make an order, as the case may be—

        (i) quashing the acquittal in the Crown Court and ordering the defendant to be retried for the offence, or

        (ii) declaring whether the acquittal outside the United Kingdom is a bar to the defendant's trial in England and Wales and, if it is, whether that acquittal shall not be such a bar.

(2) Such a prosecutor must—

    (a) apply in writing;

    (b) serve the application on the Registrar;

    (c) not more than 2 business days later serve on the defendant who was acquitted—

        (i) the application, and

        (ii) a notice charging the defendant with the offence, unless the defendant has already been arrested and charged under section 87 of the Criminal Justice Act 2003 (arrest, under warrant or otherwise, and charge [*ibid.*, §§ 3-174, 7-292]).

(3) The application must—

    (a) give details, with relevant facts and dates, of the defendant's acquittal;

    (b) explain—

        (i) what new and compelling evidence there is against the defendant, and

        (ii) why in all the circumstances it would be in the interests of justice for the court to make the order sought;

    (c) include or attach any application for the following, with reasons—

        (i) an order under section 80(6) of the Criminal Justice Act 2003 (procedure and evidence) [*ibid.*, § 7-285] for the production of any document, exhibit or other thing which in the prosecutor's opinion is necessary for the determination of the application,

        (ii) an order under that section for the attendance before the court of any witness who would be a compellable witness at the trial the prosecutor wants the court to order,

        (iii) an order for a reporting restriction under section 82 of the Criminal Justice Act 2003 (restrictions on publication in the interests of justice) [*ibid.*, § 7-287]; and

    (d) attach—

        (i) written witness statements of the evidence on which the prosecutor relies as new and compelling evidence against the defendant,

        (ii) relevant documents from the trial at which the defendant was acquitted, including a record of the offence or offences charged and of the evidence given, and

        (iii) any other document or thing that the prosecutor thinks the court will need to decide the application.

Respondent's notice

27.5.—(1) A defendant on whom a prosecutor serves an application may serve a respondent's **B-381** notice, and must do so if the defendant wants to make representations to the court.

(2) Such a defendant must serve the respondent's notice on—

    (a) the Registrar; and

    (b) the prosecutor,

not more than 28 days after service of the application.

(3) The respondent's notice must—

    (a) give the date on which the respondent was served with the prosecutor's application;

    (b) summarise any relevant facts not contained in that application;

    (c) explain the defendant's grounds for opposing that application;

    (d) include or attach any application for the following, with reasons—

        (i) an extension of time within which to serve the respondent's notice,

        (ii) bail pending the hearing of the prosecutor's application, if the defendant is in custody,

(iii) a direction to attend in person any hearing that the defendant could attend by live link, if the defendant is in custody,

(iv) an order under section 80(6) of the Criminal Justice Act 2003 (procedure and evidence) for the production of any document, exhibit or other thing which in the defendant's opinion is necessary for the determination of the prosecutor's application,

(v) an order under that section for the attendance before the court of any witness who would be a compellable witness at the trial the prosecutor wants the court to order; and

(e) attach or identify any other document or thing that the defendant thinks the court will need to decide the application.

Application to Crown Court for summons or warrant

B-382   **27.6.**–(1) This rule applies where—

(a) the prosecutor has served on the Registrar an application under rule 27.4 (application for order for retrial);

(b) the defendant is not in custody as a result of arrest under section 88 of the Criminal Justice Act 2003 (bail and custody before application [*ibid.*, § 3-175]); and

(c) the prosecutor wants the Crown Court to issue—

(i) a summons requiring the defendant to appear before the Court of Appeal at the hearing of the prosecutor's application, or

(ii) a warrant for the defendant's arrest

under section 89 of the 2003 Act (bail and custody before hearing [*ibid.*, § 7-294]).

(2) The prosecutor must—

(a) apply in writing; and

(b) serve the application on the Crown Court officer.

(3) The application must—

(a) explain what the case is about, including a brief description of the defendant's acquittal, the new evidence and the stage that the application to the Court of Appeal has reached;

(b) specify—

(i) the decision that the prosecutor wants the Crown Court to make,

(ii) each offence charged, and

(iii) any relevant previous bail decision and the reasons given for it;

(c) propose the terms of any suggested condition of bail.

Application of other rules about procedure in the Court of Appeal

B-383   **27.7.** On an application under rule 27.4 (application for order for retrial)—

(a) the rules in Part 36 (appeal to the Court of Appeal: general rules) apply with the necessary modifications;

(b) rules 39.8, 39.9 and 39.10 (bail and bail conditions in the Court of Appeal) apply as if the references in those rules to appeal included references to an application under rule 27.4; and

(c) rule 39.14 (renewal or setting aside of order for retrial) applies as if the reference to section 7 of the Criminal Appeal Act 1968 [*ibid.*, § 7-111] were a reference to section 84 of the Criminal Justice Act 2003 (retrial [[*ibid.*, § 7-289]]).

Criminal Procedure Rules 2015 (S.I. 2015 No. 1490), Pt 28

SENTENCING PROCEDURES IN SPECIAL CASES

Reasons for not following usual sentencing requirements

B-384   **28.1.**–(1) This rule applies where the court decides—

(a) not to follow a relevant sentencing guideline;

(b) not to make, where it could—

(i) a reparation order (unless it passes a custodial or community sentence),

(ii) a compensation order,

(iii) a slavery and trafficking reparation order, or

(iv) a travel restriction order;

(c) not to order, where it could—

(i) that a suspended sentence of imprisonment is to take effect,

    (ii)   the endorsement of the defendant's driving record, or

    (iii) the defendant's disqualification from driving, for the usual minimum period or at all;

  (d) to pass a lesser sentence than it otherwise would have passed because the defendant has assisted, or has agreed to assist, an investigator or prosecutor in relation to an offence.

(2) The court must explain why it has so decided, when it explains the sentence that it has passed.

(3) Where paragraph (1)(d) applies, the court must arrange for such an explanation to be given to the defendant and to the prosecutor in writing, if the court thinks that it would not be in the public interest to explain in public.

Notice of requirements of suspended sentence and community, etc. orders

28.2.–(1) This rule applies where the court–   **B-385**

  (a) makes a suspended sentence order;

  (b) imposes a requirement under–

    (i)   a community order,

    (ii)   a youth rehabilitation order, or

    (iii) a suspended sentence order; or

  (c) orders the defendant to attend meetings with a supervisor.

(2) The court officer must notify–

  (a) the defendant of–

    (i)   the length of the sentence suspended by a suspended sentence order, and

    (ii)   the period of the suspension;

  (b) the defendant and, where the defendant is under 14, an appropriate adult, of–

    (i)   any requirement or requirements imposed, and

    (ii)   the identity of any responsible officer or supervisor, and the means by which that person may be contacted;

  (c) any responsible officer or supervisor, and, where the defendant is under 14, the appropriate qualifying officer (if that is not the responsible officer), of–

    (i)   the defendant's name, address and telephone number (if available),

    (ii)   the offence or offences of which the defendant was convicted, and

    (iii) the requirement or requirements imposed; and

  (d) the person affected, where the court imposes a requirement–

    (i)   for the protection of that person from the defendant, or

    (ii)   requiring the defendant to reside with that person.

(3) If the court imposes an electronic monitoring requirement, the monitor of which is not the responsible officer, the court officer must–

  (a) notify the defendant and, where the defendant is under 16, an appropriate adult, of the monitor's name, and the means by which the monitor may be contacted; and

  (b) notify the monitor of–

    (i)   the defendant's name, address and telephone number (if available),

    (ii)   the offence or offences of which the defendant was convicted,

    (iii) the place or places at which the defendant's presence must be monitored,

    (iv) the period or periods during which the defendant's presence there must be monitored, and

    (v)   the identity of the responsible officer, and the means by which that officer may be contacted.

Notification requirements

28.3.–(1) This rule applies where, on a conviction, sentence or order, legislation requires the   **B-386** defendant–

  (a) to notify information to the police; or

  (b) to be included in a barred list.

(2) The court must tell the defendant that such requirements apply, and under what legislation.

Variation of sentence

28.4.–(1) This rule–   **B-387**

  (a) applies where a magistrates' court or the Crown Court can vary or rescind a sentence or order, other than an order to which rule 24.18 applies (setting aside a conviction or varying a costs etc. order); and

  (b) authorises the Crown Court, in addition to its other powers, to do so within the period of 56 days beginning with another defendant's acquittal or sentencing where–

     (i)   defendants are tried separately in the Crown Court on the same or related facts alleged in one or more indictments, and

     (ii) one is sentenced before another is acquitted or sentenced.

(2) The court may exercise its power—

   (a) on application by a party, or on its own initiative; or

   (b) at a hearing, in public or in private, or without a hearing.

(3) A party who wants the court to exercise that power must—

   (a) apply in writing as soon as reasonably practicable after—

     (i)   the sentence or order that that party wants the court to vary or rescind, or

     (ii) where paragraph (1)(b) applies, the other defendant's acquittal or sentencing;

   (b) serve the application on—

     (i)   the court officer, and

     (ii) each other party; and

   (c) in the application—

     (i)   explain why the sentence should be varied or rescinded,

     (ii) specify the variation that the applicant proposes, and

     (iii) if the application is late, explain why.

(4) The court must not exercise its power in the defendant's absence unless—

   (a) the court makes a variation—

     (i)   which is proposed by the defendant, or

     (ii) the effect of which is that the defendant is no more severely dealt with under the sentence as varied than before; or

   (b) the defendant has had an opportunity to make representations at a hearing (whether or not the defendant in fact attends).

(5) The court may—

   (a) extend (even after it has expired) the time limit under paragraph (3), unless the court's power to vary or rescind the sentence cannot be exercised; and

   (b) allow an application to be made orally.

Application to vary or discharge a compensation, etc. order

B-388   28.5.—(1) This rule applies where on application by the defendant a magistrates' court can vary or discharge—

   (a) a compensation order; or

   (b) a slavery and trafficking reparation order.

(2) A defendant who wants the court to exercise that power must—

   (a) apply in writing as soon as practicable after becoming aware of the grounds for doing so;

   (b) serve the application on the magistrates' court officer;

   (c) where the order was made in the Crown Court, serve a copy of the application on the Crown Court officer; and

   (d) in the application, specify the order that the defendant wants the court to vary or discharge and explain (as applicable)—

     (i)   what civil court finding shows that the injury, loss or damage was less than it had appeared to be when the order was made,

     (ii) in what circumstances the person for whose benefit the order was made has recovered the property for the loss of which it was made,

     (iii) why a confiscation order, unlawful profit order or slavery and trafficking reparation order makes the defendant now unable to pay compensation or reparation in full, or

     (iv) in what circumstances the defendant's means have been reduced substantially and unexpectedly, and why they seem unlikely to increase for a considerable period.

(3) The court officer must serve a copy of the application on the person for whose benefit the order was made.

(4) The court must not vary or discharge the order unless—

   (a) the defendant, and the person for whose benefit it was made, each has had an opportunity to make representations at a hearing (whether or not either in fact attends); and

   (b) where the order was made in the Crown Court, the Crown Court has notified its consent.

Application to remove, revoke or suspend a disqualification or restriction

B-389   28.6.—(1) This rule applies where, on application by the defendant, the court can remove, revoke or suspend a disqualification or restriction included in a sentence (except a disqualification from driving).

(2) A defendant who wants the court to exercise such a power must –

    (a) apply in writing, no earlier than the date on which the court can exercise the power;

    (b) serve the application on the court officer; and

    (c) in the application–

        (i) specify the disqualification or restriction, and

        (ii) explain why the defendant wants the court to remove, revoke or suspend it.

(3) The court officer must serve a copy of the application on the chief officer of police for the local justice area.

Application for a restitution order by the victim of a theft

28.7.–(1) This rule applies where, on application by the victim of a theft, the court can order a **B-390** defendant to give that person goods obtained with the proceeds of goods stolen in that theft.

(2) A person who wants the court to exercise that power if the defendant is convicted must–

    (a) apply in writing as soon as practicable (without waiting for the verdict);

    (b) serve the application on the court officer; and

    (c) in the application–

        (i) identify the goods, and

        (ii) explain why the applicant is entitled to them.

(3) The court officer must serve a copy of the application on each party.

(4) The court must not determine the application unless the applicant and each party has had an opportunity to make representations at a hearing (whether or not each in fact attends).

(5) The court may–

    (a) extend (even after it has expired) the time limit under paragraph (2); and

    (b) allow an application to be made orally.

Requests for medical reports, etc.

28.8.–(1) This rule applies where the court– **B-391**

    (a) requests a medical examination of the defendant and a report; or

    (b) requires information about the arrangements that could be made for the defendant where the court is considering–

        (i) a hospital order, or

        (ii) a guardianship order.

(2) Unless the court otherwise directs, the court officer must, as soon as practicable, serve on each person from whom a report or information is sought a note that–

    (a) specifies the power exercised by the court;

    (b) explains why the court seeks a report or information from that person; and

    (c) sets out or summarises any relevant information available to the court.

Information to be supplied on admission to hospital or guardianship

28.9.–(1) This rule applies where the court– **B-392**

    (a) orders the defendant's detention and treatment in hospital; or

    (b) makes a guardianship order.

(2) Unless the court otherwise directs, the court officer must, as soon as practicable, serve on (as applicable) the hospital or the guardian–

    (a) a record of the court's order;

    (b) such information as the court has received that appears likely to assist in treating or otherwise dealing with the defendant, including information about–

        (i) the defendant's mental condition,

        (ii) the defendant's other circumstances, and

        (iii) the circumstances of the offence.

Information to be supplied on committal for sentence, etc.

28.10.–(1) This rule applies where a magistrates' court or the Crown Court convicts the defendant **B-393** and–

    (a) commits or adjourns the case to another court–

        (i) for sentence, or

        (ii) for the defendant to be dealt with for breach of a deferred sentence, a conditional discharge, or a suspended sentence of imprisonment, imposed by that other court;

    (b) deals with a deferred sentence, a conditional discharge, or a suspended sentence of imprisonment, imposed by another court; or

    (c) makes an order that another court is, or may be, required to enforce.

  (2) Unless the convicting court otherwise directs, the court officer must, as soon as practicable—

    (a) where paragraph (1)(a) applies, arrange the transmission from the convicting to the other court of a record of any relevant—

      (i) certificate of conviction,

      (ii) magistrates' court register entry,

      (iii) decision about bail, for the purposes of section 5 of the Bail Act 1976 [§ 3-28 in the main work],

      (iv) note of evidence,

      (v) statement or other document introduced in evidence,

      (vi) medical or other report,

      (vii) representation order or application for such order, and

      (viii) interim driving disqualification;

    (b) where paragraph (1)(b) or (c) applies, arrange—

      (i) the transmission from the convicting to the other court of notice of the convicting court's order, and

      (ii) the recording of that order at the other court;

    (c) in every case, notify the defendant and, where the defendant is under 14, an appropriate adult, of the location of the other court.

Application to review sentence because of assistance given or withheld

B-394   **28.11.**—(1) This rule applies where the Crown Court can reduce or increase a sentence on application by a prosecutor in a case in which—

    (a) since being sentenced, the defendant has assisted, or has agreed to assist, an investigator or prosecutor in relation to an offence; or

    (b) since receiving a reduced sentence for agreeing to give such assistance, the defendant has failed to do so.

  (2) A prosecutor who wants the court to exercise that power must—

    (a) apply in writing as soon as practicable after becoming aware of the grounds for doing so;

    (b) serve the application on—

      (i) the court officer, and

      (ii) the defendant; and

    (c) in the application—

      (i) explain why the sentence should be reduced, or increased, as appropriate, and

      (ii) identify any other matter relevant to the court's decision, including any sentencing guideline or guideline case.

  (3) The general rule is that the application must be determined by the judge who passed the sentence, unless that judge is unavailable.

  (4) The court must not determine the application in the defendant's absence unless the defendant has had an opportunity to make representations at a hearing (whether or not the defendant in fact attends).

Criminal Procedure Rules 2015 (S.I. 2015 No. 1490), Pt 29

Road Traffic Penalties

Representations about obligatory disqualification or endorsement

B-395   **29.1.**—(1) This rule applies—

    (a) where the court—

      (i) convicts the defendant of an offence involving obligatory disqualification from driving and section 34(1) of the Road Traffic Offenders Act 1988 (disqualification for certain offences [§ 32-249 in the main work]) applies,

      (ii) convicts the defendant of an offence where section 35 of the 1988 Act (disqualification for repeated offences [*ibid.*, § 32-264]) applies, or

      (iii) convicts the defendant of an offence involving obligatory endorsement of the defendant's driving record and section 44 of the 1988 Act (orders for endorsement [*ibid.*, § 32-292]) applies;

    (b) unless the defendant is absent.

    (a) where paragraph (1)(a)(i) applies (obligatory disqualification under section 34)—

(i) that the court must order the defendant to be disqualified from driving for a minimum of 12 months (or 2 or 3 years, as the case may be, according to the offence and the defendant's driving record), unless the court decides that there are special reasons to order disqualification for a shorter period, or not to order disqualification at all, and

(ii) if applicable, that the period of disqualification will be reduced by at least 3 months if, by no later than 2 months before the end of the reduced period, the defendant completes an approved driving course;

(2) The court must explain, in terms the defendant can understand (with help, if necessary)—

(b) where paragraph (1)(a)(ii) applies (disqualification under section 35)—

(i) that the court must order the defendant to be disqualified from driving for a minimum of 6 months (or 1 or 2 years, as the case may be, according to the defendant's driving record), unless, having regard to all the circumstances, the court decides to order disqualification for a shorter period, or not to order disqualification at all, and

(ii) that circumstances of which the court cannot take account in making its decision are any that make the offence not a serious one; hardship (other than exceptional hardship); and any that during the last 3 years already have been taken into account by a court when ordering disqualification for less than the usual minimum period, or not at all, for repeated driving offences;

(c) where paragraph (1)(a)(iii) applies (obligatory endorsement), that the court must order the endorsement of the defendant's driving record unless the court decides that there are special reasons not to do so;

(d) in every case, as applicable—

(i) that the court already has received representations from the defendant about whether any such special reasons or mitigating circumstances apply and will take account of them, or

(ii) that the defendant may make such representations now, on oath or affirmation.

(3) Unless the court already has received such representations from the defendant, before it applies rule 24.11 (magistrates' court procedure if the court convicts) or rule 25.16 (Crown Court procedure if the court convicts), as the case may be, the court must—

(a) ask whether the defendant wants to make any such representations; and

(b) if the answer to that question is "yes", require the defendant to take an oath or affirm and make them.

Application to remove a disqualification from driving
29.2.–(1) This rule applies where, on application by the defendant, the court can remove a disqualification from driving. **B-396**

(2) A defendant who wants the court to exercise that power must—

(a) apply in writing, no earlier than the date on which the court can exercise the power;

(b) serve the application on the court officer; and

(c) in the application—

(i) specify the disqualification that the defendant wants the court to remove, and

(ii) explain why.

(3) The court officer must serve a copy of the application on the chief officer of police for the local justice area.

Information to be supplied on order for endorsement of driving record, etc.
29.3.–(1) This rule applies where the court— **B-397**

(a) convicts the defendant of an offence involving obligatory endorsement, and orders there to be endorsed on the defendant's driving record (and on any counterpart licence, if other legislation requires)—

(i) particulars of the conviction,

(ii) particulars of any disqualification from driving that the court imposes, and

(iii) the penalty points to be attributed to the offence;

(b) disqualifies the defendant from driving for any other offence; or

(c) suspends or removes a disqualification from driving.

(2) The court officer must, as soon as practicable, serve on the Secretary of State notice that includes details of—

(a) where paragraph (1)(a) applies—

     (i)   the local justice area in which the court is acting,

     (ii)   the dates of conviction and sentence,

     (iii)   the offence, and the date on which it was committed,

     (iv)   the sentence, and

     (v)   the date of birth, and sex, of the defendant, where those details are available;

  (b) where paragraph (1)(b) applies—

     (i)   the date and period of the disqualification,

     (ii)   the power exercised by the court;

  (c) where paragraph (1)(c) applies—

     (i)   the date and period of the disqualification,

     (ii)   the date and terms of the order for its suspension or removal,

     (iii)   the power exercised by the court, and

     (iv)   where the court suspends the disqualification pending appeal, the court to which the defendant has appealed.

Statutory declaration to avoid fine after fixed penalty notice

B-398   **29.4.**–(1) This rule applies where—

  (a) a chief officer of police, or the Secretary of State, serves on the magistrates' court officer a certificate registering, for enforcement as a fine, a sum payable by a defendant after failure to comply with a fixed penalty notice;

  (b) the court officer notifies the defendant of the registration; and

  (c) the defendant makes a statutory declaration with the effect that there become void—

     (i)   the fixed penalty notice, or any associated notice sent to the defendant as owner of the vehicle concerned, and

     (ii)   the registration and any enforcement proceedings.

  (2) The defendant must serve that statutory declaration not more than 21 days after service of notice of the registration, unless the court extends that time limit.

  (3) The court officer must—

  (a) serve a copy of the statutory declaration on the person by whom the certificate was registered;

  (b) cancel any endorsement on the defendant's driving record (and on any counterpart licence, if other legislation requires); and

  (c) notify the Secretary of State of any such cancellation.

Application for declaration about a course or programme certificate decision

B-399   **29.5.**–(1) This rule applies where the court can declare unjustified—

  (a) a course provider's failure or refusal to give a certificate of the defendant's satisfactory completion of an approved course; or

  (b) a programme provider's giving of a certificate of the defendant's failure fully to participate in an approved programme.

  (2) A defendant who wants the court to exercise that power must—

  (a) apply in writing, not more than 28 days after—

     (i)   the date by which the defendant was required to complete the course, or

     (ii)   the giving of the certificate of failure fully to participate in the programme;

  (b) serve the application on the court officer; and

  (c) in the application, specify the course or programme and explain (as applicable)—

     (i)   that the course provider has failed to give a certificate,

     (ii)   where the course provider has refused to give a certificate, why the defendant disagrees with the reasons for that decision, or

     (iii)   where the programme provider has given a certificate, why the defendant disagrees with the reasons for that decision.

  (3) The court officer must serve a copy of the application on the course or programme provider.

  (4) The court must not determine the application unless the defendant, and the course or programme provider, each has had an opportunity to make representations at a hearing (whether or not either in fact attends).

Appeal against recognition of foreign driving disqualification

B-400   **29.6.**–(1) This rule applies where—

  (a) a Minister gives a disqualification notice under section 57 of the Crime (International Co operation) Act 2003; and

(b)   the person to whom it is given wants to appeal under section 59 of the Act to a magistrates' court.

(2) That person ("the appellant") must serve an appeal notice on –

(a)   the court officer, at a magistrates' court in the local justice area in which the appellant lives; and

(b)   the Minister, at the address given in the disqualification notice.

(3) The appellant must serve the appeal notice within the period for which section 59 of the 2003 Act provides.

(4) The appeal notice must—

(a)   attach a copy of the disqualification notice;

(b)   explain which of the conditions in section 56 of the 2003 Act is not met, and why section 57 of the Act therefore does not apply; and

(c)   include any application to suspend the disqualification, under section 60 of the Act.

(5) The Minister may serve a respondent's notice, and must do so if—

(a)   the Minister wants to make representations to the court; or

(b)   the court so directs.

(6) The Minister must—

(a)   unless the court otherwise directs, serve any such respondent's notice not more than 14 days after—

(i)   the appellant serves the appeal notice, or

(ii)   a direction to do so;

(b)   in any such respondent's notice—

(i)   identify the grounds of opposition on which the Minister relies,

(ii)   summarise any relevant facts not already included in the disqualification and appeal notices, and

(iii)   identify any other document that the Minister thinks the court will need to decide the appeal (and serve any such document with the notice).

(7) Where the court determines an appeal, the general rule is that it must do so at a hearing (which must be in public, unless the court otherwise directs).

(8) The court officer must serve on the Minister—

(a)   notice of the outcome of the appeal;

(b)   notice of any suspension of the disqualification; and

(c)   the appellant's driving licence, if surrendered to the court officer.

Criminal Procedure Rules 2015 (S.I. 2015 No. 1490), Pt 30

ENFORCEMENT OF FINES AND OTHER ORDERS FOR PAYMENT

[*Not set out in this work*]. **B-401**

Criminal Procedure Rules 2015 (S.I. 2015 No. 1490), Pt 31

BEHAVIOUR ORDERS

When this part applies

31.1.–(1) This part applies where— **B-402**

(a)   a magistrates' court or the Crown Court can make, vary or revoke a civil order—

(i)   as well as, or instead of, passing a sentence, or in any other circumstances in which other legislation allows the court to make such an order, and

(ii)   that requires someone to do, or not do, something;

(b)   a magistrates' court or the Crown Court can make a European protection order;

(c)   a magistrates' court can give effect to a European protection order made in another European Union member State.

(2) A reference to a "behaviour order" in this part is a reference to any such order.

(3) A reference to "hearsay evidence" in this part is a reference to evidence consisting of hearsay within the meaning of section 1(2) of the Civil Evidence Act 1995 [§ 11-58 in the main work].

Behaviour orders: general rules

31.2.–(1) The court must not make a behaviour order unless the person to whom it is directed has **B-403** had an opportunity—

(a)   to consider—

    (i)   what order is proposed and why, and

    (ii) the evidence in support; and

  (b) to make representations at a hearing (whether or not that person in fact attends).

(2) That restriction does not apply to making—

  (a) an interim behaviour order, but unless other legislation otherwise provides such an order has no effect unless the person to whom it is directed—

    (i)   is present when it is made, or

    (ii) is handed a document recording the order not more than 7 days after it is made;

  (b) a restraining order that gives effect to a European protection order, where rule 31.10 applies (giving effect to a European protection order made in another EU member State).

(3) Where the court decides not to make, where it could—

  (a) a football banning order; or

  (b) a parenting order, after a person under 16 is convicted of an offence, the court must announce, at a hearing in public, the reasons for its decision.

(4) Where the court makes an order which imposes one or more of the prohibitions or restrictions listed in rule 31.9(1), the court must arrange for someone to explain to the person who benefits from that protection—

  (a) that that person may apply for a European protection order, if he or she decides to reside or stay in another European Union member State;

  (b) the basic conditions for making such an application; and

  (c) that it is advisable to make any such application before leaving the United Kingdom.

Application for behaviour order and notice of terms of proposed order: special rules

★B-404   **31.3.**—(1) This rule applies where—

  (a) a prosecutor wants the court to make one of the following orders if the defendant is convicted—

    (i)   an anti-social behaviour order (but this rule does not apply to an application for an interim anti-social behaviour order),

    (ii) a serious crime prevention order,

    (iii) a criminal behaviour order; or

    (iv) a prohibition order;

  (b) a prosecutor proposes, on the prosecutor's initiative or at the court's request, a sexual harm prevention order if the defendant is convicted;

  (c) a prosecutor proposes a restraining order whether the defendant is convicted or acquitted.

(2) Where paragraph (1)(a) applies (order on application) the prosecutor must serve a notice of intention to apply for such an order on—

  (a) the court officer;

  (b) the defendant against whom the prosecutor wants the court to make the order; and

  (c) any person on whom the order would be likely to have a significant adverse effect,

as soon as practicable (without waiting for the verdict).

(3) A notice under paragraph (2) must—

  (a) summarise the relevant facts;

  (b) identify the evidence on which the prosecutor relies in support;

  (c) attach any written statement that the prosecutor has not already served; and

  (d) specify the order that the prosecutor wants the court to make.

(4) A defendant served with a notice under paragraph (2) must—

  (a) serve notice of any evidence on which the defendant relies on—

    (i)   the court officer, and

    (ii) the prosecutor,

    as soon as practicable (without waiting for the verdict); and

  (b) in the notice, identify that evidence and attach any written statement that has not already been served.

(5) Where paragraph (1)(b) (sexual harm prevention order proposed) applies, the prosecutor must—

  (a) serve a draft order on the court officer and on the defendant not less than 2 business days before the hearing at which the order may be made;

  (b) in the draft order specify those prohibitions which the prosecutor proposes as necessary for the purpose of—

    (i)   protecting the public or any particular members of the public from sexual harm from the defendant, or

(ii) protecting children or vulnerable adults generally, or any particular children or vulnerable adults, from sexual harm from the defendant outside the United Kingdom.

(6) Where paragraph (1)(c) applies (restraining order proposed), the prosecutor must—

(a) serve a draft order on the court officer and on the defendant as soon as practicable (without waiting for the verdict);

(b) in the draft order specify—

(i) those prohibitions which, if the defendant is convicted, the prosecutor proposes for the purpose of protecting a person from conduct which amounts to harassment or will cause fear of violence, or

(ii) those prohibitions which, if the defendant is acquitted, the prosecutor proposes as necessary to protect a person from harassment by the defendant.

(7) Where the prosecutor wants the court to make an anti-social behaviour order, a criminal behaviour order or a prohibition order, the rules about special measures directions in Part 18 (measures to assist a witness or defendant to give evidence) apply, but—

(a) the prosecutor must apply when serving a notice under paragraph (2); and

(b) the time limits in rule 18.3(a) do not apply.

[This rule is printed as amended by the Criminal Procedure (Amendment No. 2) Rules 2016 (S.I. 2016 No. 705); and the Criminal Procedure (Amendment) Rules 2017 (S.I. 2017 No. 144).]

Evidence to assist the court: special rules

31.4.—(1) This rule applies where the court can make on its own initiative— **B-405**

(a) a football banning order;

(b) a restraining order; or

(c) an anti-social behaviour order.

(2) A party who wants the court to take account of evidence not already introduced must—

(a) serve notice on—

(i) the court officer, and

(ii) every other party,

as soon as practicable (without waiting for the verdict); and

(b) in the notice, identify that evidence; and

(c) attach any written statement containing such evidence.

[This rule is printed as amended by S.I. 2016 No. 705 (*ante*, B-404).]

Application to vary or revoke behaviour order

31.5.—(1) The court may vary or revoke a behaviour order if— **B-406**

(a) the legislation under which it is made allows the court to do so; and

(b) one of the following applies—

(i) the prosecutor,

(ii) the person to whom the order is directed,

(iii) any other person protected or affected by the order,

(iv) the relevant authority or responsible officer,

(v) the relevant Chief Officer of Police,

(vi) the Director of Public Prosecutions, or

(vii) the Director of the Serious Fraud Office.

(2) A person applying under this rule must—

(a) apply in writing as soon as practicable after becoming aware of the grounds for doing so, explaining—

(i) what material circumstances have changed since the order was made, and

(ii) why the order should be varied or revoked as a result; and

(b) serve the application on—

(i) the court officer,

(ii) as appropriate, the prosecutor or defendant, and

(iii) any other person listed in paragraph (1)(b), if the court so directs.

(3) A party who wants the court to take account of any particular evidence before making its decision must, as soon as practicable—

(a) serve notice on—

(i) the court officer,

(ii) as appropriate, the prosecutor or defendant, and

        (iii)   any other person listed in paragraph (1)(b) on whom the court directed the application to be served; and

    (b) in that notice identify the evidence and attach any written statement that has not already been served.

(4) The court may decide an application under this rule with or without a hearing.

(5) But the court must not—

    (a) dismiss an application under this rule unless the applicant has had an opportunity to make representations at a hearing (whether or not the applicant in fact attends); or

    (b) allow an application under this rule unless everyone required to be served, by this rule or by the court, has had at least 14 days in which to make representations, including representations about whether there should be a hearing.

(6) The court officer must—

    (a) serve the application on any person, if the court so directs; and

    (b) give notice of any hearing to—

        (i)   the applicant, and

        (ii) any person required to be served, by this rule or by the court.

[This rule is printed as amended by S.I. 2016 No. 705 (*ante*, B-404).]

Notice of hearsay evidence

B-407   **31.6.**–(1) A party who wants to introduce hearsay evidence must—

    (a) serve notice on—

        (i)   the court officer, and

        (ii) every other party directly affected; and

    (b) in that notice—

        (i)   explain that it is a notice of hearsay evidence,

        (ii) identify that evidence,

        (iii) identify the person who made the statement which is hearsay, or explain why if that person is not identified, and

        (iv) explain why that person will not be called to give oral evidence.

(2) A party may serve one notice under this rule in respect of more than one notice [*sic*] and more than one witness.

[This rule is printed as amended by S.I. 2016 No. 705 (*ante*, B-404).]

Cross-examination of maker of hearsay statement

B-408   **31.7.**–(1) This rule applies where a party wants the court's permission to cross-examine a person who made a statement which another party wants to introduce as hearsay.

(2) The party who wants to cross-examine that person must—

    (a) apply in writing, with reasons, not more than 7 days after service of the notice of hearsay evidence; and

    (b) serve the application on—

        (i)   the court officer,

        (ii) the party who served the hearsay evidence notice, and

        (iii) every party on whom the hearsay evidence notice was served.

(3) The court may decide an application under this rule with or without a hearing.

(4) But the court must not—

    (a) dismiss an application under this rule unless the applicant has had an opportunity to make representations at a hearing (whether or not the applicant in fact attends); or

    (b) allow an application under this rule unless everyone served with the application has had at least 7 days in which to make representations, including representations about whether there should be a hearing.

Credibility and consistency of maker of hearsay statement

B-409   **31.8.**–(1) This rule applies where a party wants to challenge the credibility or consistency of a person who made a statement which another party wants to introduce as hearsay.

(2) The party who wants to challenge the credibility or consistency of that person must—

    (a) serve notice of intention to do so on—

        (i)   the court officer, and

        (ii) the party who served the notice of hearsay evidence

not more than 7 days after service of that hearsay evidence notice; and

    (b) in the notice, identify any statement or other material on which that party relies.

(3) The party who served the hearsay notice—

    (a) may call that person to give oral evidence instead; and

    (b) if so, must serve notice of intention to do so on—

        (i)   the court officer, and

        (ii)   every party on whom the hearsay notice was served

    not more than 7 days after service of the notice under paragraph (2).

[[This rule is printed as amended by S.I. 2016 No. 705 (*ante*, B-404).]

European protection order to be given effect in another EU member State

    31.9.—(1) This rule applies where—   **B-410**

    (a) a person benefits from the protection of one or more of the following prohibitions or restrictions imposed on another person by an order of a court in England and Wales when dealing with a criminal cause or matter—

        (i)   a prohibition from entering certain localities, places or defined areas where the protected person resides or visits,

        (ii)   a prohibition or restriction of contact with the protected person by any means (including by telephone, post, facsimile transmission or electronic mail),

        (iii)   a prohibition or restriction preventing the other person from approaching the protected person whether at all or to within a particular distance; and either

    (b) that protected person wants the Crown Court or a magistrates' court to make a European protection order to supplement such an order; or

    (c) the court varies or revokes such a prohibition or restriction in such an order and correspondingly amends or revokes a European protection order already made.

(2) Such a protected person—

    (a) may apply orally or in writing to the Crown Court at the hearing at which the order imposing the prohibition or restriction is made by that court; or

    (b) in any other case, must apply in writing to a magistrates' court and serve the application on the court officer.

(3) The application must—

    (a) identify the prohibition or restriction that the European protection order would supplement;

    (b) identify the date, if any, on which that prohibition or restriction will expire;

    (c) specify the European Union member State in which the applicant has decided to reside or stay, or in which he or she already is residing or staying;

    (d) indicate the length of the period for which the applicant intends to reside or stay in that member State;

    (e) explain why the applicant needs the protection of that measure while residing or staying in that member State; and

    (f) include any other information of which the applicant wants the court to take account.

(4) Where the court makes or amends a European protection order, the court officer must—

    (a) issue an order in the form required by Directive 2011/99/EU;

    (b) serve on the competent authority of the European Union member State in which the protected person has decided to reside or stay—

        (i)   a copy of that form, and

        (ii)   a copy of the form translated into an official language of that member State, or into an official language of the European Union if that member State has declared that it will accept a translation in that language.

(5) Where the court revokes a European protection order, the court officer must without delay so inform that authority.

(6) Where the court refuses to make a European protection order, the court officer must arrange for the protected person to be informed of any available avenue of appeal or review against the court's decision.

Giving effect to a European protection order made in another EU member State

    31.10.—(1) This rule applies where the Lord Chancellor serves on the court officer—   **B-411**

    (a) a request by an authority in another European Union member State to give effect to a European protection order;

(b) a request by such an authority to give effect to a variation of such an order; or

(c) notice by such an authority of the revocation or withdrawal of such an order.

(2) In the case of a request to which paragraph (1) refers, the court officer must, without undue delay—

    (a) arrange for the court to consider the request;

    (b) serve on the requesting authority—

        (i) notice of any further information required by the court, and

        (ii) subject to any such requirement and any response, notice of the court's decision;

    (c) where the court gives effect to the European protection order—

        (i) include in the notice served on the requesting authority the terms of the restraining order made by the court,

        (ii) serve notice of those terms, and of the potential legal consequences of breaching them, on the person restrained by the order made by the court and on the person protected by that order, and

        (iii) serve notice on the Lord Chancellor of any breach of the restraining order which is reported to the court;

    (d) where the court refuses to give effect to the European protection order—

        (i) include in the notice served on the requesting authority the grounds for the refusal,

        (ii) where appropriate, inform the protected person, or any representative or guardian of that person, of the possibility of applying for a comparable order under the law of England and Wales, and

        (iii) arrange for that person, representative or guardian to be informed of any available avenue of appeal or review against the court's decision.

(3) In the case of a notice to which paragraph (1) refers, the court officer must, as soon as possible, arrange for the court to act on that notice.

(4) Unless the court otherwise directs, the court officer must omit from any notice served on a person against whom a restraining order may be, or has been, made the address or contact details of the person who is the object of the European protection order.

Court's power to vary requirements under this part

31.11. Unless other legislation otherwise provides, the court may—

B-412

    (a) shorten a time limit or extend it (even after it has expired);

    (b) allow a notice or application to be given in a different form, or presented orally.

Criminal Procedure Rules 2015 (S.I. 2015 No. 1490), Pt 32

Breach, Revocation and Amendment of Community and Other Orders

When this Part applies

32.1. This Part applies where—

B-413

    (a) the person responsible for a defendant's compliance with an order to which applies—

        (i) Schedule 3, 5, 7 or 8 to the Powers of Criminal Courts (Sentencing) Act 2000,

        (ii) Schedule 8 or 12 to the Criminal Justice Act 2003,

        (iii) Schedule 2 to the Criminal Justice and Immigration Act 2008, or

        (iv) the Schedule to the Street Offences Act 1959,

    wants the court to deal with that defendant for failure to comply;

    (b) one of the following wants the court to exercise any power it has to revoke or amend such an order—

        (i) the responsible officer or supervisor,

        (ii) the defendant, or

        (iii) where the legislation allows, a person affected by the order; or

    (c) the court considers exercising on its own initiative any power it has to revoke or amend such an order.

For Schedule 3 to the 2000 Act, see §§ 5-228 *et seq.* in the supplements to the 2012 edition of this work; for Schedule 5 to the 2000 Act, see *ante*, §§ 5-342 *et seq.*; for Schedule 7 to the 2000 Act, see §§ 5-371 *et seq.* in the supplements to the 2012 edition of this work; for Schedule 8 to the 2000 Act, see §§ 5-700 *et seq.* in the main work; for Schedule 8 to the 2003 Act, see *ibid.*, §§ 5-312 *et seq.*; for Schedule 12 to the 2003 Act, see *ibid.*, §§ 5-535 *et seq.*; for Schedule 2 to the 2008 Act, see *ibid.*, §§ 5-348 *et seq.* The schedule to the 1959 Act is not set out in this work.

Application by responsible officer or supervisor

32.2.–(1) This rule applies where–   **B-414**

    (a) the responsible officer or supervisor wants the court to–

        (i)   deal with a defendant for failure to comply with an order to which this Part applies, or

        (ii) revoke or amend such an order; or

    (b) the court considers exercising on its own initiative any power it has to–

        (i)   revoke or amend such an order, and

        (ii) summon the defendant to attend for that purpose.

(2) Rules 7.2 to 7.4, which deal, among other things, with starting a prosecution in a magistrates' court by information and summons, apply–

    (a) as if–

        (i)   a reference in those rules to an allegation of an offence included a reference to an allegation of failure to comply with an order to which this Part applies, and

        (ii) a reference to the prosecutor included a reference to the responsible officer or supervisor; and

    (b) with the necessary consequential modifications.

Application by defendant or person affected

32.3.–(1) This rule applies where–   **B-415**

    (a) the defendant wants the court to exercise any power it has to revoke or amend an order to which this Part applies; or

    (b) where the legislation allows, a person affected by such an order wants the court to exercise any such power.

(2) That defendant, or person affected, must–

    (a) apply in writing, explaining why the order should be revoked or amended; and

    (b) serve the application on–

        (i)   the court officer,

        (ii) the responsible officer or supervisor, and

        (iii) as appropriate, the defendant or the person affected.

Procedure on application by responsible officer or supervisor

32.4.–(1) Except for rules 24.8 (written guilty plea: special rules) and 24.9 (single justice procedure: **B-416** special rules), the rules in Part 24, which deal with the procedure at a trial in a magistrates' court, apply–

    (a) as if–

        (i)   a reference in those rules to an allegation of an offence included a reference to an allegation of failure to comply with an order to which this Part applies,

        (ii) a reference to the court's verdict included a reference to the court's decision to revoke or amend such an order, or to exercise any other power it has to deal with the defendant, and

        (iii) a reference to the court's sentence included a reference to the exercise of any such power; and

    (b) with the necessary consequential modifications.

(2) The court officer must serve on each party any order revoking or amending an order to which this Part applies.

CPD VII Sentencing

[For CPD VII Sentencing A (Pleas of guilty in the Crown Court), see § 4-175 in the main work.]   **B-417**

[For CPD VII Sentencing B (Determining the factual basis of sentence), see § 5-99 (para. 1), § 4-175 (paras 2-4), §§ 5-100 *et seq.* (paras 7-26) in the main work.]

[For CPD VII Sentencing C (Indications of sentence: *R. v. Goodyear*), see § 5-127 in the main work.]

[For CPD VII Sentencing D (Facts to be stated on pleas of guilty), see § 5-123 in the main work.]

[For CPD VII Sentencing E (Concurrent and consecutive sentences), see § 5-558 in the main work.]

[For CPD VII Sentencing F (Victim personal statements), see § 5-117 in the main work.]

[For CPD VII Sentencing G (Families bereaved by homicide and other criminal conduct), see § 5-118 in the main work.]

[For CPD VII Sentencing H (Community impact statements), see § 5-448 in the main work.]

[For CPD VII Sentencing I (Impact statements for businesses), see § 5-121 in the main work.]

[For CPD VII Sentencing J (Binding over orders and conditional discharge), see §§ 5-221 *et seq.* (paras 1-18), § 5-1305 (para. 19), and § 5-209 (para. 20).]

[For CPD VII Sentencing K (Committal for sentence), see § 5-48 in the main work.]

[For CPD VII Sentencing L (Imposition of life sentences), see § 5-515 in the main work.]

[For CPD VII Sentencing M (Mandatory life sentences), see § 5-408 in the main work.]

[For CPD VII Sentencing N (Transitional arrangements for sentences where the offence was committed before December 18, 2003), see *ante*, §§ 5-409 *et seq.*]

[For CPD VII Sentencing P (Procedure for announcing the minimum term in open court), see § 5-414 in the main work.]

[For CPD VII Sentencing Q (Financial, etc. information required for sentencing), see § 5-662 in the main work.]

Criminal Procedure Rules 2015 (S.I. 2015 No. 1490), Pt 33

CONFISCATION AND RELATED PROCEEDINGS

General rules

Interpretation

B-418   **33.1.** In this Part:

"document" means anything in which information of any description is recorded;

"hearsay evidence" means evidence consisting of hearsay within the meaning of section 1(2) of the Civil Evidence Act 1995 [§ 11-58 in the main work];

"restraint proceedings" means proceedings under sections 42 and 58(2) and (3) of the Proceeds of Crime Act 2002 [*ibid.*, §§ 5-817 *et seq.*];

"receivership proceedings" means proceedings under sections 48, 49, 50, 51, 54(4), 59(2) and (3), 62 and 63 of the 2002 Act;

"witness statement" means a written statement signed by a person which contains the evidence, and only that evidence, which that person would be allowed to give orally; and

words and expressions used have the same meaning as in Part 2 of the 2002 Act.

Calculation of time

B-419   **33.2.**–(1) This rule shows how to calculate any period of time for doing any act which is specified by this Part for the purposes of any proceedings under Part 2 of the Proceeds of Crime Act 2002 or by an order of the Crown Court in restraint proceedings or receivership proceedings.

(2) A period of time expressed as a number of days shall be computed as clear days.

(3) In this rule "clear days" means that in computing the number of days—

(a) the day on which the period begins; and

(b) if the end of the period is defined by reference to an event, the day on which that event occurs,

are not included.

(4) Where the specified period is 5 days or less and includes a day which is not a business day that day does not count.

Court office closed

B-420   **33.3.** When the period specified by this Part, or by an order of the Crown Court under Part 2 of the Proceeds of Crime Act 2002, for doing any act at the court office falls on a day on which the office is closed, that act shall be in time if done on the next day on which the court office is open.

Application for registration of Scottish or Northern Ireland order

B-421   **33.4.**–(1) This rule applies to an application for registration of an order under article 6 of the Proceeds of Crime Act 2002 (enforcement in different parts of the United Kingdom) Order 2002.

(2) The application may be made without notice.

(3) The application must be in writing and may be supported by a witness statement which must—

(a)   exhibit the order or a certified copy of the order; and

(b)   to the best of the witness's ability, give full details of the realisable property located in England and Wales in respect of which the order was made and specify the person holding that realisable property.

(4) If the court registers the order, the applicant must serve notice of the registration on—

(a)   any person who holds realisable property to which the order applies; and

(b)   any other person whom the applicant knows to be affected by the order.

(5) The permission of the Crown Court under rule 33.10 (service outside the jurisdiction) is not required to serve the notice outside England and Wales.

Application to vary or set aside registration

33.5.–(1) An application to vary or set aside registration of an order under article 6 of the   **B-422**
Proceeds of Crime Act 2002 (enforcement in different parts of the United Kingdom) Order 2002 may be made to the Crown Court by—

(a)   any person who holds realisable property to which the order applies; and

(b)   any other person affected by the order.

(2) The application must be in writing and may be supported by a witness statement.

(3) The application and any witness statement must be lodged with the Crown Court.

(4) The application must be served on the person who applied for registration at least 7 days before the date fixed by the court for hearing the application, unless the Crown Court specifies a shorter period.

(5) No property in England and Wales may be realised in pursuance of the order before the Crown Court has decided the application.

Register of orders

33.6.–(1) The Crown Court must keep, under the direction of the Lord Chancellor, a register of   **B-423**
the orders registered under article 6 of the Proceeds of Crime Act 2002 (enforcement in different parts of the United Kingdom) Order 2002.

(2) The register must include details of any variation or setting aside of a registration under rule 33.5 and of any execution issued on a registered order.

(3) If the person who applied for registration of an order which is subsequently registered notifies the Crown Court that the court which made the order has varied or discharged the order, details of the variation or discharge, as the case may be, must be entered in the register.

Statements of truth

33.7.–(1) Any witness statement required to be served by this part must be verified by a statement   **B-424**
of truth contained in the witness statement.

(2) A statement of truth is a declaration by the person making the witness statement to the effect that the witness statement is true to the best of his knowledge and belief and that he made the statement knowing that, if it were tendered in evidence, he would be liable to prosecution if he wilfully stated in it anything which he knew to be false or did not believe to be true.

(3) The statement of truth must be signed by the person making the witness statement.

(4) If the person making the witness statement fails to verify the witness statement by a statement of truth, the Crown Court may direct that it shall not be admissible as evidence.

Use of witness statements for other purposes

33.8.–(1) Except as provided by this rule, a witness statement served in proceedings under Part 2   **B-425**
of the Proceeds of Crime Act 2002 may be used only for the purpose of the proceedings in which it is served.

(2) Paragraph (1) does not apply if and to the extent that—

(a)   the witness gives consent in writing to some other use of it;

(b)   the Crown Court gives permission for some other use; or

(c)   the witness statement has been put in evidence at a hearing held in public.

Service of documents

33.9.–(1) Rule 49.1 (notice required to accompany process served outside the United Kingdom   **B-426**
and translations) shall not apply in restraint proceedings and receivership proceedings.

(2) An order made in restraint proceedings or receivership proceedings may be enforced against the defendant or any other person affected by it notwithstanding that service of a copy of the order has not been effected in accordance with Part 4 if the Crown Court is satisfied that the person had notice of the order by being present when the order was made.

Service outside the jurisdiction

B-427
33.10.–(1) Where this Part requires a document to be served on someone who is outside England and Wales, it may be served outside England and Wales with the permission of the Crown Court.

(2) Where a document is to be served outside England and Wales it may be served by any method permitted by the law of the country in which it is to be served.

(3) Nothing in this rule or in any court order shall authorise or require any person to do anything in the country where the document is to be served which is against the law of that country.

(4) Where this Part requires a document to be served a certain period of time before the date of a hearing and the recipient does not appear at the hearing, the hearing must not take place unless the Crown Court is satisfied that the document has been duly served.

Certificates of service

B-428
33.11.–(1) Where this Part requires that the applicant for an order in restraint proceedings or receivership proceedings serve a document on another person, the applicant must lodge a certificate of service with the Crown Court within 7 days of service of the document.

(2) The certificate must state—
    (a)   the method of service;
    (b)   the date of service; and
    (c)   if the document is served under rule 4.9 (service by another method), such other information as the court may require when making the order permitting service by that method.

(3) Where a document is to be served by the Crown Court in restraint proceedings and receivership proceedings and the court is unable to serve it, the court must send a notice of nonservice stating the method attempted to the party who requested service.

External requests and orders

B-429
33.12.–(1) The rules in this Part and in Part 42 (appeal to the Court of Appeal in confiscation and related proceedings) apply with the necessary modifications to proceedings under the Proceeds of Crime Act 2002 (External Requests and Orders) Order 2005 in the same way that they apply to corresponding proceedings under Part 2 of the Proceeds of Crime Act 2002.

(2) This table shows how provisions of the 2005 Order correspond with provisions of the 2002 Act.

Article of the Proceeds of Crime Act 2002 (External Requests and Orders) Order 2005	Section of the Proceeds of Crime Act 2002
8	41
9	42
10	43
11	44
15	48
16	49
17	58
23	31
27	50
28	51
41	62
42	63
44	65
45	66

Confiscation proceedings

Statements in connection with confiscation orders

B-430
33.13.–(1) This rule applies where—
    (a)   the court can make a confiscation order; and

    (b) the prosecutor asks the court to make such an order, or the court decides to make such an order on its own initiative.

(2) Within such periods as the court directs—

    (a) if the court so orders, the defendant must give such information, in such manner, as the court directs;

    (b) the prosecutor must serve a statement of information relevant to confiscation on the court officer and the defendant;

    (c) if the court so directs—

        (i) the defendant must serve a response notice on the court officer and the prosecutor, and

        (ii) the parties must identify what is in dispute.

(3) Where it appears to the court that a person other than the defendant holds, or may hold, an interest in property held by the defendant which property is likely to be realised or otherwise used to satisfy a confiscation order—

    (a) the court must not determine the extent of the defendant's interest in that property unless that other person has had a reasonable opportunity to make representations; and

    (b) the court may order that other person to give such information, in such manner and within such a period, as the court directs.

(4) The court may—

    (a) shorten or extend a time limit which it has set;

    (b) vary, discharge or supplement an order which it has made;

    (c) postpone confiscation proceedings without a hearing.

(5) A prosecutor's statement of information must—

    (a) identify the maker of the statement and show its date;

    (b) identify the defendant in respect of whom it is served;

    (c) specify the conviction which gives the court power to make the confiscation order, or each conviction if more than one;

    (d) if the prosecutor believes the defendant to have a criminal lifestyle, include such matters as the prosecutor believes to be relevant in connection with deciding—

        (i) whether the defendant has such a lifestyle,

        (ii) whether the defendant has benefited from his or her general criminal conduct,

        (iii) the defendant's benefit from that conduct, and

        (iv) whether the court should or should not make such assumptions about the defendant's property as legislation permits;

    (e) if the prosecutor does not believe the defendant to have a criminal lifestyle, include such matters as the prosecutor believes to be relevant in connection with deciding—

        (i) whether the defendant has benefited from his or her particular criminal conduct, and

        (ii) the defendant's benefit from that conduct;

    (f) in any case, include such matters as the prosecutor believes to be relevant in connection with deciding—

        (i) whether to make a determination about the extent of the defendant's interest in property in which another person holds, or may hold, an interest, and

        (ii) what determination to make, if the court decides to make one.

(6) A defendant's response notice must—

    (a) indicate the extent to which the defendant accepts the allegations made in the prosecutor's statement of information; and

    (b) so far as the defendant does not accept an allegation, give particulars of any matters on which the defendant relies,

in any manner directed by the court.

(7) The court must satisfy itself that there has been explained to the defendant, in terms the defendant can understand (with help, if necessary)—

    (a) that if the defendant accepts to any extent an allegation in a prosecutor's statement of information, then the court may treat that as conclusive for the purposes of deciding whether the defendant has benefited from general or particular criminal conduct, and if so by how much;

    (b) that if the defendant fails in any respect to comply with a direction to serve a response notice, then the court may treat that as acceptance of each allegation to which the defendant has not replied, except the allegation that the defendant has benefited from general or particular criminal conduct; and

(c)   that if the defendant fails without reasonable excuse to comply with an order to give information, then the court may draw such inference as it believes is appropriate.

Application for compliance order

33.14.–(1) This rule applies where—

    (a)   the prosecutor wants the court to make a compliance order after a confiscation order has been made;

    (b)   the prosecutor or a person affected by a compliance order wants the court to vary or discharge the order.

(2) Such a prosecutor or person must—

    (a)   apply in writing; and

    (b)   serve the application on—

        (i)   the court officer, and

        (ii)   as appropriate, the prosecutor and any person who is affected by the compliance order (or who would be affected if it were made), unless the court otherwise directs.

(3) The application must—

    (a)   specify—

        (i)   the confiscation order,

        (ii)   the compliance order, if it is an application to vary or discharge that order;

    (b)   if it is an application for a compliance order—

        (i)   specify each measure that the prosecutor proposes to ensure that the confiscation order is effective, including in particular any restriction or prohibition on the defendant's travel outside the United Kingdom, and

        (ii)   explain why each such measure is appropriate;

    (c)   if it is an application to vary or discharge a compliance order, as appropriate—

        (i)   specify any proposed variation, and

        (ii)   explain why it is appropriate for the order to be varied or discharged;

    (d)   attach any material on which the applicant relies;

    (e)   propose the terms of the order; and

    (f)   ask for a hearing, if the applicant wants one, and explain why it is needed.

(4) A person who wants to make representations about the application must—

    (a)   serve the representations on—

        (i)   the court officer, and

        (ii)   the applicant;

    (b)   do so as soon as reasonably practicable after service of the application;

    (c)   attach any material on which that person relies; and

    (d)   ask for a hearing, if that person wants one, and explain why it is needed.

(5) The court—

    (a)   may determine the application at a hearing (which must be in private unless the court otherwise directs), or without a hearing;

    (b)   may dispense with service on any person of a prosecutor's application for a compliance order if, in particular—

        (i)   the application is urgent, or

        (ii)   there are reasonable grounds for believing that to give notice of the application would cause the dissipation of property that otherwise would be available to satisfy the confiscation order.

Application for reconsideration

33.15.–(1) This rule applies where the prosecutor wants the court, in view of fresh evidence—

    (a)   to consider making a confiscation order where the defendant was convicted but no such order was considered;

    (b)   to reconsider a decision that the defendant had not benefited from criminal conduct;

    (c)   to reconsider a decision about the amount of the defendant's benefit.

(2) The application must—

    (a)   be in writing and give—

        (i)   the name of the defendant,

        (ii)   the date on which and the place where any relevant conviction occurred,

        (iii)   the date on which and the place where any relevant confiscation order was made or varied,

    (iv)   details of any slavery and trafficking reparation order made by virtue of any relevant confiscation order,

    (v)   the grounds for the application, and

    (vi) an indication of the evidence available to support the application; and

  (b) where the parties are agreed on the terms of the proposed order include, in one or more documents—

    (i)   a draft order in the terms proposed, and

    (ii) evidence of the parties' agreement.

(3) The application must be served on—

  (a) the court officer; and

  (b) the defendant.

(4) The court—

  (a) may determine the application without a hearing where the parties are agreed on the terms of the proposed order;

  (b) must determine the application at a hearing in any other case.

(5) Where this rule or the court requires the application to be heard, the court officer must arrange for the court to hear it no sooner than the eighth day after it was served unless the court otherwise directs.

[This rule is printed as amended by the Criminal Procedure (Amendment) Rules 2017 (S.I. 2017 No. 144).]

Application for new calculation of available amount

33.16.—(1) This rule applies where the prosecutor or a receiver wants the court to make a new calculation of the amount available for confiscation. **★B-433**

(2) The application—

  (a) must be in writing and may be supported by a witness statement;

  (b) must identify any slavery and trafficking reparation order made by virtue of the confiscation order; and

  (c) where the parties are agreed on the terms of the proposed order, must include in one or more documents—

    (i)   a draft order in the terms proposed, and

    (ii) evidence of the parties' agreement.

(3) The application and any witness statement must be served on the court officer.

(4) The application and any witness statement must be served on—

  (a) the defendant;

  (b) the receiver, if the prosecutor is making the application and a receiver has been appointed; and

  (c) the prosecutor, if the receiver is making the application.

(5) The court—

  (a) may determine the application without a hearing where the parties are agreed on the terms of the proposed order;

  (b) must determine the application at a hearing in any other case.

(6) Where this rule or the court requires the application to be heard, the court officer must arrange for the court to hear it no sooner than the eighth day after it was served unless the court otherwise directs.

[This rule is printed as amended by the Criminal Procedure (Amendment) Rules 2017 (S.I. 2017 No. 144).]

Variation of confiscation order due to inadequacy of available amount

33.17.—(1) This rule applies where the defendant, the prosecutor or a receiver wants the court to vary a confiscation order because the amount available is inadequate. **★B-434**

(2), (3) [*Identical to r.33.16(2), (3), ante, B-433.*]

(4) The application and any witness statement must be served on—

  (a) the prosecutor;

  (b) the defendant, if the receiver is making the application; and

  (c) the receiver, if the defendant is making the application and a receiver has been appointed.

(5), (6) [*Identical to r.33.16(5), (6), ante, B-433.*]

[This rule is printed as amended by the Criminal Procedure (Amendment) Rules 2017 (S.I. 2017 No. 144).]

Application by magistrates' court officer to discharge confiscation order

33.18.–(1) This rule applies where a magistrates' court officer wants the court to discharge a confiscation order because the amount available is inadequate or the sum outstanding is very small.

(2) The application must be in writing and give details of—

   (a) the confiscation order;

   (b) any slavery and trafficking reparation order made by virtue of the confiscation order;

   (c) the amount outstanding under the order; and

   (d) the grounds for the application.

(3) The application must be served on—

   (a) the defendant;

   (b) the prosecutor; and

   (c) any receiver.

(4) The court may determine the application without a hearing unless a person listed in paragraph (3) indicates, within 7 days after the application was served, that he or she would like to make representations.

(5) If the court makes an order discharging the confiscation order, the court officer must, at once, send a copy of the order to—

   (a) the magistrates' court officer who applied for the order;

   (b) the defendant;

   (c) the prosecutor; and

   (d) any receiver.

Application for variation of confiscation order made against an absconder

33.19.–(1) This rule applies where the defendant wants the court to vary a confiscation order made while the defendant was an absconder.

(2) The application must be in writing and supported by a witness statement which must give details of—

   (a) the confiscation order;

   (b) any slavery and trafficking reparation order made by virtue of the confiscation order;

   (c) the circumstances in which the defendant ceased to be an absconder;

   (d) the defendant's conviction of the offence or offences concerned; and

   (e) the reason why the defendant believes the amount required to be paid under the confiscation order was too large.

(3) The application and witness statement must be served on the court officer.

(4) The application and witness statement must be served on the prosecutor at least 7 days before the date fixed by the court for hearing the application, unless the court specifies a shorter period.

Application for discharge of confiscation order made against an absconder

33.20.–(1) This rule applies where the defendant wants the court to discharge a confiscation order made while the defendant was an absconder and—

   (a) the defendant since has been tried and acquitted of each offence concerned; or

   (b) the prosecution has not concluded or is not to proceed.

(2) The application must be in writing and supported by a witness statement which must give details of—

   (a) the confiscation order;

   (b) the date on which the defendant ceased to be an absconder;

   (c) the acquittal of the defendant if he or she has been acquitted of the offence concerned; and

   (d) if the defendant has not been acquitted of the offence concerned—

      (i) the date on which the defendant ceased to be an absconder,

      (ii) the date on which the proceedings taken against the defendant were instituted and a summary of steps taken in the proceedings since then, and

      (iii) any indication that the prosecutor does not intend to proceed against the defendant.

(3), (4) [*Identical to r.33.19(3), (4), ante, § B-436.*]

(5) If the court orders the discharge of the confiscation order, the court officer must serve notice on any other court responsible for enforcing the order.

Application for increase in term of imprisonment in default

33.21.–(1) This rule applies where—

   (a) a court varies a confiscation order; and

    (b) the prosecutor wants the court in consequence to increase the term of imprisonment to be served in default of payment.

(2) The application must be made in writing and give details of—

    (a) the name and address of the defendant;

    (b) the confiscation order;

    (c) the grounds for the application; and

    (d) the enforcement measures taken, if any.

(3) On receipt of the application, the court officer must—

    (a) at once, send to the defendant and any other court responsible for enforcing the order, a copy of the application; and

    (b) fix a time, date and place for the hearing and notify the applicant and the defendant of that time, date and place.

(4) If the court makes an order increasing the term of imprisonment in default, the court officer must, at once, send a copy of the order to—

    (a) the applicant;

    (b) the defendant;

    (c) where the defendant is in custody at the time of the making of the order, the person having custody of the defendant; and

    (d) any other court responsible for enforcing the order.

Compensation - general

    33.22.—(1) This rule applies where a person who held realisable property wants the court to award   **B-439** compensation for loss suffered in consequence of anything done in relation to that property in connection with confiscation proceedings.

(2) The application must be in writing and may be supported by a witness statement.

(3) The application and any witness statement must be served on the court officer.

(4) The application and any witness statement must be served on—

    (a) the person alleged to be in default; and

    (b) the person or authority by whom the compensation would be payable,

at least 7 days before the date fixed by the court for hearing the application, unless the court directs otherwise.

Compensation - confiscation order made against absconder

    33.23.—(1) This rule applies where—   **B-440**

    (a) the court varies or discharges a confiscation order made against an absconder;

    (b) a person who held realisable property suffered loss as a result of the making of that confiscation order; and

    (c) that person wants the court to award compensation for that loss.

(2) The application must be in writing and supported by a witness statement which must give details of—

    (a) the confiscation order;

    (b) the variation or discharge of the confiscation order;

    (c) the realisable property to which the application relates; and

    (d) the loss suffered by the applicant as a result of the confiscation order.

(3), (4) [*Identical to r.33.19(3), (4), ante, § B-436.*]

Payment of money in bank or building society account in satisfaction of confiscation order

    33.24.—(1) An order under section 67 of the Proceeds of Crime Act 2002 [§ 5-866 in the main   **B-441** work] requiring a bank or building society to pay money to a magistrates' court officer ("a payment order") shall—

    (a) be directed to the bank or building society in respect of which the payment order is made;

    (b) name the person against whom the confiscation order has been made;

    (c) state the amount which remains to be paid under the confiscation order;

    (d) state the name and address of the branch at which the account in which the money ordered to be paid is held and the sort code of that branch, if the sort code is known;

    (e) state the name in which the account in which the money ordered to be paid is held and the account number of that account, if the account number is known;

    (f) state the amount which the bank or building society is required to pay to the court officer under the payment order;

(g) give the name and address of the court officer to whom payment is to be made; and

(h) require the bank or building society to make payment within a period of 7 days beginning on the day on which the payment order is made, unless it appears to the court that a longer or shorter period would be appropriate in the particular circumstances.

(2) In this rule "confiscation order" has the meaning given to it by section 88(6) of the Proceeds of Crime Act 2002 [*ibid.*, § 5-897].

Application to realise seized property

B-442   **33.25.**–(1) This rule applies where–

(a) property is held by a defendant against whom a confiscation order has been made;

(b) the property has been seized by or produced to an officer; and

(c) an officer who is entitled to apply wants a magistrates' court–

   (i) to make an order under section 67A of the Proceeds of Crime Act 2002 [*ibid.*, § 5-867] authorising the realisation of the property towards satisfaction of the confiscation order, or

   (ii) to determine any storage, insurance or realisation costs in respect of the property which may be recovered under section 67B of the 2002 Act [*ibid.*, § 5-868].

(2) Such an officer must–

(a) apply in writing; and

(b) serve the application on–

   (i) the court officer, and

   (ii) any person whom the applicant believes would be affected by an order.

(3) The application must–

(a) specify the property;

(b) explain–

   (i) the applicant's entitlement to apply,

   (ii) how the proposed realisation meets the conditions prescribed by section 67A of the 2002 Act, and

   (iii) how any storage, etc. costs have been calculated;

(c) attach any material on which the applicant relies; and

(d) propose the terms of the order.

(4) The court may–

(a) determine the application at a hearing, or without a hearing;

(b) consider an application made orally instead of in writing;

(c) consider an application which has not been served on a person likely to be affected by an order.

(5) If the court authorises the realisation of the property, the applicant must–

(a) notify any person affected by the order who was absent when it was made; and

(b) serve on the court officer a list of those so notified.

Appeal about decision on application to realise seized property

B-443   **33.26.**–(1) This rule applies where on an application under rule 33.25 for an order authorising the realisation of property–

(a) a magistrates' court decides not to make such an order and an officer who is entitled to apply wants to appeal against that decision to the Crown Court, under section 67C(1) of the Proceeds of Crime Act 2002 [*ibid.*, § 5-869];

(b) a magistrates' court makes such an order and a person who is affected by that decision, other than the defendant against whom the confiscation order was made, wants to appeal against it to the Crown Court, under section 67C(2) of the 2002 Act;

(c) a magistrates' court makes a decision about storage, etc. costs and an officer who is entitled to apply wants to appeal against that decision to the Crown Court, under section 67C(4) of the 2002 Act.

(2) The appellant must serve an appeal notice–

(a) on the Crown Court officer and on any other party;

(b) not more than 21 days after the magistrates' court's decision, or, if applicable, service of notice under rule 33.25(5).

(3) The appeal notice must–

(a) specify the decision under appeal;

(b) where paragraph (1)(a) applies, explain why the property should be realised;

(c) in any other case, propose the order that the appellant wants the court to make, and explain why.

(4) Rule 34.11 (constitution of the Crown Court) applies on such an appeal.

Application for direction about surplus proceeds

33.27.–(1) This rule applies where–   **B-444**

  (a) on an application under rule 33.25, a magistrates' court has made an order authorizing an officer to realise property;

  (b) an officer so authorised holds proceeds of that realisation;

  (c) the confiscation order has been fully paid; and

  (d) the officer, or a person who had or has an interest in the property represented by the proceeds, wants a magistrates' court or the Crown Court to determine under section 67D of the Proceeds of Crime Act 2002 [*ibid.*, § 5-870] –

    (i) to whom the remaining proceeds should be paid, and

    (ii) in what amount or amounts.

(2) Such a person must–

  (a) apply in writing; and

  (b) serve the application on–

    (i) the court officer, and

    (ii) as appropriate, the officer holding the proceeds, or any person to whom such proceeds might be paid.

(3) The application must–

  (a) specify the property which was realised;

  (b) explain the applicant's entitlement to apply;

  (c) describe the distribution proposed by the applicant and explain why that is proposed;

  (d) attach any material on which the applicant relies; and

  (e) ask for a hearing, if the applicant wants one, and explain why it is needed.

(4) A person who wants to make representations about the application must–

  (a) serve the representations on–

    (i) the court officer,

    (ii) the applicant, and

    (iii) any other person to whom proceeds might be paid;

  (b) do so as soon as reasonably practicable after service of the application;

  (c) attach any material on which that person relies; and

  (d) ask for a hearing, if that person wants one, and explain why it is needed.

(5) The court–

  (a) must not determine the application unless the applicant and each person on whom it was served–

    (i) is present, or

    (ii) has had an opportunity to attend or to make representations;

  (b) subject to that, may determine the application–

    (i) at a hearing (which must be in private unless the court otherwise directs), or without a hearing,

    (ii) in the absence of any party to the application.

Seizure and detention proceedings

Application for approval to seize property or to search

33.28.–(1) This rule applies where an officer who is entitled to apply wants the approval of a **B-445** magistrates' court, under section 47G of the Proceeds of Crime Act 2002–

  (a) to seize property, under section 47C of that Act;

  (b) to search premises or a person or vehicle for property to be seized, under section 47D, 47E or 47F of that Act.

(2) Such an officer must–

  (a) apply in writing; and

  (b) serve the application on the court officer.

(3) The application must–

  (a) explain–

> (i) the applicant's entitlement to apply, and
>
> (ii) how the proposed seizure meets the conditions prescribed by sections 47B, 47C and, if applicable, 47D, 47E or 47F of the 2002 Act;
>
> (b) if applicable, specify any premises, person or vehicle to be searched;
>
> (c) attach any material on which the applicant relies; and
>
> (d) propose the terms in which the applicant wants the court to give its approval.
>
> (4) The court—
>
> (a) must determine the application—
>
> (i) at a hearing, which must be in private unless the court otherwise directs, and
>
> (ii) in the applicant's presence;
>
> (b) may consider an application made orally instead of in writing.

For sections 47A *et seq.* of the 2002 Act, see §§ 5-826 *et seq.* in the main work.

Application to extend detention period

B-446

33.29.—(1) This rule applies where an officer who is entitled to apply, or the prosecutor, wants a magistrates' court to make an order, under section 47M of the Proceeds of Crime Act 2002, extending the period for which seized property may be detained.

> (2) Such an officer or prosecutor must—
>
> (a) apply in writing; and
>
> (b) serve the application on—
>
> (i) the court officer, and
>
> (ii) any person whom the applicant believes would be affected by an order.
>
> (3) The application must—
>
> (a) specify—
>
> (i) the property to be detained, and
>
> (ii) whether the applicant wants it to be detained for a specified period or indefinitely;
>
> (b) explain—
>
> (i) the applicant's entitlement to apply, and
>
> (ii) how the proposed detention meets the conditions prescribed by section 47M of the 2002 Act;
>
> (c) attach any material on which the applicant relies; and
>
> (d) propose the terms of the order.
>
> (4) The court—
>
> (a) must determine the application—
>
> (i) at a hearing, which must be in private unless the court otherwise directs, and
>
> (ii) in the applicant's presence;
>
> (b) may—
>
> (i) consider an application made orally instead of in writing,
>
> (ii) require service of the application on the court officer after it has been heard, instead of before.
>
> (5) If the court extends the period for which the property may be detained, the applicant must—
>
> (a) notify any person affected by the order who was absent when it was made; and
>
> (b) serve on the court officer a list of those so notified.

Application to vary or discharge order for extended detention

B-447

33.30.—(1) This rule applies where an officer who is entitled to apply, the prosecutor, or a person affected by an order to which rule 33.29 applies, wants a magistrates' court to vary or discharge that order, under section 47N of the Proceeds of Crime Act 2002.

> (2) Such a person must—
>
> (a) apply in writing; and
>
> (b) serve the application on—
>
> (i) the court officer, and
>
> (ii) as appropriate, the applicant for the order, or any person affected by the order.
>
> (3) The application must—
>
> (a) specify the order and the property detained;
>
> (b) explain—
>
> (i) the applicant's entitlement to apply,
>
> (ii) why it is appropriate for the order to be varied or discharged,

     (iii)   if applicable, on what grounds the court must discharge the order;
   (c) attach any material on which the applicant relies;
   (d) if applicable, propose the terms of any variation; and
   (e) ask for a hearing, if the applicant wants one, and explain why it is needed.
 (4) A person who wants to make representations about the application must—
   (a) serve the representations on—
     (i)   the court officer, and
     (ii) the applicant;
   (b) do so as soon as reasonably practicable after service of the application;
   (c) attach any material on which that person relies; and
   (d) ask for a hearing, if that person wants one, and explain why it is needed.
 (5) The court—
   (a) must not determine the application unless the applicant and each person on whom it was served—
     (i)   is present, or
     (ii) has had an opportunity to attend or to make representations;
   (b) subject to that, may determine the application—
     (i)   at a hearing (which must be in private unless the court otherwise directs), or without a hearing,
     (ii) in the absence of any party to the application.

Appeal about property detention decision

B-448

33.31.—(1) This rule applies where—
   (a) on an application under rule 33.29 for an order extending the period for which property may be detained—
     (i)   a magistrates' court decides not to make such an order, and
     (ii) an officer who is entitled to apply for such an order, or the prosecutor, wants to appeal against that decision to the Crown Court under section 47O(1) of the Proceeds of Crime Act 2002;
   (b) on an application under rule 33.30 to vary or discharge an order under rule 33.29—
     (i)   a magistrates' court determines the application, and
     (ii) a person who is entitled to apply under that rule wants to appeal against that decision to the Crown Court under section 47O(2) of the 2002 Act.
 (2) The appellant must serve an appeal notice—
   (a) on the Crown Court officer and on any other party;
   (b) not more than 21 days after the magistrates' court's decision, or, if applicable, service of notice under rule 33.29(5).
 (3) The appeal notice must—
   (a) specify the decision under appeal;
   (b) where paragraph (1)(a) applies, explain why the detention period should be extended;
   (c) where paragraph (1)(b) applies, propose the order that the appellant wants the court to make, and explain why.
 (4) Rule 34.11 (constitution of the Crown Court) applies on such an appeal.

Restraint and receivership proceedings: rules that apply generally

Taking control of goods and forfeiture

B-449

33.32.—(1) This rule applies to applications under sections 58(2) and (3) and 59(2) and (3) of the Proceeds of Crime Act 2002 [§§ 5-587, 5-858 in the main work] for leave of the Crown Court to take control of goods or levy distress against property, or to exercise a right of forfeiture by peaceable re-entry in relation to a tenancy, in circumstances where the property or tenancy is the subject of a restraint order or a receiver has been appointed in respect of the property or tenancy.
 (2) The application must be made in writing to the Crown Court.
 (3) The application must be served on—
   (a) the person who applied for the restraint order or the order appointing the receiver; and
   (b) any receiver appointed in respect of the property or tenancy,
at least 7 days before the date fixed by the court for hearing the application, unless the Crown Court specifies a shorter period.

Joining of applications

B-450   **33.33.** An application for the appointment of a management receiver or enforcement receiver under rule 33.56 may be joined with–

    (a) an application for a restraint order under rule 33.51; and

    (b) an application for the conferral of powers on the receiver under rule 33.57.

Applications to be dealt with in writing

    33.34. Applications in restraint proceedings and receivership proceedings are to be dealt with without a hearing, unless the Crown Court orders otherwise.

Business in chambers

    33.35. Restraint proceedings and receivership proceedings may be heard in chambers.

Power of court to control evidence

B-451   **33.36.**–(1) When hearing restraint proceedings and receivership proceedings, the Crown Court may control the evidence by giving directions as to–

    (a) the issues on which it requires evidence;

    (b) the nature of the evidence which it requires to decide those issues; and

    (c) the way in which the evidence is to be placed before the court.

    (2) The court may use its power under this rule to exclude evidence that would otherwise be admissible.

    (3) The court may limit cross-examination in restraint proceedings and receivership proceedings.

Evidence of witnesses

B-452   **33.37.**–(1) The general rule is that, unless the Crown Court orders otherwise, any fact which needs to be proved in restraint proceedings or receivership proceedings by the evidence of a witness is to be proved by their evidence in writing.

    (2) Where evidence is to be given in writing under this rule, any party may apply to the Crown Court for permission to cross-examine the person giving the evidence.

    (3) If the Crown Court gives permission under paragraph (2) but the person in question does not attend as required by the order, his evidence may not be used unless the court gives permission.

Witness summons

    33.38.–(1) Any party to restraint proceedings or receivership proceedings may apply to the Crown Court to issue a witness summons requiring a witness to–

    (a) attend court to give evidence; or

    (b) produce documents to the court.

    (2) Rule 17.3 (application for summons, warrant or order: general rules) applies to an application under this rule as it applies to an application under section 2 of the Criminal Procedure (Attendance of Witnesses) Act 1965 [§ 8-1 in the main work].

Hearsay evidence

B-453   **33.39.** Section 2(1) of the Civil Evidence Act 1995 (duty to give notice of intention to rely on hearsay evidence [*ibid.*, § 11-59]) does not apply to evidence in restraint proceedings and receivership proceedings.

Disclosure and inspection of documents

B-454   **33.40.**–(1) This rule applies where, in the course of restraint proceedings or receivership proceedings, an issue arises as to whether property is realisable property.

    (2) The Crown Court may make an order for disclosure of documents.

    (3) Part 31 of the Civil Procedure Rules 1998 as amended from time to time shall have effect as if the proceedings were proceedings in the High Court.

Court documents

B-455   **33.41.**–(1) Any order which the Crown Court issues in restraint proceedings or receivership proceedings must–

    (a) state the name and judicial title of the person who made it;

    (b) bear the date on which it is made; and

    (c) be sealed by the Crown Court.

    (2) The Crown Court may place the seal on the order–

(a) by hand; or

(b) by printing a facsimile of the seal on the order whether electronically or otherwise.

(3) A document purporting to bear the court's seal shall be admissible in evidence without further proof.

Consent orders

33.42.–(1) This rule applies where all the parties to restraint proceedings or receivership proceed- **B-456** ings agree the terms in which an order should be made.

(2) Any party may apply for a judgment or order in the terms agreed.

(3) The Crown Court may deal with an application under paragraph (2) without a hearing.

(4) Where this rule applies—

(a) the order which is agreed by the parties must be drawn up in the terms agreed;

(b) it must be expressed as being "By Consent"; and

(c) it must be signed by the legal representative acting for each of the parties to whom the order relates or by the party if he is a litigant in person.

(5) Where an application is made under this rule, then the requirements of any other rule as to the procedure for making an application do not apply.

Slips and omissions

33.43.–(1) The Crown Court may at any time correct an accidental slip or omission in an order **B-457** made in restraint proceedings or receivership proceedings.

(2) A party may apply for a correction without notice.

Supply of documents from court records

33.44.–(1) No document relating to restraint proceedings or receivership proceedings may be supplied from the records of the Crown Court for any person to inspect or copy unless the Crown Court grants permission.

(2) An application for permission under paragraph (1) must be made on notice to the parties to the proceedings.

Disclosure of documents in criminal proceedings

33.45.–(1) This rule applies where— **B-458**

(a) proceedings for an offence have been started in the Crown Court and the defendant has not been either convicted or acquitted on all counts; and

(b) an application for a restraint order under section 42(1) of the Proceeds of Crime Act 2002 [§ 5-817 in the main work] has been made.

(2) The judge presiding at the proceedings for the offence may be supplied from the records of the Crown Court with documents relating to restraint proceedings and any receivership proceedings.

(3) Such documents must not otherwise be disclosed in the proceedings for the offence.

Preparation of documents

33.46.–(1) Every order in restraint proceedings or receivership proceedings must be drawn up by **B-459** the Crown Court unless—

(a) the Crown Court orders a party to draw it up;

(b) a party, with the permission of the Crown Court, agrees to draw it up; or

(c) the order is made by consent under rule 33.42.

(2) The Crown Court may direct that—

(a) an order drawn up by a party must be checked by the Crown Court before it is sealed; or

(b) before an order is drawn up by the Crown Court, the parties must lodge an agreed statement of its terms.

(3) Where an order is to be drawn up by a party—

(a) he must lodge it with the Crown Court no later than 7 days after the date on which the court ordered or permitted him to draw it up so that it can be sealed by the Crown Court; and

(b) if he fails to lodge it within that period, any other party may draw it up and lodge it.

(4) Nothing in this rule shall require the Crown Court to accept a document which is illegible, has not been duly authorised, or is unsatisfactory for some other similar reason.

Order for costs

33.47.–(1) This rule applies where the Crown Court is deciding whether to make an order for **B-460** costs in restraint proceedings or receivership proceedings.

(2) The court has discretion as to—

    (a) whether costs are payable by one party to another;

    (b) the amount of those costs; and

    (c) when they are to be paid.

(3) If the court decides to make an order about costs—

    (a) the general rule is that the unsuccessful party must be ordered to pay the costs of the successful party; but

    (b) the court may make a different order.

(4) In deciding what order (if any) to make about costs, the court must have regard to all of the circumstances, including—

    (a) the conduct of all the parties; and

    (b) whether a party has succeeded on part of an application, even if he has not been wholly successful.

(5) The orders which the court may make include an order that a party must pay—

    (a) a proportion of another party's costs;

    (b) a stated amount in respect of another party's costs;

    (c) costs from or until a certain date only;

    (d) costs incurred before proceedings have begun;

    (e) costs relating to particular steps taken in the proceedings;

    (f) costs relating only to a distinct part of the proceedings; and

    (g) interest on costs from or until a certain date, including a date before the making of an order.

(6) Where the court would otherwise consider making an order under paragraph (5)(f), it must instead, if practicable, make an order under paragraph (5)(a) or (c).

(7) Where the court has ordered a party to pay costs, it may order an amount to be paid on account before the costs are assessed.

Assessment of costs

B-461   **33.48.**—(1) Where the Crown Court has made an order for costs in restraint proceedings or receivership proceedings it may either—

    (a) make an assessment of the costs itself; or

    (b) order assessment of the costs under rule 45.11.

(2) In either case, the Crown Court or the assessing authority, as the case may be, must—

    (a) only allow costs which are proportionate to the matters in issue; and

    (b) resolve any doubt which it may have as to whether the costs were reasonably incurred or reasonable and proportionate in favour of the paying party.

(3) The Crown Court or the assessing authority, as the case may be, is to have regard to all the circumstances in deciding whether costs were proportionately or reasonably incurred or proportionate and reasonable in amount.

(4) In particular, the Crown Court or the assessing authority must give effect to any orders which have already been made.

(5) The Crown Court or the assessing authority must also have regard to—

    (a) the conduct of all the parties, including in particular, conduct before, as well as during, the proceedings;

    (b) the amount or value of the property involved;

    (c) the importance of the matter to all the parties;

    (d) the particular complexity of the matter or the difficulty or novelty of the questions raised;

    (e) the skill, effort, specialised knowledge and responsibility involved;

    (f) the time spent on the application; and

    (g) the place where and the circumstances in which work or any part of it was done.

Time for complying with an order for costs

B-462   **33.49.** A party to restraint proceedings or receivership proceedings must comply with an order for the payment of costs within 14 days of—

    (a) the date of the order if it states the amount of those costs;

    (b) if the amount of those costs is decided later under rule 45.11, the date of the assessing authority's decision; or

    (c) in either case, such later date as the Crown Court may specify.

Application of costs rules

33.50. Rules 33.47, 33.48 and 33.49 do not apply to the assessment of costs in proceedings to the extent that section 11 of the Access to Justice Act 1999 applies and provisions made under that Act make different provision.

Restraint proceedings

Application for restraint order or ancillary order

33.51.–(1) This rule applies where the prosecutor, or an accredited financial investigator, makes **B-463** an application under section 42 of the Proceeds of Crime Act 2002 [§ 5-817 in the main work] for—

(a) a restraint order, under section 41(1) of the 2002 Act [*ibid.*, § 5-807]; or

(b) an ancillary order, under section 41(7) of that Act, for the purpose of ensuring that a restraint order is effective.

(2) The application may be made without notice if the application is urgent or if there are reasonable grounds for believing that giving notice would cause the dissipation of realisable property which is the subject of the application.

(3) An application for a restraint order must be in writing and supported by a witness statement which must—

(a) give the grounds for the application;

(b) to the best of the witness' ability, give full details of the realisable property in respect of which the applicant is seeking the order and specify the person holding that realisable property;

(c) include the proposed terms of the order.

(4) An application for an ancillary order must be in writing and supported by a witness statement which must—

(a) give the grounds for, and full details of, the application;

(b) include, if appropriate—

(i) any request for an order for disclosure of documents to which rule 33.40 applies (disclosure and inspection of documents),

(ii) the identity of any person whom the applicant wants the court to examine about the extent or whereabouts of realisable property,

(iii) a list of the main questions that the applicant wants to ask any such person, and

(iv) a list of any documents to which the applicant wants to refer such a person; and

(c) include the proposed terms of the order.

(5) An application for a restraint order and an application for an ancillary order may (but need not) be made at the same time and contained in the same documents.

(6) An application by an accredited financial investigator must include a statement that, under section 68 of the 2002 Act [*ibid.*, § 5-871], the applicant has authority to apply.

Restraint and ancillary orders

33.52.–(1) The Crown Court may make a restraint order subject to exceptions, including, but not **B-464** limited to, exceptions for reasonable living expenses and reasonable legal expenses, and for the purpose of enabling any person to carry on any trade, business or occupation.

(2) But the Crown Court must not make an exception for legal expenses where this is prohibited by section 41(4) of the Proceeds of Crime Act 2002.

(3) An exception to a restraint order may be made subject to conditions.

(4) The Crown Court must not require the applicant for a restraint order to give any undertaking relating to damages sustained as a result of the restraint order by a person who is prohibited from dealing with realisable property by the restraint order.

(5) The Crown Court may require the applicant for a restraint order to give an undertaking to pay the reasonable expenses of any person, other than a person who is prohibited from dealing with realisable property by the restraint order, which are incurred in complying with the restraint order.

(6) An order must include a statement that disobedience of the order, either by a person to whom the order is addressed, or by another person, may be contempt of court and the order must include details of the possible consequences of being held in contempt of court.

(7) Unless the Crown Court otherwise directs, an order made without notice has effect until the court makes an order varying or discharging it.

(8) The applicant for an order must—

(a) serve copies of the order and of the witness statement made in support of the application on the defendant and any person who is prohibited by the order from dealing with realisable property; and

(b) notify any person whom the applicant knows to be affected by the order of its terms.

Application for discharge or variation of restraint or ancillary order by a person affected by the order

B-465   **33.53.**—(1) This rule applies where a person affected by a restraint order makes an application to the Crown Court under section 42(3) of the Proceeds of Crime Act 2002 to discharge or vary the restraint order or any ancillary order made under section 41(7) of the Act.

(2) The application must be in writing and may be supported by a witness statement.

(3) The application and any witness statement must be lodged with the Crown Court.

(4) The application and any witness statement must be served on the person who applied for the restraint order and any person who is prohibited from dealing with realisable property by the restraint order (if he is not the person making the application) at least 2 days before the date fixed by the court for hearing the application, unless the Crown Court specifies a shorter period.

Application for variation of restraint or ancillary order by the person who applied for the order

B-466   **33.54.**—(1) This rule applies where the applicant for a restraint order makes an application under section 42(3) of the Proceeds of Crime Act 2002 to the Crown Court to vary the restraint order or any ancillary order made under section 41(7) of the 2002 Act (including where the court has already made a restraint order and the applicant is seeking to vary the order in order to restrain further realisable property).

(2) The application may be made without notice if the application is urgent or if there are reasonable grounds for believing that giving notice would cause the dissipation of realizable property which is the subject of the application.

(3) The application must be in writing and must be supported by a witness statement which must—

(a) give the grounds for the application;

(b) where the application is for the inclusion of further realisable property in a restraint order give full details, to the best of the witness's ability, of the realisable property in respect of which the applicant is seeking the order and specify the person holding that realisable property;

(c) where the application is to vary an ancillary order, include, if appropriate—

(i) any request for an order for disclosure of documents to which rule 33.40 applies (disclosure and inspection of documents),

(ii) the identity of any person whom the applicant wants the court to examine about the extent or whereabouts of realisable property,

(iii) a list of the main questions that the applicant wants to ask any such person, and

(iv) a list of any documents to which the applicant wants to refer such a person; and

(d) include the proposed terms of the variation.

(4) An application by an accredited financial investigator must include a statement that, under section 68 of the 2002 Act [§ 5-871 in the main work], the applicant has authority to apply.

(5) The application and witness statement must be lodged with the Crown Court.

(6) Except where, under paragraph (2), notice of the application is not required to be served, the application and witness statement must be served on any person who is prohibited from dealing with realisable property by the restraint order at least 2 days before the date fixed by the court for hearing the application, unless the Crown Court specifies a shorter period.

(7) If the court makes an order for the variation of a restraint or ancillary order, the applicant must serve copies of the order and of the witness statement made in support of the application on—

(a) the defendant;

(b) any person who is prohibited from dealing with realisable property by the restraint order (whether before or after the variation); and

(c) any other person whom the applicant knows to be affected by the order.

Application for discharge of restraint or ancillary order by the person who applied for the order

B-467   **33.55.**—(1) This rule applies where the applicant for a restraint order makes an application under section 42(3) of the Proceeds of Crime Act 2002 to discharge the order or any ancillary order made under section 41(7) of the 2002 Act.

(2) The application may be made without notice.

(3) The application must be in writing and must state the grounds for the application.

(4) If the court makes an order for the discharge of a restraint or ancillary order, the applicant must serve copies of the order on—

(a) the defendant;

(b) any person who is prohibited from dealing with realisable property by the restraint order (whether before or after the discharge); and (c)　any other person whom the applicant knows to be affected by the order.

Receivership proceedings

Application for appointment of a management or an enforcement receiver
　33.56.—(1) This rule applies to an application for the appointment of a management receiver　**B-468**
under section 48(1) of the Proceeds of Crime Act 2002 [§ 5-845 in the main work] and an application for the appointment of an enforcement receiver under section 50(1) of the 2002 Act [*ibid.*, §
5-849].
　(2) The application may be made without notice if—
　　(a)　the application is joined with an application for a restraint order under rule 33.51 (applica-
　　　　tion for restraint order or ancillary order);
　　(b)　the application is urgent; or
　　(c)　there are reasonable grounds for believing that giving notice would cause the dissipation of
　　　　realisable property which is the subject of the application.
　(3) The application must be in writing and must be supported by a witness statement which must—
　　(a)　give the grounds for the application;
　　(b)　give full details of the proposed receiver;
　　(c)　to the best of the witness' ability, give full details of the realisable property in respect of
　　　　which the applicant is seeking the order and specify the person holding that realisable
　　　　property;
　　(d)　where the application is made by an accredited financial investigator, include a statement
　　　　that, under section 68 of the 2002 Act [*ibid.*, § 5-871], the applicant has authority to apply;
　　　　and
　　(e)　if the proposed receiver is not a person falling within section 55(8) of the 2002 Act [*ibid.*, §
　　　　5-854] and the applicant is asking the court to allow the receiver to act—
　　　　(i)　without giving security, or
　　　　(ii)　before he has given security or satisfied the court that he has security in place,
　　　　　　explain the reasons why that is necessary.
　(4) Where the application is for the appointment of an enforcement receiver, the applicantn must
provide the Crown Court with a copy of the confiscation order made against the defendant.
　(5) The application and witness statement must be lodged with the Crown Court.
　(6) Except where, under paragraph (2), notice of the application is not required to be served, the
application and witness statement must be lodged with the Crown Court and served on—
　　(a)　the defendant;
　　(b)　any person who holds realisable property to which the application relates; and
　　(c)　any other person whom the applicant knows to be affected by the application,
at least 7 days before the date fixed by the court for hearing the application, unless the Crown Court
specifies a shorter period.
　(7) If the court makes an order for the appointment of a receiver, the applicant must serve copies
of the order and of the witness statement made in support of the application on—
　　(a)　the defendant;
　　(b)　any person who holds realisable property to which the order applies; and
　　(c)　any other person whom the applicant knows to be affected by the order.

Application for conferral of powers on a management receiver or an enforcement receiver
　33.57.—(1) This rule applies to an application for the conferral of powers on a management　**B-469**
receiver under section 49(1) of the Proceeds of Crime Act 2002 [*ibid.*, § 5-847] or an enforcement
receiver under section 51(1) of the 2002 Act [*ibid.*, § 5-850].
　(2) The application may be made without notice if the application is to give the receiver power to
take possession of property and—
　　(a)　the application is joined with an application for a restraint order under rule 33.51 (applica-
　　　　tion for restraint order or ancillary order);
　　(b)　the application is urgent; or
　　(c)　there are reasonable grounds for believing that giving notice would cause the dissipation of
　　　　the property which is the subject of the application.
　(3) The application must be made in writing and supported by a witness statement which must—
　　(a)　give the grounds for the application;
　　(b)　give full details of the realisable property in respect of which the applicant is seeking the
　　　　order and specify the person holding that realisable property;

(c) where the application is made by an accredited financial investigator, include a statement that, under section 68 of the 2002 Act, the applicant has authority to apply; and

(d) where the application is for power to start, carry on or defend legal proceedings in respect of the property, explain—

    (i) what proceedings are concerned, in what court, and

    (ii) what powers the receiver will ask that court to exercise.

(4) Where the application is for the conferral of powers on an enforcement receiver, the applicant must provide the Crown Court with a copy of the confiscation order made against the defendant.

(5) The application and witness statement must be lodged with the Crown Court.

(6) Except where, under paragraph (2), notice of the application is not required to be served, the application and witness statement must be served on—

(a) the defendant;

(b) any person who holds realisable property in respect of which a receiver has been appointed or in respect of which an application for a receiver has been made;

(c) any other person whom the applicant knows to be affected by the application; and

(d) the receiver (if one has already been appointed),

at least 7 days before the date fixed by the court for hearing the application, unless the Crown Court specifies a shorter period.

(7) If the court makes an order for the conferral of powers on a receiver, the applicant must serve copies of the order on—

(a) the defendant;

(b) any person who holds realisable property in respect of which the receiver has been appointed; and

(c) any other person whom the applicant knows to be affected by the order.

Applications for discharge or variation of receivership orders, and applications for other orders

B-470   33.58.—(1) This rule applies to applications under section 62(3) of the Proceeds of Crime Act 2002 [*ibid.*, § 5-861] for orders (by persons affected by the action of receivers) and applications under section 63(1) of the 2002 Act [*ibid.*, § 5-862] for the discharge or variation of orders relating to receivers.

(2) The application must be made in writing and lodged with the Crown Court.

(3) The application must be served on the following persons (except where they are the person making the application)—

(a) the person who applied for appointment of the receiver;

(b) the defendant;

(c) any person who holds realisable property in respect of which the receiver has been appointed;

(d) the receiver; and

(e) any other person whom the applicant knows to be affected by the application,

at least 7 days before the date fixed by the court for hearing the application, unless the Crown Court specifies a shorter period.

(4) If the court makes an order for the discharge or variation of an order relating to a receiver under section 63(2) of the 2002 Act, the applicant must serve copies of the order on any persons whom he knows to be affected by the order.

Sums in the hands of receivers

B-471   33.59.—(1) This rule applies where the amount payable under a confiscation order has been fully paid and any sums remain in the hands of an enforcement receiver.

(2) The receiver must make an application to the Crown Court for directions as to the distribution of the sums in his hands.

(3) The application and any evidence which the receiver intends to rely on in support of the application must be served on—

(a) the defendant; and

(b) any other person who held (or holds) interests in any property realised by the receiver,

at least 7 days before the date fixed by the court for hearing the application, unless the Crown Court specifies a shorter period.

(4) If any of the provisions listed in paragraph (5) (provisions as to the vesting of funds in a trustee in bankruptcy) apply, then the Crown Court must make a declaration to that effect.

(5) These are the provisions—

(a) section 31B of the Bankruptcy (Scotland) Act 1985;

(b) section 306B of the Insolvency Act 1986; and

(c) article 279B of the Insolvency (Northern Ireland) Order 1989.

Security

33.60.–(1) This rule applies where the Crown Court appoints a receiver under section 48 or 50 of the Proceeds of Crime Act 2002 [*ibid.*, §§ 5-845, 5-849] and the receiver is not a person falling within section 55(8) [*ibid.*, § 5-854] of the 2002 Act (and it is immaterial whether the receiver is a permanent or temporary member of staff or on secondment from elsewhere). **B-472**

(2) The Crown Court may direct that before the receiver begins to act, or within a specified time, he must either—

(a) give such security as the Crown Court may determine; or

(b) file with the Crown Court and serve on all parties to any receivership proceedings evidence that he already has in force sufficient security,

to cover his liability for his acts and omissions as a receiver.

(3) The Crown Court may terminate the appointment of a receiver if he fails to—

(a) give the security; or

(b) satisfy the court as to the security he has in force,

by the date specified.

Remuneration

33.61.–(1) [*Identical to r.33.60(1), ante, § B-472.*] **B-473**

(2) The receiver may only charge for his services if the Crown Court—

(a) so directs; and

(b) specifies the basis on which the receiver is to be remunerated.

(3) Unless the Crown Court orders otherwise, in determining the remuneration of the receiver, the Crown Court shall award such sum as is reasonable and proportionate in all the circumstances and which takes into account—

(a) the time properly given by him and his staff to the receivership;

(b) the complexity of the receivership;

(c) any responsibility of an exceptional kind or degree which falls on the receiver in consequence of the receivership;

(d) the effectiveness with which the receiver appears to be carrying out, or to have carried out, his duties; and

(e) the value and nature of the subject matter of the receivership.

(4) The Crown Court may refer the determination of a receiver's remuneration to be ascertained by the taxing authority of the Crown Court and rules 45.11 (assessment and reassessment) to 45.14 (application for an extension of time) shall have effect as if the taxing authority was ascertaining costs.

(5) A receiver appointed under section 48 of the 2002 Act is to receive his remuneration by realising property in respect of which he is appointed, in accordance with section 49(2)(d) of the 2002 Act [*ibid.*, § 5-847].

(6) A receiver appointed under section 50 of the 2002 Act is to receive his remuneration by applying to the magistrates' court officer for payment under section 55(4)(b) of the 2002 Act.

Accounts

33.62.–(1) The Crown Court may order a receiver appointed under section 48 or 50 of the Proceeds of Crime Act 2002 to prepare and serve accounts. **B-474**

(2) A party to receivership proceedings served with such accounts may apply for an order permitting him to inspect any document in the possession of the receiver relevant to those accounts.

(3) Any party to receivership proceedings may, within 14 days of being served with the accounts, serve notice on the receiver—

(a) specifying any item in the accounts to which he objects;

(b) giving the reason for such objection; and

(c) requiring the receiver within 14 days of receipt of the notice, either—

(i) to notify all the parties who were served with the accounts that he accepts the objection, or

(ii) if he does not accept the objection, to apply for an examination of the accounts in relation to the contested item.

(4) When the receiver applies for the examination of the accounts he must at the same time lodge with the Crown Court—

(a) the accounts; and

(b) a copy of the notice served on him under this section of the rule.

(5) If the receiver fails to comply with paragraph (3)(c) of this rule, any party to receivership proceedings may apply to the Crown Court for an examination of the accounts in relation to the contested item.

(6) At the conclusion of its examination of the accounts the court must certify the result.

Non-compliance by receiver

B-475   **33.63.**–(1) If a receiver appointed under section 48 or 50 of the Proceeds of Crime Act 2002 fails to comply with any rule, practice direction or direction of the Crown Court, the Crown Court may order him to attend a hearing to explain his non-compliance.

(2) At the hearing, the Crown Court may make any order it considers appropriate, including–

(a) terminating the appointment of the receiver;

(b) reducing the receiver's remuneration or disallowing it altogether; and

(c) ordering the receiver to pay the costs of any party.

Statements, etc. relevant to making confiscation orders

B-476   **33.64.**–(1) Where a prosecutor or defendant–

(a) serves on the magistrates' court officer any statement or other document under section 73 of the Criminal Justice Act 1988 in any proceedings in respect of an offence listed in Schedule 4 to that Act; or

(b) serves on the Crown Court officer any statement or other document under section 11 of the Drug Trafficking Act 1994 or section 73 of the 1988 Act in any proceedings in respect of a drug trafficking offence or in respect of an offence to which Part VI of the 1988 Act applies,

that party must serve a copy as soon as practicable on the defendant or the prosecutor, as the case may be.

(2) Any statement tendered by the prosecutor to the magistrates' court under section 73 of the 1988 Act or to the Crown Court under section 11(1) of the 1994 Act or section 73(1A) of the 1988 Act must include the following particulars–

(a) the name of the defendant;

(b) the name of the person by whom the statement is made and the date on which it was made;

(c) where the statement is not tendered immediately after the defendant has been convicted, the date on which and the place where the relevant conviction occurred; and

(d) such information known to the prosecutor as is relevant to the determination as to whether or not the defendant has benefited from drug trafficking or relevant criminal conduct and to the assessment of the value of any proceeds of drug trafficking or, as the case may be, benefit from relevant criminal conduct.

(3) Where, in accordance with section 11(7) of the 1994 Act or section 73(1C) of the 1988 Act, the defendant indicates in writing the extent to which he or she accepts any allegation contained within the prosecutor's statement, the defendant must serve a copy of that reply on the court officer.

(4) Expressions used in this rule have the same meanings as in the 1994 Act or, where appropriate, the 1988 Act.

Postponed determinations

B-477   **33.65.**–(1) Where an application is made by the defendant or the prosecutor–

(a) to a magistrates' court under section 72A(5)(a) of the Criminal Justice Act 1988 asking the court to exercise its powers under section 72A(4) of that Act; or

(b) to the Crown Court under section 3(5)(a) of the Drug Trafficking Act 1994 asking the court to exercise its powers under section 3(4) of that Act, or under section 72A(5)(a) of the 1988 Act asking the court to exercise its powers under section 72A(4) of the 1988 Act,

the application must be in writing and the applicant must serve a copy on the prosecutor or the defendant, as the case may be.

(2) A party served with a copy of an application under paragraph (1) must, within 28 days of the date of service, notify the applicant and the court officer, in writing, whether or not that party opposes the application, giving reasons for any opposition.

(3) After the expiry of the period referred to in paragraph (2), the court may determine an application under paragraph (1)–

(a) without a hearing; or

(b) at a hearing at which the parties may be represented.

Confiscation orders - revised assessments

33.66.—(1) Where the prosecutor makes an application under section 13, 14 or 15 of the Drug **B-478**
Trafficking Act 1994 or section 74A, 74B or 74C of the Criminal Justice Act 1988, the application
must be in writing and a copy must be served on the defendant.

(2) The application must include the following particulars —

    (a)   the name of the defendant;

    (b)   the date on which and the place where any relevant conviction occurred;

    (c)   the date on which and the place where any relevant confiscation order was made or, as the
case may be, varied;

    (d)   the grounds on which the application is made; and

    (e)   an indication of the evidence available to support the application.

Application to the Crown Court to discharge or vary order to make material available

33.67.—(1) Where an order under section 93H of the Criminal Justice Act 1988 (order to make **B-479**
material available) or section 55 of the Drug Trafficking Act 1994 (order to make material available
[§ 15-291 in the main work]) has been made by the Crown Court, any person affected by it may apply in writing to the court officer for the order to be discharged or varied, and on hearing such an
application the court may discharge the order or make such variations to it as the court thinks fit.

(2) Subject to paragraph (3), where a person proposes to make an application under paragraph (1)
for the discharge or variation of an order, that person must give a copy of the application, not later
than 48 hours before the making of the application—

    (a)   to a constable at the police station specified in the order; or

    (b)   to the office of the appropriate officer who made the application, as specified in the order,
in either case together with a notice indicating the time and place at which the application for
discharge or variation is to be made.

(3) The court may direct that paragraph (2) need not be complied with if satisfied that the person
making the application has good reason to seek a discharge or variation of the order as soon as possible and it is not practicable to comply with that paragraph.

(4) In this rule:

    "constable" includes a person commissioned by the Commissioners for Her Majesty's Revenue
and Customs;

    "police station" includes a place for the time being occupied by Her Majesty's Revenue and
Customs.

Application to the Crown Court for increase in term of imprisonment in default of payment

33.68.—(1) This rule applies to applications made, or that have effect as made, to the Crown Court **B-480**
under section 10 of the Drug Trafficking Act 1994 and section 75A of the Criminal Justice Act 1988
(interest on sums unpaid under confiscation orders).

(2) Notice of an application to which this rule applies to increase the term of imprisonment or
detention fixed in default of payment of a confiscation order by a person ("the defendant") must be
made by the prosecutor in writing to the court officer.

(3) A notice under paragraph (2) shall—

    (a)   state the name and address of the defendant;

    (b)   specify the grounds for the application;

    (c)   give details of the enforcement measures taken, if any; and

    (d)   include a copy of the confiscation order.

(4) On receiving a notice under paragraph (2), the court officer must —

    (a)   forthwith send to the defendant and the magistrates' court required to enforce payment of
the confiscation order under section 140(1) of the Powers of Criminal Courts (Sentencing)
Act 2000 [*ibid.*, § 5-651.], a copy of the said notice; and

    (b)   notify in writing the applicant and the defendant of the date, time and place appointed for
the hearing of the application.

(5) Where the Crown Court makes an order pursuant to an application mentioned in paragraph
(1) above, the court officer must send forthwith a copy of the order—

    (a)   to the applicant;

    (b)   to the defendant;

    (c)   where the defendant is at the time of the making of the order in custody, to the person
having custody of him or her; and

    (d)   to the magistrates' court mentioned in paragraph (4)(a).

Drug trafficking - compensation on acquittal in the Crown Court

B-481   **33.69.** Where the Crown Court cancels a confiscation order under section 22(2) of the Drug Trafficking Act 1994, the Crown Court officer must serve notice to that effect on the High Court officer
and on the court officer of the magistrates' court which has responsibility for enforcing the order.

Contempt proceedings

Application to punish for contempt of court

B-482   **33.70.**–(1) This rule applies where a person is accused of disobeying–

(a) a compliance order made for the purpose of ensuring that a confiscation order is effective;

(b) a restraint order; or

(c) an ancillary order made for the purpose of ensuring that a restraint order is effective.

(2) An applicant who wants the Crown Court to exercise its power to punish that person for
contempt of court must comply with the rules in Part 48 (contempt of court).

Criminal Procedure Rules 2015 (S.I. 2015 No. 1490), Pt 34

APPEAL TO THE CROWN COURT

When this Part applies

B-483   **34.1.**–(1) This Part applies where–

(a) a defendant wants to appeal under–

(i)   section 108 of the Magistrates' Courts Act 1980,

(ii)   section 45 of the Mental Health Act 1983,

(iii) paragraph 10 of Schedule 3 to the Powers of Criminal Courts (Sentencing) Act 2000,
or paragraphs 9(8) or 13(5) of Schedule 8 to the Criminal Justice Act 2003,

(iv)   section 42 of the Counter-Terrorism Act 2008;

(b) the Criminal Cases Review Commission refers a defendant's case to the Crown Court under
section 11 of the Criminal Appeal Act 1995;

(c) a prosecutor wants to appeal under–

(i)   section 14A(5A) of the Football Spectators Act 1989, or

(ii)   section 147(3) of the Customs and Excise Management Act 1979; or

(d) a person wants to appeal under–

(i)   section 1 of the Magistrates' Courts (Appeals from Binding Over Orders) Act 1956,

(ii)   section 12(5) of the Contempt of Court Act 1981,

(iii) regulation 3C or 3H of the Costs in Criminal Cases (General) Regulations 1986,

(iv)   section 22 of the Football Spectators Act 1989, or

(v)   section 10(4) or (5) of the Crime and Disorder Act 1998.

(2) A reference to an "appellant" in this Part is a reference to such a party or person.

For section 108 of the 1980 Act, see § 2-95 in the main work; for section 45 of the 1983 Act,
see *ibid.*, § 2-103; for Schedule 3 to the 2000 Act, see §§ 5-228 *et seq.* in the supplements to the
2012 edition of this work; for Schedule 8 to the 2003 Act, see §§ 5-312 *et seq.* in the main work;
for section 11 of the 1995 Act, see *ibid.*, § 2-107; for section 14A of the 1989 Act, see *ibid.*, §
5-1095; for section 147 of the 1979 Act, see *ibid.*, § 25-449; for section 1 of the 1956 Act, see *ibid.*,
§ 2-97; for section 12 of the 1981 Act, see *ibid.*, § 28-81; for regulations 3C and 3H of the 1986
regulations, see *ibid.*, §§ 6-60, 6-65; for section 22 of the 1989 Act, see *ibid.*, § 2-99; and for section 10 of the 1998 Act, see *ibid.*, § 5-1308. Section 42 of the 2008 Act is not set out in this work.

Service of appeal notice

B-484   **34.2.**–(1) An appellant must serve an appeal notice on–

(a) the magistrates' court officer; and

(b) every other party.

(2) The appellant must serve the appeal notice–

(a) as soon after the decision appealed against as the appellant wants; but

(b) not more than 21 days after–

(i)   sentence or the date sentence is deferred, whichever is earlier, if the appeal is against
conviction or against a finding of guilt,

(ii)   sentence, if the appeal is against sentence, or

    (iii)   the order or failure to make an order about which the appellant wants to appeal, in any other case.

(3) The appellant must serve with the appeal notice any application for the following, with reasons—

    (a)   an extension of the time limit under this rule, if the appeal notice is late;

    (b)   bail pending appeal, if the appellant is in custody;

    (c)   the suspension of any disqualification imposed in the case, where the magistrates' court or the Crown Court can order such a suspension pending appeal.

(4) Where both the magistrates' court and the Crown Court can grant bail or suspend a disqualification pending appeal, an application must indicate by which court the appellant wants the application determined.

[This rule is printed as amended by the Criminal Procedure (Amendment No. 2) Rules 2016 (S.I. 2016 No. 705).]

Form of appeal notice

34.3. The appeal notice must be in writing and must—   **B-485**

    (a)   specify—

        (i)   the conviction or finding of guilt,

        (ii)   the sentence, or

        (iii)   the order, or the failure to make an order,

        about which the appellant wants to appeal;

    (b)   summarise the issues;

    (c)   in an appeal against conviction—

        (i)   identify the prosecution witnesses whom the appellant will want to question if they are called to give oral evidence, and

        (ii)   say how long the trial lasted in the magistrates' court and how long the appeal is likely to last in the Crown Court;

    (d)   in an appeal against a finding that the appellant insulted someone or interrupted proceedings in the magistrates' court, attach—

        (i)   the magistrates' court's written findings of fact, and

        (ii)   the appellant's response to those findings;

    (e)   say whether the appellant has asked the magistrates' court to reconsider the case; and

    (f)   include a list of those on whom the appellant has served the appeal notice.

Duty of magistrates' court officer

34.4. The magistrates' court officer must—   **B-486**

    (a)   as soon as practicable serve on the Crown Court officer—

        (i)   the appeal notice and any accompanying application served by the appellant,

        (ii)   details of the parties including their addresses,

        (iii)   a copy of each magistrates' court register entry relating to the decision under appeal and to any application for bail pending appeal, and

        (iv)   any report received for the purposes of sentencing;

    (b)   keep any document or object exhibited in the proceedings in the magistrates' court, or arrange for it to be kept by some other appropriate person, until—

        (i)   6 weeks after the conclusion of those proceedings, or

        (ii)   the conclusion of any proceedings in the Crown Court that begin within that 6 weeks;

    (c)   provide the Crown Court with any document, object or information for which the Crown Court officer asks, within such period as the Crown Court officer may require; and

    (d)   arrange for the magistrates' court to hear as soon as practicable any application to that court under rule 34.2(3)(c) (suspension of disqualification pending appeal).

Duty of person keeping exhibit

34.5. A person who, under arrangements made by the magistrates' court officer, keeps a document   **B-487** or object exhibited in the proceedings in the magistrates' court must—

    (a)   keep that exhibit until—

        (i)   6 weeks after the conclusion of those proceedings, or

        (ii)   the conclusion of any proceedings in the Crown Court that begin within that 6 weeks, unless the magistrates' court or the Crown Court otherwise directs; and

    (b)   provide the Crown Court with any such document or object for which the Crown Court officer asks, within such period as the Crown Court officer may require.

Reference by the Criminal Cases Review Commission

B-488   **34.6.**–(1) The Crown Court officer must, as soon as practicable, serve a reference by the Criminal Cases Review Commission on—

    (a) the appellant;

    (b) every other party; and

    (c) the magistrates' court officer.

  (2) The appellant may serve an appeal notice on—

    (a) the Crown Court officer; and

    (b) every other party,

not more than 21 days later.

  (3) The Crown Court must treat the reference as the appeal notice if the appellant does not serve an appeal notice.

Application to introduce further evidence or for ruling on procedure, evidence or other question of law

B-489   **34.7.**–(1) Paragraph (2) of this rule applies where—

    (a) a party wants to introduce evidence which was not introduced by either party in the magistrates' court; and

    (b) one of these Parts applies—

        (i) Part 18 (measures to assist a witness or defendant to give evidence),

        (ii) Part 20 (hearsay evidence),

        (iii) Part 21 (evidence of bad character), or

        (iv) Part 22 (evidence of a complainant's previous sexual behaviour).

  (2) Such a party must serve the notice or application to introduce evidence required by that Part not more than 14 days after service of the appeal notice.

  (3) Paragraph (4) of this rule applies to an application—

    (a) about—

        (i) case management, or any other question of procedure, or

        (ii) the introduction or admissibility of evidence, or any other question of law;

    (b) that has not been determined before the hearing of the appeal begins.

  (4) The application is subject to any other rule that applies to it (for example, as to the time and form in which the application must be made).

[This rule is printed as amended by the Criminal Procedure (Amendment) Rules 2016 (S.I. 2016 No. 120).]

Hearings and decisions

B-490   **34.8.**–(1) The Crown Court as a general rule must hear in public an appeal or reference to which this Part applies, but—

    (a) may order any hearing to be in private; and

    (b) where a hearing is about a public interest ruling, must hold that hearing in private.

  (2) The Crown Court officer must give as much notice as reasonably practicable of every hearing to—

    (a) the parties;

    (b) any party's custodian; and

    (c) any other person whom the Crown Court requires to be notified.

  (3) The Crown Court officer must serve every decision on—

    (a) the parties;

    (b) any other person whom the Crown Court requires to be served; and

    (c) the magistrates' court officer and any party's custodian, where the decision determines an appeal.

  (4) But where a hearing or decision is about a public interest ruling, the Crown Court officer must not—

    (a) give notice of that hearing to; or

    (b) serve that decision on,

anyone other than the prosecutor who applied for that ruling, unless the court otherwise directs.

Abandoning an appeal

B-491   **34.9.**–(1) The appellant—

    (a) may abandon an appeal without the Crown Court's permission, by serving a notice of abandonment on—

    (i)   the magistrates' court officer,

    (ii) the Crown Court officer, and

    (iii) every other party

    before the hearing of the appeal begins; but

  (b) after the hearing of the appeal begins, may only abandon the appeal with the Crown Court's permission.

(2) A notice of abandonment must be signed by or on behalf of the appellant.

(3) Where an appellant who is on bail pending appeal abandons an appeal—

  (a) the appellant must surrender to custody as directed by the magistrates' court officer; and

  (b) any conditions of bail apply until then.

Court's power to vary requirements under this Part

34.10. The Crown Court may—   **B-492**

  (a) shorten or extend (even after it has expired) a time limit under this Part;

  (b) allow an appellant to vary an appeal notice that that appellant has served;

  (c) direct that an appeal notice be served on any person; (d) allow an appeal notice or a notice of abandonment to be in a different form to one set out in the Practice Direction, or to be presented orally.

Constitution of the Crown Court

34.11. (1) On the hearing of an appeal the general rule is that—   ★**B-493**

  (a) the Crown Court must comprise—

    (i)   a judge of the High Court, a Circuit judge, a Recorder or a qualifying judge advocate, and

    (ii) no less than two and no more than four justices of the peace, none of whom took part in the decision under appeal; and

  (b) if the appeal is from a youth court, each justice of the peace must be qualified to sit as a member of a youth court

(2) Despite the general rule—

  (a) the Crown Court may include only one justice of the peace if—

    (i)   the presiding judge decides that otherwise the start of the appeal hearing will be delayed unreasonably, or

    (ii) one or more of the justices of the peace who started hearing the appeal is absent; and

  (b) the Crown Court may comprise only a judge of the High Court, a Circuit judge, a Recorder or a qualifying judge advocate if—

    (i)   the appeal is against conviction, under section 108 of the Magistrates' Courts Act 1980, and

    (ii) the respondent agrees that the court should allow the appeal, under section 48(2) of the Senior Courts Act 1981 [§ 2-114 in the main work].

(3) Before the hearing of an appeal begins—

  (a) the Crown Court may comprise only a judge of the High Court, a Circuit judge, a Recorder or a qualifying judge advocate; and

  (b) so constituted, the court may, among other things, exercise the powers to which the rules in this Part and in Part 3 (case management) apply.

[This rule is printed as substituted by the Criminal Procedure (Amendment) Rules 2016 (S.I. 2016 No. 120); and as subsequently amended by the Criminal Procedure (Amendment) Rules 2017 (S.I. 2017 No. 144).]

CPD IX Appeal 34A: Appeals to the Crown Court

34A.1 CrimPR 34.4 applies when a defendant appeals to the Crown Court against conviction or **B-494** sentence and specifies the information and documentation that must be provided by the magistrates' court.

34A.2 On an appeal against conviction, the reasons given by the magistrates for their decision should not be included with the documents; the appeal hearing is not a review of the magistrates' court's decision but a re-hearing.

34A.3 On an appeal against sentence, the magistrates' court's reasons and factual finding leading to the finding of guilt should be included, but any reasons for the sentence imposed should be omitted as the Crown Court will be conducting a fresh sentencing exercise.

Criminal Procedure Rules 2015 (S.I. 2015 No. 1490), Pt 35

APPEAL TO THE HIGH COURT BY CASE STATED

When this Part applies

B-495   **35.1.–** This Part applies where a person wants to appeal to the High Court by case stated–

(a)   under section 111 of the Magistrates' Courts Act 1980 [§ 2-108 in the main work], against a decision of a magistrates' court; or

(b)   under section 28 of the Senior Courts Act 1981 [*ibid.*, § 7-2], against a decision of the Crown Court.

Application to state a case

B-496   **35.2.–**(1) A party who wants the court to state a case for the opinion of the High Court must–

(a)   apply in writing, not more than 21 days after the decision against which the applicant wants to appeal; and

(b)   serve the application on–

(i)   the court officer, and

(ii)   each other party.

(2) The application must–

(a)   specify the decision in issue;

(b)   specify the proposed question or questions of law or jurisdiction on which the opinion of the High Court will be asked; (c) indicate the proposed grounds of appeal; and

(d)   include or attach any application for the following, with reasons–

(i)   if the application is to the Crown Court, an extension of time within which to apply to state a case,

(ii)   bail pending appeal,

(iii)   the suspension of any disqualification imposed in the case, where the court can order such a suspension pending appeal.

(3) A party who wants to make representations about the application must–

(a)   serve the representations on–

(i)   the court officer, and

(ii)   each other party; and

(b)   do so not more than 14 days after service of the application.

(4) The court may determine the application without a hearing.

(5) If the court decides not to state a case, the court officer must serve on each party–

(a)   notice of that decision; and

(b)   the court's written reasons for that decision, if not more than 21 days later the applicant asks for those reasons.

Preparation of case stated

35.3–(1) This rule applies where the court decides to state a case for the opinion of the High Court.

(2) The court officer must serve on each party notice of–

(a)   the decision to state a case, and

(b)   any recognizance ordered by the court.

(3) Unless the court otherwise directs, not more than 21 days after the court's decision to state a case–

(a)   in a magistrates court, the court officer must serve a draft case on each party;

(b)   in the Crown Court, the applicant must serve a draft case on the court officer and each other party.

(4) The draft case must–

(a)   specify the decision in issue;

(b)   specify the question(s) of law or jurisdiction on which the opinion of the High Court will be asked;

(c)   include a succinct summary of–

(i)   the nature and history of the proceedings,

  (ii) the court's relevant findings of fact, and

  (iii) the relevant contentions of the parties;

 (d) if a question is whether there was sufficient evidence on which the court reasonably could reach a finding of fact—

  (i) specify that finding, and

  (ii) include a summary of the evidence on which the court reached that finding.

(5) Except to the extent that paragraph (4)(d) requires, the draft case must not include an account of the evidence received by the court.

(6) A party who wants to make representations about the content of the draft case, or to propose a revised draft, must—

 (a) serve the representations, or revised draft, on—

  (i) the court officer, and

  (ii) each other party; and

 (b) do so not more than 21 days after service of the draft case.

(7) The court must state the case not more than 21 days after the time for service of representations under paragraph (6) has expired.

(8) A case stated for the opinion of the High Court must—

 (a) comply with paragraphs (4) and (5); and

 (b) identify—

  (i) the court that stated it, and

  (ii) the court office for that court.

(9) The court officer must serve the case stated on each party.

Duty of justices' legal adviser

35.4.–(1) This rule applies—   **B-497**

 (a) only in a magistrates' court; and

 (b) unless the court—

  (i) includes a District Judge (Magistrates' Courts), and

  (ii) otherwise directs.

(2) A justices' legal adviser must—

 (a) give the court legal advice; and

 (b) if the court so requires, assist it by—

  (i) preparing and amending the draft case, and

  (ii) completing the case stated.

Court's power to vary requirements under this Part

35.5.–(1) The court may shorten or extend (even after it has expired) a time limit under this Part. **B-498**

(2) A person who wants an extension of time must –

 (a) apply when serving the application, representations or draft case for which it is needed; and

 (b) explain the delay.

Criminal Procedure Rules 2015 (S.I. 2015 No. 1490), Pt 36

APPEAL TO THE COURT OF APPEAL: GENERAL RULES

When this Part applies

36.1.–(1) This Part applies to all the applications, appeals and references to the Court of Appeal **B-499**
to which Parts 37, 38, 39, 40, 41 and 43 apply.

(2) In this Part and in those, unless the context makes it clear that something different is meant "court" means the Court of Appeal or any judge of that court.

Case management in the Court of Appeal

36.2.–(1) The court and the parties have the same duties and powers as under Part 3 (case **B-500**
management).

(2) The Registrar—

 (a) must fulfil the duty of active case management under rule 3.2; and

 (b) in fulfilling that duty may exercise any of the powers of case management under—

  (i) rule 3.5 (the court's general powers of case management),

  (ii) rule 3.10(3) (requiring a certificate of readiness), and

(iii)   rule 3.11 (requiring a party to identify intentions and anticipated requirements) subject to the directions of the court.

(3) The Registrar must nominate a case progression officer under rule 3.4.

Power to vary requirements

B-501   **36.3.** The court or the Registrar may—

(a)   shorten a time limit or extend it (even after it has expired) unless that is inconsistent with other legislation;

(b)   allow a party to vary any notice that that party has served;

(c)   direct that a notice or application be served on any person;

(d)   allow a notice or application to be in a different form, or presented orally.

Application for extension of time

B-502   **36.4.** A person who wants an extension of time within which to serve a notice or make an application must—

(a)   apply for that extension of time when serving that notice or making that application; and

(b)   give the reasons for the application for an extension of time.

Renewing an application refused by a judge or the Registrar

B-503   **36.5.**–(1) This rule applies where a party with the right to do so wants to renew—

(a)   to a judge of the Court of Appeal an application refused by the Registrar; or

(b)   to the Court of Appeal an application refused by a judge of that court.

(2) That party must—

(a)   renew the application in the form set out in the Practice Direction, signed by or on behalf of the applicant;

(b)   serve the renewed application on the Registrar not more than 14 days after—

(i)   the refusal of the application that the applicant wants to renew; or

(ii)   the Registrar serves that refusal on the applicant, if the applicant was not present in person or by live link when the original application was refused.

Hearings

B-504   **36.6.**–(1) The general rule is that the Court of Appeal must hear in public—

(a)   an application, including an application for permission to appeal; and

(b)   an appeal or reference,

but it may order any hearing to be in private.

(2) Where a hearing is about a public interest ruling that hearing must be in private unless the court otherwise directs.

(3) Where the appellant wants to appeal against an order restricting public access to a trial the court—

(a)   may decide without a hearing—

(i)   an application, including an application for permission to appeal, and

(ii)   an appeal; but

(b)   must announce its decision on such an appeal at a hearing in public.

(4) Where the appellant wants to appeal or to refer a case to the Supreme Court the court—

(a)   may decide without a hearing an application—

(i)   for permission to appeal or to refer a sentencing case, or

(ii)   to refer a point of law; but

(b)   must announce its decision on such an application at a hearing in public.

(5) A judge of the Court of Appeal and the Registrar may exercise any of their powers—

(a)   at a hearing in public or in private; or

(b)   without a hearing.

Notice of hearings and decisions

B-505   **36.7.**–(1) The Registrar must give as much notice as reasonably practicable of every hearing to—

(a)   the parties;

(b)   any party's custodian;

(c)   any other person whom the court requires to be notified; and

(d)   the Crown Court officer, where Parts 37, 38 or 40 apply.

(2) The Registrar must serve every decision on—

(a) the parties;

(b) any other person whom the court requires to be served; and

(c) the Crown Court officer and any party's custodian, where the decision determines an appeal or application for permission to appeal.

(3) But where a hearing or decision is about a public interest ruling, the Registrar must not—

(a) give notice of that hearing to; or

(b) serve that decision on,

anyone other than the prosecutor who applied for that ruling, unless the court otherwise directs.

Duty of Crown Court officer

36.8.–(1) The Crown Court officer must provide the Registrar with any document, object or **B-506** information for which the Registrar asks within such period as the Registrar may require.

(2) Where someone may appeal to the Court of Appeal, the Crown Court officer must keep any document or object exhibited in the proceedings in the Crown Court, or arrange for it to be kept by some other appropriate person, until—

(a) 6 weeks after the conclusion of those proceedings; or

(b) the conclusion of any appeal proceedings that begin within that 6 weeks,

unless the court, the Registrar or the Crown Court otherwise directs.

(3) Where Part 37 applies (appeal to the Court of Appeal against ruling at preparatory hearing), the Crown Court officer must as soon as practicable serve on the appellant a transcript or note of—

(a) each order or ruling against which the appellant wants to appeal; and

(b) the decision by the Crown Court judge on any application for permission to appeal.

(4) Where Part 38 applies (appeal to the Court of Appeal against ruling adverse to prosecution), the Crown Court officer must as soon as practicable serve on the appellant a transcript or note of—

(a) each ruling against which the appellant wants to appeal;

(b) the decision by the Crown Court judge on any application for permission to appeal; and

(c) the decision by the Crown Court judge on any request to expedite the appeal.

(5) Where Part 39 applies (appeal to the Court of Appeal about conviction or sentence), the Crown Court officer must as soon as practicable serve on the Registrar—

(a) the appeal notice and any accompanying application that the appellant serves on the Crown Court officer;

(b) any Crown Court judge's certificate that the case is fit for appeal;

(c) the decision on any application at the Crown Court centre for bail pending appeal;

(d) such of the Crown Court case papers as the Registrar requires; and

(e) such transcript of the Crown Court proceedings as the Registrar requires.

(6) Where Part 40 applies (appeal to the Court of Appeal regarding reporting or public access) and an order is made restricting public access to a trial, the Crown Court officer must—

(a) immediately notify the Registrar of that order, if the appellant has given advance notice of intention to appeal; and

(b) as soon as practicable provide the applicant for that order with a transcript or note of the application.

Duty of person transcribing proceedings in the Crown Court

36.9. A person who transcribes a recording of proceedings in the Crown Court under arrange- **B-507** ments made by the Crown Court officer must provide the Registrar with any transcript for which the Registrar asks within such period as the Registrar may require.

Duty of person keeping exhibit

36.10. A person who under arrangements made by the Crown Court officer keeps a document or **B-508** object exhibited in the proceedings in the Crown Court must—

(a) keep that exhibit until—

(i) 6 weeks after the conclusion of the Crown Court proceedings, or

(ii) the conclusion of any appeal proceedings that begin within that 6 weeks, unless the court, the Registrar or the Crown Court otherwise directs; and

(b) provide the Registrar with any such document or object for which the Registrar asks within such period as the Registrar may require.

Registrar's duty to provide copy documents for appeal or reference

36.11. Unless the court otherwise directs, for the purposes of an appeal or reference— **B-509**

    (a) the Registrar must—
        (i)   provide a party with a copy of any document or transcript held by the Registrar for such purposes, or
        (ii) allow a party to inspect such a document or transcript on payment by that party of any charge fixed by the Treasury; but
    (b) the Registrar must not provide a copy or allow the inspection of—
        (i)   a document provided only for the court and the Registrar, or
        (ii) a transcript of a public interest ruling or of an application for such a ruling.

Declaration of incompatibility with a Convention right

B-510
    36.12.—(1) This rule applies where a party—
    (a) wants the court to make a declaration of incompatibility with a Convention right under section 4 of the Human Rights Act 1998 [§ 16-19 in the main work]; or
    (b) raises an issue that the Registrar thinks may lead the court to make such a declaration.
    (2) The Registrar must serve notice on—
    (a) the relevant person named in the list published under section 17(1) of the Crown Proceedings Act 1947; or
    (b) the Treasury Solicitor, if it is not clear who is the relevant person.
    (3) That notice must include or attach details of—
    (a) the legislation affected and the Convention right concerned;
    (b) the parties to the appeal; and
    (c) any other information or document that the Registrar thinks relevant.
    (4) A person who has a right under the 1998 Act to become a party to the appeal must—
    (a) serve notice on—
        (i)   the Registrar, and
        (ii) the other parties,
      if that person wants to exercise that right; and
    (b) in that notice—
        (i)   indicate the conclusion that that person invites the court to reach on the question of incompatibility, and
        (ii) identify each ground for that invitation, concisely outlining the arguments in support.
    (5) The court must not make a declaration of incompatibility—
    (a) less than 21 days after the Registrar serves notice under paragraph (2); and
    (b) without giving any person who serves a notice under paragraph (4) an opportunity to make representations at a hearing.

Abandoning an appeal

B-511
    36.13.—(1) This rule applies where an appellant wants to—
    (a) abandon—
        (i)   an application to the court for permission to appeal, or
        (ii) an appeal; or
    (b) reinstate such an application or appeal after abandoning it.
    (2) The appellant—
    (a) may abandon such an application or appeal without the court's permission by serving a notice of abandonment on—
        (i)   the Registrar, and
        (ii) any respondent
      before any hearing of the application or appeal; but
    (b) at any such hearing, may only abandon that application or appeal with the court's permission.
    (3) A notice of abandonment must be in the form set out in the Practice Direction, signed by or on behalf of the appellant.
    (4) On receiving a notice of abandonment the Registrar must—
    (a) date it;
    (b) serve a dated copy on—
        (i)   the appellant,
        (ii) the appellant's custodian, if any,
        (iii) the Crown Court officer, and
        (iv) any other person on whom the appellant or the Registrar served the appeal notice; and

    (c) treat the application or appeal as if it had been refused or dismissed by the Court of Appeal.

(5) An appellant who wants to reinstate an application or appeal after abandoning it must—

    (a) apply in writing, with reasons; and

    (b) serve the application on the Registrar.

Abandoning a ground of appeal or opposition

36.14.–(1) If the court gives permission to appeal then unless the court otherwise directs the decision indicates that— ★**B-512**

    (a) the appellant has permission to appeal on every ground identified by the appeal notice; and

    (b) the court finds reasonably arguable each ground on which the appellant has permission to appeal.

(2) If the court gives permission to appeal but not on every ground identified by the appeal notice the decision indicates that—

    (a) at the hearing of the appeal the court will not consider representations that address any ground thus excluded from argument; and

    (b) an appellant who wants to rely on such an excluded ground needs the court's permission to do so.

(3) An appellant who wants to rely at the hearing of an appeal on a ground of appeal excluded from argument by a judge of the Court of Appeal when giving permission to appeal must—

    (a) apply in writing, with reasons, and identify each such ground;

    (b) serve the application on—

        (i) the Registrar, and

        (ii) any respondent;

    (c) serve the application not more than 14 days after—

        (i) the giving of permission to appeal, or

        (ii) the Registrar serves notice of that decision on the applicant, if the applicant was not present in person or by live link when permission to appeal was given.

(4) Paragraph (5) applies where a party wants to abandon—

    (a) a ground of appeal on which that party has permission to appeal; or

    (b) a ground of opposition identified in a respondent's notice.

(5) Such a party must serve notice on—

    (a) the Registrar; and

    (b) each other party,

before any hearing at which that ground will be considered by the court.

[This rule is printed as substituted by the Criminal Procedure (Amendment) Rules 2017 (S.I. 2017 No. 144).]

Criminal Procedure Rules 2015 (S.I. 2015 No. 1490), Pt 37

Appeal to the Court of Appeal Against a Ruling at a Preparatory Hearing

When this Part applies

37.1.–(1) This Part applies where a party wants to appeal under— **B-513**

    (a) section 9(11) of the Criminal Justice Act 1987 [§ 7-309 in the main work] or section 35(1) of the Criminal Procedure and Investigations Act 1996 [*ibid.*, §§ 4-137, 7-313]; or

    (b) section 47(1) of the Criminal Justice Act 2003 [*ibid.*, § 4-335].

(2) A reference to an "appellant" in this Part is a reference to such a party.

Service of appeal notice

37.2.–(1) An appellant must serve an appeal notice on— **B-514**

    (a) the Crown Court officer;

    (b) the Registrar; and

    (c) every party directly affected by the order or ruling against which the appellant wants to appeal.

(2) The appellant must serve the appeal notice not more than 5 business days after—

    (a) the order or ruling against which the appellant wants to appeal; or

    (b) the Crown Court judge gives or refuses permission to appeal.

Form of appeal notice

B-515   **37.3.**–(1) An appeal notice must be in the form set out in the Practice Direction.

(2) The appeal notice must—

(a)   specify each order or ruling against which the appellant wants to appeal;

(b)   identify each ground of appeal on which the appellant relies, numbering them consecutively (if there is more than one) and concisely outlining each argument in support;

(c)   summarise the relevant facts;

(d)   identify any relevant authorities;

(e)   include or attach any application for the following, with reasons—

(i)   permission to appeal, if the appellant needs the court's permission,

(ii)   an extension of time within which to serve the appeal notice,

(iii) a direction to attend in person a hearing that the appellant could attend by live link, if the appellant is in custody;

(f)   include a list of those on whom the appellant has served the appeal notice; and

(g)   attach—

(i)   a transcript or note of each order or ruling against which the appellant wants to appeal,

(ii)   all relevant skeleton arguments considered by the Crown Court judge,

(iii) any written application for permission to appeal that the appellant made to the Crown Court judge,

(iv)   a transcript or note of the decision by the Crown Court judge on any application for permission to appeal, and

(v)   any other document or thing that the appellant thinks the court will need to decide the appeal.

Crown Court judge's permission to appeal

B-516   **37.4.**–(1) An appellant who wants the Crown Court judge to give permission to appeal must—

(a)   apply orally, with reasons, immediately after the order or ruling against which the appellant wants to appeal; or

(b)   apply in writing and serve the application on—

(i)   the Crown Court officer, and

(ii)   every party directly affected by the order or ruling

not more than 2 business days after that order or ruling.

(2) A written application must include the same information (with the necessary adaptations) as an appeal notice.

Respondent's notice

B-517   **37.5.**–(1) A party on whom an appellant serves an appeal notice may serve a respondent's notice, and must do so if—

(a)   that party wants to make representations to the court; or

(b)   the court so directs.

(2) Such a party must serve the respondent's notice on—

(a)   the appellant;

(b)   the Crown Court officer;

(c)   the Registrar; and

(d)   any other party on whom the appellant served the appeal notice.

(3) Such a party must serve the respondent's notice not more than 5 business days after—

(a)   the appellant serves the appeal notice; or

(b)   a direction to do so.

(4) The respondent's notice must be in the form set out in the Practice Direction.

(5) The respondent's notice must—

(a)   give the date on which the respondent was served with the appeal notice;

(b)   identify each ground of opposition on which the respondent relies, numbering them consecutively (if there is more than one), concisely outlining each argument in support and identifying the ground of appeal to which each relates;

(c)   summarise any relevant facts not already summarised in the appeal notice;

(d)   identify any relevant authorities;

(e)   include or attach any application for the following, with reasons—

(i)   an extension of time within which to serve the respondent's notice,

    (ii)   a direction to attend in person any hearing that the respondent could attend by live link, if the respondent is in custody;

  (f)   identify any other document or thing that the respondent thinks the court will need to decide the appeal.

Powers of Court of Appeal judge

37.6. A judge of the Court of Appeal may give permission to appeal as well as exercising the pow- **B-518** ers given by other legislation (including these rules).

Renewing applications

37.7. Rule 36.5 (renewing an application refused by a judge or the Registrar) applies with a time **B-519** limit of 5 business days.

Right to attend hearing

37.8.–(1) A party who is in custody has a right to attend a hearing in public. **B-520**

(2) The court or the Registrar may direct that such a party is to attend a hearing by live link.

Criminal Procedure Rules 2015 (S.I. 2015 No. 1490), Pt 38

APPEAL TO THE COURT OF APPEAL AGAINST RULING ADVERSE TO PROSECUTION

When this Part applies

38.1.–(1) This Part applies where a prosecutor wants to appeal under section 58(2) of the Criminal **B-521** Justice Act 2003 [§ 7-247 in the main work].

(2) A reference to an "appellant" in this Part is a reference to such a prosecutor.

Decision to appeal

38.2.–(1) An appellant must tell the Crown Court judge of any decision to appeal– **B-522**

  (a) immediately after the ruling against which the appellant wants to appeal; or

  (b) on the expiry of the time to decide whether to appeal allowed under paragraph (2).

(2) If an appellant wants time to decide whether to appeal–

  (a) the appellant must ask the Crown Court judge immediately after the ruling; and

  (b) the general rule is that the judge must not require the appellant to decide there and then but instead must allow until the next business day.

Service of appeal notice

38.3.–(1) An appellant must serve an appeal notice on– **B-523**

  (a) the Crown Court officer;

  (b) the Registrar; and

  (c) every defendant directly affected by the ruling against which the appellant wants to appeal.

(2) The appellant must serve the appeal notice not later than–

  (a) the next business day after telling the Crown Court judge of the decision to appeal, if the judge expedites the appeal; or

  (b) 5 business days after telling the Crown Court judge of that decision, if the judge does not expedite the appeal.

Form of appeal notice

38.4.–(1) An appeal notice must be in the form set out in the Practice Direction. **B-524**

(2) The appeal notice must–

  (a) specify each ruling against which the appellant wants to appeal;

  (b) identify each ground of appeal on which the appellant relies, numbering them consecutively (if there is more than one) and concisely outlining each argument in support;

  (c) summarise the relevant facts;

  (d) identify any relevant authorities;

  (e) include or attach any application for the following, with reasons–

    (i)   permission to appeal, if the appellant needs the court's permission,

    (ii) an extension of time within which to serve the appeal notice,

    (iii) expedition of the appeal, or revocation of a direction expediting the appeal;

  (f) include a list of those on whom the appellant has served the appeal notice;

  (g) attach–

(i)   a transcript or note of each ruling against which the appellant wants to appeal,

(ii)   all relevant skeleton arguments considered by the Crown Court judge,

(iii)   any written application for permission to appeal that the appellant made to the Crown Court judge,

(iv)   a transcript or note of the decision by the Crown Court judge on any application for permission to appeal,

(v)   a transcript or note of the decision by the Crown Court judge on any request to expedite the appeal, and

(vi)   any other document or thing that the appellant thinks the court will need to decide the appeal; and

(h) attach a form of respondent's notice for any defendant served with the appeal notice to complete if that defendant wants to do so.

Crown Court judge's permission to appeal

B-525   38.5.–(1) An appellant who wants the Crown Court judge to give permission to appeal must—

(a) apply orally, with reasons, immediately after the ruling against which the appellant wants to appeal; or

(b) apply in writing and serve the application on—

(i)   the Crown Court officer, and

(ii)   every defendant directly affected by the ruling

on the expiry of the time allowed under rule 38.2 to decide whether to appeal.

(2) A written application must include the same information (with the necessary adaptations) as an appeal notice.

(3) The Crown Court judge must allow every defendant directly affected by the ruling an opportunity to make representations.

(4) The general rule is that the Crown Court judge must decide whether or not to give permission to appeal on the day that the application for permission is made.

[This rule is printed as amended by the Criminal Procedure (Amendment) Rules 2016 (S.I 2016 No. 120).]

Expediting an appeal

B-526   38.6.–(1) An appellant who wants the Crown Court judge to expedite an appeal must ask, giving reasons, on telling the judge of the decision to appeal.

(2) The Crown Court judge must allow every defendant directly affected by the ruling an opportunity to make representations.

(3) The Crown Court judge may revoke a direction expediting the appeal unless the appellant has served the appeal notice.

Respondent's notice

B-527   38.7.–(1) A defendant on whom an appellant serves an appeal notice may serve a respondent's notice, and must do so if—

(a) the defendant wants to make representations to the court; or

(b) the court so directs.

(2) Such a defendant must serve the respondent's notice on—

(a) the appellant;

(b) the Crown Court officer;

(c) the Registrar; and

(d) any other defendant on whom the appellant served the appeal notice.

(3) Such a defendant must serve the respondent's notice—

(a) not later than the next business day after—

(i)   the appellant serves the appeal notice, or

(ii)   a direction to do so

if the Crown Court judge expedites the appeal; or

(b) not more than 5 business days after—

(i)   the appellant serves the appeal notice, or

(ii)   a direction to do so

if the Crown Court judge does not expedite the appeal.

(4) The respondent's notice must be in the form set out in the Practice Direction.

(5) The respondent's notice must—

(a) give the date on which the respondent was served with the appeal notice;

(b) identify each ground of opposition on which the respondent relies, numbering them consecutively (if there is more than one), concisely outlining each argument in support and identifying the ground of appeal to which each relates;

(c) summarise any relevant facts not already summarised in the appeal notice;

(d) identify any relevant authorities;

(e) include or attach any application for the following, with reasons–

   (i) an extension of time within which to serve the respondent's notice,

   (ii) a direction to attend in person any hearing that the respondent could attend by live link, if the respondent is in custody;

(f) identify any other document or thing that the respondent thinks the court will need to decide the appeal.

Public interest ruling

38.8.–(1) This rule applies where the appellant wants to appeal against a public interest ruling. **B-528**

(2) The appellant must not serve on any defendant directly affected by the ruling–

(a) any written application to the Crown Court judge for permission to appeal; or

(b) an appeal notice

if the appellant thinks that to do so in effect would reveal something that the appellant thinks ought not be disclosed.

(3) The appellant must not include in an appeal notice–

(a) the material that was the subject of the ruling; or

(b) any indication of what sort of material it is

if the appellant thinks that to do so in effect would reveal something that the appellant thinks ought not be disclosed.

(4) The appellant must serve on the Registrar with the appeal notice an annex–

(a) marked to show that its contents are only for the court and the Registrar;

(b) containing whatever the appellant has omitted from the appeal notice, with reasons; and

(c) if relevant, explaining why the appellant has not served the appeal notice.

(5) Rules 38.5(3) and 38.6(2) do not apply.

Powers of Court of Appeal judge

38.9. A judge of the Court of Appeal may– **B-529**

(a) give permission to appeal;

(b) revoke a Crown Court judge's direction expediting an appeal; and

(c) where an appellant abandons an appeal, order a defendant's acquittal, his release from custody and the payment of his costs,

as well as exercising the powers given by other legislation (including these Rules).

Renewing applications

38.10. Rule 36.5 (renewing an application refused by a judge or the Registrar) applies with a time **B-530**
limit of 5 business days.

Right to attend hearing

38.11.–(1) A respondent who is in custody has a right to attend a hearing in public. **B-531**

(2) The court or the Registrar may direct that such a respondent is to attend a hearing by live link.

Criminal Procedure Rules 2015 (S.I. 2015 No. 1490), Pt 39

<small>APPEAL TO THE COURT OF APPEAL ABOUT CONVICTION OR SENTENCE</small>

When this Part applies

39.1.–(1) This Part applies where– **B-532**

(a) a defendant wants to appeal under–

   (i) Part 1 of the Criminal Appeal Act 1968 [§§ 7-37 *et seq.* in the main work], or

   (ii) section 274(3) of the Criminal Justice Act 2003;

   (iii) paragraph 14 of Schedule 22 to the Criminal Justice Act 2003;

   (iv) section 42 of the Counter-Terrorism Act 2008;

(b) the Criminal Cases Review Commission refers a case to the Court of Appeal under section 9 of the Criminal Appeal Act 1995;

    (c) a prosecutor wants to appeal to the Court of Appeal under section 14A(5A) of the Football Spectators Act 1989 [*ibid.*, § 5-1095];

    (d) a party wants to appeal under section 74(8) of the Serious Organised Crime and Police Act 2005 [*ibid.*, § 5-156];

    (e) a person found to be in contempt of court wants to appeal under section 13 of the Administration of Justice Act 1960 [*ibid.*, § 28-130] and section 18A of the Criminal Appeal Act 1968 [*ibid.*, § 7-162]; or

    (f) a person wants to appeal to the Court of Appeal under—

        (i) section 24 of the Serious Crime Act 2007 [*ibid.*, § 5-1179], or

        (ii) regulation 3C or 3H of the Costs in Criminal Cases (General) Regulations 1986 [*ibid.*, §§ 6-60, 6-65].

(2) A reference to an "appellant" in this Part is a reference to such a party or person.

Service of appeal notice

B-533   **39.2.**–(1) The general rule is that an appellant must serve an appeal notice—

    (a) on the Crown Court officer at the Crown Court centre where there occurred—

        (i) the conviction, verdict, or finding,

        (ii) the sentence, or

        (iii) the order, or the failure to make an order

        about which the appellant wants to appeal; and

    (b) not more than—

        (i) 28 days after that occurred, or

        (ii) 21 days after the order, in a case in which the appellant appeals against a wasted or third party costs order.

(2) But an appellant must serve an appeal notice—

    (a) on the Registrar instead where—

        (i) the appeal is against a minimum term review decision under section 274(3) of, or paragraph 14 of Schedule 22 to, the Criminal Justice Act 2003, or

        (ii) the Criminal Cases Review Commission refers the case to the court; and

    (b) not more than 28 days after—

        (i) the minimum term review decision about which the appellant wants to appeal, or

        (ii) the Registrar serves notice that the Commission has referred a conviction.

Form of appeal notice

B-534   **39.3.**–(1) An appeal notice must be in the form set out in the Practice Direction.

(2) The appeal notice must—

    (a) specify—

        (i) the conviction, verdict, or finding,

        (ii) the sentence, or

        (iii) the order, or the failure to make an order

        about which the appellant wants to appeal;

    (b) identify each ground of appeal on which the appellant relies, numbering them consecutively (if there is more than one) and concisely outlining each argument in support;

    (c) identify the transcript that the appellant thinks the court will need, if the appellant wants to appeal against a conviction;

    (d) identify the relevant sentencing powers of the Crown Court, if sentence is in issue;

    (e) where the Criminal Cases Review Commission refers a case to the court, explain how each ground of appeal relates (if it does) to the reasons for the reference;

    (f) summarise the relevant facts;

    (g) identify any relevant authorities;

    (h) include or attach any application for the following, with reasons—

        (i) permission to appeal, if the appellant needs the court's permission,

        (ii) an extension of time within which to serve the appeal notice,

        (iii) bail pending appeal,

        (iv) a direction to attend in person a hearing that the appellant could attend by live link, if the appellant is in custody,

        (v) the introduction of evidence, including hearsay evidence and evidence of bad character,

        (vi) an order requiring a witness to attend court,

    (vii)   a direction for special measures for a witness,

    (viii)   a direction for special measures for the giving of evidence by the appellant;

  (i)   identify any other document or thing that the appellant thinks the court will need to decide the appeal.

Crown Court judge's certificate that case is fit for appeal.

39.4.–(1) An appellant who wants the Crown Court judge to certify that a case is fit for appeal must—   **B-535**

  (a) apply orally, with reasons, immediately after there occurs—

    (i)   the conviction, verdict, or finding,

    (ii)   the sentence, or

    (iii)   the order, or the failure to make an order

    about which the appellant wants to appeal; or

  (b) apply in writing and serve the application on the Crown Court officer not more than 14 days after that occurred.

(2) A written application must include the same information (with the necessary adaptations) as an appeal notice.

Reference by Criminal Cases Review Commission

39.5.–(1) The Registrar must serve on the appellant a reference by the Criminal Cases Review Commission.   **B-536**

(2) The court must treat that reference as the appeal notice if the appellant does not serve such a notice under rule 39.2.

Respondent's notice

39.6.–(1) The Registrar—   **B-537**

  (a) may serve an appeal notice on any party directly affected by the appeal; and

  (b) must do so if the Criminal Cases Review Commission refers a conviction, verdict, finding or sentence to the court.

(2) Such a party may serve a respondent's notice, and must do so if—

  (a) that party wants to make representations to the court; or

  (b) the court or the Registrar so directs.

(3) Such a party must serve the respondent's notice on—

  (a) the appellant;

  (b) the Registrar; and

  (c) any other party on whom the Registrar served the appeal notice.

(4) Such a party must serve the respondent's notice—

  (a) not more than 14 days after the Registrar serves—

    (i)   the appeal notice, or

    (ii)   a direction to do so; or

  (b) not more than 28 days after the Registrar serves notice that the Commission has referred a conviction.

(5) The respondent's notice must be in the form set out in the Practice Direction.

(6) The respondent's notice must—

  (a) give the date on which the respondent was served with the appeal notice;

  (b) identify each ground of opposition on which the respondent relies, numbering them consecutively (if there is more than one), concisely outlining each argument in support and identifying the ground of appeal to which each relates;

  (c) identify the relevant sentencing powers of the Crown Court, if sentence is in issue;

  (d) summarise any relevant facts not already summarised in the appeal notice;

  (e) identify any relevant authorities;

  (f) include or attach any application for the following, with reasons—

    (i)   an extension of time within which to serve the respondent's notice,

    (ii)   bail pending appeal,

    (iii)   a direction to attend in person a hearing that the respondent could attend by live link, if the respondent is in custody,

    (iv)   the introduction of evidence, including hearsay evidence and evidence of bad character,

    (v)   an order requiring a witness to attend court,

    (vi)   a direction for special measures for a witness; and

    (g) identify any other document or thing that the respondent thinks the court will need to decide the appeal.

Introducing evidence

★B-538   **39.7.**–(1) The following Parts apply with such adaptations as the court or the Registrar may direct–

    (a) Part 16 (written witness statements);

    (b) Part 18 (measures to assist a witness or defendant to give evidence);

    (c) Part 19 (expert evidence);

    (d) Part 20 (hearsay evidence);

    (e) Part 21 (evidence of bad character); and

    (f) Part 22 (evidence of a complainant's previous sexual behaviour).

(2) But the general rule is that–

    (a) a respondent who opposes an appellant's application or notice to which one of those Parts applies must do so in the respondent's notice, with reasons;

    (b) an appellant who opposes a respondent's application or notice to which one of those Parts applies must serve notice, with reasons, on–

        (i) the Registrar, and

        (ii) the respondent

        not more than 14 days after service of the respondent's notice; and

    (c) the court or the Registrar may give directions with or without a hearing.

(3) A party who wants the court to order the production of a document, exhibit or other thing connected with the proceedings must–

    (a) identify that item; and

    (b) explain–

        (i) how it is connected with the proceedings,

        (ii) why its production is necessary for the determination of the case, and

        (iii) to whom it should be produced (the court, appellant or respondent, or any two or more of them).

(4) A party who wants the court to order a witness to attend to be questioned must–

    (a) identify the proposed witness; and

    (b) explain–

        (i) what evidence the proposed witness can give,

        (ii) why that evidence is capable of belief,

        (iii) if applicable, why that evidence may provide a ground for allowing the appeal,

        (iv) on what basis that evidence would have been admissible in the case which is the subject of the application for permission to appeal or appeal, and

        (v) why that evidence was not introduced in that case.

(5) Where the court orders a witness to attend to be questioned, the witness must attend the hearing of the application for permission to appeal or of the appeal, as applicable, unless the court otherwise directs.

(6) Where the court orders a witness to attend to be questioned before an examiner on the court's behalf, the court must identify the examiner and may give directions about–

    (a) the time and place, or times and places, at which that questioning must be carried out;

    (b) the manner in which that questioning must be carried out, in particular as to–

        (i) the service of any report, statement or questionnaire in preparation for the questioning,

        (ii) the sequence in which the parties may ask questions, and

        (iii) if more than one witness is to be questioned, the sequence in which those witnesses may be questioned; and

    (c) the manner in which, and when, a record of the questioning must be submitted to the court.

(7) Where the court orders the questioning of a witness before an examiner, the court may delegate to that examiner the giving of directions under paragraph (6)(a), (b) and (c).

[This rule is printed as substituted by the Criminal Procedure (Amendment) Rules 2017 (S.I. 2017 No. 144).]

Application for bail pending appeal or retrial

B-539   **39.8.**–(1) This rule applies where a party wants to make an application to the court about bail pending appeal or retrial.

(2) That party must serve an application in the form set out in the Practice Direction on—

    (a)   the Registrar, unless the application is with the appeal notice; and

    (b)   the other party.

(3) The court must not decide such an application without giving the other party an opportunity to make representations, including representations about any condition or surety proposed by the applicant.

(4) This rule and rule 14.16 (bail condition to be enforced in another European Union member State) apply where the court can impose as a condition of bail pending retrial a requirement—

    (a)   with which a defendant must comply while in another European Union member State; and

    (b)   which that other member State can monitor and enforce.

Conditions of bail pending appeal or retrial

39.9.—(1) This rule applies where the court grants a party bail pending appeal or retrial subject to   **B-540** any condition that must be met before that party is released.

(2) The court may direct how such a condition must be met.

(3) The Registrar must serve a certificate in the form set out in the Practice Direction recording any such condition and direction on—

    (a)   that party;

    (b)   that party's custodian; and

    (c)   any other person directly affected by any such direction.

(4) A person directly affected by any such direction need not comply with it until the Registrar serves that person with that certificate.

(5) Unless the court otherwise directs, if any such condition or direction requires someone to enter into a recognizance it must be—

    (a)   in the form set out in the Practice Direction and signed before—

        (i)   the Registrar,

        (ii)   the custodian, or

        (iii)   someone acting with the authority of the Registrar or custodian;

    (b)   copied immediately to the person who enters into it; and

    (c)   served immediately by the Registrar on the appellant's custodian or vice versa, as appropriate.

(6) Unless the court otherwise directs, if any such condition or direction requires someone to make a payment, surrender a document or take some other step—

    (a)   that payment, document or step must be made, surrendered or taken to or before—

        (i)   the Registrar,

        (ii)   the custodian, or

        (iii)   someone acting with the authority of the Registrar or custodian;

    (b)   the Registrar or the custodian, as appropriate, must serve immediately on the other a statement that the payment, document or step has been made, surrendered or taken, as appropriate.

(7) The custodian must release the appellant where it appears that any condition ordered by the court has been met.

(8) For the purposes of section 5 of the Bail Act 1976 (record of decision about bail [§ 3-28 in the main work]), the Registrar must keep a copy of—

    (a)   any certificate served under paragraph (3);

    (b)   a notice of hearing given under rule 36.7(1); and

    (c)   a notice of the court's decision served under rule 36.7(2).

(9) Where the court grants bail pending retrial the Registrar must serve on the Crown Court officer copies of the documents kept under paragraph (8).

Forfeiture of a recognizance given as a condition of bail

39.10.—(1) This rule applies where—   **B-541**

    (a)   the court grants a party bail pending appeal or retrial; and

    (b)   the bail is subject to a condition that that party provides a surety to guarantee that he will surrender to custody as required; but

    (c)   that party does not surrender to custody as required.

(2) The Registrar must serve notice on—

    (a)   the surety; and

    (b)   the prosecutor

of the hearing at which the court may order the forfeiture of the recognizance given by that surety.

(3) The court must not forfeit a surety's recognizance—

    (a) less than 7 days after the Registrar serves notice under paragraph (2); and

    (b) without giving the surety an opportunity to make representations at a hearing.

Right to attend hearing

★**B-542**   **39.11.** A party who is in custody has a right to attend a hearing in public unless—

    (a) it is a hearing preliminary or incidental to an appeal, including the hearing of an application for permission to appeal;

    (b) it is the hearing of an appeal and the court directs that-

        (i) the appeal involves a question of law alone, and

        (ii) for that reason the appellant has no permission to attend; or

    (c) that party is in custody in consequence of—

        (i) a verdict of not guilty by reason of insanity, or

        (ii) a finding of disability.

[This rule is printed as amended by the Criminal Procedure (Amendment) Rules 2017 (S.I. 2017 No. 144).]

Power to vary determination of appeal against sentence

B-543   **39.12.**—(1) This rule applies where the court decides an appeal affecting sentence in a party's absence.

(2) The court may vary such a decision if it did not take account of something relevant because that party was absent.

(3) A party who wants the court to vary such a decision must—

    (a) apply in writing, with reasons;

    (b) serve the application on the Registrar not more than 7 days after—

        (i) the decision, if that party was represented at the appeal hearing, or

        (ii) the Registrar serves the decision, if that party was not represented at that hearing.

Directions about re-admission to hospital on dismissal of appeal

B-544   **39.13.**—(1) This rule applies where—

    (a) an appellant subject to—

        (i) an order under section 37(1) of the Mental Health Act 1983 (detention in hospital on conviction [§ 5-1249 in the main work]), or

        (ii) an order under section 5(2) of the Criminal Procedure (Insanity) Act 1964 (detention in hospital on finding of insanity or disability [*ibid.*, § 4-239])

        has been released on bail pending appeal; and

    (b) the court—

        (i) refuses permission to appeal,

        (ii) dismisses the appeal, or

        (iii) affirms the order under appeal.

(2) The court must give appropriate directions for the appellant's—

    (a) re-admission to hospital; and

    (b) if necessary, temporary detention pending re-admission.

Renewal or setting aside of order for retrial

B-545   **39.14.**—(1) This rule applies where—

    (a) a prosecutor wants a defendant to be arraigned more than 2 months after the court ordered a retrial under section 7 of the Criminal Appeal Act 1968 [*ibid.*, § 7-111]; or

    (b) a defendant wants such an order set aside after 2 months have passed since it was made.

(2) That party must apply in writing, with reasons, and serve the application on—

    (a) the Registrar;

    (b) the other party.

CPD IX Appeal 39A: Appeals Against Conviction and Sentence—the Provision of Notice to the Prosecution

B-546   **39A.1** When an appeal notice served under rule 39.2 is received by the Registrar of Criminal Appeals, the registrar will notify the relevant prosecution authority, giving the case name, reference number and the trial or sentencing court.

39A.2 If the court or the registrar directs, or invites, the prosecution authority to serve a respondent's notice under rule 39.6, prior to the consideration of leave, the registrar will also at that time serve on the prosecution authority the appeal notice containing the grounds of appeal and the transcripts, if available. If the prosecution authority is not directed or invited to serve a respondent's notice but wishes to do so, the authority should request the grounds of appeal and any existing transcript from the Criminal Appeal Office. Any respondent's notice received prior to the consideration of leave will be made available to the single judge.

39A.3 The Registrar of Criminal Appeals will notify the relevant prosecution authority in the event that:

(a) leave to appeal against conviction or sentence is granted by the single judge; or

(b) the single judge or the registrar refers an application for leave to appeal against conviction or sentence to the full court for determination; or

(c) there is to be a renewed application for leave to appeal against sentence only.

If the prosecution authority has not yet been served with the appeal notice and transcript, the registrar will serve these with the notification, and if leave is granted, the registrar will also serve the authority with the comments of the single judge.

39A.4 The prosecution should notify the registrar without delay if they wish to be represented at the hearing. The prosecution should note that the registrar will not delay listing to await a response from the prosecution as to whether they wish to attend. Prosecutors should note that occasionally, for example, where the single judge fixes a hearing date at short notice, the case may be listed very quickly.

39A.5 If the prosecution wishes to be represented at any hearing, the notification should include details of counsel instructed and a time estimate. An application by the prosecution to remove a case from the list for counsel's convenience, or to allow further preparation time, will rarely be granted.

39A.6 There may be occasions when the Court of Appeal ... will grant leave to appeal to an unrepresented applicant and proceed forthwith with the appeal in the absence of the appellant and counsel. The prosecution should not attend any hearing at which the appellant is unrepresented (*Nasteska v. The former Yugoslav Republic of Macedonia (Application No.23152/05)*). As a court of review, the Court of Appeal ... would expect the prosecution to have raised any specific matters of relevance with the sentencing judge in the first instance.

CPD IX Appeal 39B: Listing of Appeals Against Conviction and Sentence in the Court of Appeal Criminal Division (CACD)

39B.1 Arrangements for the fixing of dates for the hearing of appeals will be made by the **B-547** Criminal Appeal Office Listing Officer, under the superintendence of the Registrar of Criminal Appeals who may give such directions as he deems necessary.

39B.2 Where possible, regard will be had to an advocate's existing commitments. However, in relation to the listing of appeals, the Court of Appeal takes precedence over all lower courts, including the Crown Court. Wherever practicable, a lower court will have regard to this principle when making arrangements to release an advocate to appear in the Court of Appeal. In case of difficulty the lower court should communicate with the Registrar. In general an advocate's commitment in a lower court will not be regarded as a good reason for failing to accept a date proposed for a hearing in the Court of Appeal.

39B.3 Similarly when the Registrar directs that an appellant should appear by video link, the prison must give precedence to video-links to the Court of Appeal over video-links to the lower courts, including the Crown Court.

39B.4 The copy of the Criminal Appeal Office summary provided to advocates will contain the summary writer's time estimate for the whole hearing including delivery of judgment. It will also contain a time estimate for the judges' reading time of the core material. The listing officer will rely on those estimates, unless the advocate for the appellant or the Crown provides different time estimates to the listing officer, in writing, within 7 days of the receipt of the summary by the advocate. Where the time estimates are considered by an advocate to be inadequate, or where the estimates have been altered because, for example, a ground of appeal has been abandoned, it is the duty of the advocate to inform the court promptly, in which event the Registrar will reconsider the time estimates and inform the parties accordingly.

39B.5 [*Provides for the following target times to run from receipt of an appeal by the listing officer as being ready for hearing: in the case of sentence appeals, 14 days from receipt by listing officer to fixing a hearing date, and 14 days from fixing the date to the date of hearing; in the case of conviction appeals, the corresponding times would be 21 and 42 days respectively; and, where a witness is to attend, the times would be 28 and 52 days respectively; where legal vacations impinge on those periods, they might be extended, and where expedition was required they might be abridged; and, for these purposes, "appeal" includes an application for leave to appeal which requires an oral hearing.*]

CPD IX Appeal 39C: Appeal Notices Containing Grounds of Appeal (as amended by Criminal Practice Directions 2015 (Amendment No. 1), unreported, March 23, 2016, Lord Thomas C.J.)

B-548

39C.1 The requirements for the service of notices of appeal and the time limits for doing so are as set out in Part 39 of the Criminal Procedure Rules. The court must be provided with an appeal notice as a single document which sets out the grounds of appeal. Advocates should not provide the court with an advice addressed to lay or professional clients. Any appeal notice or grounds of appeal served on the court will usually be provided to the respondent.

39C.2 Advocates should not settle grounds unless they consider that they are properly arguable. Grounds should be carefully drafted; the court is not assisted by grounds of appeal which are not properly set out and particularised. Should leave to amend the grounds be granted, it is most unlikely that further grounds will be entertained.

39C.3 Where the appellant wants to appeal against conviction, transcripts must be identified in accordance with CrimPR 39.3(c) [*sic*]. This includes specifying the date and time of transcripts in the notice of appeal. Accordingly, the date and time of the summing up should be provided, including both parts of a split summing up. Where relevant, the date and time of additional transcripts (such as rulings or early directions) should be provided. Similarly, any relevant written materials (such as route to verdict) should be identified.

CPD IX Appeal 39D: Respondents' Notices

B-549

39D.1 The requirements for the service of respondents' notices and the time limits for doing so are as set out in CrimPR, Pt 39. Any respondent's notice served should be in accordance with CrimPR 39.6. The court does not require a response to the respondent's notice.

CPD IX Appeal 39E: Loss of Time

B-550

39E.1 Both the court and the single judge have power, in their discretion ... to direct that part of the time during which an applicant is in custody after lodging his notice of application for leave to appeal should not count towards sentence. Those contemplating an appeal should seek advice and should remember that a notice of appeal without grounds is ineffective and that grounds should be substantial and particularised and not a mere formula. When leave to appeal has been refused by the single judge, it is often of assistance to consider the reasons given by the single judge before making a decision whether to renew the application. Where an application devoid of merit has been refused by the single judge he may indicate that the full court should consider making a direction for loss of time on renewal of the application. However, the full court may make such a direction whether or not such an indication has been given by the single judge.

39E.2 Applicants and counsel are reminded of the warning given by the Court of Appeal in *R. v. Hart; R. v. George; R. v. Clarke; R. v. Brown* [§ 7-227 in the main work] and should "heed the fact that this court is prepared to exercise its power ... The mere fact that counsel has advised that there are grounds of appeal will not always be a sufficient answer to the question as to whether or not an application has indeed been brought which was totally without merit."

CPD IX Appeal 39F: Skeleton Arguments

B-551

39F.1 Advocates should always ensure that the court, and any other party as appropriate, has a single document containing all of the points that are to be argued. The appeal notice must comply with the requirements of Part 68. In cases of an appeal against conviction, advocates must serve a skeleton argument when the appeal notice does not sufficiently outline the grounds of the appeal, particularly in cases where a complex or novel point of law has been raised. In an appeal against sentence it may be helpful for an advocate to serve a skeleton argument when a complex issue is raised.

39F.2 The appellant's skeleton argument, if any, must be served no later than 21 days before the hearing date, and the respondent's skeleton argument, if any, no later than 14 days before the hearing date, unless otherwise directed by the court.

39F.3 A skeleton argument, if provided, should contain a numbered list of the points the advocate intends to argue, grouped under each ground of appeal, and stated in no more than one or two sentences. It should be as succinct as possible. Advocates should ensure that the correct Criminal Appeal Office number and the date on which the document was served appears at the beginning of any document and that their names are at the end.

CPD IX Appeal 39G: Criminal Appeal Office Summaries

B-552

39G.1 To assist the court the Criminal Appeal Office prepares summaries of the cases coming before it. These are entirely objective and do not contain any advice about how the court should deal with the case or any view about its merits. They consist of two parts.

39G.2 Part I, which is provided to all of the advocates in the case, generally contains (a) particulars of the proceedings in the Crown Court, including representation and details of any co-accused, (b) particulars of the proceedings in the Court of Appeal (Criminal Division), (c) the facts of the case, as drawn from the transcripts, appeal notice, respondent's notice, witness statements and/or the exhibits, (d) the submissions and rulings, summing up and sentencing remarks. Should an advocate not want any factual material in his advice taken into account this should be stated in the advice.

39G.3 The contents of the summary are a matter for the professional judgment of the writer, but an advocate wishing to suggest any significant alteration to Part I should write to the Registrar of Criminal Appeals. If the registrar does not agree, the summary and the letter will be put to the court for decision. The court will not generally be willing to hear oral argument about the content of the summary.

39G.4 Advocates may show Part I of the summary to their professional or lay clients (but to no one else) if they believe it would help to check facts or formulate arguments, but summaries are not to be copied or reproduced without the permission of the Criminal Appeal Office; permission for this will not normally be given in cases involving children or sexual offences or where the Crown Court has made an order restricting reporting.

39G.5 Unless a judge of the High Court or the Registrar of Criminal Appeals gives a direction to the contrary in any particular case involving material of an explicitly salacious or sadistic nature, Part I will also be supplied to appellants who seek to represent themselves before the full court or who renew to the full court their applications for leave to appeal against conviction or sentence.

39G.6 Part II, which is supplied to the court alone, contains (a) a summary of the grounds of appeal and (b) in appeals against sentence (and applications for such leave), summaries of the antecedent histories of the parties and of any relevant pre-sentence, medical or other reports.

39G.7 All of the source material is provided to the court and advocates are able to draw attention to anything in it which may be of particular relevance.

Criminal Procedure Rules 2015 (S.I. 2015 No. 1490), Pt 40

APPEAL TO THE COURT OF APPEAL ABOUT REPORTING OR PUBLIC ACCESS RESTRICTION

When this Part applies
40.1.–(1) This Part applies where a person directly affected by an order to which section 159(1) of the Criminal Justice Act 1988 [§ 7-323 in the main work] applies wants to appeal against that order. **B-553**
(2) A reference to an "appellant" in this Part is a reference to such a party.

Service of appeal notice
40.2.–(1) An appellant must serve an appeal notice on— **B-554**
(a) the Crown Court officer;
(b) the Registrar;
(c) the parties; and
(d) any other person directly affected by the order against which the appellant wants to appeal.
(2) The appellant must serve the appeal notice not later than—
(a) the next business day after an order restricting public access to the trial;
(b) 10 business days after an order restricting reporting of the trial.

Form of appeal notice
40.3.–(1) An appeal notice must be in the form set out in the Practice Direction. **B-555**
(2) The appeal notice must—
(a) specify the order against which the appellant wants to appeal;
(b) identify each ground of appeal on which the appellant relies, numbering them consecutively (if there is more than one) and concisely outlining each argument in support;
(c) summarise the relevant facts;
(d) identify any relevant authorities;
(e) include or attach, with reasons—
(i) an application for permission to appeal,
(ii) any application for an extension of time within which to serve the appeal notice,
(iii) any application for a direction to attend in person a hearing that the appellant could attend by live link, if the appellant is in custody,

> (iv)   any application for permission to introduce evidence, and
>
> (v)   a list of those on whom the appellant has served the appeal notice; and
>
> (f)   attach any document or thing that the appellant thinks the court will need to decide the appeal.

Advance notice of appeal against order restricting public access

B-556   **40.4.**—(1) This rule applies where the appellant wants to appeal against an order restricting public access to a trial.

(2) The appellant may serve advance written notice of intention to appeal against any such order that may be made.

(3) The appellant must serve any such advance notice—

> (a)   on—
>
> > (i)   the Crown Court officer,
> >
> > (ii)   the Registrar,
> >
> > (iii)   the parties, and
> >
> > (iv)   any other person who will be directly affected by the order against which the appellant intends to appeal, if it is made; and
>
> (b)   not more than 5 business days after the Crown Court officer displays notice of the application for the order.

(4) The advance notice must include the same information (with the necessary adaptations) as an appeal notice.

(5) The court must treat that advance notice as the appeal notice if the order is made.

Duty of applicant for order restricting public access

B-557   **40.5.**—(1) This rule applies where the appellant wants to appeal against an order restricting public access to a trial.

(2) The party who applied for the order must serve on the Registrar—

> (a)   a transcript or note of the application for the order; and
>
> (b)   any other document or thing that that party thinks the court will need to decide the appeal.

(3) That party must serve that transcript or note and any such other document or thing as soon as practicable after—

> (a)   the appellant serves the appeal notice; or
>
> (b)   the order, where the appellant served advance notice of intention to appeal.

Respondent's notice on appeal against reporting restriction

B-558   **40.6.**—(1) This rule applies where the appellant wants to appeal against an order restricting the reporting of a trial.

(2) A person on whom an appellant serves an appeal notice may serve a respondent's notice, and must do so if—

> (a)   that person wants to make representations to the court; or
>
> (b)   the court so directs.

(3) Such a person must serve the respondent's notice on—

> (a)   the appellant;
>
> (b)   Crown Court officer;
>
> (c)   the Registrar;
>
> (d)   the parties; and
>
> (e)   any other person on whom the appellant served the appeal notice.

(4) Such a person must serve the respondent's notice not more than 3 business days after—

> (a)   the appellant serves the appeal notice; or
>
> (b)   a direction to do so.

(5) The respondent's notice must be in the form set out in the Practice Direction.

(6) The respondent's notice must—

> (a)   give the date on which the respondent was served with the appeal notice;
>
> (b)   identify each ground of opposition on which the respondent relies, numbering them consecutively (if there is more than one), concisely outlining each argument in support and identifying the ground of appeal to which each relates;
>
> (c)   summarise any relevant facts not already summarised in the appeal notice;
>
> (d)   identify any relevant authorities;
>
> (e)   include or attach any application for the following, with reasons
>
> > (i)   an extension of time within which to serve the respondent's notice,

    (ii)   a direction to attend in person any hearing that the respondent could attend by live link, if the respondent is in custody,

    (iii) permission to introduce evidence; and

  (f) identify any other document or thing that the respondent thinks the court will need to decide the appeal.

Renewing applications

40.7. [*Identical to r.37.7, ante, § B-519.*]   **B-559**

Right to introduce evidence

40.8. No person may introduce evidence without the court's permission.   **B-560**

Right to attend hearing

40.9.–(1) A party who is in custody has a right to attend a hearing in public of an appeal against **B-561**
an order restricting the reporting of a trial.

(2) The court or the Registrar may direct that such a party is to attend a hearing by live link.

Criminal Procedure Rules 2015 (S.I. 2015 No. 1490), Pt 41

REFERENCE TO THE COURT OF APPEAL OF POINT OF LAW OR UNDULY LENIENT SENTENCING

When this Part applies

41.1. This Part applies where the Attorney General wants to—   **B-562**

  (a) refer a point of law to the Court of Appeal under section 36 of the Criminal Justice Act 1972 [§ 7-437 in the main work]; or

  (b) refer a sentencing case to the Court of Appeal under section 36 of the Criminal Justice Act 1988 [*ibid.*, § 7-442].

Service of notice of reference and application for permission

41.2.–(1) The Attorney General must—   **B-563**

  (a) serve on the Registrar—

    (i)   any notice of reference, and

    (ii) any application for permission to refer a sentencing case; and

  (b) with a notice of reference of a point of law, give the Registrar details of—

    (i)   the defendant affected,

    (ii) the date and place of the relevant Crown Court decision, and

    (iii) the relevant verdict and sentencing.

(2) The Attorney General must serve an application for permission to refer a sentencing case not more than 28 days after the last of the sentences in that case.

Form of notice of reference and application for permission

41.3.–(1) A notice of reference and an application for permission to refer a sentencing case must **B-564**
be in the appropriate form set out in the Practice Direction, giving the year and number.

(2) A notice of reference of a point of law must—

  (a) specify the point of law in issue and indicate the opinion that the Attorney General invites the court to give;

  (b) identify each ground for that invitation, numbering them consecutively (if there is more than one) and concisely outlining each argument in support;

  (c) exclude any reference to the defendant's name and any other reference that may identify the defendant;

  (d) summarise the relevant facts; and

  (e) identify any relevant authorities.

(3) An application for permission to refer a sentencing case must—

  (a) give details of—

    (i)   the defendant affected,

    (ii) the date and place of the relevant Crown Court decision, and

    (iii) the relevant verdict and sentencing;

  (b) explain why that sentencing appears to the Attorney General unduly lenient, concisely outlining each argument in support; and

  (c) include the application for permission to refer the case to the court.

(4) A notice of reference of a sentencing case must—

    (a)   include the same details and explanation as the application for permission to refer the case;

    (b)   summarise the relevant facts; and

    (c)   identify any relevant authorities.

(5) Where the court gives the Attorney General permission to refer a sentencing case, it may treat the application for permission as the notice of reference.

Registrar's notice to defendant

B-565   41.4.–(1) The Registrar must serve on the defendant—

    (a)   a notice of reference;

    (b)   an application for permission to refer a sentencing case.

(2) Where the Attorney General refers a point of law, the Registrar must give the defendant notice that—

    (a)   the outcome of the reference will not make any difference to the outcome of the trial; and

    (b)   the defendant may serve a respondent's notice.

(3) Where the Attorney General applies for permission to refer a sentencing case, the Registrar must give the defendant notice that—

    (a)   the outcome of the reference may make a difference to that sentencing, and in particular may result in a more severe sentence; and

    (b)   the defendant may serve a respondent's notice.

Respondent's notice

B-566   41.5.–(1) A defendant on whom the Registrar serves a reference or an application for permission to refer a sentencing case may serve a respondent's notice, and must do so if—

    (a)   the defendant wants to make representations to the court; or

    (b)   the court so directs.

(2) Such a defendant must serve the respondent's notice on—

    (a)   the Attorney General; and

    (b)   the Registrar.

(3) Such a defendant must serve the respondent's notice—

    (a)   where the Attorney General refers a point of law, not more than 28 days after—

        (i)   the Registrar serves the reference, or

        (ii)   a direction to do so;

    (b)   where the Attorney General applies for permission to refer a sentencing case, not more than 14 days after—

        (i)   the Registrar serves the application, or

        (ii)   a direction to do so.

(4) Where the Attorney General refers a point of law, the respondent's notice must—

    (a)   identify each ground of opposition on which the respondent relies, numbering them consecutively (if there is more than one), concisely outlining each argument in support and identifying the Attorney General's ground or reason to which each relates;

    (b)   summarise any relevant facts not already summarised in the reference;

    (c)   identify any relevant authorities; and

    (d)   include or attach any application for the following, with reasons—

        (i)   an extension of time within which to serve the respondent's notice,

        (ii)   permission to attend a hearing that the respondent does not have a right to attend,

        (iii)   a direction to attend in person a hearing that the respondent could attend by live link, if the respondent is in custody.

(5) Where the Attorney General applies for permission to refer a sentencing case, the respondent's notice must—

    (a)   say if the respondent wants to make representations at the hearing of the application or reference; and

    (b)   include or attach any application for the following, with reasons—

        (i)   an extension of time within which to serve the respondent's notice,

        (ii)   permission to attend a hearing that the respondent does not have a right to attend,

        (iii)   a direction to attend in person a hearing that the respondent could attend by live link, if the respondent is in custody.

Variation or withdrawal of notice of reference or application for permission

B-567   41.6.–(1) This rule applies where the Attorney General wants to vary or withdraw—

    (a)   a notice of reference; or

(b) an application for permission to refer a sentencing case.

(2) The Attorney General—

    (a) may vary or withdraw the notice or application without the court's permission by serving notice on—

        (i)   the Registrar, and

        (ii) the defendant

    before any hearing of the reference or application; but

    (b) at any such hearing, may only vary or withdraw that notice or application with the court's permission.

Right to attend hearing

41.7.—(1) A respondent who is in custody has a right to attend a hearing in public unless it is a   **B-568** hearing preliminary or incidental to a reference, including the hearing of an application for permission to refer a sentencing case.

(2) The court or the Registrar may direct that such a respondent is to attend a hearing by live link.

Anonymity of defendant on reference of point of law

41.8. Where the Attorney General refers a point of law, the court must not allow anyone to   **B-569** identify the defendant during the proceedings unless the defendant gives permission.

Criminal Procedure Rules 2015 (S.I. 2015 No. 1490), Pt 42

APPEAL TO THE COURT OF APPEAL IN CONFISCATION AND RELATED PROCEEDINGS

General rules

Extension of time

42.1.—(1) An application to extend the time limit for giving notice of application for permission to   **B-570** appeal under Part 2 of the Proceeds of Crime Act 2002 must—

    (a) be included in the notice of appeal; and

    (b) state the grounds for the application.

(2) The parties may not agree to extend any date or time limit set by this Part or by the Proceeds of Crime Act 2002 (Appeals under Part 2) Order 2003 [§ 5-989 *et seq.* in the main work].

Other applications

42.2. Rule 39.3(2)(h) (form of appeal notice) applies in relation to an application—   **B-571**

    (a) by a party to an appeal under Part 2 of the Proceeds of Crime Act 2002 that, under article 7 of the Proceeds of Crime Act 2002 (Appeals under Part 2) Order 2003, a witness be ordered to attend or that the evidence of a witness be received by the Court of Appeal; or

    (b) by the defendant to be given permission by the court to be present at proceedings for which permission is required under article 6 of the 2003 Order,

as it applies in relation to applications under Part I of the Criminal Appeal Act 1968 and the form in which rule 39.3 requires notice to be given may be modified as necessary.

Examination of witness by court

42.3. Rule 36.7 (notice of hearings and decisions) applies in relation to an order of the court   **B-572** under article 7 of the Proceeds of Crime Act 2002 (Appeals under Part 2) Order 2003 to require a person to attend for examination as it applies in relation to such an order of the court under Part I of the Criminal Appeal Act 1968.

Supply of documentary and other exhibits

42.4. Rule 36.11 (registrar's duty to provide copy documents for appeal or reference) applies in   **B-573** relation to an appellant or respondent under Part 2 of the Proceeds of Crime Act 2002 as it applies in relation to an appellant and respondent under Part I of the Criminal Appeal Act 1968.

Registrar's power to require information from court of trial

42.5. The Registrar may require the Crown Court to provide the Court of Appeal with any as-   **B-574** sistance or information which it requires for the purposes of exercising its jurisdiction under Part 2 of the Proceeds of Crime Act 2002, the Proceeds of Crime Act 2002 (Appeals under Part 2) Order 2003 or this Part.

Hearing by single judge

42.6. Rule 36.6(5) (hearings) applies in relation to a judge exercising any of the powers referred to in article 8 of the Proceeds of Crime Act 2002 (Appeals under Part 2) Order 2003 or the powers in rules 42.12(3) and (4) (respondent's notice), 42.15(2) (notice of appeal) and 42.16(6) (respondent's notice), as it applies in relation to a judge exercising the powers referred to in section 31(2) of the Criminal Appeal Act 1968.

Determination by full court

B-576 **42.7.** Rule 36.5 (renewing an application refused by a judge or the Registrar) applies where a single judge has refused an application by a party to exercise in that party's favour any of the powers listed in article 8 of the Proceeds of Crime Act 2002 (Appeals under Part 2) Order 2003, or the power in rule 42.12(3) or (4) as it applies where the judge has refused to exercise the powers referred to in section 31(2) of the Criminal Appeal Act 1968 [*ibid.*, § 7-233].

Notice of determination

B-577 **42.8.**–(1) This rule applies where a single judge or the Court of Appeal has determined an application or appeal under the Proceeds of Crime Act 2002 (Appeals under Part 2) Order 2003 or under Part 2 of the Proceeds of Crime Act 2002.

(2) The Registrar must, as soon as practicable, serve notice of the determination on all of the parties to the proceedings.

(3) Where a single judge or the Court of Appeal has disposed of an application for permission to appeal or an appeal under section 31 of the 2002 Act [*ibid.*, § 5-795], the Registrar must also, as soon as practicable, serve the order on a court officer of the court of trial and any magistrates' court responsible for enforcing any confiscation order which the Crown Court has made.

Record of proceedings and transcripts

B-578 **42.9.** Rule 5.5 (recording and transcription of proceedings in the Crown Court) and rule 36.9 (duty of person transcribing proceedings in the Crown Court) apply in relation to proceedings in respect of which an appeal lies to the Court of Appeal under Part 2 of the Proceeds of Crime Act 2002 as they apply in relation to proceedings in respect of which an appeal lies to the Court of Appeal under Part I of the Criminal Appeal Act 1968.

Appeal to the Supreme Court

B-579 **42.10.**–(1) An application to the Court of Appeal for permission to appeal to the Supreme Court under Part 2 of the Proceeds of Crime Act 2002 must be made–

(a) orally after the decision of the Court of Appeal from which an appeal lies to the Supreme Court; or

(b) in the form set out in the Practice Direction, in accordance with article 12 of the Proceeds of Crime Act 2002 (Appeals under Part 2) Order 2003 [*ibid.*, § 5-1002] and served on the Registrar.

(2) The application may be abandoned at any time before it is heard by the Court of Appeal by serving notice in writing on the Registrar.

(3) Rule 36.6(5) (hearings) applies in relation to a single judge exercising any of the powers referred to in article 15 of the 2003 Order [*ibid.*, § 5-1004], as it applies in relation to a single judge exercising the powers referred to in section 31(2) of the Criminal Appeal Act 1968.

(4) Rule 36.5 (renewing an application refused by a judge or the Registrar) applies where a single judge has refused an application by a party to exercise in that party's favour any of the powers listed in article 15 of the 2003 Order as they apply where the judge has refused to exercise the powers referred to in section 31(2) of the 1968 Act.

(5) The form in which rule 36.5(2) requires an application to be made may be modified as necessary.

Confiscation: appeal by prosecutor or by person with interest in property

Notice of appeal

B-580 **42.11.**–(1) Where an appellant wishes to apply to the Court of Appeal for permission to appeal under section 31 of the Proceeds of Crime Act 2002 [*ibid.*, § 5-795], the appellant must serve a notice of appeal in the form set out in the Practice Direction on–

(a) the Crown Court officer; and

(b) the defendant.

(2) When the notice of a prosecutor's appeal about a confiscation order is served on the defendant,

it must be accompanied by a respondent's notice in the form set out in the Practice Direction for the defendant to complete and a notice which—

   (a) informs the defendant that the result of an appeal could be that the Court of Appeal would increase a confiscation order already imposed, make a confiscation order itself or direct the Crown Court to hold another confiscation hearing;

   (b) informs the defendant of any right under article 6 of the Proceeds of Crime Act 2002 (Appeals under Part 2) Order 2003 [*ibid.*, § 5-993] to be present at the hearing of the appeal, although in custody;

   (c) invites the defendant to serve any notice on the Registrar—

      (i) to apply to the Court of Appeal for permission to be present at proceedings for which such permission is required under article 6 of the 2003 Order [*ibid.*, § 5-993], or

      (ii) to present any argument to the Court of Appeal on the hearing of the application or, if permission is given, the appeal, and whether the defendant wishes to present it in person or by means of a legal representative;

   (d) draws to the defendant's attention the effect of rule 42.4 (supply of documentary and other exhibits); and

   (e) advises the defendant to consult a solicitor as soon as possible.

   (3) The appellant must provide the Crown Court officer with a certificate of service stating that the appellant has served the notice of appeal on the defendant in accordance with paragraph (1) or explaining why it has not been possible to do so.

Respondent's notice

   42.12.—(1) This rule applies where a defendant is served with a notice of appeal under rule 42.11. **B-581**

   (2) If the defendant wishes to oppose the application for permission to appeal, the defendant must, not more than 14 days after service of the notice of appeal, serve on the Registrar and on the appellant a notice in the form set out in the Practice Direction—

   (a) stating the date on which the notice of appeal was served;

   (b) summarising the defendant's response to the arguments of the appellant; and

   (c) specifying the authorities which the defendant intends to cite.

   (3) The time for giving notice under this rule may be extended by the Registrar, a single judge or by the Court of Appeal.

   (4) Where the Registrar refuses an application under paragraph (3) for the extension of time, the defendant is entitled to have the application determined by a single judge.

   (5) Where a single judge refuses an application under paragraph (3) or (4) for the extension of time, the defendant is entitled to have the application determined by the Court of Appeal.

Amendment and abandonment of appeal

   42.13.—(1) The appellant may amend a notice of appeal served under rule 42.11 or abandon an **B-582** appeal under section 31 of the Proceeds of Crime Act 2002—

   (a) without the permission of the court at any time before the Court of Appeal has begun hearing the appeal; and

   (b) with the permission of the court after the Court of Appeal has begun hearing the appeal, by serving notice in writing on the Registrar.

   (2) Where the appellant serves a notice abandoning an appeal under paragraph (1), the appellant must send a copy of it to—

   (a) the defendant;

   (b) a court officer of the court of trial; and

   (c) the magistrates' court responsible for enforcing any confiscation order which the Crown Court has made.

   (3) Where the appellant serves a notice amending a notice of appeal under paragraph (1), the appellant must send a copy of it to the defendant.

   (4) Where an appeal is abandoned under paragraph (1), the application for permission to appeal or appeal must be treated, for the purposes of section 85 of the 2002 Act (conclusion of proceedings [*ibid.*, § 5-893]), as having been refused or dismissed by the Court of Appeal.

Appeal about compliance, restraint or receivership order

Permission to appeal

   42.14.—(1) Permission to appeal to the Court of Appeal under section 13B, section 43 or section **B-583** 65 [*ibid.*, §§ 5-769, 5-819, 5-864] of the Proceeds of Crime Act 2002 may only be given where—

    (a) the Court of Appeal considers that the appeal would have a real prospect of success; or

    (b) there is some other compelling reason why the appeal should be heard.

(2) An order giving permission to appeal may limit the issues to be heard and be made subject to conditions.

Notice of appeal

B-584   **42.15.**—(1) Where an appellant wishes to apply to the Court of Appeal for permission to appeal under section 13B, 43 or 65 of the Proceeds of Crime Act 2002 Act, the appellant must serve a notice of appeal in the form set out in the Practice Direction on the Crown Court officer.

(2) Unless the Registrar, a single judge or the Court of Appeal directs otherwise, the appellant must serve the notice of appeal, accompanied by a respondent's notice in the form set out in the Practice Direction for the respondent to complete, on—

    (a) each respondent;

    (b) any person who holds realisable property to which the appeal relates; and

    (c) any other person affected by the appeal,

as soon as practicable and in any event not later than 5 business days after the notice of appeal is served on the Crown Court officer.

(3) The appellant must serve the following documents with the notice of appeal—

    (a) four additional copies of the notice of appeal for the Court of Appeal;

    (b) four copies of any skeleton argument;

    (c) one sealed copy and four unsealed copies of any order being appealed;

    (d) four copies of any witness statement or affidavit in support of the application for permission to appeal;

    (e) four copies of a suitable record of the reasons for judgment of the Crown Court; and

    (f) four copies of the bundle of documents used in the Crown Court proceedings from which the appeal lies.

(4) Where it is not possible to serve all of the documents referred to in paragraph (3), the appellant must indicate which documents have not yet been served and the reasons why they are not currently available.

(5) The appellant must provide the Crown Court officer with a certificate of service stating that the notice of appeal has been served on each respondent in accordance with paragraph (2) and including full details of each respondent or explaining why it has not been possible to effect service.

Respondent's notice

B-585   **42.16.**—(1) This rule applies to an appeal under section 13B, 43 or 65 of the Proceeds of Crime Act 2002.

(2) A respondent may serve a respondent's notice on the Registrar.

(3) A respondent who—

    (a) is seeking permission to appeal from the Court of Appeal; or

    (b) wishes to ask the Court of Appeal to uphold the decision of the Crown Court for reasons different from or additional to those given by the Crown Court,

must serve a respondent's notice on the Registrar.

(4) A respondent's notice must be in the form set out in the Practice Direction and where the respondent seeks permission to appeal to the Court of Appeal it must be requested in the respondent's notice.

(5) A respondent's notice must be served on the Registrar not later than 14 days after—

    (a) the date the respondent is served with notification that the Court of Appeal has given the appellant permission to appeal; or

    (b) the date the respondent is served with notification that the application for permission to appeal and the appeal itself are to be heard together.

(6) Unless the Registrar, a single judge or the Court of Appeal directs otherwise, the respondent serving a respondent's notice must serve the notice on the appellant and any other respondent—

    (a) as soon as practicable; and

    (b) in any event not later than 5 business days,

after it is served on the Registrar.

Amendment and abandonment of appeal

B-586   **42.17.**—(1) The appellant may amend a notice of appeal served under rule 42.15 or abandon an appeal under section 13B, 43 or 65 of the Proceeds of Crime Act 2002—

(a) without the permission of the court at any time before the Court of Appeal has begun hearing the appeal; and

(b) with the permission of the court after the Court of Appeal has begun hearing the appeal,

by serving notice in writing on the Registrar.

(2) Where the appellant serves a notice under paragraph (1), the appellant must send a copy of it to each respondent.

Stay

42.18. Unless the Court of Appeal or the Crown Court orders otherwise, an appeal under section 13B, 43 or 65 of the Proceeds of Crime Act 2002 does not operate as a stay of any order or decision of the Crown Court.

B-587

Striking out appeal notices and setting aside or imposing conditions on permission to appeal

42.19.—(1) The Court of Appeal may—

(a) strike out the whole or part of a notice of appeal served under rule 42.15; or

(b) impose or vary conditions upon which an appeal under section 13B, 43 or 65 of the Proceeds of Crime Act 2002 may be brought.

B-588

(2) The Court of Appeal may only exercise its powers under paragraph (1) where there is a compelling reason for doing so.

(3) Where a party is present at the hearing at which permission to appeal was given, that party may not subsequently apply for an order that the Court of Appeal exercise its powers under paragraph (1)(b).

Hearing of appeals

42.20.—(1) This rule applies to appeals under section 13B, 43 or 65 of the Proceeds of Crime Act 2002.

B-589

(2) Every appeal must be limited to a review of the decision of the Crown Court unless the Court of Appeal considers that in the circumstances of an individual appeal it would be in the interests of justice to hold a re-hearing.

(3) The Court of Appeal may allow an appeal where the decision of the Crown Court was—

(a) wrong; or

(b) unjust because of a serious procedural or other irregularity in the proceedings in the Crown Court.

(4) The Court of Appeal may draw any inference of fact which it considers justified on the evidence.

(5) At the hearing of the appeal a party may not rely on a matter not contained in that party's notice of appeal unless the Court of Appeal gives permission.

Criminal Procedure Rules 2015 (S.I. 2015 No. 1490), Pt 43

Appeal or Reference to the Supreme Court

When this Part applies

43.1.—(1) This Part applies where—

B-590

(a) a party wants to appeal to the Supreme Court after—

(i) an application to the Court of Appeal to which Part 27 applies (retrial following acquittal), or

(ii) an appeal to the Court of Appeal to which applies Part 37 (appeal to the Court of Appeal against ruling at preparatory hearing), Part 38 (appeal to the Court of Appeal against ruling adverse to prosecution), or Part 39 (appeal to the Court of Appeal about conviction or sentence); or

(b) a party wants to refer a case to the Supreme Court after a reference to the Court of Appeal to which Part 41 applies (reference to the Court of Appeal of point of law or unduly lenient sentencing).

(2) A reference to an "appellant" in this Part is a reference to such a party.

Application for permission or reference

43.2.—(1) An appellant must—

B-591

(a) apply orally to the Court of Appeal—

(i) for permission to appeal or to refer a sentencing case, or

    (ii)   to refer a point of law immediately after the court gives the reasons for its decision; or
  (b) apply in writing and serve the application on the Registrar and every other party not more than—
    (i)   14 days after the court gives the reasons for its decision if that decision was on a sentencing reference to which Part 41 applies (Attorney General's reference of sentencing case), or
    (ii) 28 days after the court gives those reasons in any other case.

(2) An application for permission to appeal or to refer a sentencing case must—
  (a) identify the point of law of general public importance that the appellant wants the court to certify is involved in the decision; and
  (b) give reasons why—
    (i)   that point of law ought to be considered by the Supreme Court, and
    (ii) the court ought to give permission to appeal.

(3) An application to refer a point of law must give reasons why that point ought to be considered by the Supreme Court.

(4) An application must include or attach any application for the following, with reasons—
  (a) an extension of time within which to make the application for permission or for a reference,
  (b) bail pending appeal,
  (c) permission to attend any hearing in the Supreme Court, if the appellant is in custody.

(5) A written application must be in the form set out in the Practice Direction.

[This rule is printed as amended by the Criminal Procedure (Amendment) Rules 2016 (S.I 2016 No. 120).]

Determination of detention pending appeal, etc.

B-592   **43.3.** On an application for permission to appeal the Court of Appeal must—
  (a) decide whether to order the detention of a defendant who would have been liable to be detained but for the decision of the court; and
  (b) determine any application for—
    (i)   bail pending appeal,
    (ii) permission to attend any hearing in the Supreme Court, or
    (iii) a representation order.

Bail pending appeal

B-593   **43.4.** Rules 39.8 (application for bail pending appeal or retrial), 39.9 (conditions of bail pending appeal or retrial) and 39.10 (forfeiture of a recognizance given as a condition of bail) apply.

Criminal Procedure Rules 2015 (S.I. 2015 No. 1490), Pt 44

Request to the European Court for a Preliminary Ruling

When this Part applies

B-594   **44.1.** This Part applies where the court can request the Court of Justice of the European Union ("the European Court") to give a preliminary ruling, under Article 267 of the Treaty on the Functioning of the European Union.

Preparation of request

B-595   **44.2.**—(1) The court may—
  (a) make an order for the submission of a request—
    (i)   on application by a party, or
    (ii) on its own initiative;
  (b) give directions for the preparation of the terms of such a request.

(2) The court must—
  (a) include in such a request—
    (i)   the identity of the court making the request,
    (ii) the parties' identities,
    (iii) a statement of whether a party is in custody,
    (iv) a succinct statement of the question on which the court seeks the ruling of the European Court,
    (v) a succinct statement of any opinion on the answer that the court may have expressed in any judgment that it has delivered,

    (vi) a summary of the nature and history of the proceedings, including the salient facts
and an indication of whether those facts are proved, admitted or assumed,

    (vii) the relevant rules of national law,

    (viii) a summary of the relevant contentions of the parties,

    (ix) an indication of the provisions of European union law that the European Court is
asked to interpret, and

    (x) an explanation of why a ruling of the European Court is requested;

  (b) express the request in terms that can be translated readily into other languages; and

  (c) set out the request in a schedule to the order.

Submission of request

44.3.–(1) The court officer must serve the order for the submission of the request on the Senior **B-596**
Master of the Queen's Bench Division of the High Court.

(2) The Senior Master must—

  (a) submit the request to the European Court; but

  (b) unless the court otherwise directs, postpone the submission of the request until—

    (i) the time for any appeal against the order has expired, and

    (ii) any appeal against the order has been determined.

CPD IX Appeal 44A: References to the European Court of Justice

44A.1 Further to rule 44.3 of the Criminal Procedure Rules, the order containing the reference **B-597**
shall be filed with the Senior Master of the Queen's Bench Division of the High Court for onward
transmission to the Court of Justice of the European Union. The order should be marked for the attention of Mrs Isaac and sent to the Senior Master, c/o Queen's Bench Division Associates Dept,
Room WG03, Royal Courts of Justice, Strand, London, WC2A 2LL.

44A.2 There is no longer a requirement that the relevant court file be sent to the Senior Master.
The parties should ensure that all appropriate documentation is sent directly to the European Court
at the following address: The Registrar, Court of Justice of the European Union, Kirchberg, L-2925
Luxemburg.

44A.3 There is no prescribed form for use but the following details must be included in the back
sheet to the order: (i) solicitor's full address; (ii) solicitor's and court references; (iii) solicitor's e-mail
address.

44A.4 The European Court of Justice regularly updates its recommendation to national courts and
tribunals in relation to the initiation of preliminary ruling proceedings. The current recommendation is 2012/C338/01: http://eurlex.europa.eu/LexUriServ/LexUriServ.do?uri=OJ:C:2012:338:
0001: 0006:EN:PDF.

44A.5 The referring court may request the Court of Justice of the European Union to apply its
urgent preliminary ruling procedure where the referring court's proceedings relate to a person in
custody. For further information see Council Decision 2008/79/EC [2008] OJ L24/42: http://eurle
x.europa.eu/LexUriServ/LexUriServ.do?uri=OJ:L:2008:024:0042:0043:EN:PDF.

44A.6 Any such request must be made in a document separate from the order or in a covering letter and must set out: (i) the matters of fact and law which establish the urgency; (ii) the reasons why
the urgent preliminary ruling procedure applies; and (iii) in so far as possible, the court's view on the
answer to the question referred to the Court of Justice of the European Union for a preliminary
ruling.

44A.7 Any request to apply the urgent preliminary ruling procedure should be filed with the
Senior Master as described above.

Criminal Procedure Rules 2015 (S.I. 2015 No. 1490), Pt 45

G ENERAL

Costs

When this Part applies

45.1.–(1) This Part applies where the court can make an order about costs under— **B-598**

  (a) Part II of the Prosecution of Offences Act 1985 and Part II, IIA or IIB of the Costs in
Criminal Cases (General) Regulations 1986;

  (b) section 109 of the Magistrates' Courts Act 1980;

(c)   section 52 of the Senior Courts Act 1981 and rule 45.6 or rule 45.7;

(d)   section 8 of the Bankers Books Evidence Act 1879;

(e)   section 2C(8) of the Criminal Procedure (Attendance of Witnesses) Act 1965;

(f)   section 36(5) of the Criminal Justice Act 1972;

(g)   section 159(5) and Schedule 3, paragraph 11, of the Criminal Justice Act 1988;

(h)   section 14H(5) of the Football Spectators Act 1989;

(i)   section 4(7) of the Dangerous Dogs Act 1991;

(j)   Part 3 of the Serious Crime Act 2007 (Appeals under Section 24) Order 2008; or

(k)   Part 1 or 2 of the Extradition Act 2003.

(2) In this Part, "costs" means—

(a)   the fees payable to a legal representative;

(b)   the disbursements paid by a legal representative; and

(c)   any other expenses incurred in connection with the case.

[This rule is printed as amended by the Criminal Procedure (Amendment) Rules 2016 (S.I. 2016 No. 120).]

For Part II of the 1985 Act, see §§ 6-1 *et seq.* in the main work; for Parts II, IIA and IIB of the 1986 regulations, see *ibid.*, §§ 6-56 *et seq.*; for section 109 of the 1980 Act, see *ibid.*, § 2-113; for section 8 of the 1879 Act, see *ibid.*, § 11-66; for section 2C of the 1965 Act, see *ibid.*, § 8-5; for section 37 of the 1972 Act, see *ibid.*, § 7-437; for section 159 of the 1988 Act, see *ibid.*, § 7-324; for Schedule 3 to the 1988 Act, see *ibid.*, § 7-452; for section 14H of the 1989 Act, see *ibid.*, § 5-1105; for section 4 of the 1991 Act, see *ibid.*, § 31-38; and for Part 3 of the 2008 order, see *ibid.*, §§ 7-349 *et seq.* The 2003 Act is outside the scope of this work.

Costs orders: general rules

B-599

45.2.–(1) The court must not make an order about costs unless each party and any other person directly affected—

(a)   is present; or

(b)   has had an opportunity—

(i)   to attend, or

(ii)   to make representations.

(2) The court may make an order about costs—

(a)   at a hearing in public or in private; or

(b)   without a hearing.

(3) In deciding what order, if any, to make about costs, the court must have regard to all the circumstances, including—

(a)   the conduct of all the parties; and

(b)   any costs order already made.

(4) If the court makes an order about costs, it must—

(a)   specify who must, or must not, pay what, to whom; and

(b)   identify the legislation under which the order is made, where there is a choice of powers.

(5) The court must give reasons if it—

(a)   refuses an application for a costs order; or

(b)   rejects representations opposing a costs order.

(6) If the court makes an order for the payment of costs—

(a)   the general rule is that it must be for an amount that is sufficient reasonably to compensate the recipient for costs—

(i)   actually, reasonably and properly incurred, and

(ii)   reasonable in amount; but

(b)   the court may order the payment of—

(i)   a proportion of that amount,

(ii)   a stated amount less than that amount,

(iii)   costs from or until a certain date only,

(iv)   costs relating only to particular steps taken, or

(v)   costs relating only to a distinct part of the case.

(7) On an assessment of the amount of costs, relevant factors include—

(a)   the conduct of all the parties;

(b)   the particular complexity of the matter or the difficulty or novelty of the questions raised;

   (c)   the skill, effort, specialised knowledge and responsibility involved;

   (d)   the time spent on the case;

   (e)   the place where and the circumstances in which work or any part of it was done; and

   (f)   any direction or observations by the court that made the costs order.

  (8) If the court orders a party to pay costs to be assessed under rule 45.11, it may order that party to pay an amount on account.

  (9) An order for the payment of costs takes effect when the amount is assessed, unless the court exercises any power it has to order otherwise.

Court's power to vary requirements under Sections 2, 3 and 4

  45.3.–(1) Unless other legislation provides, the court may–   **B-600**

   (a)   extend a time limit for serving an application or representations under rules 45.4 to 45.10, even after it has expired; and

   (b)   consider an application or representations–

      (i)   made in a different form to one set out in the Practice Direction, or

      (ii)   made orally instead of in writing.

  (2) A person who wants an extension of time must–

   (a)   apply when serving the application or representations for which it is needed; and

   (b)   explain the delay.

[This rule is printed as amended by S.I. 2016 No. 120 (*ante*, B-598).]

Costs out of central funds

Costs out of central funds

  45.4.–(1) This rule applies where the court can order the payment of costs out of central funds.   **B-601**

  (2) In this rule, costs–

   (a)   include–

      (i)   on an appeal, costs incurred in the court that made the decision under appeal, and

      (ii)   at a retrial, costs incurred at the initial trial and on any appeal; but

   (b)   do not include costs met by legal aid.

  (3) The court may make an order–

   (a)   on application by the person who incurred the costs; or

   (b)   on its own initiative.

  (4) Where a person wants the court to make an order that person must–

   (a)   apply as soon as practicable; and

   (b)   outline the type of costs and the amount claimed, if that person wants the court to direct an assessment; or

   (c)   specify the amount claimed, if that person wants the court to assess the amount itself.

  (5) The general rule is that the court must make an order, but–

   (a)   the court may decline to make a defendant's costs order if, for example–

      (i)   the defendant is convicted of at least one offence, or

      (ii)   the defendant's conduct led the prosecutor reasonably to think the prosecution case stronger than it was; and

   (b)   the court may decline to make a prosecutor's costs order if, for example, the prosecution was started or continued unreasonably.

  (6) If the court makes an order–

   (a)   the court may direct an assessment under, as applicable–

      (i)   Part III of the Costs in Criminal Cases (General) Regulations 1986 [[§ 6-67 *et seq.* in the main work]], or

      (ii)   Part 3 of the Serious Crime Act 2007 (Appeals under Section 24) Order 2008;

   (b)   the court may assess the amount itself in a case in which either–

      (i)   the recipient agrees the amount, or

      (ii)   the court decides to allow a lesser sum than that which is reasonably sufficient to compensate the recipient for expenses properly incurred in the proceedings;

   (c)   an order for the payment of a defendant's costs which includes an amount in respect of fees payable to a legal representative, or disbursements paid by a legal representative, must include a statement to that effect.

  (7) If the court directs an assessment, the order must specify any restriction on the amount to be paid that the court considers appropriate.

(8) If the court assesses the amount itself, it must do so subject to any restriction on the amount to be paid that is imposed by regulations made by the Lord Chancellor.

Payment of costs by one party to another

Costs on conviction and sentence, etc.

B-602   **45.5.**–(1) This rule applies where the court can order a defendant to pay the prosecutor's costs if the defendant is—

(a) convicted or found guilty;

(b) dealt with in the Crown Court after committal for sentence there;

(c) dealt with for breach of a sentence; or

(d) in an extradition case—

(i) ordered to be extradited, under Part 1 of the Extradition Act 2003, or

(ii) sent for extradition to the Secretary of State, under Part 2 of that Act, or

(iii) unsuccessful on an appeal by the defendant to the High Court, or on an application by the defendant for permission to appeal from the High Court to the Supreme Court.

(2) The court may make an order—

(a) on application by the prosecutor; or

(b) on its own initiative.

(3) Where the prosecutor wants the court to make an order—

(a) the prosecutor must—

(i) apply as soon as practicable, and

(ii) specify the amount claimed; and

(b) the general rule is that the court must make an order if it is satisfied that the defendant can pay.

(4) A defendant who wants to oppose an order must make representations as soon as practicable.

(5) If the court makes an order, it must assess the amount itself.

Costs on appeal

B-603   **45.6.**–(1) This rule—

(a) applies where a magistrates' court, the Crown Court or the Court of Appeal can order a party to pay another person's costs on an appeal, or an application for permission to appeal;

(b) authorises the Crown Court, in addition to its other powers, to order a party to pay another party's costs on an appeal to that court, except on an appeal under—

(i) section 108 of the Magistrates' Courts Act 1980 [§ 2-95 in the main work], or

(ii) section 45 of the Mental Health Act 1983 [*ibid.*, § 2-103].

(2) In this rule, costs include—

(a) costs incurred in the court that made the decision under appeal; and

(b) costs met by legal aid.

(3) [*Identical to r.45.4(3), ante, B-601.*]

(4) A person who wants the court to make an order must—

(a) apply as soon as practicable;

(b) notify each other party;

(c) specify—

(i) the amount claimed, and

(ii) against whom; and

(d) where an appellant abandons an appeal to the Crown Court by serving a notice of abandonment—

(i) apply in writing not more than 14 days later, and

(ii) serve the application on the appellant and on the Crown Court officer.

(5) A party who wants to oppose an order must—

(a) make representations as soon as practicable; and

(b) where the application was under paragraph (4)(d), serve representations on the applicant, and on the Crown Court officer, not more than 7 days after it was served.

(6) Where the application was under paragraph (4)(d), the Crown Court officer may—

(a) submit it to the Crown Court; or

(b) serve it on the magistrates' court officer, for submission to the magistrates' court.

(7) If the court makes an order, it may direct an assessment under rule 45.11, or assess the amount itself where—

(a) the appellant abandons an appeal to the Crown Court;

(b) the Crown Court decides an appeal, except an appeal under—

(i) section 108 of the Magistrates' Courts Act 1980, or

(ii) section 45 of the Mental Health Act 1983; or

(c) the Court of Appeal decides an appeal to which Part 40 applies (appeal to the Court of Appeal regarding reporting or public access restriction).

(8) If the court makes an order in any other case, it must assess the amount itself.

[This rule is printed as amended by the Criminal Procedure (Amendment No. 2) Rules 2016 (S.I. 2016 No. 705).]

Costs on an application

45.7.–(1) This rule— **B-604**

(a) applies where the court can order a party to pay another person's costs in a case in which—

(i) the court decides an application for the production in evidence of a copy of a bank record,

(ii) a magistrates' court or the Crown Court decides an application to terminate a football banning order,

(iii) a magistrates' court or the Crown Court decides an application to terminate a disqualification for having custody of a dog,

(iv) the Crown Court allows an application to withdraw a witness summons, or

(v) the Crown Court decides an application relating to a deferred prosecution agreement under rule 11.5 (breach), rule 11.6 (variation) or rule 11.7 (lifting suspension of prosecution);

(b) authorises the Crown Court, in addition to its other powers, to order a party to pay another party's costs on an application to that court under rule 11.5, 11.6 or 11.7.

(2) [*Identical to r.45.4(3), ante, B-601*]

(3) A person who wants the court to make an order must—

(a) apply as soon as practicable;

(b) notify each other party; and

(c) specify—

(i) the amount claimed, and

(ii) against whom.

(4) A party who wants to oppose an order must make representations as soon as practicable.

(5) If the court makes an order, it may direct an assessment under rule 45.11, or assess the amount itself.

Costs resulting from unnecessary or improper act, etc.

45.8.–(1) This rule applies where the court can order a party to pay another party's costs incurred **B-605** as a result of an unnecessary or improper act or omission by or on behalf of the first party.

(2) In this rule, costs include costs met by legal aid.

(3) The court may make an order—

(a) on application by the party who incurred such costs; or

(b) on its own initiative.

(4) A party who wants the court to make an order must—

(a) apply in writing as soon as practicable after becoming aware of the grounds for doing so, and in any event no later than the end of the case;

(b) serve the application on—

(i) the court officer (or, in the Court of Appeal, the Registrar), and

(ii) each other party;

(c) in that application specify—

(i) the party by whom costs should be paid,

(ii) the relevant act or omission,

(iii) the reasons why that act or omission meets the criteria for making an order,

(iv) the amount claimed, and

(v) those on whom the application has been served.

(5) Where the court considers making an order on its own initiative, it must—

    (a)   identify the party against whom it proposes making the order; and

    (b)   specify—

        (i)   the relevant act or omission,

        (ii)   the reasons why that act or omission meets the criteria for making an order, and

        (iii)   with the assistance of the party who incurred the costs, the amount involved.

(6) A party who wants to oppose an order must—

    (a)   make representations as soon as practicable; and

    (b)   in reply to an application, serve representations on the applicant and on the court officer (or Registrar) not more than 7 days after it was served.

(7) If the court makes an order, it must assess the amount itself.

(8) To help assess the amount, the court may direct an enquiry by—

    (a)   the Lord Chancellor, where the assessment is by a magistrates' court or by the Crown Court; or

    (b)   the Registrar, where the assessment is by the Court of Appeal.

(9) In deciding whether to direct such an enquiry, the court must have regard to all the circumstances including—

    (a)   any agreement between the parties about the amount to be paid;

    (b)   the amount likely to be allowed;

    (c)   the delay and expense that may be incurred in the conduct of the enquiry; and

    (d)   the particular complexity of the assessment, or the difficulty or novelty of any aspect of the assessment.

(10) If the court directs such an enquiry—

    (a)   paragraphs (3) to (8) inclusive of rule 45.11 (assessment and re-assessment) apply as if that enquiry were an assessment under that rule (but rules 45.12 (appeal to a costs judge) and 45.13 (appeal to a High Court judge) do not apply);

    (b)   the authority that carries out the enquiry must serve its conclusions on the court officer as soon as reasonably practicable after following that procedure; and

    (c)   the court must then assess the amount to be paid.

[This rule is printed as amended by the Criminal Procedure (Amendment) Rules 2016 (S.I. 2016 No. 120); and the Criminal Procedure (Amendment No. 2) Rules 2016 (S.I. 2016 No. 705).]

Other costs orders

Costs against a legal representative

B-606   **45.9.**—(1) This rule applies where—

    (a)   a party has incurred costs—

        (i)   as a result of an improper, unreasonable or negligent act or omission by a legal or other representative or representative's employee, or

        (ii)   which it has become unreasonable for that party to have to pay because of such an act or omission occurring after those costs were incurred; and

    (b)   the court can—

        (i)   order the representative responsible to pay such costs, or

        (ii)   prohibit the payment of costs to that representative.

(2) In this rule, costs include costs met by legal aid.

(3) [*Identical to r.45.8(3), ante, B-605.*]

(4) A party who wants the court to make an order must—

    (a)   apply in writing as soon as practicable after becoming aware of the grounds for doing so, and in any event no later than the end of the case;

    (b)   serve the application on—

        (i)   the court officer (or, in the Court of Appeal, the Registrar),

        (ii)   the representative responsible,

        (iii)   each other party, and

        (iv)   any other person directly affected;

    (c)   in that application specify—

        (i)   the representative responsible,

        (ii)   the relevant act or omission,

        (iii)   the reasons why that act or omission meets the criteria for making an order,

    (iv)   the amount claimed, and

    (v)   those on whom the application has been served.

(5) Where the court considers making an order on its own initiative, it must—

    (a)   identify the representative against whom it proposes making that order; and

    (b)   [*identical to r.45.8(5)(b)*, ante, *B-605*].

(6) A representative who wants to oppose an order must—

    (a)   [*identical to r.45.8(6)(a)*, ante, *B-605*];

    (b)   [*identical to r.45.8(6)(b)*, ante, *B-605*].

(7) If the court makes an order—

    (a)   the general rule is that it must do so without waiting until the end of the case, but it may postpone making the order; and

    (b)   it must assess the amount itself.

(8)-(10) [*Identical to r.45.8(8)-(10)*, ante, *B-605*.]

(11) Instead of making an order, the court may make adverse observations about the representative's conduct for use in an assessment where—

    (a)   a party's costs are—

        (i)   to be met by legal aid, or

        (ii)   to be paid out of central funds; or

    (b)   there is to be an assessment under rule 45.11.

[This rule is printed as amended by the Criminal Procedure (Amendment) Rules 2016 (S.I. 2016 No. 120), r.14(d); and the Criminal Procedure (Amendment No. 2) Rules 2016 (S.I. 2016 No. 705), r.14(c).]

Costs against a third party

45.10.–(1) This rule applies where—   **B-607**

    (a)   there has been serious misconduct by a person who is not a party; and

    (b)   the court can order that person to pay a party's costs.

(2) In this rule, costs include costs met by legal aid.

(3) [*Identical to r.45.4(3)*, ante, *B-601*.]

(4) A party who wants the court to make an order must—

    (a)   apply in writing as soon as practicable after becoming aware of the grounds for doing so;

    (b)   serve the application on—

        (i)   the court officer (or, in the Court of Appeal, the Registrar),

        (ii)   the person responsible,

        (iii)   each other party, and

        (iv)   any other person directly affected;

    (c)   in that application specify—

        (i)   the person responsible,

        (ii)   the relevant misconduct,

        (iii)   the reasons why the criteria for making an order are met,

        (iv)   the amount claimed, and

        (v)   those on whom the application has been served.

(5) Where the court considers making an order on its own initiative, it must—

    (a)   identify the person against whom it proposes making that order; and

    (b)   specify—

        (i)   the relevant misconduct,

        (ii)   the reasons why the criteria for making an order are met, and

        (iii)   with the assistance of the party who incurred the costs, the amount involved.

(6) A person who wants to oppose an order must—

    (a)   [*identical to r.45.8(6)(a)*, ante, *B-605*];

    (b)   [*identical to r.45.8(6)(b)*, ante, *B-605*].

(7) If the court makes an order—

    (a)   the general rule is that it must do so at the end of the case, but it may do so earlier; and

    (b)   it must assess the amount itself.

(8)-(10) [*Identical to r.45.8(8)-(10)*, ante, *B-605*].

[This rule is printed as amended by the Criminal Procedure (Amendment) Rules 2016 (S.I. 2016 No. 120), r.14(e); and the Criminal Procedure (Amendment No. 2) Rules 2016 (S.I. 2016 No. 705), r.14(d).]

Assessment of costs

Assessment and re-assessment

B-608

45.11.–(1) This rule applies where the court directs an assessment under–

(a) rule 33.48 (confiscation and related proceedings – restraint and receivership proceedings: rules that apply generally – assessment of costs);

(b) rule 45.6 (costs on appeal); or

(c) rule 45.7 (costs on an application).

(2) The assessment must be carried out by the relevant assessing authority, namely–

(a) the Lord Chancellor, where the direction was given by a magistrates' court or by the Crown Court; or

(b) the Registrar of Criminal Appeals, where the direction was given by the Court of Appeal.

(3) The party in whose favour the court made the costs order ("the applicant") must–

(a) apply for an assessment–

(i) in writing, in any form required by the assessing authority, and

(ii) not more than 3 months after the costs order; and

(b) serve the application on–

(i) the assessing authority, and

(ii) the party against whom the court made the costs order ("the respondent").

(4) The applicant must–

(a) summarise the work done;

(b) specify–

(i) each item of work done, giving the date, time taken and amount claimed,

(ii) any disbursements or expenses, including the fees of any advocate, and

(iii) any circumstances of which the applicant wants the assessing authority to take particular account; and

(c) supply–

(i) receipts or other evidence of the amount claimed, and

(ii) any other information or document for which the assessing authority asks, within such period as that authority may require.

(5) A respondent who wants to make representations about the amount claimed must–

(a) do so in writing; and

(b) serve the representations on the assessing authority, and on the applicant, not more than 21 days after service of the application.

(6) The assessing authority must–

(a) if it seems likely to help with the assessment, obtain any other information or document;

(b) resolve in favour of the respondent any doubt about what should be allowed; and

(c) serve the assessment on the parties.

(7) Where either party wants the amount allowed re-assessed–

(a) that party must–

(i) apply to the assessing authority, in writing and in any form required by that authority,

(ii) serve the application on the assessing authority, and on the other party, not more than 21 days after service of the assessment,

(iii) explain the objections to the assessment,

(iv) supply any additional supporting information or document, and

(v) ask for a hearing, if that party wants one; and

(b) a party who wants to make representations about an application for re-assessment must–

(i) do so in writing,

(ii) serve the representations on the assessing authority, and on the other party, not more than 21 days after service of the application, and

(iii) ask for a hearing, if that party wants one;

(c) the assessing authority–

(i) must arrange a hearing, in public or in private, if either party asks for one,

(ii) subject to that, may re-assess the amount allowed with or without a hearing,

(iii) must re-assess the amount allowed on the initial assessment, taking into account the reasons for disagreement with that amount and any other representations,

(iv) may maintain, increase or decrease the amount allowed on the assessment,

(v) must serve the re-assessment on the parties, and

    (vi)   must serve reasons on the parties, if not more than 21 days later either party asks for such reasons.

(8) A time limit under this rule may be extended even after it has expired—

    (a) by the assessing authority, or

    (b) by the Senior Costs Judge, if the assessing authority declines to do so.

[This rule is printed as amended by the Criminal Procedure (Amendment No. 2) Rules 2016 (S.I. 2016 No. 705).]

Appeal to a costs judge

45.12.–(1) This rule applies where—   **B-609**

    (a) the assessing authority has re-assessed the amount allowed under rule 45.11; and

    (b) either party wants to appeal against that amount.

(2) That party must—

    (a) serve an appeal notice on—

        (i)   the Senior Costs Judge,

       (ii)   the other party, and

     (iii)   the assessing authority

       not more than 21 days after service of the written reasons for the re-assessment;

    (b) explain the objections to the re-assessment;

    (c) serve on the Senior Costs Judge with the appeal notice—

        (i)   the applications for assessment and re-assessment,

       (ii)   any other information or document considered by the assessing authority,

     (iii)   the assessing authority's written reasons for the re-assessment, and

     (iv)   any other information or document for which a costs judge asks, within such period as the judge may require; and

    (d) ask for a hearing, if that party wants one.

(3) A party who wants to make representations about an appeal must—

    (a) serve representations in writing on—

        (i)   the Senior Costs Judge, and

       (ii)   the applicant

       not more than 21 days after service of the appeal notice; and

    (b) ask for a hearing, if that party wants one.

(4) Unless a costs judge otherwise directs, the parties may rely only on—

    (a) the objections to the amount allowed on the initial assessment; and

    (b) any other representations and material considered by the assessing authority.

(5) A costs judge—

    (a) must arrange a hearing, in public or in private, if either party asks for one;

    (b) subject to that, may determine an appeal with or without a hearing;

    (c) may—

        (i)   consult the assessing authority,

       (ii)   consult the court which made the costs order, and

     (iii)   obtain any other information or document;

    (d) must reconsider the amount allowed by the assessing authority, taking into account the objections to the re-assessment and any other representations;

    (e) may maintain, increase or decrease the amount allowed on the re-assessment;

    (f) may provide for the costs incurred by either party to the appeal; and

    (g) must serve reasons for the decision on—

        (i)   the parties, and

       (ii)   the assessing authority.

(6) A costs judge may extend a time limit under this rule, even after it has expired.

Appeal to a High Court judge

45.13.–(1) This rule applies where—   **B-610**

    (a) a costs judge has determined an appeal under rule 45.12; and

    (b) either party wants to appeal against the amount allowed.

(2) A party who wants to appeal—

    (a) may do so only if a costs judge certifies that a point of principle of general importance was involved in the decision on the review; and

(b) must apply in writing for such a certificate and serve the application on—
    (i) the costs judge,
    (ii) the other party
not more than 21 days after service of the decision on the review.
(3) That party must—
(a) appeal to a judge of the High Court attached to the Queen's Bench Division as if it were an appeal from the decision of a master under Part 52 of the Civil Procedure Rules 1998); and
(b) serve the appeal not more than 21 days after service of the costs judge's certificate under paragraph (2).
(4) A High Court judge—
(a) may extend a time limit under this rule even after it has expired;
(b) has the same powers and duties as a costs judge under rule 45.12; and
(c) may hear the appeal with one or more assessors.

Application for an extension of time
B-611   **45.14.**–(1) A party who wants an extension of time under rule 45.11, 45.12 or 45.13 must—
(a) apply in writing;
(b) explain the delay; and
(c) attach the application, representations or appeal for which the extension of time is needed.

For the criminal costs practice direction, see §§ 6-123 *et seq.* in the main work.

Criminal Procedure Rules 2015 (S.I. 2015 No. 1490), Pt 46

REPRESENTATIVES

Functions of representatives and their supporters
B-612   **46.1**–(1) Under these rules, anything that a party may or must do may be done—
(a) by a legal representative on that party's behalf;
(b) by a person with the corporation's written authority, where that corporation is a defendant;
(c) with the help of a parent, guardian or other suitable supporting adult where that party is a defendant—
    (i) who is under 18, or
    (ii) whose understanding of what the case involves is limited
unless other legislation (including a rule) otherwise requires.
(2) A member, officer or employee of a prosecutor may, on the prosecutor's behalf—
(a) serve on the magistrates' court officer, or present to a magistrates' court, an information under section 1 of the Magistrates' Courts Act 1980; or
(b) issue a written charge and requisition, or single justice procedure notice, under section 29 of the Criminal Justice Act 2003.

Notice of appointment, etc. of legal representative: general rules
B-613   **46.2.**–(1) This rule applies—
(a) in relation to a party who does not have legal aid for the purposes of a case;
(b) where such a party—
    (i) appoints a legal representative for the purposes of the case, or
    (ii) dismisses such a representative, with or without appointing another;
(c) where a legal representative for such a party withdraws from the case.
(2) Where paragraph (1)(b) applies, that party must give notice of the appointment or dismissal to—
(a) the court officer;
(b) each other party; and
(c) where applicable, the legal representative who has been dismissed,
as soon as practicable and in any event within 5 business days.
(3) Where paragraph (1)(c) applies, that legal representative must, as soon as practicable, give notice to—
(a) the court officer;
(b) the party whom he or she has represented; and

(c) each other party.

(4) Any such notice—

    (a) may be given orally, but only if—

        (i) it is given at a hearing, and

        (ii) it specifies no restriction under paragraph (5)(b) (restricted scope of appointment);

    (b) otherwise, must be in writing.

(5) A notice of the appointment of a legal representative—

    (a) must identify—

        (i) the legal representative who has been appointed, with details of how to contact that representative, and

        (ii) all those to whom the notice is given;

    (b) may specify a restriction, or restrictions, on the purpose or duration of the appointment; and

    (c) if it specifies any such restriction, may nonetheless provide that documents may continue to be served on the represented party at the representative's address until—

        (i) further notice is given under this rule, or

        (ii) that party obtains legal aid for the purposes of the case.

(6) A legal representative who is dismissed by a party or who withdraws from representing a party must, as soon as practicable, make available to that party such documents in the representative's possession as have been served on that party.

Application to change legal representative: legal aid

46.3.—(1) This rule applies—   **B-614**

    (a) in relation to a party who has legal aid for the purposes of a case;

    (b) where such a party wants to select a legal representative in place of the representative named in the legal aid representation order.

(2) Such a party must—

    (a) apply in writing as soon as practicable after becoming aware of the grounds for doing so; and

    (b) serve the application on—

        (i) the court officer, and

        (ii) the legal representative named in the legal aid representation order.

(3) The application must—

    (a) explain what the case is about, including what offences are alleged, what stage it has reached and what is likely to be in issue at trial;

    (b) explain how and why the applicant chose the legal representative named in the legal aid representation order;

    (c) if an advocate other than that representative has been instructed for the applicant, explain whether the applicant wishes to replace that advocate;

    (d) explain, giving relevant facts and dates—

        (i) in what way, in the applicant's opinion, there has been a breakdown in the relationship between the applicant and the current representative such that neither the individual representing the applicant nor any colleague of his or hers any longer can provide effective representation, or

        (ii) what other compelling reason, in the applicant's opinion, means that neither the individual representing the applicant nor any colleague of his or hers any longer can provide effective representation;

    (e) give details of any previous application by the applicant to replace the legal representative named in the legal aid representation order;

    (f) state whether the applicant—

        (i) waives the legal professional privilege attaching to the applicant's communications with the current representative, to the extent required to allow that representative to respond to the matters set out in the application, or

        (ii) declines to waive that privilege and acknowledges that the court may draw such inferences as it thinks fit in consequence;

    (g) explain how and why the applicant has chosen the proposed new representative;

    (h) include or attach a statement by the proposed new representative which—

        (i) confirms that that representative is eligible and willing to conduct the case for the applicant,

        (ii) confirms that that representative can and will meet the current timetable for the case, including any hearing date or dates that have been set, if the application succeeds,

   (iii) explains what, if any, dealings that representative has had with the applicant before the present case; and

  (i) ask for a hearing, if the applicant wants one, and explain why it is needed.

 (4) The legal representative named in the legal aid representation order must—

  (a) respond in writing no more than 5 business days after service of the application; and

  (b) serve the response on—

   (i) the court officer,

   (ii) the applicant, and

   (iii) the proposed new representative.

 (5) The response must—

  (a) explain which, if any, of the matters set out in the application the current representative disputes;

  (b) explain, as appropriate, giving relevant facts and dates—

   (i) whether, and if so in what way, in the current representative's opinion, there has been a breakdown in the relationship with the applicant such that neither the individual representing the applicant nor any colleague of his or hers any longer can provide effective representation,

   (ii) whether, in the current representative's opinion, there is some other compelling reason why neither the individual representing the applicant nor any colleague of his or hers any longer can provide effective representation, and if so what reason,

   (iii) whether the current representative considers there to be a duty to withdraw from the case in accordance with professional rules of conduct, and if so the nature of that duty, and

   (iv) whether the current representative no longer is able to represent the applicant through circumstances outside the representative's control, and if so the particular circumstances that render the representative unable to do so;

  (c) explain what, if any, dealings the current representative had had with the applicant before the present case; and

  (d) ask for a hearing, if the current representative wants one, and explain why it is needed.

 (6) The court may determine the application—

  (a) without a hearing, as a general rule; or

  (b) at a hearing, which must be in private unless the court otherwise directs.

 (7) Unless the court otherwise directs, any hearing must be in the absence of each other party and each other party's representative and advocate (if any).

 (8) If the court allows the application, as soon as practicable—

  (a) the current representative must make available to the new representative such documents in the current representative's possession as have been served on the applicant party; and

  (b) the new representative must serve notice of appointment on each other party.

 (9) Paragraph (10) applies where—

  (a) the court refuses the application;

  (b) in response to that decision—

   (i) the applicant declines further representation by the current representative or asks for legal aid to be withdrawn, or

   (ii) the current representative declines further to represent the applicant; and

  (c) the court in consequence withdraws the applicant's legal aid.

 (10) The court officer must serve notice of the withdrawal of legal aid on—

  (a) the applicant; and

  (b) the current representative.

Criminal Procedure Rules 2015 (S.I. 2015 No. 1490), Pt 47 (as substituted by the Criminal Procedure (Amendment) Rules 2016 (S.I. 2016 No. 120), r.15)

INVESTIGATION ORDERS AND WARRANTS

Section 1: General rules

When this Part applies

B-615 **47.1.** This Part applies to the exercise of the powers listed in each of rules 47.4, 47.24, 47.35, 47.42, 47.46, 47.51 and 47.54.

[This rule is printed as amended by the Criminal Procedure (Amendment No. 2) Rules 2016 (S.I. 2016 No. 705); and the Criminal Procedure (Amendment) Rules 2017 (S.I. 2017 No. 144).]

Meaning of "court", "applicant" and "respondent"

47.2. In this Part— **B-616**

   (a) a reference to the "court" includes a reference to any justice of the peace or judge who can exercise a power to which this Part applies;

   (b) "applicant" means a person who, or an authority which, can apply for an order or warrant to which this Part applies; and

   (c) "respondent" means any person—

      (i) against whom such an order is sought or made, or

     (ii) on whom an application for such an order is served.

Documents served on the court officer

47.3.–(1) Unless the court otherwise directs, the court officer may— **B-617**

   (a) keep a written application; or

   (b) arrange for the whole or any part to be kept by some other appropriate person, subject to any conditions that the court may impose.

(2) Where the court makes an order when the court office is closed, the applicant must, not more than 72 hours later, serve on the court officer—

   (a) a copy of the order; and

   (b) any written material that was submitted to the court.

(3) Where the court issues a warrant—

   (a) the applicant must return it to the court officer as soon as practicable after it has been executed, and in any event not more than 3 months after it was issued (unless other legislation otherwise provides); and

   (b) the court officer must—

      (i) keep the warrant for 12 months after its return, and

     (ii) during that period, make it available for inspection by the occupier of the premises to which it relates, if that occupier asks to inspect it.

Section 2: Investigation orders

When this Section applies

47.4. This Section applies where— **B-618**

   (a) a Circuit judge can make, vary or discharge an order for the production of, or for giving access to, material under paragraph 4 of Schedule 1 to the Police and Criminal Evidence Act 1984 [§ 15-109 in the main work], other than material that consists of or includes journalistic material;

   (b) for the purposes of a terrorist investigation, a Circuit judge can make, vary or discharge—

      (i) an order for the production of, or for giving access to, material, or for a statement of its location, under paragraphs 5 and 10 of Schedule 5 to the Terrorism Act 2000 [*ibid.*, §§ 25-105, 25-106],

     (ii) an explanation order, under paragraphs 10 and 13 of Schedule 5 to the 2000 Act [*ibid.*, §§ 25-110, 25-113],

     (iii) a customer information order, under paragraphs 1 and 4 of Schedule 6 to the 2000 Act;

   (c) for the purposes of a terrorist investigation, a Circuit judge can make, and the Crown Court can vary or discharge, an account monitoring order, under paragraphs 2 and 4 of Schedule 6A to the 2000 Act *ibid.*, §§ 25-117, 25-119;

   (d) for the purposes of an investigation to which Part 8 of the Proceeds of Crime Act 2002 or the Proceeds of Crime Act 2002 (External Investigations) Order 2014 applies, a Crown Court judge can make, and the Crown Court can vary or discharge—

      (i) a production order, under sections 345 and 351 of the 2002 Act [*ibid.*, §§ 15-315, 15-322] or under articles 6 and 12 of the 2014 Order,

     (ii) an order to grant entry, under sections 347 [*ibid.*, § 15-318] and 351 of the 2002 Act or under articles 8 and 12 of the 2014 Order,

     (iii) a disclosure order, under sections 357 and 362 of the 2002 Act [*ibid.*, §§ 15-330, 15-336] or under articles 16 and 21 of the 2014 Order,

    (iv) a customer information order, under sections 363 and 369 of the 2002 Act [*ibid.*, §§ 15-337, 15-344] or under articles 22 and 28 of the 2014 Order,

    (v) an account monitoring order, under sections 370, 373 and 375 of the 2002 Act [*ibid.*, §§ 15-345, 15-348, 15-350] or under articles 29, 32 and 34 of the 2014 Order;

(e) in connection with an extradition request, a Circuit judge can make an order for the production of, or for giving access to, material under section 157 of the Extradition Act 2003.

Exercise of court's powers

B-619   **47.5.**—(1) Subject to paragraphs (2), (3) and (4), the court may determine an application for an order, or to vary or discharge an order—

(a) at a hearing (which must be in private unless the court otherwise directs), or without a hearing; and

(b) in the absence of—

    (i) the applicant,

    (ii) the respondent (if any),

    (iii) any other person affected by the order.

(2) The court must not determine such an application in the applicant's absence if—

(a) the applicant asks for a hearing; or

(b) it appears to the court that—

    (i) the proposed order may infringe legal privilege, within the meaning of section 10 of the Police and Criminal Evidence Act 1984 [*ibid.*, § 15-126], section 348 or 361 of the Proceeds of Crime Act 2002 [*ibid.*, §§ 15-319, 15-335] or article 9 of the Proceeds of Crime Act 2002 (External Investigations) Order 2014,

    (ii) the proposed order may require the production of excluded material, within the meaning of section 11 of the 1984 Act [*ibid.*, § 15-129], or

    (iii) for any other reason the application is so complex or serious as to require the court to hear the applicant.

(3) The court must not determine such an application in the absence of any respondent or other person affected, unless—

(a) the absentee has had at least 2 business days in which to make representations; or

(b) the court is satisfied that—

    (i) the applicant cannot identify or contact the absentee,

    (ii) it would prejudice the investigation if the absentee were present,

    (iii) it would prejudice the investigation to adjourn or postpone the application so as to allow the absentee to attend, or

    (iv) the absentee has waived the opportunity to attend.

(4) The court must not determine such an application in the absence of any respondent who, if the order sought by the applicant were made, would be required to produce or give access to journalistic material, unless that respondent has waived the opportunity to attend.

(5) The court officer must arrange for the court to hear such an application no sooner than 2 business days after it was served, unless—

(a) the court directs that no hearing need be arranged; or

(b) the court gives other directions for the hearing.

(6) The court must not determine an application unless satisfied that sufficient time has been allowed for it.

(7) If the court so directs, the parties to an application may attend a hearing by live link or telephone.

(8) The court must not make, vary or discharge an order unless the applicant states, in writing or orally, that to the best of the applicant's knowledge and belief—

(a) the application discloses all the information that is material to what the court must decide; and

(b) the content of the application is true.

(9) Where the statement required by paragraph (8) is made orally—

(a) the statement must be on oath or affirmation, unless the court otherwise directs; and

(b) the court must arrange for a record of the making of the statement.

(10) The court may—

(a) shorten or extend (even after it has expired) a time limit under this Section;

(b) dispense with a requirement for service under this Section (even after service was required); and

(c)   consider an application made orally instead of in writing.

(11) A person who wants an extension of time must—

(a)   apply when serving the application for which it is needed; and

(b)   explain the delay.

Application for order: general rules

47.6.–(1) This rule applies to each application for an order to which this Section applies.   **B-620**

(2) The applicant must—

(a)   apply in writing and serve the application on the court officer;

(b)   demonstrate that the applicant is entitled to apply, for example as a constable or under legislation that applies to other officers;

(c)   give the court an estimate of how long the court should allow—

(i)   to read the application and prepare for any hearing, and

(ii)   for any hearing of the application;

(d)   attach a draft order in the terms proposed by the applicant;

(e)   serve notice of the application on the respondent, unless the court otherwise directs;

(f)   serve the application on the respondent to such extent, if any, as the court directs.

(3) A notice served on the respondent must—

(a)   specify the material or information in respect of which the application is made; and

(b)   identify—

(i)   the power that the applicant invites the court to exercise, and

(ii)   the conditions for the exercise of that power which the applicant asks the court to find are met.

(4) The applicant must serve any order made on the respondent.

Application containing information withheld from a respondent or other person

47.7.–(1) This rule applies where an application includes information that the applicant thinks   **B-621** ought to be revealed only to the court.

(2) The application must—

(a)   identify that information; and

(b)   explain why that information ought not to be served on the respondent or another person.

(3) At a hearing of an application to which this rule applies—

(a)   the general rule is that the court must consider, in the following sequence—

(i)   representations first by the applicant and then by the respondent and any other person, in the presence of them all, and then

(ii)   further representations by the applicant, in the others' absence; but

(b)   the court may direct other arrangements for the hearing.

Application to vary or discharge an order

47.8.–(1) This rule applies where one of the following wants the court to vary or discharge an   **B-622** order to which a rule in this Section refers—

(a)   an applicant;

(b)   the respondent; or

(c)   a person affected by the order.

(2) That applicant, respondent or person affected must—

(a)   apply in writing as soon as practicable after becoming aware of the grounds for doing so;

(b)   serve the application on—

(i)   the court officer, and

(ii)   the respondent, applicant, or any person known to be affected, as applicable;

(c)   explain why it is appropriate for the order to be varied or discharged;

(d)   propose the terms of any variation; and

(e)   ask for a hearing, if one is wanted, and explain why it is needed.

Application to punish for contempt of court

47.9.–(1) This rule applies where a person is accused of disobeying—   **B-623**

(a)   a production order made under paragraph 4 of Schedule 1 to the Police and Criminal Evidence Act 1984;

(b)   a production etc. order made under paragraph 5 of Schedule 5 to the Terrorism Act 2000;

(c)   an explanation order made under paragraph 13 of that Schedule;

(d)   an account monitoring order made under paragraph 2 of Schedule 6A to that Act;

(e)   a production order made under section 345 of the Proceeds of Crime Act 2002 or article 6 of the Proceeds of Crime Act 2002 (External Investigations) Order 2014;

(f)   an account monitoring order made under section 370 of the 2002 Act or article 29 of the 2014 Order; or

(g)   a production order made under section 157 of the Extradition Act 2003.

(2) An applicant who wants the court to exercise its power to punish that person for contempt of court must comply with the rules in Part 48 (contempt of court).

Orders under the Police and Criminal Evidence Act 1984

Application for a production order under the Police and Criminal Evidence Act 1984

B-624   **47.10.**–(1) This rule applies where an applicant wants the court to make an order to which rule 47.4(a) refers.

(2) As well as complying with rule 47.6 (application for order: general rules), the application must, in every case–

(a)   specify the offence under investigation (and see paragraph (3)(a));

(b)   describe the material sought;

(c)   identify the respondent;

(d)   specify the premises on which the material is believed to be, or explain why it is not reasonably practicable to do so;

(e)   explain the grounds for believing that the material is on the premises specified, or (if applicable) on unspecified premises of the respondent;

(f)   specify the set of access conditions on which the applicant relies (and see paragraphs (3) and (4)); and

(g)   propose–
    (i)   the terms of the order, and
    (ii)   the period within which it should take effect.

(3) Where the applicant relies on paragraph 2 of Schedule 1 to the Police and Criminal Evidence Act 1984 ("the first set of access conditions": general power to gain access to special procedure material), the application must–

(a)   specify the indictable offence under investigation;

(b)   explain the grounds for believing that the offence has been committed;

(c)   explain the grounds for believing that the material sought–
    (i)   is likely to be of substantial value to the investigation (whether by itself, or together with other material),
    (ii)   is likely to be admissible evidence at trial for the offence under investigation, and
    (iii)   does not consist of or include items subject to legal privilege or excluded material;

(d)   explain what other methods of obtaining the material–
    (i)   have been tried without success, or
    (ii)   have not been tried because they appeared bound to fail; and

(e)   explain why it is in the public interest for the respondent to produce the material, having regard to–
    (i)   the benefit likely to accrue to the investigation if the material is obtained, and
    (ii)   the circumstances under which the respondent holds the material.

(4) Where the applicant relies on paragraph 3 of Schedule 1 to the Police and Criminal Evidence Act 1984 ("the second set of access conditions": use of search warrant power to gain access to excluded or special procedure material), the application must–

(a)   state the legislation under which a search warrant could have been issued, had the material sought not been excluded or special procedure material (in this paragraph, described as "the main search power");

(b)   include or attach the terms of the main search power;

(c)   explain how the circumstances would have satisfied any criteria prescribed by the main search power for the issue of a search warrant; and

(d)   explain why the issue of such a search warrant would have been appropriate.

Orders under the Terrorism Act 2000

Application for an order under the Terrorism Act 2000

B-625   **47.11.**–(1) This rule applies where an applicant wants the court to make one of the orders to which rule 47.4(b) and (c) refers.

(2) As well as complying with rule 47.6 (Application for order: general rules), the application must—

    (a) specify the offence under investigation;

    (b) explain how the investigation constitutes a terrorist investigation within the meaning of the Terrorism Act 2000;

    (c) identify the respondent; and

    (d) give the information required by whichever of rules 47.12 to 47.16 applies.

Content of application for a production etc. order under the Terrorism Act 2000

47.12. As well as complying with rules 47.6 and 47.11, an applicant who wants the court to make **B-626** an order for the production of, or for giving access to, material, or for a statement of its location, must—

    (a) describe that material;

    (b) explain why the applicant thinks the material is—

        (i) in the respondent's possession, custody or power, or

        (ii) expected to come into existence and then to be in the respondent's possession, custody or power within 28 days of the order;

    (c) explain how the material constitutes or contains excluded material or special procedure material;

    (d) confirm that none of the material is expected to be subject to legal privilege;

    (e) explain why the material is likely to be of substantial value to the investigation;

    (f) explain why it is in the public interest for the material to be produced, or for the applicant to be given access to it, having regard to—

        (i) the benefit likely to accrue to the investigation if it is obtained, and

        (ii) the circumstances in which the respondent has the material, or is expected to have it; and

    (g) propose—

        (i) the terms of the order, and

        (ii) the period within which it should take effect.

Content of application for an order to grant entry under the Terrorism Act 2000

47.13. An applicant who wants the court to make an order to grant entry in aid of a production **B-627** order must—

    (a) specify the premises to which entry is sought;

    (b) explain why the order is needed; and

    (c) propose the terms of the order.

Content of application for an explanation order under the Terrorism Act 2000

47.14. As well as complying with rules 47.6 and 47.11, an applicant who wants the court to make **B-628** an explanation order must—

    (a) identify the material that the applicant wants the respondent to explain;

    (b) confirm that the explanation is not expected to infringe legal privilege; and

    (c) propose the terms of the order.

Content of application for a customer information order under the Terrorism Act 2000

47.15. As well as complying with rules 47.6 and 47.11, an applicant who wants the court to make a **B-629** customer information order must—

    (a) explain why it is desirable for the purposes of the investigation to trace property said to be terrorist property within the meaning of the Terrorism Act 2000;

    (b) explain why the order will enhance the effectiveness of the investigation; and

    (c) propose the terms of the order.

Content of application for an account monitoring order under the Terrorism Act 2000

47.16. As well as complying with rules 47.6 and 47.11, an applicant who wants the court to make **B-630** an account monitoring order must—

    (a) specify—

        (i) the information sought,

        (ii) the period during which the applicant wants the respondent to provide that information (to a maximum of 90 days), and

    (iii) where, when and in what manner the applicant wants the respondent to provide that information;

(b) explain why it is desirable for the purposes of the investigation to trace property said to be terrorist property within the meaning of the Terrorism Act 2000;

(c) explain why the order will enhance the effectiveness of the investigation; and

(d) propose the terms of the order.

Orders under the Proceeds of Crime Act 2002

Application for an order under the Proceeds of Crime Act 2002

B-631
    47.17. (1) This rule applies where an applicant wants the court to make one of the orders to which rule 47.4(d) refers.

(2) As well as complying with rule 47.6 (application for order: general rules), the application must—

(a) identify—
    (i) the respondent, and
    (ii) the person or property the subject of the investigation;

(b) in the case of an investigation in the United Kingdom, explain why the applicant thinks that—
    (i) the person under investigation has benefitted from criminal conduct, in the case of a confiscation investigation, or committed a money laundering offence, in the case of a money laundering investigation, or
    (ii) the cash involved is property obtained through unlawful conduct, or is intended to be used in unlawful conduct, in the case of a detained cash investigation;

(c) in the case of an investigation outside the United Kingdom, explain why the applicant thinks that—
    (i) there is an investigation by an overseas authority which relates to a criminal investigation or to criminal proceedings (including proceedings to remove the benefit of a person's criminal conduct following that person's conviction), and
    (ii) the investigation is into whether property has been obtained as a result of or in connection with criminal conduct, or into the extent or whereabouts of such property;

(d) give the additional information required by whichever of rules 47.18 to 47.22 applies.

Content of application for a production order under the Proceeds of Crime Act 2002

B-632
    47.18. As well as complying with rules 47.6 and 47.17, an applicant who wants the court to make an order for the production of, or for giving access to, material, must—

(a) describe that material;

(b) explain why the applicant thinks the material is in the respondent's possession or control;

(c) confirm that none of the material is—
    (i) expected to be subject to legal privilege, or
    (ii) excluded material;

(d) explain why the material is likely to be of substantial value to the investigation;

(e) explain why it is in the public interest for the material to be produced, or for the applicant to be given access to it, having regard to—
    (i) the benefit likely to accrue to the investigation if it is obtained, and
    (ii) the circumstances in which the respondent has the material; and

(f) propose—
    (i) the terms of the order, and
    (ii) the period within which it should take effect, if 7 days from the date of the order would not be appropriate.

Content of application for an order to grant entry under the Proceeds of Crime Act 2002

B-633
    47.19. An applicant who wants the court to make an order to grant entry in aid of a production order must—

(a) specify the premises to which entry is sought;

(b) explain why the order is needed; and

(c) propose the terms of the order.

Content of application for a disclosure order under the Proceeds of Crime Act 2002

B-634
    47.20. As well as complying with rules 47.6 and 47.17, an applicant who wants the court to make a disclosure order must—

(a) describe in general terms the information that the applicant wants the respondent to provide;

(b) confirm that none of the information is—

   (i) expected to be subject to legal privilege, or

   (ii) excluded material;

(c) explain why the information is likely to be of substantial value to the investigation;

(d) explain why it is in the public interest for the information to be provided, having regard to the benefit likely to accrue to the investigation if it is obtained; and

(e) propose the terms of the order.

Content of application for a customer information order under the Proceeds of Crime Act 2002

47.21. As well as complying with rules 47.6 and 47.17, an applicant who wants the court to make a customer information order must—   **B-635**

(a) explain why customer information about the person under investigation is likely to be of substantial value to that investigation;

(b) explain why it is in the public interest for the information to be provided, having regard to the benefit likely to accrue to the investigation if it is obtained; and

(c) propose the terms of the order.

Content of application for an account monitoring order under the Proceeds of Crime Act 2002

47.22. As well as complying with rules 47.6 and 47.17, an applicant who wants the court to make an account monitoring order for the provision of account information must—   **B-636**

(a) specify—

   (i) the information sought,

   (ii) the period during which the applicant wants the respondent to provide that information (to a maximum of 90 days), and

   (iii) when and in what manner the applicant wants the respondent to provide that information;

(b) explain why the information is likely to be of substantial value to the investigation;

(c) explain why it is in the public interest for the information to be provided, having regard to the benefit likely to accrue to the investigation if it is obtained; and

(d) propose the terms of the order.

Orders under the Extradition Act 2003

47.23. [*Application for a production order under the Extradition Act 2003.*]   **B-637**

Section 3: Investigation warrants

When this Section applies

47.24. This Section applies where—   **B-638**

(a) a justice of the peace can issue a warrant under—

   (i) section 8 of the Police and Criminal Evidence Act 1984 [§ 15-101 in the main work],

   (ii) section 2 of the Criminal Justice Act 1987 [*ibid.*, § 1-470];

(b) a Circuit judge can issue a warrant under—

   (i) paragraph 12 of Schedule 1 to the Police and Criminal Evidence Act 1984[*ibid.*, § 15-111],

   (ii) paragraph 11 of Schedule 5 to the Terrorism Act 2000 [*ibid.*, § 25-111],

   (iii) section 160 of the Extradition Act 2003;

(c) a Crown Court judge can issue a warrant under—

   (i) section 352 of the Proceeds of Crime Act 2002 [*ibid.*, § 15-323], or

   (ii) article 13 of the Proceeds of Crime Act 2002 (External Investigations) Order 2014;

(d) a court to which these Rules apply can issue a warrant to search for and seize articles or persons under a power not listed in paragraphs (a), (b) or (c).

Exercise of court's powers

47.25. (1) The court must determine an application for a warrant—   **B-639**

(a) at a hearing, which must be in private unless the court otherwise directs;

(b) in the presence of the applicant; and

(c) in the absence of any person affected by the warrant, including any person in occupation or control of premises which the applicant wants to search.

649

(2) If the court so directs, the applicant may attend the hearing by live link or telephone.

(3) The court must not determine an application unless satisfied that sufficient time has been allowed for it.

(4) The court must not determine an application unless the applicant confirms, on oath or affirmation, that to the best of the applicant's knowledge and belief—

    (a) the application discloses all the information that is material to what the court must decide, including any circumstances that might reasonably be considered capable of undermining any of the grounds of the application; and

    (b) the content of the application is true.

(5) If the court requires the applicant to answer a question about an application—

    (a) the applicant's answer must be on oath or affirmation;

    (b) the court must arrange for a record of the gist of the question and reply; and

    (c) if the applicant cannot answer to the court's satisfaction, the court may—

        (i) specify the information the court requires, and

        (ii) give directions for the presentation of any renewed application.

(6) Unless to do so would be inconsistent with other legislation, on an application the court may issue—

    (a) a warrant in respect of specified premises;

    (b) a warrant in respect of all premises occupied or controlled by a specified person;

    (c) a warrant in respect of all premises occupied or controlled by a specified person which specifies some of those premises; or

    (d) more than one warrant—

        (i) each one in respect of premises specified in the warrant,

        (ii) each one in respect of all premises occupied or controlled by a person specified in the warrant (whether or not such a warrant also specifies any of those premises), or

        (iii) at least one in respect of specified premises and at least one in respect of all premises occupied or controlled by a specified person (whether or not such a warrant also specifies any of those premises).

Application for warrant: general rules

B-640   47.26.–(1) This rule applies to each application to which this Section applies.

(2) The applicant must—

    (a) apply in writing;

    (b) serve the application on—

        (i) the court officer, or

        (ii) if the court office is closed, the court;

    (c) demonstrate that the applicant is entitled to apply, for example as a constable or under legislation that applies to other officers;

    (d) give the court an estimate of how long the court should allow—

        (i) to read and prepare for the application, and

        (ii) for the hearing of the application; and

    (e) tell the court when the applicant expects any warrant issued to be executed.

(3) The application must disclose anything known or reported to the applicant that might reasonably be considered capable of undermining any of the grounds of the application.

(4) Where the application includes information that the applicant thinks should not be supplied under rule 5.7 (supply to a party of information or documents from records or case materials) to a person affected by a warrant, the applicant may—

    (a) set out that information in a separate document, marked accordingly; and

    (b) in that document, explain why the applicant thinks that that information ought not to be supplied to anyone other than the court.

(5) The application must include—

    (a) a declaration by the applicant that to the best of the applicant's knowledge and belief—

        (i) the application discloses all the information that is material to what the court must decide, including anything that might reasonably be considered capable of undermining any of the grounds of the application, and

        (ii) the content of the application is true; and

    (b) a declaration by an officer senior to the applicant that the senior officer has reviewed and authorised the application.

(6) The application must attach a draft warrant or warrants in the terms proposed by the applicant.

Information to be included in a warrant

47.27. (1) A warrant must identify— **B-641**

    (a) the person or description of persons by whom it may be executed;

    (b) any person who may accompany a person executing the warrant;

    (c) so far as practicable, the material, documents, articles or persons to be sought;

    (d) the legislation under which it was issued;

    (e) the name of the applicant;

    (f) the court that issued it, unless that is otherwise recorded by the court officer;

    (g) the court office for the court that issued it; and

    (h) the date on which it was issued.

(2) A warrant must specify—

    (a) either—

        (i) the premises to be searched, where the application was for authority to search specified premises, or

        (ii) the person in occupation or control of premises to be searched, where the application was for authority to search any premises occupied or controlled by that person; and

    (b) the number of occasions on which specified premises may be searched, if more than one.

(3) A warrant must include, by signature, initial, or otherwise, an indication that it has been approved by the court that issued it.

(4) Where a warrant comprises more than a single page, each page must include such an indication.

(5) A copy of a warrant must include a prominent certificate that it is such a copy.

Application for warrant under section 8 of the Police and Criminal Evidence Act 1984

47.28. (1) This rule applies where an applicant wants a magistrates' court to issue a warrant or war- **B-642**
rants under section 8 of the Police and Criminal Evidence Act 1984.

(2) As well as complying with rule 47.26, the application must—

    (a) specify the offence under investigation (and see paragraph (3));

    (b) so far as practicable, identify the material sought (and see paragraph (4));

    (c) specify the premises to be searched (and see paragraphs (5) and (6));

    (d) state whether the applicant wants the premises to be searched on more than one occasion (and see paragraph (7)); and

    (e) state whether the applicant wants other persons to accompany the officers executing the warrant or warrants (and see paragraph (8)).

(3) In relation to the offence under investigation, the application must—

    (a) state whether that offence is—

        (i) an indictable offence, or

        (ii) a relevant offence as defined in section 28D of the Immigration Act 1971; and

    (b) explain the grounds for believing that the offence has been committed.

(4) In relation to the material sought, the application must explain the grounds for believing that that material—

    (a) is likely to be of substantial value to the investigation (whether by itself, or together with other material);

    (b) is likely to be admissible evidence at trial for the offence under investigation; and

    (c) does not consist of or include items subject to legal privilege, excluded material or special procedure material.

(5) In relation to premises which the applicant wants to be searched and can specify, the application must—

    (a) specify each set of premises;

    (b) in respect of each set of premises, explain the grounds for believing that material sought is on those premises; and

    (c) in respect of each set of premises, explain the grounds for believing that—

        (i) it is not practicable to communicate with any person entitled to grant entry to the premises,

        (ii) it is practicable to communicate with such a person but it is not practicable to communicate with any person entitled to grant access to the material sought,

        (iii) entry to the premises will not be granted unless a warrant is produced, or

        (iv) the purpose of a search may be frustrated or seriously prejudiced unless a constable arriving at the premises can secure immediate entry to them.

(6) In relation to premises which the applicant wants to be searched but at least some of which the applicant cannot specify, the application must—

    (a) explain the grounds for believing that—
        (i) because of the particulars of the offence under investigation it is necessary to search any premises occupied or controlled by a specified person, and
        (ii) it is not reasonably practicable to specify all the premises which that person occupies or controls which might need to be searched;
    (b) specify as many sets of premises as is reasonably practicable;
    (c) in respect of each set of premises, whether specified or not, explain the grounds for believing that material sought is on those premises; and
    (d) in respect of each specified set of premises, explain the grounds for believing that—
        (i) it is not practicable to communicate with any person entitled to grant entry to the premises,
        (ii) it is practicable to communicate with such a person but it is not practicable to communicate with any person entitled to grant access to the material sought,
        (iii) entry to the premises will not be granted unless a warrant is produced, or
        (iv) the purpose of a search may be frustrated or seriously prejudiced unless a constable arriving at the premises can secure immediate entry to them.

(7) In relation to any set of premises which the applicant wants to be searched on more than one occasion, the application must—

    (a) explain why it is necessary to search on more than one occasion in order to achieve the purpose for which the applicant wants the court to issue the warrant; and
    (b) specify any proposed maximum number of occasions.

(8) In relation to any set of premises which the applicant wants to be searched by the officers executing the warrant with other persons authorised by the court, the application must—

    (a) identify those other persons, by function or description; and
    (b) explain why those persons are required.

Application for warrant under section 2 of the Criminal Justice Act 1987

B-643   **47.29.** (1) This rule applies where an applicant wants a magistrates' court to issue a warrant or warrants under section 2 of the Criminal Justice Act 1987.

(2) As well as complying with rule 47.26, the application must—

    (a) describe the investigation being conducted by the Director of the Serious Fraud Office and include—
        (i) an explanation of what is alleged and why, and
        (ii) a chronology of relevant events;
    (b) specify the document, documents or description of documents sought by the applicant (and see paragraphs (3) and (4)); and
    (c) specify the premises which the applicant wants to be searched (and see paragraph (5)).

(3) In relation to each document or description of documents sought, the application must—

    (a) explain the grounds for believing that each such document—
        (i) relates to a matter relevant to the investigation, and
        (ii) could not be withheld from disclosure or production on grounds of legal professional privilege; and
    (b) explain the grounds for believing that—
        (i) a person has failed to comply with a notice by the Director to produce the document or documents,
        (ii) it is not practicable to serve such a notice, or
        (iii) the service of such a notice might seriously impede the investigation.

(4) In relation to any document or description of documents which the applicant wants to be preserved but not seized under a warrant, the application must—

    (a) specify the steps for which the applicant wants the court's authority in order to preserve and prevent interference with the document or documents; and
    (b) explain why such steps are necessary.

(5) In respect of each set of premises which the applicant wants to be searched, the application must explain the grounds for believing that a document or description of documents sought by the applicant is on those premises.

(6) If the court so directs, the applicant must make available to the court material on which is based the information given under paragraph (2).

Application for warrant under paragraph 12 of Schedule 1 to the Police and Criminal Evidence Act 1984

47.30. (1) This rule applies where an applicant wants a Circuit judge to issue a warrant or warrants under paragraph 12 of Schedule 1 to the Police and Criminal Evidence Act 1984. **B-644**

(2) As well as complying with rule 47.26, the application must—

(a) specify the offence under investigation (and see paragraph (3)(a));

(b) specify the set of access conditions on which the applicant relies (and see paragraphs (3) and (4));

(c) so far as practicable, identify the material sought;

(d) specify the premises to be searched (and see paragraphs (6) and (7)); and

(e) state whether the applicant wants other persons to accompany the officers executing the warrant or warrants (and see paragraph (8)).

(3) Where the applicant relies on paragraph 2 of Schedule 1 to the Police and Criminal Evidence Act 1984 ("the first set of access conditions": general power to gain access to special procedure material), the application must—

(a) specify the indictable offence under investigation;

(b) explain the grounds for believing that the offence has been committed;

(c) explain the grounds for believing that the material sought—

(i) is likely to be of substantial value to the investigation (whether by itself, or together with other material),

(ii) is likely to be admissible evidence at trial for the offence under investigation, and

(iii) does not consist of or include items subject to legal privilege or excluded material;

(d) explain what other methods of obtaining the material—

(i) have been tried without success, or

(ii) have not been tried because they appeared bound to fail; and

(e) explain why it is in the public interest to obtain the material, having regard to—

(i) the benefit likely to accrue to the investigation if the material is obtained, and

(ii) the circumstances under which the material is held.

(4) Where the applicant relies on paragraph 3 of Schedule 1 to the Police and Criminal Evidence Act 1984 ("the second set of access conditions": use of search warrant power to gain access to excluded or special procedure material), the application must—

(a) state the legislation under which a search warrant could have been issued, had the material sought not been excluded or special procedure material (in this paragraph, described as "the main search power");

(b) include or attach the terms of the main search power;

(c) explain how the circumstances would have satisfied any criteria prescribed by the main search power for the issue of a search warrant;

(d) explain why the issue of such a search warrant would have been appropriate.

(5) Where the applicant relies on the second set of access conditions and on an assertion that a production order made under paragraph 4 of Schedule 1 to the 1984 Act in respect of the material sought has not been complied with—

(a) the application must—

(i) identify that order and describe its terms, and

(ii) specify the date on which it was served; but

(b) the application need not comply with paragraphs (6) or (7).

(6) In relation to premises which the applicant wants to be searched and can specify, the application must (unless paragraph (5) applies)—

(a) specify each set of premises;

(b) in respect of each set of premises, explain the grounds for believing that material sought is on those premises; and

(c) in respect of each set of premises, explain the grounds for believing that—

(i) it is not practicable to communicate with any person entitled to grant entry to the premises,

(ii) it is practicable to communicate with such a person but it is not practicable to communicate with any person entitled to grant access to the material sought,

(iii) the material sought contains information which is subject to a restriction on disclosure or an obligation of secrecy contained in an enactment and is likely to be disclosed in breach of the restriction or obligation if a warrant is not issued, or

(iv) service of notice of an application for a production order under paragraph 4 of Schedule 1 to the 1984 Act may seriously prejudice the investigation.

(7) In relation to premises which the applicant wants to be searched but at least some of which the applicant cannot specify, the application must (unless paragraph (5) applies)—

   (a) explain the grounds for believing that—

      (i) because of the particulars of the offence under investigation it is necessary to search any premises occupied or controlled by a specified person, and

     (ii) it is not reasonably practicable to specify all the premises which that person occupies or controls which might need to be searched;

   (b) specify as many sets of premises as is reasonably practicable;

   (c) in respect of each set of premises, whether specified or not, explain the grounds for believing that material sought is on those premises; and

   (d) in respect of each specified set of premises, explain the grounds for believing that—

      (i) it is not practicable to communicate with any person entitled to grant entry to the premises,

     (ii) it is practicable to communicate with such a person but it is not practicable to communicate with any person entitled to grant access to the material sought,

    (iii) the material sought contains information which is subject to a restriction on disclosure or an obligation of secrecy contained in an enactment and is likely to be disclosed in breach of the restriction or obligation if a warrant is not issued, or

    (iv) service of notice of an application for a production order under paragraph 4 of Schedule 1 to the 1984 Act may seriously prejudice the investigation.

(8) In relation to any set of premises which the applicant wants to be searched by the officers executing the warrant with other persons authorised by the court, the application must—

   (a) identify those other persons, by function or description; and

   (b) explain why those persons are required.

Application for warrant under paragraph 11 of Schedule 5 to the Terrorism Act 2000

B-645   **47.31.**—(1) This rule applies where an applicant wants a Circuit judge to issue a warrant or warrants under paragraph 11 of Schedule 5 to the Terrorism Act 2000.

(2) As well as complying with rule 47.26, the application must—

   (a) specify the offence under investigation;

   (b) explain how the investigation constitutes a terrorist investigation within the meaning of the Terrorism Act 2000;

   (c) so far as practicable, identify the material sought (and see paragraph (4));

   (d) specify the premises to be searched (and see paragraph (5)); and

   (e) state whether the applicant wants other persons to accompany the officers executing the warrant or warrants (and see paragraph (6)).

(3) Where the applicant relies on an assertion that a production order made under paragraph 5 of Schedule 5 to the 2000 Act in respect of material on the premises has not been complied with—

   (a) the application must—

      (i) identify that order and describe its terms, and

     (ii) specify the date on which it was served; but

   (b) the application need not comply with paragraphs (4) or (5)(b).

(4) In relation to the material sought, unless paragraph (3) applies the application must explain the grounds for believing that—

   (a) the material consists of or includes excluded material or special procedure material but does not include items subject to legal privilege;

   (b) the material is likely to be of substantial value to a terrorist investigation (whether by itself, or together with other material); and

   (c) it is not appropriate to make an order under paragraph 5 of Schedule 11 to the 2000 Act in relation to the material because—

      (i) it is not practicable to communicate with any person entitled to produce the material,

     (ii) it is not practicable to communicate with any person entitled to grant access to the material or entitled to grant entry to premises to which the application for the warrant relates, or

    (iii) a terrorist investigation may be seriously prejudiced unless a constable can secure immediate access to the material.

(5) In relation to the premises which the applicant wants to be searched, the application must—

   (a) specify—

      (i) where paragraph (3) applies, the respondent and any premises to which the production order referred, or

(ii)   in any other case, one or more sets of premises, or any premises occupied or controlled
by a specified person (which may include one or more specified sets of premises); and

(b)   unless paragraph (3) applies, in relation to premises which the applicant wants to be
searched but cannot specify, explain why—

(i)   it is necessary to search any premises occupied or controlled by the specified person,
and

(ii)   it is not reasonably practicable to specify all the premises which that person occupies
or controls which might need to be searched;

(c)   explain the grounds for believing that material sought is on those premises.

(6) In relation to any set of premises which the applicant wants to be searched by the officers
executing the warrant with other persons authorised by the court, the application must—

(a)   identify those other persons, by function or description; and

(b)   explain why those persons are required.

Application for warrant under section 352 of the Proceeds of Crime Act 2002

47.32.—(1) This rule applies where an applicant wants a Crown Court judge to issue a warrant or   **B-646**
warrants under—

(a)   section 352 of the Proceeds of Crime Act 2002; or

(b)   article 13 of the Proceeds of Crime Act 2002 (External Investigations) Order 2014 (S.I.
2014 No. 1893).

(2) As well as complying with rule 47.26, the application must—

(a)   explain whether the investigation is a confiscation investigation, a money laundering
investigation, a detained cash investigation or an external investigation;

(b)   in the case of an investigation in the United Kingdom, explain why the applicant suspects
that—

(i)   the person under investigation has benefited from criminal conduct, in the case of a
confiscation investigation, or committed a money laundering offence, in the case of a
money laundering investigation, or

(ii)   the cash involved is property obtained through unlawful conduct, or is intended to be
used in unlawful conduct, in the case of a detained cash investigation;

(c)   in the case of an investigation outside the United Kingdom, explain why the applicant
believes that—

(i)   there is an investigation by an overseas authority which relates to a criminal investigation or to criminal proceedings (including proceedings to remove the benefit of a
person's criminal conduct following that person's conviction), and

(ii)   the investigation is into whether property has been obtained as a result of or in connection with criminal conduct, or into the extent or whereabouts of such property;

(d)   indicate what material is sought (and see paragraphs (4) and (5));

(e)   specify the premises to be searched (and see paragraph (6)); and

(f)   state whether the applicant wants other persons to accompany the officers executing the
warrant or warrants (and see paragraph (7)).

(3) Where the applicant relies on an assertion that a production order made under sections 345
and 351 of the 2002 Act or under articles 6 and 12 of the 2014 Order has not been complied with—

(a)   the application must—

(i)   identify that order and describe its terms,

(ii)   specify the date on which it was served, and

(iii)   explain the grounds for believing that the material in respect of which the order was
made is on the premises specified in the application for the warrant; but

(b)   the application need not comply with paragraphs (4) or (5).

(4) Unless paragraph (3) applies, in relation to the material sought the application must—

(a)   specify the material; or

(b)   give a general description of the material and explain the grounds for believing that it
relates to the person under investigation and—

(i)   in the case of a confiscation investigation, relates to the question whether that person
has benefitted from criminal conduct, or to any question about the extent or
whereabouts of that benefit,

(ii)   in the case of a money laundering investigation, relates to the question whether that
person has committed a money laundering offence,

(iii)   in the case of a detained cash investigation into the derivation of cash, relates to the
question whether that cash is recoverable property,

(iv) in the case of a detained cash investigation into the intended use of the cash, relates to the question whether that cash is intended by any person to be used in unlawful conduct,

(v) in the case of an investigation outside the United Kingdom, relates to that investigation.

(5) Unless paragraph (3) applies, in relation to the material sought the application must explain also the grounds for believing that—

(a) the material consists of or includes special procedure material but does not include excluded material or privileged material;

(b) the material is likely to be of substantial value to the investigation (whether by itself, or together with other material); and

(c) it is in the public interest for the material to be obtained, having regard to—

(i) other potential sources of information,

(ii) the benefit likely to accrue to the investigation if the material is obtained.

(6) In relation to the premises which the applicant wants to be searched, unless paragraph (3) applies the application must—

(a) explain the grounds for believing that material sought is on those premises;

(b) if the application specifies the material sought, explain the grounds for believing that it is not appropriate to make a production order under sections 345 and 351 of the 2002 Act or under articles 6 and 12 of the 2014 Order because—

(i) it is not practicable to communicate with any person against whom the production order could be made,

(ii) it is not practicable to communicate with any person who would be required to comply with an order to grant entry to the premises, or

(iii) the investigation might be seriously prejudiced unless an appropriate person is able to secure immediate access to the material;

(c) if the application gives a general description of the material sought, explain the grounds for believing that—

(i) it is not practicable to communicate with any person entitled to grant entry to the premises,

(ii) entry to the premises will not be granted unless a warrant is produced, or

(iii) the investigation might be seriously prejudiced unless an appropriate person arriving at the premises is able to secure immediate access to them;

(7) In relation to any set of premises which the applicant wants to be searched by those executing the warrant with other persons authorised by the court, the application must—

(a) identify those other persons, by function or description; and

(b) explain why those persons are required.

B-647   **47.33.** [*Application for warrant under section 160 of the Extradition Act 2003.*]

Application for warrant under any other power

B-648   **47.34.**–(1) This rule applies—

(a) where an applicant wants a court to issue a warrant or warrants under a power (in this rule, "the relevant search power") to which rule 47.24(d) (other powers) refers; but

(b) subject to any inconsistent provision in legislation that applies to the relevant search power.

(2) As well as complying with rule 47.26, the application must—

(a) demonstrate the applicant's entitlement to apply;

(b) identify the relevant search power (and see paragraph (3));

(c) so far as practicable, identify the articles or persons sought (and see paragraph (4));

(d) specify the premises to be searched (and see paragraphs (5) and (6));

(e) state whether the applicant wants the premises to be searched on more than one occasion, if the relevant search power allows (and see paragraph (7)); and

(f) state whether the applicant wants other persons to accompany the officers executing the warrant or warrants, if the relevant search power allows (and see paragraph (8)).

(3) The application must—

(a) include or attach the terms of the relevant search power; and

(b) explain how the circumstances satisfy the criteria prescribed by that power for making the application.

(4) In relation to the articles or persons sought, the application must explain how they satisfy the criteria prescribed by the relevant search power about such articles or persons.

(5) In relation to premises which the applicant wants to be searched and can specify, the application must—

(a) specify each set of premises; and

(b) in respect of each, explain how the circumstances satisfy any criteria prescribed by the relevant search power—

   (i) for asserting that the articles or persons sought are on those premises, and

   (ii) for asserting that the court can exercise its power to authorise the search of those particular premises.

(6) In relation to premises which the applicant wants to be searched but at least some of which the applicant cannot specify, the application must—

(a) explain how the relevant search power allows the court to authorise such searching;

(b) specify the person who occupies or controls such premises;

(c) specify as many sets of such premises as is reasonably practicable;

(d) explain why—

   (i) it is necessary to search more premises than those specified, and

   (ii) it is not reasonably practicable to specify all the premises which the applicant wants to be searched;

(e) in respect of each set of premises, whether specified or not, explain how the circumstances satisfy any criteria prescribed by the relevant search power for asserting that the articles or persons sought are on those premises; and

(f) in respect of each specified set of premises, explain how the circumstances satisfy any criteria prescribed by the relevant search power for asserting that the court can exercise its power to authorise the search of those premises.

(7) In relation to any set of premises which the applicant wants to be searched on more than one occasion, the application must—

(a) explain how the relevant search power allows the court to authorise such searching;

(b) explain why the applicant wants the premises to be searched more than once; and

(c) specify any proposed maximum number of occasions.

(8) In relation to any set of premises which the applicant wants to be searched by the officers executing the warrant with other persons authorised by the court, the application must—

(a) identify those other persons, by function or description; and

(b) explain why those persons are required.

Section 4: Orders for the retention or return of property

When this Section applies

47.35.–(1) This Section applies where—   **B-649**

(a) under section 1 of the Police (Property) Act 1897, a magistrates' court can—

   (i) order the return to the owner of property which has come into the possession of the police or the National Crime Agency in connection with an investigation of a suspected offence, or

   (ii) make such order with respect to such property as the court thinks just, where the owner cannot be ascertained;

(b) a Crown Court judge can—

   (i) order the return of seized property under section 59(4) of the Criminal Justice and Police Act 2001 [§ 15-172 in the main work], or

   (ii) order the examination, retention, separation or return of seized property under section 59(5) of the Act.

(2) In this Section, a reference to a person with "a relevant interest" in seized property means someone from whom the property was seized, or someone with a proprietary interest in the property, or someone who had custody or control of it immediately before it was seized.

Exercise of court's powers

47.36.–(1) The court may determine an application for an order—   **B-650**

(a) at a hearing (which must be in private unless the court otherwise directs), or without a hearing;

(b) in a party's absence, if that party—

   (i) applied for the order, or

   (ii) has had at least 14 days in which to make representations.

(2) The court officer must arrange for the court to hear such an application no sooner than 14 days after it was served, unless—

   (a) the court directs that no hearing need be arranged; or

   (b) the court gives other directions for the hearing.

(3) If the court so directs, the parties to an application may attend a hearing by live link or telephone.

(4) The court may—

   (a) shorten or extend (even after it has expired) a time limit under this Section;

   (b) dispense with a requirement for service under this Section (even after service was required); and

   (c) consider an application made orally instead of in writing.

(5) A person who wants an extension of time must—

   (a) apply when serving the application or representations for which it is needed; and

   (b) explain the delay.

B-651   **47.37.** [*Application for an order under section 1 of the Police (Property) Act 1897.*]

Application for an order under section 59 of the Criminal Justice and Police Act 2001

B-652   **47.38.**—(1) This rule applies where an applicant wants the court to make an order to which rule 47.35(1)(b) refers.

(2) The applicant must apply in writing and serve the application on—

   (a) the court officer; and

   (b) as appropriate—

     (i) the person who for the time being has the seized property,

     (ii) each person whom the applicant knows or believes to have a relevant interest in the property.

(3) In each case, the application must—

   (a) explain the applicant's interest in the property (either as a person with a relevant interest, or as possessor of the property in consequence of its seizure, as appropriate);

   (b) explain the circumstances of the seizure of the property and identify the power that was exercised to seize it (or which the person seizing it purported to exercise, as appropriate); and

   (c) include or attach a list of those on whom the applicant has served the application.

(4) On an application for an order for the return of property under section 59(4) of the Criminal Justice and Police Act 2001, the application must explain why any one or more of these applies—

   (a) there was no power to make the seizure;

   (b) the property seized is, or contains, an item subject to legal privilege which is not an item that can be retained lawfully in the circumstances listed in section 54(2) of the Act [§ 15-167 in the main work];

   (c) the property seized is, or contains, excluded or special procedure material which is not material that can be retained lawfully in the circumstances listed in sections 55 and 56 of the Act;

   (d) the property seized is, or contains, something taken from premises under section 50 of the Act [[*ibid.*, § 15-162], or from a person under section 51 of the Act [*ibid.*, § 15-163], in the circumstances listed in those sections and which cannot lawfully be retained on the conditions listed in the Act.

(5) On an application for an order for the examination, retention, separation or return of property under section 59(5) of the 2001 Act, the application must—

   (a) specify the direction that the applicant wants the court to make, and explain why;

   (b) if applicable, specify each requirement of section 53(2) of the Act (examination and return of property [*ibid.*, § 15-166]) which is not being complied with;

   (c) if applicable, explain why the retention of the property by the person who now has it would be justified on the grounds that, even if it were returned, it would immediately become appropriate for that person to get it back under—

     (i) a warrant for its seizure, or

     (ii) a production order made under paragraph 4 of Schedule 1 to the Police and Criminal Evidence Act 1984, section 20BA of the Taxes Management Act 1970 or paragraph 5 of Schedule 5 to the Terrorism Act 2000.

Application containing information withheld from another party

★B-652a   **47.39.**—(1) This rule applies where—

   (a) an applicant serves an application to which rule 47.37 (application for an order under section 1 of the Police (Property) Act 1897) or rule 47.38 (application for an order under section 59 of the Criminal Justice and Police Act 2001) applies; and

(b) the application includes information that the applicant thinks ought not be revealed to another party.

(2) The applicant must—

(a) omit that information from the part of the application that is served on that other party;

(b) mark the other part to show that, unless the court otherwise directs, it is only for the court; and

(c) in that other part, explain why the applicant has withheld that information from that other party.

(3) If the court so directs, any hearing of an application to which this rule applies may be, wholly or in part, in the absence of a party from whom information has been withheld.

(4) At any hearing of an application to which this rule applies—

(a) the general rule is that the court must consider, in the following sequence—

(i) representations first by the applicant and then by each other party, in all the parties' presence, and then

(ii) further representations by the applicant, in the absence of a party from whom information has been withheld; but

(b) the court may direct other arrangements for the hearing.

[This rule was inserted by the Criminal Procedure (Amendment) Rules 2017 (S.I. 2017 No. 144).]

Representations in response

47.40.—(1) This rule applies where a person wants to make representations about an application under rule 47.37 or rule 47.38. **★B-653**

(2) Such a person must—

(a) serve the representations on—

(i) the court officer, and

(ii) the applicant and any other party to the application;

(b) do so not more than 14 days after service of the application; and

(c) ask for a hearing, if that person wants one.

(3) Representations in opposition to an application must explain why the grounds on which the applicant relies are not met.

(4) Where representations include information that the person making them thinks ought not be revealed to another party, that person must—

(a) omit that information from the representations served on that other party;

(b) mark the information to show that, unless the court otherwise directs, it is only for the court; and

(c) with that information include an explanation of why it has been withheld from that other party.

[This rule is printed as amended and as re-numbered by the Criminal Procedure (Amendment) Rules 2017 (S.I. 2017 No. 144).]

Application to punish for contempt of court

47.41.—(1) This rule applies where a person is accused of disobeying an order under section 59 of the Criminal Justice and Police Act 2001. **★B-654**

(2) A person who wants the court to exercise its power to punish that person for contempt of court must comply with the rules in Part 48 (contempt of court).

[This rule is printed as re-numbered by the Criminal Procedure (Amendment) Rules 2017 (S.I. 2017 No. 144).]

Section 5: Orders for the retention of fingerprints, etc.

When this Section applies

47.42. This Section applies where— **★B-655**

(a) a District Judge (Magistrates' Court) can make an order under—

(i) section 63F(7) or 63R(6) of the Police and Criminal Evidence Act 1984 [§ 15-273, 15-274 in the main work], or

(ii)   paragraph 20B(5) or 20G(6) of Schedule 8 to the Terrorism Act 2000 [*ibid.*, §§ 25-145b, 12-145g];

(b)   the Crown Court can determine an appeal under–

(i)   section 63F(10) of the Police and Criminal Evidence Act 1984, or

(ii)   paragraph 20B(8) of Schedule 8 to the Terrorism Act 2000.

[This rule is printed as re-numbered by the Criminal Procedure (Amendment) Rules 2017 (S.I. 2017 No. 144).]

Exercise of court's powers

★B-656   47.43.–(1) The court must determine an application under rule 47.43, and an appeal under rule 47.44–

(a)   at a hearing, which must be in private unless the court otherwise directs; and

(b)   in the presence of the applicant or appellant.

(2) The court must not determine such an application or appeal unless any person served under those rules–

(a)   is present; or

(b)   has had an opportunity–

(i)   to attend, or

(ii)   to make representations.

[This rule is printed as re-numbered by the Criminal Procedure (Amendment) Rules 2017 (S.I. 2017 No. 144).]

Application to extend retention period

★B-657   47.44.–(1) This rule applies where a magistrates' court can make an order extending the period for which there may be retained material consisting of–

(a)   fingerprints taken from a person–

(i)   under a power conferred by Part V of the Police and Criminal Evidence Act 1984,

(ii)   with that person's consent, in connection with the investigation of an offence by the police, or

(iii)   under a power conferred by Schedule 8 to the Terrorism Act 2000[*ibid.*, §§ 25-134] *et seq.* in relation to a person detained under section 41 of that Act [*ibid.*, § 25-52];

(b)   a DNA profile derived from a DNA sample so taken; or

(c)   a sample so taken.

(2) A chief officer of police who wants the court to make such an order must–

(a)   apply in writing–

(i)   within the period of 3 months ending on the last day of the retention period, where the application relates to fingerprints or a DNA profile, or

(ii)   before the expiry of the retention period, where the application relates to a sample;

(b)   in the application–

(i)   identify the material,

(ii)   state when the retention period expires,

(iii)   give details of any previous such application relating to the material, and

(iv)   outline the circumstances in which the material was acquired;

(c)   serve the application on the court officer, in every case; and

(d)   serve the application on the person from whom the material was taken, where–

(i)   the application relates to fingerprints or a DNA profile, or

(ii)   the application is for the renewal of an order extending the retention period for a sample.

(3) An application to extend the retention period for fingerprints or a DNA profile must explain why that period should be extended.

(4) An application to extend the retention period for a sample must explain why, having regard to the nature and complexity of other material that is evidence in relation to the offence, the sample is likely to be needed in any proceedings for the offence for the purposes of–

(a)   disclosure to, or use by, a defendant; or

(b)   responding to any challenge by a defendant in respect of the admissibility of material that is evidence on which the prosecution proposes to rely.

(5) On an application to extend the retention period for fingerprints or a DNA profile, the applicant must serve notice of the court's decision on any respondent where–

(a) the court makes the order sought; and

(b) the respondent was absent when it was made.

[This rule is printed as re-numbered by the Criminal Procedure (Amendment) Rules 2017 (S.I. 2017 No. 144).]

Appeal

47.45.–(1) This rule applies where, under rule 47.43, a magistrates' court determines an applica- ★**B-658** tion relating to fingerprints or a DNA profile and—

(a) the person from whom the material was taken wants to appeal to the Crown Court against an order extending the retention period; or

(b) a chief officer of police wants to appeal to the Crown Court against a refusal to make such an order.

(2) The appellant must—

(a) serve an appeal notice—

(i) on the Crown Court officer and on the other party, and

(ii) not more than 21 days after the magistrates' court's decision, or, if applicable, service of notice under rule 47.43(5); and

(b) in the appeal notice, explain, as appropriate, why the retention period should, or should not, be extended.

(3) Rule 34.11 (constitution of the Crown Court) applies on such an appeal.

[This rule is printed as re-numbered by the Criminal Procedure (Amendment) Rules 2017 (S.I. 2017 No. 144).]

When this Section applies

47.46. This Section applies where— ★**B-659**

(a) a justice of the peace can make or discharge an investigation anonymity order, under sections 76 and 80(1) of the Coroners and Justice Act 2009 [§ 2-106, in the main work];

(b) a Crown Court judge can determine an appeal against –

(i) a refusal of such an order, under section 79 of the 2009 Act,

(ii) a decision on an application to discharge such an order, under section 80(6) of the 2009 Act.

[This rule is printed as re-numbered by the Criminal Procedure (Amendment) Rules 2017 (S.I. 2017 No. 144).]

Exercise of court's powers

47.47.–(1) The court may determine an application for an investigation anonymity order, and any ★**B-660** appeal against the refusal of such an order—

(a) at a hearing (which must be in private unless the court otherwise directs); or

(b) without a hearing.

(2) The court must determine an application to discharge an investigation anonymity order, and any appeal against the decision on such an application—

(a) at a hearing (which must be in private unless the court otherwise directs); and

(b) in the presence of the person specified in the order, unless—

(i) that person applied for the discharge of the order,

(ii) that person has had an opportunity to make representations, or

(iii) the court is satisfied that it is not reasonably practicable to communicate with that person.

(3) The court may consider an application or an appeal made orally instead of in writing.

[This rule is printed as re-numbered by the Criminal Procedure (Amendment) Rules 2017 (S.I. 2017 No. 144).]

Application for an investigation anonymity order

47.48.–(1) This rule applies where an applicant wants a magistrates' court to make an investigation ★**B-661** anonymity order.

(2) The applicant must—

(a) apply in writing;

(b) serve the application on the court officer;

    (c) identify the person to be specified in the order, unless–

        (i) the applicant wants the court to determine the application at a hearing, or

        (ii) the court otherwise directs;

    (d) explain how the proposed order meets the conditions prescribed by section 78 of the Coroners and Justice Act 2009;

    (e) say if the applicant intends to appeal should the court refuse the order;

    (f) attach any material on which the applicant relies; and

    (g) propose the terms of the order.

  (3) At any hearing of the application, the applicant must–

    (a) identify to the court the person to be specified in the order, unless–

        (i) the applicant has done so already, or

        (ii) the court otherwise directs; and

    (b) unless the applicant has done so already, inform the court if the applicant intends to appeal should the court refuse the order.

[This rule is printed as re-numbered by the Criminal Procedure (Amendment) Rules 2017 (S.I. 2017 No. 144).]

Application to discharge an investigation anonymity order

★B-662   **47.49.**–(1) This rule applies where one of the following wants a magistrates' court to discharge an investigation anonymity order–

    (a) an applicant; or

    (b) the person specified in the order.

  (2) That applicant or the specified person must–

    (a) apply in writing as soon as practicable after becoming aware of the grounds for doing so;

    (b) serve the application on–

        (i) the court officer, and as applicable

        (ii) the applicant for the order, and

        (iii) the specified person;

    (c) explain–

        (i) what material circumstances have changed since the order was made, or since any previous application was made to discharge it, and

        (ii) why it is appropriate for the order to be discharged; and

    (d) attach–

        (i) a copy of the order, and

        (ii) any material on which the applicant relies.

  (3) A party must inform the court if that party intends to appeal should the court discharge the order.

[This rule is printed as re-numbered by the Criminal Procedure (Amendment) Rules 2017 (S.I. 2017 No. 144).]

Appeal

★B-663   **47.50.**–(1) This rule applies where one of the following ("the appellant") wants to appeal to the Crown Court–

    (a) the applicant for an investigation anonymity order, where a magistrates' court has refused to make the order;

    (b) a party to an application to discharge such an order, where a magistrates' court has decided that application.

  (2) The appellant must–

    (a) serve on the Crown Court officer a copy of the application to the magistrates' court; and

    (b) where the appeal concerns a discharge decision, notify each other party,

not more than 21 days after the decision against which the appellant wants to appeal.

  (3) The Crown Court must hear the appeal without justices of the peace.

[This rule is printed as re-numbered by the Criminal Procedure (Amendment) Rules 2017 (S.I. 2017 No. 144).]

Section 7: Investigation approval orders under the Regulation of Investigatory Powers Act 2000

When this Section applies

47.51.–(1) This Section applies where a justice of the peace can make an order approving– ★**B-664**

(a) the grant or renewal of an authorisation, or the giving or renewal of a notice, under section 23A of the Regulation of Investigatory Powers Act 2000 [§ 25-401a, in the main work];

(b) the grant or renewal of an authorisation under section 32A of the 2000 Act.

[This rule is printed as re-numbered by the Criminal Procedure (Amendment) Rules 2017 (S.I. 2017 No. 144).]

Exercise of court's powers

47.52.–(1) This rule applies where a magistrates' court refuses to approve the grant, giving or ★**B-665** renewal of an authorisation or notice.

(2) The court must not exercise its power to quash that authorisation or notice unless the applicant has had at least 2 business days from the date of the refusal in which to make representations.

[This rule is printed as re-numbered by the Criminal Procedure (Amendment) Rules 2017 (S.I. 2017 No. 144).]

Application for approval for authorisation or notice

47.53.–(1) This rule applies where an applicant wants a magistrates' court to make an order ap- ★**B-666** proving–

(a) under sections 23A and 23B [*ibid.*, § 25-401b,] of the Regulation of Investigatory Powers Act 2000–

(i) an authorisation to obtain or disclose communications data, under section 22(3) of the 2000 Act, or

(ii) a notice that requires a postal or telecommunications operator if need be to obtain, and in any case to disclose, communications data, under section 22(4) of the 2000 Act [*ibid.*, § 25-400,];

(b) under sections 32A and 32B of the Regulation of Investigatory Powers Act 2000, an authorisation for–

(i) the carrying out of directed surveillance, under section 28 of the 2000 Act, or

(ii) the conduct or use of a covert human intelligence source, under section 29 of the 2000 Act.

(2) The applicant must–

(a) apply in writing and serve the application on the court officer;

(b) attach the authorisation or notice which the applicant wants the court to approve;

(c) attach such other material (if any) on which the applicant relies to satisfy the court–

(i) as required by section 23A(3) and (4) of the 2000 Act, in relation to communications data,

(ii) as required by section 32A(3) and (4) of the 2000 Act, in relation to directed surveillance, or

(iii) as required by section 32A(5) and (6), and, if relevant, section 43(6A), of the 2000 Act, in relation to a covert human intelligence source; and

(d) propose the terms of the order.

[This rule is printed as re-numbered by the Criminal Procedure (Amendment) Rules 2017 (S.I. 2017 No. 144).]

Section 8: Orders for access to documents, etc. under the Criminal Appeal Act 1995

When this Section applies

47.54. This section applies where the Crown Court can order a person to give the Criminal Cases ★**B-667** Review Commission access to a document or other material under section 18A of the Criminal Appeal Act 1995.

[This rule was inserted by the Criminal Procedure (Amendment No. 2) Rules 2016 (S.I. 2016 No. 705). It is printed as re-numbered by the Criminal Procedure (Amendment) Rules 2017 (S.I. 2017 No. 144).]

Exercise of court's powers

47.55.–(1) Subject to paragraphs (2), (3) and (4), the court may determine an application by the ★**B-668** Criminal Cases Review Commission for an order–

  (a) at a hearing (which must be in private unless the court otherwise directs), or without a hearing; and

  (b) in the absence of—

    (i) the Commission,

    (ii) the respondent,

    (iii) any other person affected by the order.

(2) The court must not determine such an application in the Commission's absence if—

  (a) the Commission asks for a hearing; or

  (b) it appears to the court that the application is so complex or serious as to require the court to hear the Commission.

(3) The court must not determine such an application in the absence of any respondent or other person affected, unless—

  (a) the absentee has had at least 2 business days in which to make representations; or

  (b) the court is satisfied that—

    (i) the Commission cannot identify or contact the absentee,

    (ii) it would prejudice the exercise of the Commission's functions to adjourn or postpone the application so as to allow the absentee to attend, or

    (iii) the absentee has waived the opportunity to attend.

(4) The court must not determine such an application in the absence of any respondent who, if the order sought by the Commission were made, would be required to produce or give access to journalistic material, unless that respondent has waived the opportunity to attend.

(5) The court officer must arrange for the court to hear such an application no sooner than 2 business days after it was served, unless—

  (a) the court directs that no hearing need be arranged; or

  (b) the court gives other directions for the hearing.

(6) The court must not determine an application unless satisfied that sufficient time has been allowed for it.

(7) If the court so directs, the parties to an application may attend a hearing by live link or telephone.

(8) The court must not make an order unless an officer of the Commission states, in writing or orally, that to the best of that officer's knowledge and belief—

  (a) the application discloses all the information that is material to what the court must decide; and

  (b) the content of the application is true.

(9) Where the statement required by paragraph (8) is made orally—

  (a) the statement must be on oath or affirmation, unless the court otherwise directs; and

  (b) the court must arrange for a record of the making of the statement.

(10) The court may shorten or extend (even after it has expired) a time limit under this section.

[This rule was inserted by S.I. 2016 No. 705 (*ante*, B-667). It is printed as re-numbered by S.I. 2017 No. 144 (*ante*, B-667).]

Application for an order for access

★**B-669** **47.56.**—(1) Where the Criminal Cases Review Commission wants the court to make an order for access to a document or other material, the Commission must—

  (a) apply in writing and serve the application on the court officer;

  (b) give the court an estimate of how long the court should allow—

    (i) to read the application and prepare for any hearing, and

    (ii) for any hearing of the application;

  (c) attach a draft order in the terms proposed by the Commission; and

  (d) serve the application and draft order on the respondent.

(2) The application must—

  (a) identify the respondent;

  (b) describe the document, or documents, or other material sought;

  (c) explain the reasons for thinking that—

    (i) what is sought is in the respondent's possession or control, and

    (ii) access to what is sought may assist the Commission in the exercise of any of its functions; and

  (d) explain the Commission's proposals for—

    (i)   the manner in which the respondent should give access, and

    (ii)   the period within which the order should take effect.

(3) The Commission must serve any order made on the respondent.

[This rule was inserted by S.I. 2016 No. 705 (*ante*, B-667). It is printed as re-numbered by S.I. 2017 No. 144 (*ante*, B-667).]

Application containing information withheld from a respondent or other person

47.57.–(1) This rule applies where–   **★B-670**

    (a)   the Criminal Cases Review Commission serves an application under rule 47.55 (application for an order for access); and

    (b)   the application includes information that the Commission thinks ought not be revealed to a recipient.

(2) The Commission must–

    (a)   omit that information from the part of the application that is served on that recipient;

    (b)   mark the other part, to show that it is only for the court; and

    (c)   in that other part, explain why the Commission has withheld it from that recipient.

(3) A hearing of an application to which this rule applies may take place, wholly or in part, in the absence of that recipient and any other person.

(4) At a hearing of an application to which this rule applies–

    (a)   the general rule is that the court must consider, in the following sequence–

        (i)   representations first by the Commission and then by the other parties, in the presence of them all, and then

        (ii)   further representations by the Commission, in the others' absence; but

    (b)   the court may direct other arrangements for the hearing.

[This rule was inserted by S.I. 2016 No. 705 (*ante*, B-667). It is printed as re-numbered by S.I. 2017 No. 144 (*ante*, B-667).]

Application to punish for contempt of court

47.58.–(1) This rule applies where a person is accused of disobeying an order for access made   **★B-671** under section 18A of the Criminal Appeal Act 1995.

(2) An applicant who wants the court to exercise its power to punish that person for contempt of court must comply with the rules in Part 48 (contempt of court).

[This rule was inserted by S.I. 2016 No. 705 (*ante*, B-667). It is printed as re-numbered by S.I. 2017 No. 144 (*ante*, B-667).]

CPD XI Other Proceedings 47A: Investigation Orders and Warrants

47A.1 Powers of entry, search and seizure, and powers to obtain banking and other confidential   **B-672** information, are among the most intrusive that investigators can exercise. Every application must be carefully scrutinised with close attention paid to what the relevant statutory provision requires of the applicant and to what it permits. CrimPR, Pt 47 must be followed, and the accompanying forms must be used. These are designed to prompt applicants, and the courts, to deal with all of the relevant criteria.

47A.2 The issuing of a warrant or the making of such an order is never to be treated as a formality and it is therefore essential that the judge or magistrate considering the application is given, and must take, sufficient time for the purpose. The prescribed forms require the applicant to provide a time estimate, and listing officers and justices' legal advisers should take account of these.

47A.3 Applicants for orders and warrants owe the court duties of candour and truthfulness. On any application made without notice to the respondent, and so on all applications for search warrants, the duty of frank and complete disclosure is especially onerous. The applicant must draw the court's attention to any information that is unfavourable to the application. The existence of unfavourable information will not necessarily lead to the application being refused; it will be a matter for the court what weight to place on each piece of information.

47A.4 Where an applicant supplements an application with additional oral or written information, on questioning by the court or otherwise, it is essential that the court keeps an adequate record. What is needed will depend upon the circumstances. The rules require that a record of the 'gist' be retained. The purpose of such a record is to allow the sufficiency of the court's reasons for its decision subsequently to be assessed. The gravity of such decisions requires that their exercise should be susceptible to scrutiny and to explanation by reference to all of the information that was taken into account.

47A.5 The forms that accompany CrimPR, Pt 47 provide for the most frequently encountered applications. However, there are some hundreds of powers of entry, search and seizure, supplied by a corresponding number of legislative provisions. In any criminal matter, if there is no form designed for the particular warrant or order sought, the forms should still be used, as far as is practicable, and adapted as necessary. The applicant should pay particular attention to the specific legislative requirements for the granting of such an application to ensure that the court has all of the necessary information, and, if the court might be unfamiliar with the legislation, should provide a copy of the relevant provisions. Applicants must comply with the duties of candour and truthfulness, and include in their application the declarations required by the Rules and must make disclosure of any unfavourable information to the court.

Criminal Procedure Rules 2015 (S.I. 2015 No. 1490), Pt 48

CONTEMPT OF COURT

General rules

When this Part applies

B-673 **48.1**–(1) This Part applies where the court can deal with a person for conduct—

    (a) in contempt of court; or

    (b) in contravention of the legislation to which rules 48.5 and 48.9 refer.

(2) In this Part, "respondent" means any such person.

Exercise of court's power to deal with contempt of court

B-674 **48.2**–(1) The court must determine at a hearing—

    (a) an enquiry under rule 48.8;

    (b) an allegation under rule 48.9.

(2) The court must not proceed in the respondent's absence unless—

    (a) the respondent's behaviour makes it impracticable to proceed otherwise; or

    (b) the respondent has had at least 14 days' notice of the hearing, or was present when it was arranged.

(3) If the court hears part of an enquiry or allegation in private, it must announce at a hearing in public—

    (a) the respondent's name;

    (b) in general terms, the nature of any conduct that the respondent admits, or the court finds proved; and

    (c) any punishment imposed.

Notice of suspension of imprisonment by Court of Appeal or Crown Court

B-675 **48.3**–(1) This rule applies where—

    (a) the Court of Appeal or the Crown Court suspends an order of imprisonment for contempt of court; and

    (b) the respondent is absent when the court does so.

(2) The respondent must be served with notice of the terms of the court's order—

    (a) by any applicant under rule 48.9; or

    (b) by the court officer, in any other case.

Application to discharge an order for imprisonment

B-676 **48.4**–(1) This rule applies where the court can discharge an order for a respondent's imprisonment for contempt of court.

(2) A respondent who wants the court to discharge such an order must—

    (a) apply in writing, unless the court otherwise directs, and serve any written application on—

        (i) the court officer, and

        (ii) any applicant under rule 48.9 on whose application the respondent was imprisoned;

    (b) in the application—

        (i) explain why it is appropriate for the order for imprisonment to be discharged, and

        (ii) give details of any appeal, and its outcome; and

    (c) ask for a hearing, if the respondent wants one.

Contempt of court by obstruction, disruption, etc.

Initial procedure on obstruction, disruption, etc.

48.5–(1) This rule applies where the court observes, or someone reports to the court–   **B-677**

(a) in the Court of Appeal or the Crown Court, obstructive, disruptive, insulting or intimidating conduct, in the courtroom or in its vicinity, or otherwise immediately affecting the proceedings;

(b) in the Crown Court, a contravention of–

    (i) section 3 of the Criminal Procedure (Attendance of Witnesses) Act 1965 (disobeying a witness summons [§ 8-26, in the main work]);

    (ii) section 20 of the Juries Act 1974 (disobeying a jury summons[*ibid.*, § 28-41,]);

    (iii) section 8 of the Contempt of Court Act 1981 (obtaining details of a jury's deliberations, etc.);

(c) in a magistrates' court, a contravention of–

    (i) section 97(4) of the Magistrates' Courts Act 1980 (refusing to give evidence), or

    (ii) section 12 of the Contempt of Court Act 1981 (insulting or interrupting the court, etc. [*ibid.*, § 28-81,]);

(d) a contravention of section 9 of the Contempt of Court Act 1981 (without the court's permission, recording the proceedings, etc. [*ibid.*, § 28-74,]);

(e) any other conduct with which the court can deal as, or as if it were, a criminal contempt of court, except failure to surrender to bail under section 6 of the Bail Act 1976 [*ibid.*, § 3-31,].

(2) Unless the respondent's behaviour makes it impracticable to do so, the court must–

(a) explain, in terms the respondent can understand (with help, if necessary)–

    (i) the conduct that is in question,

    (ii) that the court can impose imprisonment, or a fine, or both, for such conduct,

    (iii) (where relevant) that the court has power to order the respondent's immediate temporary detention, if in the court's opinion that is required,

    (iv) that the respondent may explain the conduct,

    (v) that the respondent may apologise, if he or she so wishes, and that this may persuade the court to take no further action, and

    (vi) that the respondent may take legal advice; and

(b) allow the respondent a reasonable opportunity to reflect, take advice, explain and, if he or she so wishes, apologise.

(3) The court may then–

(a) take no further action in respect of that conduct;

(b) enquire into the conduct there and then; or

(c) postpone that enquiry (if a magistrates' court, only until later the same day).

Review after temporary detention

48.6–(1) This rule applies in a case in which the court has ordered the respondent's immediate   **B-678**
temporary detention for conduct to which rule 48.5 applies.

(2) The court must review the case–

(a) if a magistrates' court, later the same day;

(b) in the Court of Appeal or the Crown Court, no later than the next business day.

(3) On the review, the court must–

(a) unless the respondent is absent, repeat the explanations required by rule 48.5(2)(a); and

(b) allow the respondent a reasonable opportunity to reflect, take advice, explain and, if he or she so wishes, apologise.

(4) The court may then–

(a) take no further action in respect of the conduct;

(b) if a magistrates' court, enquire into the conduct there and then; or

(c) if the Court of Appeal or the Crown Court–

    (i) enquire into the conduct there and then, or

    (ii) postpone the enquiry, and order the respondent's release from such detention in the meantime.

Postponement of enquiry

48.7–(1) This rule applies where the Court of Appeal or the Crown Court postpones the enquiry.   **B-679**

(2) The court must arrange for the preparation of a written statement containing such particulars of the conduct in question as to make clear what the respondent appears to have done.

(3) The court officer must serve on the respondent—

    (a) that written statement;

    (b) notice of where and when the postponed enquiry will take place; and

    (c) a notice that—

        (i) reminds the respondent that the court can impose imprisonment, or a fine, or both, for contempt of court, and

        (ii) warns the respondent that the court may pursue the postponed enquiry in the respondent's absence, if the respondent does not attend.

Procedure on enquiry

B-680   **48.8**–(1) At an enquiry, the court must—

    (a) ensure that the respondent understands (with help, if necessary) what is alleged, if the enquiry has been postponed from a previous occasion;

    (b) explain what the procedure at the enquiry will be; and

    (c) ask whether the respondent admits the conduct in question.

(2) If the respondent admits the conduct, the court need not receive evidence.

(3) If the respondent does not admit the conduct, the court must consider—

    (a) any statement served under rule 48.7;

    (b) any other evidence of the conduct;

    (c) any evidence introduced by the respondent; and

    (d) any representations by the respondent about the conduct.

(4) If the respondent admits the conduct, or the court finds it proved, the court must—

    (a) before imposing any punishment for contempt of court, give the respondent an opportunity to make representations relevant to punishment;

    (b) explain, in terms the respondent can understand (with help, if necessary)—

        (i) the reasons for its decision, including its findings of fact, and

        (ii) the punishment it imposes, and its effect; and

    (c) if a magistrates' court, arrange for the preparation of a written record of those findings.

(5) The court that conducts an enquiry—

    (a) need not include the same member or members as the court that observed the conduct; but

    (b) may do so, unless that would be unfair to the respondent.

Contempt of court by failure to comply with court order, etc.

Initial procedure on failure to comply with court order, etc.

B-681   **48.9**–(1) This rule applies where—

    (a) a party, or other person directly affected, alleges—

        (i) in the Crown Court, a failure to comply with an order to which applies rule 33.70 (compliance order, restraint order or ancillary order), rule 47.13 (certain investigation orders under the Terrorism Act 2000) or rule 47.22 (certain investigation orders under the Proceeds of Crime Act 2002),

        (ii) in the Court of Appeal or the Crown Court, any other conduct with which that court can deal as a civil contempt of court, or

        (iii) in the Crown Court or a magistrates' court, unauthorised use of disclosed prosecution material under section 17 of the Criminal Procedure and Investigations Act 1996 [§ 12-88, in the main work];

    (b) the court deals on its own initiative with conduct to which paragraph (1)(a) applies.

(2) Such a party or person must—

    (a) apply in writing and serve the application on the court officer; and

    (b) serve on the respondent—

        (i) the application, and

        (ii) notice of where and when the court will consider the allegation (not less than 14 days after service).

(3) The application must—

    (a) identify the respondent;

    (b) explain that it is an application for the respondent to be dealt with for contempt of court;

    (c) contain such particulars of the conduct in question as to make clear what is alleged against the respondent; and

(d) include a notice warning the respondent that the court—
  (i) can impose imprisonment, or a fine, or both, for contempt of court, and
  (ii) may deal with the application in the respondent's absence, if the respondent does not attend the hearing.
(4) A court which acts on its own initiative under paragraph (1)(b) must—
  (a) arrange for the preparation of a written statement containing the same information as an application; and
  (b) arrange for the service on the respondent of—
  (i) that written statement, and
  (ii) notice of where and when the court will consider the allegation (not less than 14 days after service).

Procedure on hearing

48.10–(1) At the hearing of an allegation under rule 48.9, the court must— **B-682**
  (a) ensure that the respondent understands (with help, if necessary) what is alleged;
  (b) explain what the procedure at the hearing will be; and
  (c) ask whether the respondent admits the conduct in question.
(2) If the respondent admits the conduct, the court need not receive evidence.
(3) If the respondent does not admit the conduct, the court must consider—
  (a) the application or written statement served under rule 48.9;
  (b) any other evidence of the conduct;
  (c) any evidence introduced by the respondent; and
  (d) any representations by the respondent about the conduct.
(4) If the respondent admits the conduct, or the court finds it proved, the court must—
  (a) [*identical to r.48.8(4)(a)*, ante, *B-680*];
  (b) [*identical to r.48.8(4)(b)*, ante, *B-680*]; and
  (c) in a magistrates' court, arrange for the preparation of a written record of those findings.

Introduction of written witness statement or other hearsay

48.11–(1) Where rule 48.9 applies, an applicant or respondent who wants to introduce in evidence **B-683** the written statement of a witness, or other hearsay, must—
  (a) serve a copy of the statement, or notice of other hearsay, on—
  (i) the court officer, and
  (ii) the other party; and
  (b) serve the copy or notice—
  (i) when serving the application under rule 48.9, in the case of an applicant, or
  (ii) not more than 7 days after service of that application or of the court's written statement, in the case of the respondent.
(2) Such service is notice of that party's intention to introduce in evidence that written witness statement, or other hearsay, unless that party otherwise indicates when serving it.
(3) A party entitled to receive such notice may waive that entitlement.

Content of written witness statement

48.12–(1) This rule applies to a written witness statement served under rule 48.11. **B-684**
(2) Such a written witness statement must contain a declaration by the person making it that it is true to the best of that person's knowledge and belief.

Content of notice of other hearsay

48.13–(1) This rule applies to a notice of hearsay, other than a written witness statement, served **B-685** under rule 48.11.
(2) Such a notice must—
  (a) set out the evidence, or attach the document that contains it; and
  (b) identify the person who made the statement that is hearsay.

Cross-examination of maker of written witness statement or other hearsay

48.14–(1) This rule applies where a party wants the court's permission to cross-examine a person **B-686** who made a statement which another party wants to introduce as hearsay.
(2) The party who wants to cross-examine that person must—

    (a) apply in writing, with reasons; and

    (b) serve the application on—

        (i) the court officer, and

        (ii) the party who served the hearsay.

(3) A respondent who wants to cross-examine such a person must apply to do so not more than 7 days after service of the hearsay by the applicant.

(4) An applicant who wants to cross-examine such a person must apply to do so not more than 3 days after service of the hearsay by the respondent.

(5) The court—

    (a) may decide an application under this rule without a hearing; but

    (b) must not dismiss such an application unless the person making it has had an opportunity to make representations at a hearing.

Credibility and consistency of maker of written witness statement or other hearsay

B-687   **48.15**–(1) This rule applies where a party wants to challenge the credibility or consistency of a person who made a statement which another party wants to introduce as hearsay.

(2) The party who wants to challenge the credibility or consistency of that person must—

    (a) serve notice of intention to do so on—

        (i) the court officer, and

        (ii) the party who served the hearsay; and

    (b) in it, identify any statement or other material on which that party relies.

(3) A respondent who wants to challenge such a person's credibility or consistency must serve such a notice not more than 7 days after service of the hearsay by the applicant.

(4) An applicant who wants to challenge such a person's credibility or consistency must serve such a notice not more than 3 days after service of the hearsay by the respondent.

(5) The party who served the hearsay—

    (a) may call that person to give oral evidence instead; and

    (b) if so, must serve notice of intention to do so on—

        (i) the court officer, and

        (ii) the other party

    as soon as practicable after service of the notice under paragraph (2).

[This rule is printed as amended by the Criminal Procedure (Amendment No. 2) Rules 2016 (S.I. 2016 No. 705).]

Magistrates' courts' powers to adjourn, etc.

B-688   **48.16**–(1) This rule applies where a magistrates' court deals with unauthorised disclosure of prosecution material under sections 17 and 18 of the Criminal Procedure and Investigations Act 1996 [§§ 12-88, 12-91 in the main work].

(2) The sections of the Magistrates' Courts Act 1980 listed in paragraph (3) apply as if in those sections—

    (a) "complaint" and "summons" each referred to an application or written statement under rule 48.9;

    (b) "complainant" meant an applicant; and

    (c) "defendant" meant the respondent.

(3) Those sections are—

    (a) section 51 (issue of summons on complaint);

    (b) section 54 (adjournment);

    (c) section 55 (non-appearance of defendant);

    (d) section 97(1) (summons to witness);

    (e) section 121(1) (constitution and place of sitting of court);

    (f) section 123 (defect in process).

(4) Section 127 of the 1980 Act (limitation of time) does not apply.

Court's power to vary requirements

B-689   **48.17**–(1) The court may shorten or extend (even after it has expired) a time limit under rule 48.11, 48.14 or 48.15.

(2) A person who wants an extension of time must—

    (a) apply when serving the statement, notice or application for which it is needed; and

(b) explain the delay.

CPD XI Other Proceedings 48A: Contempt in the Face of the Magistrates' Court

48A [*Refers to Contempt of Court Act 1981, s.12 [§ 28-81 in the main work]; advises that, in the majority of* **B-690** *cases, an apology and a promise as to future conduct should be enough to secure a person's release; but there are likely to be cases where the nature and seriousness of the conduct will require the court to consider using its powers under s.12(2) to fine or commit to custody; before imposing a penalty, the court should offer the offender a further opportunity to apologise, and should follow the procedure in rule 48.8(4) of the Criminal Procedure Rules; in deciding how to deal with the offender, regard should be had to the period during which he has been detained, whether the conduct was admitted and its seriousness; and period of committal should be as short as possible commensurate with the interests of preserving good order in the administration of justice.*]

Criminal Procedure Rules 2015 (S.I. 2015 No. 1490), Pt 49

INTERNATIONAL CO-OPERATION

[*Not set out in this work*]. **B-691**

Criminal Procedure Rules 2015 (S.I. 2015 No. 1490), Pt 50

EXTRADITION

[*Not set out in this work*]. **B-692**

CPD XI Other Proceedings 50A-50F: Extradition (as substituted by Criminal Practice Directions 2015 (Amendment No. 4), unreported, March 28, 2017, Lord Thomas C.J.)

[*Not set out in this work*].

CPD XII General Application

[For CPD XII General Application A (Court dress), see § 2-29 in the main work.] **B-693**

[For CPD XII General Application B (Modes of address and titles of judges and magistrates), see § 2-14 (paras 1 and 2). Paragraph 3 is not set out in this work.]

[CPD XII General Application C (Availability of judgments given in the Court of Appeal and High Court) is not set out in this work (but see § 7-33 in the main work).]

[For CPD XII General Application D (Citation of authority and provision of copies of judgments to the court), see §§ 7-200a *et seq.* in the main work]

[CPD XII General Application E (Preparation of judgments: neutral citation) is not set out in this work.]

[For CPD XII General Application F (Citation of Hansard), see § 9-38 in the main work.]

CPD XIII Listing

[CPD XIII Listing A to G are set out in full at § 2-22 *et seq.* in the main work]. **B-694**

CPD XIII Listing: Annex 1 General Principles for the Deployment of the Judiciary in the Magistrates' Court

This distils the full deployment guidance issued in November 2012. The relevant sections dealing **B-695** specifically with the allocation of work within the magistrates' court have been incorporated into this practice direction. It does not seek to replace the guidance in its entirety.

Presumptions

1 The presumptions which follow are intended to provide an acceptable and flexible framework **B-696** establishing the deployment of the district judges (magistrates' courts) and magistrates. The system must be capable of adaptation to meet particular needs, whether of locality or caseload. In any event, the presumptions which follow are illustrative not exhaustive.

2 District judges (magistrates' courts) should generally (not invariably) be deployed in accordance with the following presumptions ("the presumptions"): (a) Cases involving complex points of law and evidence; (b) cases involving complex procedural issues; (c) long cases (included on grounds of practicality); (d) interlinked cases (given the need for consistency, together with their likely complexity and novelty); (e) cases for which armed police officers are required in court, such as high end firearms cases; (f) a share of the more routine business of the court, including case management and pre-trial reviews, (for a variety of reasons, including the need for district judges (magistrates' courts) to have competence in all areas of work and the desirability of an equitable division of work between magistrates and district judges (magistrates' courts), subject always to the interests of the administration of justice); (g) where appropriate, in supporting the training of magistrates; (h) occasionally, in mixed benches of district judges (magistrates' courts) and magistrates (with a particular view both to improving the case management skills of magistrates and to improving the culture of collegiality); (i) in the short-term tackling of particular local backlogs ("backlog busting"), sometimes in combination with magistrates from the local or (with the senior presiding judge's approval) adjoining benches.

3 In accordance with current arrangements certain classes of cases necessarily require district judges (magistrates' courts) and have therefore been excluded from the above presumptions; these are as follows: (a) extradition; (b) terrorism; (c) prison adjudications; (d) sex cases in the youth court as per Annex 2; (e) cases where the defendant is likely to be sentenced to a very large fine: see Annex 3; (f) the special jurisdiction of the Chief Magistrate.

4 In formulating the presumptions, the following considerations have been taken into account.

(a) The listing of cases is here, as elsewhere, a judicial function: see *CPD XIII Listing A*, para. 10. In the magistrates' courts the Judicial Business Group, subject to the supervision of the presiding judges of the circuit, is responsible for determining the day-to-day listing practice in that area. The day-to-day operation of that listing practice is the responsibility of the justices' clerk with the assistance of the listing officer.

(b) Equally, providing the training of magistrates is a responsibility of justices' clerks.

(c) It is best not to treat "high profile" cases as a separate category but to consider their listing in the light of the principles and presumptions. The circumstances surrounding high profile cases do not permit ready generalisation, save that they are likely to require especially sensitive handling. Listing decisions involving such cases will often benefit from good communication at a local level between the justices' clerk, the district judge (magistrates' courts) and the bench chairman.

(d) Account must be taken of the need to maintain the competences of all members of the judiciary sitting in the magistrates' court.

CPD XIII Listing: Annex 2 Sexual Offences in the Youth Court

Introduction

1 This annex sets out the procedure to be applied in the youth court in all cases involving allegations of sexual offences which are capable of being sent for trial at the Crown Court under the grave crime provisions.

2 This applies to all cases involving such charges, irrespective of the gravity of the allegation, the age of the defendant and/or the antecedent history of the defendant. (So, for example, every allegation of sexual touching, under s.3 of the SOA 2003, is covered by this protocol.)

3 This does not alter the test (set out in the Sentencing Guidelines Council's definitive guideline, entitled "Overarching Principles–Sentencing Youths" [Appendix S-15 *et seq.*]) that the youth court must apply when determining whether a case is a "grave crime".

4 In the Crown Court, cases involving allegations of sexual offences frequently involve complex and sensitive issues and only those circuit judges and recorders who have been specifically authorised and who have attended the appropriate Judicial College course may try this type of work.

5 A number of district judges (magistrates' courts) have now undertaken training in dealing with these difficult cases and have been specifically authorised to hear cases involving serious sexual offences which fall short of requiring to be sent to the Crown Court ("an authorised district judge (magistrates' courts)"). As such, a procedure similar to that of the Crown Court will now apply to allegations of sexual offences in the youth court.

Procedure

6 The determination of venue in the youth court is governed by section 51 of the CDA 1998 [§ 1-24 in the main work], which provides that the youth must be tried summarily unless charged with such a grave crime that long-term detention is a realistic possibility (s.24(1) of the MCA 1980 [*ibid.*, § 1-83]), or that one of the other exceptions to this presumption arises.

7 Wherever possible such cases should be listed before an authorised district judge (magistrates' courts), to decide whether the case falls within the grave crime provisions and should therefore be sent for trial. If jurisdiction is retained and the allegation involves actual, or attempted, penetrative activity, the case must be tried by an authorised district judge (magistrates' courts). In all other cases, the authorised district judge (magistrates' courts) must consider whether the case is so serious and/or complex that it must be tried by an authorised district judge (magistrates' courts), or whether the case can be heard by any district judge (magistrates' courts) or any youth court bench.

8 If it is not practicable for an authorised district judge (magistrates' courts) to determine venue, any district judge (magistrates' courts) or any youth court bench may consider that issue. If jurisdiction is retained, appropriate directions may be given but the case papers, including a detailed case summary and a note of any representations made by the parties, must be sent to an authorized district judge (magistrates' courts) to consider. As soon as possible the authorised district judge (magistrates' courts) must decide whether the case must be tried by an authorised district judge (magistrates' courts) or whether the case is suitable to be heard by any district judge (magistrates' courts) or any youth court bench; however, if the case involves actual, or alleged, penetrative activity, the trial must be heard by an authorised district judge (magistrates' courts).

9 Once an authorised district judge (magistrates' courts) has decided that the case is one which must be tried by an authorised district judge (magistrates' courts), and in all cases involving actual or alleged penetrative activity, all further procedural hearings should, so far as practicable, be heard by an authorised district judge (magistrates' courts).

10 All cases which are remitted for sentence from the Crown Court to the youth court should be listed for sentence before an authorised district judge (magistrates' courts).

Arrangements for an authorised district judge (magistrates' courts) to be appointed
11 Where a case is to be tried by an authorised district judge (magistrates' courts) but no such **B-699** judge is available, the bench legal adviser should contact the Chief Magistrate's office for an authorised district judge (magistrates' courts) to be assigned.

CPD Listing: Annex 3 Cases Involving Very Large Fines in the Magistrates' Court

1 [*Applies following commencement of LASPOA 2012, s.85 (§ 1·120 in the main work).*] **B-700**
2 An authorised district judge (magistrates' courts) must deal with any allocation decision, trial and sentencing hearing in the following types of cases which are triable either way: (a) cases involving death or significant, life changing injury or a high risk of death or significant, life-changing injury; (b) cases involving substantial environmental damage or polluting material of a dangerous nature; (c) cases where major adverse effect on human health or quality of life, animal health or flora has resulted; (d) cases where major costs through clean-up, site restoration or animal rehabilitation have been incurred; (e) cases where the defendant corporation has a turnover in excess of £10m but does not exceed £250m, and has acted in a deliberate, reckless or negligent manner; (f) cases where the defendant corporation has a turnover in excess of £250m; (g) cases where the court will be expected to analyse complex company accounts; (h) high profile cases or ones of an exceptionally sensitive nature.

3 The prosecution agency must notify the justices' clerk where practicable of any case of the type mentioned in paragraph 2 ..., no less than seven days before the first hearing to ensure that an authorised district judge (magistrates' courts) is available at the first hearing.

4 The justices' clerk shall contact the office of the Chief Magistrate to ensure that an authorised district judge (magistrates' courts) can be assigned to deal with such a case if there is not such a person available in the courthouse. The justices' clerk shall also notify a presiding judge of the circuit that such a case has been listed.

5 Where an authorised district judge (magistrates' courts) is not appointed at the first hearing the court shall adjourn the case. The court shall ask the accused for an indication of his plea, but shall not allocate the case nor, if the accused indicates a guilty plea, sentence him, commit him for sentence, ask for a pre-sentence report or give any indication as to likely sentence that will be imposed. The justices' clerk shall ensure an authorised district judge (magistrates' courts) is appointed for the following hearing and notify the presiding judge of the circuit that the case has been listed.

6 When dealing with sentence, section 3 of the PCC(S)A 2000 [§ 5-29 in the main work] can be invoked where, despite the magistrates' court having maximum fine powers available to it, the offence or combination of offences make it so serious that the Crown Court should deal with it as though the person had been convicted on indictment.

7 An authorised district judge (magistrates' courts) should consider allocating the case to the Crown Court or committing the accused for sentence.

CPD Listing: Annex 4 The Management of Terrorism Cases

Application
1 This annex applies to "terrorism cases". For the purposes of this annex a case is a "terrorism **B-701** case" where:

    (a) one of the offences charged against any of the defendants is indictable only and it is alleged by the prosecution that there is evidence that it took place during an act of terrorism or for the purposes of terrorism as defined in section 1 of the Terrorism Act 2000

[§ 25-13 in the main work]; this may include, but is not limited to:
(i) murder;
(ii) manslaughter;
(iii) an offence under section 18 of the Offences against the Person Act 1861 (wounding with intent);
(iv) an offence under section 23 or 24 of that Act (administering poison etc);
(v) an offence under section 28 or 29 of that Act (explosives);
(vi) an offence under section 2, 3 or 5 of the Explosive Substances Act 1883 (causing explosions);
(vii) an offence under section 1 (2) of the Criminal Damage Act 1971 (endangering life by damaging property);
(viii) an offence under section 1 of the Biological Weapons Act 1974 (biological weapons);
(ix) an offence under section 2 of the Chemical Weapons Act 1996 (chemical weapons);
(x) an offence under section 56 of the Terrorism Act 2000 (directing a terrorist organisation);
(xi) an offence under section 59 of that Act (inciting terrorism overseas);
(xii) offences under (v), (vii) and (viii) above given jurisdiction by virtue of section 62 of that Act (terrorist bombing overseas); and
(xiii) an offence under section 5 of the Terrorism Act 2006 (preparation of terrorism acts);
(b) one of the offences charged is indictable only and includes an allegation by the prosecution of serious fraud that took place during an act of terrorism or for the purposes of terrorism as defined in section 1 of the Terrorism Act 2000 and the prosecutor gives a notice under section 51B of the CDA 1998 (notices in serious or complex fraud cases) [§ 1-26 in the main work]:
(c) one of the offences charged is indictable only, which includes an allegation that a defendant conspired, incited or attempted to commit an offence under sub-paragraphs (1)(a) or (b) above; or
(d) it is a case (which can be indictable only or triable either way) that a judge of the terrorism cases list (see paragraph 2(a) below) considers should be a terrorism case.
In deciding whether a case not covered by sub-paragraphs (1)(a), (b) or (c) above should be a terrorism case, the judge may hear representations from the CPS.

The terrorism cases list

B-702
2 (a) All terrorism cases, wherever they originate in England and Wales, will be managed in a list known as the "terrorism cases list" by such judges of the High Court as are nominated by the President of the Queen's Bench Division.
(b) Such cases will be tried, unless otherwise directed by the President of the Queen's Bench Division, by a judge of the High Court as nominated by the President of the Queen's Bench Division.

3 The judges managing the terrorism cases referred to in paragraph 2(a) will be supported by the London and South Eastern Regional Co-ordinator's Office (the "Regional Co-ordinator's Office"). An official of that office or an individual nominated by that office will act as the case progression officer for cases in that list for the purposes of rule 3.4 of the Criminal Procedure Rules.

Procedure after charge

B-703
4 Immediately after a person has been charged in a terrorism case, anywhere in England and Wales, a representative of the CPS will notify the person on the 24-hour rota for special jurisdiction matters at Westminster Magistrates' Court of the following information:
(a) the full name of each defendant and the name of his solicitor of other legal representative, if known;
(b) the charges laid;
(c) the name and contact details of the crown prosecutor with responsibility for the case, if known; and
(d) confirmation that the case is a terrorism case.

5 The person on the 24-hour rota will then ensure that all terrorism cases wherever they are charged in England and Wales are listed before the Chief Magistrate or other District Judge designated under the Terrorism Act 2000. Unless the Chief Magistrate or other District Judge designated under the Terrorism Act 2000 directs otherwise, the first appearance of all defendants accused of terrorism offences will be listed at Westminster Magistrates' Court.

6 In order to comply with section 46 of the PACE Act 1984 [§ 3-164 in the main work], if a

defendant in a terrorism case is charged at a police station within the local justice area in which Westminster Magistrates' Court is situated, the defendant must be brought before Westminster Magistrates' Court as soon as is practicable and in any event not later than the first sitting after he is charged with the offence. If a defendant in a terrorism case is charged in a police station outside the local justice area in which Westminster Magistrates' Court is situated, unless the Chief Magistrate or other designated judge directs otherwise, the defendant must be removed to that area as soon as is practicable. He must then be brought before [that court] as soon as is practicable after his arrival in the area and in any event not later than the first sitting of [that court] after his arrival in that area.

7 As soon as is practicable after charge a representative of the CPS will also provide the Regional Listing Co-ordinator's Office with the information listed in paragraph 4 above.

8 The Regional Co-ordinator's Office will then ensure that the Chief Magistrate and the Legal Aid Agency have the same information.

Cases to be sent to the Crown Court under section 51 of the Crime and Disorder Act 1998 [§ 1-24 in the main work]

9 The court should ordinarily direct that the plea and trial preparation hearing should take place about 14 days after charge. **B-704**

10 The sending magistrates' court should contact the Regional Listing Co-ordinator's Office who will be responsible for notifying the magistrates' court as to the relevant Crown Court to which to send the case.

11 In all terrorism cases, the magistrates' court case progression form for cases sent to the Crown Court under section 51 of the [1998 Act] should not be used. Instead of the automatic directions set out in that form, the magistrates' court shall make the following directions to facilitate the preliminary hearing at the Crown Court:

    (a) three days prior to the preliminary hearing in the terrorism cases list, the prosecution must serve upon each defendant and the Regional Listing Co-ordinator:

       (i) a preliminary summary of the case;

       (ii) the names of those who are to represent the prosecution, if known;

       (iii) an estimate of the length of the trial;

       (iv) a suggested provisional timetable which should generally include:

          • the general nature of further enquiries being made by the prosecution,

          • the time needed for the completion of such enquiries,

          • the time required by the prosecution to review the case,

          • a timetable for the phased service of the evidence,

          • the time for the provision by the Attorney-General for his consent if necessary,

          • the time for service of the detailed defence case statement,

          • the date for the case management hearing, and

          • the estimated trial date;

       (v) a preliminary statement of the possible disclosure issues setting out the nature and scale of the problem, including the amount of unused material, the manner in which the prosecution seeks to deal with these matters and a suggested timetable for discharging their statutory duty; and

       (vi) any information relating to bail and custody time limits;

    (b) one day prior to the preliminary hearing in the terrorist cases list, each defendant must serve in writing on the Regional Listing Co-ordinator and the prosecution:

       (i) the proposed representation;

       (ii) observations on the timetable; and

       (iii) an indication of plea and the general nature of the defence.

Cases to be sent to the Crown Court after the prosecutor gives notice under section 51D of the Crime and Disorder Act 1998 [§ 1-28 in the main work]

12 If a terrorism case is to be sent to the Crown Court after the prosecutor gives a notice under section 51B of the CDA 1998 [§ 1-26 in the main work] the magistrates' court should proceed as in paragraphs 9–11 above. **B-705**

13 When a terrorism case is so sent the case will go into the terrorism list and be managed by a judge as described in paragraph 2(a) above.

The preliminary hearing at the Crown Court

14 At the plea and trial preparation hearing, the judge will determine whether the case is one to remain in the terrorism list and if so, give directions setting the provisional timetable. **B-706**

15 The Legal Aid Agency must attend the hearing by an authorised officer to assist the court.

Use of video links

B-707

16 Unless a judge otherwise directs, all Crown Court hearings prior to the trial will be conducted by video link for all defendants in custody.

Security

B-708

17 The police service and the prison service will provide the Regional Listing Co-ordinator's Office with an initial joint assessment of the security risks associated with any court appearance by the defendants within 14 days of charge. Any subsequent changes in circumstances or the assessment of risk which have the potential to impact upon the choice of trial venue will be notified to the Regional Listing Co-ordinator's Office immediately.

CPD Listing: Annex 5 Management of Cases from the Organised Crime Division of the Crown Prosecution Service

B-709

1 The Organised Crime Division (OCD) of the CPS is responsible for prosecution of cases from the National Crime Agency (NCA). Typically, these cases involve more than one defendant, are voluminous and raise complex and specialised issues of law. It is recognised that if not closely managed, such cases have the potential to cost vast amounts of public money and take longer than necessary.

2 This annex applies to all cases handled by the OCD.

Designated court centres

B-710

3 Subject to the overriding discretion of the presiding judges of the circuit, OCD cases should normally be heard at Designated Court Centres (DCC). The process of designating court centres for this purpose has taken into account geographical factors and the size, security and facilities of those court centres. The designated court centres are:

    (a) Northern Circuit: Manchester, Liverpool and Preston;

    (b) North Eastern Circuit: Leeds, Newcastle and Sheffield;

    (c) Western Circuit: Bristol and Winchester;

    (d) South Eastern Circuit (not including London): Reading, Luton, Chelmsford, Ipswich, Maidstone, Lewes and Hove;

    (e) South Eastern Circuit (London only): Southwark, Blackfriars, Kingston, Woolwich, Croydon and the Central Criminal Court;

    (f) Midland Circuit: Birmingham, Leicester and Nottingham;

    (g) Wales Circuit: Cardiff, Swansea and Mold.

Selection of designated court centres

B-711

4 If arrests are made in different parts of the country and the OCD seeks to have all defendants tried by one Crown Court, the OCD will, at the earliest opportunity, write to the relevant court cluster manager with a recommendation as to the appropriate designated court centre, requesting that the decision be made by the relevant presiding judges. In the event that the designated court centre within one region is unable to accommodate a case, for example, as a result of a custody time limit expiry date, consideration may be given to transferring the case to a DCC in another region with the consent of the relevant presiding judges.

5 There will be a single point of contact person at the OCD for each HMCTS region, to assist listing co-ordinators.

6 The single contact person for each HMCTS region will be the relevant cluster manager, with the exception of the South Eastern Circuit, where the appropriate person will be the Regional Listing Co-ordinator.

Designation of the trial judge

B-712

7 The trial judge will be assigned by the Presiding Judge at the earliest opportunity, and in accordance with *CPD XIII Listing E* [§ 2-22j in the main work]. Where the trial judge is unable to continue with the case, all further pre-trial hearings should be by a single judge until a replacement has been assigned.

Procedure after charge

B-713

8 Within 24 hours of the laying of a charge, a representative of the OCD will notify the relevant cluster manager of the following information to enable an agreement to be reached between that cluster manager and the reviewing CPS lawyer before the first appearance as to the DCC to which the case should be sent:

(a) the full name of each defendant and the name of his legal representatives, if known;

(b) the charges laid; and

(c) the name and contact details of the crown prosecutor with responsibility for the case.

Exceptions

9 Where it is not possible to have a case dealt with at a DCC, the OCD should liaise closely with **B-714**
the relevant cluster manager and the presiding judges to ensure that the cases are sent to the most
appropriate court centre. This will, among other things, take into account the location of the likely
source of the case, convenience of the witnesses, travelling distance for OCD staff and facilities at the
court centres.

10 In the event that it is allocated to a non-designated court centre, the OCD should be permitted
to make representations in writing to the presiding judges within 14 days as to why the venue is not
suitable. The presiding judges will consider the reasons and, if necessary, hold a hearing. The CPS
may renew their request at any stage where further reasons come to light that may affect the original
decision on venue.

11 Nothing in this annex should be taken to remove the right of the defence to make representations as to the venue.

Criminal Costs Practice Direction (2015)

For the *Criminal Costs Practice Direction (2015)*, see §§ 6-124 *et seq.* in the main work. **B-715**

APPENDIX C
The Duties of Advocates

I. CODE OF CONDUCT

The second edition of the Bar Standards Board Handbook came into force on April 30, 2015. **C-1** It contains (in Part 2) the ninth edition of the Code of Conduct for the Bar of England and Wales. Part 1 of the handbook is an introduction. Parts 3 and 4 contain the scope of practice rules and the qualification rules. Part 5 comprises the enforcement regulations and Part 6 provides for the interpretation of terms used throughout the handbook.

Within the code, there are "core duties", "outcomes", "rules" and "guidance". The significance of each is explained in the introductory section of the handbook. Thus the core duties (italicised words and expressions are defined in Part 6)—

"underpin the entire regulatory framework and set the mandatory standards that all *BSB regulated persons* are required to meet. They also define the core elements of professional conduct. Disciplinary proceedings may be taken against a *BSB regulated person* if the *Bar Standards Board* believes there has been a breach by that person of the Core Duties set out in this *Handbook* and that such action would be in accordance with the *Enforcement Policy*."

The outcomes—

"explain the reasons for the regulatory scheme and what it is designed to achieve. They are derived from the *regulatory objectives* as defined in the *LSA* and the risks which must be managed if those objectives are to be achieved. They are not themselves mandatory rules, but they are factors which *BSB regulated persons* should have in mind when considering how the Core Duties, Conduct Rules or Qualification Rules (as appropriate) should be applied in particular circumstances. The *Bar Standards Board* will take into account whether or not an Outcome has, or might have been, adversely affected when considering how to respond to alleged breaches of the Core Duties, Conduct Rules or Qualification Rules."

The conduct rules (*i.e.* those in the code of conduct)—

"supplement the Core Duties and are mandatory. Disciplinary proceedings may be taken against a *BSB regulated person* if the *Bar Standards Board* believes there has been a breach by that person of the Conduct Rules set out in Part 2 of this *Handbook* and that it would be in accordance with the *Enforcement policy* to take such action. However, the Conduct Rules are not intended to be exhaustive. In any situation where no specific Rule applies, reference should be made to the Core Duties. In situations where specific Rules do apply, it is still necessary to consider the Core Duties, since compliance with the Rules alone will not necessarily be sufficient to comply with the Core Duties."

The guidance is self-explanatory, its principal purpose being to assist in the interpretation of the core duties and rules.

The code of conduct itself is divided into four sections: A - Application, B - The Core Duties, **C-2** C - The Conduct Rules, and D - Rules Applying to Particular Groups of Regulated Persons. The conduct rules are themselves divided into five sections, *viz.* C1 "You and the court", C2 "Behaving ethically", C3 "You and your client", C4 "You and your regulator" and C5 "You and your practice". So far as practice in court is concerned, the most important rules are contained in section C1. These, together with the core duties, are set in full, *post.* The handbook runs to a total of 277 pages and space precludes the inclusion of more detail. However it should be noted that C2 (behaving ethically) contains provisions relating to honesty, integrity and independence, referral fees, undertakings, discrimination and foreign work, and that C3 (you and your client) has rules relating to "best interests of each client, provision of a competent standard of work, and confidentiality", "not misleading clients and potential clients", "personal responsibility", "accepting instructions", "defining terms or basis on which instructions are accepted", "returning instructions", "requirement not to discriminate", "the 'cab-rank rule'" and the "quality assurance scheme for advocates rules".

Core duties

CD1	You must observe your duty to the court in the administration of justice.
CD2	You must act in the best interests of each client.
CD3	You must act with honesty and integrity.
CD4	You must maintain your independence.
CD5	You must not behave in a way which is likely to diminish the trust and confidence which the public places in you or in the profession.
CD6	You must keep the affairs of each client confidential.
CD7	You must provide a competent standard of work and service to each client.
CD8	You must not discriminate unlawfully against any person.
CD9	You must be open and co-operative with your regulators.
CD10	You must take reasonable steps to manage your practice, or carry out your role within your practice, competently and in such a way as to achieve compliance with your legal and regulatory obligations.

Guidance to the core duties

gC1 The Core Duties are not presented in order of precedence, subject to the following:

.1 CD1 overrides any other core duty, if and to the extent the two are inconsistent. Rules C3.5 and C4 deal specifically with the relationship between CD1, CD2 and CD6 and you should refer to those rules and to the related Guidance;

.2 in certain other circumstances set out in this Code of Conduct one Core Duty overrides another. Specifically, Rule C16 provides that CD2 (as well as being subject to CD1) is subject to your obligations under CD3, CD4 and CD8.

gC2 Your obligation to take reasonable steps to manage your *practice*, or carry out your role within your *practice*, competently and in such a way as to achieve compliance with your legal and regulatory obligations (CD10) includes an obligation to take all reasonable steps to mitigate the effects of any breach of those legal and regulatory obligations once you become aware of the same.

The Conduct Rules

C.1 You and the court

Outcomes

oC1 The *court* is able to rely on information provided to it by those conducting litigation and by advocates who appear before it.

oC2 The proper administration of justice is served.

oC3 The interests of *clients* are protected to the extent compatible with outcomes oC1 and oC2 and the Core Duties.

oC4 Both those who appear before the *court* and *clients* understand clearly the extent of the duties owed to the *court* by advocates and those conducting litigation and the circumstances in which duties owed to *clients* will be overridden by the duty owed to the *court*.

oC5 *The public* has confidence in the administration of justice and in those who serve it.

Rules

rC3 You owe a duty to the *court* to act with independence in the interests of justice. This duty overrides any inconsistent obligations which you may have (other than obligations under the criminal law). It includes the following specific obligations which apply whether you are acting as an advocate or are otherwise involved in the conduct of litigation in whatever role (with the exception of Rule C3.1 below, which applies when acting as an advocate):

.1 you must not knowingly or recklessly mislead or attempt to mislead the *court*;

.2 you must not abuse your role as an advocate;

.3 you must take reasonable steps to avoid wasting the *court's* time;

.4 you must take reasonable steps to ensure that the *court* has before it all relevant decisions and legislative provisions;

.5 you must ensure that your ability to act independently is not compromised.

rC4 Your duty to act in the best interests of each *client* is subject to your duty to the *court*.

rC5 Your duty to the *court* does not require you to act in breach of your duty to keep the affairs of each *client* confidential.

Not misleading the court

rC6 Your duty not to mislead the *court* or to permit the *court* to be misled will include the following obligations: **C-7**

.1 you must not:

.a make submissions, representations or any other statement; or

.b ask questions which suggest facts to witnesses

which you know, or are instructed, are untrue or misleading.

.2 you must not call witnesses to give evidence or put affidavits or witness statements to the *court* which you know, or are *instructed*, are untrue or misleading, unless you make clear to the *court* the true position as known by or instructed to you.

Not abusing your role as an advocate

rC7 Where you are acting as an advocate, your duty not to abuse your role includes the following obligations: **C-8**

.1 you must not make statements or ask questions merely to insult, humiliate or annoy a witness or any other person;

.2 you must not make a serious allegation against a witness whom you have had an opportunity to cross-examine unless you have given that witness a chance to answer the allegation in cross-examination;

.3 you must not make a serious allegation against any person, or suggest that a person is guilty of a crime with which your *client* is charged unless:

.a you have reasonable grounds for the allegation; and

.b the allegation is relevant to your *client's* case or the credibility of a witness; and

.c where the allegation relates to a third party, you avoid naming them in open *court* unless this is reasonably necessary.

.4 you must not put forward to the *court* a personal opinion of the facts or the law unless you are invited or required to do so by the *court* or by law.

Guidance

Guidance on Rules C3 - C6 and relationship to CD1 and CD2

gC3 Rules C3 - C6 set out some specific aspects of your duty to the *court* (CD1). See CD1 and associated Guidance at gC1. **C-9**

gC4 Knowingly misleading the *court* includes inadvertently misleading the *court* if you later realise that you have misled the *court*, and you fail to correct the position. Recklessness means being indifferent to the truth, or not caring whether something is true or false. The duty continues to apply for the duration of the case.

gC5 Your duty under Rule C3.3 includes drawing to the attention of the *court* any decision or provision which may be adverse to the interests of your *client*. It is particularly important where you are appearing against a litigant who is not legally represented.

gC6 You are obliged by CD2 to promote and to protect your *client's* interests so far as that is consistent with the law and with your overriding duty to the *court* under CD1. Your duty to the *court* does not prevent you from putting forward your *client's* case simply because you do not believe that the facts are as your *client* states them to be (or as you, on your *client's* behalf, state them to be), as long as any positive case you put forward accords with your *instructions* and you do not mislead the *court*. Your role when acting as an advocate or conducting litigation is to present your *client's* case, and it is not for you to decide whether your *client's* case is to be believed.

gC7 For example, you are entitled and it may often be appropriate to draw to the witness's attention other evidence which appears to conflict with what the witness is saying and you are entitled to indicate that a *court* may find a particular piece of evidence difficult to accept. But if the witness maintains that the evidence is true, it should be recorded in the witness statement and you will not be misleading the *court* if you call the witness to confirm their witness statement. Equally, there may be circumstances where you call a hostile witness whose evidence you are instructed is untrue. You will not be in breach of Rule C6 if you make the position clear to the *court*. See further the guidance at gC14.

gC8 As set out in Rule C4, your duty to the *court* does not permit or require you to disclose confidential information which you have obtained in the course of your *instructions* and which your *client* has not authorised you to disclose to the *court*. However, Rule C6 requires you not knowingly to mislead the *court* or to permit the *court* to be misled. There may be situations where you have obligations under both these rules.

gC9 Rule C3.5 makes it clear that your duty to act in the best interests of your *client* is subject to your duty to the *court*. For example, if your *client* were to tell you that he had committed the crime with which he was charged, in order to be able to ensure compliance with Rule C4 on the one hand and Rule C3 and Rule C6 on the other:

.1 you would not be entitled to disclose that information to the *court* without your *client's* consent; and

.2 you would not be misleading the *court* if, after your *client* had entered a plea of "not guilty", you were to test in cross-examination the reliability of the evidence of the prosecution witnesses and then address the jury to the effect that the prosecution had not succeeded in making them sure of your *client's* guilt.

gC10 However, you would be misleading the *court* and would therefore be in breach of Rules C3 and C6 if you were to set up a positive case inconsistent with the confession, as for example by:

.1 suggesting to prosecution witnesses, calling your *client* or your witnesses to show; or submitting to the *jury*, that your *client* did not commit the crime; or

.2 suggesting that someone else had done so; or

.3 putting forward an alibi.

gC11 If there is a risk that the *court* will be misled unless you disclose confidential information which you have learned in the course of your *instructions*, you should ask the client for permission to disclose it to the *court*. If your *client* refuses to allow you to make the disclosure you must cease to act, and return your *instructions*: see Rules C25 to C27 below. In these circumstances you must not reveal the information to the *court*.

gC12 For example, if your *client* tells you that he has previous *convictions* of which the prosecution is not aware, you may not disclose this without his consent. However, in a case where mandatory sentences apply, the non-disclosure of the previous *convictions* will result in the *court* failing to pass the sentence that is required by law. In that situation, you must advise your *client* that if consent is refused to your revealing the information you will have to cease to act. In situations where mandatory sentences do not apply, and your *client* does not agree to disclose the previous *convictions*, you can continue to represent your *client* but in doing so must not say anything that misleads the *court*. This will constrain what you can say in mitigation. For example, you could not advance a positive case of previous good character knowing that there are undisclosed prior *convictions*. Moreover, if the *court* asks you a direct question you must not give an untruthful answer and therefore you would have to withdraw if, on your being asked such a question, your *client* still refuses to allow you to answer the question truthfully. You should explain this to your *client*.

gC13 Similarly, if you become aware that your *client* has a document which should be disclosed but has not been disclosed, you cannot continue to act unless your *client* agrees to the disclosure of the document. In these circumstances you must not reveal the existence or contents of the document to the *court*.

[The next paragraph is C-20.]

II. BAR COUNCIL GUIDANCE

Written standards of work

C-20   The Bar Council issued written standards for the conduct of professional work together with the eighth edition of the code of conduct. They did not form part of the code, but paragraph 701(d) obliged a barrister "to have regard to any relevant written standards." They can still be found on the website of the Bar Standards Board, but it does not appear that they are intended to have any continuing effect as there is a statement at the top of the page to the effect that, as from January 6, 2014, barristers should refer to the board's handbook (as to which, see *ante*, C-1) for rules and guidance on their conduct as such.

[The next paragraph is C-45.]

Criticism of previous counsel

In consequence of observations made by the Court of Appeal in *R. v. Clarke and Jones, The*   **C-45**
Times, August 19, 1994, and *R. v. Bowler, The Times*, May 9, 1995, the following guidance was approved by Lord Taylor C.J. and the Bar Council. It is still to be found on the website of the Bar
Council, but it is emphasised there that it is not "guidance" for the purposes of the Bar Standards
Board's handbook (as to which, see *ante*, C-1)), and it is accompanied by a disclaimer to the effect
that it does not constitute legal advice and a statement to the effect that it was prepared by the Bar
Council to assist barristers on matters of professional conduct and ethics.

1. Allegations against former counsel may receive substantial publicity whether accepted or
   rejected by the court. Counsel should not settle or sign grounds of appeal unless he is
   satisfied that they are reasonable, have some real prospect of success and are such that he
   is prepared to argue before the court (Guide to Proceedings in the Court of Appeal
   Criminal Division, para. A2-6 [*post*, Appendix J-5]). When such allegations are properly
   made however, in accordance with the Code of Conduct counsel newly instructed must
   promote and protect fearlessly by all proper and lawful means his lay client's best interests
   without regard to others, including fellow members of the legal profession (Code, para.
   303(a)).

2. When counsel newly instructed is satisfied that such allegations are made, and a waiver of
   privilege is necessary, he should advise the lay client fully about the consequences of
   waiver and should obtain a waiver of privilege in writing signed by the lay client relating to
   communications with, instructions given to and advice given by former counsel. The allegations should be set out in the Grounds of Application for Leave of Appeal. Both
   waiver and grounds should be lodged without delay; the grounds may be perfected if
   necessary in due course.

3. On receipt of the waiver and grounds, the Registrar of Criminal Appeals will send both to
   former counsel with an invitation on behalf of the court to respond to the allegations
   made.

4. If former counsel wishes to respond and considers the time for doing so insufficient, he
   should ask the Registrar for further time. The court will be anxious to have full information and to give counsel adequate time to respond.

5. The response should be sent to the Registrar. On receipt, he will send it to counsel newly
   instructed who may reply to it. The grounds and the responses will go before the single
   judge.

6. The Registrar may have received grounds of appeal direct from the applicant, and obtained
   a waiver of privilege before fresh counsel is assigned. In those circumstances, when assigning counsel, the Registrar will provide copies of the waiver, the grounds of appeal and any
   response from former counsel.

7. This guidance covers the formal procedures to be followed. It is perfectly proper for
   counsel newly instructed to speak to former counsel as a matter of courtesy before grounds
   are lodged to inform him of the position.

As to the need to follow the Bar Council's guidance, see *R. v. Nasser, The Times*, February 19,
1998, CA.

Preparation of defence statements

As to guidance regarding the duties of counsel in relation to the preparation of defence state-   **C-46**
ments, see § 12-122 in the main work.

III. MISCELLANEOUS AUTHORITIES ON DUTIES OF ADVOCATES

(1) Return of brief or instructions

Members of the criminal bar have a personal responsibility for compliance with provisions of   **C-47**
the Code of Conduct relating to the return of instructions, of which their clerks should be aware.
It is open to a court concerned with a problem caused by a late return of a brief to send a
complaint to the Professional Conduct Committee of the Bar Council: *R. v. Sutton JJ., ex p. DPP*,
95 Cr.App.R. 180, DC, *per* Brooke J., at p. 186 (decided in relation to paragraphs 507 and 508 of
the fifth edition of the Code of Conduct).

The absence of what counsel would regard as sufficient time for preparation does not constitute an exception to the cab-rank rule requiring him to act for his client: see *R. v. Ulcay* (§ 4-67 in the main work).

(2) Duty not to accept certain instructions

C-48   Counsel should not appear for the prosecution in a case where the defendant is a person he has previously represented; para. 501(f) of the Code of Conduct for the Bar (6th ed.) referred to the risk that the barrister might have considential information or special knowledge disadvantageous to the defendant, his former client; it is contrary to the spirit of the code that a barrister should put himself in a position where such a risk might be perceived: *R. v. Dann* [1997] Crim.L.R. 46, CA. As to *Dann*, see further *Re T. and A. (Children) (Risk of Disclosure)* [2002] 1 F.L.R. 859, CA (Civ.Div.).

(3) Duty in relation to the giving of advice and taking of instructions

C-48a   Although not laid down in prescriptive form in the codes of conduct governing barristers and solicitors, solicitors and counsel should make a brief note of the advice given and the instructions received in conference on important issues as to the conduct of the defence (such as discussions relating to strategy, including as to whether the defendant should give evidence); such a note would be to the benefit of the client, in that it will serve to ensure that he has been given the appropriate advice; it would also serve to protect the advocate and his instructing solicitors from criticism based on assertions made after the event by a dissatisfied client: *R. v. Anderson, The Times,* December 23, 2010, CA.

(4) Duty of counsel to acquaint themselves with the terms of the indictment

C-49   See *R. v. Peckham*, 25 Cr.App.R. 125, CCA (prosecution), and *R. v. Olivo*, 28 Cr.App.R. 173, CCA (defence).

(5) Duty concerning recent legislation

C-50   In *R. v. Isaacs, The Times,* February 9, 1990, the Court of Appeal said that when presenting cases at first instance or in appellate courts, counsel have a positive duty to inform the court of all relevant commencement dates of recent legislation.

(6) Duty of counsel to inform themselves of the sentencing powers of the court

C-51   The Court of Appeal has repeatedly emphasised the duty of both counsel to inform themselves before the commencement of proceedings in the Crown Court of the sentencing powers of the court, including powers in relation to ancillary orders, such as costs, compensation, etc. The starting point is *R. v. Clarke (R.W.W.)*, 59 Cr.App.R. 298, CA. Lawton L.J. concluded the judgment of the court with the following general observations and guidance. His Lordship's remarks are even more apposite today than when they were made: legislation in relation to sentence has become ever more complex. Sections 28 and 29 of the MCA 1952 were replaced by sections 37 and 38 respectively of the MCA 1980, which have themselves since been subject to extensive amendment. Section 37 was eventually repealed by the CDA 1998, and section 38 was repealed and replaced by section 3 of the PCC(S)A 2000.

> "We adjudge that counsel as a matter of professional duty to the Court, and in the case of defending counsel to their client, should always before starting a criminal case satisfy themselves as to what the maximum sentence is. There can be no excuse for counsel not doing this and they should remember that the performance of this duty is particularly important in a case where a man has been committed to the Crown Court for sentencing pursuant to the provisions of sections 28 and 29 of the Magistrates' Courts Act 1952, and section 56 of the Criminal Justice Act 1967. Those statutory provisions are pregnant with dangers for court and for counsel and above all for accused persons...
>
> Secondly, those who administer the Crown Court should act as follows. Before the Crown Court came into existence..., it was the practice of many clerks of assize and many clerks of the peace to make a note on the documents put before the trial judge of the maximum sentence which could be passed and of the paragraphs in *Archbold's Criminal Pleading, Evidence and Practice* which dealt with the offence. In some Crown Courts this former practice has been followed. On the other hand it is clear from this case and from inquiries which we have made that it is not always

followed. It should be; and it is particularly important that it should be when judges are asked to deal with cases committed for sentence under the statutory provisions to which I have already referred" (at pp. 301–302).

A reminder of the duty of counsel for both sides to ensure that sentences imposed, and orders made, are within the powers of the court, and to invite the court to vary a sentence if on subsequent consideration it appears to be unlawful, was given in *R. v. Komsta and Murphy*, 12 Cr.App.R.(S.) 63. Turner J. commented that it could not be too clearly understood that there was positive obligation on counsel, both for the prosecution and the defence, to ensure that no order was made that the court had no power to make. The PCC(S)A 2000, s. 155(1) (see § 5-1312 in the main work) allowed the Crown Court to alter or vary any sentence or order, within the period of 28 [now 56] days of the making of the order. If it appeared to either counsel that the order was one which the court had no power to make, counsel should not hesitate to invite the court to exercise such powers.

See also *R. v. Richards*, The Times, April 1, 1993, CA, *R. v. Hartrey* [1993] Crim.L.R. 230, CA, *R. v. Johnstone (D.)*, The Times, June 18, 1996, CA, *R. v. Bruley* [1996] Crim.L.R. 913, CA, *R. v. McDonnell* [1996] Crim.L.R. 914, CA, *R. v. Street*, 161 J.P. 28, CA, *R. v. Blight* [1999] Crim.L.R. 426, CA and, most recently, *R. v. Cain* [2007] 2 Cr.App.R.(S.) 25, CA. In *Blight*, it was said that counsel do not discharge their duty simply by having a copy of *Archbold* "to hand"; it is the duty of both counsel to be aware in advance of the powers of the court so that any error may be recited immediately; as to the defence counsel, it was said to be very difficult to see how mitigation can be done properly without having in the very front of the mind the powers within which the judge must exercise his duty. In *R. v. Cain*, it was said that defence advocates should ascertain and be prepared to assist the judge with any relevant legal restrictions on sentence, and the prosecution advocate should ensure that the sentencer does not, through inadvertence, impose an unlawful sentence; in particular, prosecution advocates should always be ready to assist the court by drawing attention to any statutory provisions that govern the court's sentencing powers and to any sentencing guidelines or guideline decisions of the Court of Appeal.

In *R. v. Reynolds* [2007] 2 Cr.App.R.(S.) 87, CA, it was said that prosecuting and defence **C-52** advocates must ensure that they are fully aware of the potential impact of the provisions of the dangerous offender provisions in Chapter 5 of Part 12 of the CJA 2003 (§§ 5-473 *et seq.* in the main work), that they are able to assist the sentencer in that respect and are alert to any mistakes made in passing sentence so that any problem can be resolved before it is too late.

(7) Defendant absconding

See generally, §§ 3-222 *et seq.* in the main work, and *R. v. Shaw*, 70 Cr.App.R. 313, CA (§ 7-87 **C-53** in the main work).

(8) Defendant not giving evidence

In *R. v. Bevan*, 98 Cr.App.R. 354, CA, it was held that where a defendant decides not to give **C-54** evidence, it should be the invariable practice of counsel to record that decision and to cause the defendant to sign that record, indicating clearly first, that he has, of his own free will, decided not to give evidence and, secondly, that he has so decided bearing in mind the advice given to him by counsel. In the light of section 35 of the CJPOA 1994 (§ 4-377 in the main work), the advice of the Court of Appeal in *Bevan* is likely to become of greater importance than at the time of the decision. As to this, see also *Ebanks (Kurt) v. The Queen* [2006] 1 W.L.R. 1827, PC (§ 4-382 in the main work).

R. v. Bevan, ante, was considered in *R. v. Good (Alfie)*, unreported, May 17, 2016, CA ([2016] ★ EWCA Crim. 1054). It was said that counsel's advice on the question whether to give evidence or not should include advice as to the likely direction to the jury on the issue and of the adverse inference that they might draw in light of that direction (pursuant to s.35 of the 1994 Act); and attention should also be drawn, where required, to the fact that, without evidence from the defendant, there will be no evidence to substantiate his case. Where a defendant decides not to give evidence, whether following advice or notwithstanding advice, the court said that it should be the invariable practice for counsel to make a record of the decision with a summary of the reasons; he should read this out to the defendant, who should then be asked to sign it; and that should be done before the time when the judge gives the warning about not giving evidence set out in section 35(2) of the 1994 Act; a photocopy of the endorsement should be made in chambers or in the office of an advocate as a record of the advice and the decision.

(9) Duties in relation to cross-examination

C-55   See §§ 8-216, 8-219 *et seq.* in the main work and, in relation to defence counsel's duty when cross-examining a co-defendant, see *R. v. Fenlon*, 71 Cr.App.R. 307, CA, see § 8-297 in the main work.

(10) Duties in relation to the summing up

C-56   See §§ 4-433 *et seq.* in the main work.

(11) Duties in relation to appeal

C-57   As to the duty to advise in relation to the possibility of an appeal against conviction or sentence, see §§ 7-165 *et seq.* in the main work.

As to counsel's general duty in relation to the drafting of grounds of appeal, see § 7-168 in the main work. As to criticism of former counsel, see § 7-83 in the main work and *ante*, and C-45, *ante.*

As to the duty of counsel for the prosecution, see § 7-201 in the main work.

The duty of a barrister to present his client's case before the Court of Appeal could not extend to advancing the client's assertion, unsubstantiated by any evidence, that the trial judge was corrupt or biased. A barrister's duty in such circumstances is either to decline to comply with the instructions or to withdraw from the case: *Thatcher v. Douglas, The Times,* January 8, 1996, CA (Civ. Div.).

(12) Duties of prosecuting counsel

C-58   Apart from the matters mentioned above, see also (a) *The Role and Responsibilities of the Prosecution Advocate, post,* E-15 *et seq.*; (b) *R. v. Herbert*, 94 Cr.App.R. 230, CA (§ 4-173 in the main work) and *R. v. Richards and Stober*, 96 Cr.App.R. 258, CA (§ 19-103 in the main work), in relation to "plea-bargaining" and the acceptance of pleas, with particular reference to cases where there are two or more defendants; (c) §§ 4-342 *et seq.* in the main work, in relation to the opening of a case generally, and *R. v. Hobstaff*, 14 Cr.App.R.(S.) 605, CA, in relation to opening the facts on a plea of guilty; and (d) the Attorney-General's guidelines on the acceptance of pleas and the prosecutor's role in the sentencing exercise (*ante*, Appendix A-276 *et seq.*).

(13) Advocate as witness

C-59   In *R. v. Jacquith (or Jaquith) and Emode* [1989] Crim.L.R. 508 and 563, CA, junior counsel for one defendant has been called on his behalf to rebut a suggestion of recent invention made against him. The Court of Appeal said that the evidence on this point was admissible but it was very undesirable for counsel to give evidence on this point in court. In addition to the effect on the jury it caused embarrassment and difficulty to other members of the Bar who had to set about cross-examining a colleague.

May L.J. said that the suggestion had been made that the court give some indication of its views concerning evidence given by counsel and also where a client alleged an attempt to pervert the court of justice by a co-defendant. their Lordships considered, however, that the right course would be to list points for consideration by the Bar Council and the Law Society. It was not sought to lay these maters down as ones of principle; their Lordships merely thought they deserved consideration.

1. No advocate should ever give evidence if that could possibly be avoided. 2. Where it was not possible for an advocate to avoid giving evidence, he should take no further part in the case. It necessarily followed that, if he was not being led, the trial must stop and a retrial be ordered. 3. There was a duty on counsel to anticipate circumstances in which he might be called upon to give evidence. Experienced counsel ought to be able to anticipate whether such a situation might arise. Where such a situation was anticipated, or envisaged even as a possibility, he should withdraw from the case. 4. Where it came to the notice of a legal adviser, through an accused person, that one of his co-defendants had attempted to pervert the court of justice, there was a duty on the

legal adviser, usually the instructing solicitor, to take a detailed proof at once to provide a record and for further investigation. 5. Where the giving of evidence by an advocate caused real embarrassment or inhibition or difficulty regarding cross-examination by other advocates, the judge should exercise his discretion to discharge the jury and order a retrial.

(14) Co-habiting counsel

It is generally undesirable for husband and wife, or other partners living together, to appear as **C-60** counsel on opposite sides in the same criminal matter since it might give rise to an apprehension that the proper conduct of the case had been in some way affected by that personal relationship: *R. v. Batt, The Times,* May 30, 1996, CA. See also *Re L. (Minors) (Care Proceedings: Solicitors)* [2001] 1 W.L.R. 100, Fam D. (Wilson J.).

APPENDIX D
Forms for use at Plea and Trial Preparation Hearings

PLEA AND TRIAL PREPARATION HEARINGS

Introduction and Guidance
Revised December 2015

All cases sent to the Crown Court after 5th January 2016 will be sent to a Plea and Trial Preparation Hearing

This Introduction and Guidance note has been revised to include the information published by the SPJ's office and draws on the experience of the six early adopter courts.

Why the Change?

There has been a widely held perception that Preliminary Hearings in cases where not guilty pleas are expected have been held too early in the process for the court to give more than perfunctory orders and that Plea and Case Management Hearings are either unnecessary or not held at a time when active case management could be most effective. The result has been a multiplicity of hearings.

There have also been differing local practices and protocols, and differing methods of recording court orders. The result has been failings of compliance when orders made have not always been communicated clearly to those who must act upon them.

The new Plea and Trial Preparation Hearing (PTPH) and related procedures will provide a single national process to be used in all Crown Courts. It builds on the Transforming Summary Justice initiative in the Magistrates' Courts.

The PTPH:

- Takes place a little later in the process than Preliminary Hearings, generally 28 days after sending unless, in individual cases, the Resident Judge orders otherwise;

- Occurs after the prosecution will have provided available information about the case and obtained details of the availability of likely prosecution witnesses. In all but complex cases this should be sufficient to enable the court to case manage effectively without the need for a Further Case Management Hearing (FCMH) before trial.

- Presumes that the parties will have communicated with each other prior to the PTPH in accordance with the duty of engagement now found in CrimPR 3 and will continue to do so thereafter.

The overarching aims	The overarching aims are: • A single national process • Robust case management • A reduced number of hearings • The earlier resolution of pleas and the identification of the issues in the case • The maximum participation and engagement by every participant within the system • Effective compliance with the Criminal Procedure Rules (CrimPR); Practice and Court Directions. The CrimPR and CrimPD are available to view at: http://www.justice.gov.uk/courts/procedure-rules/criminal/
Implementation	**All cases sent after 5th January 2016 will be sent to a PTPH hearing.** The chain of implementation is this. There is a National Implementation Team setting national requirements reflected in this Guidance. Each circuit has a Circuit Implementation Team (the South Eastern Circuit has two) and most Crown Courts will need to establish their own Crown Court Implementation Team (Local LITs) chaired by the Resident Judge as a means to inform court users and respond to their questions and to liaise with the Circuit Implementation Team so as to ensure continuity across the Circuit. The judicial leads for the Circuits Implementation Teams are: London: HHJ Hilliard QC supported by HHJ Kinch QC Midlands: HHJ Dean QC North East: HHJ Collier QC Northern: HHJ Goldstone QC South East: HHJ Holt supported by HHJ Cutts QC Wales: HHJ Rees Western: HHJ Ford QC. National guidance and resources is available for the Circuit Implementation Teams and the Court Implementation teams.
Digital Case System	Parallel with the introduction of the PTPH is the provision of the Digital Case System (DCS) to all Crown Courts before the end of March 2016. The DCS is already operating in Leeds, Southwark, Portsmouth, Liverpool, and Merthyr Tydfil. Reading, Isleworth and Leicester will commence using DCS in November. When the DCS is fully rolled out there will be **no paper files in the Crown Court.** The documents relied on in criminal cases such as the indictment, statements, paper exhibits, defence statement, applications and written orders will be uploaded onto the DCS and will be accessible on computers, tablets and even smartphones. Paper copies will continue to be required for unrepresented parties and jurors. Documents will be "served" when they are uploaded onto the system AND a notification is sent, by e mail, to the other party or parties.

Thus any paperwork handed over during a hearing will only be deemed to have been "filed" when it is uploaded onto the DCS. These elements of the new approach are reflected in the new CrimPR 4.6.

More information about DCS may be found At:

http://www.justice.gov.uk/about/criminal-justice-system-efficiency-programme

PTPH and the DCS

Therefore some courts will have DCS before 5th January and others will only start DCS after 5th January.

- Whilst the PTPH and DCS are complementary to each other the key message is that courts do not need to have the DCS up and running to implement BCM or to use the PTPH form effectively.
- The PTPH does centre around the PTPH form as the primary record of the hearing and the orders made. Arrangements are in hand to put the PTPH form on the DCS so that it can be completed by the parties online. This will be of particular assistance in multi-defendant cases. Those arrangements are not expected to be in place by 5th January so all courts will be starting without that element.

The early adopter courts

There are six early adopter courts using the PTPH. They are Isleworth; Leicester; Merthyr Tydfil; Portsmouth; Reading and Woolwich. Liverpool and Leeds start soon after. Some started with cases sent from 5th October. Their reports indicate that the system is working. At each court there was effective engagement with the court users and, whilst not everything has gone smoothly at all times, the hearings are constructive and legal representatives have embraced the prospect of reducing the number of pre-trial hearings by making effective use of the PTPH. Early and effective engagement with court users and court staff at all levels seems to be the key to success. Whilst it is too early for a statistical analysis more guilty pleas have occurred than might have been expected at Preliminary Hearings.

The experiences of the early adopter courts identify problems and will inform decisions on national implementation.

The Expedited Case Management Initiative

It was recognised that the move to BCM would result in a bulge of work where the two systems overlapped. As a result the CPS has had in place an Expedited Case Management Initiative ("the Blitz") at all Crown Courts from October to December 2015 to review cases of assault, theft, fraud and drugs to confirm whether or not they should proceed; whether further work is required; and whether they might be resolved by guilty pleas.

The duty of engagement

The new CrimPR 3.3 requires the parties to communicate at the first available opportunity, and in any event no later than the beginning of the day of the first hearing, and then thereafter until the conclusion of

PTPH – INTRODUCTION AND GUIDANCE

the case. By that communication the parties are required to establish whether the defendant is likely to plead guilty or not guilty, what is agreed and what is likely to be disputed, what information, or other material, is required by on party or another and why; and what is to be done, by whom and when.

The parties are required to report on that communication to the court at the first hearing and then thereafter as directed by the court.

The role of Magistrates on Sending

When a case is to be sent for PTPH to the Crown Court the Magistrates should expect the parties to provide information on any relevant communications between them in accordance with the duty of engagement (CrimPR 3.3).

Where **guilty pleas** are indicated the Magistrates should consider ordering a PSR. Separate guidance on this has been published.

Where **not-guilty pleas** are indicated the magistrates should explore with the parties:

- Whether the defendant is prepared to plead to other offences?
- In brief terms what are the issues in the case, what evidence and issues are agreed and what is likely to be disputed?
- What information, or other material, is required by either of the parties to facilitate an effective PTPH?

In most cases, it is very unlikely that the magistrates will need to make any directions. The duties of the parties are already clear and set out in the rules. Standard directions will not be appropriate or necessary at this stage.

Where directions are sought by the parties, magistrates should expect an explanation as to why such directions would be necessary and appropriate in the circumstances.

It is anticipated that directions will usually only be sought where one party considers that the other has not complied with their duties under the rules, or it is likely to assist in ensuring that the PTPH is effective.

If either party objects to the direction being made, the magistrates should not make the order, but refer the matter to the Crown Court, for the judge to resolve at the PTPH.

A copy of any order made must be given to the parties.

The BCM questionnaire will be completed to record the outcome of the magistrates' court hearing, and sent to the Crown Court and parties by E mail. It is very important to identify linked cases or linked defendants.

When Common Platform (the stage beyond DCS) is available, all relevant information will be passed from the magistrates' court to the

PTPH – INTRODUCTION AND GUIDANCE

Crown Court digitally. In the meantime the magistrates' court will continue to use LIBRA in order to send information such as the case details, the Notice of Sending, and, from 16 November 2015, whether a PSR was ordered. Work is ongoing to establish the most efficient way to advise the Crown Court of any issues identified and directions given by the magistrates to assist the PTPH.

The role of the Crown Court at PTPH

At an effective PTPH the defendant will be arraigned unless there is good reason not to.

In the event of a guilty plea the defendant should, if possible, be sentenced on that day.

In the event of a not guilty plea the court will;
- set the trial date;
- identify, so far as can be determined at that stage, the issues for trial;
- Consider with the parties the witness requirements that can be determined at that stage.
- provide a timetable for the necessary pre-trial preparation and give appropriate directions for an effective trial;
- make provision for any Further Case Management hearing that is actually required to take place at the time when it can be of maximum effectiveness. A FCMH will only be needed in complex cases.

Engagement between the parties and with the court should ensure that these elements can be achieved.

If the parties indicate that there is an issue that prevents arraignment such as a prospective application to dismiss or doubt as to fitness to plead the court will expect nevertheless to give directions to a trial date if it is needed but catering by way of a FCMH for the resolution of the issue – usually timed at around Stage 2 (see below)

What is the timing of the PTPH?

Cases sent to the Crown Court should be listed for PTPH within 28 days.

When cases have to be listed to take into account Saturdays, Bank holidays and court closure days then they should be adjourned beyond 28 days as opposed to being listed earlier than 28 days. This will give the prosecution maximum opportunity to ensure the case is properly prepared and the PTPH effective.

The National Implementation Team (NIT) has agreed that each Circuit may establish listing practices which result in the listing of a PTPH exceeding 28 days, so long as it is not more than 35 days from the sending provided that any such arrangements are consistent across the Circuit.

This will:
- accommodate smaller courts by allowing them to group their newly sent cases into hearings on only one or two days per week; or
- accommodate the listing patterns of larger court centres where the volume of sent cases are better handled if they

PTPH – INTRODUCTION AND GUIDANCE

can list a similar number of cases per day across the week;
or

- enable the trial advocate to attend the PTPH.

BCM timescales and processes **do not apply** to these exceptional cases:

- Witnesses under 10 years;
- Section 28 hearings (pre recorded video cross examination of vulnerable witnesses being piloted in certain courts);
- Terrorism cases;
- Murder cases.

With the exception of terrorism cases which have their own specific process and expectations the other exceptional cases listed above should still be subject to BCM principles.

The NIT Working Group will produce detailed guidance to explain how these exception cases should be dealt with in the magistrates' court to avoid confusion with BCM.

Why the form? The form must be used for all cases sent to the Crown Court after 5th January 2016 where not guilty pleas are anticipated unless expressly exempted by the CrimPR or CrimPD.
The form is to be regarded as the primary record of orders made so that there is no room for error or dispute The form is intended to:

- gather necessary information from the parties;
- monitor the extent to which the prosecution provide information prior to the PTPH;
- Obtain a clear early indication of the prosecution witnesses likely to be required for trial.
- allow the court to make, record and distribute clear orders timetabling the preparation of the case for trial. This is particularly important as it will address the need for those who have to act upon the orders to know exactly what the judge ordered.
- allow the court to provide for further hearings when they are going to be necessary and most useful.

Judges are invited to make standard orders within a single national process. This is of great assistance to court users. Judges remain free to make bespoke orders where it is considered they are required as long as they are made within the PTPH structure. Time spent ensuring a clear set of case management orders at PTPH should allow the case to proceed without the need for additional hearings.

Using the PTPH form prior to DCS No less than 7 day before the PTPH the prosecution should prepare a form tailored to the number of defendants and send it electronically to the defence representatives. In single defendant cases the Defence should complete the information required and send it electronically to the Court AND the prosecutor in time that it can be available in electronic form for the Judge on the day of the hearing.

PTPH – INTRODUCTION AND GUIDANCE

In multi-handed cases the parties are encouraged to pass the form sequentially but it is accepted that this process can be complex. Therefore if the process would be less complex and more timely then it may be convenient for advocates to co-operate at court to complete a single form electronically or in exceptional cases the form can be completed on paper. If it is completed on paper please keep in mind that the document will be scanned for distribution.

After the hearing the court will make copies available to the parties (either electronically or on paper).

A form on the DCS

This is in preparation. This will enable the PTPH form to be edited within the system but will not be available until around **February 2016.**

The key features of this improved functionality will be:

- The PTPH form will be completed by the parties within the DCS, and it will be possible to do this simultaneously and collaboratively, thereby producing a single composite version. This is particularly helpful for multi-handed cases.
- The DCS will automatically record the time, date and the reason for any amendments to the form, thereby providing an audit trail.
- Any earlier versions of the form will be retained and can be viewed, if required.
- The final completed form may be viewed on the DCS.

It will be necessary to enable the system to deal with:

- A single case with multiple defendants
- A single defendant with many cases
- Merging and splitting cases.

The Officer in the Case will not have access to the DCS so a form completed on the DCS will have to be copied to the OIC by the CPS.

Until the editable PTPH form is available in the DCS the following process has been adopted by some early adopter areas:

- CPS complete their sections of the PTPH form and upload into Section S – PTPH Form. An email is sent to the defence advising the form has been uploaded, this should take place no later than 7 days prior to the PTPH hearing.
- Defence download the PTPH Form from DCS, complete their sections and upload into Section S – PTPH Form. There will be 2 versions of the form at this time, for assurance purposes both should be retained. It is recommended this is uploaded at least 1 day prior to the PTPH.
- The Judge will download the latest version of the PTPH Form and complete the necessary sections and at the end of the case will upload into Section S – PTPH Form for all parties to access.
- For more details see PTPH- Use in DCS – Interim Guidance.

PTPH – INTRODUCTION AND GUIDANCE

Unrepresented Defendants

Unrepresented defendants will not have access to the DCS. The prosecutor should provided a paper form with the usual prosecution materials and after the hearing the court must provided a paper copy of the final completed form.

Contact Information

This follows on the requirement that prosecution and defence seek to identify case owners who will engage with each other at the earliest opportunity. The provision of contact information is vital to allow proper communication between participants. The form expressly reminds participants of their duties under the CrimPR. Individual names are required but it is acceptable to provide group email addresses provided they are properly monitored and acted upon. Parties must ensure effective cover for sickness or absence.

What the Prosecution will serve prior to the PTPH

The usefulness of the PTPH depends on:
- The lodging no less than seven days prior to the PTPH of a draft indictment; and
- service prior to the hearing of the principal parts of the prosecution case then available. The summary required will, in police cases, usually be the MG5. The prosecution material is to be served:
  - If the defendant is on bail – by the sending hearing in the Magistrates' Court;
  - If the defendant is in custody – no less than seven days before the PTPH.

Details of what is expected to be served are set out in the CrimPD 3A.12 and 3A.20 and a breakdown appears in the form so that compliance can be monitored.

There may be good reasons why the prosecution has not served all the materials listed prior to the PTPH but the court will usually expect to proceed with the hearing rather than adjourn it.

What if the Defendant decides to plead guilty?

The form is intended for those who will be pleading not guilty.

If, after sending, the defendant decides to plead guilty the defendant should not wait for the PTPH but instead inform the court and, if so advised, apply for the preparation of a Fast Delivery Pre-sentence report, or a Standard Delivery Pre-sentence report and/or a DRR assessment. In each case reasons why a report is justified are required. The court will consider that request administratively and may adjourn the case for a Plea and Sentence hearing on a date by which any report that has been ordered will be available. A court ordering the preparation of a Pre-sentence Report will usually direct a short format report unless good reason for a full report has been identified.

Four Stages

In most cases the court will be able to set just four dates for the parties to complete their pre-trial preparation and therefore the Judge or court will need only to insert the dates for the four stages

PTPH – INTRODUCTION AND GUIDANCE

and, if it would be useful, delete any orders that are not required. The draft orders have been grouped in a way intended to facilitate such an approach.

The setting of a multiplicity of dates is recognised as the enemy of compliance but where necessary individual dates can be set.

The four stages are:

- **Stage 1** – for the service of the bulk of prosecution materials. This date will ordinarily be 50 days (custody cases) or 70 days (bail cases) after the sending. This is in line with the timetable for the service of the prosecution case provided in the Crime and Disorder Act (Services of Prosecution Evidence) Regulations 2005. The court does not have power to abridge this time (without consent) but does have power to extend it.
- **Stage 2** – for the service of the defence response. This date will ordinarily be 28 days after Stage 1 reflecting the time provided for the service of a Defence Statement
- **Stage 3** – for the prosecution response to the Defence Statement and other defence items. This date will ordinarily be 14 or 28 days after Stage 2 depending on the anticipated date of trial.
- **Stage 4** - for the defence to provide final materials or make applications that will commonly arise out of prosecution disclosure.

In cases involving witnesses aged under 10 a different timetable will be required to conform to the Protocol to Expedite Cases of 19th Jan 2015.

The Court's Directions

The form includes standard directions. These have been approved by the Lord Chief Justice and will apply unless the Court expressly orders otherwise.

Directions are numbered and a two or three letter code appears alongside the directions as a visual prompt, and, following the re-numbering exercise this year, there are references to the Criminal Procedure Rules 2015.

In individual cases the court may revise the standard directions or make other bespoke orders as necessary. However the form is designed so that the numbering of standard orders will not alter.

It is accepted that individual courts have developed systems that have, for them, worked well and may find that not all of the elements of their current systems are present in this form. However the use of a national form with standard directions will greatly assist both prosecution and defence in developing systems to respond to them. This is why local forms and protocols can no longer continue to be used.

Non-contentious orders

There will be considerable savings of resources for all parties if non-contentious orders, such as some special measures orders, are made at the PTPH without further formality. At the early adopter and, if it would be useful, delete any orders that are not required. The draft orders have been grouped in a way intended to facilitate such an approach.

The setting of a multiplicity of dates is recognised as the enemy of compliance but where necessary individual dates can be set.

The four stages are:

- **Stage 1** – for the service of the bulk of prosecution materials. This date will ordinarily be 50 days (custody cases) or 70 days (bail cases) after the sending. This is in line with the timetable for the service of the prosecution case provided in the Crime and Disorder Act (Services of Prosecution Evidence) Regulations 2005. The court does not have power to abridge this time (without consent) but does have power to extend it.
- **Stage 2** – for the service of the defence response. This date will ordinarily be 28 days after Stage 1 reflecting the time provided for the service of a Defence Statement
- **Stage 3** – for the prosecution response to the Defence Statement and other defence items. This date will ordinarily be 14 or 28 days after Stage 2 depending on the anticipated date of trial.
- **Stage 4** - for the defence to provide final materials or make applications that will commonly arise out of prosecution disclosure.

In cases involving witnesses aged under 10 a different timetable will be required to conform to the Protocol to Expedite Cases of 19th Jan 2015.

The Court's Directions

The form includes standard directions. These have been approved by the Lord Chief Justice and will apply unless the Court expressly orders otherwise.

Directions are numbered and a two or three letter code appears alongside the directions as a visual prompt, and, following the re-numbering exercise this year, there are references to the Criminal Procedure Rules 2015.

In individual cases the court may revise the standard directions or make other bespoke orders as necessary. However the form is designed so that the numbering of standard orders will not alter.

It is accepted that individual courts have developed systems that have, for them, worked well and may find that not all of the elements of their current systems are present in this form. However the use of a national form with standard directions will greatly assist both prosecution and defence in developing systems to respond to them. This is why local forms and protocols can no longer continue to be used.

Non-contentious orders

There will be considerable savings of resources for all parties if non-contentious orders, such as some special measures orders, are made at the PTPH without further formality. At the early adopter

PTPH – INTRODUCTION AND GUIDANCE

but usually will do so only in one of the following cases:

- Class 1 cases[1];
- Class 2 cases which carry a maximum penalty of 10 years or more;
- Cases involving death by driving (whether dangerous or careless), or death in the workplace;
- Cases involving a vulnerable witness;
- Cases in which the defendant is a child or otherwise under a disability, or requires special assistance;
- Cases in which there is a corporate defendant or an unrepresented defendant;
- Cases in which the expected length of the trial is such that a FCMH is desirable and any case in which the trial is likely to last longer than four weeks;
- Cases in which expert evidence is to be introduced;
- Cases in which there are likely to be linked criminal and care directions in accordance with the 2013 Protocol.

The Court may also order a FCMH:

- Where the defendant requests a hearing to enter a guilty plea;
- Cases in which an application to dismiss or stay has been made;
- Cases in which arraignment has not taken place for any reason.

See CrimPD I. 3A.21

Issues such as Abuse; Fitness to Plead; Dismissal; Joinder and Severance

Where there is an abuse of process or fitness to plead issue or a possible dismissal application it will not be possible to arraign the defendant at PTPH. Experience at the early adopter courts is that the best way forward is to give full PTPH directions towards a trial but to make provision for a FCMH at the time of Stage 2 to resolve these issues. A similar approach may also be appropriate to resolve issues of joinder or severance.

Certificates of Readiness

Unless otherwise ordered the prosecution and each defendant must file a Certificate of Readiness (in standard form) no less than 28 days before the day set for trial (or the beginning of the warned list). The certificate is available on the MoJ Criminal Procedure Forms page.

This Certificate is of considerable importance to a structure which aims to minimise the number of court hearings. It follows that parties will be expected to give it careful thought.

The Certificates should be completed by each party (outside of DCS in MS Word format), then simply uploaded to the DCS (PTPH Section) and email notification given to the Court.

---

[1] For classification of cases see Criminal Practice Direction XIII Listing B: Classification.

PTPH – Introduction and Guidance – Revised December   2015 - Page 11 of 12

PTPH – INTRODUCTION AND GUIDANCE

Compliance

Parties are expected to comply with the timetables set. If, exceptionally, an element required by a particular stage is not available that is not to be regarded as a reason for not serving the remainder.

If a party had been directed to serve, for example, a special measures application by a certain date but later decides not to pursue such an application it is not necessary to file any formal notice that the matter will not be pursued.

Parties are reminded that all participants have a duty to prepare and conduct the case in accordance with the overriding objective; to comply with the Criminal Procedure Rules, Practice Directions and directions of the Court; and at once to inform the court and all parties of any significant failure (CrimPR1.2)

Generally parties are expected to resolve issues of compliance by engagement to resolve matters between themselves.

Administrative Directions

Where the parties have not succeeded in resolving matters between themselves and further directions are required from the court pre-trial the court will usually expect to give administrative directions without the need for an oral hearing.

Compliance Courts

If a party fails to comply with a case management direction then that party may be required to attend the court to explain the failure. This should be used when other means to gain compliance have failed and/or a pattern of failure is identified. Unless otherwise directed a defendant and other parties to the case will not usually be expected to attend such a hearing (CrimPD I 3A.23; 26-28)

The future – The Common Platform

The introduction of the PTPH and this form is a step towards electronic case management and the electronic monitoring of compliance which will be possible with the introduction of the Common Platform. This will have huge advantages for all. The use of a single national process with largely standard directions is essential to the future development of systems for the court, prosecution and defence that work one with another.

Improving the Form

Court users who would like to propose adjustments to the form or to suggest additional, or re-phrased, standard directions are encouraged to make suggestions to BCM.info@judiciary.gsi.gov.uk.

> Signed: Lord Chief Justice
>
> Senior Presiding Judge
>
> President

D-2

FORM - PTPH NG 1

PLEA AND TRIAL PREPARATION HEARING
PARTIES PRE-HEARING INFORMATION FORM
The pre-hearing information form must be completed for all cases sent to the Crown Court
where a trial is anticipated unless the case is expressly exempted by the CrimPR or CrimPD.

Crown Court at:		T:		PTI URN:	

	Defendant	DOB	Principal Charge(s)	Remand Status	Custody Time Limit	
D1				☐Unconditional Bail ☐Conditional Bail ☐ Custody ☐Youth Det. Remand		

	Real Issues and Time Estimate: Defence to set out below, so far as known, the real issues in the case - CrimPR 3.2;3.3;3.11- and provide provisional time estimate for overall trial length	*Streamlined Forensic Reports:* Are the conclusions of any served Streamlined Forensics Report (SFR1) admitted as fact. If not identify the disputed issues concerning that conclusion? CrimPR 19.3. Make clear what is admitted and what is not admitted.
D1		Choose Disputed Issues:

Other Proceedings:	
Particulars of any associated CRIMINAL proceedings?	
Particulars of any linked FAMILY proceedings?	

Contact Information:

The parties must provide the information required below at the PTPH or if not then available it must promptly be provided to the court and other parties in writing. The court and other parties must be informed of any change and effective cover must be provided for sickness or absence. Legal professionals and investigators must provide CJSM emails. The names of individuals must be given but it is acceptable to provide group email addresses provided that they are effectively monitored and acted upon.

If the prosecution or defence have not allocated a trial advocate then the advocate at a hearing or, the prosecution Reviewing Lawyer or the defence solicitor is required to respond to issues in place of the trial advocate.

Court Case Progression	*Name:*	*Phone:*	*Email:*
Case Progression Officer:			

Prosecution Information	*Name:*	*Phone:*	*Email:*
Advocate at PTPH			
Advocate for trial			
Reviewing Lawyer			
Case Progression Officer (usually Paralegal)			
Officer in the Case (or equivalent)			

Defence Information		*Name and Address for Service:*	*Phone:*	*CJSM Email for service:*
D1	Defence Solicitors (or unrepresented defendant)			
	Case Progression Officer			
	Funding – Tick ☑	Private Funding ☐; Legal Rep applied for ☐; Legal Rep Order granted ☐ or Unrepresented ☐		
		Name:	*Phone:*	*CJSM Email:*
	Advocate at PTPH			
	Advocate for trial			

STATE OF PREPARATION AT PTPH

PROSECUTION		Yes/No/N/A	*If not yet served they can be served by/Notes:*
IND	Draft Indictment	*Choose*	
SUM	Summary of circumstances of the offence(s) and of any account given by defendant(s) in interview (this may be in Form MG5).	*Choose*	
EVI	Statements identified by prosecution as being of importance for the purpose of plea and initial case management.	*Choose*	
EVI	Exhibits identified by prosecution as being of importance for the	*Choose*	

FORM - PTPH NG 1

	purpose of plea and initial case management.		
TV	Relevant CCTV that would be relied upon by prosecution at trial.	*Choose*	
EXP	Streamlined Forensic Report(s) or indication of scientific evidence that the prosecution is likely to introduce.	*Choose*	
EXP	Indication of medical evidence that the prosecution is likely to introduce.	*Choose*	
EXP	Indication of other expert evidence that the prosecution is likely to introduce.	*Choose*	
BC	Indication of bad character evidence to be relied on.	*Choose*	
HS	Indication of any hearsay evidence to be relied on.	*Choose*	
SM	Indication of special measures to be sought.	*Choose*	
CRO	Defendant's criminal record if any.	*Choose*	
VPS	Victim Personal Statement if any.	*Choose*	

DEFENCE		Yes/No/N/A	Particulars
ABU FTP	Are there preliminary issues such as Abuse of Process or Fitness to Plead?	*Choose*	
DMS	Is an application for Dismissal anticipated after time for service elapses?	*Choose*	
SEV	Is an application for Severance anticipated? CrimPR 3.21	*Choose*	
ARR	Can the defendant be arraigned at PTPH? If not set out the reason.	*Choose*	
ALT	Is the defendant willing to offer a plea to another offence and/or a plea on a limited basis?	*Choose*	
DS	Is a Defence Statement available at this stage?	*Choose*	
PNC	Where there are joint defendants does this defendant agree to cross-disclosure of lists of previous convictions (the PNC print out)	*Choose*	
DS	Where there are joint defendants does this defendant agree to cross-disclosure of Defence Statements (If agreed Defence Statements may be uploaded on the Joint DCS file, If not agreed they will have to be served separately)	*Choose*	

THIRD PARTY DISCLOSURE		Yes/No/N/A	Particulars
TPD	Is it believed that any third party holds potentially disclosible material?	*Choose*	
TPD	Will the prosecution be making enquiries to review that material?	*Choose*	

WITNESS REQUIREMENTS KNOWN AT PTPH: To be populated with names of prosecution witnesses known at PTPH.

Prosecution to indicate any witness who the Prosecution intend to call live regardless of Defence requirements (write "**P**" in the "Required by" column.

Each Defendant is required to identify which prosecution witnesses it can be predicted will be required to give evidence and those whose evidence is not disputed by that defendant (write "**D1**" etc as appropriate in the relevant column AND where a witness is required identify the relevant disputed issue for **that** defendant.

Parties are expected to provide a considered list and must not simply indicate "all witnesses". Where a witness is named but no statement has been provided parties are not expected to indicate requirements.

Witness Orders: The judge will review the witness requirements and the witness orders will be given in the Judge's

PLEA AND TRIAL PREPARATION HEARING FORM for DCS – Page 3 of 12

Orders therefore the names listed here must be repeated there. A witness will not be warned unless he or she is shown as required in the Judge's orders section. **Unless otherwise ordered the Defence must also complete the Standard Witness Table at Stage 2.**				
Name of witness	Required by:	Not disputed by:	Relevant disputed issue etc.	Mark if availability known ☐
				☐
				☐
				☐
				☐
				☐
				☐
				☐
				☐
				☐
				☐
				☐
				☐

PLEA AND TRIAL PREPARATION HEARING FORM for DCS – Page 4 of 12

FORM - PTPH NG 1

PLEA AND TRIAL PREPARATION HEARING JUDICIAL ORDERS This form is the primary record of all orders made at PTPH and all orders of the court at PTPH must be incorporated. Any subsequent variation must be by further order.	

Crown Court at:	T:	PTI URN:

PLEAS

1	Judicial warning and notes of judicial comment (if any)	☐ Credit for Plea
2	Pleas entered at PTPH:	
3	Reason if not arraigned at PTPH:	

PRE-ARRAIGNMENT FCMH IF REQUIRED	Date:		⏲ Time Estimate
4 **Pre-Arraignment Further Case Management Hearing to resolve ☑:** ☐ Abuse of Process; ☐ Dismissal application; ☐ Joinder/Severance. ☐ Other:		☐ Defendant not required ☐ Defendant must attend ☐ Suitable for PVL ☐ Application/skeleton and supporting materials by: ☐ Response and supporting materials by:	minutes hours

PRE-ARRAIGNMENT FCMH ON FITNESS TO PLEAD	Date:	☑	⏲ Time Estimate
☐ Fitness to Plead;		☐ Defendant not required ☐ Defendant must attend ☐ Suitable for PVL or Hospital Link ☐ Defence first medical report by: ☐ Prosecution to notify defence if the prosecution do OR do not intend to obtain medical report within 7 days or by: ☐ If Prosecution are to serve medical report then to be served by;	minutes hours

PLEA AND TRIAL PREPARATION HEARING FORM for DCS – Page 5 of 12

		☐ If Prosecution are not to serve medical report then defence to serve any second medical report by:

WITNESS REQUIREMENTS KNOWN AT PTPH and JUDGE'S WITNESS ORDERS THAT CAN BE MADE AT PTPH WITHOUT FURTHER FORMALITY

To be populated with witness names as in Part 1.

The Court has agreed that prosecution witnesses marked confirmed are likely to be required to give evidence.

Where it can be done justly without further formality the judge may make orders such as:

SMEAS – Special measures in which case the Court should specify which special measures are provided for;

SUMM – ordering the issue of a witness summons for the witness where grounds are made out;

UKLINK – ordering a UK live link <u>if available</u> – for example for police officers, other investigators, or experts to give evidence remotely;

SAT – ordering a satellite link from abroad.

Unless otherwise ordered the Defence must also complete the Standard Witness Table at Stage 2.

Name of witness	Confirmed by Court	SMEAS etc.	Details/Relevant disputed issue/ Judge's additional directions or observations

STANDARD ORDERS FOR WITNESSES

5	SM	Where Special measures are provided above:	In respect of any witness who has provided an ABE interview, the ABE interview as edited by agreement or by order of the court shall stand as that witness' evidence in chief unless otherwise ordered.
			Any witness who has provided an ABE interview shall view that interview in the week preceding the trial in the presence of the officer in the case (or equivalent) or other suitable police officer (or investigator equivalent) who shall record any comment the witness shall make and pass that record to the prosecutor.
			Any application for screens or live link shall be made after a court visit and shall include the witness' reasons for the preference.
			The attendance of any such witness at trial must be timetabled for the time when the witness is expected to commence examination.
6	WIT	Young or vulnerable witnesses CrimPR 18 & 3.9(7)	Young or vulnerable witnesses to which an Advocates' Gateway toolkit applies are to be examined and cross-examined in accordance with that toolkit unless that is superseded by specific ground rules.

PLEA AND TRIAL PREPARATION HEARING FORM for DCS – Page 6 of 12

7	SAT	Where provision is made for a witness by UKLINK or SAT:	Particulars of the link must be provided not less than three weeks before trial - CrimPD 18.23-4):
8	EXP	Expert witnesses – CrimPR 19	Expert witnesses of comparable disciplines must liaise and serve on the parties and the Court a statement of the points on which they agree and disagree with reasons no less than 14 days prior to the trial OR by such date as may be inserted here:
9		Other orders about witnesses:	

YJCEA 1999 s.28 CASES (where implemented)

10	A s.28 direction is made for the following witnesses and their ABE interviews shall stand as their evidence in chief and they shall be cross examined in advance of the trial: Witnesses:				
	The intermediary's report shall be filed by:				

		Date:	*Time:*		⏱ *Time Estimate*
11	Ground Rules Hearing			Ground Rules Form filed by: ☐ Defendant not required ☐ Defendant must attend ☐ Suitable for PVL ☐ The intermediary shall attend the Ground Rules Hearing	minutes hours
12	s.28 Cross-examination Hearing			☐ Defendant not required ☐ Defendant must attend	minutes hours

13	**Supplemental Orders for s.28 cases**
	Any intermediary shall attend the hearing.
	Date for witness to refresh their memory [date]:
	The officer in the case or another suitable police officer (or investigator equivalent) shall attend during the memory refreshing and make a note of anything said by the witness
	The judge (and advocates) shall meet the witness on [date}:...
	The advocates are not to meet the witness without the judge.
	s.4 Contempt of Court Act 1981 order has been made for ☐ the Ground Rules Hearing ☐ s.28 hearing
	The case is allocated to [Judge]: The future management of the case will be under the supervision of the trial judge.
	Other:

TRIAL	Date:		☑ *Facilities required:*		⏱ *Time Estimate*
14		☐ Fixture ☐ Backer ☐ Fixed Floater ☐ Warned List commencing.	☐ CCTV ☐ Live Link ☐ Satellite Link from: ☐ Interpreter for defendant(s) (language): ☐ Other		days weeks

PLEA AND TRIAL PREPARATION HEARING FORM for DCS – Page 7 of 12

FORM - PTPH NG 1

15		Certificates of Readiness to be filed by all parties (If no date is inserted then to be 28 days before trial date)	⊠

STAGE 1 - UNLESS INDIVIDUAL DATES ARE PROVIDED THE PROSECUTION SHALL SERVE THE FOLLOWING BY: Ordinarily 50 days (custody cases) or 70 days (bail cases) after sending.			**Date:**
		ITEM	Date :	Additional requirements/particulars/directions if any:

		ITEM	Date :	Additional requirements/particulars/directions if any:
16	EVI	Service of prosecution case.		To include making available ABE transcripts and recordings.
17	DCL	Initial disclosure (if not yet served).		
18	TV	CCTV relied upon.		To be served in format compatible with systems available at court. Otherwise party to provide system.
19	IV	Written record of defendant's taped Interview(s) (ROTI).		Unless otherwise ordered where there is a substantially "no comment" interview a short summary rather than a full transcript is sufficient. In any event the parties are expected to engage pre-trial to agree a summary or editing.
20	IV	Audio recording of defendant's tape interviews(s).		
21	999	999 call transcript(s) and recording(s) relied upon.		
22	TEL	Telephone records to be relied upon.		
23	FOR	Service of forensic statements (SFR 2 or MG11) that can be served by Stage 1 CrimPR 19.3.		This order only applies where, in relation to SFR1 (or other served summary of expert's conclusions), the defendant has identified on the PTPH form a conclusion that is not admitted and what the disputed issues are. The SFR2 or MG11 will be limited to those identified issues.
24	BC	Bad character notice(s) CrimPR 21		To include, if to be relied upon, evidence of facts of bad character.
25	HSY	Hearsay application(s) CrimPR 20		
26	SM	Special measures application(s) CrimPR 18		
27		Other:		
28		Other:		

THIRD PARTY DISCLOSURE: It is ordered:			**Date:**
	TPD	The following areas of third party material have been identified:	
29	TPD	Prosecution shall either make requests to third party, OR notify defence in writing that it does not intend to make any application for third party disclosure by:	
30	TPD	Prosecution to apply for any necessary third party disclosure summons by:	
	TPD	Prosecution to make any application required to the Family Court by:	
31	TPD	If the prosecution is to pursue third party disclosure then the prosecution must serve a report in writing on the outcome of efforts to identify potentially disclosable materials held by third	

PLEA AND TRIAL PREPARATION HEARING FORM for DCS – Page 8 of 12

FORM - PTPH NG 1

		parties and any ongoing enquiries not yet completed by:		
32	TPD	Any disclosable third party disclosure shall be served on the defence by:		
		Other:		

STAGE 2 - UNLESS INDIVIDUAL DATES ARE PROVIDED IT IS ORDERED THAT THE DEFENCE SHALL SERVE THE FOLLOWING BY: Ordinarily 28 days after Stage 1.				**DATE:**
		ITEM	*Date:*	*Additional requirements/particulars/directions:*
33	DS	Defence Statement. (In single defendant cases to be uploaded. In multi-defendant cases to be uploaded if cross-service was agreed and if not to be served separately)		To include particulars of alibi; and requests for disclosure, describing the material and explaining, by reference to the issues in the case, why it is disclosible.
34	WIT	Final list of prosecution witnesses required to give live evidence; defence witnesses and interpreter requirements.		To be submitted in the Standard Witness Table with time estimates.
35	FOR	Response to Summary of Expert Conclusions (SFR1)		Stating which, if any, of the expert's conclusions are admitted as fact and where a conclusion is not admitted stating what are the disputed issues concerning that conclusion. A defendant who did not identify such issues on the PTPH form and does not serve such a response is taken to admit as fact the conclusions of the summary (SFR1).
36	SM	Special measures application for defendant or defence witnesses.		Any reply from prosecution or other party to be served within 14 days.
37	ABE	List of editing requests or objections to ABE interview recording.		
38	IV	List of editing requests for the Defendant's ROTI (if any).		
39	BC	Response to prosecution bad character notice(s) - CrimPR 21.		
40	HSY	Response to prosecution hearsay application(s) – CrimPR 20.		
41	SM	Response to prosecution special measures application(s) - CrimPR 18.		
42	EXP	Defence expert evidence to be relied upon - CrimPR 19.		
43		Other:		
44		Other:		

STAGE 3 – UNLESS INDIVIDUAL DATES ARE PROVIDED IT IS ORDERED THAT THE PROSECUTION SHALL SERVE THE FOLLOWING BY: Ordinarily 14 or 28 days after Stage 2			**DATE:**
	ITEM	*Date for Service*	*Additional requirements/particulars/directions:*

PLEA AND TRIAL PREPARATION HEARING FORM for DCS – Page 9 of 12

45	DCL	Further disclosure.		Items required to be disclosed under CPIA resulting from or requested by the Defence Statement.
46	EVI	Further evidence to be relied upon that could not be served by Stage 1.		
47	FOR	Forensic science statements (SFR2 or MG11) required as a result of the Defence response to a summary of conclusions (SFR1) - CrimPR 19.3		
48	EXP	Expert medical evidence.		
49	EXP	Psychiatric evidence.		
50	EXP	Other (specify) expert evidence.		
51	SAT	Satellite/Live link application(s) CrimPD 18.23-24		
52	TEL	Cell site analysis.		
53	INT	Intermediary report(s) with draft specific Ground Rules if required. CrimPR 18 & 3.9(7)		For Witness:
54		Other:		
55		Other:		

STAGE 4 – UNLESS INDIVIDUAL DATES ARE GIVEN IT IS ORDERED THAT THE DEFENCE SHALL SERVE THE FOLLOWING BY: Ordinarily 14 or 28 days after Stage 3.				DATE:
		ITEM	*Date:*	*Additional requirements/particulars/directions:*
56	DCL	Complaint about prosecution non-disclosure		To comply with s.8 CPIA and CrimPR 15.5.
57	DCL	Application(s) for witness summons for Third Party Disclosure if the prosecution indicates at PTPH that it will not be pursuing any TPD issues OR any Defendant is dissatisfied with the outcome of prosecution enquiries.		To comply with CrimPR 17.5
58	EXP	Defence expert evidence to be relied upon that could not be served by Stage 2 - CrimPR 19		
59	BC	s.100 or 101 bad character of non-defendant application - CrimPR 21		Any reply from prosecution or other party to be served within 14 days
60	SXB	s.41 Evidence of sexual behaviour application - CrimPR 22		Any reply from prosecution or other party to be served within 14 days
61	SM	Response to prosecution intermediary Report(s) - CrimPR 18		
62	INT	Intermediary report for defendant or defence witnesses with draft Ground Rules		Any reply from prosecution or other party to be served within 14 days

PLEA AND TRIAL PREPARATION HEARING FORM for DCS – Page 10 of 12

FORM - PTPH NG 1

45	DCL	Further disclosure.		Items required to be disclosed under CPIA resulting from or requested by the Defence Statement.
46	EVI	Further evidence to be relied upon that could not be served by Stage 1.		
47	FOR	Forensic science statements (SFR2 or MG11) required as a result of the Defence response to a summary of conclusions (SFR1) - CrimPR 19.3		
48	EXP	Expert medical evidence.		
49	EXP	Psychiatric evidence.		
50	EXP	Other (specify) expert evidence.		
51	SAT	Satellite/Live link application(s) CrimPD 18.23-24		
52	TEL	Cell site analysis.		
53	INT	Intermediary report(s) with draft specific Ground Rules if required. CrimPR 18 & 3.9(7)		For Witness:
54		Other:		
55		Other:		

STAGE 4 – UNLESS INDIVIDUAL DATES ARE GIVEN IT IS ORDERED THAT THE DEFENCE SHALL SERVE THE FOLLOWING BY: Ordinarily 14 or 28 days after Stage 3.			DATE:	
		ITEM	Date:	Additional requirements/particulars/directions:
56	DCL	Complaint about prosecution non-disclosure		To comply with s.8 CPIA and CrimPR 15.5.
57	DCL	Application(s) for witness summons for Third Party Disclosure if the prosecution indicates at PTPH that it will not be pursuing any TPD issues OR any Defendant is dissatisfied with the outcome of prosecution enquiries.		To comply with CrimPR 17.5
58	EXP	Defence expert evidence to be relied upon that could not be served by Stage 2 - CrimPR 19		
59	BC	s.100 or 101 bad character of non-defendant application - CrimPR 21		Any reply from prosecution or other party to be served within 14 days
60	SXB	s.41 Evidence of sexual behaviour application - CrimPR 22		Any reply from prosecution or other party to be served within 14 days
61	SM	Response to prosecution intermediary Report(s) - CrimPR 18		
62	INT	Intermediary report for defendant or defence witnesses with draft Ground Rules		Any reply from prosecution or other party to be served within 14 days

PLEA AND TRIAL PREPARATION HEARING FORM for DCS – Page 10 of 12

		Statement may count against the Defendant
		☐ Failure to attend is a separate offence
		☐ Trial in absence in which case advocates may withdraw
		☐ Other:

Parties are reminded that:

All participants have a duty to prepare and conduct the case in accordance with the overriding objective; to comply with the CrimPR, practice directions and directions of the court; and at once to inform the court and all parties of any significant failure - CrimPR1.2.

Prosecution and Defence Case Progression Officers are reminded of their duties to monitor compliance with directions; make sure the court is kept informed of events that may affect the progress of the case; make sure that he or she can be contacted promptly about the case during ordinary business hours; act promptly and reasonably in response to communications about the case and, if he or she will be unavailable appoint a substitute to fulfil his or her duties and inform the other Case Progression Officers - CrimPR3.4.

Parties must actively assist the court to fulfil the overriding objective and engage with other parties to further the overriding objective without or if necessary with a direction - CrimPR3.3. Provided they promptly inform the court Case Progression Officer parties may agree to vary a time limit fixed by a direction if the variation will not affect the date of any hearing that has been fixed or significantly affect the progress of the case in any other way -CrimPR 3.7

After the hearing Case Progression Officers and OICs must ensure that they receive and act upon the orders made.

JUDICIAL SIGNATURE Where the Judge him or herself has made the entries on the DCS it is not necessary to enter a name	
73	HHJ/Recorder:	Date:

HOW TO USE
THE ONLINE PTPH FORM

The ONLINE PTPH form will be available for use from 10 March 2016

Introduction and Guidance December 2015

This guidance is supplemental to the PTPH Introduction and Guidance Notes updated in December 2015. That document outlines the elements of BCM and the principles behind the PTPH and can be found on the MoJ forms site here https://www.justice.gov.uk/courts/procedure-rules/criminal/forms-2015
Guidance on how to use the PTPH form within the DCS can be found at: https://www.gov.uk/government/uploads/system/uploads/attachment_data/file/506930/crown-court-digital-case-system-user-guide-manage-pre-trial-preparation-form.pdf

What is changing

The new form will be much easier to use, particularly in multi-defendant cases, and the opportunity has been taken to draw on the experiences of the early adopters to re-order and improve the form. The key changes are:

- The online form does not need to be downloaded and uploaded. Parties and the court can complete information within the DCS – even simultaneously.
- The form can be auto-populated with information from the CPS computers improving speed and accuracy.
- Some more information is required from the parties – this reflects issues that arose with the early adopters.
- The court's section has been re-ordered the better to reflect the sequence of events during a PTPH. Some of the standard orders have been revised and additional orders added following requests from the early adopters. These are explained in more detail below.

What about non-DCS courts or non-DCS prosecutors?

Although non-DCS courts will not be able to use the online form the CPS will put into use the revised format in place of the original. Non-CPS prosecutors, such as local authorities, will need to use the revised PTPH form available from the Ministry of Justice website at https://www.justice.gov.uk/courts/procedure-rules/criminal/forms-2015 or links there and circulate it by email. The site provides forms for up to 10 defendants. The revised form is generally referred to at the ONLINE form to distinguish it from the original PTPH form.

What about defendants

Defendants in person will not have access to the DCS. It follows that the CPS and other prosecutors will serve papers (including a part complete PTPH form) on paper.
The court will complete the online PTPH form with the orders and print a

PTPH – How to use the ONLINE form –11 March 2016 - Page 1 of 5

PTPH – HOW TO USE THE ONLINE FORM

in person? copy for defendants in person.

How to use the Online form

Users of the DCS will be familiar with the green menu of buttons. When the online PTPH form is available you will find a green button labelled PTPH. Click on that to bring up an editable PTPH screen. This has the same information as the "paper" form but is formatted differently to assist with online completion.

The Prosecutor will populate the prosecution information 7 days before the hearing. For the CPS this will involve completing the PTPH form in the CPS computer and uploading it into the PTPH section on DCS at which point the green PTPH button will become functional. This transfer of information will insert the names of the prosecution witnesses into the witness list in the parties section and the judge's section. In a multi-defendant case the form will be tailored to the number of defendants. (Non-DCS prosecutors will circulate a form tailored to the number of defendants by email).

Each defence representative should complete their information by two days before the hearing although changes can be made up to and during the hearing.

The court will complete the orders section including the stage dates.

At the end of the hearing the form – with its orders will be fixed as that represents the orders made by the court at that hearing.

There is a button on the editable PTPH screen that enables the user to download it as a PDF document and keep it in their own system. The finalized PTPH form will be viewable in the PTPH section of DCS and the PTPH Part 2 of the form will be viewable in the Judges' Orders section of the Bundle.

Emphasis on issues

The experience of the early adopters is that time spent identifying the real issues in the case was worthwhile. Parties are expected to identify the issues in very broad terms at the Magistrates' sending hearings and rather more information is to be expected by the time the PTPH form is completed. This can then inform the discussion about witness requirements.

Witness Requirements

Experience so far is that time spent sorting out the real witness requirements at PTPH is well worth while. It avoids a host of witnesses being warned when their evidence is not really in dispute and means that the witness warning teams can concentrate on those whose attendance is really necessary.

The revised form prompts and facilitates this examination with tables in the parties section and in the court's section.

PTPH – HOW TO USE THE ONLINE FORM

Parties: The table in the parties section will be pre-populated with names of witnesses by the prosecutor. Each defendant will have to indicate those witnesses who are required to attend for cross examination (in which case an indication of the relevant disputed issue must be provided) and which witnesses are not disputed.

The Court: The court will complete a parallel table in the second section. This will already have been pre-populated with the same list of witnesses as in the parties section and the court can then confirm which witnesses are to be warned for trial. On the same table the court can conveniently make specific orders for those witnesses where these can be made without further formality.

Thus a court might make a special measures order by inserting SMEAS and providing details of the type – eg ABE and Screens. Other orders that might be made are for the use of satellite links, UK remote links or for witness summonses.

It remains the case that defendants must still submit a **Standard Witness Table** at Stage 2. The defence cannot be expected to provide final witness requirements before they have had a chance to consider the case as served at Stage 1. It will be the Standard Witness Table that finally determines the witnesses to be called at trial.

Other changes

There are a range of other changes and additions. For example:

- There is provision for s.28 YJCEA 1999 hearings (pre-recorded cross-examination of vulnerable witnesses)
- The orders to identify issues with streamlined forensics and whether a full forensic report is needed have been improved.
- There are changes to the standard orders for vulnerable witnesses.
- Better provision is made for orders where fitness to plead is raised as an issue.
- More detailed orders are provided to address third party disclosure issues.
- There is provision for a judge, in an appropriate case, to direct the provision of, for example, an opening note, draft agreed facts or a jury bundle index.

Why is the form longer not shorter?

The form is longer than before. Each change has been proposed from the experience of the early adopters and the subject of debate and no addition has been made without careful scrutiny.

It is recognised that the court will necessarily take some time to complete the form but that will provide clear written orders to take the case towards trial.

Some courts are still concerned that it is necessary to put in a date for each of the staged orders individually. Even before we have dates inserted

PTPH – How to use the ONLINE form –11 March 2016 - Page 3 of 5

automatically users should keep in mind that inserting a single date for eg. Stage 1 applies to all the Stage 1 orders unless otherwise provided.

It assists the CPS if orders that are definitely able to be ruled out at PTPH are marked as such. This is because the CPS will be tracking all the directions in this section, unless otherwise indicated.

The response of the CPS, Investigators and Defence to the forms during the early adoption period has been extremely positive and it is clear that some time spent in court ensuing clear and clearly recorded orders is of immense value in securing accurate and timely compliance.

The form retains a fair amount of explanatory wording. The form is read and used by a range of people from experienced judges and advocates to clerical staff who may have limited knowledge of rules and procedures.

Why can't the PTPH orders be edited after the hearing ?

There will be occasions when either prosecution or defence make justified applications, for example to extend time. Often those will be dealt with by adjusting the stage dates to accommodate the need for extra time or by making individual orders. Many would like to do that by editing the dates on the PTPH orders rather than by stand alone order. At this stage that cannot be done. The reason is that it would not be workable or practicable for the CPS or Defence solicitors to pick up the alterations from an edited PTPH form.

Therefore any order made subsequent to the PTPH (including variations to the PTPH orders) must be made as a separate stand alone order.

Making further Orders

Any further orders must be prepared as a word document and entered into the "Orders" section

Where an order is made in the absence of the parties (such as an administrative order) and uploaded to the DCS the parties will need to be notified, usually by email, that the order has been made. (See CrimPR 4.6 on service).

The future

The working and content of the online PTPH form will be under review. One revision already being considered is that within the ORDERS section the stage dates (based on the date of sending and whether a defendant is in custody or on bail) will be auto- populated, although it will be capable of being changed by the judge as necessary. It is also hoped that there will be a green ORDERS button similar to that for PTPH which will make it easier for the judge/court to post written orders.

Expect a 6 monthly review. Piecemeal changes are not realistic because of

PTPH – How to use the ONLINE form –11 March 2016 - Page 4 of 5

PTPH – HOW TO USE THE ONLINE FORM

the linkage between the DCS and other computer systems.

In the future the Common Platform project will provide more opportunity for linkage, for more electronic case management and monitoring, and for more sophisticated listing.

Improving the Form

Court users who would like to propose adjustments to the form or to suggest additional, or re-phrased, standard directions are encouraged to make suggestions to BCM.info@judiciary.gsi.gov.uk.

<blockquote>
Signed: Lord Chief Justice

Senior Presiding Judge

President
</blockquote>

APPENDIX E
Crown Prosecution Service

I. CODE FOR CROWN PROSECUTORS

A. INTRODUCTION

The Crown Prosecution Service is the principal public prosecuting authority for England and **E-1** Wales and is headed by the Director of Public Prosecutions, who is to discharge his functions under the superintendence of the Attorney-General (Prosecution of Offences Act 1985, s.3(1)). The Attorney-General is accountable to Parliament for the Service.

The Crown Prosecution Service is a national organisation consisting of 42 areas. Each area is headed by a Chief Crown Prosecutor and corresponds to a single police force area, with one for London. It was set up in 1986 to prosecute cases investigated by the police.

Although the Crown Prosecution Service works closely with the police, it is independent of them. The independence of crown prosecutors is of fundamental constitutional importance. Casework decisions taken with fairness, impartiality and integrity help deliver justice for victims, witnesses, defendants and the public.

The Crown Prosecution Service co-operates with the investigating and prosecuting agencies of other jurisdictions.

The Director of Public Prosecutions is responsible for issuing a Code for Crown Prosecutors under section 10 of the Prosecution of Offences Act 1985, giving guidance on the general principles to be applied when making decisions about prosecutions. This is the seventh edition of the code and replaces all earlier versions. It was issued on January 28, 2013.

B. THE CODE

1. INTRODUCTION

1.1 The Code for Crown Prosecutors (the code) is issued by the Director of Public Prosecutions **E-2** (DPP) under section 10 of the Prosecution of Offences Act 1985. This is the seventh edition of the code and replaces all earlier versions.

1.2 The DPP is the head of the Crown Prosecution Service (CPS), which is the principal public prosecution service for England and Wales. The DPP operates independently, under the superintendence of the Attorney-General who is accountable to Parliament for the work of the CPS.

1.3 The code gives guidance to prosecutors on the general principles to be applied when making decisions about prosecutions. The code is issued primarily for prosecutors in the CPS, but other prosecutors follow the code either through convention or because they are required to do so by law.

1.4 In this code, the term "suspect" is used to describe a person who is not yet the subject of formal criminal proceedings; the term "defendant" is used to describe a person who has been charged or summonsed; and the term "offender" is used to describe a person who has admitted his or her guilt to a police officer or other investigator or prosecutor, or who has been found guilty in a court of law.

2. GENERAL PRINCIPLES

2.1 The decision to prosecute or to recommend an out-of-court disposal is a serious step that af- **E-3** fects suspects, victims, witnesses and the public at large and must be undertaken with the utmost care.

2.2 It is the duty of prosecutors to make sure that the right person is prosecuted for the right offence and to bring offenders to justice wherever possible. Casework decisions taken fairly, impartially and with integrity help to secure justice for victims, witnesses, defendants and the public. Prosecutors must ensure that the law is properly applied; that relevant evidence is put before the court; and that obligations of disclosure are complied with.

2.3 Although each case must be considered on its own facts and on its own merits, there are general principles that apply in every case.

2.4 Prosecutors must be fair, independent and objective. They must not let any personal views about the ethnic or national origin, gender, disability, age, religion or belief, political views, sexual orientation, or gender identity of the suspect, victim or any witness influence their decisions. Neither must prosecutors be affected by improper or undue pressure from any source. Prosecutors must always act in the interests of justice and not solely for the purpose of obtaining a conviction.

2.5 The CPS is a public authority for the purposes of current, relevant equality legislation. Prosecutors are bound by the duties set out in this legislation.

2.6 Prosecutors must apply the principles of the European Convention on Human Rights, in accordance with the Human Rights Act 1998, at each stage of a case. Prosecutors must also comply with any guidelines issued by the Attorney-General; with the *Criminal Procedure Rules* currently in force; and have regard to the obligations arising from international conventions. They must follow the policies and guidance of the CPS issued on behalf of the DPP and available for the public to view on the CPS website.

3. The Decision Whether to Prosecute

E-4

3.1 In more serious or complex cases, prosecutors decide whether a person should be charged with a criminal offence and, if so, what that offence should be. They make their decisions in accordance with this code and the DPP's guidance on charging. The police apply the same principles in deciding whether to start criminal proceedings against a person in those cases for which they are responsible.

3.2 The police and other investigators are responsible for conducting enquiries into any alleged crime and for deciding how to deploy their resources. This includes decisions to start or continue an investigation and on the scope of the investigation. Prosecutors often advise the police and other investigators about possible lines of inquiry and evidential requirements, and assist with pre-charge procedures. In large scale investigations the prosecutor may be asked to advise on the overall investigation strategy, including decisions to refine or narrow the scope of the criminal conduct and the number of suspects under investigation. This is to assist the police and other investigators to complete the investigation within a reasonable period of time and to build the most effective prosecution case. However, prosecutors cannot direct the police or other investigators.

3.3 Prosecutors should identify and, where possible, seek to rectify evidential weaknesses, but, subject to the threshold test (see section 5), they should swiftly stop cases which do not meet the evidential stage of the full code test (see section 4) and which cannot be strengthened by further investigation, or where the public interest clearly does not require a prosecution (see section 4). Although prosecutors primarily consider the evidence and information supplied by the police and other investigators, the suspect or those acting on his or her behalf may also submit evidence or information to the prosecutor via the police or other investigators, prior to charge, to help inform the prosecutor's decision.

3.4 Prosecutors must only start or continue a prosecution when the case has passed both stages of the full code test (see section 4). The exception is when the threshold test (see section 5) may be applied where it is proposed to apply to the court to keep the suspect in custody after charge, and the evidence required to apply the full code test is not yet available.

3.5 Prosecutors should not start or continue a prosecution which would be regarded by the courts as oppressive or unfair and an abuse of the court's process.

3.6 Prosecutors review every case they receive from the police or other investigators. Review is a continuing process and prosecutors must take account of any change in circumstances that occurs as the case develops, including what becomes known of the defence case. Wherever possible, they should talk to the investigator when thinking about changing the charges or stopping the case. Prosecutors and investigators work closely together, but the final responsibility for the decision whether or not a case should go ahead rests with the CPS.

3.7 Parliament has decided that a limited number of offences should only be taken to court with the agreement of the DPP. These are called consent cases. In such cases the DPP, or prosecutors acting on his or her behalf, apply the code in deciding whether to give consent to a prosecution. There are also certain offences that should only be taken to court with the consent of the Attorney-General. Prosecutors must follow current guidance when referring any such cases to the Attorney-General. Additionally, the Attorney-General will be kept informed of certain cases as part of his or her superintendence of the CPS and accountability to Parliament for its actions.

4. The Full Code Test

E-5

4.1 The full code test has two stages: (i) the evidential stage; followed by (ii) the public interest stage.

4.2 In most cases, prosecutors should only decide whether to prosecute after the investigation has been completed and after all the available evidence has been reviewed. However there will be cases where it is clear, prior to the collection and consideration of all the likely evidence, that the public interest does not require a prosecution. In these instances, prosecutors may decide that the case should not proceed further.

4.3 Prosecutors should only take such a decision when they are satisfied that the broad extent of the criminality has been determined and that they are able to make a fully informed assessment of the public interest. If prosecutors do not have sufficient information to take such a decision, the investigation should proceed and a decision taken later in accordance with the full code test set out in this section.

The evidential stage

4.4 Prosecutors must be satisfied that there is sufficient evidence to provide a realistic prospect of   **E-6** conviction against each suspect on each charge. They must consider what the defence case may be, and how it is likely to affect the prospects of conviction. A case which does not pass the evidential stage must not proceed, no matter how serious or sensitive it may be.

4.5 The finding that there is a realistic prospect of conviction is based on the prosecutor's objective assessment of the evidence, including the impact of any defence and any other information that the suspect has put forward or on which he or she might rely. It means that an objective, impartial and reasonable jury or bench of magistrates or judge hearing a case alone, properly directed and acting in accordance with the law, is more likely than not to convict the defendant of the charge alleged. This is a different test from the one that the criminal courts themselves must apply. A court may only convict if it is sure that the defendant is guilty.

4.6 When deciding whether there is sufficient evidence to prosecute, prosecutors should ask themselves the following:

Can the evidence be used in court?

Prosecutors should consider whether there is any question over the admissibility of certain evidence. In doing so, prosecutors should assess:

    (a) the likelihood of that evidence being held as inadmissible by the court; and

    (b) the importance of that evidence in relation to the evidence as a whole.

Is the evidence reliable?

Prosecutors should consider whether there are any reasons to question the reliability of the evidence, including its accuracy or integrity.

Is the evidence credible?

Prosecutors should consider whether there are any reasons to doubt the credibility of the evidence.

The public interest stage

4.7 In every case where there is sufficient evidence to justify a prosecution, prosecutors must go   **E-7** on to consider whether a prosecution is required in the public interest.

4.8 It has never been the rule that a prosecution will automatically take place once the evidential stage is met. A prosecution will usually take place unless the prosecutor is satisfied that there are public interest factors tending against prosecution which outweigh those tending in favour. In some cases the prosecutor may be satisfied that the public interest can be properly served by offering the offender the opportunity to have the matter dealt with by an out-of-court disposal rather than bringing a prosecution.

4.9 When deciding the public interest, prosecutors should consider each of the questions set out below in paragraphs 4.12(a) to (g) so as to identify and determine the relevant public interest factors tending for and against prosecution. These factors, together with any public interest factors set out in relevant guidance or policy issued by the DPP, should enable prosecutors to form an overall assessment of the public interest.

4.10 The explanatory text below each question in paragraphs 4.12(a) to (g) provides guidance to prosecutors when addressing each particular question and determining whether it identifies public interest factors for or against prosecution. The questions identified are not exhaustive, and not all the questions may be relevant in every case. The weight to be attached to each of the questions, and the factors identified, will also vary according to the facts and merits of each case.

4.11 It is quite possible that one public interest factor alone may outweigh a number of other factors which tend in the opposite direction. Although there may be public interest factors tending against prosecution in a particular case, prosecutors should consider whether nonetheless a prosecution should go ahead and those factors put to the court for consideration when sentence is passed.

4.12 Prosecutors should consider each of the following questions:

(a) *How serious is the offence committed?*

The more serious the offence, the more likely it is that a prosecution is required. When deciding the level of seriousness of the offence committed, prosecutors should include amongst the factors for consideration the suspect's culpability and the harm to the victim by asking themselves the questions at (b) and (c).

(b) *What is the level of culpability of the suspect?*

The greater the suspect's level of culpability, the more likely it is that a prosecution is required. Culpability is likely to be determined by the suspect's level of involvement; the extent to which the offending was premeditated and/or planned; whether they have previous criminal convictions and/or out-of-court disposals and any offending whilst on bail or whilst subject to a court order; whether the offending was or is likely to be continued, repeated or escalated; and the suspect's age or maturity (see paragraph (d) below for suspects under 18). Prosecutors should also have regard when considering culpability as to whether the suspect is, or was at the time of the offence, suffering from any significant mental or physical ill-health as in some circumstances this may mean that it is less likely that a prosecution is required. However, prosecutors will also need to consider how serious the offence was, whether it is likely to be repeated and the need to safeguard the public or those providing care to such persons.

(c) *What are the circumstances of and the harm caused to the victim?*

The circumstances of the victim are highly relevant. The greater the vulnerability of the victim, the more likely it is that a prosecution is required. This includes where a position of trust or authority exists between the suspect and victim. A prosecution is also more likely if the offence has been committed against a victim who was at the time a person serving the public. Prosecutors must also have regard to whether the offence was motivated by any form of discrimination against the victim's ethnic or national origin, gender, disability, age, religion or belief, sexual orientation or gender identity; or the suspect demonstrated hostility towards the victim based on any of those characteristics. The presence of any such motivation or hostility will mean that it is more likely that prosecution is required. In deciding whether a prosecution is required in the public interest, prosecutors should take into account the views expressed by the victim about the impact that the offence has had. In appropriate cases, this may also include the views of the victim's family. Prosecutors also need to consider if a prosecution is likely to have an adverse effect on the victim's physical or mental health, always bearing in mind the seriousness of the offence. If there is evidence that prosecution is likely to have an adverse impact on the victim's health it may make a prosecution less likely, taking into account the victim's views. However, the CPS does not act for victims or their families in the same way as solicitors act for their clients, and prosecutors must form an overall view of the public interest.

(d) *Was the suspect under the age of 18 at the time of the offence?*

The criminal justice system treats children and young people differently from adults and significant weight must be attached to the age of the suspect if they are a child or young person under 18. The best interests and welfare of the child or young person must be considered including whether a prosecution is likely to have an adverse impact on his or her future prospects that is disproportionate to the seriousness of the offending. Prosecutors must have regard to the principal aim of the youth justice system which is to prevent offending by children and young people. Prosecutors must also have regard to the obligations arising under the United Nations 1989 Convention on the Rights of the Child. As a starting point, the younger the suspect, the less likely it is that a prosecution is required. However, there may be circumstances which mean that notwithstanding the fact that the suspect is under 18, a prosecution is in the public interest. These include where the offence committed is serious, where the suspect's past record suggests that there are no suitable alternatives to prosecution, or where the absence of an admission means that out-of-court disposals which might have addressed the offending behaviour are not available.

(e) *What is the impact on the community?*

The greater the impact of the offending on the community, the more likely it is that a prosecution is required. In considering this question, prosecutors should have regard to how community is an inclusive term and is not restricted to communities defined by location.

(f) *Is prosecution a proportionate response?*

Prosecutors should also consider whether prosecution is proportionate to the likely outcome, and in so doing the following may be relevant to the case under consideration:

- the cost to the CPS and the wider criminal justice system, especially where it could be regarded as excessive when weighed against any likely penalty (prosecutors should not decide the public interest on the basis of this factor alone; it is essential that regard is also given to the public interest factors identified when considering the other questions in paragraphs 4.12(a) to (g), but cost is a relevant factor when making an overall assessment of the public interest);
- cases should be capable of being prosecuted in a way that is consistent with principles of effective case management; for example, in a case involving multiple suspects, prosecution might be reserved for the main participants in order to avoid excessively long and complex proceedings.

(g) *Do sources of information require protecting?*

In cases where public interest immunity does not apply, special care should be taken when proceeding with a prosecution where details may need to be made public that could harm sources of information, international relations or national security. It is essential that such cases are kept under continuing review.

5. The Threshold Test

5.1 The threshold test may only be applied where the suspect presents a substantial bail risk and **E-8** not all the evidence is available at the time when he or she must be released from custody unless charged.

When the threshold test may be applied

5.2 Prosecutors must determine whether the following conditions are met: **E-8a**
   (a) there is insufficient evidence currently available to apply the evidential stage of the full code test; and
   (b) there are reasonable grounds for believing that further evidence will become available within a reasonable period; and
   (c) the seriousness or the circumstances of the case justifies the making of an immediate charging decision; and
   (d) there are continuing substantial grounds to object to bail in accordance with the Bail Act 1976 and in all the circumstances of the case it is proper to do so.

5.3 Where any of the above conditions is not met, the threshold test cannot be applied and the suspect cannot be charged. The custody officer must determine whether the person may continue to be detained or released on bail, with or without conditions.

5.4 There are two parts to the evidential consideration of the threshold test.

The first part of the threshold test–is there reasonable suspicion?

5.5 Prosecutors must be satisfied that there is at least a reasonable suspicion that the person to be charged has committed the offence.

5.6 In determining this, prosecutors must consider the evidence then available. This may take the form of witness statements, material or other information, provided the prosecutor is satisfied that:
   (a) it is relevant; and
   (b) it is capable of being put into an admissible format for presentation in court; and
   (c) it would be used in the case.

5.7 If satisfied on this the prosecutor should then consider the second part of the threshold test.

The second part of the threshold test - can further evidence be gathered to provide a realistic prospect of conviction?

5.8 Prosecutors must be satisfied that there are reasonable grounds for believing that the continuing investigation will provide further evidence, within a reasonable period of time, so that all the evidence together is capable of establishing a realistic prospect of conviction in accordance with the full code test.

5.9 The further evidence must be identifiable and not merely speculative.

5.10 In reaching this decision prosecutors must consider:
   (a) the nature, extent and admissibility of any likely further evidence and the impact it will have on the case;
   (b) the charges that all the evidence will support;
   (c) the reasons why the evidence is not already available;
   (d) the time required to obtain the further evidence and whether any consequential delay is reasonable in all the circumstances.

5.11 If both parts of the threshold test are satisfied, prosecutors must apply the public interest stage of the full code test based on the information available at that time.

Reviewing the threshold test

E-9   5.12 A decision to charge under the threshold test must be kept under review. The evidence must be regularly assessed to ensure that the charge is still appropriate and that continued objection to bail is justified. The full code test must be applied as soon as is reasonably practicable and in any event before the expiry of any applicable custody time limit.

6. SELECTION OF CHARGES

E-10   6.1 Prosecutors should select charges which:

    (a) reflect the seriousness and extent of the offending supported by the evidence;

    (b) give the court adequate powers to sentence and impose appropriate post-conviction orders; and

    (c) enable the case to be presented in a clear and simple way.

6.2 This means that prosecutors may not always choose or continue with the most serious charge where there is a choice.

6.3 Prosecutors should never go ahead with more charges than are necessary just to encourage a defendant to plead guilty to a few. In the same way, they should never go ahead with a more serious charge just to encourage a defendant to plead guilty to a less serious one.

6.4 Prosecutors should not change the charge simply because of the decision made by the court or the defendant about where the case will be heard.

6.5 Prosecutors must take account of any relevant change in circumstances as the case progresses after charge.

7. OUT-OF-COURT DISPOSALS

E-11   7.1 An out-of-court disposal may take the place of a prosecution in court if it is an appropriate response to the offender and/or the seriousness and consequences of the offending.

7.2 Prosecutors must follow any relevant guidance when asked to advise on or authorise a simple caution, a conditional caution, any appropriate regulatory proceedings, a punitive or civil penalty, or other disposal. They should ensure that the appropriate evidential standard for the specific out-of-court disposal is met including, where required, a clear admission of guilt, and that the public interest would be properly served by such a disposal.

8. MODE OF TRIAL

E-12   8.1 Prosecutors must have regard to the current guidelines on sentencing and allocation when making submissions to the magistrates' court about where the defendant should be tried.

8.2 Speed must never be the only reason for asking for a case to stay in the magistrates' court. But prosecutors should consider the effect of any likely delay if a case is sent to the Crown Court, and the possible effect on any victim or witness if the case is delayed.

Venue for trial in cases involving youths

8.3 Prosecutors must bear in mind that youths should be tried in the youth court wherever possible. It is the court which is best designed to meet their specific needs. A trial of a youth in the Crown Court should be reserved for the most serious cases or where the interests of justice require a youth to be jointly tried with an adult.

9. ACCEPTING GUILTY PLEAS

E-12a   9.1 Defendants may want to plead guilty to some, but not all, of the charges. Alternatively, they may want to plead guilty to a different, possibly less serious, charge because they are admitting only part of the crime.

9.2 Prosecutors should only accept the defendant's plea if they think the court is able to pass a sentence that matches the seriousness of the offending, particularly where there are aggravating features. Prosecutors must never accept a guilty plea just because it is convenient.

9.3 In considering whether the pleas offered are acceptable, prosecutors should ensure that the interests and, where possible, the views of the victim, or in appropriate cases the views of the victim's family, are taken into account when deciding whether it is in the public interest to accept the plea. However, the decision rests with the prosecutor.

9.4 It must be made clear to the court on what basis any plea is advanced and accepted. In cases where a defendant pleads guilty to the charges but on the basis of facts that are different from the prosecution case, and where this may significantly affect sentence, the court should be invited to hear evidence to determine what happened, and then sentence on that basis.

9.5 Where a defendant has previously indicated that he or she will ask the court to take an offence into consideration when sentencing, but then declines to admit that offence at court, prosecutors will consider whether a prosecution is required for that offence. Prosecutors should explain to the defence advocate and the court that the prosecution of that offence may be subject to further review, in consultation with the police or other investigators wherever possible.

9.6 Particular care must be taken when considering pleas which would enable the defendant to avoid the imposition of a mandatory minimum sentence. When pleas are offered, prosecutors must also bear in mind the fact that ancillary orders can be made with some offences but not with others.

10. Reconsidering a Prosecution Decision

10.1 People should be able to rely on decisions taken by the CPS. Normally, if the CPS tells a **E-12b** suspect or defendant that there will not be a prosecution, or that the prosecution has been stopped, the case will not start again. But occasionally there are reasons why the CPS will overturn a decision not to prosecute or to deal with the case by way of an out-of-court disposal or when it will restart the prosecution, particularly if the case is serious.

10.2 These reasons include:

(a) cases where a new look at the original decision shows that it was wrong and, in order to maintain confidence in the criminal justice system, a prosecution should be brought despite the earlier decision;

(b) cases which are stopped so that more evidence which is likely to become available in the fairly near future can be collected and prepared; in these cases, the prosecutor will tell the defendant that the prosecution may well start again;

(c) cases which are stopped because of a lack of evidence but where more significant evidence is discovered later; and

(d) cases involving a death in which a review following the findings of an inquest concludes that a prosecution should be brought, notwithstanding any earlier decision not to prosecute.

© Crown Copyright 2013

C. Authorities

Charging of youths

Whereas the code for crown prosecutors requires consideration to be given to the interests of a **E-12c** child or young person when deciding whether it is in the public interest to prosecute (see now para. 4.12(d), *ante*, E-7), there is no requirement that a crown prosecutor should obtain a risk assessment from the youth offending services or that he should contact the potential defendant's school: *R. (A.) v. South Yorkshire Police and CPS*, 171 J.P. 465, DC.

In *D. and B. v. Commr of Police for the Metropolis, CPS, Croydon JJ.* [2008] A.C.D. 47, DC, it was held that it was permissible for a crown prosecutor to decide that the combination of the seriousness of an offence and the public interest warranted prosecution, despite the fact that the particular circumstances of the offence would normally, in accordance with the guidance issued under section 65 of the CDA 1998, be such as to justify only a final warning.

Charging victims of human trafficking

What follows will have to be considered in the light of the defence provided by section 45 of **E-12d** the Modern Slavery Act 2015 (§ 19-464 in the main work).

Where it is possible that a defendant or potential defendant is a victim of human trafficking, a prosecutor should take cognisance of the CPS guidance on (i) the prosecution of defendants charged with immigration offences who might be victims of trafficking, and (ii) the prosecution of young offenders charged with offences who might be such victims; in particular, under (i), when deciding whether to prosecute, or to continue to prosecute, a "credible trafficked victim" for immigration offences, prosecutors should consider whether this would serve the public interest; and under (ii), a case should be discontinued on evidential grounds where there is clear evidence that a youth has a credible defence of duress, but, if the evidence is less certain, further details should be sought from the police and youth offender teams; the defence, on the other hand, should make inquiries wherever there is credible material showing that the defendant might have been a trafficked victim, especially if the client is young; as a signatory to the Council of Europe Convention on Action against Trafficking in Human Beings, the United Kingdom is required to identify and protect victims of trafficking, and, whereas the CPS guidance supports the purpose of the convention, a trial which had failed to have proper regard to it was not fair, either under the principles of the common law or under the principles enshrined in the ECHR: *R. v. O., The Times*, October 2, 2008, CA ([2008] EWCA Crim. 2835).

R. v. O. and the issues arising from it were further considered in *R. v. M. (L.), B. (M.) and G. (D.); R. v. Tabot; R. v. Tijani* [2011] 1 Cr.App.R. 12, CA. It was held that one way in which the duty under Article 26 of the Council of Europe Convention (to avoid the imposition of penalties on victims of human trafficking for their involvement in unlawful activities to the extent that they were compelled to become so involved) is met in England and Wales, is by means of the guidance given to prosecutors considering whether charges should be brought against those who are or may be victims of trafficking (the court pointed out that whilst the guidance is now set out in the context of immigration offences only, it should be taken to apply whatever the nature of the allegation). The effect of the CPS's guidance, according to the court, is to require of prosecutors a three-stage exercise, asking, first, whether there is reason to believe that the person has been trafficked, secondly, whether there is clear evidence of a common law defence (in which case, any proceedings will be discontinued on evidential grounds) and, thirdly, where there is no such evidence, but the offence may have been committed as a result of compulsion arising from the trafficking, whether the public interest requires a prosecution. It was said that Article 26 does not require a blanket immunity from prosecution for trafficked victims, and that there will normally be no reason not to prosecute a victim of trafficking if the offence appears to have been committed out-with any reasonable nexus of compulsion occasioned by the trafficking. The court said that material considerations for the prosecutor when deciding whether to pursue a prosecution will be the gravity of the offence, the degree of continuing compulsion and the alternatives reasonably available to the defendant. As to this case, see also § 17-119 in the main work.

R. v. O. and *R. v. M. (L.), B. (M.) and G. (D.); R. v. Tabot; R. v. Tijani* were further considered in *R. v. N. (A.); R. v. Le* [2012] 1 Cr.App.R. 35, CA. It was held that: (i) implementation of Article 26 is normally achieved by the proper exercise of the prosecutorial discretion which enables the Crown, however strong the evidence, to decide that it would be inappropriate to prosecute, or to continue with the prosecution of, a defendant who is unable to advance duress as a defence, but who falls within the protective ambit of that article; this requires a judgment to be made in the light of all the available evidence; the responsibility is not that of the court but of the prosecution; but the court may intervene if its process is abused by using the "ultimate sanction" of a stay; the burden of establishing an improper exercise of the discretion rests on the defendant; that the context is the United Kingdom's convention obligation does not involve the creation of any new principles; apart from the specific jurisdiction to stay proceedings, the court may also, in the exercise of its sentencing responsibilities, implement Article 26 in the language of the article itself, by discharging the defendant absolutely or conditionally; (ii) the only publication likely to be relevant to an inquiry into an alleged abuse is the CPS's guidance on human trafficking and smuggling as it was in force at the time when the relevant decisions were made; unless it is to be argued that the guidance itself is open to question because it has failed to keep itself regularly updated in light of developing knowledge, for the purposes of the court considering an alleged abuse for which the prosecution are responsible, it is that guidance that should be the starting, and in the overwhelming majority of cases, the finishing point; (iii) expert evidence is unlikely to assist on the issue of the correctness of the decision to prosecute; (iv) a defendant has one opportunity to give his instructions to his legal advisers; it is only most exceptionally that the court would, on appeal, consider it appropriate to allow a defendant to advance fresh instructions about the facts; and there is no special category of exceptionality in the context of Article 26; and (v) an abuse argument founded on the convention that is advanced long after conviction is most unlikely to succeed on the basis that subsequent events show that, if the decision whether to prosecute were to be taken now, the result might have been different from the decision actually taken in the light of the standards and guidance existing at the time it was taken.

These issues were further considered in *R. v. L. (C.); R. v. N. (H.V.); R. v. N. (T.H.); R. v. T. (H.D.) (Children's Commr for England and Equality and Human Rights Commission Intervening)* [2013]

2 Cr.App.R. 23, CA. It was held that: (i) whereas Article 8 of European Parliament and Council Directive 2011/36/EU obliges member states to "take the necessary measures to ensure that competent national authorities are entitled not to prosecute or impose penalties on victims of trafficking ... for their involvement in criminal activities which they have been compelled to commit as a direct consequence of being subjected" to trafficking, the courts will give effect to this obligation by reviewing decisions to prosecute, staying inappropriate prosecutions and discharging defendants where prosecution was appropriate but punishment inappropriate; as to the review of the decision to prosecute, this is no mere *Wednesbury* review (*Associated Picture Houses Ltd v. Wednesbury Corporation* [1948] 1 K.B. 223, CA); the court must reach its own conclusion on the evidence presented to it; (ii) if it is found that the defendant is a victim of trafficking, the next question is the extent to which the offences with which he is charged were integral to, or consequent on, the exploitation of which he was the victim; in some cases the facts will show that he was under levels of compulsion that mean that, in reality, culpability was extinguished; if so, a stay is likely to be granted; in other cases, more likely in the case of a defendant who is no longer a child (18 plus), culpability may be diminished but nevertheless be significant; for these individuals, prosecution may well be appropriate, with due allowance to be made in any sentencing decision for their diminished culpability; in yet other cases, the fact that the defendant was a victim of trafficking will provide no more than a colourable excuse for criminality that is unconnected to and does not arise from their victimisation; (iii) as to the question whether the defendant was indeed a victim of trafficking, where there has been a referral to one of the two competent authorities (the U.K. Border Agency and the U.K. Human Tracking Centre), if their conclusion is that the defendant is a victim of trafficking, the court is likely to adopt that view although it is not bound by it, as it is the court that has the ultimate responsibility for making the decision with all the relevant evidence bearing on the issues of trafficking, exploitation, age and culpability being addressed; while there is no obligation to seek assistance from experts in the field, the court may adjourn for further information on the subject, and indeed may require the assistance of various authorities; and (iv) where the defendant is under 18, his best interests are not the only consideration, but they are a primary consideration; and where there is any doubt about whether or not the defendant is under that age, "due inquiry" must be made (CYPA 1933, s.99(1) (§ 19-412 in the main work)); this requires much more than superficial observation of the defendant in the dock; the court must be provided with all the relevant evidence that bears on the issue of age; if, at the end of the inquiry, his age remains in doubt and there are reasons to believe that he is under the age of 18, he must be presumed to be under that age.

The cases discussed in the three preceding paragraphs were all further considered in *R. v.* ★ *Joseph and conjoined appeals, ante*, § 19-464.

The full code test/evidential stage

When applying the "realistic prospect of conviction" test, a prosecutor should adopt a "merits **E-12e** based" approach, imagining himself to be the fact finder and asking himself, whether, on balance, the evidence is sufficient to merit a conviction, taking into account what he knows about the defence case, rather than a predictive "bookmaker's" approach, based on past experience of similar cases; questions of how a jury are likely to see a case are not relevant at this stage but at a later stage, under the public interest test in paragraphs 5.6 to 5.13 of the code: *R. (F.B.) v. DPP* [2009] 1 Cr.App.R. 38, DC. As to this case, see also §§ 1-337, 16-48 in the main work.

For a decision of the Grand Chamber of the European Court of Human Rights in relation to the evidential test, see *Armani Da Silva v. U.K., The Times*, April 26, 2016, ECtHR (Grand Chamber) (§ 1-420 in the main work)

II. LEGAL GUIDANCE AND CHARGING STANDARDS

Apart from the code for crown prosecutors, the CPS has prepared legal guidance to prosecu- **E-13** tors and caseworkers in relation to many criminal offences and procedural issues. It has never been suggested that such guidance has the force of law, or even parity of standing with the code. It is merely, in the words of the CPS website (where it is available to the public), "an aid to guide crown prosecutors and associate prosecutors in the use of their discretion in making decisions in cases", which "does not create any rights enforceable at law, in any legal proceedings", and is subject to the principles as set out in the code for crown prosecutors.

E-14   Incorporated within the guidance are various "charging standards" for various offences or groups of offences, such as offences against the person, driving offences, drug offences, public order offences and theft. They contain a mixture of propositions of law (as to the ingredients of the various offences, maximum penalties, available alternative verdicts, etc.) and guidance as to the various factors that should be taken into consideration in deciding which offence to charge. The standards emphasise that they:

    (a) are not to be used in the determination of any pre-charge decision, such as the decision to arrest;

    (b) do not override any guidance issued on the use of appropriate alternative forms of disposal short of charge, such as cautioning;

    (c) do not override the principles set out in the code for crown prosecutors;

    (d) do not override the need for consideration to be given in every case as to whether a charge or prosecution is in the public interest;

    (e) do not override particular policy guidance involving hate crimes; and

    (f) do not remove the need for each case to be considered on its individual merits or fetter the discretion of the police to charge and the CPS to prosecute the most appropriate offence depending on the particular facts of the case in question.

The following recitation of general charging principles is common to all the standards:

    (a) the charge or charges preferred should accurately reflect the extent of the defendant's involvement and responsibility, thereby allowing the courts the discretion to sentence appropriately;

    (b) the choice of charges should ensure the clear and simple presentation of the case, particularly where there is more than one defendant;

    (c) it is wrong to encourage a defendant to plead guilty to a few charges by selecting more charges than are necessary;

    (d) it is wrong to select a more serious charge which is not supported by the evidence in order to encourage a plea of guilty to a lesser allegation.

III. THE ROLE AND RESPONSIBILITIES OF THE PROSECUTION ADVOCATE

Foreword

E-15   The prosecution advocate plays an important public role and as such may be considered a cornerstone of an open and fair criminal justice system. The principles so well articulated by Farquharson L.J. and his committee as to the role of the prosecution advocate have served us well since they were published in 1986. However, the time has come for new guidance which, whilst building on the established principles, reflects the changes that have occurred in the criminal courts, at the Bar and within the Crown Prosecution Service over recent years.

    I welcome and commend the new Guidelines which, whilst not legally binding unless expressly approved by the Court of Appeal, nonetheless provide important practical guidance for practitioners involved in the prosecution process.

    Lord Woolf C.J.

Introduction

E-16   The work undertaken in 1986 by the committee chaired by Farquharson L.J. has, for over 15 years, provided valuable guidance as to role [*sic*] of the prosecution advocate and their relationship with the Crown Prosecution Service (CPS).

    However, the ever-evolving criminal justice system, changes at the Bar and developments in the CPS brought about by the implementation of Sir Iain Glidewell's Review, mean that the environment in which we all operate has radically changed since the original report was published.

    Whilst the principles established by Farquharson L.J.'s committee have been enormously helpful and will continue to apply, the time has come for new guidance that reflects the changes and emphasises the new relationship that is developing between CPS Areas and the local Bar.

The new Guidelines have therefore been developed to take account of the changes and are the result of the Bar and CPS working in partnership and in consultation with the judiciary, Bar Council and Law Society.

We commend the Guidelines as providing valuable guidance and a framework within which the Bar and the CPS can work effectively together.

Lord Goldsmith Q.C., Attorney General

David Calvert-Smith Q.C., Director of Public Prosecutions

1. Pre-trial preparation

Farquharson

(a) *It is the duty of prosecution counsel to read the Instructions delivered to him expeditiously and to advise or confer with those instructing him on all aspects of the case well before its commencement.*   **E-17**

1.1 The Crown Prosecution Service (CPS) will deliver instructions at a stage in the proceedings **E-18** that allows sufficient time for the prosecution advocate adequately to consider, prepare and advise on the evidence before the court hearing or draft/agree the indictment.

1.2 Where a CPS higher court advocate represents the prosecution at a Plea and Directions Hearing (PDH), the CPS will deliver instructions to the trial advocate no later than 10 working days after the date of the PDH.

1.3 The CPS will deliver instructions which:

    i. address the issues in the case including any strategic decisions that have been or may need to be made;

    ii. identify relevant case law;

    iii. explain the basis and rationale of any decision made in relation to the disclosure of unused material;

    iv. where practical, provide specific guidance or indicate parameters on acceptable plea(s); and

    v. where a case is an appeal either to the Crown Court from the magistrates' court or is before the Court of Appeal, Divisional Court or House of Lords, address the issues raised in the notice of appeal, case stated, application for judicial review or petition.

Action on receipt of instructions

1.4 On receipt of instructions the prosecution advocate will consider the papers and advise the **E-19** CPS, ordinarily in writing, or orally in cases of urgency where:

    i. the prosecution advocate forms a different view to that expressed by the CPS (or where applicable a previous prosecution advocate) on acceptability of plea;

    ii. the indictment as preferred requires amendment;

    iii. additional evidence is required;

    iv. there is an evidential deficiency (which cannot be addressed by the obtaining of further evidence) and, applying the Code for Crown Prosecutors, there is no longer a realistic prospect of conviction; or the prosecution advocate believes that it is not in the public interest to continue the prosecution;

    v. in order to expedite and simplify proceedings certain formal admissions should be made;

    vi. the prosecution advocate, having reviewed previous disclosure decisions, disagrees with a decision that has been made; or is not satisfied that he or she is in possession of all relevant documentation; or considers that he or she has not been fully instructed regarding disclosure matters;

    vii. a case conference is required (particularly where there is a sensitive issue, *e.g.* informant/ PII/ disclosure etc);

    viii. the presentation of the case to the court requires special preparation of material for the jury or presentational aids.

1.5 The prosecution advocate will endeavour to respond within five working days of receiving **E-20** instructions, or within such period as may be specified or agreed where the case is substantial or the issues complex.

1.6 Where the prosecution advocate is to advise on a specific aspect of the case other than 1.4 (i-viii), the advocate should contact the CPS and agree a realistic timescale within which advice is to be provided.

1.7 The prosecution advocate will inform the CPS without delay where the advocate is unlikely to be available to undertake the prosecution or advise within the relevant timescale.

1.8 When returning a brief, the advocate originally instructed must ensure that the case is in good order and should discuss outstanding issues or potential difficulties with the advocate receiving the brief. Where the newly instructed advocate disagrees with a decision or opinion reached by the original advocate, the CPS should be informed so that the matter can be discussed.

Case summaries

E-21

1.9 When a draft case summary is prepared by the CPS, the prosecution advocate will consider the summary and either agree the contents or advise the CPS of any proposed amendment.

1.10 In cases where the prosecution advocate is instructed to settle the case summary or schedules, the document(s) will be prepared and submitted to the CPS without delay.

Case management plan

E-22

1.11 On receipt of a case management plan the prosecution advocate, having considered the papers, will contact the Crown Prosecutor within seven days, or such period as may be specified or agreed where the case is substantial or the issues complex, to discuss and agree the plan. The plan will be maintained and regularly reviewed to reflect the progress of the case.

Keeping the prosecution advocate informed

E-23

1.12 The CPS will inform the prosecution advocate of developments in the case without delay and, where a decision is required which may materially affect the conduct and presentation of the case, will consult with the prosecution advocate prior to that decision.

1.3 Where the CPS is advised by the defence of a plea(s) of guilty or there are developments which suggest that offering no evidence on an indictment or count therein is an appropriate course, the matter should always be discussed with the prosecution advocate without delay unless to do so would be wholly impracticable.

Victims and witnesses

E-24

1.14 When a decision whether or not to prosecute is based on the public interest, the CPS will always consider the consequences of that decision for the victim and will take into account any views expressed by the victim or the victim's family.

1.15 The prosecution advocate will follow agreed procedures and guidance on the care and treatment of victims and witnesses, particularly those who may be vulnerable or have special needs.

Appeals

E-25

1.16 Where the prosecution advocate forms a different view to that expressed by the CPS on the conduct/approach to the appeal, the advocate should advise the CPS within FIVE working days of receiving instructions or such period as may be specified or agreed where the case is substantial or the issues complex.

PDH and other preliminary hearings

E-26

1.17 The principles and procedures applying to trials as set out in the following paragraphs will be equally applicable where the prosecution advocate is conducting a PDH or other preliminary hearing.

2. Withdrawal of instructions

Farquharson

E-27

(b) *A solicitor who has briefed counsel to prosecute may withdraw his instructions before the commencement of the trial up to the point when it becomes impracticable to do so, if he disagrees with the advice given by Counsel or for any other proper professional reason.*

2.1 The CPS will consult and take all reasonable steps to resolve any issue or disagreement and will only consider withdrawing instructions from a prosecution advocate as a last resort.

2.2 If the prosecution advocate disagrees with any part of his or her instructions the advocate should contact the responsible Crown Prosecutor to discuss the matter. Until the disagreement has been resolved the matter will remain confidential and must not be discussed by the prosecution advocate with any other party to the proceedings.

"Proper professional reason"

E-28

2.3 The prosecution advocate will keep the CPS informed of any personal concerns, reservations or ethical issues that the advocate considers have the potential to lead to possible conflict with his or her instructions.

2.4 Where the CPS identifies the potential for professional embarrassment or has concerns about the prosecution advocate's ability or experience to present the case effectively to the court, the CPS reserves the right to withdraw instructions.

Timing

2.5 It is often difficult to define when, in the course of a prosecution it becomes impracticable to **E-29** withdraw instructions as circumstances will vary according to the case. The nature of the case, its complexity, witness availability and the view of the court will often be factors that will influence the decision.

2.6 In the majority of prosecutions it will not be practicable to withdraw instructions once the judge has called the case before the court as a preliminary step to the swearing of the jury.

2.7 If instructions are withdrawn, the prosecution advocate will be informed in writing and reasons will be given.

2.8 Instructions may only be withdrawn by or with the consent of the Chief Crown Prosecutor, Assistant Chief Crown Prosecutor, Head of a CPS Trials Unit or, in appropriate cases, Head of a CPS Criminal Justice Unit.

2.9 In relation to cases prosecuted by the CPS Casework Directorate, the decision may only be taken by the Director Casework or Head of Division.

3. Presentation and conduct

Farquharson

(c) *While he remains instructed it is for counsel to take all necessary decisions in the presentation and general* **E-30** *conduct of the prosecution.*

3.1 The statement at 3(c) applies when the prosecution advocate is conducting the trial, PDH or any other preliminary hearing, but is subject to the principles and procedures relating to matters of policy set out in section 4 below.

Disclosure of material

3.2 Until the conclusion of the trial the prosecution advocate and CPS have a continuing duty to **E-31** keep under review decisions regarding disclosure. The prosecution advocate should in every case specifically consider whether he or she can satisfactorily discharge the duty of continuing review on the basis of the material supplied already, or whether it is necessary to inspect further material or to reconsider material already inspected.

3.3 Disclosure of material must always follow the established law and procedure. Unless consultation is impracticable or cannot be achieved without a delay to the hearing, it is desirable that the CPS, and where appropriate the disclosure officer are consulted over disclosure decisions.

4. Policy decisions

Farquharson

(d) *Where matters of policy[1] fall to be decided after the point indicated in (b) above (including offering no* **E-32** *evidence on the indictment or on a particular count, or on the acceptance of pleas to lesser counts), it is the duty of Counsel to consult his Instructing Solicitor/Crown Prosecutor whose views at this stage are of crucial importance.*

(e) *In the rare case where counsel and his instructing solicitor are unable to agree on a matter of policy, it is, subject to (g) below, for prosecution counsel to make the necessary decisions.*

Policy issues arising at trial

4.1 The prosecution advocate should alert the CPS at the first opportunity if a matter of policy is **E-33** likely to arise.

4.2 The prosecution advocate must not give an indication or undertaking which binds the prosecution without first discussing the issue with the CPS.

---

[1] "Policy" decisions should be understood as referring to non-evidential decisions on: the acceptance of pleas of guilty to lesser counts or groups of counts or available alternatives; offering no evidence on particular counts; consideration of a retrial; whether to lodge an appeal; certification of a point of law; and the withdrawal of the prosecution as a whole.

CPS representation at Crown Court

E-34
4.3 Whenever possible, an experienced Crown Prosecutor will be available at the Crown Court to discuss and agree any issue involving the conduct or progress of the case.

4.4 When it is not possible to provide a Crown Prosecutor at court, an experienced caseworker will attend and facilitate communication between the prosecution advocate and the Crown Prosecutor having responsibility for the case.

4.5 In exceptional circumstances where it is not possible to contact a Crown Prosecutor, the prosecution advocate should ask the court to adjourn the hearing for a realistic period in order to consult with the CPS. Where an adjournment is refused, the prosecution advocate may make the decision but should record his or her reasons in writing.

Referral to senior CPS representative

E-35
4.6 Where an issue remains unresolved following consultation with a Crown Prosecutor; or where the case/issue under consideration is substantial, sensitive or complex; or the prosecution advocate disagrees with the advice of the Crown Prosecutor, the matter may be referred to the Chief Crown Prosecutor, the Director Casework or to a senior Crown Prosecutor with delegated authority to act on their behalf.

4.7 In order to ensure consultation takes place at the highest level appropriate to the circumstances and nature of the case, the court should be asked to adjourn if necessary. When an adjournment is sought, the facts leading to the application should be placed before the court only in so far as they are relevant to that application.

4.8 Where a Chief Crown Prosecutor has been directly involved in the decision making process and the issue remains unresolved, the matter may be referred to the Director of Public Prosecutions.

Farquharson

E-36
(f) *Where counsel has taken a decision on a matter of policy with which his Instructing Solicitor has not agreed, then it would be appropriate for the Attorney General to require Counsel to submit to him a written report of all the circumstances, including his reasons for disagreeing with those who instruct him.*

4.9 It will only be in exceptional circumstances that the Attorney General will require a written report. The prosecution advocate will first discuss the decision with the Chief Crown Prosecutor or the Director, Casework. Where, by agreement, the issue remains one that either party considers should be drawn to the attention of the Director of Public Prosecutions the prosecution advocate will, on request, provide a written report for submission to the Director of Public Prosecutions. If he considers it appropriate to do so, the Director of Public Prosecutions may refer the matter to the Attorney General.

4.10 Where there has been a disagreement on a matter of policy, provided that the CPS is satisfied that the prosecution advocate followed the principles set out in this document, the professional codes of conduct and was not *Wednesbury* unreasonable, the CPS will not apply sanctions in respect of any future work solely as a result of the decision in a particular case.

5. Change of advice

Farquharson

E-37
(g) *When counsel has had the opportunity to prepare his brief and to confer with those instructing him, but at the last moment before trial unexpectedly advises that the case should not proceed or that pleas to lesser offences should be accepted, and his Instructing Solicitor does not accept such advice, counsel should apply for an adjournment if instructed so to do.*

E-38
5.1 The CPS and the prosecution advocate should agree a period of adjournment that would allow a newly instructed advocate to prepare for trial. The period should be realistic and acknowledge that in such circumstances a case conference will usually be required.

5.2 The facts leading to the application for the adjournment should be placed before the court only in so far as they are relevant to that application.

6. Prosecution advocate's role in decision making at trial

Farquharson

E-39
(h) *Subject to the above, it is for prosecution counsel to decide whether to offer no evidence on a particular count or on the indictment as a whole and whether to accept pleas to a lesser count or counts.*

6.1 The prosecution advocate may ask the defence advocate as to whether a plea will be forthcoming but at this initial stage should not suggest or indicate a plea that might be considered acceptable to the prosecution before a plea is offered.

6.2 Where the defence advocate subsequently offers details of a plea, the prosecution advocate may discuss the matter with a view to establishing an acceptable plea that reflects the defendant's criminality and provides the court with sufficient powers to sentence appropriately.

Responsibility of prosecution advocate to consult

6.3 Where the prosecution advocate forms the view that the appropriate course is to accept a plea **E-40** before proceedings commence or continue, or to offer no evidence on the indictment or any part of it, the prosecution advocate should:

    i. whenever practicable, speak with the victim or victim's family attending court to explain the position;

    ii. ensure that the interests of the victim or any views expressed by the victim or victim's family are taken into account as part of the decision making process; and

    iii. keep the victim or victim's family attending court informed and explain decisions as they are made.

6.4 Where appropriate the prosecution advocate may seek an adjournment of the court hearing in order to facilitate discussion with the victim or victim's family.

6.5 The prosecution advocate should always comply with paragraph 6.3 and, where practicable, discuss the matter with the CPS before informing the defence advocate or the court that a plea is acceptable.

6.6 Where the defendant indicates an acceptable plea, unless the issue is simple, the defence should reduce the basis of the plea to writing. The prosecution advocate should show the CPS any written record relating to the plea and agree with the CPS the basis on which the case will be opened to the court.

6.7 It is the responsibility of the prosecution advocate to ensure that the defence advocate is aware of the basis on which the plea is accepted by the prosecution and the way in which the prosecution case will be opened to the court.

6.8 It will not be necessary for the prosecution advocate to consult the CPS where the plea or course of action accords with the written instructions received from the CPS, although paragraph 6.3 may still apply.

Prosecution advocate's role in sentencing

6.9 The prosecution advocate should always draw the court's attention to any matters, including ag- **E-41** gravating or mitigating features, that might affect sentence. Additionally, the advocate should be in a position to assist the court, if requested, with any statutory provisions or sentencing guidelines and should always draw attention to potential sentencing errors.

6.10 Where a discussion on plea and sentence takes place, the prosecution advocate must adhere to the Attorney General's Guidelines on the Acceptance of Pleas published on 7 December 2000.

7. Seeking judicial approval

Farquharson

    (i) *If prosecution counsel invites the Judge to approve the course he is proposing to take, then he must abide by* **E-42** *the judge's decision.*

7.1 A discussion with the judge about the acceptability of a plea or conduct of the case should be held in the presence of the defendant unless exceptional circumstances apply.[2]

7.2 In exceptional circumstances, where the prosecution advocate considers it appropriate to communicate with the judge or seek the judge's view in chambers, the CPS should be consulted before such a step is taken.

7.3 Where discussions take place in chambers it is the responsibility of the prosecution advocate to remind the judge, if necessary, that an independent record must always be kept.

7.4 The prosecution advocate should also make a full note of such an event, recording all deci-

---

[2] For the purposes of these guidelines, "exceptional circumstances" would include the following:

    (i) Where there is material or information which should not be made public, *e.g.* a police text, or for some other compelling reason such as a defendant or witness suffering, unkown to them, from a serious or terminal illness; or

    (ii) There are sensitivities surrounding a prosecution decision or proposed action which need to be explained in chambers with a view to obtaining judicial approval. Such approval may be given in open court where it is necessary to explain a prosecution decision or action in order to maintain public confidence in the criminal justice system.

sions and comments. This note should be made available to the CPS.

Farquharson

E-43

(j) *If prosecution counsel does not invite the judge's approval of his decision it is open to the judge to express his dissent with the course proposed and invite counsel to reconsider the matter with those instructing him, but having done so, the final decision remains with counsel.*

7.5 Where a judge expresses a view based on the evidence or public interest, the CPS will carry out a further review of the case.

7.6 The prosecution advocate will inform the CPS in a case where the judge has expressed a dissenting view and will agree the action to be taken. Where there is no CPS representative at court, the prosecution advocate will provide a note of the judge's comments.

7.7 The prosecution advocate will ensure that the judge is aware of all factors that have a bearing on the prosecution decision to adopt a particular course. Where there is a difference of opinion between the prosecution advocate and the CPS the judge will be informed as to the nature of the disagreement.

Farquharson

E-44

(k) *In an extreme case where the judge is of the opinion that the course proposed by counsel would lead to serious injustice, he may decline to proceed with the case until counsel has consulted with either the Director or the Attorney General as may be appropriate.*

7.8 As a preliminary step, the prosecution advocate will discuss the judge's observations with the Chief Crown Prosecutor in an attempt to resolve the issue. Where the issue remains unresolved the Director of Public Prosecutions will be consulted. In exceptional circumstances the Director of Public Prosecutions may consult the Attorney General.

E-45

Note: These Guidelines are subject to the Code of Conduct of the Bar of England and Wales (barrister advocates) and The Law Society's The Guide to the Professional Conduct of Solicitors (solicitor advocates). Whilst reference is made in the guidelines to the CPS and levels of authority within the Service, the guidelines may be adopted as best practice, with consequential amendments to levels of authority, by other prosecuting authorities.

These Guidelines may be amended at any time and copyright is waived.

These Guidelines are also available on the CPS Website: www.cps.gov.uk.

APPENDIX F
Interpretation Act 1978

General provisions as to enactment and operation

Words of enactment

1. Every section of an Act takes effect as a substantive enactment without introductory words.   **F-1**

Amendment or repeal in same Session

2. Any Act may be amended or repealed in the Session of Parliament in which it is passed.   **F-2**

Judicial notice

3. Every Act is a public Act to be judicially noticed as such, unless the contrary is expressly **F-3**
provided by the Act.

Time of commencement

4. An Act or provision of an Act comes into force–   **F-4**
- (a) where provision is made for it to come into force on a particular day, at the beginning of
  that day;
- (b) where no provision is made for its coming into force, at the beginning of the day on which
  the Act receives the Royal Assent.

Interpretation and construction

Definitions

5. In any Act, unless the contrary intention appears, words and expressions listed in Schedule 1 to **F-5**
this Act are to be construed according to that Schedule.

Gender and number

6. In any Act, unless the contrary intention appears,–   **F-6**
- (a) words importing the masculine gender include the feminine;
- (b) words importing the feminine gender include the masculine;
- (c) words in the singular include the plural and words in the plural include the singular.

References to service by post

7. Where an Act authorises or requires any document to be served by post (whether the expression **F-7**
"serve" or the expression "give" or "send" or any other expression is used) then, unless the contrary
intention appears, the service is deemed to be effected by properly addressing, prepaying and posting
a letter containing the document and, unless the contrary is proved, to have been effected at the time
at which the letter would be delivered in the ordinary course of post.

References to distance

8. In the measurement of any distance for the purposes of an Act, that distance shall, unless the **F-8**
contrary intention appears, be measured in a straight line on a horizontal plane.

References to time of day

9. Subject to section 3 of the Summer Time Act 1972 (construction of references to points of time **F-9**
during the period of summer time), whenever an expression of time occurs in an Act, the time
referred to shall, unless it is otherwise specifically stated, be held to be Greenwich mean time.

References to Sovereign

10. In any Act a reference to the Sovereign reigning at the time of the passing of the Act is to be **F-10**
construed, unless the contrary intention appears, as a reference to the Sovereign for the time being.

Construction of subordinate legislation

11. Where an Act confers power to make subordinate legislation, expressions used in that legisla- **F-11**
tion have, unless the contrary intention appears, the meaning which they bear in the Act.

Statutory powers and duties

Continuity of powers and duties

12.–(1) Where an Act confers a power or imposes a duty it is implied, unless the contrary inten- **F-12**
tion appears, that the power may be exercised, or the duty is to be performed, from time to time as
occasion requires.

(2) Where an Act confers a power or imposes a duty on the holder of an office as such, it is
implied, unless the contrary intention appears, that the power may be exercised, or the duty is to be
performed, by the holder for the time being of the office.

Anticipatory exercise of powers

13. Where an Act which (or any provision of which) does not come into force immediately on its **F-13**

passing confers power to make subordinate legislation, or to make appointments, give notices, prescribe forms or do any other thing for the purposes of the Act, then, unless the contrary intention appears, the power may be exercised, and any instrument made thereunder may be made so as to come into force, at any time after the passing of the Act so far as may be necessary or expedient for the purpose—

    (a) of bringing the Act or any provision of the Act into force; or

    (b) of giving full effect to that Act or any such provision at or after the time when it comes into force.

Implied power to amend

F-14   **14.** Where an Act confers power to make—

    (a) rules, regulations or byelaws; or

    (b) Orders in Council, orders or other subordinate legislation to be made by statutory instrument,

it implies, unless the contrary intention appears, a power exercisable in the same manner and subject to the same conditions or limitations, to revoke, amend or re-enact any instrument made under the power.

Power to include sunset and review provisions in subordinate legislation

F-14a   **14A.**—(1) This section applies where an Act confers a power or a duty on a person to make subordinate legislation except to the extent that—

    (a) the power or duty is exercisable by the Scottish Ministers, or

    (b) the power or duty is exercisable by any other person within devolved competence (within the meaning of the Scotland Act 1998).

    (2) The subordinate legislation may include—

    (a) provision requiring the person to review the effectiveness of the legislation within a specified period or at the end of a specified period;

    (b) provision for the legislation to cease to have effect at the end of a specified day or a specified period;

    (c) if the power or duty is being exercised to amend other subordinate legislation, provision of the kind mentioned in paragraph (a) or (b) in relation to that other legislation.

    (3) The provision that may be made by virtue of subsection (2)(a) includes provision requiring the person to consider whether the objectives which it was the purpose of the legislation to achieve remain appropriate and, if so, whether they could be achieved in another way.

    (4) Subordinate legislation including provision of a kind mentioned in subsection (2) may make such provision generally or only in relation to specified provisions of the legislation or specified cases or circumstances.

    (5) Subordinate legislation including provision of a kind mentioned in subsection (2) may make transitional, consequential, incidental or supplementary provision or savings in connection with such provision.

    (6) In this section "specified" means specified in the subordinate legislation.

[This section was inserted by the Enterprise and Regulatory Reform Act 2013, s.59(1) and (2).]

Repealing enactments

Repeal of repeal

F-15   **15.** Where an Act repeals a repealing enactment, the repeal does not revive any enactment previously repealed unless words are added reviving it.

General savings

F-16   **16.**—(1) Without prejudice to section 15, where an Act repeals an enactment, the repeal does not, unless the contrary intention appears,—

    (a) revive anything not in force or existing at the time at which the repeal takes effect;

    (b) affect the previous operation of the enactment repealed or anything duly done or suffered under that enactment;

    (c) affect any right, privilege, obligation or liability acquired, accrued or incurred under that enactment;

    (d) affect any penalty, forfeiture or punishment incurred in respect of any offence committed against that enactment;

    (e) affect any investigation, legal proceeding or remedy in respect of any such right, privilege, obligation, liability, penalty, forfeiture or punishment;

and any such investigation, legal proceeding or remedy may be instituted, continued or enforced, and any such penalty, forfeiture or punishment may be imposed, as if the repealing Act had not been passed.

(2) This section applies to the expiry of a temporary enactment as if it were repealed by an Act.

[Considered in *R. v. West London Stipendiary Magistrate, ex p. Simeon* [1983] A.C. 234, HL. See also *Hough v. Windus* (1884) 12 Q.B.D. 224, and *R. v. Fisher (Charles)* [1969] 1 W.L.R. 8, CA.]

Repeal and re-enactment

17.–(1) Where an Act repeals a previous enactment and substitutes provisions for the enactment **F-17** repealed, the repealed enactment remains in force until the substitute provisions come into force.

(2) Where an Act repeals and re-enacts, with or without modification, a previous enactment then, unless the contrary intention appears,–

(a) any reference in any other enactment to the enactment so repealed shall be construed as a reference to the provision re-enacted;

(b) in so far as any subordinate legislation made or other thing done under the enactment so repealed, or having effect as if so made or done, could have been made or done under the provision re-enacted, it shall have effect as if made or done under that provision.

Miscellaneous

Duplicated offences

18. Where an act or omission constitutes an offence under two or more Acts, or both under an Act **F-18** and at common law, the offender shall, unless the contrary intention appears, be liable to be prosecuted and punished under either or any of those Acts or at common law, but shall not be liable to be punished more than once for the same offence.

See in the main work, § 4-189.

Citation of other Acts

19. Where an Act cites another Act by year, statute, session or chapter, or a section or other por- **F-19** tion of another Act by number or letter, the reference shall, unless the contrary intention appears, be read as referring—

(a) in the case of Acts included in any revised edition of the statutes printed by authority, to that edition;

(b) in the case of Acts not so included but included in the edition prepared under the direction of the Record Commission, to that edition;

(c) in any other case, to the Acts printed by the Queen's Printer, or under the superintendence or authority of Her Majesty's Stationery Office.

(2) An Act may continue to be cited by the short title authorised by any enactment notwithstanding the repeal of that enactment.

References to other enactments

20.–(1) Where an Act describes or cites a portion of an enactment by referring to words, sections **F-20** or other parts from or to which or from and to which the portion extends, the portion described or cited includes the words, sections or other parts referred to unless the contrary intention appears.

(2) Where an Act refers to an enactment, the reference unless the contrary intention appears, is a reference to that enactment as amended, and includes a reference thereto as extended or applied, by or under any other enactment, including any other provision of that Act.

References to EU instruments

20A. Where an Act passed after the commencement of this section refers to a EU instrument that **F-20a** has been amended, extended or applied by another such instrument, the reference, unless the contrary intention appears, is a reference to that instrument as so amended, extended or applied.

[This section was inserted by the Legislative and Regulatory Reform Act 2006, s.25(1). It is printed as amended by the European Union (Amendment) Act 2008, s.3, and Sched., Pt 2.]

Supplementary

Interpretation, etc.

F-21   **21.**–(1) In this Act "Act" includes a local and personal or private Act; and "subordinate legislation" means Orders in Council, orders, rules, regulations, schemes, warrants, byelaws and other instruments made or to be made under any Act.

(2) This Act binds the Crown.

Application to Acts and Measures

F-22   **22.**–(1) This Act applies to itself, to any Act passed after the commencement of this Act (subject, in the case of section 20A, to the provision made in that section) and, to the extent specified in Part I of Schedule 2, to Acts passed before the commencement of this Act.

(2) In any of the foregoing provisions of this Act a reference to an Act is a reference to an Act to which that provision applies; but this does not affect the generality of references to enactments or of the references in section 19(1) to other Acts.

(3) This Act applies to Measures of the General Synod of the Church of England (and, so far as it relates to Acts passed before the commencement of this Act, to Measures of the Church Assembly passed after May 28, 1925) as it applies to Acts.

[This section is printed as amended by the Legislative and Regulatory Reform Act 2006, s.25(2).]

Application to other instruments

F-23   **23.**–(1) The provisions of this Act, except sections 1 to 3 and 4(b), apply, so far as applicable and unless the contrary intention appears, to subordinate legislation made after the commencement of this Act and, to the extent specified in Part II of Schedule 2, to subordinate legislation made before the commencement of this Act, as they apply to Acts.

(2) In the application of this Act to Acts passed or subordinate legislation made after the commencement of this Act, all references to an enactment include an enactment comprised in subordinate legislation whenever made, and references to the passing or repeal of an enactment are to be construed accordingly.

(3) Sections 9 and 19(1) also apply to deeds and other instruments and documents as they apply to Acts and subordinate legislation; and in the application of section 17(2)(a) to Acts passed or subordinate legislation made after the commencement of this Act, the reference to any other enactment includes any deed or other instrument or document.

(4) Subsections (1) and (2) of this section do not apply to Orders in Council made under section 5 of the Statutory Instruments Act 1946, section 1(3) of the Northern Ireland (Temporary Provisions) Act 1972 or Schedule 1 to the Northern Ireland Act 1974.

F-23a   **23A.** [*Acts of the Scottish Parliament,*] etc.
F-23b   **23B.** [*Measures and Acts of the National Assembly for Wales,*] etc.
F-24   **24.** [*Application to Northern Ireland.*]

Repeals and savings

F-25   **25.**–(1) The enactments described in Schedule 3 are repealed to the extent specified in the third column of that Schedule.

(2) Without prejudice to section 17(2)(a), a reference to the Interpretation Act 1889, to any provision of that Act or to any other enactment repealed by this Act whether occurring in another Act, in subordinate legislation, in Northern Ireland legislation or in any deed or other instrument or document, shall be construed as referring to this Act, or to the corresponding provision of this Act, as it applies to Acts passed at the time of the reference.

(3) The provisions of this Act relating to Acts passed after any particular time do not affect the construction of Acts passed before that time, though continued or amended by Acts passed thereafter.

F-26   **26.** [*Commencement.*]
F-27   **27.** [*Short title.*]

SCHEDULE 1

WORDS AND EXPRESSIONS DEFINED

F-28   *Note*: The years or dates which follow certain entries in this Schedule are relevant for the purposes of paragraph 4 of Schedule 2 (application to existing enactments).

Definitions

... .

"Bank of England" means, as the context requires, the Governor and Company of the Bank of England or the bank of the Governor and Company of the Bank of England.

... .

"British Islands" means the United Kingdom, the Channel Islands and the Isle of Man. [1889]

"British possession" means any part of Her Majesty's dominions outside the United Kingdom; and where parts of such dominions are under both a central and local legislature, all parts under the central legislature are deemed, for the purposes of this definition, to be one British possession. [1889]

... .

"Central funds", in an enactment providing in relation to England and Wales for the payment of costs out of central funds, means money provided by Parliament.

... .

"Civil partnership" means a civil partnership which exists under or by virtue of the Civil Partnership Act 2004 (and any reference to a civil partner is to be read accordingly).

[This definition is inserted by the Civil Partnership Act 2004, s.261(1), and Sched. 27, para. 59.]

"Colonial legislature", and "legislature" in relation to a British possession, mean the authority, other than the Parliament of the United Kingdom or Her Majesty in Council, competent to make laws for the possession. [1889]

"Colony" means any part of Her Majesty's dominions outside the British Islands except—

    (a) countries having fully responsible status within the Commonwealth;

    (b) territories for whose external relations a country other than the United Kingdom is responsible;

    (c) associated states; and where parts of such dominions are under both a central and a local legislature, all parts under the central legislature are deemed for the purposes of this definition to be one colony. [1889]

"Commencement", in relation to an Act or enactment, means the time when the Act or enactment comes into force.

"The EU", or "the EU Treaties" and other expressions defined by section 1 of and Schedule 1 to the European Communities Act 1972 have the meanings prescribed by that Act.

[This definition is printed as amended by the European Union (Amendment) Act 2008, s.3, and Sched., Pt 2.]

... .

"Consular officer" has the meaning assigned by Article 1 of the Vienna Convention set out in Schedule 1 to the Consular Relations Act 1968.

... .

"County Court" means—

    (a) in relation to England and Wales, the County Court established under section A1 of the County Courts Act 1984;

    (b) [*Northern Ireland*].

[This definition is printed as amended by the County Courts Act 1984, Sched. 2; and the Crime and Courts Act 2013, s.17(5), and Sched. 9. para. 94.]

"Court of Appeal" means—

    (a) in relation to England and Wales, Her Majesty's Court of Appeal in England;

    (b) in relation to Northern Ireland, Her Majesty's Court of Appeal in Northern Ireland.

"Court of summary jurisdiction", "summary conviction" and "Summary Jurisdiction Acts", in relation to Northern Ireland, have the same meanings as in Measures of the Northern Ireland Assembly and Acts of the Parliament of Northern Ireland.

"Crown Court" means—

    (a) in relation to England and Wales, the Crown Court constituted by section 4 of the Courts Act 1971;

    (b) [*Northern Ireland*].

... .

"EEA agreement" means the agreement on the European Economic Area signed at Oporto on 2nd May 1992, together with the Protocol adjusting that Agreement signed at Brussels on 17th March 1993, as modified or supplemented from time to time. [The date of the coming into force of this paragraph.]

"EEA state", in relation to any time, means—

    (a) a state which at that time is a member State; or

    (b) any other state which at that time is a party to the EEA agreement. [The date of the coming into force of this paragraph.]

[These two definitions were inserted, as from January 8, 2007, by the Legislative and Regulatory Reform Act 2006, s.26(1).]

"England" means, subject to any alteration of boundaries under Part IV of the Local Government Act 1972, the area consisting of the counties established by section 1 of that Act, Greater London and the Isles of Scilly. [1st April 1974]

... .

"Governor-General" includes any person who for the time being has the powers of the Governor-General, and "Governor", in relation to any British possession, includes the officer for the time being administering the government of that possession. [1889]

"Her Majesty's Revenue and Customs" has the meaning given by section 4 of the Commissioners for Revenue and Customs Act 2005.

[This definition was inserted by the Commissioners for Revenue and Customs Act 2005, s.4(3).]

"High Court" means—

    (a) in relation to England and Wales, Her Majesty's High Court of Justice in England;

    (b) in relation to Northern Ireland, Her Majesty's High Court of Justice in Northern Ireland.

... .

"Land" includes buildings and other structures, land covered with water, and any estate, interest, easement, servitude or right in or over land. [1st January 1979]

... .

"Local policing body" has the meaning given by section 101(1) of the Police Act 1996.

[This definition was inserted by the Police Reform and Social Responsibility Act 2011, s.97(1) and (2).]

"London borough" means a borough described in Schedule 1 to the London Government Act 1963, "inner London borough" means one of the boroughs so described and numbered from 1 to 12 and "outer London borough" means one of the boroughs so described and numbered 13 to 32, subject (in each case) to any alterations made under Part IV of the Local Government Act 1972 or Part II of the Local Government Act 1992.

[This definition is printed as amended by the Local Government Act 1992, s.27(1), and Sched. 3, para. 21.]

"Lord Chancellor" means the Lord High Chancellor of Great Britain.

"Magistrates' court" has the meaning assigned to it—

    (a) in relation to England and Wales, by section 148 of the Magistrates' Courts Act 1980;

    (b) [*Northern Ireland*].

[This definition is printed as amended by the MCA 1980, s.154, and Sched. 7, para. 169.]

"Month" means calendar month. [1850]

... .

"Oath" and "affidavit" include affirmation and declaration, and "swear" includes affirm and declare.

"Officer of Revenue and Customs" has the meaning given by section 2(1) of the Commissioners for Revenue and Customs Act 2005.

[This definition was inserted by the Commissioners for Revenue and Customs Act 2005, s.2(7).]

"Ordnance Map" means a map made under powers conferred by the Ordnance Survey Act 1841 or the Boundary Survey (Ireland) Act 1854.

"Parliamentary Election" means the election of a Member to serve in Parliament for a constituency. [1889]

"Person" includes a body of persons corporate or unincorporate. [1889]

"Police and crime commissioner" means a police and crime commissioner established under section 1 of the Police Reform and Social Responsibility Act 2011.

[This definition was inserted by the Police Reform and Social Responsibility Act 2011, s.97(1) and (3).]

"Police area" ... and other expressions relating to the police have the meaning or effect described—
(a) in relation to England and Wales, by section 101(1) of the Police Act 1996; ...

[This definition is printed as amended by the Police Act 1996, Sched. 7, para. 32; the Police Reform and Social Responsibility Act 2011, s.97(1) and (4); and the Police and Fire Reform (Scotland) Act 2012 (Consequential Provisions and Modifications) Order 2013 (S.I. 2013 No. 602).]

"The Privy Council" means the Lords and others of Her Majesty's Most Honourable Privy Council.
"Registered" in relation to nurses, midwives and health visitors, means registered in the register maintained by the United Kingdom Central Council for Nursing, Midwifery and Health Visiting by virtue of qualifications in nursing, midwifery or health visiting, as the case may be.

[This definition was inserted by the Nurses, Midwives and Health Visitors Act 1979, s.23(4), and Sched. 7, para. 30.]

"Registered medical practitioner" means a fully registered person within the meaning of the Medical Act 1983 who holds a licence to practise under that Act. [1st January 1979]

[This definition is printed as amended by the Medical Act 1983, s.56(1), and Sched. 5, para. 18; and the Medical Act 1983 (Amendment) Order 2002 (S.I 2002 No. 3135), Sched.1, para. 10.]

"Rules of Court" in relation to any court means rules made by the authority having power to make rules or orders regulating the practice and procedure of that court, and in Scotland includes Acts of Adjournal and Acts of Sederunt; and the power of the authority to make rules of court (as above defined) includes power to make such rules for the purpose of any Act which directs or authorises anything to be done by rules of court. [1889]
"Secretary of State" means one of Her Majesty's Principal Secretaries of State.
"Senior Courts" means the Senior Courts of England and Wales.

[This definition was inserted by the Constitutional Reform Act 2005, s.59(5), and Sched. 11, para. 24.]

"Sent for trial" means, in relation to England and Wales, sent by a magistrates' court to the Crown Court for trial pursuant to section 51 or 51A of the Crime and Disorder Act 1998.

[This definition was inserted by the CJA 2003, s.41, and Sched. 3, para. 49(b).]

... .

"The standard scale", with reference to a fine or penalty for an offence triable only summarily,—
(a) in relation to England and Wales, has the meaning given by section 37 of the Criminal Justice Act 1982;
(b) [*Scotland*];
(c) [*Northern Ireland*].

[This definition was inserted by the CJA 1988, s.170(1), and Sched. 15, para. 58(a). (For s.37 of the 1982 Act, see the main work, § 5-659.)]

"Statutory declaration" means a declaration made by virtue of the Statutory Declarations Act 1835.
"Statutory maximum", with reference to a fine or penalty on summary conviction for an offence—
(a) in relation to England and Wales, means the prescribed sum within the meaning of section 32 of the Magistrates' Courts Act 1980;
(b) [*Scotland*]; and
(c) [*Northern Ireland*].

[This definition was inserted by the CJA 1988, s.170(1), and Sched. 15, para. 58(b). (For s.32 of the 1980 Act, see the main work, § 1-119.)]

"Supreme Court" means the Supreme Court of the United Kingdom.

[This definition is printed as amended by the Constitutional Reform Act 2005, s.59(5), and Sched. 11, para. 24.]

"The Treasury" means the Commissioners of Her Majesty's Treasury.

"United Kingdom" means Great Britain and Northern Ireland. [12th April 1927]

"Wales" means the combined area of the counties which were created by section 20 of the Local Government Act 1972, as originally enacted, but subject to any alteration made under section 73 of that Act (consequential alteration of boundary following alteration of watercourse) [1st April 1974]

[This definition was substituted by the Local Government (Wales) Act 1994, Sched. 2, para. 9.]

... .

"Writing" includes typing, printing, lithography, photography and other modes of representing or reproducing words in a visible form, and expressions referring to writing are construed accordingly.

Construction of certain expressions relating to offences

In relation to England and Wales—

(a) "indictable offence" means an offence which, if committed by an adult, is triable on indictment, whether it is exclusively so triable or triable either way;

(b) "summary offence" means an offence which, if committed by an adult, is triable only summarily;

(c) "offence triable either way" means an offence, other than an offence triable on indictment only by virtue of Part V of the Criminal Justice Act 1988 which, if committed by an adult, is triable either on indictment or summarily;

and the terms "indictable", "summary" and "triable either way", in their application to offences are to be construed accordingly.

In the above definitions references to the way or ways in which an offence is triable are to be construed without regard to the effect, if any, of section 22 of the Magistrates' Courts Act 1980 on the mode of trial in a particular case.

[This para. is printed as amended by the MCA 1980, Sched. 7; and the CJA 1988, Sched. 15, para. 59.]

Construction of certain references to relationships

In relation to England and Wales—

(a) references (however expressed) to any relationship between two persons;

(b) references to a person whose father and mother were or were not married to each other at the time of his birth; and

(c) references cognate with references falling within paragraph (b) above,

shall be construed in accordance with section 1 of the Family Law Reform Act 1987. [The date of the coming into force of that section.]

[This para. was added by Schedule 2 to the Family Law Reform Act 1987.]

Construction of certain expressions relating to the police: Scotland

In relation to Scotland—

(a) references to a police force include references to the Police Service of Scotland;

(b) references to a chief officer of police include references to the chief constable of the Police Service of Scotland;

(c) "police authority" means the Scottish Police Authority;

(d) the "police area" of the Police Service of Scotland is Scotland and references to a police force or police authority for any area include references to the Police Service of Scotland or, as the case may be, the Scottish Police Authority;

(e) references to a constable or chief constable of, or appointed for, any area are to be construed as references to a constable or, as the case may be, the chief constable of, or appointed for, the Police Service of Scotland.

[This para. was added by the Police and Fire Reform (Scotland) Act 2012 (Consequential Provisions and Modifications) Order 2013 (S.I. 2013 No. 602).]

NOTE: the definitions of the following expressions have been omitted: "Associated state", "Bank of Ireland", "Building regulations", "Charity Commissioners", "Comptroller and Auditor

General", "Consular officer", "The Corporation Tax Acts", "Crown Estate Commissioners", "Financial year", "The Income Tax Acts", "Lands Clauses Act", "National Debt Commissioners", "Northern Ireland legislation", "Sewerage undertaker", "Sheriff", "The Tax Acts" and "Water undertaker".

SCHEDULE 2

APPLICATION OF ACT TO EXISTING ENACTMENTS

PART I

ACTS

1. The following provisions of this Act apply to Acts whenever passed:— **F-29**

    Section 6(a) and (c) so far as applicable to enactments relating to offences punishable on indictment or on summary conviction

    Section 9

    Section 10

    Section 11 so far as it relates to subordinate legislation made after the year 1889

    Section 14A

    Section 18

    Section 19(2).

[Para. 1 is printed as amended by the Enterprise and Regulatory Reform Act 2013, s.59(1) and (3).]

2. The following apply to Acts passed after the year 1850:—

    Section 1

    Section 2

    Section 3

    Section 6(a) and (c) so far as not applicable to such Acts by virtue of paragraph 1

    Section 15

    Section 17(1).

3. The following apply to Acts passed after the year 1889:—

    Section 4

    Section 7

    Section 8

    Section 12

    Section 13

    Section 14 so far as it relates to rules, regulations or byelaws

    Section 16(1)

    Section 17(2)(a)

    Section 19(1)

    Section 20(1).

4.—(1) Subject to the following provisions of this paragraph—

    (a) paragraphs of Schedule 1 at the end of which a year or date is specified or described apply, so far as applicable, to Acts passed on or after the date, or after the year, so specified or described; and

    (b) paragraphs of that Schedule at the end of which no year or date is specified or described apply, so far as applicable, to Acts passed at any time.

(2) The definition of "British Islands", in its application to Acts passed after the establishment of the Irish Free State but before the commencement of this Act, includes the Republic of Ireland.

(3) The definition of "colony", in its application to an Act passed at any time before the commencement of this Act, includes—

    (a) any colony within the meaning of section 18(3) of the Interpretation Act 1889 which was excluded, but in relation only to Acts passed at a later time, by any enactment repealed by this Act;

    (b) any country or territory which ceased after that time to be part of Her Majesty's dominions but subject to a provision for the continuation of existing law as if it had not so ceased;

and paragraph (b) of the definition does not apply.

(4) The definition of "Lord Chancellor" does not apply to Acts passed before 1st October 1921 in which that expression was used in relation to Ireland only.

(5) The definition of "person", so far as it includes bodies corporate, applies to any provision of an Act whenever passed relating to an offence punishable on indictment or on summary conviction.

(6) This paragraph applies to the National Health Service Reorganisation Act 1973 and the Water Act 1973 as if they were passed after 1st April 1974.

[Para. 4 is printed as amended by the Family Law Reform Act 1987, Scheds 2 and 4.]

5. The following definitions shall be treated as included in Schedule 1 for the purposes specified in this paragraph—

    (a) in any Act passed before 1st April 1974, a reference to England includes Berwick upon Tweed and Monmouthshire and, in the case of an Act passed before the Welsh Language Act 1967, Wales;

    (b) in any Act passed before the commencement of this Act and after the year 1850, "land" includes messuages, tenements and hereditaments, houses and buildings of any tenure;

    (c) [*Scotland*].

PART II

SUBORDINATE LEGISLATION

F-30   6. Sections 4(a), 9 and 19(1), and so much of Schedule 1 as defines the following expressions, namely—

    England;
    Local land charges register and appropriate local land charges register;
    in relation to Scotland, expressions relating to the police;
    United Kingdom;
    Wales;

apply to subordinate legislation made at any time before the commencement of this Act as they apply to Acts passed at that time.

[Para. 6 is printed as amended by the British Nationality Act 1981, Sched. 9; and the Police and Fire Reform (Scotland) Act 2012 (Consequential Provisions and Modifications) Order 2013 (S.I. 2013 No. 602).]

7. The definition in Schedule 1 of "county court", in relation to England and Wales, applies to Orders in Council made after the year 1846.

APPENDIX G
Guidelines on Claims for Fees under a Crown Court Representation Order and in the Court of Appeal

A. SUMMARY OF SOURCE MATERIAL

Legislation

As from April 2, 2001 the relevant provisions of the Legal Aid in Criminal and Care Proceed- **G-1** ings (Costs) Regulations 1989 (S.I. 1989 No. 343), as amended, were superseded, virtually unamended, by the Criminal Defence Service (Funding) Order 2001 (S.I. 2001 No. 855) ("the Funding Order 2001"). This was significantly amended by a series of amending orders until it was revoked and replaced, in relation to representation orders granted on or after April 30, 2007, by the Criminal Defence Service (Funding) Order 2007 (S.I. 2007 No. 1174). The 2007 order was itself amended on many occasions over the following six years, until it lapsed on April 1, 2013, with the commencement of the repeal of its enabling legislation by the LASPOA 2012, s.39(1), and Sched. 5, para. 39. Full details of all the amending instruments for both the 2001 order and the 2007 order may be found in the second supplement to the 2013 edition of this work, together with the full text of the 2007 order (as amended).

The Criminal Legal Aid (Remuneration) Regulations 2013 (S.I. 2013 No. 435) (set out in full, *post*, G-6 *et seq.*) came into force on April 1, 2013. The substance of the 2013 regulations is almost identical to that of the 2007 order as it read at the time it lapsed, and many, if not all, the authorities that related to the 2007 order at that time will simply carry across. Where they are referred to *post* in this appendix, references to provisions of the former legislation have simply been updated to refer to the corresponding provision of the 2013 regulations.

As to the transitional arrangements in connection with the repeal of the relevant provisions of the Access to Justice Act 1999 and the commencement of the relevant provisions of the 2012 Act, see *ante*, § 6-173.

A challenge to the 8.75 per cent reduction in litigators' fees effected by amendments to Schedules 2, 3 and 4 to S.I. 2013 No. 435 (*ante*) in the Criminal Legal Aid (Remuneration) (Amendment) Regulations 2014 (S.I. 2013 No. 415) (as to which, see *post*, G-71, G-71a, G-72, G-72a, G-73, G-75a, G-80, G-86, G-92a) was rejected in *R. (London Criminal Courts Solicitors' Association) v. Lord Chancellor* [2015] Costs L.R. 7, QBD (Burnett J.).

Recent amendments

S.I. 2013 No. 435 (*ante*) was amended by two further instruments in the second half of 2015. **G-1a** The first of these was the Criminal Legal Aid (Remuneration etc.) (Amendment) Regulations 2015 (S.I. 2015 No. 1369). Part 2 (reg. 3) and Schedules 1 to 3 amended the principal regulations so as further to reduce the fees payable to litigators under Schedules 2 (graduated fee scheme for Crown Court work), 3 (proceedings in the Court of Appeal) and 4 (advice and assistance, representation in a magistrates' court, and certain other work). The remainder of the amendments (in Pt 3 (regs 4-7, and Scheds 4 to 13)) were originally due to come into force on January 11, 2016. However, this was first delayed to April 1, 2016, by amendments effected by the Criminal Legal Aid (Remuneration etc.) (Amendment) (No. 2) Regulations 2015 (S.I. 2015 No. 2049). Then, on January 28, 2016, the Justice Secretary announced in a ministerial statement that it is no longer intended to bring these amendments into force and that the July, 2015, decrease in fees would be suspended for one year from April 1, 2016. As to how this is being achieved, see the summary of S.I. 2016 No. 313 (*post*).

The amendments made by Part 2 apply to matters in which a determination under section 13 (advice and assistance for individuals in custody (§ 6-209 in the main work)), 15 (advice and assistance for criminal proceedings (*ibid.*, § 6-211)) or 16 (representation for criminal proceedings (*ibid.*, § 6-212)) of the 2012 Act was made after June 30, 2015 (reg. 2(1)). Part 2 came into force on July 1, 2015.

The second measure was the Civil and Criminal Legal Aid (Amendment) (No. 2) Regulations 2015 (S.I. 2015 No. 1678). The majority of the amendments were overdue amendments that were consequential on the abolition of committals and transfers for trial. The remainder were consequential on new rules on preparation for trial in the Crown Court under the Criminal Procedure Rules 2015 (S.I. 2015 No. 1490). In particular, certain references to a plea and case management hearing (no longer mandatory) have been omitted, with the regulations now making provision by reference to the occurrence, or result, of the first hearing at which the assisted person enters a plea instead. According to the explanatory memorandum "This reflects the fact that for purposes of remuneration ..., it is the type of plea which is relevant, not the name of the hearing at which it is entered."

There is transitional provision in relation to committal proceedings that have been discontinued or withdrawn, in relation to committals and transfers that occurred before the abolition of committals and transfers and in relation to payment for preparation of a plea and case management hearing questionnaire where no oral hearing takes place. These regulations came into force in stages on October 5, 2015, and November 1, 2015.

With effect from March 31, 2016, the Criminal Legal Aid (Remuneration) (Amendment) Regulations 2016 (S.I. 2016 No. 313) revoked, subject to exceptions, regulations 1(2)(b) (commencement), 2(2) (transitional provision), and Part 3 (regs 4-7) of, and Schedules 4 to 13 to, S.I. 2015 No. 1369 (*ante*), and S.I. 2015 No. 2049 (*ante*), so that neither the fixed fee schemes for the remuneration of criminal legal aid services provided for by Part 3 of S.I. 2015 No. 1369, nor the amendments that were consequential on the intended introduction of new contracts for the provision of criminal legal aid, will come into force.

The exceptions are set out in regulation 3, which provides that some minor amendments of regulations 17A (*post*, G-21a), 21(4)(d) (*post*, G-26), and 28(1)(c)(i) (*post*, G-34) of, and of paragraph 1(1) of Schedule 2 (*post*, G-69), and paragraph 5 of Schedule 4 (*post*, G-92a), to, S.I. 2013 No. 435 (*ante*) in regulation 6 of S.I. 2015 No. 1369 are not revoked. The detail of those amendments are set out in the relevant paragraphs (post). Whilst the commencement provisions governing Part 3 of S.I. 2015 No. 1369 were revoked in their entirety from March 31, 2016, and there is, therefore, no commencement provision at all in relation to what is left of regulation 6, as things stood (at the date of the making of S.I. 2016 No. 313), the saved amendments were to come into force on April 1, 2016. It can only be assumed that the intention was to imply that the commencement date of the saved amendments was to be saved as well.

In addition, Schedules 2 to 4 to S.I. 2013 No. 435 (Appendix G-69 *et seq.*) are amended by S.I. 2016 No. 313 to increase the fees for advice, assistance and representation made available under sections 13 (see § 6-209 in the main work), 15 (*ibid.*, § 6-211) and 16 (*ibid.*, § 6-212) of the 2012 Act, by amending the existing fee schemes for the remuneration of criminal legal aid services, for work done pursuant to a legal aid determination made on or after April 1, 2016. This is achieved by simply reversing the fee reduction introduced by Part 2 of S.I. 2015 No. 1369 in July, 2015. This reversal only applies to services made available pursuant to a determination made on or after April 1, 2016, under section 13, 15 or 16 of the LASPOA 2012 (*ante*).

★   The latest amendments to S.I. 2013 No. 435 were effected by the Criminal Legal Aid (Standard Crime Contract) (Amendment) Regulations 2017 (S.I. 2017 No. 311). The amendments to regulation 8 and Schedule 4 replace references to the 2010 Standard Crime Contract with references to the 2017 Standard Crime Contract, which replaced the former on April 17, 2017. An amendment to regulation 3 ensures that regulation 9 (payments from other sources (*post*, G-16)) applies to proceedings in magistrates' courts as well as in the Crown Court and Court of Appeal.

The current regimes

G-2   Apart from a handful of historical cases which will be governed by the former provisions for *ex post facto* taxation (as to which see Appendix G-200 *et seq.* in the supplements to the 2010 edition of this work), advocates' fees in the Crown Court effectively fall into one of two regimes:

(i) *Graduated fees.* These were first introduced in 1997 for trials lasting up to 10 days, appeals and other minor Crown Court business: Legal Aid in Criminal and Care Proceedings (Costs) Regulations 1989 (S.I. 1989 No. 343), Sched. 3. The scheme was then extended to cover trials of up to 25 days and, as from 2005, of trials up to 40 days. As from April 30, 2007, it was intended that the scheme would cover all Crown Court work save for those cases contracted under the Very High Costs Case provisions: Criminal Defence Service (Funding) Order 2007 (S.I. 2007 No. 1174), art. 3(6A), and Sched. 1, para. 2(1). The 2007 scheme is sometimes referred to as the Revised Advocacy Graduated Fee Scheme (RAGFS). The details were contained in Schedule 1 to the 2007 order, which replaced Schedule 4 to the Criminal Defence Service (Funding) Order 2001 (S.I. 2001 No. 855). The 2007 scheme (as amended) is now to be found in Schedule 1 to the Criminal Legal Aid (Remuneration) Regulations 2013 (S.I. 2013 No. 435).

(ii) *Very High Cost Cases (VHCC).* This regime came into effect on October 29, 2001. All cases estimated to last more than 24 days are capable of being subject to a VHCC contract. As to the current VHCC regime, see *post*, G-181 *et seq.*

Notes for guidance

(a) Graduated fees

The Ministry of Justice's *Crown Court Fee Guidance (GFSG)* is updated at regular intervals. In **G-3** addition, guidance notes have been issued by the Criminal Bar Association, and are available on both the Criminal Bar Association's and the Courts Service's National Taxing Team's websites. The GFSG includes references to costs judges' decisions which are given and commonly referred to and indexed by their "X" references. For convenience these references are used hereafter. The guidance may be cited by advocates when asking for a re-determination: GFSG, Preface. However, while interesting and instructive, it is simply the department's gloss on the wording of the regulations, and does not bind costs judges: *R. v. Phillips*, X1, SCTO 594/97.

The Bar Council has also introduced a *Graduated Fee Payment Protocol.* This is an essential part of the mechanism by which advocates will be remunerated in future, and sets out arrangements to ensure that substitute advocates are paid by instructed advocates. The protocol falls outside the immediate scope of this work. It is available on both the Bar Council's and the Criminal Bar Association's websites.

(b) Very High Cost Cases

Very High Cost Cases are governed by the Very High Cost (Crime) Cases Arrangements 2013 **G-4** (see *post*, G-181 *et seq.*). Additional guidance is contained in the 2013 VHCC Guidance (published by the Legal Aid Agency, an executive agency of the Ministry of Justice).

Contract Appeals Committee decisions

Summaries of decisions of the Contract Appeals Committee have been collated and appear on **G-5** the website of the Legal Aid Agency's section of the Ministry of Justice's website.

B. THE REMUNERATION REGULATIONS

Criminal Legal Aid (Remuneration) Regulations 2013 (S.I. 2013 No. 435)

Citation and commencement

1. These Regulations may be cited as the Criminal Legal Aid (Remuneration) Regulations 2013 **G-6** and shall come into force on 1st April 2013.

Interpretation

2.–(1) In these Regulations– **G-7**

    "the Act" means the Legal Aid, Sentencing and Punishment of Offenders Act 2012;

    "advocate" means a barrister, a solicitor advocate or a solicitor who is exercising their automatic rights of audience in the Crown Court;

    "appropriate officer" means–

(a) in the case of proceedings in the civil division of the Court of Appeal, the head of the civil appeals office;

(b) in the case of proceedings in the criminal division of the Court of Appeal, the registrar of criminal appeals;

(c) in the case of proceedings in the Crown Court, the Lord Chancellor;

(d) in respect of advice or assistance as to an appeal from the Crown Court to the Court of Appeal (except in the case of an appeal under section 9(11) of the Criminal Justice Act 1987 (preparatory hearings)) where, on the advice of any representative instructed, notice of appeal is given, or application for leave to appeal is made, whether or not such appeal is later abandoned, the registrar of criminal appeals;

(e) in respect of advice or assistance as to an appeal to the Courts-Martial Appeal Court, the registrar of criminal appeals;

(f) in respect of advice or assistance as to an appeal from the Court of Appeal to the Supreme Court, where the appeal is not lodged with the Supreme Court, the registrar of criminal appeals; and

(g) in any other case, the Lord Chancellor,

and, in any case, includes an officer designated by the person who is the appropriate officer by virtue of paragraphs (a) to (g) to act on his behalf for the purposes of these Regulations;

"assisted person" means an individual in whose favour a section 16 determination has been made;

"fee earner" means a litigator, or person employed by a litigator, who undertakes work on a case;

"instructed advocate" means—

(a) where the section 16 determination provides for representation by a single advocate, the first barrister or solicitor advocate instructed in the case, who has primary responsibility for the case; or

(b) where the section 16 determination provides for representation by more than one advocate, each of—

(i) the leading instructed advocate; and

(ii) the led instructed advocate;

"leading instructed advocate" means the first leading barrister or solicitor advocate instructed in the case who has primary responsibility for those aspects of a case undertaken by a leading advocate;

"led instructed advocate" means the first led barrister or solicitor advocate instructed in the case who has primary responsibility for those aspects of the case undertaken by a led advocate;

"litigator" means the person referred to in the representation order as representing an assisted person, being a solicitor, firm of solicitors or other appropriately qualified person.

"main hearing" means—

(a) in relation to a case which goes to trial, the trial;

(b) in relation to a guilty plea (within the meaning of Schedule 1), the hearing at which pleas are taken or, where there is more than one such hearing, the last such hearing;

(c) in relation to a cracked trial (within the meaning of Schedule 1), the hearing at which—

(i) the case becomes a cracked trial by meeting the conditions in the definition of a cracked trial, whether or not any pleas were taken at that hearing; or

(ii) a formal verdict of not guilty was entered as a result of the prosecution offering no evidence, whether or not the parties attended the hearing;

(d) in relation to an appeal against conviction or sentence in the Crown Court, the hearing of the appeal;

(e) in relation to proceedings arising out of a committal for sentence in the Crown Court, the sentencing hearing; and

(f) in relation to proceedings arising out of an alleged breach of an order of the Crown Court, the hearing at which those proceedings are determined;

"related proceedings" means—

(a) two or more sets of proceedings involving the same defendant which are prepared, heard or dealt with together; or

(b) proceedings involving more than one defendant which arise out of the same incident, so that the defendants are charged, tried or disposed of together;

"relevant order" means whichever of the 2015 Duty Provider Crime Contract or the 2015 Own Client Crime Contract governs the provision of advice and assistance made available under sections 13 or 15 of the Act, for which remuneration is claimed;

"representation order" means a document which records a section 16 determination;

"representative" means a litigator or an advocate including, where appropriate, an instructed advocate or trial advocate;

"section 16 determination" means a determination made under section 16 of the Act that an individual qualities for representation for the purposes of criminal proceedings;

"senior solicitor" means a solicitor who, in the judgement of the appropriate officer, has the skill, knowledge and experience to deal with the most difficult and complex cases;

"solicitor advocate" means a solicitor who has obtained a higher courts advocacy qualification in accordance with regulations and rules of conduct of the Law Society;

"solicitor, legal executive or fee earner of equivalent experience" means a solicitor, Fellow of the Institute of Legal Executives or equivalent senior fee earner who, in the judgement of the appropriate officer, has good knowledge and experience of the conduct of criminal cases;

"trainee solicitor or fee earner of equivalent experience" means a trainee solicitor or other fee earner who is not a Fellow of the Institute of Legal Executives, who, in the judgement of the appropriate officer, carries out the routine work on a case;

"trial advocate" means, unless otherwise provided, an advocate instructed pursuant to a section 16 determination to represent the assisted person at the main hearing in any case;

"Very High Cost Case" means a case in which a section 16 determination has been made and which the Director classifies as a Very High Cost Case on the grounds that—

    (a) in relation to fees claimed by litigators—

        (i) if the case were to proceed to trial, the trial would in the opinion of the Director be likely to last for more than 40 days and the Director considers that there are no exceptional circumstances which make it unsuitable to be dealt with under an individual case contract for Very High Cost Cases made by the Lord Chancellor under section 2(1) of the Act; or

        (ii) if the case were to proceed to trial, the trial would in the opinion of the Director be likely to last no fewer than 25 and no more than 40 days and the Director considers that there are circumstances which make it suitable to be dealt with under an individual case contract for Very High Cost Cases made by the Lord Chancellor under section 2(1) of the Act;

    (b) in relation to fees claimed by advocates, if the case were to proceed to trial, the trial would in the opinion of the Director be likely to last for more than 60 days and the Director considers that there are no exceptional circumstances which make it unsuitable to be dealt with under an individual case contract for Very High Cost Cases made by the Lord Chancellor under section 2(1) of the Act;

"Very High Cost Case contract" means the 2013 VHCC contract between the Lord Chancellor and a representative for the provision of representation under section 16 of the Act (criminal legal aid).

(2) The fees and rates set out in the Schedules to these Regulations are exclusive of value added tax.

(3) A function of the Lord Chancellor or Director under these Regulations may be exercised by, or by an employee of, a person authorised for that purpose by the Lord Chancellor or Director respectively.

[This regulation is printed as amended (insertion of definition of "Very High Cost Case contract") by the Criminal Legal Aid (Remuneration) (Amendment) Regulations 2013 (S.I. 2013 No. 2803), reg. 3(1) and (3). The amendment applies in relation to fees for work undertaken on or after December 2, 2013: *ibid.*, reg. 4. It is also printed as further amended by the Criminal Legal Aid (Remuneration) (Amendment) Regulations 2015 (S.I. 2015 No. 882), reg. 2(1) and (2) (insertion of definitions of "main hearing" and "trial advocate", and inclusion of words "or trial advocate" at the end of the definition of "representative"). The amendments apply to criminal proceedings in the Crown Court in which a determination under the LASPOA 2012, s.16 (§ 6-212 in the main work) is made on or after May 5, 2015.]

Scope

3.—(1) Regulations 5(2), 10 and 14(1) apply to proceedings in magistrates' courts and to proceed- **★G-8**
ings in the Crown Court.

(2) Regulation 8 and Schedule 4 apply to proceedings in magistrates' courts, to proceedings in the County Court, to proceedings in the Crown Court and to proceedings in the High Court.

(3) Regulations 16 and 31 and Schedule 5 apply to proceedings in magistrates' courts, to proceedings in the Crown Court and to proceedings in the Court of Appeal.

(4) Regulations 4, 5(1) and (3) to (8), 13, 14(2) to (9), 15, 17 to 24 and 28 to 30 and Schedules 1 and 2 apply to proceedings in the Crown Court only.

(5) Regulations 11 and 25 to 27, apply to proceedings in the Crown Court and to proceedings in the Court of Appeal.

(5A) Regulation 9 applies to proceedings in magistrates' courts, to proceedings in the Crown Court and to proceedings in the Court of Appeal.

(6) Regulation 6 and Schedule 3 apply to proceedings in the Court of Appeal only.

(7) Regulation 7 applies to proceedings in the Supreme Court only.

(8) With the exception of regulations 12 and 12A and paragraphs 13(8) and (9) of Schedule 2 and Schedule 6, these regulations do not apply to Very High Cost Cases.

(9) For the purpose of these regulations, any reference to the Court of Appeal includes as appropriate a reference to—

    (a)   the criminal division of the Court of Appeal;

    (b)   the civil division of the Court of Appeal;

    (c)   the Courts-Martial Appeal Court; and

    (d)   a Divisional Court of the High Court.

[This regulation is printed as amended (insertion of references to reg. 12A and Sched. 6) by the Criminal Legal Aid (Remuneration) (Amendment) Regulations 2013 (S.I. 2013 No. 2803), reg. 3(1) and (4). The amendment applies in relation to fees for work undertaken on or after December 2, 2013: *ibid.*, reg. 4. It is also printed as further amended by the Civil and Criminal Legal Aid (Remuneration) (Amendment) Regulations 2015 (S.I. 2015 No. 325), reg. 3(1) and (2); and the Criminal Legal Aid (Standard Crime Contract) (Amendment) Regulations 2017 (S.I. 2017 No. 311).]

[The next paragraph is G-10.]

Claims for fees by advocates–Crown Court

G-10   **4.**–(1) Claims for fees by a trial advocate in proceedings in the Crown Court must be made and determined in accordance with the provisions of Schedule 1 to these Regulations.

(2) A claim for fees under this regulation and Schedule 1 must be made by each trial advocate.

(3) Subject to regulation 31, a claim by a trial advocate for fees in respect of work done pursuant to a section 16 determination must not be entertained unless the trial advocate submits it within three months of the conclusion of the proceedings to which it relates.

(4) A trial advocate must submit a claim for fees to the appropriate officer in such form and manner as the appropriate officer may direct.

(5) A trial advocate must supply such further information and documents as the appropriate officer may require.

(6) Where a confiscation hearing under Part 2 of the Proceeds of Crime Act 2002 (confiscation: England and Wales), section 2 of the Drug Trafficking Act 1994 (confiscation orders) or section 71 of the Criminal Justice Act 1988 (confiscation orders) is to be held more than 28 days after—

    (a)   the conclusion of the trial to which the section 16 determination relates; or

    (b)   the entering of a guilty plea,

a trial advocate may submit any claim for fees in respect of the trial or guilty plea as soon as the trial has concluded or the guilty plea has been entered.

(7) Where the section 16 determination provides for representation by—

    (a)   a single advocate other than a QC; or

    (b)   two or more advocates other than QC,

and a QC agrees to appear as the single advocate or as a leading junior, that QC must be treated for all the purposes of these Regulations as having been instructed in relation to that determination, and the remuneration of that QC must be determined as if the advocate were not a QC.

(8) In this regulation, where the main hearing is a trial, "trial advocate" means an advocate who—

    (a)   is instructed pursuant to a section 16 determination to represent the assisted person at the trial, and

    (b)   attends the first day of the trial.

[This regulation is printed as amended, with effect from May 5, 2015, by the Criminal Legal Aid (Remuneration) (Amendment) Regulations 2015 (S.I. 2015 No. 882), reg. 2(3)(a), (4)(a), (5)(a), (6)(a) and (7). For the transitional provision, see *ante*, G-7.]

Claims for fees and disbursements by litigators–Crown Court

5.–(1) Claims for fees by litigators in proceedings in the Crown Court must be made and **G-11** determined in accordance with the provisions of Schedule 2 to these Regulations.

(2) Claims for disbursements by litigators in proceedings in the Crown Court or in proceedings in a magistrates' court which are subsequently sent for trial to the Crown Court must be made and determined in accordance with the provisions of regulations 14 to 17.

(3) Subject to regulation 31, a claim by a litigator for fees in respect of work done pursuant to a section 16 determination must not be entertained unless the litigator submits it within three months of the conclusion of the proceedings to which it relates.

(4) Subject to paragraph (5), a claim by a litigator for fees in proceedings in the Crown Court must be submitted to the appropriate officer in such form and manner as the appropriate officer may direct and must be accompanied by the representation order and any receipts or other documents in support of any disbursement claimed.

(5) A claim under paragraph 20 or 26 of Schedule 2 to these Regulations must—

(a) summarise the items of work done by a fee earner in respect of which fees are claimed according to the classes specified in paragraph 26(2) of Schedule 2;

(b) state, where appropriate, the dates on which the items of work were done, the time taken, the sums claimed and whether the work was done for more than one assisted person;

(c) specify, where appropriate, the level of fee earner who undertook each of the items of work claimed; and

(d) give particulars of any work done in relation to more than one indictment or a retrial.

(6) Where the litigator claims that paragraph 29 of Schedule 2 applies in relation to an item of work, the litigator must give full particulars in support of the claim.

(7) The litigator must specify any special circumstances which the litigator considers should be drawn to the attention of the appropriate officer.

(8) The litigator must supply such further information and documents as the appropriate officer may require.

[This regulation is printed as amended by S.I. 2015 No. 1678 (as to which, see *ante*, G-1a).]

[The next paragraph is G-13.]

Proceedings in the Court of Appeal

6. Claims for fees by representatives in proceedings in the Court of Appeal must be made and **G-13** determined in accordance with the provisions of Schedule 3 to these Regulations.

Proceedings in the Supreme Court

7.–(1) In proceedings in the Supreme Court, the fees payable to a representative in respect of **G-14** advice and assistance or representation made available to an individual in accordance with sections 15 or 16 of the Act must be determined by such officer as may be prescribed by order of the Supreme Court.

(2) Subject to paragraph (1), these Regulations do not apply to proceedings in the Supreme Court.

Claims for fees for certain categories of work to which the Standard Crime Contract applies

8.–(1) This regulation applies to— ★**G-15**

(a) advice and assistance provided pursuant to a determination made under section 13 or section 15 of the Act;

(b) representation in proceedings in a magistrates' court pursuant to a section 16 determination;

(c) representation pursuant to a section 16 determination in proceedings prescribed as criminal proceedings under section 14(h) of the Act; and

(d) representation in appeals by way of case stated to the High Court.

(2) Claims for fees in cases to which this regulation applies must—

(a) be made and determined in accordance with the 2017 Standard Crime Contract; and

(b) be paid in accordance with the rates set out in Schedule 4.

(3) In this regulation and in Schedule 4, "2017 Standard Crime Contract" means the contract so named between the Lord Chancellor and a person with whom the Lord Chancellor has made an arrangement under section 2(1) of the Act for the provision of advice, assistance and representation made available under sections 13, 15 and 16 of the Act.

[This regulation is printed as amended by the Criminal Legal Aid (Standard Crime Contract) (Amendment) Regulations 2017 (S.I. 2017 No. 311).]

Payments from other sources

9. Where representation is provided in respect of any proceedings, the representative, whether acting pursuant to a section 16 determination or otherwise, must not receive or be a party to the making of any payment for work done in connection with those proceedings, except such payments as may be made—

    (a) by the Lord Chancellor; or

    (b) in respect of any expenses or fees incurred in—

        (i)   preparing, obtaining or considering any report, opinion or further evidence, whether provided by an expert witness or otherwise; or

        (ii) obtaining any transcripts or recordings,

where an application under regulation 13 for an authority to incur such fees or expenses has been refused by a committee appointed under arrangements made by the Lord Chancellor to deal with, amongst other things, appeals of, or review of, assessment of costs.

In connection with regulation 9, see *R. v. Banfield, ante,* § 7-165.

Cases sent for trial to the Crown Court

G-17

10.–(1) Where a case is sent for trial to the Crown Court, the payment in relation to work carried out in the magistrates' court is included within the applicable fee payable under Schedule 1 or Schedule 2.

(2) Paragraph (1) does not apply where the case is remitted to a magistrates' court.

[This regulation is printed as amended by S.I. 2015 No. 1678 (*ante*, G-1a).]

Proceedings for contempt

G-18

11. Where representation is provided in proceedings referred to in section 14(g) of the Act (proceedings for contempt in the face of a court), the Lord Chancellor may only pay remuneration for services in accordance with Schedules 1, 2 and 3.

Notification of Very High Cost Cases

G-18a

12.–(1) A litigator who has conduct of a case which is, or is likely to be classified as, a Very High Cost Case, must notify the Lord Chancellor in writing as soon as practicable.

(2) Where a litigator fails to comply with this regulation without good reason, and as a result there is a loss to public funds, the Lord Chancellor may refuse payment of the litigator's costs up to the extent of such loss.

(3) The Lord Chancellor must not refuse payment under paragraph (2) unless the litigator has been given a reasonable opportunity to show why the payment should not be refused.

Fees in Very High Cost Cases

12A. Where services consisting of representation made available under section 16 of the Act (criminal legal aid) are provided in a case which is the subject of a Very High Cost Case contract, fees for that case must be paid—

    (a) in accordance with the terms of that contract; and

    (b) at the rates set out for the appropriate category and level of representative set out in Schedule 6 to these Regulations.

[This regulation was inserted by the Criminal Legal Aid (Remuneration) (Amendment) Regulations 2013 (S.I. 2013 No. 2803), reg. 3(1) and (5). It applies in relation to fees for work undertaken on or after December 2, 2013: *ibid.*, reg. 4.]

Authorisation of expenditure

G-18b

13.–(1) Where it appears to a litigator necessary for the proper conduct of proceedings in the Crown Court for costs to be incurred in relation to representation by taking any of the following steps—

    (a) obtaining a written report or opinion of one or more experts;

    (b) employing a person to provide a written report or opinion (otherwise than as an expert);

    (c) obtaining any transcripts or recordings; or

    (d) performing an act which is either unusual in its nature or involves unusually large expenditure,

the litigator may apply to the Lord Chancellor for prior authority to do so.

(2) Where the Lord Chancellor authorises the taking of any step referred to in paragraph (1), the Lord Chancellor shall also authorise the maximum to be paid in respect of that step.

(3) A representative assigned to an assisted person in any proceedings in the Crown Court may apply to the Lord Chancellor for prior authority for the incurring of travelling and accommodation expenses in order to attend at the main hearing in those proceedings.

[This regulation is printed as amended, with effect from May 5, 2015, by the Criminal Legal Aid (Remuneration) (Amendment) Regulations 2015 (S.I. 2015 No. 882), reg. 2(8). For the transitional provision, see *ante*, G-7.]

The following authorities were decided under the corresponding provisions in earlier legal aid legislation: see, in particular, regulation 54 of the Legal Aid in Criminal and Care Proceedings (General) Regulations 1989 (S.I. 1989 No. 344).

In *R. v. Silcott, Braithwaite and Raghip, The Times*, December 9, 1991, the Court of Appeal said that all members of the legal profession were under a duty not to involve the legal aid fund in unnecessary expenditure. If an expert consulted by the defence was hostile to the accused's case or his solicitor considered the opinion to be wrong or defective it was most unlikely that legal aid authority would be given on application by the solicitor to consult more than one expert and certainly no more than two. In the instant case, the opinions of two experts had been obtained on behalf of one defendant. They were adverse to the defendant. Neither expert was called, but both changed their views in the light of the opinion of a third expert, who had been consulted after the trial's conclusion. This demonstrated that a third opinion had been necessary in the interests of justice. "Expert shopping" was to be discouraged, but there were exceptional cases where the need for a further expert opinion could be demonstrated. In such cases counsel should be asked to advise on evidence in support of an extension of the legal aid certificate, if he thought it right to do so. The courts and those responsible for the legal aid fund must rely on proper professional standards being observed by all the lawyers concerned.

A judge has no power to authorise the incurring of costs under a legal aid order for an expert witness, although he may express his opinion as to the desirability of legal aid being so extended: *R. v. Donnelly* [1998] Crim.L.R. 131, CA.

14.–(1) A litigator may submit a claim to the appropriate officer for payment of a disbursement **G-19** for which the litigator has incurred liability in proceedings in the Crown Court, or in proceedings in a magistrates' court which are subsequently sent for trial to the Crown Court, in accordance with the provisions of this regulation.

(2) A claim for payment under paragraph (1) may be made where—

(a) a litigator has obtained prior authority to incur expenditure of £100 or more under regulation 13; and

(b) the litigator has incurred such a liability.

(3) Without prejudice to regulation 17(4) and (5) a claim for payment under paragraph (1) must not exceed the maximum amount authorised under the prior authority.

(4) A claim for payment under paragraph (1) may be made at any time before the litigator submits a claim for fees under regulation 5.

(5) A claim for payment under paragraph (1) must be submitted to the appropriate officer in such form and manner as the appropriate officer may direct and must be accompanied by the authority to incur expenditure and any invoices or other documents in support of the claim.

(6) Subject to regulation 16, the appropriate officer must allow the disbursement subject to the limit in paragraph (3) if it appears to have been reasonably incurred in accordance with the prior authority.

(7) The appropriate officer must notify the litigator and, where the disbursement claimed includes the fees or charges of any person, may notify that person of the appropriate officer's decision.

(8) Where the appropriate officer allows the disbursement, the appropriate officer must notify the litigator and, where the disbursement includes the fees or charges of any person, may notify that person, of the amount payable, and must authorise payment to the litigator accordingly.

(9) Regulations 28 to 30 do not apply to a payment under this regulation.

[This regulation is printed as amended by S.I. 2015 No. 1678 (*ante*, G-1a).]

Interim disbursements and final determination of fees
15.–(1) On a final determination of fees, regulations 5(2) and 17 apply notwithstanding that a pay- **G-20** ment has been made under regulation 14.

(2) Where the amount found to be due under regulation 17 in respect of a disbursement is less

than the amount paid under regulation 14 ("the interim payment"), the appropriate officer must deduct the difference from the sum otherwise payable to the litigator on the determination of fees, and where the amount due under regulation 17 exceeds the interim payment, the appropriate officer must add the difference to the amount otherwise payable to the litigator.

Expert services

G-20a   16.–(1) Subject to paragraph (2), the Lord Chancellor may provide for the payment of expert services only at the fixed fees or at rates not exceeding the rates set out in Schedule 5.

(2) The appropriate officer may, in relation to a specific claim, increase the fixed fees or rates set out in Schedule 5 if that officer considers it reasonable to do so in exceptional circumstances.

(3) For the purposes of paragraph (2), exceptional circumstances are where the expert's evidence is key to the client's case and either—

> (a)   the complexity of the material is such that an expert with a high level of seniority is required; or
>
> (b)   the material is of such a specialised and unusual nature that only very few experts are available to provide the necessary evidence.

Determination of litigators' disbursements

G-21   17.–(1) Subject to paragraphs (2) to (5), the appropriate officer must allow such disbursements claimed under regulation 5(2) as appear to the appropriate officer to have been reasonably incurred.

(2) If the disbursements claimed are abnormally large by reason of the distance of the court or the assisted person's residence or both from the litigator's place of business, the appropriate officer may limit reimbursement of the disbursements to what otherwise would, having regard to all the circumstances, be a reasonable amount.

(3) No question as to the propriety of any step or act in relation to which prior authority has been obtained under regulation 13 may be raised on any determination of disbursements, unless the litigator knew or ought reasonably to have known that the purpose for which the authority was given had failed or had become irrelevant or unnecessary before the disbursements were incurred.

(4) Where disbursements are reasonably incurred in accordance with and subject to the limit imposed by a prior authority given under regulation 13, no question may be raised on any determination of fees as to the amount of the payment to be allowed for the step or act in relation to which the authority was given.

(5) Where disbursements are incurred in taking any steps or doing any act for which authority may be given under regulation 13, without such authority having been given or in excess of any fee so authorised, payment in respect of those disbursements may nevertheless be allowed on a determination of disbursements payable under regulation 5.

(6) Paragraph (7) applies where the Lord Chancellor receives a request for funding of an expert service of a type not listed in Schedule 5.

(7) In considering the rate at which to fund the expert service the Lord Chancellor—

> (a)   must have regard to the rates set out in Schedule 5; and
>
> (b)   may require more than one quotation for provision of the service to be submitted to the Lord Chancellor.

Interim payment of litigators' fees

G-21a   17A.–(1) A litigator may make a claim to the appropriate officer for an interim payment of the litigator's fees, in relation to proceedings in the Crown Court, in accordance with this regulation.

(2) Subject to paragraphs (3) to (6), a litigator may make a claim for an interim payment under this regulation in relation to one or more of the following stages in the proceedings—

> (a)   after the first hearing at which the assisted person enters a plea of not guilty;
>
> (b)   where representation is transferred to the litigator following the ordering of a retrial, after the date for the retrial has been set; and
>
> (c)   after commencement of a trial which is listed for 10 days or more.

(3) A litigator may not make a claim for an interim payment under paragraph (2)(a) or (b) in relation to a case committed or sent for trial to the Crown Court on the election of a defendant where the magistrates' court has determined the case to be suitable for summary trial.

(4) Subject to paragraphs (5) and (6), a litigator may make only one claim in relation to each of the stages in the proceedings set out in paragraph (2).

(5) A litigator may not make a claim for an interim payment under paragraph (2)(a) or (b) at the same time as, or after, that litigator has made a claim for an interim payment under paragraph (2)(c).

(6) A litigator may not make a claim for an interim payment under paragraph (2)(c) if the trial in question is a retrial and the litigator was the litigator for the first or a previous trial.

(7) A litigator may not make a claim for an interim payment at the same time as, or after, that litigator has made a claim under regulation 5.

(8) A litigator must make a claim for an interim payment to the appropriate officer in such form and manner as the appropriate officer may direct.

(9) A litigator must supply such information and documents as the appropriate officer may require to determine the claim for interim payment.

(10) Where a claim for an interim payment is made in accordance with this regulation, the appropriate officer must authorise payment.

(11) Where the claim is made under paragraph (2)(a) the amount of the interim payment is the sum of—

   (a)   the fee which, on a final determination of fees, would be paid to the litigator if paragraph 13 of Schedule 2 and the scenario "Before trial transfer (original litigator)" set out in the table following that paragraph applied; and

   (b)   any additional payments which, on a final determination of fees, would be paid to the litigator under paragraph 12 of Schedule 2.

(12) Where the claim is made under paragraph (2)(b), the amount of the interim payment is the sum of—

   (a)   the fee which, on a final determination of fees, would be paid to the litigator under paragraph 13 of Schedule 2 and the scenario "Transfer before cracked retrial (new litigator)" set out in the table following that paragraph; and

   (b)   any additional payments which, on a final determination of fees, would be paid to the litigator under paragraph 12 of Schedule 2.

(13) Where the claim is made under paragraph (2)(c), the amount of the interim payment is—

   (a)   the sum of—

      (i)   the fee determined in accordance with paragraph (14) on the basis that the trial length is one day; and

      (ii)   any additional payments which, on a final determination of fees, must be paid to the litigator under paragraph 12 of Schedule 2;

   (b)   less any amount paid to the litigator, in the proceedings in question, for a claim under paragraph (2)(a) or (b).

(14) The fee referred to in paragraph (13)(a)(i) is—

   (a)   where the number of pages of prosecution evidence is less than or equal to the PPE Cut-off specified in the table following paragraph 5(2) of Schedule 2, the basic fee specified in the table following paragraph 7(2) of that Schedule as appropriate to the offence with which the assisted person is charged and the number of pages of prosecution evidence served on the court;

   (b)   where the pages of prosecution evidence exceeds the PPE Cut-off specified in the table following paragraph 5(2) of Schedule 2, the final fee as calculated in accordance with paragraph 9(2) of that Schedule as appropriate to the offence with which the assisted person is charged and the number of pages of prosecution evidence served on the court.

(15) For purposes of paragraphs (11) to (14)—

   (a)   the number of defendants;

   (b)   the number of pages of prosecution evidence served on the court; and

   (c)   the offence with which the assisted person is charged are determined as at the date of the claim for the interim payment.

(16) Where a litigator has received a hardship payment under regulation 21, the amount of that hardship payment must be deducted from any interim payment payable to that litigator under this regulation.

(17) Where a litigator has already received one or more interim payments under this regulation, the amount to be deducted under paragraph (16) excludes any hardship payment already deducted from any earlier interim payment.

(18) Regulations 28 to 30 do not apply to a payment under this regulation.

(19) In this regulation, "cracked trial", "guilty plea" and "PPE cut-off" have the meaning given in Schedule 2.

(20) For the purpose of this regulation, the number of pages of prosecution evidence served on the court must be determined in accordance with paragraph 1(3) to (5) of Schedule 2.

[This regulation was inserted by the Criminal Legal Aid (Remuneration) (Amendment) (No. 2) Regulations 2014 (S.I. 2014 No. 2422), reg. 2(3), and Sched., with effect from October 2, 2014. The amendments made by those regulations apply to criminal proceedings in which a determina-

tion under the LASPOA 2012, s.16 (§ 6-212 in the main work) was made on or after October 2
2014: reg. 3. It is printed as further amended by S.I. 2015 No. 1369 (*ante,* G-1a); and S.I. 2015
No. 1678 (*ante,* G-1a).]

Interim payments in cases awaiting determination of fees

G-22   18.–(1) The appropriate officer must authorise an interim payment in respect of a claim for fees
in proceedings in the Crown Court in accordance with this regulation.

(2) Entitlement to a payment arises in respect of a claim for fees by a trial advocate, where—

    (a) the graduated fee claimed in accordance with Schedule 1 is £4,000 or more (exclusive of
value added tax); and

    (b) the claim for fees is for less than the amount mentioned in sub-paragraph (a) but is related
to any claim for fees falling under sub-paragraph (a).

(3) For the purposes of this regulation, the following claims for fees are related to each other—

    (a) the claims of trial advocates acting in the same proceedings for a defendant; and

    (b) the claims of any instructed advocate acting for any assisted person in related proceedings.

(4) Entitlement to a payment under paragraph (1) does not arise until three months have elapsed
from the earlier of—

    (a) the date on which the claim for fees is received by the appropriate officer for determina-
tion, except that where there are related claims for fees, the date on which the last claim is
received by the appropriate officer; or

    (b) three months after the conclusion of the last of any related proceedings.

(5) A trial advocate may submit a claim for an interim payment under this regulation where—

    (a) no payment has been made under paragraph (1); and

    (b) six months have elapsed from the conclusion of the proceedings against the assisted person.

(6) Subject to regulation 31, payment must not be made under this regulation unless the trial
advocate has submitted a claim for fees in accordance with regulation 4(3).

(7) In this regulation, where the main hearing is a trial, "trial advocate" means an advocate who—

    (a) is instructed pursuant to a section 16 determination to represent the assisted person at the
trial, and

    (b) attends the first day of the trial.

[This regulation is printed as amended, with effect from May 5, 2015, by the Criminal Legal
Aid (Remuneration) (Amendment) Regulations 2015 (S.I. 2015 No. 882), reg. 2(3)(b), (4)(b),
(5)(b) and (9). For the transitional provision, see *ante,* G-7.]

Amount of interim payments in cases awaiting determination of fees

G-23   19.–(1) Where entitlement to an interim payment arises under regulation 18, the amount payable
is 40% of the total claim for fees, less any sum already paid.

(2) Regulations 28 to 30 do not apply to an interim payment under this regulation.

Staged payments in long Crown Court proceedings

G-24   20.–(1) An instructed advocate may submit a claim to the appropriate officer for a staged payment
of the instructed advocate's fees in relation to proceedings in the Crown Court.

(2) Where a claim is submitted in accordance with this regulation, a staged payment must be allowed where the appropriate officer is satisfied—

    (a) that the claim relates to fees for a period of preparation of 100 hours or more, for which
the instructed advocate will, subject to final determination of the fees payable, be entitled
to be paid in accordance with Schedule 1; and

    (b) that the period from sending for trial (or from the date of the section 16 determination, if
later) to the conclusion of the Crown Court proceedings is likely to exceed 12 months, having regard, amongst other matters, to the number of defendants, the anticipated pleas and
the weight and complexity of the case.

(3) In this regulation, "preparation" means—

    (a) reading the papers in the case;

    (b) contact with prosecutors;

    (c) written or oral advice on plea;

    (d) researching the law, preparation for examination of witnesses and preparation of oral
submissions;

    (e) viewing exhibits or undisclosed material at police stations;

 (f) written advice on evidence;

 (g) preparation of written submissions, notices or other documents for use at the trial;

 (h) attendance at views at the scene of the alleged offence,

and is limited to preparation done before the trial, except in proceedings in which a preparatory hearing has been ordered under section 8 of the Criminal Justice Act 1987 (commencement of trial and arraignment), in which case it is limited to preparation done before the date on which the jury is sworn (or on which it became certain, by reason of pleas of guilty or otherwise, that the matter would not proceed to trial).

(4) The amount allowed for preparation falling within paragraph (3) must be determined by reference to the number of hours of preparation which it appears to the appropriate officer, without prejudice to the final determination of the fees payable, has been reasonably done, multiplied by the hourly rate for special preparation as set out in the table following paragraph 24 of Schedule 1, as appropriate to the category of advocate.

(5) A claim for staged payment of fees under this regulation must be made to the appropriate officer in such form and manner as the appropriate officer may direct, including such case plan as the appropriate officer may require for the purposes of paragraph (2)(a).

(6) An instructed advocate may claim further staged payments in accordance with this regulation in respect of further periods of preparation exceeding 100 hours which were not included in an earlier claim.

(7) Regulations 28 to 30 do not apply to a payment under this regulation.

[This regulation is printed as amended by S.I. 2015 No. 1678 (*ante*, G-1a).]

[The next paragraph is G-26.]

Hardship payments

 21.–(1) Subject to paragraphs (5) and (6), the appropriate officer may allow a hardship payment to **G-26** a representative in the circumstances set out in paragraph (2).

 (2) Those circumstances are that the representative–

 (a) represents the assisted person in proceedings in the Crown Court;

 (b) applies for such payment, in such form and manner as the appropriate officer may direct, not less than six months after the representative was first instructed in those proceedings, or in related proceedings if the representative was instructed in those proceedings earlier than in the proceedings to which the application relates;

 (c) is unlikely to receive final payment in respect of the proceedings, as determined under Schedule 1 or 2, within the three months following the application for the hardship payment; and

 (d) satisfies the appropriate officer that, by reason of the circumstance in sub-paragraph (c), the representative is likely to suffer financial hardship.

(3) Every application for a hardship payment by an advocate must be accompanied by such information and documents as the appropriate officer may require as evidence of–

 (a) the work done by the advocate in relation to the proceedings up to the date of the application; and

 (b) the likelihood of financial hardship.

(4) Every application for a hardship payment by a litigator must be accompanied by such information and documents as the appropriate officer may require as evidence of–

 (a) the Class of Offence with which the assisted person is charged, in accordance with Part 7 of Schedule 1;

 (b) the length of trial, where appropriate;

 (c) the number of pages of prosecution evidence, determined in accordance with paragraph 1(2) of Schedule 2;

 (d) the total number of defendants in the proceedings who are represented by the litigator, where appropriate;

 (e) the likelihood of financial hardship.

(5) The amount of any hardship payment is at the discretion of the appropriate officer, but must not exceed such sum as would be reasonable remuneration for the work done by the representative in the proceedings up to the date of the application.

(6) A hardship payment must not be made if it appears to the appropriate officer that the sum which would be reasonable remuneration for the representative, or the sum required to relieve the representative's financial hardship, is less than £5,000 (excluding value added tax).

(7) Subject to paragraphs (9) and (10) where the appropriate officer allows a hardship payment under paragraph (1), the appropriate officer must authorise payment accordingly.

(8) Where the application for a hardship payment is made by an advocate other than a trial advocate, and the appropriate officer allows a hardship payment under paragraph (1)–

    (a)   payment must be made to the–

        (i)   appropriate trial advocate who attends the first day of trial, where the trial has commenced;

        (ii)   appropriate trial advocate, where a trial has not commenced, or

        (iii) appropriate instructed advocate, where there is no trial advocate, and;

    (b)   the appropriate officer must notify the advocate who made the application that payment has been made to the appropriate trial advocate or the appropriate instructed advocate.

(9) Where a litigator has received an interim payment under regulation 17A, the amount of that interim payment must be deducted from any hardship payment payable to that litigator under this regulation.

(10) Where a litigator has already received one or more hardship payments under this regulation, the amount deducted under paragraph (9) excludes any interim payment already deducted from any earlier hardship payment.

(11) In paragraph (8)–

    "appropriate instructed advocate" means–

        (a)   where the section 16 determination provides for representation by a single advocate, the instructed advocate, or

        (b)   where the section 16 determination provides for representation by more than one advocate, the leading instructed advocate or the led instructed advocate, as appropriate, and

    "appropriate trial advocate" means–

        (a)   where the section 16 determination provides for representation by a single advocate, the trial advocate, or

        (b)   where the section 16 determination provides for representation by more than one advocate, the leading trial advocate or the led trial advocate, as appropriate.

[This regulation is printed as amended by S.I. 2014 No. 2422 (*ante*, G-21a). For the transitional provision, see *ante*, G-21a. It is printed as further amended, with effect from May 5, 2015, by the Criminal Legal Aid (Remuneration) (Amendment) Regulations 2015 (S.I. 2015 No. 882), reg. 2(3)(c) and (10) (for transitional provision, see *ante*, G-7); and, with effect from April 1, 2016, by S.I. 2015 No. 1369 (*ante*, G-1a).]

Computation of final claim where an interim payment has been made

G-27   **22.**–(1) At the conclusion of a case in which one or more payments have been made to an instructed advocate, a trial advocate or a litigator under regulations 17A to 21, the trial advocate or litigator must submit a claim under regulation 4 or 5 for the determination of the overall remuneration, whether or not such a claim will result in any payment additional to those already made.

(2) In the determination of the amount payable to a trial advocate or litigator under regulation 4 or 5–

    (a)   the appropriate officer must deduct the amount of any payment made under regulations 17A to 21 in respect of the same case from the amount that would otherwise be payable; and

    (b)   if the amount of the interim payment is greater than the amount that would otherwise be payable, the appropriate officer may recover the amount of the difference, either by way of repayment by the trial advocate or litigator or by way of deduction from any other amount that may be due to the trial advocate or litigator.

(3) In this regulation, where the main hearing is a trial, "trial advocate" means an advocate who–

    (a)   is instructed pursuant to a section 16 determination to represent the assisted person at the trial, and

    (b)   attends the first day of the trial.

[This regulation is printed as amended by S.I. 2014 No. 2422 (*ante*, G-21a). For the transitional provision, see *ante*, G-21a. It is also printed as further amended, with effect from May 5, 2015, by the Criminal Legal Aid (Remuneration) (Amendment) Regulations 2015 (S.I. 2015 No. 882), reg. 2(3)(d), (6)(b) and (11). For the transitional provision, see *ante*, G-7.]

Payment of fees to advocates–Crown Court

G-28   **23.**–(1) Having determined the fees payable to each trial advocate, in accordance with Schedule 1, the appropriate officer must notify each trial advocate of the fees payable and authorise payment accordingly.

(2) Where, as a result of any redetermination or appeal made or brought pursuant to regulations 28 to 30, the fees payable under paragraph (1) are altered—

(a) if they are increased, the appropriate officer must authorise payment of the increase; or

(b) if they are decreased, the trial advocate must repay the amount of such decrease.

(3) Where the payment of any fees of a trial advocate is ordered under regulation 29(12) or regulation 30(8), the appropriate officer must authorise payment.

(4) In this regulation, where the main hearing is a trial, "trial advocate" means an advocate who—

(a) is instructed pursuant to a section 16 determination to represent the assisted person at the trial, and

(b) attends the first day of the trial.

[This regulation is printed as amended, with effect from May 5, 2015, by the Criminal Legal Aid (Remuneration) (Amendment) Regulations 2015 (S.I. 2015 No. 882), reg. 2(3)(e), (5)(c), (6)(c) and (12). For the transitional provision, see *ante*, G-7.]

Payment of fees to litigators–Crown Court

24.—(1) Having determined the fees payable to a litigator in accordance with Schedule 2, the ap- **G-29** propriate officer must authorise payment accordingly.

(2) Where the appropriate officer determines that the fees payable under paragraph (1) are greater than or less than the amount claimed by the litigator under regulation 5(1), the appropriate officer must notify the litigator of the amount the appropriate officer has determined to be payable.

(3) Where, as a result of any redetermination or appeal made or brought pursuant to regulations 28 to 30, the fees payable under paragraph (1) are altered—

(a) if they are increased, the appropriate officer must authorise payment of the increase; or

(b) if they are decreased, the litigator must repay the amount of such decrease.

(4) Where the payment of any fees of the litigator is ordered under regulation 29(12) or regulation 30(8), the appropriate officer must authorise payment.

[The next paragraph is G-31.]

Recovery of overpayments

25.—(1) This regulation applies where a representative is entitled to be paid a certain sum ("the **G-31** amount due") by virtue of the provisions of Schedule 1, 2 or 3 and, for whatever reason, the representative is paid an amount greater than that sum.

(2) Where this regulation applies, the appropriate officer may—

(a) require immediate repayment of the amount in excess of the amount due ("the excess amount"); or

(b) deduct the excess amount from any other sum which is or becomes payable to the representative by virtue of the provisions of Schedule 1, 2 or 3,

and where sub-paragraph (a) applies the representative must repay the excess amount to the appropriate officer.

(3) The appropriate officer may proceed under paragraph (2)(b) without first proceeding under paragraph (2)(a).

(4) Paragraph (2) applies notwithstanding that the representative to whom the excess amount was paid is exercising, or may exercise, a right under regulations 28 to 30.

(5) In this regulation, where the main hearing is a trial, "trial advocate" means, for the purposes of the meaning of "representative", the advocate who—

(a) is instructed pursuant to a section 16 determination to represent the assisted person at the trial, and

(b) attends the first day of the trial.

[This regulation is printed as amended, with effect from May 5, 2015, by the Criminal Legal Aid (Remuneration) (Amendment) Regulations 2015 (S.I. 2015 No. 882), reg. 2(13). For the transitional provision, see *ante*, G-7.]

Adverse observations

26.—(1) Where in any proceedings to which Schedule 1, 2 or 3 applies, the court makes adverse **G-32**

observations concerning a representative's conduct of the proceedings, the appropriate officer may reduce any fee which would otherwise be payable in accordance with Schedule 1, 2 or 3 by such proportion as the appropriate officer considers reasonable.

(2) Before reducing the fee payable to a representative in accordance with the provisions of paragraph (1), the appropriate officer must give the representative the opportunity to make representations about whether it is appropriate to reduce the fee and the extent to which the fee should be reduced.

Wasted costs orders

G-33
27.–(1) Subject to paragraph (2), where the court has disallowed the whole or any part of any wasted costs under section 19A of the Prosecution of Offences Act 1985 (costs against legal representatives etc), the appropriate officer, in determining fees in respect of work done by the representative against whom the wasted costs order was made, may deduct the amount in the wasted costs order from the amount otherwise payable in accordance with these Regulations.

(2) Where the appropriate officer, in accordance with this regulation, is minded to disallow any amount of a claim for work done to which the wasted costs order relates, the appropriate officer must disallow that amount or the amount of the wasted costs order, whichever is the greater.

Redetermination of fees by appropriate offcer

G-34
28.–(1) Where—

    (a) an advocate in proceedings in the Crown Court is dissatisfied with the decision not to allow any of the following fees, or with the number of hours allowed in the calculation of such a fee, namely—

        (i) a special preparation fee under paragraph 17 of Schedule 1; or

        (ii) a wasted preparation fee under paragraph 18 of Schedule 1; or

    (b) a trial advocate in proceedings in the Crown Court is dissatisfied with—

        (i) the decision not to allow an hourly fee in respect of attendance at conferences or views at the scene of the alleged offence under paragraph 19 of Schedule 1, or with the number of hours allowed in the calculation of such a fee;

        (ii) the calculation by the appropriate officer of the fee payable to the trial advocate in accordance with Schedule 1; or

        (iii) the decision of the appropriate officer under paragraph 3(3) of Schedule 1 (reclassification of an offence not specifically listed in the relevant Table of Offences and so deemed to fall within Class H); or

    (c) a litigator is dissatisfied with—

        (i) the determination by the appropriate officer of the fee payable to the litigator in accordance with Schedule 2; or

        (ii) the decision of the appropriate officer under paragraph 3(3) of Schedule 2 (reclassification of an offence not specifically listed in the relevant Table of Offences and so deemed to fall within Class H),

the advocate, trial advocate or litigator, as the case may be, may apply to the appropriate officer to redetermine those fees, to review that decision or to reclassify the offence, as appropriate.

(2) An application under paragraph (1) may not challenge the quantum of any of the fees set out in Schedule 1 or Schedule 2.

(3) Subject to regulation 31, an application under paragraph (1), or paragraph 11(1) of Schedule 3, must be made—

    (a) within 21 days of the receipt of the fees payable under regulation 23, regulation 24 or paragraph 10 of Schedule 3, as appropriate;

    (b) by giving notice in writing to the appropriate officer, specifying the matters in respect of which the application is made and the grounds of objection; and

    (c) in such form and manner as the appropriate officer may direct.

(4) The notice of application must be accompanied by the information and documents supplied under regulation 4, regulation 5 or Schedule 3, as appropriate.

(5) The notice of application must state whether the applicant wishes to appear or to be represented and, if the applicant so wishes, the appropriate officer must notify the applicant of the hearing date and time.

(6) The applicant must supply such further information and documents as the appropriate officer may require.

(7) The appropriate officer must, in the light of the objections made by the applicant or on behalf of the applicant—

   (a)   redetermine the fees, whether by way of confirmation, or increase or decrease in the
amount previously determined;

   (b)   confirm the classification of the offence within Class H; or

   (c)   reclassify the offence,

as the case may be, and must notify the applicant of his decision.

(8) Where the applicant so requests, the appropriate officer must give reasons in writing for the
appropriate officer's decision.

(9) Subject to regulation 31, any request under paragraph (8) must be made within 21 days of
receiving notification of the appropriate officer's decision under paragraph (7).

(10) In this regulation, where the main hearing is a trial, "trial advocate" means an advocate who—

   (a)   is instructed pursuant to a section 16 determination to represent the assisted person at the
trial, and

   (b)   attends the first day of the trial.

[This regulation is printed as amended, with effect from May 5, 2015, by the Criminal Legal
Aid (Remuneration) (Amendment) Regulations 2015 (S.I. 2015 No. 882), reg. 2(14) (for
transitional provision, see *ante*, G-7; and, with effect from April 1, 2016, by S.I. 2015 No. 1369
(ante, G-1a)).]

Appeals to a costs judge

29.—(1) Where the appropriate officer has given his reasons for his decision under regulation   **G-35**
28(8), a representative who is dissatisfied with that decision may appeal to a costs judge.

(2) Subject to regulation 31, an appeal under paragraph (1) or paragraph 11(2) of Schedule 3
must be instituted within 21 days of the receipt of the appropriate officer's reasons, by giving notice
in writing to the Senior Costs Judge.

(3) The appellant must send a copy of any notice of appeal given under paragraph (2) to the appropriate officer.

(4) The notice of appeal must be accompanied by—

   (a)   a copy of any written representations given under regulation 28(3);

   (b)   the appropriate officer's reasons for the appropriate officer's decision given under regulation 28(8); and

   (c)   the information and documents supplied to the appropriate officer under regulation 28.

(5) The notice of appeal must—

   (a)   be in such form as the Senior Costs Judge may direct;

   (b)   specify separately each item appealed against, showing (where appropriate) the amount
claimed for the item, the amount determined and the grounds of the objection to the
determination; and

   (c)   state whether the appellant wishes to appear or to be represented or whether the appellant
will accept a decision given in the appellant's absence.

(6) The Senior Costs Judge may, and if so directed by the Lord Chancellor either generally or in a
particular case must, send to the Lord Chancellor a copy of the notice of appeal together with copies
of such other documents as the Lord Chancellor may require.

(7) With a view to ensuring that the public interest is taken into account, the Lord Chancellor may
arrange for written or oral representations to be made on the Lord Chancellor's behalf and, if the
Lord Chancellor intends to do so, the Lord Chancellor must inform the Senior Costs Judge and the
appellant.

(8) Any written representations made on behalf of the Lord Chancellor under paragraph (7) must
be sent to the Senior Costs Judge and the appellant and, in the case of oral representations, the
Senior Costs Judge and the appellant must be informed of the grounds on which such representations will be made.

(9) The appellant must be permitted a reasonable opportunity to make representations in reply.

(10) The costs judge must inform the appellant (or the person representing him) and the Lord
Chancellor, where representations have been or are to be made on the Lord Chancellor's behalf, of
the date of any hearing and, subject to the provisions of this regulation, may give directions as to the
conduct of the appeal.

(11) The costs judge may consult the trial judge or the appropriate officer and may require the appellant to provide any further information which the costs judge requires for the purpose of the appeal and, unless the costs judge otherwise directs, no further evidence may be received on the hearing of the appeal and no ground of objection may be raised which was not raised under regulation
28.

(12) The costs judge has the same powers as the appropriate officer under these Regulations and, in the exercise of such powers, may alter the redetermination of the appropriate officer in respect of any sum allowed, whether by increasing or decreasing it, as the costs judge thinks fit.

(13) The costs judge must communicate his decision and the reasons for it in writing to the appellant, the Lord Chancellor and the appropriate officer.

(14) Where the costs judge increases the sums redetermined under regulation 28, the costs judge may allow the appellant a sum in respect of part or all of any reasonable costs incurred by the appellant in connection with the appeal (including any fee payable in respect of an appeal).

Appeals to the High Court

G-36   **30.**–(1) A representative who is dissatisfied with the decision of a costs judge on an appeal under regulation 29 may apply to a costs judge to certify a point of principle of general importance.

(2) Subject to regulation 31, an application under paragraph (1) or paragraph 11(3) of Schedule 3 must be made within 21 days of receiving notification of a costs judge's decision under regulation 29(13).

(3) Where a costs judge certifies a point of principle of general importance the appellant may appeal to the High Court against the decision of a costs judge on an appeal under regulation 29, and the Lord Chancellor must be a respondent to such an appeal.

(4) Subject to regulation 31, an appeal under paragraph (3) must be instituted within 21 days of receiving notification of a costs judge's certificate under paragraph (1).

(5) Where the Lord Chancellor is dissatisfied with the decision of a costs judge on an appeal under regulation 29, the Lord Chancellor may, if no appeal has been made by an appellant under paragraph (3), appeal to the High Court against that decision, and the appellant must be a respondent to the appeal.

(6) Subject to regulation 31, an appeal under paragraph (5) must be instituted within 21 days of receiving notification of the costs judge's decision under regulation 29(13).

(7) An appeal under paragraph (3) or (5) must—

    (a) be brought in the Queen's Bench Division;

    (b) subject to paragraph (4), follow the procedure set out in Part 52 of the Civil Procedure Rules 1998; and

    (c) be heard and determined by a single judge whose decision will be final.

(8) The judge has the same powers as the appropriate officer and a costs judge under these Regulations and may reverse, affirm or amend the decision appealed against or make such other order as the judge thinks fit.

Time limits

G-37   **31.**–(1) Subject to paragraph (2), the time limit within which any act is required or authorised to be done under these Regulations may, for good reason, be extended—

    (a) in the case of acts required or authorised to be done under regulations 29 or 30, by a costs judge or the High Court as the case may be; and

    (b) in the case of acts required or authorised to be done by a representative under any other regulation, by the appropriate officer.

(2) Where a representative without good reason has failed (or, if an extension were not granted, would fail) to comply with a time limit, the appropriate officer, a costs judge or the High Court, as the case may be, may, in exceptional circumstances, extend the time limit and must consider whether it is reasonable in the circumstances to reduce the fees payable to the representative under regulations 4, 5 or 6, provided that the fees must not be reduced unless the representative has been allowed a reasonable opportunity to show cause orally or in writing why the fees should not be reduced.

(3) A representative may appeal to a costs judge against a decision made under this regulation by an appropriate officer and such an appeal must be instituted within 21 days of the decision being given by giving notice in writing to the Senior Costs Judge specifying the grounds of appeal.

(4) In this regulation, where the main hearing is a trial, "trial advocate" means, for the purposes of the meaning of "representative", the advocate who—

    (a) is instructed pursuant to a section 16 determination to represent the assisted person at the trial, and

    (b) attends the first day of the trial.

[This regulation is printed as amended, with effect from May 5, 2015, by the Criminal Legal Aid (Remuneration) (Amendment) Regulations 2015 (S.I. 2015 No. 882), reg. 2(15). For the transitional provision, see *ante*, G-7.]

[The next paragraph is G-39.]

Regulation 4   SCHEDULE 1

ADVOCATES' GRADUATED FEE SCHEME

PART 1

DEFINITIONS AND SCOPE

Interpretation

1.–(1) In this Schedule–   **G-39**

"case" means proceedings in the Crown Court against any one assisted person–

   (a) on one or more counts of a single indictment;

   (b) arising out of a single notice of appeal against conviction or sentence, or a single committal for sentence, whether on one or more charges; or

   (c) arising out of a single alleged breach of an order of the Crown Court,

and a case falling within paragraph (c) must be treated as a separate case from the proceedings in which the order was made;

"cracked trial" means a case on indictment in which–

   (a) the assisted person enters a plea of not guilty to one or more counts at the first hearing at which he or she enters a plea and–

      (i) the case does not proceed to trial (whether by reason of pleas of guilty or for other reasons) or the prosecution offers no evidence; and

      (ii) either–

         (aa) in respect of one or more counts to which the assisted person pleaded guilty, the assisted person did not so plead at the first hearing at which he or she entered a plea; or

         (bb) in respect of one or more counts which did not proceed, the prosecution did not, before or at the first hearing at which the assisted person entered a plea, declare an intention of not proceeding with them; or

   (b) the case is listed for trial without a hearing at which the assisted persons enters a plea;

"excluded hearing" means–

   (a) the first hearing at which the assisted person enters a plea;

   (b) any hearing which forms part of the main hearing, or

   (c) any hearing for which a fee is payable under a provision of this Schedule other than paragraph 12(2);

"guilty plea" means a case on indictment which–

   (a) is disposed of without a trial because the assisted person pleaded guilty to one or more counts; and

   (b) is not a cracked trial;

"*Newton* hearing" means a hearing at which evidence is heard for the purpose of determining the sentence of a convicted person in accordance with the principles of *R. v. Newton* (1982) 77 Cr.App.R. 13;

"standard appearance" means an appearance by the trial advocate or substitute advocate in any of the following hearings unless it is an excluded hearing–

   (a) a plea and case management hearing;

   (b) a pre-trial review;

   (ba) a pre-trial preparation hearing;

   (bb) a case management hearing;

   (c) the hearing of a case listed for plea which is adjourned for trial;

   (d) any hearing (except a trial, the first hearing at which the assisted person enters a plea or a hearing referred to in paragraph 2(1)(b)) which is listed but cannot proceed because of the failure of the assisted person or a witness to attend, the unavailability of a pre-sentence report or other good reason;

   (e) custody time limit applications;

   (f) bail and other applications (except where any such applications take place in the course of a hearing referred to in paragraph 2(1)(b));

   (g) the hearing of the case listed for mention only, including applications relating to the date of the trial (except where an application takes place in the course of a hearing referred to in paragraph 2(1)(b));

   (h) a sentencing hearing other than one falling within paragraph 2(1)(b)(ii), paragraph 15(1) or paragraph 34;

(i) a preliminary hearing; or

(j) a hearing, whether contested or not, relating to breach of bail, failure to surrender to bail or execution of a bench warrant,

provided that a fee is not payable elsewhere under this Schedule in respect of the hearing;

"substitute advocate" means an advocate who is not an instructed advocate or the trial advocate but who undertakes work on the case; ... .

(2) For the purposes of this Schedule, the number of pages of prosecution evidence served on the court must be determined in accordance with sub-paragraphs (3) to (5).

(3) The number of pages of prosecution evidence includes all—

(a) witness statements;

(b) documentary and pictorial exhibits;

(c) records of interviews with the assisted person; and

(d) records of interviews with other defendants,

which form part of the served prosecution documents or which are included in any notice of additional evidence.

(4) Subject to sub-paragraph (5), a document served by the prosecution in electronic form is included in the number of pages of prosecution evidence.

(5) A documentary or pictorial exhibit which—

(a) has been served by the prosecution in electronic form; and

(b) has never existed in paper form,

is not included within the number of pages of prosecution evidence unless the appropriate officer decides that it would be appropriate to include it in the pages of prosecution evidence taking into account the nature of the document and any other relevant circumstances.

(6) In proceedings on indictment in the Crown Court initiated otherwise than by sending for trial, the appropriate officer must determine the number of pages of prosecution evidence in accordance with sub-paragraphs (2) to (5) or as nearly in accordance with those sub-paragraphs as possible as the nature of the case permits.

(7) A reference to the Table of Offences in this Schedule is to the Table of Offences in Part 7 and a reference to a Class of Offence in this Schedule is to the Class in which that offence is listed in the Table of Offences.

[This paragraph is printed as amended, with effect from May 5, 2015, by the Criminal Legal Aid (Remuneration) (Amendment) Regulations 2015 (S.I. 2015 No. 882), reg. 2(16)(a). For the transitional provision, see *ante*, G-7. It is printed as further amended by S.I. 2015 No. 1678 (*ante*, G-1a).]

Application

G-40
2.—(1) Subject to sub-paragraphs (2) to (11), this Schedule applies to—

(a) every case on indictment; and

(b) the following proceedings in the Crown Court—

(i) an appeal against conviction or sentence;

(ii) a sentencing hearing following a committal for sentence to the Crown Court; and

(iii) proceedings arising out of an alleged breach of an order of the Crown Court (whether or not this Schedule applies to the proceedings in which the order was made).

(2) Sub-paragraphs (3) and (4) apply where, following a trial, an order is made for a new trial and the same trial advocate appears at both trials where—

(a) the defendant is an assisted person at both trials; or

(b) the defendant is an assisted person at the new trial only; or

(c) the new trial is a cracked trial or guilty plea.

(3) Subject to sub-paragraph (4), in respect of a new trial, or if the trial advocate so elects, in respect of the first trial, the graduated fee payable to the trial advocate must be calculated in accordance with Part 2 or Part 3, as appropriate, except that the fee must be reduced by—

(a) 30%, where the new trial started within one month of the conclusion of the first trial;

(b) 20%, where the new trial did not start within one month of the conclusion of the first trial;

(c) 40%, where the new trial becomes a cracked trial or guilty plea within one month of the conclusion of the first trial; or

(d) 25% where the new trial becomes a cracked trial or guilty plea more than one month after the conclusion of the first trial.

(4) Where—

(a) in relation to the first trial, the case was sent for trial to the Crown Court on the election of a defendant where the magistrates' court had determined the case to be suitable for summary trial; and

   (b) the new trial becomes a cracked trial or guilty plea,

the fee payable to the trial advocate must be

      (i) the graduated fee calculated in accordance with Part 2, in respect of the first trial; and

      (ii) the fixed fee set out in paragraph 10 in respect of the new trial.

(5) Sub-paragraphs (6) and (7) apply in the circumstances set out in sub-paragraph (2) but where a different trial advocate appears for the assisted person at each trial.

(6) Subject to sub-paragraph (7), in respect of each trial, the graduated fee payable to the trial advocate must be calculated in accordance with Part 2 or Part 3 as appropriate.

(7) Where—

   (a) in relation to the first trial, the case was sent for trial to the Crown Court on the election of a defendant where the magistrates' court had determined the case to be suitable for summary trial; and

   (b) the new trial becomes a cracked trial or guilty plea,

the fee payable to the trial advocate at the first trial must be the graduated fee, calculated in accordance with Part 2 and the fee payable to the trial advocate at the new trial must be the fixed fee set out in paragraph 10.

(8) Where following a case on indictment a *Newton* hearing takes place—

   (a) for the purposes of this Schedule the case is to be treated as having gone to trial;

   (b) the length of the trial is to be taken to be the combined length of the main hearing and the *Newton* hearing;

   (c) the provisions of this Schedule relating to cracked trials and guilty pleas do not apply; and

   (d) no fee is payable under paragraph 15 in respect of the *Newton* hearing.

(10) Where, at any time after proceedings are sent for trial to the Crown Court they are—

   (a) discontinued by a notice served under section 23A of the Prosecution of Offences Act 1985 (discontinuance of proceedings after accused has been sent for trial), or

   (b) dismissed pursuant to paragraph 2 of Schedule 3 to the Crime and Disorder Act 1998 (applications for dismissal),

the provisions of paragraph 22 apply.

(11) For the purposes of this Schedule, a case on indictment which discontinues at or before the first hearing at which the assisted person enters a plea otherwise than—

   (a) by reason of a plea of guilty being entered; or

   (b) in accordance with sub-paragraph (10),

must be treated as a guilty plea.

[Para. 2 is printed as amended by S.I. 2015 No. 1678 (*ante*, G-1a).]

Class of offences

3.—(1) For the purposes of this Schedule—   **G-41**

   (a) every indictable offence falls within the Class under which it is listed in the Table of Offences and, subject to sub-paragraph (2), indictable offences not specifically so listed are deemed to fall within Class H;

   (b) conspiracy to commit an indictable offence contrary to section 1 of the Criminal Law Act 1977 (the offence of conspiracy), incitement to commit an indictable offence and attempts to commit an indictable offence contrary to section 1 of the Criminal Attempts Act 1981 (attempting to commit an offence) fall within the same Class as the substantive offence to which they relate;

   (c) where the Table of Offences specifies that the Class within which an offence falls depends on whether the value involved exceeds a stated limit, the value must be presumed not to exceed that limit unless the advocate making the claim under regulation 4 proves otherwise to the satisfaction of the appropriate officer;

   (d) where more than one count of the indictment is for an offence in relation to which the Class depends on the value involved, that value must be taken to be the total value involved in all those offences, but where two or more counts relate to the same property, the value of that property must be taken into account once only;

   (e) where an entry in the Table of Offences specifies an offence as being contrary to a statutory provision, then subject to any express limitation in the entry that entry includes every offence contrary to that statutory provision whether or not the words of description in the entry are appropriate to cover all such offences;

(f) where in a case on indictment there is a hearing to determine the question of whether an assisted person is unfit to plead or unfit to stand trial, the trial advocate must elect whether that hearing falls within the same Class as the indictable offence to which it relates or within Class D; and

(g) where in a case on indictment a restriction order is made under section 41 of the Mental Health Act 1983 (power of higher courts to restrict discharge from hospital), the offence falls within Class A, regardless of the Class under which the offence would be listed in the Table of Offences but for this paragraph.

(2) Where an advocate in proceedings in the Crown Court is dissatisfied with the classification within Class H of an indictable offence not listed in the Table of Offences, the advocate may apply to the appropriate officer when lodging the claim for fees to reclassify the offence.

(3) The appropriate officer must, in light of the objections made by the advocate–

(a) confirm the classification of the offence within Class H; or

(b) reclassify the offence,

and must notify the advocate of the decision.

As to this paragraph, see *post*, G-119.

PART 2

GRADUATED FEES FOR TRIAL

Calculation of graduated fees

G-42
4. The amount of the graduated fee for a single trial advocate representing one assisted person being tried on one indictment in the Crown Court in a trial lasting one to 40 days must be calculated in accordance with the following formula–

$$G = B + (d \times D) + (e \times E) + (w \times W)$$

Where–

- **G** is the amount of the graduated fee;
- **B** is the basic fee specified in the table following paragraph 5 as appropriate to the offence for which the assisted person is tried and the category of trial advocate;
- **d** is the number of days or parts of a day on which the advocate attends at court by which the trial exceeds 2 days but does not exceed 40 days;
- **D** is the fee payable in respect of daily attendance at court for the number of days by which the trial exceeds 2 days but does not exceed 40 days, as appropriate to the offence for which the assisted person is tried and the category of trial advocate;
- **e** is the number of pages of prosecution evidence excluding the first 50, up to a maximum of 10,000;
- **E** is the evidence uplift specified in the table following paragraph 5 as appropriate to the offence for which the assisted person is tried and the category of trial advocate;
- **w** is the number of prosecution witnesses excluding the first 10;
- **W** is the witness uplift specified in the table following paragraph 5 as appropriate to the offence for which the assisted person is tried and the category of trial advocate.

Table of fees

G-43
5. For the purposes of paragraph 4 the basic fee (B), the daily attendance fee (D), the evidence uplift (E) and the witness uplift (W) appropriate to any offence are those specified in the table following this paragraph in accordance with the Class within which that offence falls.

TABLE OF FEES AND UPLIFTS

Class of Offence	Basic Fee (B) (£)	Daily attendance fee (D) (£)	Evidence uplift (E) (£)	Witness uplift (W) (£)
QC				
A	2,856	979	1.63	6.53
B	2,529	857	1.63	6.53
C	1,968	816	1.63	6.53
D	2,284	816	1.63	6.53
E	1,514	612	1.63	6.53
F	1,514	612	1.63	6.53

Class of Offence	Basic Fee (B) (£)	Daily attendance fee (D) (£)	Evidence uplift (E) (£)	Witness uplift (W) (£)
G	1,514	612	1.63	6.53
H	1,903	816	1.63	6.53
I	2,122	816	1.63	6.53
J	2,856	979	1.63	6.53
K	2,856	979	1.63	6.53
Leading Junior				
A	2,142	734	1.23	4.9
B	1,897	643	1.23	4.9
C	1,476	612	1.23	4.9
D	1,714	612	1.23	4.9
E	1,136	459	1.23	4.9
F	1,136	459	1.23	4.9
G	1,136	459	1.23	4.9
H	1,427	612	1.23	4.9
I	1,592	612	1.23	4.9
J	2,142	734	1.23	4.9
K	2,142	734	1.23	4.9
Led Junior				
A	1,632	490	0.81	3.26
B	1,265	428	0.81	3.26
C	898	408	0.81	3.26
D	1,125	408	0.81	3.26
E	694	306	0.81	3.26
F	694	306	0.81	3.26
G	694	306	0.81	3.26
H	816	408	0.81	3.26
I	979	408	0.81	3.26
J	1,632	490	0.81	3.26
K	1,428	490	0.81	3.26
Junior alone				
A	1,632	530	0.98	4.9
B	1,305	469	0.98	4.9
C	898	408	0.98	4.9
D	1,125	408	0.98	4.9
E	653	326	0.98	4.9
F	694	326	0.98	4.9
G	694	326	0.98	4.9
H	816	408	0.98	4.9
I	979	408	0.98	4.9
J	1,632	530	0.98	4.9
K	1,632	530	0.98	4.9

PART 3

GRADUATED FEES FOR GUILTY PLEAS AND CRACKED TRIALS

Scope of Part 3

G-44 6.–(1) Subject to sub-paragraph (2) and to paragraph 22, this Part does not apply to a case sent for trial to the Crown Court on the election of a defendant where the magistrates' court has determined the case to be suitable for a summary trial.

(2) This Part applies in all cases where the trial is a cracked trial because the prosecution offer no evidence on all counts against a defendant and the judge directs that a not guilty verdict be entered.

[This paragraph was substituted by S.I. 2014 No. 2422 (*ante*, G-21a). For the transitional provision, see *ante*, G-21a. It is printed as amended by S.I. 2015 No. 1678 (*ante*, G-1a).]

Calculation of graduated fees in guilty pleas and cracked trials

G-44a 7.–(1) The amount of the graduated fee for a single trial advocate representing one assisted person in a guilty plea or cracked trial is—

    (a) where the case is a guilty plea or a trial which cracks in the first third—

        (i) the basic fee specified in Table A following paragraph 8 as appropriate to the offence with which the assisted person is charged, and the category of trial advocate; and

        (ii) the evidence uplift, as appropriate to the number of pages of prosecution evidence, calculated in accordance with that table; and

    (b) where the case is a trial which cracks in the second or last third—

        (i) the basic fee specified in Table B following paragraph 8 as appropriate to the offence with which the assisted person is charged and the category of trial advocate; and

        (ii) the evidence uplift, as appropriate to the number of pages of prosecution evidence, calculated in accordance with that table.

(2) Where—

    (a) the trial of a case does not commence on the date first fixed; or

    (b) the case is not taken and disposed of from the first warned list in which it is entered,

the basic fee and evidence uplift for the offence are those specified for the last third in Table B following paragraph 8.

(3) In this paragraph, and in the tables following paragraph 8, references to the first, second and last third are references to the first, second and last third—

    (a) where a case is first listed for trial on a fixed date, of the period of time beginning with the day after the date on which the case is so listed and ending with the day before the date so fixed;

    (b) where the case is first placed in a warned list, of the period of time beginning with the day after the date on which the case is so placed and ending with the day before the date of the start of that warned list,

and where the number of days in this period of time cannot be divided by three equally, any days remaining after such division must be added to the last third.

(4) Where a graduated fee is calculated in accordance with this Part for the purposes of paragraph 2(3), the fee must be calculated as if the trial had cracked in the last third.

Tables of fees

G-45 8. Subject to paragraph 7, the basic fee and evidence uplift appropriate to any offence are specified in the tables following this paragraph in accordance with the Class within which that offence falls, the category of trial advocate and whether the case is a guilty plea, a trial which cracks in the first third or a trial which cracks in the second or last third.

TABLE A: FEES AND UPLIFTS IN GUILTY PLEAS AND TRIALS WHICH CRACK IN THE FIRST THIRD

Class of Offence	Basic fee (£)	Evidence uplift per page of prosecution evidence (pages 1 to 1,000) (£)	Evidence uplift per page of prosecution evidence (1,001 to 10,000) (£)
QC			
A	1,714	2.85	1.43
B	1,305	1.8	0.9
C	1,224	1.28	0.64

Class of Offence	Basic fee (£)	Evidence uplift per page of prosecution evidence (pages 1 to 1,000) (£)	Evidence uplift per page of prosecution evidence (1,001 to 10,000) (£)
D	1,305	2.85	1.43
E	1,081	0.92	0.46
F	1,081	1.2	0.61
G	1,081	1.2	0.61
H	1,224	1.65	0.82
I	1,224	1.61	0.8
J	1,714	2.85	1.43
K	1,714	1.59	0.8
Leading Junior			
A	1,285	2.15	1.07
B	979	1.35	0.67
C	918	0.96	0.48
D	979	2.15	1.07
E	811	0.69	0.35
F	811	0.9	0.46
G	811	0.9	0.46
H	918	1.24	0.61
I	918	1.21	0.6
J	1,285	2.15	1.07
K	1,285	1.19	0.6
Led Junior			
A	857	1.43	0.72
B	653	0.9	0.45
C	612	0.64	0.32
D	653	1.43	0.72
E	541	0.46	0.23
F	541	0.61	0.3
G	541	0.61	0.3
H	612	0.83	0.42
I	612	0.8	0.4
J	857	1.43	0.72
K	857	0.8	0.4
Junior Alone			
A	979	1.19	0.59
B	694	0.81	0.41
C	449	0.6	0.3
D	694	1.19	0.59
E	408	0.35	0.17
F	408	0.54	0.27
G	408	0.54	0.27
H	490	0.54	0.28
I	571	0.42	0.22
J	979	1.19	0.59

Class of Offence	Basic fee (£)	Evidence uplift per page of prosecution evidence (pages 1 to 1,000) (£)	Evidence uplift per page of prosecution evidence (1,001 to 10,000) (£)
K	979	1.02	0.51

TABLE B: FEES AND UPLIFTS IN TRIALS WHICH CRACK IN THE SECOND OR FINAL THIRD

Class of Offence	Basic Fee (£)	Evidence uplift per page of prosecution evidence (pages 1 to 250) (£)	Evidence up lift per page of prosecutionevidence (pages 251-1000) (£)	Evidence uplift per page of prosecution evidence (pages 1,001 to 10,000) (£)
QC				
A	2,324	5.07	1.27	1.68
B	1,743	3.2	0.8	1.06
C	1,520	2.27	0.57	0.75
D	1,743	5.07	1.27	1.68
E	1,232	1.63	0.41	0.54
F	1,232	2.14	0.54	0.71
G	1,232	2.14	0.54	0.71
H	1,540	2.93	0.73	0.96
I	1,598	2.87	0.71	0.94
J	2,324	5.07	1.27	1.68
K	2,324	2.83	0.71	0.94
Leading Junior				
A	1,744	3.8	0.95	1.26
B	1,307	2.4	0.6	0.8
C	1,140	1.7	0.43	0.56
D	1,307	3.8	0.95	1.26
E	924	1.22	0.31	0.41
F	924	1.6	0.41	0.53
G	924	1.6	0.41	0.53
H	1,155	2.2	0.54	0.72
I	1,198	2.14	0.53	0.71
J	1,744	3.8	0.95	1.26
K	1,744	2.13	0.53	0.71
Led Junior				
A	1162	2.54	0.64	0.84
B	871	1.6	0.4	0.53
C	760	1.14	0.28	0.37
D	871	2.54	0.64	0.84
E	616	0.82	0.2	0.27
F	616	1.07	0.27	0.36
G	616	1.07	0.27	0.36
H	770	1.46	0.37	0.48
I	798	1.43	0.36	0.48
J	1162	2.54	0.64	0.84
K	1162	1.42	0.36	0.47

Class of Offence	Basic Fee (£)	Evidence uplift per page of prosecution evidence (pages 1 to 250) (£)	Evidence up lift per page of prosecutionevidence (pages 251-1000) (£)	Evidence uplift per page of prosecution evidence (pages 1,001 to 10,000) (£)
Junior alone				
A	1307	4.52	2.1	0.69
B	908	3.11	1.45	0.48
C	581	2.31	1.07	0.36
D	808	4.52	2.1	0.69
E	508	1.34	0.63	0.2
F	508	2.08	0.96	0.32
G	508	2.08	0.96	0.32
H	618	2.08	0.97	0.32
I	726	1.63	0.76	0.25
J	1307	4.52	2.1	0.69
K	1234	3.91	1.82	0.60

PART 4

FIXED FEE FOR GUILTY PLEAS AND CRACKED TRIALS

Scope of Part 4

9.–(1) Subject to sub-paragraph (2), this Part applies to a case sent for trial to the Crown Court on **G-46** the election of a defendant where the magistrates' court has determined the case to be suitable for summary trial.

(2) This Part does not apply where the trial is a cracked trial because the prosecution offer no evidence on all counts against a defendant and the judge directs that a not guilty verdict be entered.

[This paragraph was substituted by S.I. 2014 No. 2422 (*ante*, G-21a). For the transitional provision, see *ante*, G-21a. It is printed as amended by S.I. 2015 No. 1678 (*ante*, G-1a).]

Fixed fee for guilty pleas or cracked trials

10. The fee payable to an advocate in relation to a guilty plea or cracked trial to which this Part applies is £194 per proceedings.

PART 5

FIXED FEES

General provisions

11.–(1) All work undertaken by an advocate in a case to which Part 4 applies is included within **G-46a** the fee set out in paragraph 10 except for attendance at a confiscation hearing to which paragraph 14 applies.

(2) Except as provided under this Part, all work undertaken by an advocate in a case to which Part 3 applies is included within the basic fee (B) specified in the table following paragraph 5, or that following paragraph 8, as appropriate to—

(a) the offence for which the assisted person is tried;

(b) the category of advocate; and

(c) whether the case is a cracked trial, guilty plea or trial.

Fees for standard appearance

12.–(1) The fee payable in respect of— **G-47**

(a) an appearance by the trial advocate or substitute advocate at the first hearing at which the assisted person enters a plea; and

(b) up to four standard appearances by the trial advocate or substitute advocate,

is included within the basic fee (B) specified in the table following paragraph 5, or that following paragraph 8, as appropriate to the offence for which the assisted person is tried and the category of trial advocate.

(2) The fee payable in respect of an appearance by the trial advocate or substitute advocate at a

standard appearance not included in sub-paragraph (1) is specified in the table following paragraph 24 as appropriate to the category of trial advocate or substitute advocate.

(4) This paragraph does not apply to a standard appearance which is or forms part of the main hearing in a case or to a hearing for which a fee is payable elsewhere under this Schedule.

[Para. 12 is printed as amended by S.I. 2015 No. 1678 (*ante*, G-1a).]

As to whether any appearances can be remunerated under paragraph 12(2) where no basic fee is payable, see *R. v. Metcalf* and *R. v. Muoka*, *post*, G-129.

Fees for abuse of process, disclosure, admissibility and withdrawal of plea hearings

G-48   13.–(1) This paragraph applies to—

(a) the hearing of an application to stay the case on indictment or any count on the ground that the proceedings constitute an abuse of the process of the court;

(b) any hearing relating to the question of whether any material should be disclosed by the prosecution to the defence or the defence to the prosecution (whether or not any claim to public interest immunity is made);

(c) the hearing of an application under section 2(1) of the Criminal Procedure (Attendance of Witnesses) Act 1965 (issue of witness summons on application to Crown Court) for disclosure of material held by third parties;

(d) any hearing relating to the question of the admissibility as evidence of any material; and

(e) the hearing of an application to withdraw a plea of guilty where the application is—

(i)   made by an advocate other than the advocate who appeared at the hearing at which the plea of guilty was entered; and

(ii) unsuccessful.

(2) Where a hearing to which this paragraph applies is held on any day of the main hearing of a case on indictment, no separate fee is payable in respect of attendance at the hearing, but the hearing is included in the length of the main hearing for the purpose of calculating the fees payable.

(3) Where a hearing to which this paragraph applies is held prior to the first or only day of the main hearing, it is not included in the length of the main hearing for the purpose of calculating the fees payable and the trial advocate or substitute advocate must be remunerated for attendance at such a hearing—

(a) in respect of any day where the hearing begins before and ends after the luncheon adjournment, at the daily rate set out in the table following paragraph 24 as appropriate to the category of trial advocate or substitute advocate; or

(b) in respect of any day where the hearing begins and ends before the luncheon adjournment, or begins after the luncheon adjournment, at the half-daily rate set out in the table following paragraph 24 as appropriate to the category of trial advocate or substitute advocate.

Fees for confiscation hearings

G-49   14.–(1) This paragraph applies to—

(a) a hearing under Part 2 of the Proceeds of Crime Act 2002 (confiscation: England and Wales);

(b) a hearing under section 2 of the Drug Trafficking Act 1994 (confiscation orders); and

(c) a hearing under section 71 of the Criminal Justice Act 1988 (confiscation orders).

(2) A hearing to which this paragraph applies is not included in the length of the main hearing or of any sentencing hearing for the purpose of calculating the fees payable, and the trial advocate or substitute advocate must be remunerated in respect of such a hearing—

(a) where the number of pages of evidence is fewer than 51, for attendance—

(i)   in respect of any day when the hearing begins before and ends after the luncheon adjournment, at the daily rate set out in the first section of the table following this sub-paragraph; or

(ii) in respect of any day when the hearing begins and ends before the luncheon adjournment, or begins after the luncheon adjournment, at the half-daily rate set out in the first section of that table,

as appropriate to the category of trial advocate or substitute advocate;

(b) where the number of pages of evidence is between 51 and 1000—

(i)   at the rates for the relevant number of pages set out in the second section of the table following this sub-paragraph; and

(ii) where the hearing lasts for more than one day, for attendance on subsequent days or half-days at the daily rate or half-daily rate set out in the first section of that table,

as appropriate to the category of trial advocate or substitute advocate; or

(c) where the number of pages of evidence exceeds 1000–

 (i) at the rates for 751 to 1000 pages set out in the second section of the table following this sub-paragraph;

 (ii) with such fee as the appropriate officer considers reasonable for preparation in respect of the pages in excess of 1000, at the hourly rates for preparation set out in the third section of that table; and

 (iii) where the hearing lasts for more than one day, for attendance on subsequent days or half-days at the daily rate or half-daily rate set out in the first section of that table,

as appropriate to the category of trial advocate or substitute advocate.

FEES FOR CONFISCATION HEARINGS

	Fee for QC (£)	Fee for leading junior (£)	Fee for junior alone (£)	Fee for led junior (£)
1. Daily and half-daily rates				
Half-daily rate	260	195	130	130
Daily rate	497	346	238	238
2. Pages of evidence				
51–250	649	541	433	324
251–500	973	811	649	486
501–750	1,298	1,081	865	649
751–1000	1,946	1,622	1,298	973
3. Preparation				
Hourly rates	74	56	39	39

(3) In sub-paragraph (2) "evidence" means–

(a) the statement of information served under section 16 of the Proceeds of Crime Act 2002 and relied on by the prosecution for the purposes of a hearing under Part 2 of that Act, or a similar statement served and so relied on for the purposes of a hearing under section 2 of the Drug Trafficking Act 1994 or under section 71 of the Criminal Justice Act 1988 and, in each case, any attached annexes and exhibits;

(b) any other document which–

 (i) is served as a statement or an exhibit for the purposes of the trial;

 (ii) is specifically referred to in, but not served with, a statement mentioned in paragraph (a); and

 (iii) the prosecution state that they intend to rely on in the hearing; and

(c) any written report of an expert obtained with the prior authority of the Lord Chancellor under regulation 13 or allowed by the appropriate officer under these Regulations, and any attached annexes and exhibits, other than documents contained in such annexes or exhibits which have also been served under paragraph (a) or (b) or which consist of financial records or similar data.

Fees for sentencing hearings

15.–(1) This paragraph applies to a sentencing hearing following a case on indictment to which **G-50** this Schedule applies, where sentence has been deferred under section 1 of the Powers of Criminal Courts (Sentencing) Act 2000 (deferment of sentence).

(2) The fee payable to an advocate for appearing at a hearing to which this paragraph applies is that set out in the table following paragraph 24 as appropriate to the category of trial advocate or substitute advocate and the circumstances of the hearing.

Fees for ineffective trials

16. The fee set out in the table following paragraph 24 as appropriate to the category of trial **G-51** advocate is payable in respect of each day on which the case was listed for trial but did not proceed on the day for which it was listed, for whatever reason.

Fees for special preparation

17.–(1) This paragraph applies where, in any case on indictment in the Crown Court in respect of **G-52** which a graduated fee is payable under Part 2 or Part 3–

(a) it has been necessary for an advocate to do work by way of preparation substantially in

excess of the amount normally done for cases of the same type because the case involves a
very unusual or novel point of law or factual issue;

   (b) the number of pages of prosecution evidence, as defined in paragraph 1(2), exceeds 10,000
and the appropriate officer considers it reasonable to make a payment in excess of the
graduated fee payable under this Schedule; or

   (c) a documentary or pictorial exhibit is served by the prosecution in electronic form where—

      (i) the exhibit has never existed in paper form; and

      (ii) the appropriate officer—

         (aa) does not consider it appropriate to include the exhibit in the pages of prosecu-
tion evidence; and

         (bb) considers it reasonable to make a payment in respect of the exhibit in excess of
the graduated fee.

(2) Where this paragraph applies, a special preparation fee may be paid, in addition to the graduated fee payable under Part 2 or Part 3.

(3) The amount of the special preparation fee must be calculated—

   (a) where sub-paragraph (1)(a) applies, from the number of hours preparation in excess of the
amount the appropriate officer considers reasonable for cases of the same type;

   (b) where sub-paragraph (1)(b) applies, from the number of hours which the appropriate officer considers reasonable to read the excess pages; and

   (c) where sub-paragraph (1)(c) applies, from the number of hours which the appropriate officer considers reasonable to view the prosecution evidence,

and in each case using the hourly fee rates set out in the table following paragraph 24 as appropriate
to the category of trial advocate.

(4) Any claim for a special preparation fee under this paragraph must be made by a trial advocate,
whether or not the trial advocate did the work claimed for.

(5) A trial advocate claiming a special preparation fee must supply such information and documents as may be required by the appropriate officer in support of the claim.

(6) In determining a claim under this paragraph, the appropriate officer must take into account all
the relevant circumstances of the case, including, where special preparation work has been undertaken
by more than one advocate, the benefit of such work to the trial advocate.

(7) In sub-paragraphs (4) and (5), where the main hearing is a trial, "trial advocate" means the
advocate who—

   (a) is instructed pursuant to a section 16 determination to represent the assisted person at the
trial, and

   (b) attends the first day of the trial.

[This paragraph is printed as amended, with effect from May 5, 2015, by the Criminal Legal
Aid (Remuneration) (Amendment) Regulations 2015 (S.I. 2015 No. 882), reg. 2(3)(f), (4)(c),
(6)(d), and (16)(b). For the transitional provision, see *ante*, G-7.]

Fees for wasted preparation

G-53   18.—(1) A wasted preparation fee may be claimed where a trial advocate in any case to which this
paragraph applies is prevented from representing the assisted person in the main hearing by any of
the following circumstances—

   (a) the trial advocate is instructed to appear in other proceedings at the same time as the main
hearing in the case and has been unable to secure a change of date for either the main
hearing or the other proceedings;

   (b) the date fixed for the main hearing is changed by the court despite the trial advocate's
objection;

   (c) the trial advocate has withdrawn from the case with the leave of the court because of the
trial advocate's professional code of conduct or to avoid embarrassment in the exercise of
the trial advocate's profession;

   (d) the trial advocate has been dismissed by the assisted person or the litigator; or

   (e) the trial advocate is obliged to attend at any place by reason of a judicial office held by the
trial advocate or other public duty.

(2) This paragraph applies to every case on indictment to which this Schedule applies provided
that—

   (a) the case goes to trial, and the trial lasts for five days or more; or

   (b) the case is a cracked trial, and the number of pages of prosecution evidence exceeds 150.

(3) The amount of the wasted preparation fee must be calculated from the number of hours of

preparation reasonably carried out by the trial advocate, using the hourly fee rates set out in the table following paragraph 24 as appropriate to the category of trial advocate, but no such fee is payable unless the number of hours of preparation is eight or more.

(4) Any claim for a wasted preparation fee under this paragraph must be made by a trial advocate, whether or not the trial advocate did the work claimed for.

(5) A trial advocate claiming a wasted preparation fee must supply such information and documents as may be required by the appropriate officer as proof of the circumstances in which the advocate was prevented from representing the assisted person and of the number of hours of preparation.

(6) In sub-paragraphs (4) and (5), where the main hearing is a trial, "trial advocate" means an advocate who—

(a) is instructed pursuant to a section 16 determination to represent the assisted person at the trial, and

(b) attends the first day of the trial.

[This paragraph is printed as amended, with effect from May 5, 2015, by the Criminal Legal Aid (Remuneration) (Amendment) Regulations 2015 (S.I. 2015 No. 882), reg. 2(4)(c), (6)(d) and (16)(c). For the transitional provision, see *ante*, G-7.]

Fees for conferences and views

G-54

19.—(1) This paragraph applies to the following types of work—

(a) attendance by the trial advocate at pre-trial conferences with prospective or actual expert witnesses not held at court;

(b) attendance by the trial advocate at views at the scene of the alleged offence;

(c) attendance by the trial advocate at pre-trial conferences with the assisted person not held at court;

(d) reasonable travelling time by the trial advocate for the purpose of attending a view at the scene of the alleged offence; or

(e) reasonable travelling time by the trial advocate for the purpose of attending a pre-trial conference with the assisted person or prospective or actual expert witness, where the appropriate officer is satisfied that the assisted person or prospective or actual expert witness was unable or could not reasonably have been expected to attend a conference at the trial advocate's chambers or office.

(2) The fees payable in respect of attendance at the first three pre-trial conferences or views, as set out in sub-paragraph (1)(a) to (c), are included in the basic fee (B) specified in the table following paragraph 5, or that following paragraph 8, as appropriate to the offence for which the assisted person is tried, the category of trial advocate and whether the case is a guilty plea, cracked trial or trial, provided that the trial advocate satisfies the appropriate officer that the work was reasonably necessary.

(3) The fee specified in the table following paragraph 24 as appropriate to the category of trial advocate is payable in the following circumstances, provided that the trial advocate satisfies the appropriate officer that the work was reasonably necessary—

(a) for trials lasting not less than 21 and not more than 25 days, and cracked trials where it was accepted by the court at the first hearing at which the assisted person entered a plea that the trial would last not less than 21 days and not more than 25 days, one further pre-trial conference or view not exceeding two hours;

(b) for trials lasting not less than 26 and not more than 35 days, and cracked trials where it was accepted by the court at the first hearing at which the assisted person entered a plea that the trial would last not less than 26 days and not more than 35 days, two further pre-trial conferences or views each not exceeding two hours; and

(c) for trials lasting not less than 36 days, and cracked trials where it was accepted by the court at the first hearing at which the assisted person entered a plea that the trial would last not less than 36 days and not more than 40 days, three further pre-trial conferences or views each not exceeding two hours.

(4) Travel expenses must be paid for all conferences and views set out in sub-paragraph (1)(a) to (c), provided that the trial advocate satisfies the appropriate officer that they were reasonably incurred.

(5) Travelling time must be paid for all conferences and views set out in sub-paragraph (1)(a) to (c), provided that the trial advocate satisfies the appropriate officer that it was reasonable.

[Para. 19 is printed as amended by S.I. 2015 No. 1678 (*ante*, G-1a).]

Fees for appeals, committals for sentence and breach hearings

20.—(1) Subject to sub-paragraphs (4) and (5) and paragraph 26 the fee payable to a trial advocate **G-55** in any of the hearings referred to in paragraph 2(1)(b) is the fixed fee specified in the table following paragraph 24.

(2) Where a hearing referred to in paragraph 2(1)(b) is listed but cannot proceed because of the failure of the assisted person or a witness to attend, the unavailability of a pre-sentence report, or other good reason, the fee payable to the advocate is the fixed fee specified in the table following paragraph 24.

(3) Where—

    (a) a bail application;

    (b) a mention hearing; or

    (c) any other application,

takes place in the course of a hearing referred to in paragraph 2(1)(b), the fee payable to the advocate is the fixed fee specified in the table following paragraph 24.

(4) Where it appears to the appropriate officer that the fixed fee allowed under sub-paragraph (1) would be inappropriate taking into account all of the relevant circumstances of the case the appropriate officer may instead allow fees of such amounts as appear to the appropriate officer to be reasonable remuneration for the relevant work in accordance with sub-paragraph (5).

(5) The appropriate officer may allow any of the following classes of fees to an advocate in respect of work allowed by the appropriate officer under this paragraph—

    (a) a fee for preparation including, where appropriate, the first day of the hearing including, where they took place on that day—

        (i) short conferences;

        (ii) consultations;

        (iii) applications and appearances (including bail applications);

        (iv) views at the scene of the alleged offence; and

        (v) any other preparation;

    (b) a refresher fee for any day or part of a day for which a hearing continued, including, where they took place on that day—

        (i) short conferences;

        (ii) consultations;

        (iii) applications and appearances (including bail applications);

        (iv) views at the scene of the alleged offence; and

        (v) any other preparation; and

    (c) subsidiary fees for—

        (i) attendance at conferences, consultations and views at the scene of the alleged offence not covered by paragraph (a) or (b);

        (ii) written advice on evidence, plea, appeal, case stated or other written work; and

        (iii) attendance at applications and appearances (including bail applications and adjournments for sentence) not covered by paragraph (a) or (b).

Fees for contempt proceedings

G-55a

21.—(1) Subject to sub-paragraph (2), remuneration for advocates in proceedings referred to in section 14(g) of the Act in the Crown Court must be at the rates specified in the table following this sub-paragraph.

Category of advocate	Payment rates (£ per day)
QC	300
Leading junior	225
Led junior or junior acting alone	150

(2) Where an advocate and a litigator are instructed in proceedings referred to in section 14(g) of the Act, remuneration must be at the rates specified in the table following this sub-paragraph, as appropriate to the category of advocate.

Category of advocate	Payment rates (£ per day)
QC	175
Leading junior	125
Led junior or junior acting alone	100

Discontinuance or dismissal of proceedings

G-56

22.—(1) This paragraph applies to proceedings which are sent for trial in the Crown Court.

(2) Where proceedings referred to in sub-paragraph (1) are discontinued by a notice served under section 23A of the Prosecution of Offences Act 1985 (discontinuance of proceedings after accused has been sent for trial) at any time before the prosecution serves its evidence in accordance with the Crime and Disorder Act 1998 (Service of Prosecution Evidence) Regulations 2005 the advocate must be paid 50% of the basic fee (B) for a guilty plea, as specified in the table following paragraph 8 as appropriate to the offence for which the assisted person is charged and the category of advocate.

(3) Where proceedings referred to in sub-paragraph (1) are discontinued by a notice served under section 23A of the Prosecution of Offences Act 1985 (discontinuance of proceedings after accused has been sent for trial) at any time after the prosecution serves its evidence in accordance with the Crime and Disorder Act 1998 (Service of Prosecution Evidence) Regulations 2005, the advocate must be paid a graduated fee calculated in accordance with paragraph 7, as appropriate for representing an assisted person in a guilty plea.

(5) Where, at or before the first hearing at which the assisted person enters a plea—

(a)   the prosecution offers no evidence and the assisted person is discharged; or

(b)   the case is remitted to the magistrates' court in accordance with paragraph 10(3)(a), 13(2) or 15(3)(a) of Schedule 3 to the Crime and Disorder Act 1998,

the advocate instructed in the proceedings must be paid a graduated fee calculated in accordance with paragraph 7, as appropriate for representing an assisted person in a guilty plea.

(6) Where an application for dismissal is made under paragraph 2 of Schedule 3 to the Crime and Disorder Act 1998, the advocate must be remunerated for attendance at the hearing of the application for dismissal—

(a)   in respect of any day where the hearing begins before and ends after the luncheon adjournment, at the daily rate set out in the table following paragraph 24 as appropriate to the category of advocate; or

(b)   in respect of any day where the hearing begins and ends before the luncheon adjournment, or begins after the luncheon adjournment, at the half-daily rate set out in that table as appropriate to the category of advocate,

provided that a fee is not payable elsewhere under this Schedule in respect of any day of the hearing.

(7) Where an application for dismissal is made under paragraph 2 of Schedule 3 to the Crime and Disorder Act 1998, and—

(a)   the charge, or charges, are dismissed and the assisted person is discharged; or

(b)   the case is remitted to the magistrates' court in accordance with paragraph 10(3)(a), 13(2) or 15(3)(a) of Schedule 3 to the Crime and Disorder Act 1998,

in respect of the first day of the hearing of the application to dismiss, the advocate instructed in the proceedings must be paid a graduated fee calculated in accordance with paragraph 7, as appropriate for representing an assisted person in a guilty plea.

(8) Where an advocate represents more than one assisted person in proceedings referred to in sub-paragraph (1), the advocate must be paid a fixed fee of 20% of—

(a)   the fee specified in sub-paragraph (2) where that sub-paragraph applies; or

(b)   the basic fee (B) specified in the table following paragraph 8 where sub-paragraph (3), (4) or (5) applies, as appropriate for the circumstances set out in the relevant sub-paragraph,

in respect of each additional assisted person the advocate represents.

[Para. 22 is printed as amended by S.I. 2015 No. 1678 (*ante*, G-1a).]

Noting brief fees

23. The fee payable to an advocate retained solely for the purpose of making a note of any hearing must be the daily fee set out in the table following paragraph 24.   **G-57**

Fixed fees

24. The table following this paragraph sets out the fixed fees payable in relation to the category of work specified in the first column of the table.   **G-57a**

FIXED FEES

Category of work	Paragraph providing for fee	Fee for QC £	Fee for leading junior £	Fee for led junior or junior alone £
Standard appearance	9(2)	173 per day	130 per day	87 per day

Category of work	Paragraph providing for fee	Fee for QC £	Fee for leading junior £	Fee for led junior or junior alone £
Abuse of process hearing	10(1)(a)	260 Half day	195 Half day	130 Half day
		497 Full day	346 Full day	238 Full day
Hearings relating to disclosure	10(1)(b) and (c)	260 Half day	195 Half day	130 Half day
		497 Full day	346 Full day	238 Full day
Hearings relating to the admissibility of evidence	10(1)(d)	260 Half day	195 Half day	130 Half day
		497 Full day	346 Full day	238 Full day
Hearings on withdrawal of guilty plea	10(1)(e)	260 Half day	195 Half day	130 Half day
		497 Full day	346 Full day	238 Full day
Deferred sentencing hearing	12(1)(a)	324 per day	238 per day	173 per day
Ineffective trial payment	13	281 per day	195 per day	130 per day
Special preparation	14	74 per hour	56 per hour	39 per hour
Wasted preparation	15	74 per hour	56 per hour	39 per hour
Conferences and views	16	74 per hour	56 per hour	39 per hour
Appeals to the Crown Court against conviction	17(1)	260 per day	195 per day	130 per day
Appeals to the Crown Court against sentence	17(1)	216 per day	151 per day	108 per day
Proceedings relating to breach of an order of the Crown Court	17(1)	216 per day	151 per day	108 per day
Committal for sentence	17(1)	260 per day	195 per day	130 per day
Adjourned appeals, committals for sentence and breach hearings	17(2)	173 per day	130 per day	87 per day
Bail applications, mentions and other applications in appeals, committals for sentence and breach hearings	17(3)	173 per day	130 per day	87 per day
Second and subsequent days of an application to dismiss	18(6)	260 Half day	195 Half day	130 Half day
		497 Full day	346 Full day	238 Full day
Noting brief	19	–	–	108 per day
Hearing for mitigation of sentence	29	260 per day	173 per day	108 per day

[The table is printed as amended by S.I. 2015 No. 1678 (*ante*, G-1a).]

Part 6

Miscellaneous

Identity of instructed advocate

25.–(1) Where an instructed advocate is appointed before the first hearing at which the assisted **G-58** person enters a plea, the instructed advocate must notify the Court in writing as soon as the appointment is made and, where appropriate, must confirm whether the instructed advocate is the leading instructed advocate or the led instructed advocate.

(2) Where the section 16 determination provides for representation by a single advocate and no instructed advocate has been notified to the Court in accordance with sub-paragraph (1)–

    (a) the barrister or solicitor advocate who attends the first hearing at which the assisted person enters a plea is deemed to be the instructed advocate; and

    (b) the Court must make a written record of this fact.

(3) Where the section 16 determination provides for representation by a single advocate and no barrister or solicitor advocate attends the first hearing at which the assisted person enters a plea–

    (a) the barrister or solicitor advocate who attends the next hearing in the case is deemed to be the instructed advocate; and

    (b) the Court must make a written record of this fact.

(4) Where the section 16 determination provides for representation by more than one advocate, and no leading instructed advocate has been notified to the Court in accordance with sub-paragraph (1), the leading advocate who attends–

    (a) the first hearing at which the assisted person enters a plea; or

    (b) where no leading advocate attends the first hearing at which the assisted person enters a plea, the next hearing in the case attended by a leading advocate,

is deemed to be the leading instructed advocate, and the Court must make a written record of this fact.

(5) Where the section 16 determination provides for representation by more than one advocate, and no led instructed advocate has been notified to the Court in accordance with sub-paragraph (1), the led advocate who attends–

    (a) the first hearing at which the assisted person enters a plea; or

    (b) where no led advocate attends the first hearing at which the assisted person enters a plea, the next hearing in the case attended by a led advocate,

is deemed to be the led instructed advocate, and the Court must make a written record of this fact.

(6) Where a section 16 determination is amended after the first hearing at which the assisted person enters a plea to provide for representation by more than one advocate–

    (a) the additional instructed advocate must notify the Court in writing of the additional instructed advocate's appointment within 7 days of the date on which the section 16 determination is amended; and

    (b) each instructed advocate must notify the Court whether that instructed advocate is the leading instructed advocate or the led instructed advocate.

(7) Where no additional instructed advocate has been notified to the Court in accordance with sub-paragraph (6)(a), the advocate who attends the next hearing in the case is deemed to be an instructed advocate and the Court must record in writing whether that instructed advocate is the leading instructed advocate or the led instructed advocate, as appropriate to the circumstances of the case.

(8) Where–

    (a) a case ceases to be a Very High Cost Case (in relation to fees claimed by advocates); and

    (b) none of sub-paragraphs (1) to (7) applies,

the instructed advocate must notify the Court in writing of the instructed advocate's appointment within 7 days of the case ceasing to be a Very High Cost Case.

(9) The Court must attach–

    (a) any notice received under sub-paragraph (1), (6) or (8); and

    (b) any record made by it under sub-paragraph (2), (3), (4), (5) or (7),

to the representation order.

(10) An instructed advocate must remain as instructed advocate at all times, except where–

    (a) a date for trial is fixed at or before the first hearing at which the assisted person enters a plea and the instructed advocate is unable to conduct the trial due to the instructed advocate's other pre-existing commitments;

    (b) the instructed advocate is dismissed by the assisted person or the litigator; or

(c)   the instructed advocate is required to withdraw because of his professional code of conduct.

(11) Where, in accordance with sub-paragraph (10), an instructed advocate withdraws, the instructed advocate must—

(a)   immediately notify the court of the withdrawal—

(i)   in writing; or

(ii)   where the withdrawal takes place at a hearing, orally; and

(b)   within 7 days of the date of the withdrawal, notify the court in writing of the identity of a replacement instructed advocate, who must fulfil all the functions of an instructed advocate in accordance with these Regulations.

(12) This paragraph does not apply to a claim for fees under paragraph 32, 33 or 34.

[Para. 25 is printed as amended by S.I. 2015 No. 1678 (*ante*, G-1a).]

Payment of fees to trial advocate

G-59   26.–(1) In accordance with regulation 23 the appropriate officer must notify each trial advocate of the total fees payable and authorise payment to the trial advocate accordingly.

(2) Payment of the fees in accordance with sub-paragraph (1) must be made to each trial advocate.

(3) Where the section 16 determination provides for representation by a single advocate, the trial advocate is responsible for arranging payment of fees to the instructed advocate and any substitute advocate who has undertaken work on the case.

(4) Where there are two trial advocates for an assisted person, payment must be made to each trial advocate individually, and—

(a)   the leading trial advocate is responsible for arranging payment of fees to the instructed advocate and any substitute advocate who have undertaken work on the case of a type for which a leading advocate is responsible; and

(b)   the led trial advocate is responsible for arranging payment of fees to the instructed advocate and any substitute advocate who have undertaken work on the case of a type for which a led advocate is responsible.

(4A) In this paragraph, where the main hearing is a trial, "trial advocate" means an advocate who—

(a)   is instructed pursuant to a section 16 determination to represent the assisted person at the trial, and

(b)   attends the first day of the trial.

(5) This paragraph does not apply to a claim for fees under paragraph 32, 33 or 34.

[This paragraph is printed as amended, with effect from May 5, 2015, by the Criminal Legal Aid (Remuneration) (Amendment) Regulations 2015 (S.I. 2015 No. 882), reg. 2(5)(d) and (16)(d). For the transitional provision, see *ante*, G-7.]

Additional charges and additional cases

G-60   27.–(1) Where an assisted person is charged with more than one offence on one indictment, the fee payable to the trial advocate under this Schedule must be based on whichever of those offences the trial advocate selects.

(2) Where two or more cases to which this Schedule applies involving the same trial advocate are heard concurrently (whether involving the same or different assisted persons)—

(a)   the trial advocate must select one case ("the principal case"), which must be treated for the purposes of remuneration in accordance with this Schedule;

(b)   in respect of the main hearing in each of the other cases the trial advocate must be paid a fixed fee of 20% of—

(i)   the basic fee (B) specified in the table following paragraph 5 or that following paragraph 8, as appropriate, for the principal case, where that is a case falling within paragraph 2(1)(a); or

(ii)   the fixed fee for the principal case, where that is a case falling within paragraph 2(1)(b) or paragraph 10.

(3) Nothing in sub-paragraphs (4) to (6) permits a fixed fee under Part 5, other than one to which paragraph 14 applies, to be paid in a case to which Part 4 applies.

(4) Where a trial advocate or substitute advocate appears at a hearing specified in paragraph 12, 13, 14, 15 or 16, forming part of two or more cases involving different assisted persons, the trial advocate or substitute advocate must be paid—

(a)   in respect of the first such case, the fixed fee for that hearing specified in the table following paragraph 24; and

(b)   in respect of each of the other cases, 20% of that fee.

(5) Subject to sub-paragraphs (1) to (4), where a trial advocate or substitute advocate appears at a hearing forming part of two or more cases, the trial advocate or substitute advocate must be paid the fixed fee for that hearing specified in the table following paragraph 24 in respect of one such case, without any increase in respect of the other cases.

(6) Where a trial advocate selects—

    (a)   one offence, in preference to another offence, under sub-paragraph (1); or

    (b)   one case as the principal case, in preference to another case, under sub-paragraph (2),

that selection does not affect the trial advocate's right to claim any of the fees set out in the table following paragraph 24 to which the trial advocate would otherwise have been entitled.

Multiple advocates

28. Where a section 16 determination provides for representation by three advocates in a case the **G-61** provisions of this Schedule apply, and the fees payable to the led juniors in accordance with Part 2 or Part 3 are payable to each led junior who is instructed in the case.

Non-local appearances

29. Where an advocate is instructed to appear in a court which is not within 40 kilometres of the **G-62** advocate's office or chambers, the appropriate officer may allow an amount for travelling and other expenses incidental to that appearance, provided that the amount must not be greater than the amount, if any, which would be payable to a trial advocate from the nearest local Bar or the nearest advocate's office (whichever is the nearer) unless the advocate instructed to appear has obtained prior approval under regulation 13 for the incurring of such expenses or can justify the attendance having regard to all the relevant circumstances of the case.

Trials lasting over 40 days

30. Where a trial exceeds 40 days, the trial advocate must be paid a fee as set out in the table following this paragraph, as appropriate to the category of trial advocate and the Class of Offence, for each day by which the trial exceeds 40 days on which the trial advocate attends at court. **G-63**

DAILY RATES PAYABLE WHERE A TRIAL LASTS OVER 40 DAYS

Class of Offence	Daily rate payable for days 41 to 50 (£)	Daily rate payable for days 51 and over (£)
QC		
A–K	387	414
Leading Junior		
A–K	331	356
Led Junior		
A–K	221	237
Junior Acting Alone		
A	266	285
B	247	265
C	247	265
D	266	285
E	225	241
F	225	241
G	225	241
H	247	265
I	247	265
J	266	285
K	266	285

Assisted person unfit to plead or stand trial

31. Where in any case a hearing is held to determine the question of whether the assisted person is **G-64** unfit to plead or to stand trial (a "fitness hearing")—

    (a)   if a trial on indictment is held, or continues, at any time thereafter, the length of the fitness hearing is included in determining the length of the trial for the calculation of the graduated fee in accordance with Part 2 or Part 3;

(b) if a trial on indictment is not held, or does not continue, thereafter by reason of the assisted person being found unfit to plead or to stand trial, the trial advocate must be paid—

(i) a graduated fee calculated in accordance with paragraph 4 as appropriate to the combined length of—

(aa) the fitness hearing; and

(bb) any hearing under section 4A of the Criminal Procedure (Insanity) Act 1964 (finding that the accused did the act or made the omission charged against him); or

(ii) a graduated fee calculated in accordance with paragraph 7 as appropriate for representing an assisted person in a cracked trial,

whichever the trial advocate elects; and

(c) if at any time the assisted person pleads guilty to the indictable offence, the trial advocate must be paid either—

(i) a graduated fee calculated in accordance with paragraph 4 as appropriate to the length of the fitness hearing; or

(ii) a graduated fee calculated in accordance with paragraph 7 as appropriate for representing an assisted person in a guilty plea,

whichever the trial advocate elects.

Cross examination of witness

G-65   32.—(1) Where in any case on indictment an advocate is retained solely for the purpose of cross-examining a witness under section 38 of the Youth Justice and Criminal Evidence Act 1999 (defence representation for purposes of cross-examination), the advocate must be paid a graduated fee calculated in accordance with paragraph 4.

(2) For the purposes of this paragraph the daily attendance fee (D) is as set out in the table following paragraph 5 as appropriate to the number of days of attendance at court by the advocate.

Provision of written or oral advice

G-66   33.—(1) Where in any case on indictment an advocate is assigned pursuant to a section 16 determination solely for the purpose of providing written or oral advice, the advocate must be paid for the reasonable number of hours of preparation for that advice using the hourly fee rates for special preparation set out in the table following paragraph 24 as appropriate to the category of trial advocate.

(2) An advocate claiming a fee for advice under this paragraph may apply to the appropriate officer to redetermine the fee under regulation 28 and the advocate must supply such information and documents as may be required by the appropriate officer as proof of the number of hours of preparation.

Mitigation of sentence

G-67   34.—(1) Where in any case on indictment an advocate is assigned pursuant to a section 16 determination to appear at a sentencing hearing solely for the purpose of applying to the court to mitigate the assisted person's sentence, the advocate must be paid in respect of that appearance the fee specified in the table following paragraph 24 together with a fee calculated from the reasonable number of hours of preparation for that appearance using the hourly fee rates for special preparation set out in the table following paragraph 24 as appropriate to the category of trial advocate.

(2) An advocate claiming an hourly preparation fee under this paragraph may apply to the appropriate officer to redetermine such hourly fee under regulation 28 and the advocate must supply such information and documents as may be required by the appropriate officer as proof of the number of hours of preparation.

Table of offences

G-68   At the end of Schedule 1 to the regulations (in Pt 7), there is a table of offences. For the effect thereof, see *post*, G-119, G-168 *et seq.*

Regulation 5   SCHEDULE 2

LITIGATORS' GRADUATED FEE SCHEME

PART 1

DEFINITION AND SCOPE

Interpretation

G-69   1.—(1) In this Schedule—

"case" means proceedings in the Crown Court against any one assisted person—

    (a) on one or more counts of a single indictment;

    (b) arising out of a single notice of appeal against conviction or sentence, or a single committal for sentence, whether on one or more charges; or

    (c) arising out of a single alleged breach of an order of the Crown Court,

and a case falling within paragraph (c) must be treated as a separate case from the proceedings in which the order was made;

"cracked trial" means a case on indictment in which—

    (a) the assisted person enters a plea of not guilty to one or more counts at the first hearing at which he or she enters a plea and

        (i) the case does not proceed to trial (whether by reason of pleas of guilty or for other reasons) or the prosecution offers no evidence; and

        (ii) either—

            (aa) in respect of one or more counts to which the assisted person pleaded guilty, the assisted person did not so plead at the first hearing at which he or she entered a plea; or

            (bb) in respect of one or more counts which did not proceed, the prosecution did not, before or at the first hearing at which the assisted person entered a plea, declare an intention of not proceeding with them; or

    (b) the case is listed for trial without a hearing at which the assisted persons enters a plea;

"guilty plea" means a case on indictment which—

    (a) is disposed of without a trial because the assisted person pleaded guilty to one or more counts; and

    (b) is not a cracked trial;

"main hearing" means—

    (a) in relation to a case which goes to trial, the trial;

    (b) in relation to a guilty plea, the hearing at which pleas are taken or, where there is more than one such hearing, the last such hearing;

    (c) in relation to a cracked trial, the hearing at which—

        (i) the case becomes a cracked trial by meeting the conditions in the definition of a cracked trial, whether or not any pleas were taken at that hearing; or

        (ii) a formal verdict of not guilty was entered as a result of the prosecution offering no evidence, whether or not the parties attended the hearing;

    (d) in relation to an appeal against conviction or sentence in the Crown Court, the hearing of the appeal;

    (e) in relation to proceedings arising out of a committal for sentence in the Crown Court, the sentencing hearing; and

    (f) in relation to proceedings arising out of an alleged breach of an order of the Crown Court, the hearing at which those proceedings are determined;

"*Newton* hearing" means a hearing at which evidence is heard for the purpose of determining the sentence of a convicted person in accordance with the principles of *R. v. Newton* (1982) 77 Cr.App.R. 13;

"PPE Cut-off" means the number of pages of prosecution evidence for use in determining the fee payable to a litigator under this Schedule, as set out in the tables following paragraph 5(1) and (2).

(2) For the purposes of this Schedule, the number of pages of prosecution evidence served on the court must be determined in accordance with sub-paragraphs (3) to (5).

(3) The number of pages of prosecution evidence includes all—

    (a) witness statements;

    (b) documentary and pictorial exhibits;

    (c) records of interviews with the assisted person; and

    (d) records of interviews with other defendants,

which form part of the served prosecution documents or which are included in any notice of additional evidence.

(4) Subject to sub-paragraph (5), a document served by the prosecution in electronic form is included in the number of pages of prosecution evidence.

(5) A documentary or pictorial exhibit which—

    (a) has been served by the prosecution in electronic form; and

(b)   has never existed in paper form,

is not included within the number of pages of prosecution evidence unless the appropriate officer decides that it would be appropriate to include it in the pages of prosecution evidence taking into account the nature of the document and any other relevant circumstances.

(6) In proceedings on indictment in the Crown Court initiated otherwise than by sending for trial, the appropriate officer must determine the number of pages of prosecution evidence in accordance with sub-paragraphs (2) to (5) or as nearly in accordance with those sub-paragraphs as possible as the nature of the case permits.

(7) A reference to the Table of Offences in this Schedule is to the Table of Offences in Part 7 of Schedule 1 and a reference to a Class of Offence in this Schedule is to the Class in which that offence is listed in the Table of Offences.

[Para. 1 is printed as amended by S.I. 2015 No. 1678 (*ante,* G-1a); and S.I. 2015 No. 1369 (*ante,* G-1a).]

Application

G-69a

2.–(1) Subject to sub-paragraphs (2) to (7), this Schedule applies to—

(a)   every case on indictment;

(b)   the following proceedings in the Crown Court—

(i)   an appeal against conviction or sentence from the magistrates' court;

(ii)   a sentencing hearing following a committal for sentence to the Crown Court;

(iii) proceedings arising out of an alleged breach of an order of the Crown Court (whether or not this Schedule applies to the proceedings in which the order was made);

(c)   a sentencing hearing following a case on indictment to which this Schedule applies, where sentence has been deferred under section 1 of the Powers of Criminal Courts (Sentencing) Act 2000 (deferment of sentence);

(d)   any other post-sentence hearing.

(3) Where, at any time after proceedings are sent for trial to the Crown Court they are—

(a)   discontinued by a notice served under section 23A of the Prosecution of Offences Act 1985 (discontinuance of proceedings after accused has been sent for trial); or

(b)   dismissed pursuant to paragraph 2 of Schedule 3 to the Crime and Disorder Act 1998 (applications for dismissal),

the provisions of paragraphs 21 and 22 apply.

(4) Where, following a case on indictment, a *Newton* hearing takes place—

(a)   for the purposes of this Schedule the case is to be treated as having gone to trial;

(b)   the length of the trial is to be taken to be the combined length of the main hearing and the *Newton* hearing; and

(c)   the provisions of this Schedule relating to cracked trials and guilty pleas will not apply.

(5) For the purposes of this Schedule, a case on indictment which discontinues at or before the first hearing at which the assisted person enters a plea otherwise than—

(a)   by reason of a plea of guilty being entered; or

(b)   in accordance with sub-paragraph (3),

must be treated as a guilty plea.

(6) For the purposes of this Schedule, where a trial that is not a Very High Cost Case (in relation to fees claimed by litigators) lasts over 200 days, it must be treated as if it had lasted 200 days.

(7) For the purposes of this Schedule, where the number of pages of prosecution evidence in a case which is not a Very High Cost Case (in relation to fees claimed by litigators) exceeds—

(a)   the PPE Cut-off figure specified in the table following paragraph 5(2) as appropriate to the offence for which the assisted person is to be tried and the length of trial; and

(b)   10,000,

the case must be treated as though it had 10,000 pages of prosecution evidence.

[Para. 2 is printed as amended by S.I. 2015 No. 1678 (*ante,* G-1a).]

Class of offences

G-70

3.–(1) For the purposes of this Schedule—

(a)   every indictable offence falls within the Class under which it is listed in the Table of Offences and, subject to sub-paragraph (2), indictable offences not specifically so listed are deemed to fall within Class H;

(b)   conspiracy to commit an indictable offence contrary to section 1 of the Criminal Law Act 1977 (the offence of conspiracy), incitement to commit an indictable offence and attempts to commit an indictable offence contrary to section 1 of the Criminal Attempts Act 1981 (attempting to commit an offence) fall within the same Class as the substantive offence to which they relate;

(c)   where the Table of Offences specifies that the Class within which an offence falls depends on whether the value involved exceeds a stated limit, the value must be presumed not to exceed that limit unless the litigator making the claim under regulation 5 proves otherwise to the satisfaction of the appropriate officer;

(d)   where more than one count of the indictment is for an offence in relation to which the Class depends on the value involved, that value must be taken to be the total value involved in all those offences, but where two or more counts relate to the same property, the value of that property must be taken into account once only;

(e)   where an entry in the Table of Offences specifies an offence as being contrary to a statutory provision, then subject to any express limitation in the entry that entry includes every offence contrary to that statutory provision whether or not the words of description in the entry are appropriate to cover all such offences;

(f)   where in a case on indictment there is a hearing to determine the question of whether an assisted person is unfit to plead or unfit to stand trial, the litigator must elect whether that hearing falls within the same Class as the indictable offence to which it relates or within Class D;

(g)   where in a case on indictment a restriction order is made under section 41 of the Mental Health Act 1983 (power of higher courts to restrict discharge from hospital), the offence falls within Class A, regardless of the Class under which the offence would be listed in the Table of Offences, but for this paragraph.

(2) Where a litigator in proceedings in the Crown Court is dissatisfied with the classification within Class H of an indictable offence not listed in the Table of Offences, the litigator may apply to the appropriate officer, when lodging the claim for fees, to reclassify the offence.

(3) The appropriate officer must, in light of the objections made by the litigator—

(a)   confirm the classification of the offence within Class H; or

(b)   reclassify the offence,

and must notify the litigator of the decision.

As to this paragraph, see *post*, G-119.

PART 2

GRADUATED FEES FOR GUILTY PLEAS, CRACKED TRIALS AND TRIALS

Scope

4.–(1) Subject to sub-paragraph (2) and to paragraph 21, this Part does not apply to a guilty plea **G-70a** or cracked trial in a case sent for trial to the Crown Court on the election of a defendant where the magistrates' court has determined the case to be suitable for summary trial.

(2) This Part applies in all cases where the trial is a cracked trial because the prosecution offer no evidence on all counts against a defendant and the judge directs that a not guilty verdict be entered.

[This paragraph was substituted by S.I. 2014 No. 2422 (*ante*, G-21a). For the transitional provision, see *ante*, G-21a. It is printed as amended by S.I. 2015 No. 1678 (*ante*, G-1a).]

Pages of prosecution evidence

5.–(1) For the purposes of this Part, the PPE Cut-off figures in a cracked trial or guilty plea are **G-70b** specified in the table following this sub-paragraph, as appropriate to the offence with which the assisted person is charged.

PPE CUT-OFF FIGURES IN CRACKED TRIALS AND GUILTY PLEAS

Type of case	Class of offence										
	A	B	C	D	E	F	G	H	I	J	K
Cracked trial or guilty plea	80	70	40	80	40	50	50	40	40	80	120

(2) For the purposes of this Part, the PPE Cut-off figures in a trial are specified in the table following this sub-paragraph, as appropriate to the offence for which the assisted person is tried and the length of trial.

PPE Cut-off figures in trials

Trial length in days	PPE Cut off A	PPE Cut off B	PPE Cut off C	PPE Cut off D	PPE Cut off E	PPE Cut off F	PPE Cut off G	PPE Cut off H	PPE Cut off I	PPE Cut off J	PPE Cut off K
1	80	70	40	80	40	50	50	40	40	80	120
2	80	70	40	80	40	50	50	40	40	80	120
3	95	105	81	95	120	138	138	122	134	95	186
4	126	139	120	126	158	173	173	157	185	126	252
5	156	170	157	156	195	206	206	191	232	156	314
6	186	203	193	186	229	240	240	225	281	186	372
7	218	238	230	218	265	276	276	260	329	218	433
8	257	274	267	257	301	310	310	301	376	257	495
9	293	306	301	293	333	342	342	338	420	293	550
10	330	338	339	330	365	373	373	374	464	330	606
11	367	370	378	367	399	405	405	412	509	367	663
12	404	402	417	404	433	437	437	449	554	404	721
13	440	434	455	440	467	470	470	486	598	440	779
14	477	465	493	477	500	501	501	523	642	477	836
15	514	497	531	514	532	533	533	559	686	514	894
16	551	535	569	551	565	564	564	596	730	551	951
17	587	573	607	587	598	596	596	637	774	587	1,007
18	624	611	646	624	646	627	627	687	818	624	1,063
19	661	649	684	661	696	659	659	736	862	661	1,119
20	697	687	722	697	746	690	690	786	907	697	1,174
21	742	722	753	742	787	720	720	826	943	742	1,230
22	786	757	785	786	828	752	752	867	980	786	1,286
23	830	792	819	830	868	784	784	908	1,017	830	1,341
24	874	826	857	874	908	816	816	948	1,053	874	1,396
25	917	860	894	917	948	848	848	988	1,088	917	1,451
26	961	895	931	961	988	880	880	1,028	1,124	961	1,505

Trial length in days	PPE Cut off A	PPE Cut off B	PPE Cut off C	PPE Cut off D	PPE Cut off E	PPE Cut off F	PPE Cut off G	PPE Cut off H	PPE Cut off I	PPE Cut off J	PPE Cut off K
27	1,005	935	967	1,005	1,028	912	912	1,068	1,160	1,005	1,560
28	1,049	975	1,004	1,049	1,068	944	944	1,107	1,196	1,049	1,615
29	1,099	1,016	1,041	1,099	1,108	976	976	1,147	1,231	1,099	1,670
30	1,150	1,057	1,077	1,150	1,148	1,007	1,007	1,187	1,267	1,150	1,725
31	1,200	1,098	1,114	1,200	1,188	1,039	1,039	1,226	1,303	1,200	1,780
32	1,251	1,138	1,151	1,251	1,228	1,070	1,070	1,266	1,349	1,251	1,835
33	1,301	1,179	1,187	1,301	1,268	1,102	1,102	1,307	1,394	1,301	1,889
34	1,352	1,220	1,224	1,352	1,308	1,133	1,133	1,357	1,439	1,352	1,944
35	1,402	1,261	1,262	1,402	1,347	1,165	1,165	1,407	1,485	1,402	1,999
36	1,453	1,302	1,303	1,453	1,435	1,196	1,196	1,457	1,530	1,453	2,054
37	1,503	1,348	1,345	1,503	1,526	1,228	1,228	1,507	1,575	1,503	2,109
38	1,554	1,395	1,386	1,554	1,617	1,259	1,259	1,557	1,621	1,554	2,164
39	1,604	1,441	1,428	1,604	1,708	1,291	1,291	1,607	1,666	1,604	2,219
40	1,652	1,484	1,444	1,652	1,745	1,314	1,314	1,629	1,704	1,652	2,271
41	1,700	1,527	1,461	1,700	1,782	1,338	1,338	1,651	1,742	1,700	2,324
42	1,748	1,570	1,477	1,748	1,820	1,361	1,361	1,673	1,780	1,748	2,377
43	1,796	1,613	1,494	1,796	1,857	1,384	1,384	1,695	1,818	1,796	2,430
44	1,844	1,656	1,511	1,844	1,895	1,410	1,410	1,716	1,856	1,844	2,483
45	1,892	1,699	1,527	1,892	1,932	1,440	1,440	1,738	1,894	1,892	2,536
46	1,939	1,742	1,544	1,939	1,970	1,470	1,470	1,760	1,932	1,939	2,589
47	1,987	1,785	1,560	1,987	2,007	1,501	1,501	1,782	1,970	1,987	2,642
48	2,039	1,828	1,577	2,039	2,045	1,531	1,531	1,804	2,008	2,039	2,695
49	2,091	1,871	1,594	2,091	2,082	1,561	1,561	1,826	2,046	2,091	2,749
50	2,144	1,914	1,610	2,144	2,120	1,591	1,591	1,848	2,084	2,144	2,802
51	2,196	1,957	1,627	2,196	2,158	1,622	1,622	1,870	2,122	2,196	2,855
52	2,249	2,000	1,644	2,249	2,195	1,652	1,652	1,892	2,160	2,249	2,908
53	2,301	2,043	1,660	2,301	2,233	1,682	1,682	1,914	2,198	2,301	2,962
54	2,354	2,086	1,677	2,354	2,271	1,712	1,712	1,936	2,236	2,354	3,015

Trial length in days	PPE Cut off A	PPE Cut off B	PPE Cut off C	PPE Cut off D	PPE Cut off E	PPE Cut off F	PPE Cut off G	PPE Cut off H	PPE Cut off I	PPE Cut off J	PPE Cut off K
55	2,406	2,129	1,694	2,406	2,308	1,743	1,743	1,958	2,275	2,406	3,068
56	2,459	2,172	1,710	2,459	2,346	1,773	1,773	1,980	2,313	2,459	3,121
57	2,512	2,215	1,727	2,512	2,384	1,803	1,803	2,002	2,351	2,512	3,175
58	2,564	2,258	1,744	2,564	2,422	1,833	1,833	2,024	2,389	2,564	3,228
59	2,617	2,301	1,760	2,617	2,459	1,864	1,864	2,046	2,427	2,617	3,281
60	2,669	2,345	1,777	2,669	2,497	1,894	1,894	2,068	2,465	2,669	3,335
61	2,722	2,388	1,794	2,722	2,535	1,924	1,924	2,090	2,503	2,722	3,388
62	2,775	2,431	1,811	2,775	2,572	1,959	1,959	2,112	2,542	2,775	3,442
63	2,827	2,474	1,827	2,827	2,610	2,020	2,020	2,134	2,580	2,827	3,495
64	2,880	2,517	1,844	2,880	2,648	2,081	2,081	2,156	2,618	2,880	3,549
65	2,933	2,561	1,861	2,933	2,686	2,141	2,141	2,178	2,656	2,933	3,602
66	2,985	2,604	1,877	2,985	2,723	2,202	2,202	2,200	2,694	2,985	3,656
67	3,038	2,647	1,894	3,038	2,761	2,263	2,263	2,222	2,776	3,038	3,709
68	3,091	2,690	1,911	3,091	2,799	2,323	2,323	2,244	2,865	3,091	3,763
69	3,144	2,734	1,927	3,144	2,836	2,384	2,384	2,266	2,954	3,144	3,816
70	3,196	2,777	1,944	3,196	2,874	2,445	2,445	2,288	3,043	3,196	3,870
71	3,249	2,820	1,961	3,249	2,912	2,506	2,506	2,310	3,132	3,249	3,923
72	3,302	2,864	1,978	3,302	2,950	2,566	2,566	2,332	3,221	3,302	3,977
73	3,355	2,907	1,994	3,355	2,987	2,627	2,627	2,354	3,310	3,355	4,031
74	3,407	2,950	2,016	3,407	3,025	2,688	2,688	2,376	3,399	3,407	4,084
75	3,460	2,994	2,040	3,460	3,063	2,749	2,749	2,398	3,488	3,460	4,138
76	3,513	3,037	2,064	3,513	3,101	2,809	2,809	2,420	3,577	3,513	4,192
77	3,566	3,080	2,089	3,566	3,138	2,870	2,870	2,442	3,666	3,566	4,245
78	3,619	3,124	2,113	3,619	3,176	2,931	2,931	2,464	3,755	3,619	4,299
79	3,672	3,167	2,137	3,672	3,214	2,992	2,992	2,486	3,844	3,672	4,353
80	3,724	3,211	2,161	3,724	3,251	3,052	3,052	2,508	3,933	3,724	4,406
81	3,777	3,254	2,185	3,777	3,289	3,113	3,113	2,530	4,023	3,777	4,460
82	3,830	3,297	2,210	3,830	3,327	3,174	3,174	2,552	4,112	3,830	4,514

Trial length in days	PPE Cut off A	PPE Cut off B	PPE Cut off C	PPE Cut off D	PPE Cut off E	PPE Cut off F	PPE Cut off G	PPE Cut off H	PPE Cut off I	PPE Cut off J	PPE Cut off K
83	3,883	3,341	2,234	3,883	3,365	3,235	3,235	2,575	4,201	3,883	4,568
84	3,936	3,384	2,258	3,936	3,402	3,295	3,295	2,597	4,290	3,936	4,622
85	3,989	3,428	2,282	3,989	3,440	3,356	3,356	2,619	4,379	3,989	4,675
86	4,042	3,471	2,307	4,042	3,478	3,417	3,417	2,641	4,469	4,042	4,729
87	4,095	3,515	2,331	4,095	3,516	3,478	3,478	2,663	4,558	4,095	4,783
88	4,148	3,558	2,355	4,148	3,553	3,539	3,539	2,685	4,647	4,148	4,837
89	4,201	3,602	2,379	4,201	3,591	3,599	3,599	2,707	4,737	4,201	4,891
90	4,254	3,645	2,404	4,254	3,629	3,660	3,660	2,729	4,826	4,254	4,945
91	4,307	3,689	2,428	4,307	3,666	3,721	3,721	2,751	4,915	4,307	4,999
92	4,360	3,733	2,452	4,360	3,704	3,782	3,782	2,774	5,005	4,360	5,053
93	4,413	3,776	2,477	4,413	3,742	3,843	3,843	2,796	5,094	4,413	5,107
94	4,466	3,820	2,501	4,466	3,780	3,903	3,903	2,818	5,183	4,466	5,161
95	4,519	3,863	2,525	4,519	3,817	3,964	3,964	2,840	5,273	4,519	5,215
96	4,572	3,907	2,549	4,572	3,855	4,025	4,025	2,862	5,362	4,572	5,269
97	4,625	3,951	2,574	4,625	3,893	4,086	4,086	2,884	5,452	4,625	5,323
98	4,679	3,994	2,598	4,679	3,930	4,147	4,147	2,906	5,541	4,679	5,377
99	4,732	4,038	2,622	4,732	3,968	4,207	4,207	2,929	5,631	4,732	5,431
100	4,785	4,082	2,647	4,785	4,006	4,268	4,268	2,951	5,720	4,785	5,485
101	4,838	4,125	2,671	4,838	4,044	4,329	4,329	2,973	5,810	4,838	5,539
102	4,891	4,169	2,695	4,891	4,081	4,390	4,390	2,995	5,899	4,891	5,593
103	4,944	4,213	2,720	4,944	4,119	4,451	4,451	3,032	5,989	4,944	5,647
104	4,997	4,257	2,744	4,997	4,157	4,512	4,512	3,073	6,079	4,997	5,702
105	5,051	4,300	2,768	5,051	4,195	4,573	4,573	3,114	6,168	5,051	5,756
106	5,104	4,344	2,793	5,104	4,232	4,633	4,633	3,155	6,258	5,104	5,810
107	5,157	4,388	2,817	5,157	4,270	4,694	4,694	3,196	6,348	5,157	5,864
108	5,210	4,432	2,841	5,210	4,308	4,755	4,755	3,237	6,437	5,210	5,918
109	5,264	4,475	2,866	5,264	4,345	4,816	4,816	3,278	6,527	5,264	5,973
110	5,317	4,519	2,890	5,317	4,383	4,877	4,877	3,319	6,617	5,317	6,027

Trial length in days	PPE Cut off A	PPE Cut off B	PPE Cut off C	PPE Cut off D	PPE Cut off E	PPE Cut off F	PPE Cut off G	PPE Cut off H	PPE Cut off I	PPE Cut off J	PPE Cut off K
111	5,370	4,563	2,914	5,370	4,421	4,938	4,938	3,361	6,706	5,370	6,081
112	5,423	4,607	2,939	5,423	4,459	4,999	4,999	3,402	6,796	5,423	6,135
113	5,477	4,650	2,963	5,477	4,496	5,059	5,059	3,443	6,886	5,477	6,189
114	5,530	4,694	2,987	5,530	4,534	5,120	5,120	3,484	6,976	5,530	6,244
115	5,583	4,738	3,012	5,583	4,572	5,181	5,181	3,525	7,066	5,583	6,298
116	5,637	4,782	3,036	5,637	4,610	5,242	5,242	3,566	7,155	5,637	6,352
117	5,690	4,826	3,060	5,690	4,647	5,303	5,303	3,607	7,245	5,690	6,406
118	5,743	4,869	3,085	5,743	4,685	5,364	5,364	3,648	7,335	5,743	6,460
119	5,797	4,913	3,109	5,797	4,723	5,425	5,425	3,689	7,425	5,797	6,514
120	5,850	4,957	3,133	5,850	4,760	5,486	5,486	3,730	7,515	5,850	6,569
121	5,904	5,001	3,158	5,904	4,798	5,547	5,547	3,771	7,605	5,904	6,623
122	5,956	5,044	3,182	5,956	4,836	5,607	5,607	3,812	7,693	5,956	6,677
123	6,009	5,088	3,206	6,009	4,874	5,668	5,668	3,853	7,782	6,009	6,731
124	6,061	5,131	3,230	6,061	4,911	5,729	5,729	3,895	7,871	6,061	6,785
125	6,114	5,175	3,254	6,114	4,949	5,789	5,789	3,936	7,959	6,114	6,839
126	6,167	5,218	3,278	6,167	4,987	5,850	5,850	3,977	8,048	6,167	6,892
127	6,219	5,261	3,302	6,219	5,025	5,911	5,911	4,017	8,137	6,219	6,945
128	6,272	5,304	3,326	6,272	5,062	5,971	5,971	4,058	8,225	6,272	6,999
129	6,324	5,347	3,350	6,324	5,100	6,032	6,032	4,098	8,314	6,324	7,052
130	6,377	5,390	3,374	6,377	5,138	6,093	6,093	4,139	8,403	6,377	7,106
131	6,430	5,433	3,398	6,430	5,175	6,153	6,153	4,179	8,491	6,430	7,159
132	6,482	5,476	3,422	6,482	5,213	6,214	6,214	4,219	8,580	6,482	7,212
133	6,535	5,520	3,446	6,535	5,251	6,274	6,274	4,260	8,669	6,535	7,266
134	6,588	5,563	3,470	6,588	5,289	6,335	6,335	4,300	8,757	6,588	7,319
135	6,640	5,606	3,494	6,640	5,326	6,396	6,396	4,341	8,846	6,640	7,373
136	6,693	5,649	3,518	6,693	5,364	6,456	6,456	4,381	8,935	6,693	7,426
137	6,745	5,692	3,542	6,745	5,402	6,517	6,517	4,422	9,023	6,745	7,479
138	6,798	5,735	3,566	6,798	5,439	6,578	6,578	4,462	9,112	6,798	7,533

Trial length in days	PPE Cut off A	PPE Cut off B	PPE Cut off C	PPE Cut off D	PPE Cut off E	PPE Cut off F	PPE Cut off G	PPE Cut off H	PPE Cut off I	PPE Cut off J	PPE Cut off K
139	6,851	5,778	3,590	6,851	5,477	6,638	6,638	4,503	9,201	6,851	7,586
140	6,903	5,821	3,614	6,903	5,515	6,699	6,699	4,543	9,289	6,903	7,639
141	6,956	5,864	3,638	6,956	5,553	6,760	6,760	4,584	9,378	6,956	7,693
142	7,008	5,908	3,662	7,008	5,590	6,820	6,820	4,624	9,467	7,008	7,746
143	7,061	5,951	3,686	7,061	5,628	6,881	6,881	4,664	9,555	7,061	7,800
144	7,114	5,994	3,709	7,114	5,666	6,942	6,942	4,705	9,644	7,114	7,853
145	7,166	6,037	3,733	7,166	5,704	7,002	7,002	4,745	9,733	7,166	7,906
146	7,219	6,080	3,757	7,219	5,741	7,063	7,063	4,786	9,821	7,219	7,960
147	7,272	6,123	3,781	7,272	5,779	7,124	7,124	4,826	9,910	7,272	8,013
148	7,324	6,166	3,805	7,324	5,817	7,184	7,184	4,867	9,999	7,324	8,067
149	7,377	6,209	3,829	7,377	5,854	7,245	7,245	4,907	10,087	7,377	8,120
150	7,429	6,252	3,853	7,429	5,892	7,305	7,305	4,948	10,176	7,429	8,173
151	7,482	6,296	3,877	7,482	5,930	7,366	7,366	4,988	10,265	7,482	8,227
152	7,535	6,339	3,901	7,535	5,968	7,427	7,427	5,029	10,353	7,535	8,280
153	7,587	6,382	3,925	7,587	6,005	7,487	7,487	5,069	10,442	7,587	8,333
154	7,640	6,425	3,949	7,640	6,043	7,548	7,548	5,110	10,531	7,640	8,387
155	7,692	6,468	3,973	7,692	6,081	7,609	7,609	5,150	10,619	7,692	8,440
156	7,745	6,511	3,997	7,745	6,119	7,669	7,669	5,190	10,708	7,745	8,494
157	7,798	6,554	4,021	7,798	6,156	7,730	7,730	5,231	10,797	7,798	8,547
158	7,850	6,597	4,045	7,850	6,194	7,791	7,791	5,271	10,885	7,850	8,600
159	7,903	6,641	4,069	7,903	6,232	7,851	7,851	5,312	10,974	7,903	8,654
160	7,956	6,684	4,093	7,956	6,269	7,912	7,912	5,352	11,063	7,956	8,707
161	8,008	6,727	4,117	8,008	6,307	7,973	7,973	5,393	11,151	8,008	8,760
162	8,061	6,770	4,141	8,061	6,345	8,033	8,033	5,433	11,240	8,061	8,814
163	8,113	6,813	4,165	8,113	6,383	8,094	8,094	5,474	11,329	8,113	8,867
164	8,166	6,856	4,189	8,166	6,420	8,155	8,155	5,514	11,417	8,166	8,921
165	8,219	6,899	4,213	8,219	6,458	8,215	8,215	5,555	11,506	8,219	8,974
166	8,271	6,942	4,237	8,271	6,496	8,276	8,276	5,595	11,595	8,271	9,027

Trial length in days	PPE Cut off A	PPE Cut off B	PPE Cut off C	PPE Cut off D	PPE Cut off E	PPE Cut off F	PPE Cut off G	PPE Cut off H	PPE Cut off I	PPE Cut off J	PPE Cut off K
167	8,324	6,985	4,261	8,324	6,534	8,337	8,337	5,636	11,683	8,324	9,081
168	8,376	7,029	4,285	8,376	6,571	8,397	8,397	5,676	11,772	8,376	9,134
169	8,429	7,072	4,309	8,429	6,609	8,458	8,458	5,716	11,861	8,429	9,188
170	8,482	7,115	4,333	8,482	6,647	8,518	8,518	5,757	11,949	8,482	9,241
171	8,534	7,158	4,357	8,534	6,684	8,579	8,579	5,797	12,038	8,534	9,294
172	8,587	7,201	4,380	8,587	6,722	8,640	8,640	5,838	12,127	8,587	9,348
173	8,639	7,244	4,404	8,639	6,760	8,700	8,700	5,878	12,215	8,639	9,401
174	8,692	7,287	4,428	8,692	6,798	8,761	8,761	5,919	12,304	8,692	9,454
175	8,745	7,330	4,452	8,745	6,835	8,822	8,822	5,959	12,393	8,745	9,508
176	8,797	7,373	4,476	8,797	6,873	8,882	8,882	6,000	12,481	8,797	9,561
177	8,850	7,417	4,500	8,850	6,911	8,943	8,943	6,040	12,570	8,850	9,615
178	8,903	7,460	4,524	8,903	6,948	9,004	9,004	6,081	12,659	8,903	9,668
179	8,955	7,503	4,548	8,955	6,986	9,064	9,064	6,121	12,747	8,955	9,721
180	9,008	7,546	4,572	9,008	7,024	9,125	9,125	6,162	12,836	9,008	9,775
181	9,060	7,589	4,596	9,060	7,062	9,186	9,186	6,202	12,925	9,060	9,828
182	9,113	7,632	4,620	9,113	7,099	9,246	9,246	6,242	13,013	9,113	9,881
183	9,166	7,675	4,644	9,166	7,137	9,307	9,307	6,283	13,102	9,166	9,935
184	9,218	7,718	4,668	9,218	7,174	9,368	9,368	6,323	13,191	9,218	9,988
185	9,271	7,762	4,692	9,271	7,211	9,428	9,428	6,364	13,279	9,271	10,042
186	9,323	7,805	4,716	9,323	7,248	9,489	9,489	6,404	13,368	9,323	10,095
187	9,376	7,848	4,740	9,376	7,285	9,549	9,549	6,445	13,457	9,376	10,148
188	9,429	7,891	4,764	9,429	7,322	9,610	9,610	6,485	13,545	9,429	10,202
189	9,481	7,934	4,788	9,481	7,360	9,671	9,671	6,526	13,634	9,481	10,255
190	9,534	7,977	4,812	9,534	7,397	9,731	9,731	6,566	13,723	9,534	10,309
191	9,587	8,020	4,836	9,587	7,434	9,792	9,792	6,607	13,811	9,587	10,362
192	9,639	8,063	4,860	9,639	7,471	9,853	9,853	6,647	13,900	9,639	10,415
193	9,692	8,106	4,884	9,692	7,508	9,913	9,913	6,687	13,988	9,692	10,469
194	9,744	8,150	4,908	9,744	7,545	9,974	9,974	6,728	14,077	9,744	10,522

Trial length in days	PPE Cut off A	PPE Cut off B	PPE Cut off C	PPE Cut off D	PPE Cut off E	PPE Cut off F	PPE Cut off G	PPE Cut off H	PPE Cut off I	PPE Cut off J	PPE Cut off K
195	9,797	8,193	4,932	9,797	7,582	10,035	10,035	6,768	14,166	9,797	10,575
196	9,850	8,236	4,956	9,850	7,620	10,095	10,095	6,809	14,254	9,850	10,629
197	9,902	8,279	4,980	9,902	7,657	10,156	10,156	6,849	14,343	9,902	10,682
198	9,955	8,322	5,004	9,955	7,694	10,217	10,217	6,890	14,432	9,955	10,736
199	10,007	8,365	5,028	10,007	7,731	10,277	10,277	6,930	14,520	10,007	10,789
200	10,060	8,408	5,051	10,060	7,768	10,338	10,338	6,971	14,609	10,060	10,842

Cracked trial or guilty plea where the number of pages of prosecution evidence is less than or equal to the PPE Cut-off

G-70c

6.–(1) Where in a cracked trial or guilty plea the number of pages of prosecution evidence is less than or equal to the PPE Cut-off specified in the table following paragraph 5(1) as appropriate to the Class of Offence with which the assisted person is charged, the total fee payable to the litigator is—

(a) the basic fee, calculated in accordance with the table following sub-paragraph (2) of this paragraph;

(b) the defendant uplift, if any, calculated in accordance with the table following paragraph 12; and

(c) the adjustment for transfers and retrials, if any, calculated in accordance with paragraph 13.

(2) For the purposes of sub-paragraph (1), the basic fee appropriate to a cracked trial or a guilty plea is specified in the table following this sub-paragraph, in accordance with the type of case and Class of Offence with which the assisted person is charged.

BASIC FEES FOR CRACKED TRIALS AND GUILTY PLEAS (£)

Type of case	Class of Offence										
	A	B	C	D	E	F	G	H	I	J	K
Cracked trial	904.58	707.32	524.83	859.35	233.03	224.23	224.23	237.00	253.67	904.58	773.86
Guilty plea	680.39	556.11	442.91	646.36	184.70	195.81	195.81	190.97	174.60	680.39	640.84

[The table following para. 6(2) is printed as substituted by S.I. 2016 No. 313 (*ante*, G-1a).

Trial where the number of pages of prosecution evidence is less than or equal to the PPE Cut-off

G-71

7.–(1) Where in a trial the number of pages of prosecution evidence is less than or equal to the PPE Cut-off specified in the table following paragraph 5(2) as appropriate to the offence for which the assisted person is tried and the length of trial, the total fee payable to the litigator is—

(a) the basic fee, calculated in accordance with the table following sub-paragraph (2);

(b) the length of trial proxy, if any, calculated in accordance with the table following subparagraph (3);

(c) the defendant uplift, if any, calculated in accordance with the table following paragraph 12; and

(d) the adjustment for transfers and retrials, if any, calculated in accordance with paragraph 13.

(2) For the purposes of sub-paragraph (1), the basic fee appropriate to a trial is specified in the table following this sub-paragraph, in accordance with the offence for which the assisted person is tried.

Class of Offence										
Type of case	A	B	C	D	E	F	G	H	I	J	K
Trial	1,467.58	1,097.66	739.59	1394.20	352.72	357.60	357.60	357.75	357.44	1,467.58	1,031.82

(3) For the purposes of sub-paragraph (1), the length of trial proxy is specified in the table following this sub-paragraph, in accordance with the offence for which the assisted person is tried and the length of trial.

Trial Length in Days	Trial length proxy A	Trial length proxy B	Trial length proxy C	Trial length proxy D	Trial length proxy E	Trial length proxy F	Trial length proxy G	Trial length proxy H	Trial length proxy I	Trial length proxy J	Trial length proxy K
1	0.00	0.00	0.00	0.00	0.00	0.00	0.00	0.00	0.00	0.00	0.00
2	0.00	0.00	0.00	0.00	0.00	0.00	0.00	0.00	0.00	0.00	0.00
3	252.54	452.88	432.51	239.92	716.58	644.94	644.94	703.69	862.39	252.54	574.13
4	769.79	879.65	843.33	731.30	1,033.65	898.77	898.77	1,009.83	1,320.93	769.79	1,140.63
5	1,261.16	1,285.08	1,233.61	1,198.10	1,334.86	1,139.90	1,139.90	1,300.64	1,756.54	1,261.16	1,678.81
6	1,761.17	1,695.98	1,621.20	1,673.12	1,617.11	1,386.43	1,386.43	1,589.05	2,200.59	1,761.17	2,181.04
7	2,253.87	2,102.22	2,011.03	2,141.18	1,915.45	1,632.83	1,632.83	1,879.51	2,637.65	2,253.87	2,713.26
8	2,746.56	2,508.44	2,400.87	2,609.24	2,213.79	1,875.25	1,875.25	2,169.97	3,074.70	2,746.56	3,245.48
9	3,210.92	2,874.04	2,751.71	3,050.38	2,482.29	2,093.45	2,093.45	2,431.38	3,473.43	3,210.92	3,724.49
10	3,675.29	3,239.65	3,102.56	3,491.52	2,750.81	2,311.64	2,311.64	2,692.79	3,872.17	3,675.29	4,203.48
11	4,143.10	3,605.74	3,462.93	3,935.94	3,031.66	2,536.06	2,536.06	2,961.38	4,279.02	4,143.10	4,703.99
12	4,607.74	3,971.38	3,823.47	4,377.35	3,312.59	2,760.47	2,760.47	3,229.64	4,686.22	4,607.74	5,204.80
13	5,072.39	4,337.02	4,175.80	4,818.77	3,593.15	2,983.98	2,983.98	3,492.07	5,086.28	5,072.39	5,705.63
14	5,537.03	4,702.67	4,528.13	5,260.19	3,865.07	3,203.34	3,203.34	3,754.51	5,486.32	5,537.03	6,206.43
15	6,001.68	5,068.31	4,880.46	5,701.59	4,136.15	3,422.69	3,422.69	4,016.95	5,886.37	6,001.68	6,707.21
16	6,466.32	5,433.96	5,232.79	6,143.00	4,407.26	3,642.05	3,642.05	4,279.39	6,286.42	6,466.32	7,207.20
17	6,930.96	5,799.60	5,585.12	6,584.42	4,678.35	3,861.41	3,861.41	4,541.82	6,686.47	6,930.96	7,693.86
18	7,395.60	6,165.24	5,937.45	7,025.83	4,949.45	4,080.76	4,080.76	4,804.26	7,086.52	7,395.60	8,180.52
19	7,860.25	6,530.88	6,289.77	7,467.24	5,220.54	4,300.12	4,300.12	5,066.69	7,486.57	7,860.25	8,667.17
20	8,324.89	6,896.53	6,642.11	7,908.66	5,491.63	4,519.48	4,519.48	5,329.13	7,886.63	8,324.89	9,153.84
21	8,798.40	7,234.27	6,931.61	8,358.47	5,715.66	4,698.94	4,698.94	5,544.96	8,215.37	8,798.40	9,640.50
22	9,271.81	7,571.99	7,221.19	8,808.22	5,939.70	4,878.48	4,878.48	5,760.90	8,544.12	9,271.81	10,127.16
23	9,737.21	7,909.69	7,510.79	9,250.36	6,157.06	5,058.02	5,058.02	5,976.83	8,872.90	9,737.21	10,613.82
24	10,202.62	8,239.72	7,800.39	9,692.49	6,374.43	5,237.57	5,237.57	6,192.76	9,198.07	10,202.62	11,100.48
25	10,668.04	8,569.74	8,088.48	10,134.63	6,591.80	5,417.10	5,417.10	6,405.21	9,519.15	10,668.04	11,587.14
26	11,133.44	8,899.77	8,371.53	10,576.78	6,809.17	5,596.65	5,596.65	6,615.99	9,840.24	11,133.44	12,073.81
27	11,598.84	9,229.80	8,654.60	11,018.90	7,026.53	5,776.19	5,776.19	6,826.76	10,161.33	11,598.84	12,560.46

Trial Length in Days	Trial length proxy A	Trial length proxy B	Trial length proxy C	Trial length proxy D	Trial length proxy E	Trial length proxy F	Trial length proxy G	Trial length proxy H	Trial length proxy I	Trial length proxy J	Trial length proxy K
28	12,064.25	9,559.83	8,937.65	11,461.05	7,243.91	5,955.73	5,955.73	7,037.54	10,482.41	12,064.25	13,047.13
29	12,529.67	9,889.86	9,220.70	11,903.18	7,461.27	6,133.18	6,133.18	7,248.30	10,803.51	12,529.67	13,533.78
30	12,995.07	10,219.88	9,503.75	12,345.31	7,678.63	6,309.59	6,309.59	7,459.07	11,124.59	12,995.07	14,020.44
31	13,460.48	10,549.91	9,786.81	12,787.46	7,896.01	6,486.01	6,486.01	7,669.85	11,445.67	13,460.48	14,507.11
32	13,925.88	10,879.95	10,069.87	13,229.59	8,113.38	6,662.43	6,662.43	7,880.61	11,766.76	13,925.88	14,993.76
33	14,391.30	11,209.97	10,352.92	13,671.73	8,330.74	6,838.84	6,838.84	8,091.39	12,087.84	14,391.30	15,480.43
34	14,856.70	11,540.00	10,635.97	14,113.87	8,548.11	7,015.26	7,015.26	8,302.16	12,408.93	14,856.70	15,967.09
35	15,322.11	11,870.03	10,919.03	14,556.01	8,765.48	7,191.68	7,191.68	8,512.93	12,730.02	15,322.11	16,453.75
36	15,787.52	12,200.05	11,202.09	14,998.14	8,982.84	7,368.10	7,368.10	8,723.70	13,051.10	15,787.52	16,940.41
37	16,252.93	12,530.09	11,485.14	15,440.28	9,200.22	7,544.51	7,544.51	8,934.48	13,372.19	16,252.93	17,427.07
38	16,718.33	12,860.11	11,768.20	15,882.42	9,417.58	7,720.93	7,720.93	9,145.25	13,693.28	16,718.33	17,913.73
39	17,183.74	13,190.13	12,051.25	16,324.55	9,634.94	7,897.35	7,897.35	9,356.02	14,014.36	17,183.74	18,400.40
40	17,622.38	13,492.13	12,163.57	16,741.26	9,722.09	8,027.76	8,027.76	9,447.16	14,282.00	17,622.38	18,865.89
41	18,063.40	13,796.43	12,277.13	17,160.24	9,811.54	8,158.44	8,158.44	9,539.40	14,551.22	18,063.40	19,334.83
42	18,504.54	14,100.82	12,390.73	17,579.32	9,901.04	8,289.12	8,289.12	9,631.68	14,820.51	18,504.54	19,803.93
43	18,945.79	14,405.31	12,504.33	17,998.51	9,990.58	8,419.82	8,419.82	9,723.97	15,089.84	18,945.79	20,273.20
44	19,387.15	14,709.89	12,617.96	18,417.79	10,080.16	8,550.52	8,550.52	9,816.28	15,359.23	19,387.15	20,742.61
45	19,828.61	15,014.56	12,731.61	18,837.18	10,169.77	8,681.22	8,681.22	9,908.63	15,628.69	19,828.61	21,212.18
46	20,270.18	15,319.32	12,845.28	19,256.68	10,259.43	8,811.94	8,811.94	10,000.97	15,898.19	20,270.18	21,681.91
47	20,711.85	15,624.18	12,958.98	19,676.26	10,349.13	8,942.66	8,942.66	10,093.35	16,167.76	20,711.85	22,151.80
48	21,153.65	15,929.14	13,072.69	20,095.97	10,438.87	9,073.39	9,073.39	10,185.75	16,437.38	21,153.65	22,621.84
49	21,595.54	16,234.19	13,186.44	20,515.76	10,528.64	9,204.12	9,204.12	10,278.16	16,707.05	21,595.54	23,092.04
50	22,037.53	16,539.33	13,300.19	20,935.66	10,618.45	9,334.88	9,334.88	10,370.61	16,976.79	22,037.53	23,562.39
51	22,479.65	16,844.56	13,413.98	21,355.67	10,708.32	9,465.63	9,465.63	10,463.06	17,246.59	22,479.65	24,032.91
52	22,921.86	17,149.88	13,527.78	21,775.77	10,798.21	9,596.40	9,596.40	10,555.54	17,516.43	22,921.86	24,503.58
53	23,364.19	17,455.30	13,641.60	22,195.99	10,888.15	9,727.16	9,727.16	10,648.04	17,786.33	23,364.19	24,974.41
54	23,806.62	17,760.82	13,755.44	22,616.29	10,978.13	9,857.94	9,857.94	10,740.56	18,056.29	23,806.62	25,445.40
55	24,249.16	18,066.42	13,869.31	23,036.69	11,068.14	9,988.72	9,988.72	10,833.10	18,326.31	24,249.16	25,916.54

Trial Length in Days	Trial length proxy A	Trial length proxy B	Trial length proxy C	Trial length proxy D	Trial length proxy E	Trial length proxy F	Trial length proxy G	Trial length proxy H	Trial length proxy I	Trial length proxy J	Trial length proxy K
56	24,691.80	18,372.13	13,983.20	23,457.22	11,158.20	10,119.52	10,119.52	10,925.66	18,596.39	24,691.80	26,387.85
57	25,134.56	18,677.92	14,097.11	23,877.83	11,248.29	10,250.32	10,250.32	11,018.24	18,866.52	25,134.56	26,859.31
58	25,577.42	18,983.81	14,211.04	24,298.55	11,338.39	10,381.13	10,381.13	11,110.84	19,136.71	25,577.42	27,330.92
59	26,020.39	19,289.79	14,325.00	24,719.38	11,428.49	10,511.95	10,511.95	11,203.47	19,406.96	26,020.39	27,802.70
60	26,463.47	19,595.86	14,438.97	25,140.29	11,518.59	10,642.77	10,642.77	11,296.10	19,677.26	26,463.47	28,274.63
61	26,906.66	19,902.03	14,552.97	25,561.32	11,608.70	10,773.60	10,773.60	11,388.77	19,947.62	26,906.66	28,746.72
62	27,349.94	20,208.30	14,666.99	25,982.45	11,698.80	10,904.44	10,904.44	11,481.46	20,218.04	27,349.94	29,218.96
63	27,793.35	20,514.64	14,781.02	26,403.69	11,788.90	11,035.28	11,035.28	11,574.16	20,488.52	27,793.35	29,691.37
64	28,236.86	20,821.10	14,895.09	26,825.02	11,879.00	11,166.14	11,166.14	11,666.89	20,759.04	28,236.86	30,163.93
65	28,680.48	21,127.63	15,009.17	27,246.45	11,969.10	11,297.01	11,297.01	11,759.62	21,029.63	28,680.48	30,636.65
66	29,124.20	21,434.28	15,123.28	27,667.99	12,059.20	11,427.88	11,427.88	11,852.39	21,300.28	29,124.20	31,109.52
67	29,568.03	21,741.01	15,237.40	28,089.63	12,149.30	11,558.76	11,558.76	11,945.17	21,570.97	29,568.03	31,582.55
68	30,011.97	22,047.83	15,351.55	28,511.37	12,239.40	11,689.65	11,689.65	12,037.98	21,841.73	30,011.97	32,055.74
69	30,456.02	22,354.74	15,465.72	28,933.21	12,329.50	11,820.54	11,820.54	12,130.81	22,112.55	30,456.02	32,529.08
70	30,900.17	22,661.76	15,579.91	29,355.16	12,419.60	11,951.45	11,951.45	12,223.66	22,383.42	30,900.17	33,002.60
71	31,344.44	22,968.86	15,694.12	29,777.22	12,509.70	12,082.36	12,082.36	12,316.53	22,654.35	31,344.44	33,476.26
72	31,788.81	23,276.06	15,808.35	30,199.37	12,599.80	12,213.28	12,213.28	12,409.42	22,925.33	31,788.81	33,950.08
73	32,233.28	23,583.35	15,922.61	30,621.63	12,689.90	12,344.21	12,344.21	12,502.32	23,196.37	32,233.28	34,424.05
74	32,677.87	23,890.74	16,036.89	31,043.98	12,780.00	12,475.14	12,475.14	12,595.26	23,467.47	32,677.87	34,898.19
75	33,122.56	24,198.21	16,151.19	31,466.43	12,870.10	12,606.09	12,606.09	12,688.21	23,738.63	33,122.56	35,372.48
76	33,567.36	24,505.78	16,265.50	31,889.00	12,960.20	12,737.03	12,737.03	12,781.18	24,009.84	33,567.36	35,846.92
77	34,012.28	24,813.45	16,379.85	32,311.66	13,050.30	12,867.99	12,867.99	12,874.16	24,281.10	34,012.28	36,321.53
78	34,457.29	25,121.21	16,494.21	32,734.43	13,140.40	12,998.95	12,998.95	12,967.17	24,552.43	34,457.29	36,796.30
79	34,902.42	25,429.06	16,608.60	33,157.30	13,230.50	13,129.94	13,129.94	13,060.21	24,823.82	34,902.42	37,271.22
80	35,347.65	25,737.00	16,723.00	33,580.26	13,320.60	13,260.92	13,260.92	13,153.27	25,095.26	35,347.65	37,746.29
81	35,792.99	26,045.04	16,837.42	34,003.35	13,410.70	13,391.90	13,391.90	13,246.34	25,366.75	35,792.99	38,221.52
82	36,238.43	26,353.17	16,951.88	34,426.52	13,500.80	13,522.90	13,522.90	13,339.43	25,638.30	36,238.43	38,696.92
83	36,683.99	26,661.40	17,066.35	34,849.80	13,590.90	13,653.90	13,653.90	13,432.55	25,909.92	36,683.99	39,172.47

Trial Length in Days	Trial length proxy A	Trial length proxy B	Trial length proxy C	Trial length proxy D	Trial length proxy E	Trial length proxy F	Trial length proxy G	Trial length proxy H	Trial length proxy I	Trial length proxy J	Trial length proxy K
84	37,129.65	26,969.72	17,180.83	35,273.17	13,681.01	13,784.93	13,784.93	13,525.68	26,181.58	37,129.65	39,648.18
85	37,575.42	27,278.13	17,295.35	35,696.65	13,771.11	13,915.94	13,915.94	13,618.83	26,453.30	37,575.42	40,124.04
86	38,021.30	27,586.64	17,409.90	36,120.24	13,861.21	14,046.97	14,046.97	13,712.01	26,725.09	38,021.30	40,600.06
87	38,467.29	27,895.23	17,524.45	36,543.93	13,951.31	14,178.01	14,178.01	13,805.21	26,996.93	38,467.29	41,076.24
88	38,913.39	28,203.93	17,639.03	36,967.72	14,041.41	14,309.06	14,309.06	13,898.42	27,268.82	38,913.39	41,552.58
89	39,359.59	28,512.71	17,753.63	37,391.61	14,131.51	14,440.10	14,440.10	13,991.66	27,540.77	39,359.59	42,029.07
90	39,805.90	28,821.60	17,868.25	37,815.60	14,221.61	14,571.17	14,571.17	14,084.91	27,812.78	39,805.90	42,505.73
91	40,252.32	29,130.57	17,982.89	38,239.70	14,311.71	14,702.24	14,702.24	14,178.20	28,084.84	40,252.32	42,982.53
92	40,698.83	29,439.63	18,097.56	38,663.90	14,401.81	14,833.32	14,833.32	14,271.49	28,356.97	40,698.83	43,459.49
93	41,145.47	29,748.80	18,212.24	39,088.20	14,491.91	14,964.40	14,964.40	14,364.81	28,629.15	41,145.47	43,936.62
94	41,592.21	30,058.05	18,326.95	39,512.60	14,582.01	15,095.49	15,095.49	14,458.15	28,901.38	41,592.21	44,413.90
95	42,039.06	30,367.40	18,441.68	39,937.10	14,672.11	15,226.59	15,226.59	14,551.52	29,173.67	42,039.06	44,891.33
96	42,486.02	30,676.84	18,556.44	40,361.72	14,762.22	15,357.69	15,357.69	14,644.89	29,446.03	42,486.02	45,368.93
97	42,933.08	30,986.38	18,671.21	40,786.43	14,852.32	15,488.81	15,488.81	14,738.25	29,718.43	42,933.08	45,846.68
98	43,380.25	31,296.01	18,786.00	41,211.24	14,942.42	15,619.94	15,619.94	14,831.63	29,990.89	43,380.25	46,324.60
99	43,827.53	31,605.73	18,900.82	41,636.15	15,032.52	15,751.07	15,751.07	14,925.00	30,263.42	43,827.53	46,802.66
100	44,274.91	31,915.55	19,015.65	42,061.17	15,122.62	15,882.21	15,882.21	15,018.37	30,535.98	44,274.91	47,280.88
101	44,722.41	32,225.46	19,130.51	42,486.29	15,212.72	16,013.36	16,013.36	15,111.74	30,808.63	44,722.41	47,759.26
102	45,170.01	32,535.45	19,245.39	42,911.51	15,302.82	16,144.51	16,144.51	15,205.11	31,081.31	45,170.01	48,237.80
103	45,617.73	32,845.55	19,360.30	43,336.84	15,392.92	16,275.67	16,275.67	15,298.48	31,354.06	45,617.73	48,716.50
104	46,065.54	33,155.74	19,475.21	43,762.27	15,483.02	16,406.84	16,406.84	15,391.85	31,626.86	46,065.54	49,195.35
105	46,513.46	33,466.03	19,590.12	44,187.79	15,573.12	16,538.02	16,538.02	15,485.22	31,899.72	46,513.46	49,674.36
106	46,961.50	33,776.40	19,705.04	44,613.42	15,663.22	16,669.21	16,669.21	15,578.59	32,172.64	46,961.50	50,153.43
107	47,409.64	34,086.84	19,819.95	45,039.15	15,753.32	16,800.40	16,800.40	15,671.96	32,445.62	47,409.64	50,632.48
108	47,857.89	34,397.27	19,934.87	45,465.00	15,843.43	16,931.60	16,931.60	15,765.33	32,718.65	47,857.89	51,111.54
109	48,306.24	34,707.71	20,049.78	45,890.93	15,933.53	17,062.82	17,062.82	15,858.70	32,991.74	48,306.24	51,590.60
110	48,754.70	35,018.15	20,164.69	46,316.97	16,023.63	17,194.03	17,194.03	15,952.07	33,264.88	48,754.70	52,069.66
111	49,203.28	35,328.59	20,279.60	46,743.12	16,113.73	17,325.26	17,325.26	16,045.44	33,538.08	49,203.28	52,548.71

Trial Length in Days	Trial length proxy A	Trial length proxy B	Trial length proxy C	Trial length proxy D	Trial length proxy E	Trial length proxy F	Trial length proxy G	Trial length proxy H	Trial length proxy I	Trial length proxy J	Trial length proxy K
112	49,651.95	35,639.02	20,394.51	47,169.36	16,203.83	17,456.49	17,456.49	16,138.81	33,811.34	49,651.95	53,027.77
113	50,100.74	35,949.45	20,509.43	47,595.72	16,293.93	17,587.73	17,587.73	16,232.18	34,084.66	50,100.74	53,506.84
114	50,549.63	36,259.89	20,624.34	48,022.16	16,384.03	17,718.99	17,718.99	16,325.55	34,358.03	50,549.63	53,985.89
115	50,998.64	36,570.33	20,739.25	48,448.70	16,474.13	17,850.24	17,850.24	16,418.92	34,631.46	50,998.64	54,464.95
116	51,447.75	36,880.77	20,854.17	48,875.36	16,564.23	17,981.51	17,981.51	16,512.29	34,904.94	51,447.75	54,944.01
117	51,896.97	37,191.20	20,969.08	49,302.12	16,654.33	18,112.78	18,112.78	16,605.66	35,178.49	51,896.97	55,423.07
118	52,346.29	37,501.64	21,083.99	49,728.98	16,744.43	18,244.06	18,244.06	16,699.03	35,452.09	52,346.29	55,902.12
119	52,795.73	37,812.07	21,198.91	50,155.94	16,834.53	18,375.35	18,375.35	16,792.40	35,725.74	52,795.73	56,381.19
120	53,245.27	38,122.51	21,313.82	50,583.00	16,924.63	18,506.65	18,506.65	16,885.77	35,999.46	53,245.27	56,860.25
121	53,694.91	38,432.95	21,428.73	51,010.17	17,014.73	18,637.95	18,637.95	16,979.14	36,273.23	53,694.91	57,339.30
122	54,137.91	38,743.38	21,543.64	51,431.02	17,104.83	18,768.69	18,768.69	17,072.51	36,543.17	54,137.91	57,818.36
123	54,580.90	39,053.82	21,658.55	51,851.87	17,194.93	18,899.43	18,899.43	17,165.88	36,813.11	54,580.90	58,297.42
124	55,023.91	39,360.61	21,771.79	52,272.71	17,285.03	19,030.16	19,030.16	17,259.25	37,083.05	55,023.91	58,775.55
125	55,466.90	39,666.39	21,884.98	52,693.55	17,375.13	19,160.90	19,160.90	17,352.62	37,353.00	55,466.90	59,247.42
126	55,909.89	39,972.16	21,998.17	53,114.41	17,465.23	19,291.63	19,291.63	17,445.93	37,622.93	55,909.89	59,719.29
127	56,352.90	40,277.95	22,111.36	53,535.25	17,555.33	19,422.37	19,422.37	17,537.91	37,892.88	56,352.90	60,191.17
128	56,795.89	40,583.73	22,224.55	53,956.10	17,645.43	19,553.11	19,553.11	17,629.88	38,162.82	56,795.89	60,663.04
129	57,238.88	40,889.51	22,337.74	54,376.94	17,735.53	19,683.85	19,683.85	17,721.85	38,432.76	57,238.88	61,134.92
130	57,681.88	41,195.29	22,450.92	54,797.79	17,825.63	19,814.58	19,814.58	17,813.82	38,702.70	57,681.88	61,606.79
131	58,124.87	41,501.07	22,564.12	55,218.63	17,915.74	19,945.32	19,945.32	17,905.79	38,972.65	58,124.87	62,078.65
132	58,567.87	41,806.85	22,677.30	55,639.48	18,005.84	20,076.06	20,076.06	17,997.76	39,242.58	58,567.87	62,550.53
133	59,010.87	42,112.63	22,790.49	56,060.32	18,095.94	20,206.79	20,206.79	18,089.73	39,512.53	59,010.87	63,022.41
134	59,453.86	42,418.40	22,903.68	56,481.17	18,186.04	20,337.53	20,337.53	18,181.70	39,782.47	59,453.86	63,494.28
135	59,896.86	42,724.19	23,016.87	56,902.01	18,276.14	20,468.27	20,468.27	18,273.66	40,052.42	59,896.86	63,966.15
136	60,339.86	43,029.97	23,130.07	57,322.86	18,366.24	20,599.01	20,599.01	18,365.63	40,322.36	60,339.86	64,438.02
137	60,782.85	43,335.75	23,243.25	57,743.70	18,456.34	20,729.74	20,729.74	18,457.60	40,592.30	60,782.85	64,909.90
138	61,225.85	43,641.53	23,356.44	58,164.56	18,546.44	20,860.48	20,860.48	18,549.57	40,862.24	61,225.85	65,381.77
139	61,668.84	43,947.30	23,469.63	58,585.40	18,636.54	20,991.22	20,991.22	18,641.54	41,132.19	61,668.84	65,853.64

Trial Length in Days	Trial length proxy A	Trial length proxy B	Trial length proxy C	Trial length proxy D	Trial length proxy E	Trial length proxy F	Trial length proxy G	Trial length proxy H	Trial length proxy I	Trial length proxy J	Trial length proxy K
140	62,111.84	44,253.09	23,582.82	59,006.25	18,726.64	21,121.95	21,121.95	18,733.52	41,402.13	62,111.84	66,325.52
141	62,554.83	44,558.86	23,696.01	59,427.09	18,816.74	21,252.69	21,252.69	18,825.48	41,672.07	62,554.83	66,797.38
142	62,997.82	44,864.65	23,809.20	59,847.94	18,906.84	21,383.43	21,383.43	18,917.46	41,942.01	62,997.82	67,269.26
143	63,440.83	45,170.43	23,922.38	60,268.79	18,996.95	21,514.17	21,514.17	19,009.43	42,211.96	63,440.83	67,741.13
144	63,883.82	45,476.21	24,035.58	60,689.64	19,087.05	21,644.90	21,644.90	19,101.39	42,481.89	63,883.82	68,213.00
145	64,326.82	45,781.99	24,148.77	61,110.47	19,177.15	21,775.64	21,775.64	19,193.36	42,751.84	64,326.82	68,684.88
146	64,769.82	46,087.77	24,261.95	61,531.33	19,267.25	21,906.38	21,906.38	19,285.32	43,021.78	64,769.82	69,156.75
147	65,212.81	46,393.55	24,375.15	61,952.17	19,357.35	22,037.11	22,037.11	19,377.30	43,291.72	65,212.81	69,628.62
148	65,655.81	46,699.32	24,488.33	62,373.03	19,447.45	22,167.85	22,167.85	19,469.27	43,561.66	65,655.81	70,100.49
149	66,098.81	47,005.10	24,601.52	62,793.86	19,537.55	22,298.59	22,298.59	19,561.24	43,831.61	66,098.81	70,572.37
150	66,541.80	47,310.89	24,714.71	63,214.71	19,627.65	22,429.33	22,429.33	19,653.21	44,101.54	66,541.80	71,044.25
151	66,984.79	47,616.67	24,827.90	63,635.56	19,717.75	22,560.06	22,560.06	19,745.18	44,371.49	66,984.79	71,516.11
152	67,427.79	47,922.44	24,941.09	64,056.41	19,807.85	22,690.80	22,690.80	19,837.15	44,641.43	67,427.79	71,987.98
153	67,870.78	48,228.23	25,054.28	64,477.25	19,897.95	22,821.54	22,821.54	19,929.12	44,911.37	67,870.78	72,459.86
154	68,313.78	48,534.00	25,167.46	64,898.10	19,988.05	22,952.27	22,952.27	20,021.09	45,181.32	68,313.78	72,931.73
155	68,756.78	48,839.79	25,280.66	65,318.94	20,078.16	23,083.01	23,083.01	20,113.05	45,451.26	68,756.78	73,403.61
156	69,199.78	49,145.56	25,393.84	65,739.79	20,168.26	23,213.74	23,213.74	20,205.02	45,721.20	69,199.78	73,875.48
157	69,642.77	49,451.34	25,507.03	66,160.63	20,258.36	23,344.49	23,344.49	20,297.00	45,991.14	69,642.77	74,347.34
158	70,085.77	49,757.13	25,620.22	66,581.48	20,348.46	23,475.22	23,475.22	20,388.96	46,261.09	70,085.77	74,819.22
159	70,528.77	50,062.91	25,733.41	67,002.33	20,438.56	23,605.96	23,605.96	20,480.93	46,531.02	70,528.77	75,291.10
160	70,971.76	50,368.69	25,846.61	67,423.17	20,528.66	23,736.70	23,736.70	20,572.91	46,800.97	70,971.76	75,762.97
161	71,414.76	50,674.46	25,959.79	67,844.02	20,618.76	23,867.43	23,867.43	20,664.87	47,070.91	71,414.76	76,234.84
162	71,857.75	50,980.24	26,072.98	68,264.86	20,708.86	23,998.17	23,998.17	20,756.85	47,340.85	71,857.75	76,706.71
163	72,300.74	51,286.02	26,186.17	68,685.72	20,798.96	24,128.91	24,128.91	20,848.82	47,610.79	72,300.74	77,178.59
164	72,743.74	51,591.80	26,299.36	69,106.56	20,889.06	24,259.64	24,259.64	20,940.78	47,880.74	72,743.74	77,650.46
165	73,186.74	51,897.59	26,412.55	69,527.40	20,979.16	24,390.38	24,390.38	21,032.75	48,150.67	73,186.74	78,122.33
166	73,629.73	52,203.37	26,525.74	69,948.25	21,069.26	24,521.12	24,521.12	21,124.72	48,420.62	73,629.73	78,594.21
167	74,072.73	52,509.14	26,638.92	70,369.10	21,159.36	24,651.85	24,651.85	21,216.69	48,690.56	74,072.73	79,066.07

Trial Length in Days	Trial length proxy A	Trial length proxy B	Trial length proxy C	Trial length proxy D	Trial length proxy E	Trial length proxy F	Trial length proxy G	Trial length proxy H	Trial length proxy I	Trial length proxy J	Trial length proxy K
168	74,515.73	52,814.93	26,752.12	70,789.95	21,249.46	24,782.59	24,782.59	21,308.66	48,960.50	74,515.73	79,537.95
169	74,958.72	53,120.70	26,865.30	71,210.79	21,339.56	24,913.33	24,913.33	21,400.63	49,230.44	74,958.72	80,009.83
170	75,401.72	53,426.48	26,978.49	71,631.63	21,429.66	25,044.06	25,044.06	21,492.60	49,500.39	75,401.72	80,481.69
171	75,844.72	53,732.26	27,091.68	72,052.49	21,519.76	25,174.81	25,174.81	21,584.57	49,770.33	75,844.72	80,953.57
172	76,287.71	54,038.04	27,204.87	72,473.33	21,609.86	25,305.54	25,305.54	21,676.54	50,040.28	76,287.71	81,425.44
173	76,730.70	54,343.83	27,318.06	72,894.18	21,699.96	25,436.28	25,436.28	21,768.51	50,310.22	76,730.70	81,897.32
174	77,173.70	54,649.60	27,431.25	73,315.02	21,790.06	25,567.02	25,567.02	21,860.48	50,580.16	77,173.70	82,369.19
175	77,616.70	54,955.38	27,544.44	73,735.87	21,880.16	25,697.75	25,697.75	21,952.44	50,850.10	77,616.70	82,841.06
176	78,059.69	55,261.16	27,657.63	74,156.71	21,970.26	25,828.49	25,828.49	22,044.41	51,120.05	78,059.69	83,312.94
177	78,502.69	55,566.94	27,770.82	74,577.56	22,060.36	25,959.23	25,959.23	22,136.39	51,389.98	78,502.69	83,784.80
178	78,945.69	55,872.72	27,884.00	74,998.40	22,150.47	26,089.96	26,089.96	22,228.35	51,659.93	78,945.69	84,256.68
179	79,388.68	56,178.50	27,997.20	75,419.25	22,240.57	26,220.70	26,220.70	22,320.32	51,929.87	79,388.68	84,728.55
180	79,831.68	56,484.28	28,110.38	75,840.09	22,330.67	26,351.44	26,351.44	22,412.30	52,199.81	79,831.68	85,200.42
181	80,274.68	56,790.07	28,223.58	76,260.94	22,420.77	26,482.17	26,482.17	22,504.26	52,469.75	80,274.68	85,672.30
182	80,717.67	57,095.84	28,336.77	76,681.78	22,510.87	26,612.91	26,612.91	22,596.24	52,739.70	80,717.67	86,144.17
183	81,160.67	57,401.62	28,449.95	77,102.64	22,599.68	26,743.65	26,743.65	22,688.21	53,009.63	81,160.67	86,616.04
184	81,603.66	57,707.40	28,563.15	77,523.48	22,688.43	26,874.38	26,874.38	22,780.17	53,279.58	81,603.66	87,087.91
185	82,046.65	58,013.18	28,676.33	77,944.32	22,777.18	27,005.13	27,005.13	22,872.14	53,549.52	82,046.65	87,559.79
186	82,489.66	58,318.96	28,789.52	78,365.17	22,865.93	27,135.86	27,135.86	22,964.11	53,819.46	82,489.66	88,031.67
187	82,932.65	58,624.74	28,902.71	78,786.02	22,954.68	27,266.60	27,266.60	23,056.08	54,089.40	82,932.65	88,503.53
188	83,375.65	58,930.52	29,015.90	79,206.87	23,043.43	27,397.34	27,397.34	23,148.05	54,359.35	83,375.65	88,975.40
189	83,818.64	59,236.30	29,129.09	79,627.71	23,132.18	27,528.06	27,528.06	23,240.02	54,629.29	83,818.64	89,447.28
190	84,261.64	59,542.08	29,242.28	80,048.55	23,220.93	27,658.81	27,658.81	23,331.99	54,899.23	84,261.64	89,919.15
191	84,704.64	59,847.86	29,355.46	80,469.41	23,309.68	27,789.55	27,789.55	23,423.96	55,169.18	84,704.64	90,391.03
192	85,147.63	60,153.64	29,468.66	80,890.25	23,398.43	27,920.28	27,920.28	23,515.94	55,439.11	85,147.63	90,862.90
193	85,590.63	60,459.41	29,581.84	81,311.10	23,487.18	28,051.02	28,051.02	23,607.90	55,709.06	85,590.63	91,334.76
194	86,033.62	60,765.20	29,695.03	81,731.94	23,575.92	28,181.76	28,181.76	23,699.87	55,979.00	86,033.62	91,806.64
195	86,476.61	61,070.98	29,808.22	82,152.79	23,664.67	28,312.49	28,312.49	23,791.84	56,248.94	86,476.61	92,278.52

Trial Length in Days	Trial length proxy A	Trial length proxy B	Trial length proxy C	Trial length proxy D	Trial length proxy E	Trial length proxy F	Trial length proxy G	Trial length proxy H	Trial length proxy I	Trial length proxy J	Trial length proxy K
196	86,919.61	61,376.76	29,921.41	82,573.64	23,753.42	28,443.23	28,443.23	23,883.80	56,518.88	86,919.61	92,750.39
197	87,362.61	61,682.54	30,034.60	82,994.48	23,842.17	28,573.96	28,573.96	23,975.78	56,788.83	87,362.61	93,222.26
198	87,805.60	61,988.32	30,147.79	83,415.33	23,930.92	28,704.70	28,704.70	24,067.75	57,058.76	87,805.60	93,694.13
199	88,248.61	62,294.10	30,260.97	83,836.17	24,019.67	28,835.45	28,835.45	24,159.72	57,328.71	88,248.61	94,166.01
200	88,691.60	62,599.87	30,374.17	84,257.02	24,108.42	28,966.17	28,966.17	24,251.69	57,598.65	88,691.60	94,637.88

[The tables following sub-paras 7(2) and (3) are printed as substituted by the S.I. 2016 No. 313 (*ante*, G-1a).]

Cracked trials and guilty pleas where the number of pages of prosecution evidence exceeds the PPE cut-off

8.–(1) Where in a cracked trial or guilty plea the number of pages of prosecution evidence **G-72**
exceeds the PPE Cut-off specified in the table following paragraph 5(1) as appropriate to the offence
with which the assisted person is charged, the total fee payable to the litigator is—

(a) the final fee, calculated in accordance with sub-paragraph (2) of this paragraph;

(b) the defendant uplift, if any, calculated in accordance with the table following paragraph
12; and

(c) the adjustment for transfers and retrials, if any, calculated in accordance with paragraph
13.

(2) For the purposes of sub-paragraph (1), the final fee payable to a litigator in a cracked trial or
guilty plea is calculated in accordance with the following formula—

$$F = I + (D \times i)$$

Where—

• **F** is the amount of the final fee;

• **I** is the initial fee specified in the tables following this paragraph, as appropriate to the type of
case, the offence with which the assisted person is charged and the number of pages of prosecution evidence;

• **D** is the difference between—

(i)   the number of pages of prosecution evidence in the case; and

(ii) the lower number in the PPE range as specified in the tables following this paragraph, as
appropriate to the type of case, the offence with which the assisted person is charged and
the number of pages of prosecution evidence in the case;

• **i** is the incremental fee per page of prosecution evidence specified in the tables following this
paragraph, as appropriate to the type of case, the offence with which the assisted person is
charged and the number of pages of prosecution evidence in the case.

TABLE OF FINAL FEES IN CRACKED TRIALS

Class of Offence	PPE Range	Initial fee (£)	Incremental fee per page of prosecution evidence (£)
A and J	0–79	904.58	0
A and J	80–249	904.58	10.70
A and J	250–999	2,722.89	6.71
A and J	1000–2799	7,757.90	3.92
A and J	2800–4599	14,820.75	3.92
A and J	4600–6399	21,883.61	3.11
A and J	6400–8199	27,490.35	3.11
A and J	8200–9999	33,097.09	3.11
A and J	10,000	38,700.71	0
B	0–69	709.15	0
B	70–249	709.15	7.83
B	250–999	2,117.67	3.66
B	1000–2799	4,864.56	2.44
B	2800–4599	9,255.51	2.44
B	4600–6399	13,646.46	2.05
B	6400–8199	17,338.49	2.05
B	8200–9999	21,030.50	2.05
B	10,000	24,720.46	0
C	0–39	524.84	0
C	40–249	524.84	3.92

Class of Offence	PPE Range	Initial fee (£)	Incremental fee per page of prosecution evidence (£)
C	250–999	1,348.77	2.25
C	1000–2799	3,033.06	1.43
C	2800–4599	5,607.48	1.43
C	4600–6399	8,181.89	1.43
C	6400–8199	10,756.31	1.43
C	8200–9999	13,330.74	1.43
C	10,000	15,903.73	0
D	0–79	859.35	0
D	80–249	859.35	10.14
D	250–999	2,582.50	6.11
D	1000–2799	7,163.76	3.61
D	2800–4599	13,655.74	3.61
D	4600–6399	20,147.71	2.96
D	6400–8199	25,474.79	2.96
D	8200–9999	30,801.87	2.96
D	10,000	36,125.98	0
E	0–39	233.03	0
E	40–249	233.03	4.60
E	250–999	1,199.43	1.46
E	1000–2799	2,291.54	0.61
E	2800–4599	3,390.26	0.61
E	4600–6399	4,488.97	0.61
E	6400–8199	5,587.69	0.61
E	8200–9999	6,686.41	0.61
E	10,000	7,784.51	0
F and G	0–49	224.22	0
F and G	50–249	224.22	4.42
F and G	250–999	1,107.53	1.79
F and G	1000–2799	2,450.39	0.70
F and G	2800–4599	3,704.67	0.70
F and G	4600–6399	4,958.94	0.70
F and G	6400–8199	6,213.21	0.70
F and G	8200–9999	7,467.49	0.70
F and G	10,000	8,721.06	0
H	0–39	237.00	0
H	40–249	237.00	4.26
H	250–999	1,131.61	1.56
H	1000–2799	2,298.20	0.70
H	2800–4599	3,550.79	0.70
H	4600–6399	4,803.37	0.70
H	6400–8199	6,055.96	0.70
H	8200–9999	7,308.55	0.70
H	10,000	8,560.44	0

Class of Offence	PPE Range	Initial fee (£)	Incremental fee per page of prosecution evidence (£)
I	0–39	253.68	0
I	40–249	253.68	5.92
I	250–999	1,496.80	2.31
I	1000–2799	3,231.91	0.90
I	2800–4599	4,847.36	0.90
I	4600–6399	6,462.79	0.90
I	6400–8199	8,078.23	0.90
I	8200–9999	9,693.67	0.90
I	10,000	11,308.20	0
K	0–119	773.86	0
K	120–249	773.86	6.55
K	250–999	1,624.85	5.02
K	1000–2799	5,388.98	4.39
K	2800–4599	13,299.04	4.39
K	4600–6399	21,209.12	3.75
K	6400–8199	27,954.29	3.75
K	8200–9999	34,699.46	3.75
K	10,000	41,440.89	0

TABLE OF FINAL FEES IN GUILTY PLEAS

Class of Offence	PPE Range	Initial fee (£)	Incremental fee per page of prosecution evidence (£)
A and J	0–79	680.39	0
A and J	80–399	680.39	5.62
A and J	400–999	2,478.29	2.96
A and J	1000–2799	4,256.09	1.89
A and J	2800–4599	7,666.89	1.89
A and J	4600–6399	11,077.68	1.12
A and J	6400–8199	13,090.60	1.12
A and J	8200–9999	15,103.53	1.12
A and J	10,000	17,115.33	0
B	0–69	556.11	0
B	70–399	556.11	4.52
B	400–999	2,046.59	2.28
B	1000–2799	3,411.75	1.45
B	2800–4599	6,025.92	1.45
B	4600–6399	8,640.11	1.06
B	6400–8199	10,555.35	1.06
B	8200–9999	12,470.60	1.06
B	10,000	14,384.78	0
C	0–39	442.91	0
C	40–399	442.91	2.66
C	400–999	1,401.88	1.46

Class of Offence	PPE Range	Initial fee (£)	Incremental fee per page of prosecution evidence (£)
C	1000–2799	2,276.27	0.79
C	2800–4599	3,699.93	0.79
C	4600–6399	5,123.61	0.79
C	6400–8199	6,547.28	0.79
C	8200–9999	7,970.95	0.79
C	10,000	9,393.82	0
D	0–79	646.36	0
D	80–399	646.36	5.23
D	400–999	2,320.66	2.75
D	1000–2799	3,968.37	1.71
D	2800–4599	7,046.20	1.71
D	4600–6399	10,124.03	1.06
D	6400–8199	12,036.98	1.06
D	8200–9999	13,949.91	1.06
D	10,000	15,861.79	0
E	0–39	184.70	0
E	40–399	184.70	2.92
E	400–999	1,237.24	1.25
E	1000–2799	1,989.07	0.46
E	2800–4599	2,819.70	0.46
E	4600–6399	3,650.33	0.46
E	6400–8199	4,480.96	0.46
E	8200–9999	5,311.59	0.46
E	10,000	6,141.75	0
F and G	0–49	195.81	0
F and G	50–399	195.81	2.83
F and G	400–999	1,187.73	0.99
F and G	1000–2799	1,781.21	0.32
F and G	2800–4599	2,354.07	0.32
F and G	4600–6399	2,926.93	0.32
F and G	6400–8199	3,499.78	0.32
F and G	8200–9999	4,072.64	0.32
F and G	10,000	4,645.18	0
H	0–39	190.97	0
H	40–399	190.97	2.79
H	400–999	1,196.59	0.99
H	1000–2799	1,790.74	0.32
H	2800–4599	2,359.85	0.32
H	4600–6399	2,928.98	0.32
H	6400–8199	3,498.10	0.32
H	8200–9999	4,067.22	0.32
H	10,000	4,636.00	0
I	0–39	174.60	0

Class of Offence	PPE Range	Initial fee (£)	Incremental fee per page of prosecution evidence (£)
I	40–399	174.60	3.12
I	400–999	1,298.52	1.36
I	1000–2799	2,116.29	0.51
I	2800–4599	3,033.02	0.51
I	4600–6399	3,949.75	0.51
I	6400–8199	4,866.48	0.51
I	8200–9999	5,783.22	0.51
I	10,000	6,699.45	0
K	0–119	640.84	0
K	120–399	640.84	5.26
K	400–999	2,113.13	2.93
K	1000–2799	3,869.24	2.73
K	2800–4599	8,775.55	2.73
K	4600–6399	13,681.86	2.08
K	6400–8199	17,423.28	2.08
K	8200–9999	21,164.71	2.08
K	10,000	24,904.04	0

[The above table is printed as substituted by S.I. 2016 No. 313 (*ante*, G-1a).]

Trials where the number of pages of prosecution evidence exceeds the PPE Cut-off

9.–(1) Where in a trial the number of pages of prosecution evidence exceeds the PPE Cut-off **G-72a** figure specified in the table following paragraph 5(2) as appropriate to the offence for which the assisted person is tried and the length of trial, the total fee payable to the litigator is—

(a) the final fee, calculated in accordance with sub-paragraph (2) of this paragraph;

(b) the defendant uplift, if any, calculated in accordance with the table following paragraph 12; and

(c) the adjustment for transfers and retrials, if any, calculated in accordance with paragraph 13.

(2) For the purposes of sub-paragraph (1), the final fee is calculated in accordance with the following formula—

$$F = I + (D \times i)$$

Where—

• **F** is the amount of the final fee;

• **I** is the initial fee specified in the table following this paragraph as appropriate to the offence for which the assisted person is tried and the number of pages of prosecution evidence;

• **D** is the difference between—

(i) the number of pages of prosecution evidence in the case; and

(ii) the lower number in the PPE range as specified in the table following this paragraph, as appropriate to the offence for which the assisted person is tried and the number of pages of prosecution evidence in the case;

• **i** is the incremental fee per page of prosecution evidence specified in the table following this paragraph, as appropriate to the offence for which the assisted person is tried and the number of pages of prosecution evidence in the case.

TABLE OF FINAL FEES IN TRIALS

Offence Class	PPE Range	Initial Fee	Incremental fee per page
A and J	0–79	1,467.58	0
A and J	80–209	1,467.58	16.58
A and J	210–699	3,622.54	12.66

Offence Class	PPE Range	Initial Fee	Incremental fee per page
A and J	700–1049	9,824.91	10.62
A and J	1050–1999	13,543.42	9.21
A and J	2000–3599	22,295.42	8.42
A and J	3600–5199	35,767.03	8.42
A and J	5200–6799	49,238.64	8.42
A and J	6800–8399	62,710.26	8.42
A and J	8400–9999	76,181.87	8.42
A and J	10,000	89,645.06	0
B	0–69	1,097.66	0
B	70–199	1,097.66	12.81
B	200–499	2,762.60	11.44
B	500–899	6,195.38	9.63
B	900–1299	10,048.21	8.09
B	1300–1999	13,285.03	7.09
B	2000–3299	18,249.51	7.09
B	3300–4999	27,469.24	7.09
B	5000–5999	39,525.82	7.09
B	6000–7999	46,617.93	7.09
B	8000–8999	60,802.14	7.09
B	9000–9999	67,894.24	7.09
B	10,000	74,979.26	0
C	0–39	739.59	0
C	40–299	739.59	10.57
C	300–799	3,486.54	9.23
C	800–1249	8,101.74	7.73
C	1250–1999	11,578.09	6.83
C	2000–3199	16,700.93	4.72
C	3200–4559	22,368.79	4.72
C	4560–5919	28,792.38	4.72
C	5920–7279	35,215.96	4.72
C	7280–8639	41,639.54	4.72
C	8640–9999	48,063.12	4.72
C	10,000	54,482.00	0
D	0–79	1,394.20	0
D	80–209	1,394.20	15.75
D	210–699	3,441.41	12.03
D	700–1049	9,333.67	10.09
D	1050–1999	12,866.25	8.75
D	2000–3599	21,180.65	8.00
D	3600–5199	33,978.67	8.00
D	5200–6799	46,776.70	8.00
D	6800–8399	59,574.74	8.00
D	8400–9999	72,372.77	8.00
D	10,000	85,162.80	0
E	0–39	352.72	0

Offence Class	PPE Range	Initial Fee	Incremental fee per page
E	40–69	352.72	9.52
E	70–129	638.20	8.57
E	130–599	1,152.58	8.29
E	600–1349	5,049.74	5.44
E	1350–2999	9,131.96	2.39
E	3000–4749	13,072.77	2.39
E	4750–6499	17,252.41	2.39
E	6500–8249	21,432.04	2.39
E	8250–9999	25,611.69	2.39
E	10,000	29,788.93	0
F and G	0–49	357.60	0
F and G	50–229	357.60	7.31
F and G	230–699	1,673.21	6.96
F and G	700–1399	4,946.64	5.60
F and G	1400–1949	8,865.80	4.32
F and G	1950–3549	11,242.37	2.16
F and G	3550–5149	14,691.41	2.16
F and G	5150–6749	18,140.45	2.16
F and G	6750–8349	21,589.49	2.16
F and G	8350–9999	25,038.53	2.16
F and G	10,000	28,593.21	0
H	0–39	357.75	0
H	40–249	357.75	8.60
H	250–619	2,162.92	7.15
H	620–1299	4,807.79	5.31
H	1300–2999	8,418.74	4.21
H	3000–4999	15,583.59	2.27
H	5000–5999	20,129.84	2.27
H	6000–6999	22,402.90	2.27
H	7000–7999	24,676.03	2.27
H	8000–8999	26,949.15	2.27
H	9000–9999	29,222.28	2.27
H	10,000	31,493.13	0
I	0–39	357.44	0
I	40–369	357.44	9.14
I	370–799	3,373.66	9.09
I	800–1299	7,282.43	8.99
I	1300–2699	11,779.02	7.08
I	2700–4199	21,697.63	3.04
I	4200–5359	26,264.52	3.04
I	5360–6519	29,796.25	3.04
I	6520–7679	33,327.97	3.04
I	7680–8839	36,859.71	3.04
I	8840–9999	40,391.43	3.04
I	10,000	43,920.11	0

Offence Class	PPE Range	Initial Fee	Incremental fee per page
K	0–119	1,031.82	0
K	120–734	1,031.82	8.66
K	735–1289	6,356.06	8.72
K	1290–2399	11,193.67	8.87
K	2400–4499	21,042.53	8.84
K	4500–7999	39,605.74	8.84
K	8000–8399	70,544.40	8.84
K	8400–8799	74,080.24	8.84
K	8800–9199	77,616.08	8.84
K	9200–9599	81,151.94	8.84
K	9600–9999	84,687.78	8.84
K	10,000	88,214.79	0

[The table in para. 9 is printed as substituted by S.I. 2016 No. 313 (*ante*, G-1a).]

PART 3

FIXED FEE FOR GUILTY PLEAS AND CRACKED TRIALS

Scope of Part 3

G-73   10.–(1) Subject to sub-paragraph (2), this Part applies to a case sent for trial to the Crown Court on the election of a defendant where the magistrates' court has determined the case to be suitable for summary trial.

(2) This Part does not apply where the trial is a cracked trial because the prosecution offer no evidence on all counts against a defendant and the judge directs that a not guilty verdict be entered.

[This paragraph was substituted by S.I. 2014 No. 2422 (*ante*, G-21a). For the transitional provision, see *ante*, G-21a. It is printed as amended by S.I. 2015 No. 1678 (*ante*, G-1a).]

Fixed fee for guilty pleas or cracked trials

11. The fee payable to a litigator in relation to a guilty plea or cracked trial to which this Part applies is £330.33 per proceedings.

[Para. 11 is printed as amended by S.I. 2016 No. 303 (*ante*, G-1a).]

PART 4

DEFENDANT UPLIFTS, RETRIALS AND TRANSFERS

Defendant uplifts

G-73a   12.–(1) The defendant uplift payable to a litigator is calculated in accordance with the table following this paragraph.

(2) Only one defendant uplift is payable in each case.

(3) In the table following this paragraph, the total fee means—

(a) in a cracked trial or guilty plea where the number of pages of prosecution evidence does not exceed the PPE Cut-off specified in the table following paragraph 5(1), the basic fee specified in the table following paragraph 6(2);

(b) in a trial where the number of pages of prosecution evidence does not exceed the PPE Cut-off specified in the table following paragraph 5(2), the basic fee specified in the table following paragraph 7(2) plus the length of trial proxy specified in the table following paragraph 7(3);

(c) in a cracked trial or guilty plea where the number of pages of prosecution evidence exceeds the PPE Cut-off specified in the table following paragraph 5(1), the final fee, as calculated in accordance with paragraph 8(2); and

(d) in a trial where the number of pages of prosecution evidence exceeds the PPE Cut-off specified in the table following paragraph 5(2), the final fee, as calculated in accordance with paragraph 9(2);

(e) where appropriate, the fee set out in paragraph 11.

(4) In a case where the representation of one defendant would attract a fixed fee under Part 3 and

the representation of one or more of the other defendants would attract a graduated fee under Part 2, the total fee is the fee falling within whichever of paragraphs (a) to (d) of sub-paragraph (3) is appropriate.

DEFENDANT UPLIFTS

Total number of defendants represented by litigator	Percentage uplift to total fee
2–4	20%
5+	30%

Retrials and transfers

13.—(1) Where following a trial an order is made for a retrial and the same litigator acts for the   **G-73b**
assisted person at both trials the fee payable to that litigator is—

    (a) in respect of the first trial, a fee calculated in accordance with the provisions of this Schedule; and

    (b) in respect of the retrial, 25% of the fee, as appropriate to the circumstances of the retrial, in accordance with the provisions of this Schedule.

(2) Where—

    (a) a case is transferred to a new litigator; or

    (b) a retrial is ordered and a new litigator acts for the assisted person at the retrial,

the fee payable to the original litigator and the new litigator is a percentage of the total fee, calculated in accordance with the table following this paragraph, as appropriate to the circumstances and timing of the retrial, transfer or withdrawal of the section 16 determination.

(3) In sub-paragraph (2), "transfer" includes the making of a section 16 determination in favour of an individual who, immediately before the making of the section 16 determination—

    (a) had represented themselves; or

    (b) had been represented (otherwise than pursuant to a section 16 determination) by the litigator named in the order,

    and for the purposes of that sub-paragraph the litigator is to be treated as a new litigator.

(4) For the purposes of sub-paragraph (2), a case is not transferred to a new litigator where—

    (a) a firm of solicitors is named as litigator in the representation order and the solicitor or other appropriately qualified person with responsibility for the case moves to another firm;

    (b) a firm of solicitors is named as litigator in the representation order and the firm changes (whether by merger or acquisition or in some other way), but so that the new firm remains closely related to the firm named in the order; or

    (c) a solicitor or other appropriately qualified person is named as litigator in the representation order and responsibility for the case is transferred to another solicitor or appropriately qualified person in the same firm or a closely related firm.

(5) For the purposes of sub-paragraph (2), where a case which has been transferred to a new litigator is transferred again, that new litigator—

    (a) must be treated as the original litigator, where the transfer takes place at any time before the trial or any retrial;

    (b) must be treated as a new litigator, where the transfer takes place during the trial or any retrial; and

    (c) must not receive any fee, where the transfer takes place after the trial or any retrial but before the sentencing hearing.

(6) Where a section 16 determination is withdrawn before the case ends, a litigator must receive a percentage of the total fee, in accordance with the table following this paragraph, as appropriate to the circumstances and timing of a transfer.

(7) In the table following this paragraph, the total fee means—

    (a) in a cracked trial or guilty plea in a case to which Part 2 applies, where the number of pages of prosecution evidence is less than or equal to the PPE Cut-off specified in the table following paragraph 5(1), the basic fee as set out in the table following paragraph 6(2);

    (b) in a trial where the number of pages of prosecution evidence is less than or equal to the PPE Cut-off specified in the table following paragraph 5(2), the basic fee specified in the table following paragraph 7(2) plus the length of trial proxy specified in the table following paragraph 7(3);

    (c) in a cracked trial or guilty plea in a case to which Part 2 applies, where the number of pages of prosecution evidence exceeds the PPE Cut-off specified in the table following paragraph 5(1), the final fee as calculated in accordance with paragraph 8(2);

    (d) in a trial where the number of pages of prosecution evidence exceeds the PPE Cut-off specified in the table following paragraph 5(2), the final fee, as calculated in accordance with paragraph 9(2);

    (e) in a cracked trial or guilty plea in a case to which Part 3 applies, the fixed fee set out in paragraph 11.

(8) Where a case becomes a Very High Cost Case after a section 16 determination has been made and is transferred from the litigator named on the representation order to a new litigator—

    (a) the original litigator must be remunerated in accordance with the individual Very High Cost Case contract entered into by that litigator; and

    (b) the new litigator must be remunerated in accordance with the individual Very High Cost Case contract entered into by that litigator.

(9) Where a case becomes a Very High Cost Case after a section 16 determination has been made and the section 16 determination is withdrawn before the end of the case, the litigator must be remunerated in accordance with the table following this paragraph as appropriate to the circumstances and timing of the withdrawal.

(10) Sub-paragraph (11) applies where—

    (a) the case is a case to which Part 3 would apply if it resulted in a cracked trial or guilty plea; and

    (b) at the time the case is transferred to a new litigator in accordance with sub-paragraph (2) it is not known whether the case would result in a cracked trial or guilty plea or whether it would proceed to trial.

(11) Where this sub-paragraph applies—

    (a) for the purpose of a claim by the original litigator at the time of the transfer of the case, "total fee" in the table following this paragraph, means the fixed fee set out in paragraph 11;

    (b) the original litigator may, if the case proceeds to trial, claim the difference between the payment received at the time of transfer of the case and the payment that would have been due at that time if that payment had been based on the case proceeding to trial.

(12) A litigator may not be treated both as an original litigator and as a new litigator in a case.

RETRIALS AND TRANSFERS

Scenario	Percentage of the total fee	Case type used to determine total fee	Claim period
Cracked trial before retrial, where there is no change of litigator	25%	Cracked trial	—
Retrial, where there is no change of litigator	25%	Trial	—
Up to and including plea and case management hearing transfer (original litigator)	25%	Cracked trial	—
Transfer at or before the first hearing at which the assisted person enters a plea – guilty plea (new litigator)	100%	Guilty plea	—
Transfer at or before the first hearing at which the assisted person enters a plea – cracked trial (new litigator)	100%	Cracked trial	—
Transfer at or before the first hearing at which the assisted person enters a plea – trial (new litigator)	100%	Trial	—
Before trial transfer (original litigator)	75%	Cracked trial	—

Scenario	Percentage of the total fee	Case type used to determine total fee	Claim period
Before trial transfer – cracked trial (new litigator)	100%	Cracked trial	–
Before trial transfer – trial (new litigator)	100%	Trial	–
During trial transfer (original litigator)	100%	Trial	Claim up to and including the day before the transfer
During trial transfer (new litigator)	50%	Trial	Claim for the full trial length
Transfer after trial or guilty plea and before sentencing hearing (original litigator)	100%	Trial, cracked trial or guilty plea as appropriate	Claim for the full trial length, excluding the length of the sentencing hearing
Transfer after trial or guilty plea and before sentencing hearing (new litigator)	10%	Trial	Claim for one day, or for the length of the sentencing hearing if longer than one day
Transfer before retrial (original litigator)	25%	Cracked trial	–
Transfer before cracked retrial (new litigator)	50%	Cracked trial	
Transfer before retrial (new litigator)	50%	Trial	Claim for the full retrial length
Transfer during retrial (original litigator)	25%	Trial	Claim up to and including the day before the transfer
Transfer during retrial (new litigator)	50%	Trial	Claim for the full retrial length
Transfer after retrial or cracked retrial and before sentencing hearing (original litigator)	25%	Trial or cracked trial as appropriate	Claim for the full retrial length, excluding the length of the sentencing hearing
Transfer after retrial or cracked retrial and before sentencing hearing (new litigator)	10%	Trial	Claim for one day, or for the length of the sentencing hearing if longer than one day

[Para. 13 is printed as amended by S.I. 2015 No. 1678 (*ante*, G-1a).]

PART 5

FIXED FEES

General provisions

14.—(1) All work undertaken by a litigator in a case to which Part 3 applies is included within the **G-74** fee set out in paragraph 11 except for a defendant uplift as provided for in paragraph 22.

(2) Except as provided under this Part, remuneration for all work undertaken by a litigator in a case to which Part 2 applies is included within the fee set out in Part 2 in this Schedule as appropriate to—

    (a)   the offence for which the assisted person is charged or tried;

    (b)   whether the case is a cracked trial, guilty plea or trial; and

    (c)   the number of pages of prosecution evidence.

Fees for appeals and committals for sentence hearings

15. The fee payable to a litigator instructed in—   **G-74a**

    (a)   an appeal against conviction from a magistrates' court;

    (b)   an appeal against sentence from a magistrates' court; or

(c)   a sentencing hearing following a committal for sentence to the Crown Court,

is that set out in the table following paragraph 19.

Fees for hearing subsequent to sentence

G-74b   16.–(1) The fee payable to a litigator instructed in relation to a hearing under an enactment listed in sub-paragraph (2) is that set out in the table following paragraph 19.

(2) The enactments are–

(a)   section 1CA of the Crime and Disorder Act 1998 (variation and discharge of orders under section 1C);

(b)   section 155 of the Powers of Criminal Courts (Sentencing) Act 2000 (alteration of Crown Court sentence);

(c)   section 74 of the Serious Organised Crime and Police Act 2005 (assistance by defendant: review of sentence).

Fees for contempt proceedings

G-75   17.–(1) This paragraph applies to proceedings referred to in section 14(g) of the Act in the Crown Court.

(2) Where, in proceedings to which this paragraph applies, the contempt is alleged to have been committed by a person other than a defendant in a case to which this Schedule applies, remuneration for litigators must be at the rate set out in the table following paragraph 19.

(3) Where, in proceedings to which this paragraph applies, the contempt is alleged to have been committed by the defendant in a case to which this Schedule applies, all work undertaken by the litigator is included within–

(a)   the fee payable under Part 2 of this Schedule, or

(b)   in proceedings under paragraph 15 or paragraph 18, the fixed fee set out in the table following paragraph 19.

Fees for alleged breaches of a Crown Court order

G-75a   18.–(1) This paragraph applies to proceedings in the Crown Court against one assisted person arising out of a single alleged breach of an order of the Crown Court.

(3) The fee payable to the litigator in respect of the proceedings to which this paragraph applies is that set out in the table following paragraph 19.

Fixed Fees

19. The table following this paragraph sets out the fixed fees payable in relation to the category of work specified in the first column of the table.

Types of proceedings	Paragraph providing for fee	Fee payable – (£ per proceedings)
Appeal against sentence from a magistrates' court	15	155.32
Appeal against conviction from a magistrates' court	15	349.47
Committal for sentence	15	232.98
Hearing subsequent to sentence	16	155.32
Contempt proceedings (where contempt is alleged to have been committed by a person other than the defendant)	17(2)	116.49
Alleged breach of a Crown Court order	18(2)	77.66

[The table in para. 19 is printed as substituted by S.I. 2016 No. 313 (*ante*, G-1a).]

Fees for special preparation

G-76   20.–(1) This paragraph applies in any case on indictment in the Crown Court–

(a)   where a documentary or pictorial exhibit is served by the prosecution in electronic form and–

(i)   the exhibit has never existed in paper form; and

(ii)   the appropriate officer does not consider it appropriate to include the exhibit in the pages of prosecution evidence; or

(b)   in respect of which a fee is payable under Part 2 (other than paragraph 7), where the number of pages of prosecution evidence, as so defined, exceeds 10,000, and the appropriate officer considers it reasonable to make a payment in excess of the fee payable under Part 2.

(2) Where this paragraph applies, a special preparation fee may be paid, in addition to the fee payable under Part 2.

(3) The amount of the special preparation fee must be calculated from the number of hours which the appropriate officer considers reasonable—

    (a) where sub-paragraph (1)(a) applies, to view the prosecution evidence; and

    (b) where sub-paragraph (1)(b) applies, to read the excess pages,

and in each case using the rates specified in the table following paragraph 27.

(4) A litigator claiming a special preparation fee must supply such information and documents as may be required by the appropriate officer in support of the claim.

(5) In determining a claim under this paragraph, the appropriate officer must take into account all the relevant circumstances of the case.

Discontinuance or dismissal of proceedings

    21.–(1) This paragraph applies to proceedings which are sent for trial to the Crown Court.   **G-76a**

(2) Where proceedings to which this paragraph applies are discontinued by a notice served under section 23A of the Prosecution of Offences Act 1985 (discontinuance of proceedings after accused has been sent for trial) at any time before the prosecution serves its evidence in accordance with the Crime and Disorder Act 1998 (Service of Prosecution Evidence) Regulations 2005 the litigator must be paid 50% of the basic fee for a guilty plea, as specified in the table following paragraph 6, as appropriate to the offence for which the assisted person is charged.

(3) Where proceedings to which this paragraph applies are discontinued by a notice served under section 23A of the Prosecution of Offences Act 1985 (discontinuance of proceedings after accused has been sent for trial) at any time after the prosecution serves its evidence in accordance with the Crime and Disorder Act 1998 (Service of Prosecution Evidence) Regulations 2005, the litigator must be paid a fee calculated in accordance with paragraph 6, or, where appropriate, paragraph 8, as appropriate for representing an assisted person in a guilty plea.

(4) Where an application for dismissal is made under paragraph 2 of Schedule 3 to the Crime and Disorder Act 1998, section 6 of the Criminal Justice Act 1987 or paragraph 5 of Schedule 6 to the Criminal Justice Act 1991, and—

    (a) the charge, or charges are dismissed and the assisted person is discharged; or

    (b) the case is remitted to the magistrates' court in accordance with paragraph 10(3)(a), 13(2) or 15(3)(a) of Schedule 3 to the Crime and Disorder Act 1998,

the litigator instructed in the proceedings must be paid a fee calculated in accordance with paragraph 6, or where appropriate, paragraph 8, as appropriate for representing an assisted person in a guilty plea.

(6) Where, at or before the first hearing at which the assisted person enters a plea—

    (a) the prosecution offers no evidence and the assisted person is discharged; or

    (b) the case is remitted to the magistrates' court in accordance with paragraph 10(3)(a), 13(2) or 15(3)(a) of Schedule 3 to the Crime and Disorder Act 1998,

the litigator must be paid a fee calculated in accordance with paragraph 6 or where appropriate paragraph 8, as appropriate for representing an assisted person in a guilty plea.

[Para. 21 is printed as amended by S.I. 2015 No. 1678 (*ante*, G-1a).]

Defendant uplifts

    22.–(1) Where a litigator represents more than one assisted person in proceedings referred to in   **G-77** paragraph 21(2), (3), (4) or (5), a defendant uplift is payable.

(2) The defendant uplift must be calculated in accordance with the table following this paragraph.

(3) In the table following this paragraph, the total fee means—

    (a) the fee specified in sub-paragraph (2) of paragraph 21 where that sub-paragraph applies;

    (b) the basic fee (B) specified in the table following paragraph 6, or, where appropriate, the initial fee specified in paragraph 8, where paragraph 21(3), (4) or (5) applies, as appropriate for the circumstances set out in that sub-paragraph; or

    (c) where appropriate the fee set out in paragraph 11.

(4) In a case where the representation of one defendant would attract a fixed fee under Part 3 and the representation of one or more of the other defendants would attract a graduated fee under Part 2, the total fee in the table following this paragraph means the fee falling within sub-paragraph (3)(b).

DEFENDANT UPLIFTS

Total number of defendants represented by litigator	Percentage uplift to total fee
2–4	20%
5+	30%

Warrant for arrest

G-77a   23.–(1) This paragraph applies where–

(a)   the assisted person fails to attend a hearing;

(b)   at that hearing the court issues a warrant for the arrest of the assisted person, pursuant to section 7(1) of the Bail Act 1976 ("the warrant"); and

(c)   the case does not proceed in the absence of the assisted person.

(2) Where in a case on indictment the warrant is not executed within three months of the date on which it was issued, the fee payable to the litigator is–

(a)   where the warrant is issued at or before the first hearing at which the assisted person enters a plea, the fee payable for a guilty plea in accordance with paragraph 6 or where appropriate paragraph 8;

(b)   where the warrant is issued after the first hearing at which the assisted person enters a plea but before the trial, the fee payable for a cracked trial in accordance with paragraph 6 or where appropriate paragraph 8, as appropriate to the Class of Offence with which the assisted person is charged; and

(c)   where the warrant is issued during the trial, and the trial is aborted as a result, the fee payable for a trial as if the trial had ended on the day the warrant was issued.

(3) Where the warrant is issued during the course of proceedings referred to in paragraph 15 or 18 the fee payable to the litigator is the fee set out in the table following paragraph 19, as appropriate to the type of proceedings.

(4) Sub-paragraph (5) applies where–

(a)   a fee has been paid, or is payable, to the litigator in accordance with sub-paragraph (2);

(b)   the warrant is executed within 15 months of the date on which it was issued;

(c)   the case proceeds after the warrant has been executed; and

(d)   the litigator submits a claim for fees for the determination of the litigator's overall remuneration in the case, in accordance with regulation 5.

(5) Where this sub-paragraph applies–

(a)   the appropriate officer must deduct the amount paid or payable in accordance with sub-paragraph (2) from the amount payable to the litigator on the final determination of fees in the case; and

(b)   if the fee paid or payable in accordance with sub-paragraph (2) is greater than the amount payable to the litigator on the final determination of fees in the case, the appropriate officer may recover the amount of the difference by way of repayment by the litigator.

[Para. 23 is printed as amended by S.I. 2015 No. 1678 (*ante*, G-1a).]

PART 6

MISCELLANEOUS

Additional charges

G-78   24.–(1) Where an assisted person is charged with more than one offence on one indictment, the fee payable to the litigator under this Schedule must be based on whichever of those offences the litigator selects.

(2) Where a litigator selects one offence, in preference to another offence, under sub-paragraph (1) that selection does not affect the litigator's right to claim any of the fees provided for in Part 5 of this Schedule to which the litigator would otherwise have been entitled.

Assisted person unfit to plead or stand trial

G-78a   25. Where in any case a hearing is held to determine the question of whether the assisted person is unfit to plead or to stand trial (a "fitness hearing")–

(a)   if a trial on indictment is held, or continues, at any time thereafter, the length of the fitness hearing is included in determining the length of the trial for the calculation of the fee in accordance with Part 2;

(b)   if a trial on indictment is not held, or does not continue, thereafter by reason of the assisted person being found unfit to plead or to stand trial, the litigator must be paid–

    (i)   a fee calculated in accordance with paragraph 7 or where appropriate paragraph 9, as appropriate to the combined length of—

        (aa) the fitness hearing; and

        (bb) any hearing under section 4A of the Criminal Procedure (Insanity) Act 1964 (finding that the accused did the act or made the omission charged against him); or

    (ii) a fee calculated in accordance with paragraph 6, or where appropriate paragraph 8, as appropriate, for representing an assisted person in a cracked trial,

whichever the litigator elects; and

  (c) if at any time the assisted person pleads guilty to the indictable offence, the litigator must be paid either—

    (i)   a fee calculated in accordance with paragraph 7 or, where appropriate, paragraph 9, as appropriate to the length of the fitness hearing; or

    (ii) a fee calculated in accordance with paragraph 6 or, where appropriate, paragraph 8, as appropriate for representing an assisted person in a guilty plea,

whichever the litigator elects.

Fees for confiscation proceedings

G-79

26.—(1) This paragraph applies to—

  (a) proceedings under Part 2 of the Proceeds of Crime Act 2002 (confiscation: England and Wales);

  (b) proceedings under section 2 of the Drug Trafficking Act 1994 (confiscation orders); and

  (c) proceedings under section 71 of the Criminal Justice Act 1988 (confiscation orders).

(2) Where this paragraph applies, the appropriate officer may allow work done in the following classes by a litigator—

  (a) preparation, including taking instructions, interviewing witnesses, ascertaining the prosecution case, preparing and perusing documents, dealing with letters and telephone calls, instructing an advocate and expert witnesses, conferences, consultations and work done in connection with advice on appeal;

  (b) attending at court where an advocate is instructed, including conferences with the advocate at court;

  (c) travelling and waiting; and

  (d) writing routine letters and dealing with routine telephone calls.

(3) The appropriate officer must consider the claim, any further particulars, information or documents submitted by the litigator under regulation 5 and any other relevant information and must allow such work as appears to him to have been reasonably done in the proceedings.

(4) Subject to sub-paragraph (3), the appropriate officer must allow fees under this paragraph in accordance with paragraph 27.

(5) The appropriate officer must allow fees in accordance with paragraphs 27 to 29 as appropriate to such of the following grades of fee earner as the appropriate officer considers reasonable—

  (a) senior solicitor;

  (b) solicitor, legal executive or fee earner of equivalent experience; or

  (c) trainee or fee earner of equivalent experience.

Prescribed fee rates

G-80

27. Subject to paragraphs 28 and 29, for proceedings in the Crown Court to which paragraph 26 applies the appropriate officer must allow fees for work under paragraph 26(2) at the following prescribed rates—

Class of work	Grade of fee earner	Rate	Variations
Preparation	Senior solicitor	£48.36 per hour	£50.87 per hour for a fee hour earner whose office is situated within the City of London or a London borough
	Solicitor, legal executive or fee earner	£41.06 per hour	£43.12 per hour for a fee earner whose office

Class of work	Grade of fee earner	Rate	Variations
	of equivalent experience		is situated within the City of London or a London borough
	Trainee or fee earner of equivalent experience	£27.15 per hour	£31.03 per hour for a fee earner whose office is situated within the City of London or a London borough
Attendance at court where more than one representative instructed	Senior solicitor	£38.55 per hour	
	Solicitor, legal executive or fee earner of equivalent experience	£31.03 per hour	
	Trainee or fee earner of equivalent experience	£18.71 per hour	
Travelling and waiting	Senior solicitor	£22.58 per hour	
	Solicitor, legal executive or fee earner of equivalent experience	£22.58 per hour	
	Trainee or fee earner of equivalent experience	£11.41 per hour	
Writing routine letters and dealing with routine telephone calls		£3.15 per item	£3.29 per item for a fee earner whose office is situated within the City of London or a London borough.

[The table in para. 27 is printed as substituted by S.I. 2016 No. 313 (*ante*, G-1a).]

Allowing fees at less than the prescribed rates

G-81　28. In respect of any item of work, the appropriate officer may allow fees at less than the relevant prescribed rate specified in paragraph 27 where it appears to the appropriate officer reasonable to do so having regard to the competence and despatch with which the work was done.

Allowing fees at more than the prescribed rates

G-81a　29.–(1) Upon a determination the appropriate officer may, subject to the provisions of this paragraph, allow fees at more than the relevant prescribed rate specified in paragraph 27 for preparation, attendance at court where more than one representative is instructed, routine letters written and routine telephone calls, in respect of offences in Class A, B, C, D, G, I, J or K in the Table of Offences.

(2) The appropriate officer may allow fees at more than the prescribed rate where it appears to the appropriate officer, taking into account all the relevant circumstances of the case, that—

　(a)　the work was done with exceptional competence, skill or expertise;

　(b)　the work was done with exceptional despatch; or

　(c)　the case involved exceptional complexity or other exceptional circumstances.

(3) Paragraph 3 of Schedule 1 applies to litigators in respect of proceedings in the Crown Court as it applies to advocates.

(4) Where the appropriate officer considers that any item or class of work should be allowed at more than the prescribed rate, the appropriate officer must apply to that item or class of work a percentage enhancement in accordance with the following provisions of this paragraph.

(5) In determining the percentage by which fees should be enhanced above the prescribed rate the appropriate officer must have regard to—

   (a)   the degree of responsibility accepted by the fee earner;

   (b)   the care, speed and economy with which the case was prepared; and

   (c)   the novelty, weight and complexity of the case.

   (6) The percentage above the relevant prescribed rate by which fees for work may be enhanced must not exceed 100%.

   (7) The appropriate officer may have regard to the generality of proceedings to which these Regulations apply in determining what is exceptional within the meaning of this paragraph.

   In *R. v. Farrell and Selby* [2007] Costs L.R. 495, it was held in relation to the provisions of **G-81b** paragraph 4 of Part 1 of Schedule 2 to the Criminal Defence Service (Funding) Order 2001 (S.I. 2001 No. 855) for paying enhanced rates to solicitors, (i) it was open to a determining officer to apply different rates of enhancement to different items of work; since a determining officer was required, in deciding on the rate of enhancement, to have regard, *inter alia*, to the "degree of responsibility accepted by the solicitor and his staff", it was permissible for a determining officer to apply a lesser rate of enhancement to work of a routine nature done by Grade B fee earners than that applied to the senior fee earners to whom they reported; (ii) when enhancement was appropriate, a determining officer should first assess what enhanced rate would have been applied if legal aid had been granted prior to October 1, 1994 (the date of commencement of the revised rules as to enhancement introduced by the Legal Aid in Criminal and Care Proceedings (Costs) (Amendment) (No. 3) Regulations 1994 (S.I. 1994 No. 2218)), *viz.* the hourly broad average direct cost rate plus an appropriate uplift for care and conduct, and then he should adjust the resulting figure upwards to allow for subsequent inflation; he should then decide on a rate of enhancement such as would match this figure; where, however, the figure exceeded the maximum enhanced rate under the 2001 order, then the determining officer should apply the maximum enhanced rate. Since the provisions under consideration corresponded to those of paragraph 6 of Schedule 2 to the Criminal Defence Service (Funding) Order 2007 (S.I. 2007 No. 1174) (prior to amendment), it could safely be taken that this decision carried across to that order (prior to amendment) with the effect—as in this case—that, wherever enhanced rates are appropriate, the rate of enhancement is always going to be 100 per cent because the 1994 hourly direct cost plus uplift for care and attention, plus uplift for inflation is always going to exceed twice the current hourly rates, which have remained unchanged for many years. This was confirmed in *R. v. Bowles* [2007] Costs L.R. 514. Whilst the provision for payment at enhanced rates under the 2013 regulations relates only to fees payable under paragraph 26, the provisions of paragraph 29 correspond to paragraph 6 of the unamended Schedule 2, and it would appear that the decision in *Farrell and Selby* will carry across to this paragraph in the same way that it carried across to paragraph 6.

Regulation 6   SCHEDULE 3

PROCEEDINGS IN THE COURT OF APPEAL

General provisions

   1.—(1) The provisions of this Schedule apply to proceedings in the Court of Appeal.   **G-82**

   (2) In determining fees the appropriate officer must, subject to the provisions of this Schedule—

   (a)   take into account all the relevant circumstances of the case including the nature, importance, complexity or difficulty of the work and the time involved; and

   (b)   allow a reasonable amount in respect of all work actually and reasonably done.

Claims for fees and disbursements by litigators

   2.—(1) Subject to regulation 31, no claim by a litigator for fees and disbursements in respect of work done in proceedings in the Court of Appeal pursuant to a section 16 determination must be entertained unless the litigator submits it within three months of the conclusion of the proceedings to which it relates.

   (2) Subject to sub-paragraph (3), a claim for fees in proceedings in the Court of Appeal must be submitted to the appropriate officer in such form and manner as the appropriate officer may direct and must be accompanied by the representation order and any receipts or other documents in support of any disbursement claimed.

   (3) A claim must—

   (a)   summarise the items of work done by a fee earner in respect of which fees are claimed according to the classes specified in paragraph 3(1);

   (b)   state, where appropriate, the dates on which the items of work were done, the time taken, the sums claimed and whether the work was done for more than one assisted person;

(c) specify, where appropriate, the level of fee earner who undertook each of the items of work claimed;

(d) give particulars of any work done in relation to more than one indictment or a retrial; and

(e) specify any disbursements claimed, the circumstances in which they were incurred and the amounts claimed in respect of them.

(4) Where the litigator claims that paragraph 8(1) applies in relation to an item of work, the litigator must give full particulars in support of the claim.

(5) The litigator must specify any special circumstances which the litigator considers should be drawn to the attention of the appropriate officer.

(6) The litigator must supply such further information and documents as the appropriate officer may require.

(7) Where a retrospective section 16 determination has been made under regulations made under section 19 of the Act in respect of any proceedings where an appellant has been successful on appeal and granted a defendant's costs order under section 16(4) of the Prosecution of Offences Act 1985 (defence costs), the litigator must certify that no claim for fees incurred before the retrospective section 16 determination was made has been or will be made from central funds in relation to that work.

Determination of litigators' fees

G-83 3.–(1) The appropriate officer may allow work done in the following classes by fee earners–

(a) preparation, including taking instructions, interviewing witnesses, ascertaining the prosecution case, advising on plea and mode of trial, preparing and perusing documents, dealing with letters and telephone calls which are not routine, preparing for advocacy, instructing an advocate and expert witnesses, conferences, consultations, views and work done in connection with advice on appeal;

(b) advocacy, including applications for bail and other applications to the court;

(c) attending at court where an advocate is assigned, including conferences with the advocate at court;

(d) travelling and waiting; and

(e) writing routine letters and dealing with routine telephone calls.

(2) The appropriate officer must consider the claim, any further information or documents submitted by the fee earner under paragraph 2 and any other relevant information and must allow–

(a) such work as appears to the appropriate officer to have been reasonably done pursuant to the section 16 determination (including any representation or advice which is deemed to be work done pursuant to that determination) by a fee earner, classifying such work according to the classes specified in sub-paragraph (1) as the appropriate officer considers appropriate; and

(b) such time in each class of work allowed by him (other than routine letters written and routine telephone calls) as the appropriate officer considers reasonable.

(3) The fees allowed in accordance with this Schedule are those appropriate to such of the following grades of litigator as the appropriate officer considers reasonable–

(a) senior solicitor;

(b) solicitor, legal executive or fee earner of equivalent experience; or

(c) trainee or fee earner of equivalent experience.

Determination of litigators' disbursements

G-84 4. The appropriate officer must allow such disbursements claimed under paragraph 2 as appear to the appropriate officer to have been reasonably incurred, provided that–

(a) if they are abnormally large by reason of the distance of the court or the assisted person's residence or both from the litigator's place of business, the appropriate officer may limit reimbursement of the disbursements to what otherwise would, having regard to all the circumstances, be a reasonable amount; and

(b) the cost of a transcript, or any part thereof, of the proceedings in the court from which the appeal lies obtained otherwise than through the registrar must not be allowed except where the appropriate officer considers that it is reasonable in all the circumstances for such disbursement to be allowed.

Claims for fees by advocates

5.–(1) Subject to regulation 31, a claim by an advocate for fees for work done in proceedings in the Court of Appeal pursuant to a section 16 determination must not be entertained unless the advocate submits it within three months of the conclusion of the proceedings to which the section 16 determination relates.

(2) Where the advocate claims that paragraph 9(4) applies in relation to an item of work the advocate must give full particulars in support of his claim.

(3) Subject to sub-paragraph (4), a claim for fees by an advocate in proceedings in the Court of Appeal must be submitted to the appropriate officer in such form and manner as the appropriate officer may direct.

(4) A claim must—

    (a)   summarise the items of work done by an advocate in respect of which fees are claimed according to the classes specified in paragraph 6(2);

    (b)   state, where appropriate, the dates on which the items of work were done, the time taken, the sums claimed and whether the work was done for more than one assisted person; and

    (c)   give particulars of any work done in relation to more than one indictment or a retrial.

(5) The advocate must specify any special circumstances which the advocate considers should be drawn to the attention of the appropriate officer.

(6) The advocate must supply such further information and documents as the appropriate officer may require.

Determination of advocate's fees

6.—(1) The appropriate officer must consider the claim, any further particulars and information   **G-85** submitted by an advocate under paragraph 5 and any other relevant information and must allow such work as appears to the appropriate officer to have been reasonably done.

(2) The appropriate officer may allow any of the following classes of fee to an advocate in respect of work allowed by him under this paragraph—

    (a)   a basic fee for preparation including preparation for a pre-trial review and, where appropriate, the first day's hearing including, where they took place on that day, short conferences, consultations, applications and appearances (including bail applications), views and any other preparation;

    (b)   a refresher fee for any day or part of a day during which a hearing continued, including, where they took place on that day, short conferences, consultations, applications and appearances (including bail applications), views at the scene of the alleged offence and any other preparation;

    (c)   subsidiary fees for—

        (i)   attendance at conferences, consultations and views at the scene of the alleged offence not covered by paragraph (a) or (b);

        (ii)   written advice on evidence, plea or appeal or other written work; and

        (iii)   attendance at pre-trial reviews, applications and appearances (including bail applications and adjournments for sentence) not covered by paragraph (a) or (b).

(3) Where a section 16 determination provides for representation by—

    (a)   a single advocate other than a QC; or

    (b)   two advocates other than QC,

and a QC agrees to appear as the single advocate or as a leading junior, that QC must be treated for all the purposes of this Schedule as having been instructed pursuant to that section 16 determination, and the remuneration of the QC must be determined as if the advocate were not a QC.

In connection with this paragraph, see *R. v. Bromige, post,* G-160.

Litigators' fees for proceedings in the Court of Appeal

7.—(1) For proceedings in the Court of Appeal the appropriate officer must allow fees for work by   **G-86** litigators at the following prescribed rates

Class of work	Grade of fee earner	Rate	Variations
Preparation	Senior solicitor	£48.36 per hour	£50.87 per hour for a litigator whose office is situated within the City of London or a London borough
	Solicitor, legal executive or fee earner	£41.06 per hour	£43.12 per hour for a litigator whose office is

Class of work	Grade of fee earner	Rate	Variations
	of equivalent experience		situated within the City of London or a London borough
	Trainee or fee earner of equivalent experience	£27.15 per hour	£31.03 per hour for a litigator whose office is situated within the City of London or a London borough
Advocacy	Senior solicitor	£58.40 per hour	
	Solicitor	£51.10 per hour	
Attendance at court where more than one representative assigned	Senior solicitor	£38.55 per hour	
	Solicitor, legal executive or fee earner of equivalent experience	£31.03 per hour	
	Trainee or fee earner of equivalent experience	£18.71 per hour	
Travelling and waiting	Senior solicitor	£22.58 per hour	
	Solicitor, legal executive or fee earner of equivalent experience	£22.58 per hour	
	Trainee or fee earner of equivalent experience	£11.41 per hour	
Routine letters written and routine telephone calls		£3.15 per item	£3.29 per item for a litigator whose office is situated within the City of London or a London borough.

(2) In respect of any item of work, the appropriate officer may allow fees at less than the relevant prescribed rate specified in the table following sub-paragraph (1) where it appears to the appropriate officer reasonable to do so having regard to the competence and despatch with which the work was done.

[The table in para. 7 is printed as substituted by S.I. 2016 No. 313 (*ante*, G-1a).]

Allowance of litigators' fees at more than the prescribed rate

G-87
8.–(1) Upon a determination of fees the appropriate officer may, subject to the provisions of this paragraph, allow fees at more than the relevant prescribed rate specified in paragraph 7 for preparation, advocacy, attendance at court where more than one representative is assigned, routine letters written and routine telephone calls, in respect of offences in Class A, B, C, D, G, I, J or K in the Table of Offences in Part 7 of Schedule 1.

(2) The appropriate officer may allow fees at more than the prescribed rate where it appears to the appropriate officer, taking into account all the relevant circumstances of the case, that—

(a) the work was done with exceptional competence, skill or expertise;

(b) the work was done with exceptional despatch; or

(c) the case involved exceptional complexity or other exceptional circumstances.

(3) Paragraph 3 of Schedule 1 applies to litigators in respect of proceedings in the Court of Appeal as it applies to advocates.

(4) Where the appropriate officer considers that any item or class of work should be allowed at more than the prescribed rate, the appropriate officer must apply to that item or class of work a percentage enhancement in accordance with the following provisions of this paragraph.

(5) In determining the percentage by which fees should be enhanced above the prescribed rate the appropriate officer may have regard to—

    (a) the degree of responsibility accepted by the fee earner;

    (b) the care, speed and economy with which the case was prepared; and

    (c) the novelty, weight and complexity of the case.

(6) The percentage above the relevant prescribed rate by which fees for work may be enhanced must not exceed 100%.

(7) The appropriate officer may have regard to the generality of proceedings to which these Regulations apply in determining what is exceptional within the meaning of this paragraph.

Advocates' fees for proceedings in the Court of Appeal

    9.—(1) Subject to sub-paragraph 9(4), for proceedings in the Court of Appeal the appropriate of- **G-88** ficer must allow fees for work by advocates at the following prescribed rates—

JUNIOR COUNSEL

Type of proceedings	Basic fee	Full day refresher	Subsidiary fees		
			Attendance at consultation, conferences and views	Written work	Attendance at pretrial reviews, applications and other appearances
All appeals	Maximum amount: £545.00 per case	Maximum amount: £178.75 per day	£33.50 per hour, minimum amount: £16.75	Maximum amount: £58.25 per item	Maximum amount: £110 per appearance

QC

Type of proceedings	Basic fee	Full day refresher	Subsidiary fees		
			Attendance at consultation, conferences and views	Written work	Attendance at pretrial reviews, applications and other appearances
All appeals	Maximum amount: £5,400.00 per case	Maximum amount: £330.50 per day	£62.50 per hour, minimum amount: £32.00	Maximum amount: £119.50 per item	Maximum amount: £257.50 per appearance

(2) Where an hourly rate is specified in the table following sub-paragraph (1), the appropriate officer must determine any fee for such work in accordance with that hourly rate, provided that the fee determined must not be less than the minimum amount specified.

(3) Where a refresher fee is claimed in respect of less than a full day, the appropriate officer must allow such fee as appears to the appropriate officer reasonable having regard to the fee which would be allowable for a full day.

(4) Where it appears to the appropriate officer, taking into account all the relevant circumstances of the case, that owing to the exceptional circumstances of the case the amount payable by way of fees in accordance with the table following sub-paragraph (1) would not provide reasonable remuneration for some or all of the work the appropriate officer has allowed, the appropriate officer may allow such amounts as appear to the appropriate officer to be reasonable remuneration for the relevant work.

[The next paragraph is G-91.]

Payment of fees

    10.—(1) Having determined the fees payable to a representative in accordance with the terms of **G-91** this Schedule, the appropriate officer must notify the representative of the fees payable and authorise payment accordingly.

(2) Where, as a result of any redetermination or appeal made or brought pursuant to paragraph 11, the fees payable under paragraph (1) are altered—

    (a) if they are increased, the appropriate officer must authorise payment of the increase; and

    (b) if they are decreased, the representative must repay the amount of such decrease.

(3) Where the payment of any fees of the representative is ordered under regulation 29(12) or regulation 30(8), the appropriate officer must authorise payment.

Redeterminations and appeals

G-92   11.—(1) Where a representative is dissatisfied with—

    (a) the fees determined in accordance with the provisions of this Schedule; or

    (b) the decision of the appropriate officer under paragraph 3(3) of Schedule 1,

he may apply to the appropriate officer to redetermine those fees or reclassify the offence, in accordance with the provisions of regulation 28(3) to (9).

(2) Where—

    (a) a representative has made an application to the appropriate officer under sub-paragraph (1); and

    (b) the appropriate officer has given his reasons for a decision under regulation 28(7),

a representative who is dissatisfied with that decision may appeal to a costs judge, in accordance with the provisions of regulation 29(2) to (14).

(3) A representative who is dissatisfied with the decision of a costs judge on an appeal under subparagraph (2) may apply to a costs judge to certify a point of principle of general importance, and the provisions of regulation 30(2) to (8) apply.

Regulation 8   SCHEDULE 4

RATES PAYABLE FOR THE CLAIMS SPECIFIED IN REGULATION 8

★G-92a   [*Sets out the rates payable for proceedings in a magistrates' court and certain other work to which the 2015 Duty Provider Contract or the 2015 Own Client Contract applies. It has been amended by the Criminal Legal Aid (Remuneration) (Amendment) Regulations 2013 (S.I. 2013 No. 2803), the Criminal Legal Aid (Remuneration) (Amendment) Regulations 2014 (S.I. 2014 No. 415), the Civil and Criminal Legal Aid (Remuneration) Regulations 2015 (S.I. 2015 No. 325), the Criminal Legal Aid (Remuneration etc.) (Amendment) Regulations 2015 (S.I. 2015 No. 1369), the Criminal Legal Aid (Remuneration) (Amendment) Regulations 2016 (S.I. 2016 No. 313), and the Criminal Legal Aid (Standard Crime Contract) (Amendment) Regulations 2017 (S.I. 2017 No. 311).*]

Regulation 16   SCHEDULE 5

EXPERTS' FEES AND RATES

G-92b

Expert	Non-London - hourly rate unless stated to be a fixed fee	London - hourly rate unless stated to be a fixed fee
A&E consultant	£100.80	£108
Accident reconstruction	£72	£54.40
Accountant	£64	£64
Accountant (general staff)	£40	£40
Accountant (manager)	£86.40	£86.40
Accountant (partner)	£115.20	£115.20
Anaesthetist	£108	£72
Architect	£79.20	£72
Back calculations	£144 fixed fee	£151.20 fixed fee
Benefit expert	£72	£72
Cardiologist	£115.20	£72
Cell telephone site analysis	£72	£72
Child psychiatrist	£108	£72
Child psychologist	£100.80	£72
Computer expert	£72	£72
Consultant engineer	£72	£54.40

Expert	Non-London - hourly rate unless stated to be a fixed fee	London - hourly rate unless stated to be a fixed fee
Dentist	£93.60	£72
Dermatologist	£86.40	£72
Disability consultant	£54.40	£54.40
DNA (testing of sample)	£252 per test	£252 per test
DNA (preparation of report)	£72	£72
Doctor (GP)	£79.20	£72
Drug expert	£72	£72
Employment consultant	£54.40	£54.40
Enquiry agent	£25.60	£18.40
ENT surgeon	£100.80	£72
Facial mapping	£108	£72
Fingerprint expert	£72	£37.60
Fire investigation	£72	£54.40
Firearm expert	£72	£72
Forensic scientist	£90.40	£72
General surgeon	£108	£72
Geneticist	£86.40	£72
GP (records report)	£50.40 fixed fee	£72 fixed fee
Gynaecologist	£108	£72
Haematologist	£97.60	£72
Handwriting expert	£72	£72
Interpreter	£28	£25
Lip reader/Signer	£57.60	£32.80
Mediator	£100.80	£100.80
Medical consultant	£108	£72
Medical microbiologist	£108	£72
Medical report	£79.20	£72
Meteorologist	£100.80	£144 fixed fee
Midwife	£72	£72
Neonatologist	£108	£72
Neurologist	£122.40	£72
Neuropsychiatrist	£126.40	£72
Neuroradiologist	£136.80	£72
Neurosurgeon	£136.80	£72
Nursing expert	£64.80	£64.80
Obstetrician	£108	£72
Occupational therapist	£54.40	£54.40
Oncologist	£112	£72
Orthopaedic surgeon	£115.20	£72
Paediatrician	£108	£72
Pathologist	£122.40	£432 fixed fee
Pharmacologist	£97.60	£72
Photographer	£25.60	£18.40
Physiotherapist	£64.80	£64.80

Expert	Non-London - hourly rate unless stated to be a fixed fee	London - hourly rate unless stated to be a fixed fee
Plastic surgeon	£108	£72
Process server	£25.60	£18.40
Psychiatrist	£108	£72
Psychologist	£93.60	£72
Radiologist	£108	£72
Rheumatologist	£108	£72
Risk assessment expert	£50.40	£50.40
Speech therapist	£79.20	£72
Surgeon	£108	£72
Surveyor	£40	£40
Telecoms expert	£72	£72
Toxicologist	£108	£72
Urologist	£108	£72
Vet	£72	£72
Voice recognition	£93.60	£72

[Schedule 5 is printed as substituted by the Criminal Legal Aid (Remuneration) (Amendment) Regulations 2013 (S.I. 2013 No. 2803), reg. 3(1) and (7), and Sched. 1.]

SCHEDULE 6

FEES IN VERY HIGH COST CASES

PART 1

INTERPRETATION AND APPLICATION

Interpretation

G-92c   1.–(1) In this Schedule—

(a)   a reference to a level is a reference to that level as defined in the Very High Cost Case contract;

(b)   a reference to a category is a reference to that category as defined in that contract;

(c)   the standard rates apply to work as described in the Very High Cost Case contract Guide; and

(d)   the preliminary hearing, half day and full day rates apply as described in the Very High Cost Case contract Guide.

(2) In this Part—

(a)   "Task List" has the meaning given in the Very High Cost Case contract;

(b)   "parties" means the representative who has signed the Very High Cost Case contract and the Lord Chancellor.

(3) In Table 2, a junior may be either a barrister or a solicitor-advocate.

Application

G-92d   2.–(1) This paragraph makes provision in relation to the application of this Schedule to work done in a case which is the subject of a Very High Cost Case contract signed by the parties before 2nd December 2013.

(2) Part 2 of this Schedule applies to work done pursuant to any Task List agreed between the parties before 2nd December 2013.

(3) Subject to sub-paragraph (4), Part 3 of this Schedule applies to work done pursuant to any Task List agreed between the parties on or after 2nd December 2013.

(4) Part 2 of this Schedule applies to work done in a case in which—

(a)   the court has set a trial date before 2nd December 2013; and

(b)   that trial date is on or before 31st March 2014.

(5) For the purpose of sub-paragraph (4), any adjournment or postponement of a trial which takes place after the trial date is set must be disregarded.

3. Part 3 of this Schedule applies to work done in a case which is the subject of a Very High Cost Case contract signed by the parties on or after 2nd December 2013.

PART 2

TABLE 1: PREPARATION (HOURLY RATES)

	Category 1 (£)	Category 2 (£)	Category 3 (£)	Category 4 (£)	Standard Rates (£)
Litigator					
Level A	145.00	113.00	91.00	91.00	55.75
Level B	127.00	100.00	79.00	79.00	47.25
Level C	84.00	65.00	51.00	51.00	34.00
Pupil/junior	45.00	36.00	30.00	30.00	
Barrister					
QC	145.00	113.00	91.00	91.00	
Leading junior	127.00	100.00	79.00	79.00	
Led junior	91.00	73.00	61.00	61.00	
Junior alone	100.00	82.00	70.00	70.00	
2nd Led junior	63.00	50.00	43.00	43.00	
Solicitor Advocate					
Leading level A	145.00	113.00	91.00	91.00	
Led level A	127.00	100.00	79.00	79.00	
Leading level B	127.00	100.00	79.00	79.00	
Led level B	104.00	86.00	66.00	66.00	
Level A alone	131.00	109.00	88.00	88.00	
Level B alone	113.00	95.00	75.00	75.00	
Second advocate	63.00	50.00	43.00	43.00	

G-92e

TABLE 2: ADVOCACY RATES

	Preliminary hearing (£)	Half day (£)	Full day (£)
QC	113.00	238.00	476.00
Leading junior	86.00	195.00	390.00
Led junior	58.00	126.00	252.00
Junior alone	67.00	143.00	285.00
2nd Led junior	34.00	64.00	128.00
Noting junior	29.00	55.00	109.00

G-92f

TABLE 3: ATTENDANCE AT COURT WITH ADVOCATE (HOURLY RATES FOR LITIGATORS)

	£
Level A	42.25
Level B	34.00
Level C	20.50

G-92g

TABLE 4: TRAVELLING, WAITING AND MILEAGE

	£
Travelling (hourly rates)	25.00 (up to a maximum of 4 hours in one day)

G-92h

	£
Waiting (hourly rates)	25.00
Mileage	00.45 per mile

PART 3

TABLE 1: PREPARATION (HOURLY RATES)

G-92i

	Category 1 (£)	Category 2 (£)	Category 3 (£)	Category 4 (£)	Standard Rates (£)
Litigator					
Level A	101.50	79.10	63.70	63.70	39.03
Level B	88.90	70.00	55.30	55.30	33.08
Level C	58.80	45.50	35.70	35.70	24.50
Pupil/junior	31.50	25.20	21.00	21.00	
Barrister					
QC	101.50	79.10	63.70	63.70	
Leading junior	88.90	70.00	55.30	55.30	
Led junior	63.70	51.10	42.70	42.70	
Junior alone	70.00	57.40	49.00	49.00	
2nd Led junior	44.10	35.00	30.10	30.10	
Solicitor Advocate					
Leading level A	101.50	79.10	63.70	63.70	
Led level A	88.90	70.00	55.30	55.30	
Leading level B	88.90	70.00	55.30	55.30	
Led level B	72.80	60.20	46.20	46.20	
Level A alone	91.70	76.30	61.60	61.60	
Level B alone	79.10	66.50	52.50	52.50	
Second advocate	44.10	35.00	30.10	30.10	

TABLE 2: ADVOCACY RATES

G-92j

	Preliminary hearing (£)	Half day (£)	Full day (£)
QC	79.10	166.60	333.20
Leading junior	60.20	136.50	273.00
Led junior	40.60	88.20	176.40
Junior alone	46.90	100.10	199.50
2nd Led junior	23.80	44.80	89.60
Noting junior	20.30	38.50	76.30

TABLE 3: ATTENDANCE AT COURT WITH ADVOCATE (HOURLY RATES FOR LITIGATORS)

G-92k

	£
Level A	29.58
Level B	23.80
Level C	14.35

TABLE 4: TRAVELLING, WAITING AND MILEAGE

	£
Travelling (hourly rates)	25.00 (up to a maximum of 4 hours in one day)
Waiting (hourly rates)	25.00
Mileage	00.45 per mile

[Schedule 6 was inserted by the Criminal Legal Aid (Remuneration) (Amendment) Regulations 2013 (S.I. 2013 No. 2803), reg. 3(1) and (8), and Sched. 2. It applies in relation to fees for work undertaken on or after December 2, 2013: *ibid.*, reg. 4.]

C. REPRESENTATION ORDERS

Representatives are entitled to claim and be remunerated only for work done in respect of **G-93** Crown Court proceedings in accordance with the provisions of the schedules to the remuneration regulations: S.I. 2013 No. 435, regs 4, 5 and 9.

Existence of a valid representation order

Payment can only be made for work done under a representation order. There is no power **G-94** under the legislation to make a payment in respect of work actually and reasonably undertaken by counsel in the genuine but mistaken belief that the appropriate order was in existence.

Solicitors are obliged to enclose a copy of the representation order with counsel's instructions, and to inform counsel of any subsequent amendments: *General Criminal Contract: Contract Specification*, Part B, para. 5.4. It is, however, incumbent upon counsel to check whether the appropriate order exists. If it is not with his instructions, then it is his duty, if he seeks to look to the legal aid fund thereafter for remuneration, to see that the appropriate authority is obtained and supplied to him: *Hunt v. East Dorset Health Authority* [1992] 1 W.L.R. 785 at 788 (Hobhouse J.); and *R. v. Welsby* [1998] 1 Cr.App.R. 197, Crown Court (Ebsworth J.) (counsel has a professional duty to ensure that he is covered by appropriate certificate).

Determining the effective date of a representation order

The effective date of a representation order for the purposes of determining which regulations **G-95** apply is the date upon which representation was first granted to counsel's instructing solicitors and not the date of the later representation order under which they instructed counsel: *R. v. Hadley* [2005] Costs L.R. 548.

Orders made ultra vires

Representation orders assigning solicitors or counsel which are made *ultra vires* are invalid, and **G-96** work done under such an order cannot be remunerated. However, where it is possible to construe an order as *intra vires*, that construction should be adopted: *R. v. O'Brien and Oliffe*, 81 Cr.App.R. 25 at 30 (Hobhouse J.). There is no power to backdate a representation order: *R. v. Welsby, ante*; *R. v. Conroy* [2004] Costs L.R. 182.

Representation by an advocate

As to when a representation order may include representation by one or more advocates or by a **G-97** Queen's Counsel, see regulations 16 to 20 of the Criminal Legal Aid (Determinations by a Court and Choice of Representative) Regulations 2013 (S.I. 2013 No. 614) (*ante*, §§ 6-263f *et seq.*).

It is submitted that a leading junior would not be entitled to any remuneration where he acts under a certificate granted for Queen's Counsel. A leading junior who acted under an unamended legal aid certificate granted to cover Queen's Counsel was not covered by the certificate and could not be remunerated under the order or by a defendant's costs order under section 16 of the Prosecution of Offences Act 1985: *R. v. Liverpool Crown Court, ex p. The Lord Chancellor, The Times*, April 22, 1993, DC. However, a Queen's Counsel must be remunerated at the appropriate rate for junior counsel where he agrees to act as a sole advocate or as a leading junior: S.I. 2013 No. 435, reg. 4(7).

[The next paragraph is G-100.]

Orders for Queen's Counsel acting alone

G-100   Where prior authority has been obtained to instruct a Queen's Counsel alone, the propriety of the order may not be challenged on the determination of Queen's Counsel's fees unless the solicitor knew or ought reasonably to have known that the purpose for which the authority had been given had failed or become irrelevant or unnecessary before the fees were incurred: S.I. 2013 No. 435, reg. 17(3).

Work done under the order

G-101   The work claimed for must have been done under the order. Work done before the date of commencement of the representation order cannot be claimed or allowed: *R. v. Clarke* (1991) Costs L.R. 496. An order cannot be backdated in respect of proceedings in the Crown Court: *R. v. North Staffordshire JJ., ex p. O'Hara* [1994] C.O.D. 248, DC; *R. v. Welsby* [1998] 1 Cr.App.R. 197, Crown Court (Ebsworth J.).

"Topping up"

G-102   An assisted person's solicitor or advocate is prohibited from receiving or being party to the making of any payment for work done in connection with the proceedings in respect of which the representation order was made other than payments by the Lord Chancellor or in respect of various specified disbursements: S.I. 2013 No. 435, reg. 9. These provisions are designed to prevent "topping" up of fees, rather than to prevent counsel from receiving payment for private fees incurred before the representation order was granted or *ex gratia* payments from solicitors who wrongly instructed counsel in the mistaken belief that he was covered by a representation order. However, once a representation order has been granted, the prohibition applies to all solicitors and advocates and not merely those persons acting under the representation order: *R. v. Grant* [2006] Costs L.R. 173.

D. Reasonable Remuneration

G-103   The basic principle of remuneration under the former *ex post facto* regime was that counsel should receive reasonable remuneration for work actually and reasonably undertaken by him. Assessment of the work undertaken and the remuneration claimed was made in each case after the event by experienced officers appointed by the Lord Chancellor's department and subject to the appellate and expert supervision of costs judges and the High Court.

G-104   Graduated fees are calculated by reference to pre-determined fixed fees. Although allowances are made for different classes of case and for the length and size of each case, the scheme necessarily embraces a "swings and roundabouts" principle. Save in exceptional cases, graduated fees draw no distinction between straightforward and complex cases of the same length, class and size.

When they were introduced in 1997, it was intended that they would be cost neutral. The extension of fees to cover 25 to 40 day cases represented a diminution in fees for defence work, balanced by an increase in the fees of prosecution counsel who are now subject to a similar scheme. The further extension of the scheme in 2007 to all trials on indictment save for those covered by VHCC contracts was a far remove from its original ambit, and may give rise to some serious underfunding of cases or aspects of cases.

Very High Cost Cases are remunerated by an hourly preparation fee and refreshers which fall within prescribed bands. The categorisation of the class of case, rates of remuneration, refreshers and the number of hours of preparation allowed to counsel must be agreed before the work is undertaken.

E. Interim Fees and other Pre-assessment Payments

(1) Staged payments for preparation in long cases

G-105   Where the period from sending to the Crown Court to the conclusion of the proceedings is likely to exceed 12 months, a legal representative may apply for staged payments (*i.e.* interim fees for the preparation of a case) in respect of each period of preparation of 100 hours or more undertaken before trial or, in serious fraud cases, before the empanelling of a jury. Preparation in this context is widely defined and includes, *inter alia*, conferences with the defendant, written advice on evidence or plea, legal research and preparation for oral or written submissions: S.I. 2013 No. 435, reg. 20.

[The next paragraph is G-110.]

(2) Interim payment of expenses

A litigator may make a claim for an interim payment of disbursements in accordance with the **G-110** provisions of regulation 14 of S.I. 2013 No. 435.

(3) Interim payment pending determination

Entitlement

In certain circumstances, an advocate may claim an interim payment of 40 per cent of the total **G-111** claim less any sum already paid: S.I. 2013 No. 435, reg. 19(1). Such payments may only be made where, (a) the basic fee claimed by counsel, or the total costs claimed by a solicitor in a related claim, or the basic fee claimed by counsel in a related claim, exceeds £4,000 (exclusive of VAT); and (b) three months have elapsed from either the date on which the bill is ready to tax or, if earlier, three months after the conclusion of the last of any related proceedings. A bill is deemed to be ready to tax on the date of receipt of the last bill in a related claim. Related claims are claims for costs of solicitors and counsel in the same proceedings acting for the same defendant or acting in related proceedings. Related proceedings are those involving the same defendant which are prepared, heard, or dealt with together, or proceedings involving more than one defendant arising out of the same incident so that the defendants are charged, tried, or disposed of together: S.I. 2013 No. 435, reg. 18.

There is no right of re-determination or appeal against the interim award: S.I. 2013 No. 435, reg. 19(2).

Claims

An advocate may submit a claim for interim payment where, (a) he is entitled to such payment; **G-112** (b) no payment has been made; (c) six months have elapsed since the conclusion of the proceedings against the defendant he represented; and (d) counsel has submitted a proper claim under regulation 4(3) (three-month time limit for the submission of claims): S.I. 2013 No. 435, reg. 18(2)-(6).

(4) Hardship payments

A discretionary hardship payment may be made on proof of the likelihood of financial **G-113** hardship. The proof required is left to the discretion of taxing officers. Counsel are advised to contact their circuit representative, before submitting a claim, to determine the form of proof likely to be acceptable. The sum paid cannot exceed the amount which is likely to be eventually paid, but payment will not be made for sums less than £5,000. Claims may only be made, (a) at least six months after the legal representative was first instructed, and (b) where final payment is unlikely to be made within the next three months by reason of which the applicant is likely to suffer financial hardship: S.I. 2013 No. 435, reg. 21.

(5) Obligations to submit claims

Any person who has received a staged, interim or hardship payment must submit a claim under **G-114** the appropriate regulation for final determination of his overall remuneration: S.I. 2013 No. 435, reg. 22(1). Any such payment will be set off against the overall remuneration on final determination and excess payments can be recovered: *ibid.*, reg. 22(2).

F. GRADUATED FEES

(1) Introduction

As to the introduction of the scheme for graduated fees, see *ante*, G-2. **G-115**

The scheme determines the taxation and payment of fees for advocacy and preparation in something of a mechanistic or formulaic way: *Meeke and Taylor v. Secretary of State for Constitutional Affairs* [2006] Costs L.R. 1. It is a comprehensive scheme which must be applied by examining the particular wording of the legislation: *R. v. Kemp*, X15 363/99. There is no "equity" in the regulations; they have to be construed and given effect however hard the result might be: *R. v. Riddell*, X3, SCCO 319/98, even where payment is morally due: see *R. v. Dhaliwal* [2004] Costs L.R. 689. Conversely, as was pointed out in *R. v. Chubb* [2002] Costs L.R. 333:

> "As has often been said, when the graduated fee system was introduced, it was on a principle which was expressed as being 'swings and roundabouts'. It is perfectly reasonable where the system operates against the Lord Chancellor's Department, that an appeal should be launched. There are many occasions, in my experience, when the graduated fee system has operated very much to the disadvantage of members of the bar and there is no reason why the bar should not take advantage when it operates in their favour."

References within this section to paragraphs are references to paragraphs in Schedule 1 to S.I. 2013 No. 435 (unless otherwise stated).

[The next paragraph is G-118.]

(2) Cases on indictment

Scheduled offences

G-118   A "case" includes proceedings in the Crown Court against any one assisted person on one or more counts of a single indictment: S.I. 2013 No. 435, Sched. 1, para. 1(1). Where counts or defendants are severed and dealt with separately, then each separate indictment is a separate case. Conversely, indictments which are joined should be treated as one case: GFSG: A1, A2: *R. v. Chubb* [2002] Costs L.R. 333. A "case" should not be confused with a trial; there may be two trials in one case: *R. v. Bond* [2005] Costs L.R. 533.

All cases on indictment now fall within the scheme unless specifically excluded: S.I. 2013 No. 435, Sched. 1, para. 2. As to pre-indictment hearings, see *post*, G-121a.

In *R. v. Hussain* [2011] Costs L.R. 689, after one defendant was committed for trial and a plea and case management hearing was conducted in relation to a single-count indictment, a second defendant was committed for trial, as a result of which a second indictment was preferred which included the allegation against the first defendant in the single-count indictment, and the defendants were in due course tried on the second indictment. It was held that: (i) whereas paragraph 1(1) of Schedule 2 to S.I. 2013 No. 435 (*ante*, G-69) provides that "'case' means proceedings in the Crown Court against any one assisted person—(a) on one or more counts of a single indictment ...", there were two "cases"; (ii) in respect of the second indictment, the solicitors were entitled to a graduated fee for trial, together with the appropriate uplift for representing more than one defendant; and (iii) in respect of the first indictment, they were entitled to a graduated fee for a cracked trial. The costs judge observed that whilst it might be thought that the solicitors had obtained something of a windfall for, in layman's terms, this was really only one case, the regulations must be applied mechanistically.

Table of offences

G-119   The table of offences in Schedule 1 to S.I. 2013 No. 435 contains offences listed by statute with a description set out only for convenience. The statutory reference includes every offence contrary to that reference, whether or not the description of the offence is apt to describe the offence actually charged: S.I. 2013 No. 435, Sched. 1, para. 3(1)(e). Cases which do not appear in the table of offences are deemed to fall within Class H: S.I. 2013 No. 435, Sched. 1, para. 3(1)(a). An advocate who is dissatisfied with that deemed classification may apply to the appropriate officer to reclassify the offence: S.I. 2013 No. 435, Sched. 1, para. 3(2).

The offences are divided into the following classes:

Class A	Homicide and related grave offences
Class B	Offences involving serious violence or damage and serious drug offences
Class C	Lesser offences involving violence or damage, and less serious drug offences
Class D	Sexual offences and offences against children
Class E	Burglary and going equipped
Class F	Other offences of dishonesty including those where the value does not exceed £30,000
Class G	Other more serious offences of dishonesty including those where the value exceeds £30,000 but does not exceed £100,000
Class H	Miscellaneous lesser offences
Class I	Offences against public justice and similar offences
Class J	Serious sexual offences
Class K	The most serious offences of dishonesty and other offences where the value exceeds £100,000

Where counts of differing classes appear in the same indictment, the fee is based upon the class selected by the advocate: S.I. 2013 No. 435, Sched. 1, para. 27(1). Once counsel has chosen which count to use as the basis of a claim, that choice is irrevocable: *R. v. Buoniauto*, X25, SCCO 483/2000. Where an indictment is drafted in such a way that the offence charged could fall into either of two different classes in the table of offences, the advocate may choose the class to which the case is to be assigned for the purpose of calculating the fees payable: *Lord Chancellor v. Ahmed* [2014] Costs L.R. 21, QBD (Andrews J.). Where two or more advocates appear for the same defendant, the grounds of each claim must be the same: *R. v. Powell*, X8, SCTO 336/98.

The offences are summarised and listed alphabetically by statute: *post*, G-168 *et seq.*

Conspiracy, incitement or attempt to commit an offence fall within the same class as the **G-120** substantive offence: S.I. 2013 No. 435, Sched. 1, para. 3(1)(b). Conspiracy to defraud at common law does not appear in the table of offences. It will accordingly fall within Class H: S.I. 2013 No. 435, Sched. 1, para. 3(1)(a). Where the appropriate class depends upon a value, the lower value is presumed unless the claimant "proves otherwise to the satisfaction of the appropriate authority": S.I. 2013 No. 435, Sched. 1, para. 3(1)(c). This may be done by extracts from the indictment or witness statements. Values relating to offences taken into consideration should be excluded from the computation: GFSG: E10. The proof required is proof on a balance of probabilities, and the appropriate officer must take a common sense approach in deciding whether the burden has been discharged: *R. v. Garness* [2014] Costs L.R. 201.

In *R. v. O'Donnell and Fawley* [2012] Costs L.R. 431, it was held that the scheme is mechanistic and that there is no discretion for the court to say that, because the defendants may have been shown to have committed offences in a different class, which would attract a higher fee, it is permissible to reclassify the offence actually charged accordingly.

The calculation of values

The property values of each count falling within the same class may be aggregated, provided **G-121** the same property is not counted twice: S.I. 2013 No. 435, Sched. 1, para. 3(1)(d). However, offences taken into consideration are excluded from the calculation, even where it is agreed that the counts on the indictment are to be treated merely as sample counts: *R. v. Knight*, X35, SCCO 34/2003.

In *R. v. Wei* [2010] Costs L.R. 846, it was held that "value", for the purposes of paragraph 3 of Schedule 2 to S.I. 2013 No. 435 and the table of offences in Part 7 of Schedule 1 (*ante*, G-68, G-70; *post*, G-168 *et seq.*), must, in the context of an offence of dishonesty, such as possession of articles for use in fraud, mean the value of the dishonest enterprise, and not the value of the particular articles. The court said that the obvious intention was to provide greater remuneration for more complex and lengthy cases within the confines of the formulaic graduated fee system.

Preliminary hearings

In *Lord Chancellor v. Shapiro* [2010] Costs L.R. 769, QBD (Sweeney J.), it was held that for a **G-121a** first hearing in the Crown Court of a case sent for trial under section 51 of the CDA 1998 (§ 1-24 in the main work) to fall within the graduated fee scheme there must be an indictment in existence at the time. It was said that since the order makes no specific provision for such hearings, it follows that they fall to be remunerated as part of the basic fee if there is an indictment in existence at the time, and, if there is not, there is no provision for payment; in particular, the order making no provision for *ex post facto* taxation (except in strictly limited circumstances), there is no power to make a payment on an *ex post facto* basis. For criticism of this decision, see the commentary in CLW/10/38/8.

Pleas and directions hearings and pre-trial reviews

G-122   Pleas and directions hearings are not defined under the regulations. Accordingly if a matter is listed as a pleas and directions hearing, it will be so treated. There is nothing to prevent a pleas and directions hearing from being adjourned, or there being more than one or even a series of such hearings: *R. v. Beecham*, X11, QBD (Ebsworth J.). However, the listing of the case is not necessarily determinative. For example, although a case may be listed as a pleas and directions hearing, if a defendant pleads at that hearing and is sentenced, it cannot be said that a pleas and directions hearing has taken place: *R. v. Johnson*, SCCO 51/06. Pleas and directions hearings (other than those which form part of the main hearing) and pre-trial reviews are payable at a fixed rate. Any pre-trial hearings to determine, for example, the admissibility of evidence, fall outside the main hearing and are remunerated as standard appearance fees: *R. v. Rahman*, X21, SCCO 119/2000; *R. v. Carter*, X18, SCCO 384/99.

Fees for oral hearings which fall within the definition of a standard appearance are deemed to be included in the basic fee: see *post*, G-129. Case management hearings which are not standard appearances are remunerated according to the fees set out in the table following paragraph 24: S.I. 2013 No. 435, Sched. 1, para. 12(2). As to standard appearances, see *post*, G-129.

The start of the main hearing

G-123   In *Lord Chancellor v. Ian Henery Solicitors Ltd* [2012] Costs L.R. 205, QBD (Spencer J.), it was held that when considering the question whether, and if so on what date, a case has proceeded to trial, the following principles apply: (i) whether or not a jury have been sworn is not conclusive; (ii) there can be no doubt that a trial will have begun if the jury have been sworn, the case has been opened, and evidence has been called; (iii) a trial will also have begun if the jury have been sworn and the case has been opened to any extent, even if only for a few minutes (*Meeke and Taylor v. Secretary of State for Constitutional Affairs* [2006] Costs L.R. 1, QBD (David Clarke J.)); (iv) a trial will not have begun, even if the jury have been sworn (and whether or not the defendant has been put in the charge of the jury), if there has been no trial in a meaningful sense, *e.g.* because, before the case can be opened, the defendant pleads guilty (*R. v. Brook* [2004] Costs L.R. 178, *R. v. Baker and Fowler* [2004] Costs L.R. 693, and *R. v. Sanghera* [2008] Costs L.R. 823); (v) a trial will have begun, even if there has been no empanelment of a jury, if submissions have begun in a continuous process resulting in the empanelling of a jury, the opening of the case, and the leading of evidence (considering *R. v. Wembo* [2011] Costs L.R. 926, *R. v. Bullingham* [2011] Costs L.R. 1078, and an unreported decision of Mitting J. in December, 2005, in the case of *R. v. Smith*); (vi) if, in accordance with modern practice in long cases, a jury have been selected but not sworn, then provided the court is dealing with substantial matters of case management it may well be that the trial has begun in a meaningful sense; and (vii) where there is likely to be any difficulty in deciding whether a trial has begun, and if so when it began, the judge should be prepared, upon request, to indicate his view on the matter for the benefit of the parties and the determining officer, in the light of these principles.

In *R. v. Budai* [2011] Costs L.R. 1073, the costs judge acknowledged the principle in (v), *ante*, but held that this did not cover a case where, on the day listed for trial, all that was done was that interpreters were sworn, a potential panel of 18 jurors was selected (prior to their being sent away until the following day to assess their availability for a lengthy trial) and there was a direction made regarding the amendment of the indictment. On the other side of the line are *R. v. Wembo*, *ante* (where, immediately prior to a jury being empanelled, counsel had attended two days of hearings that related to a witness anonymity order, those days had formed part of the trial for the purposes of calculating the graduated fee); and *R. v. Bullingham*, *ante* (where a jury had not been empanelled, but the judge directed that there should be a *voire dire* to determine the admissibility of evidence which the prosecution wanted to open to the jury, and there was such a *voire dire* at which evidence was called, the trial started with the giving of that direction even though the effect of the ruling on the *voire dire* was that the prosecution decided to accept pleas to lesser offences in consequence of which the defendant pleaded guilty and there was no requirement for a jury). The reasoning in *Bullingham* was expressly approved in *Lord Chancellor v. Ian Henery Solicitors Ltd, ante*, but it is submitted that the result is difficult to justify, not least for its failure to give effect to the obvious purpose of paragraph 13 of Schedule 1 (*ante*, § G-48), which the costs judge did not even refer to. Sub-paragraph (1)(d) expressly contemplates that a hearing as to the admissibility of evidence may take place before the main hearing of a case (trial or cracked trial), and if it does, it is to be remunerated in accordance with that paragraph. The decision of the costs judge effectively emasculates this by converting the admissibility hearing into the main hearing. See also the commentary in CLW/12/01/14.

The start of a preparatory hearing is the commencement of the trial for the purposes of the regulations: *R. v. Jones*, X17, SCCO 527/99: GFSG: B8, B8A.

Calculating the length of the main hearing

Length of the main hearing means the number of days of the main hearing together with the **G-124** number of days of any *Newton* hearing in relation to the assisted person whose trial is under consideration: S.I. 2013 No. 435, reg. 2(1), and Sched. 1, para. 2(8). Thus, where counsel successfully submits that there is no case to answer, the main hearing ceases, despite the fact that the trial may continue against the co-defendants: *Secretary of State for Constitutional Affairs v. Stork, The Times*, October 7, 2005, QBD (Gray J.). This can lead to harsh anomalies, as where a defendant pleads guilty shortly after a jury have been sworn during an estimated three-week trial; despite preparation for a three-week trial, counsel will be remunerated as for a one day trial: *Meeke and Taylor v. Secretary of State for Constitutional Affairs, ante*. Non-sitting days cannot be included: *R. v. Nassir*, X13, SCCO 703/98. Where a jury are sworn, but discharged the same day for some reason other than the private or professional convenience of counsel, with a new jury sworn the following day, there may be sufficient continuity to conclude that the trial did in fact proceed, and start of the trial is the date on which the first jury were sworn: *R. v. Gussman*, X14, SCTO 40/99, but part of a day counts as a whole day: S.I. 2013 No. 435, Sched. 1, para. 4. Applications relating to abuse of process, disclosure and witness summonses are to be treated as part of the main hearing where they are heard during the main hearing: S.I. 2013 No. 435, Sched. 1, para. 13(2). The length of a fitness hearing which precedes a trial on indictment must also be included in determining the length of the trial: S.I. 2013 No. 435, Sched. 1, para. 31(a). Confiscation proceedings are excluded from the computation: S.I. 2013 No. 435, Sched. 1, para. 14(2).

Where, during the currency of a trial, there had been a day when one juror could not attend, but the judge had directed all counsel to attend in order that agreement should be reached as to how to reduce one section of the evidence, counsel was not entitled to count that day as a day of the trial; although the judge had indicated he would be available in case there was some issue on which agreement could not be reached, it had not been necessary to involve the judge and the case had not been called on in court; counsel was, however, entitled to a non-effective hearing fee for that day (under Sched. 1, para. 16 (*ante*, G-51)); the case was listed for that day, counsel had been obliged to attend, but in fact the trial did not proceed on that day: *R. v. Budai, ante*.

Fees for contested trials

The calculation of any graduated fee involves arcane formulae: S.I. 2013 No. 435, Sched. 1, **G-125** para. 4. To calculate the correct fee, the appropriate figures should be substituted from the tables of fees and uplifts: S.I. 2013 No. 435, Sched. 1, para. 5.

[The next paragraph is G-129.]

Standard appearances

Standard appearances are defined in S.I. 2013 No. 435 as appearances which do not form part **G-129** of the main hearing, and constitute (i) plea and case management hearings; (ii) pre-trial reviews and pre-trial preparation hearings; (iii) the hearing of a case listed for plea which is adjourned for trial; (iv) custody time limit, bail and other applications; (v) mentions, including applications relating to the date of trial; (vi) a sentencing hearing other than one following a committal for sentence to the Crown Court, or one where sentence has been deferred under the PCC(S)A 2000, s.1, or one where the advocate has been instructed solely for the purposes of entering a plea in mitigation under paragraph 34 of Schedule 1; (vii) a hearing, whether contested or not, relating to breach of bail, failure to surrender to bail or execution of a bench warrant; and (viii) any hearing (except a trial, the first hearing at which the assisted person enters a plea, appeal against conviction or sentence, sentencing hearing following a committal for sentence to the Crown Court, or proceedings arising out of an alleged breach of an order of the Crown Court) which is listed but cannot proceed because of the failure of the assisted person or a witness to attend, the unavailability of a pre-sentence report or other good reason: Sched. 1, para. 1(1). Under S.I. 2013 No. 435, an advocate's fees payable for the first plea and case management hearing or pre-trial review and up to four standard appearances are deemed to be included in the basic fee and are not subject to separate remuneration: Sched. 1, para. 12 (*ante*, G-47). The fifth and subsequent standard appearances are remunerated as set out in the table following paragraph 24: *ibid.*, para. 12(2).

Where an advocate made three appearances at non-effective hearings, the first two of which had been listed as a plea and case management hearing and the third of which had been listed for an anticipated plea of guilty to be taken, where the third hearing was ineffective because the defendant had absconded, and where a bench warrant had been issued which remained outstanding, paragraph 12(1) did not apply as no basic fee had become payable (and thus it did not prevent payment in respect of the three appearances); payment could be made under paragraph 12(2); there was no authority in the legislation for a statement in the graduated fee scheme guidance that suggested that no fee could be paid so long as a bench warrant was outstanding: *R. v. Metcalf* [2010] Costs L.R. 646; and, to similar effect, see *R. v. Muoka* [2013] Costs L.R. 523.

Trial of Bail Act offences

G-130   The trial of any Bail Act 1976 offence in the Crown Court entitles counsel who attends to apply for a new "trial" fee for the contested trial or plea: *R. v. Shaw* [2005] Costs L.R. 326; *R. v. Despres* [2005] Costs L.R. 750.

Sendings to the Crown Court

G-131   Where cases are sent to the Crown Court under the CDA 1998, s.51, and are discontinued before the prosecution serve their evidence, the advocate is entitled to 50 per cent of the fee calculated on the basis of a guilty plea: S.I. 2013 No. 435, Sched. 1, para. 22(2), together with an additional 20 per cent of that fee for each additional person represented: para. 22(8)(a). Once the prosecution have served their evidence, discontinuance, the offering of no evidence at a pleas and case management hearing, or the remitting of the case to the magistrates' court at such hearing because the indictment contains no indictable offence, is treated for the purposes of calculating the relevant fee as if each was a guilty plea: *ibid.*, para. 22(3) and (5). An advocate representing more than one person in the latter circumstances is entitled to 20 per cent of the appropriate basic fee for each additional person he represents: para. 22(8)(b).

Dismissal hearings

G-132   Where a successful application for dismissal is made under the CDA 1998, Sched. 3, para. 2, with the result that the case is dismissed or remitted back to the magistrates' court, the fee is calculated as if the matter had been disposed of by a guilty plea, together with an attendance fee based upon the total number of days and half days occupied by the hearing: S.I. 2013 No. 435, Sched. 1, para. 22(6) and (7). A full day's hearing is any court day which begins before and ends after the luncheon adjournment: para. 22(6)(a). An advocate representing more than one person in such circumstances is entitled to 20 per cent of the appropriate basic fee for each additional person he represents: para. 22(8)(b).

Transfers

G-133   A case will be "transferred" to a new litigator for the purposes of paragraph 13(2)(a) of

Schedule 2 to the Criminal Legal Aid (Remuneration) Regulations 2013 (S.I. 2013 No. 435) (*ante*, G-73b) where the representation order has been amended to substitute the new litigator and the new litigator has agreed to accept the instructions and has carried out a conflicts check; an amended representation order will not be effective to transfer a case to a new litigator who has not carried out a conflicts check because it is incumbent upon any firm of solicitors to carry out such a check before accepting instructions and, therefore, in such circumstances, it cannot be said that the new litigator has been "instructed" until that duty has been discharged: *Tuckers Solicitors v. Lord Chancellor* [2014] Costs L.R. 29, QBD (Andrews J.) (considering a corresponding provision in the Criminal Defence Service (Funding) Order 2007 (S.I. 2007 No. 1174), and observing that, in practice, it would be desirable if, when the Crown Court sends information to the putative new litigator, it were to include the indictment, witness list and, if available, the case summary, rather than leaving it to the former solicitors to do so).

In *R. v. Rayan* [2010] Costs L.R. 969, it was held that, for the purposes of paragraph 13(2) of Schedule 2 to S.I. 2013 No. 435 (*ante*, G-73b), which provides that where a case is transferred from one litigator to another, the original litigator is entitled to 25 per cent of the cracked trial fee where the transfer took place "up to and including plea and case management hearing" or a fee of 75 per cent of the cracked trial fee for a "before trial transfer", the reference to a "plea and case management hearing" must be taken to be a reference to an effective such hearing. An effective hearing, it was held, requires there to have been a plea, and for case management directions of sufficient substance to have been made such that the hearing could be described as a plea and case management hearing.

Retrials

A standard graduated fee is paid for retrials, where the same advocate appears, subject to the **G-134** following discounts based upon the time elapsed from the conclusion of the first trial to the start of the retrial: S.I. 2013 No. 435, para. 2(3):

30 per cent	retrial starts within one month
20 per cent	retrial starts after one month
40 per cent	retrial is cracked or becomes a guilty plea within one month
25 per cent	retrial is cracked or becomes a guilty plea after one month.

No discounts are applied where the advocate who conducts the retrial is not the advocate who conducted the original trial: *ibid.*, para. 2(5) and (6).

In *R. v. Connors* [2014] Costs L.R. 942 it was held that under the graduated fee scheme for advocates as set out in Schedule 1 to the Criminal Defence Service (Funding) Order 2007 (S.I. 2007 No. 1174), where there is a trial followed by a retrial with the same advocate acting in both trials, the advocate does not have to wait until the conclusion of the second trial to claim payment for the first trial. Furthermore, an advocate need not wait until the conclusion of the second trial before electing to have the reduced fee applied to the first trial under paragraph 2(4) of Schedule 1 to the 2007 order (now under Sched. 1, para. 2(2) and (3), to S.I. 2013 No. 435 (*ante*, G-40)). If it turned out that there should have been a greater reduction than the one actually applied, the Legal Aid Agency could recoup any excess payment via article 26 of the 2007 order (now via reg. 25 of S.I. 2013 No. 435 (Appendix G-31)): *ibid.*

Where the case was sent to the Crown Court on the election of the defendant where the magistrates' court had determined the case to be suitable for summary trial, and the new trial becomes a cracked trial or guilty plea, the advocate will receive a graduated fee for the first trial and a fixed fee for the second trial: S.I. 2013 No. 435, Sched. 1, para. 2(4). This also applies where the trial advocate is different at the second trial: S.I. 2013 No. 435, Sched. 1, para. 2(5) and (7).

Where a defence advocate was initially retained privately but, the jury at the first trial having **G-134a** been unable to agree on a verdict, was then instructed for the retrial under a representation order, the defendant having run out of money, and where the defendant was acquitted at the retrial with a defendant's costs order being made in his favour, no payment could be made under the defendant's costs order out of central funds in respect of work done in preparation for the retrial between the date of the first trial and the grant of the representation order; the graduated fee payable for a retrial under the Criminal Defence Service (Funding) Order 2001 (S.I. 2001 No. 855) was intended to allow for all preparation carried out for that retrial; to have authorised the payment would have resulted in a double payment out of public funds effectively in respect of the same work: *R. v. Long* [2009] Costs L.R. 151. The result would be the same under S.I. 2013 No. 435.

In *Lord Chancellor v. Purnell and McCarthy* [2010] Costs L.R. 81, QBD (Sir Christopher Holland), where a full trial had been conducted in which the jury had acquitted the defendant on the main charge of murder, but had been unable to agree on an alternative charge of manslaughter and on another count of violent disorder, where a date for a retrial had been fixed, where the prosecution eventually decided to offer no evidence, and where it was clear that counsel had not, meanwhile, been standing by awaiting a decision by the prosecution whether to proceed (it was not the case that the matter had been adjourned after trial to allow the prosecution time to decide whether they intended to proceed further) but, on the contrary, had begun preparing for the retrial, it was held that counsel were entitled to a graduated fee for a "cracked trial". They had every reason to expect and prepare for a retrial, as the case was serious and had so far featured a finding by at least three jurors that manslaughter had been proved against the defendant to the criminal standard. Under the 2001 order, there was no provision for any percentage reduction of the fee in such cases. This, however, has since been remedied: see now S.I. 2013 No. 435, Sched. 1, para. 2(2) and (3) (*ante*, G-40).

In *R. v. Seivwright* [2011] Costs L.R. 327, it was held that paragraph 13(1) of Schedule 2 to S.I. 2013 No. 435 (*ante*, G-73b) applies only where the retrial follows a trial and an order has been made for a retrial following appeal or where a jury have failed to reach a verdict, and that "retrial" for this purpose means a new trial which is not part of the same procedural and temporal matrix as the first trial. It was said that whilst this conclusion might be thought to conflict with the Litigator Graduated Fee Scheme Guidance published by the Legal Services Commission, that was merely guidance and not a source of law that was binding. On the facts, it was held that where the trial had commenced on a Monday, the jury had been discharged on the Thursday, the matter was listed for mention on the Friday when it was agreed that a new jury would be empanelled on the following Monday, and where they were so empanelled, there was but one trial.

In *R. v. Nettleton* [2014] Costs L.R. 387, it was held that where the question arises whether "an order [was] made for a retrial", this is not to be confined to cases where one jury are discharged following a disagreement and an order for a new trial is made before a different jury, but it does not extend to every interruption to the trial process, even if it involves the discharge of one jury and the empanelment of a fresh jury. The question is whether the new proceeding was part of the same procedural and temporal matrix as the prior proceeding (see *Seivwright, ante*). If there is a continuous process, even a long gap will not necessarily render the second proceeding a "retrial", and the fact that additional evidence has been served by the prosecution, including from one or more new witnesses, will not *per se* render the new proceeding a retrial. In this case, it was held that it was clear that there had been a trial and a retrial where the jury at the original hearing had been discharged following the arrest of the judge, and there had then been a four-month gap before the second proceeding began with a new judge, new jury and, in the case of some defendants, new counsel.

Guilty pleas

G-135   S.I. 2013 No. 435 defines a guilty plea as a case on indictment which is disposed of without trial because of the guilty plea, and is not a cracked trial: Sched. 1, para. 1(1). Cases which result in a *Newton* hearing are excluded: *ibid.*, para. 2(8)(c); and see *post*, G-147.

The graduated fee for guilty pleas is calculated by reference to the basic fee, together with the appropriate evidence uplift per page as set out in the table of fees and uplifts: S.I. 2013 No. 435, Sched. 1, paras 7 and 8 (and Table A).

Graduated fees for guilty pleas under Part 3 of Schedule 1 to S.I. 2013 No. 435 no longer apply to cases committed to the Crown Court on the election of the defendant where the magistrates' court determined that the case was suitable for summary trial: S.I. 2013 No. 435, Sched. 1, para. 6.

In *R. v. Agbobu* [2009] Costs L.R. 374, it was held that even though a case may not be a "guilty plea" within the definition in paragraph 1(1) of Schedule 2 to S.I. 2013 No. 435 (*ante*, G-69), paragraph 21(4) of Part 3 of that schedule (*ante*, G-76a) nevertheless provides that "where an application for dismissal is made ... and–(a) the charge, or charges are dismissed and the assisted person is discharged; ... the litigator instructed in the proceedings must be paid a fee calculated in accordance with paragraph 6, or where appropriate, paragraph 8, as appropriate for representing an assisted person in a guilty plea". Accordingly, the fee payable for a litigator representing a defendant against whom charges were dismissed was that payable for a guilty plea and not a cracked trial.

Cracked trials

A cracked trial is a case on indictment in which (a) the assisted person enters a plea of not **G-136** guilty to one or more counts at the first hearing at which he or she enters a plea and (i) the case does not proceed to trial (whether by reason of pleas of guilty or for other reasons) or the prosecution offer no evidence; and (ii) either (aa) in respect of one or more counts to which the assisted person pleaded guilty, he did not so plead at the first hearing at which he entered a plea; or (bb) in respect of one or more counts which did not proceed, the prosecution did not, before or at the first hearing at which the assisted person entered a plea, declare an intention of not proceeding with them; or (b) the case is listed for trial without hearing at which the assisted persons enters a plea: S.I. 2013 No. 435, Sched. 1, para. 1(1) (the definition is defective in that in (b) there is no reference to the case not proceeding to trial (read literally it would cover cases that go to trial where no plea and case management hearing took place)). The rationale for the cracked trial fee is that it provides some element of compensation for the loss of refreshers and trial length increments which otherwise would have been payable: *R. v. Frampton* [2005] Costs L.R. 527. Graduated fees for guilty pleas under Part 3 of Schedule 1 to S.I. 2013 No. 435 no longer apply to cases committed to the Crown Court on the election of the defendant where the magistrates' court determined that the case was suitable for summary trial: S.I. 2013 No. 435, Sched. 1, para. 6.

The essence of a cracked trial is that after the conclusion of a pleas and directions hearing there are still counts on which the prosecution and defence do not agree so that a trial remains a real possibility: *R. v. Minster*, X23, SCTO 647/99; *R. v. Mohammed*, X27, SCCO 210/2000. A case listed for a plea and directions hearing is ultimately defined by what actually happens at that hearing. If a defendant pleads guilty at what is listed as a plea and directions hearing, the plea obviates the need for such a hearing. Accordingly, an advocate is entitled to a fee for a cracked trial: *R. v. Johnson* [2006] Costs L.R. 852 (*sed quaere*, as this flies in the face of the definition of a "cracked trial": see (a), *ante*). Where an indictment containing two counts was listed for trial following a plea and directions hearing, but the defendant pleaded guilty to one count, which was acceptable to the prosecution, whereupon the case was put back for sentence, and where, at the adjourned hearing, a formal not guilty verdict was entered on the other count and where the defendant was represented by different counsel on the two occasions, it was counsel who represented him on the first occasion who was entitled to the "cracked trial" fee as what happened on that occasion came within the definition of a "cracked trial" (*viz.* case was one in which a plea and directions hearing took place, the case did not proceed to trial, but the guilty plea was not entered at that hearing): *R. v. Johnson (Craig)* [2007] Costs L.R. 316. Once a meaningful trial has started, a change of plea cannot convert the trial into a cracked trial: *R. v. Maynard*, X19, SCCO 461/99; *R. v. Karra*, X19A, SCCO 375/99; and *Meeke and Taylor v. Secretary of State for Constitutional Affairs* [2006] Costs L.R. 1, QBD (David Clarke J.). Where a jury were discharged on the second day of a trial on a three count indictment, and on the following working day the prosecution added a new lesser count, and, before a new jury were sworn, the defendant offered sufficient pleas to the indictment, counsel was entitled to a fee for the first (abortive) trial, and a cracked trial fee for the later hearing at which pleas were tendered: *Frampton, ante.*

Cracked trial fees do not apply where a person pleads not guilty at a pleas and directions hearing, but later the same day changes his plea; a guilty plea fee is appropriate: *R. v. Baxter*, X22, SCCO 375/99.

The fee for a cracked trial is calculated by reference to when the case cracked, *i.e.* in the first, second or third part of a period calculated from the date when the court first fixed the date of trial or first ordered that the case should be placed into a warned list, to the date of that first fixture or the date of the start of that warned list. The fact that the fixture might later be broken, or the case moved to another warned list is immaterial and does not affect the calculation. Where the number of days in the period cannot be equally divided by three, the remainder is simply added to the last third of the period: S.I. 2013 No. 435, Sched. 1, paras 7 and 8. The fee is payable to the advocate who appeared at the hearing where pleas were entered or the last such hearing if there was more than one: *R. v. Faulkner*, X33, SCCO 201/02.

In *R. v. Carty* [2009] Costs L.R. 500, it was held that where the prosecution of one of several defendants was stayed, the case fell within the definition of a "cracked trial". The fact that the defendant's advocate had not been present on the occasion of the stay (which had been ordered at a hearing when the principal defendant, being before the court on a separate indictment, had then entered acceptable pleas to the indictment in question) did not preclude payment. Moreover, since 1996, there had been an administrative practice which permitted the prosecution to offer no evidence and an acquittal to be pronounced in open court without the legal representatives being present, and paragraph F.11 of the Graduated Fee Guidance Manual permitted a cracked trial fee to be paid in such circumstances. For this purpose, there was no reason to differentiate between a cracked trial arising from the prosecution offering no evidence and one arising from a stay.

In *R. v. Harris* [2009] Costs L.R. 507, where the defendant had pleaded guilty at a pleas and directions hearing to various offences, but where his "benefit" for the purpose of confiscation proceedings under the CJA 1988 had not yet been agreed, and where sentence and those proceedings had therefore been adjourned, the matter was held not to fall within the definition of a "cracked trial" in paragraph 9(3) of Schedule 4 to the Criminal Defence Service (Funding) Order 2001 (S.I. 2001 No. 855) (which corresponds to the current definition), and the hearing at which the confiscation order was eventually made was said not to fall within the definition of a *Newton* hearing (*R. v. Newton*, 77 Cr.App.R. 13, CA) under paragraph 1(1) (corresponding to the definition in para. 1(1) of Sched. 1 to S.I. 2013 No. 435) for the purposes of paragraph 2(6) (see now para. 2(6) of Sched. 1 to S.I. 2013 No. 435, *ante*, G-40). The prosecution had accepted the basis of the defendant's guilty plea, but in the knowledge that it would take further time, and in all likelihood another hearing, to work out the defendant's benefit. The matter, therefore, fell within the definition of "guilty plea" under paragraph 9(5).

As to the distinction between a "trial" and a "cracked trial", see also *ante*, G-123.

Calculating the pages of prosecution evidence

G-137   Prosecution evidence includes all witness statements, documentary and pictorial exhibits and records of interview with any defendant served on the defence pursuant to the Crime and Disorder Act 1998 (Service of Prosecution Evidence) Regulations 2005 (S.I. 2005 No. 902) (§§ 1-51, 1-52 in the main work), or included in any notice of additional evidence, and now includes documents served in electronic form, except for a documentary or pictorial exhibit which has never existed in paper form, unless the appropriate officer decides that it would be appropriate to include it in the page count taking into account the nature of the document and any other relevant circumstances: S.I. 2013 No. 435, Sched. 1, para. 1(2) to (5), and Sched. 2, para. 1(2) to (5). The first 50 pages must be excluded for the purposes of the calculation: S.I. 2013 No. 435, Sched. 1, para. 4. Additional documents cannot be included in the computation unless accompanied by a written notice of additional evidence: *R. v. Sturdy*, X9, December 18, 1998, SCTO 714/98; *R. v. Gkampos* [2011] Costs L.R. 142 (pages of antecedent materials relating to the defendant); and *R. v. Ward* [2012] Costs L.R. 605; but see *R. v. Qu* [2012] Costs L.R. 599 (evidence served by prosecution during trial and on which they intended to rely to be included in page count, though not accompanied by formal notice of additional evidence (see CLW/12/26/12 for the suggestion that the costs judge arrived at the correct result, but not necessarily for the right reasons)). Where one or more notices of additional evidence have been served, a page count should include the contents of all such notices, unless all sides are agreed that service of a particular notice was an administrative error; and it is irrelevant when a notice was served, or whether it was requested by the defence or prosecution: *R. v. Taylor* [2005] Costs L.R. 712 (notice served on day jury retired). A prosecution notice of intention to adduce bad character evidence does not fall within the term "any notice of additional evidence": *R. v. McCall* [2011] Costs L.R. 914 (but for a critique of the reasoning, see CLW/11/40/5). Where the Crown have exhibited and served tapes of interview, and defence counsel considers that a transcript of the interview is necessary, the pages of transcript should be included in the computation: *R. v. Brazier*, X5, SCTO 810/97. Taxing officers have been directed to include the fullest transcript produced, together with the version in the transfer bundle (if shorter), and also to include any video evidence transcripts requested by the judge: GFSG A4, A4A. Taxing officers have been directed to exclude title and separator pages: GFSG: A4A; and any additional edited versions of transcripts placed before a jury: GFSG: A5. Fax front sheets which are no more than title pages, duplicate witness statements, whether typed or hand-written, and very short lists of (*e.g.* two) exhibits should not be counted: *R. v. El Treki*, X26, SCCO 431/2000. And nor should pages comprising admissions and a jury bundle consisting of, *inter alia*, an index and details of the defendants: *R. v. Wei* [2010] Costs L.R. 846. No allowance is made for small or large typefaces or for line spacing. Unused material is also excluded.

Whereas paragraph 1(3) of Schedule 2 to S.I. 2013 No. 435 (*ante*, G-69) lists the documents that may be included when calculating the "pages of prosecution evidence" for the purposes of determining a litigator's fee under the graduated fee scheme, the list is to be taken to be exhaustive, notwithstanding that it does not include documents which will have to be read in most cases or even referred to in court (such as the indictment, custody records, correspondence, crime reports, and unused material): *R. v. Tucker* [2010] Costs L.R. 850.

In *R. v. Jalibaghodelehzi* [2014] Costs L.R. 781, it was held that when deciding whether a documentary or pictorial exhibit fell within paragraph 1(2C) of Schedule 1 to the Criminal Defence Service (Funding) Order 2007 (S.I. 2007 No. 1174) (see now the corresponding provision in paragraph 1(5) of Schedules 1 and 2 to S.I. 2013 No. 435 (*ante*, G-39, G-69)), such exhibits should be included if they required a similar degree of consideration to evidence served on paper. Thus, if thousands of pages of raw telephone data were served and the task of the defence lawyers was simply to see whether their client's mobile phone number appeared anywhere (a task more easily done by electronic search), it would be difficult to conclude that the pages should be treated as part of the page count. However, if the evidence served electronically was an important part of the prosecution case, it would be difficult to conclude that the pages should not be included in the page count.

A submission that *R. v. Jalibaghodelehzi* (*ante*) was wrongly decided was rejected in *R. v. Napper* [2014] Costs L.R. 947. In that case it was held that any documentary or pictorial exhibit served electronically is to be included in the page count where it previously existed in paper form. Where it had not previously existed in paper form, or it was impossible to determine whether it had previously existed in paper form, then determining officers are required to consider the nature of the documents and all the relevant circumstances, including the significance of the documents in the case as a whole. The court said that the task of a determining officer under paragraph 1(2C) of Schedule 1 to the 2007 order (*ante*) was not merely to make a determination as to whether such evidence would in practice have been served in paper form prior to the amendments made by the Criminal Defence Service (Funding) (Amendment) Order 2012 (S.I. 2012 No. 750). However, where the litigator and the advocate are one and the same person, this is a circumstance to be taken into account. It was stated that in such a case, if it is appropriate to include exhibits falling within paragraph (2C) in the page count for the purposes of calculating the litigator's fee, it will not be appropriate to include them again when calculating the fee payable under Schedule 1.

R. v. Jalibaghodelehzi and *R. v. Napper* (*ante*) were approved and followed in *R. v. Dodd* [2014] Costs L.R. 1131; and the factual narrative revealed in *R. v. Sana* [2014] Costs L.R. 1143, suggests that, in that case at least, the Legal Aid Agency had accepted and applied the approach in *R. v. Jalibaghodelehzi* and *R. v. Napper*. In *R. v. Furniss* [2015] Costs L.R. 151, Crown Court at Nottingham, Haddon-Cave J. (i) approved *R. v. Jalibaghodelehzi*, (ii) said that cell site, telephone, and similar material served by the prosecution in digital form must be included as pages of prosecution evidence for graduated fee purposes, irrespective of how important or central it is to the prosecution case (thus going further than the costs judges in *R. v. Jalibaghodelehzi*, *R. v. Napper* and *R. v. Dodd*), and (iii) opined that the page-count limit of 10,000 pages in the graduated fee scheme for advocates constituted an artificial cap on their remuneration irrespective of the work actually done, and that, whilst it was possible to divine a pragmatic reason for a rough-and-ready cap where the actual page count was not significantly above the maximum (say 20–30 per cent), where it vastly exceeded 10,000 pages, such a restriction was manifestly disproportionate and could not rationally have been intended to apply. However, it appears that no argument to the contrary was advanced (and certainly none on behalf of the Lord Chancellor), and it is submitted that his Lordship's remarks (which included gratuitous suggestions as to the computation of the page count in confiscation proceedings and as to costs against the Legal Aid Agency on an indemnity basis if advocates have to bring further appeals on these points to costs judges), made in the context of a Crown Court trial and wholly outside the legislative framework for the determination of legal aid fees, are of doubtful authoritative status (as to which, see the commentary in CLW/15/05/8).

It was held in *R. v. Thompson* [2015] Costs L.R. 173 that *R. v. Furniss* (*ante*) is binding on costs judges. However, it was further held that *Furniss* was only concerned with cases in which the representation order was granted before April 1, 2012 (the date on which the amendments to the Criminal Defence Service (Funding) Order 2007 (S.I. 2007 No. 1174) effected by the Criminal Defence Service (Funding) (Amendment) Order 2012 (S.I. 2012 No. 750), came into force), and that where a representation order was granted before that date (as in the instant case), costs judges had no discretion to include the material referred to in *Furniss* in the page count. In the instant appeal, the Lord Chancellor did not appear but made a written submission in which he pointed out that, on any view, *Furniss* did not apply to the case, and more generally, he took issue with the status of *Furniss*.

In *R. v Manning*, unreported, April 3, 2015, Crown Court at Manchester (H.H. Judge Mansell Q.C.), the judge found that *R. v. Furniss* was not only not binding on the Crown Court, but that the reasoning was flawed for the reasons given in the commentary in CLW/15/05/8. The judge further found that it is no part of the function of a trial judge to dictate to the prosecution how to serve their evidence or to direct them to make agreements with the defence so as to affect the calculation of defence graduated fees (or to dictate to the determining officer how fees are to be calculated under the Criminal Legal Aid (Remuneration) Regulations 2013 (S.I. 2013 No. 435) (*ante*, G-6 *et seq.*) in any given case).

The most recent addition to this saga is *R. v. Jagelo*, unreported, January 6, 2016, in which Costs Judge Rowley held that *Furniss* is not binding on costs judges, and that the provision for the graduated fee payable for a given case to be supplemented by a payment under the special preparation arrangements where the number of pages exceeded 10,000 was compatible with the right of a defendant, under Article 6(3)(c) of the ECHR (§ 16-72 in the main work), to receive representation that was adequately remunerated, such that there was no need to read down paragraph 2(7) of Schedule 2 (*ante*, G-69a) to remove or restrict the cap; the special preparation process is neither arbitrary nor irrational in principle.

The decisions of the costs judges in *R. v. O'Cuneff* [2010] Costs L.R. 476, *R. v. Burbidge* [2010] Costs L.R. 639, and *R. v. Ibefune*, unreported, June 24, 2010, evidence a conflict as between them and the Legal Services Commission as to the weight to be given to the number of pages of prosecution evidence agreed between the parties and the Crown Court at the end of the case. The commission's stance of not accepting this figure without additional objective evidence has now, however, been fully vindicated by *Criminal Practice Direction I (General matters) 3B* (*ante*, Appendix B-19). This inserts new requirements relating to the pagination and indexing of served evidence (as to which, see § 4-344 in the main work). It was plainly no coincidence that, in doing so, the practice direction adopted the (then) definition of "pages of prosecution evidence" contained in the Criminal Defence Service (Funding) Order 2007 (S.I. 2007 No. 1174). Compliance with the requirements of the new provisions by the prosecution will supply the commission (and costs judges) with an objective measure of the number of pages of prosecution evidence.

In *R. v. Greenwood* [2010] Costs L.R. 268, it was held that whereas paragraph 13(2) of Schedule 2 to S.I. 2013 No. 435 (*ante*, G-73b) provides that "where ...a case is transferred to a new litigator ... the fee payable to the original litigator and the new litigator is a percentage of the total fee, calculated in accordance with the table following this paragraph, as appropriate to the circumstances and timing of the ... transfer", and whereas the table provides that where a case is transferred prior to the plea and case management hearing the original litigator should receive 25 per cent of a cracked trial fee, in calculating that fee, the number of pages of prosecution evidence should be taken to be the number of such pages served on the court as at the date of transfer.

Images and photographs

G-138   See now paragraphs 1(2) to (5) of Schedules 1 and 2 to S.I. 2013 No. 435. For authorities on the former provision, which will still apply where the representation order was granted before April 1, 2012, see *R. v. Rigelsford* [2006] Costs L.R. 518, and *R. v. Austin* [2006] Costs L.R. 857.

Fees for leading and junior counsel

Under S.I. 2013 No. 435, fees payable to Queen's Counsel, leading juniors and led juniors are **G-139** not directly related, and are calculated from the relevant tables: see, for example, the tables following paragraphs 5 and 8 of Schedule 1. Where two or more led juniors are instructed in the same case, each is paid as if they were the sole junior: Sched. 1, para. 28.

In *R. v. Newport* [2009] Costs L.R. 983, where two juniors appeared for the defendant when **G-140** the representation order authorised instruction of junior counsel and Queen's Counsel, it was held that whilst a strict approach would lead to the conclusion that the leading junior was entitled to no payment, such an outcome would be unjust. Justice demanded that some payment should be made, especially given that the representation order had contemplated payment of two counsel. However, it was said that payment should be at the rate applicable to a leading junior. As to this case, see also *post*, G-269.

Advocates instructed for limited purposes

Advocates retained for a limited purpose are remunerated according to the specific provisions **G-141** of S.I. 2013 No. 435. The limited purposes are:

(a) the cross-examination of witnesses under the YJCEA 1999, s.38, which is remunerated as if for trial, save that the daily attendance fee is calculated by reference to the number of days the advocate actually attended court, instead of the number of days of the trial itself: S.I. 2013 No. 435, Sched. 1, para. 32;

(b) the provision of written or oral advice: see *post*, G-160;

(c) mitigation of sentence on indictment, which is remunerated as for a sentencing hearing together with a fee based on the fixed hourly special preparation rate according to the "reasonable number of hours" taken: S.I. 2013 No. 435, Sched. 1, para. 34(1); and an advocate who is discontented with the fee paid may seek a redetermination: para. 34(2).

[The next paragraph is G-143.]

Instructed and substitute advocates

An instructed advocate is the first advocate instructed in the case who has primary responsibil- **G-143** ity for the case, or, where a representation order provides for more than one advocate, it means both the first advocate instructed who has primary responsibility for those aspects of a case undertaken by a leading advocate and the first advocate instructed who has primary responsibility for those aspects of a case undertaken by a led advocate: S.I. 2013 No. 435, reg. 2(1).

The new scheme (RAGFS) places great emphasis on continuity of representation. It seeks to achieve this partly by identifying an "instructed advocate" who is responsible for advocacy services and partly by paying the total fee for advocacy to the instructed advocate. An instructed advocated remains an instructed advocate at all times, although provision is made for the instructed advocate to be changed, where, for example, he is unable to conduct the trial because of a clash of commitments, is dismissed by the client, or professionally embarrassed: see Sched. 1, para. 25(10). If the instructed advocate cannot attend a preliminary hearing, and sends a substitute advocate, he nevertheless remains responsible both for the conduct of the case and the ultimate payment of the substitute advocate.

Instructed advocates appointed before the pleas and directions hearing must in writing inform the court of their appointment as soon as they are appointed, otherwise the advocate who attends the pleas and directions hearing will be deemed to be the instructed advocate. If no advocate attends the plea and directions hearing, the advocate who attends the next hearing will be deemed to be and will be recorded by the court as the instructed advocate: see Sched. 1, para. 25(1)-(6). Where the representation order is amended after a plea and case management hearing to include a second advocate, each advocate must notify the court in writing whether they are the led or leading advocate. Where no additional instructed advocate is notified to the court in writing within seven days of the plea and case management hearing, the advocate to appear at the next hearing is deemed to be the instructed advocate and the court will record in writing whether he is the leading instructed advocate or the led instructed advocate, as appropriate to the circumstances of the case: *ibid.*, para. 25(7).

To give effect to the scheme, emphasise the continuity of representation, and ensure that all substitute advocates are paid for any RAGFS work they undertake, the Bar Council has introduced a *Graduated Fee Payment Protocol.* The protocol is an essential part of the mechanism by which advocates will be remunerated in future, but it falls outside the immediate scope of this work. It is available on both the Bar Council's and the Criminal Bar Association's websites.

Sentencing hearings in cases on indictment

G-144　　　　Any person appearing at a sentencing hearing in a case on indictment is entitled to a fixed fee where sentence has been deferred: S.I. 2013 No. 435, Sched. 1, para. 15.

A contested application for an anti-social behaviour order at a sentencing hearing does not attract a separate or additional fee: *R. v. Brinkworth* [2006] Costs L.R. 512.

Under S.I. 2013 No. 435, an advocate instructed solely for the purpose of mitigation shall be paid the fee payable under paragraph 15 together with a fee calculated by reference to the reasonable number of hours of preparation for that appearance multiplied by the hourly rate set out in the table following paragraph 24 which is appropriate to the category of trial advocate: Sched. 1, para. 34(1). The advocate may apply for redetermination of such fee and shall supply such information and documents as may be required by the appropriate officer as proof of the number of hours of preparation: *ibid.*, para. 34(2).

Fitness hearings

G-145　　　　A fitness hearing is a hearing to determine whether a defendant is fit to plead or stand trial: S.I. 2013 No. 435, Sched. 1, para. 31. If there is a trial on indictment at any time thereafter, the length of the fitness hearing shall be included in determining the length of the trial: *ibid.*, para. 31(a). Where a person pleads guilty at any time after a fitness hearing is held, the advocate may elect to be paid either as if the fitness hearing was a trial or for the guilty plea: *ibid.*, para. 31(c). Where a person is found to be unfit, the trial advocate may elect to treat the fitness hearing either as a trial or as a cracked trial: *ibid.*, para. 31(b).

Cross-examination of vulnerable witnesses

G-146　　　　Where an advocate is retained solely for the purpose of cross-examining a vulnerable witness under section 38 of the YJCEA 1999, the graduated fee shall be assessed as though the matter was a trial, with the length of trial uplift and refresher calculated by reference to the number of days the advocate attended court: S.I. 2013 No. 435, Sched. 1, para. 32.

Newton hearings

G-147　　　　Where a *Newton* hearing takes place following a trial on indictment the provisions relating to cracked trials, guilty pleas and sentencing hearings do not apply. The hearing is remunerated as for a contested trial. For the purposes of computation, the length of the *Newton* hearing is added to the main hearing: S.I. 2013 No. 435, Sched. 1, para. 2(8). Thus the main hearing starts on the day the plea is entered, even if this occurred during a pleas and directions hearing: *R. v. Gemeskel,* X2, SCTO 180/98. The advocate who attended the main hearing should claim the whole fee and remunerate the other advocate (if any) who attended the *Newton* hearing: GFSG: B12, 13.

Where a *Newton* hearing does not take place because the basis of plea was subsequently agreed, the case reverts to a guilty plea or cracked trial as appropriate: *R. v. Riddell,* X3, SCTO 318/98. If the hearing is aborted, the usual rules apply: see *post,* G-162, and *R. v. Ayres* [2002] Costs L.R. 330.

In *R. v. Newton,* 77 Cr.App.R. 13, the Court of Appeal clearly envisaged circumstances in which a sentencing judge could reach a conclusion without hearing evidence. However, the regulations define a *Newton* hearing as one at which evidence is heard for the purpose of determining the sentence of a convicted person in accordance with the *Newton* principles. Accordingly, a *Newton* hearing at which no evidence is called can only be remunerated by a standard appearance fee as it is not a *Newton* hearing for the purposes of the regulations: *R. v. Hunter-Brown*, X29, SCCO, 164/2001.

Evidence given by a defendant, who had already pleaded guilty, in the trial of a co-defendant (with cross-examination on his basis of plea), and which was referred to by the judge when giving reasons for rejecting his basis of plea when he later passed sentence, was not a *Newton* hearing within sub-paragraph 1(1) of Schedule 2 to S.I. 2013 No. 435 (*ante*, G-39); the evidence had not been given for the purpose of determining sentence as required by that provision: *R. v. Hunt* [2016] Costs L.R. 429.

Where a *Newton* hearing is held on a committal for sentence, the only fee payable under Schedule 2 to S.I. 2013 No. 435 is the fixed fee payable for a committal for sentence: *R. v. Holden* [2010] Costs L.R. 851.

Adverse judicial comment and reduction of graduated or fixed fees

Where a trial judge makes adverse observations concerning an advocate's conduct of a gradu- **G-148** ated or fixed fee case, the appropriate authority may reduce the fee by such proportion as it "considers reasonable", having first given the advocate the opportunity to make representations about the extent of the reduction: S.I. 2013 No. 435, reg. 26. See also *post*, G-220.

(3) Additional fees

Confiscation proceedings

Hearings under section 2 of the DTA 1994, section 71 of the CJA 1988 or Part 2 of the PCA **G-149** 2002 are excluded from the length computation of the main hearing and are remunerated separately as work for which a daily or half-daily fee is payable: S.I. 2013 No. 435, Sched. 1, para. 14(1) and (2). Entitlement to the daily fee arises where the hearing begins before but ends after the luncheon adjournment; a half-daily fee is paid where the hearing ends before or begins after the luncheon adjournment: S.I. 2013 No. 435, Sched. 1, para. 14(2). The appropriate rates are set out in the table following paragraph 14(2).

Abuse of process, disclosure and witness summonses' etc.

Applications relating to abuse of process, disclosure or witness summonses heard before the **G-150** main hearing are paid at the daily rates set out in the table following paragraph 24: S.I. 2013 No. 435, Sched. 1, para. 13(2). As to remuneration for such applications where they take place as part of the main hearing, see *ante*, G-124. A hearing merely relating to the failure of the prosecution to comply with an earlier disclosure order attracts only a standard appearance fee: GFSG: 12.

In respect of representation orders granted on or after April 30, 2007, these provisions were extended to include applications relating to the admissibility of evidence, and an unsuccessful application to withdraw a guilty plea made by an advocate other than the advocate who appeared at the hearing where the plea was tendered: see now S.I. 2013 No. 435, Sched. 1, para. 13(1)(d) and (e).

[The next paragraph is G-152.]

Conferences and views

The first three pre-trial conferences or views are not separately remunerated; the fees are **G-152** deemed to be included in the basic fee: Sched. 1, para. 19(2). Thereafter, the permitted number of further conferences or views (each not exceeding two hours) is as follows:

1 conference	trials of more than 20 but less than 26 days
2 conferences	trials of more than 25 days but less than 36 days
3 conferences	trials of more than 35 days

The number of further conferences allowed in respect of cracked trials is similar, save that the anticipated length of trial is that accepted by the court at the plea and case management hearing (save that, on a literal reading of the legislation, three conferences will only be paid for where it was accepted that the trial would last not more than 40 days): Sched. 1, para. 19(3).

G-153   Conferences include conferences with expert witnesses: S.I. 2013 No. 435, Sched. 1, para. 19(1)(a). Travel expenses and the time taken in travelling, including time taken to travel to a conference with a defendant who could not reasonably be expected to attend counsel's chambers, are remunerated at the specified hourly rate: *ibid.*, para. 19(5). Where such fees are allowed, reasonable travelling expenses may also be claimed: *ibid.*, para. 19(4). The local bar rule has no application to such fees: *R. v. Carlyle* [2002] Costs L.R. 192.

[The next paragraph is G-156.]

Special preparation

G-156   Special preparation is preparation substantially in excess of the amount normally done for cases of the type in question and undertaken because the case involves "a very unusual or novel point of law or factual issue": S.I. 2013 No. 435, Sched. 1, para. 17(1)(a). "Very" qualifies both "unusual" and "novel" and the phrase "very unusual or novel" qualifies both the expressions "point of law" and "factual issue": *Meeke and Taylor v. Secretary of State for Constitutional Affairs* [2006] Costs L.R. 1, QBD (David Clarke J.). Remuneration is calculated at an hourly rate for "the number of hours preparation in excess of the amount the appropriate officer considers reasonable for cases of the same type": S.I. 2013 No. 435, Sched. 1, para. 17(3)(a); and with no enhancement under paragraph 29 of Schedule 2: *Lord Chancellor v. McLarty & Co. Solicitors* [2012] Costs L.R. 190, QBD (Burnett J.).

What falls to be compensated is the extra work caused by the unusual or novel point by comparison with the sort of case involved without the unusual or novel point; as the term is used in relation to the quantification of fees, "type" in this context should be defined as an indication of weight; but the exercise does not include any consideration of the reasonableness of the time claimed; thus, once the determining officer has resolved that the case qualifies for a special preparation fee, he must assess the number of hours worked in excess of the norm and compensate for those hours at the prescribed hourly rate: *R. v. Goodwin* [2008] Costs L.R. 497.

R. v. Goodwin, ante, was considered in *R. v. Kholi* [2010] Costs L.R. 982, in which it was held that under paragraph 52(i) of the Guidance Manual for the CPS Graduated Fee Scheme (which is in materially identical terms to para. 17(1)(a) of Sched. 1 to S.I. 2013 No. 435 (*ante*, G-53)), it is only those hours of work attributable to the unusual or novel point of law or factual issue which was involved, which fall to be remunerated as special preparation; it is not the case that all time spent by the advocate in preparation over and above the norm for the type of case should be so remunerated.

The concept of "normal preparation" done for a case of the same type is wholly artificial. Other than in routine cases of burglary and theft, in virtually all other crimes in the criminal calendar, the circumstances vary infinitely: *R. v. Briers* [2005] Costs L.R. 146. The test is "What is the normal preparation for this offence?" not "What is the normal preparation for a case exhibiting these particular facts": *Briers, ante; R. v. Ward-Allen* [2005] Costs L.R. 745.

It is for counsel to differentiate between what he considers to be the normal preparation for a case of that type and the actual preparation that he has carried out: *Briers, ante; R. v. Marandola* [2006] Costs L.R. 184.

Very unusual or novel points of law have an obvious meaning, namely a point of law which either has never been raised or decided (novel) or which is outwith the usual professional experience (very unusual): *R. v. Ward-Allen, ante.* Some further assistance can be found in *Perry v. Lord Chancellor, The Times,* May 26, 1994, although it should be noted that that case was not concerned with these regulations.

Very unusual or novel factual issues have a similar meaning, namely a factual issue which either has never been raised or which is outwith the usual professional experience: *R. v. Ward-Allen, ante.* Such issues might cover extremely rare medical conditions, such as Munchausen's Syndrome by Proxy or "pubic symphysitis dysfunction", the exceptional, if not unique, nature of which was held in *R. v. Bishop* [2008] Costs L.R. 808, to justify a special preparation fee where it had contributed to prosecution material of over 600 pages (not served as part of the page count); novel issues might, for example have included DNA fingerprinting when it was introduced, but it would not qualify now. A case involving "shaken baby syndrome" does not necessarily attract a special preparation fee, unless there are additional medical complications: *R. v. Khair* [2005] Costs L.R. 542. A special preparation fee was allowed in *R. v. Thompson* [2006] Costs L.R. 668 where the defendant was accused of murdering her husband 10 years earlier. Counsel had to consider not only pathology and toxicology reports, but also a psychiatric profile on the husband prepared by a psychiatrist who had never met him, and issues arising in diabetology and physiology. Transcripts of the original coroner's inquest and the defendant's previous trials for theft and attempted murder of another husband were also served.

The novelty of the bad character provisions of the CJA 2003 did not provide grounds for claiming a special preparation fee; the criminal law is constantly changing: *R. v. Christie* [2010] 4 Costs L.R. 634.

A special preparation fee would be reasonable where counsel had to check a sample of over 33,000 original photographs of which the prosecution had only copied a representative fraction for use at trial: *R. v. Rigelsford* [2006] Costs L.R. 523; and see *ante*, G-138. But the mere fact that preparation properly undertaken for a complex three-week rape trial was "wasted" because the defendant decided to plead guilty during the prosecution opening did not justify a special preparation fee: *Meeke and Taylor v. Secretary of State for Constitutional Affairs, ante.*

A large quantity of unused material does not of itself give rise to a novel or unusual factual issue even where it is accepted that detailed examination of the material was necessary: *R. v. Lawrence* [2007] Costs L.R. 138; and even where the trial judge has extended a representation order to allow two juniors to peruse such material: *R. v. Dhaliwal* [2004] Costs L.R. 689. Such work is not remunerated under the graduated fee scheme or indeed at all: *ibid.* Nor does the mere failure of the scheme to accommodate unused material amount to a breach of the principle of equality of arms: *R. v. Marandola, ante.*

An advocate can also claim a special preparation fee where the prosecution evidence exceeds 10,000 pages and the appropriate officer considers that it is reasonable to make a payment in excess of the graduated fee which would otherwise be payable; the fee is calculated by reference to the number of hours which the appropriate officer considers reasonable to read the excess pages, using the current hourly fee rate: S.I. 2013 No. 435, Sched. 1, para. 17(1)(b), (2) and (3)(b); and Sched. 2, para. 20(1)(b). As to this particular provision, see *R. v. Furniss* and *R. v. Jagelo, ante,* G-137.

An advocate making a claim for special preparation should provide the Legal Aid Agency with dates, times and descriptions of the work completed, and the page count of any material considered, and any documents produced as a result of the special preparation should be annexed to the claim form, and the claim should relate each item of special preparation to the very unusual or novel point of law or fact that gave rise to the need for special preparation in the first place: *R. v. French* [2014] Costs L.R. 786.

An advocate's failure to keep a contemporaneous work log may result in rejection of a claim for a special preparation fee: *R. v. Dunne* [2013] Costs L.R. 1031 (considering the corresponding provision in the Criminal Defence Service (Funding) Order 2007 (S.I. 2007 No. 1174).

Evidence served electronically

A special preparation fee may also be claimed where a documentary or pictorial exhibit, which **G-157** has never existed in paper form, is served by the prosecution in electronic form, and the appropriate officer does not consider it appropriate to include it in the pages of prosecution evidence; and such fee may be paid if the appropriate officer considers it reasonable to make a payment in excess of the fee otherwise payable under the graduated fee scheme, with the amount of the payment depending on the number of hours which the appropriate officer considers reasonable to view the exhibit: see Sched. 1, para. 17(1)(c) and (2), and Sched. 2, para. 20(1)(a) and (2). The drafting of these provisions in the two schedules is slightly different, but it is submitted that the intent is the same. As to the drafting, this – taken at face value – gives the appropriate officer a discretion whether to make a payment even where he considers it reasonable to do so. It is submitted, however, that the legislation is unlikely to be so construed: if the appropriate officer considers it reasonable to make a payment, then it is likely to be held that he should do so. The revised wording of these provisions (introduced by the Criminal Defence Service (Funding) (Amendment) Order 2001 (S.I. 2012 No. 750)) was doubtless intended to avoid the difficulties caused by the former wording and which gave rise to a series of decisions, such as *R. v. Rigelsford* [2006] Costs L.R. 518, *R. v. Austin* [2006] Costs L.R. 857, *Lord Chancellor v. Michael J. Reed Ltd* [2010] Costs L.R. 72, QBD (Penry-Davey J.), *Lord Chancellor v. McLarty & Co. Solicitors* [2012] Costs L.R. 190, QBD (Burnett J.), and *R. v. Jones* [2010] Costs L.R. 469. For details of these authorities, which will still have application to cases in which a representation order was granted before April 1, 2012, see previous supplements.

Lord Chancellor v. Michael J. Reed Ltd (*ante*) was followed in *R. v. Osoteko* [2014] Costs L.R. 190, but the costs judge certified a point of principle of general importance, *viz.* whether that case had created too narrow a definition of pages of prosecution evidence. The appeal to the High Court (see *Maclaverty Cooper Atkins v. Lord Chancellor* [2014] Costs L.R. 629, QBD (Akenhead J.)) was dismissed, the court approving and following *Lord Chancellor v. Michael J. Reed Ltd.*

[The next paragraph is G-159.]

Listening to or viewing tapes

G-159   There is now no provision for any separate payment for listening to or viewing tapes. These are now treated as being rolled up within the whole of the graduated fee.

Provision of written or oral advice

G-160   Any advocate instructed solely to provide written or oral advice shall be paid a fee calculated from the reasonable number of hours of preparation for that advice using the appropriate hourly rate in the table following paragraph 24 of Schedule 1 to S.I. 2013 No. 435: see Sched. 1, para. 33(1). The advocate may apply for re-determination of such fee under regulation 28, and he shall supply such information and documents as may be required by the appropriate officer as proof of the number of hours of preparation: *ibid.*, para. 33(2).

As to whether a solicitor may properly instruct counsel other than counsel who appeared at trial to advise on the question of appeal where trial counsel has advised in the negative, see *R. v. Umezie*, § 7-165 in the main work.

R. v. Umezie was considered in *R. v. Bromige* [2011] Costs L.R. 145, in which it was held that where solicitors, on receipt of trial counsel's negative advice as to the prospects of a successful appeal against sentence, instructed fresh counsel to advise on the question, trial counsel's negative advice (whether written or oral) did not terminate the representation order; paragraph A1-2 of the Guide to Commencing Proceedings in the Court of Appeal (Criminal Division) (*post*, Appendix J-4) did not preclude payment of a fee for subsequent advice given by fresh counsel in relation to the appeal, because that paragraph was only concerned with the amendment of representation orders, and no amendment to the representation order granted by the magistrates' court was necessary to instruct fresh counsel to advise; however, fresh counsel's claim for a fee for his advice could only fall within paragraph 6 of Schedule 3 to S.I. 2013 No. 435 (*ante*, G-85), which provides, that upon the determination of an advocate's fees in proceedings in the Court of Appeal, "the appropriate officer must consider the claim ... and must allow such work as appears to him to have been reasonably done"; as a general principle it will not be reasonable to obtain advice on a point that has already been the subject of advice, with the obvious exceptions to this principle being if the initial advice is incompetent or ambiguous, or if there is a change in circumstances or if new evidence has come to light; the reason given in this case for seeking further advice, *viz.* that the solicitors were not convinced as to the correctness of the negative oral advice from trial counsel, was not sufficient; therefore the work done by fresh counsel was not reasonably done for the purposes of paragraph 6 because no good reason had been shown for instructing him to give advice on a point that had already been the subject of advice. For the submission that the costs judge's reliance on paragraph 6 of Schedule 3 is unsustainable, see CLW/11/08/45.

(4) Acting for more than one defendant, or in more than one "case"

G-161   The definition of "case" in paragraph 1(1) of Schedule 2 (*ante*, G-69) could not possibly lead to the conclusion that if a litigator represents more than one defendant charged and tried on the same indictment that litigator is then entitled to be paid on the basis that there are as many cases as there are defendants: *Lord Chancellor v. Eddowes Perry and Osbourne Ltd* [2011] Costs L.R. 498, QBD (Spencer J.). As to this case, see also *post*, G-273.

An uplift of one-fifth for each additional defendant represented may only be claimed where the regulations so provide: S.I. 2013 No. 435, Sched. 1, para. 27(2). Where an advocate acts for more than one defendant, the advocate must select the case on which remuneration is to be based (the principal case). Claims for such uplifts may be made for pleas and directions hearings, some aborted hearings, main hearings, appeals against conviction, committals for sentence, proceedings for a breach of a Crown Court order, disclosure, abuse and witness summons hearings, and confiscation proceedings: S.I. 2013 No. 435, Sched. 1, para. 27(4). But no uplifts for these hearings, with the exception of confiscation proceedings, are payable in cases that were committed to the Crown Court on the election of the defendant, where the magistrates' court had determined that the case was suitable for summary trial: *ibid.*, para. 27(3). In respect of a trial, the uplift is limited to one-fifth of the basic fee and not the basic fee enhanced by reference to the prosecution evidence, witnesses and length of trial uplift: *ibid.*, para. 27(2)(b), *i.e.* where the main hearing in each case was heard concurrently: *R. v. Fletcher*, X6, SCTO 815/97.

The above provisions also apply where the advocate conducts two or more cases concurrently: S.I. 2013 No. 435, Sched. 1, para. 27(2). Proceedings arising out of a single notice of appeal against conviction or sentence, or single committal for sentence, constitute a separate "case": para. 1(1) of Schedule 1 to S.I. 2013 No. 435. However, a committal for sentence together with a committal for breach of a community service order constituted two separate "cases" as the latter was a committal for breach of an earlier order: *R. v. Hines*, X24, SCCO 337/2000. As a case means proceedings on one or more counts of a single indictment, it is submitted that two trials arising from a severed indictment give rise to two separate graduated fees, as the trials are not heard concurrently.

In *R. v. Fury* [2011] Costs L.R. 919, it was said that if a hearing deals with one case then another, independently of each other, it will be hearing them consecutively; hearings will be concurrent only if they are combined or conjoined or somehow interlinked; this will be so where the main hearings of a number of cases against the same defendant are listed together and the defendant either pleads guilty or is to be sentenced in all of the cases; the cases will impact on each other either as to the directions that are given for sentencing or as to the sentences that are imposed; they will not be considered independently of each other. For criticism of the actual decision in this case (cases were not heard concurrently where, as part of an agreed package, defendant pleaded guilty to one indictment and prosecution offered no evidence on the other, all counts having originally been in the same indictment), see CLW/11/40/3.

In *R. v. Sturmer and Lewis* [2009] Costs L.R. 364, it was said that the combined effect of paragraph 15 and the table in paragraph 19 of Schedule 2 to S.I. 2013 No. 435 (*ante*, G-74a, G-75a) is that where a litigator is "instructed in ... a sentencing hearing following a committal for sentence to the Crown Court", the "fee payable ... is that set out in the table" (para. 15), *i.e.* "£210.64" per proceedings (the table). "Proceedings" can involve more than one defendant and, if there is only one "proceedings", only one fee will be payable, however many defendants are represented by the litigator.

[The next paragraph is G-163.]

(5) Abortive hearings

The payment of fixed fees for abortive hearings is limited to ineffective trials: see Sched. 1,   **G-163**
para. 16. As to this, see *R. v. Budai, ante*, G-124.

(6) Wasted preparation

Wasted preparation occurs where an advocate does not represent his client because of (a) a   **G-164**
clash of listings and the advocate has been unable to secure a change of date for either hearing;
or (b) a fixture for a main hearing is altered by the court despite the advocate's objection; or (c)
the advocate withdraws with leave of the court because of professional embarrassment; or (d) the

advocate is dismissed by the client; or (e) the advocate is obliged to undertake judicial or other public duties: S.I. 2013 No. 435, Sched. 1, para. 18(1). A representation order replacing a single junior with Queen's Counsel acting alone does not entitle junior counsel to claim a wasted preparation fee in respect of the preparation reasonably and properly undertaken; counsel has no redress under the scheme: *R. v. Schultz*, X10, SCTO 552/98. The hourly fee may be claimed only where eight or more hours of preparation have been undertaken, and (a) the trial lasted for five days or more, or (b) in the case of a cracked trial, there are more than 150 pages of prosecution evidence: S.I. 2013 No. 435, Sched. 1, para. 18(2). The wasted preparation fee is calculated by reference to the number of hours of preparation reasonably carried out by the advocate, who must supply such information and documents in support of the claim as may be required: S.I. 2013 No. 435, Sched. 1, para. 18(3) and (5).

The requirements of paragraph 18(1) were satisfied where, following the vacation of the trial date by the trial judge and his proposal of a new date, counsel had written objecting to the new date (on the grounds that he had booked and paid for a holiday abroad that started within 10 days of the new date), but where, despite that objection, the trial had gone ahead on the proposed date, with the result that counsel had had to return the brief: *R. v. Ghaffar* [2009] Costs L.R. 980. The fact that counsel's objection was to the new date, and not to the vacation of the original fixture, was not a valid ground for refusing a wasted preparation fee in respect of the substantial preparation done by counsel prior to the vacation of the original fixture. Changing a fixture is a process and an objection to part of that process is therefore an objection to the change. There was nothing in paragraph 18(1)(b) that restricted it to counsel's professional commitments.

(7) Appeals, pleas before venue, committals and other fees

G-165   Graduated fixed fees are also payable in respect of committals for sentence (which include plea before venue cases), appeals from magistrates' courts and breach of Crown Court orders: S.I. 2013 No. 435, Sched. 1, para. 20; noting briefs: *ibid.*, para. 23; bail and other applications, and mentions when not forming part of a main hearing or other hearing for which a fixed fee is provided: *ibid.*, para. 20(3). The appropriate rate is that listed in the table following paragraph 24. After the Crown Court is seized of a case, any bail applications, or executions of bench warrants made in a magistrates' court are remunerated as if made in the Crown Court: *R. v. Bailey*, X16, 378/99. As to trials of Bail Act 1976 offences, see *ante*, G-130.

(8) Contempt proceedings

G-166   Remuneration for proceedings for contempt in the face of the court is fixed at discrete daily rates: S.I. 2013 No. 435, reg. 11, and Sched. 1, para. 21. The fees are fixed and there is no discretion to allow *ex post facto* payment, however regrettable and unfair the result may be: *R. v. Russell* [2006] Costs L.R. 841. Such payments do not fall within the graduated fee scheme and, therefore, such hearings do not form part of the main hearing or the sentencing hearing.

(9) Travel expenses

G-167   Travel and hotel expenses may be claimed subject to the usual 40 kilometre local bar rule: S.I. 2013 No. 435, Sched. 1, para. 29 (see generally *post*, G-253). Expenses should not be paid in respect of conferences for which advocates are not entitled to be remunerated, unless the conference was abortive due to circumstances beyond the advocate's control: *R. v. Pickett*, X39.

(10) Table of offences

G-168   The effect of the table of offences at the end of Schedule 1 to S.I. 2013 No. 435 (as amended by the Protection of Freedoms Act 2012 (Consequential Amendments) Order 2013 (S.I. 2013 No. 862)) is set out in the following paragraphs. Offences are divided into those below £30,000, those where the value is £30,000 or more, but less than £100,000, and those where the value involved is £100,000 or more. As to the method of calculation for the purposes of determining value, see *ante*, G-121. As to conspiracy, incitement and attempt, see *ante*, G-120. It should be noted that there are various errors in the table: for example, it refers to section 39 (rather than section 139) of the CJA 1988 (this has been corrected below) and it refers to various measures that have been repealed and replaced, including the Post Office Act 1953, the Merchant Shipping Act 1970 and the Air Navigation Order 2005 (S.I. 2005 No. 1970)).

An "armed robbery" (see the Theft Act 1968 entries) arises where the offender was armed with a firearm or imitation firearm, or was thought by the victim to have been so armed, or was armed with an offensive weapon: *R. v. Stables*, X12, SCTO 102/99.

Where a judge proposes to try an offence under the Bail Act 1976, s.6, in respect of a defendant who is first brought up before him for non-attendance, then there is a trial or guilty plea under the graduated fee scheme: *R. v. Shaw* [2005] Costs L.R. 326.

As several statutes are listed under more than one class, the following is a list of the statutes **G-169** and orders featured in the table, with the classes in which they appear–

Air Navigation Order 2005 (S.I. 2005 No. 1970)	H
Aviation Security Act 1982	B
Bail Act 1976	H
Bribery Act 2010	I
Child Abduction Act 1984	C
Children and Young Persons Act 1933	B, J
Cremation Act 1902	I
Crime and Disorder Act 1998	B, C, H
Criminal Damage Act 1971	B, C
Criminal Justice Act 1961	C
Criminal Justice Act 1967	I
Criminal Justice Act 1988	H
Criminal Justice Act 1991	B
Criminal Justice (International Co-operation) Act 1990	B
Criminal Justice (Terrorism and Conspiracy) Act 1998	I
Criminal Justice and Public Order Act 1994	I
Criminal Law Act 1967	I
Criminal Law Act 1977	C
Customs and Excise Management Act 1979	B, C, F, G, H, K
Dangerous Dogs Act 1991	C
Disorderly Houses Act 1751	H
Domestic Violence, Crime and Victims Act 2004	B
Drug Trafficking Act 1994	B, I
Drug Trafficking Offences Act 1986	C
European Communities Act 1972	I
Explosive Substances Act 1883	A, B
Firearms Act 1968	B, C
Firearms (Amendment) Act 1988	C
Forgery Act 1861	F, I
Forgery and Counterfeiting Act 1981	F, G, K
Fraud Act 2006	F, G, K
Hallmarking Act 1973	F, G, K
Identity Cards Act 2006	F
Immigration Act 1971	C
Indecency with Children Act 1960	J
Indecent Displays (Control) Act 1981	H
Infant Life (Preservation) Act 1929	A

Infanticide Act 1938	A
Insolvency Act 1986	G
Magistrates' Courts Act 1980	I
Malicious Damage Act 1861	H
Mental Health Act 1959	J
Mental Health Act 1983	D
Merchant Shipping Act 1970	H
Misuse of Drugs Act 1971	B, C, H
Nuclear Material (Offences) Act 1983	B
Obscene Publications Act 1959	H
Offences against the Person Act 1861	A, B, C, H
Perjury Act 1911	I
Post Office Act 1953	H
Prevention of Corruption Act 1906	I
Prevention of Crime Act 1953	H
Prison Act 1952	C
Prison Security Act 1992	B
Proceeds of Crime Act 2002	B
Prohibition of Female Circumcision Act 1985	C
Protection from Eviction Act 1977	H
Protection from Harassment Act 1997	H
Protection of Children Act 1978	J
Public Bodies Corrupt Practices Act 1889	I
Public Order Act 1986	B, C, H
Public Passenger Vehicles Act 1981	H
Road Traffic Act 1960	H
Road Traffic Act 1988	B, H
Road Traffic Regulation Act 1984	H
Sexual Offences Act 1956	D, H, J
Sexual Offences Act 1967	D, H
Sexual Offences Act 2003	D, J
Sexual Offences (Amendment) Act 2000	D
Stamp Duties Management Act 1891	F, G, K
Submarine Telegraph Act 1885	C
Suicide Act 1961	B
Taking of Hostages Act 1982	B
Terrorism Act 2000	B, C
Theatres Act 1968	H
Theft Act 1968	B, C, E, F, G, H, K
Theft Act 1978	F, G, H, K
Trade Descriptions Act 1968	H, I
Treason Act 1842	C
Value Added Tax Act 1994	F, G, K
Vehicle Excise and Registration Act 1994	H

Class A: homicide and related grave offences

(i) *Common law offences*

    Murder and manslaughter   **G-170**

(ii) *Offences created by primary or secondary legislation*

    Those contrary to the following provisions:

        Explosive Substances Act 1883, ss.2 and 3;

        Infant Life (Preservation) Act 1929, s.1(1);

        Infanticide Act 1938, s.1(1);

        Offences against the Person Act 1861, s.4.

Class B: offences involving serious violence or damage, and serious drugs offences

(i) *Common law offences*

    Kidnapping and false imprisonment   **G-171**

(ii) *Offences created by primary or secondary legislation*

    Those contrary to the following provisions:

        Aviation Security Act 1982, s.2(1)(b);

        Crime and Disorder Act 1998, s.30(1);

        Children and Young Persons Act 1933, s.1;

        Criminal Damage Act 1971, s.1(2) and (where the value exceeds £30,000) s.1(3);

        Criminal Justice Act 1991, s.90;

        Criminal Justice (International Co-operation) Act 1990, ss.12 and 18;

        Customs and Excise Management Act 1979, s.50 (Class A or B drugs), s.85, s.170(2)(b) or (c) (in relation to Class A or B drugs);

        Domestic Violence, Crime and Victims Act 2004, s.5;

        Drug Trafficking Act 1994, ss.49, 50, 51, 52 and 53;

        Explosive Substances Act 1883, s.4(1);

        Firearms Act 1968, ss.5, 16, 17 and 18;

        Misuse of Drugs Act 1971, s.4 (Class A or B drug), s.5(3) (Class A or B drug), ss.6, 8, 9, 12 and 13;

        Nuclear Material (Offences) Act 1983, s.2;

        Offences against the Person Act 1861, ss.16, 17, 18, 21, 22, 23, 28, 29, 30, 32, 33, 34 and 58;

        Prison Security Act 1992, s.1;

        Proceeds of Crime Act 2002, ss.327, 328, 329, 330, 331, 332, 333, 339(1A);

        Public Order Act 1986, ss.1, 2 and 38;

        Road Traffic Act 1988, ss.1, 3A and 22A;

        Suicide Act 1961, s.2;

        Taking of Hostages Act 1982, s.1;

        Terrorism Act 2000, ss.11, 12, 13, 15, 16, 17, 18, 39, 54, 56, 57, 58 and 59;

        Theft Act 1968, s.8(1) (if "armed"), s.8(2) (if "with weapon"), s.10, s.12A (if resulting in death) and 21.

Class C: lesser offences involving violence or damage, and less serious drugs offences

(i) *Common law offences*

    Permitting an escape, rescue, breach of prison and escaping from lawful custody without **G-172** force

(ii) *Offences created by primary or secondary legislation*

    Those contrary to the following provisions:

Child Abduction Act 1984, ss.1 and 2;

Crime and Disorder Act 1998, ss.29(1) and 30(1);

Criminal Damage Act 1971, s.1(1) and, where the offence does not also fall within section 1(2) and where the value of the damage is less than £30,000, s.1(3), s.2 and s.3;

Criminal Justice Act 1961, s.22;

Criminal Law Act 1977, s.51;

Customs and Excise Management Act 1979, s.50 (in relation to Class C drugs), s.68A(1) and (2), s.86, s.170(2)(b), (c) (in relation to Class C drugs);

Dangerous Dogs Act 1991, s.3;

Drug Trafficking Offences Act 1986, ss.26B and 26C;

Firearms Act 1968, ss.1, 2, 3, 4, 19, 20, 21(4), 21(5) and 42;

Firearms (Amendment) Act 1988, s.6(1);

Immigration Act 1971, s.25;

Misuse of Drugs Act 1971, s.4 (Class C drug), s.5(2) (Class A drug), s.5(3) (Class C drug);

Offences against the Person Act 1861, ss.20, 24, 26, 27, 31, 37, 47, 59, 60 and 64;

Prison Act 1952, s.39;

Prohibition of Female Circumcision Act 1985, s.1;

Public Order Act 1986, ss.18 to 23;

Submarine Telegraph Act 1885, s.3;

Terrorism Act 2000, s.19;

Theft Act 1968, s.8(1) (other than when "armed");

Treason Act 1842, s.2.

Class D: sexual offences and offences against children

Offences created by primary or secondary legislation

G-173   Those contrary to the following provisions:

Criminal Law Act 1977, s.54;

Mental Health Act 1983, s.127;

Sexual Offences Act 1956, s.4, s.9, s.10 (other than by man with girl under 13), s.11, s.13 (between male aged 21 or over and male under 16), ss.14, 15, 19, 21, 23, 27, 29, 30 and 31;

Sexual Offences Act 1967, s.5;

Sexual Offences Act 2003, s.3, s.4 (without penetration), ss.11 to 13, 15 to 19, 32, 33, 36, 37, 40, 41, 52, 53, 61 to 67, 69 and 70;

Sexual Offences (Amendment) Act 2000, s.3.

Class E: burglary, etc.

Offences created by primary or secondary legislation

G-174   Those contrary to the following provisions:

Theft Act 1968, ss.9 and 25

Classes F, G and K: other offences of dishonesty (offences always in Class F)

Offences created by primary or secondary legislation

G-175   Those contrary to the following provisions:

Forgery Act 1861, ss.36, 37;

Identity Cards Act 2006, s.25(1), (3) and (5).

Classes F, G and K: other offences of dishonesty (offences always in Class G)

Offences created by primary or secondary legislation

G-176   Those contrary to the following provisions:

Customs and Excise Management Act 1979, s.50 (counterfeit notes or coins), s.170(2)(b) or (c) (counterfeit notes or coins);

Forgery and Counterfeiting Act 1981, ss.14 to 17;
Insolvency Act 1986, s.360.

Classes F, G and K: other offences of dishonesty (offences in Class G if value exceeds £30,000, in Class K if value exceeds £100,000 and otherwise in Class F)

Offences created by primary or secondary legislation
    Those contrary to the following provisions: **G-177**
        Customs and Excise Management Act 1979, s.50 (to the extent not specified elsewhere), s.168, s.170(1)(b), s.170(2)(b), (c) (to the extent not specified elsewhere);
        Forgery and Counterfeiting Act 1981, ss.1 to 5;
        Fraud Act 2006, ss.2, 3, 4, 6, 7, 9 and 11;
        Hallmarking Act 1973, s.6;
        Stamp Duties Management Act 1891, s.13;
        Theft Act 1968, ss.1, 11, 13, 15, 16, 17 and 22;
        Theft Act 1978, ss.1 and 2;
        Value Added Tax Act 1994, s.72(1)-(8).

Class H: miscellaneous other offences

(i) *Common law offences*
        Keeping a disorderly house, outraging public decency   **G-178**

(ii) *Offences created by primary or secondary legislation*
    Those contrary to the following provisions:
        Air Navigation Order 2005 (S.I. 2005 No. 1970), art. 75;
        Bail Act 1976, s.9(1);
        Crime and Disorder Act 1998, ss.1(10), 2(8), 31(1) and 32(1);
        Criminal Justice Act 1988, s.139;
        Customs and Excise Management Act 1979, ss.13 and 16;
        Disorderly Houses Act 1751, s.8;
        Indecent Displays (Control) Act 1981, s.1;
        Malicious Damage Act 1861, s.36;
        Merchant Shipping Act 1970, s.27;
        Misuse of Drugs Act 1971, s.5(2) (Class B or C drug); s.11;
        Obscene Publications Act 1959, ss.1 and 2;
        Offences against the Person Act 1861, ss.35 and 38;
        Post Office Act 1953, s.11;
        Prevention of Crime Act 1953, s.1;
        Protection from Eviction Act 1977, s.1;
        Protection from Harassment Act 1997, ss.3(6), 4(1) and 5(5);
        Public Order Act 1986, s.3;
        Public Passenger Vehicles Act 1981, s.65;
        Road Traffic Act 1960, s.233;
        Road Traffic Act 1988, ss.2 and 173;
        Road Traffic Regulation Act 1984, s.115;
        Sexual Offences Act 1956, ss.2, 3, 12, 13 (other than where one participant over 21 and the other under 16), 22, 24 and 32;
        Sexual Offences Act 1967, s.4;
        Theatres Act 1968, s.2;
        Theft Act 1968, s.12A (but not where death results);
        Theft Act 1978, s.3;
        Trade Descriptions Act 1968, ss.1, 8, 9, 12, 13 and 14;

Vehicle Excise and Registration Act 1994, s.44.

Class I: offences against public justice and similar offences

(i) *Common law offences*

G-179   Embracery, fabrication of evidence with intent to mislead tribunal, perverting the course of justice and personation of jurors

(ii) *Offences created by primary or secondary legislation*
    Those contrary to the following provisions:
        Bribery Act 2010, ss.1, 2 and 6;
        Cremation Act 1902, s.8(2);
        Criminal Justice Act 1967, s.89;
        Criminal Justice (Terrorism and Conspiracy) Act 1998, s.5;
        Criminal Justice and Public Order Act 1994, ss.51(1) and (2), 75(1) and (2);
        Criminal Law Act 1967, ss.4(1) and 5;
        Drug Trafficking Act 1994, s.58(1);
        European Communities Act 1972, s.11;
        Forgery Act 1861, s.34;
        Magistrates' Courts Act 1980, s.106;
        Perjury Act 1911, ss.1 to 7(2);
        Prevention of Corruption Act 1906, s.1;
        Public Bodies Corrupt Practices Act 1889, s.1;
        Trade Descriptions Act 1968, s.29(2).

Class J: serious sexual offences

Offences created by primary or secondary legislation

G-180   Those contrary to the following provisions:
        Children and Young Persons Act 1933, ss.25, 26;
        Indecency with Children Act 1960, s.1(1);
        Protection of Children Act 1978, s.1;
        Sexual Offences Act 1956, ss.1(1), 5, 6, 7, 10, 12 (of person under 16), 16, 17, 20, 25, 26
            and 28;
        Sexual Offences Act 2003, ss.1, 2, 4 (activity involving penetration), 5 to 10, 14, 25, 26, 30,
            31, 34, 35, 38, 39, 47 to 50 and 57 to 59A.

G. VERY HIGH COST CASES

Definition

G-181   For the definition of a "Very High Cost Case", see regulation 2 of S.I. 2013 No. 435 (*ante*, G-7). Regulation 3(8) (*ante*, G-8) provides that the regulations (with the exception of reg. 12 and para. 13(8) and (9) of Schedule 2) do not apply to Very High Costs Cases.

Background

G-182   Unlike the former scheme for the *ex post facto* taxation of fees (as to which, see Appendix G in the supplements to the 2010 edition of this work) and the graduated fee scheme, the Very High Cost Case ("VHCC") regime is not concerned with fee assessment after the completion of a case. VHCCs operate under a contract-based system where litigators' and advocates' tasks and the time allotted for each task are agreed or determined before the work is undertaken. They are managed by the Complex Crime Unit of the Legal Aid Agency (an executive agency of the Ministry of Justice).

Notification and classification

G-183   Litigators (referred to by the Legal Aid Agency as "organisations") are required to notify the Legal Aid Agency of any case which is, or is likely to be, a VHCC: S.I. 2013 No. 435, reg. 12.

Notification is effected by submitting a VHCC Notification Request Form 2013, which is available on the agency's website. If a case qualifies, or if an organisation is in any doubt about this, the organisation should make the notification within five business days of the earliest hearing at which the court sets a trial estimate, or the organisation identifying that the case will be or is likely to be a VHCC, or the organisation receiving a VHCC notification request form 2013 from the agency. If the notification requirements are not met, and the agency is likely to or will suffer financial loss as a result, it may, in discharging its functions under the LASPOA 2012: (a) impose any sanction on the organisation in accordance with any other legal aid agreement or contract; (b) exclude the organisation from undertaking VHCC work or Individual Case Contract work on the case that it failed to notify; (c) where it persistently breaches this duty, exclude the organisation from undertaking future VHCC work or Individual Case Contract Work or reduce or refuse any payment to the organisation in relation to the case.

Part A of the current (2013) arrangements sets out the obligations and processes for notification and classification for all cases which may be classified as VHCCs on or after April 1, 2013. Part B applies to cases which fall to be classified on or after that date and where the trial would in the opinion of the Director of Legal Aid Casework be likely to last for more than 60 days (para. 1.4). Part C applies to cases which fall to be classified on or after that date where the case satisfies the definition of a Very High Cost Case (in reg. 2(1) of S.I. 2013 No. 435 (*ante*, G-7)) and the trial would in the opinion of the agency be likely to last for less than 61 days. Paragraph 5.4 of the arrangements states that where it is the opinion of the agency that a case will last no fewer than 25 days and no more than 40 days, it will only be classified as a Very High Cost Case if it is prosecuted by the Serious Fraud Office or it is a terrorism case.

Where a case satisfies the definition of a VHCC for organisations, the agency will issue a VHCC decision letter. If the case is one which in the director's opinion will last more than 60 days, the agency will issue a 2013 VHCC Contract (for organisations). In other cases, the agency will issue a 2013 Individual Case Contract (for organisations).

Where the case satisfies the definition of a VHCC for advocates, and a self-employed advocate has been instructed, the agency will issue a VHCC decision letter and a 2013 VHCC contract (for self-employed advocates) to the self-employed advocate. Exceptional circumstances apart, organisations and advocates must meet the eligibility criteria set out in the arrangements before they can undertake work on a Very High Cost Case.

For information as to the working of earlier arrangements, see the second supplement to the 2013 edition of this work.

Paragraph 13(9) of Schedule 2 is not to be construed literally; where, therefore, a very high cost case panel firm was instructed under the representation order prior to the case being classified as a very high cost case, where it continued to act after such classification and where, after the defendant had pleaded guilty and been put back for sentence, the representation order was withdrawn (apparently on the application of the solicitors) by order of the court, solicitors and counsel fell to be remunerated under the very high cost cases regime, not the graduated fee regime; paragraph 13(9) had no application to this situation; rather, it was intended to deal with the remuneration of a non-panel firm where a case is reclassified as a very high cost case whereupon the representation order is withdrawn (rather than being transferred to another litigator, in which case para. 13(8) is engaged): *Lord Chancellor v. Alexander Johnson & Co. Solicitors and McCarthy* [2011] Costs L.R. 987, QBD (Davis J.).

[The next paragraph is G-187.]

Remuneration

Once a case is classified as a VHCC, the Legal Aid Agency will assign it to one of four categories **G-187** against the criteria contained in clause 4.21 of the VHCC Specification (see also §§ 4.12 *et seq.* in the VHCC Guidance). For this purpose, the contracted organisation is required to submit a completed VHCC category assessment sheet within 15 business days of the decision letter: Arrangements, para. 8.2(c). The category to which the case is assigned determines the hourly rate payable for preparatory work undertaken by litigators. Advocacy rates are non-category specific.

Self-employed advocates are remunerated directly by the Legal Aid Agency: clause 5.21 of the

VHCC Specification (for organisations). Where the VHCC has been classified both as a VHCC for organisations and for advocates, self-employed advocates must claim under their VHCC contract. Where the case is a VHCC for organisations but has not been classified as a VHCC for advocates, any self-employed advocate must claim under the advocates' graduated fee scheme. Employed advocates must claim payment through their organisation, whether under the graduated fee scheme (where the VHCC has not been classified as a VHCC for advocates) or under the VHCC scheme (where the VHCC is a VHCC in relation to both organisations and advocates).

As to rates of payments, these are now determined by regulation 12A of, and Schedule 6 (*ante*, G-18a, G-92c, *et seq.*) to the Criminal Legal Aid (Remuneration) Regulations 2013 (S.I. 2013 No. 435) for cases subject to the 2013 VHCC contract, and by the provisions of the Criminal Defence Service (Very High Cost Cases) (Funding) Order 2013 (S.I. 2013 No. 2804) for work undertaken on or after December 2, 2013 (unless the trial date was set before that date and is before April, 2014), in a "pre-commencement case" (as to which, see the Legal Aid, Sentencing and Punishment of Offenders Act 2012 (Consequential, Transitional and Saving Provisions) Regulations 2013 (S.I. 2013 No. 534), reg. 2) that was the subject of a contract made between the Legal Services Commission and members of the (now abolished) Very High Cost Case (Crime) Panel (art. 3 and Sched. 1) or was the subject of a 2010 VHCC contract (art. 4 and Sched. 2). S.I. 2013 No. 2804 also amended paragraph 25 (Very High Cost Cases) of Schedule 2 (litigators' graduated fee scheme) to the Criminal Defence Service (Funding) Order 2007 (S.I. 2007 No. 1174) (which was revoked by the Criminal Defence Service (Funding) (Amendment) Order 2011 (S.I. 2011 No. 2065) in relation to proceedings in which a representation order was granted on or after October 3, 2011) to provide for reduced fees for work done on or after December 2, 2013 (unless the trial date was set before that date and is before April, 2014), in a Very High Costs Case where a litigator instructed an advocate who was not a member of the Very High Cost Case (Crime) Panel.

[The next paragraph is G-195.]

H. Preparation and Submission of Claims

(1) The preparation of claims

G-195   There is no mandatory graduated fee form. The use of computer-generated forms is permitted and this allows only the relevant data to be submitted. As to graduated fees generally, see *ante*, G-115 *et seq.*

(2) Time limits for the submission of claims

G-196   No claim by an advocate for fees for work done shall be entertained unless submitted within three months of the conclusion of the proceedings to which it relates: S.I. 2013 No. 435, reg. 4(3). However, where a confiscation hearing under section 2 of the DTA 1994, section 71 of the CJA 1988 or Part 2 of the PCA 2002 is held more than 28 days after a person has been found or pleaded guilty, a graduated fee claim can be submitted despite the fact that the proceedings have not yet been completed: *ibid.*, reg. 4(6). The time limit may be extended for "good reason": *ibid.*, reg. 31(1); for example, where the claim is particularly complicated and difficult to prepare, where a co-defendant's case is awaiting disposal, or because there is a genuine misunderstanding about the submission of a claim. Extensions should be sought before the time limit expires.

G-197   Where there are no good reasons, the time may be extended in "exceptional circumstances", in which case the appropriate authority shall consider whether it is reasonable to reduce the fee: S.I. 2013 No. 435, reg. 31(2). An advocate should be given a reasonable opportunity to show cause why his costs should not be reduced (*ibid.*). Any reduction may be challenged by appeal to the taxing master: *post*, G-269. As to what may constitute "good reason" or "exceptional circumstances", see *post*, G-269.

Notwithstanding that a representation order may be expressed to cover proceedings in the Crown Court "and in the event of [the defendant] being convicted or sentenced ..., advice and assistance in regard to the making of an appeal", the legislation is clear as to the need for a claim in relation to work done in the Crown Court to be submitted within three months of the conclusion of the proceedings in that court, rather than within three months of the date on which an application for leave to appeal to the Court of Appeal was refused: *R. v. White* [2008] Costs L.R. 479.

In *R. v. Dumbaya* [2012] Costs L.R. 976, the costs judge took a different view and held that since "representation" for the purposes of Part I of the Access to Justice Act 1999, "includes ... subject to any time limits which may be prescribed, advice and assistance as to any appeal" (the 1999 Act, s.26), proceedings should not be regarded as "concluded" until any such advice or assistance has been given. For corresponding provision in the LASPOA 2012, see section 42(1).

The Legal Services Commission disagreed with the judge in *Dumbaya*. Its November, 2012, guidance provides that (i) the "conclusion of the proceedings" for litigators is the date on which the defendant was acquitted or sentenced; where confiscation proceedings follow sentence, these will be treated as separate proceedings; (ii) the "conclusion of the proceedings" for advocates is the date on which the defendant was acquitted or sentenced or on which confiscation proceedings are concluded; (iii) the commission is currently seeking clarification (in light of conflicting authorities) on whether the time taken, following conviction, to obtain and provide advice on appeal can be taken into account when determining when proceedings conclude, but, pending clarification, proposes to use the date of sentence or acquittal as the conclusion of proceedings; advocates or litigators who risk not meeting the three-month time limit as a result of obtaining or providing advice on appeal should contact the commission for an extension; (iv) bereavement, serious illness, burglary, and flooding in an office, are examples of what are likely to constitute "good reason", but delay in obtaining evidence (including prosecution page counts) and administrative errors will not; (v) those who believe that they are unlikely to meet the time limit should email requesting an extension as soon as possible with grounds; advocates, if appropriate, should provide the name of any firm that is refusing to provide relevant documents; (vi) while the disallowance of the entirety of a claim might constitute a disproportionate sanction and, accordingly, an "exceptional" circumstance, as might the length of the delay and the amount of money involved, a rigid framework for imposing financial penalties is not suitable, and claims must instead be assessed on a case-by-case basis; (vii) accordingly, litigators and advocates who submit claims out of time without "good reason" should provide an explanation as to the impact on them of a total disallowance or reduction of fees for the specific case; although the amount of detail need not be equivalent to that provided when asking for payments to be expedited on hardship grounds, it must be sufficient to enable the determining officer to understand the impact of any decision to disallow or reduce fees.

It is submitted that the commission's stance that proceedings conclude upon acquittal or sentence is to be preferred to the approach of the costs judge in *Dumbaya, ante.* As there is no provision under the 2007 order for payment for advice or assistance on appeal, there seems little point in delaying the date on which the proceedings may be said to have concluded. Any other view also introduces uncertainty.

(3) Submitting an amended claim

Where a genuine error is made in submitting a graduated fee claim, counsel should not be **G-198** precluded for all time from submitting an amended claim where the refusal to permit him to do so could result in his being deprived of fees to which he would have been entitled had the claim been advanced correctly in the first place: *R. v. Hann* [2009] Costs L.R. 833. Where, therefore, counsel, as a result of a genuine error, had submitted a claim for a cracked trial where the case was disposed of as a guilty plea (albeit there had been a long delay between plea and sentence, throughout which it had been on the cards that a *Newton* hearing (*R. v. Newton*, 77 Cr.App.R. 13, CA) would eventually be required), it was held that counsel (who had been paid the appropriate graduated fee for a guilty plea) should be granted an extension of time in which to submit an amended claim for a guilty plea plus a special preparation fee (under what is now S.I. 2013 No. 435, Sched. 1 para. 17). See also *R. v. Lafayette* [2010] 4 Costs L.R. 650 (there is no good reason why a lawyer who has submitted a claim should not be permitted to amend it before it has been determined).

[The next paragraph is G-251.]

I. Disbursements and Expenses

(1) Disbursements

G-251　　A barrister is not entitled to claim for disbursements or expenses other than those permitted under S.I. 2013 No. 435.

For an example of the Legal Services Commission successfully questioning, pursuant to regulation 17 of S.I. 2013 No. 435 (*ante*, G-21), the propriety of incurring costs where the defence had sought, and obtained, prior authority to incur those costs, see *R. v. Ward* [2012] Costs L.R. 605. The costs related to the printing of a large quantity of documentation that had been contained on two computer discs and a memory stick. The solicitors had obtained authority on the ground that the files were inaccessible electronically, or that the software would corrupt their own network or that specialist software was needed to download and read the material. However, this only applied to the documents on the memory stick, and when the decision was taken not to print off the material on the memory stick, the solicitors "knew or ought reasonably to have known that the purpose for which authority had been given had failed or had become irrelevant or unnecessary before the disbursements were incurred." It had not been reasonable to incur the considerable costs when the prosecution did not intend to print the material off, and when there was no real difficulty in accessing it electronically. However, it was held that the purchase of a hard drive used by a computer expert instructed to analyse computers that had been seized was reasonable; it was inevitable that the contents would have to be copied on to a new drive, rather than a previously used drive, to avoid contamination, and such a purchase would not be part of the expert's overheads because once the drive was used, it could not be re-used for the same purpose.

(2) Travelling and accommodation expenses

Entitlement under the regulations

G-252　　Travel and other expenses incidental to appearance at court may be claimed provided the court is not within 40 kilometres of the advocate's office or chambers. Unless prior approval for the expenditure has been obtained under the regulations, or unless the advocate can justify his attendance having regard to all the relevant circumstances of the case, the amount payable shall not be greater than that, if any, payable to a trial advocate from the nearest local Bar or the nearest advocate's office (whichever is the nearer): S.I. 2013 No. 435, Sched. 1, para. 29. As to interim payment of travel and accommodation expenses, see *ante*, G-110.

Local bars

G-253　　In *R. v. Comer* [2009] Costs L.R. 972, it was said that in paragraph 29 of Schedule 1 to S.I. 2013 No. 435 (*ante*, G-62), the juxtaposition of the phrase "local Bar" with the phrase "advocate's office" suggests that a fairly modest number of practitioners can constitute a local bar. The existence of a bar mess is not a prerequisite, and whether the barristers based in an area constitute a local bar will be a question of feel. In this case, the view of the resident judge that "there is a healthy local bar" was considered to be the best evidence of such a bar. As to this case, see also *post*, G-258.

An advocate may be able to justify his attendance in a distant court which is usually serviced by a local bar where:

(a) the instruction of local counsel might lead to suspicion of prejudice, lack of independence or lack of objectivity (*e.g.* cases of local notoriety involving public figures or officials);

(b) there are insufficient local counsel whom instructing solicitors consider are sufficiently experienced to undertake the case in question so as to give the client a reasonable choice;

(c) the services of an advocate who has specialised experience and knowledge of the type of case of an unusual or technical nature are required;

(d) the advocate has previously been instructed in related matters which would assist him in the presentation or preparation of the case in question: *R. v. Conboy* (1990) Costs L.R. 493; and see *R. v. Gussman*, X14, SCTO 40/99 (counsel had represented his client seven years earlier on a charge of murder; his knowledge of his client's earlier medical condition was relevant to the current charges of rape, and this amounted to special circumstances justifying his attendance).

It is submitted that a further justification arises where an advocate is forced to follow a particular judge on circuit who is seized of his case and it was not reasonable to instruct another local advocate for that particular hearing. Where an advocate is instructed from outside a local bar for any of the above reasons it is advisable that he obtains a letter from his instructing solicitor explaining why he was instructed, and for his clerk to obtain prior approval for incurring such expenses from the court. This applies also to Queen's Counsel practising off-circuit: *post*, G-256.

[The next paragraph is G-256.]

Queen's Counsel and local bars

Queen's Counsel should not be regarded as being "local" to any particular bar, even though his **G-256** chambers are in one particular place. Where Queen's Counsel practises on circuit, he should as a general rule receive an amount in respect of travelling and hotel expenses actually and reasonably incurred and necessarily and exclusively attributable to his attendance at a court on the circuit on which he practises: *R. v. Thomas; R. v. Davidson; R. v. Hutton* (1985) Costs L.R. 469. Where Queen's Counsel practises outside his circuit, the "local bar" rules apply: *ante*, G-253.

Expenses reasonably incurred

The reasonableness of an advocate's claim for travel and hotel expenses should be judged not **G-257** by reference to the expenses incurred by other advocates in the same case, but in relation to the demands upon the advocate in putting forward his lay client's case and his own particular circumstances in relation to the conduct of the trial: *R. v. Plews* (1984) Costs L.R. 466; *post*, G-260.

The regulations refer to expenditure "reasonably incurred", whereas earlier regulations referred to expenses "actually and reasonably incurred". In *R. v. Conboy* (1990) Costs L.R. 493, the taxing master observed that the current wording is wider. It is submitted that the alteration acknowledges an advocate's entitlement to recover a reasonable amount in respect of expenses necessarily and exclusively attributable to attendance at court. Thus, where the expense incurred was reasonable, an advocate should recover in full. Where the travel undertaken or accommodation used was reasonable but the cost incurred was excessive, an advocate may only claim for and recover a reasonable amount being a sum no greater than that which he would have incurred had his expenses been reasonable.

Travel to court

In determining what is actually and reasonably incurred the relevant travel is that between **G-258** court and an advocate's chambers: *R. v. Khan*, January 1989, TC C/13. Actual expenses incurred in travelling from an advocate's home to court will only be allowed if his home is nearer to court than his chambers, otherwise his journey is deemed to start from chambers: *R. v. Slessor* (1984) Costs L.R. 438. And, in such a case, he will only be entitled to travelling expenses actually incurred, *i.e.* from home to court: *R. v. Comer* [2009] Costs L.R. 972 (as to which, see also *ante*, G-253).

(i) *Public transport expenses*

Where expenses are recoverable, travel costs are generally limited to the cost of public transport **G-259** actually incurred, together with the expense incurred in getting from the starting point to the railhead or coach station and the expense incurred from getting from the terminal to the court: *Slessor, ante.*

(ii) *Car expenses*

Where an advocate chooses to journey by car, the expenses allowed will not exceed the **G-260** equivalent cost of public transport: *Slessor, ante; Conboy, ante.* The expenses of travel by car will be allowed where public transport is not available or is not reasonably convenient. What is "not reasonably convenient" is a matter for the discretion of the taxing officer. What may be convenient in one case may not be convenient in another. The time spent in getting from the starting point to the railhead, and from the terminus to court is always relevant: if it is considerable, the use of a car may be justified. Taxing officers have been urged to adopt a flexible and broad approach to the problem: *Slessor, ante.* Where the case papers are heavy and bulky, an advocate may be justified in using a car (an example given by the taxing officer in argument in *Conboy, ante*). In *R. v. Plews* (1984) Costs L.R. 466, counsel would have had to catch a 7.15 a.m. train from London to allow him to arrive at court in sufficient time to robe, see his client and solicitor, and to hold any pre-hearing discussions. It was therefore reasonable for counsel, bearing in mind that he had to travel from his home to the station and was faced with a full day in court, to travel by car.

(iii) *Expenses for reasonable travel by car*

G-261   In *Plews, ante,* counsel's claim, based on a mileage rate less than that prescribed for medical practitioners in regulations then current, was considered reasonable, the taxing master observing that a claim based upon the equivalent rate would have been allowed. The usual means of estimating the expenses of travel by car is the standard mileage rate which is calculated by reference to the average cost of running a motor car, including such matters as depreciation, insurance, maintenance, etc., which are referable to the running of a car of the relevant engine capacity. Although the rate is not a precise measure of the actual cost of a particular form of transport, it is intended to provide a mechanism for reimbursing expenses incurred when travelling by car: *Conboy, ante.* Where it is reasonable to incur the expense of travelling by car it must also be reasonable to incur necessary and consequential costs of car parking (if any).

The Legal Services Commission announced an increase in its rates for civil solicitors from 36p per mile to 45p per mile as from April 2, 2001. It is submitted that it is reasonable that similar rates should apply to criminal advocates.

Accommodation expenses

G-262   Hotel or accommodation expenses cannot be divorced from travelling expenses. They should be paid instead of travelling expenses where an advocate reasonably chooses, or by reason of distance is obliged, to stay near a court distant from his chambers rather than travel daily. If travelling expenses are not payable then neither are hotel or accommodation expenses: *R. v. Khan,* January 1989, TC C/13. Where an advocate claims expenses for overnight accommodation and the cost equals or is less than that of the daily travel for which he would be entitled to be reimbursed, such expenses should be allowed. Where the hotel expenses are more than the cost of daily travel, they should be allowed if, having regard to the demands of the case on an advocate, including the need for conferences after court and overnight preparation, the advocate could not have returned home at a reasonable hour: *Plews, ante.*

Conference travel expenses and travel time

G-263   Travel expenses reasonably incurred and necessarily and exclusively attributable to attending a conference should be reimbursed where an advocate attends a conference in prison where the authorities will only produce the client at the place of detention; the same principle applies when the client is a patient in a psychiatric hospital: *R. v. Hindle* (1987) Costs L.R. 486.

J. PROCEEDINGS IN THE COURT OF APPEAL

General principles

G-264   Payment for proceedings in the Court of Appeal is governed by Schedule 3 to S.I. 2013 No. 435 (*ante,* G-82 *et seq.*), which provides for *ex post facto* taxation, the overriding principles being that the appropriate officer should, in determining fees, allow a "reasonable amount" in respect of all work "actually and reasonably done".

Advice on appeal

G-265   As to this, see, in particular, *R. v. Umezie,* § 7-165 in the main work, and *R. v. Bromige, ante,* G-160.

Solicitor advocates

G-266   In *R. v. Mansell* [2011] Costs L.R. 531, it was held that: (i) under S.I. 2013 No. 435, the fees of a solicitor advocate in the Court of Appeal fall to be determined under Schedule 3 as if he were an advocate, and not a litigator; (ii) a solicitor advocate is an "advocate" for all proceedings covered by S.I. 2013 No. 435, including in the Court of Appeal (see the definition of "advocate" in reg. 2, *ante*, G-7); and (iii) that paragraph 3 of Schedule 3 (determination of litigators' fees (*ante*, G-83)), which permits payment of advocacy by litigators, does not mean that all advocacy by solicitors is payable under that paragraph.

K. Determinations and Appeals

(1) The taxing authorities

Graduated fee claims are determined by Crown Court taxing officers and should usually be **G-267** paid within 10 working days of receipt of the claim.

Applications for re-determination are addressed to the chief clerk of the Crown Court or the regional taxation director as appropriate. The re-determination does not have to be carried out by the original officer, although this is usually the case. Where difficult points of principle arise or large sums are in dispute the matter is referred to the regional taxing director or his assistant. Appeals from re-determinations are heard by costs judges appointed by the Lord Chancellor.

(2) Guide to the process of determination and appeal

A brief outline of the various stages of the determination of an advocate's fees is set out below. **G-268** The regulations referred to are those of S.I. 2013 No. 435 (*ante*, §§ G-6 *et seq.*). The table below is merely intended as a guide to the relevant procedures.

As to the circumstances in which an advocate or a litigator may apply to the appropriate officer for a redetermination of his fees, for a review of specified decisions or for an offence to be reclassified, see regulation 28 of S.I. 2013 No. 435 (*ante*, G-34).

The references in the last column in the tables below are references to regulations of S.I. 2013 No. 435.

Stage	*Description*	*reg.*
Submission of Claim		4
Time limit	Within 3 months of conclusion of proceedings (see *ante*, G-196)	4(3)
Particulars submitted in all cases	In the form and manner directed by the appropriate officer	4(3)
Interim payments (40% of total claim less any sum paid)		19
Definition	Payable where:	18
	(a) the basic fee claimed by any counsel in any related proceedings exceeds £4,000, and	18(2)
	(b) 3 months have elapsed from the date of the conclusion of related proceedings or the date on which the bill is ready to tax, whichever is earlier.	18(4)
Related proceedings	Proceedings involving the same defendant heard or dealt with together or proceedings involving more than one defendant arising out of the same incident so that defendants are charged, tried or disposed of together.	18(3)
When the bill is ready to tax	Date of receipt of last bill in related proceedings.	18(4)
Entitlement	Where counsel is entitled to an interim payment but no interim payment has been made and counsel has submitted his claim.	18(4), (5)
Time limit	6 months after the conclusion of proceedings against the defendant represented.	18(5)

Stage	Description	reg.
Determination and notification of costs; authorisation of payment		
	Costs determined in accordance with Schedule 1.	23(1)
	Counsel notified of costs payable and payment authorised.	23(1)
Re-calculation of graduated fee or re-determination of decision to allow special or wasted preparation fee, or classification of offence		
Time limit	Within 21 days of receipt or notification of costs payable.	28(3)
Particulars to be submitted	(a) Written notice specifying matters in respect of which application is made, grounds of objection and whether counsel wishes to appear or to be represented.	28(3), (5)
	(b) Documents and information supplied with submission of claim.	28(4)
	(c) Further information, particulars and documents as required by the appropriate officer.	28(6)
Re-determination of decision not to allow conference fee (time limit and particulars as above)		28(1)(b)
Re-determination by the appropriate officer		28(7)
Application for written reasons		28(8)
Time limit	21 days of notification of the decision	28(8), (9)
Appeal to costs judge		29(1)
Time limit	21 days of receipt of written reasons.	29(2)
Particulars to be submitted to costs judge and appropriate officer	(a) Copy of written representations on application for re-determination.	29(4)
	(b) Appropriate officer's written reasons.	
	(c) All documents supplied hereto.	
Form of notice of appeal	(a) As directed by the costs judge.	29(5)
	(b) Specifying separately each item appealed against, showing amount claimed and determined for each item and the ground of objection.	
	(c) Stating whether appellant wishes to appear or to be represented.	
Lord Chancellor's written representations	Where the Lord Chancellor makes written representations, counsel shall have a reasonable opportunity to make representations in reply.	29(9)
Notification of hearing	The costs judge shall inform counsel of hearing date and give directions as to conduct of appeal.	29(10)
No further evidence	Unless costs judge otherwise directs no other evidence shall be raised at the hearing nor objection taken which was not raised at redetermination.	29(11)
Notification of costs judge's decision		29(13)
Costs	Costs may be awarded where the appeal is allowed.	29(14)

Stage	Description	reg.
Appeals to the High Court		30
Right of appeal	Right of appeal to single QBD judge from costs judge's decision on a point of principle of public importance.	30(7)
Application for costs judge's certificate	Counsel may apply to the costs judge to certify a point of principle of general importance.	30(1)
Time limit for application	Within 21 days of notification of costs judge's decision.	30(2)
Time limit for appeal	Within 21 days from receipt of costs judge's certificate.	
Appeal by Lord Chancellor	Within 21 days of notification of costs judge's decision, the Lord Chancellor may appeal the decision if counsel does not do so.	30(5)

(3) The enforcement and extension of time limits

Time limits may be extended for good reason by the appropriate authority, *i.e.* the appropriate **G-269** officer, costs judge, or the High Court: S.I. 2013 No. 435, reg. 31(1). Where for no good reason the time limit is not adhered to, the appropriate authority may in exceptional circumstances extend the time limit and shall consider whether it is reasonable in the circumstances to reduce the costs, subject to granting the advocate a reasonable opportunity to state either orally or in writing why the costs should not be reduced: *ibid.*, reg. 31(2). A decision not to extend time, or to reduce costs for claims out of time may be appealed by notice in writing to the senior costs judge specifying the grounds of appeal. The appeal must be instituted within 21 days of the decision being given: *ibid.*, reg. 31(3); and see *ante*, G-198. For the latest guidance from the Legal Services Commission on the submission of late claims and what may or may not be treated as "good reason" or "exceptional circumstances", see *ante*, G-197.

It was held in *R. v. Mahmood* [2008] Costs L.R. 326, that where a 10 per cent penalty was imposed following a delay of over two months in submitting a claim for costs, but where the representative had only received a notice, prior to the case being tried, stating that all late claims would be the subject of a penalty unless there was a good reason, this did not constitute notice to show cause why the claim should not be reduced. The determining officer had clearly not considered the circumstances of the particular case on its own merits.

In *R. v. Roberts* [2008] Costs L.R. 323, the oversight of two fee earners, the holiday of one of those fee-earners (even if well-deserved), and a subsequent systematic firm-wide failure did not constitute "good reason" or "exceptional circumstances" so as to justify an extension of time, following a delay of 17 months in submitting a claim for costs. Nor did previous good character constitute "exceptional circumstances", although it was said that it might amount to mitigating circumstances when considering the extent of any reduction in costs (were an extension to be granted). This was the case despite a general softening in the attitude to the delay.

A misunderstanding of the legislation cannot amount to "good reason", but could amount to "exceptional circumstances" where the evidence was that other bills that had been submitted late for like reason in the past had been accepted: *R. v. White* [2008] Costs L.R. 479. But a simple failure to follow up a case could rarely constitute "good reason" or "exceptional circumstances", and it made no difference that the firm in question had generally had a good record for submitting claims in time: *R. v. Johnson* [2008] Costs L.R. 983.

Neither "mere oversight" on the part of leading counsel nor a mistaken belief on the part of junior counsel that leading counsel's clerk was dealing with their fees could amount to "good reason" for not submitting their claims on time; but disallowance of fees *in toto* may be so disproportionate as to amount to "exceptional circumstances": see *R. v. Lafayette* [2010] 4 Costs L.R. 650.

In *R. v. Griffin* [2008] Costs L.R. 483, leading counsel had been under the mistaken impression that his junior was going to prepare a taxation note to be agreed between them before submission. However, in the event, his junior submitted his own claim independently and sent a copy of his taxation note to his leader, such note making it plain that he had submitted a claim and asserting, mistakenly, that leading counsel had already submitted his own claim. It was held that as this was already seven months out of time, and leading counsel only submitted his own claim after a further two years, neither the misunderstanding as between leader and junior, nor extreme pressure of work plus some personal pressure over the two years that followed discovery of the fact that his junior had submitted his own claim, could amount to "good reason" for the failure to submit the claim within the three-month time limit; nor could they amount to "exceptional circumstances" so as to justify an extension of time despite the absence of good reason. There had been no obligation on the determining officer to remind counsel that his claim was late and the absence, at the time, of published criteria to be applied to the submission of late claims, did not avail counsel. What was critical to the outcome was the fact that two years before his eventual submission of his claim, he had been alerted by his junior's note to the fact that he would need to submit his own claim and he had failed then to take any steps to address the situation.

G-270   In *R. v. Islami* [2009] Costs L.R. 988, following a ruling that total disallowance of a claim by solicitors for £58,060.13 (including disbursements and travelling expenses) due to delay (of three years and nine months) would be so disproportionate (because of the substantial effect that this would have on the firm's profits) as to amount to "exceptional circumstances" and that the claim should be re-submitted, albeit that a five per cent penalty should be applied to the sum ultimately allowed, it was held that the fact that an administrative officer at the firm had then not complied with her instructions to submit the relevant documents for taxation, and the fact that this was only discovered during her ensuing extensive sick leave, did not amount to a "good reason" for a further delay of nine months in re-submitting the claim. In these circumstances, total disallowance of the claim, and the ensuing effect on the firm's profits, was no longer a disproportionate penalty sufficient to constitute "exceptional circumstances". Had the sum been needed with the urgency suggested at the original hearing, the firm would have ensured that the claim was re-submitted immediately and carefully tracked. Instead, the administrative problems identified at the original hearing had clearly not been resolved. However, it was said that this conclusion should be applied only to the profit costs and that the claim, so far as it related to disbursements (which had long since been paid out by the firm), should still be determined (without penalty), provided that the necessary papers were lodged within 14 days.

     A reduction of an out-of-time claim to zero is not automatically to be regarded as so disproportionate as to give rise to "exceptional circumstances", but the shortness of the delay, the amount of money involved and the impact on the advocate or litigator involved are capable of constituting exceptional circumstances; each case must, however, turn on its own facts; there can be no hard and fast rules or pre-set scales: *R. v. Grigoropolou* [2012] Costs L.R. 982.

G-271   In *R. v. Newport* [2009] Costs L.R. 983, it was said that, although it has often been stated that barristers must have suitable systems in place to ensure that claims for fees and requests for redeterminations are made within the relevant time limits, and although the delay in this particular case was significant (over three years after the determining officer had refused payment), "exceptional circumstances" for extending the time to apply for a redetermination had been made out where counsel had trusted his senior clerk to ensure that the claim and any appeal procedure was appropriately and punctually concluded, but where he had been deliberately misled by the clerk, who failed, despite counsel's regular enquiries, to inform counsel that his claim had been refused *in toto*. This was found to be a rare and regrettable situation and not akin to an argument that "pressures of work" constituted exceptional circumstances (which would not be successful).

(4) Re-determinations and appeals

Graduated fees

G-272   An advocate may only seek re-determination or appeal in respect of graduated fees where, (a) the issue is either whether the graduated fee scheme applied to the relevant proceedings, or (b) complaint is made as to the calculation of the remuneration payable, or (c) where the advocate is dissatisfied with a refusal to allow a special preparation fee or the number of hours allowed in the calculation of such fee; or (d) where the advocate is dissatisfied with the classification of an offence which does not appear in the Table of offences: S.I. 2013 No. 435, reg. 28(3). Under S.I. 2013 No. 435 a re-determination may also be sought in respect of a decision not to allow an hourly fee in respect of attendance at conferences or views at the scene of the alleged offence, or of the number of hours allowed in the calculation of such a fee: see reg. 28(1)(b)(i).

Re-determination

On an application for re-determination an advocate shall specify the grounds of his objection **G-273** to all or any part of the determination (S.I. 2013 No. 435, reg. 28(3)(b)) and may appear in person or through another to make representations: S.I. 2013 No. 435, reg. 28(5). An advocate is not obliged to provide fresh information or material to assist the determining officer in the redetermination. If no additional information is provided, the determining officer has a duty to redetermine on the basis of the information already supplied: *R. v. O'Brien* [2003] Costs L.R. 625. Many appeals which might otherwise have succeeded have failed because the representations made to the appropriate officer have been perfunctory and inexplicit: *R. v. Davies* (1985) Costs L.R. 472.

As from January 1, 1994, the General Council of the Bar has agreed that all requests for fees to be re-determined or for written reasons to be provided should be signed by counsel personally.

Re-determination should, where possible, be carried out by the officer who determined costs. Where cases are cited in support of the re-determination, sufficient references must be given to allow an advocate to identify and look them up: *R. v. Pelepenko*, X27A, SCCO 186/2001.

Where the Legal Aid Agency makes a decision to recover an overpayment of fees pursuant to regulation 25 of S.I. 2013 No. 435 (*ante*, G-31) and the litigator requests a review, a subsequent confirmation by the commission of its decision to recoup constitutes a redetermination within the meaning of regulation 28 (*ante*, G-34), so as to allow the litigator to appeal to a costs judge pursuant to regulation 29(1) (*ante*, G-35): *Lord Chancellor v. Eddowes Perry and Osbourne Ltd* [2011] Costs L.R. 498, QBD (Spencer J.) (disapproving *R. v. Charlery*; *R. v. Small* [2011] Costs L.R. 331). As to this case, see also *ante*, G-161.

Further evidence on appeal and supplemental written reasons

On appeal before a costs judge no further evidence shall be received and no ground of objection **G-274** shall be valid which was not raised on the application for re-determination unless the costs judge otherwise directs: S.I. 2013 No. 435, reg. 29(11). These provisions are strictly applied. A costs judge will rarely accede to a request to adduce further evidence or allow a fresh objection to be raised. Where written reasons do not address a point raised in the claim, counsel cannot pursue the matter in the appeal. The proper method of dealing with such an omission is to seek supplemental written reasons from the appropriate officer.

Appeals

The right of appeal to a costs judge is effectively limited in that no appeal lies against a **G-275** determination unless the advocate has applied for a re-determination and, thereafter, for written reasons under S.I. 2013 No. 435, reg. 29(1).

An advocate wishing to appeal must have regard to, and be familiar with, the provisions of Part 5 of the *Criminal Costs Practice Directions* (2015) (*ante*, Appendix B-270 *et seq.*) (§§ 6-146 *et seq.*

Representation, costs and expenses of appeal

For the purposes of an appeal to a costs judge, an advocate is treated as the appellant and can **G-276** elect to be represented at the hearing. A successful appellant may be awarded a sum in respect of part or all of any reasonable costs incurred in connection with the appeal: S.I. 2013 No. 435, reg. 29(14); and see *R. v. Boswell*; *R. v. Halliwell* [1987] 1 W.L.R. 705 (Leggatt J.).

A barrister without the intervention of a solicitor may accept a brief or instructions, with or without fee, directly from, and represent, another barrister on that other barrister's appeal as to his fees before a costs judge: see *Code of Conduct*, 8th ed., para. 401 (Appendix C-7, *ante*). A professional fee payable by one barrister to another for conducting the former's appeal is capable of constituting part of the costs incurred by the appellant counsel: *R. v. Boswell*; *R. v. Halliwell*, *ante*. In assessing such costs the costs judge is entitled to take account of time and skill expended by the appellant or his counsel in the drawing of grounds and preparation of the appeal, and the conduct of the hearing, and travel and subsidence costs: *ibid*. Costs incurred in instructing other counsel are clearly reasonable where there is some technical question on the applicability of some part of the regulations or other issue which legitimately deserves the attention of specialist costs counsel. Costs are not reasonably incurred if trial counsel is available, could easily have represented himself and the only real issue is the weight of the case or the value of a particular item of work undertaken: *Jackson v. Lord Chancellor* [2003] Costs L.R. 395; and *R. v. Martin* [2007] Costs L.R. 128. A successful appellant will ordinarily be entitled to the return of the fee payable in respect of the appeal.

Appeals to the single judge

G-277   As to appeals from a costs judge to the High Court, see S.I. 2013 No. 435, reg. 30. The ambit of an appeal is strictly limited to the point of principle certified by the costs judge as being of general importance (such certificate being a pre-condition to an appeal): *Patten v. Lord Chancellor*, 151 N.L.J. 851, QBD (Leveson J.), not following *Harold v. Lord Chancellor* [1999] Costs L.R. 14. Although *Patten* was concerned with the interpretation of regulation 16 of the Legal Aid in Criminal and Care Proceedings (Costs) Regulations 1989 (S.I. 1989 No. 343), regulation 29 of S.I. 2013 No. 435 is worded in almost identical terms. A refusal of a costs judge to certify that the matter raises a point of principle of general importance is not susceptible to judicial review: *R. v. Supreme Court Taxing Office, exp. John Singh & Co* [1997] 1 Costs L.R. 49, CA (Civ. Div). As to the limited scope for a challenge, by way of judicial review, to the substantive decision of a costs judge where a certificate has been refused, see § 6-75 in the main work.

(5) Recovery of overpayment

G-278   Where an advocate receives a sum in excess of his entitlement, the taxing authority may either require immediate repayment of that excess, or deduct the excess from any other sum payable to the advocate under the regulations: S.I. 2013 No. 435, reg. 25. These provisions apply notwithstanding the fact that a re-determination or appeal has been or may be requested: S.I. 2013 No. 435, reg. 25(4).

(6) Appeals under VHCCs

G-279   Under the arrangements that came into force on April 1, 2013 (*ante*, G-181 *et seq.*), both the VHCC Specification for organisations and that for advocates provide for a right of appeal to the VHCC Appeals Panel. The details are set out in paragraph 6 of the specifications, with paragraph 6.4 listing the issues in relation to which there is a right of appeal (*e.g.* the category to which a case has been assigned) and paragraph 6.5 listing those issues in relation to which there is no right of appeal. The appeal process, including time limits, is provided for by paragraphs 6.6 to 6.30. The appeal will normally be determined by a single adjudicator but may be referred to an appeals committee. The decision of the adjudicator or committee is final (para. 6.28), but is binding only in relation to the particular appeal (para. 6.29). Anonymised versions of decisions will be published on the Legal Aid Agency's website (para. 6.30).

APPENDIX H
Sexual Offences (The Law as at April 30, 2004)

A. I<small>NTRODUCTION</small>

The history of the sexual offences legislation since 1956 is set out in detail at §§ 20-1 *et seq.* in **H-1** the main work. All the statutory provisions contained in this appendix were repealed with effect from May 1, 2004, by the SOA 2003, but, as stated in the main work, they have continuing effect in relation to conduct occurring prior to that date. It should be borne in mind that this appendix states the law as at April 30, 2004, and that, therefore, there may yet be prosecutions for offences committed prior to even earlier material changes in the law: see, in particular, the amendments effected by the SOA 1985 and the CJPOA 1994 (summarised at §§ 20-2, 20-3 in the main work).

B. S<small>EXUAL</small> O<small>FFENCES</small> A<small>CT</small> 1956

(1) Rape

(a) *Introduction*

Section 1 of the 1956 Act made rape an offence. Section 1(1) of the Sexual Offences (Amend- **H-2** ment) Act 1976 provided a statutory definition of rape in terms designed to give effect to the Report of the Advisory Group on the Law of Rape (Cmnd. 6352) and the views expressed by the House of Lords in *DPP v. Morgan* [1976] A.C. 182. Section 1(1) was repealed by the CJPOA 1994, which also substituted a new section 1 in the 1956 Act. The effect of this was to adopt the 1976 definition, but to extend it so as to cover anal intercourse with a woman or a man. In addition, the new provision referred simply to "sexual intercourse" whereas the 1976 Act referred to "unlawful sexual intercourse". The omission of the word "unlawful" made clear Parliament's adoption of the decision of the House of Lords in *R. v. R.* [1992] A.C. 599, that a man may rape his wife.

Section 7(2) of the 1976 Act (as amended by the CJA 1988, s.158(1) and (6)) provided that in that Act "a rape offence":

> "means any of the following, namely rape, attempted rape, aiding, abetting, counselling and procuring rape or attempted rape, incitement to commit rape, conspiracy to rape and burglary with intent to rape."

(b) *Statute*

Sexual Offences Act 1956, s.1

Rape of woman or man

1.–(1) It is an offence for a man to rape a woman or another man. **H-3**

(2) A man commits rape if—

(a) he has sexual intercourse with a person (whether vaginal or anal) who at the time of the intercourse does not consent to it; and

(b) at the time he knows that the person does not consent to the intercourse or is reckless as to whether that person consents to it.

(3) A man also commits rape if he induces a married woman to have sexual intercourse with him by impersonating her husband.

(4) Subsection (2) applies for the purposes of any enactment.

[This section is printed as substituted (from November 3, 1994) by the CJPOA 1994, s.142.]

Sexual Offences (Amendment) Act 1976, s.1

1.–(1) [*Repealed by Criminal Justice and Public Order Act 1994, s.168(3) and Sched. 11.*] **H-4**

(2) It is hereby declared that if at a trial for a rape offence the jury has to consider whether a man believed that a woman or man was consenting to sexual intercourse, the presence or absence of reasonable grounds for such a belief is a matter to which the jury is to have regard, in conjunction with any other relevant matters, in considering whether he so believed.

[Subs. (2) is printed as amended by the CJPOA 1994, s.168(2), and Sched. 10, para. 35(1), (2).]

As to the use of the words "man" and "woman", see *post*, H-222. As to the meaning of "a rape offence", see *ante*, H-2.

In the case of a summary trial or a trial by court-martial, the references to the jury in section 1(2) of the 1976 Act are to be construed as references to the court: *ibid.*, s.7(3).

(c) *Anonymity*

H-5   See §§ 20-257 *et seq.* in the main work.

(d) *Indictment*

Statement of Offence

H-6   *Rape, contrary to section 1(1) of the Sexual Offences Act 1956.*

Particulars of Offence

A B on the __ day of __, 20_, had sexual intercourse with C D who at the time of the said intercourse did not consent to it, the said A B either knowing that the said C D did not so consent or being reckless as to whether she [or he] so consented.

Where the victim is a woman, the intercourse may be vaginal or anal: s.1(1) of the 1956 Act, *ante*, H-3. It is unnecessary to specify in the indictment whether the allegation is of vaginal or anal intercourse, but there will be cases where it is of assistance to do so. This can be done by adding the words "*per vaginam*" or "*per anum*" after the words "sexual intercourse". The addition of these words will be particularly useful where it is alleged that a woman was raped both vaginally and anally; the counts will reflect this and will ensure, in the event of a conviction on one count only, that the court is aware of the basis of the jury's verdict. As to where it is unclear on the evidence whether penetration was of the vagina or the anus, see *R. v. K. (Robert)* [2009] 1 Cr.App.R. 24, CA (§ 20-20 in the main work).

Good practice does not require that, where the prosecution rely on recklessness as an alternative to knowledge, there should be separate counts (alleging respectively knowledge and recklessness): *R. v. Flitter* [2001] Crim.L.R. 328, CA.

Allegation of joint offence

H-7   Where a person has been raped by more than one man on the same occasion, all the accused should be charged in one count of rape, with no mention of aiders and abettors: see the direction of the House of Lords in *DPP v. Merriman* [1973] A.C. 584. This enables the jury to be told that it matters not whether an individual accused physically committed the act of rape, or assisted or encouraged someone else to; thus, several accused may be convicted where the jury is satisfied only that each played a guilty part, but not as to who committed the physical act.

(e) *Mode of trial and class of offence*

H-8   This offence and an attempt to commit it are triable on indictment only: SOA 1956, s.37(2), and Sched. 2, para. 1. As to the classification of offences, see § 2-22c in the main work.

(f) *Alternative verdicts*

H-9   On a count of rape, the accused may be convicted of procurement of a woman by threats (s.2) or false pretences (s.3) or of administering drugs to obtain or facilitate intercourse (s.4): SOA 1956, s.37(4), and Sched. 2, para. 1.

As to alternative verdicts generally, see §§ 4-524 *et seq.* in the main work. Where the alleged victim was a girl under 16 years of age, then whether or not her age is averred in the indictment, a jury may not convict the accused under section 6(3) of the CLA 1967 (§ 4-525 in the main work) of an offence contrary to section 6 of the SOA 1956 (unlawful intercourse with a girl under

16): *R. v. Fisher* [1969] 2 Q.B. 114, Assizes (Cusack J.); *R. v. Mochan*, 54 Cr.App.R. 5, Assizes (Cusack J.), approved in *R. v. Hodgson* [1973] Q.B. 565, 57 Cr.App.R. 502, CA.

As every charge of rape contains the essential ingredients of indecent assault (*viz.* an assault and indecency), it follows that where a man is acquitted of rape on the ground of the victim's consent, it is open to the jury to convict him where the victim is under 16, of indecent assault, because the consent which provided a defence to a charge of rape cannot, by virtue of the SOA 1956, ss.14(2) and 15(2), provide a defence to a charge of indecent assault. Age is not an ingredient of, nor an essential averment in the framing of a count of indecent assault: *R. v. Hodgson, ante.*

In *R. v. Timmins* [2006] 1 Cr.App.R. 18, CA, it was held that the effect of the decision in *R. v. J.* [2005] 1 A.C. 562, HL (on a true construction of the 1956 Act, it was impermissible to prosecute a charge of indecent assault under section 14(1) (*post*, H-117) in circumstances where the only conduct upon which the charge was based was an act of unlawful sexual intercourse with a girl under the age of 16 in respect of which no prosecution could be commenced under section 6(1) (*post*, H-50) by virtue of the time bar contained in section 37(2) of, and Schedule 2 to, the Act) was not such as to preclude a judge from leaving it to a jury to convict of indecent assault as an alternative to a charge of rape, under section 6(3) of the CLA 1967 (*ante*), where they were satisfied as to the act of sexual intercourse and as to the fact that the girl was under 16 at the time, and where they acquitted of rape on the ground that they were not satisfied as to lack of consent, and this was so notwithstanding that the proceedings for rape had been begun over 12 months after the alleged offence; the decision in *J.* had turned on the words of Schedule 2 to the 1956 Act, which provided that "A prosecution may not be commenced more than 12 months after the offence charged."; leaving a possible alternative verdict to a jury could not be described as a "commencement" of proceedings for the offence; but it would be an abuse of process to bring a charge of rape against a person against whom there was no evidence whatever of rape (in particular lack of consent) in order to circumvent a time limit.

In the earlier case of *R. v. Rabbitts* (2005) 149 S.J. 890, CA, it was held that, *R. v. J.* having decided that, as a matter of statutory construction, it was not open to the prosecution to bring a charge of indecent assault where the conduct on which the prosecution was based was an act of consensual sexual intercourse with a girl under 16, and where the purpose was to circumvent the statutory time limit of 12 months on prosecutions for unlawful sexual intercourse with a girl of that age, it made no difference that the count of indecent assault was included in the indictment as an alternative to a charge of rape to cater for the possibility that the jury would not be satisfied as to lack of consent.

In *R. v. Cottrell; R. v. Fletcher* [2008] 1 Cr.App.R. 7, CA, it was said that to the extent that *Timmins* and *Rabbitts* were inconsistent, they should be followed as they apply to the facts of the individual case. As to the flawed nature of the decision in *Timmins*, see CLW/05/43/4.

(g) *Autrefois acquit and convict*

For the general principles, see §§ 4-183 *et seq.* in the main work.   **H-10**

An acquittal upon an indictment for rape was held to be no bar to a subsequent indictment on the same facts for a common assault: *R. v. Dungey* (1864) 4 F. & F. 99 (and see now s.6(3A) of the CLA 1967 (§ 4-525 in the main work), reversing the effect of *R. v. Mearns* [1991] 1 Q.B. 82, 91 Cr.App.R. 312, CA).

An acquittal on an indictment for rape cannot be successfully pleaded as a bar to a subsequent indictment for assault with intent to commit rape: *R. v. Gisson* (1847) 2 C. & K. 781, or, in certain circumstances, to a subsequent indictment for attempted rape, see *R. v. Hearn* [1970] Crim.L.R. 175, CA (§ 4-203 in the main work).

However, it should be noted that there was (as at April 30, 2004), in all probability, no longer an offence of assault with intent to rape, contrary to common law. It did not survive the creation of an identical statutory offence in the Offences against the Person Act 1861, s.38, which was in turn abolished by virtue of section 10 of, and Schedule 3 to, the Criminal Law Act 1967: *R. v. P.* [1990] Crim.L.R. 323, Crown Court (Pill J.) (but note the commentary and reference, by Professor J. C. Smith, to the opposite view expressed by Turner J. in *R. v. J.*, unreported, June 9, 1986). *Cf.* section 16 of the 1956 Act (assault with intent to commit buggery), *post*, H-138.

(h) *Sentence*

Maximum

H-11 Rape: life imprisonment–SOA 1956, s.37(3), and Sched. 2, para. 1(a).

Attempted rape: life imprisonment–SOA 1956, s.37(3), and Sched. 2, para. 1(a) (as amended by the SOA 1985, s.3).

Guidelines

H-12 In *R. v. H.* [2012] 2 Cr.App.R.(S.) 21, CA, it was said that in the search for principle, it is impossible to reconcile all the authorities that purport to provide guidance on sentencing for historic sexual offending; that the following considerations, derived from statute (general provisions about sentencing in the CJA 2003, Pt 12, Chap. 1 (ss.142–176), and the Coroners and Justice Act 2009, s.125 (sentencing guidelines: duty of court (§ 5-180 in the main work))) and case law, should be treated as guidance; and that reference to earlier decisions (with the exception of *R. v. Millberry; R. v. Morgan; R. v. Lackenby* [2003] 1 Cr.App.R. 25, CA) is unlikely to be helpful and is to be discouraged. First, sentence will be imposed on the basis of the legislative provisions current at the time of sentence, and by measured reference to any definitive sentencing guidelines relevant to the situation revealed by the established facts. Secondly, although sentence must be limited to the maximum permissible at the date when the offence was committed, it is wholly unrealistic to attempt an assessment of sentence by seeking to identify today what the sentence was likely to have been if the offence had come to light at or shortly after its commission. Thirdly, the particular circumstances in which the offence was committed and its seriousness must be the main focus; due allowance for the passage of time may be appropriate; the date may have a considerable bearing on the offender's culpability; for example, if he was young and immature at the time, that remains a continuing feature of the sentencing decision; similarly, if the allegations had come to light many years earlier, and the offender admitted them, but, for whatever reason, the complaint had not been drawn to the attention of, or investigated by, the police, or had been investigated but had not then been pursued to trial, these too would be relevant matters. Fourthly, careful judgment of the harm done to the victim is always a critical feature of the sentencing decision; simultaneously, equal care needs to be taken to assess the true extent of the offender's criminality by reference to what he actually did and the circumstances in which he did it. Fifthly, the passing of the years may demonstrate aggravating features if, for example, the offender has continued to commit sexual crime or he represents a continuing risk to the public; on the other hand, mitigation may be found in an unblemished life over the intervening years, particularly if accompanied by evidence of positive good character. Sixthly, early admissions and a guilty plea are of particular importance in historic cases; given that it is tempting to lie about events long ago, it is greatly to the offender's credit if he makes early admissions; even more powerful mitigation is available to the offender who, out of a sense of guilt and remorse, reports himself to the authorities. The court considered, *inter alia, R. v. Bowers* [1999] 2 Cr.App.R.(S.) 97, CA, *R. v. Fowler* [2002] 2 Cr.App.R.(S.) 99, CA, *Att.-Gen.'s References (Nos 37, 38, 44, 54, 51, 53, 35, 40, 43, 45, 41 and 42 of 2003)* [2004] 1 Cr.App.R.(S.) 84, CA, *R. v. McKendrick* [2005] 2 Cr.App.R.(S.) 68, CA, *R. v. Patterson* [2006] 2 Cr.App.R.(S.) 48, CA, *Att.-Gen.'s Reference (No. 39 of 2006) (R. v. J. (Rodney Clive))* [2007] 1 Cr.App.R.(S.) 34, CA, *R. v. Moon* [2011] 1 Cr.App.R.(S.) 34, CA, *R. v. Hartley (Practice Note)* [2012] 1 Cr.App.R. 7, CA, and *Att.-Gen.'s Reference (No. 78 of 2010)* [2011] 2 Cr.App.R.(S.) 109, CA.

This approach to sentencing historic sexual offences was specifically endorsed by the Sentencing Council for England and Wales: see Annex B to its definitive guideline on sexual offences (Appendix S-20.155). But for more recent guidance from the Court of Appeal (suggesting that there was now only very limited need to refer to *R. v. H.*), see Appendix S-1053.

R. v. H. was considered in *Att.-Gen.'s Reference (No. 32 of 2016) (R. v. B.)* [2016] 2 Cr.App.R.(S.) 20, CA, in which it was said that there was no principle of sentencing that all historic sexual offences had to be met by immediate terms of imprisonment, whatever the circumstances; the Sentencing Council's guideline on sexual offences (Appendix S-20) made it clear that there may be exceptional cases where a non-custodial sentence was appropriate; the passage of time since an offence, the age of the offender at the time he committed an offence and the fact he had not been convicted of any offence in the interim were all factors to be considered when assessing

sentence generally, and there was no good reason why they could not be relevant to the question
of suspension.

(i) *Ingredients of the offence*

A "man"

The common law presumption that a boy under the age of 14 was incapable of sexual   **H-13**
intercourse was abolished (for both natural and unnatural intercourse) by the SOA 1993, ss.1,
2(2), (3).

A woman may be convicted as an aider and abettor: *R. v. Ram* (1893) 17 Cox 609 at 610n.

A man may be convicted of raping his wife: *R. v. R.* [1992] 1 A.C. 599, HL (confirmed by the
revised definition of "rape" introduced by the CJPOA 1994, *ante*, § H-3).

Sexual intercourse

Where it is necessary to prove sexual intercourse (whether natural or unnatural), it shall not be   **H-14**
necessary to prove the completion of the intercourse by the emission of seed, but it shall be
deemed complete upon proof of penetration only: SOA 1956, s.44 (*post*, § H-219). "Unnatural"
intercourse in section 44 means buggery (including bestiality): *R. v. Gaston*, 73 Cr.App.R. 164,
CA.

The amendment of section 1 of the 1956 Act by the 1994 Act (§ 20-3 in the main work, and
ante, H-3) did not alter the law (whereunder even the slightest penetration would be sufficient:
see *R. v. R'Rue* (1838) 8 C. & P. 641; *R. v. Allen* (1839) 9 C. & P. 31) so as to make penetration of
the vagina, properly so-called, an essential ingredient of "vaginal" rape; it is sufficient that there
was any degree of penetration by the penis within the labia of the pudendum of the complainant;
the word "vaginal" in section 1 is used in comparison with, or in addition to, "anal", and not so as
to indicate that the word is being used in the medical sense, rather than the general sense of the
female genitalia: *R. v. J.F.*, unreported, December 16, 2002, CA ([2002] EWCA Crim. 2936).

Sexual intercourse is a continuing act; it follows that consensual intercourse will become rape if
the woman (or man) ceases to consent during the intercourse, and the man (other man), with the
necessary *mens rea*, continues the act: *Kaitamaki v. R.* [1985] A.C. 147, PC (decided on the corresponding New Zealand legislation). It should be noted that these were not the facts in *Kaitamaki*;
the facts were that the defendant claimed he only realised the woman was not consenting after
intercourse had begun. As to this aspect of the decision, see *post*, H-20. However, the foregoing
proposition appears to follow as a matter of logic from the Board's decision on the narrower
point.

Absence of consent

General

It must be proved that the accused had sexual intercourse with the complainant without her or   **H-15**
his consent: s.1(2)(a) of the 1956 Act, *ante*, H-3. This applies even where the offence is alleged to
have been committed on a person under the age of 16, though sometimes in such a case the
prosecution will not need to prove much more than the age of the victim: *R. v. Harling*, 26
Cr.App.R. 127, CCA. It is not, however, necessary to support a charge of rape that there is
evidence that the complainant demonstrated her lack of consent or communicated it to the accused; the minimum requirement is evidence of lack of consent in fact, which might take many
forms; the most obvious is the complainant's simple assertion, which may or may not be backed
up by evidence of force or threats; alternatively, it may consist of evidence that by reason of drink,
drugs, sleep, age or mental handicap the complainant was unaware of what was occurring and/or
incapable of giving consent; or it may consist of evidence that the complainant was deceived as to
the identity of the man with whom she had intercourse: *R. v. Malone* [1998] 2 Cr.App.R. 447,
CA. As to intercourse with a woman known to be asleep, see *R. v. Mayers* (1872) 12 Cox 311; *R. v.
Young* (1878) 14 Cox 114.

Lack of consent will have been established if the jury are satisfied that although the complainant did not dissent, her understanding and lack of knowledge were such, whether on account of
age, the consumption of drink or drugs or mental handicap, that she was incapable of giving

consent or of exercising any judgment on the matter: see *R. v. Howard*, 50 Cr.App.R. 56, CCA (age); *R. v. Lang*, 62 Cr.App.R. 50, CA (drink); *R. v. Fletcher* (1859) Bell 63; *R. v. Ryan* (1846) 2 Cox 115; *R. v. Fletcher* (1866) L.R. 1 C.C.R. 39; *R. v. Barratt* (1873) L.R. 2 C.C.R. 81; *R. v. Pressy* (1867) 10 Cox 635, CCR (mental handicap). To the extent that they suggest that where no force, threat or deceit was used, there must be evidence of some resistance on the part of the complainant, *Howard* and *Lang* should no longer be taken to represent the law: *Malone, ante.*

Evidence of resistance may, of course, be highly relevant to the separate issue of the defendant's knowledge or recklessness in relation to the lack of consent.

H-16   Although juries should be told that "consent" in the context of the offence of rape is a word which must be given its ordinary meaning, it is sometimes necessary for the judge to go further. For example, he should point out, if necessary, that there is a difference between consent and submission (as to which, see also § 20-10 in the main work). In cases where intercourse took place after threats not involving violence, or the fear of it, a jury should be directed to concentrate on the state of mind of the victim immediately before the act of intercourse. The jury should be reminded too of the wide spectrum of states of mind which consent could comprehend and that where a dividing line had to be drawn between real consent and mere submission they should apply their combined good sense, experience and knowledge of human nature and modern behaviour to all the relevant facts of the case: *R. v. Olugboja*, 73 Cr.App.R. 344, CA (*cf. R. v. McAllister* [1997] Crim.L.R. 233, CA, *post*, H-124). The word "want" should not be used in directing a jury on the issue of consent, there being a clear difference between "wanting" to have intercourse and "consenting" to it: *R. v. T. (D.)* [2000] 7 *Archbold News* 3, CA.

As to evidence about the lack of sexual experience of a complainant, see § 20-11 in the main work.

As to intercourse with a defective, see also the SOA 1956, ss.7 and 45 (*post*, H-64, H-68).

Intercourse by false pretences

H-17   The only types of fraud which vitiate consent for the purposes of the law of rape are frauds as to the nature of the act or as to the identity of the person doing the act: *R. v. Linekar* [1995] 2 Cr.App.R. 49, CA. As to frauds as to the nature of the act, see *R. v. Case* (1850) 1 Den. 580, and *R. v. Flattery* (1877) 2 Q.B.D. 410, where the consent was induced by the pretence that the act of intercourse was a form of medical treatment, and *R. v. Williams* [1923] 1 K.B. 340, 17 Cr.App.R. 56, CCA, where a choirmaster pretended to be testing a girl's breathing powers with an instrument. As to fraud as to the identity of the perpetrator of the Act, section 1(3) of the SOA 1956 (*ante*, H-3) makes express provision for the case of a man inducing a married woman to have sexual intercourse with him by impersonating her husband. This provision was first introduced by the Criminal Law Amendment Act 1885 for the purpose of reversing the decision in *R. v. Barrow* (1868) L.R. 1 C.C.R. 156. As to other instances of impersonation, it is possible that the principle in *Barrow* will still prevail; but it was dissented from in *R. v. Dee* (1884) 15 Cox C.C. 57, and doubt about the correctness of the decision was expressed in *Flattery*. What was said in *Linekar* as to fraud as to identity vitiating consent was *obiter*, the case not concerning mistake as to identity at all, but it is submitted that the view of the Court of Appeal represents the modern and better view.

See also section 3 of the SOA 1956 (*post*, H-27) in relation to false pretences of a less fundamental character; and *R. v. Tabassum* [2000] 2 Cr.App.R. 328, CA (*post*, H-124) in which it was held that a deception as to the quality of the act vitiated consent in a case of indecent assault.

Recent complaint

H-18   See § 20-12 in the main work.

Distress of victim

H-19   See § 20-13 in the main work.

Mens rea

General

H-20   It must be proved that at the time of the non-consensual intercourse, the defendant either knew that the victim was not consenting or that he was reckless as to whether she or he was consenting: see s.1(2)(b) of the SOA 1956, *ante*, H-3. If the tribunal of fact has to consider whether the defendant believed that a person was consenting to intercourse, the presence or absence of reasonable grounds for such a belief is a matter to which the tribunal is to have regard, in conjunction with any other relevant matters, in considering whether he so believed: Sexual Offences (Amendment) Act 1976, s.1(2), *ante*, H-4.

Sexual intercourse is a continuing act, which ends upon withdrawal. If, therefore, a man becomes aware that the other person is not consenting after intercourse has commenced and he does not desist, he will be guilty of rape from the moment that he realises that she or he is not consenting: *Kaitamaki v. R.* [1985] A.C. 147, PC. This case was decided on sections 127 and 128 of the New Zealand Crimes Act 1961, which are to the same effect as section 44 of the 1956 Act (*post*, H-219) and section 1 of the 1956 Act (*ante*, H-3). As to the situation where the victim was in fact consenting at the outset, but ceases to consent, see *ante*, H-14. This will also be rape provided that the man was aware of the change or was reckless in respect thereof.

Recklessness

Substantive offences. In *R. v. Satnam and Kewal*, 78 Cr.App.R. 149, CA, earlier confusion was **H-21** resolved. The authorities having been reviewed, it was held that any direction as to the definition of rape should be based upon section 1 of the Sexual Offences (Amendment) Act 1976 (see now s.1(2) of the SOA 1956, *ante*, H-3) and upon *DPP v. Morgan* [1976] A.C. 182, HL (§ 17-10 in the main work). The court suggested that a practical definition of recklessness in sexual cases had been given in *R. v. Kimber*, 77 Cr.App.R. 225, CA (a case of indecent assault), namely if the jury were sure that the defendant had been indifferent to the feelings and wishes of the victim, aptly described colloquially as "couldn't care less" then that in law was "reckless". Thus (see pp. 154-155), in summing up a case of rape which involves the issue of consent, the judge should, in dealing with the state of mind of the defendant, direct the jury that before they can convict, the Crown must have proved either that he knew the woman did not consent to sexual intercourse, or that he was reckless as to whether she consented. If the jury are sure he knew she did not consent, they will find him guilty of rape knowing there to be no consent. If they are not sure about that, they will go on to consider reckless rape. If he may genuinely have believed that she did consent, even though he was mistaken in that belief he must be acquitted: see s.1(2) of the 1976 Act, *ante*, H-4. In considering whether his belief may have been genuine, the jury should take into account all the relevant circumstances (including presence or absence of reasonable grounds: see s.1(2)). If, after considering them, the jury are sure that the defendant had no genuine belief that the woman consented to have intercourse, then they will convict. He will be guilty because that finding of fact would mean that his mental state was such that either he knew she was not consenting or he was reckless as to whether she was consenting. If the jury are sure that he could not have cared less whether she wanted to have sexual intercourse or not, but pressed on regardless, then he would have been reckless and could not have believed that she wanted to.

In *R. v. Taylor (Robert)*, 80 Cr.App.R. 327, CA, Lord Lane C.J. said (at p. 332) that in rape, the defendant is reckless if he does not believe the woman is consenting and could not care less whether she is consenting or not but presses on regardless. *Taylor* was followed and applied in *R. v. Adkins* [2000] 2 All E.R. 185, CA, where it was held to be unnecessary to give a direction as to honest belief in every case where consent is in issue; such a direction is only required when, on the evidence in the case, there is room for the possibility of a genuine mistaken belief that the victim had consented; equally, the question of honest belief does not necessarily arise where reckless rape is in issue, for the defendant might have failed to address his mind to the question whether or not there was consent, or have been indifferent as to whether or not there was consent, in circumstances where, if he had addressed his mind to the question, he could not genuinely have believed that there was consent; where, therefore, the defence case was not merely that the complainant consented but that she actively facilitated intercourse, there was no scope for a genuine, but mistaken, belief as to consent.

Attempts. In *R. v. Khan*, 91 Cr.App.R. 29, the Court of Appeal held that precisely the same **H-22** analysis can be made of the offence of attempted rape as that of the full offence, namely: (a) the intention of the offender is to have sexual intercourse with another person; (b) the offence is committed if, but only if, the circumstances are that: (i) the other person does not consent; *and* (ii) the defendant knows that he or she is not consenting or is reckless as to that fact.

Drunkenness and mistake of fact

H-23   It is clear from both *DPP v. Majewski* [1977] A.C. 443, HL (§ 17-107 in the main work) and *R. v. Caldwell* [1982] A.C. 341, HL (§ 17-112 in the main work) that "recklessness" as a consequence of voluntarily induced intoxication cannot amount to a defence.

If the accused was, or may have been, genuinely mistaken as to fact (see generally, §§ 17-10 *et seq.* in the main work, and H-21, *ante*), for example, if he thought or may have thought that the complainant was consenting to sexual intercourse, and the jury are sure that that mistake was a consequence of intoxication, what then is the position? It appears to be this: implicit in such a finding is the finding that but for the voluntary consumption of drink the jury are sure that the accused would have known either that the complainant was not consenting or, at the very least, that there was a risk that she was not consenting. Whatever the true scope of the meaning of "reckless" in the context of sexual offences, it is plain (see *ante*, H-21) that to proceed knowing that there was a risk that the complainant was not consenting and not caring whether she consented or not is to act recklessly. It therefore follows that if the jury are sure that by virtue of drink (or drugs) the accused was not alerted, at the very least to the existence of that risk, that in itself constitutes the necessary recklessness for the purposes of the offence, see *Majewski* (§ 17-109 in the main work); and a genuine mistake as to fact in such circumstances constitutes no defence. This approach is borne out by the decision of the Court of Appeal in *R. v. Woods (W.),* 74 Cr.App.R. 312. It was conceded on behalf of W that, but for section 1(2) of the Sexual Offences (Amendment) Act 1976 (*ante*, H-4), the principles in *Majewski* and *Caldwell* (as to the relevance of drink to recklessness) would apply and that accordingly a genuine mistake as to fact as a consequence of drink could found no defence. However, it was argued that section 1(2) of the 1976 Act permitted the jury to take into account a defendant's drunken state as a possible reasonable ground for his belief that a woman was consenting to intercourse. The submission was roundly rejected. "Relevant" in that subsection means "*legally* relevant". W's drunkenness was not a matter that the jury were entitled to take into consideration in deciding whether or not reasonable grounds existed for W's belief that the woman consented to intercourse.

The question was considered again in *R. v. Fotheringham,* 88 Cr.App.R. 206, CA, in which the defendant was charged with rape. His defence was that he was so drunk at the time that he believed he was having intercourse with his wife. Applying *Majewski, Caldwell, Woods, ante,* and *R. v. O'Grady* [1987] Q.B. 995, 85 Cr.App.R. 315, CA (§ 17-16 in the main work), the court held that "in rape, self-induced intoxication is no defence, whether the issue be intention, consent or, as here, mistake as to the identity of the victim" (at p. 212).

(j) *Liability of accessories*

H-24   As to indicting accessories to rape, see *ante*, H-7; and as to their liability to conviction, notwithstanding the acquittal of the alleged principal, see *R. v. Cogan and Leak* [1976] Q.B. 217, 61 Cr.App.R. 217, CA (§ 20-26 in the main work).

(k) *Attempts*

H-25   See § 20-27 in the main work, and, in relation to the *mens rea* of an attempt, see *ante*, H-22.

(2) Procurement of intercourse by threats or false pretences

(a) *Statute*

Sexual Offences Act 1956, ss.2, 3

H-26   **2.**–(1) It is an offence for a person to procure a woman, by threats or intimidation, to have ... sexual intercourse in any part of the world.

(2) [*Repealed by CJPOA 1994, s.33(1).*]

[Subs. (1) is printed as repealed in part by the CJPOA 1994, s.168(1) and (3), and Scheds 9, para. 2, and 11.]

H-27   **3.**–(1) It is an offence for a person to procure a woman, by false pretences or false representations, to have ... sexual intercourse in any part of the world.

(2) [*Repealed by Criminal Justice and Public Order Act 1994, s.33(1).*]

[Subs. (1) is printed as repealed in part by the CJPOA 1994, s.168(1) and (3), and Scheds 9, para. 2, and 11.]

As to the meaning of "sexual intercourse", see *post*, H-219; as to the use of the word "woman", see *post*, H-222.

For anonymity provisions, see §§ 20-257 *et seq.* in the main work.

(b) *Indictment*

Statement of Offence

<table><tr><td>*Procuration, contrary to section 3(1) of the Sexual Offences Act 1956.*</td><td>**H-28**</td></tr></table>

Particulars of Offence

A B, on the ___ day of ___, 20_, procured J N, a woman, to have sexual intercourse with himself [or *with E F, as the case may be*] *by falsely pretending or representing to her that* [state in ordinary language the false pretence or representation].

The false pretences must be set out: *R. v. Field* (1892) 116 CCC Sess.Pap. 1891–1892, 757; but they need not be expressly negatived: *R. v. Clarke*, 59 J.P. 248.

An indictment for an offence contrary to section 2 may easily be framed from the above specimen.

(c) *Mode of trial and classification of offences*

The offence contrary to section 2 and an attempt to commit it are triable on indictment only: **H-29** SOA 1956, s.37(2), and Sched. 2, para. 7(a), (b).

The offence contrary to section 3 is triable on indictment only: SOA 1956, s.37(2), and Sched. 2, para. 8.

As to the classification of offences, see § 2-22c in the main work.

(d) *Alternative verdicts*

As to the possibility of a conviction of either of these offences on a charge of rape, see *ante*, **H-30** H-9.

(e) *Sentence*

Either offence, or an attempt to commit the offence contrary to section 2: imprisonment not **H-31** exceeding two years–SOA 1956, s.37(3), and Sched. 2, paras 7(a), (b), and 8.

(f) *Ingredients of the offences*

"Procure"

See *post*, H-171. **H-32**

False pretences

Seduction by a married man of a woman under promise of marriage by false representation **H-33** was held to be within section 3(2) of the Criminal Law Amendment Act 1885 (*rep.*), of which section 3(1) of the Act of 1956 was a replacement: *R. v. Williams*, 62 J.P. 310. It is immaterial whether the intercourse was procured with the defendant or with another: *ibid.*, and see *R. v. Jones* [1896] 1 Q.B. 4.

(3) Administering drugs to obtain or facilitate intercourse

(a) *Statute*

Sexual Offences Act 1956, s.4

4.–(1) It is an offence for a person to apply or administer to, or cause to be taken by, a woman any **H-34** drug, matter or thing with intent to stupefy or overpower her so as thereby to enable any man to have unlawful sexual intercourse with her.

(2) [*Repealed by Criminal Justice and Public Order Act 1994, s.33(1).*]

As to the meaning of "sexual intercourse", see *post*, H-219; as to the use of the words "man" and "woman", see *post*, H-222.

For anonymity provisions, see *post*, §§ 20-257 *et seq.* in the main work.

(b) *Mode of trial and class of offence*

H-35   This offence is triable only on indictment: SOA 1956, s.37(2), and Sched. 2, para. 9. As to the classification of offences, see § 2-22c in the main work.

(c) *Alternative verdicts*

H-36   As to the possibility of a conviction of this offence on a charge of rape, see *ante*, H-9.

(d) *Sentence*

H-37   Imprisonment not exceeding two years: SOA 1956, s.37(3), and Sched. 2, para. 9.

(e) *Ingredients of the offence*

H-38   "Unlawful" sexual intercourse means illicit sexual intercourse, *i.e.* outside the bond of marriage: *R. v. Chapman* [1959] 1 Q.B. 100, 42 Cr.App.R. 257, CCA (considering s.19 of the 1956 Act, *post*, H-148).

The essence of the offence is the administering of the drug. If there has been only one administration, there can be only one offence, even though the intention of the administration was to enable more than one man to have intercourse with the woman: *R. v. Shillingford and Vanderwall*, 52 Cr.App.R. 188, CA.

(4) Sexual intercourse with girl under 13

(a) *Statute*

Sexual Offences Act 1956, s.5

H-39   **5.** It is an offence for a man to have unlawful sexual intercourse with a girl under the age of thirteen.

[This section is printed as effectively amended by the CLA 1967, s.12(5)(a).]

As to the meaning of "sexual intercourse", see *post*, H-219; as to the use of the words "man" and "girl", see *post*, H-222.

For anonymity provisions, see §§ 20-257 *et seq.* in the main work.

(b) *Indictment*

Statement of Offence

H-40   *Sexual intercourse with a girl under 13, contrary to section 5 of the Sexual Offences Act 1956.*

Particulars of Offence

A B, on the ___ day of ___, 20_, had sexual intercourse with J N, a girl under the age of 13 years.

(c) *Mode of trial and classification of offences*

H-41   This offence and an attempt to commit it are triable only on indictment: SOA 1956, s.37(2), and Sched. 2, para. 2(a), (b). As to the classification of offences, see § 2-22c in the main work.

(d) *Alternative verdicts*

H-42   Indecent assault, contrary to section 14(1) of the 1956 Act (*post*, H-117): *R. v. McCormack* [1969] 2 Q.B. 442, 53 Cr.App.R. 514, CA. As to alternative verdicts generally, see §§ 4-524 *et seq.* in the main work.

(e) *Sentence*

The full offence: life imprisonment–SOA 1956, s.37(2), and Sched. 2, para. 2(a).   **H-43**

Attempt: imprisonment not exceeding seven years–*ibid.*, para. 2(b).

Custodial sentences are normally imposed, unless the offender is psychologically abnormal or of limited intelligence (see in particular *Att.-Gen.'s Reference (No. 20 of 1994)*, 16 Cr.App.R.(S.) 578, CA.). Some guidance may be obtained from the guideline of the Sentencing Council in relation to offences under the SOA 2003 (Appendix S-20); and for guidance as to how to sentence historic offences, see Appendix S-1053.

(f) *Ingredients of the offence*

Man

As to the abolition of the presumption that a boy under 14 is incapable of sexual intercourse,   **H-44**
see *ante*, H-13.

Consent immaterial

The evidence is the same as in rape, with the exception that it is immaterial whether the act   **H-45**
was done with or without the consent of the girl. If it was in fact without her consent, an indictment for rape will lie, notwithstanding the age of the child: *R. v. Dicken* (1877) 14 Cox 8; *R. v. Harling*, 26 Cr.App.R. 127, CCA; *R. v. Howard*, 50 Cr.App.R. 56, CCA, *ante*, H-15. So, where the defendant was indicted for an attempt to commit the offence, and the evidence was that he had attempted to have sexual intercourse with the girl, but that she had consented to the attempt, it was held that the fact of her consent was immaterial, and that the defendant was properly convicted: *R. v. Beale* (1865) L.R. 1 C.C.R. 10.

Knowledge of age immaterial

A mistake as to the age of the girl, even if based on reasonable grounds, will not avail a   **H-46**
defendant: *R. v. Prince* (1875) L.R. 2 C.C.R. 154 (*post*, H-161); *R. v. K.* [2002] 1 A.C. 462, HL; and see the specific defence provided by section 6(3) in relation to the less serious offence of intercourse with a girl under 16 (*post*, H-50).

(g) *Evidence*

Recent complaint

See § 20-12 in the main work.   **H-47**

Distress of victim

See § 20-13 in the main work.   **H-48**

Age

The provisions of section 99(2) of the CYPA 1933 (§ 19-412 in the main work), as to presump-   **H-49**
tion and determination of age do not apply: see the proviso to Schedule 1 to the 1933 Act (whilst the proviso was repealed by the SOA 2003 (see § 19-412 in the main work), its effect in relation to any prosecution for an offence under the 1956 Act will be saved by virtue of the Interpretation Act 1978, s.16 (*ante*, Appendix F-16)). The girl must be proved to have been under 13 years of age when the offence was committed. The best way of doing this is to produce a duly certified copy of the certificate of birth, coupled with evidence of identity; but the age may be proved by any other legal means: *R. v. Cox* [1898] 1 Q.B. 179 (age could be proved by persons who had seen the child and by a teacher at an elementary school which the child attended). Where a certificate of birth is put in, there must be evidence of identity as well: see *R. v. Nicholls* (1867) 10 Cox 476; *R. v. Bellis*, 6 Cr.App.R. 283, CCA; *R. v. Rogers*, 10 Cr.App.R. 276, CCA.

In the case of an adopted child, the date of birth may be proved by a certified copy of an entry in the Adopted Children Register: Adoption and Children Act 2002, s.77(5).

(5) Sexual intercourse with a girl under 16

(a) *Statute*

Sexual Offences Act 1956, s.6

H-50   **6.**–(1) It is an offence, subject to the exceptions mentioned in this section, for a man to have unlawful sexual intercourse with a girl ... under the age of sixteen.

(2) Where a marriage is invalid under section two of the Marriage Act 1949, or section one of the Age of Marriage Act 1929 (the wife being a girl under the age of sixteen), the invalidity does not make the husband guilty of an offence under this section because he has sexual intercourse with her, if he believes her to be his wife, and has reasonable cause for the belief.

(3) A man is not guilty of an offence under this section because he has unlawful sexual intercourse with a girl under the age of sixteen, if he is under the age of twenty-four and has not previously been charged with a like offence, and he believes her to be of the age of sixteen or over and has reasonable cause for the belief.

In this subsection "a like offence" means an offence under this section or an attempt to commit one, or an offence under paragraph (1) of section five of the Criminal Law Amendment Act 1885 (the provision replaced for England and Wales by this section).

[This section is printed as repealed in part by the CLA 1967, s.10(1), and Sched. 2, para. 14.]

As to the meaning of "sexual intercourse", see *post*, H-219; as to the use of the words "man" and "girl", see *post*, H-222.

As to the proof of exceptions, see the SOA 1956, s.47, *post*, H-225.

For anonymity provisions, see §§ 20-257 *et seq.* in the main work.

Marriage Act 1949, s.2

Marriages of persons under sixteen
H-51   **2.** A marriage solemnized between persons either of whom is under the age of sixteen shall be void.

(b) *Indictment*

Statement of Offence

H-52   *Sexual intercourse with a girl under 16, contrary to section 6(1) of the Sexual Offences Act 1956.*

Particulars of Offence

A B, on the ___ day of ___, 20_, had sexual intercourse with J N, a girl under the age of 16 years.

(c) *Mode of trial and classification of offences*

H-53   This offence and an attempt to commit it are triable either way: MCA 1980, s.17(1), and Sched. 1 (§ 1-125 in the main work). As to the classification of offences, see § 2-22c in the main work.

(d) *Alternative verdicts*

H-54   Indecent assault, contrary to section 14(1) of the 1956 Act (*post*, H-117): *R. v. McCormack* [1969] 2 Q.B. 442, 53 Cr.App.R. 514, CA. As to alternative verdicts generally, see §§ 4-524 *et seq.* in the main work.

(e) *Time limit on prosecutions*

H-55   Prosecutions for an offence under section 6 or an attempt to commit such offence may not be commenced more than 12 months after the offence charged: SOA 1956, s.37(2), and Sched. 2, para. 10(a), (b).

As to what is a commencement of the prosecution, see *R. v. West* [1898] 1 Q.B. 174; *R. v. Wakely* [1920] 1 K.B. 688, 14 Cr.App.R. 121, CCA.

In appropriate circumstances, evidence of prior offences by the defendant against the same girl committed outside the 12 months' time limit will be admissible: *R. v. Shellaker* [1914] 1 K.B. 414, 9 Cr.App.R. 240, CCA; *cf. R. v. Hewitt*, 19 Cr.App.R. 64, CCA; *R. v. Adams, The Times*, April 8, 1993, CA.

As to the impropriety of bringing a prosecution for indecent assault, based on an act of consensual sexual intercourse, where a prosecution under section 6 is time barred, see *R. v. J.*, *post*, H-118.

(f) *Sentence*

The full offence, or an attempt to commit it: imprisonment not exceeding two years' SOA 1956, **H-56** s.37(3), and Sched. 2, para. 10(a), (b). The penalty on summary conviction is governed by section 32 of the MCA 1980 (§ 1-119 in the main work).

In *R. v. Taylor*, 64 Cr.App.R. 182, CA, the court laid down guidelines for the sentencing of persons convicted of having unlawful sexual intercourse with a girl under the age of 16. Lawton L.J. distinguished between cases where "virtuous friendship" between young people of about the same age ended in sexual intercourse, and cases where a man in a supervisory capacity set out to seduce a girl under 16 who was in his charge. In the first type of case, sentences of a punitive nature were not required; in the second, sentences near the maximum of two years should be passed.

In *R. v. Bayliss* [2000] 1 Cr.App.R.(S.) 412, CA, it was said that attitudes to teenage prostitution had changed since *Taylor*, and that there was a greater appreciation that this offence and that of taking indecent photographs of children, contrary to the Protection of Children Act 1978 (§§ 31-107 *et seq.* in the main work), had been put on the statute book for the protection of children, including against themselves.

(g) *Ingredients of the offence*

Man

As to the abolition of the presumption that a boy under 14 is incapable of sexual intercourse, **H-57** see *ante*, H-13.

A girl under 16 cannot be indicted for "abetting" or "inciting" a man to have unlawful sexual intercourse with herself: *R. v. Tyrrell* [1894] 1 Q.B. 710.

As to doctors who prescribe contraceptive pills to girls under 16, see *Gillick v. West Norfolk and Wisbech Area Health Authority* [1986] A.C. 112, HL, *post*, H-196.

Consent immaterial

See *ante*, H-45, and *R. v. Ratcliffe* (1882) 10 Q.B.D. 74. **H-58**

"Unlawful" sexual intercourse

See *R. v. Chapman*, *ante*, H-38. **H-59**

(h) *Evidence*

Recent complaint

See § 20-12 in the main work. **H-60**

Distress of victim

See § 20-13 in the main work. **H-61**

Age

See *ante*, H-49, the contents of which apply, *mutatis mutandis*, to the offence under section 6. **H-62**

(i) *Defences*

In the case of a man under the age of 24, the presence of reasonable cause to believe that the **H-63** girl was over the age of 16 years is a valid defence provided that the defendant has not previously been charged with a like offence: SOA 1956, s.6(3) (*ante*, H-50). As to the meaning of the expression "a like offence", see *ibid.* The defence is not incompatible with Article 6 (right to fair trial (§

16-72 in the main work)) or 14 (prohibition on discrimination (§ 16-177 in the main work)) of the ECHR as being discriminatory on the grounds that, (a) a woman who had sexual intercourse with a boy under 16 would, if prosecuted, be charged with indecent assault, in relation to which she would have a defence, whatever her age, of genuine belief that the boy was 16 or more, and (b) it was restricted to men under the age of 24; as to (b), even though the choice of age was arbitrary, it did not introduce an element of disproportionality into the offence: *R. v. Kirk and Russell* [2002] Crim.L.R. 756, CA.

In *R. v. Rider*, 37 Cr.App.R. 209, Assizes, Streatfeild J. had to construe the wording of the Criminal Law Amendment Act 1922. The proviso to section 2 of that Act gave a man under 24 years of age a defence to a charge of unlawful sexual intercourse with a girl under 16 years of age if at the time of the intercourse he had reasonable cause to believe that the girl was over the age of 16; but the defence was only available "on the first occasion on which he is charged with" such an offence. It was held that "charged" in this context meant "appeared before a court with jurisdiction to deal with the matter". The defendant had been committed for trial on two separate occasions in respect of like allegations relating to different girls. Both allegations were joined in the same indictment and it was held that appearance before the assize was the first occasion on which he appeared before a court with jurisdiction to deal with the matter and, therefore, the defence was available in respect of both counts. Streatfeild J. said, however, that had the magistrates refused to commit for trial in respect of the first matter, the appearance at the assize on the second matter would have been the second occasion. This result seems illogical. It should be borne in mind that at the time of *Rider*, the offence in question could be tried only on indictment. It is now triable either way and it is respectfully submitted that the defence should only be available to a person who at the time of the alleged offence has not been before a court (magistrates' court, whether or not the matter is to be tried summarily, Crown Court or service court) on a charge of such an offence. This gives due effect to the actual decision in *Rider* to the revised formulation of the defence in the 1956 Act and to the changes in the legislation relating to mode of trial. It is also consistent with the rationale underlying the restriction on the defence, *viz.* that once the serious nature of such conduct has been brought to the attention of a man, he can legitimately be expected to be more careful about a girl's age.

To constitute a defence under this proviso, where it applies, the defendant must have reasonable cause to believe, and, in fact, must have believed that the girl was over the age of 16 years: *R. v. Banks* [1916] 2 K.B. 621, 12 Cr.App.R. 74, CCA; *R. v. Harrison*, 26 Cr.App.R. 166, CCA. The question of the existence of reasonable cause to believe is one for the jury: *R. v. Forde* [1923] 2 K.B. 400, 17 Cr.App.R. 99, CCA.

The defence is available not only where intercourse has taken place, but also where it has been merely attempted: *R. v. Collier* [1960] Crim.L.R. 204, Assizes (Streatfeild J.).

As to the burden of proof of the "exceptions" (defences) in subsections (2) and (3) of section 6, see section 47 of the 1956 Act, *post*, H-225.

(6) Intercourse with defectives

(a) *Statute*

Sexual Offences Act 1956, ss.7, 9

Intercourse with defective

H-64
    7.–(1) It is an offence, subject to the exception mentioned in this section, for a man to have unlawful sexual intercourse with a woman who is a defective.

    (2) A man is not guilty of an offence under this section because he has unlawful sexual intercourse with a woman if he does not know and has no reason to suspect her to be a defective.

[This section is printed as substituted by the MHA 1959, s.127(1)(a).]

Procurement of defective

H-65
    9.–(1) It is an offence, subject to the exception mentioned in this section, for a person to procure a woman who is a defective to have unlawful sexual intercourse in any part of the world.

    (2) A person is not guilty of an offence under this section because he procures a defective to have unlawful sexual intercourse, if he does not know and has no reason to suspect her to be a defective.

As to the meaning of "sexual intercourse", see *post*, H-219 as to the use of the words "man" and "woman", see *post*, H-222; as to the meaning of "defective", see *post*, H-68.

For anonymity provisions, see §§ 20-257 *et seq.* in the main work.

As to the burden of proof in relation to the exception in subsection (2) of both sections, see section 47 of the Act, *post*, H-225.

(b) *Mode of trial and classification of offences*

Offences against sections 7 and 9, and attempts to commit them, are triable only on indictment: **H-66**
SOA 1956, s.37(2), and Sched. 2, paras 11(a), (b), and 13(a), (b). As to the classification of offences, see § 2-22c in the main work.

(c) *Sentence*

Offences against sections 7 and 9, and attempts to commit them: imprisonment not exceeding **H-67**
two years–SOA 1956, s.37(3), and Sched. 2, paras 11(a), (b), and 13(a), (b). For an illustrative
example, see *R. v. Adcock* [2000] 1 Cr.App.R.(S.) 563, CA.

(d) *Ingredients of the offences*

"Defective"

Sexual Offences Act 1956, s.45

Meaning of defective

45. In this Act "defective" means a person suffering from a state of arrested or incomplete **H-68**
development of mind which includes severe impairment of intelligence and social functioning.

[This section is printed as substituted by the MHA 1959, s.127(1); and as amended by the
Mental Health (Amendment) Act 1982, Sched. 3.]

The words "severe impairment of intelligence and social functioning" are ordinary English
words and not words of art; they were inserted in the definition to protect women, if defectives,
from exploitation. Severe impairment is to be measured against the standards of normal persons:
R. v. Hall (J.H.), 86 Cr.App.R. 159, CA. The trial judge's direction that it was for them to decide
on all the evidence whether the victim was severely impaired within the ordinary meaning of
those words was correct.

"Unlawful" sexual intercourse

See *R. v. Chapman, ante*, H-38.　　　　　　　　　　　　　　　　　　　**H-69**

"Procure"

See *post*, H-171.　　　　　　　　　　　　　　　　　　　　　　　**H-70**

(7) Incest by a man

(a) *Statute*

Sexual Offences Act 1956, s.10

10.–(1) It is an offence for a man to have sexual intercourse with a woman whom he knows to be **H-71**
his grand-daughter, daughter, sister or mother.

(2) In the foregoing subsection "sister" includes half-sister and for the purposes of that subsection
any expression importing a relationship between two people shall be taken to apply notwithstanding
that the relationship is not traced through lawful wedlock.

As to the meaning of "sexual intercourse", see *post*, H-219; as to the use of the words "man"
and "woman", see *post*, § H-222.

For anonymity provisions, see §§ 20-257 *et seq.* in the main work.

(b) *Indictment*

Statement of Offence

H-72　　　　　　*Incest, contrary to section 10(1) of the Sexual Offences Act 1956.*

Particulars of Offence

A B, being a male person, on the ___ day of ___, 20_, had sexual intercourse with J N, whom he knew to be his daughter [if under the age of 13, add her age].

An indictment which charged the offence as having been committed "on divers days" between two specified dates was held to be bad for duplicity: *R. v. Thompson* [1914] 2 K.B. 99, 9 Cr.App.R. 252, CCA.

Where a brother and sister were charged in separate counts of the same indictment with committing incest and were tried separately, with the result that the brother was convicted and the sister acquitted, it was held that the acquittal of the sister did not make the conviction of the brother bad: *R. v. Gordon*, 19 Cr.App.R. 20, CCA. As to inconsistent verdicts generally, see §§ 7-70 *et seq.* in the main work.

(c) *Mode of trial and classification of offences*

H-73　　This offence, and an attempt to commit it, are triable only on indictment: SOA 1956, s.37(2), and Sched. 2, para. 14(a), (b). As to the classification of offences, see § 2-22c in the main work.

(d) *Alternative verdicts*

H-74　　On a charge of the full offence, unlawful sexual intercourse with a girl under 13 (s.5) or with a girl under 16 (s.6): SOA 1956, s.37(4), and Sched. 2, para. 14(a). Where the girl is under 16, indecent assault (whether or not the indictment avers her age): *R. v. Rogina*, 64 Cr.App.R. 79, CA. This possibility arises by virtue of the combination of section 37(5) (*post*, H-226) and the specific provision in Schedule 2 for a conviction of an offence under either section 5 or 6 (indecent assault being an alternative on an indictment charging either of those offences, *ante*, H-42, H-54).

(e) *Restriction on prosecution*

H-75　　A prosecution for this offence, or an attempt to commit it, may not be commenced except by or with the consent of the DPP: SOA 1956, s.37(2), and Sched. 2, para. 14(a), (b).

(f) *Sentence*

Maximum

H-76　　The full offence and an attempt to commit it: if with a girl under 13, and so charged in the indictment, life imprisonment, otherwise imprisonment not exceeding seven years– SOA 1956, s.37(3), and Sched. 2, para. 14(a), (b).

Basis of sentence

H-77　　See *R. v. Huchison*, 56 Cr.App.R. 307, CA.

Guidelines

H-78　　In *Att.-Gen.'s Reference (No. 1 of 1989)*, 90 Cr.App.R. 141, the Court of Appeal laid down guidelines for sentencing in cases of incest by a father against a daughter. The court made the following suggestions "as a broad guide" to the level of sentence for various categories of the crime of incest. All were on the assumption that there had been no plea of guilty. They should be read subject to *Practice Statement (Crime: Sentencing)* [1992] 1 W.L.R. 948. See, in particular, paragraph 10 thereof.

(i) *Girl aged over 16 years*

H-79　　A range from three years' imprisonment down to a nominal penalty would be appropriate depending in particular on the one hand whether force was used and the degree of harm if any, to the girl, and, on the other, the desirability where it existed of keeping family disruption to a minimum. The older the girl the greater the possibility that she might have been willing or even the instigating party, a factor which would be reflected in the sentence.

(ii) *Girl aged from 13 to 16 years*

A sentence between about five years' and three years' imprisonment would be appropriate.   **H-80** Much the same principles would apply as in the case of the girl over 16 years, though the likelihood of corruption increased in inverse proportion to the age of the girl.

(iii) *Girl aged under 13 years*

It was here that the widest range of sentences was likely to be found. If any case of incest could   **H-81** properly be described as the "ordinary" type of case, it would be one where the sexual relationship between husband and wife had broken down; the father had probably resorted to excessive drinking and the eldest daughter was gradually, by way of familiarities, indecent acts and suggestions made the object of the father's frustrated inclinations. If the girl was not far short of her thirteenth birthday and there were no particularly adverse or favourable features, a term of about six years' imprisonment would seem to be appropriate. The younger the girl when the sexual approach was started, the more likely it would be that the girl's will was overborne and, accordingly, the more serious would be the crime.

(iv) *Aggravating factors*

Whatever the age of the girl, the following, *inter alia*, would aggravate the offence: **H-82**
- (a) physical or psychological suffering from the offence;
- (b) the incest taking place at frequent intervals or over a long period;
- (c) the use of threats or violence, or the girl being otherwise terrified of her father;
- (d) the incest being accompanied by perversions abhorrent to the girl, such as buggery or *fellatio*;
- (e) the girl becoming pregnant; and
- (f) the commission of similar offences against more than one girl.

(v) *Mitigating features*

Possible mitigating features were, *inter alia*:   **H-83**
- (a) a plea of guilty;
- (b) genuine affection on the defendant's part rather than the intention to use the girl simply as an outlet for his sexual inclinations;
- (c) previous sexual experience by the girl; and
- (d) deliberate attempts at seduction by the girl.

In relation to a plea of guilty, the court said that such a plea was seldom not entered and it should be met by an appropriate discount, depending on the usual considerations, that is, how promptly the defendant confessed, the degree of contrition and so on. The court also said that occasionally a shorter term of imprisonment than would otherwise be imposed might be justified as being of benefit to the victim and the family.

For cases illustrating the application of these guidelines, see CSP B4-2. For cases of incest by a brother with a sister, see *ibid.*, B4-2.3D; for a case of incest by a mother with her young son, see *ibid.*, B4-2.3E.

(g) *Effect of adoption*

The prohibition contained in section 10(1) applies notwithstanding the adoption of one of the   **H-84** parties: Adoption and Children Act 2002, s.74(1)(b) (whilst this provision was amended to substitute a reference to sections 64 and 65 of the SOA 2003 for the references to sections 10 and 11 of the 1956 Act, its previous operation will be saved by virtue of section 16 of the Interpretation Act 1978 (*ante*, Appendix F-16)).

(h) *Ingredients of the offence*

If a man makes a genuine mistake as to the identity of the person with whom he has intercourse,   **H-85** he will not commit the offence: *R. v. Baillie-Smith*, 64 Cr.App.R. 76, CA (intercourse with daughter, thinking her to be his wife).

As to the abolition of the common law presumption that a boy under 14 is incapable of sexual intercourse, see *ante*, H-13.

(i) *Evidence*

H-86   The relationship between the parties may be proved by oral evidence or by certificates of marriage and birth, coupled with identification. An admission by the defendant that the person with whom the offence had been committed was his daughter may be sufficient evidence of the relationship: *R. v. Jones (Evan)*, 24 Cr.App.R. 55, CCA.

Evidence tending to show pre-existent sexual passion between the parties is admissible: *R. v. Ball* [1911] A.C. 47, HL.

The defendant was charged with incest with S, who was alleged to be his daughter. His defence was that he had no knowledge that S *was* his daughter. He desired to give evidence:

    (a) that he had been told by his first wife (the mother of S) that S had been begotten by another man and that he believed that statement to be true;

    (b) that he had told his second wife that he was not the father of S;

    (c) explaining statements which he had made on certain occasions acknowledging S to be his daughter.

It was held (on appeal) that this evidence was relevant to the issue whether the defendant *knew* that S was his daughter and that he was entitled to give any evidence relevant to that issue, including evidence of an admission by his first wife: *R. v. Carmichael* [1940] 1 K.B. 630, 27 Cr.App.R. 183, CCA.

(8) Incitement to incest of girls under 16

H-87   See the CLA 1977, s.54, *post*, H-239.

(9) Incest by a woman

(a) *Statute*

Sexual Offences Act 1956, s.11

H-88   **11.**–(1) It is an offence for a woman of the age of sixteen or over to permit a man whom she knows to be her grandfather, father, brother or son to have sexual intercourse with her by her consent.

    (2) In the foregoing subsection "brother" includes half-brother, and for the purposes of that subsection any expression importing a relationship between two people shall be taken to apply notwithstanding that the relationship is not traced through lawful wedlock.

As to the meaning of "sexual intercourse", see *post*, H-219; as to the use of the words "woman" and "man", see *post*, H-222.

For anonymity provisions, see §§ 20-257 *et seq.* in the main work.

(b) *Indictment*

Statement of Offence

H-89   *Incest, contrary to section 11(1) of the Sexual Offences Act 1956.*

Particulars of Offence

A B, being a female person of the age of 18, on the ___ day of ___, 20_, with her consent permitted J N, whom she knew to be her father, to have sexual intercourse with her.

As to the form of the indictment, see also *R. v. Thompson*, *ante*, H-72.

(c) *Mode of trial and classification of offences*

H-90   This offence, and an attempt to commit it, are triable only on indictment: SOA 1956, s.37(2), and Sched. 2, para. 15(a), (b). As to the classification of offences, see § 2-22c in the main work.

(d) *Restriction on prosecution*

A prosecution for this offence or an attempt to commit it may not be commenced except by or **H-91**
with the consent of the DPP: SOA 1956, s.37(2), and Sched. 2, para. 15(a), (b).

(e) *Sentence*

The full offence: imprisonment not exceeding seven years–SOA 1956, s.37(3), and Sched. 2, **H-92**
para. 15(a).
Attempt: imprisonment not exceeding two years–*ibid.*, para. 15(b).

(f) *Effect of adoption*

The prohibition contained in section 11(1) applies notwithstanding the adoption of one of the **H-93**
parties: Adoption and Children Act 2002, s.74(1)(b) (as to which, see *ante*, H-84).

(g) *Ingredients of offence*

The common law presumption as to incapacity in relation to boys under 14 years of age (*ante*, **H-94**
H-13) had no application where a woman was charged with committing incest with such a boy: *R.
v. Pickford* [1995] 1 Cr.App.R. 420, CA.

(10) Buggery

(a) *Introduction*

The SOA 1956 contains two "unnatural offences", namely buggery (with a person or with an **H-95**
animal) and gross indecency between men. There are time limits and requirements as to the
consent of the DPP in respect of both offences in certain circumstances.

The SOA 1967 amended the law by providing, in particular, that consenting men over the age
of 21 (reduced to 18 by the CJPOA 1994, and to 16 by the Sexual Offences (Amendment) Act
2000) who commit buggery or gross indecency in private, do not commit an offence (s.1, *post*,
H-97). There are different rules regarding the lawfulness of procuration of buggery and gross
indecency (s.4, *post*, H-236). Section 11(3) provides that section 46 of the 1956 Act (use of words
"man", "boy" and other expressions) shall apply for the purposes of the provisions of the 1967
Act as it applies for the purposes of the provisions of that Act. For section 46, see *post*, H-222.

The CJPOA 1994 effected further changes in the law. Apart from reducing the age of consent
for homosexual acts to 18 (*ante*), it redefined the offence of rape to include non-consensual anal
intercourse with a man or a woman (*ante*, H-3). Non-consensual buggery should, therefore, be
charged as rape. Consensual buggery between two people will not be an offence if the act takes
place in private and both parties have achieved the age of 16.

As to the offences of indecent assault on a man and assault with intent to commit buggery,
which may be on a man or a woman (categorised in the 1956 Act as "assault" offences rather than
as "unnatural offences"), see sections 15, *post*, H-127, and 16, *post*, H-138.

(b) *Statute*

Sexual Offences Act 1956, s.12

12.–(1) It is an offence for a person to commit buggery with another person otherwise than in the **H-96**
circumstances first described in subsection (1A) or (1AA) below or with an animal.

(1A) The circumstances referred to in subsection (1) are that the act of buggery takes place in
private and both parties have attained the age of sixteen.

(1AA) The other circumstances so referred to are that the person is under the age of sixteen and
the other person has attained that age.

(1B) An act of buggery by one man with another shall not be treated as taking place in private if it
takes place—

(a) when more than two persons take part or are present; or
(b) in a lavatory to which the public have or are permitted to have access, whether on payment
or otherwise.

(1C) In any proceedings against a person for buggery with another person it shall be for the prosecutor to prove that the act of buggery took place otherwise than in private or that one of the parties to it had not attained the age of sixteen.

(2), (3) [*Repealed by Police and Criminal Evidence Act 1984, Sched. 7.*]

[Subs. (1) is printed as amended by the CLA 1967, s.12(5)(a); the CJPOA 1994, s.143(1), (2); and the Sexual Offences (Amendment) Act 2000, s.2(1)(a) and (b); subss. (1A), (1B) and (1C) were inserted by the 1994 Act, s.143(1), (3); and are printed as amended by the 2000 Act, s.1(1); subs. (1AA) was inserted by the 2000 Act, s.2(1)(c).]

For anonymity provisions, see §§ 20-257 *et seq.* in the main work.

As to conspiracy or incitement to commit this offence, see *R. v. Boulton* (1871) 12 Cox 87.

Sexual Offences Act 1967, s.1

Amendment of law relating to homosexual acts in private

H-97   **1.**–(1) Notwithstanding any statutory or common law provision, ...

(a) a homosexual act in private shall not be an offence provided that the parties consent thereto and have attained the age of sixteen years; and

(b) a homosexual act by any person shall not be an offence if he is under the age of sixteen and the other party has attained that age.

(2) An act which would otherwise be treated for the purposes of this Act as being done in private shall not be so treated if done—

(a) when more than two persons take part or are present; or

(b) in a lavatory to which the public have or are permitted to have access, whether on payment or otherwise.

(3) A man who is suffering from severe mental handicap cannot in law give any consent which, by virtue of subsection (1) of this section, would prevent a homosexual act from being an offence, but a person shall not be convicted, on account of the incapacity of such a man to consent, of an offence consisting of such an act if he proves that he did not know and had no reason to suspect that man to be suffering from severe mental handicap.

(3A) In subsection (3) of this section "severe mental handicap" means a state of arrested or incomplete development of mind which includes severe impairment of intelligence and social functioning.

(4) Section 128 of the Mental Health Act 1959 (prohibition on men on the staff of a hospital, or otherwise having responsibility for mental patients, having sexual intercourse with women patients) shall have effect as if any reference therein to having unlawful sexual intercourse with a woman included a reference to committing buggery or an act of gross indecency with another man.

(5) [*Repealed by CJPOA 1994, s.168(3) and Sched. 11.*]

(6) It is hereby declared that where in any proceedings it is charged that a homosexual act is an offence the prosecutor shall have the burden of proving that the act was done otherwise than in private or otherwise than with the consent of the parties or that any of the parties had not attained the age of sixteen years.

(7) For the purposes of this section a man shall be treated as doing a homosexual act if, and only if, he commits buggery with another man or commits an act of gross indecency with another man or is a party to the commission by a man of such an act.

[This section is printed as amended and repealed in part by the Mental Health (Amendment) Act 1982, s.65(1), (2), and Scheds 3, para. 34, and 4; the CJPOA 1994, ss.146(1) and 168(3), and Sched. 11; and the Sexual Offences (Amendment) Act 2000, ss.1(2)(a) and 2(3)(a) and (b).]

As to the use of the word "man", see *post*, H-222.

For section 128 of the MHA 1959, see *post*, H-228.

(c) *Indictment for buggery with a person*

Statement of Offence

H-98   *Buggery, contrary to section 12(1) of the Sexual Offences Act 1956.*

Particulars of Offence

A B, a person of [or over] the age of 21 years, on the ___ day of ___, 20_, committed buggery with J N, a person under the age of 18 years.

Because the penalty provisions have the effect of creating a number of separate offences (see *post*, H-103), the particulars should be clear as to which offence is alleged; in the specimen set out above, it is a five year offence that is alleged. Alternative counts may be laid, where appropriate: see *R. v. Reakes* [1974] Crim.L.R. 615, CA.

As to the correct practice where old offences are charged, see *R. v. R.* [1993] Crim.L.R. 541, CA; *R. v. B.*, *ibid.* As to the need for special caution where extremely old offences are alleged, *i.e.* dating back to the period prior to the passing of the SOA 1967 (July 27, 1967), see *R. v. D.* [1993] Crim.L.R. 542, CA.

As to the particulars which need to be averred on a charge of attempted buggery, see *R. v. D.*, *ante.* The principles are the same as for the full offence.

(d) *Indictment for buggery with an animal (bestiality)*

Statement of Offence

Buggery, contrary to section 12(1) of the Sexual Offences Act 1956. **H-99**

Particulars of Offence

A B, a person of [or over] the age of 21 years, on the ___ day of ___, 20_, committed buggery with a cow [or as the case may be].

(e) *Mode of trial and classification of offences*

This offence, and an attempt to commit it, are triable only on indictment: SOA 1956, s.37(2), **H-100** and Sched. 2, para. 3(a), (b). As to the classification of offences, see § 2-22c in the main work.

(f) *Time limits*

Sexual Offences Act 1967, s.7

7.–(1) No proceedings for an offence to which this section applies shall be commenced after the **H-101** expiration of twelve months from the date on which that offence was committed.

(2) This section applies to—

    (a) any offence under section 13 of the Act of 1956 (gross indecency between men);

    (b) [*repealed by Criminal Law Act 1977, Sched. 13*];

    (c) any offence of buggery by a man with another man not amounting to an assault on that other man and not being an offence by a man with a boy under the age of 16.

For section 13 of the 1956 Act, see *post,* H-107.

Where it was unclear upon the evidence given at the trial whether the offence charged had been committed within the 12 month period prior to the commencement of proceedings for the offence, the court quashed the conviction: *R. v. Lewis,* 68 Cr.App.R. 310, CA. A judge need not in every case to which section 7(1) applies direct the jury that they must be sure the offence was committed within the prescribed period. However, he must do so where an issue under the subsection is raised by the defence, or where it clearly arises on the evidence given at the trial: *ibid.*

(g) *Restriction on prosecutions*

Sexual Offences Act 1967, s.8

8. No proceedings shall be instituted except by or with the consent of the Director of Public **H-102** Prosecutions against any man for the offence of buggery with, or gross indecency with, another man ... or for aiding, abetting, counselling, procuring or commanding its commission where either of those men was at the time of its commission under the age of sixteen.

[This section is printed as amended by the Sexual Offences (Amendment) Act 2000, s.1(2)(b); and as repealed in part by the Criminal Jurisdiction Act 1975, s.14(5), and Sched. 6, Pt I; and the Criminal Attempts Act 1981, s.10, and Sched., Pt I.]

Failure to obtain the consent of the DPP will lead to the quashing of the conviction: *R. v. Angel,* 52 Cr.App.R. 280, CA; *Secretary of State for Defence v. Warn* [1970] A.C. 394, HL (proceedings before court-martial).

Section 8 does not apply to proceedings under the Indecency with Children Act 1960 (*post,* H-230): CJA 1972, s.48.

(h) *Sentence*

Maximum

H-103   The full offence, or an attempt to commit it: if with a person under the age of 16 or with an animal, life imprisonment; if the accused is of or over the age of 21 and the other person is under the age of 18, imprisonment not exceeding five years; otherwise, imprisonment not exceeding two years—SOA 1956, s.37(3), and Sched. 2, para. 3(a), (b) (as substituted by the CJPOA 1994, s.144(1), (2)). (For an offence of non-consensual buggery with a male over 15 committed before the commencement of the amendments effected by the 1994 Act (November 3, 1994), the maximum remains at 10 years: *Att.-Gen.'s Reference (No. 48 of 1994) (R. v. Jeffrey)*, 16 Cr.App.R.(S.) 980, CA.)

The effect of the different penalty provisions is to create distinct offences: see *R. v. Courtie* [1984] A.C. 463, HL.

Absence of consent not being an ingredient of the offence, it is not open to a judge to sentence on the basis that there was lack of consent; if lack of consent is alleged, there should be a charge of rape: *R. v. Davies* [1998] 1 Cr.App.R.(S.) 380, CA; *R. v. D. (Anthony)* [2000] 1 Cr.App.R.(S.) 120, CA.

Guidelines

H-104   The bracket of sentencing in cases of homosexual offences against boys with neither aggravating nor mitigating factors was set out in *R. v. Willis*, 60 Cr.App.R. 146, CA, as being from three to five years. The court in that case also identified the principal aggravating and mitigating features. In *R. v. A. and W.* [2001] 2 Cr.App.R. 18, CA, the court specifically said that the guidelines in *Willis* remained the starting point. In *R. v. Patterson* [2006] 2 Cr.App.R.(S.) 48, however, the Court of Appeal said that sentences in historic cases of buggery should now be determined as if the offence were one of rape in accordance with the guidelines in *R. v. Millberry; R. v. Morgan; R. v. Lackenby* [2003] 1 Cr.App.R. 25, CA, instead of by reference to the *Willis* guidelines. The court said that it is important that the sentence should reflect the gravity of the offence rather than the particular label attached to it, and since there is no distinction in principle or in essential gravity made in the *Millberry* guidelines between rape of a male and rape of a female, it would be wrong for a sentence of buggery to be imposed on any other basis. This approach was taken further in *R. v. Kearns* [2009] 1 Cr.App.R.(S.) 107, CA, where it was applied to what was apparently a case of consensual buggery of a 15-year-old boy. For criticism of the *Patterson/Kearns* approach, see the commentaries at CLW/06/34/24 and CLW/09/16/8. Whilst this criticism remains valid, sentencers dealing with historic offending should now be guided, as to general principles, by the judgment of the Court of Appeal in *R. v. Forbes* [2016] 2 Cr.App.R.(S.) 44 (as to which, see Appendix S-1053).

(i) *Ingredients of the offence*

H-105   The definition of the offence derives from the common law. It consists of sexual intercourse (*per anum—R. v. Jacobs* (1817) R. & R. 331) by man with man or, in the same manner, by man with woman (*R. v. Wiseman* (1718) Fortescue K.B. 91; Fost. 91), or by man or woman in any manner (*R. v. Bourne*, 36 Cr.App.R. 125, CCA) with beast (also referred to as bestiality): see 1 Hale 669; 1 Hawk. c. 4; 1 East P.C. 480; 1 Russ. Cr., 12th ed., 735. Once penetration is proved, both parties (if consenting) are equally guilty.

Penetration, without emission, is sufficient: *R. v. Reekspear* (1832) 1 Mood. 342.

As to the abolition of the common law presumption that a boy under 14 is incapable of sexual intercourse, see *ante*, H-13.

The offence of bestiality does not depend on consent but on the commission of a particular act: *R. v. Bourne, ante* (defendant convicted of aiding and abetting his wife to commit buggery with a dog, it being assumed that she would have been entitled to an acquittal on the ground of duress).

The following direction on the question of privacy (1967 Act, s.1, *ante*) has been approved by the Court of Appeal: "you look at all the circumstances, the time of night, the nature of the place including such matters as lighting and you consider further the likelihood of a third person coming upon the scene": *R. v. Reakes* [1974] Crim.L.R. 615.

In relation to subsection (3A) of section 1 of the 1967 Act, it is open to the prosecution to prove severe mental handicap without calling medical evidence but by inviting the jury to observe the behaviour and reactions of the complainant and to draw what they consider to be an appropriate inference: *R. v. Robbins* [1988] Crim.L.R. 744, CA.

(j) *Evidence*

The rule as to the admissibility of recent complaints was held to apply in the case of buggery **H-106** with a youth of 19: *R. v. Wannell,* 17 Cr.App.R. 53, CCA.

(11) Gross indecency

(a) *Statute*

Sexual Offences Act 1956, s.13

13. It is an offence for a man to commit an act of gross indecency with another man otherwise **H-107** than in the circumstances described below, whether in public or private, or to be a party to the commission by a man of an act of gross indecency with another man, or to procure the commission by a man of an act of gross indecency with another man.

The circumstances referred to above are that the man is under the age of sixteen and the other man has attained that age.

[This section is printed as amended by the Sexual Offences (Amendment) Act 2000, s.2(2)(a) and (b).]

Gross indecency is no longer an offence where the act takes place in private and both parties consent thereto and both have attained the age of 16: see SOA 1967, s.1 (as amended by the Sexual Offences (Amendment) Act 2000, s.1(2)(a)), *ante,* H-97.

Furthermore, it is not an offence under this section for a man to procure the commission by another man of an act of gross indecency with himself which by reason of section 1 of the 1967 Act is not an offence under this section: see section 4(3) of the 1967 Act, *post,* H-236. As to procuration of gross indecency, see further H-113, *post.*

As to the use of the word "man", see *post,* H-222.

(b) *Indictment*

Statement of Offence

Gross indecency, contrary to section 13 of the Sexual Offences Act 1956. **H-108**

Particulars of Offence

A B, on the ___ day of ___, 20_, being a male person, committed an act of gross indecency with J N, a male person otherwise than in private [or *with J N, a male person under the age of 16 years, namely, of the age of ___ years*].

(c) *Mode of trial and classification of offences*

Offences contrary to section 13, and an attempt to procure the commission by a man of an act **H-109** of gross indecency with another man, are triable either way: MCA 1980, s.17(1), and Sched. 1 (§ 1-125 in the main work). As to the classification of offences, see § 2-22c in the main work.

(d) *Time limits and restrictions on prosecutions*

See *ante,* H-101, H-102. **H-110**

(e) *Sentence*

Offences contrary to section 13: if by a man of or over the age of 21 with a man under the age **H-111** of 16, imprisonment not exceeding five years, otherwise two years—SOA 1956, s.37(3), and Sched. 2, para. 16(a) (as amended by the CJPOA 1994, s.144(1), (3), and the Sexual Offences (Amendment) Act 2000, s.1(1)).

An attempt to procure the commission by a man of an act of gross indecency with another man: as for the full offences—SOA 1956, s.37(3), and Sched. 2, para. 16(b) (as amended by the CJPOA 1994, s.144(1), (3), and the Sexual Offences (Amendment) Act 2000, s.1(1)).

Penalties on summary conviction are provided for by the MCA 1980, s.32 (§ 1-119 in the main work).

An attempt to commit any other offence than the one specifically provided for by the 1956 Act will be punishable in accordance with the Criminal Attempts Act 1981, ss.1 and 4 (§§ 33-128 *et seq.* in the main work).

(f) *Ingredients of the offences*

Gross indecency

H-112   If there is an agreement whereby two male persons act in concert to behave in a grossly indecent manner, as, for example, to make a grossly indecent exhibition, the offence is committed even though there has been no actual physical contact: *R. v. Hunt*, 34 Cr.App.R. 135, CCA.

An offence of indecency between men is not committed unless both men participate in the indecency. "With another man" in section 13 cannot be construed as meaning "against" or "directed towards" a person who did not consent: *R. v. Preece and Howells* [1977] Q.B. 370, 63 Cr.App.R. 28, CA, and see *R. v. Hornby and Peaple*, 32 Cr.App.R. 1, CCA, and *R. v. Hunt, ante*.

Where two persons are jointly indicted for an offence under the section, one may be convicted and the other acquitted: *R. v. Jones* [1896] 1 Q.B. 4; *R. v. Pearce*, 35 Cr.App.R. 17, CCA; but see *R. v. Batten, The Times,* March 16, 1990, CA, where two men were charged with committing an act of gross indecency with each other. The jury convicted one defendant, but failed to agree in respect of the other and were discharged. The Court of Appeal quashed the conviction: the issue was the same in the case of both men and it was not a case where there was some evidence such as a confession, implicating one man but not the other. If both are to be convicted, it is important that the jury should be directed that, to establish the offence, it must be proved that there was an act of gross indecency by the one defendant with the other and that the two defendants were acting in concert: *R. v. Hornby and Peaple, ante*.

A conviction for attempting to commit an act of gross indecency may be maintained where one of the persons implicated alone has been charged and the other has not been charged but has been called as a witness for the prosecution and swears that he did not consent to any act of indecency: *R. v. Pearce, ante*.

Procuring gross indecency

H-113   It is an offence within section 13 for a male person to procure the commission with himself of an act of gross indecency by another male person: *R. v. Jones, ante; R. v. Cope*, 16 Cr.App.R. 77, CCA. But, if the act itself is not an offence by virtue of section 1 of the SOA 1967, the procuration thereof will not be an offence either: *ibid.*, s.4(3). See *ante*, H-97, and *post*, H-236.

If a male person persuades, or attempts to persuade, a boy to handle him indecently, such person alone may be charged and convicted under this section. In a case where indecent assault may be difficult or impossible to prove, because no threat or hostile act by the defendant towards the boy can easily be established, the proper charge is that of procuring or attempting to procure (as the case may be) an act of gross indecency with the defendant himself: *R. v. Burrows*, 35 Cr.App.R. 180, CCA.

On a charge of incitement to procure an act of gross indecency, it is not necessary that there should be, at the time of the incitement, an ascertained person with whom the act was to be committed: *R. v. Bentley* [1923] 1 K.B. 403, CCA.

As to the meaning of "procure", see also *post*, H-171.

Attempting to procure an act of gross indecency

H-114   Procuring the commission of an act of gross indecency under section 13 of the 1956 Act is itself a substantive offence. Section 1(4)(b) of the Criminal Attempts Act 1981 (§ 33-128 in the main work) does not preclude the charging of an attempt to procure an act of gross indecency under section 1(1) of the 1981 Act because section 1(4)(b) applies in circumstances when the alleged procurement is additional to and not part of the substantive offence: *Chief Constable of*

Hampshire v. Mace, 84 Cr.App.R. 40, DC. (The penalty for such attempt is specifically provided for by the 1956 Act: see *ante*, H-111.)

What conduct will be sufficient to constitute an attempt will depend on the application of the formula in section 1(1) of the 1981 Act: was what was done "more than merely preparatory to the commission of the offence"?

Authorities decided prior to the 1981 Act can be no more than illustrative: see *R. v. Cope, ante; R. v. Woods*, 22 Cr.App.R. 41, CCA; *R. v. Miskell*, 37 Cr.App.R. 214, Ct-MAC.

(g) *Evidence*

Guilty plea by one defendant

See *R. v. Mattison* [1990] Crim.L.R. 117, CA (§ 9-90 in the main work). **H-115**

Recent complaint

The rule as to admissibility of recent complaints was held not to apply to this offence on the **H-116** ground that consent of the other male person is immaterial: *R. v. Hoodless*, 64 J.P. 282.

(12) Indecent assault on a woman

(a) *Statute*

Sexual Offences Act 1956, s.14

Indecent assault on a woman
14.–(1) It is an offence, subject to the exception mentioned in subsection (3) of this section, for a **H-117** person to make an indecent assault on a woman.

(2) A girl under the age of sixteen cannot in law give any consent which would prevent an act being an assault for the purposes of this section.

(3) Where a marriage is invalid under section two of the Marriage Act 1949, or section one of the Age of Marriage Act 1929 (the wife being a girl under the age of sixteen), the invalidity does not make the husband guilty of any offence under this section by reason of her incapacity to consent while under that age, if he believes her to be his wife and has reasonable cause for the belief.

(4) A woman who is a defective cannot in law give any consent which would prevent an act being an assault for the purposes of this section, but a person is only to be treated as guilty of an indecent assault on a defective by reason of that incapacity to consent, if that person knew or had reason to suspect her to be a defective.

As to the use of the words "woman" and "girl", see *post*, H-222.

As to the meaning of "defective", see *ante*, H-68.

For the Marriage Act 1949, s.2, see *ante*, H-51.

For the burden of proof of exceptions, see section 47 of the 1956 Act, *post*, H-225.

For anonymity provisions, see *post*, §§ 20-257 *et seq.* in the main work.

(b) *Indictment*

Statement of Offence

Indecent assault, contrary to section 14(1) of the Sexual Offences Act 1956. **H-118**

Particulars of Offence

A B, on the ___ day of ___, 20_, indecently assaulted J N, a woman.

Age is not an essential ingredient of, nor an essential averment in, the framing of a count under section 14(1): *R. v. Hodgson* [1973] Q.B. 565, 57 Cr.App.R. 502, CA. As to the need, however, to specify the age of the girl in certain old cases, see *post*, H-120.

Where the prosecution case leaves it open to the jury to convict on either of two distinct factual bases, it will be necessary for the judge to direct them as to the need for unanimity as to the basis of any verdict of guilty: see *R. v. Turner* [2000] Crim.L.R. 325, CA, and *R. v. D.* [2001] 1 Cr.App.R. 13, CA.

In *R. v. J.* [2005] 1 A.C. 562, HL, it was held that, on a true construction of the SOA 1956, it is impermissible to prosecute a charge of indecent assault under section 14(1) in circumstances where the only conduct upon which that charge was based was an act of unlawful sexual intercourse with a girl under the age of 16 in respect of which no prosecution might be commenced under section 6(1) (*ante*, H-50) by virtue of the time bar of 12 months contained in section 37(2) of, and Schedule 2, para. 10, to, the Act (as to which, see *ante*, H-55). Their Lordships held that the court was under a duty to give effect to a statute which was plain and unambiguous; it must have been intended that the prohibition in paragraph 10 would have some meaningful effect, otherwise there would have been no possible purpose in prohibiting prosecution under section 6 after a lapse of 12 months if exactly the same conduct could thereafter be prosecuted, with exposure to the same penalty (at the time of enactment), under section 14; but this did not prevent a prosecution being properly founded on independent acts other than sexual intercourse itself or conduct inherent in or forming part of it. As to the effect of this decision in relation to indecent assault as a possible alternative verdict on a charge of rape, see the cases cited at H-9, *ante*.

(c) *Mode of trial and class of offence*

H-119   This offence is triable either way: MCA 1980, s.17(1), and Sched. 1 (§ 1-125 in the main work). As to the classification of offences, see § 2-22c in the main work.

(d) *Sentence*

H-120   Imprisonment, not exceeding 10 years: SOA 1956, s.37, and Sched. 2, para. 17 (as amended by the SOA 1985, s.3(3)). The 1985 amendment took effect on September 16, 1985: prior to that, the maximum penalty was two years' imprisonment, save where the girl was under 13 and was so stated in the indictment, in which case the maximum was five years' imprisonment. In relation to cases where the facts date back beyond September 16, 1985, see *R. v. R.* [1993] Crim.L.R. 541, CA; *R. v. B.*, *ibid.*

Where a defendant charged with rape of a girl under 16 is acquitted of rape, but convicted of indecent assault on the basis that consent is no defence, the sentence should not exceed the maximum for an offence of unlawful sexual intercourse with a girl under 16 (as to which, see *ante*, H-56): *R. v. Iles* [1998] 2 Cr.App.R.(S.) 63, CA.

The fact that the victim had been abused on a previous occasion does not reduce, but might increase, the gravity of further offending by an adult thereafter. If, however, by reason of being corrupted or precocious, or both, the victim instigated offences against herself, that was an aspect which the judge was entitled to take into account. But it was mitigation only in a negative sense, namely that the child was not being treated in a way which she was personally resisting or found repugnant: *Att.-Gen.'s Reference (No. 36 of 1995) (R. v. Dawson)* [1996] 2 Cr.App.R.(S.) 50, CA.

There is no sentencing principle which precludes the imposition of a custodial sentence on a first conviction of a persistent indecent assault (on a female on an underground train): *R. v. Townsend*, 16 Cr.App.R.(S.) 553, CA, *R. v. Tanyildiz* [1998] 1 Cr.App.R.(S.) 362, CA, and *R. v. Diallo* [2000] 1 Cr.App.R.(S.) 426, CA (not following *R. v. Neem*, 14 Cr.App.R.(S.) 18, CA).

Cases decided prior to the increase in the statutory maximum effected by the SOA 1985 could not be regarded as authoritative in relation to the tariff after the increase; the conclusion in *R. v. Demel* [1997] 2 Cr.App.R.(S.) 5, CA, that the upper end of the tariff for a single incident involving a breach of trust following a trial was in the range of 13 to 18 months' imprisonment should not be followed as the authorities relied on were decided in relation to a different statutory framework or had been decided without apparent appreciation of the effect of the 1985 Act: *R. v. L.* [1999] 1 Cr.App.R. 117, CA (two years' imprisonment following trial for "grave" breach of trust by 52-year-old man on nine-year-old girl upheld; declining to issue guidelines, but observing that in most cases the personal circumstances of the offender would have to take second place to the duty of the court to protect victims). See also *R. v. Wellman* [1999] 2 Cr.App.R.(S.) 162, CA.

For cases of indecent assault, see CSP B4-6.

As to the non-applicability of the Sentencing Guidelines Council's guideline on sexual offences to offences under the 1956 Act, see *Att.-Gen.'s Reference (No. 78 of 2010)* [2011] 2 Cr.App.R.(S.) 109, CA (pointing out that offences under the SOA 2003 are differently defined and have different (more severe) maximum penalties); but see Appendix S-1053 as to the approach to sentencing for historic offences generally.

In *R. v. Clifford* [2015] 1 Cr.App.R.(S.) 32, CA, the appellant (71/ no convictions) was convicted on eight counts of indecent assault, contrary to section 14(1) of the 1956 Act, in respect of four victims, in relation to offences committed between 1977 and 1984 when the statutory maximum was two years' imprisonment. It was held (considering *R. v. H.*, *ante*, H-12) that the judge had been entitled in the course of his sentencing remarks to observe that some of the offending would now be charged as rape or assault by penetration, and had been entitled to impose consecutive sentences to reflect the overall criminality involved according to modern standards and attitudes (as reflected in the Sentencing Council for England and Wales's guideline on sexual offences (Appendix S-20)). However, the judge had been wrong to take into account when passing sentence the appellant's assertions of innocence (which did not directly impugn the victims (by way of distinction from *Att.-Gen.'s Reference (No. 38 of 2013) (R. v. Hall)* [2014] 1 Cr.App.R.(S.) 61, CA)), his vehement complaints about the fact that the victims were entitled to anonymity, and the fact that he had stood behind a television reporter on camera outside the court, mimicking the reporter's actions (where there was no evidence that the victims were aware of this conduct and the matter had not been dealt with as a contempt of court).

(e) *Ingredients of the offence*

General

For a full exposition of the elements of the offence, see *R. v. Court* [1989] A.C. 28, HL. **H-121**

  (a) Most indecent assaults will be clearly of a sexual nature. Some may have only sexual undertones. The jury must decide whether "right-minded persons would consider the conduct indecent or not". The test is whether what occurred was so offensive to contemporary standards of modesty and privacy as to be indecent.

  (b) If the circumstances of the assault are *incapable* of being regarded as indecent, then the undisclosed intention of the accused could not make the assault an indecent one: see *R. v. George* [1956] Crim.L.R. 52, Assizes (Streatfeild J.).

  (c) The victim need not be aware of the circumstances of indecency or apprehended indecency.

  (d) Cases which ordinarily present no problem are those in which the facts, *devoid of explanation*, will give rise to the irresistible inference that the defendant intended to assault his victim in a manner which right-minded persons would clearly think was indecent. Where the circumstances are such as only to be *capable* of constituting an indecent assault, in order to determine whether or not right-minded persons might think that the assault was indecent the following factors are relevant:

    (i) the relationship of the defendant to the victim (relative, friend, stranger);

    (ii) how the defendant had come to embark on this conduct and why he was so behaving. Such information helps a jury to answer the vital question: are we sure that the defendant not only intended to commit an assault but an assault which was indecent? Any evidence which tends to explain the reason for the defendant's conduct is relevant to establish whether or not he intended to commit not only an assault but an indecent one.

  (e) The prosecution must prove: (i) that the accused intentionally assaulted the victim; (ii) that the assault, or the assault and the circumstances accompanying it, are capable of being considered by right-minded persons as indecent; and (iii) that the accused intended to commit such an assault as is referred to in (ii) above.

The above propositions are founded upon Lord Ackner's speech (at p.36), with which the other members of the House concurred, except Lord Goff, who dissented from the decision. It follows that no offence will be committed where the man believes that the woman is consenting to his conduct, whether his belief is based on reasonable grounds or not: this was the effect of the earlier Court of Appeal decision in *R. v. Kimber*, 77 Cr.App.R. 225.

R. v. Court was considered in *R. v. C.* [1992] Crim.L.R. 642, CA, in which it was held that where an assault was indecent in itself, it was unnecessary to establish a specific indecent intent. In *Court*, the issue of whether or not what had occurred amounted to an indecent assault turned on motive and, therefore, specific intent had been necessary to the verdict. Where there was no question whether what had occurred was indecent or not, the basic intent of assault was sufficient. The law before *Court* remained the law and indecent assault remained an offence of basic intent;

self-induced voluntary intoxication is not a defence. See also *DPP v. H.* [1992] C.O.D. 266, an earlier decision of the Divisional Court to the same effect.

Court and *George, ante,* were referred to in *R. v. Price* [2004] 1 Cr.App.R. 12, CA, in which it was held that stroking a woman's legs over trousers and below the knee was capable of amounting to an indecent assault.

In *R. v. Kumar* (2006) 150 S.J. 1053, CA, it was said that whilst *Court* was authority for the proposition that a doctor who obtained sexual satisfaction from a necessary medical examination properly conducted was not guilty of indecent assault where the prosecution case was limited to an allegation that he had carried out a medical examination in appropriate circumstances but in an inappropriate way and as a cloak for his own sexual gratification, where the issue had been as to the manner in which the defendant had carried out the examination (*i.e.* in an appropriate way in the presence of a chaperon or in an inappropriate way in the absence of a chaperon), there had been no need to direct the jury as to the remote theoretical possibility suggested in *Court.*

Person

H-122   A woman may be guilty of an offence under this section: *R. v. Hare* [1934] 1 K.B. 354, 24 Cr.App.R. 108, CCA.

Assault

H-123   As to this, see generally, §§ 19-221 *et seq.* in the main work.

In *Fairclough v. Whipp,* 35 Cr.App.R. 138, DC, the respondent exposed himself in the presence of a girl aged nine and invited her to touch his exposed person, which she did. *Held,* an invitation to another person to touch the invitor could not amount to an assault on the invitee, and that therefore there had been no assault and consequently no indecent assault by the respondent: applied in *DPP v. Rogers,* 37 Cr.App.R. 137, DC; and *R. v. Dunn* [2015] 2 Cr.App.R 13, CA; but *cf. Beal v. Kelley,* 35 Cr.App.R. 128, DC, and *R. v. Sargeant,* 161 J.P. 127, CA, *post,* H-133. See also *R. v. Sutton,* 66 Cr.App.R. 21, CA, *post,* H-134, and the Indecency with Children Act 1960, *post,* H-230 *et seq.*

If a man inserts his finger into the vagina of a girl under 16, this is an indecent assault, however willing or co-operative the girl may be: *R. v. McCormack* [1969] 2 Q.B. 442, 53 Cr.App.R. 514, CA.

Consent

H-124   If the person assaulted is under 16, her consent is no defence: SOA 1956, s.14(2) (*ante,* H-117).

Where the woman's consent was procured by fraud as to the nature (*R. v. Case* (1850) 4 Cox 220) or quality (*R. v. Tabassum* [2000] 2 Cr.App.R. 328, CA) of the act, such consent constitutes no defence. See also § 19-233 in the main work, and *ante,* H-17.

Where a jury asked for the difference between consent and submission to be defined, it was not incumbent on the judge to direct the jury that reluctant acquiescence amounted to consent; it was for the jury to decide whether there was consent and their good sense and experience should lead them to the right conclusion: *R. v. McAllister* [1997] Crim.L.R. 233, CA (*cf. R. v. Olugboja,* 73 Cr.App.R. 344, CA, *ante,* H-16).

Consent cannot be a defence where the indecent assault consists in the infliction of blows intended or likely to cause bodily harm: *R. v. Donovan* [1934] 2 K.B. 498, 25 Cr.App.R. 1, CCA; approved and applied by the House of Lords in *R. v. Brown (Anthony)* [1994] 1 A.C. 212. (As to *Brown,* see also § 19-233 in the main work.) *Donovan* was also referred to in *R. v. Boyea* [1992] Crim.L.R. 574, CA, in which it was held that an assault which was intended or likely to cause bodily harm, and which was accompanied by indecency, constituted the offence of indecent assault regardless of consent, provided that the injury was not "transient or trifling". However, the tribunal of fact must take account of changing social attitudes, particularly in the field of sexual relations between adults. As a generality, the level of vigour in sexual congress which was generally acceptable, and therefore the voluntarily accepted risk of incurring some injury was probably higher now than in 1934, when *Donovan* was decided. It followed that the phrase "transient or trifling" must be understood in the light of current conditions. *Boyea* was approved in *Brown (Anthony), ante.* (See also *R. v. Wilson (A.)* [1996] 2 Cr.App.R. 241, CA (§ 19-235 in the main work).)

Bona fide belief as to age of girl

Where the complainant was under the age of 16 at the time of the alleged offence, the   **H-125**
defendant's genuine belief that she was in fact 16 or over at the time will negative criminal liability if the complainant in fact consented or the defendant genuinely believed that she was
consenting: *R. v. K.* [2002] 1 A.C. 462, HL.

Indecent assault within marriage

A man may be guilty of indecent assault upon his wife: *R. v. Kowalski*, 86 Cr.App.R. 339, CA.   **H-126**

(13) Indecent assault on a man

(a) *Statute*

Sexual Offences Act 1956, s.15

  15.–(1) It is an offence for a person to make an indecent assault on a man.   **H-127**
  (2) A boy under the age of sixteen cannot in law give any consent which would prevent an act being an assault for the purposes of this section.
  (3) A man who is a defective cannot in law give any consent which would prevent an act being an
assault for the purposes of this section, but a person is only to be treated as guilty of an indecent assault on a defective by reason of that incapacity to consent, if that person knew or had reason to
suspect him to be a defective.
  (4), (5) [*Repealed by Police and Criminal Evidence Act 1984, Sched. 7.*]

As to the use of the words "man" and "boy", see *post*, H-222.
As to the meaning of "defective", see *ante*, H-68.
For anonymity provisions, see §§ 20-257 *et seq.* in the main work.

(b) *Indictment*

Statement of Offence

Indecent assault on male person, contrary to section 15(1) of the Sexual Offences Act 1956.   **H-128**

Particulars of Offence

A B, on the ___ day of ___, 20_, indecently assaulted J N, a male person.

In practice, the age of the alleged victim, if he was under the age of 16, was usually averred.

(c) *Mode of trial and class of offence*

This offence is triable either way: MCA 1980, s.17(1), and Sched. 1 (§ 1-125 in the main work).   **H-129**
As to the classification of offences, see § 2-22c in the main work.

(d) *Sentence*

Imprisonment not exceeding 10 years: SOA 1956, s.37(3), and Sched. 2, para. 18.   **H-130**
  As to the approach to sentencing for historic offences, see *R. v. Forbes* [2016] 2 Cr.App.R.(S.)
44, CA (as to which, see Appendix S-1053).

(e) *Ingredients of the offence*

General

See *R. v. Court* and *R. v. C.*, *ante*, H-121, which, it is submitted, apply equally to this offence.   **H-131**

Person

A woman may be guilty of this offence: *R. v. Hare*, *ante*, H-122.   **H-132**

Assault

As to assaults generally, see §§ 19-221 *et seq.* in the main work.   **H-133**

An offence under section 15 is committed when a woman immediately prior to having sexual intercourse with a 14-year-old boy holds his penis. The act alleged to constitute the assault is an indecent act, consent is therefore no defence (s.15(2)–see *R. v. Sutton*, 66 Cr.App.R. 21, CA): *Faulkner v. Talbot*, 74 Cr.App.R. 1, DC.

Semble, an allegation of sexual intercourse by a woman with a boy under 16, *per se* connotes an allegation of indecent assault: see *R. v. McCormack* [1969] 2 Q.B. 442, 53 Cr.App.R. 514, CA; *Faulkner v. Talbot, ante*.

If there is an assault committed in circumstances of indecency, then there need not be an indecent touching: see *Beal v. Kelly*, 35 Cr.App.R. 128, DC (when boy refused to touch defendant's penis when asked to do so, defendant pulled boy towards him, but let him go); and *R. v. Sargeant*, 161 J.P. 127, CA (grabbed boy, then used threat of further force to compel boy to masturbate himself). *Cf. Fairclough v. Whipp, ante*, H-123.

H-134 In order to constitute an assault against a child under 16, the act complained of either must itself be inherently indecent or it must be one that is hostile or threatening or an act which the child is demonstrably reluctant to accept (see *DPP v. Rogers*, 37 Cr.App.R. 137, DC, and *Williams v. Gibbs* [1958] Crim.L.R. 127, DC). Although sections 14(2) and 15(2) of the 1956 Act bar the child's consent from preventing an act being an indecent assault, consent does avail to prevent the act being an assault if the act is not inherently indecent. The proper course where there is an act which could not conceivably be called an assault but which takes place in an indecent situation, is to prosecute under the Indecency with Children Act 1960 (*post*, H-230 *et seq.*): *R. v. Sutton*, 66 Cr.App.R. 21, CA. The defendant photographed partially clothed and unclothed boys, intending to sell the photographs to magazines. In order to arrange poses, he touched the boys on the hands, legs and torso; the actions were not threatening or hostile and the boys consented to them. His convictions under section 15(1) were quashed: touching merely to indicate a pose was not of itself indecent and was consented to. Consent did therefore avail to prevent the acts having been assaults and the question of indecency did not arise.

Consent

H-135 Consent is a defence as it negatives the assault: see *R. v. Wollaston* (1872) 12 Cox 180, CCR. See also *ante*, H-124.

A boy under the age of 16 cannot in law give any consent which would prevent an act being an assault for the purposes of the section: s.15(2), *ante*, H-127; but see the cases cited in the previous paragraph.

Bona fide belief as to age of boy

H-136 See *R. v. K.* [2002] 1 A.C. 462, HL, *ante*, H-125; and *R. v. Fernandez, The Times*, June 26, 2002, CA (confirming that the decision of the House of Lords applies equally to this offence).

(f) *Evidence*

H-137 The rule as to the admissibility of recent complaints (§§ 8-207 *et seq.* in the main work) was held to apply in the case of an indecent assault upon a boy of 15: *R. v. Camelleri* [1922] 2 K.B. 122, 16 Cr.App.R. 162, CCA.

(14) Assault with intent to commit buggery

(a) *Statute*

Sexual Offences Act 1956, s.16

H-138 **16.**–(1) It is an offence for a person to assault another person with intent to commit buggery.

(2)-(3) [*Repealed by Police and Criminal Evidence Act 1984, Sched. 7.*]

As to the offence of buggery, see *ante*, H-96 *et seq.*

As to assault, see generally, §§ 19-221 *et seq.* in the main work.

For anonymity provisions, see §§ 20-257 *et seq.* in the main work.

(b) *Indictment*

Statement of Offence

Assault with intent to commit buggery, contrary to section 16(1) of the Sexual Offences Act 1956. **H-139**

Particulars of Offence

A B, on the ___ day of ___, 20_, assaulted J N with intent to commit buggery with the said J N.

(c) *Mode of trial and class of offence*

This offence is triable only on indictment: SOA 1956, s.37(2), and Sched. 2, para. 19. As to the **H-140** classification of offences, see § 2-22c in the main work.

(d) *Sentence*

Imprisonment not exceeding 10 years: SOA 1956, s.37(3), and Sched. 2, para. 19. **H-141**

(e) *Effect of Criminal Justice and Public Order Act 1994*

It seems that no thought could have been given to the effect on this offence of the redefinition **H-142** of rape to include non-consensual anal intercourse. The logical solution would have been to substitute "rape" for "buggery" at the end of subsection (1). The offence consisting of an assault allied to a specific intent suggests non-consensual buggery, but because of the bizarre nature of the amendments to section 12, not all nonconsensual buggery (*e.g.* both parties over 18 and the act takes place in private) constitutes the *offence* of buggery, although it will always be rape. It is submitted that the proper interpretation is that an offence under section 16 is committed where there is an assault accompanied by the requisite intent regardless of whether or not the act itself, if completed, would constitute the offence of buggery. This does, of course, lead to anomalous results; it would be an offence contrary to this provision to assault a woman intending to have anal intercourse with her but it would not be an offence to do so intending to have vaginal intercourse, although both acts, if completed, would constitute rape. The alternative interpretation would be to confine the offence to the commission of an assault with intent to commit buggery in circumstances which would make the act, if completed, an offence contrary to section 12. Because of the assault ingredient, this would effectively confine the offence to assaults on persons under 18. This seems to be an unwarranted restriction of the scope of the offence; Parliament having, if anything, deemed non-consensual buggery to be a more serious offence than it was previously, it would be an extremely curious result of the legislation if someone who committed an assault with the intention of committing that more serious offence should no longer be guilty of an offence under section 16.

As to whether there was a common law offence of assault with intent to rape, see *ante*, H-10.

(15) Abduction of woman by force or for the sake of her property

(a) *Statute*

Sexual Offences Act 1956, s.17

17.—(1) It is an offence for a person to take away or detain a woman against her will with the **H-143** intention that she shall marry or have unlawful sexual intercourse with that or any other person, if she is so taken away or detained either by force or for the sake of her property or expectations of property.

(2) In the foregoing subsection, the reference to a woman's expectations of property relates only to property of a person to whom she is next of kin or one of the next of kin, and "property" includes any interest in property.

[This section is printed as effectively amended by the CLA 1967, s.12(5)(a).]

As to the meaning of "sexual intercourse", see *post*, H-219; as to the use of the word "woman", see *post*, H-222.

(b) *Indictment*

Statement of Offence

H-144   *Abduction, contrary to section 17(1) of the Sexual Offences Act 1956.*

Particulars of Offence

A B, on the ___ day of ___, 20_, took away [or *detained*] *J N against her will and by force* [or *for the sake of her property or expectations of property*] *with the intention that she should have unlawful sexual intercourse with him the said A B or with another* [or *with the intention that she should marry him the said A B or another*].

(c) *Mode of trial and class of offence*

H-145   This offence is triable on indictment only: SOA 1956, s.37(2), and Sched. 2, para. 4. As to the classification of offences, see § 2-22c in the main work.

(d) *Sentence*

H-146   Imprisonment not exceeding 14 years: SOA 1956, s.37(3), and Sched. 2, para. 4.

(e) *Ingredients of the offence*

H-147   As to the meaning of "unlawful" sexual intercourse, see *ante*, H-38.

If the woman is taken away with her own consent, but afterwards refuses to continue further with the offender, and is forcibly detained by him, this is within the statute: see 1 Hawk. c.41 (*Forcible Marriage*), s.7.

(16) Abduction of unmarried girl under 18 from parent or guardian

(a) *Statute*

Sexual Offences Act 1956, s.19

H-148   19.—(1) It is an offence, subject to the exception mentioned in this section, for a person to take an unmarried girl under the age of eighteen out of the possession of her parent or guardian against his will, if she is taken with the intention that she shall have unlawful sexual intercourse with men or with a particular man.

(2) A person is not guilty of an offence under this section because he takes such a girl out of the possession of her parent or guardian as mentioned above, if he believes her to be of the age of eighteen or over and has reasonable cause for the belief.

(3) In this section "guardian" means any person having the parental responsibility for or care of the girl.

[This section is printed as amended by the Children Act 1989, s.108(4), and Sched. 12, para. 11.]

As to the meaning of "sexual intercourse", see *post*, H-219; as to the use of the words "girl" and "man", see *post*, H-222; as to the meaning of "parental responsibility", see *post*, H-224.

For the burden of proof of exceptions, see section 47 of the 1956 Act, *post*, H-225.

(b) *Indictment*

Statement of Offence

H-149   *Abduction of girl, contrary to section 19(1) of the Sexual Offences Act 1956.*

Particulars of Offence

A B, on the ___ day of ___, 20_, unlawfully took or caused to be taken J N, an unmarried girl under the age of 18, out of the possession and against the will of her father [or *mother or of C D then having parental responsibility for or care of her*] *with an intent unlawfully to have sexual intercourse with her* [or *that she should have unlawful sexual intercourse with E F or generally*].

(c) *Mode of trial and class of offence*

H-150   This offence is triable on indictment only: SOA 1956, s.37(2), and Sched. 2, para. 20. As to the classification of offences, see § 2-22c in the main work.

(d) *Sentence*

Imprisonment not exceeding two years: SOA 1956, s.37(3), and Sched. 2, para. 20. **H-151**

(e) *Ingredients of the offence*

For the evidence necessary to support this indictment, see *post*, H-157 *et seq.*, *mutatis mutandis.* **H-152**
As to the meaning of "unlawful" sexual intercourse, see *ante*, H-38.

Upon an indictment under this section for taking a girl out of the possession of her father, it was proved that at the time of the commission of the alleged offence she was employed by another person as barmaid at a distance from her father's home. It was held that she was under the lawful charge of her employer and not in the possession of her father, and that therefore the defendant could not be convicted of the offence with which he was charged: *R. v. Henkers* (1886) 16 Cox 257. The age of the girl must be proved by the prosecution, as *ante*, H-49. The presumption of the CYPA 1933, s.99, does not apply to this offence: see the proviso to Schedule 1 to the 1933 Act (as to which see *ante*, H-49).

(17) Abduction of unmarried girl under 16 from parent or guardian

(a) *Statute*

Sexual Offences Act 1956, s.20

20.–(1) It is an offence for a person acting without lawful authority or excuse to take an unmar- **H-153**
ried girl under the age of sixteen out of the possession of her parent or guardian against his will.
(2) In the foregoing subsection "guardian" means any person having parental responsibility for or care of the girl.

[This section is printed as amended by the Children Act 1989, s.108(4), and Sched. 12, para. 12.]

As to the use of the word "girl", see *post*, H-222; as to the meaning of "parental responsibility", see *post*, H-224.

See now section 2 of the Child Abduction Act 1984 (§ 19-397 in the main work) which covers much the same ground and is not limited to the abduction of girls.

(b) *Indictment*

Statement of Offence

Abduction of a girl, contrary to section 20(1) of the Sexual Offences Act 1956. **H-154**

Particulars of Offence

A B, on the ___ day of ___, 20_, unlawfully took or caused to be taken J N, an unmarried girl aged 14, out of the possession and against the will of her father [or *mother or of E F then having parental responsibility for or care of her*].

(c) *Mode of trial and class of offence*

This offence is triable on indictment only: SOA 1956, s.37(2), and Sched. 2, para. 21. As to the **H-155**
classification of offences, see § 2-22c in the main work.

(d) *Sentence*

Imprisonment not exceeding two years: SOA 1956, s.37(3), and Sched. 2, para. 21. **H-156**

(e) *Ingredients of the offence*

That the girl was in the possession of her father, etc.

This is a question for the jury: *R. v. Mace*, 50 J.P. 776. A girl will still be in the possession of **H-157**
her parent/guardian even while she is away from home if she intends to return; and if, when so

out of the house, the defendant induces her to run away with him, he is guilty: *R. v. Mycock* (1871) 12 Cox 28. See also *R. v. Baillie* (1859) 8 Cox 238; *R. v. Green* (1862) 3 F. & F. 274; and *R. v. Miller* (1876) 13 Cox 179.

The taking

H-158   The taking need not be by force, either actual or constructive, and it is immaterial whether the girl consents or not: *R. v. Manktelow* (1853) 6 Cox 143, and see *R. v. Kipps* (1850) 4 Cox 167; *R. v. Booth* (1872) 12 Cox 231; and *R. v. Robins* (1844) 1 C. & K. 456 (where the girl positively encouraged the defendant).

The words "taking out of the possession and against the will" of the parent mean some conduct amounting to a substantial interference with the possessory relationship of parent and child: *R. v. Jones (J.W.)* [1973] Crim.L.R. 621 (Swanwick J.)—attempt to take girls (aged 10) for a walk with a view to indecently assaulting them held not to constitute an attempt to commit the offence. (*Cf. R. v. Leather*, 98 Cr.App.R. 179, CA, decided on the Child Abduction Act 1984 (§ 19-398 in the main work).)

It is no defence that the defendant acted in concert with the girl and had no intention of keeping her away from her home permanently: *R. v. Timmins* (1860) 8 Cox 401; *R. v. Frazer and Norman*, ibid. at 446. See also *R. v. Baillie*, ibid. at 238.

Instead of a taking, it can be shown that a girl left her parent or guardian, in consequence of some persuasion, inducement or blandishment held out to her by the defendant: *R. v. Henkers* (1886) 16 Cox 257, following *R. v. Olifier* (1866) 10 Cox 402.

H-159   Where a man induces a girl, by promise of what he will do for her, to leave her father's house and live with him, he may be convicted, although he is not actually present or assisting her at the time when she leaves her father's roof: *R. v. Robb* (1864) 4 F. & F. 59. If the girl leaves her father, without any persuasion, inducement or blandishment held out to her by the defendant, so that she has got fairly away from home, and then goes to him, although it may be his moral duty to return her to her father's custody, yet his not doing so is no infringement of this statute, for the statute does not say he shall restore, but only that he shall not take her away: *R. v. Olifier, ante,* and this is so even though it be proved that before she so left he had taken her about to places of amusement and had intercourse with her: *R. v. Kauffman*, 68 J.P. 189. If the suggestion to go away with the defendant comes from the girl only, and he takes merely the passive part of yielding to her suggestion, he is entitled to an acquittal: *R. v. Jarvis* (1903) 20 Cox 249. It is submitted that the ruling to the contrary in *R. v. Biswell* (1847) 2 Cox 279 is not law. For a discussion of the authorities, see *R. v. Mackney* (1903) 29 Vict.L.R. 22, where the English cases are considered.

Against the will, etc.

H-160   If the defendant induced the parents, by false and fraudulent representations, to allow him to take the child away, this is an abduction: *R. v. Hopkins* (1842) C. & Mar. 254.

Where the girl's mother had encouraged her in a lax course of life, by permitting her to go out alone at night and dance at public-houses, from one of which she went away with the defendant, Cockburn C.J. ruled that she could not be said to be taken away against her mother's will: *R. v. Primelt* (1858) 1 F. & F. 50.

To prove this element of the offence, it has been said that the parent or guardian must be called: *R. v. Nash, The Times,* July 2, 1903. *Sed quaere.*

Under 16, etc.

H-161   Prove that she was under the age of 16 years and unmarried. As to the power of a court to presume her age from her appearance, see the CYPA 1933, s.99(2) (§ 19-412 in the main work) and Sched. 1 (§ 19-408 in the main work (prior to its repeal by the SOA 2003, the proviso to Sched. 1 stipulated that s.99(2) did apply to offences under s.20)). It is no defence that the defendant did not know her to be under 16, or might suppose from her appearance that she was older: *R. v. Olifier, ante; R. v. Mycock, ante; R. v. Booth, ante;* or even that the defendant bona fide believed and had reasonable grounds for believing that she was over 16: *R. v. Prince* (1875) L.R. 2 C.C.R. 154. Doubts about *Prince* were expressed by the House of Lords in *B. (a Minor) v. DPP* [2000] 2 A.C. 428 (*post*, H-235) and *R. v. K.* [2002] 1 A.C. 462 (*ante*, H-125), but its correctness did not fall to be decided upon. Those expressions of doubt are likely to found a challenge to *Prince*, but it is submitted that the express provision of a defence based on mistake as to age in relation to the offence contrary to section 19 (*ante*, H-148) makes it abundantly clear that Parliament intended that there should be no corresponding defence in relation to the abduction of a girl under 16.

Mens rea

The act of abduction is positively prohibited, and therefore the absence of a corrupt motive is **H-162** no answer to the charge: see *R. v. Booth*, *ante*.

If the defendant, at the time he took the girl away, did not know, and had no reason to know, that she was subject to the parental responsibility and care of her father, mother or some other person, he is not guilty of this offence: *R. v. Hibbert* (1869) L.R. 1 C.C.R. 184.

Without lawful authority or excuse

The defendant must show that he had either lawful authority or a lawful excuse; motive is **H-163** irrelevant: *R. v. Tegerdine*, 75 Cr.App.R. 298, CA (statutory history reviewed). It is submitted that the burden on the defendant is merely an evidential one, which is discharged if there is sufficient evidence to raise an issue on the matter: *cf.* the specific provision in section 47 (*post*, H-225) in relation to "exceptions" under the Act. And see generally, §§ 4-444 *et seq.* in the main work.

(18) Abduction of defective from parent or guardian

(a) *Statute*

Sexual Offences Act 1956, s.21

21.—(1) It is an offence, subject to the exception mentioned in this section, for a person to take a **H-164** woman who is a defective out of the possession of her parent or guardian against his will, if she is so taken with the intention that she shall have unlawful sexual intercourse with men or with a particular man.

(2) A person is not guilty of an offence under this section because he takes such a woman out of the possession of her parent or guardian as mentioned above, if he does not know and has no reason to suspect her to be a defective.

(3) In this section "guardian" means any person having parental responsibility for or care of the woman.

[This section is printed as amended by the Children Act 1989, s.108(4), and Sched. 12, para. 13.]

As to the meaning of "sexual intercourse", see *post*, H-219; as to the meaning of "unlawful" sexual intercourse, see *ante*, H-38; as to the use of the words "man" and "woman", see *post*, H-222; as to the meaning of "defective", see *ante*, H-68; as to the meaning of "parental responsibility", see *post*, H-224.

For the burden of proof of exceptions, see section 47 of the 1956 Act, *post*, H-225.

(b) *Mode of trial and class of offence*

This offence is triable on indictment only: SOA 1956, s.37(2), and Sched. 2, para. 22. As to the **H-165** classification of offences, see § 2-22c in the main work.

(c) *Sentence*

Imprisonment not exceeding two years: SOA 1956, s.37(3), and Sched. 2, para. 22.   **H-166**

(19) Causing prostitution of women

(a) *Statute*

Sexual Offences Act 1956, s.22

22.—(1) It is an offence for a person—   **H-167**

(a) to procure a woman to become, in any part of the world, a common prostitute; or

(b) to procure a woman to leave the United Kingdom, intending her to become an inmate of or frequent a brothel elsewhere; or

(c) to procure a woman to leave her usual place of abode in the United Kingdom, intending her to become an inmate of or frequent a brothel in any part of the world for the purposes of prostitution.

(2) [*Repealed by Criminal Justice and Public Order Act 1994, s.33(1).*]

As to the use of the word "woman", see *post*, H-222.

(b) *Indictment*

Statement of Offence

H-168   *Procuring a woman to become a common prostitute, contrary to section 22(1)(a) of the Sexual Offences Act 1956.*

Particulars of Offence

A B, on or about the ___ day of ___ , 20_, at ___ procured C D, a woman, to become a common prostitute.

(c) *Mode of trial and classification of offences*

H-169   This offence, and an attempt to commit it, are triable on indictment only: SOA 1956, s.37(2), and Sched. 2, para. 23(a), (b). As to the classification of offences, see § 2-22c in the main work.

(d) *Sentence*

H-170   The full offence, and an attempt to commit it: imprisonment not exceeding two years: SOA 1956, s.37(3), and Sched. 2, para. 23(a), (b).

(e) *Ingredients of the offence*

"Procure"

H-171   As to the meaning of the word "procure" in general, see §§ 18-22, 18-23 in the main work, and see *Att.-Gen.'s Reference (No. 1 of 1975)* [1975] Q.B. 773, 61 Cr.App.R. 118, CA; *Re Royal Victoria Pavilion, Ramsgate* [1961] Ch. 581, Ch D, and *Blakely v. DPP* [1991] R.T.R. 405, DC. In the first of these authorities, Lord Widgery C.J. said that to procure, "means to produce by endeavour. You procure a thing by setting out to see that it happens and taking the appropriate steps to produce that happening" (at pp.779, 121). In *Re Royal Victoria Pavilion, Ramsgate*, Pennycuick J. (at p.587) defined "to procure" as "to obtain by care and effort" or "to see to it".

In *R. v. Broadfoot*, 64 Cr.App.R. 71, CA, the court described *Att.-Gen's Reference (No. 1 of 1975)*, *ante*, as a useful guide. Whilst saying that the interpretation of the word was a matter of common sense for the jury to determine in the light of the particular facts, the court appears to have approved (see p.74) the suggestion of Shaw L.J., during argument, that it could be regarded as bringing about a course of conduct which the woman in question would not have embarked upon of her own volition. *R. v. Christian* (1913) 23 Cox 541, was distinguished. It was there held that procuration could be negatived by evidence showing the girl was not really procured, because she needed no procuring, and acted of her own free will.

If a woman is already a common prostitute she cannot become one and accordingly cannot be procured to become one. It follows that if there is evidence of procuration but "the woman" is a police officer it is a good defence to a charge of attempting to procure a woman to become a prostitute contrary to section 1(1) of the Criminal Attempts Act 1981, that the defendant thought that "the woman" he was attempting to procure was already a prostitute. If he believed (or might have believed) that, it could not be said that he was trying to procure her to become that which he believed she already was. Section 1(3) of the 1981 Act (§ 33-128 in the main work) is concerned with the converse case where the woman is a common prostitute but the defendant believes she is not. In such circumstances, he may be convicted of an attempt even though the commission of the offence is impossible: *R. v. Brown (R.A.)*, 80 Cr.App.R. 36, CA.

As to "attempting to do the impossible", see also § 33-137 in the main work.

"Common prostitute"

H-172   This includes a woman who offiers her body commonly for acts of lewdness for payment

although there is no act or offer of an act of ordinary sexual intercourse: *R. v. De Munck* [1918] 1
K.B. 635, 13 Cr.App.R. 113, CCA. The word "common" in the term "common prostitute" is not
mere surplusage—a common prostitute is any woman who offers herself commonly for lewdness
for reward. Whether or not the performance by a woman of a single act of lewdness with a man
on one occasion for reward constitutes the woman a prostitute, it plainly does not make her a
woman who offers herself commonly for lewdness. That must be someone who is prepared for
reward to engage in acts of lewdness with all and sundry or with anyone who may hire her for
that purpose: *R. v. Morris-Lowe*, 80 Cr.App.R. 114, CA, applying *R. v. De Munck, ante*.

It is not necessary that she should have submitted to acts of lewdness in a passive way. Active
acts of indecency by the woman herself, *e.g.* masturbation by her of clients when acting as a mas-
seuse will fall within the section: *R. v. Webb* [1964] 1 Q.B. 357, 47 Cr.App.R. 265, CCA.

In *R. v. McFarlane* [1994] Q.B. 419, 99 Cr.App.R. 8, CA, it was held in relation to a prosecution under section 30 of the 1956 Act (*post*, H-197) that the essence of prostitution is the making
of an offer of sexual services for reward, and that it is immaterial that the person making the offer does not intend to perform them and does not do so. It is obviously desirable that "prostitution" is given the same meaning wherever it appears in a statute; accordingly, this decision is likely
to be applied to section 22. For a criticism of this decision, see the 1996 edition of this work.

(20) Procuration of girl under 21

(a) *Statute*

Sexual Offences Act 1956, s.23

H-173   **23.**—(1) It is an offence for a person to procure a girl under the age of twenty-one to have unlawful sexual intercourse in any part of the world with a third person.
(2) [*Repealed by Criminal Justice and Public Order Act 1994, s.33(1).*]

As to the meaning of "sexual intercourse", see *post*, H-219; as to the use of the word "girl", see
post, H-222.

(b) *Mode of trial and classification of offences*

H-174   This offence, and an attempt to commit it, are triable on indictment only: SOA 1956, s.37(2),
and Sched. 2, para. 24(a), (b). As to the classification of offences, see § 2-22c in the main work.

(c) *Sentence*

H-175   The full offence, and an attempt to commit it: imprisonment not exceeding two years; SOA
1956, s.37(3), and Sched. 2, para. 24(a), (b).

(d) *Ingredients of the offence*

H-176   As to the meaning of "procure", see *ante*, H-171. As to the meaning of "unlawful" sexual
intercourse, see *ante*, H-38.

Before the defendant can be found guilty of an offence contrary to this section, it is necessary
to prove that unlawful sexual intercourse did take place; if intercourse is not proved to have taken
place but procurement with the intention that it should take place is proved, there may be a
conviction of an attempt to commit the full offence: *R. v. Johnson* [1964] 2 Q.B. 404, 48 Cr.App.R.
25, CCA. As to the difference between an attempt and an intention, see *R. v. Landow*, 8 Cr.App.R.
218, CCA. As to conspiracy with the procurer, see *R. v. Mackenzie and Higginson*, 6 Cr.App.R. 64,
CCA.

(21) Detention of a woman in brothel or other premises

(a) *Statute*

Sexual Offences Act 1956, s.24

H-177   **24.**—(1) It is an offence for a person to detain a woman against her will on any premises with the intention that she shall have unlawful sexual intercourse with men or with a particular man, or to detain a woman against her will in a brothel.

(2) Where a woman is on any premises for the purpose of having unlawful sexual intercourse or is in a brothel, a person shall be deemed for the purpose of the foregoing subsection to detain her there if, with the intention of compelling or inducing her to remain there, he either withholds from her her clothes or any other property belonging to her or threatens her with legal proceedings in the event of her taking away clothes provided for her by him or on his directions.

(3) A woman shall not be liable to any legal proceedings, whether civil or criminal, for taking away or being found in possession of any clothes she needed to enable her to leave premises on which she was for the purpose of having unlawful sexual intercourse or to leave a brothel.

As to the meaning of "sexual intercourse", see *post*, H-219; as to the use of the words "man" and "woman", see *post*, H-222.

(b) *Indictment*

Statement of Offence

H-178   *Detaining a woman against her will for unlawful sexual intercourse* [or *in a brothel*], *contrary to section 24(1) of the Sexual Offences Act 1956.*

Particulars of Offence

A B, on or about the ___ day of ___, 20_, detained C D, a woman, against her will at ___ intending her to have unlawful sexual intercourse with men [or *with E F, a man*] [or *detained C D, a woman, against her will at ___, a brothel*].

(c) *Mode of trial and class of offence*

H-179   This offence is triable on indictment only: SOA 1956, s.37(2), and Sched. 2, para. 25. As to the classification of offences, see § 2-22c in the main work.

(d) *Sentence*

H-180   Imprisonment not exceeding two years: SOA 1956, s.37(3), and Sched. 2, para. 25.

(e) *Ingredients of offence*

Unlawful sexual intercourse

H-181   See *ante*, H-38.

"Brothel"

H-182   See §§ 20-233 *et seq.* in the main work.

(f) *Evidence*

H-183   See § 20-235 in the main work.

(22) Allowing premises to be used for intercourse

(a) *Statute*

Sexual Offences Act 1956, ss.25, 26, 27

Permitting girl under thirteen to use premises for intercourse

H-184   **25.** It is an offence for a person who is the owner or occupier of any premises, or who has, or acts or assists in, the management or control of any premises, to induce or knowingly suffer a girl under the age of thirteen to resort to or be on those premises for the purpose of having unlawful sexual intercourse with men or with a particular man.

[This section is printed as effectively amended by the CLA 1967, s.12(5)(a).]

Permitting girl between thirteen and sixteen to use premises for intercourse

H-185   **26.** It is an offence for a person who is the owner or occupier of any premises, or who has, or acts or assists in, the management or control of any premises, to induce or knowingly suffer a girl ... under the age of sixteen, to resort to or be on those premises for the purpose of having unlawful sexual intercourse with men or with a particular man.

[The words omitted were repealed by the CLA 1967, s.10(1), and Sched. 2, para. 14. This repeal renders the marginal note misleading.]

Permitting defective to use premises for intercourse

27.–(1) It is an offence, subject to the exception mentioned in this section, for a person who is the **H-186** owner or occupier of any premises, or who has, or acts or assists in, the management or control of any premises, to induce or knowingly suffer a woman who is a defective to resort to or be on those premises for the purpose of having unlawful sexual intercourse with men or with a particular man.

(2) A person is not guilty of an offence under this section because he induces or knowingly suffers a defective to resort to or be on any premises for the purpose mentioned, if he does not know and has no reason to suspect her to be a defective.

As to the meaning of "sexual intercourse", see *post*, H-219; as to the use of the words "man", "woman" and "girl", see *post*, H-222; as to the meaning of "defective", see *ante*, H-68.

For the burden of proof of exceptions, see section 47 of the 1956 Act, *post*, H-225.

(b) *Mode of trial and classification of offences*

Section 25– this offence is triable only on indictment: SOA 1956, s.37(2), and Sched. 2, para. **H-187** 6.

Section 26–this offence is triable either way: MCA 1980, s.17(1), and Sched. 1 (§ 1-125 in the main work).

Section 27–this offence is triable only on indictment: SOA 1956, s.37(2), and Sched. 2, para. 27.

As to the classification of offences, see § 2-22c in the main work.

(c) *Sentence*

Section 25–life imprisonment: SOA 1956, s.37(3), and Sched. 2, para. 6. **H-188**

Section 26–imprisonment not exceeding two years: SOA 1956, s.37(3), and Sched. 2, para. 26. The penalty on summary conviction is provided for by the MCA 1980, s.32 (§ 1-119 in the main work).

Section 27–imprisonment not exceeding two years: SOA 1956, s.37(3), and Sched. 2, para. 27.

(d) *Ingredients of the offences*

"Management", "assists in the management"

See the following cases, decided in relation to section 33 of the 1956 Act ("assisting in the **H-189** management of a brothel"): *Abbott v. Smith* [1965] 2 Q.B. 662, DC (meaning of "management"); *Gorman v. Standen; Palace-Clark v. Standen* [1964] 1 Q.B. 294, 48 Cr.App.R. 30, DC; *Jones and Wood v. DPP*, 96 Cr.App.R. 130, DC; and *Elliott v. DPP; Dublides v. DPP, The Times,* January 19, 1989, DC ("assisting in the management"). In the last of these cases, the court appears to have accepted a distinction between assisting in the management of premises and assisting the management of premises.

"Unlawful" sexual intercourse

See *ante*, H-38. **H-190**

"Knowingly suffer"

In *R. v. Webster* (1885) 16 Q.B.D. 134, it was held that the words "knowingly suffer" mean that **H-191** the defendant knew of the girl's purpose in being on the premises and did not prevent the unlawful sexual intercourse from occurring when it was in his power to do so. The girl was the defendant's daughter, and the premises were her home, where she resided with the defendant. But see *R. v. Merthyr Tydfil JJ.* (1894) 10 T.L.R. 375, where a mother was held not within the section, who for the purposes of obtaining conclusive evidence against a man who had seduced her daughter, permitted him to come to her house to repeat his unlawful intercourse.

(23) **Causing or encouraging prostitution, etc.**

(a) *Statute*

Sexual Offences Act 1956, ss.28, 29

Causing or encouraging prostitution of, intercourse with, or indecent assault on, girl under sixteen

28.–(1) It is an offence for a person to cause or encourage the prostitution of, or the commission **H-192**

of unlawful sexual intercourse with, or of an indecent assault on, a girl under the age of sixteen for whom he is responsible.

(2) Where a girl has become a prostitute, or has had unlawful sexual intercourse, or has been indecently assaulted, a person shall be deemed for the purposes of this section to have caused or encouraged it, if he knowingly allowed her to consort with, or to enter or continue in the employment of, any prostitute or person of known immoral character.

(3) The persons who are to be treated for the purposes of this section as responsible for a girl are (subject to subsection (4) of this section)—

    (a) her parents;

    (b) any person who is not a parent of hers but who has parental responsibility for her; and

    (c) any person who has care of her.

(4) An individual falling within subsection (3)(a) or (b) of this section is not to be treated as responsible for a girl if—

    (a) a residence order under the Children Act 1989 is in force with respect to her and he is not named in the order as the person with whom she is to live; or

    (aa) a special guardianship order under that Act is in force with respect to her and he is not her special guardian; or

    (b) a care order under that Act is in force with respect to her.

(5) If, on a charge of an offence against a girl under this section, the girl appears to the court to have been under the age of sixteen at the time of the offence charged, she shall be presumed for the purposes of this section to have been so, unless the contrary is proved.

[This section is printed as amended by the Children Act 1989, s.108(4), and Sched. 12, para. 14; and the Adoption and Children Act 2002, s.139(1), and Sched. 3, para. 8.]

Causing or encouraging prostitution of defective

H-193
    29.–(1) It is an offence, subject to the exception mentioned in this section, for a person to cause or encourage the prostitution in any part of the world of a woman who is a defective.

(2) A person is not guilty of an offence under this section because he causes or encourages the prostitution of such a woman, if he does not know and has no reason to suspect her to be a defective.

As to the meaning of "sexual intercourse", see *post*, H-219; as to the use of the words "woman" and "girl", see *post*, H-222; as to the meaning of "parental responsibility", see *post*, H-224; as to the meaning of "defective", see *ante*, H-68.

For the burden of proof of exceptions, see section 47 of the 1956 Act, *post*, § H-225.

(b) *Mode of trial and classification of offences*

H-194
    These offences are triable only on indictment: SOA 1956, s.37(2), and Sched. 2, paras 28 and 29. As to the classification of offences, see § 2-22c in the main work.

(c) *Sentence*

H-195
    Sections 28 and 29—imprisonment not exceeding two years: SOA 1956, s.37(3), and Sched. 2, paras 28 and 29.

(d) *Ingredients of the offences*

H-196
    As to what constitutes "causing" or "encouraging", see *R. v. Ralphs*, 9 Cr.App.R. 86, CCA; *R. v. Chainey* [1914] 1 K.B. 137, 9 Cr.App.R. 175, CCA.

In *R. v. Drury*, 60 Cr.App.R. 195, CA, it was held that there was evidence on which it could be held that a girl (aged 14) was in the care of the defendant where, at the time of the assault by a friend of the defendant, she was babysitting for him. The case was decided on the original wording of section 28(3)(c), *viz.* "any other person who has the custody, charge or care of her". The 1989 amendment (*ante*) would not appear to affect this point. As to encouragement, the court said that there must be encouragement in fact and an intention to encourage.

A doctor who in the exercise of his clinical judgment gives contraceptive advice and treatment to a girl under 16 without her parents' consent does not commit an offence under section 6 or 28 of the 1956 Act, because the bona fide exercise by the doctor of his clinical judgment negates the *mens rea* which is an essential ingredient of those offences: *Gillick v. West Norfolk and Wisbech Area Health Authority* [1986] A.C. 112, HL.

As to the meaning of "unlawful" sexual intercourse, see *ante*, H-38.

(24) Man living on earnings of prostitution

(a) *Statute*

Sexual Offences Act 1956, s.30

30.—(1) It is an offence for a man knowingly to live wholly or in part on the earnings of   **H-197**
prostitution.

(2) For the purposes of this section a man who lives with or is habitually in the company of a
prostitute, or who exercises control, direction or influence over a prostitute's movements in a way
which shows he is aiding, abetting or compelling her prostitution with others, shall be presumed to
be knowingly living on the earnings of prostitution, unless he proves the contrary.

As to the use of the word "man", see *post*, H-222.

(b) *Indictment*

Statement of Offence

Living on prostitution, contrary to section 30(1) of the Sexual Offences Act 1956.   **H-198**

Particulars of Offence

*A B, being a man, on the ___ day of ___, 20_, and on other days between that date and the ___ day of ___,
20_, knowingly lived wholly or in part on the earnings of the prostitution of J N.*

In an indictment for this offence a person may be charged with having committed the offence
on one specified day only: *R. v. Hill*, 10 Cr.App.R. 56, CCA. Evidence is admissible to show what
the defendant's relations with the woman in question had been either before or after the day
specified in the indictment: *ibid.*

As to the application of the alibi notice provisions to this offence, see *R. v. Hassan*, 54 Cr.App.R.
56, CA (§ 12-66 in the main work).

(c) *Mode of trial and class of offence*

This offence is triable either way: SOA 1956, s.37(2), and Sched. 2, para. 30. As to the clas-   **H-199**
sification of offences, see § 2-22c in the main work.

(d) *Sentence*

Maximum

On conviction on indictment, imprisonment not exceeding seven years; on summary convic-   **H-200**
tion, six months, or a fine not exceeding £5,000: SOA 1956, s.37(3), and Sched. 2, para. 30 (as
amended by the Street Offences Act 1959, s.4), and the MCA 1980, ss.32, 34(3)(a).

Guidelines

A sentence exceeding two years should be reserved for cases where there is some evidence of   **H-201**
physical or mental coercion of the prostitutes involved, or of corruption. The existence of such
coercion or corruption is the crucial sentencing factor: *R. v. Farrugia*, 69 Cr.App.R. 108, CA. See
also *R. v. Thomas*, 5 Cr.App.R.(S.) 138, CA; *R. v. El-Gazzar*, 8 Cr.App.R.(S.) 182, CA; *R. v. Malik*
[1998] 1 Cr.App.R.(S.) 115, CA; and CSP B5-1.

(e) *Ingredients of the offence*

"Man"

In *R. v. Tan* [1983] Q.B. 1053, 76 Cr.App.R. 300, CA, it was held that a person who was born a   **H-202**
man and who remained biologically a man was a man for all purposes although he had undergone
hormone treatment and surgical treatment consisting of sex-change operations and had become
philosophically or psychologically female (applying *Corbett v. Corbett* [1971] P. 83).

Prostitution

H-203 As to what constitutes "prostitution", see *ante*, H-172. As to proving that at the material time the woman was a prostitute, see § 20-235 in the main work, and *R. v. Wilson (D.T.)*, 78 Cr.App.R. 247, CA, in which *Woodhouse v. Hall*, 72 Cr.App.R. 39, DC, was applied in the context of a prosecution under section 30.

Knowingly living on earnings of prostitution

H-204 There are three distinct foundations upon which the prosecution can rely in order to raise a presumption that an offence has been committed under section 30(2) (*ante*, H-197):

   (a) proof that the accused was at the material time living with the prostitute;

   (b) proof that he was habitually at the material time in her company;

   (c) proof that he exercised control, direction or influence over her movements in a way which showed him to be aiding or abetting her prostitution.

Once evidence giving rise to the presumption has been led, it then has two facets: (a) it is presumed that he is living on immoral earnings; and (b) it is presumed that he is doing so knowingly: *R. v. Clarke*, 63 Cr.App.R. 16, CA. It is not necessary to prove that he was living with or habitually in the company of such a prostitute in a way which showed that he was aiding, abetting or compelling her prostitution with others: *ibid.* See also *R. v. Lawrence, post*, H-206.

H-205 In *R. v. Stewart*, 83 Cr.App.R. 327, CA, the court was referred to *R. v. Silver*, 40 Cr.App.R. 32, CCC (Judge Maude); *R. v. Thomas*, 41 Cr.App.R. 121, CCA; *Shaw v. DPP* [1962] A.C. 220, HL; *R. v. Calderhead and Bidney*, 68 Cr.App.R. 37, CA; and *R. v. Wilson (D.T.), ante.* Mustill L.J. said, in giving the court's judgment:

> "What we collect from them is as follows: according to the literal meaning of the section any person who supplies goods or services to a prostitute is in one sense living off the earnings of prostitution: for in part he earns his livelihood from payments which the woman would not be able to make but for her trade. This cannot be the right view. There has to be a closer connection between the receipt of money and the trade before the recipient commits an offence. We doubt whether it is possible to devise a definition of the type and closeness of the necessary connection which will deal with all the circumstances which may arise; and, indeed, it is dangerous to treat words or phrases from judgments delivered in relation to one set of facts, as if they provided a statutory gloss which can be reliably applied to facts of a quite different nature ... .
>
> Subject to this reservation, we believe that an approach which will often be useful is to identify for the jury the flavour of the words 'living off', and then to express this general concept in the shape of guidance more directly referable to the case in hand. In our judgment, the word 'parasite' (to be found in the speech of Lord Reid in *Shaw v. DPP* ...), or some expanded equivalent, provides a useful starting point for this exercise, and does express a concept which accounts for all the reported cases except for *Silver*.
>
> Adopting this general approach, and dealing specifically with a defendant who supplies goods or services to a prostitute, a good working test, sufficient to deal with many cases, is whether the fact of supply means that the supplier and the prostitute were engaged in the business of prostitution together: and 'the fact of supply' will include the scale of supply, the price charged and the nature of the goods or services. It will be impossible to say in advance that certain categories of supplies must necessarily fall outside the section, any more than that other categories must be within it, but the idea of participation in the prostitute's business will enable the jury to distinguish readily between (say) the supplier of groceries on the one hand and the publisher of prostitutes' advertisements on the other. There will remain a residue of more difficult cases, and these include the situation where premises are let at a market rent with knowledge of the purpose to which they are to be put. We see no room here for any rule of thumb distinction between premises which are or are not let at abnormally high rates. Certainly, the jury will find it easier to infer in the former case that the lessor participates in the woman's earnings. ... We can, however, see no logic in the suggestion that the lessor cannot be convicted unless the rent is exorbitant and indeed the judgment of Ashworth J. in *Shaw v. DPP* (at p.230) and the speech of Lord Simonds in the same case (at p.265 ... see the words 'whatever the rent') are authority for the view that the presence or absence of this factor is not conclusive. Nor in our opinion is the question whether the premises are occupied or capable of occupation as residential premises to be taken as the touchstone.
>
> Instead, the judge must bear in mind when framing his direction the distinction between the offence under section 30(1), and the offences under sections 34, 35 and 36, and must not allow

the jury to believe that knowledge of use to which the premises are put will be sufficient in itself to found a conviction. He must draw the attention of the jury to whatever factors are material to the individual case. These will often include, but not be limited to, the nature and location of the premises, the involvement of the lessor in adapting, furnishing or outfitting the premises for prostitution, the duration of the letting, the hours during which the premises are occupied, the rent at which they are let, the method of payment of rent, the fact that the prostitute does or does not live as well as work at the premises, the presence or absence of a personal relationship between the lessor and the lessee, the steps taken by the lessor to remove the prostitutes from his premises, and the steps taken by the lessor to disguise his relationship with the premises and the persons working there. Having presented the facts to the jury, the judge will invite them to consider whether they are sure that the lessor was involved together with the prostitute in the business of prostitution" (at pp.332–333).

Mustill L.J. then said that in the opinion of the court, the judge's direction, that where a letting **H-206** was referable to prostitution and nothing else it was immaterial whether the letting was at a higher than normal rent, was correct, and to the extent that *Silver, ante,* is a decision to the contrary, it should not be followed.

It is essential that a jury should receive a clear and careful direction with regard to this offence and the burden of proof in relation to it. In particular, where the prosecution rely on subsection (2) (*ante,* H-197), the jury's attention should be directed to the various alternatives contained in the subsection, and to any evidence relating to any of those alternatives: *R. v. Lawrence,* 47 Cr.App.R. 72, CCA.

In *R. v. Howard,* 94 Cr.App.R. 89, CA, Lord Lane C.J. said that what is required is a simple direction based primarily on what was said in *Shaw v. DPP, ante,* and *Stewart, ante,* adjusted to the facts of the particular case.

(f) *Evidence*

That the defendant knowingly lived wholly or in part on the earnings of prostitution is usually **H-207** proved by evidence that the prostitute paid the rent of rooms where both were living together, or paid for his food, or supplied him with money, or paid for drink consumed by him in public-houses, or the like. Whether conversation and association with a prostitute amounts to proof that the defendant was habitually in her company is a question of fact for the jury: *R. v. Ptohopoulos,* 52 Cr.App.R. 47, CA.

There need not be proof that the prostitute handed money to the defendant if the evidence establishes that what the defendant received was earned by the prostitute (see *Calvert v. Mayes* [1954] 1 Q.B. 242, approved in *Shaw*). Nor, as was held in *R. v. Ansell* [1975] Q.B. 215, 60 Cr.App.R. 45, CA, if the money comes from the men with whom the prostitutes are dealing and not from the prostitutes themselves, does that fact in law prevent the money being the earnings of prostitution: see, for example, *R. v. Farrugia,* 69 Cr.App.R. 108, CA.

(25) Woman exercising control over prostitute

(a) *Statute*

Sexual Offences Act 1956, s.31

31. It is an offence for a woman for purposes of gain to exercise control, direction or influence **H-208** over a prostitute's movements in a way which shows she is aiding, abetting or compelling her prostitution.

As to the use of the word "woman", see *post,* H-222. As to the meaning of "prostitution", see *ante,* H-172.

(b) *Mode of trial and class of offence*

This offence is triable either way: SOA 1956, s.37(2), and Sched. 2, para. 31. As to the clas- **H-209** sification of offences, see § 2-22c in the main work.

(c) *Sentence*

On conviction on indictment, imprisonment not exceeding seven years; on summary convic- **H-210** tion, six months, or a fine not exceeding £5,000: SOA 1956, s.37(3), and Sched. 2, para. 31 (as amended by the Street Offences Act 1959, s.4), and the MCA 1980, ss.32, 34(3)(a).

(26) Solicitation for immoral purposes

(a) *Statute*

Sexual Offences Act 1956, s.32

H-211 **32.** It is an offence for a man persistently to solicit or importune in a public place for immoral purposes.

As to the use of the word "man", see *post*, H-222.

(b) *Mode of trial and class of offence*

H-212 This offence is triable either way: SOA 1956, s.37(2), and Sched. 2, para. 32. As to the classification of offences, see *ante*, Appendix B-209.

(c) *Sentence*

H-213 On conviction on indictment, imprisonment not exceeding two years; on summary conviction, six months, or a fine not exceeding £5,000: SOA 1956, s.37(3), and Sched. 2, para. 32, and the MCA 1980, ss.32, 34(3)(a).

(d) *Ingredients of the offence*

"persistently"

H-214 Two separate acts of importuning within the period named in the information or indictment are sufficient to render the importuning persistent: *Dale v. Smith* [1967] 1 W.L.R. 700, DC (justices entitled to treat the use of the word "Hello" by the defendant to a youth in a public lavatory as an act of importuning, in view of the fact that the same word had been used by the defendant to another youth on the previous evening and had been followed by an undoubted act of importuning, *viz.* an invitation to look at indecent photographs).

"solicit"

H-215 In *Behrendt v. Burridge*, 63 Cr.App.R. 202, DC, the defendant was observed for about 50 minutes sitting on a high stool in the bay window of a house. She sat silent and motionless, dressed in a low cut top and mini-skirt. The bay window was illuminated by a red light. She was charged with soliciting for the purpose of prostitution, contrary to section 1 of the Street Offences Act 1959. The Divisional Court said that the fact that her behaviour could be described as an explicit form of advertising was not decisive in her favour: advertising and soliciting are not mutually exclusive. It was clear that she was soliciting in the sense of tempting or allowing prospective customers to come in for the purposes of prostitution.

See also *Horton v. Mead* [1913] 1 K.B. 154, DC, and *Burge v. DPP* [1962] 1 W.L.R. 265, DC.

"importune"

H-216 See *Dale v. Smith, ante,* H-214.

"public place"

H-217 No definition appears in the 1956 Act, but it is a frequently used expression in legislation: see, for example, the Public Order Act 1936, s.9 (§ 25-329 in the main work), the Prevention of Crime Act 1953, s.1(4) (§ 24-165 in the main work) and the Firearms Act 1968, s.57(4) (§ 24-120 in the main work).

"for immoral purposes"

H-218 An immoral purpose within section 32 has to be some kind of sexual activity: *Crook v. Edmondson* [1966] 2 Q.B. 81, DC; *R. v. Kirkup*, 96 Cr.App.R. 352, CA.

Section 32 applies both to heterosexual and homosexual behaviour: *R. v. Goddard*, 92 Cr.App.R. 185, CA.

Although section 1 of the SOA 1967 (*ante*, H-97) prevents homosexual practices in private between consenting parties who have attained the age of 16 from being a criminal offence, the 1967 Act did not change the law to the extent of preventing approaches for such purposes from being the offence of persistently importuning for "immoral purposes": *R. v. Ford*, 66 Cr.App.R. 46, CA. The judge correctly ruled that the conduct complained of could amount to an offence and correctly left the jury to decide whether the conduct was or was not immoral.

Similarly, in *R. v. Goddard, ante*, the unchallenged evidence of two young women was that they had had explicit sexual invitations made to them by G. It was held: (a) that it did not matter that the proposed sexual activity may be within the law; and (b) that it was a matter for the jury to decide, whether the invitations were for sexually immoral purposes, considering the circumstances in which the overtures were made and the nature of the overtures. This decision effectively overruled that part of the majority decision in *Crook v. Edmondson, ante*, which had held that "immoral purposes" was to be confined to purposes declared to be offences under other provisions of the 1956 Act.

The correct procedure is for the trial judge to rule whether the acts complained of could amount to an offence and, provided they are so capable, to leave it to the jury to decide whether the conduct, in fact, involved an immoral purpose, applying contemporary standards of morality: *R. v. Goddard, ante*.

(27) Interpretation

(a) *Meaning of "sexual intercourse"*

Sexual Offences Act 1956, s.44

44. Where, on the trial of any offence under this Act, it is necessary to prove sexual intercourse **H-219** (whether natural or unnatural), it shall not be necessary to prove the completion of the intercourse by the emission of seed, but the intercourse shall be deemed complete upon proof of penetration only.

See further, *ante*, H-14.

Boys under the age of 14

As to the abolition of the common law presumption that a boy under the age of 14 is incapable **H-220** of sexual intercourse, see *ante*, H-13. The presumption did not apply to a charge of aiding and abetting the commission of an offence: 1 Hale 630; *R. v. Williams* [1893] 1 Q.B. 320. Nor would it apply where the boy was not the defendant: see *R. v. Pickford* [1995] 1 Cr.App.R. 420, CA (*ante*, H-94).

(b) *Meaning of "defective"*

See section 45 of the SOA 1956, *ante*, H-68. **H-221**

(c) *Use of words "man", "boy", "woman" and "girl"*

Sexual Offences Act 1956, s.46

46. The use in any provision of this Act of the word "man" without the addition of the word **H-222** "boy", or *vice versa*, shall not prevent the provision applying to any person to whom it would have applied if both words had been used, and similarly with the words "woman" and "girl".

As to the use of the word "man", see *R. v. Tan* [1983] Q.B. 1053, 76 Cr.App.R. 300, CA, *ante*, H-202.

Section 46 applies for the purposes of the provisions of the SOA 1967 as it applies for the purposes of the provisions of the 1956 Act: SOA 1967, s.11(3). It also has effect as if the reference to the 1956 Act included a reference to the Sexual Offences (Amendment) Act 1976: Sexual Offences (Amendment) Act 1976, s.7(2).

(d) *Meaning of "parental responsibility"*

Sexual Offences Act 1956, s.46A

H-223   **46A.** In this Act "parental responsibility" has the same meaning as in the Children Act 1989.

[This section was inserted by the Children Act 1989, s.108(4), and Sched. 12, para. 17.]

Section 105(1) of the Act of 1989 provides that in that Act "parental responsibility" has the meaning given by section 3.

Children Act 1989, s.3

H-224   **3.**–(1) In this Act "parental responsibility" means all the rights, duties, powers, responsibilities and authority which by law a parent of a child has in relation to the child and his property.

(2) It also includes the rights, powers and duties which a guardian of the child's estate (appointed, before the commencement of section 5, to act generally) would have had in relation to the child and his property.

(3) The rights referred to in subsection (2) include, in particular, the right of the guardian to receive or recover in his own name, for the benefit of the child, property of whatever description and wherever situated which the child is entitled to receive or recover.

(4) The fact that a person has, or does not have, parental responsibility for a child shall not affect—

    (a) any obligation which he may have in relation to the child (such as a statutory duty to maintain the child); or

    (b) any rights which, in the event of the child's death, he (or any other person) may have in relation to the child's property.

(5) A person who—

    (a) does not have parental responsibility for a particular child; but

    (b) has care of the child,

may (subject to the provisions of this Act) do what is reasonable in all the circumstances of the case for the purpose of safeguarding or promoting the child's welfare.

Further reference may need to be made to sections 2 (parental responsibility for children) and 12 (residence orders and parental responsibility) of the 1989 Act.

(28) Proof of exceptions

Sexual Offences Act 1956, s.47

H-225   **47.** Where in any of the foregoing sections the description of an offence is expressed to be subject to exceptions mentioned in the section, proof of the exception is to lie on the person relying on it.

(29) Powers and procedure for dealing with offenders

Sexual Offences Act 1956, s.37

Prosecution and punishment of offences

H-226   **37.**–(1) The Second Schedule to this Act shall have effect, subject to and in accordance with the following provisions of this section, with respect to the prosecution and punishment of the offences listed in the first column of the Schedule, being the offences under this Act and attempts to commit certain of those offences.

(2) The second column in the Schedule shows, for any offence, if it may be prosecuted on indictment or summarily, or either ... and what special restrictions (if any) there are on the commencement of a prosecution.

(3) The third column in the Schedule shows, for any offence, the punishments which may be imposed on conviction on indictment or on summary conviction, a reference to a period giving the maximum term of imprisonment and a reference to a sum of money the maximum fine.

(4) The fourth column in the Schedule contains provisions which are either supplementary to those in the second or third column or enable a person charged on indictment with the offence specified in the first column to be found guilty of another offence if the jury are not satisfied that he is guilty of the offence charged or of an attempt to commit it, but are satisfied that he is guilty of the other offence.

(5) A provision in the fourth column of the Schedule enabling the jury to find the accused guilty of an offence specified in that provision authorises them, if not satisfied that he is guilty of the of-

fence so specified, to find him guilty of any other offence of which they could find him guilty if he had been indicted for the offence so specified.

(6) Where in the Schedule there is used a phrase descriptive of an offence or group of offences followed by a reference to a section by its number only, the reference is to a section of this Act, and the phrase shall be taken as referring to any offence under the section mentioned.

(7) Nothing in this section or in the Second Schedule to this Act shall exclude the application to any of the offences referred to in the first column of the Schedule—

(a) of section 24 of the Magistrates' Courts Act 1980 (which relates to the summary trial of young offenders for indictable offences); or

(b) of subsection (5) of section 121 of the Magistrates' Courts Act 1980 (which limits the punishment which may be imposed by a magistrates' court sitting in an occasional courthouse); or

(c) of any enactment or rule of law restricting a court's power to imprison; or

(d) of any enactment or rule of law authorising an offender to be dealt with in a way not authorised by the enactments specially relating to his offence; or

(e) of any enactment or rule of law authorising a jury to find a person guilty of an offence other than that with which he is charged.

[This section is printed as amended by the MCA 1980, Sched. 7, para. 17; and as repealed in part by the Courts Act 1971, s.56(4), and Sched. 11, Pt IV.]

Subsection (5) was considered in *R. v. Rogina*, 64 Cr.App.R. 79, CA, *ante*, H-74.

Attempts

Schedule 2 to the 1956 Act is not set out in this appendix. All relevant provisions thereof are referred to in the context of the individual offences, *ante*. Some of the paragraphs in the Schedule specifically refer to an attempt to commit a particular offence (sometimes with a different penalty to the full offence, sometimes with the same penalty). Wherever there is specific reference to an attempt in the schedule, this is referred to in the text in relation to the offence in question; where there is no such reference in the text, this is because there is no separate reference to an attempt in the schedule. In such cases, the Criminal Attempts Act 1981 will exclusively determine liability to prosecution and punishment for an attempt: for the 1981 Act, see §§ 33-128 *et seq.* in the main work.

H-227

C. Mental Health Act 1959

Mental Health Act 1959, s.128

Sexual intercourse with patients

128.—(1) Without prejudice to section seven of the Sexual Offences Act 1956, it shall be an offence, subject to the exception mentioned in this section,—

(a) for a man who is an officer on the staff of or is otherwise employed in, or is one of the managers of, a hospital independent hospital or care home to have unlawful sexual intercourse with a woman who is for the time being receiving treatment for mental disorder in that hospital or home, or to have such intercourse on the premises of which the hospital or home forms part with a woman who is for the time being receiving such treatment there as an outpatient;

(b) for a man to have unlawful sexual intercourse with a woman who is a mentally disordered patient and who is subject to his guardianship under the Mental Health Act 1983 or is otherwise in his custody or care under the Mental Health Act 1983 or in pursuance of arrangements under ... Part III of the National Assistance Act 1948 ... or the National Health Service Act 1977, or as a resident in a care home.

H-228

(2) It shall not be an offence under this section for a man to have sexual intercourse with a woman if he does not know and has no reason to suspect her to be a mentally disordered patient.

(3) Any person guilty of an offence under this section shall be liable on conviction on indictment to imprisonment for a term not exceeding two years.

(4) No proceedings shall be instituted for an offence under this section except by or with the consent of the Director of Public Prosecutions.

(5) This section shall be construed as one with the Sexual Offences Act 1956; and section 47 of that Act (which relates to the proof of exceptions) shall apply to the exception mentioned in this section.

(6) In this section "independent hospital" and "care home" have the same meaning as in the Care Standards Act 2000.

[This section is printed as amended by the National Health Service Act 1977, s.129, Sched. 15, para. 29, and Sched. 16; the MHA 1983, s.148, and Sched. 3, para. 15; the Registered Homes Act 1984, s.57, and Sched. 1, para. 2; and the Care Standards Act 2000, s.116, and Sched. 4, para. 2.]

H-229　As to the meaning of "sexual intercourse", see *ante*, H-219; as to the meaning of "unlawful" sexual intercourse, see *R. v. Chapman, ante*, H-38; as to the use of the words "man" and "woman", see *ante*, H-222.

For anonymity provisions, see §§ 20-257 *et seq.* in the main work.

For section 47 of the 1956 Act (burden of proof of exceptions), see *ante*, H-225.

By section 1(4) of the Sexual Offences Act 1967, section 128 is to have effect as if any reference therein to having unlawful sexual intercourse with a woman included a reference to committing buggery or an act of gross indecency with another man.

In connection with the offences created by this section, see *R. v. Davies and Poolton* [2000] Crim.L.R. 297, CA (§ 19-363 in the main work), decided in relation to the similarly worded section 127 of the 1959 Act.

D. INDECENCY WITH CHILDREN ACT 1960

(1) Statute

Indecency with Children Act 1960, s.1(1)

H-230　**1.**–(1) Any person who commits an act of gross indecency with or towards a child under the age of sixteen, or who incites a child under that age to such an act with him or another, shall be liable on conviction on indictment to imprisonment for a term not exceeding ten years, or on summary conviction to imprisonment for a term not exceeding six months, to a fine not exceeding the prescribed sum, or to both.

(2) [*Repealed by Police and Criminal Evidence Act 1984, Sched. 7.*]

(3) References in the Children and Young Persons Act 1933 ... to the offences mentioned in the First Schedule to that Act shall include offences under this section.

(4) offences under this section shall be deemed to be offences against the person for the purpose of section three of the Visiting Forces Act 1952 (which restricts the trial by United Kingdom courts of offenders connected with visiting forces).

[Subs. (1) is printed as amended by the C(S)A 1997, s.52 (substitution of "ten" for "two"); and the CJCSA 2000, s.39 (substitution of "sixteen" for "fourteen"). The first of these amendments took effect on October 1, 1997, but does not apply to offences committed before that date: Crime (Sentences) Act (Commencement No. 2 and Transitional Provisions) Order 1997 (S.I. 1997 No. 2200). The second amendment took effect on January 11, 2001: Criminal Justice and Court Services Act 2000 (Commencement No. 1) Order 2000 (S.I. 2000 No. 3302).]

As to Schedule 1 to the CYPA 1933, see § 19-408 in the main work.

For anonymity provisions, see §§ 20-257 *et seq.* in the main work.

(2) Indictment

Statement of Offence

H-231　*Indecency with a child, contrary to section 1(1) of the Indecency with Children Act 1960.*

Particulars of offence

A B, on the ___ day of ___, 20_, committed an act of gross indecency with [or towards] J N, a child of the age of 10 years [or incited J N, a child of the age of 10 years to commit an act of gross indecency with him the said A B (or with Y Z)].

It is a prerequisite of a conviction contrary to section 1 that the child was under the age of 16 at the time of the act or incitement: the child's age is an ingredient of the offence about which the jury must be satisfied and, unless age is admitted, calls for an appropriate direction from the judge: see *R. v. Goss and Goss*, 90 Cr.App.R. 400, CA, and *R. v. Radcliffe* [1990] Crim.L.R. 524, CA.

As to the propriety of preferring a charge of outraging public decency although the facts are covered by section 1(1), see *R. v. May (J.)*, 91 Cr.App.R. 157, CA (§ 20-238 in the main work).

(3) Mode of trial and class of offence

This offence is triable either way: s.1(1), *ante*. As to the classification of offences, see § 2-22c in the main work.

(4) Sentence

See section 1(1), *ante*. As to "the prescribed sum", see section 32 of the MCA 1980 (§ 1-119 in the main work).

(5) Consent of Director of Public Prosecutions

Section 8 of the SOA 1967 (no proceedings shall be instituted except by or with the consent of the Director against any man for gross indecency or certain other offences where any person involved is under 21) shall not apply to proceedings under the Indecency with Children Act 1960: CJA 1972, s.48.

(6) Ingredients of the offence

In *R. v. Speck*, 65 Cr.App.R. 161, CA, it was held that section 1 was contravened where S passively permitted a child to keep her hand on his penis for so long (in this case about five minutes) that his inactivity amounted to an invitation to her to continue the activity. If such an invitation could properly be inferred, it would constitute an "act" within section 1(1). Apart from allowing the child's hand to remain where she had placed it, S did nothing to encourage the child. A proper direction to the jury in such circumstances would be that the defendant's conduct might constitute an offence under section 1(1) if it amounted to an invitation from the defendant to the child to continue the activity in question. If they took that view (*i.e.* that there had been an "act") then they should go on to determine whether the act was an act of gross indecency. See also *R. v. B.* [1999] Crim.L.R. 594, CA.

Section 1(1) creates one offence of gross indecency, namely, the committing of an act of gross indecency involving a child; that is, "with or towards a child" is to be read as a phrase: *DPP v. Burgess* [1971] Q.B. 432, DC; *R. v. Francis*, 88 Cr.App.R. 127, CA. In *Francis*, the court considered the circumstances in which a man contravened section 1(1) if he masturbated in the presence of a child: the act had to be directed towards the child, the offender at the very least deriving satisfaction from the knowledge that the child was watching what he was doing.

As to the age of the victim being an essential ingredient of the offence, see *ante*, H-220; and it is necessary for the prosecution to prove the absence of a genuine belief on the part of the defendant that the victim was 16 years or above: *B. (a Minor) v. DPP* [2000] 2 A.C. 428, HL. The presence or absence of reasonable grounds for such belief goes only to whether such belief was genuinely held: *ibid.*

E. Sexual Offences Act 1967

(1) Procuring others to commit homosexual acts

Sexual Offences Act 1967, s.4

4.—(1) A man who procures another man to commit with a third man an act of buggery which by reason of section 1 of this Act is not an offence shall be liable on conviction on indictment to imprisonment for a term not exceeding two years.

(2) [*Repealed by Criminal Law Act 1977, Sched. 13.*]

(3) It shall not be an offence under section 13 of the Act of 1956 for a man to procure the commission by another man of an act of gross indecency with the first-mentioned man which by reason of section 1 of this Act is not an offence under the said section 13.

The offence under subsection (1) is triable either way: MCA 1980, s.17(1), and Sched. 1 (§ 1-119 in the main work).

As to the use of the word "man", see *ante*, H-222.

As to the offence of buggery, see *ante*, H-95 *et seq.*

For section 13 of the 1956 Act, see *ante*, H-107.

As to "procures", see *ante*, H-171.

(2) Living on earnings of male prostitution

Sexual Offences Act 1967, s.5

H-237   5.–(1) A man or woman who knowingly lives wholly or in part on the earnings of prostitution of another man shall be liable–

       (a)   on summary conviction to imprisonment for a term not exceeding six months, or

       (b)   on conviction on indictment to imprisonment for a term not exceeding seven years.

     (2) [*Repealed by Criminal Law Act 1977, Sched. 13.*]

     (3) Anyone may arrest without a warrant a person found committing an offence under this section.

H-238   As to the use of the words "man" and "woman", see *ante*, H-222 and–in relation to "man"–see *R. v. Tan* [1983] Q.B. 1053, 76 Cr.App.R. 300, CA, *ante*, H-202.

     As to the classification of offences, see § 2-22c in the main work.

     Subsection (3) has ceased to have effect by virtue of the PACE Act 1984, s.26(1) (§ 15-197 in the main work).

F. Criminal Law Act 1977

Criminal Law Act 1977, s.54

Incitement of girls under 16

H-239   54.–(1) It is an offence for a man to incite to have sexual intercourse with him a girl under the age of sixteen whom he knows to be his grand-daughter, daughter or sister.

     (2) In the preceding subsection "man" includes boy, "sister" includes half-sister, and for the purposes of that subsection any expression importing a relationship between two people shall be taken to apply notwithstanding that the relationship is not traced through lawful wedlock.

     (3) The following provisions of section 1 of the Indecency with Children Act 1960, namely–

     ...

     subsection (3) (references in Children and Young Persons Act 1933 to the offences mentioned in Schedule 1 to that Act to include offences under that section);

     subsection (4) (offences under that section to be deemed offences against the person for the purpose of section 3 of the Visiting Forces Act 1952),

     shall apply in relation to offences under this section.

     (4) A person guilty of an offence under this section shall be liable–

       (a)   on summary conviction, to imprisonment for a term not exceeding six months or to a fine not exceeding the prescribed sum or both;

       (b)   on conviction on indictment to imprisonment for a term not exceeding two years.

     [This section is printed as effectively amended by the MCA 1980, s.32(2) (substitution of reference to "the prescribed sum"); and as repealed in part by the PACE Act 1984, Sched. 7.]

H-240   As to Schedule 1 to the CYPA 1933, see § 19-408 in the main work.

     As to "the prescribed sum", see the MCA 1980, s.32(2) and (9) (§ 1-119 in the main work).

     For anonymity provisions, see §§ 20-257 *et seq.* in the main work.

     Section 54 filled a *lacuna* in the law, identified in *R. v. Whitehouse* [1977] Q.B. 868, 65 Cr.App.R. 33, CA.

     As to incitement at common law, see *ante*, §§ 33-74 *et seq.*

G. Sexual Offences (Amendment) Act 2000

(1) Statute

Sexual Offences (Amendment) Act 2000, ss.3, 4

Abuse of position of trust

H-241   3.–(1) Subject to subsections (2) and (3) below, it shall be an offence for a person aged 18 or over–

       (a)   to have sexual intercourse (whether vaginal or anal) with a person under that age; or

       (b)   to engage in any other sexual activity with or directed towards such a person,

     if (in either case) he is in a position of trust in relation to that person.

     (2) Where a person ("A") is charged with an offence under this section of having sexual intercourse with, or engaging in any other sexual activity with or directed towards, another person ("B"), it shall be a defence for A to prove that, at the time of the intercourse or activity–

    (a)   he did not know, and could not reasonably have been expected to know, that B was under 18;

    (b)   he did not know, and could not reasonably have been expected to know, that B was a person in relation to whom he was in a position of trust; or

    (c)   he was lawfully married to B.

(3) It shall not be an offence under this section for a person ("A") to have sexual intercourse with, or engage in any other sexual activity with or directed towards, another person ("B") if immediately before the commencement of this Act—

    (a)   A was in a position of trust in relation to B; and

    (b)   a sexual relationship existed between them.

(4) A person guilty of an offence under this section shall be liable—

    (a)   on summary conviction, to imprisonment for a term not exceeding six months, or to a fine not exceeding the statutory maximum, or to both;

    (b)   on conviction on indictment, to imprisonment for a term not exceeding five years, or to a fine, or to both.

(5) In this section, "sexual activity"—

    (a)   does not include any activity which a reasonable person would regard as sexual only with knowledge of the intentions, motives or feelings of the parties; but

    (b)   subject to that, means any activity which such a person would regard as sexual in all the circumstances.

As to "the commencement of this Act", see the Sexual Offences (Amendment) Act 2000 (Commencement No. 1) Order 2000 (S.I. 2000 No. 3303), which brought the Act into force on January 8, 2001.

Meaning of "position of trust"

4.—(1) For the purposes of section 3 above, a person aged 18 or over ("A") is in a position of trust   **H-242** in relation to a person under that age ("B") if any of the four conditions set out below, or any condition specified in an order made by the Secretary of State by statutory instrument, is fulfilled.

(2) The first condition is that A looks after persons under 18 who are detained in an institution by virtue of an order of a court or under an enactment, and B is so detained in that institution.

(3) The second condition is that A looks after persons under 18 who are resident in a home or other place in which—

    (a)   accommodation and maintenance are provided by an authority under section 23(2) of the Children Act 1989 or Article 27(2) of the Children (Northern Ireland) Order 1995;

    (b)   accommodation is provided by a voluntary organisation under section 59(1) of that Act or Article 75(1) of that Order; or

    (c)   accommodation is provided by an authority under section 26(1) of the Children (Scotland) Act 1995,

and B is resident, and is so provided with accommodation and maintenance or accommodation, in that place.

(4) The third condition is that A looks after persons under 18 who are accommodated and cared for in an institution which is—

    (a)   a hospital;

    (b)   a residential care home, nursing home, mental nursing home or private hospital;

    (c)   a community home, voluntary home, children's home or residential establishment; or

    (d)   a home provided under section 82(5) of the Children Act 1989,

and B is accommodated and cared for in that institution.

(5) The fourth condition is that A looks after persons under 18 who are receiving full-time education at an educational institution, and B is receiving such education at that institution.

(6) No order shall be made under subsection (1) above unless a draft of the order has been laid before and approved by a resolution of each House of Parliament.

(7) A person looks after persons under 18 for the purposes of this section if he is regularly involved in caring for, training, supervising or being in sole charge of such persons.

(8) For the purposes of this section a person receives full-time education at an educational institution if—

    (a)   he is registered or otherwise enrolled as a full-time pupil or student at the institution; or

    (b)   he receives education at the institution under arrangements with another educational institution at which he is so registered or otherwise enrolled.

(9) In this section, except where the context otherwise requires—

    "authority" means—

(a) in relation to Great Britain, a local authority; and

(b) [*Northern Ireland*];

"children's home" has—

(a) in relation to England and Wales, the meaning which would be given by subsection (3) of section 63 of the Children Act 1989 if the reference in paragraph (a) of that subsection to more than three children were a reference to one or more children; and

(b) [*Northern Ireland*];

"community home" has the meaning given by section 53(1) of the Children Act 1989;

"hospital" has—

(a) in relation to England and Wales, the meaning given by section 128(1) of the National Health Service Act 1977;

(b) [*Scotland*]; and

(c) [*Northern Ireland*];

"mental nursing home" has, in relation to England and Wales, the meaning given by section 22(1) of the Registered Homes Act 1984

"nursing home"—

(a) in relation to England and Wales, has the meaning given by section 21(1) of the Registered Homes Act 1984;

(b) [*Scotland*];

(c) [*Northern Ireland*];

"private hospital" has—

(a) [*Scotland*]; and

(b) [*Northern Ireland*];

"residential care home"—

(a) in relation to England and Wales, has the meaning given by section 1(2) of the Registered Homes Act 1984;

(b) [*Scotland*]; and

(c) [*Northern Ireland*];

"residential establishment" has the meaning given by section 93(1) of the Children (Scotland) Act 1995 as the meaning of that expression in Scotland;

"voluntary home" has—

(a) in relation to England and Wales, the meaning given by section 60(3) of the Children Act 1989; and

(b) [*Northern Ireland*].

(2) Indictment

Statement of Offence

H-243   *Abuse of a position of trust, contrary to section 3(1)(a) of the Sexual Offences (Amendment) Act 2000.*

Particulars of Offence

A B, on the ___ day of ___, 20_, being a person of the age of at least 18 years, had sexual intercourse with J N, being a person under the age of 18 years, and being at the time in a position of trust in relation to J N, in that at the time he looked after persons under the age of 18 years who were receiving full-time education at ___ school, and J N was at the time in receipt of such education at the aforesaid school.

(3) Mode of trial and class of offence

H-244   This offence is triable either way: s.3(4), *ante.* As to the classification of offences, see § 2-22c in the main work.

(4) Sentence

H-245   See s.3(4), *ante.*

The setting out of the various positions of trust in section 4(2) to (5) is not to be taken as indicative of descending seriousness: *R. v. Hubbard* [2002] 2 Cr.App.R.(S.) 101, CA.

APPENDIX J
A Guide to Commencing Proceedings in the Court of Appeal (Criminal Division)

NOTE: the text of the guide that follows has been subjected to some editorial revision (in relation to such matters as punctuation, use of upper and lower case, abbreviations, manner of citation of legislative references and authorities, and in order to correct a small number of obvious, minor errors). None of these revisions has any effect on the sense of the guide.

A GUIDE TO COMMENCING PROCEEDINGS IN THE COURT OF APPEAL (CRIMINAL DIVISION)

Foreword by the Lord Chief Justice of England and Wales

In recent years the Court of Appeal Criminal Division has faced increased complexity in appeals, not only against conviction but also against sentence, particularly in the light of the plethora of recent sentencing legislation. Additionally, the jurisdiction of the court has expanded to encompass a variety of diverse applications and appeals by the defence, the Crown and other interested parties. **J-1**

This guide provides invaluable advice as to the initial steps for commencing proceedings in the Court of Appeal Criminal Division generally and in relation to perhaps unfamiliar provisions.

The first and most important step is, of course, the preparation of the grounds of appeal. The rules prescribe the form and content of the Notice and Grounds of Appeal. Practitioners are also required to summarise the facts and outline their arguments concisely. Well drafted grounds of appeal assist the single judge when considering leave and serve to shorten any hearing before the full court. Ill-prepared and prolix documents necessarily lead to wasted time spent on preparation and unnecessarily protracted hearings.

It is important that we all take seriously our responsibility to ensure the effective progression of cases and keep delay to a minimum. Once an application or appeal is commenced, the responsible officer at the Criminal Appeal Office will be available to assist with any queries on practice or procedure.

The court could not deal with this volume of work efficiently without the support of the Registrar and his staff in the Criminal Appeal Office. Their experience and expertise is invaluable and can always be relied on by those who use the court, not least those who are unfamiliar with its practice and procedures.

Judge C.J.
October 2008

Introduction

Since the publication of the last Guide to Proceedings in the Court of Appeal (Criminal Division), the court's jurisdiction has increased. It hears appeals not only against conviction and sentence, but also against various interlocutory rulings, as well as other appeals and applications. **J-2**

This guide provides practical information about how to commence and conduct proceedings before the court. Once proceedings are commenced, an application will have its own unique reference number and a case progression officer who can help with any difficulties or queries about procedure.

The guide is set out as follows:

A. General principles of practice and procedure when applying for leave to appeal conviction and sentence.

B. Guidance on appeals against rulings made in preparatory hearings.

C. Guidance on prosecution appeals against 'terminating' rulings.

D. Brief guidance on other appeals in bullet point form showing:
  * the type of appeal,
  * the relevant section of the statute
  * the relevant Criminal Procedure Rules
  * who can apply
  * the forms to be used and time limits
  * respondents' notices,
  * whether representation orders are available
  * whether leave to appeal is required

E. Guidance on applications for a retrial for a serious offence.

A list of all up to date forms referred to in this guide may be accessed from the HMCS website at www.hmcourts-service.gov.uk or the Criminal Procedure Rules Committee website at www.justice.gov.uk/criminal/procrules. Where the Criminal Procedure Rules do not provide for a specific form, this guide indicates the appropriate form to be used.

This guide was prepared under my direction by the staff of the Criminal Appeal Office, but principally by Ms Alix Beldam and Ms Susan Holdham. It describes the law and practice of the Court as at 1st October 2008.

Master Venne

Registrar of Criminal Appeals

Terminology

J-3   The Criminal Appeal Act 1968 refers to "leave to appeal". This is now referred to as "permission to appeal" in the Criminal Procedure Rules 2007. This guide keeps to the terminology used by the Act.

Also consistently with the Act, an "appellant" is referred to without distinction, but it should be borne in mind that it is the accepted practice of the Criminal Appeal Office (CAO) to refer to a person who has served notice of appeal but not been granted leave to appeal as an "applicant" and use the term "appellant" to refer to a person who has been granted leave to appeal.

Any reference to counsel should be read as including a solicitor advocate as appropriate.

A. General Principles of Practice and Procedure when Applying for Leave to Appeal Conviction and Sentence

A1 Advice and assistance

J-4   A1-1 Provision for advice or assistance on appeal is included in the trial representation order issued by the Crown Court. Solicitors should not wait to be asked for advice by the defendant. Immediately following the conclusion of the case, the legal representatives should see the defendant and counsel should express orally his final view as to the prospects of a successful appeal (whether against conviction or sentence or both). If there are no reasonable grounds of appeal, that should be confirmed in writing and a copy provided then, or as soon as practicable thereafter, to the defendant by the solicitor. If there are reasonable grounds, grounds of appeal should be drafted, signed and sent to instructing solicitors as soon as possible. Solicitors should immediately send a copy of the documents received from counsel to the defendant.

A1-2 Prior to the lodging of the notice and grounds of appeal by service of Form NG, the Registrar has no power to grant a representation order. Also, the Crown Court can only amend a representation order in favour of fresh legal representatives if advice on appeal has not been given by trial legal representatives and it is necessary and reasonable for another legal representative to be instructed. Where advice on appeal has been given by trial legal representatives, application for funding may only be made to the Legal Services Commission (LSC).

A1-3 Once the Form NG has been lodged, the Registrar is the authority for decisions about representation orders, in accordance with the principle that the court before which there are proceedings is the court with power to grant a right to representation (Access to Justice Act 1999, Sched. 3, affirmed by regulation 10 of the Criminal Defence Service (General) (No. 2) Regulations 2001 (S.I. 2001 No. 1437)).

A1-4 Where, in order to settle grounds of appeal, work of an exceptional nature is contemplated or where the expense will be great, legal representatives should submit a Form NG with provisional grounds of appeal and with a note to the Registrar requesting a representation order to cover the specific work considered necessary to enable proper grounds of appeal to be settled.

A2 Form NG and grounds of appeal

J-5   A2-1 Where counsel has advised an appeal, solicitors should forward the signed grounds of appeal to the Crown Court accompanied by Form NG and such other forms as may be appropriate. It should be noted that Form NG and grounds of appeal are required to be served within the relevant time limit in all cases, whether or not leave to appeal is required (*e.g.* where a trial judge's certificate has been granted). However, on a reference by the Criminal Cases Review Commission (CCRC), if no Form NG and grounds are served within the required period, then the reference shall be treated as the appeal notice: rule 68.5(2).

A2-2 Grounds must be settled with sufficient particularity to enable the Registrar, and subsequently the court, to identify clearly the matters relied upon. A mere formula such as "the conviction is unsafe" or "the sentence is in all the circumstances too severe" will be ineffective as grounds and time will continue to run against the defendant.

A2-3 Rule 68.3(1) sets out the information that must be contained in the appeal notice. The notice must ... [*see § 7-382 in the main work*].

A2-4 There is now a requirement for the grounds of appeal to set out the relevant facts and nature of the proceedings concisely in one all encompassing document, not separate grounds and advice. The intended readership of this document is the court and not the lay or professional client. Its purpose is to enable the single judge to grasp quickly the facts and issues in the case. In appropriate cases, draft grounds of appeal may be perfected before submission to the single judge (*see further below para. A5*).

A2-5 Any document mentioned in the grounds should be identified clearly, by exhibit number or otherwise. Similarly, if counsel requires an original exhibit or shorthand writer's tape recording, he should say so well in advance of any determination or hearing.

A2-6 Counsel should not settle or sign grounds unless they are reasonable, have some real prospect of success and are such that he is prepared to argue them before the court. Counsel should not settle grounds he cannot support because he is "instructed" to do so by a defendant.

A2-7 Procedure in relation to particular grounds of appeal

A2-7.1 *Applications to call fresh evidence*

A Form W and a statement from the witness in the form prescribed by section 9 of the CJA 1967 should be lodged in respect of each witness it is proposed to call. The Form W should indicate whether there is an application for a witness order. The Registrar or the single judge may direct the issue of a witness order, but only the court hearing the appeal may give leave for a witness to be called.

The court will require a cogent explanation for the failure to adduce the evidence at trial. A supporting witness statement or affidavit from the appellant's solicitor should be lodged in this regard (*R. v. Gogana, The Times,* July 12, 1999).

If there is to be an application to adduce hearsay and/or evidence of bad character or for special measures, then the appropriate forms should be lodged: rule 68.7(1).

A2-7.2 *Complaints against trial counsel as a ground of appeal*

Where a ground of appeal explicitly criticises trial counsel and/or trial solicitors, the Registrar will institute the "waiver of privilege" procedure. The appellant will be asked to "waive privilege" in respect of instructions to and advice at trial from legal representatives. If he does waive privilege, the grounds of appeal are sent to the appropriate trial representative(s) and they are invited to respond. Any response will be sent to the appellant or his fresh legal representatives for comment. All these documents will be sent to the single judge when considering the application for leave. The single judge may draw inferences from any failure to participate in the process. "Waiver of privilege" is a procedure that should be instigated by the Registrar and not by fresh legal representatives, who should go no further than obtaining a waiver of privilege from the appellant: *R. v. Doherty and McGregor* [1997] 2 Cr.App.R. 218.

A2-7.3 *Insufficient weight given to assistance to prosecution authorities*

Where a ground of appeal against sentence is that the judge has given insufficient weight to the assistance given to the prosecution authorities, the "text" which had been prepared for the sentencing judge is obtained by the Registrar. Grounds of appeal should be drafted in an anodyne form with a note to the Registrar alerting him to the existence of a "text". The single judge will have seen the "text" when considering leave as will the full court before the appeal hearing and it need not be alluded to in open court.

A3 Time limits

A3-1 Notice and grounds should reach the Crown Court within 28 days from the date of the conviction in the case of an application for leave to appeal against conviction and within 28 days from the date of sentence in the case of an application for leave to appeal against sentence [CAA 1968, s.18 and rule 68.2(1)]. On a reference by the CCRC, Form NG and grounds should be served on the Registrar not more than 56 days after the Registrar has served notice that the CCRC has referred a conviction and not more than 28 days in the case of a sentence referral: rule 68.2(2).

A3-2 A confiscation order (whether made under the CJA 1988, the DTA 1994 or the PCA 2002) is a sentence [CAA 1968, s.50]. Where sentences are passed in separate proceedings on different dates there may be two appeals against sentence. Thus, there may be an appeal against the custodial part of a sentence and an appeal against a confiscation order (*R. v. Neal* [1999] 2 Cr.App.R.(S.) 352).

A3-3 An application for extension of the 28 day period in which to give notice of application for

J-6

leave to appeal or notice of appeal must always be supported by reasons why the application for leave was not submitted in time. It is not enough merely to tick the relevant box on Form NG.

A3-4 Such an application should be submitted when the application for leave to appeal against either conviction or sentence is made and not in advance. Notwithstanding the terms of section 18(3) of the CAA 1968, it has long been the practice of the Registrar to require the extension of time application to be made at the time of service of the notice and grounds of appeal. This practice is now reflected by Criminal Procedure Rule 65.4.

A4 Transcript and notes of evidence

J-7   A4-1 In conviction cases, transcripts of the summing up and proceedings up to and including verdict are obtained as a matter of course. Similarly, the transcript of the prosecution opening of facts on a guilty plea and the judge's observations on passing sentence are usually obtained in sentence cases. There is now an obligation under rule 68.3(2) for counsel to identify any further transcript which counsel considers the court will need and to provide a note of names, dates and times to enable an order to be placed with the shorthand writers. Whether or not any further transcript is required is a matter for the judgment of the Registrar or his staff.

A4-2 Transcript should only be requested if it is essential for the proper conduct of the appeal in the light of the grounds. If the Registrar and counsel are unable to agree the extent of the transcript to be obtained, the Registrar may refer that matter to a judge. In some cases the Registrar may propose that counsel agree a note in place of transcript.

A4-3 In certain circumstances the costs of unnecessary transcript could be ordered to be paid by the appellant. Where transcript is obtained otherwise than through the Registrar, he may disallow the cost on taxation of public funding.

A5 Perfection of grounds of appeal

J-8   A5-1 The purpose of perfection is (a) to save valuable judicial time by enabling the court to identify at once the relevant parts of the transcript and (b) to give counsel the opportunity to reconsider his original grounds in the light of the transcript. Perfected grounds should consist of a fresh document which supersedes the original grounds of appeal and contains *inter alia* references by page number and letter (or paragraph number) to all relevant passages in the transcript.

A5-2 In conviction or confiscation cases, the Registrar will almost certainly invite counsel to perfect grounds in the light of the transcript obtained, to assist the single judge or full court. Where counsel indicates a wish to perfect grounds of appeal against sentence, the Registrar will consider the request and will only invite perfection where he considers it necessary for the assistance of the single judge or full court.

A5-3 If perfection is appropriate, counsel will be sent a copy of the transcript and asked to perfect his grounds within 14 days. In the absence of any response from counsel, the existing notice and grounds of appeal will be placed before the single judge or the court without further notice. If counsel does not wish to perfect his grounds, the transcript should be returned with a note to that effect.

A5-4 If, having considered the transcript, counsel is of opinion that there are no valid grounds, he should set out his reasons in a further advice and send it to his instructing solicitors. He should inform the Registrar that he has done so, but should not send him a copy of that advice. Solicitors should send a copy to the appellant and obtain instructions, at the same time explaining that if the appellant persists with his application the court may consider whether to make a loss of time order (*see further below A-13*).

A6 Respondent's notice

J-9   A6-1 The Criminal Procedure Rules 2005 provide for the service of a respondent's notice. Under rule 68.6(1) the Registrar may serve the appeal notice on any party directly affected by the appeal (usually the prosecution) and must do so in a CCRC case. That party may then serve a respondent's notice if it wishes to make representations and must do so if the Registrar so directs: rule 68.6(2). The respondent's notice should be served within 14 days (rule 68.6(4)) on the appellant, the Registrar and any other party on whom the Registrar served the appeal notice (rule 68.6(3)). The respondent's notice must be in the specified form [Form RN], in which a respondent should set out the grounds of opposition (rule 68.6(5)) and which must include the information set out in rule 68.6(6).

A6-2 In practice, this procedure primarily applies prior to consideration of leave by the single judge in both conviction and sentence cases. The Attorney General and the Registrar, following consultation with representatives from the Crown Prosecution Service (CPS) and the Revenue and Customs Prosecution Office (RCPO), have agreed guidance on types of cases and/or issues where the Registrar should consider whether to serve an appeal notice and direct or invite a party to serve a respondent's notice before the consideration of leave by the single judge. Examples of when the Registrar might **direct** a respondent's notice include where the grounds concern matters which were the subject of public interest immunity (PII), allegations of jury irregularity, criticism of the conduct of the judge and complex frauds. Cases where it might be appropriate for the Registrar to **invite** a respondent's notice include, for example, homicide offences, serious sexual offences, cases with national profile or high media interest, cases of violence or domestic violence.

A6-3 In conviction cases where leave has been granted or where the application for leave has been referred to the full court, the Crown is briefed to attend the hearing and required to submit a respondent's notice/skeleton argument. In relation to sentence cases where leave has been granted, referred or an appellant is represented on a renewed application, the sentence protocol set out in paragraph II.1 of the consolidated criminal practice direction [see now *Criminal Practice Direction (Appeal) 68A* [2013] 1 W.L.R. 3164 (§ 7-203 in the main work)] will apply. In those cases, a respondent's notice/skeleton argument will have to be served when the Crown indicates a wish to attend or when the Registrar invites or directs the Crown to attend.

A7 Referral by the Registrar

A7-1 Leave to appeal is required in all cases except where the trial judge or sentencing judge has certified that the case is fit for appeal (CAA 1968, ss.1(2) and 11(1A)) or where the case has been referred by the CCRC. The appellant must obtain leave to pursue grounds not related to the Commission's reasons for referral: CAA 1995, s.14(4B). **J-10**

A7-2 Where leave to appeal is required and the Registrar has obtained the necessary documents, he will refer the application(s) either (a) to a single judge for decision under section 31 of the CAA 1968 or (b) directly to the full court, in which case a representation order is usually granted for the hearing. However, the Registrar will not grant a representation order when the presence of counsel is not required, *e.g.* where the application refers solely to an amendment of the number of days to be credited as "remand time" and the figure is agreed by the parties. Where an application is referred to the full court by the Registrar because an unlawful sentence has been passed or other procedural error identified, a representation order will ordinarily be granted, but counsel should be aware that the court may make observations for the attention of the determining officer that a full fee should not be allowed on taxation.

A7-3 Where leave to appeal is not required, *e.g.* on appeal by certificate of the trial judge, the Registrar will usually grant a representation order for the hearing. On a reference from the CCRC, it is the Registrar's usual practice to grant a representation order in the first instance, to solicitors for them to nominate and instruct counsel to settle grounds of appeal. Once counsel's details are known, a further representation order will be granted to cover the preparation (including settling grounds) and presentation of the appeal by counsel and further work by solicitors, as necessary in light of the grounds.

A8 Bail pending appeal

A8-1 Bail may be granted (a) by a single judge or the full court or (b) by a trial or sentencing judge who has certified the case fit for appeal. In the latter case, bail can only be granted within 28 days of the conviction or sentence which is the subject of the appeal and may not be granted if an application for bail has already been made to the Court of Appeal. **J-11**

A8-2 An application to the Court of Appeal for bail must be supported by a completed Form B, whether or not the application is made at the same time as the notice and grounds are served. The completed Form B must be served on the Registrar and the prosecution at least 24 hours before any application is made to enable the Crown to make representations (either written or oral) about the application and any conditions.

A8-3 An application for bail will not be considered by a single judge or the court until notice of application for leave to appeal or notice of appeal has first been given. In practice, judges will also require the relevant transcripts to be available so they may take a view as to the merits of the substantive application.

A8-4 It is the practice of the court, if bail is granted, to require a condition of residence. An application for variation of conditions of bail may be determined by the Registrar (if unopposed) or a single judge.

A9 Consideration of the applications by single judge

A9-1 Normally a single judge will consider the application for leave to appeal together with any ancillary applications, *e.g.* for bail or representation order, without hearing oral argument. Counsel may request an oral hearing, but it is only in very rare circumstances that the Registrar would consider it appropriate to grant a representation order for the proceedings before a single judge at an **J-12** oral hearing, but counsel may appear to argue the applications before the single judge where instructed to do so, usually appearing either *pro bono* or privately funded. Oral applications for leave and bail are usually heard at 9.30 a.m. before the normal court sittings. Counsel appears unrobed. If counsel considers that an application may take longer than 20 minutes, the Registrar must be informed.

A10 Powers of the single judge

J-13   A10-1 The single judge may grant the application for leave, refuse it or refer it to the full court. In conviction cases and in sentence cases where appropriate, the single judge may grant limited leave, *i.e.* leave to argue some grounds but not others. If the grounds upon which leave has been refused are to be renewed before the full court, counsel must notify the Registrar within 14 days. In the absence of any notification of renewal, it will be assumed that the grounds upon which leave was refused will not be pursued.

The single judge may also grant, refuse or refer any ancillary application.

A11 Grant of leave or reference to full court

J-14   A11-1 Where the single judge grants leave or refers an application to the court, it is usual to grant a representation order for the preparation and presentation of the appeal. This is usually limited to the services of counsel only, in which event counsel will be assigned by the Registrar. In such a case the Registrar will provide a brief but does not act as an appellant's solicitor. Counsel who settled grounds of appeal will usually be assigned. However, the Registrar may assign one counsel to represent more than one appellant if appropriate. If it is considered that a representation order for two counsel and/or solicitors is required, counsel should notify the Registrar and provide written justification in accordance with the Criminal Defence Service (General) (No. 2) Regulations 2001.

A11-2 If solicitors are assigned, it should be noted that by virtue of regulation 13 of the Criminal Defence Service (General) (No. 2) Regulations 2001, a representation order can only be issued to a solicitor if he holds a General Criminal Contract (Crime Franchise) with the LSC. A solicitor not holding such a franchise may apply to the LSC for an individual case contract (by virtue of which the solicitor is employed on behalf of the LSC to represent an appellant in a given case). Such a contract is sufficient for the purposes of regulation 13.

A11-3 In some circumstances, the Registrar may refer an application to the full court. This may be because there is a novel point of law or because in a sentence case, the sentence passed is unlawful and regardless of the merits, the sentence should be amended. A representation order for counsel is usually granted. Counsel for the prosecution usually attends a Registrar's referral.

A12 Refusal by the single judge

J-15   A12-1 Where the single judge refuses leave to appeal, the Registrar sends a notification of the refusal, including any observations which the judge may have made, to the appellant, who is informed that he may require the application to be considered by the court by serving a renewal notice [Form SJ-Renewal] upon the Registrar within 14 days from the date on which the notice of refusal was served on him.

A12-2 A refused application which is not renewed within 14 days lapses. An appellant may apply for an extension of time in which to renew his application for leave: CAA 1968, s.31, and rule 65.5(2). The Registrar will normally refer such an application to the court to be considered at the same time as the renewed application for leave to appeal. An application for extension for time in which to renew must be supported by cogent reasons.

A12-3 If it is intended that counsel should represent the appellant at the hearing of the renewed application for leave to appeal, whether privately instructed or on a *pro bono* basis, such intention must be communicated to the CAO in writing as soon as that decision has been made. Whilst a representation order is not granted by the Registrar in respect of a renewed application for leave, counsel may apply at the hearing to the court for a representation order to cover that appearance. In practice, this is only granted where the application for leave is successful.

A13 Directions for loss of time

J-16   A13-1 The CAA 1968, s. 29, empowers the court to direct that time spent in custody as an appellant shall not count as part of the term of any sentence to which the appellant is for the time being subject. The court will do so where it considers that an application is wholly without merit. Such an order may not be made where leave to appeal or a trial judge's certificate has been granted, on a reference by the CCRC or where an appeal has been abandoned.

A13-2 The mere fact that counsel has advised that there are grounds of appeal will not be a sufficient answer to the question as to whether or not an application has indeed been brought which was wholly without merit: *R. v. Hart; R. v. George; R. v. Clarke; R. v. Brown* [2007] 1 Cr.App.R. 31.

A13-3 The Form SJ, on which the single judge records his decisions, and the reverse of which is used by appellants to indicate their wish to renew, includes:

- a box for the single judge to initial to indicate that that the full court should consider loss of time if the application is renewed and
- a box for the applicant to give reasons why such an order should not be made, whether or not an indication has been given by a single judge.

A14 Abandonment

A14-1 An appeal or application may be abandoned at any time before the hearing without leave by completing and lodging Form A. An oral instruction or letter indicating a wish to abandon is insufficient.   **J-17**

A14-2 At the hearing, an application or appeal can only be abandoned with the permission of the court: rule 65.13(2). An appeal or application which is abandoned is treated as having been dismissed or refused by the full court, as the case may be: rule 65.13(4)(c).

A14-3 A notice of abandonment cannot be withdrawn nor can it be conditional. A person who wants to reinstate an application or appeal after abandonment must apply in writing with reasons: rule 65.13(5). The court has power to allow reinstatement only where the purported abandonment can be treated as a nullity (see *R. v. Medway*, 62 Cr.App.R. 85; *R. v. Burt, The Independent*, December 3, 2004; *R. v. Grant* (2005) 149 S.J. 1186).

A15 Case management duties

A15-1 Rule 65.2 gives the court and parties the same powers and duties of case management as in Part 3 of the rules. In accordance with those duties, for each application received, the Registrar nominates a case progression officer (the "responsible officer"). There is also a duty on the parties actively to assist the court to progress cases. Close contact between counsel and solicitors and the responsible officer is encouraged in order to facilitate the efficient preparation and listing of appeals, especially in complex cases and those involving witnesses.   **J-18**

A15-2 Powers exercisable by the single judge and the Registrar are contained in the CAA 1968, s.31. These powers include the power to make procedural directions for the efficient and effective preparation of an application or appeal and the power to make an order under section 23(1)(a) of the 1968 Act for the production of evidence etc. necessary for the determination of the case.

A15-3 Procedural directions given by the Registrar may be appealed to a single judge. Those given by a single judge, including a single Lord Justice, are final.

B. Interlocutory Appeals against Rulings in Preparatory Hearings

Appeal against a ruling under section 9 of the Criminal Justice Act 1987 or a decision under section 35 of the Criminal Procedure and Investigations Act 1996 [Part 66 Criminal Procedure Rules 2007]

B1 Where a judge has ordered a preparatory hearing, he may make a ruling as to the admissibility of evidence; any other question of law relating to the case or any question as to the severance or joinder of charges. (s.9(3)(b), (c) and (d) of the 1987 Act/s.31(3)(a), (b) and (c) of the 1996 Act)   **J-19**

B2 Under section 9(11) of the 1987 Act/section 35(1) of the 1996 Act the defence or the prosecution may appeal to the CACD (and ultimately to the House of Lords) against such a ruling, but only with the leave of the trial judge, single judge or the full court. As to the scope of a judge's powers in relation to a preparatory hearing and thus the extent of appeal rights, see *R. v. H* (§ 7-310 in the main work).

B3 If the trial date is imminent and the application is urgent, the Registrar should be notified so that he may consider referring the application directly to the full court and make arrangements for listing.

B4 If an application for leave to appeal is made to the trial judge, it should be made orally immediately after the ruling, or within two business days by serving a notice of an application on the appropriate officer of the Crown Court and all parties directly affected: rule 66.4. Notice of appeal or application for leave to appeal [Form NG (Prep)] is to be served on the Registrar, the Crown Court and the parties within five business days of the ruling or the trial judge's decision whether to grant leave: rule 66.2.

B5 The notice and grounds of appeal having been served on the other parties, grounds of opposition should be served in a respondent's notice [Form RN (Prep)] within five business days of service of the appeal notice: rule 66.5.

B6 Defence representatives are usually covered by the Crown Court representation order if one is in force (Access to Justice Act 1999, Sched. 3, para. 2(2)).

B7 If the relevant time limits are not complied with, the court has power to grant an extension of time, but cogent grounds in support of the application will be required. Where a single judge refuses leave to appeal or an extension of time within which to serve a notice, the application may be renewed for determination by the full court by serving the notice of refusal, appropriately completed, upon the Registrar within five business days of the refusal being served (rule 66.7).

C. APPEALS BY A PROSECUTOR AGAINST A "TERMINATING" RULING

Criminal Justice Act 2003, s.58 [Part 67 Criminal Procedure Rules 2007]

J-20

C1 Section 58 of the 2003 Act gives the prosecution a right of appeal in relation to a "terminating" ruling: in effect where the prosecution agrees to the defendant's acquittal if the appeal against the ruling is not successful (*R. v. Y.* [2008] 1 Cr.App.R. 34). This is wide enough to encompass a case management decision (*R. v. Clarke* [2008] 1 Cr.App.R. 33).

C2 There is no right of appeal in respect of a ruling that the jury be discharged or a ruling in respect of which there is a right of appeal to the Court of Appeal by virtue of another enactment (s.57(2)). The prosecution should therefore consider whether there is a right of appeal under section 9 of the CJA 1987 or section 35 of the CPIA 1996.

C3 The prosecution must inform the court that it intends to appeal or request an adjournment to consider whether to appeal (s.58(4)), which will be until the next business day (rule 67.2(2)). The judge has a discretion to adjourn for longer if there is a real reason for doing so (*R. v. H.* [2008] EWCA Crim. 483). The prosecution can then ask the trial judge to grant leave to appeal (rule 67.5), although leave to appeal can be granted by the trial judge, the single judge or the full court. The Crown must give the undertaking (as to the defendant's acquittal if the appeal is abandoned or leave to appeal is not obtained) at the time when it informs the court of its intention to appeal. The failure to give it then is fatal to an application to the Court of Appeal for leave: s.58(8); *R. v. Arnold* [2008] R.T.R. 25.

C4 Whether or not leave is granted, the trial judge must then decide if the appeal is to be expedited and if so, adjourn the case. If he decides that the appeal should not be expedited, then he can adjourn the case or discharge the jury (s.59). Leave should be granted only where the trial judge considers there is a real prospect of success and not in an attempt to speed up the hearing of the appeal (*R. v. J.G.* [2006] EWCA Crim. 3276).

C5 Whether the appeal is expedited or not affects the time limits for service of the notice of appeal [Form NG (Pros)] and respondent's notice [Form RN (Pros)]. If expedited, the appeal notice must be served the next business day after the decision, if not expedited, it must be served within five business days. Similar time limits apply to the service of the respondent's notice. Defence representatives are usually covered by the Crown Court representation order if one is in force (such proceedings being considered incidental within the Access to Justice Act 1999, Sched. 3, para. 2(2)). If the relevant time limits are not complied with, the court has power to grant an extension of time.

C6 Expedition does not impose time limits on the Registrar or Court of Appeal. However, if leave has not been granted by the trial judge, the application may be referred to the full court by the Registrar to enable the application and appeal to be heard together to ensure that the matter is dealt with quickly.

C7 The Registrar endeavours to list prosecution appeals where a jury has not been discharged as quickly as possible. He is unlikely to be able to list an appeal in less than a week from the ruling because it is necessary for the prosecution to obtain transcripts, papers to be copied and the judges to read their papers. It is of great assistance if it is anticipated that there is to be an appeal against a ruling where the jury has not been discharged, that a telephone call is made to the Registrar or CAO general office (020 7947 6011) notifying the office even before the appeal notice is sent, so that the list office may be put on notice. The listing of an urgent appeal invariably means that other cases have to be removed from the list.

D. OTHER APPEALS

D1 Prosecution appeal against the making of a confiscation order or where the court declines to make one (save on reconsideration of benefit)

J-21
- S.31 of the PCA 2002.
- Parts 71 and 72 of the Criminal Procedure Rules.
- From April 1, 2008 only the prosecution can appeal
- Proceedings are commenced by serving a Form PoCA 1 on the defendant and the Crown Court within 28 days of the decision appealed against. [Proceeds of Crime Act (Appeals under Part 2) Order 2003, art. 3(2)(a).]

- A respondent's notice PoCA 2 is to be served on the Registrar of Criminal Appeals and the appellant not later than 14 days after receiving PoCA 1.
- An undischarged Crown Court representation order will cover advice and assistance on the merits of opposing the appeal and drafting the respondent's notice, otherwise an application for a representation order can be made to the Registrar [Access to Justice Act 1999, ss.12(2)(b), 26]. In any event, where an application for a representation order is made on PoCA 2, the Registrar will consider a representation order for the hearing.
- Leave to appeal can be granted by a single judge or the full court.

D2 Appeal in relation to a restraint order

- S.43 of the PCA 2002.

- Parts 71 and 73 of the Criminal Procedure Rules.
- The prosecution or an accredited financial investigator can appeal a refusal to make a restraint order. A person who applied for an order or who is affected by the order can apply to the Crown Court to vary or discharge the order and then appeal that decision to the Court of Appeal.
- Proceedings are commenced by serving a form PoCA 3 on the Crown Court within 14 days of the decision being appealed. PoCA 3 must then be served on any respondent, and on any person who holds realisable property to which the appeal relates, or is affected by the appeal, not later than seven days after the form is lodged at the Crown Court. The documents which are to be served with PoCA 3 are set out in rule 73.2(3).
- A respondent's notice PoCA 4 is to be served on the Registrar not later than 14 days after the respondent is notified that the appellant has leave to appeal or notified that the application for leave and any appeal are to be heard together. PoCA 4 is then to be served on the appellant and any other respondent as soon as is practicable and not later than seven days after it was served on the Registrar.
- An application for a restraint order can be made as soon as a criminal investigation has begun. The proposed defendant may not have been charged: PCA 2002, s.40. This affects the type of public funding.
- If a defendant has been charged with a criminal offence connected to the restraint order then the restraint proceedings are regarded as incidental to the criminal proceedings and are treated as criminal proceedings for funding purposes [Criminal Defence Service (General) (No. 2) Regulations 2001, reg.3(3)(c)] and the Registrar can grant a representation order if a defendant appeals a decision on an application to vary or discharge the restraint order.
- If the prosecution apply for a restraint order in the Crown Court before the subject of the restraint order has been charged with a criminal offence and the subject of that order wishes to appeal a decision on an application to vary or discharge the restraint order then civil legal aid may be available as these proceedings fall within the Access to Justice Act 1999, Sched. 2, para. 3. The Legal Services Commission should be contacted for funding within the Community Legal Service scheme.
- Similarly, a person affected by the order who wishes to appeal a decision on an application to vary or discharge the restraint order should apply to the Legal Services Commission for funding within the Community Legal Service scheme.
- Leave to appeal can be granted by a single judge or full court.

D3 Appeal in relation to a receivership order

- S.65 of the PCA 2002.

- Parts 71 and 73 of the Criminal Procedure Rules.
- An appeal can be brought by:
  (a) the person who applied for the order,
  (b) a person who is affected by the order or,
  (c) the receiver.
  The orders against which an appeal will lie are:
  (1) the appointment or non-appointment of a receiver,
  (2) the powers of a receiver,
  (3) an order giving a direction to a receiver, and
  (4) the variation or discharge of a receivership order.
- Proceedings are commenced by serving a Form PoCA 3 on the Crown Court within 14 days of the decision being appealed. PoCA 3 must then be served on any respondent and

on any person who holds realisable property to which the appeal relates, or is affected by the appeal, not later than seven days after the form is lodged at the Crown Court. The documents which are to be served with PoCA 3 are set out in rule 73.2(3).

- A respondent's notice PoCA 4 is to be served on the Registrar not later than 14 days after the respondent is notified that the appellant has leave to appeal or is notified that the application for leave and any appeal are to be heard together. PoCA 4 is then to be served on the appellant and any other respondent as soon as is practicable and not later than seven days after it was served on the Registrar.
- If a defendant has been charged with a criminal offence connected to a receivership order then the receivership proceedings are regarded as incidental to the criminal proceedings and are treated as criminal proceedings for funding purposes [Criminal Defence Service (General) (No. 2) Regulations 2001, reg.3(3)(c)] and the Registrar can grant a representation order if a defendant appeals a decision relating to a receivership order.
- If a management receivership order or an application for such an order is made in the Crown Court before a criminal offence has been charged and a person affected by the order (including the proposed defendant) wishes to appeal a decision then civil legal aid may be available as these proceedings fall within Access to Justice Act 1999, Sched. 2, para. 3. The Legal Services Commission should be contacted for funding within the Community Legal Service scheme.
- Leave to appeal can be granted by a single judge or the full court.

D4 Appeal against an order of the Crown Court in the exercise of its jurisdiction to punish for contempt – usually a finding of contempt or sentence for contempt

J-24
- S.13 of the Administration of Justice Act 1960.
- Part 68 of the Criminal Procedure Rules.
- Anyone dealt with by the Crown Court for contempt may appeal.
- Proceedings are commenced by lodging a Form NG at the Crown Court not more than 28 days after the order to be appealed.
- The Registrar may direct a respondent's notice Form RN or the Crown may serve one if they wish to make representations to the court.
- An undischarged Crown Court representation order will cover advice and assistance on appeal. The Registrar will usually grant a representation order for the hearing: Access to Justice Act 1999, s.12(2)(b).
- No leave to appeal is required. The appeal is as of right.
- Appeals occur most frequently when an appellant wishes to appeal a sentence for failing to appear at the Crown Court as the failing to appear is dealt with as if it were contempt.

D5 Appeal against a minimum term set or reviewed by a High Court judge

J-25
- Para. 14 of Schedule 22 to the CJA 2003
- Part 68 of the Criminal Procedure Rules
- A defendant with a mandatory life sentence imposed before December 18, 2003 who has had his minimum term set or reviewed by a High Court judge can appeal.
- Proceedings are commenced by service of Form NG (MT) on the Registrar not more than 28 days after the decision.
- The Registrar may direct a respondent's notice Form RN or the Crown may serve one if they wish to make representations to the court.
- An application for a representation order can be made to the Registrar [Access to Justice Act 1999, s.12(2)(b)].
- Leave to appeal is required and can be granted by the full court or a single judge: Criminal Justice Act 2003 (Mandatory Life Sentences: Appeals in Transitional Cases) Order 2005 (S.I. 2005 No. 2798), art. 8.

D6 Attorney General's reference of an unduly lenient sentence

J-26
- S.36 of the CJA 1988.
- Part 70 of the Criminal Procedure Rules.
- The Attorney General can refer sentences only in relation to specific offences or sentences [CJA 1988, ss.35, 36, and Criminal Justice Act 1988 (Reviews of Sentencing) Order 2006] including a minimum term, set or reviewed by a High Court judge [CJA 2003, Sched. 22, para. 15].

- Although rule 70.3(1) implies there is a specific form to commence proceedings, in practice a standard letter with supporting documents is sent by the Attorney General's office no more than 28 days after sentence.
- If the defendant wishes to make representations to the court he must serve a respondent's notice within 14 days of the Registrar serving the application upon him. Again, there is no specific form designated.
- Representation orders are not issued to respond to an Attorney General's reference but a defendant who appears by counsel is entitled to his reasonable costs from central funds. The cost of instructing leading counsel in addition to or instead of junior counsel is generally not considered reasonable unless there is a compelling reason. It is advisable to consult with the Registrar before leading counsel is instructed.
- The leave of the Court of Appeal is required.

D7 Attorney General's reference of a point of law on an acquittal

J-27

- S.36 of the CJA 1972.
- Part 70 of the Criminal Procedure Rules.
- The Attorney General can refer a point of law to the Court of Appeal for an opinion on the acquittal on indictment of the defendant.
- Although rule 70.3(1) implies there is a specific form to commence proceedings, there is no such form and rule 70.3 sets out what should be included in the reference. The defendant should not be identified.
- There is no time limit.
- If the defendant wishes to make representations to the court he must serve a respondent's notice within 28 days of the Registrar serving the application upon him. Again there is no specific form.
- Representation orders are not issued to respond to an Attorney General's reference but a defendant who appears by counsel is entitled to his reasonable costs from central funds.
- Leave is not required.

D8 Appeal against a finding of unfitness to plead or a finding that the accused did the act or made the omission charged

J-28

- S.15 of the CAA 1968.
- Part 68 of the Criminal Procedure Rules.
- The accused can appeal (by the person appointed to represent the accused) against
  - a finding of unfitness to plead (but not fitness to plead as the defendant can appeal any subsequent conviction in the usual way on the basis he was not fit to plead) or
  - that he did the act or made the omission charged or
  - both findings.

  The appeal does not lie until both findings have been made.
- Proceedings are commenced by the service of Form NG on the Crown Court not more than 28 days after the finding made which the accused wishes to appeal.
- The Crown should serve a respondent's notice Form RN if directed by the Registrar or if they wish to make representations to the court.
- There does not appear to be any statutory provision empowering the grant of a representation order. The Prosecution of Offences Act 1985, s.19, refers to costs from central funds being available to cover the fees of a person appointed by the Crown Court under section 4A of the Criminal Procedure (Insanity) Act 1964. In *R. v. Antoine* ([1999] 2 Cr.App.R 225, CA) this was interpreted to include the costs of an appeal. The Prosecution of Offences Act 1985, s.16(4) provides that where the Court of Appeal allows an appeal under Part 1 of the CAA 1968 against a finding under the Criminal Procedure (Insanity) Act 1964 that the appellant is under a disability, or that he did the act or made the omission charged against him the court may make a defendant's costs order in favour of the accused.
- Leave to appeal may be granted by the Crown Court judge, a single judge or the full court.

D9 Appeal against a verdict of not guilty by reason of insanity

J-29

- S.12 of the CAA 1968.
- Part 68 of the Criminal Procedure Rules.
- The defendant can appeal a verdict of not guilty by reason of insanity.

- Proceedings are commenced by the service of Form NG on the Crown Court not more than 28 days after the verdict.
- The Crown should serve a respondent's notice Form RN if directed by the Registrar or if they wish to make representations to the court.
- There does not appear to be any statutory provision empowering the grant of a representation order. The Prosecution of Offences Act 1985, s.16(4), provides that where the Court of Appeal <u>allows an appeal</u> then the court may make a defendant's costs order. If the appeal is not allowed costs from central funds should be available on the same basis as was allowed in *Antoine* (*ante*) in the absence of any statutory provision.
- Leave to appeal may be granted by the Crown Court judge, a single judge or the full court.

D10 Appeal against the order following a verdict of not guilty by reason of insanity or a finding of unfitness to plead

J-30
- S.16A of the CAA 1968.
- Part 68 of the Criminal Procedure Rules.
- An accused who, as a result of a verdict of not guilty by reason of insanity or a finding of fitness to plead has a hospital order, interim hospital order or supervision order made against him may appeal against the order.
- Proceedings are commenced by the service of Form NG on the Crown Court not more than 28 days after the order.
- [As D9, *ante*.]
- [As D9, *ante*.]
- [As D9, *ante*.]

D11 Appeal against review of sentence

J-31
- S.74(8) of the SOCPA 2005.
- Part 68 of the Criminal Procedure Rules.
- A defendant or specified prosecutor may appeal.
- Proceedings are commenced by serving a Form NG (RD) on the Crown Court not more than 28 days after the review.
- A respondent's notice Form RN should be served if directed by the Registrar or if the respondent wishes to make representations to the Court.
- An application for a representation order can be made to the Registrar: Access to Justice Act 1999, s.12(2)(b).
- Leave to appeal can be granted by the single judge or full court [Serious Organised Crime and Police Act 2005 (Appeals under section 74) Order 2006 (S.I. 2006 No. 2135)].

D12 Appeal against an order for trial by jury of sample counts

J-32
- S.18 of the Domestic Violence, Crime and Victims Act 2004.
- Part 66 of the Criminal Procedure Rules.
- The defendant can appeal.
- An application for the jury to try some counts as sample counts and the judge to try the remainder if the jury convict, must be determined at a preparatory hearing and section 18 confers rights of interlocutory appeal. A Form NG (Prep) must be served on the Crown Court, the Registrar and any party directly affected not more than five business days after the order or the Crown Court judge granting or refusing leave. (*For applications to the Crown Court judge, see Part B above.*)
- A respondent's notice Form RN (Prep) should be served if the court directs or the Crown (or any party affected) wants to make representations to the court.
- Defence representatives are usually covered by the Crown Court representation order if one is in force [Access to Justice Act 1999, Sched. 3, para. 2(2)].
- The Crown Court Judge, single judge or full court can grant leave to appeal.

D13 Appeal against an order relating to a trial to be conducted without a jury where there is a danger of jury tampering

J-33
- S.9(11) of the CJA 1987 and s.35(1) of the CPIA 1996.
- Part 66 of the Criminal Procedure Rules.
- The prosecution can appeal the refusal to make an order; the defence can appeal the making of an order.

- A Form NG (Prep) must be served on the Crown Court, the Registrar and any party directly affected not more than five business days after the order or the Crown Court judge grants or refuses leave. (*For applications to the Crown Court judge, see Part B above.*)
- A respondent's notice Form RN (Prep) should be served if the court directs or the Crown (or any party affected) wants to make representations to the court.
- Defence representatives are usually covered by the Crown Court representation order if one is in force [Access to Justice Act 1999, Sched. 3, para.2 (2)].
- Leave is required. The Crown Court judge, single judge or full court can grant leave to appeal.

D14 Appeal against an order that a trial should continue without a jury or a new trial take place without a jury after jury tampering

- S.47 of the CJA 2003.   **J-34**
- Part 66 of the Criminal Procedure Rules (relating to appeals against an order made in a preparatory hearing notwithstanding the ruling will not have been in the context of a preparatory hearing).
- The defendant can appeal.
- As D13, *ante*
- As D13, *ante*
- As D13, *ante*
- As D13, *ante*

D15 Appeal against orders restricting or preventing reports or restricting public access

- S.159 of the CJA 1988   **J-35**
- Part 69 of the Criminal Procedure Rules
- A person aggrieved may appeal.
- Applications against orders <u>restricting reporting</u> shall be made within 10 business days after the date on which the order was made by serving Form NG (159) on the Registrar, the Crown Court, the prosecutor and defendant and any other affected person. Applications against orders to <u>restrict public access</u> must be made the next business day after the order was made. If advance notice of an order restricting public access is given, then advance notice of an intention to appeal may be made not more than five business days after the advance notice is displayed.
- A person on whom an appeal notice is served should serve a respondent's notice Form RN (159) within three business days if he wishes to make representations to the court or the court so directs.
- The court may make such order as to costs as it thinks fit (CJA 1988, s.159(5)(c)), but not out of central funds - *Holden v. CPS (No. 2)* [1994] 1 A.C. 22, HL.
- A single judge or the full court can grant leave to appeal: CAA 1968, s.31(2B).
- Applications for leave to appeal and appeals in relation to reporting restrictions <u>may</u> be heard in private (rule 65.6 (1)). Applications for leave to appeal and appeals relating to restricting public access must be determined <u>without</u> a hearing (rule 65.6(3)).

D16 Appeal against a wasted costs order and appeal against a third party costs order

- Regulation 3C (costs wasted) and 3E (third party costs) of the Costs in Criminal Cases   **J-36** (General) Regulations 1986.
- A legal or other representative against whom a wasted costs order has been made in the Crown Court or a third party against whom a third party costs order has been made may appeal.
- Notice of appeal should be served on the Crown Court within 21 days of the order being made. There is no specific form. The notice should be served on any interested party (including, if appropriate, the Ministry of Justice).
- Any interested party can make representations orally or in writing.
- There is no power to grant a representation order or to order costs out of central funds as these proceedings are civil in nature.
- Leave to appeal is not required.

D17 Appeal relating to serious crime prevention orders

- S.24 of the SCA 2007.   **J-37**

- Part 68 of the Criminal Procedure Rules.
- A person subject to the order, an applicant authority or anyone given the opportunity to make representations at the Crown Court about the making, refusal to make, variation or non-variation of an order may appeal.
- Proceedings are commenced by the service of Form NG (SCPO) on the Crown Court not more than 28 days after the order.
- A respondent's notice Form RN (SCPO) should be served if directed by the Registrar or if the respondent wishes to make representations to the court.
- Proceedings before the Crown Court or the Court of Appeal relating to serious crime prevention orders and arising by virtue of section 19, 20, 21 or 24 of the SCA 2007 are criminal proceedings for the purposes of section 12(2)(g) of the Access to Justice Act 1999 [see the Criminal Defence Service (General) (No. 2) (Amendment) Regulations (S.I. 2008 No. 725)]. Accordingly, the Registrar may grant a representation order to a person subject to the order. A person who made representations at the Crown Court can apply to the LSC for funding. The court has discretion to order costs as it thinks fit [Serious Crime Act 2007 (Appeals under section 24) Order 2008 (S.I. 2008 No. 1863), Pt 3].
- Leave to appeal can be granted by the Crown Court judge, full court or single judge [S.I. 2008 No. 1863, art. 9].

D18 Appeal against the non-making of a football banning order

J-38
- S.14A(5A) of the Football Spectators Act 1989.
- Part 68 of the Criminal Procedure Rules.
- The prosecution can appeal.
- The appeal notice should be served on the Crown Court within 28 days of the decision not to make an order. However, there is no designated form.
- A respondent's notice should be served if directed by the Registrar or if the respondent wishes to make representations to the court. However, again there is no designated form.
- An application for a representation order may be made to the Registrar - Access to Justice Act 1999, s.12(2)(b).
- Currently, the Court of Appeal has been given no powers to deal with these appeals.

E. APPLICATION FOR A RETRIAL FOR A SERIOUS OFFENCE

E1 Application by a prosecutor to quash an acquittal and seek a retrial for a qualifying offence

S.76(1) of the Criminal Justice Act 2003 [Part 41 of the Criminal Procedure Rules]

J-39
E1-1 There must be new and compelling evidence and it must be in the interests of justice for the acquitted person to be retried for a qualifying offence as listed in the CJA 2003, Sched. 5, Pt 1 (CJA 2003, ss.78, 79: see *R. v. Dunlop* [2007] 1 Cr.App.R. 8, and *R. v. Miell* [2008] 1 Cr.App.R. 23).

E1-2 Proceedings can begin in one of two ways.

(1) By serving notice of the application under section 76 on the Court of Appeal and within two days serving the notice on the acquitted person (s.80). This notice charges him with the offence. It requires the personal written consent of the Director of Public Prosecutions (DPP) (s.76(3)). If the acquitted person is not in custody the prosecution can ask the Crown Court to issue:

   (i) a summons for the acquitted person to appear before the Court of Appeal for the hearing of the application or

   (ii) a warrant for his arrest (s.89(3)).

   Once arrested on the warrant the acquitted person must be brought before the Crown Court within 48 hours (s.89(6)).

(2) An acquitted person may be charged with the offence before an application under section 76 has been made. This may be after an arrest in an investigation authorised by the DPP (s.85(2)) or where no authorisation has been given, after arrest under a warrant issued by a justice of the peace (s.87(1)). Having been charged, the acquitted person must be brought before the Crown Court to consider bail within 24 hours (s.88(2)). He can then be remanded in custody or on bail for 42 days whilst an application under s.76 is prepared: s.88(6) unless an extension is granted under subsection (8). Once a notice of application under section 76 has been served, stating that the acquitted person has previously been charged with the offence, the acquitted person must be brought before the Crown Court to consider bail within 48 hours of the notice being given to the Registrar, if the acquitted person is already in custody under secton 88 (*ante*) (s.89(2)).

E1-3 Thus in either case, bail is dealt with largely by the Crown Court. The Court of Appeal only considers bail on the adjournment of the hearing of the application under section 76 (s.90(1)).

E1-4 The notice ["Notice of a s.76 application required by s.80(1) Criminal Justice Act 2003"] should where practicable be accompanied by the witness statements which are relied on as the new and compelling evidence, the original witness statements, unused statements, indictment, paper exhibits from the original trial, any relevant transcripts from the original trial and any other documents relied on: rule 41.2(2).

E1-5 An acquitted person who wants to oppose a section 76 application must serve a response ["Response of the acquitted person under s.80 Criminal Justice Act 2003"] not more than 28 days after receiving the notice: rule 41.3(2).

E2 Application by a prosecutor for a determination whether a foreign acquittal is a bar to a trial and if so, an order that it not be a bar

S. 76(2) of the Criminal Justice Act 2003 [Part 41 of the Criminal Procedure Rules]

E2-1 The prosecution can apply, with the personal written consent of the DPP (s.76(3)) for a **J-40** determination whether an acquittal outside the UK is a bar to the acquitted person being tried in England and Wales and if it is found to be so, an order that the acquittal not be a bar. Proceedings can begin in the same way as for an application under section 76(1).

E3 Application for restrictions on publication relating to an application under section 76

S. 82 of the Criminal Justice Act 2003 [Part 41 of the Criminal Procedure Rules]

E3-1 An application can be made by the DPP for reporting restrictions. This can be made after a **J-41** notice of an application for a retrial has been made and may also be made by the court of its own motion (s.82(5)). An application can also be made by the DPP for reporting restrictions *before* a notice of an application for a retrial if an investigation has been commenced: s.82(6). The application for reporting restrictions must be served on the Registrar ["Application for restrictions on publication under s.82 Criminal Justice Act 2003"] and (usually) the acquitted person (rule 41.8(1)).

E3-2 A party who wants to vary or revoke an order for restrictions on publication under section 82(7) may apply to the Court of Appeal in writing at any time after the order was made (rule 41.9(1)).

E4 Representation orders

E4-1 The Registrar will usually grant a representation order to the acquitted person for solicitors **J-42** and counsel to respond to any of the above applications.

APPENDIX N
Protocols

A. Cᴏɴᴛʀᴏʟ ᴀɴᴅ Mᴀɴᴀɢᴇᴍᴇɴᴛ ᴏꜰ Hᴇᴀᴠʏ Fʀᴀᴜᴅ ᴀɴᴅ ᴏᴛʜᴇʀ Cᴏᴍᴘʟᴇx Cʀɪᴍɪɴᴀʟ Cᴀsᴇs

A protocol issued by the Lord Chief Justice of England and Wales   **N-1**

22 March 2005

Introduction

The investigation

        The role of the prosecuting authority and the judge

        Interviews

        The prosecution and defence teams

        Initial consideration of the length of a case

        Notification of cases likely to last more than 8 weeks

        Notification of cases likely to last more than 8 weeks

        Venue

Designation of the trial judge

        The assignment of a judge

Case management

        Objectives

        The assignment of a judge

Case management

        Objectives

        Fixing the trial date

        The first hearing for the giving of initial directions

        The first Case Management Hearing

        Further Case Management Hearings

        Consideration of the length of the trial

        The exercise of the powers

        Fixing the trial date

        The first hearing for the giving of initial directions

        The first Case Management Hearing

        Further Case Management Hearings

        Consideration of the length of the trial

        The exercise of the powers

        Expert Evidence

        Surveillance Evidence

Disclosure

Abuse of process

The trial

        The particular hazard of heavy fraud trials

        Judicial mastery of the case

        The order of the evidence

        Case management sessions

Controlling prolix cross-examination
Electronic presentation of evidence
Use of interviews
Jury Management
Maxwell hours
Livenote

Other issues

Defence representation and defence costs
Assistance to the Judge
Jury Management
Maxwell hours
Livenote

Other issues

Defence representation and defence costs
Assistance to the Judge

Introduction

N-2   There is a broad consensus that the length of fraud and trials of other complex crimes must be controlled within proper bounds in order:

(i) To enable the jury to retain and assess the evidence which they have heard. If the trial is so long that the jury cannot do this, then the trial is not fair either to the prosecution or the defence.

(ii) To make proper use of limited public resources: see *Jisl* [2004] EWCA Crim. 696 at [113]-[121].

There is also a consensus that no trial should be permitted to exceed a given period, save in exceptional circumstances; some favour 3 months, others an outer limit of 6 months. Whatever view is taken, it is essential that the current length of trials is brought back to an acceptable and proper duration.

This Protocol supplements the Criminal Procedure Rules and summarises good practice which experience has shown may assist in bringing about some reduction in the length of trials of fraud and other crimes that result in complex trials. Flexibility of application of this Protocol according to the needs of each case is essential; it is designed to inform but not to proscribe.

This Protocol is primarily directed towards cases which are likely to last eight weeks or longer. It should also be followed, however, in all cases estimated to last more than four weeks. This Protocol applies to trials by jury, but many of the principles will be applicable if trials without a jury are permitted under s.43 of the Criminal Justice Act 2003.

The best handling technique for a long case is continuous management by an experienced Judge nominated for the purpose.

It is intended that this Protocol be kept up to date; any further practices or techniques found to be successful in the management of complex cases should be notified to the office of the Lord Chief Justice.

1. The investigation

(i) The role of the prosecuting authority and the judge

N-3   (a) Unlike other European countries, a judge in England and Wales does not directly control the investigation process; that is the responsibility of the Investigating Authority, and in turn the Prosecuting Authority and the prosecution advocate. Experience has shown that a prosecution lawyer (who must be of sufficient experience and who will be a member of the team at trial) and the prosecution advocate, if different, should be involved in the investigation as soon as it appears that a heavy fraud trial or other complex criminal trial is likely to ensue. The costs that this early preparation will incur will be saved many times over in the long run.

(b) The judge can and should exert a substantial and beneficial influence by making it clear that, generally speaking, trials should be kept within manageable limits. In most cases 3 months should be the target outer limit, but there will be cases where a duration of 6 months, or in exceptional circumstances, even longer may be inevitable.

(ii) Interviews

(a) At present many interviews are too long and too unstructured. This has a knock-on effect on the length of trials. Interviews should provide an opportunity for suspects to respond to the allegations against them. They should not be an occasion to discuss every document in the case. It should become clear from judicial rulings that interviews of this kind are a waste of resources. **N-4**

(b) The suspect must be given sufficient information before or at the interview to enable them to meet the questions fairly and answer them honestly; the information is not provided to give him the opportunity to manufacture a false story which fits undisputable facts.

(c) It is often helpful if the principal documents are provided either in advance of the interview or shown as the interview progresses; asking detailed questions about events a considerable period in the past without reference to the documents is often not very helpful.

(iii) The prosecution and defence teams

(a) **The Prosecution Team**

While instructed it is for the lead advocate for the prosecution to take all necessary decisions in the presentation and general conduct of the prosecution case. The prosecution lead advocate will be treated by the court as having that responsibility. **N-5**

However, in relation to policy decisions the lead advocate for the prosecution must not give an indication or undertaking which binds the prosecution without first discussing the issue with Director of the Prosecuting authority or other senior officer.

"Policy" decisions should be understood as referring to non-evidential decisions on: the acceptance of pleas of guilty to lesser counts or groups of counts or available alternatives: offering no evidence on particular counts; consideration of a re-trial; whether to lodge an appeal; certification of a point of law; and the withdrawal of the prosecution as a whole (for further information see the "Farquharson Guidelines" on the role and responsibilities of the prosecution advocate).

(b) **The Defence Team**

In each case, the lead advocate for the defence will be treated by the court as having responsibility to the court for the presentation and general conduct of the defence case.

(c) In each case, a case progression officer must be assigned by the court, prosecution and defence from the time of the first hearing when directions are given (as referred to in paragraph 3(iii)) until the conclusion of the trial.

(d) In each case where there are multiple defendants, the LSC will need to consider carefully the extent and level of representation necessary.

(iv) Initial consideration of the length of a case

If the prosecutor in charge of the case from the Prosecuting Authority or the lead advocate for the prosecution consider that the case as formulated is likely to last more than 8 weeks, the case should be referred in accordance with arrangements made by the Prosecuting Authority to a more senior prosecutor. The senior prosecutor will consider whether it is desirable for the case to be prosecuted in that way or whether some steps might be taken to reduce its likely length, whilst at the same time ensuring that the public interest is served. **N-6**

Any case likely to last 6 months or more must be referred to the Director of the Prosecuting Authority so that similar considerations can take place.

(v) Notification of cases likely to last more than 8 weeks

Special arrangements will be put in place for the early notification by the CPS and other Prosecuting Authorities, to the LSC and to a single designated officer of the Court in each Region (Circuit) of any case which the CPS or other Prosecuting Authority consider likely to last over 8 weeks. **N-7**

(vi) Venue

The court will allocate such cases and other complex cases likely to last 4 weeks or more to a specific venue suitable for the trial in question, taking into account the convenience to witnesses, the parties, the availability of time at that location, and all other relevant considerations. **N-8**

2. Designation of the trial judge

The assignment of a judge

N-9

(a) In any complex case which is expected to last more than four weeks, the trial judge will be assigned under the direction of the Presiding Judges at the earliest possible moment.

(b) Thereafter the assigned judge should manage that case "from cradle to grave"; it is essential that the same judge manages the case from the time of his assignment and that arrangements are made for him to be able to do so. It is recognised that in certain court centres with a large turnover of heavy cases (*e.g.* Southwark) this objective is more difficult to achieve. But in those court centres there are teams of specialist judges, who are more readily able to handle cases which the assigned judge cannot continue with because of unexpected events; even at such courts, there must be no exception to the principle that one judge must handle all the pre-trial hearings until the case is assigned to another judge.

3. Case management

(i) Objectives

N-10

(a) The number, length and organisation of case management hearings will, of course, depend critically on the circumstances and complexity of the individual case. However, thorough, well-prepared and extended case management hearings will save court time and costs overall.

(b) Effective case management of heavy fraud and other complex criminal cases requires the judge to have a much more detailed grasp of the case than may be necessary for many other Plea and Case Management Hearings (PCMHs). Though it is for the judge in each case to decide how much pre-reading time he needs so that the judge is on top of the case, it is not always a sensible use of judicial time to allocate a series of reading days, during which the judge sits alone in his room, working through numerous boxes of ring binders.

See paragraph 3(iv)(e) below

(ii) Fixing the trial date

N-11

Although it is important that the trial date should be fixed as early as possible, this may not always be the right course. There are two principal alternatives:

(a) The trial date should be fixed at the first opportunity—*i.e.* at the first (and usually short) directions hearing referred to in The first hearing for the giving of initial directions. From then on everyone must work to that date. All orders and pre-trial steps should be timetabled to fit in with that date. All advocates and the judge should take note of this date, in the expectation that the trial will proceed on the date determined.

(b) The trial date should not be fixed until the issues have been explored at a full case management hearing (referred to in The first Case Management Hearing), after the advocates on both sides have done some serious work on the case. Only then can the length of the trial be estimated.

Which is apposite must depend on the circumstances of each case, but the earlier it is possible to fix a trial date, by reference to a proper estimate and a timetable set by reference to the trial date, the better.

It is generally to be expected that once a trial is fixed on the basis of the estimate provided, that it will not be **increased** if, and only if, the party seeking to extend the time justifies why the original estimate is no longer appropriate.

(iii) The first hearing for the giving of initial directions

N-12

At the first opportunity the assigned judge should hold a short hearing to give initial directions. The directions on this occasion might well include:

(a) That there should be a full case management hearing on, or commencing on, a specified future date by which time the parties will be properly prepared for a meaningful hearing and the defence will have full instructions.

(b) That the prosecution should provide an outline written statement of the prosecution case at least one week in advance of that case management hearing, outlining in simple terms:

(i) the key facts on which it relies;

(ii) the key evidence by which the prosecution seeks to prove the facts.

The statement must be sufficient to permit the judge to understand the case and for the defence to appreciate the basic elements of its case against each defendant. The prosecution may be invited to highlight the key points of the case orally at the case management hearing by way of a short mini-opening. The outline statement should not be considered binding, but it will serve the essential purpose in telling the judge, and everyone else, what the case is really about and identifying the key issues.

(c) That a core reading list and core bundle for the case management hearing should be delivered at least one week in advance.

(d) Preliminary directions about disclosure: see paragraph 4.

(iv) The first case management hearing

(a) At the first case management hearing: **N-13**

    (1) the prosecution advocate should be given the opportunity to highlight any points from the prosecution outline statement of case (which will have been delivered at least a week in advance;

    (2) each defence advocate should be asked to outline the defence.

If the defence advocate is not in a position to say what is in issue and what is not in issue, then the case management hearing can be adjourned for a short and limited time and to a fixed date to enable the advocate to take instructions; such an adjournment should only be necessary in exceptional circumstances, as the defence advocate should be properly instructed by the time of the first case management hearing and in any event is under an obligation to take sufficient instructions to fulfil the obligations contained in sections 33–39 of Criminal Justice Act 2003.

(b) There should then be a real dialogue between the judge and all advocates for the purpose of identifying:

    (i) the focus of the prosecution case;

    (ii) the common ground;

    (iii) the real issues in the case. (Rule 3.2 of the Criminal Procedure Rules.)

(c) The judge will try to generate a spirit of co-operation between the court and the advocates on all sides. The expeditious conduct of the trial and a focussing on the real issues must be in the interests of **all** parties. It cannot be in the interests of any defendant for his good points to become lost in a welter of uncontroversial or irrelevant evidence.

(d) In many fraud cases the primary facts are not seriously disputed. The real issue is what each defendant knew and whether that defendant was dishonest. Once the judge has identified what is in dispute and what is not in dispute, the judge can then discuss with the advocate how the trial should be structured, what can be dealt with by admissions or agreed facts, what uncontroversial matters should be proved by concise oral evidence, what timetabling can be required under Rule 3.10 Criminal Procedure Rules, and other directions.

(e) In particularly heavy fraud or complex cases the judge may possibly consider it necessary to allocate a whole week for a case management hearing. If that week is used wisely, many further weeks of trial time can be saved. In the gaps which will inevitably arise during that week (for example while the advocates are exploring matters raised by the judge) the judge can do a substantial amount of informed reading. The case has come "alive" at this stage. Indeed, in a really heavy fraud case, if the judge fixes one or more case management hearings on this scale, there will be need for fewer formal reading days. Moreover a huge amount can be achieved in the pre-trial stage, if all trial advocates are gathered in the same place, focussing on the case **at the same time**, for several days consecutively.

(f) Requiring the defence to serve proper case statements may enable the court to identify

    (i) what is common ground and

    (ii) the real issues.

It is therefore important that proper defence case statements be provided as required by the Criminal Procedure Rules; judges will use the powers contained in ss.28–34 of the Criminal Proceedings and Evidence Act 1996 [*sic*] (and the corresponding provisions of the CJA 1987, ss.33 and following of the Criminal Justice Act 2003) and the Criminal Procedure Rules to ensure that realistic defence case statements are provided.

(g) Likewise this objective may be achieved by requiring the prosecution to serve draft admissions by a specified date and by requiring the defence to respond within a specified number of weeks.

(v) Further case management hearings

(a) The date of the next case management hearing should be fixed at the conclusion of the **N-14** hearing so that there is no delay in having to fix the date through listing offices, clerks and others.

(b) If one is looking at a trial which threatens to run for months, pre-trial case management on an intensive scale is essential.

(vi) Consideration of the length of the trial

N-15

(a) Case management on the above lines, the procedure set out in paragraph 1(iv), may still be insufficient to reduce the trial to a manageable length; generally a trial of 3 months should be the target, but there will be cases where a duration of 6 months or, in exceptional circumstances, even longer may be inevitable.

(b) If the trial is not estimated to be within a manageable length, it will be necessary for the judge to consider what steps should be taken to reduce the length of the trial, whilst still ensuring that the prosecution has the opportunity of placing the full criminality before the court.

(c) To assist the judge in this task,

(i) the lead advocate for the prosecution should be asked to explain why the prosecution have rejected a shorter way of proceeding; they may also be asked to divide the case into sections of evidence and explain the scope of each section and the need for each section;

(ii) the lead advocates for the prosecution and for the defence should be prepared to put forward in writing, if requested, ways in which a case estimated to last more than three months can be shortened, including possible severance of counts or defendants, exclusions of sections of the case or of evidence or areas of the case where admissions can be made.

(d) One course the judge may consider is pruning the indictment by omitting certain charges and/or by omitting certain defendants. The judge must not usurp the function of the prosecution in this regard, and he must bear in mind that he will, at the outset, know less about the case than the advocates. The aim is achieve [*sic*] fairness to all parties

(e) Nevertheless, the judge does have two methods of pruning available for use in appropriate circumstances:

(i) persuading the prosecution that it is not worthwhile pursuing certain charges and/or certain defendants;

(ii) severing the indictment. Severance for reasons of case management alone is perfectly proper, although judges should have regard to any representations made by the prosecution that severance would weaken their case. Indeed the judge's hand will be strengthened in this regard by rule 1.1(2)(g) of the Criminal Procedure Rules. However, before using what may be seen as a blunt instrument, the judge should insist on seeing full defence statements of all affected defendants. Severance may be unfair to the prosecution if, for example, there is a cut-throat defence in prospect. For example, the defence of the principal defendant may be that the defendant relied on the advice of his accountant or solicitor that what was happening was acceptable. The defence of the professional may be that he gave no such advice. Against that background, it might be unfair to the prosecution to order separate trials of the two defendants.

(vii) The exercise of the powers

N-16

(a) The Criminal Procedure Rules require the court to take a more active part in case management. These are salutary provisions which should bring to an end interminable criminal trials of the kind which the Court of Appeal criticised in *Jisl* [2004] EWCA 696 at [113]-[121].

(b) Nevertheless these salutary provisions do not have to be used on every occasion. Where the advocates have done their job properly, by narrowing the issues, pruning the evidence and so forth, it may be quite inappropriate for the judge to "weigh in" and start cutting out more evidence or more charges of his own volition. It behoves the judge to make a careful assessment of the degree of judicial intervention which is warranted in each case.

(c) The note of caution in the previous paragraph is supported by certain experience which has been gained of the Civil Procedure Rules (on which the Criminal Procedure Rules are based). The CPR contain valuable and efficacious provisions for case management by the judge on his own initiative which have led to huge savings of court time and costs. Surveys by the Law Society have shown that the CPR have been generally welcomed by court users and the profession, but there have been reported to have been isolated instances in which the parties to civil litigation have faithfully complied with both the letter and the spirit of the CPR, and have then been aggrieved by what was perceived to be unnecessary intermeddling by the court.

(viii) Expert evidence

(a) Early identification of the subject matter of expert evidence to be adduced by the prosecution and the defence should be made as early as possible, preferably at the directions hearing. **N-17**

(b) Following the exchange of expert evidence, any areas of disagreement should be identified and a direction should generally be made requiring the experts to meet and prepare, after discussion, a joint statement identifying points of agreement and contention and areas where the prosecution is put to proof on matters of which a positive case to the contrary is not advanced by the defence. After the statement has been prepared it should be served on the court, the prosecution and the defence. In some cases, it might be appropriate to provide that to the jury.

(ix) Surveillance evidence

(a) Where a prosecution is based upon many months' observation or surveillance evidence and it appears that it is capable of effective presentation based on a shorter period, the advocate should be required to justify the evidence of such observations before it is permitted to be adduced, either substantially or in its entirety. **N-18**

(b) Schedules should be provided to cover as much of the evidence as possible and admissions sought.

4. Disclosure

[*Replaced by the 2013 judicial protocol on disclosure: see post, N-52 et seq.*] **N-19**

5. Abuse of process

(i) Applications to stay or dismiss for abuse of process have become a normal feature of heavy and complex cases. Such applications may be based upon delay and the health of defendants. **N-20**

(ii) Applications in relation to absent special circumstances [*sic*] tend to be unsuccessful and not to be pursued on appeal. For this reason there is comparatively little Court of Appeal guidance: but see: *Harris and Howells* [2003] EWCA Crim. 486. It should be noted that abuse of process is not there to discipline the prosecution or the police.

(iii) The arguments on both sides must be reduced to writing. Oral evidence is seldom relevant.

(iv) The judge should direct full written submissions (rather than "skeleton arguments") on any abuse application in accordance with a timetable set by him; these should identify any element of prejudice the defendant is alleged to have suffered.

(v) The judge should normally aim to conclude the hearing within an absolute maximum limit of one day, if necessary in accordance with a timetable. The parties should therefore prepare their papers on this basis and not expect the judge to allow the oral hearing to be anything more than an occasion to highlight concisely their arguments and answer any questions the court may have of them; applications will not be allowed drag on.

6. The trial

(i) The particular hazard of heavy fraud trials

A heavy fraud or other complex trial has the potential to lose direction and focus. This is a disaster for three reasons: **N-21**

(a) the jury will lose track of the evidence, thereby prejudicing both prosecution and defence;

(b) the burden on the defendants, the judge and indeed all involved will become intolerable;

(c) scarce public resources are wasted. Other prosecutions are delayed or—worse—may never happen. Fraud which is detected but not prosecuted (for resource reasons) undermines confidence.

(ii) Judicial mastery of the case

(a) It is necessary for the judge to exercise firm control over the conduct of the trial at all stages. **N-22**

(b) In order to do this the judge must read the witness statements and the documents, so that the judge can discuss case management issues with the advocates on—almost—an equal footing.

(c) To this end, the judge should not set aside weeks or even days for pre-reading (see paragraph 3(i)(b)). Hopefully the judge will have gained a good grasp of the evidence during the case management hearings. Nevertheless, realistic reading time must be provided for the judge in advance of trial.

(d) The role of the judge in a heavy fraud or other complex criminal trial is different from his/ her role in a "conventional" criminal trial. So far as possible, the judge should be freed from other duties and burdens, so that he/she can give the high degree of commit-ment which a heavy fraud trial requires. This will pay dividends in terms of saving weeks or months of court time.

(iii) The order of the evidence

N-23

(a) By the outset of the trial at the latest (and in most cases very much earlier) the judge must be provided with a schedule, showing the sequence of prosecution (and in an appropriate case defence) witnesses and the dates upon which they are expected to be called. This can only be prepared by discussion between prosecution and defence which the judge should expect, and say he/she expects, to take place: See: Criminal Procedure Rule 3.10. The schedule should, in so far as it relates to prosecution witnesses, be developed in consulta-tion with the witnesses, via the witness care units, and with consideration given to their personal needs. Copies of the schedule should be provided for the Witness Service.

(b) The schedule should be kept under review by the trial judge and by the parties. If a case is running behind or ahead of schedule, each witness affected must be advised by the party who is calling that witness at the earliest opportunity.

(c) If an excessive amount of time is allowed for any witness, the judge can ask why. The judge may probe with the advocates whether the time envisaged for the evidence-in-chief or cross-examination (as the case may be) of a particular witness is really necessary.

(iv) Case management sessions

N-24

(a) The order of the evidence may have legitimately to be departed from. It will, however, be a useful for tool for monitoring the progress of the case. There should be periodic case management sessions, during which the judge engages the advocates upon a stock-taking exercise: asking, amongst other questions, "where are we going?" and "what is the relevance of the next three witnesses?". This will be a valuable means of keeping the case on track. Rule 3.10 of the Criminal Procedure Rules will again assist the judge.

(b) The judge may wish to consider issuing the occasional use of "case management notes" to the advocates, in order to set out the judge's tentative views on where the trial may be go-ing off track, which areas of future evidence are relevant and which may have become ir-relevant (*e.g.* because of concessions, admissions in cross-examination and so forth). Such notes from the judge plus written responses from the advocates can, cautiously used, provide a valuable focus for debate during the periodic case management reviews held during the course of the trial.

(v) Controlling prolix cross-examination

N-25

(a) Setting **rigid** time limits in advance for cross-examination is rarely appropriate—as experi-ence has shown in civil cases; but a timetable is essential so that the judge can exercise control and so that there is a clear target to aim at for the completion of the evidence of each witness. Moreover the judge can and should indicate when cross-examination is ir-relevant, unnecessary or time wasting. The judge may limit the time for further cross-examination of a particular witness.

(vi) Electronic presentation of evidence

N-26

(a) Electronic presentation of evidence (EPE) has the potential to save huge amounts of time in fraud and other complex criminal trials and should be used more widely.

(b) HMCS is providing facilities for the easier use of EPE with a standard audio visual facility. Effectively managed, the savings in court time achieved by EPE more than justify the cost.

(c) There should still be a core bundle of those documents to which frequent reference will be made during the trial. The jury may wish to mark that bundle or to refer back to particular pages as the evidence progresses. EPE can be used for presenting all docu-ments not contained in the core bundle.

(d) Greater use of other modern forms of graphical presentations should be made wherever possible.

(vii) Use of interviews

The judge should consider extensive editing of self serving interviews, even when the defence **N-27** want the jury to hear them in their entirety; such interviews are not evidence of the truth of their contents but merely of the defendant's reaction to the allegation.

(viii) Jury management

(a) The jury should be informed as early as possible in the case as to what the issues are in a **N-28** manner directed by the Judge.

(b) The jury must be regularly updated as to the trial timetable and the progress of the trial, subject to warnings as to the predictability of the trial process.

(c) Legal argument should be heard at times that causes the least inconvenience to jurors.

(d) It is useful to consider with the advocates whether written directions should be given to the jury and, if so, in what form.

(ix) Maxwell hours

(a) Maxwell hours should only be permitted after careful consideration and consultation **N-29** with the Presiding Judge.

(b) Considerations in favour include:

(i) legal argument can be accommodated without disturbing the jury;

(ii) there is a better chance of a representative jury;

(iii) time is made available to the judge, advocates and experts to do useful work in the afternoons

(c) Considerations against include:

(i) the lengthening of trials and the consequent waste of court time;

(ii) the desirability of making full use of the jury once they have arrived at court;

(iii) shorter trials tend to diminish the need for special provisions *e.g.* there are fewer difficulties in empanelling more representative juries;

(iv) they are unavailable if any defendant is in custody.

(d) It may often be the case that a maximum of one day of Maxwell hours a week is sufficient; if so, it should be timetabled in advance to enable all submissions by advocates, supported by skeleton arguments served in advance, to be dealt with in the period after 1:30 pm on that day.

(x) Livenote

If Livenote is used, it is important that all users continue to take a note of the evidence, otherwise **N-30** considerable time is wasted in detailed reading of the entire daily transcript.

7. Other issues

(i) Defence representation and defence costs

(a) Applications for change in representation in complex trials need special consideration; **N-31** the ruling of HH Judge Wakerley QC (as he then was) in *Asghar Ali* has been circulated by the JSB.

(b) Problems have arisen when the Legal Services Commission have declined to allow advocates or solicitors to do certain work; on occasions the matter has been raised with the judge managing or trying the case.

(c) The Legal Services Commission has provided guidance to judges on how they can obtain information from the LSC as to the reasons for their decisions; further information in relation to this can be obtained from *Nigel Field, Head of the Complex Crime Unit, Legal Services Commission, 29-37 Red Lion Street, London, WC1R 4PP.*

(ii) Assistance to the judge

Experience has shown that in some very heavy cases, the judge's burden can be substantially offset **N-32** with the provision of a judicial assistant or other support and assistance.

[The next paragraph is N-52.]

B. Disclosure of Unused Material in Criminal Cases

Foreword

N-52   [*Identical to the foreword to the Attorney-General's guidelines: ante, § A-242a.*]

Introduction

N-53   This protocol is prescribed for use by CPD IV Disclosure 22A: Disclosure of Unused Material. It is applicable in all the criminal courts of England and Wales, including the Crown Court, the Court Martial[1] and the magistrates' courts. It replaces the previous judicial document 'Disclosure: a Protocol for the Control and Management of Unused Material in the Crown Court'[2] and it also replaces section 4 'Disclosure' of the Lord Chief Justice's Protocol on the Control and Management of Heavy Fraud and Other Complex Criminal Cases, dated 22 March 2005.[3]

This protocol is intended to provide a central source of guidance for the judiciary, although that produced by the Attorney General also requires attention.

In summary, this judicial protocol sets out the principles to be applied to, and the importance of, disclosure; the expectations of the court and its role in disclosure, in particular in relation to case management; and the consequences if there is a failure by the prosecution or defence to comply with their obligations.

Readers should note that a review of disclosure in the magistrates' courts is currently being undertaken by H.H.J. Kinch Q.C. and the Chief Magistrate, on behalf of Lord Justice Gross, the Senior Presiding Judge. Amendments may therefore be made following the recommendations of that review, and in accordance with other forthcoming changes to the criminal justice system.

The importance of disclosure for fair trials

N-54   1. Disclosure remains one of the most important – as well as one of the most misunderstood and abused – of the procedures relating to criminal trials. Lord Justice Gross' review has reemphasised the need for all those involved to understand the statutory requirements and to undertake their roles with rigour, in a timely manner.

2. The House of Lords stated in *R. v. H.* [2004] UKHL 3; [2004] 2 A.C. 134; [2004] 2 Cr.App.R. 10:

> "Fairness ordinarily requires that any material held by the prosecution which weakens its case or strengthens that of the defendant, if not relied on as part of its formal case against the defendant, should be disclosed to the defence. Bitter experience has shown that miscarriages of justice may occur where such material is withheld from disclosure. The golden rule is that full disclosure of such material should be made" ([2004] 2 A.C. 134, at 147).

The Criminal Cases Review Commission has recently noted that failure to disclose material to the defence to which they were entitled remains the biggest single cause of miscarriages of justice.

3. However, it is also essential that the trial process is not overburdened or diverted by erroneous and inappropriate disclosure of unused prosecution material or by misconceived applications. Although the drafters of the Criminal Procedure and Investigations Act 1996 ('CPIA 1996') cannot have anticipated the vast increase in the amount of electronic material that has been generated in recent years, nevertheless the principles of that Act still hold true. Applications by the parties or decisions by judges based on misconceptions of the law or a general laxity of approach (however well-intentioned) which result in an improper application of the disclosure regime have, time and again, proved unnecessarily costly and have obstructed justice. As Lord Justice Gross noted, the burden of disclosure must not be allowed to render the prosecution of cases impracticable.

4. The overarching principle is that unused prosecution material will fall to be disclosed if, and only if, it satisfies the test for disclosure applicable to the proceedings in question, subject to any over-

---

[1] The timetables given here may vary in the Court Martial and reference should be made to the Criminal Procedure and Investigations Act 1996 (Application to the Armed Forces) Order 2009 and to any practice note issued by the Judge Advocate General.

[2] The previous judicial protocol was endorsed by the Court of Appeal in *R. v. K.* [2006] EWCA Crim. 724; [2006] 2 All ER 552 (Note).

[3] This protocol also replaces the Protocol for the Provision of Advance Information, Prosecution Evidence and Disclosure of Unused Material in the Magistrates' Courts, dated 12 May 2006, which was adopted as part of the Stop Delaying Justice initiative.

riding public interest considerations. The test for disclosure will depend on the date the criminal investigation in question commenced, as this will determine whether the common law disclosure regime applies, or either of the two disclosure regimes under the CPIA 1996.

5. The test for disclosure under section 3 of the CPIA 1996 as amended will be applicable in nearly every case and all those involved in the process will need to be familiar with it. Material fulfils the test if – but only if – it "might reasonably be considered capable of undermining the case for the prosecution ... or of assisting the case for the accused."

6. The disclosure process must be led by the prosecution so as to trigger comprehensive defence engagement, supported by robust judicial case management. Active participation by the court in the disclosure process is a critical means of ensuring that delays and adjournments are avoided, given failures by the parties to comply with their obligations may disrupt and (in some cases) frustrate the course of justice.

Disclosure of unused material in criminal cases

7. The court should keep the timetable for prosecution and defence disclosure under review from the first hearing. Judges should as a matter of course ask the parties to identify the issues in the case, and invite the parties to indicate whether further disclosure is sought, and on what topics. For example, it is not enough for the judge to rely on the content of the PCMH form. Proper completion of the disclosure process is a vital part of case preparation, and it may well affect the progress of the case. The court will expect disclosure to have been considered from the outset; the prosecution and defence advocates need to be aware of any potential problems and substantive difficulties should be explained to the judge; and the parties should propose a sensible timetable. Realism is preferable to optimistic but unachievable deadlines which may dislocate the court schedule and imperil the date of trial. It follows that judges should not impose deadlines for service of the case papers or disclosure until they are confident that the prosecution advocate has taken instructions from the individuals who are best placed to evaluate the work to be undertaken.

N-55

8. The advocates – both prosecution and defence – must be kept fully informed throughout the course of the proceedings as to any difficulties which may prevent them from complying with their disclosure obligations. When problems arise or come to light after directions have been given, the advocates should notify the court and the other party (or parties) immediately rather than waiting until the date set by the court for the service of the material is imminent or has passed, and they must provide the court with a suggested timetable in order to resolve the problem. The progress of the disclosure process should be reviewed at every hearing. There remains no basis in practice or law for counsel to counsel disclosure.

9. If there is a preliminary hearing the judge should seize the opportunity to impose an early timetable for disclosure and to identify any likely problems including as regards third party material and material that will require an application to the Family Court. In an appropriate case the court should consider holding a joint criminal/care directions hearing. See "Material held by Third Parties", from paragraph 44 below.

10. For the PCMH to be effective, the defence must have a proper opportunity to review the case papers and consider initial disclosure, with a view to preparing a properly completed defence statement which will inform the judge's conduct of the PCMH, and inform the prosecution of the matters required by sections 5, 6A and 6C of the CPIA. As the Court of Appeal noted in *R. v. Newell* [2012] EWCA Crim. 650; [2012] 2 Cr.App.R. 10, "a typed defence statement must be provided before the PCMH. If there is no defence statement by the time of the PCMH, then a judge will usually require the trial advocate to see that such a statement is provided and not proceed with the PCMH until that is done. In the ordinary case the trial advocate will be required to do that at the court and the PCMH resumed later in the day to avoid delay". There may be some instances when there will be a well-founded defence application to extend the 28-day time limit for serving a proper defence statement. In a proper case (but never routinely), it may be appropriate to put the PCMH back by a week or more, to enable an appropriate defence statement to be filed.

11. The defence statement can be admitted into evidence under section 6E(4) of the CPIA 1996. However, information included on the PCMH form (which is primarily an administrative form) will not usually be admitted in evidence when the defence advocate has complied with the letter and the spirit of the Criminal Procedure Rules.[4] Introducing the PCMH form (or part of it) during the trial is likely to be an exceptional event. The status of the trial preparation form in the magistrates' court is somewhat different, as discussed below.

12. The court should not extend time lightly or as a matter of course. If an extension is sought, it ought to be accompanied by an appropriate explanation. For instance, it is not sufficient for the prosecutor merely to say that the investigator has delivered the papers late: the underlying reasons are

---

[4] *R. v. Newell* [2012] EWCA Crim. 650; [2012] 2 Cr.App.R. 10.

to be provided to the court. The same applies if the defence statement is delayed. Whichever party is at fault, realistic proposals for service are to be set out.

13. Judges should not allow the prosecution to avoid their statutory responsibility for reviewing the unused material by the expedient of permitting the defence to have access to (or providing the defence with copies of) the material listed in the schedules of non-sensitive unused prosecution material irrespective of whether it satisfies, wholly or in part, the relevant test for disclosure. Additionally, it is for the prosecutor to decide on the manner of disclosure, and it does not have to mirror the form in which the information was originally recorded. Rose L.J. gave guidance on case management issues in this context in *R. v. CPS (Interlocutory Application under sections 35/36 CPIA)* [2005] EWCA Crim. 2342. Allowing the defence to inspect items that fulfil the disclosure test is also a valid means of providing disclosure.

14. The larger and more complex the case, the more important it is for the prosecution to adhere to the overarching principle and ensure that sufficient prosecution attention and resources are allocated to the task. Handing the defendant the "keys to the warehouse" has been the cause of many gross abuses in the past, resulting in considerable expenditure by the defence without any material benefit to the course of justice. The circumstances relating to large and complex cases are outlined below.

15. The court will require the defence to engage and assist in the early identification of the real issues in the case and, particularly in the larger and more complex cases, to contribute to the search terms to be used for, and the parameters of, the review of any electronically held material (which can be very considerable). Any defence criticisms of the prosecution approach to disclosure should be timely and reasoned; there is no place for disclosure "ambushes" or for late or uninformative defence statements. Admissions should be used so far as possible to narrow the real issues in dispute.

16. A constructive approach to disclosure is a necessary part of professional best practice, for the defence and prosecution. This does not undermine the defendant's legitimate interests, it accords with his or her obligations under the rules and it ensures that all the relevant material is provided. Delays and failures by the prosecution and the defence are equally damaging to a timely, fair and efficient trial, and judges should be vigilant in preventing and addressing abuses. Accordingly, whenever there are potential failings by either the defence or the prosecution, judges, in exercising appropriate oversight of disclosure, should carefully investigate the suggested default and give timely directions.

17. In the Crown Court, the defence statement is to be served within 28 days of the date when the prosecution complies with its duty of initial disclosure (or purports to do so) and whenever section 5(5) of the CPIA applies to the proceedings, and the defence statement must comply with section 6A of the CPIA. Service of the defence statement is a most important stage in the disclosure process, and timely service is necessary to facilitate proper consideration of the disclosure issues well in advance of the trial date. Judges expect a defence statement to contain a clear and detailed exposition of the issues of fact and law. Defence statements that merely rehearse the suggestion that the defendant is innocent do not comply with the requirements of the CPIA.

18. The prosecutor should consider the defence statement carefully and promptly provide a copy to the disclosure officer, to assist the prosecution in its continuing disclosure obligations. The court expects the Crown to identify any suggested deficiencies in the defence statement, and to draw these to the attention of the defence and the court; in particular in large and complex cases, it will assist the court if this is in writing. Although the prosecution's ability to request, and the court's jurisdiction to give, an adverse inference direction under section 11 of CPIA is not contingent on the prosecution having earlier identified any suggested deficiencies, nevertheless the prosecutor must provide a timely written explanation of its position.

19. Judges should examine the defence statement with care to ensure that it complies with the formalities required by the CPIA. As stated in *R. v. H.* (*supra*) (para. 35):

> "If material does not weaken the prosecution case or strengthen that of the defendant, there is no requirement to disclose it. For this purpose the parties' respective cases should not be restrictively analysed. But they must be carefully analysed, to ascertain the specific facts the prosecution seek to establish and the specific grounds on which the charges are resisted. The trial process is not well served if the defence are permitted to make general and unspecified allegations and then seek far-reaching disclosure in the hope that material may turn up to make them good. Neutral material or material damaging to the defendant need not be disclosed and should not be brought to the attention of the court."

20. If no defence statement – or an inadequate defence statement – is served within the relevant time limits, the judge should investigate the position. At every PCMH where there is no defence statement, including those where an extension has been given, or the time for filing has not yet expired, the defence should be warned in appropriate terms that pursuant to section 6E(2) of the

CPIA an adverse inference may be drawn during the trial, and this result is likely if there is no justification for the deficiency. The fact that a warning has been given should be noted.

21. An adverse inference may be drawn under section 11 of the CPIA if the accused fails to discharge his or her disclosure obligations. Whenever the amended CPIA regime applies, the prosecution may comment on any failure in defence disclosure (except where the failure relates to a point of law) without leave of the court, but counsel should use a measure of judgment as to whether it is wise to embark on cross-examination about such a failure.[5] If the accused is cross-examined about discrepancies between his evidence and his defence statement, or if adverse comment is made, the judge must give appropriate guidance to the jury.[6]

22. In order to secure a fair trial, it is vital that the prosecution is mindful of its continuing duty of disclosure. Once the defence statement has been received, the Crown must review disclosure in the light of the issues identified in the defence statement. In cases of complexity, the following steps are then likely to be necessary:

    i. service by the prosecution of any further material due to the defence following receipt of the defence statement;

    ii. any defence request to the prosecution for service of additional specific items; as discussed below, these requests must be justified by reference to the defence statement and they should be submitted on the section 8 form;

    iii. prosecution response to the defence request;

    iv. if the defence considers that disclosable items are still outstanding, a section 8 application should be made using the appropriate form.

23. It follows that all requests by the defence to the prosecution for disclosure should be made on the section 8 application form, even if no hearing is sought in the first instance. Discussion and co-operation between the parties outside of court is encouraged in order to ensure that the court is only asked to issue a ruling when strictly necessary. However, use of the section 8 form will ensure that focussed requests are clearly set out in one place.

24. The judge should set a date as part of the timetabling exercise by which any application under section 8 is to be made, if this appears to be a likely eventuality.

25. The court will require the section 8 application to be served on the prosecution well in advance of the hearing – indeed, prior to requesting the hearing – to enable the Crown to identify and serve any items that meet the test for disclosure.

26. Service of a defence statement is an essential precondition for an application under section 8, and applications should not be heard or directions for disclosure issued in the absence of a properly completed statement (see Part 22 of the Criminal Procedure Rules). In particular, blanket orders in this context are inconsistent with the statutory framework for disclosure laid down by the CPIA and the decision of the House of Lords in *R. v. H.* (*supra*). It follows that defence requests for disclosure of particular pieces of unused prosecution material which are not referable to any issue in the case identified in the defence statement should be rejected.

27. Judges must ensure that defendants are not prejudiced on account of the failures of their lawyers, and, when necessary, the professions should be reminded that if justice is to be done, and if disclosure is to be dealt with fairly in accordance with the law, a full and careful defence statement and a reasoned approach to section 8 applications are essential. In exploring the adequacy of the defence statement, a judge should always ask what the issues are and upon what matters of fact the defendant intends to rely[7] and on what matters of fact the defendant takes issue.

Listing

28. Sufficient time is necessary for the judge properly to undertake the PCMH, and this is a **N-56** paramount consideration when listing cases. Unless the court is able to sit early, judges who are part heard on trials are probably not best placed to conduct PCMHs.

29. Cases that raise particularly difficult issues of disclosure should be referred to the resident judge for directions (unless a trial judge has been allocated) and, for trials of real complexity, the trial judge should be identified at an early stage, prior to the PCMH if possible. Listing officers, working in consultation with the resident judge and, if allocated, the trial judge, should ensure that sufficient time is allowed for judges to prepare and deal with prosecution and defence applications relating to disclosure, particularly in the more complex cases.

Magistrates' courts (including the youth court)

30. The principles relating to disclosure apply equally in the magistrates' courts. It follows that **N-57**

---

[5] *R. v. Essa* [2009] EWCA Crim. 43, para. 22.
[6] *R. v. Hanyes* [2011] EWCA Crim. 3281.
[7] *R. v. Rochford* [2010] EWCA Crim. 1928; [2011] 1 Cr.App.R. 11.

whilst disclosure of unused material in compliance with the statutory test is undoubtedly essential in order to achieve justice, it is critical that summary trials are not delayed or made over-complicated by misconceived applications for, or inappropriate disclosure of, prosecution material.

31. Magistrates will rely on their legal advisers for guidance, and the latter should draw the attention of the parties and the court to the statutory provisions and the applicable case law. Cases raising disclosure issues of particular complexity should be referred to a District Judge (Magistrates' Courts), if available.

32. Although service of a defence statement is voluntary for summary trials (s.6 CPIA), the defendant cannot make an application for specific disclosure under section 8 CPIA, and the court cannot make any orders in this regard, unless a proper defence statement has been provided. It follows that although providing a defence statement is not mandatory, it remains a critical stage in the disclosure process. If disclosure issues are to be raised by the defence, a defence statement must be served well in advance of the trial date. Any section 8 application must be made in strict compliance with the rules.

33. The case-management forms used in the magistrates' courts fulfil some of the functions of a defence statement, and the prosecution must take into account the information provided as to the defence case when conducting its on-going review of unused material. As the Court of Appeal noted in *R. v. Newell* (*supra*), admissions can be made in the trial preparation form and the defence is able to identify the matters that are not in issue. Admissions made in these circumstances may be admissible during the trial. However, other information on the form that does not come within the section relating to admissions should be treated in the same way as the contents of a PCMH form in the Crown Court and it should not generally be introduced as part of the evidence at trial. However, the contents of the trial preparation form do not replace the need to serve a defence statement if the defendant seeks to apply for disclosure under section 8 CPIA.

34. The standard directions require that any defence statement is to be served within 14 days of the date upon which the prosecution has complied with, or purported to comply with, the duty to provide initial disclosure. There may be some instances when there will be a wellfounded defence application to extend the 14-day time limit for serving the defence statement. These applications must be made in accordance with the Criminal Procedure Rules, in writing and before the time limit expires.

35. Although CCTV footage frequently causes difficulties, it is to be treated as any other category of unused material and it should only be disclosed if the material meets the appropriate test for disclosure under the CPIA. The defence should either be provided with copies of the sections of the CCTV or afforded an opportunity to view them. If the prosecution refuses to disclose CCTV material that the defence considers to be discloseable, the courts should not make standard or general directions requiring the prosecutor to disclose material of this kind in the absence of an application under section 8. When potentially relevant CCTV footage is not in the possession of the police, the guidance in relation to third party material will apply, although the police remain under a duty to pursue all reasonable lines of inquiry, including those leading away from a suspect, whether or not defence requests are made.

36. The previous convictions of witnesses and any disciplinary findings against officers in the case are frequently discloseable and care should be taken to disclose them as appropriate. Documents such as crime reports or records of emergency calls should not be provided on a routine basis, for instance as part of a bundle of disclosed documents, irrespective of whether the material satisfies the appropriate test for disclosure. Defence advocates should not request this material in standard or routine correspondence, and instead focussed consideration should be given to the circumstances of the particular case. Unjustified requests for disclosure of material of this kind are routinely made, frequently leading to unnecessary delays and adjournments. The prosecution should always consider whether the request is properly made out.

37. The supervisory role of the courts is critical in this context, and magistrates must guard against granting unnecessary adjournments and issuing unjustified directions.

Large and complex cases in the Crown Court

N-58

38. Disclosure is a particular problem with the larger and more complex cases, which require a scrupulous approach by the parties and robust case management by the judiciary. If possible, the trial judge should be identified at the outset.

39. The legal representatives need to fulfil their duties in this context with care and efficiency; they should co-operate with the other party (or parties) and the court; and the judge and the other party (or parties) are to be informed of any difficulties, as soon as they arise. The court should be provided with an up-to-date timetable for disclosure whenever there are material changes in this regard. A disclosure-management document, or similar, prepared by the prosecution will be of particular assistance to the court in large and complex cases.

40. Judges should be prepared to give early guidance as to the prosecution's approach to disclosure, thereby ensuring early engagement by the defence.

41. Cases of this nature frequently include large volumes of digitally stored material. The Attorney General's 2011 guidance (now included as an annex to the Attorney General's Guidelines on Disclosure 2013) is of particular relevance and assistance in this context.

42. Applications for witness anonymity orders require particular attention; as the Court of Appeal noted in *R. v. Mayers* [2008] EWCA Crim. 2989; [2009] 1 Cr.App.R. 30, in making such an application, the prosecution's obligations of disclosure "go much further than the ordinary duties of disclosure".

43. If the judge considers that there are reasonable grounds to doubt the good faith of the investigation, he or she will be concerned to see that there has been independent and effective appraisal of the documents contained in the disclosure schedule and that its contents are adequate. In appropriate cases where this issue has arisen and there are grounds which show there is a real issue, consideration should be given to receiving evidence on oath from the senior investigating officer at an early case management hearing.

Material held by third parties

44. Where material is held by a third party such as a local authority, a social services department, **N-59** hospital or business, the investigators and the prosecution may need to make enquiries of the third party, with a view to inspecting the material and assessing whether the relevant test for disclosure is met and determining whether any or all of the material should be retained, recorded and, in due course, disclosed to the accused. If access by the prosecution is granted, the investigators and the prosecution will need to establish whether the custodian of the material intends to raise PII issues, as a result of which the material may have to be placed before the court for a decision. This does not obviate the need for the defence to conduct its own enquiries as appropriate. Speculative enquiries without any proper basis in relation to third party material – whether by the prosecution or the defence – are to be discouraged, and, in appropriate cases, the court will consider making an order for costs where an application is clearly unmeritorious and misconceived.

45. The 2013 Protocol and Good Practice Model on Disclosure of Information in Cases of Alleged Child Abuse and Linked Criminal and Care Directions Hearings has recently been published. It provides a framework and timetable for the police and CPS to obtain discloseable material from local authorities, and for applications to be made to the Family Court. It is applicable to all cases of alleged child abuse where the child is aged 17 years or under. It is not binding on local authorities, but it does represent best practice and therefore should be consulted in all such cases. Delays in obtaining this type of material have led to unacceptable delays to trials involving particularly vulnerable witnesses and every effort must be made to ensure that all discloseable material is identified at an early stage so that any necessary applications can be made and the defence receive material to which they are entitled in good time.

46. There is no specific procedure for disclosure of material held by third parties in criminal proceedings, although the procedure established under section 2 of the Criminal Procedure (Attendance of Witnesses) Act 1965 or section 97 of the Magistrates' Courts Act 1980 is often used for this purpose. Where the third party in question declines to allow inspection of the material, or requires the prosecution to obtain an order before providing copies, the prosecutor will need to consider whether it is appropriate to obtain a witness summons under either section 2 of the Criminal Procedure (Attendance of Witnesses) Act 1965 or section 97 of the Magistrates' Courts Act 1980. Part 28 of the Criminal Procedure Rules and paragraphs 3.5 and 3.6 of the Code of Practice under the CPIA 1996 should be followed.

47. Applications for third party disclosure must identify the documents that are sought and provide full details of why they are discloseable. This is particularly relevant when access is sought to the medical records of those who allege they are victims of crime. It should be appreciated that a duty to assert confidentiality may arise when a third party receives a request for disclosure, or the right to privacy may be claimed under Article 8 of the ECHR (see in particular Crim. P.R., Pt 28.6). Victims do not waive the confidentiality of their medical records, or their right to privacy under Article 8 of the ECHR, by making a complaint against the accused. The court, as a public authority, must ensure that any interference with the right to privacy under Article 8 is in accordance with the law, and is necessary in pursuit of a legitimate public interest. General and unspecified requests to trawl through such records should be refused. Confidentiality rests with the subject of the material, not with the authority holding it. The subject is entitled to service of the application and has the right to make representations: Criminal Procedure Rule 22.3 and *R. (B.) v. Stafford Combined Court* [2006] EWHC 1645 (Admin.); [2006] 2 Cr.App.R. 34. The 2013 Protocol and Good Practice Model at paragraph 13 should be followed. It is likely that the judge will need to issue directions when issues of this kind are raised (*e.g.* whether enquiries with the third party are likely to be appropriate;

who is to make the request; what material is to be sought, and from whom; and a timetable should be set).

48. The judge should consider whether to take any steps if a third party fails, or refuses, to comply with a request for disclosure, including suggesting that either of the parties pursue the request and, if necessary, make an application for a witness summons. In these circumstances, the court will need to set an appropriate timetable for compliance with Part 28 of the rules. Any failure to comply with the timetable must immediately be referred back to the court for further directions, although a hearing will not always be necessary. Generally, it may be appropriate for the defence to pursue requests of this kind when the prosecution, for good reason, decline to do so and the court will need to ensure that this procedure does not delay the trial.

49. There are very limited circumstances in which information relating to Family Court proceedings (*e.g.* where there have been care proceedings in relation to a child who has complained to the police of mistreatment) may be communicated without a court order: see the Family Procedure Rules 12.73. Reference should be made to the 2013 Protocol and Good Practice Model. In most circumstances, a court order will be required and paragraph 11 of the Protocol which sets out how an application should be made should be followed.

Other government departments

N-60

50. Material held by other government departments or other Crown agencies will not be prosecution material for the purposes of section 3(2) or section 8(4) of the CPIA if it has not been inspected, recorded and retained during the course of the relevant criminal investigation. The *CPIA Code of Practice and the Attorney General's Guidelines on Disclosure*, however, impose a duty upon the investigators and the prosecution to pursue all reasonable lines of inquiry and that may involve seeking disclosure from the relevant body.

International matters

N-61

51. The obligations of the Crown in relation to relevant third-party material held overseas are as set out in *R. v. Flook* [2009] EWCA Crim. 682; [2010] 1 Cr.App.R. 30: the Crown must pursue reasonable lines of enquiry and if it appears there is relevant material, all reasonable steps must be taken to obtain it, whether formally or otherwise. To a great extent, the success of these enquiries will depend on the laws of the country where the material is held and the facts of the individual case. It needs to be recognised that when the material is held in a country outside of the European Union, the power of the Crown and the courts of England and Wales to obtain third-party material may well be limited. If informal requests are unsuccessful, the avenues are limited to the Crime (International Co-operation) Act 2003 and any applicable international conventions. It cannot, in any sense, be guaranteed that a request to a foreign government, court or body will produce the material sought. Additionally, some foreign authorities may be prepared to show the material in question to the investigating officers, whilst refusing to allow the material to be copied or otherwise made available.

52. As the Court of Appeal observed in *R. v. Khyam* [2008] EWCA Crim. 1612; [2009] 1 Cr.App.R.(S.) 77:

"The prosecuting authorities in this jurisdiction simply cannot compel authorities in a foreign country to acknowledge, let alone comply with, our disclosure principles" (at [37]).

The obligation is therefore to take reasonable steps. Whether the Crown has complied with that obligation is for the courts to judge in each case.

53. It is, therefore, important that the prosecution sets out the position clearly in writing, including any inability to inspect or retrieve any material that potentially ought to be disclosed, along with the steps that have been taken.

Applications for non-disclosure in the public interest

N-62

54. Applications in this context, whenever possible, should be considered by the trial judge. The House of Lords in *R. v. H.* (*supra*) has provided useful guidance as to the proper approach to be applied (para. [36]):

"When any issue of derogation from the golden rule of full disclosure comes before it, the court must address a series of questions:
    (1) What is the material which the prosecution seek to withhold? This must be considered by the court in detail.
    (2) Is the material such as may weaken the prosecution case or strengthen that of the defence? If No, disclosure should not be ordered. If Yes, full disclosure should (subject to (3), (4) and (5) below) be ordered.

(3) Is there a real risk of serious prejudice to an important public interest (and, if so, what) if full disclosure of the material is ordered? If No, full disclosure should be ordered.

(4) If the answer to (2) and (3) is Yes, can the defendant's interest be protected without disclosure or disclosure be ordered to an extent or in a way which will give adequate protection to the public interest in question and also afford adequate protection to the interests of the defence?

> This question requires the court to consider, with specific reference to the material which the prosecution seek to withhold and the facts of the case and the defence as disclosed, whether the prosecution should formally admit what the defence seek to establish or whether disclosure short of full disclosure may be ordered. This may be done in appropriate cases by the preparation of summaries or extracts of evidence, or the provision of documents in an edited or anonymised form, provided the documents supplied are in each instance approved by the judge. In appropriate cases the appointment of special counsel may be a necessary step to ensure that the contentions of the prosecution are tested and the interests of the defendant protected (see para. [22] above). In cases of exceptional difficulty the court may require the appointment of special counsel to ensure a correct answer to questions (2) and (3) as well as (4).

(5) Do the measures proposed in answer to (4) represent the minimum derogation necessary to protect the public interest in question? If No, the court should order such greater disclosure as will represent the minimum derogation from the golden rule of full disclosure.

(6) If limited disclosure is ordered pursuant to (4) or (5), may the effect be to render the trial process, viewed as a whole, unfair to the defendant? If Yes, then fuller disclosure should be ordered even if this leads or may lead the prosecution to discontinue the proceedings so as to avoid having to make disclosure.

(7) If the answer to (6) when first given is No, does that remain the correct answer as the trial unfolds, evidence is adduced and the defence advanced?

It is important that the answer to (6) should not be treated as a final, once-and-for-all, answer but as a provisional answer which the court must keep under review."

55. In this context, the following matters are to be emphasised:

a. the procedure for making applications to the court is set out in the Criminal Procedure Rules, Pt 22;

b. when the PII application is a Type 1 or Type 2 application, proper notice to the defence is necessary to enable the accused to make focused submissions to the court and the notice should be as specific as the nature of the material allows; it is appreciated that in some cases only the generic nature of the material can be identified; in some wholly exceptional cases (Type 3 cases) it may be justified to give no notice at all; the judge should always ask the prosecution to justify the form of notice (or the decision to give no notice at all);

c. the prosecution should be alert to the possibility of disclosing a statement in a redacted form by, for example, simply removing personal details; this may obviate the need for a PII application, unless the redacted material satisfies the test for disclosure;

d. except when the material is very short (for instance only a few sheets), or for reasons of sensitivity, the prosecution should supply securely sealed copies to the judge in advance, together with a short statement explaining the relevance of each document, how it satisfies the disclosure test and why it is suggested that disclosure would result in a real risk of serious prejudice to an important public interest; in undertaking this task, the use of merely formulaic expressions is to be discouraged; in any case of complexity a schedule of the material should be provided, identifying the particular objection to disclosure in relation to each item, and leaving a space for the judge's decision;

e. the application, even if held in private or in secret, should be recorded; the judge should give some short statement of reasons; this is often best done document by document as the hearing proceeds;

f. the recording, copies of the judge's orders (and any copies of the material retained by the court) should be clearly identified, securely sealed and kept in the court building in a safe or locked cabinet consistent with its security classification, and there should be a proper register of the contents; arrangements should be made for the return of the material to the prosecution once the case is concluded and the time for an appeal has elapsed.

Conclusion

56. Historically, disclosure was viewed essentially as being a matter to be resolved between the par- **N-63**

ties, and the court only became engaged if a particular issue or complaint was raised. That perception is now wholly out of date. The regime established under the Criminal Justice Act 2003 and the Criminal Procedure Rules gives judges the power – indeed, it imposes a duty on the judiciary – actively to manage disclosure in every case. The efficient, effective and timely resolution of these issues is a critical element in meeting the overriding objective of the Criminal Procedure Rules of dealing with cases justly.

APPENDIX S
Sentencing Guidelines and Related Authorities

I. GUIDELINES

2. NEW SENTENCES: CRIMINAL JUSTICE ACT 2003

S-2 The Sentencing Council for England and Wales has issued a definitive guideline (*post*, S-27) relating to the imposition of community and custodial sentences. It applies to all offenders over the age of 18 falling to be sentenced on or after February 1, 2017, regardless of the date of the offence. Specifically, the guideline deals with (i) the imposition of community orders, (ii) the imposition of custodial sentences, and (iii) suspended sentences (general guidance). There is also a sentencing decision flowchart, and an annex setting out the fine bands. Whilst not explicitly stated, the guideline is presumably intended to replace everything in the guideline on "*New Sentences: Criminal Justice Act* 2003" (see the sentencing supplement *et seq.*), that relates to the imposition of community or custodial sentences, but not such parts of it as relate to dealing with breaches of such sentences or the deferment of sentence. As to breaches, however, see *post.*

The Sentencing Council for England and Wales has issued a consultation guideline on sentencing for, *inter alia*, breaches of community orders and suspended sentence orders. From the wording of the consultation document (see pages 10 and 14) it is assumed that the proposed guideline would replace the relevant parts of the guideline on "*New Sentences: Criminal Justice Act 2003*" (*ibid.*). The consultation closed on January 25, 2017. For the full text of the guideline, see www.sentencingcouncil.org.uk.

4. ROBBERY (SENTENCING GUIDELINES COUNCIL)

★S-4 As to a new guideline on the sentencing of those aged under 18 for, *inter alia*, robbery, see *post*, S-15, S-29, S-31 *et seq.*

5. DOMESTIC VIOLENCE

★S-5 The Sentencing Council for England and Wales has issued a consultation guideline on, *inter alia*, domestic abuse (covering all offences that occur within a domestic context such as assault, sexual offences or criminal damage). The definitive guideline will replace the Sentencing Guidelines Council's guideline on domestic violence. The consultation closed on June 30, 2017.

6. BREACH OF A PROTECTIVE ORDER

S-6 The Sentencing Council for England and Wales has issued a consultation guideline on sentencing for, *inter alia*, breaches of protective orders, which would replace the current guideline (see the sentencing supplement *et seq.*). The consultation closed on January 25, 2017. For the full text of the guideline, see www.sentencingcouncil.org.uk.

7. SEXUAL OFFENCES (SENTENCING GUIDELINES COUNCIL)

★S-7 As to a new guideline on the sentencing of those aged under 18 for, *inter alia*, sexual offences, see *post*, S-15, S-29 *et seq.*

8. Reduction in Sentence for a Guilty Plea

★**S-8**   The Sentencing Council for England and Wales has issued a new guideline on reduction in sentence for a guilty plea, replacing that issued by the Sentencing Guidelines Council. It applies equally in magistrates' courts and the Crown Court, to all individual offenders aged 18 and older, and to organisations, in cases where the first hearing is after May 31, 2017, regardless of the date of the offence. For the detail, see *post*, S-28 *et seq.*

9. Fail to Surrender to Bail

S-9   The Sentencing Council for England and Wales has issued a consultation guideline on sentencing for, *inter alia*, failing to surrender to bail. From the wording of the consultation document on page 40, it is assumed that the proposed guideline would replace the current guideline (see the sentencing supplement *et seq.*). The consultation closed on January 25, 2017. For the full text of the guideline, see www.sentencingcouncil.org.uk.

11. Magistrates' Court Sentencing Guidelines

S-11   The Sentencing Council for England and Wales has issued new sentencing guidelines for magistrates' courts, which revise, in relation to certain summary offences, the Sentencing Guidelines Council's guidelines. The guidelines apply to all offenders aged 18 or over who are sentenced on or after April 24, 2017, regardless of the date of the offence. Of the guidelines set out in Appendix S in the sentencing supplement, the following are updated: vehicle-taking without consent (Theft Act 1968, s.12 (§ 21-141 in the main work, Appendix S-11.110)), careless driving (RTA 1988, s.3 (§ 32-58 in the main work, Appendix S-11.117)), driving whilst disqualified (1988 Act, s.103 (§ 32-164 in the main work, Appendix S-11.122)), excess alcohol offences (1988 Act, s.5(1)(a) (driving/attempting to drive) and (1)(b) (in charge) (§ 32-89 in the main work, Appendix S-11.124, S-11.126)), failure to a provide specimen for analysis (1988 Act, s.7(6) (drive/attempt/in charge) (§ 32-126 in the main work, Appendix S-11.128, S-11.129)), and driving, attempting to drive, or being in charge of a vehicle when unfit through drink or drugs (1988 Act, s.4(1) and (2) (§ 32-77 in the main work, Appendix S-11.134)).

The Sentencing Council for England and Wales has issued a consultation guideline on sentencing for failures to surrender to bail or to comply with notification requirements, and breaches of community orders, suspended sentence orders, post-sentence supervision, protective orders (*i.e.* restraining and non-molestation orders), criminal behaviour orders and anti-social behaviour orders, sexual harm prevention orders and sexual offences prevention orders, and disqualifications from acting as a director or from keeping an animal. It is assumed that the proposed guideline would replace the relevant parts of the magistrates' court guideline (see the sentencing supplement *et seq.*). The consultation closed on January 25, 2017. For the full text of the guidelines, see www.sentencingcouncil.org.uk.

Taking conveyance without consent

S-11.110   The Sentencing Council for England and Wales has issued new sentencing guidelines for magistrates' courts, which revise, in relation to, *inter alia*, the offence under section 12 of the Theft Act 1968 (§ 21-141 in the main work), the Sentencing Guidelines Council's guidelines. The guidelines apply to all offenders aged 18 or over who are sentenced on or after April 24, 2017, regardless of the date of the offence. The format is the same as for other offence-specific guidelines issued by the council. At step 1, the court should determine which of three categories applies. Category 1 involves higher culpability and greater harm, category 2 involves one or the other, but not both, and category 3 involves neither. The sole indicators of higher culpability are: "a leading role where offending is part of a group activity", "involvement of others through coercion, intimidation or exploitation", "sophisticated nature of offence/significant planning", "abuse of position of power or trust or responsibility" and "commission of offence in association with or to further other criminal activity". Indicators of lower culpability are: "performed limited function under direction", "involved through coercion, intimidation or exploitation", "limited awareness or understanding of offence", "exceeding authorised use of *e.g.* employer's or relative's vehicle" and "retention of hire car for short period beyond return date". The indicator of greater harm are: "vehicle later burnt", "vehicle belonging to elderly/disabled person", "emergency services vehicle", "medium to large goods vehicle", "passengers carried", "damage to lock/

ignition" and "vehicle taken from private premises". All other cases are "lesser harm" cases. For a category 1 case, the starting point is a high level community order, the range is a medium level community order to 26 weeks' custody, and disqualification of between nine and 12 months should be considered. For a category 2 offence, the starting point is a medium level community order, the range is a community order and disqualification of between five and eight months should be considered. For a category 3 offence, the starting point is a low level community order, the range is from a band B fine to a medium level community order, and disqualification should be considered. Having identified a sentence within the range, the court should adjust this for any aggravating or mitigating factors (a non-exhaustive list being included in the guideline) and then go through the other standard steps required by any offence-specific guideline, *viz.* consider the SOCPA 2005, ss.73 and 74 (assistance by defendants: reduction or review of sentence (§§ 5-155, 5-156 in the main work)), credit for a guilty plea, the totality principle, the question of compensation and any appropriate ancillary orders, the need to give reasons and (where relevant) to make any appropriate allowance for time spent on bail (CJA 2003, s.240A (*ibid.*, § 5-604)).

Driving without due care and attention

The Sentencing Council for England and Wales has issued new sentencing guidelines for **S-11.117** magistrates' courts, which revise, in relation to, *inter alia*, the offence under section 3 of the RTA 1988 (§ 32-58 in the main work), the Sentencing Guidelines Council's guidelines. The guidelines apply to all offenders aged 18 or over who are sentenced on or after April 24, 2017, regardless of the date of the offence. The format is the same as for other offence-specific guidelines issued by the council. At step 1, the court should determine which of three categories applies. Category 1 involves higher culpability and greater harm, category 2 involves one or the other, but not both, and category 3 involves neither. The sole indicators of higher culpability are: "excessive speed or aggressive driving", "carrying out other tasks while driving", "vehicle used for carriage of heavy goods or of passengers for reward", "driving when tired or unwell", and "driving contrary to medical advice (including written advice from a drug manufacturer not to drive when taking any medicine)". The sole indicators of greater harm are "injury to others, "damage to vehicles or property" and "high level of traffic or pedestrians in vicinity". Where none of these indicators are present, the case is one of lower culpability and/or lesser harm. The starting point and range for a category 1 case is a band C fine, for a category 2 case, a band B fine, and for a category 3 case, a band A fine. For a category 1 case, disqualification should be considered; if not ordered, then endorsement of between seven and nine penalty points should be ordered. For a category 2 case, the offender's licence should be endorsed with five or six penalty points; and for a category 3 case, endorsement of three or four penalty points should be ordered. Having identified a sentence within the range, the court should adjust this for any aggravating or mitigating factors (a non-exhaustive list being included in the guideline) and then go through the other standard steps required by any offence-specific guideline, *viz.* consider the SOCPA 2005, ss.73 and 74 (assistance by defendants: reduction or review of sentence (§§ 5-155, 5-156 in the main work)), credit for a guilty plea, the totality principle, the question of compensation and any appropriate ancillary orders, and the need to give reasons.

Driving whilst disqualified

The Sentencing Council for England and Wales has issued new sentencing guidelines for **S-11.122** magistrates' courts, which revise, in relation to, *inter alia*, the offence under section 103 of the RTA 1988 (§ 32-164 in the main work), the Sentencing Guidelines Council's guidelines. The guidelines apply to all offenders aged 18 or over who are sentenced on or after April 24, 2017, regardless of the date of the offence. The format is the same as for other offence-specific guidelines issued by the council. At step 1, the court should determine which of three categories applies. Category 1 involves higher culpability and greater harm, category 2 involves one or the other, but not both, and category 3 involves neither. The sole indicators of higher culpability are: "driving shortly after disqualification imposed", "vehicle obtained during disqualification period", and "driving for reward". The sole indicators of greater harm are "significant distance driven" and "evidence of associated bad driving". Where none of these indicators are present, the case is one of lower culpability and/or lesser harm. For a category 1 case, the starting point is 12 weeks' custody, the range is a high level community order to 26 weeks' custody, and disqualification should be ordered for between 12 and 18 months beyond the expiry of the current ban. For a category 2 offence, the starting point is a high level community order, the range is a medium level community order to 12 weeks' custody and disqualification should be ordered for between six and 12 months beyond the expiry of the current ban. For a category 3 offence, the starting point is a low level community order, the range is a band C fine to a medium level community order, and disqualification should be ordered for between three and six months beyond the expiry of the current ban, or, if no disqualification order, then endorsement with six penalty points should be ordered. Having identified a sentence within the range, the court should adjust this for any aggravating or mitigating factors (a non-exhaustive list being included in the guideline) and then go through the other standard steps required by any offence-specific guideline, *viz.* consider the SOCPA 2005, ss.73 and 74 (assistance by defendants: reduction or review of sentence (§§ 5-155, 5-156 in the main work)), credit for a guilty plea, the totality principle, the question of compensation and any appropriate ancillary orders, the need to give reasons and (where relevant) to make any appropriate allowance for time spent on bail (CJA 2003, s.240A (*ibid.*, § 5-604)).

Excess alcohol (drive/attempt to drive)

S-11.124   For guidance on sentencing for the offence of driving, attempting to drive, or being in charge of, a motor vehicle with a specified controlled drug in the body above the specified limit (RTA 1988, s.5A (§ 32-105 in the main work)), which considers whether the guideline for driving or attempting to drive with excess alcohol (see the sentencing supplement) can apply to that offence, see *ante*, § 32-108.

The Sentencing Council for England and Wales has issued new sentencing guidelines for magistrates' courts, which revise, in relation to, *inter alia*, the offence under section 5(1)(a) of the RTA 1988 (§ 32-89 in the main work), the Sentencing Guidelines Council's guidelines. The guidelines apply to all offenders aged 18 or over who are sentenced on or after April 24, 2017, regardless of the date of the offence. The format is the same as for other offence-specific guidelines issued by the council, save that steps 1 and 2 are combined with the starting point and range being based on a table in identical form to that in the Sentencing Guidelines Council's table (see the sentencing supplement). As to the content of the table, there are just two differences. These relate to the two lowest ranges, with the lowest range now being a band B fine to a band C fine, and the second lowest range now being a band C fine to a low level community order. Having identified a sentence within the range, the court should adjust this for any aggravating or mitigating factors (a non-exhaustive list being included in the guideline) and then go through the other standard steps required by any offence-specific guideline, *viz.* consider the SOCPA 2005, ss.73 and 74 (assistance by defendants: reduction or review of sentence (§§ 5-155, 5-156 in the main work)), credit for a guilty plea, the totality principle, the question of compensation and any appropriate ancillary orders, the need to give reasons and (where relevant) to make any appropriate allowance for time spent on bail (CJA 2003, s.240A (*ibid.*, § 5-604)).

Excess alcohol (in charge)

S-11.126   The Sentencing Council for England and Wales has issued new sentencing guidelines for magistrates' courts, which revise, in relation to, *inter alia*, the offence under section 5(1)(b) of the RTA 1988 (§ 32-89 in the main work), the Sentencing Guidelines Council's guidelines. The guidelines apply to all offenders aged 18 or over who are sentenced on or after April 24, 2017, regardless of the date of the offence. The format is the same as for other offence-specific guidelines issued by the council, save that steps 1 and 2 are combined with the starting point and range being based on a table in identical form to that in the Sentencing Guidelines Council's table (see the sentencing supplement). As to the content of the table, there are just two differences. These relate to the two lowest ranges, with the lowest range now being a band A fine to a band B fine, and the second lowest range now being a band B fine to a band C fine. Having identified a sentence within the range, the court should adjust this for any aggravating or mitigating factors (a non-exhaustive list being included in the guideline) and then go through the other standard steps required by any offence-specific guideline, *viz.* consider the SOCPA 2005, ss.73 and 74 (assistance by defendants: reduction or review of sentence (§§ 5-155, 5-156 in the main work)), credit for a guilty plea, the totality principle, the question of compensation and any appropriate ancillary orders, the need to give reasons and (where relevant) to make any appropriate allowance for time spent on bail (CJA 2003, s.240A (*ibid.*, § 5-604)).

Failure to provide specimen for analysis (drive/attempt to drive)

S-11.128 The Sentencing Council for England and Wales has issued new sentencing guidelines for magistrates' courts, which revise, in relation to, *inter alia*, the offence under section 7(6) of the RTA 1988 (§ 32-126 in the main work), the Sentencing Guidelines Council's guidelines. As the offence under section 7(6) carries different maximum penalties according to whether the offender was driving or attempting to drive at the relevant time, the former guidelines and the new guidelines are split into two (for other cases, see *post*, S-11.129). The guidelines apply to all offenders aged 18 or over who are sentenced on or after April 24, 2017, regardless of the date of the offence. The format is the same as for other offence-specific guidelines issued by the council. At step 1, the court should determine which of three categories applies. Category 1 involves higher culpability and greater harm, category 2 involves one or the other, but not both, and category 3 involves neither. The sole indicator of higher culpability is: "deliberate refusal/failure". The one indicator of greater harm is: "high level of impairment". Where none of these indicators are present, the case is one of lower culpability and/or lesser harm. The starting points, ranges and recommended disqualification periods are exactly as in the table in the Sentencing Guidelines Council's guideline (see the sentencing supplement), save that (i) the starting point for a category 2 offence is a medium level community order, (ii) the range for such an offence is a community order, and (iii) the range for a category 3 offence is a band B fine to a low level community order. Having identified a sentence within the range, the court should adjust this for any aggravating or mitigating factors (a non-exhaustive list being included in the guideline) and then go through the other standard steps required by any offence-specific guideline, *viz.* consider the SOCPA 2005, ss.73 and 74 (assistance by defendants: reduction or review of sentence (§§ 5-155, 5-156 in the main work)), credit for a guilty plea, the totality principle, the question of compensation and any appropriate ancillary orders, the need to give reasons and (where relevant) to make any appropriate allowance for time spent on bail (CJA 2003, s.240A (*ibid.*, § 5-604)).

Failure to provide specimen for analysis (in charge)

S-11.129 The Sentencing Council for England and Wales has issued new sentencing guidelines for magistrates' courts, which revise, in relation to, *inter alia*, the offence under section 7(6) of the RTA 1988 (§ 32-126 in the main work), the Sentencing Guidelines Council's guidelines. As the offence under section 7(6) carries different maximum penalties according to whether the offender was driving or attempting to drive at the relevant time, the former guidelines and the new guidelines are split into two (for cases where the offender was driving or attempting to drive, see *ante*, S-11.128). The guidelines apply to all offenders aged 18 or over who are sentenced on or after April 24, 2017, regardless of the date of the offence. The format is the same as for other offence-specific guidelines issued by the council. At step 1, the court should determine which of three categories applies. Category 1 involves higher culpability and greater harm, category 2 involves one or the other, but not both, and category 3 involves neither. The sole indicator of higher culpability is: "deliberate refusal/failure". Indicators of lower culpability are: "honestly held belief but unreasonable excuse", "genuine attempt to comply" and "all other cases". The one indicator of greater harm is: "high level of impairment". Where this is not present, the case is one of lesser harm. The starting points, ranges and recommended disqualification periods are exactly as in the table in the Sentencing Guidelines Council's guideline (see the sentencing supplement) subject to one minor difference: for a category 2 case, the new guideline says, in relation to disqualification "Disqualify up to six months or 10 points". Having identified a sentence within the range, the court should adjust this for any aggravating or mitigating factors (a non-exhaustive list being included in the guideline) and then go through the other standard steps required by any offence-specific guideline, *viz.* consider the SOCPA 2005, ss.73 and 74 (assistance by defendants: reduction or review of sentence (§§ 5-155, 5-156 in the main work)), credit for a guilty plea, the totality principle, the question of compensation and any appropriate ancillary orders, the need to give reasons and (where relevant) to make any appropriate allowance for time spent on bail (CJA 2003, s.240A (*ibid.*, § 5-604)).

Unfit through drink or drugs

S-11.134 The Sentencing Council for England and Wales has issued new sentencing guidelines for magistrates' courts, which revise, in relation to, *inter alia*, the offences under section 4 of the RTA

1988 (§ 32-77 in the main work), the Sentencing Guidelines Council's guidelines. The guidelines apply to all offenders aged 18 or over who are sentenced on or after April 24, 2017, regardless of the date of the offence. The format for the two guidelines is the same as for other offence-specific guidelines issued by the council. At step 1, the court should determine which of three categories applies. Category 1 involves higher culpability and greater harm, category 2 involves one or the other, but not both, and category 3 involves neither. In the driving/attempting to drive guideline, the sole indicators of higher culpability are: "driving LGV, HGV or PSV, *etc.*", and "driving for reward". The sole indicator of greater harm is "high level of impairment". For the "in charge" guideline, the sole indicators of higher culpability are: "high likelihood of driving", "in charge of LGV, HGV or PSV, *etc.*" and "offering to drive for hire or reward". The sole indicator of greater harm is again "high level of impairment". Where none of these indicators are present, the case is one of lower culpability and/or lesser harm.

The starting points, ranges and recommendations in relation to disqualification are as follows for a case of driving or attempting to drive. For a category 1 case, the starting point is 12 weeks' custody, the range is a high level community order to 26 weeks' custody and disqualification should be ordered for between 29 and 36 months, or for between 36 and 60 months in the case of a second offence in 10 years. For a category 2 offence, the starting point is a medium level community order, the range is a community order and disqualification should be ordered for between 17 and 28 months, or for between 36 and 52 months in the case of a second offence in 10 years. For a category 3 offence, the starting point is a band C fine, the range is a band B fine to a low level community order and disqualification should be ordered for between 12 and 16 months, or for between 36 and 40 months in the case of a second offence in 10 years.

The starting points, ranges and recommendations in relation to disqualification are as follows for a case of being unfit whilst in charge. For a category 1 case, the starting point is a high level community order, the range is a medium level community order to 12 weeks' custody, and the court should consider disqualification or, if not disqualifying, order endorsement of 10 penalty points. For a category 2 offence, the starting point is a band C fine, the range is a band B fine to a medium level community order, and the court should consider disqualification or, if not disqualifying, order endorsement of 10 penalty points. For a category 3 offence, the starting point and range is a band B fine, and the court should order the endorsement of 10 penalty points.

Having identified a sentence within the appropriate range, the court should adjust this for any aggravating or mitigating factors (a non-exhaustive list being included in the guideline) and then go through the other standard steps required by any offence-specific guideline, *viz.* consider the SOCPA 2005, ss.73 and 74 (assistance by defendants: reduction or review of sentence (§§ 5-155, 5-156 in the main work)), credit for a guilty plea, the totality principle, the question of compensation and any appropriate ancillary orders, the need to give reasons and (where relevant) to make any appropriate allowance for time spent on bail (CJA 2003, s.240A (*ibid.*, § 5-604)).

13. Breach of an Anti-Social Behaviour Order

S-13   The Sentencing Council for England and Wales has issued a consultation guideline on sentencing for, *inter alia*, breach of a criminal behaviour order, and of anti-social behaviour orders during the transitional period of those orders. From the wording of the consultation document on page 33, it is assumed that the proposed guideline would replace the current guideline (see the sentencing supplement *et seq.*). The consultation closed on January 25, 2017. For the full text of the guideline, see www.sentencingcouncil.org.uk.

15. Sentencing Youths

★S-15   The Sentencing Council for England and Wales has issued a definitive guideline relating to the overarching principles for sentencing those aged under 18 at the date of conviction (Pt 1), and to the sentencing of such persons for sexual offences and robbery (Pts 2 & 3). It applies to all offenders who are sentenced after May 31, 2017, regardless of the date of the offence. For the details, see *post*, S-29 *et seq.*

20. Sexual Offences (Sentencing Council for England and Wales)

★S-20   As to a new guideline on the sentencing of those aged under 18 for, *inter alia*, sexual offences, see *ante*, S-15, and *post*, S-30 *et seq.*

25. Robbery (Sentencing Council for England and Wales)

As to a new guideline on the sentencing of those aged under 18 for, *inter alia*, robbery, see *ante*, S-15, and *post*, S-31 *et seq.* ★**S-25**

27. Imposition of Community Orders and Custodial Sentences

The Sentencing Council for England and Wales has issued a definitive guideline relating to the imposition of community and custodial sentences. It applies to all offenders over the age of 18 falling to be sentenced on or after February 1, 2017, regardless of the date of the offence. **S-27**

Specifically, the guideline deals with (i) the imposition of community orders, (ii) the imposition of custodial sentences, and (iii) suspended sentences (general guidance). There is also a sentencing decision flowchart, and an annex setting out the fine bands.

Community orders

General principles

A community order must not be imposed unless the offence is serious enough to warrant such **S-27a** a sentence (CJA 2003, s.148(1) (§ 5-78 in the main work)). Where an offender is being sentenced for a non-imprisonable offence, there is no power to make a community order (2003 Act, s.150A (*ibid.*, § 5-238)). Sentencers must consider all available disposals at the time of sentence: even where the threshold for a community sentence has been passed, a fine or discharge may be an appropriate penalty. In particular, a Band D fine may be an appropriate alternative to a community order. The court must ensure that the restriction on the offender's liberty is commensurate with the seriousness of the offence (s.148(2)(b)) and that the requirements imposed are the most suitable for the offender (s.148(2)(a)). Sentences should not necessarily escalate from one community order range to the next on each sentencing occasion. The decision as to the appropriate range of community order should be based upon the seriousness of the new offence (taking into account any previous convictions).

Community order levels

The seriousness of the offence should be the initial factor in determining which requirements **S-27b** to include in a community order. Offence-specific guidelines refer to three sentencing levels within the community order band based on offence seriousness (low, medium and high). The culpability and harm present in the offence/offences should be considered to identify which of the three sentencing levels within the community order band (low, medium and high) is appropriate (see the below table for non-exhaustive examples of requirements that may be appropriate in each). At least one requirement must be imposed for the purpose of punishment and/or a fine imposed in addition to the community order, unless there are exceptional circumstances that relate to the offence or the offender that would make it unjust in all the circumstances to do so (2003 Act, s.177(2A) and (2B) (*ibid.*, § 5-240)).

Low	Medium	High
Offences only just cross community order threshold, where the seriousness of the offence or the nature of the offender's record means that a discharge or fine is inappropriate In general, only one requirement will be appropriate and the length may be curtailed if additional requirements are necessary	Offences that obviously fall within the community order band	Offences only just fall below the custody threshold or the custody threshold is crossed but a community order is more appropriate in the circumstances More intensive sentences that combine two or more requirements may be appropriate

Low	Medium	High
Suitable requirements might include: • Any appropriate rehabilitative requirement(s) • 40-80 hours of unpaid work • Curfew requirement within the lowest range (for example, up to 16 hours per day for a few weeks) • Exclusion requirement, for a few months • Prohibited activity requirement • Attendance centre requirement (where available)	*Suitable requirements might include:* • Any appropriate rehabilitative requirement(s) • Greater number of hours of unpaid work (for example 80-150 hours) • Curfew requirement within the middle range (for example up to 16 hours for two-three months) • Exclusion requirement lasting in the region of six months • Prohibited activity requirement	*Suitable requirements might include:* • Any appropriate rehabilitative requirement(s) • 150-300 hours of unpaid work • Curfew requirement up to 16 hours per day for 4-12 months • Exclusion order lasting in the region of 12 months
* If order does not contain a punitive requirement, suggested fine levels are indicated below:		
Band A fine	*Band B fine*	*Band C fine*

Specific considerations in determining requirements

S-27c
   (i) Where two or more requirements are included, they must be compatible with one another and must not be excessive.
   (ii) Any requirement must not conflict with an offender's religious beliefs or with the requirements of any other order to which he may be subject. Interference with an offender's attendance at work or educational establishment should also be avoided.
   (iii) The particular requirements imposed must be suitable for the individual offender and will be influenced by a range of factors, including the stated purposes of the sentence, the risk of re-offending, the ability of the offender to comply and the availability of the requirements in the local area.

Requirements

S-27d
Community orders consist of one or more of the following requirements:

Unpaid work requirement	40-300 hours to be completed within 12 months
Rehabilitation activity requirement	provides flexibility for responsible officers in managing an offender's rehabilitation; the court does not prescribe the activities to be included but will specify the maximum number of activity days the offender must complete; where appropriate, this requirement should be made in addition to, and not in place of, other requirements; sentencers should ensure the length of a rehabilitation activity requirement is suitable and proportionate
Programme requirement	specify the number of days
Prohibited activity requirement	must consult National Probation Service
Curfew requirement	2-16 hours in any 24 hours, for a maximum term of 12 months, and those likely to be affected must be considered (and see *post* on electronic monitoring)

Exclusion requirement	from a specified place/places, for a maximum period of two years, which may be continuous or only during specified periods (and see *post* on electronic monitoring)
Residence requirement	at a place specified or as directed by the responsible officer
Foreign travel prohibition requirement	not to exceed 12 months
Mental health treatment requirement	may be residential/non-residential; must be by/ under the direction of a registered medical practitioner or chartered psychologist; the court must be satisfied that (a) the mental condition of the offender is such as requires, and may be susceptible to, treatment but is not such as to warrant the making of a hospital or guardianship order, (b) arrangements for treatment have been made, and (c) the offender has expressed willingness to comply
Drug rehabilitation requirement	the court must be satisfied that the offender is dependent on, or has a propensity to, misuse drugs that requires or is susceptible to treatment; the offender must consent; treatment can be residential or non-residential, and reviews must be attended by the offender (subject to application for amendment) at intervals of not less than a month (discretionary on requirements of up to 12 months, mandatory on requirements of over 12 months)
Alcohol treatment requirement	residential or non-residential; must have the offender's consent; and the court must be satisfied that the offender is dependent on alcohol and that the dependency is susceptible to treatment
Alcohol abstinence and monitoring requirement	where available
Attendance centre requirement	12-36 hours; only available for offenders aged under 25

Pre-sentence reports

Whenever the court reaches the provisional view that a community order may be appropriate, it **S-27e** should request a pre-sentence report (whether written or oral) unless the court is of the opinion that a report is unnecessary in all the circumstances of the case. It may be helpful to indicate to the National Probation Service the court's preliminary opinion as to which of the three sentencing ranges is relevant and the purpose/purposes of sentencing that the package of requirements is expected to fulfil. Ideally, a pre-sentence report should be completed on the same day to avoid adjourning the case. If an adjournment cannot be avoided, the information should be provided to the National Probation Service in written form and a copy retained on the court file for the benefit of the sentencing court. However, the court must make clear to the offender that all sentencing options remain open including, in appropriate cases, committal for sentence to the Crown Court.

Electronic monitoring

The court must impose an electronic monitoring requirement where it makes a community **S-27f** order with a curfew or exclusion requirement (2003 Act, s.177(3) (*ibid.*, § 5-240)) save where (i) there is a person (other than the offender) without whose co-operation it will not be practicable to secure the monitoring and that person does not consent (2003 Act, s.215(2) (*ibid.*, § 5-266)), and/ or (ii) electronic monitoring is unavailable and/ or impractical (2003 Act, s.218(4) (*ibid.*, § 5-270)), and/ or (iii) in the particular circumstances of the case, it considers it inappropriate to do so (s.177(3)(b)).

The court may impose electronic monitoring in all other cases, which should be used with the primary purpose of promoting and monitoring compliance with other requirements in circumstances where the punishment of the offender and/ or the need to safeguard the public and prevent re-offending are the most important concerns.

Custodial sentences

S-27g   The approach to the imposition of a custodial sentence should be as follows:

Has the custody threshold been passed?

S-27h   A custodial sentence must not be imposed unless the offence or the combination of the offence and one or more offences associated with it was so serious that neither a fine alone nor a community sentence can be justified for the offence. As to the custody threshold (there being no general definition thereof), the circumstances of the individual offence and the factors assessed by offence-specific guidelines will determine whether an offence is so serious that neither a fine alone nor a community sentence can be justified. Where no offence-specific guideline is available to determine seriousness, the harm caused by the offence, the culpability of the offender and any previous convictions will be relevant to the assessment. The clear intention of the threshold test is to reserve prison as a punishment for the most serious offences.

Is it unavoidable that a sentence of imprisonment be imposed?

S-27i   Passing the custody threshold does not mean that a custodial sentence should be deemed inevitable. Custody should not be imposed where a community order could provide sufficient restriction on an offender's liberty (by way of punishment) while addressing the rehabilitation of the offender to prevent future crime. For offenders on the cusp of custody, imprisonment should not be imposed where there would be an impact on dependants that would make a custodial sentence disproportionate to achieving the aims of sentencing.

What is the shortest term commensurate with the seriousness of the offence?

S-27j   In considering this, the court must not consider any licence or post-sentence supervision requirements that may subsequently be imposed upon the offender's release.

Can the sentence be suspended?

S-27k   A suspended sentence must not be imposed as a more severe form of community order. A suspended sentence is a custodial sentence, and sentencers should be clear that they would impose an immediate custodial sentence if the power to suspend were not available. If not, a non-custodial sentence should be imposed.

The following factors should be weighed when considering whether it is possible to suspend the sentence:

Factors indicating that it would not be appropriate to suspend a custodial sentence	Factors indicating that it may be appropriate to suspend a custodial sentence
Offender presents a risk/ danger to the public	Realistic prospect of rehabilitation
Appropriate punishment can only be achieved by immediate custody	Strong personal mitigation
History of poor compliance with court orders	Immediate custody will result in significant harmful impact upon others

To ensure that the overall terms of the suspended sentence are commensurate with offence seriousness, care must be taken to ensure requirements imposed are not excessive. A court wishing to impose onerous or intensive requirements should reconsider whether a community sentence might be more appropriate.

Pre-sentence report

S-27l   Whenever the court reaches the provisional view that the custody threshold has been passed, and as to the length of imprisonment that represents the shortest term commensurate with the seriousness of the offence, it should obtain a pre-sentence report, whether oral or written, unless it considers a report to be unnecessary. Ideally, this should be completed on the same day to avoid adjourning the case.

Magistrates should consult their legal adviser before deciding to impose a custodial sentence without having obtained a pre-sentence report.

Suspended sentences

The guidance regarding pre-sentence reports (see *ante*) applies if suspending custody. **S-27m**

Where the court imposes a term of imprisonment of between 14 days and two years, it may suspend the sentence for between six months and two years (the operational period). The time for which a sentence is suspended should reflect the length of the sentence (up to 12 months might normally be appropriate for a suspended sentence of up to six months).

Where the court imposes two or more sentences to be served consecutively, it may suspend the sentence where the aggregate of the terms is between 14 days and two years.

When the court suspends a sentence, it may impose one or more requirements for the offender to undertake in the community (which are identical to those available for community orders (see *ante*)).

A custodial sentence that is suspended should be for the same term that would have applied if the sentence was to be served immediately.

For the full text of the guidelines, see www.sentencingcouncil.org.uk.

28. REDUCTION IN SENTENCE FOR A GUILTY PLEA

The Sentencing Council for England and Wales has issued a new guideline, replacing that is- **★S-28** sued by the Sentencing Guidelines Council (S-8 in the sentencing supplement). It applies equally in magistrates' courts and the Crown Court, to all individual offenders aged 18 and older, and to organisations, in cases where the first hearing is after May 31, 2017, regardless of the date of the offence.

The purpose of the guideline is to encourage those who are going to plead guilty to do so as **★S-28a** early in the court process as possible, but nothing in it should be used to put pressure on a defendant to plead guilty. It makes a clear distinction between the reduction in sentence available where the plea is entered or indicated at the first stage of the proceedings and that which is available where it is only entered or indicated at a later stage. In particular, (i) the plea should be considered independently of the offender's personal mitigation; (ii) factors such as admissions at interview, co-operation with the investigation and demonstrations of remorse should be considered separately and prior to any guilty plea reduction, as potential mitigation; (iii) the benefits of a plea (*viz.* normally reduces impact of crime on victims, saves victims and witnesses having to testify, saves time and money) apply regardless of the strength of the evidence, which, therefore, should not be taken into account when determining the level of reduction; (iv) the guideline applies only to the punitive elements of the sentence and has no impact on ancillary orders, including orders of disqualification from driving.

The five-stage approach should be to determine the appropriate sentence for the offence in ac- **★S-28b** cordance with any offence-specific guideline (1), to determine the level of reduction for the plea (2), to state the amount of that reduction (3), to apply it to the appropriate sentence (4), and to follow any further steps in the offence-specific guideline to determine the final sentence (5).

The maximum reduction of one-third should be awarded for a guilty plea indicated at the first **★S-28c** stage of proceedings. The first stage will normally be the first hearing at which a plea or indication of plea is sought and recorded by the court. Where a defendant is given the opportunity to enter a guilty plea without attending a court hearing, doing so within the required time limits will constitute a plea at the first stage of proceedings. After the first stage, the maximum level of reduction is one-quarter. The reduction should be decreased from one-quarter to a maximum of one-tenth on the first day of trial, having regard to the time when the guilty plea is first indicated to the court, relative to the progress of the case and the trial date. The reduction should normally be decreased further, even to zero, if the plea is entered during the course of the trial. Where there is pre-recorded cross-examination, the trial will be deemed to have begun at that point.

Where the reduction in sentence leads to the imposition of one type of sentence rather than **★S-28d** another, *e.g.* community sentence in lieu of custodial sentence, or fine in lieu of community sentence, there should normally be no further reduction on account of the plea. When dealing with more than one summary offence, where the aggregate sentence is limited to a maximum of six months and where, allowing for a reduction for each guilty plea, consecutive sentences might result in the imposition of the maximum six-month sentence, the court may make a modest additional reduction to the overall sentence to reflect the benefits derived from the pleas. Reducing a custodial sentence to reflect a guilty plea may enable a magistrates' court to retain jurisdiction of an either-way offence rather than committing the case for sentence to the Crown Court.

★S-28e   The final section of the guideline sets out exceptions. First, where the court is satisfied that there were particular circumstances that significantly reduced the defendant's ability to understand what was alleged or otherwise made it unreasonable to expect him to indicate a guilty plea sooner than was done, a reduction of one-third should still be made. Courts should distinguish between cases in which it is necessary to receive advice and/ or have sight of evidence in order to understand whether the defendant is in fact and law guilty of the offence charged, and cases in which a defendant merely delays his plea in order to assess the strength of the prosecution case and the prospects of conviction or acquittal. Secondly, where an offender's version of events is rejected at a *Newton* (*R. v. Newton,* 77 Cr.App.R. 13, CA (§ 5-110 in the main work)) or "special reasons" hearing, the reduction that would have been available at the stage of the proceedings the plea was indicated should normally be halved. Where witnesses are called at such a hearing, it may be appropriate further to decrease the reduction. Thirdly, if an offender is convicted of a lesser or different offence from that originally charged, and has earlier made an unequivocal indication of a guilty plea to this lesser or different offence to the prosecution and the court, the court should give the level of reduction that is appropriate to the stage in the proceedings at which this indication of plea (to the lesser or different offence) was made, taking into account any other of these exceptions that apply. In the Crown Court where the offered plea is a permissible alternative on the indictment as charged, the offender will not be treated as having given an unequivocal indication unless he has entered that plea. Fourthly, the provisions of the guideline are subordinate to statutory provisions relating to minimum sentences for certain offences: see, in particular, the Firearms Act 1968, s.51A (*ibid.,* § 5-425), and the CJA 2003, s.144 (*ibid.,* § 5-122).

★S-28f   Special consideration has to be given to a murder case to ensure that the minimum term properly reflects the seriousness of the offence. Whilst the general principles continue to apply (both that a guilty plea should be encouraged and that the extent of any reduction should reduce if the indication of plea is later than the first stage of the proceedings), the process of determining the level of reduction is different. When deciding whether it is appropriate to order a whole-life term, the court should consider the fact that the offender has pleaded guilty to murder. Where a whole-life term is not to be imposed, (i) the court should weigh carefully the overall length of the minimum term, taking into account other reductions for which the offender may be eligible so as to avoid a combination leading to an inappropriately short term, (ii) where it is appropriate to reduce the minimum term having regard to a plea of guilty, the reduction should not exceed one-sixth and should never exceed five years, and (iii) the maximum reduction should only be given when a guilty plea has been indicated at the first stage of the proceedings and lesser reductions should be given for guilty pleas after that point, with a maximum of one-twentieth being given for a plea on the day of trial. The first and second exceptions apply to murder cases.

★S-28g   The appendices are illustrative flowcharts that do not form part of the guideline.

29. Sentencing Children and Young People

★S-29   The Sentencing Council for England and Wales has issued a definitive guideline relating to the overarching principles for sentencing those aged under 18 at the date of conviction (Pt 1), and to the sentencing of such persons for sexual offences and robbery (Pts 2 & 3). It applies to all offenders who are sentenced after May 31, 2017, regardless of the date of the offence.

Part 1 (overarching principles)

SECTION ONE: general approach

Sentencing principles

★S-29a   A court must have regard to the CDA 1998, s.37(1) (aim of the youth justice system (§ 5-73 in the main work)), and the CYPA 1933, s.44(1) (general considerations (*ibid.*, § 5-74)). While the seriousness of the offence will be the starting point, the focus should be on the offender, rather than the offence, with rehabilitation being the aim, where possible. The effect the sentence is likely to have on the offender (both positive and negative), as well as any underlying factors contributing to the offending behaviour, should be borne in mind.

It is important to avoid "criminalising" children and young people unnecessarily. The primary aim should be to encourage offenders to take responsibility for their actions and to promote their re-integration into society rather than to punish. Restorative justice may be of particular value. The extent to which the offender was acting impulsively and whether his conduct was affected by inexperience, emotional volatility or negative influences should be considered. Emotional and developmental age is at least as relevant as chronological age.

Young offenders should, if possible, be given the opportunity to learn from their mistakes without undue penalisation or stigma, especially as a court sanction might have a significant effect on their prospects and opportunities, and hinder their re-integration into society. The sentence should not result in their alienation from society if that can be avoided. The fact that penal interventions may interfere with their education should be borne in mind. Any restriction on liberty must be commensurate with the seriousness of the offence.

Pending the commencement of section 9 (inserting s.142A (purposes of sentencing: offenders under 18 (*ibid.*, § 5-76)) into the CJA 2003) of the CJIA, deterrence can be a factor in sentencing, although normally it should be restricted to serious offences and can, and often will, be outweighed by welfare considerations.

Welfare

In discharging its statutory obligation to have regard to the welfare of the offender (s.44 of the 1933 Act), a court should ensure that it is alert to (i) any mental health problems or learning difficulties/ disabilities, (ii) any brain injury or traumatic life experience (including exposure to drug and alcohol abuse), and the developmental impact this may have had, (iii) any speech and language difficulties and the effect this may have on the ability of the offender (or any accompanying adult) to communicate with the court, to understand the sanction imposed or to fulfil the obligations resulting from that sanction, (iv) vulnerability to self-harm, particularly within a custodial environment, and (v) the effect of experiences of neglect and/ or abuse. **★S-29b**

The court should ensure that it has access to information about how best to identify and respond to factors that are regularly present in the background of young offenders (deprived homes, poor parental employment records, low educational attainment, early experience of offending by other family members, abuse and/or neglect, negative peer influences and the misuse of drugs and/or alcohol), and that a proper assessment has taken place to enable the most appropriate sentence to be imposed.

A court should bear in mind the various reasons why offenders may conduct themselves inappropriately in court (*e.g.* nervousness, a belief that they will be discriminated against, peer pressure, *etc.*).

When dealing with an offender who is "looked after" (*i.e.* in care), a court should bear in mind the additional complex vulnerabilities that are likely to be present in his background (little or no contact with family and/or friends, special educational needs and/or emotional and behavioural problems, exposure to criminal peers, likely to be in care as a result of abuse, neglect or parental absence due to bereavement, imprisonment or desertion). A court should bear in mind that the level of parental-type support that an offender in care receives throughout the criminal justice process may be limited. Sentencers will need to consider any impact a custodial sentence may have on leaving care rights and whether this is proportionate to the seriousness of the offence. For those who are in the process of leaving care or have recently left care, sentencers should bear in mind any effect this may have had on their behaviour.

When having regard to the welfare principle, the particular factors that arise in the case of minority ethnic children and young people need to be taken into account.

The welfare principle is subject to the obligation to impose only those restrictions on liberty that are commensurate with the seriousness of the offence. Accordingly, a court should not impose greater restrictions because of other factors in the offender's life.

When considering an offender who may be particularly vulnerable, sentencers should consider which disposal is best able to support the individual and which disposals could potentially exacerbate any underlying issues. This is particularly important when considering custody as there are concerns about the effect of being in closed conditions, with significant risks of self-harm, including suicide. The vulnerability factors that are often present in an offender's background should also be considered in light of the offending behaviour itself.

These principles do not undermine the fact that the sentence should reflect the seriousness of the offence.

SECTION TWO: allocation (see also the allocation charts at pp.11-13 of the guideline)

★**S-29c**   Trial in the Crown Court should be reserved for the most serious cases (*R. (H., A. and O.) v. Southampton Youth Court* (§ 1-88 in the main work)).

Dangerousness

★**S-29d**   In considering whether to commit a defendant to the Crown Court for trial under section 51A(2) and (3)(d) (*ibid.*, § 1-25) of the CDA 1998 (the offence is a specified offence and it appears to the court that, if the defendant is found guilty, the criteria for the imposition of a sentence under s.226B (*ibid.*, § 5-479) of the CJA 2003 would be met), in anything but the most serious cases, it may be impossible for the court to form a view as to whether the defendant would meet the criteria of the dangerous offender provisions without greater knowledge of the circumstances of the offence and the defendant. In those circumstances, jurisdiction should be retained in the youth court. If, following conviction, the dangerousness criteria appear to be met then the offender should be committed for sentence.

Grave crimes

★**S-29e**   As there is now a power to commit grave crimes (*i.e.* those within s.91 (*ibid.*, § 5-587) of the PC-C(S)A 2000) for sentence (2000 Act, s.3B (*ibid.*, § 5-31)), the court should no longer take the prosecution case at its highest when deciding whether to retain jurisdiction. In most cases it is likely to be impossible to decide whether there is a real prospect that a sentence in excess of two years' detention will be imposed (*R. (H., A. and O.) v. Southampton Youth Court, ante*), without knowing more about the facts of the case and the circumstances of the child or young person. In such circumstances, the youth court should retain jurisdiction and commit for sentence if it is of the view, having heard more about the facts and the circumstances of the offender, that its powers of sentence are insufficient.

Where the court decides that the case is suitable to be dealt with in the youth court, it must warn the defendant that all available sentencing options remain open and, if found guilty, he may be committed to the Crown Court for sentence.

Therefore, defendants should only be sent for trial or committed for sentence when charged with, or found guilty of, an offence of such gravity that a custodial sentence substantially exceeding two years is a realistic possibility. For children aged 10 or 11, and aged 12 to 14 who are not persistent offenders, the court should take into account the normal prohibition on imposing custodial sentences.

Charged alongside an adult

★**S-29f**   Where a child or young person is jointly charged with an adult and the adult is sent for trial to the Crown Court, the court should conclude that the child or young person must be tried separately in the youth court unless it is in the interests of justice for him to be tried jointly. Factors to consider include whether separate trials will cause injustice to witnesses or to the case as a whole (consideration should be given to the YJCEA 1999, ss.27 (*ibid.*, § 8-89) and 28 (*ibid.*, § 8-93)), the age of the child or young person (the younger, the greater the desirability that he be tried in the youth court), the age gap (a substantial gap militates in favour of trial in the youth court), lack of maturity, the relative alleged culpability of the child or young person compared with the adult, whether the alleged role played by the child or young person was minor, and his criminal record, if any.

Remittal from the Crown Court for sentence

★**S-29g**   Whereas, if a child or young person is convicted before the Crown Court of an offence other than homicide, the court must remit the case to a youth court, unless it would be undesirable to do so (2000 Act, s.8 (*ibid.*, § 5-51)), in considering whether remittal would be undesirable, a court should balance the need for expertise in the sentencing of children and young people with the benefits of the sentence being imposed by the court that determined guilt. Particular attention should be given to those who are appearing before the Crown Court only because they were jointly charged with an adult. Referral orders are generally not available in the Crown Court, but may be the most appropriate sentence.

SECTION THREE: parental responsibilities

Where a court finds that it would be unreasonable to adhere to the requirement that parents or guardians attend all stages of the proceedings, extra care must be taken to ensure the outcomes are clearly communicated to and understood by the defendant. As to binding over parents under the 2000 Act, s.150 (*ibid.*, § 5-1305), and parenting orders under the 1998 Act, ss.8 and 9 (*ibid.*, §§ 5-1306, 5-1307), in most circumstances a parenting order is likely to be more appropriate than a parental bind over. ★**S-29h**

SECTION FOUR: determining the sentence

Key considerations are: (i) the principal aim of the youth justice system, (ii) the welfare of the offender, (iii) the age of the offender (chronological, developmental and emotional), (iv) the seriousness of the offence, (v) the likelihood of further offences being committed, and (vi) the harm likely to result from any further offences. ★**S-29i**

The seriousness of the offence

When offence-specific guidance for children and young persons is available, this should be referred to. Whilst the seriousness of the offence should be the starting point, sentencing should always be individualistic. ★**S-29j**

In assessing culpability, the court should consider the extent to which the offence was planned, the role of the offender, and the awareness that he had of his actions and their possible consequences. There is an expectation that, in general, a youth will be dealt with less severely than an adult.

Harm should be assessed in accordance with section 143 of the 2003 Act (*ante*).

The court should also consider any aggravating or mitigating factors that may affect the overall seriousness of the offence.

Aggravating factors:

Statutory aggravating factors (see the 2003 Act, ss.143(2) and (3), 145 and 146 (*ibid.*, §§ 5-78, 5-140, 5-141)) ★**S-29k**

Other aggravating factors (non-exhaustive):
- steps taken to prevent victim reporting or obtaining assistance ★**S-29l**
- steps taken to prevent victim from assisting or supporting the prosecution
- victim is particularly vulnerable due to factors such as age or mental or physical disability
- restraint, detention or additional degradation of victim
- prolonged nature of offence
- attempts to conceal/dispose of evidence
- established evidence of community/ wider impact
- failure to comply with current court orders
- attempt to conceal identity
- involvement of others through peer pressure, bullying, coercion or manipulation
- commission of offence whilst under the influence of alcohol or drugs
- history of antagonising or bullying victim
- deliberate humiliation of victim, including by filming of the offence, deliberately committing the offence before a group of peers with the intention of causing additional distress or circulating details/ photos/ videos, *etc.*, on social media or within peer groups

Factors reducing seriousness or reflecting personal mitigation (non-exhaustive):
- no convictions or no relevant/recent convictions ★**S-29m**
- remorse, particularly where evidenced by voluntary reparation to victim
- good character and/or exemplary conduct

- unstable upbringing including, but not limited to:
  - time in care
  - lack of familial presence or support
  - disrupted experiences in accommodation or education
  - exposure to drug/alcohol abuse, familial criminal behaviour or domestic abuse
  - victim of neglect or abuse, or exposure to neglect or abuse of others
  - experience of trauma or loss
- participated in offence due to bullying, peer pressure, coercion or manipulation
- limited understanding of effect on victim
- serious medical condition requiring urgent, intensive or long-term treatment
- communication or learning disabilities, or mental health concerns
- in education, work or training
- particularly young or immature (where it affects responsibility)
- determination and/or demonstration of steps taken to address addiction or offending behaviour

Age and maturity of the child or young person

★**S-29n**   The consideration of age requires a different approach to that which would be adopted in relation to the age of an adult. Even within the category of child or young person, the response of a court is likely to be very different depending on where the defendant sits in the age bracket. Although chronological age dictates in some instances what sentence can be imposed, the developmental and emotional age of the offender is of at least equal importance as his chronological age. It is important to consider whether the offender has the necessary maturity to appreciate fully the consequences of his conduct, the extent to which he was acting impulsively and whether his conduct was affected by inexperience, emotional volatility or negative influences.

SECTION FIVE: guilty plea

★**S-29o**   This section applies regardless of the date of the offence where the first hearing is after May 31, 2017. It largely corresponds to the guideline on reduction in sentence for a guilty plea (*ante*, S-28 *et seq.*), the main differences being that (i) the five-stage approach should be used to determine the appropriate sentence in accordance with this guideline (as well as any offence-specific guideline), (ii) whereas a detention and training order can only be imposed for four, six, eight, 10, 12, 18 or 24 months, if the reduction in sentence for a guilty plea results in a sentence that falls between two prescribed periods, the court must impose the lesser of those two periods, which may result in a reduction greater than a third, in order that the full reduction is given and a lawful sentence imposed, (iii) a detention and training order of up to 24 months may be imposed on a child or young person if the offence is one which, but for the plea, would have attracted a sentence of detention in excess of 24 months under section 91 of the 2000 Act (*ante*), and (iv) as a referral order is only available upon pleading guilty, there should be no further reduction of the sentence to reflect the plea.

SECTION SIX: available sentences

Crossing a significant age threshold between commission of offence and sentence

★**S-29p**   When an increase in the age of a child or young person results in the maximum sentence on the date of conviction being greater than that available on the date of the offence, the starting point should be the sentence likely to have been imposed on the date of the offence. When any significant age threshold is passed, it will rarely be appropriate that a more severe sentence than the maximum that the court could have imposed at the time the offence was committed should be imposed. However, a sentence at or close to that maximum may be appropriate.

Persistent offenders

★**S-29q**   A child or young person must be classed as a persistent offender in order for certain orders to be made. A defendant who has committed one previous offence cannot reasonably be classed as a persistent offender, and one who has committed two or more previous offences should not necessarily be assumed to be one. To determine if the behaviour is persistent, the nature of the previous offences and the lapse of time between them need to be considered. When an offender is being sentenced in a single appearance for a series of separate, comparable offences, committed over a short space of time, then the court could justifiably consider him to be a persistent offender, despite the fact that there may be no previous convictions. In these cases, the court should consider whether the offender has had a prior opportunity to address his offending behaviour before imposing one of the sentences available for persistent offenders only. Where the court determines that he has not had such an opportunity and believes that an alternative sentence has a reasonable prospect of preventing re-offending, then this alternative should be imposed. The court may also wish to consider any evidence of a reduction in the level of offending when taking into account previous offending behaviour. Young offenders may be unlikely to desist from committing crime in a clear-cut manner, but there may be changes in patterns of behaviour (*e.g.* committing fewer and/or less serious offences, or longer gaps between offences) that indicate that the individual is attempting to desist from crime. Even where the defendant is a persistent offender, a court is not obliged to impose one of the optional sentences. The approach should still be individualistic.

Sentences available by age

S-29r

Sentence	Age 10-11	Age 12-14	Age 15-17	Rehabilitation period
Discharge or reparation order	Available	Available	Available	Day of sentence, save for conditional discharge (last day of period of discharge)
Financial order	Available	Available	Available	Spent six months after conviction
Referral order	Available	Available	Available	Spent on day of completion
Youth rehabilitation order	Available	Available	Available	Spent six months after the last day the order is to have effect
Youth rehabilitation order with intensive supervision and surveillance or fostering	Not available	Available (for persistent offenders only)	Available	Spent six months after the last day the order is to have effect
Detention and training order	Not available	Available (for persistent offenders only)	Available	Six months or under: spent 18 months after the sentence is completed (including supervision period) More than six months: spent 24 months after the sentence is completed (including

Sentence	Age 10-11	Age 12-14	Age 15-17	Rehabilitation period
				supervision period)
Detention for grave crimes (PCC(S)A 2000, s.91)	Available	Available	Available	More than six months - 30 months: spent 24 months after sentence completed (including licence period) More than 30 months - 48 months: spent 42 months after sentence completed (including licence period) More than 48 months: never spent
Extended sentence of detention (CJA 2003, s.226B)	Available	Available	Available	Never spent

The length of the rehabilitation period and any likely effects on the offender's future prospects should be taken into account when considering if the sentence is commensurate to the seriousness of the offence.

Breaches and the commission of further offences during the period of an order

★S-29s   If an offender is found guilty of breaching an order, or commits a further offence during the period of an order, the court will have various options available, depending upon the nature of the order (see Appendix 1 (*post*)). The primary aim should be to encourage compliance and seek to support the rehabilitation of the offender.

Discharges and reparation orders

★S-29t   An absolute discharge is appropriate when the court considers that no punishment should be imposed. A conditional discharge is appropriate when the offence is not serious enough to warrant an immediate punishment. As to reparation orders, see sections 73 and 74 of the PCC(S)A (§§ 5-696, 5-697 in the main work).

Financial order

★S-29u   In practice, given that many young offenders have limited financial resources, the court will need to determine whether imposing a fine will be the most effective disposal. It should bear in mind that young people may have money that is specifically required for travel costs to school, college or apprenticeships and lunch expenses.

Referral orders

★S-29v   In general terms, referral orders may be regarded as falling between fines and community disposals. However, bearing in mind that the principal aim of the youth justice system is to prevent children and young people offending, second or subsequent referral orders should be considered where (a) the offence is not serious enough for a youth rehabilitation order but the offender appears to require some intervention, or (b) the offence is serious enough for a youth rehabilitation order but it is felt that a referral order would be the best way to prevent further offending (*e.g.* because the offender has responded well in the past to such an order and the fresh offence is dissimilar to that for which a referral order was previously made).

Where a first offender has pleaded guilty to an offence on the cusp of the custody threshold, the youth offending team should be encouraged to convene a youth offender panel prior to sentence where the offender is asked to attend and agree an intensive contract. If that contract is placed before the sentencing court, the court can then decide whether it is sufficient to move below custody on this occasion. The proposed contract is not something the court can alter, and it will still have to decide between a referral order and custody, but can do so on the basis that, if it makes a referral order, it can have confidence in what that will entail in the particular case.

The court determines the length of the order, but a referral order panel determines the requirements of the order.

Offence seriousness	Suggested length of referral order
Low	3-5 months
Medium	5-7 months
High	7-9 months
Very high	10-12 months

Where the youth offending team propose certain requirements and their length does not correspond to the above table, if the court feels that these requirements will best achieve the aims of the youth justice system, then they may still be imposed.

Youth rehabilitation orders

As to youth rehabilitation orders, see section 1 of, and Schedule 1 to, the CJIA 2008 (*ibid.*, §§ ★**S-29w** 5-281, 5-286 *et seq.*), in addition to section 148 of the CJA 2003 (restrictions on imposing community sentences (*ibid.*, § 5-235)). A court should take care to ensure that the requirements imposed are not so onerous as to make breach almost inevitable.

When determining the nature and extent of the requirements, the court should primarily consider the likelihood of the defendant re-offending and the risk of him causing serious harm. A higher risk of re-offending does not in itself justify a greater restriction on liberty than is warranted by the seriousness of the offence (any requirements should still be commensurate with the seriousness of the offence and regard must still be had to the welfare of the offender). The youth offending team will assess this as part of their report and recommend an intervention level to the court for consideration (it is possible for the court to ask the team to consider a particular requirement).

	Child or young person profile	Requirements of order (the examples are not exclusive)
Standard	Low likelihood of re-offending and a low risk of serious harm	Primarily seek to repair harm caused through, *e.g.*: • reparation; • unpaid work; • supervision; and/or • attendance centre.
Enhanced	Medium likelihood of re-offending or a medium risk of serious harm	Seek to repair harm caused and to enable help or change through, *e.g.*: • supervision; • reparation; • requirement to address behaviour *e.g.* drug treatment, offending behaviour pro-

		gramme, education programme; and/ or • a combination of the above.
Intensive	High likelihood of re-offending or a very high risk of serious harm	Seek to ensure the control of, and enable help or change for, the offender through, *e.g.*: • supervision; • reparation; • requirement to address behaviour; • requirement to monitor or restrict movement, *e.g.* prohibited activity, • curfew, exclusion or electronic monitoring; and/ or • a combination of the above.

If the offender is assessed as presenting a high risk of re-offending or of causing serious harm, but the offence that was committed is of relatively low seriousness, then the appropriate requirements are likely to be primarily rehabilitative or for the protection of the public. Likewise, if the offender is assessed as presenting a low risk of re-offending or of causing serious harm, but the offence was of relatively high seriousness, then the appropriate requirements are likely to be primarily punitive.

Orders with intensive supervision and surveillance or with fostering

★S-29wa   As to the restrictions on the imposition of such requirements, see section 1(4) of the 2008 Act.

With intensive supervision and surveillance

★S-29wb   As to youth rehabilitation orders with intensive supervision and surveillance, see paragraphs 3 and 5 of Schedule 1 to the 2008 Act.

With fostering:

★S-29wc   As to youth rehabilitation orders with a fostering requirement, see paragraphs 4, 5, 18 and 19 of Schedule 1 to the 2008 Act. Imposition of such a requirement is likely to engage other rights (such as those under Art. 8 (to respect for private and family life (*ibid.*, § 16-137)) of the ECHR), and any interference with such rights must be proportionate. It is unlikely that the statutory criteria for the imposition of such a requirement will be met in many cases. Where they are met and the court is considering the imposition of such a requirement, care should be taken to ensure that there is a well-developed plan for the care and support of the offender throughout the period of the order and thereafter. The court will need to be provided with sufficient information, including proposals for education and training during the order and plans for the child or young person on completion of the order.

Custodial sentences

★S-29x   See section 174(8) (*ibid.*, § 5-198) of the 2003 Act as to the particular duty to give reasons for the imposition of a custodial sentence on a young offender. Any case that warrants a detention and training order of less than four months must result in a non-custodial sentence. In determining whether an offence has crossed the custody threshold, the court will need to assess the seriousness, in particular the level of harm that was caused, or was likely to have been caused, by the offence. The risk of serious harm in the future must also be assessed. The pre-sentence report will assess this criterion and must be considered before a custodial sentence is imposed, which is most likely to be unavoidable where it is necessary to protect the public from serious harm. Where the court is satisfied that the offence crosses the custody threshold, and that no other sentence is appropriate, it may, as a preliminary consideration, consult the equivalent adult guideline in order to decide upon the appropriate length of the sentence. The court may feel it appropriate to apply a sentence broadly within the region of half to two-thirds of the adult sentence for those aged 15 to 17, with a greater discount for those aged under 15. However, this is only a rough guide and must not be applied mechanistically. In most cases, when considering the appropriate reduction, the emotional and developmental age and maturity of the offender is of at least equal importance as chronological age. The individual factors relating to the offence and the offender are of the greatest importance and may constitute good reason to impose a sentence outside of this range. A court should bear in mind the negative effects a short custodial sentence can have (it disrupts education and/or training and family relationships and support, which are crucial stabilising factors for preventing re-offending).

There is an expectation that custodial sentences will be particularly rare for a child who is under 15 years. If custody is imposed, it should be for a shorter period than that which a young person aged 15 to 17 would receive. The welfare of the offender is especially important when a custodial sentence is being considered.

Detention and training order

See the PCC(S)A 2000, ss.100-107 (*ibid.*, §§ 5-507 *et seq.*). Any time spent on remand in custody or on bail subject to a qualifying curfew condition should be taken into account when calculating the length of the order. The accepted approach is to double the time spent on remand before deciding the appropriate period of detention, in order to ensure that the regime is in line with that applied to adult offenders (*R. v. Eagles* (*ibid.*, § 5-585)). After doubling the time spent on remand, the court should then adopt the nearest prescribed period available for a detention and training order.

★S-29xa

Dangerous offenders

See sections 226 and 226B (*ibid.*, §§ 5-476, 5-479) of the 2003 Act.

★S-29xb

Appendix 1 (breach of orders)

The courts' powers when an offender has breached an order are summarised in Appendix 1. In relation to breach of youth rehabilitation orders, it emphasises that the primary objective is to secure completion of the requirements imposed by the court. The court must ensure that it has sufficient information to enable it to understand why the order has been breached and should be satisfied that the youth offending team and other local authority services have taken all steps necessary to afford the offender an appropriate opportunity, and the support necessary, for compliance. This is particularly important if the court is considering a custodial sentence as a result of the breach. Where the failure arises primarily from non-compliance with reporting, or other similar, obligations and a sanction is necessary, the most appropriate response is likely to be the inclusion of (or increase in) a primarily punitive requirement, such as a curfew, unpaid work, exclusion or prohibited activity requirement, or the imposition of a fine. A continuing failure to comply is likely to lead to revocation and re-sentencing. An offender will almost certainly be considered to have "wilfully and persistently" breached a youth rehabilitation order where there have been three breaches that have demonstrated a lack of willingness to comply and have resulted in an appearance before a court, in which case additional powers are available.

★S-29y

Part 2 (sexual offences guideline)

This guideline should be read alongside Part 1. The first step is to assess the seriousness of the offence. That a sentence threshold is crossed does not necessarily mean that that sentence should be imposed.

★S-30

Step one (offence seriousness - nature of the offence)

The boxes below give examples of the type of culpability and harm factors that may indicate that a particular threshold has been crossed:

★S-30a

A non-custodial sentence* may be the most suitable disposal where one or more of the following factors apply:
Any form of non-penetrative sexual activity
Any form of sexual activity (including penetration) without coercion, exploitation or pressure, except where there is a significant disparity in age or maturity

Minimal psychological or physical harm to the victim

A custodial sentence or youth rehabilitation order with intensive supervision and surveillance* or fostering* may be justified where one or more of the following factors apply:
Any penetrative activity involving coercion, exploitation or pressure
Use or threats of violence against the victim or someone known to the victim
Prolonged detention/sustained incident
Severe psychological or physical harm to the victim

* Where the child or young person appears in a youth court, and the conditions for a compulsory referral order apply, a referral order must be made unless the court is considering a discharge, hospital order or custody.

Step two (offence seriousness - aggravating and mitigating factors)

★**S-30b**   To complete the assessment of seriousness, the court should consider the aggravating and mitigating factors relevant to the offence:

Aggravating factors
  Statutory aggravating factors (as in Pt 1, *ante*)
  Other aggravating factors (non-exhaustive):
   – Significant degree of planning
   – Acting with others
   – Use of alcohol/drugs on victim to facilitate offence
   – Abuse of trust
   – Deliberate humiliation of victim including, filming offence, deliberately committing offence before a group of peers with the intention of causing additional distress or circulating details/photos/videos, *etc.*, of offence on social media or within peer groups
   – Grooming
   – Significant disparity in age between offender and victim (measured chronologically or with reference to level of maturity) (where not taken into account at step one)
   – Victim particularly vulnerable due to factors including age or mental or physical disability
   – Any steps taken to prevent reporting incident/seeking assistance
   – Pregnancy or STI as a consequence offence
   – Blackmail
   – Use of weapon

Mitigating factors (non-exhaustive)
   – No convictions or no relevant/recent convictions
   – Good character and/or exemplary conduct
   – Participated in offence due to bullying, peer pressure, coercion or manipulation
   – Genuine belief that activity was lawful

Step three (personal mitigation)

★**S-30c**   Having assessed the offence seriousness, the court should then consider the personal mitigation. This may reduce what would otherwise be a custodial sentence to a non-custodial one, or a community sentence to a different means of disposal.

Personal mitigating factors (non-exhaustive)
Particularly young or immature (where it affects responsibility)
Communication or learning disabilities, or mental health concerns
Unstable upbringing including: • time in care • lack of familial presence or support

• disrupted experiences in accommodation or education
• exposure to drug/alcohol abuse, familial criminal behaviour or domestic abuse
• exposure by others to pornography or sexually explicit materials
• victim of neglect or abuse, or exposure to neglect or abuse of others
• experience of trauma or loss

Determination and/or demonstration of steps taken to address offending behaviour
Strong prospect of rehabilitation
In education, training or employment

Step four (reduction for guilty plea)
    See Part 1 (*ante*).   ★**S-30d**

Step five (review the sentence)
    The court must now review the sentence (in accordance with Pt 1) to ensure it is the most appropriate one for the defendant. This will include an assessment of the likelihood of reoffending and the risk of causing serious harm.   ★**S-30e**

Part three (robbery guideline)

    This should be read alongside Part 1. That a sentence threshold is crossed does not necessarily mean that that sentence should be imposed.   ★**S-31**

Step 1 (offence seriousness - nature of the offence)
    The boxes below give examples of the type of culpability and harm factors that may indicate that a particular threshold has been crossed.   ★**S-31a**

A non-custodial sentence* may be the most suitable disposal where one or more of the following factors apply:
Threat or use of minimal force
Little or no physical or psychological harm to victim
Involved through coercion, intimidation or exploitation

A custodial sentence or youth rehabilitation order with intensive supervision and surveillance* or fostering* may be justified where one or more of the following factors apply:
Use of very significant force
Threat or use of a bladed article, firearm or imitation firearm (where produced)
Significant physical or psychological harm to victim

    * Where the child or young person appears in a youth court, and the conditions for a compulsory referral order apply, a referral order must be made unless the court is considering a discharge, hospital order or custody.

Step two (offence seriousness - aggravating and mitigating factors)
    To complete the assessment of seriousness, the court should consider the aggravating and mitigating factors relevant to the offence.   ★**S-31b**

Aggravating factors
    Statutory aggravating factors (as in Pt 1, *ante*)
    Other aggravating factors (non-exhaustive):
      – Significant degree of planning
      – Deliberate humiliation of victim, including filming of offence, deliberately committing offence before a group of peers with intention of causing additional distress or circulating details/photos/video, *etc.*, of offence on social media or within peer groups
      – Threat or use of a weapon other than a bladed article, firearm or imitation firearm (whether produced or not)

- Threat to use bladed article, firearm or imitation firearm (not produced)
- Victim particularly vulnerable due to factors including age or mental or physical disability
- A leading role where offending is part of a group
- Attempt to conceal identity
- Any steps taken to prevent reporting incident/seeking assistance
- High value goods or sums targeted or obtained (includes economic, personal or sentimental)
- Restraint, detention or additional degradation of victim

Mitigating factors (non-exhaustive)
- No convictions or no relevant/recent convictions
- Good character and/or exemplary conduct
- Participated in offence due to bullying, peer pressure, coercion or manipulation
- Remorse, particularly where evidenced by voluntary reparation to victim
- Little or no planning

Steps 3-5

★**S-31c**   These correspond to those in the sexual offences guideline above (*ante*) (except, in step three (personal mitigation), a strong prospect of rehabilitation is not listed in the non-exhaustive list of mitigating factors).

II. RELATED AUTHORITIES

1. Overarching Principles: Seriousness

Deterrence/prevalence

S-103   *R. v. Bondzie (Marco) (Practice Note)* (see the sentencing supplement) is now reported at [2016] 2 Cr.App.R.(S.) 28, *sub nom. R. v. Bondzie*.

2. New Sentences: Criminal Justice Act 2003

Enforcement of community sentence in the event of breach

S-153   Where the appellant (20 when originally sentenced) admitted a single breach (of two unjustified failures to report) of a community order (with an 18-month supervision requirement, a 275-hour unpaid work requirement and a 10-month curfew requirement) for an offence of robbery, where the judge had specifically warned him that, if he breached that order, her powers would not be restricted, and he would go to prison for three years, and where the curfew had been complied with for over 40 weeks, without incident, but otherwise, compliance had been somewhat patchy (113 hours of unpaid work had, however, been completed), a sentence of 18 months' imprisonment imposed upon re-sentencing was quashed in *R. v. Aslam* [2016] 2 Cr.App.R.(S.) 29, CA. The court pointed out that there are potential dangers in being so definite as to the outcome of any possible future hearing; the extent of compliance with the order and the nature of the breach will need to be taken into account, as will the guideline on new sentences (Appendix S-2 in the sentencing supplement); the sentence departed from the approach in the guideline (*viz.* having decided that a community order is commensurate with the seriousness of the offence, the primary objective when re-sentencing for breach of the requirements is to ensure that the requirements are completed; custody should be the last resort, reserved for cases of deliberate and repeated breach, where all reasonable efforts to ensure compliance have failed); by the time of re-sentencing, substantial resources had been invested in working with the appellant, who had not re-offended; whereas it was correct that the breach report did not make good reading, it was most important that the probation service still felt able to work with the offender and there had been progress; putting an offender subject to a community order before the court in relation to a breach is an important tool available to that service to ensure that orders work effectively; there may be a reluctance to do so in circumstances such as this if the report from the probation service is not given considerable weight in deciding the manner of disposal; the service has to deal with difficult offenders whose response is often not entirely positive; what is important at a breach hearing is whether there has been any re-offending, whether the risk has been reduced, and whether the service feels its work with the offender may usefully continue; here, the failure to heed the judge's firm warnings of inevitable custody in the event of any breach did not justify a departure from the guideline.

4. ROBBERY (SENTENCING GUIDELINES COUNCIL)

Introduction

As to a new guideline on the sentencing of those aged under 18 for, *inter alia*, robbery, see *ante*, Appendix S-31 *et seq.*　　★S-250

7. SEXUAL OFFENCES (SENTENCING GUIDELINES COUNCIL)

Introduction

As to a new guideline on the sentencing of those aged under 18 for, *inter alia*, sexual offences, see *ante*, Appendix S-30 *et seq.*　　★S-400

12. CAUSING DEATH BY DRIVING

Disqualification

R. v. Needham (see the sentencing supplement) is now reported at [2016] 2 Cr.App.R. 26.　　S-657

18. DRUG OFFENCES

Categorisation of role

That an offender was effectively a sole trader in the production of cannabis does not meant that he cannot be found to have played a leading role for the purposes of the Sentencing Council's guideline on drug offences (Appendix S-18.17 in the sentencing supplement): *R. v. Handford* [2017] 1 Cr.App.R.(S.) 19, CA.　　★S-954

Community impact

R. v. Bondzie (Marco) (Practice Note) (see the sentencing supplement) is now reported at [2016] 2 Cr.App.R.(S.) 28, *sub nom. R. v. Bondzie.*　　S-956

19. OFFENCES TAKEN INTO CONSIDERATION AND TOTALITY

Totality

The Sentencing Council's guideline on totality (Appendix S-19.2 *et seq.* in the sentencing supplement) demonstrates that it is not inevitable that when a defendant is sentenced to consecutive sentences for a series of offences, particularly where each is against a different victim and forms a separate course of conduct, that he is entitled to a reduction in the total sentence where each of the individual sentences is entirely appropriate to the individual offences: *R. v. Cordle* [2017] 1 Cr.App.R.(S.) 36, CA.　　★S-1002

20. SEXUAL OFFENCES (SENTENCING COUNCIL FOR ENGLAND AND WALES)

Historic offences

R. v. Forbes; R. v. Warren; R. v. Clark; R. v. McCallen; R. v. B.D.; R. v. Rouse; R. v. Tarrant; R. v. Foulkes; R. v. Farlow (see the sentencing supplement) is now reported at [2016] 2 Cr.App.R.(S.) 44, *sub nom. R. v. Forbes.*　　S-1053

The assessment of harm and culpability generally

R. v. Forbes; R. v. Warren; R. v. Clark; R. v. McCallen; R. v. B.D.; R. v. Rouse; R. v. Tarrant; R. v.　　S-1054

Foulkes; *R. v. Farlow* (see the sentencing supplement) is now reported at [2016] 2 Cr.App.R.(S.) 44, *sub nom. R. v. Forbes.*

Indecent photographs of children

★**S-1061**   In *R. v. Pinkerton* [2017] 1 Cr.App.R.(S.) 47, CA, it was held: (i) whereas the approach under the Sentencing Council's guideline on sexual offences (Appendix S-20.75 *et seq.* in the sentencing supplement) is to take the most serious of the offending images to determine the appropriate category, whilst stating that a lower category may be appropriate if the most serious images are unrepresentative of the offender's conduct, where a defendant has large quantities of images at all levels, but the category A material (the most serious) represents a significant collection at that level and offending on a substantial scale in its own right, that does not make the category A images unrepresentative of the defendant's conduct; (ii) the guideline lays down specific types of activity as the basis for each category of offending, and it is not for police officers or indeed judges to create their own separate categories above and beyond those created by the Sentencing Council; the dangers of inconsistency and subjectivity are all too obvious; (iii) it is not necessary, save in the most exceptional circumstances, or where there is serious dispute as to the categorisation of images (which of itself should be extremely rare), for a judge to have to view the materials; a categorisation exercise properly carried out and set out in witness statements and/or schedules should obviate that; on an appeal against sentence, there should normally be no need to require an officer to attend the Court of Appeal with the material for the court to view; (iv) *R. v. Terrell* (§ 5-500 in the main work) is not authority for the proposition that this type of offending does not cause harm, nor is it authority for the proposition that a judge cannot take that harm into account when sentencing (it was concerned with the applicability of the dangerous offender provisions in the CJA 2003 in cases of this sort); there is plainly a degree of indirect harm, in that the download-ing of such images plays a part in the perpetuation of a market that will lead to further abuse of children; ordinarily, this sort of harm in a downloading case should be regarded as already being reflected in the sentencing level resulting from application of the guideline, but there is nothing wrong in judges referring to this type of harm being caused by such offending.

22. FRAUD, BRIBERY AND MONEY LAUNDERING

Fraud

★**S-1152**   In *R. v. Samuriwo* [2017] 1 Cr.App.R. (S.) 30, CA, it was said: (i) it is clear from the references to the "role" played by an offender in "group offending" in the Sentencing Council's guideline on fraud (Appendix S-22 *et seq.* in the sentencing supplement) that it is to be taken to apply to statu-tory conspiracies as well as conspiracies to defraud at common law; however (ii), the culpability as-sessment for a group of offenders may not be the same in each case; thus, an offence may have been "sophisticated" and involved "significant planning" (indicating "high culpability"), but a particular individual may have played only a "significant" role therein (indicating "medium culpability"); (iii) in a conspiracy, when assessing culpability, it is legitimate to look not only at what the particular offender did, but at what the agreement that he joined was collectively trying to do; for this reason, conspiracy offences may be more serious than a series of substantive of-fences; (iv) when it comes to the assessment of harm, it would be an error simply to look at the events on one day of the conspiracy (here, the day that the offenders were arrested, when their enterprise was undone as a result of the actions of a percipient security guard) and sentence on the basis that this resolves the harm category into which the offence is to be placed; in a conspiracy, where a sophisticated system of fraud has been set up, there is no reason to suppose that the of-fenders did not intend to carry on using it as long as they could, and the loss intended must be taken into account; where the harm intended cannot be quantified, the appropriate course is to move the case up to the corresponding point in the next category above the level of harm that has been quantified; moving categories in this way is the approach recommended in the guideline where the offence is one that creates only a risk of loss or where it has a high or medium impact on its victims; it is also in accordance with the approach in principle described in the context of the guideline on drug offences (*ibid.*, Appendix S-18 *et seq.*) in *R. v. Healey* [2013] 1 Cr.App.R.(S.) 33, CA (as to which, see § 5-184 in the main work, and Appendix S-958 in the sentencing supplement).

Revenue fraud

In *R. v. Alshateri* [2017] 1 Cr.App.R.(S.) 3, CA, it was said that it was it was not unreasonable to   **S-1152a**
use the guideline on revenue fraud (Appendix S-22.19 in the sentencing supplement) to assist in
fixing a starting point when sentencing for offences under the Trade Marks Act 1994 (because
the goods were counterfeit goods that, as a matter of fact, were subject to duty), but that there was
validity to the argument that its direct use was inappropriate (not least because there was no
evidence as to how much notional duty was involved).

23. THEFT OFFENCES

Low-value shoplifting

Where a defendant elects Crown Court trial for an offence of low-value shoplifting, section   **★S-1202**
22A of the MCA 1980 (low-value shoplifting to be a summary offence (§ 1-81 in the main work))
does not apply by virtue of subsection (2), and, when it comes to sentencing, the court is
constrained only by the Sentencing Council's guideline on theft from a shop (Appendix S-23.9 *et
seq.* in the sentencing supplement), and the statutory maximum of seven years' imprisonment; in
the context of a persistent offender for whom non-custodial methods have been tried and failed,
and where there is no current prospect of steps designed to reform and rehabilitate being effective, punishment and deterrence may justifiably come to the fore; however, the fact that there has
been previous diversionary work with an offender, which sought to prevent or reduce continued
offending, does not necessarily, if unsuccessful, preclude the court from considering that kind of
option again; if a custodial sentence has to be imposed, then it should bear a degree of
proportionality to the offence committed, albeit in the context of its aggravation by persistent offending or exhaustion of other options; and it is not the case that any custodial sentence must
inevitably be longer than the previous custodial sentence imposed for similar offending; the
maximum sentence for the matter, had it been dealt with summarily pursuant to section 22A (six
months' imprisonment), does, however, provide some assistance in fixing a proportionate sentence;
it is hard to envisage that a sentence of more than 12 months before credit for plea would ever be
appropriate for low-value, non-violent shoplifting by an individual acting alone: *R. v. Chamberlin*
[2017] 1 Cr.App.R.(S.) 46, CA.

ALMANAC

TABLE OF CONTENTS

2013

JANUARY

M	T	W	Th	F	Sa	Su
	1	2	3	4	5	6
7	8	9	10	11	12	13
14	15	16	17	18	19	20
21	22	23	24	25	26	27
28	29	30	31			

FEBRUARY

M	T	W	Th	F	Sa	Su
				1	2	3
4	5	6	7	8	9	10
11	12	13	14	15	16	17
18	19	20	21	22	23	24
25	26	27	28			

MARCH

M	T	W	Th	F	Sa	Su
				1	2	3
4	5	6	7	8	9	10
11	12	13	14	15	16	17
18	19	20	21	22	23	24
25	26	27	28	29	30	31

APRIL

M	T	W	Th	F	Sa	Su
1	2	3	4	5	6	7
8	9	10	11	12	13	14
15	16	17	18	19	20	21
22	23	24	25	26	27	28
29	30					

MAY

M	T	W	Th	F	Sa	Su
		1	2	3	4	5
6	7	8	9	10	11	12
13	14	15	16	17	18	19
20	21	22	23	24	25	26
27	28	29	30	31		

JUNE

M	T	W	Th	F	Sa	Su
					1	2
3	4	5	6	7	8	9
10	11	12	13	14	15	16
17	18	19	20	21	22	23
24	25	26	27	28	29	30

JULY

M	T	W	Th	F	Sa	Su
1	2	3	4	5	6	7
8	9	10	11	12	13	14
15	16	17	18	19	20	21
22	23	24	25	26	27	28
29	30	31				

AUGUST

M	T	W	Th	F	Sa	Su
			1	2	3	4
5	6	7	8	9	10	11
12	13	14	15	16	17	18
19	20	21	22	23	24	25
26	27	28	29	30	31	

SEPTEMBER

M	T	W	Th	F	Sa	Su
						1
2	3	4	5	6	7	8
9	10	11	12	13	14	15
16	17	18	19	20	21	22
23	24	25	26	27	28	29
30						

OCTOBER

M	T	W	Th	F	Sa	Su
	1	2	3	4	5	6
7	8	9	10	11	12	13
14	15	16	17	18	19	20
21	22	23	24	25	26	27
28	29	30	31			

NOVEMBER

M	T	W	Th	F	Sa	Su
				1	2	3
4	5	6	7	8	9	10
11	12	13	14	15	16	17
18	19	20	21	22	23	24
25	26	27	28	29	30	

DECEMBER

M	T	W	Th	F	Sa	Su
						1
2	3	4	5	6	7	8
9	10	11	12	13	14	15
16	17	18	19	20	21	22
23	24	25	26	27	28	29
30	31					

2014

JANUARY

M	T	W	Th	F	Sa	Su
		1	2	3	4	5
6	7	8	9	10	11	12
13	14	15	16	17	18	19
20	21	22	23	24	25	26
27	28	29	30	31		

FEBRUARY

M	T	W	Th	F	Sa	Su
					1	2
3	4	5	6	7	8	9
10	11	12	13	14	15	16
17	18	19	20	21	22	23
24	25	26	27	28		

MARCH

M	T	W	Th	F	Sa	Su
					1	2
3	4	5	6	7	8	9
10	11	12	13	14	15	16
17	18	19	20	21	22	23
24	25	26	27	28	29	30
31						

APRIL

M	T	W	Th	F	Sa	Su
	1	2	3	4	5	6
7	8	9	10	11	12	13
14	15	16	17	18	19	20
21	22	23	24	25	26	27
28	29	30				

MAY

M	T	W	Th	F	Sa	Su
			1	2	3	4
5	6	7	8	9	10	11
12	13	14	15	16	17	18
19	20	21	22	23	24	25
26	27	28	29	30	31	

JUNE

M	T	W	Th	F	Sa	Su
						1
2	3	4	5	6	7	8
9	10	11	12	13	14	15
16	17	18	19	20	21	22
23	24	25	26	27	28	29
30						

JULY

M	T	W	Th	F	Sa	Su
	1	2	3	4	5	6
7	8	9	10	11	12	13
14	15	16	17	18	19	20
21	22	23	24	25	26	27
28	29	30	31			

AUGUST

M	T	W	Th	F	Sa	Su
				1	2	3
4	5	6	7	8	9	10
11	12	13	14	15	16	17
18	19	20	21	22	23	24
25	26	27	28	29	30	31

SEPTEMBER

M	T	W	Th	F	Sa	Su
1	2	3	4	5	6	7
8	9	10	11	12	13	14
15	16	17	18	19	20	21
22	23	24	25	26	27	28
29	30					

OCTOBER

M	T	W	Th	F	Sa	Su
		1	2	3	4	5
6	7	8	9	10	11	12
13	14	15	16	17	18	19
20	21	22	23	24	25	26
27	28	29	30	31		

NOVEMBER

M	T	W	Th	F	Sa	Su
					1	2
3	4	5	6	7	8	9
10	11	12	13	14	15	16
17	18	19	20	21	22	23
24	25	26	27	28	29	30

DECEMBER

M	T	W	Th	F	Sa	Su
1	2	3	4	5	6	7
8	9	10	11	12	13	14
15	16	17	18	19	20	21
22	23	24	25	26	27	28
29	30	31				

2015

JANUARY
M	T	W	Th	F	Sa	Su
			1	2	3	4
5	6	7	8	9	10	11
12	13	14	15	16	17	18
19	20	21	22	23	24	25
26	27	28	29	30	31	

FEBRUARY
M	T	W	Th	F	Sa	Su
						1
2	3	4	5	6	7	8
9	10	11	12	13	14	15
16	17	18	19	20	21	22
23	24	25	26	27	28	

MARCH
M	T	W	Th	F	Sa	Su
2	3	4	5	6	7	1
2	3	4	5	6	7	8
9	10	11	12	13	14	15
16	17	18	19	20	21	22
23	24	25	26	27	28	29
30	31					

APRIL
M	T	W	Th	F	Sa	Su
		1	2	3	4	5
6	7	8	9	10	11	12
13	14	15	16	17	18	19
20	21	22	23	24	25	26
27	28	29	30			

MAY
M	T	W	Th	F	Sa	Su
				1	2	3
4	5	6	7	8	9	10
11	12	13	14	15	16	17
18	19	20	21	22	23	24
25	26	27	28	29	30	31

JUNE
M	T	W	Th	F	Sa	Su
1	2	3	4	5	6	7
8	9	10	11	12	13	14
15	16	17	18	19	20	21
22	23	24	25	26	27	28
29	30					

JULY
M	T	W	Th	F	Sa	Su
		1	2	3	4	5
6	7	8	9	10	11	12
13	14	15	16	17	18	19
20	21	22	23	24	25	26
27	28	29	30	31		

AUGUST
M	T	W	Th	F	Sa	Su
					1	2
3	4	5	6	7	8	9
10	11	12	13	14	15	16
17	18	19	20	21	22	23
24	25	26	27	28	29	30
31						

SEPTEMBER
M	T	W	Th	F	Sa	Su
	1	2	3	4	5	6
7	8	9	10	11	12	13
14	15	16	17	18	19	20
21	22	23	24	25	26	27
28	29	30				

OCTOBER
M	T	W	Th	F	Sa	Su
			1	2	3	4
5	6	7	8	9	10	11
12	13	14	15	16	17	18
19	20	21	22	23	24	25
26	27	28	29	30	31	

NOVEMBER
M	T	W	Th	F	Sa	Su
						1
2	3	4	5	6	7	8
9	10	11	12	13	14	15
16	17	18	19	20	21	22
23	24	25	26	27	28	29
30						

DECEMBER
M	T	W	Th	F	Sa	Su
	1	2	3	4	5	6
7	8	9	10	11	12	13
14	15	16	17	18	19	20
21	22	23	24	25	26	27
28	29	30	31			

2016

JANUARY

M	T	W	Th	F	Sa	Su
				1	2	3
4	5	6	7	8	9	10
11	12	13	14	15	16	17
18	19	20	21	22	23	24
25	26	27	28	29	30	31

FEBRUARY

M	T	W	Th	F	Sa	Su
1	2	3	4	5	6	7
8	9	10	11	12	13	14
15	16	17	18	19	20	21
22	23	24	25	26	27	28
29						

MARCH

M	T	W	Th	F	Sa	Su
	1	2	3	4	5	6
7	8	9	10	11	12	13
14	15	16	17	18	19	20
21	22	23	24	25	26	27
28	29	30	31			

APRIL

M	T	W	Th	F	Sa	Su
				1	2	3
4	5	6	7	8	9	10
11	12	13	14	15	16	17
18	19	20	21	22	23	24
25	26	27	28	29	30	

MAY

M	T	W	Th	F	Sa	Su
						1
2	3	4	5	6	7	8
9	10	11	12	13	14	15
16	17	18	19	20	21	22
23	24	25	26	27	28	29
30	31					

JUNE

M	T	W	Th	F	Sa	Su
		1	2	3	4	5
6	7	8	9	10	11	12
13	14	15	16	17	18	19
20	21	22	23	24	25	26
27	28	29	30			

JULY

M	T	W	Th	F	Sa	Su
				1	2	3
4	5	6	7	8	9	10
11	12	13	14	15	16	17
18	19	20	21	22	23	24
25	26	27	28	29	30	31

AUGUST

M	T	W	Th	F	Sa	Su
1	2	3	4	5	6	7
8	9	10	11	12	13	14
15	16	17	18	19	20	21
22	23	24	25	26	27	28
29	30	31				

SEPTEMBER

M	T	W	Th	F	Sa	Su
			1	2	3	4
5	6	7	8	9	10	11
12	13	14	15	16	17	18
19	20	21	22	23	24	25
26	27	28	29	30		

OCTOBER

M	T	W	Th	F	Sa	Su
					1	2
3	4	5	6	7	8	9
10	11	12	13	14	15	16
17	18	19	20	21	22	23
24	25	26	27	28	29	30
31						

NOVEMBER

M	T	W	Th	F	Sa	Su
	1	2	3	4	5	6
7	8	9	10	11	12	13
14	15	16	17	18	19	20
21	22	23	24	25	26	27
28	29	30				

DECEMBER

M	T	W	Th	F	Sa	Su
			1	2	3	4
5	6	7	8	9	10	11
12	13	14	15	16	17	18
19	20	21	22	23	24	25
26	27	28	29	30	31	

2017

JANUARY

M	T	W	Th	F	Sa	Su
2	3	4	5	6	7	1
9	10	11	12	13	14	8
16	17	18	19	20	21	15
23	24	25	26	27	28	22
30	31					29

FEBRUARY

M	T	W	Th	F	Sa	Su
6	7	1	2	3	4	5
13	14	8	9	10	11	12
20	21	15	16	17	18	19
27	28	22	23	24	25	26

MARCH

M	T	W	Th	F	Sa	Su
6	7	1	2	3	4	5
13	14	8	9	10	11	12
20	21	15	16	17	18	19
27	28	22	23	24	25	26
		29	30	31		

APRIL

M	T	W	Th	F	Sa	Su
3	4	5	6	7	1	2
10	11	12	13	14	8	9
17	18	19	20	21	15	16
24	25	26	27	28	22	23
					29	30

MAY

M	T	W	Th	F	Sa	Su
1	2	3	4	5	6	7
8	9	10	11	12	13	14
15	16	17	18	19	20	21
22	23	24	25	26	27	28
29	30	31				

JUNE

M	T	W	Th	F	Sa	Su
5	6	7	1	2	3	4
12	13	14	8	9	10	11
19	20	21	15	16	17	18
26	27	28	22	23	24	25
			29	30		

JULY

M	T	W	Th	F	Sa	Su
3	4	5	6	7	1	2
10	11	12	13	14	8	9
17	18	19	20	21	15	16
24	25	26	27	28	22	23
31					29	30

AUGUST

M	T	W	Th	F	Sa	Su
7	1	2	3	4	5	6
14	8	9	10	11	12	13
21	15	16	17	18	19	20
28	22	23	24	25	26	27
	29	30	31			

SEPTEMBER

M	T	W	Th	F	Sa	Su
4	5	6	7	1	2	3
11	12	13	14	8	9	10
18	19	20	21	15	16	17
25	26	27	28	22	23	24
				29	30	

OCTOBER

M	T	W	Th	F	Sa	Su
2	3	4	5	6	7	1
9	10	11	12	13	14	8
16	17	18	19	20	21	15
23	24	25	26	27	28	22
30	31					29

NOVEMBER

M	T	W	Th	F	Sa	Su
6	7	1	2	3	4	5
13	14	8	9	10	11	12
20	21	15	16	17	18	19
27	28	22	23	24	25	26
		29	30			

DECEMBER

M	T	W	Th	F	Sa	Su
4	5	6	7	1	2	3
11	12	13	14	8	9	10
18	19	20	21	15	16	17
25	26	27	28	22	23	24
				29	30	31

2018

JANUARY

M	T	W	Th	F	Sa	Su
1	2	3	4	5	6	7
8	9	10	11	12	13	14
15	16	17	18	19	20	21
22	23	24	25	26	27	28
29	30	31				

FEBRUARY

M	T	W	Th	F	Sa	Su
			1	2	3	4
5	6	7	8	9	10	11
12	13	14	15	16	17	18
19	20	21	22	23	24	25
26	27	28				

MARCH

M	T	W	Th	F	Sa	Su
			1	2	3	4
5	6	7	8	9	10	11
12	13	14	15	16	17	18
19	20	21	22	23	24	25
26	27	28	29	30	31	

APRIL

M	T	W	Th	F	Sa	Su
						1
2	3	4	5	6	7	8
9	10	11	12	13	14	15
16	17	18	19	20	21	22
23	24	25	26	27	28	29
30						

MAY

M	T	W	Th	F	Sa	Su
	1	2	3	4	5	6
7	8	9	10	11	12	13
14	15	16	17	18	19	20
21	22	23	24	25	26	27
28	29	30	31			

JUNE

M	T	W	Th	F	Sa	Su
				1	2	3
4	5	6	7	8	9	10
11	12	13	14	15	16	17
18	19	20	21	22	23	24
25	26	27	28	29	30	

JULY

M	T	W	Th	F	Sa	Su
						1
2	3	4	5	6	7	8
9	10	11	12	13	14	15
16	17	18	19	20	21	22
23	24	25	26	27	28	29
30	31					

AUGUST

M	T	W	Th	F	Sa	Su
		1	2	3	4	5
6	7	8	9	10	11	12
13	14	15	16	17	18	19
20	21	22	23	24	25	26
27	28	29	30	31		

SEPTEMBER

M	T	W	Th	F	Sa	Su
					1	2
3	4	5	6	7	8	9
10	11	12	13	14	15	16
17	18	19	20	21	22	23
24	25	26	27	28	29	30

OCTOBER

M	T	W	Th	F	Sa	Su
1	2	3	4	5	6	7
8	9	10	11	12	13	14
15	16	17	18	19	20	21
22	23	24	25	26	27	28
29	30	31				

NOVEMBER

M	T	W	Th	F	Sa	Su
			1	2	3	4
5	6	7	8	9	10	11
12	13	14	15	16	17	18
19	20	21	22	23	24	25
26	27	28	29	30		

DECEMBER

M	T	W	Th	F	Sa	Su
					1	2
3	4	5	6	7	8	9
10	11	12	13	14	15	16
17	18	19	20	21	22	23
24	25	26	27	28	29	30
31						

2019

JANUARY

M	T	W	Th	F	Sa	Su
	1	2	3	4	5	6
7	8	9	10	11	12	13
14	15	16	17	18	19	20
21	22	23	24	25	26	27
28	29	30	31			

FEBRUARY

M	T	W	Th	F	Sa	Su
				1	2	3
4	5	6	7	8	9	10
11	12	13	14	15	16	17
18	19	20	21	22	23	24
25	26	27	28			

MARCH

M	T	W	Th	F	Sa	Su
				1	2	3
4	5	6	7	8	9	10
11	12	13	14	15	16	17
18	19	20	21	22	23	24
25	26	27	28	29	30	31

APRIL

M	T	W	Th	F	Sa	Su
1	2	3	4	5	6	7
8	9	10	11	12	13	14
15	16	17	18	19	20	21
22	23	24	25	26	27	28
29	30					

MAY

M	T	W	Th	F	Sa	Su
		1	2	3	4	5
6	7	8	9	10	11	12
13	14	15	16	17	18	19
20	21	22	23	24	25	26
27	28	29	30	31		

JUNE

M	T	W	Th	F	Sa	Su
					1	2
3	4	5	6	7	8	9
10	11	12	13	14	15	16
17	18	19	20	21	22	23
24	25	26	27	28	29	30

JULY

M	T	W	Th	F	Sa	Su
1	2	3	4	5	6	7
8	9	10	11	12	13	14
15	16	17	18	19	20	21
22	23	24	25	26	27	28
29	30	31				

AUGUST

M	T	W	Th	F	Sa	Su
			1	2	3	4
5	6	7	8	9	10	11
12	13	14	15	16	17	18
19	20	21	22	23	24	25
26	27	28	29	30	31	

SEPTEMBER

M	T	W	Th	F	Sa	Su
						1
2	3	4	5	6	7	8
9	10	11	12	13	14	15
16	17	18	19	20	21	22
23	24	25	26	27	28	29
30						

OCTOBER

M	T	W	Th	F	Sa	Su
	1	2	3	4	5	6
7	8	9	10	11	12	13
14	15	16	17	18	19	20
21	22	23	24	25	26	27
28	29	30	31			

NOVEMBER

M	T	W	Th	F	Sa	Su
				1	2	3
4	5	6	7	8	9	10
11	12	13	14	15	16	17
18	19	20	21	22	23	24
25	26	27	28	29	30	

DECEMBER

M	T	W	Th	F	Sa	Su
						1
2	3	4	5	6	7	8
9	10	11	12	13	14	15
16	17	18	19	20	21	22
23	24	25	26	27	28	29
30	31					

2020

JANUARY

M	T	W	Th	F	Sa	Su
		1	2	3	4	5
6	7	8	9	10	11	12
13	14	15	16	17	18	19
20	21	22	23	24	25	26
27	28	29	30	31		

FEBRUARY

M	T	W	Th	F	Sa	Su
					1	2
3	4	5	6	7	8	9
10	11	12	13	14	15	16
17	18	19	20	21	22	23
24	25	26	27	28	29	

MARCH

M	T	W	Th	F	Sa	Su
						1
2	3	4	5	6	7	8
9	10	11	12	13	14	15
16	17	18	19	20	21	22
23	24	25	26	27	28	29
30	31					

APRIL

M	T	W	Th	F	Sa	Su
		1	2	3	4	5
6	7	8	9	10	11	12
13	14	15	16	17	18	19
20	21	22	23	24	25	26
27	28	29	30			

MAY

M	T	W	Th	F	Sa	Su
				1	2	3
4	5	6	7	8	9	10
11	12	13	14	15	16	17
18	19	20	21	22	23	24
25	26	27	28	29	30	31

JUNE

M	T	W	Th	F	Sa	Su
1	2	3	4	5	6	7
8	9	10	11	12	13	14
15	16	17	18	19	20	21
22	23	24	25	26	27	28
29	30					

JULY

M	T	W	Th	F	Sa	Su
		1	2	3	4	5
6	7	8	9	10	11	12
13	14	15	16	17	18	19
20	21	22	23	24	25	26
27	28	29	30	31		

AUGUST

M	T	W	Th	F	Sa	Su
					1	2
3	4	5	6	7	8	9
10	11	12	13	14	15	16
17	18	19	20	21	22	23
24	25	26	27	28	29	30
31						

SEPTEMBER

M	T	W	Th	F	Sa	Su
	1	2	3	4	5	6
7	8	9	10	11	12	13
14	15	16	17	18	19	20
21	22	23	24	25	26	27
28	29	30				

OCTOBER

M	T	W	Th	F	Sa	Su
			1	2	3	4
5	6	7	8	9	10	11
12	13	14	15	16	17	18
19	20	21	22	23	24	25
26	27	28	29	30	31	

NOVEMBER

M	T	W	Th	F	Sa	Su
						1
2	3	4	5	6	7	8
9	10	11	12	13	14	15
16	17	18	19	20	21	22
23	24	25	26	27	28	29
30						

DECEMBER

M	T	W	Th	F	Sa	Su
	1	2	3	4	5	6
7	8	9	10	11	12	13
14	15	16	17	18	19	20
21	22	23	24	25	26	27
28	29	30	31			

Archbold
paragraph
numbers

AL-8

Archbold's Criminal Pleading–2017 ed.

AL-9

Holidays and Notable Dates

Holiday, etc.	2013	2014	2015	2016	2017	2018	2019	2020
New Year's Day	Jan. 1	Jan. 1	Jan. 1	Jan. 1	Jan. 1	Jan. 1	Jan. 1	Jan. 1
New Year Holiday (England)	–	–	–	–	–	–	–	–
New Year Holiday (Scotland)	Jan. 2	Jan. 2	Jan. 2	Jan. 2	Jan. 2	Jan. 2	Jan. 2	Jan. 2
St David's Day (Wales)	Mar. 1	Mar. 1	Mar. 1	Mar. 1	Mar. 1	Mar. 1	Mar. 1	Mar. 1
St Patrick's Day (Ireland)	Mar. 17	Mar. 17	Mar. 17	Mar. 17	Mar. 17	Mar. 17	Mar. 17	Mar. 17
Good Friday	Mar. 29	Apr. 18	Apr. 3	Mar. 25	Apr. 14	Mar. 30	Apr. 19	Apr. 10
Easter Monday	Apr. 1	Apr. 21	Apr. 6	Apr. 28	Mar. 17	Apr. 2	Apr. 22	Apr. 13
St George's Day (England)	Apr. 23	Apr. 23	Apr. 23	Apr. 23	Apr. 23	Apr. 23	Apr. 23	Apr. 23
May Day Holiday	May 2	May 5	May 4	May 2	May 1	May 7	May 6	May 10
Spring Bank Holiday	May 27	May 26	May 25	May 30	May 29	May 28	May 27	May 25
August Bank Holiday	Aug. 26	Aug. 25	Aug. 24	Aug. 29	Aug. 28	Aug. 27	Aug. 26	Aug. 31
St Andrew's Day (Scotland)	Nov. 30	Nov. 30	Nov. 30	Nov. 30	Nov. 30	Nov. 30	Nov. 30	Nov. 30
Christmas Day	Dec. 25	Dec. 25	Dec. 25	Dec. 25	Dec. 25	Dec. 25	Dec. 25	Dec. 25
Boxing Day	Dec. 26	Dec. 26	Dec. 26	Dec. 26	Dec. 26	Dec. 26	Dec. 26	Dec. 26
Christmas Holiday(s)	–	–	–	Dec. 27	–	–	–	Dec. 28

Measurement Conversion Tables

The measurements set out below are based upon the following standards set by the Weights **AL-10** and Measures Act 1985, Sched. 1, Pts I to V:

YARD = 0.9144 metre; GALLON = 4.546 09 cubic decimetres or litres; POUND = 0.453 592 37 kilograms

AL-11

Measurements of Length

Imperial Units of Length		*Metric Equivalents*
Mil	1/1000 inch	0.0254 millimetres
Inch	1000 mils	2.54 centimetres
Link	7.92 inches	20.1168 centimetres
Foot	12 inches	0.3048 metres
Yard	3 feet	0.9144 metres
Fathom	6 feet	1.8288 metres
Cable	60 feet or 10 fathoms	18.288 metres
Chain	22 yards (100 links)	20.1168 metres
Furlong	220 yards	201.168 metres
Mile	1,760 yards (8 furlongs)	1.609344 kilometres
Nautical mile	6080 feet	1.853184 kilometres

Metric Units of Length		*Imperial Equivalents*
Micron	1/1000 millimetre	0.03937007 mils
Millimetre	1/1000 metre	0.03937007 inches
Centimetre	1/100 metre	0.3937 inches
Decimetre	1/10 metre	3.937 inches
Metre	Metre	1.09361329 yards
Kilometre	1000 metres	0.62137712 miles or 0.53961 nautical miles

Measurements of Area

Imperial Units of Area		*Metric Equivailents*
Square inch	1/144 square feet	6,4516 square centimetres
Square foot	1/9 square yard	929.0304 square centimetres
Square yard	Square yard	0.83613 square metres

Imperial Units of Area		*Metric Equivalents*
Square chain	484 square yards	404.685642 square metres
Rood	1,210 square yards	1011.714 square metres
Acre	4 roods or 4840 square yards	4046.85642 sq. ms or 40.4685642 acres
Square mile	640 acres	258.998811 hectares

Metric Units of Area		*Metric Equivalents*
Square millimetre	1/100 square centimetre	0.00155 square inches
Square centimetre	1/100 square decimetre	0.155 square inches
Square decimetre	1/100 metre	15.5 square inches
Square metre	Square metre	1.1959 sq. yards or 10.7639 sq. ft
Are	100 square metres	119.599 sq. yds or 0.09884 roods
Dekare	10 ares	0.2471 acres
Hectare	100 ares (1,000 square metres)	2.47105 acres
Square kilometre	100 hectares	247.105 acres or 0.3861 square miles

Measurements of Volume

Imperial Units of Volume		*Metric Equivalents*
Cubic inch		16.387064 cubic centimetres
Cubic foot	1,728 cubic inches	28.3168465 cubic decimetres
Cubic yard	27 cubic feet	0.76455485 cubic metres

Metric Units of Volume		*Imperial Equivalents*
Cubic centimetre	1,000 cubic millimetres	0.06102374 cubic inches
Cubic decimetre	1,000 cubic centimetres	0.03531466 cubic feet
Cubic metre	1,000 cubic decimetres	1.30795061 cubic yards or 35.3147 cu. ft.

Measurements of Capacity

Imperial, Apothecaries and US Units of Capacity		Metric Equivalents
Minim		0.0591938 millilitres
Fluid Drachm	60 minims	0.35516328 centilitres
Fluid ounce	8 fluid drachms	2.84130625 centilitres
US fluid ounce	1.0408 UK fluid ounces	29.573522656 millilitres
Gill	5 fluid ounces	1.42065312 decilitres
Pint	4 gills or 20 fluid ounces	0.56826125 litres
US pint	0.8327 UK pints or 16 US fluid ounces	0.47317636 litres
Quart	2 pints or 8 gills	1.1365225 litres
Gallon	4 quarts or 1.20095 US gallons	4.54609 litres
US gallon	0.08327 UK gallons	3.7854109 litres
Peck	2 gallons or 16 pints	9.09218 litres
Bushel	4 pecks or 8 gallons	36.36872 litres
Quarter	8 bushels or 36 pecks	2.909 4976 hectolitres
Chaldron	36 bushels or 4 ½ quarters	13.0927392 hectolitres

Metric Units of Capacity		Imperial Equivalents
Millilitre		0.28156064 fluid drachms
Centilitre	10 millilitres	0.35195080 fluid ounces
Decilitre	10 centilitres	0.70390160 gills
Litre	10 decilitres	1.75975398 pints or 0.21996924 UK gallons
Dekalitre	10 litres	2.1996924 UK gallons
Hectolitre	10 dekalitres or 100 litres	21.996824 UK gallons

Measurements of Weight

Imperial and Apothecaries Units of Weight		Metric Equivalents
Grain		64.79891 milligrams

Imperial and Apothecaries Units of Weight		Metric Equivalents
Scruple	20 grains	1.2959782 grams
Pennyweight	24 grains	1.55517384 grams
Drachm	3 scruples or 60 grains	3.8879346 grams
Troy ounce	8 drachms or 480 grains	31.1034768 grams
Dram	1/16 ounce	1.77184519 grams
Ounce	16 drams or 437.5 grains	28.3495231 gram
Troy pound (US)	12 troy ounces or 5,760 grains	373.241721 grams
Pound	16 ounces or 7,000 grains	453.59237 grams or 0.45359237 kilograms
Stone	14 pounds	6.35029318 kilograms
Quarter	28 pounds or 2 stone	12.7005863 kilograms
Cental	100 pounds	45.359237 kilograms
Hundredweight	4 quarters or 112 pounds	50.8023454 kilograms
Short hundredweight (US)	100 pounds	45.359237 kilograms
Ton (UK or long ton)	20 cwt or 2,240 pounds	1.0160469 metric tonnes (tonne)
Ton (US or short ton)	2,000 pounds	0.90718474 metric tonnes

Metric Units of Weight		Imperial Equivalents
Milligram	.001 grams	0.012432 grains
Centigram	.01 grams	0.15432 grains
Decigram	.1 grams	1.5432 grains
Gram	1 gram	0.03527396 ounces or 0.03215 troy ounces
Dekagram	10 grams	0.35273961 ounces
Hectogram	100 grams	3.52739619 ounces
Kilogram	1,000 grams	2.20462262 pounds
Myriagram	10 kilograms	22.0462 pounds
Quintal	100 kilograms	1.9684 hundredweight
Tonne	1,000 kilograms	0.984207 UK tons or 1.10231 US tons

Measurements of Velocity

	Per Minute	*Per Second*
Per Hour		
Mile	88 feet	17.6 inches per second
1.609344 kph	26.8224 metres	44.704 centimetres per second
Kilometres	16.6667 metres	27.7778 centimetres
0.62137 mph	54.6806 feet	10.9361 inches

Système Internationale D'unites or SI Units

1. SI units are increasingly being used to report laboratory results. They have largely replaced earlier systems such as c.g.s. units (centimetre, gram, second), m.k.s. or Giorgi units (metre, kilogram, second), and Imperial units (yard, pound, second).   **AL-16**

2. S.I. Units comprise 7 base units and 2 supplementary units. Other units are derived from these. 18 derived units are currently widely accepted.

Base SI Units

Physical Quantity	Unit	Symbol	
Length	metre	m	**AL-17**
Mass	kilogram	kg	
Time	second	s	
Electric current	ampere	A	
Temperature	kelvin	K	
Luminosity	candela	cd	
Amount of substance	mole	mol	
Plane angle*	radian*	rad	
Solid angle*	steradian*	sr	

*Supplementary Units

Derived SI Units

Physical Quantity	Unit	Symbol	
Frequency	hertz	Hz	**AL-18**
Energy	joule	J	
Force	newton	N	
Power	watt	W	
Pressure	pascal	Pa	
Electric charge	coulomb	C	
Electric potential difference	volt	V	
Electrical resistance	ohm	Ω	
Electric conductance	siemens	S	
Electric capacitance	farad	F	
Magnetic flux	weber	Wb	
Inductance	henry	H	
Magnetic flux density	tesla	T	
Luminous flux	lumen	lm	
Illuminance	lux	lx	
Absorbed dose	gray	Gy	
Activity	becquerel	Bq	
Dose Equivalence	sievert	Sv	

Multiples and Subdivisions of SI Units

Prefix	Symbol	Power	Value	
exa	E	10^{18}	1,000,000,000,000,000,000	**AL-19**
peta	P	10^{15}	1,000,000,000,000,000	

Prefix	Symbol	Power	Value
tera	T	10^{12}	1,000,000,000,000
giga	G	10^{9}	1,000,000,000
mega	M	10^{6}	1,000,000
kilo	k	10^{3}	1,000
hecto	h	10^{2}	100
deca	da	10	10
-			1
deci	d	10^{-1}	1/10
centi	c	10^{-2}	1/100
milli	m	10^{-3}	1/1,000
micro	µ	10^{-6}	1/1,000,000
nano	n	10^{-9}	1/1,000,000,000
pico	p	10^{-12}	1/1,000,000,000,000
femto	f	10^{-15}	1/1,000,000,000,000,000
atto	a	10^{-18}	1/1,000,000,000,000,000,000

International Time Differences

AL-20   The following time differences are based upon Greenwich Mean Time (GMT).
British Summer Time (BST) is one hour in advance of GMT.

Country		Hours +/-
Algeria		+1 hour
Argentina		-3 hours
Australia		
	South Australia	+9½ hours
	New South Wales	+10 hours
	Tasmania	+10 hours
	Victoria	+10 hours
Austria		+1 hour
Belgium		+1 hour
Bolivia		-4 hours
Brazil		-3 hours
Bulgaria		+2 hours
Canada		
	Newfoundland	-3½ hours
	Atlantic	-4 hours
	Eastern	-5 hours
	Central	-6 hours
	Mountain	-7 hours
	Pacific	-8 hours
	Yukon	-9 hours
Chile		-4 hours
China		+8 hours
Columbia		-5 hours
Czech Lands		+1 hour
Denmark		+1 hour
Egypt		+2 hours
Finland		+2 hours

AL-21

Country	Hours +/-
France	+1 hour
Germany	+1 hour
Ghana	
Greece	+2 hours
Holland	+1 hour
Hong Kong	+8 hours
Hungary	+1 hour
India	+5½ hours
Iraq	+3 hours
Ireland	
Israel	+2 hours
Italy	+1 hour
Jamaica	-5 hours
Japan	+9 hours
Kenya	+3 hours

Country	Hours +/-
Luxembourg	+1 hour
Malaysia	+8 hours
Malta	+1 hour
Morocco	
New Zealand	+12 hours
Nigeria	+1 hour
Norway	+1 hour
Peru	-5 hours
Philippines	+8 hours
Poland	+1 hour

Country		Hours +/-
Portugal		+2 hours
Romania		+3 hours
Russia	Moscow	+10 hours
	Vladivostock	+3 hours
Saudi Arabia		+1 hours
Serbia		+8 hours
Singapore		+2 hours
South Africa		+1 hour
Spain		+5½ hours
Sri Lanka		+1 hour
Sweden		+1 hour
Switzerland		+8 hours
Taiwan		+7 hours
Thailand		+1 hour
Tunisia		+2 hours
Turkey		+3 hours
Ukraine		+4 hours
United Arab Emirates		
United States	Eastern	-5 hours
	Central	-6 hours
	Mountain	-7 hours
	Pacific	-8 hours
Zambia		+2 hours
Zimbabwe		+2 hours

Stopping Distances

AL-22

Speed (m.p.h.)	Stopping distance (feet)
20	40
30	75
40	120
50	175
60	240
70	315

Useful Contact Details

	Telephone	Email
Courts, etc.		
House of Lords, Judicial Office	(020) 7219 3111	
Royal Courts of Justice	(020) 7947 6000	
Registrar, Criminal Appeals	(020) 7947 6103	
Criminal Appeal Office	(020) 7947 6011	Criminalappealoffice.generaloffice@hmcourts-service.x.gsi.gov.uk
Administrative Court Office	(020) 7947 6205	
Official Bodies		
Home Office	(020) 7035 4848	public.enquiries@homeoffice.gsi.gov.uk
Serious Fraud Office	(020) 7239 7272	public.enquiries@sfo.gsi.gov.uk
H.M. Revenue and Customs	0845 010 9000	Enquiries.estn@hmrc.gsi.gov.uk This address handles all enquiries related to VAT, Excise and other duties formerly administered by HM Customs and Excise (with the exception of International Trade)
New Scotland Yard	(020) 7230 1212	new.scotland.yard@met.police.uk
City of London Police	(020) 7601 2222	postmaster@cityoflondon.police.uk
British Transport Police	0800 40 50 40	
Others		
Justice	(020) 7329 5100	admin@justice.org.uk
Liberty	(020) 7403 3888	
Bar Council	(020) 7242 0082	
Bar Council Ethical Enquiries Line	(020) 7611 1307	

	Telephone	*Email*
Bar Standards Board	(020) 7611 1444	
Law Society — Lawyerline	0870 606 2588	
Law Society — Practice Advice Service	0870 606 2522	

INDEX
LEGAL TAXONOMY
FROM SWEET & MAXWELL

This index has been prepared using Sweet and Maxwell's Legal Taxonomy. Main index entries conform to keywords provided by the Legal Taxonomy except where references to specific documents or non-standard terms (denoted by quotation marks) have been included. These keywords provide a means of identifying similar concepts in other Sweet & Maxwell publications and online services to which keywords from the Legal Taxonomy have been applied. Readers may find some minor differences between terms used in the text and those which appear in the index. Suggestions to *sweetandmaxwell.taxonomy@tr.com*.

All references are to paragraph numbers.